Early Settlers of Alabama: With Notes & Genealogies Parts 1 & 2

James Edmonds Saunders, Elizabeth Saunders Blair Stubbs

BIBLIOBAZAAR

JAMES EDMONDS SAUNDERS.
Born in Virginia 1806, Died 1896.

EARLY SETTLERS OF ALABAMA.

BY

COL. JAMES EDMONDS SAUNDERS,

LAWRENCE COUNTY, ALA.

WITH

NOTES AND GENEALOGIES,

BY HIS GRANDDAUGHTER,

ELIZABETH SAUNDERS BLAIR STUBBS,

NEW ORLEANS, LA.

TWO PARTS IN ONE

PART I.

DEDICATION.

🍃 🍃 🍃

TO TWO IN HEAVEN.

🍃 🍃 🍃

In winter nights agone, two aged people sat beside December's waning fires—alone in the old home—while, without, the empty nests in the ancestral oaks were swayed by shrill blasts.

Their fledglings, too, had long since flown   *   *   *

While they sat thus communing, there was wont to enter a most quiet guest—a gentle Palmer—who sang to them only songs of HOME, and FRIENDS, and fond MEMORIES. At the enchantment of his presence they would smile and weep—often smiling through their tears.

Then the elder of the aged listeners—inspired by his Heavenly Guest—said gently to the other: "Take courage, dear Heart! I will here inscribe the old songs of Home, and Friends, and Fond Memories, ere they be lost and forgot!"

And her answer, breathed like a prayer—while the dark-bright eyes shone far into the future,—"Aye, my love—It is well—*I am comforted*." Ever, then, he wrote, and sang a Melody of Life—and she was cheered through all the long days—even to the great and solemn Night.

INTRODUCTION.

♪ ♪ ♪ ♪

Colonel Saunders began in the April numbers of the "*Moulton Advertiser*," 1880 (his county paper), a series of "letters" relating to the "*Early Settlers of Lawrence County*" (Ala.) and the Tennessee Valley.

These articles, increasing, year after year, in scope and valuable material, soon overran their limit, exacting tributary data from neighboring counties, the State, adjoining States, and only to pause in that dear "*Mother of States*" (which was his own) to note where the restless wave had tossed some immigrant ancestor of the sturdy lines of which he wrote.

The stirring recital evokes, across the beautiful Blue Ridge Mountains, to Tennessee, Alabama, and Mississippi, the warrior-emigrant. His wandering line of white wagon-tops gleams in the sunrise of the Nineteenth Century. Old Virginia lies behind him. The Indian vanishes with the smoke-wreath of his rifle's breath. He builds his wilderness-castle, *a log cabin*, and so the life of a great State begins, and Alabama looms out of territorial chaos.

Most lovingly does Colonel Saunders relate the story of her people, from the humblest mechanic at his forge, to the noble Governor in his chair of State. Her whilom ministers, merchants, lawyers, planters, statesmen, come, at his gentle summons near, and take on the semblance of the vivid life they lived. Youth and lovers, the jest, the chase—threads of gold in the noble tapestry—each play their part.

Next falls the shadow of the Texas war across the pages. And again, all too soon alas, bursts the tempest of the civil war upon the fair young manhood of our State!

Himself a veteran of veterans, he follows them all through the sad struggle to the heart-breaking surrender at Appomattox, and buries many of his young heroes —with the past—asleep in their glory! As told by him, the career of the Alabama regiments is an epitome of the war. And so, the letters, like old familiar folk-song, flowed on; while two old people lived over their lives in their pages. And, while the public clamored for publication in book form, containing, as they did, such valuable historic and genealogical matter, even then, suddenly they were *ended*, not *finished*. He wrote no more. The "*Letters*," begun in 1880, ceased in 1889. Much valuable data yet remained unwritten, lying neglected. where it had been so carefully collected. He was now eighty-four years of age, and the romantic early inspiration of his life—she who had been his child-wife at the age of fifteen—passed, chanting, into realms of Bliss; while he, benumbed with the vision of the radiance of the door through which she had passed, dreamed henceforth only of joining her who, for sixty-five years, had held the chrism of love at his family altar. His *Mary* was "in Heaven."

JAMES EDMONDS SAUNDERS.

To live parallel with a *century* is rarely allotted the span of any one human existence; but, to have appeared in the *dawn*, and lingered (with every faculty alert) late into the *evening* of *the present* era, in which men have grappled with such Titanic forces as our Civil War, and the intricacies of the age's magic progress, denotes a rare and virile ichor coursing the veins—a gift, perhaps, of some heroic ancestor—distinguishing the honored octogenarian, bravely battling with the storms of fate and militant even with time—to whom he is the noble hostage from all the ages.

Such, alas, are fast waning with the century they have so illumined. The spent eagle—still gazing at the sun—dreams, yet, of loftier heights upon which to die—and the lonely altitude of grand old age lifts it quite into the vanishing point of heaven.

James Edmonds Saunders was born in Brunswick county, Virginia, 7th of May, 1806. His ancestor, Edward Saunders, "Chirurgeon," was already seated in Northumberland county, Virginia, in 1658; and, in 1669, as one of the justices for the county, was administering both medicine and law, *pari passu*, and in drastic doses, no doubt. His commission from the Royal Governor Lord Berkeley as "*one of the king's justices for Northumberland county*" is yet preserved in the old Records at Heathsville. His descendants lived, later, in the adjoining county of Lancaster on the Wicomico river, in Wicomico parish (which was included in both counties), and record of these is preserved at Lancaster C. H.

His great-grandson, Thomas Saunders (born 1739), removed to Brunswick county, after the Revolution, in which, he, and four brothers, served with great credit in the American army, in Virginia and North Carolina.

Rev. Turner Saunders, of Tennessee, Alabama and Mississippi (born 1782), was second son of Thomas, and father of the subject of this sketch. He removed in 1808 to Franklin, Williamson county, Tenn., and with him came his brother-in-law, Maj. David Dunn, of Brunswick county, and other Virginia families, who soon formed a refined and energetic community. Descendants of some of these are, to the present day, busy making noble history for the South.

Old Harpeth Academy was near by, and here the famous Dr. Gideon Blackburn, Presbyterian minister and educator, armoured restless young energies for the stupendous battles of the new world—an hitherto unexplored realm.

And here, in the old Tennessee forest, roamed, with his boyish classmates, the young midshipman, Matthew Fontaine Maury, also a son of Virginia; the potent "*God-within*" *enthusiasm*, impelling him to speak, even thus early, of his one *life dream*, whispered him by old ocean, night and day, when his hammock swung on the sea-god's tremulous breast. Did no prophetic vision warn these lads, in their morning existence, of that hot current of life-blood which was to stain their fair land, and, unlike the warm "Gulf Stream," make desolate the hearths by which it flowed—each playing his heroic part—and *one* lifted to the very climax of fame while the world applauded?

Alabama, dusky maiden—lovely Pocahontas among her sister States—stepping out from the dawn, now beckoned evermore the weary emigrant to her "Happy Valley," where the silver Tennessee trailed its sparkling waters past wooded islands, and laughing shoals, ever crowned by the great forest monarchs! To Lawrence county, and near to the great river, came the Rev. Turner Saunders in 1821, building a commodious home between Town creek and Courtland. Other planters came—an easy-going, courteous class. Content was theirs. The morning and evening songs of their slaves, nature's merriest children (for when is the negro not a child?) echoed thousands of happy hearts.

The University of Georgia (*then* Franklin College) was the Southern *Salamanca*, and light-hearted students caracoled gaily to and from its learned shrine. (There were no railways.) The Rev. Moses Waddell was its president in 1819, another famous Presbyterian educator. The influence of Princeton College was potent at this time in the South, throwing its searchlight of knowledge far and near. To this College came young Saunders, in 1822, the spell of old Harpeth Academy still upon him, and so slight, so boyish, his comrades dubbed him "*Slim Jimmy*."

The University published in Latin, in 1858, a catalogue from the beginning (1785), in which year its *curatores* were: *Joannus* Houston, *Jacobus* Habersham, *Gulielmus* Pew, *Josephus* Clay, *Abramus* Baldwin, *Nathan* Brownson, *Joannus* Habersham, *Abiel* Holmes, *Gulielmus* Houston, Jenkin Davis, *Hugo* Lawson, *Gulielmus* Glascock and *Benjaminus* Taliaferro.

Its first president was *Josiah* Meigs, LL. D., 1801; the second, *Joannus* Brown, D. D., 1811; the third, *Robertus* Finley, D. D., 1816, and fourth, Moses Waddell, D. D., 1819.

Its alumni, beginning in 1804, include a long list of names famous in the South.

It was of the class of 1825 that the venerable president wrote so proudly, to the Rev. Turner Saunders. Their names are here given (retaining the quaint Latin nomenclature of the old catalogue): *Edmondus* Atkinson, A. M.; *Joannus* Campbell; *Gulielmus* Dougherty, A. M., curator; *Joannus* Hillyer, A. M.; *Hugo* A. Haralson, A. M., *Res. pub. Fœd. E. Cong.*; Kinchen L. Haralson, A. M.; *Jacobus* W. Harris, A. M.; *Gulielmus* L. Harris, A. M.; *Georgius* Graves, A. M.; *Joannus* J. Hunt, A. M.; *Gulielmus* L. Mitchell, A. M.. *Tutor. Curator*; *Henricus* H. Means, A. M.; *Gulielmus* C. Micou, A. M.; *Adrianus* N. Mayor, A. M.; *Henricus* J. Pope; *Benjaminus* C. Pope; *Joannus* Saukey, A. M.; *Reuben* G. Reynolds, A. M., *et Univ. Penn.*, M. D.; *Fernandus* Sims; *Albertus* C. Torrence, A. M.; *Edmundus* R. Ware, A. M., *et Univ. Penn.*, M. D.; *Georgius* J. S. Walker, A. M.; *Jacobus* B. Walker, A. M., *et Univ. Penn.*, M. D.; *Gulielmus* E. Walker, A. M.; *Gulielmus* N. Walker, *Edwardus* H. Wingfield, A. M.; *Middleton* Witt. This was the class of James E. Saunders.

ATHENS, 6th November, 1823.

REV. AND DEAR SIR—On the 9th of April last your son, James Saunders, entered as a student in the Sophomore Class of the University of Georgia. On the 1st August, his examination on the studies of the Sophomore year having been cheerfully sustained, he was cordially admitted by the Faculty to enter the Junior Class.

Since August he has been assiduously employed in pursuing the study of Belles Lettres and Criticism under my own direction, and Geometry and Mathematics under Professor Church.

It gives me great pleasure to say, with unaffected sincerity, that, although his class is a large one, thirty-five in number, his rank in scholarship is equal to that of any member in it. *I have never known a class in my life which included so much intellectual talent as the present Junior Class in this institution, to which he is attached.* But, as from your character and standing in society, I presume you would rather see your son a *good* than a *great* man, I feel a superior gratification in assuring you that his general deportment and behavior, since he has been here, has merited and met with the unqualified approbation of the members of the Faculty, as well as of the discreet citizens of this village who know him. By persisting in that course of application to study and modest conformity to the laws of College which he has hitherto pursued, until August, 1825, he can not fail to graduate with much credit to himself and to this institution, as well as with the fairest prospects of gratifying his friends, and proving highly useful to his country. This is no exaggeration. I believe that flattery is not often considered as belonging to the list of *my* infirmities. In a word, I estimate James as a youth at present of much promise.

I have spent thirty-nine years mostly in directing the minds of youth. I have experienced much pleasure and occasional pain in the management of minds of every kind. How long I shall continue in the arduous employment is, at present, very uncertain.

I should be very glad to see you here, but if that pleasure be denied, a letter occasionally would greatly gratify

Your sincere friend,   M. WADDEL.

Rev. Turner Saunders.

Other college mates were Alfred Vernon Scott, Judge Wyley W. Mason, Eugene A. Nisbet, M. C., Iverson L. Harris, Thos. J. Merriwether, James Scott, James S. Sims, M. D., Claiborne A. Watkins, M. D., Judge Augustus B. Longstreet, Judge Joseph Lumpkin, Governor George W. Crawford, Thos. A. Matthews, M. D., Hines Holt, M. C., Wm. H. Crawford, U. S. Senator, James Rembert, Abraham Walker, Judge John A. Campbell, of New Orleans, Daniel Chandler, of Mobile, Judge Robert Dougherty, of Alabama, Dr. Paul F. Eve, of Nashville, Tenn., Wm. E. Jones, M. C., Richard and James Meriwether, M. C., Wm. H. Reynolds, and other illustrious names, constellations no mists may yet obscure.

Many of these formed life-long friendships with young Saunders. *None* now survive; only a few faded letters yet remain to attest the lost fragrance of their early association. Alabama has embalmed the names of some of these in "amber immortalisation" and now "silent they rest in solemn salvatory!"

The years, like strong athletes, now ran rapid race, and into the old college curriculum, and into the heart of the dreaming youth, glided a *study* not put into the catalogue by those "most potent grave and reverend seigniors." It was the *tender passion*, whose light eclipses all other schools or courts of learning, for—

> "When all is done, all tried, all counted here * * *
> This Love just puts his hand out in a dream
> And straight out stretches all things!"

A Georgia maiden's dark eyes "held him from his rest!" The Rev. Doctor wrote to the Rev. father anxious letters, pleading for delay; but love conquers all!

ATHENS, Ga., March 31, 1824.

REVEREND AND DEAR SIR—Your son is about to leave us, and depart to yourself and his home. Never did I part with a pupil with more regret. We have conversed on the subject with the familiarity of confidential friends; and, I presume, he has disclosed to me the *weightiest of all the reasons* which urge him to the measure. Notwithstanding all his arguments, I am decidedly of the opinion that his highest earthly advantage would result from returning hither, and remaining until August, 1825. In that event, his classical and scientific education would be equal to that of any man of his age in the Southern or Western States, and the highest honors of the University of Georgia would await him. His mind would then be sufficiently mature, as well as cultivated, to enter on the study of a profession with the greatest advantage. His age would also be exactly suited to that purpose. Could he be persuaded to adopt that course, and rescind the resolution to which at present he appears so partial, I feel a confidence that he would, undoubtedly, be among the most brilliant and useful men, whose minds I have ever had the honor and pleasure of conducting. In all these assertions I am sincere. You can advise him as you think proper, as he is your son.

I am sure I wish him well; and I am confident he will, sooner or later, be convinced of the soundness of the advice I have freely and repeatedly given him on the subject.

I should be very much gratified to receive a letter from you, when you find it agreeable and convenient to write; and I am very sincerely,

Your friend, in the best bonds,

M. WADDEL.

P. S.—I inclose an extra certificate for the satisfaction of yourself and his friends.

Rev. Turner Saunders.

July 14, 1824, when eighteen years of age, he married Mary Frances Watkins (aged fifteen), eldest daughter of his neighbor, Maj. Robert H. Watkins, who had recently removed from Petersburg, Broad River, Georgia (and before that from Prince Edward county, Virginia). Major Watkins bought much land from the government through its office at Huntsville, Ala., and patents, on parchment, of many original tracts, signed by Presidents Monroe and Jackson, are preserved in the family.

The wedded pilgrimage of sixty-five years began auspiciously. The dedication of each to the other was most perfect. Love made expiation forever upon the High Altar of Life in that happy home. An Angel of Content sat at its fireside, and pointed to the precious promises whenever sorrow came to them, "*with uplifted cross on high !*" Piety was an heritage, and the family of each were of the Methodist belief.

Their neighbors (also of Virginia descent) had drifted through Tennessee, the Carolinas and Georgia to this "*Happy Valley*," where soon their children intermarried, and the common interest became welded. Young Alabama welcomed them in those "summers of long ago," and when they were tired of the "*noise of living*" folded them to her heart, sighing "Here rest, my children !"—and so fulfilled her promise to their youth—and here they sleep. And on the gravestones above them are the old familiar names—*Sherrod, Swoope, Gilchrist, Jones, Sykes, Saunders, Gath, Bynum, Clay, Ashford, Sale, Goode, Dunn, Shackelford, McMahon, Fitzgerald, Burruss, Harris, Foster, Owen, Scruggs, McGregor, Watkins,* and many others of those early settlers—long since at rest.

Again a student—the young husband was installed, in 1825, in the law office of "*Ephraim H. Foster and Francis B. Fogg*," Nashville, Tenn., working ardently at his chosen profession, ever urged onward and upward by the child-wife. Commenting upon this he said recently, with quaint humor, "We studied together, and certainly she acquired great proficiency in winning *clients,* if not cases."

The first years of practice* began in Moulton (the county seat of Lawrence*). His earliest clients, he said, were, by chance, composed mainly of widows, rich and poor, and among the former was Mrs. Leetch, the honored aunt of the future President, James K. Polk, who when visiting her in 1827, formed a friendship for young Saunders, who, in 1844, as elector, threw his powerful influence throughout the State into the presidential contest in his behalf.

In 1828 he formed a law-partnership (in Courtland, Ala.) with Judge John J. Ormond, afterward of the Supreme Bench of Alabama. At this period, their legal allies—often their friendly antagonists—were those great *northern lights* of Alabama, Judges Ligon, Hopkins, Cooper and David Hubbard, M. C., and others, of each of whom he so feelingly writes, and of all of whom the "*inverted torch*" of death now but proclaims they once lived and shone.

The old historic road, cut by Gen. Andrew Jackson as a highway through Lawrence county for his troops, runs parallel with the Memphis & Charleston Railroad for many miles. Here, three miles west of Courtland, is "*Rocky Hill,*" the family home, to which Colonel Saunders came in 1832. He built just before the war a commodious residence for his large family of children, all of whom but three, he survived (the death of one of these,

---

*STATE OF ALABAMA—88.

To All Whom It May Concern:

Know ye that we, John White and John M. Taylor, Judges of the Circuit Courts of the State of Alabama, having been satisfactorily informed of the probity, honesty and good demeanor of James E. Saunders, and having examined him touching his qualifications to practise as an attorney and counsellor at law, do by virtue of the authority in us vested hereby license and permit the said James E. Saunders to practise as an attorney and counsellor at law in the several counties and Circuit Courts of the said State of Alabama. In witness whereof we have hereunto set our hands and affixed our seals this 14th day of February, 1896.

[SEAL]   JOHN WHITE.
[SEAL]   J. M. TAYLOR.

COL. JAMES EDMONDS SAUNDERS
When a young man.
Born in Virginia 1806, died 1896.

Mrs. Mary Watkins Saunders.
Born 1809, died 1889.

Col. James Edmonds Saunders
When a young man.
Born in Virginia 1806, died 1896.

Mrs. Mary Watkins Saunders.
Born 1809, died 1889.

Mrs. Hayes, following his own within six weeks), leaving the old home, once a temple of Joy, deserted and desolate on its rocky eminence. Truly—

> They build too low,
> Who build beneath the skies!

Since Indian lads and maidens played on its gentle slopes, the old home had had but two owners, and as data is preserved, it may be of interest to note that it was first bought at the government land sales in Huntsville, Ala., in 1817, by Mr. Norment, of Virginia, who the next year built a comfortable log house on the top of the hill where now stands the stately mansion. The large rocks on that hill, he said, were then "so thickly strewn, his horse could scarce pick his way among them," hence the *miles* of rock-fences on the place. Its great old oaks of to-day were then slender saplings.

With Mr. Norment came a colony of friends and relatives from Virginia, and all settled near him—among them the Butler, Sale, Burruss, Fitzgerald and Booth families, and all from Botetourt county it was said. Of these, Rev. Freeman Fitzgerald and wife Elizabeth, became the second purchasers of "*Rocky Hill.*" His daughter was married to Dr. Thomas Watkins, of Georgia (and Austin, Texas). His brother, Mr. William Fitzgerald, and "Aunt Letty," his wife (adored by her neighbors, young and old), lived nearly opposite Capt. Charles Swoope's place, at the present Barclay home, Wheeler, Ala. Mr. William Booth was brother-in-law to the Fitzgeralds. All removed many years ago to Mississippi, Florida and Louisiana, save a few of the old people, whose dust remained in Alabama.

In the neighborhood was a little Methodist chapel, *Ebenezer*, where the Rev. Turner Saunders, and his step son-in-law, Bishop Robert Paine, sometimes preached, and there Colonel Saunders was *class leader* for many years. A roll of its early members contains some names now of prominence in the South.

Near there was *LaGrange College*, founded 1830, by the Southern Methodist Church, the *second* of its establishment (Augusta College, Kentucky, being the *first*). Its site was on the low mountain overlooking the beautiful Tennessee Valley, which was dotted over with the residences of cotton planters. Bishop Robert Paine (born 1799, died 1882) was its first president. He had married Sarah Millwater, daughter of the Rev. Turner Saunders' second wife, Mrs. Millwater. Mr. Saunders was president of the Board of Trustees from the beginning.

Rev. Edward Wardsworth was its second president (1847). Among its earliest faculty were Edward D. Sims, of Virginia (afterward of the University of Alabama); Wm. W. Hudson (afterward of the University of Alabama); Dr. Harrington (died in New Orleans); Collins D. Elliott (president of Nashville Female Academy, 1844-1861); William H. Ellison, son-in-law of Bishop Capers, and afterward president of Female College, Macon, Ga., 1836; Dr. Thomas Barbour (son of Hon. Philip S. Barbour, M. C., of Virginia), afterward professor in Medical College of St. Louis; Henry Masson, of Paris, France, and Henry Tutwiler, of Virginia, and afterward of University of Alabama. Carlos G. Smith, born in Virginia, came to La Grange in 1842, and was president of University of Alabama, 1874.

Prof. J. W. Hardee was third president of La Grange, and Rev. Richard H. Rivers, the fourth. He was instrumental in having the college removed, in 1860, to it. elegant buildings in Florence, Ala., for a further field of usefulness.

"La Grange College, during its thirty years' existence, exercised great influence throughout several States, and many of its *alumni* achieved distinction; among these were Rev. R. H. Rivers (class 1835); Rev. William R. Nicholson, now bishop in Reformed Episcopal Church; Rev. Joseph E. Douglass; Dr. C. W. Bell, distinguished minister in Cumberland Presbyterian Church; Rev. B. B. Ross, beloved professor in Agricultural and Mechanical College, Alabama, over whose chair of chemistry his son, B. B. Ross, now so ably presides; and also the beloved Prof. John T. Dunklin of the same Institution. Among the lawyers and statesmen, Edward A. O'Neal, the impetuous brigadier general of the Confederacy, able lawyer, and Governor of Alabama; David P. Lewis. lawyer, and also Governor of Alabama; Col. Henry Chambers, of Mississippi, member of Congress and statesman of distinction; Jeremiah Clemens (rival of Yancey), poet and novelist, politician and lawyer, writer and speaker and United States Senator; Judge Wm. B. Wood; Wm. M. Byrd, justice of Supreme Court, Alabama; Hon. Henry C. Jones, the eloquent advocate, and others." The above was copied from the article, by Colonel Saunders, on La Grange College (with one also on the University of Alabama), published by the United States Bureau of Education in a volume, the "History of Education in Alabama," edited by Willis G. Clark, of Mobile. "Unfortunately," continued Colonel Saunders, "no regular catalogue has been preserved which might recall to memory many other distinguished pupils of La Grange."

He was its trustee all through its noble career, and his father its virtual founder. Hence, no sketch of him would be complete without linking their combined influences for education in Alabama.

He was trustee also in that great institution, the University of Alabama, when, in 1837, the Rev. Alva Woods was succeeded as president by the charming Dr. Basil Manly, and when Dr. Barnard (afterward president of Columbia College, New York) was made professor of mathematics. He continued the life-long friend of the latter of whom he wrote most tenderly in his article on the university.

The Methodist church in Courtland, of which he was long a member, was also an object of especial care. There was always reserved a "Prophet's Chamber" at "Rocky Hill" for its pastor, and all the ministry of every denomination, and night and morning the children were gathered around the family Bible for prayer. It is the unconscious reward of such parents that these remembered prayers, like the sacred oil and spikenard, make yet a holy fragrance long years after the humble vessel is broken at the Master's feet.

Mr. Saunders was now in the Legislature, and the Democratic-Republican party (at that time so called) held irresistible sway in the South, and the little burg of Courtland was thrilled to its centre when the following invitation was issued to the popular idol.

COURTLAND, 31st August, 1839.

DEAR SIR—A meeting of the Democratic Republicans in Courtland, Ala., having tendered through us, a committee, the compliment of a public dinner to the Hon. James K. Polk, and he having accepted the invitation, Tuesday, the 17th September, has been appointed for the occasion. The grounds on which we have at this time extended this invitation are fully explained in the correspondence with him, which will appear in the public papers as soon as this will reach you, and to which we invite your attention.

The public meeting by which we were nominated made it our duty to transmit to you a special invitation to this public dinner, believing that it would be in accordance with your feelings to participate in the celebration of the late victory achieved for Democratic-Republican principles in your State. We have long felt in this section of country a strong desire to see you amongst us, and to tender to you assurances of our high esteem as a patriot and a statesman. Preserving as this communication does the most grateful remembrance of your services in the field, and coinciding with you in those great political measures which have distinguished your administration, we know of no event which would give more pleasure than your attendance at our public dinner.

With assurances of the highest consideration as individuals,

Very respectfully,

ROBT. H. WATKINS.
TR. SAUNDERS.
JAMES E. SAUNDERS.
JACK SHACKELFORD.
F. W. BYNUM.

To Gen. Andrew Jackson.

It might be well to enter here, as a *political curio* for future Alabama statesmen, the toasts offered at that famous banquet:

"1. *The President of the United States.*

"2. *Ex-President Andrew Jackson.* He had more confidence in the people and the people more in him than any man now living.

"3. *'General George Washington'* 'The honest patriot of every political creed delights to dwell upon his memory.'

"4. *The memory of Thomas Jefferson.* Let political aspirants who seek to cover themselves with his mantle learn to revere his principles.

"5. *The State of Tennessee.* Too wise to be long deceived, too pure to be corrupted and too patriotic to abandon her long cherished (Democratic) Republican principles!

"6. *Our distinguished guest, the Hon. James K. Polk.* The boldness and ability and fidelity with which he has vindicated his principles in the late contest in Tennessee as well as on every occasion command the confidence of the Republican party.

"7. *Our worthy guest and chief magistrate of the State of Alabama, A. P. Bagby,* elevated to office by his Democratic fellow-citizens, his administration has been characterized by a liberal and enlightened policy which has fully met the expectations of his friends and commanded the respect of his opponents.

"8. *The (Democratic) Republican members of Congress from the State of Tennessee.* The able and efficient contributors to the late glorious triumph which we have this day met to celebrate.

"9. *R. M. Burton and Wm. G. Childress, of Tennessee.* They have fought against fearful odds and though compelled by numbers to yield the field, they have given such a demonstration as to insure us in future an easy victory.

"10. *Wm. R. King and C. C. Clay,* our dignified Senators in Congress. Faithful sentinels on the ramparts of the Constitution.

"11. *The (Democratic) Republican members of Congress from Alabama.* The people look to them to fulfil the object of their trust.

"12. *The Hon. Wm. Smith,* a veteran Republican of the Jefferson stamp. Able defender of the doctrine of *States Rights* and strict construction of the Constitution.

"13. *The ladies* who have favored us with their company; their presence has imparted additional interest to the festivities of the day."

Thus every era shifts its panorama, and the statesmen and heroes of to-day are only the *honored shades* of to-morrow! Soon after (1845) a committee, composed of Wm. McMahon, Sr., Dr. Jack Shakelford (of Mexican war fame), Thos. Ashford, Sr., Tandy W. Walker, James E. Saunders, Wiley Galloway, Michael Mays, A. S. Bentley, Jonathan Gray and Robert Fenner, were drafting resolutions "as a public testimonial to the memory of Gen. Andrew Jackson, of our gratitude for his public services, and arrangements be made for the delivery of a *funeral discourse* upon his life and services, with such ceremony as may be suitable on so solemn an occasion, and that the Rev. Robert Paine be invited to deliver the same, in Courtland," etc.

The winter of 1840 found Col. Saunders still hard at work in the Legislature at Tuscaloosa. Judge John A. Campbell, then living in Mobile, while writing him in behalf of his friend, C. C. Haygood, takes occasion to add: "I am rather inclined to think that *our* affairs (political) are beyond legislation, and I do not hope that any will be applied that will be operative of permanent good. I however feel confident that *your* efforts will be directed to the accomplishment of the good that is possible, and for the prevention of evil that is probable. With this confidence, and to express the satisfaction I feel in seeing you in public life, I write you this hasty letter."

He writes him later, and again asking his influence for Mr. Boykin as president of Mobile Bank, adding: "He is an *Alabama-educated man,* and that, too, is in these days, when State boundaries are nearly obliterated—a consideration. I feel assured that Mr. Boykin will have no opponent comparable with him in capacity or worth, and I therefore have thought I might ask your good offices in his behalf. Your friend, John A.

Campbell." Every one knows the subsequent brilliant career of John A. Campbell, which it is superfluous here to attempt to record.

It was the year of the State bank excitement (1839), when Gov. A. P. Bagley wrote him: "I am anxious to avail the State of the benefit of your services as commissioner to examine the Branch of the Bank of the State of Alabama at Decatur, and herewith enclose your appointment," etc. The crisis was passed to the satisfaction of all, and the banks put once more on a firm basis, Col. Saunders himself taking stock.

The year 1840 found Colonel Saunders the acknowledged party leader in the Lower House of the General Assembly of Alabama. As chairman of its judiciary committee, his strength in debate, and graceful bearing, gave him great distinction throughout the State. This was in the tempestuous times known as the "*coon-skin and hard-cider campaign*," with William H. Harrison ("Tippecanoe, and Tyler too") on one side and the "Little Magician," Martin Van Buren, on the other—a long paroxysm of party frenzy on both sides. He was elector for Van Buren.

                                        TUSCUMBIA, February 23, 1841.
James E. Saunders, Esq.:

SIR—As members of the Democratic party we feel great solicitude upon the subject of the selection of a suitable candidate for this district to be placed upon the Congressional ticket to be voted for at the next August election.

It is needless, we feel assured, sir, for us to make to you professions of confidence in your ability to sustain the principles of the Democratic party, and to discharge in a satisfactory manner the duties of a Representative in Congress, and we shall therefore come directly to the object of this communication, which is to ask you to inform us whether or not you will, if nominated by the District Convention, as a candidate for this Congressional district, accept the nomination.

Permit us to add the request (and to urge your compliance) that you will attend the Circuit Court of Limestone on Monday next, and reply to General Lewis, who will address the people on that day at Athens.

                  Most respectfully, your obedient servants,
                        P. WALKER.   WM. WINSTON.
                        JOHN T. ABERNATHY.   C. COOPER.
        N. B.   C. T. BARTON.   G. W. CARROLL.

Mr. J. E. Saunders:

DEAR SIR—I have just returned from a tour through Limestone county, and find that it is the general wish of the Democratic party that you should suffer your name to be run. I assure you that, according to my opinion, you are the strongest man we have, and I hope you will suffer your name to be run. If we are beaten next August, we, as a party, are done.   Most respectfully,

                                               JOHN S. ABERNATHY.

These honors he gratefully declined. His profession, and health restricted his services within *State bounds*, and he was never afterward induced to change his decision, though repeatedly urged for public posts of great honor.

                                        ATHENS, Ala., November 7, 1843.
James E. Saunders, Esq.:

DEAR SIR—The time is approaching (and in fact it has already arrived) when it becomes necessary to make arrangements for the approaching campaign of '44. One of the important steps with our party is the selecting of electors on our ticket. In casting about over the district I can conceive of no man more suitable than yourself for that office, and I therefore have thought proper to address you on that subject. I am not alone in believing you the most fit man for that important station. My wish is to know if you will accept the appointment if tendered to you by the State convention, which is to assemble at Tuscaloosa next winter. If it should be in accordance with your inclination I should be happy for the cause's sake. There will be some hard battles to be fought next summer. I wish a man whom I have confidence in to manœuvre our forces against the artful machinations of the Federal hosts.

You will please answer this as soon as your convenience will permit.

Your friend and humble servant,

THOS. H. WILSON.

And again he became Elector for his party and for James K. Polk, his friend.

His arduous practice and public speaking had so impaired his health that in 1843 he decided to make Mobile, Ala., his *winter home*. Two years later he was appointed collector of customs of that port by Mr. Polk. He became director in the Bank of Mobile, and now formed a cotton commission house with his brother-in-law, Gen. Benj. M. Bradford, of Mississippi, which firm, when his eldest son, Robert, came of age was later known as "James E. Saunders & Son," and which transacted large business with his friends and patrons in Alabama and Mississippi, and elsewhere.

In 1852 he served his State again as elector for Pierce and King.

The South, lashed to fury, was now rallying its brightest talents, its last resources. About this time the following tribute was sent to one, afterward too weak or too indifferent, as President of the United States, to avert the storm of insult and desolation that fell upon his native South :

COURTLAND, LAWRENCE COUNTY, August 22, 1855.

SIR—Your Democratic fellow-citizens of Courtland and its vicinity have witnessed your public career with much interest, especially during the last gubernatorial canvass in your State, when, under unpropitious circumstances, you nobly defended and maintained the great principles of the Democratic-Republican party, the preservation of which we conceive to be partial to the liberty of the citizen and the perpetuation of the Union. You achieved a triumph in this struggle which reflects distinguished honor on your character as a man, and abilities as a statesman. During this contest you have had our warmest sympathies ; and as a committee appointed by a meeting of our fellow-citizens held this morning, we invite you to partake of a public dinner, at such time as may suit your personal convenience, as a testimonial of our high appreciation of your public services.

We are, with high regard, your obedient servants,

O. H. BYNUM,	WM. GRAHAM,	DRURY MAYES,
JACK SHACKELFORD,	M. I. GILCHRIST,	S. W. SHACKELFORD,
THOMAS ASHFORD,	EDWARD SHACKELFORD,	JOSEPH M. TWEEDY,
P. P. GILCHRIST,	JAMES HOLMES,	JOHN H. HARRIS,
DAVID BRIEDENTHAL,	T. T. TWEEDY,	JAMES E. SAUNDERS,
		Committee.

His Excellency Andrew Johnson, Governor of Tennessee.

In 1860 he served, once more, as elector, and for Stephen A. Douglass, in the vain hope of averting the swift-descending horrors of civil war ; President of the convention which met at Montgomery, June 4, 1860, he threw his strong influence into the cause of peace. But in vain, for, in the destiny of nations, *the hour had come!*

Then rudely was the South awakened. Bravely her sons rushed to battle. And since he could not serve his country in peace, he would defend her in war—white-haired and enfeebled as he was. From her sister States came the call to Alabama!

The grand warrior, Wallenstein, has said, "the narrow path of duty is securest." It is the martial key-note to the life of all great soldiers, whatever the struggle—safety is found nowhere else.

The defences of Mobile were rapidly pushed, and fairest hands labored making sandbags for the fortifications at Fort Morgan. With other determined citizens, he freely spent his means and energies in hurrying its progress.

Then came the War Governor's call for troops for *one year*. It sent Alabamians cheering to the front, and to the gulf coast. Close upon this followed an appeal for volunteers " to the citizens of North Alabama," from their representatives in Legislature assembled, as follows:

TO THE CITIZENS OF NORTH ALABAMA.

In pursuance of a requisition made by Gen. A. S. Johnston, under the authority of the War Department, upon Alabama for twelve months' troops, the Governor issued his late proclamation, calling upon our section of the State for volunteers, for that term. We have seen the letter of General Johnston, and believe that we are correctly advised of our true situation—of the forces of the enemy, as well as our means of resistance. We would not needlessly alarm or excite our people, but we would earnestly impress upon them the necessity of the most prompt and energetic action, by which we are confident success can be obtained; while, without such action, success is doubtful. The enemy is concentrating in heavy force upon Columbus, Ky., and if we are overwhelmed with numbers at that point, Memphis will next be invested—the contest will have to be carried on in East Tennessee, and your own valley may suffer the unspeakable horrors of invasion from a ruthless and unrelenting foe. Prudence and safety require us to meet the enemy on the threshold—to defend the outposts rather than the citadel—the door-sill rather than the hearthstone. The valley of the Tennessee has already sent forth her volunteers to defend the soil of Virginia, and to protect our gulf coast from invasion; it is necessary that they should rally now for the protection of their own families and firesides. This can best be done by defending Columbus and Memphis. Your volunteers are required at the *earliest possible moment;* no time is to be lost ! Every arrangement is made to facilitate the transportation of troops to the points where their services will be required, and to supply them with subsistence and equipments. All they want to be prepared to start, are arms !—shotguns or rifles, their bullet moulds, shot pouches and powder flasks ! Every gun which is furnished will be returned, or paid for; and no man who has one should hesitate in furnishing it to those who are to use it for his defence. The honor as well as the safety of the State is involved in promptly responding to the requisition, and thus avoiding the necessity of meeting the exigency by a draft upon the militia, which must otherwise be resorted to.

As your representatives, we have deemed it advisable, in view of the momentous interests which are involved, to address you, and most earnestly to solicit your speedy action.

Editors are requested not to publish, but to use every other means, to circulate.

R. M. PATTON (afterward J. A. WITHERSPOON, Gov.)
WM. M. JACKSON,
O. O. NELSON,
A. A. HUGHES,
R. JEMISON, JR.,
WM. H. JEMISON,
F. W. SYKES (afterward U. S. C. POSEY, S. Senator)
WM. M. GRIFFIN,
A. SNODGRASS,
G. W. MALONE,
JOHN D. MILLER,
A. R. BRINDLEY,
J. B. TALLEY,
L. W. LYNCH,

J. C. ORR,
T. M. HARDWICK,
FRANCIS W. RICE,
JONATHAN LATHAM,
T. T. COTNAM,
THOMAS J. McLELLAND,
J. P. COMAN,
JAMES SHELTON,
S. D. CABANISS,
T. L. HAMMOND,
CANNADAY BUTLER,
W. W. LITTLE,
T. A. WALKER,
S. M. CARRUTH,
S. D. McCLELLAN,

W. B. MARTIN,
R. ELLIS,
E. ALDRIDGE,
W. N. CRUMP,
A. J. COLEMAN,
JAMES MIDDLETON,
J. W. LOGAN,
M. L. DAVIS,
J. A. HILL,
WM. GRAVLEE,
L. W. LAWLER,
GEO. S. WADEN,
CHAS. CARTER,
B. W. GROCE,
R. O. PICKETT.

Montgomery, Ala., December 1, 1861.

Colonel Saunders had already returned to his beloved Tennessee Valley, earnestly studying its resources for resistance, when he received the following, (and afterwards others of its kind), so that, in all, five hundred negro men were carried to the fortifications of Forts Hindman and Henry. Each of the six valley counties, Franklin, Lawrence, Limestone, Lauderdale, Madison and Morgan, furnishing its quota, gotten up by military committees:

FROM MONTGOMERY, February 22, 1862.

To James E. Saunders, Courtland:

The Valley of the Tennessee must furnish for its defence two hundred negro fellows with the least possible delay. You are authorised as my especial aide-de-camp to call upon the people in my name and to apportion the slaves to be furnished by each county. You will report to Gen. L. P. Walker,* and the negroes will be under his orders.

JOHN GILL SHORTER, *Governor of Alabama.*

The military committee were: Wm. Cooper, Dr. Deshler and Wm. Dickson, of Franklin county; E. M. Swoope, G. Garth and F. Sykes, of Lawrence county; Dr. Dancey, Wm. Burleson and Mr. Garth, of Morgan county; S. Willis Harris and others, of Madison county; S. W. Donell, and others, of Limestone; James Ervine, G. W. Foster, and others, of Lauderdale.

See "Life of Gen. Albert Sidney Johnston," by his distinguished son, Col. Wm. Preston Johnston, for the vigorous efforts of Colonel Saunders in assisting in constructing the defences of the forts.

In meanwhile his eldest son, Major Robert T. Saunders, was serving on General Cocke's staff in Virginia.

His second son, Dr. Dudley Dunn Saunders, was at that time surgeon at the hospital post established at Chattanooga, Tenn.

And to this point had rallied many Confederate chiefs, as to the gateway of the South. Colonel Saunders was now on Gen. John Adams' staff, and the invasion of north Alabama by the enemy through Chattanooga being imminent, the Chiefs cast about for an invincible leader, and Colonel Saunders was deputised to hasten to General Beauregard, at Tupelo, and implore an able officer, as the different and *differing* officers at Chattanooga were at variance as to *who* should be chief among them.

The late Major Rambaut, of *Memphis, Tenn.*, at the time of his death (February, 1886) was preparing a series of articles on the "Campaigns of Gen. Bedford N. Forrest." It was at the urgent request of the "Confederate Historical Society," because there was no other man who had the information necessary. He was the only survivor save Dr. J. B. Cowan, who, as staff officer, was with Forrest during all of his campaigns.

His first article was upon "Forrest at *Shiloh.*" From the *second,* "Forrest at Murfreesboro," we make this extract: "Upon the retreat of General Beauregard's army from Corinth, Forrest continued in his rear and flank with the usual skirmishing and fighting. He arrived at Tupelo latter part of May, and camped just across the lagoon, from what was, then, the noted David Crockett Railway.

He was at that place (June) when Col. James E. Saunders, father of our townsman, Dr. D. D. Saunders (he being at that time on the staff of Gen. John Adams), visited Tupelo with the request that General Beauregard would assign a competent officer to the defence of Chattanooga, and asking for the assignment of *General Forrest.*

At first the request was declined, as General Beauregard appreciated the services of Forrest and did not want to give him up, but upon considering the importance of the request, and of a good officer being in command at the point named, he ordered General Forrest to take command of the same, and recommending to the War Department his promotion to Brigadier General.

*First Secretary of War.

Forrest left the next day (with Colonel Saunders), taking with him an escort* of ten picked men detailed from his own regiment (all he was allowed). Arriving at Chattanooga June 19, 1863, he at once reported to General Ledbetter, of Kirby Smith's department, and assumed command, under orders, of the brigade composed of the Eighth Texas, Col. J. A. Wheaton; First Louisiana, Col. J. W. Scott; Second Georgia, Col. J. E. Lawton; Helm's Kentucky Regiment, Lieut. Col. T. Woodward; and a battalion of Tennesseeans under Maj. Baxter Smith—the whole about 2000 men.

Colonel Scott at once raised the question as to date of commissions, claiming that he (Scott) ranked Forrest. The entire command were strangers to Forrest, and he to them, except by reputation, and they were in rather a dissatisfied condition, more especially Colonel Woodward's command, which had shortly before suffered defeat in a surprise in the Sequatchie Valley. Many little things of minor importance tended to add to their dissatisfaction.

Forrest at once set to work to equip the command by placing them, as rapidly as possible, in fighting condition—satisfied the quicker he gave battle to the enemy, the sooner the trouble would be overcome.

A few days later the question of seniority was settled by Colonel Scott being relieved, and the First Georgia battalion, Colonel Morrison, assigned instead.

This was hardly settled when another trouble arose by the expiration of the period of enlistment of the majority of the companies of *Helm's Regiment*, and all of them left except two companies (Colonel Helm was a brother-in-law of President Lincoln).

Forrest, learning there was a Federal force at Murfreesboro, determined at once to move and attack them (moving in the direction of Sparta). His forces now numbered something over 1300 men. He arrived at McMinnville on the evening of July 12. It was at this point he first made known his intention to attack the troops at Murfreesboro. Continuing his march to Woodbury, he arrived there about midnight. The streets were thronged with ladies, who stated that the evening before, the Federals had arrested and carried off to Murfreesboro nearly every man, old and young. Many wives and sisters had followed them, seeking to obtain their release. They crowded around Forrest telling of the arrest of fathers, husbands, brothers, torn away from them without notice, and pleaded with these stalwart, gallant men to befriend them. Did this inspire those true boys as they rode out of Woodbury? * * * Forrest had told them they should have their loved ones again before night had passed.

"He pushed on with his command, and arrived in the vicinity of Murfreesboro about 5 o'clock the next morning, 13th of July, sending forward a force to capture the pickets, which was done by Captains Anderson and James (the latter's home being in Murfreesboro). Scouts reported the situation of the Federal encampment, and that they were unaware of the impending danger. The Eighth Texas, under Colonel Wharton, was ordered forward, to charge them in platoons. The Second Georgians were sent through the main streets to capture the provost guard, and Federal officers and men; and to secure supplies and arms. Major Baxter Smith with his battalion, and the two companies of Kentuckians, were ordered out on the turnpike leading to Nashville and Lebanon, to cut off retreat and guard against approach from that direction, and Colonel Morrison assigned to the enemy's rear. Wharton now charged into the very heart of the Federal encampment. They were for awhile surprised in their tents, and rushed out in confusion, hotly pursued by the Texans. Their infantry rallied and made a stand. By mistaking orders, or by an accident, only some 200 men had followed Wharton in his charge, the remainder of his regiment going with the Second Georgians into the public square (which contained the court house). The Texans were brought to a halt; under a heavy fire of musketry from behind wagons, and under cover, and owing to the

---

* These ten heroes were chosen by Forrest himself for their bravery and devotion. It is remembered that six out of the ten were Maj. J. P. Strange, of Memphis; G. V. Rambaut, Wm. H. Forrest, Jos. Sheridan, Matt. Turton and Fred. Koerper, the dauntless; Capt. W. E. McGuire, the fearless scout, afterward joined them.

enemy's numbers were unable to carry the position and were forced to fall back on the McMinnville road, with a number of prisoners captured, including a cavalry force which had been detached from the infantry, and captured before they could get to their horses.

Major Baxter Smith with his battalion assisted in this capture. The remainder of the Eighth Texans and the Second Georgians had charged into the square and surrounded the court house, which was occupied by a company of Michigan infantry.

The firing had brought a large number of citizens, mostly *en deshabille*, into our lines notwithstanding the danger. The Federals were now firing from behind fences and houses, as well as from the court house, and the fire was very severe. They were twice repulsed. During the engagement we were being continually cheered by the men and women of the town.

The Texans and Georgians were now led by Forrest himself, and pressed forward notwithstanding the fire from the court house. Morrison brought up his men in the rear, and on the east side; and the doors were battered-down and the court house captured. It was here that Fred. Koeper, of Memphis (and one of the ten men of Forrest's escort) was killed. He was of daring bravery, genial and cheerful, and beloved by the old regiment. The citizen prisoners, in the court house and jail (including those from Woodbury), were promptly released, and Federal officers, and men, captured from many places of shelter sought in their flight.

Among them was Brigadier General Crittenden, who was captured by Colonel Saunders at a boarding-house on the square. As Colonel Saunders and his detachment were riding across the square, the firing being opened upon them from the court house, a ball passed through his right lung, and entirely through his body. He was carried to the residence of a citizen (Colonel Ledbetter), where he was left, supposed to be mortally wounded. Be it remembered, Colonel Saunders was the same who made the application to General Beauregard for Forrest's assignment, and was serving on Forrest's staff at the time. This gallant officer must have been 58 years of age, and was serving with distinction on Forrest's staff. I had the pleasure of meeting him only a few months ago (1895) while visiting his son, Dr. D. D. Saunders, and his daughter, Mrs. L. B. McFarland of this city, and had several pleasant hours of conversation with him, which was greatly enjoyed by both, discussing olden times. He was still well preserved, hearty and robust, though now 90 years old. He deserves to "live always and never grow old." Major Rambaut continued the narration of this brilliant victory to the end. He died (February, 1896) ere he finished his "Sketch of Forrest's Campaigns," and his old friend died the following summer. Colonel Jordan, in his "Life of General Forrest," says: "While the battle of Murfreesboro was progressing General Forrest sent Colonel Saunders with a small detachment to capture Brigadier General Crittenden, supposed to be hidden in the Inn on the public square, his headquarters. In returning from their ineffectual search a general fire from the enemy was opened upon them from the windows of the court house, and that brave and zealous gentleman received a ball which passed entirely through his right lung and body. He nevertheless sat erect in his saddle and rode several squares to the house of a citizen, into which he was taken, as all supposed, mortally wounded." * * *

The result of this campaign was an immense amount of army material and 1765 prisoners. In addition to these prisoners 102 straggling fugitive Federals came into Murfreesboro after General Forrest had left, and seeking out Colonel Saunders, who had been left in their midst, as they supposed mortally wounded, besought him to parole them, which he did in due form, desperately wounded as he was. Colonel Saunders not only got well, but got well without a fever, and after his recovery enjoyed a nearer approach to robust health than ever before. Since then he has been engaged in writing on horticulture, and in carrying on his planting interests that were so really interrupted by those eventful years when he and other patriotic souls "rode with Forrest!"

In after years, when the eagle-eyed, lion-hearted hero, Forrest, wasting with disease, was equipping his dauntless will to meet the last grim Foe, to make, alas! the great "surrender," yet again he came, weary pilgrim of life, to "Rocky Hill," his old friend's hospitable doors, where the clang and clash of his saber and spurs had often made such martial music. But now he fain would rest—and he wanted the ever-loyal and approving eyes of his old comrade to fall upon him, soothingly as of old—he in whom the "wild fever, called living" was nearly spent!

Meek—and *sublimed* to a strange gentleness, the worn victor of a hundred fields here did seem to "importune death awhile" that he might once more commune, soul to soul, with his friends, while the evening shadows closed around him. Purified of earthly dross, he knelt at the old family altar, again in heart a child, while his white-hair host and comrade, breathed over him the "*nunc dimittis*" of life's solemn close. And thus they bade each other the last farewell—and he was gone! Two weeks later the great General drifted out into the Unknown, and his aged host and hostess yet lived on, to bless their day and generation for many years.

Of the men wounded and made prisoners in the battle of Murfreesboro with Colonel Saunders, he has preserved an official list; also the killed, and those who died. It may be of value to the families of these men, and hence is published here for preserva-tion.

WOUNDED.

Davis Morris, Atlanta, Second Georgia Regiment; David McCann, Company K, Texas Rangers; Griffin B. Kennedy, Company C, Texas Rangers; S. Carter, Company K, Eighth Texas Cavalry, paroled by General Nelson; John Fenner, Company K, Eighth Texas Cavalry; Lt. James A. Collins, Company K, Eighth Texas; Nicholas Munks, Com-pany B, Eighth Texas; William H. Morgan, Company A, First Georgia Cavalry; Dr. Brock, First Georgia; John Palmer, Texas Rangers; J. F. M. Smith, Company A, First Georgia; John N. Perkins; Dr. Zuber, Company A, First Georgia: Robert Paine, Com-pany F, Second Georgia Cavalry, Robert Adams, Company F, Second Georgia Cavalry.

KILLED.

E. A. Ross, Company A, Texas Rangers (Milam county); Scott Green, Texas Rangers, Hamilton county; Wm. D. Morse, Chapel Hill, Washington county, Texas; Wm. Dallas, Cave Spring, Georgia; Dr. Williams, killed 13th of July; Henry J. Mor-ris, of Georgia; William Hale, Georgia.

DIED OF WOUNDS.

Wooten Williams, Georgia Cavalry, 14th of July, 1863; F. M. Faris, Second Georgia, died 15th of July, 1863; Samuel Mimms, Texas Rangers; Oscar Mumford, B. D. Buckner Parker, First Georgia, Vann's Valley; A. J. Duron, Georgia; Thomas Hig-don, Georgia; Jas. Hicks, Second Georgia, Randolph county; Captain Searight, Dr. H. Witcher, First Georgia; E. Scarborough, Company C, Texas Rangers; T. B. Ivie, First or Second Georgia Regiment, Russell county; Captain Crabb, died at Dr. Avent's, and removed; A. A. Thurman, Georgia Cavalry, Carable's company, 15th July; Fred. Koeper, of Memphis, died 14th July, 1862 (one of Forrest's ten picked men). *Graves without names,* seven in number.

Among Colonel Saunders' war correspondence a few notes, telegrams and letters relating to the invasion of the Tennessee Valley have been selected at random, with some others in the order of their dates (1861-1865), as throwing light on the rapidly-transpiring events of that time, and giving some additional *data* to the history of the Civil War.

They begin with a letter from Col. Edward W. Munford, of Gen. Albert Sidney Johnston's staff, relative to the general's requisition for Alabama volunteers, follo wed by a complication with Major J. W. Robertson, of the Military Academy, Marietta' Ga., as to the calling out of his "battalion of cadets," followed by letters from various officers at different posts, but always looking to the defence of his *beloved valley.* After being shot entirely through the right lung at the battle of Murfreesboro, July 13, 1863, Colonel Saunders was incapacitated for continued active duty in the field, but used ardently all other means of assisting the cause, while also directing movements as well as he could; his advice always having great weight with the various commanding officers, who trusted to his experience and his superior knowledge of every foot of ground over which they fought, as the within communications will fully attest:

> HEADQUARTERS, WESTERN DEPARTMENT, }
> BOWLING GREEN, Ky., December 2, 1861. }

Hon. James E. Saunders:

    SIR—Enclosed you will please find a letter to General Weakly. It contains the orders of General Johnston in reference to the mustering in and sending forward the volunteers from North Alabama. It was written by my hand, and I think covers every point you made in conversation with me as to transporting the volunteers and slaves from Florence.

    It is sent to you because I am not certain that Florence is Weakly's postoffice. You know, and will have the letter *put into his hands at once.* Compliments to your family.

> Your friend, etc.,
>
> ED. W. MUNFORD.

> MARIETTA, Ga., December 4, 1861.

Hon. Jas. E. Saunders:

    DEAR SIR—Your favor of the 2d inst. at hand.

    From your letter to the Governor, I infer that General Johnson does not consider the emergency sufficiently great to cause him to *use his influence* in having the proposed battalion accepted for three months. If so, I do not consider it *necessary* that I should risk breaking up the academy in order that I may serve in the field for three months.

    I also infer from your letter that General Johnson would not object to having me and my men at Fort Dixon, but would rather prefer it, as we could be of service in *drilling* the men stationed there. I can not consent to go to Fort Dixon as an *instructor* of tactics. The service to be rendered does not, in my judgment, warrant the sacrifices that would have to be made in order that the service might be rendered.

    My impression (when I consented to try and raise the battalion) was that Alabama was in danger from an invasion by the way of the river, and that men were wanted to protect laborers to be used in erecting a fortification on the river and to defend the work until it could be garrisoned. Under this impression I proposed to give my services for three months, and make any sacrifice necessary to protect the State. Your interview with General Johnson has convinced me that invasion by way of the river is at least not probable.

    I am not *seeking* service in the *field,* and was not actuated in proposing to serve three months by any *desire* for military distinction, but simply thought that a necessity for my services in the field had arisen and I would cheerfully do all in my power. I am now convinced from your interview with General Johnson that the *necessity* does *not* exist, and shall, therefore, turn to my other duties, and remain prepared to give my time, energy or life to the cause when either may be of more *use* to the country in the field than in my present position.   Very respectfully,

> J. W. ROBERTSON.

> HEADQUARTERS WESTERN DEPARTMENT, }
> BOWLING GREEN, Ky., December 22, 1861. }

Col. Jas. E. Saunders:

    DEAR SIR—I reply to your letter at my earliest opportunity after returning, and hope to make the matter of the "Battalion" of Cadets clear.

    General Johnston says he has *never,* since coming to this command, had the *slightest doubt*, nor has he any now, that to resist the threatened invasion we will need *every* man we can get; that he would be most happy to accept the services of Robertson's *battalion*, if it was put in such shape that he could do so. He has called on the Governor of Alabama for volunteers for twelve months. The Governor has issued his proclamation accordingly. The troops are being raised under the authority of that State, and when sent to the rendezvous fixed upon by the orders of the Governor they will immediately be mustered into the Confederate service, and put upon duty. He says, further, that he has *no authority whatever* to accept troops otherwise than as raised and sent to rendezvous by the States respectively embraced in his command. It is obvious, therefore, that these, or any other battalions or regiments coming from Alabama, must come *through State authority* to him, and he fears if even the Governor were to accept *volunteers* for three months (even a battalion) it would put an end to volunteering under the twelve months' call. Such a distinction he thinks the Governor would be reluctant to make. In Mississippi, the sixty-day men are raised by *special act of the Legislature*, and it is *only* another mode of getting up the militia men.

He says that it was only in consequence of the value he attached to Robertson's accomplishments as a trained and educated officer that he suggested the benefits which would result to the service from his training the volunteers fresh from home in tactics, and he supposed that no more grateful occupation for himself and the young cadets could well be imagined than that of devoting their leisure to perfecting in the military art the very men by whose sides they might be called to fight in resisting an invasion of their common homes—certainly by the suggestion he never dreamed of giving offence, nor did he misinterpret Robertson's position as one who was ambitiously seeking active service in the field. He only viewed it as a patriotic offer of his services, and appreciated it fully. He is anxious to have the services of this battalion, and never dreamed of there being no intention of invading by the Tennessee river. Indeed, he thinks the emergency *most pressing* both by that line and on this, and wants every man whom he can *lawfully* receive. Under the act of the Confederate Congress, the President *alone* can receive volunteers *for special service*. General Johnston has no such discretionary power. I have given the points. You can digest them and make a more happy answer to his letter than I feel I have done to yours.

We do not know when we will be involved in the hardest sort of fighting on this line. If the enemy would come here, his overwhelmingly superior forces would only show him how superior our comparatively few men with their convictions and feelings are to his. But they will try to turn this position and get to Nashville by another route, and we may be taken at a disadvantage of necessity. O, that we had troops—troops— troops. But they will dearly win their laurels if they win them from this army at all.

I can not, of course, give you very much information. We are getting men, but too · slowly by long odds. We need them now, and they need drilling and disciplining to make them really serviceable. However, all that human skill, energy and pluck can do under the circumstances will be done. Stir up your Alabama volunteers; make fragmentary companies, consolidate, and tell Judge Picket, for God's and his country's sake, never to say again to any mortal man when the military authorities have called for troops, that *he* "thinks they are *not needed*." You will hear of this and its consequences if you see Judge Lewis.

Good-by. Your friend,

ED. W. MUNFORD.

CORINTH, Miss., March 24, 1862.

Col. J. E. Saunders:

DEAR SIR—I wrote you from Fort Pillow. Now we are here. After a trip to Bethel, Tenn., and a detached service of guarding the railroad. I was ordered to guard a point of railroad this side of Bethel, where I spent several days in a perilous place. I, however, got on finely, having one little spat, and killing one scoundrel of the vandal tribe. Nobody hurt on my side. I am suffering a good deal from cold, both in person

and in men. I have eighty-seven men in my company. Dr. B. B. Poellnitz is sick
from cold; Capt. J. M. Rembert is standing it finely. Should you find time to visit us
call and see the Twenty-first Alabama. I would not be surprised, at any time, to receive
marching orders to go up your way, as rumor has it that the enemy is making toward
Decatur. I have no idea that they will leave their gunboats and the river so that we can
get a fight. I wish they would give us a fight here, and let us prove our strength and
determination. These are hard times; hard on men's constitution, morals and everything. I heard from home a week ago; all were well. Give my kindest regards to the
family, and believe me ready to *die or be free.*

Should we get nearer you we will expect you to visit us. How far are you from
Decatur, or Florence?

Yours,

S. S. TAYLOR,
Commanding Company E, Twenty-first Regiment, Alabama Volunteers.

NOTE.—When the following was written, Colonel Saunders was in command of the advance of
the brigade sent by General Beauregard to the relief of the Valley of the Tennessee, under Gen. John
Adams.

BRIGADE HEADQUARTERS,
CAMP TOUTE, ON CLEAR CREEK,
SIX MILES FROM CORINTH, April 30, 1862.

Colonel Saunders, on Crippled Deer Creek, Aide-de-Camp:

COLONEL—After much difficulty, I arrived here this morning with Tennessee regiment, at 7 o'clock. The roads are almost impassable. It is now raining. I fear
it will be impracticable to move more than three companies forward to-day; they can
not leave before evening.

McLelland's Tennessee battalion has been assigned to my command. As yet, I
don't know where it is. The two Louisiana companies I hope will be with me to-day or
to-morrow. I must be with you to-morrow, and will move forward as rapidly as possible. Please direct Captain Houston, as commanding officer Texas Rangers, to move his
entire command to Bear Creek. If practicable, his depot will be at Bear Creek bridge,
or Russellville.

My assistant adjutant general has not yet found me.

I fear it will be impracticable to purchase forage. Sent forward, yesterday, men,
who were not successful; will dispatch them again to-day. I have plenty of funds to
pay all. Yours, etc. JOHN ADAMS,
Colonel Commanding Brigade.

BRIGADE HEADQUARTERS, May 1, 1862.

Colonel Saunders, Aide-de-Camp:

COLONEL—I have just received the enclosed communication from General Beall, commanding, from which you will perceive I have lost Biffle and Gordon's Battalion, and, I
fear, also McLelland's Battery, and the two Louisiana companies. I shall be at Bear
Creek ("Nixon's Bridge") to-night, with Texas Rangers, and, I hope, the remainder
of Kentucky Cavalry. Please have camp selected, as also independent camp for my
headquarters.

Yours truly,

JOHN ADAMS, Com. Brig.

HEADQUARTERS CAVALRY BRIGADE,
TUSCUMBIA, Ala., May 3, 1862.

Col. J. E. Saunders:

SIR—I will arrive at Lamb's Ferry on to-morrow evening at 2 o'clock, and desire
you to make all necessary arrangements for the crossing of the river with my command
as expeditiously as possible. I may select Bainbridge, Lamb's Ferry, or a point still

higher up the river as a place for crossing. You will, by return courier, give me the information you may have, as to the facilities for crossing at Lamb's Ferry, the number and description of boats that will be in readiness. And you will also inform me concerning forage.   Respectfully,

JOHN ADAMS, *Com. Brig.*

COURTLAND, February 26, 1863.

Colonel Saunders, Decatur, Ala.:

SIR—A courier from Captain May reports the enemy from three to five hundred strong at Abernathy's. The rains will prevent them from crossing Town Creek for a day or two yet, unless they fix the railroad bridge. I sent a scout in the direction of the head of that creek, via the bridge, early this morning, also toward Bainbridge. Be so kind as to hurry up reinforcements as fast as possible. I should like much to start to-night to head the creek and bag the party at Abernathy. I could do it easily with two hundred men, and will start as soon as help arrives. "Looking the facts in the face," I think that my attempt to hold this place with the small number of men I have at present would be folly. I shall stay, however, and check their advance by such means as are in my power. If reinforcements come I wish Ferrell's Battery to return. The picket duties are heavy on my little band. I will keep you informed of all that occurs. Captain Powell started over the river this morning after the men on the other side, who, I regret to hear, having no arms have scattered much. I am doing my utmost to get all the command to the river—Lamb's Ferry.

I am, Colonel, most respectfully your obedient servant,

G. L. BAXTER.

P. S.—I have just received information from Abernathy, per Mr. W. Sherrod, who says that Abernathy was taken away a prisoner and treated very badly. I have just started a force to cut down the Town Creek railroad bridge, and scout until relieved. The vandals are acting in perfect accordance with their Hessian character, stealing everything portable and destroying what they can not carry away.

DECATUR, 27th February, 1863.

Captain Ferrill, Commanding Battery of Artillery:

SIR—A dispatch has just been received from General Bragg ordering your battery to return. Have everything ready for a movement, even to the harness on your horses.

Reinforcement will reach here in the morning.

JAMES E. SAUNDERS.

DECATUR, 27th February, 1863.

Gen. Braxton Bragg:

Your dispatch has been received; sent to Captain Ferrell, and the boats ready to convey the reinforcement.

We heard from Captain Baxter at Courtland last evening; the enemy, some 500 strong, were at Leighton—how many lower down was not known. The rains will prevent their crossing Town Creek for several days. The railroad bridge over it was broken in yesterday. Captain Baxter was advised to stay and check the advance of the enemy, and that troops would be sent. The vandals are acting in perfect accordance with their character.

JAMES E. SAUNDERS.

LA GRANGE, Ala., May 30, 1863.

Col. James E. Saunders:

DEAR SIR—Enclosed you will find the *original* pass which was given to my little

---

* NOTE.—Colonel Saunders was stationed on duty at Decatur at this time.

brother by the Federal commander during their recent raid in our county, and which, at your request, I send to you. With kind regards to yourself and wife,

I am very respectfully yours,

MRS. MOLLIE H. HUNT.

Attention, Angels, of Tenth Missouri, and Seventh Kansas Cavalry! This scion of Southern chivalry being rather adolescent for military duty is herewith permitted to return to his home and friends, and must not be molested by the destroying Angels of this command.

Done west of Tuscumbia, one mile, April 29, 1863.

FLORENCE M. COMYN,
Colonel Tenth Missouri Cavalry, Commanding Cavalry Brigade.

HEADQUARTERS EIGHTH TENNESSEE CAVALRY, }
EIGHT MILES WEST OF FLORENCE, 7 P. M., }
May 4, 1863. }

Capt. J. J. Scanlan, Esq., Tuscumbia:

DEAR SIR—I will cross the river at Garner's Ferry at as early an hour as possible, and move directly for Fulton, Miss. Being unacquainted with the country, I would be very glad if you, or Mr. Warren, would secure a guide and have him to meet me early in the morning at the ferry; we move at 4 A. M. If you have an opportunity notify General Forrest that we are over there, and that all is quiet on this side of the river. Colonel Forrest has crossed at Decatur, and is following on; I will leave a small force and artillery on this side of the river, also our baggage. Please tender Colonel Saunders my thanks for his kind suggestions and valuable information.

Very respectfully your obedient servant,

G. G. DIBRELL,
Colonel Eighth Tennessee Cavalry.

BRIGADE HEADQUARTERS, MOULTON, Ala., May 12, 1863.

COLONEL—I will be here until the morning of the 16th inst., and will then move with my command to Mississippi. Would be glad you would come up here, as I am anxious to see you before I go. Come if you possibly can.

Very respectfully your friend,

N. B. FORREST, *Brig. Gen.*

Col. James E. Saunders.

MOULTON, Ala., 12th, 1863.

COLONEL—Since writing you this morning I have received dispatches ordering me back to Tennessee. Can you meet me in Decatur, Ala., to-night or early to-morrow morning, as I wish to see you.

Respectfully your friend,

N. B. FORREST, *Brig. Gen.*

Col. J. E. Saunders.

SOUTHWESTERN TELEGRAPH COMPANY.

By Telegraph from Huntsville, Ala., March 13, 1863.

To Jas. E. Saunders:

I find it necessary for me to see General Bragg. I may return on first train. I am trying to get General Bragg to allow me to remain in valley with my brigade. I may return to Athens. Meet me there with my staff Friday or Saturday.

N. B. FORREST, *Brig. Gen.*

Col. James E. Saunders: HUNTSVILLE, Ala., May 16, 1863.

SIR—There are difficulties, in reference to the distribution of the horses and mules, captured near Rome, Georgia, with Colonel Straight's command, which will require much patience and judgment to remove.

In the rapid and long continued pursuit, which preceded this capture, the Federals first mounted (as I am informed) several hundred of their infantry who had marched on foot as far as Mt. Hope, Alabama, and afterward in the flight, whenever their horses were jaded they seized the horses of the citizens; and again, after the capture, when our cavalry were ordered to return to their rendezvous at Danville, many of their horses being completely exhausted, they had from necessity to leave them in the drove and be re-mounted on others which were fresher.

When the embarrassments connected with the separation of the interests of the Con-federate government and the citizens in this property were reported to General Bragg, he instructed me to use my own discretion as to the mode of settlement.

I therefore commit the duty of adjudicating this matter to you. You may call in citizens of high standing to assist you. Quartermasters in possession of the property shall manage and transfer it as you may direct. In deciding on the distribution, guide yourself (as far as practicable) by the following rules:

1. Where horses of citizens happen to have been taken by our cavalry, give citizens certificates of the value of the horses thus taken and pay them in stock on valuation or at public vendue.

2. Where citizens can identify their horses or mules, now in the drove, deliver the property.

3. Place in the hands of the citizens, robbed of their work animals, a sufficient num-ber of mules and horses to enable them to cultivate their crops (not to exceed two hun-dred) requiring for them receipts for the delivery of horses and mules on the first day of October at the town of Moulton, North Alabama.

4. From the residue of the drove select such as may be fit for immediate service and send them to my headquarters; and send the others to pasture—somewhere, in Giles county, Tennessee.

When you shall have performed this duty, send a report of the disposition of the property, to my headquarters.

N. B. FORREST,
Brigadier General, Commanding First Division.

To Col. James E. Saunders, Courtland, Alabama.

SOUTHWESTERN TELEGRAPH COMPANY.

By Telegraph from Tuscumbia, May 28, 1863.

To Col. J. E. Saunders: ATHENS, May 29, 1863.

Enemy in Florence and firing it. Skirmishing at Big Bear Creek.

C. B. FERRELL.

HEADQUARTERS FIRST CAVALRY DIVISION, ⎫
SPRING HILL, Tenn., May 30, 1863. ⎬

Col. James E. Saunders:

DEAR SIR—I am in receipt of your favors of the 20th and 23d inst., and have for-warded, for General Bragg's consideration and approval, the draft of letter to General Dodge, which has not yet been heard from. I have been relieved of the command of the troops in Alabama, and if General Bragg approves it he will command through Colonel Roddy.

I am glad to hear that Captain Forrest* continues to improve, and for your kindness manifested for him please accept my thanks. I presume that the dispatch of General Dodge to Colonel Straight is genuine—at any rate their calculations were all " knocked into pie."

Would be glad to hear from you in relation to the horses. From Courtland or Decatur you can write me, forwarding your letter by mail via Huntsville. From Athens use courier or persons passing to Pulaski, care of Major Falconet, Commandant of the Post, who can forward immediately to me here. The men left in charge of horses can act as couriers for you if necessary. Very respectfully,

Your friend,
N. B. FORREST,
Brigadier General Commanding.

A. Q. M. OFFICE,
DECATUR, Ala., June 9, 1863.

COLONEL—The train will come from Tuscumbia on the afternoon of the 16th and come down again on the morning of the 20th, as you request, unless the train is endangered by the appearance of the enemy. I am, sir,

Very respectfully your obedient servant,
E. W. KENNEDY,
Captain A. Q. M., C. V.

To Col. Jas. E. Saunders, Courtland, Ala.

HEADQUARTERS CAVALRY CORPS, COL. RICHARD JONES' HOUSE,
LAWRENCE COUNTY, October 15, 1863, 5:10 P. M.

COLONEL—We have just received a dispatch from General Roddy, per hands of an officer of his command, which informs us that he is at Athens, Ala. His command is safe; had a slight skirmish with a small force of the enemy, and offered him battle, which he declined. We are happy in the information, and knowing 'twould be pleasant intelligence to you, forward it. Very respectfully, colonel,

Your obedient servant,
WM. E. WAILES,
A. A. A. General.

To Colonel Saunders, at Home

HEADQUARTERS FORREST CAVALRY,
DALTON, Ga., October 31, 1863.

James E. Saunders, Esq.:

SIR—As you have no doubt learned, I have been transferred to the Mississippi river. General Bragg seemed indisposed to favor me with any facilities in my new field of operations, and I go West nearly destitute of horses, without which you know I can do nothing. It is therefore important that I collect up all the horses belonging to the government. Enclosed I send you the receipts given for horses and mules last May. If you have any other receipts or know of any other horses or mules belonging to the government I request that you will make the same known to either of my brothers, Colonel Forrest or Captain Forrest. Let me also request you to give them all the aid you can in this matter, and knowing your great zeal in the cause I believe this request will not be made in vain. Without these horses I can do nothing, and I trust the people will see how important they are to a defence of their homes and aid you in this matter. For the present my field of operations will be in West Tennessee, and any

---

* His brother, Capt. William Forrest, who was wounded, and convalescing at Colonel Saunders home.

service I may be able to render in this region will be in defence of your own unfortunate section, so often desolated by the invaders. Hoping you will attend to this matter, and thanking you for past kindness, I remain your friend and obedient servant,

N. B. FORREST, *Brig. Gen.*

HEADQUARTERS CAVALRY CORPS,
NEAR WARRENTON, Ala., October 26, 1863.

COLONEL—I am in receipt of your letter of 22d, and thank you for the suggestions
therein contained. I will endeavor to have the matter arranged accordingly.

Before leaving I directed each division commander to appoint a Board to assess the
damages done, and in addition thereto left a board of my own staff officers to see that
all damages were satisfactorily assessed. So soon as my staff join me and report, if I find
there is any dissatisfaction, I will have another board appointed to readjudge the matter.
I am determined that satisfaction shall be given and full justice done to all parties.

The manner you proposed was understood by the Boards, and I do not doubt they
have adopted the means you suggest.

I am, Colonel, very respectfully your obedient servant,

JOS. WHEELER, *Maj. Gen.*

Col. Jas. E. Saunders, near Courtland, Ala.

HEADQUARTERS FORREST CAVALRY COMMAND,
DALTON, November 1, 1863.

COLONEL—The general requests me to say that in his new field of operations he
would like very much if it become necessary for you to leave home that you would
join him. It is too laborious for you to remain with us all the time, but it would
afford us great pleasure to even have your good company occasionally.

I had the pleasure of seeing Dr. Saunders a few days ago. Himself and family
were in fine health. My best respects to your wife and the young ladies, and if I
should go through by land to Oakalona, and not by railroad, it is my intention to call
and see you and family; but I can never tell what disposition the general will make of
me until the *eleventh* hour. He is decidedly *amiable* this morning, and as *astonishing* as
it may appear, I have escaped up to the present time (ten o'clock) without one of his
peculiar blessings. Yours, with the highest regards,

J. P. STRANGE, *Staff Officer to Gen. Forrest.*

Col. James E. Saunders.

TUSCUMBIA, Ala., November 23, 1863.

COLONEL SAUNDERS—I send the boy, Tom, for my horses. I am able to sit up, and
can walk across the house on my crutches. I think of paying you a visit some time this
week if I get able to ride in a buggy. I expect to go to Oakalona as soon as I find that
I am able to get there. Captain Steele's company all mutinied, and refused to go to
Oakalona with the regiment; but both officers and men have repented, and gone to
join the regiment. Colonel, if you have any news, please write me and excuse my
short note.

Respectfully yours,

JESSE E. FORREST.*

COMO, PANOLA COUNTY, Miss., January 18, 1864.

Col. James E. Saunders:

DEAR SIR—I arrived here after several days' hard riding. I found General
Forrest here with some 4000 effective men. He has just returned from General

---

*Col. Jesse E. Forrest, a brother of the general.

Polk's headquarters; he has been put in command of North Mississippi and West Tennessee, General Lee having been transferred to South Mississippi.

This place is just forty-five miles from Memphis. We are getting plenty of forage and provisions; the general is very busily engaged in organizing his command. He has been given General Chalmers' command, with two additional Tennessee regiments. The general says he will have to station a brigade at Tupelo, and I think very likely that I will be put in command of that brigade. The general is very anxious to have you join him. General Forrest brought out about 3500 new troops and has succeeded in arming them all. My best respects to Major Watkins.

Very respectfully,

JESSE E. FORREST.

P. S.—The general has effected an exchange of prisoners with General Hulbert and I will be exchanged for immediately.

J. E. F.

ASSISTANT QUARTERMASTER'S OFFICE,
COURTLAND, Ala., December 23, 1863.

COLONEL—I would be glad if your time will permit, if you will call upon our State Commissioners as you pass through Montgomery and present two subjects for their consideration, which must be considered by them or the agents for government will be unable to supply the wants of our army.

First—The price of wool, woolen goods, leather, shoes, etc., must be advanced at least 100 per cent. Those articles sell readily at Mobile for from 300 to 500 per cent. above their rates of the 1st November.

Secondly—A discrimination must be made with this portion of Alabama and the Southern part of the State in prices. This entire district having been camped upon by our own army and that of the enemy continuously for more than twelve months, the means of subsistence is barely sufficient for its own inhabitants, and yet our army—General Roddy and others—are still camping upon them.

My next request, Colonel, is that you will call upon General Hardee and get him, if possible, to order General Wheeler to send a quartermaster and commissary to this place to receipt to the "tax in kind," collector for this district, for forage and subsistence consumed by his command during the time they camped in this valley—if not done the producers will be compelled to pay their taxes from the little left them, which will produce suffering in this valley amongst some of our best citizens, and by these officers being sent here it will save an outlay of a large amount of money to our government.

Ask Governor Watts to recommend a Military Court.

I am, Colonel, wishing you a pleasant trip,

Very respectfully, etc., your obedient servant,

S. H. RICHARDSON,
Captain and A. Q. M.

To Colonel J. E. Saunders, Rocky Hill.

TUSCUMBIA, February 11, 1864.

COLONEL SAUNDERS—Yours of the 9th is before me, and in reply I would state that I have just arrived from Tennessee, having gone as far as Jack's Creek, in which vicinity there was quite a large force of Yankees, and about twenty thousand in La Grange, Grand Junction and Bolivar, and it is believed by the citizens they are making preparations for a large raid into Mississippi. I learn from reliable source that General Forrest has fallen back to the vicinity of Jackson, Miss., and communication with him would be impossible. It is reported the Yankees are in pursuit of me; the last heard from they were in Iuka. Have sent scouts out which have not yet returned.

Very respectfully,

W. A. JOHNSON, Col. Commanding, etc.

GADSDEN, February 22, 1864.

COL. J. E. SAUNDERS—We are all off to-day for Tunnel Hill, in obedience to orders received Saturday. Nothing has been suggested to me from headquarters as to our future destination, but I have no idea that any forward move is anticipated at present, inasmuch as there is a constant stream of furloughed soldiers constantly leaving our army. Hundreds are passing daily, and I have not seen a single one returning.

I think it likely we may have some active service, as our position will likely be in front—if opportunity offers I will certainly give my men a showing at the invaders.

A late paper shows General Withers to be in command of the district of North Alabama, from latitude 32, by order of Lieutenant General Polk, and I hope sufficient protection will be thrown around our section of the State. The fear, however, is that they will consider us in the enemy's lines, and establish lines south of the mountains, but we will hope for the best.

If the citizens will do their best for me or my command I believe a very effective force can be gotten together from recruiting; and Captain Williams, whom I have left in command of the picket lines from Brown's Ferry to Decatur and Whitesburg, will be the best man for them to report to. He is a gentleman and a soldier, has my fullest confidence, and deserves to command a regiment.

I believe the leader who will take us safely through our difficulties has not yet risen to the surface. Our substance is being shamefully wasted now. We will hereafter suffer on account of the waste. These are matters of opinion, and of course private.

Colonel Foster says for me to receive all companies offering, and trust him to effect the legal organization. Yours truly,

P. D. RODDEY.

HEADQUARTERS, CAVALRY BRIGADE, }
September 23, 1864. }

DEAR COLONEL—Finding great difficulty in procuring supplies in this vicinity, I would feel much indebted if you will send by the bearers the provisions which you were kind enough to offer me this morning. Very respectfully,

Your obedient servant,
THOS. HARRISON

Colonel Saunders, near Courtland.

TUSCUMBIA, Ala., November 1, 1864.

DEAR COLONEL—I send you by the bearer the piece of tracing paper you had asked for—he is instructed to await the promised sketch.* Please make the notes which are to accompany it, as ample as your time and patience will permit.

With my kindest regards to your family, I remain yours very truly,

G. T. BEAUREGARD.

Col. Jas. E. Saunders, Rocky Hill, near Courtland, Ala.

January 4, 1865.

MR. J. E. SANDERS—I was detailed as a safe guard and sent to your residents to protect your home and family I found your familey to be Ladeies. Our soldiers behaved ungentlemanly on your premises, but it was not the falt of our officers. I was treated very kindly by your familey I would have like very much to have seen your before I went away, but scircumstances are so that I cant see you. I live in Indiana, Grant county, and am a private soldier in the 101 Indiana.

JACOB CARLL.
101st Indiana Regiment.

*Relating to the route of the army.

The limits of this sketch can follow no further the sad and glorius fortunes of the State. The lovely valley, for which he struggled in vain, overrun by cruel invasion; the forced marching of Hood's army; the generals and their gallant staffs rendezvousing at the old home; their reverses at Franklin, Tenn.; their retreat and, alas! hopeless abandonment of the valley to the enemy, and, at last, the end. And then the reign of martial law, and the *Freedman's Bureau!*

Those dark days of the *Reconstruction period* rapidly followed the horrors of civil war, and the reign of the *carpet-bagger* began, goading the people to desperation! For their protection, the younger and more reckless men of the community now formed a *secret society*, which masqueraded at night in grotesque and gruesome character, called the *Ku-Klux Klan.* Always silent and mysterious, mounted on horses they swept noiselessly by in the darkness with gleaming death's-heads skeletons and chains. It struck terror into the heart of the evil-doer, while the peaceful citizen knew a faithful patrol had guarded his premises while he slept.

Fearful that high prices would enable the South to recoup too rapidly, an iniquitous *cotton tax* was now imposed upon this prostrate industry, whose gin-houses had been burned, and fields laid waste. Colonel Saunders wrote to the Hon. Reverdy Johnson in consultation, and his reply is interesting, as it shows the sympathy of the better class of men who were then in power:

WASHINGTON, D. C., December 28, 1867.

DEAR SIR—You need not apologize for addressing me your letter of the 25th, just received. The suggestions you give me in relation to the cotton tax I will try to turn to advantage. The tax itself is, I think, objectionable, as well on grounds of expediency as want of authority in Congress to impose it. I should hope, therefore, that the amount which has been received from it in the present distressing condition of the South would be returned. If it would be impossible to find out the individual persons from whom it was received, it might be distributed among the States in the proportion of the quantity of cotton raised by each when the tax was levied; and the States be required to appropriate it to the support of their impoverished people. Or if this can not be done, justice and policy, it seems to me, alike require that the government should loan it to the States for some long period, its payment to be secured in some way within their power. I fear that Congress will not agree to repeal the tax as to the present year's crop, although I have little or no doubt that it will be repealed as to all future crops. The condition of the South gives to every American who has the happiness and reputation of his country at heart the most intense solicitude that it may soon be rendered better, and that their people may be enabled to recover their former prosperity and be restored to all the rights which the Constitution is intended to secure and guarantee, must be the wish of every man who values at their real worth the free institutions which our fathers bequeathed to us. I remain with regard,

Your obedient servant,

James E. Saunders, Esq.   REVERDY JOHNSON.

Bewildered with his emancipation, the ex-slave, always the child of nature, exercised his master's utmost patience. Colonel Saunders proceeded to establish a patriarchal *protectorate* over his own. He gave them a church on the place and organized also a plantation monthly court, where the *gray beards* among them assembled to try the derelicts. The findings of this *august body* were often ludicrous in the extreme, greatly taxing the gravity of its kind presiding officer; but, for a long time, it fulfilled its object—that of preserving law and order on the plantation, and preventing resort to the *Freedman's Bureau*, then in force throughout the South; a kind of Orphan's court, in which the *nation's ward* might appeal from his former owner directly to the indulgence of *Uncle Sam's* officials, often a trying position to the planter, when these men proved to be of the former rabid Abolition type.

Turning from the tyranny of King Cotton, as the years went on, he hoped to introduce, among the diversified industries of his neighborhood the growing of grapes, and for this purpose he induced Samuel Miller, a noted horticulturist of Missouri, to come to Rocky Hill and plant ten acres of the best adaptable varieties. In this he had also the assistance of a well-educated Austrian, or Sclavonian, by the name of Pujo, who was familiar with the processes of European culture of the vine. In that rocky soil there was no want of success in *growing* fine specimens of the best varieties, but too distant markets, large commissions, and express rates, permitted no profits. He was simply ahead of the times.

(Since then, grape growing and marketing has flourished under more favorable conditions in several colonies in Alabama.)

He wrote a bulletin on this subject, which was published by the Agricultural Department of Alabama (Judge Edward Betts, Commissioner). His library, his correspondence, his perplexing agricultural difficulties, rounded the employment of a beautiful old age, the serenity and grandeur of which is the inspiration of that virtue which is " its own exceeding great reward." At this period of his life, looking at him one might repeat—

> " There was a morning when I longed for fame,
> There was a noontime when I passed it by;
> There is an evening when I think not shame
> Its being and its substance to deny."

With him life's turmoil had now sublimed to an ecstatic calm. The Golden Wedding came in the year 1874, and still was he the lover, in whom a half-hundred years had no power to break the spell of her young eyes. Her imposing presence, versatile talents and fine social qualities always charmed him and others. A keen wound to them was her accidental laming, on 2d of January, 1873, by a fall from her horse while riding with him to visit the venerable Mrs. Benj. Sherrod, then ill at the home of her daughter, Mrs. Sam Shakelford. She was ever after restrained to a wheel-chair, but, happy Christian soul! always cheerful and making cheer for others. They were now alone. The few children left to them were married or absent. Their contemporaries, those vivid-living " early settlers" had struck their tents on the Heavenly shore ; and—

> " Those that he loved so long, and sees no more,
> Loved, and still loves—not dead, but *gone before*,
> He gathers round him."

Two old people, dreaming of the past ! And thus, for fifteen years longer, they awaited in holy communings the calm angel, who would announce, " The Master has come, and calleth for thee !" and to *her* He came *first*, as in an apocalyptic vision—literally before *the dawn;* for, when asked if she wanted more light in the room, which to her mortal vision was already darkening, she smiled, rapt in the splendor of the vision, " I shall see the Bright Light in the morning !" and so passed, softly chanting, " Jesus, lover of my soul," her hand in that of the aged husband, who, because of his desolation, would yet hold her from Heaven itself awhile. This perfect union, in which the morning had been " a song," the noon " a psalm," the evening " a prayer," had so conquered Time, that death was only a coronation for the Eternal Life beyond !

The benediction of their father's presence in their homes was yet spared his devoted children for a few years. But summer always found him, once more, at " *Rocky Hill*" among his lost saints, and ever awaiting the summons, which came to him at last, so gently, in a beloved daughter's arms, he fell asleep like a smiling child closing its eyes on a weary world. Life was now his debtor, and Love makes his grave " its oratory."

RECOLLECTIONS OF

THE EARLY SETTLERS OF NORTH ALABAMA.

> "And when he passed out of the wood, and saw the peaceful sun going down upon a wide purple prospect, he came to an old man sitting on a fallen tree. So he said to the old man, 'What do you do here?' And the old man said with a calm smile, 'I am always remembering. Come and remember with me!'
> "So the traveler sat down by the side of that old man, face to face with the serene sunset; and all his friends came softly back and stood around him. The beautiful child, the handsome boy, the young man in love, the father, the mother, and children; every one of them was there, and he had lost nothing."—*Dickens' Child's Story.*

I have intended for several years to write my Recollections of old times; and have, at length, forced myself to commence the task, before it shall be too late. I have had good opportunity of knowing the matters of which I shall treat. I came with my father's family, to Lawrence county, when I was a youth of fifteen years, and have lived here sixty years (1880).

I have resided, for years, in each of three main divisions of the county. After marriage, my first home was in Moulton, the county seat. I then moved to the Courtland Valley, and have spent many summers at the Chalybeate Springs, on the mountain (where I had a home). I knew the early settlers well, and of them I design to write; those who were here fifty or sixty years ago, or more. Of later ones I shall not speak, except they be descendants of early settlers, or incidentally connected with their history. Even confined within these limits, I foresee that my subject will become so broad, I shall have to use a simple and concise style, to bring it within proper bounds. I have taken much pains, where my own recollections were faint, to consult with the few friends of my youth, who still survive, to avoid mistakes. In speaking of the ancestors of the living, they must not expect me to picture the men as *saints*, and the women as *angels;* but such as they lived, and died on the earth.

In writing these sketches, although my most profound emotions are excited, I have not been actuated by mere sentiment; but the higher motive of being useful to the fathers and mothers, who have sons and daughters growing up. It has always been a mooted question what state of life, in respect to fortune, is best for a family. Now, as I pass the old families of the county in review before you, commencing with Moulton—passing through the Southeast section, thence to Courtland, thence around the "Valley" and back over the "Mountain"—and thence close with the Southwest section, I invoke the special attention of the young and old, to the application of the facts, to the *solution* of the question propounded. I have no desire to forestall opinion, but I predict that many parents who are compelled to make an *effort* to support and educate their children will be more content with their condition than they were.

After I shall have finished the work embraced, in the above plan, I shall write exclusively for the benefit of the boys who will read or spell through my articles, several chapters, on "Hunting and Fishing."

The Cherokee Indians.

were the earliest settlers of our county of whom we have any knowledge. They occupied, once, from Cane Creek, below Tuscumbia (where their domain joined that of the Chickasaws), up the Tennessee river, to its head-waters; and their scattered towns spread far into the Northern parts of Carolina, Georgia and Alabama. The Cherokees were the "Mountaineers" of aboriginal America, and extended over the most picturesque and salubrious region east of the Mississippi.—(Bancroft's History of the United States.) This powerful and extensive tribe came from the Eastward; and first had settlements on the Appomattox river, and were allied to the Powhatans. The Virginians drove them thence, and they retreated to the head-waters of the Holston river. Here, after having made temporary settlements, the Northern Indians compelled them to retire to the Little Tennessee river, where they established themselves permanently. About the same time a large branch of the Cherokees came from South Carolina (near Charleston), and formed towns on the main Tennessee, extending as far as the Muscle Shoals. They found all that region unoccupied, except upon the Cumberland, where was a band of roving Shawnees.—(Pickett's History of Alabama.)

Of the Cherokees in North Alabama, the earliest authentic account we have dates back to the invasion of the Spanish under De Soto, in 1540, just 340 years ago. In his wonderful march he crossed the branches of the winding and historic Coosa river; remained some time at Chiaho, where stands Rome, in Georgia; then marched down the right bank of the Coosa to Costa (the site of Gadsden, in Alabama), where lived the Cherokees. Never before had our soil been trodden by European feet. Never before had the natives beheld white faces, long beards, strange apparel, glittering armor, and, stranger than all, the singular animals bestrode by these dashing cavaliers (Pickett). The country of the Cherokees was described by the early historians as the most beautiful and romantic in the world; as abounding in delicious springs, fertile valleys, lovely rivers and lofty mountains; the woods full of game and the rivers of fish. But none of these early writers had ever seen the country about the Muscle Shoals, which was last settled and [most highly valued by these Indians. The buffaloes roamed over the plains in countless numbers. As late as 1826, *at the licks in this county, their paths, knee deep, radiated in every direction.* In 1780, the small colony which made a crop of corn that year at Nashville, Tenn., had to leave three men to prevent the buffaloes from destroying the crop, whilst the rest returned to East Tennessee for their families.—(Guild's "Old Times in Tennessee.)" Deer, wild turkeys and the smaller game continued abundant, even after the whites took possession of the country. As many as sixty deer were counted in a single herd. The Tennessee river and its affluents swarmed with fish, for there never was anywhere a better inland feeding ground for them than the Muscle Shoals. Its shallow waters stretch for fifteen miles along the channel, and spread out two or three miles wide, and produce a thick growth of aquatic plants (called moss), which come to the surface and sport the tips of their leaves on the swift, sparkling current. These plants, roots and leaves are freely eaten by fish, and wild fowls also. Of these last, swans, wild geese and ducks (which annually visited their feeding ground in old times) the number was fabulous. Added to this, the bottom of the river was strewn with mussels and periwinkles, which were not only highly relished by the fish and fowl, but by the Indians, who had in them a sure provision against starvation in times of scarcity. I could well imagine that the last prayer of the Cherokee to the Great Spirit, when he was leaving this scene of beauty and abundance, would be that he might, when he opened his eyes in the next world, be permitted to see such another hunters' paradise as this.

The males of the Cherokees, in ancient times, were larger and more robust than any other of our natives; whilst their women were tall, erect and of a delicate frame with perfect symmetry (Bartram). And on account of the pure air which they breathed, the exercise of the chase, the abundance of natural productions which their country afforded and the delicious water which was always near, they lived to an age much more advanced than the other tribes (Adair). I saw a good deal of them from 1815 to 1834, when they were removed to the West, and also had a personal knowledge of other Southern tribes, and I think this pre-eminence was maintained to modern times.

Sir Alexander Cumming, in 1730, sent an envoy who was guided by Indian traders to Neguasse, on the Little Tennessee, which was the seat of empire of all the Cherokee towns. A general assembly of the chiefs took place. They offered a chaplet, four scalps of their enemies and five eagle tails as the records of the treaty; it was proposed to them to send deputies to England. Seven chiefs were sent and a treaty was concluded, in which they promised that "*love should flow like a river and peace should endure like the mountains*," and it was kept faithfully for a generation (Bancroft). Again in 1761 this peace was confirmed, when Timberlake, a lieutenant in the Royal service, descended to the Holston in canoes and visited their towns. He returned to Charleston with three of their chiefs and sailed for England (Timberlake).

This peace, however, did not last for many years. The extension of the white settlements to East Tennessee and, shortly afterward, to Middle Tennessee roused the animosity of the Cherokees, and the Revolutionary War coming on, the emissaries of Great Britain turned their arms against the colonies they had planted, and a conflict ensued which continued nearly twenty years.

It was at this gloomy period that Gen. James Robertson, with eight others, settled at Nashville. In the fall they returned to East Tennessee for their families.. It was arranged that General Robertson should proceed, first, with a number of young men to raise the necessary buildings, and that Col. John Donelson should follow with another party of emigrants, including the women and children. To avoid the toil and peril of the route through the wilderness, Colonel Donelson conceived the idea of reaching the new settlement by water, down the Tennessee and up the Cumberland rivers. No man, white or red, had ever attempted the voyage, which was really more dangerous than the overland route, while there were equally as many Indians to be encountered. At the suck one of the boats hung upon a rock, and a hot skirmish with the Cherokees on the mountain side took place before they could extricate her. Among those who shared the dangers of this voyage was Rachel Donelson, the daughter of the leader, a black-eyed, black-haired brunette, as gay, as bold, and as handsome a lass as ever danced on the deck of a flatboat, or took the helm while her father took a shot at the Indians.—(Guild.) This lass became the wife of Gen. Andrew Jackson. I guess "he loved her for the dangers *she* had passed." What a pity there was no issue from this marriage! For what a *game* breed it would have been! This was one hundred years ago. This party of Colonel Donelson boldly shot the Muscle Shoals without a pilot. They were the first whites who ever set their eyes on the soil of Lawrence county of whom we have any account. After a voyage of four months they reached their new home, and there was a happy meeting of husbands and wives, parents and children.

To give the reader some idea of the manner in which early settlers were harassed by the Indians, it has been stated that for fifteen years they killed within seven miles of Nashville one person in about every ten days. Then, women and children were slaughtered indiscriminately, and this ruthless warfare extended to all the settlements in Middle Tennessee.—(Guild.) The Hon. Felix Grundy, who passed amidst these these perils, once alluded to them, in the United States Senate, when he spoke with touching eloquence: "I was too young to participate in these dangers and difficulties, but I can remember when death was in almost every bush, and every thicket concealed an ambuscade. If I am asked to trace my memory back, and name the first indelible impression it received, it would be the sight of my eldest brother, bleeding and dying under the wounds inflicted by the tomahawk and scalping knife. Another, and another went in the same way. I have seen a widowed mother plundered of her whole property in one night; from affluence and ease reduced to poverty in a moment, and compelled to labor with her own hands to support and educate her last and favorite son—him who now addresses you. Sir, the ancient sufferings of the West were very great. I know it. I need turn to no document to tell me what they were. They are written upon my memory—a part of them on my *heart*. Those of us who are here are but the remnant, the wreck of large families lost in the settlement of the West."

At length the patience of the settlers was completely exhausted. Moreover, they had become gradually stronger, and they determined to strike a blow which would reach the heart of the enemy, and to pursue them to their stronghold, Nickajack, from which point the Cherokees, with their allies, were accustomed to make their incursions. This was their great military station, where the warriors from the Little Tennessee above, and the Muscle Shoals below, concentrated when they meditated mischief. And here, in riotous drunkenness, they consumed the fruits of their victories. The whites had never crossed the Tennessee, and they felt secure. Suddenly General James Robertson had collected a force of 600 men, with much secrecy, and burst upon them like a thunder-bolt. They had reached the north bank of the river after dark, constructed small rafts for their guns and ammunition, and pushing them before them—sometimes wading and sometimes swimming—they reached the southern bank early in the morning, surrounded their enemies, and gained an overwhelming victory. From the numbers of the Cherokees killed, I judge there was not much quarter asked or given. The power of the tribe was completely broken. The Cherokees for the first time sued for peace, and never afterward molested the whites.

Even when Tecumseh harangued every tribe, with his fiery eloquence, from the lakes of the North to the Gulf of Mexico, the Cherokees remembered Nickajack! and the les-son written there, by the Tennesseans, in blood, and remained friendly. It was through their country that General Jackson marched his army to subdue the Creeks, in the autumn of 1813. Gen. John Coffee found a ford for his mounted men across the Muscle Shoals. They entered the river near the mouth of Blue Water creek, waded about three miles and emerged from it just below Green's Bluff; and ascending the steep and lofty bank they found themselves, in what is now, Lawrence county, but then the choice hunting grounds of the Cherokees. As they beheld the level but elevated valley, which stretched out before them, apparently, a broad prairie interspersed, thinly, with trees, it was a sad day for the poor Indian! for many a soldier's heart glowed with admiration and covetousness. There stood the leader, of gigantic stature and fine proportions, with his calm face (which I well recollect) and by his side Major Alexander McCulloch, who was his favorite aide, and had fought in many a bloody conflict, by the side of the noble Coffee. It was a strange coincident, that McCulloch, after the cession, purchased the very tract of land on which their eyes were then resting, and made it his home for many years. In its proper place, I shall give sketches of him, and his distinguished sons, Generals Ben and Henry E. McCulloch. Of the emigrants who afterward came from Middle Tennessee to this county, a large proportion had belonged to Coffee's command. During this war many of the Cherokees were our allies, and served against the Creeks. Indeed, it was owing to the fact that some friendly Indians were besieged in a small fort near Talladega, that General Jackson precipitated his march in advance of his supplies, for Old Hickory never forsook his friends, no matter what the color of their skins.

Very shortly after this war closed, I think in 1817, the Cherokees ceded land enough to form three counties, of which Lawrence was the middle one. The Indians who lived here, moved eastward, and settled with the body of the tribe. Amongst them was a chief named Melton—for whom "Melton's Bluff" was called—who settled about three miles above Guntersville.

When the whites first came to this county the cabins of the Indians were still stand-ing. Near every house was a pile of muscle and periwinkle-shells. There were monu-ments of occupation, which seemed to have existed for a long time, in mounds and forti-fications. On "Watkins' Island" at the head of the Muscle Shoals—there are a half dozen of them— and on the upper end several acres are covered with shells, as if the natives had occupied it for many ages. On the mainland, also, you can find them. One above the mouth of Town creek is very large. Near Oakville are several, one of which is very broad but flat on the top and about eight feet high. The people have a cemetery on top of it now. The settlements of the natives were most numerous on Town creek, hence the name. On Big Nance was quite a town at Courtland; and the creek is said to have been named from a very large Indian *squaw* who lived there.

There has been much conjecture of late years, in regard to the origin of the mounds, speculative visitors contending that they were made by a very ancient race they call the "Mound Builders." I agree with our historian, Pickett. He considers this a mistaken opinion, and adduces many facts to show it. He quotes extracts from Garcellasa, and other Spanish writers, who accompanied De Soto on his march, showing that the large mounds were sites for the houses of the chiefs—that they saw houses so located daily—and that the smaller ones were places of sepulture. Nearly 200 years after this, and subsequent to the settlement of Mobile by the French, the Natchez Indians were expelled on account of a massacre of the whites, from the spot now occupied by the city of that name, and settled on the Lower Washita. This was in 1730, and in only two years from that time they had mounds and fortifications, scattered over 400 acres of land, which are still to be seen. Moreover, as late as the administration of Mr. Jefferson, Lewis and Clark were sent overland to Oregon, to explore the country, and they found the Sioux, and other Western tribes, erecting earthen embankments for defence around their towns; so that the construction of these works can be easily accounted for, within the historic period.

Wonderful progress in civilization has been made by the Cherokees since the cession of their lands in this valley. This is due to Christian Missions. On the western side of the nation the Methodist Church expended much moral force in this direction. Amongst the missionaries, Rev. William McMahon, D. D., originated this mission and superintended it for many years. He had the sagacity to educate young natives to assist in the work. He has gone from earth, but has left a monument of his usefulness in the regeneration of a nation. When he was transferred to the West his mantle fell on the Rev. John B. McFerrin, D. D., who in the councils of the church was the especial friend of the Cherokee, and always encouraged their native preachers. Amongst these were Turtlefields and McIntosh. Turtlefields before his conversion was a warrior and fought under General Jackson in the Creek war. He was a hero, and was wounded in single combat with a Creek warrior. He was over six feet high, and possessed great physical force. McIntosh spoke English well, was an interpreter and excelled in that work, and became a useful minister. Dr. McFerrin is still robust (1880) and has the promise of many years to come—and yet he has seen with his own eyes savages transformed into peaceable, law-abiding Christian citizens, with all the institutions of civilised life, with learned judges, eloquent lawyers, scientific physicians and able ministers. The reason I have singled out Drs. McFerrin and McMahon is that they were identified with our county. In the proper place, I shall give sketches of them, but thought it best to speak of them in this connection before I bid farewell to the Cherokees.

The Territory of Alabama was created by a division of Mississippi Territory in 1817, with St. Stephens as its capital city. The first and second Territorial Legislature met there—the first on the 18th of January, 1818, and the second in November of the same year. This year, Cahaba was made the seat of government, but as there was no town there, and no public buildings, Huntsville was designated as the temporary capital. In Huntsville, on the 5th of July, 1819, a convention assembled to prepare a State Constitution, in which twenty-two counties were represented, viz.: Autauga, Baldwin, Blount, Cahaba, Clarke, Conecuh, Cataco, Dallas, Franklin, Lauderdale, Lawrence, Limestone, Madison, Marengo, Mobile, Montgomery, Monroe, St. Clair, Shelby, Tuscaloosa and Washington. The first General Assembly of the new State met in Huntsville, October 25, 1819, and there, on the 9th of November, Governor Bibb was inaugurated. In 1820, the government offices and archives were removed to Cahaba. In 1826, Tuscaloosa became the capital, in the administration of Gov. John Murphy, who had been chosen the year previous. In 1846, the capital was removed to Montgomery, where the General Assembly of 1847 was held. So Alabama, in fifty years, had as capitals St. Stephens, Huntsville, Cahaba, Tuscaloosa and Montgomery.

Lawrence County, Its Organization, Topography and Soil.

Lawrence county was laid off, and organized as early as the 4th of February, 1818. This was shortly after the termination of the war with Great Britain, when military fervor had not much abated, and the Legislature conferred on it the name of Lawrence. He was a naval captain, who during a bloody engagement at sea, exclaimed as he sank upon the deck, mortally wounded, "Boys! never give up the ship." This would be a good motto for the sons of Lawrence, in war and peace, throughout all time. From the start, Moulton and Courtland were rivals for the seat of justice. Both were settled as soon as the Indians were removed, and had a wonderful growth. Col. Isaac N. Owen informed me that when he came in 1821, Moulton was nearly as large as it is now, but not so well built. The law providing for a permanent seat of justice was passed 4th of December, 1819. On the same day, Moulton obtained an act of incorporation. Courtland heard of it, and on the 19th she was incorporated too; and so both these villages were made cities by law within fifteen days. In February, 1820, the election was held to fix the county seat, and the choice fell on Moulton. Arrangements were made at once for the erection of the public buildings. Maj. John Gaugett got the contract, and they were completed within two years.

Its Topography.

To enable the reader to understand the many *local* allusions I shall have to make in the course of these articles it will be necessary to speak of the physical features of this county. On the north, it is bounded by the Tennessee river, in that part of its course which includes all the Elk-River Shoals and nearly all of the Muscle Shoals. The southern boundary rests on the northern rim (which is the highest part) of a chain of mountains, which runs across the State, from east to west. Our people have been in the habit of calling these the Warrior Mountains; but the State geologist, in his report of 1879, calls them the Sand Mountains, because they are so called farther east; and we consider it best to adopt this designation. In this rim, which is several miles wide, the streams which, respectively, run south to the Gulf of Mexico, and north to the Tennessee river, take their rise; sometimes interlocking and forming narrow valleys or coves, of romantic beauty, in the bosom of towering mountains. These were settled as early as the two great valleys, by men who had been accustomed in the States from which they emigrated to ice-cold springs, and rugged scenery. They are, generally, lonely and sequestered; but in hotly contested elections, a good many people visit them.

The remainder of the county north of this broad margin of the Sand Mountains, consists of two large and fertile valleys, running east and west across the county, and divided by the Little Mountain. This is an outlying mountain, not connected with any other, some six or eight miles wide. It is not so rich as the large valleys, but has in many places a free soil, and is inhabited, sparsely, by a people who depend on cultivating the best spots, along with the natural pasturage, for a subsistence. Like the Sand Mountain, the north is the bluff side of this chain. Toward the south it gradually subsides for many miles until it meets the Moulton valley; and there one can not tell where the mountain ends, and the valley begins.

The inhabitants of our county are so familiar with it, that they seem not to be aware that the county affords some of the finest scenery east of the Rocky Mountains. Mr. Jefferson said there were men living within a half dozen miles of it who had never seen the Natural Bridge in Virginia. So it is here. The Tennessee river, in many parts of its course, presents scenes of uncommon beauty. Here is a river, tumbling with a dull roar, which can be heard for miles, over ledge after ledge of rocks, extending from bank to bank. Here are large islands, and sometimes an archipelago of small ones, with the branches of the trees trailing in the current. Here are rugged shores, deep shady nooks, cool springs, lofty precipices and ancient legends—all furnishing material for the pencil of the painter and the pen of the poet. Again, on the bluff side of the Little Mountain, all along, are scenes of great interest. Perhaps the best prospect may be had from the promontory west of Courtland, which runs, in a narrow ridge, boldly out into the valley, and terminates in a point called the " Pinnacle." It was occupied last summer (1879) by a detachment of the United States Coast Survey, which is making a geodesic survey across the continent, from the Atlantic to the Pacific Ocean. They have occupied the Monte Sano above Huntsville, and a point four miles southwest of Moulton on Sand

Mountain, as signal stations, for the purpose of triangulation and astronomic observations. From the Pinnacle the Tennessee valley can be seen to great advantage, with its broad fields, narrow skirts of timber and planters' houses dotting the scene all over. Here, where the valley wears its richest dress, the lover of the beautiful can feast his eyes by traversing a large extent of country. If he should prefer wilder scenery, he can fall back to some point on the loftier range of the Sand Mountains. Here he can not only behold a cultivated valley, with its fields and woods and homes, but can lift his eyes above the Little Mountain and see a prospect of quaint beauty, and only bounded by the power of vision; and when he tires of so much vastness and sublimity, he can descend into one of those deep, dark, green little valleys—can throw himself on the grass, beside a cool fountain, rippling from under a lofty precipice, where grow the ferns, the mosses and pendant plants, which "drop delicious coolness," and paint a pastoral scene of such beauty that it will go right to the heart of a man who is jaded with the heat and dust, cares and perplexities of a city.

The Soil

of the county when first settled, by the whites, was warm, mellow and productive. Its foundation is the St. Louis or coral limestone, which was once the bed of a sea, and the rock is full of fossil shells, which indicate the fact clearly. This rock passes under the Little Mountain and forms the floor of both the Tennessee and Moulton valleys (Geo. Report 1879). The first-mentioned valley was easily reduced to cultivation, for timber was thinly scattered over the surface, and was low and gnarled, owing to the annual fires kindled by the Indians to consume the tall grass. The production in early times, I think, would average 1200 to 1400 pounds of cotton and forty bushels of corn per acre; but the land has been worked so long, without rest or manure, that the average product now is not half what it was in old times. As long as the crops continued heavy no one cared to inquire into the nature of the soil; but since its exhaustion, and the planters have been put on short rations, there is much anxiety to know what ingredients have been lost in this long course of culture. At my request Professor Stubbs, of the Agricultural College at Auburn, Ala., has analyzed two samples of the soil, one called the new, which has never been cultivated, and another called the old, which was taken from a field which has been worked fifty-seven years. Below we present the analysis, which is the first we have ever seen, of North Alabama soil. This great Tennessee Valley, extending from Flint river, above Huntsville, to Bear creek, below Tuscumbia, is founded on the same geological stratum, the coral limestone, and the general mineral character of the soil is the same, although there may be a difference in the relative amount of humus, or vegetable mould, in localities.

ANALYSIS.

	No. 1, Old.	No. 2, New.
Insoluble matter	91.78	88.89
Soluble silica	.0906	.077
Ferric oxide (iron)	8.15	8.605
Alumina	1.90	1.995
Lime	.348	.854
Magnesia	.187	.193
Phosphoric acid	.045	.236
Sulphuric acid	.0608	.0464
Potash	.0745	.144
Soda (not determined)		.128
Soluble organic matter	1.51	3.37
Chlorine (not determined)		

INSOLUBLE MATTER.

Organic matter	3.39	7.03
Sand	87.49	81.86
Total humus	4.80	10.55

MECHANICAL ANALYSIS OF SOIL.

Clay	5.24
Fine silt	10.36
Fine sand	20.20
Coarse sand	64.20
Total	**100.00**

The foundation of the Moulton Valley is the same as that of the Tennessee Valley. But there is this difference in the soil, that there is a large proportion of fine creek land in the Moulton Valley. Town and Big-Nance creeks and Flint river rise in this valley, and their head branches spreading wide furrows to the richest alluvion. The drawback to its maximum production has always been a lack of natural drainage. Individual efforts have done something to cause the surface water to pass off, but not enough. Experience shows that land should be relieved of water for three feet below the surface. Then the frosts of winter would enter and disintegrate the soil, and the genial rays of spring sunshine would penetrate and warm it. I judge there is an obstruction at the lip of each of the three shallow basins in which these streams rise, which prevents the flow of the water, and this may be owing to the fact that the dip of the rock is toward the south. A preliminary survey might be made to ascertain the fall and the point of obstruction. Professor Smith says "the level of the Mt. Hope Valley is not much above that of the Tennessee Valley, from which it is separated by the Little Mountain.—(Geo. Report, 1879.) But he merely judged from the indications of barometer, for no instrumental survey was made. If the fall is scant there is the more necessity for a good engineer to ascertain it and lay out work. If the Moulton Valley were thoroughly drained it would be much more productive, as arable land, furnish fine meadows, and the inhabitants would be much more healthy.

Remarks of Professor Stubbs on the Analysis of North Alabama Soil.

"You see that your soil is very sandy, and has such an amount of ferric oxide (iron) as to merit the appellation of 'ferruginous sandy.' Let not the assertion that your soil is not a true clay carry dismay to your hearts. God has provided better for you than to undermine the level valley of the Tennessee with a substratum of heavy clay. Instead of that, he has given you a porous sandstone, through which the copious rains of the winter and spring may easily filter and leave the soil wholesome and sweet for the growing crops. Had you a clay soil, with your natural imperfect system of drainage, every heavy rain would convert your level fields into lagoons and your rich bottoms into lakes, and the country would become so sickly that it would be uninhabitable. Clays, it is true, absorb water and ammonia, and so does a sandy ferruginous, and in *holding* ammonia, it even excels it. The porosity of the sand permits a free passage to the water, while the iron present abstracts and retains any solid it contains. Again, the iron present not only absorbs and condenses ammonia in its pores, but also a large amount of carbonic acid gas, which the porosity of your soil enables at once to go to work as a disintegrator of rock particles and a solvent of plant food. Hence we easily see why our sand rock, with its iron compounds, has given us such valuable soils.

"In comparing the old soil, which we are now working, with the new, the great difference is, that we have lost, by fifty-seven years' cultivation, one-half the humus (or vegetable matter), one-half the potash, and, wonderful to tell, four-fifths of the phosphoric acid (bone)! Every planter who has studied the subject of soils, is ready to exclaim, 'How did this thing occur, when cotton, our principal crop, abstracts less from the soil than any other valuable crop?' It must have happened by waste, the seed having been carried away to oil mills, or fed to stock, and no return made to the lands, and the leaves, empty bolls and soft parts of the stalks, which are rich in phosphoric acid, being consumed by hungry cattle. It can be accounted for in no other way. Now what shall we do to repair the injury? The answer is obvious. First, never let a hoof go on the fields which have produced your cotton crops; secondly, suffer not a bushel of cotton seed to be carried away or wasted; thirdly, in some way add the vegetable matter which has been lost, either by resting in weeds, or clover, or by adding manure of some kind; and fourthly, mix with your manure a purer article of super-phosphate. My own experience is, that even on clover land, which is rich in humus, super-phosphate adds very materially to the product of cotton. I have tested this by the steelyards.

The Minerals

of a valuable kind were sought for very assiduously in early times. Gold! One Sunday morning when I lived in Courtland, there came a friend to my house whose mind was evidently much preoccupied. After a few minutes, he asked me to walk out with him, and when we had gotten to the bottom of the yard, he looked carefully all around, and then pulled from his pocket a hard roll with particles of something in it resembling gold, and said, 'What's that!' I answered that it looked like gold, but I did not believe it was, but if he would come in next day, I would have it tried in the crucible. He said he could not wait. I saw he was suffering, and we repaired to the silversmith. Murdock soon had the roll in the crucible, and it went off into smoke, and so did the gentleman's hopes. We went immediately to church, my friend being in a fit frame of mind to sing,

> 'How vain are all things here below,
> How false, and yet how fair.'

"This was farcical; but about a half century ago a case occurred which affected my feelings sensibly. A shy old man was seen about the bluffs on the Tennessee river digging a hole here and another there, and sleeping in the caves. This went on for a year or two. He avoided communication with anybody. No one knew whether he was seeking for gold or silver, or a hidden treasure. At length he brought to my house his mining tools, and requested me to take care of them. I asked him where he was going. He replied (and his answer was broken by a hacking cough) that he was not very well, and that he was going into some other State, to visit his kin. The poor old man never reclaimed his tools—was never heard of afterward.

"Silver! There was much muffled talk about silver mines in our county, in old times. My old friend Wyatt Cheatham was fully persuaded that there was silver in what we then called the Warrior mountains, and while he was cutting his air-line road from Moulton to Tuscaloosa, he was constantly searching for it. It was said his confidence was founded on information derived from an Indian chief, who had lived within the bounds of our county. Of course the silver mine was never found, because there was none there.

" Lead! Here too was a great search, and it was an early tradition that all the lead used by the Indians was taken from the home mines, which were kept carefully concealed from the whites. But I never heard that a lead mine was ever discovered but once, and that happened in this wise: There was a blacksmith in Courtland, Newton Smith, who was a *stormer* to work, a skilful hand to kill fish with a gig, and to blow a trumpet. He was fishing one night at the head of the Muscle Shoals, between *Watkins Island* and *Periwinkle Bar;* the very region where Rumor said the mine should be. Well! He threw his gig at a large fish with great force, it missed the fish, but struck a vein of pure lead, and ploughed a track in it several feet long, which fairly blazed in the torchlight. There was no mistake about it—it was a plain case; and having sworn his companion to secrecy, he returned to camp for the night, and reveled in dreams of untold wealth; in which a fine mansion, a beautiful wife and a broad plantation flitted before his imagination. He, next morning, returned, but never could find the spot any more. I have heard him say that he would swear to the truth of the statement on a stack of Bibles three feet high; and that was when he was duly sober, too. Of course, it was never found.

Coal! All the coal which has ever been found in North Alabama has been near the tops of the mountains. In other countries they go down into the earth for it, here we go up. Unluckily, the chain which skirts the southern boundary of our county shows but one seam of coal, and that too thin to be worked. The outcrop was purchased at an early day by Mr. Hamlin Eppes, who lived near Courtland.

Salt! There have been borings for salt and coal. On the Tennessee, near the Elk River Shoals, Mr. Daniel Gilchrist had one made 430 feet deep, in connection with the same Newton Smith who found the lead mine, without finding coal or salt. Also, Mr. Paul J. Watkins made a boring at the Tar Springs, without finding anything valuable.

Oil! Some years ago two borings were made, one of them 300 feet deep, by a company from Columbus, Miss., in search of oil; but after expending a large sum of money they abandoned the enterprise. These borings were on the waters of the Big Nance, near Mr. Joe Terry.

Our very competent State Geologist, Dr. Eugene Smith, has made several reports, from which we learn that the only coal to be found in our county is too thin to be worked; that iron is the only metal to be found that is useful; that there is no gold, silver or lead, ours not being *metal-bearing* rocks; and that it is foolish to hunt for the precious metals in our county, and that it is probable that petroleum (oil) in small quantities might be obtained.

There is a spring in the southeastern part of the county from which comes a mere rill of water with oil floating on top of it, which accumulates and sinks to the bottom in the form of a thick petroleum. It is called the Tar Spring. It is thought to be very useful as an application to rheumatic limbs. There is also an exhausted oil spring on the east side of Town creek, opposite Mr. Hartwell King's old place and belonging to his estate. Here, on the side of a mountain, is a great quantity of hardened petroleum, commonly called asphaltum.

It is said that the walls of Babylon were cemented with this substance.

The Chalybeate Springs of Lawrence deserve notice. There is one six or seven miles northeast of Moulton, which, when the valleys were unhealthful from the decay of timber, was a place of great summer resort. Six or eight families had houses there, and a framed hotel was built near the site of a Methodist church, which yet stands there. About a mile west of this sprigg was another, of the same properties, which was settled by David Hubbard, Esq. At McGee's old mill, eight miles from Courtland, on the Tuscaloosa road, is another of great excellence and delicious coolness. There a number of families used to spend their summers. In the course of my narrative I shall have to refer to these springs. There is also another small but very good spring two miles south of Mountain Spring Campground, on the old Tuscaloosa road.

Saline Springs. At White-burg, four miles south of Courtland, is a brackish spring of alkaline properties. And near Smith's old mill is another that seems in its constituents to be precisely similar to it. Both springs were noted " *licks* " for wild game when the country was first settled by the whites.

The State of Society

in a country depends on material as well as moral causes, and these must be considered together in forming a correct estimate of the character of a people. Most new countries are settled by poor men who go ahead of schools and churches, that they by years of privation and suffering achieve an independent fortune for their children. But this was not the case with our county. It is true that as soon as the Indian title was extinguished, emigrants settled sparsely in various parts of it, and it was fortunate it was so, for without the supplies they raised it would not have been possible to have sustained such a rush of people as came afterward. The inducements were great: a rich soil easily reduced to cultivation, and the price of cotton very high. The country was filled up in a short space of time by settlers, generally of high respectability and a good education; and a large proportion of whom were members of the church. Very few were wealthy. I know the general impression is to the contrary; but the large estates which have been in our county have been *made* here. A majority of the early settlers were in *good circumstances*, and hence the aggregate of wealth in our county was great. They came mostly from Tennessee, Georgia, North Carolina, and Virginia; and in many cases *in small colonies*. The immigrants brought with them all the means and appliances of civilised life—their ministers, their physicians, their merchants, their lawyers, and mechanics—and every department of business flourished. The ministers were in great force; much more so than at the present time, and the people were *church goers*. The denominations "provoked each other to good work." The Presbyteries, Associations, Conferences, and Campmeetings, were thronged. I have known more people attend the burial of a person, not known to one-tenth of the congregation, than are now to be seen on any important occasion in our towns. Were they *better* then than they are now? I doubt it very much. The truth is their motives are various, and would not bear a close scrutiny. The older people, maybe, had a curiosity to see their new neighbors; the young men may have gone to see the girls (of whom they had heard but had never seen); and the girls, I can not conceive what could have impelled *them* but pure piety! Now, the motives might not have held good "*in forum conscientiæ*," yet thereby, large assemblies were convened, and I have heard the preachers say that when this is accomplished, the main difficulty in the spread of the Gospel was removed. It is very certain, that wonderful revivals occurred during the first decade, and after the country was settled. When we come to speak, individually of the ministers you can judge better of their merits.

The physicians came in numbers, and of the first grade for that day. Moulton had an accomplished one, who took his medical diploma at Edinburgh, once the most renowned school of physics among English-speaking nations. These had mostly graduated at Philadelphia. A fair proportion of them were men of experience, and had brought reputation for skill with them. It was well their numbers were large, for thousands of acres of timber were killed by *belting*, and the trees were left to rot where they stood, and fall, limb by limb, to the ground, tainting the atmosphere with deadly miasma. The consequence was, malarial epidemics which carried off great numbers of the people. The doctors stood to their posts like heroes, and plied heroic remedies in heroic measure. These remedies were of a drastic nature, such as gamboge, scammony and tartar emetic, backed by the calomel, and the lancet. If this thorough practice did not cure the patient it was taken for granted that the case was incurable. The planters, watching the doctors and seeing that they proceeded upon the same principle as of *scouring out a rusty gun-barrel*, improved on their practice by using a mixture of tartar emetic and salts, which, combined, were supposed to produce a kind of explosion in the system, which either brought the fever to a speedy conclusion—or else the patient. Strange! the people continued to die in great numbers. There *were* physicians, here and there, who shook their heads, but said little, because the "*vox populi*" were in favor of the *heroics*. But at length a deadly sickness occurred, in the spring of 1830, about Courtland, and in spite of calomel and the lancet, with their little satellites, we lost many of our most valuable citizens: Col. Ben. Jones, Dr. Nimmo Morris, Mr. E. M. Shegog, Mr. Anderson, Mr. Carlton, and others; whilst many of our most esteemed young men were dangerously ill, amongst them John H. Harris, and his brother Richard N., who made their wills, and expected to die. It seemed evident that a change of treatment was required, but the leaders of the two parties in medicine were at enmity, and did not even speak to each other. At this critical juncture, my old friend and law partner, John J. Ormond, procured a consultation between them; one of them, however, exacting a stipulation that the other was never to speak to him after the epidemic came to an end. The consultation terminated in an agreement to try a *mild course* of treatment—and after that there were no more deaths. A revolution occurred then in the practice, but it is not *yet* entire, for there are old men and women now living who have never hauled down the flag, but will *die* by calomel.

The merchants came in as fast as their wares were wanted, and as soon as the people commenced making and selling their cotton crop an active demand sprung up. Within seven years of its first settlement, Courtland sold three hundred and twenty thousand dollars' worth of merchandise per annum. The other town, Moulton, had a large trade also. Fortunes were then made, in this line, in a few years. Merchants are the benefactors of mankind, but more especially of the ladies. The fancy side of the stores enlarged from year to year, until the finest fabrics sold in Philadelphia were found on their shelves. Goods were sold at high prices, but the quality was, uniformly, sound and good. In *old times* I never knew merchants to sell to laborers shoes made of *split* leather and *paper* soles, or any article of that class.

The lawyers who first came to the county were, generally, young, although there were a few of experience and who brought reputations with them. The profession flourished because there was great prosperity in the county. Hundreds of suits were brought to every term of the court.

This was a favorable time for lawyers of genius and learning to rise rapidly from the ranks of their profession, for the construction of the statutes had been pronounced in but few cases by the court of last resort; and so there was a broad field for the exercise of the highest order of ability. But *now*, when most points of difficulty have been adjudicated, nine-tenths of the questions are settled by counsel in chambers by referring to reports, for lawyers very properly bow to the principle "*stare decisis.*"

Owing to the above cause, and perhaps to the chastened taste of an old country, oratory is not cultivated so much as it was in early times, when lawyers indulged in a more florid and impassioned style; *now* they seem to study a precise and concise and clear diction in their argument.

Our mechanics in early times had a monopoly of all the work in the county. From the hat to the shoe, every article of dress was made at home. Capital had not learned then to manufacture every article of comfort or necessity by machinery and associated labor. Hence our mechanics were better clothed, better fed, their families better taught, and they were enabled to occupy a better position in the social scale, than they can now, in their crippled condition

Indeed the people would naturally be improved by being thrown together, from various States. Each had something to add to the common stock of information. Like the Athenians "they came to gather, to hear, and to tell some new thing. Moreover, each one had to establish his position in society anew. He had to do his first work over again. When they met socially, each one was anxious to please, and it made society charming. It is this novelty which gives life and animation to the people of a new country. From all the causes, the people of our county were the best agricultural population ever seen in a new county, and distinguished for intelligence, courtesy and hospitality.

When they met, the old men, after having their glasses of grog (which hospitality usually tendered in those times) had two unfailing topics of conversation; one was the plans of farming, and the other, the laws which prevailed, respectively, in the States from which they came. The old women (while they sipped their wine sangaree or rum toddy) one after another would rehearse what they possessed, where they came from. There was one in particular who excelled in this *game o' brag*—for she had in "old Virginia" a fine garden edged with box, a large house, in which there was not only a spacious parlor, but the *blue* room, the *pink* room, the *green* room, and the *yellow* room. When she came down with this trump the rest commonly "*threw up the sponge.*"

And the young people of that day, what did *they* talk about? When a circle of young people, of both sexes, is formed, a mysterious electric current is generated, and excites all sorts of prattle; but then, they had, in their new literature, topics of unusual interest. The Waverly novels, by the Great Unknown, were appearing number by number, in boards with uncut leaves, and everybody read them with delight. They are still standard works—with the best qualified to judge. Then we had Campbell's poetry, filling the hearts of the maidens with melodies, and the boys with patriotism. Tom Moore had, year by year, during the first quarter of this century, distributed his poetical effusions like a constellation. His "Irish Melodies" had a wonderful influence in refining the young, and his "Sacred Melodies" first enjoyed by ministers, "as bread eaten in secret," were boldly seized by Dr. Summers, and incorporated in the Methodist hymn book. Other sects have followed their example, and so the author has been canonized, and many a good old soul, who is going straight to heaven, with no library but her Bible and hymn book, thanks God that he raised up such a pious singer in Israel as Brother Moore. I could cite other poetical authors that had a great influence on character, but I am not writing a critique on poetry, and will desist.

Candor compels me now to mention some features of society in old times which are not so complimentary. People were not so temperate then as now. Public meetings were concluded by scenes of drunkenness and uproar which were revolting. The courts were disturbed by the noise in the streets. Jurors were seen in the box too stupid to perform their duties. I had not been at court for many years until the spring of last year, and the change for the better was remarkable. I felt all the time as if I was attending church. The sheriff was cool and sober, the jurors had an expression of calm intelligence, the lawyers in condition for the highest intellectual efforts, and the Judge——. You may think it unnecessary for me to say that *he* was right; but before you travel far with me in this history you will change your opinion. Lamentable to tell! old men, and sometimes members of the church, were brought to judgment for *intoxication*. Then the question was, whether the liquor "*overtuck*" *them*, or whether *they* "*overtuck*" the liquor? in plain English, whether it was accidental or intentional?

In old times we had, also, a confederacy of horse thieves, which gave the people much trouble. The league was well organised, as you will perceive by the following story: A Mr. McDaniel, who lived near Oakville, had a fine horse, which was stolen. He pursued the thief, and found him and his horse in West Tennessee. He brought them back to Moulton, and put the man on trial before two magistrates. The prisoner was a very decent looking man, of middle age, who was dressed neatly. McDaniel could prove that the prisoner sold the horse, but he had been so altered by the new cut of his mane and tail, that there was difficulty in proving his identity. There were about twenty witnesses, and about equally divided in opinion on this point. At length, McDaniel stepped forward and informed the court that he had taught his horse some tricks, amongst them to put his forefeet, when bid, on a stump, and was willing to abide by this test. The court agreed to witness the ordeal, and the whole company passed out of the court house, in some excitement and confusion, during which the prisoner was separated from the sheriff, mounted one of the horses hitched to the rack outside the court yard, and rode rapidly down the Tuscaloosa road. There were, at least, a hundred mounted men in town that day. The "hue and cry" was raised, and instant pursuit made. Such a sweepstake I never witnessed before. The cavalcade in starting was scattered all the way from the square to Spring Hill. We pedestrians waited in much impatience to hear the result, and after awhile the pursuers, one by one, began to drop in. When the full report was made, it appeared that the prisoner was superbly mounted on a filly which could beat any horse in the field, and had easily escaped. The question was then asked, to whom she belonged? But it turned out that no person had lost a horse that day; that the filly had been placed by one of his gang for the purpose of enabling the prisoner to escape, and there being no strangers in town but him, that day, that we had members of his gang in our own county. This disclosure opened the eyes of our people; every good man, after this, became a detective, and they were watched so closely, that we had but little trouble afterward.

I must concede, also, that the vice of *gambling* was much more common than it is now. For many years the professional gamblers fleeced the green young men of the county of their money, and they could not be punished, on account of the difficulty of proving that money was bet in the game. David Hubbard, Esq., who had been solicitor for many years, and knew exactly where the shoe pinched, procured the passage of an act, when he became a member of the Legislature, dispensing with the proof that money was actually bet, when a game of cards was played in a public place. This has been effectual in subduing the evils, except in private rooms.

Bennett, the Magician.

There was, however, in early times, a man called Dr. Bennett, who had a wonderful run with a simple game with *three thimbles*, placed on his knee, and a small paper ball.

He was dexterous in handling the ball, and would bet that no person could tell under which thimble the ball was left. The boys lost a good deal of their change, and even grown-up men had their curiosity excited about that tiny ball. General B. used to tell an amusing story about it. One night he and Mr. H., a rising lawyer, went to Bennett's room, not to bet on the game, but just to see how it was done. Bennett very politely agreed to perform his trick for them, as they were men of high standing. He would manœuvre the ball and they would guess where it was; very often successfully. At length, he proposed to bet Mr. H. that he could not tell where the ball was. Mr. H., who had acquired confidence, from guessing correctly, put up $25, and lost it. Bennett having tasted blood, continued to handle his thimbles, until General B. saw *exactly* where the ball was. He was a land dealer, and never had any money, but plenty of land; a quarter section was staked, and lost. The two gentlemen rose. Bennett, while politely lighting them down the steps, said: "Call in daytime, gentlemen, you will have better light." "Thank you," said the General, "we are perfectly satisfied." There was a perfect epidemic in the country in regard to the thimbles. The profits of Bennett were so great that he is said to have purchased a large part of the town of Tuscumbia, when an untoward event put an end to his harvest. At Columbia, Tenn., he won from a gawk of nineteen years of age, his horse. It belonged to the boy's father and he hesitated to deliver him to Bennett, who jerked the bridle from the boy's hand, and carried the horse to a livery stable. He was thrown into jail on a charge of robbery. He thought light of it at first, but in a few days he was convinced that the people were bent on having him hung. He sent for the great advocate, Mr. Grundy, and was acquitted. He invited the advocate to his room, and inquired the amount of his fee. Mr. G. pulled a slip of paper from his vest pocket, and answered, "$752.10." "Yes, sir," said Bennett, counting out the money and paying it over. "And now, Mr. G., *do* tell me how you arrived at the fraction in the fee?" "O! that is very simple. I had a notion of charging you $1000, but I had falling due in the Nashville Bank a note for the amount specified." "Yes, sir," answered Bennett, "you have relieved my mind."

This sleight of hand knight went to the Texan war with the invincible Davy Crockett, and fell bravely fighting the Mexican foe.

There is another feature in the state of society which has improved much of late. People, both male and female, do not shun labor, as they did in old times. Idlers were numerous then, but very few are to be seen now. Formerly, our schools, male and female, were filled with Northern teachers, although there was a large number of *our* young people of both sexes who were poor and needed such positions for a living. The people of New England were much wiser, in that generation, than we. Many of her most accomplished daughters, who were not compelled by necessity, but by a noble desire of independence, came to the South. I remember many years since, that the Hon. Freeman Smith, a senator in Congress and the chairman of the Whig National Executive Committee, came to Town Creek for his wife; and carried home a beautiful New England girl, who for the "glorious privilege of being independent" and enabling her parents the better to educate her brothers, made her home as a teacher, with the Rev. Wm. Leigh. All honor to such women! We are beginning to have them among us, and our schools are now filled with Southern teachers.

Style of Dress, and Type of Love in Early Times.

The young men in full dress wore blue cloth coats with metal buttons and swallow tails, and vests sometimes embroidered on the edges. The pants were tight about the hips and knees and loose below—of cloth in the winter and linen drill in the summer, with all the flap all in one piece. The boots sometimes had brass heels which were highly polished when the wearer was going into company. The hats were stovepipe. The face was clean shaved except that the more mature beaux sometimes wore short side-whiskers, not of the Englishcut, which hang down like the ears of a hound. The refined taste of your grandmothers would have revolted at the sight of a young man's face covered with beard; nor is there any excuse in this age for it when we have finely tempered razors. At all events the lips should be kept free from beard for *the two great purposes* for which lips were made.

As to the fashions for ladies I was afraid to venture, but called a committee of Ancients, whose report I "have adopted." The dresses had waists of natural length (they had been very short a few years before). They were pointed before and sometimes behind. The skirts were gored and tight, eight yards being sufficient for a dress; it was trimmed with festoons of satin or else a fly was worn over the dress, which was gracefully rounded from the waist, and the margin of the fly (sometimes called a tunic) had lace or edging on it. Sleeves were mutton legs, tight at the wrist and very full at the shoulders, supported there by some stiff substance. Dress material in winter was silk or Canton crêpe, and in summer, gauze, muslin or ginghams. The hair was rolled on a cushion upon the top of the head. Shoes were Prunellas. Bonnets were Leghorn flats looped up on one side and a long white ostrich feather waving over it. Very large tortoise shell combs were worn—carved and costly.

I have said before that the early settlers brought with them all the means of civilization. But their *houses* they could not bring. For many years, these (even in the richest families) consisted of two log cabins divided by a hall, and low attics above, in one of which the girls performed the mysteries of the toilet. They could stand straight, only when in the middle of the room, and in spite of these drawbacks, when the girls would descend in full dress, they would look as lovely as Venus stepping from a rosy cloud.

So you see, when the country was first settled that we had the charm of novelty in everything; *new* land, a *new* literature and *new* girls. Hence the attacks of love (like the fevers) were *inflammatory*. They are apt to be so, when the parties have never seen each other until grown up. It is unfavorable to the *grand passion*, for boys and girls to grow up together, especially in the same school. Attachments thus contracted may be very sincere, and if the parties marry, they may pull very steadily under the marriage yoke, but the feeling entertained for each other will be a sort of a Pelagian love, the beginning of which it would be impossible to specify. But in old times, when a young man saw, for the first time, the girl just budding into angelhood, the shock was absolutely electric. No past recollection of her as a school girl, with imperfect features, chewing slate pencils and gum, with disheveled hair and disordered dress, eclipsed the bright image imprinted on his imagination.

In those days a large number of enterprising young men came to the country, while many of the girls were left behind to be educated, hence the former greatly preponderated in numbers. It was no uncommon thing for a young lady to marshal in her train a half dozen gallants at the same time. Girls! you would have been sorry for your grandmothers could you have witnessed the heavy work in this line which they had to perform; so many beaux to be entertained at once, and their favors to be distributed so impartially, that no offence should be given to any one. This was a great wear on the vital energies, and you would have been truly sorry for t em! The burden was too heavy, and they generally, from sixteen years of age, had to succumb, and to select some one of their persecutors as partner, and take their revenge by persecuting him the rest of his life!

I have now finished my numbers of a *general* nature, which, as you proceed, you will find to have been necessary for the complete understanding of the *personal* histories of which I shall exclusively treat hereafter.

We now come to treat of the early settlers in person. From the great lapse of time the task is much more difficult than I supposed. Whole families have removed and no traces of them can be found. Some have become extinct, and all that can be said of them is "that they were and are not." I have taken much pains to be correct in the facts which I will lay before the public, but if I should fall into a mistake, a note from any person who knows better will secure a correction in the next number. Wherever I have reliable information I will trace the old families as far back as I can, but (as I have before said) I shall be careful in commending the living. There is much risk in writing a man's epitaph *before he dies.*

In reviewing my notes I find one thing curious, and that is that my notices of men *in private life* will not be commensurate with their merit. You can not say much of a man who is discreet and has uniformly acted with propriety. These *proper* men are hard to delineate. About as much as you can say of such men is, that in youth they were good boys—in middle age, good husbands—and in old age good Christians. Artists say that it is difficult to paint a smooth face where there are no lights and shades, but where there are prominent or eccentric features it is an easy matter. And so it is with a writer. There are many things remembered of a man of bold features, of generous virtues, and perhaps glaring faults; and therefore no lack of material. And when we finished such a character and laid it to rest, we can exclaim with Prince Hal, on the occasion of Falstaff's death, "I could have better spared a better man."

You will perhaps read many things as we proceed which may excite a smile, but I will not hold myself responsible for that. The smile will grow out of the facts graphically described, not from any levity on my part. I expect, also, that some of you, as we travel along, will get *mad.* I certainly will be careful to avoid giving offence, but if a man who has become rich "chews bad tobacco" because I truly tell of his father having been a mechanic, I can not help it. It will not make me mad, but sorry, that in his rise he should have left his common sense behind him.

The Moulton Merchants

were, in old times, John Gallagher, Moore & Norwood, Bernard M. Patterson, James Deary, Mitchell & Pryor, David Hunter, Ambrose Hunter, James M. Minis, James Elliott, the Owens, Edmund P. Anderson and Hubbard & Talmadge.

John Gallagher was a young Irishman. I never knew anything of his parentage. From his manner I judge that he had good rearing, and from his language that he had been well educated. He spoke English like an American. and with scarcely a perceptible brogue. He was not successful as a merchant, and was elected clerk of the county court in 1822, at the first election held by the people. Daniel Wright had been the first clerk, but under an appointment by the commissioner's court. Mr. Gallagher was a small man, with dark fine hair and dark-blue eyes, and always had his face clean shaved. His manners were very popular. They were easy and graceful, sufficiently dignified to maintain his own self-respect, and deferential without being at all sycophantic. They would have been a good model for any young man studying to improve himself in this respect. They seem to have pleased alike the accomplished lawyer and the sovereign of one gallows and a battered hat.

An event occurred which added greatly to his reputation, and that was the *trial of the Witch.* On Flint river there lived a poor, friendless woman, who had the misfortune of being suspected of witchcraft. At first it was spoken of in whispers, then more boldly, until it culminated in a warrant issued for her arrest by David Knott, Esq., living near Oakville. A day was fixed for the trial, and it needed no public proclamation to make it widely known. When it arrived many of the young men of Moulton went out to witness the trial. A good many witnesses were examined without a definite result, until a young woman (who was pale and seemed to be in bad health) was introduced, who swore that she was washing on the creek one day, got very tired, and sat down at the root of a beech tree to rest herself. and that the old woman, who was accused, came down the tree in the form of a squirrel with his tail curled over his back, barking at her and put a spell on her, and that she had been sick ever since, and had puked up a good many hair balls. The squire, who seemed before to have been in a brown study, seemed relieved of his perplexities, straightened up and announced that as the proof was now positive, he should send the prisoner to jail, and commenced writing the *mittimus.* An expression of dumb amazement settled on the face of every sensible man in the crowd, except Gallagher's. He was calm and self-possessed. He rose and very modestly asked permission of the court to make a single remark. The squire replied: "You can make as many remarks as you please." "Then, sir,' said Gallagher, "allow me to remind you that it would be useless to send the woman to jail, for if she is really a witch, she can escape through the key-hole; and if she should be innocent, it would be a great pity for her to be sent to prison." The old squire was in a great quandary, muttered to himself: "That's so; that's so!" and added, "but what shall we do with her?" Gallagher answered "that the case might rest just where it was until the grand jury met, and then it could be laid before them." This course was adopted, but the matter was never more moved.

The people felt that "A Daniel had come to judgment." The case was certainly managed very cleverly by the young clerk. He said just enough, and no more—he was particular not to attack the squire's belief in witchcraft, for this would have been like running against a stone wall—but he avoided a hopeless issue, made a flank movement on the old squire, and captured him completely. Now you must not conclude from the premises that Squire Knott was a very ignorant man. So far from it, he had been elected justice because he had more than average intelligence. He had a good planta- tion, negroes to work it, the dress and manner of a gentleman. I knew him and his wife well, for they were several times at our house, after we moved to Moulton. Don't be surprised that he should believe in witches. Did not New England, led by her ablest divines, rise almost *en masse*, run wild on this subject, and for several years, hang witches to the trees by dozens! Was there not a time in Old England, when her highest court had jurisdiction of witchcraft, and judgements pronounced by the Lord Chancellor himself? To come nearer home, do you not see now, gentlemen of learning (sane in every other respect) believing in ghosts as firmly as any black "Mammy" living on a dirt floor? Moreover, are there not men in our day who are esteemed great scientists, was can, with their powerful microscopes, discover many wonderful things in the construc- tion of a bug (and yet can't see the God who made it) who have given up their minds to the strange delusion that man was not *created* as we once supposed, but by a kind of transmigration through various animals, and at last when he came into the form of a monkey, obtained sufficient perfection to assume the dignity of man. You ask me if I do not believe it? Not a word of it! If this were so, would not monkeys be seen at this day in various stages of this transformation? Would you not see men who had lost every feature of the monkey except the tail? Poor fellows! How perplexing to decide what to do with them; whether to tuck them in their trousers or manage them like the devil,

> "When he comes upon earth, in a suit of blue,
> With a hole behind for his tail to come through."

While these delusions exist amongst the reputed wise men of earth, spare your smile of contempt at the country justice.

After having served in the capacity of county clerk for six years to the general satisfaction of the people, Mr. Gallagher was elected clerk of the circuit court. After this (how long I do not remember) he looked around for a wife, and found her in the daughter of Mr. Joseph Martin. He was reared in Georgia, where he married a sister of George Walton. The Martin family were plain, good people, very much respected in Georgia. They were near neighbors to the family of Dr. Thomas A. Watkins, formerly of Courtland, and Mrs. Martin was so much attached to Dr. Watkins' mother that she named one of her daughters in her honor. (Mrs. Watkins was a sister to Governor Peter Early.) Joseph Martin and George Walton moved together, and settled in Lawrence county, Mr. Martin seven miles northwest of Courtland, in sight of my father's house. They owned a small tract of land and a few slaves, and every member of the family was industrious. The loom stood under a shed at the end of the log-cabin, and the girls kept it busy. It was one of the best specimens of a family in the middle walks of life that I have ever known. The elder of the girls was Miss Caroline. She was very large but of fine proportions; very pretty, and as good as she was pretty. Many wondered why a dumpling of a man, like Gallagher, should have fallen in love with such a queenly, majestic woman. I never did. I am satisfied from observation that small men prefer large women; because it is an instinct of our nature, implanted by the Creator. Were it not so—were the large uniformly to intermarry with the small, and the small with the small, the world would be divided into two factions—the giants and the pigmies. Happily the instinct which I have mentioned preserves the average stature of man.

Several years after his marriage Mr. Gallagher was unluckily induced, by a large salary, to remove to the city of Mobile, and become an officer in a bank. Here he died, and Mrs. Gallagher brought her children back to our county, lived several years near Red Banks, thence she moved to Mississippi, and the last time her friends heard from her she was in Arkansas, and with only three living children. Before I leave the Martin family I will state that their son, Walton, a very fine young man, died in the epidemic of 1824, and Miss Rachel, a tall, beautiful girl, married Abraham Battle. They lived on the place now occupied by their son-in-law, John H. Houston. Mr. Battle died many years ago. Rachel died in 1873. We will notice Mr. Houston when we take up his family.

Among the merchants in early times were Moore & Norwood (both Methodist preachers). Moore was in fine condition, but they failed in business, and he returned to Virginia, where he spent the rest of his life in the ministry. B. M. Patterson had a store in Moulton for a while, but removed to Pulaski. James Deary and Mitchell & Pryor sold goods for a while and returned to Shelbyville, Tenn. Also James Elliott, a Scotchman, did business in Moulton at an early day, and Isaac N. Owen, then a young man, was his clerk. Elliott went to Tuscumbia. Oneill & Kelly (he was no kin to Mr. Kelly now in Moulton), when they first commenced, were in the liquor line, then added groceries and then dry goods. They made money fast. I have heard a good story of Oneill employing a man to build for them a log ware-house in the rear of their store, and when asked if he had any choice of timber he answered: "No, except the foundation logs, which I want of *good hard Hick-o-res.*"

The family of the Owens, is one of the most respectable in our county. Caleb Owen, of Camden, S. C., the ancestor, was married to Mary Nabors, of Laurens District S. C., in 1795. She was the daughter of Isaac and Mary (Boyd) Nabors. His ancestors were Welch. He moved to Madison county, Ala., in 1813. Huntsville (which had first been named Twickenham) was a very small place. He removed thence to Tuscaloosa in 1818, which was then a mere germ of a town, and afterward to Jefferson county (1821), and later Pickens county, and finally Tipton county, Tenn., where he died in 1842. I judge he was a man who "ordered his household aright," for among all his descendants, I have not found one who was not a worthy member of society. He had three sons who were merchants in our county—Isaac N., Allen G., and Franklin C. Owen, and besides these four other children.*

Isaac N. Owen,

born 1803 in South Carolina, came to Moulton in August, 1821, when quite a young man. At first he was a clerk for James Elliott; but afterward went into business on his own account. He was of fine judgment and unswerving integrity, and won the esteem and confidence of the people in a remarkable degree. His manner was dignified and somewhat reserved; except in company with his intimate friends. In person he was tall, fully six feet and spare, but broad across the shoulders. His eye was dark and his complexion sallow. In a few years he found himself in a condition to marry, and won

* NOTE.—These four children were: Jane Owen (born Darlington District, S. C., 1796; died 1848) married (1822) in Jefferson county, Ala., Percival Pickens Halbert. Their son is Prof. Henry Sale Halbert, Crawford, Miss., author and Indianologist.

Wm. Owen (born 1800, died 1841) unmarried.

Nancy Boyd Owen (born 1806) married (first) 1822, in Jefferson county, Ala., Thompson Brown; and (second) Rev. Henry Wortham Sale. Her son is Henry T. Sale, lawyer, Denver, Col.

Louisa Owen (born 1818) married (1840) Dr. B. H. Ligon, and died 1844.

The descendants of Caleb Owen have, as a rule, been church members and of pious dispositions. Eight grandsons and one great-grandson served in the Civil War, 1861.—(*Thomas M. Owen.*)

the hand of Miss Martha Craddock, 1829—a very small, beautiful, and well educated daughter of Pleasant Craddock. He kept one of the best hotels in Nashville for a long time, and his children had the advantage of the best schools, and his daughters were highly accomplished. James B. Wallace, Esq., having married the eldest daughter, Caroline, in Nashville, and settled in Moulton, Mr. Craddock sold his property in Nashville, purchased a farm east of Moulton, and moved his family also. Mrs. Craddock who was an excellent lady, suffered the most excruciating tortures from rheumatism, for many years before her death. Not long afterward her husband followed her, and I think none of the family are now living, except Mrs. Owen, and my old Tennessee schoolmate, John Craddock (1880).

Colonel Owen, during his long career as merchant, had his troubles, but they never diminished the confidence of the people; and he was able, at all times, to support his family in comfort, and have his children well educated. He had no taste for public life, although he was a decided Whig in his opinions; but in 1834 a nomination for the Legislature was thrust upon him, and he was elected by a large majority. He was a member of the Baptist Church, and one of its pillars; but had no bitter sectarian feelings toward other denominations. In short, he was a man of liberal and enlarged views. He had moved with his son-in-law, Mr. Harris, to Nashville, and his sudden death this spring, 1880, has deeply affected this community. A good man has fallen, who has been influential in his church, has reared his family well, and was dear to his friends, some of whom have known him "through sunshine and storm," for more than half a century.

He left children as follows: (1) Mary, who married Thomas C. Sale (son of Rev. Alex. Sale). He died about 1852. His daughter Anna was married to John Phelan, Esq., who, after living at Courtland for some years, removed to Chattanooga, and Mrs. Sale went with them. Later they removed to Birmingham, where Captain Phelan died; his wife and five children survive him. (2) William Franklin, went to Pine Bluff, Ark., and commenced the practice of law in company with two young men from our county—Simpson Harris and William Galloway. The firm became prominent and was doing a good business when the late war broke out. Mr. Owen became captain, and in the course of things was taken prisoner, and was confined for two years at Johnson's Island. He died a year or two after his return home. (3) Martha, who married Captain Isaac M. Jackson. They lived on Cotaco river, in Morgan county. (4) Louisa Ligon, who married Mr. Daniel Johnson of Mississippi. (5) Harriet Perkins, the youngest, who married Andrew J. Harris, long a merchant of Moulton, and now of Nashville. We will notice him again in connection with the family of his father, Wm. Harris.

Allen G. Owen was the second son of Caleb, and was born in South Carolina, 6th September, 1806. He came to Moulton February, 1829; but in 1839 moved away, and returned from Texas in 1850. He married, 1853, at Courtland a young widow, Mrs. Martha Alman, daughter of Michael Mayes, Esq. Major Owen (like his brother Isaac) is a member of the Baptist Church, and is a gentleman of singular amiability and courtesy, and much respected by all who know him. He was a merchant, for many years, in Moulton, and since 1875 has been the clerk of the Chancery Court. He has three children, Nannie, who married W. H. Hicks, of Henderson, Ky.; Frank C., who conducts a mercantile depot for General Wheeler, and Patty, an accomplished daughter, unmarried. He died in 1882.

The third son of Caleb Owen was Frank Caleb Owen, born, 1817, in Madison county; was merchant for many years in Moulton, and had a high character for integrity. He married, 1850, Lucy, a daughter of Col. Benj. Harris, of Russell's Valley, who was one of its first settlers there. He surveyed and speculated in lands a great deal. He and the Gilchrists of our county were great friends, and were partners at land sales. Colonel Harris became quite wealthy. He was the brother of Nehemiah Harris of our county. Mr. Frank Owen was greatly respected by all who knew him. Died in Moulton, 1857. His only son, Benjamin L., married Miss Watson, the daughter of a planter in Eastern

Mississippi, and lived a few miles southwest of Moulton. He finally removed to Columbus, Miss.

Mr. Edmond Pierce Anderson (born 1800), another merchant, was reared in Cumberland county, Virginia. He married Adelaide Dechaud, of Abingdon, Va., and moved to Moulton in 1823. Their oldest son, James M., was born 30th July, 1824. After a few years, this family moved to Winchester, Tenn., where Mr. Anderson died at the early age of twenty-seven, leaving his widow with two sons—the one we have mentioned and Edmond P. Jr. Col. James M. first settled at Rusk, Cherokee county, Texas, where he practised law until 1866, when he went to the flourishing city of Waco. His attention, I am informed, has been almost exclusively devoted to his profession, eschewing politics and office; never having departed from this rule but twice—he was in the secession convention of 1860 and the Legislature of 1873. He has the reputation of being one of the foremost lawyers of the State and an able legislator. He was the law partner of Senator Coke when he was elected Governor of Texas. The colonel came in 1850 to see the place of his nativity, from which I infer that he is a man of *sentiment*. We hope he will come again. If he should, we will confer on him the "the freedom of the city," and give him a welcome, as a son of Lawrence, suitable to his merits.

David and Ambrose Hunter, and James M. Minnis—all merchants—came from the same section of East Tennessee. David and Ambrose did business as partners, for some years, and made independent livings. David, the elder brother, was rather under the average height, but strongly built. He married Maria, daughter of Capt. Wm. Leetch, but she died a few years after, without issue. David was a man of fine business capacity. In addition to his merchandise, he turned a penny by horse trading. I might have forgotten this, but for an accident which happened to me when I lived at Moulton. I purchased from David a match of horses. Some little time afterward, one Sunday morning, my boy, who had been copper colored the day before, came in nearly as white as a sheet. "What's the matter, Billy?" He answered: "Why, sir, Wash and me was having a little race to see which horse was the swiftest, when my horse *frowed* me clean over a stump—and I lit on my hip upon a root—and I'm most ded, sir." Says I, "Go and lie down, and get your mammy to rub it with camphor." But Billy still lingered, and at length said: "And the horse, he's *ded too*, sir." "The ——, you say?" "Yes, sir, he stump his toe, and fell wid his hed gin the stump, and broke his neck smack off." And so it was. I never complained of David, for he didn't guarantee that the horses' head was harder than a seasoned stump. David married for his second wife a widow named Green, and from that time commenced moving about—and it was said that he moved so often that he wore out the tenons of his bedsteads.

Ambrose Hunter was a tall, well proportioned man, and a good merchant and citizen. His circumstances had improved very much since he came to this country, and he naturally felt it; but he could not get clear of the East Tennessee drawl in his pronunciation. His friend Minnis had the same infirmity; but was much the sharper man of the two, and always delighted to have a joke on his friends. He said that "Ambrose one night was attacked with a pain in the top of his head and running down into his brain. He made out to stand it until daylight, when Dr. Glover was sent for in great haste. The doctor removed a scratch, which Ambrose wore on the top of his head, secured by small slips of cloth, pasted to his head, when lo! a large cockroach made his escape. He had been feeding on the paste, and by way of variety, taking a mouthful of the flesh—and this was the sum of his brain fever." I never could tell how much of this story was true; for whenever it was alluded to in my presence, Minnis got so *merry*, and Ambrose so *mad*, that a full explanation never took place. Ambrose Hunter married Margaret Grugett, and, after her death, a lady who had an interest in the salt works in West Virginia, and I think he moved there. Minnis married also a daughter of Mrs. Grugett, a worthy woman, who should receive more special notice.

Maj. John Grugett had been the contractor for the erection of the public buildings, and after completing them built one of the largest log hotels I ever saw. It was two stories high, had four rooms on each floor and wide halls. It stood on the east side of the street leading south from the southwest corner of the square. When the major died his widow had nothing but his house, and decided to keep a hotel. She was well patronized, especially by the lawyers from other counties. Here, in olden time, could be seen the first Clay, with his eagle eye, and McKinley with his pewter eye, but so full of metaphysics that he caused George Coulter, in his agony, to exclaim, "If your Honor please, Colonel McKinley would have us believe that you was a '*Idee*' and I was an '*Idee*' and we were all '*Idees*' together;" and the fiery Cooper, who, after a long career, has no abatement of his natural force and fire, and Billy Martin, who from an East Tennessee school master raised himself to the bar, and thus educated two brothers who became governors of Alabama. But where am I going? Mrs. Grugett had a heavy burden upon her in the support of her family, and keeping her three daughters in the social position formerly held by her family. The terms of court, in which, only, she had any income, were so short and the vacations (in which she made nothing) were so long that the good lady was sometimes greatly depressed. But she was a faithful Presbyterian, and a devoted mother, and she heroically maintained the conflict with poverty. She "made every edge cut," and once when she moved her woodpile, which had been for years in the street, she utilised the rich mould by extending her fence around it, and making a fine crop of onions. This will, doubtless, excite wonder in the minds of many people, but it must be kept in mind that in those days we had only town *constables* but now we have *marshals* with batons of office, and in a case like this not only the onions but the fence around them would have been forfeited, "*pro bono publico.*"

In this conflict the poor widow was helped by her son Ben. When he got large enough to water the lawyer's horses he drew to his aid nearly all the boys in town. When mounted bare-back, Captain Ben would not lead his squadron the nearest way to the water, but the gay crowd would canter south for more than half a mile. The mothers in town were up in arms, and many a boy who wore white pants, which bore Ben's *signet*, got "*Jesse*" when he returned home. Ben got to be a stout boy, and then in the long vacations, he would go out to the woods with an ox-cart and cut and bring home a supply of wood; but one strange thing was that Ben always rode the steer *bare-back*. He seemed to be invulnerable. As he grew stronger he did all the rough work of the family. The girls were pretty and genteel. The eldest, Malonia, married Parker Alexander, who had a plantation on the Tombigbee; Margaret married Ambrose Hunter, and Iantha was courted by James M. Minnis, who had a very good living. Iantha was tall, slender, and so delicate that her friends earnestly advised her not to marry; but she dissented and was stout in maintaining her ground. The result proved that she was right, for she had ten children.

The girls having been provided for, the old lady at length hung up her arms in the Temple of Peace. And Ben—what about Ben? Poor fellow! During all these years of drudgery and labor for others he had been forgotten and his education neglected. Had his mind grown as his body he would have been a prodigy of intellect. When he was fully grown, straightened out he measured largely—over six feet. Ben went off to Mississippi and engaged in manual labor for support, and I have never heard of him but once. When war was declared with Mexico, my nephew, the late Capt. Joel T. Parrish, of the Jeff. Davis rifles, wrote informing me of his departure. I answered at once, advising him in forming his mess to include some who were inured to hard labor. On his return from Mexico he informed me that he invited Ben Grugett into his mess, and owed his life to that fact, for he fell sick and he nursed him like a brother—and morever made a splendid soldier. For my part I gave him more honor for the noble manner in which he sustained his widowed mother and helpless sisters than I would had he gained a colonel's plume in that campaign. I omitted to mention in this connection that Mr. Minnis removed his family to Aberdeen many years ago.

Circuit Judges.

Richard Ellis, Esq., was the first judge of this circuit. His residence was in Franklin county, and he was a delegate from that county to the Convention which framed the

Constitution of the State in 1819. He was a large man. with a very popular address and fine conversational powers, and was born in the State of Virginia. He was elected judge of the Fourth Circuit. It will be recollected that, from the commencement of our State government down to the year 1832, we had no separate Supreme Court, but that the circuit judges constituted this court. At the end of the term for which he was elected, by the General Assembly, Judge Ellis removed to Red River county, Texas. He was a distinguished citizen of that State, and when, in 1836, the Convention met to form a State Constitution, he was then 54 years of age. and was elected its president. He died in 1849.

John White, Esq., was elected Circuit Judge in 1825. Mr. White was a lawyer in the town of Franklin, Tennessee. He had the reputation of being a sound lawyer, although not an eloquent man. He was a man of sober, steady habits, and enjoyed the confidence of that community. He had a good, regular practice, and a respectable position at this bar—second only to that of Nashville, in the State of Tennessee. Mr. White was rather under the average stature, and had an aquiline nose and an expressive face. He married a Miss Dickenson, who was of medium size; had very fine black eyes, and was noted for her intellect; she was consumptive—the cause of the removal of the family to Courtland, where it was hoped that a milder climate would effect a cure, but she fell a victim to this disease in a few years. They built the house now occupied by E. P. Shackelford, Esq.

Soon after coming to Courtland, a partnership was formed between Mr. White and John J. Ormond, Esq., under the style of White & Ormond, which came rapidly into favor before the public. He was elected a member of the House of Representatives, in 1824, and, in the next year, judge of this circuit, and performed the duties well and faithfully. He was a member of the Presbyterian Church, and most exemplary in the performance of the duties of that relation. In Franklin, the eloquent Dr. Blackburn had been his pastor, and yet, when he came to Courtland, where that *good man*, but dull *preacher*, Mr. Barr, was in charge, he was just as punctual in attending church as he had been under the administration of his favorite Apollos. For his second wife he married Miss Southwrayed, a Northern teacher—had two children, and lived for many years at Talladega—where he died.

He left five children by his first wife—Alexander, Sidney, Robert, Ann Catherine and John. Dr. Robert, the third son, married Miss Spyker, of Franklin county, Tenn. Alexander White, whose education had been superintended with great care, by his parents, became one of the most brilliant orators of Alabama. He located at Talladega at an early day after the settlement of that part of the State, and at once took a leading rank at the bar, and was distinguished for legal attainments, and powers as a speaker and debater. He served only one term in Congress before the late war, having been elected in 1851, and was a warm supporter of General Scott for the Presidency. In 1860, Mr. White supported Mr. Bell in the contest for President. He was opposed to secession, but, after the ordinance passed, he acted with the State throughout the struggle which ensued. He was a zealous war man, and was for a time a member of a battalion organized for home defence.

Mr. White was a member of the Convention of 1865, and, of course, took a leading part, such as his eminent abilities and stirring eloquence rendered proper. His devotion to the State, his devotion to the South, was expressed in language and with emotious which consecrated him anew as a patriot. He had loved his country, he had loved the land of his birth, his native Alabama (for he was born in Lawrence) before her disasters, before she was stricken down by armed battalions; but now, that she was in her misfortanes and desolation, now that she was in chains, he loved her more than ever. I will quote in full the paragraph which contained this noble sentiment as a sample of his magnificent style:

"Mr. President: The Bonnie Blue Flag no longer reflects the light of the morning sunbeam, or kisses with its silken folds the genial breezes of our Southern clime. The hands that waved it along the crest of a hundred battle-fields, and the hearts that, for the love they bore it, no longer rally around it. Another banner waves in triumph over its closed and prostrate folds; but proud memories and glorious recollections cluster around it. Sir, I will refrain. The South needs no eulogy. The faithful record of her achievements will encircle her brow with glory bright and enduring as the diadem that crowns the night of her cloudless skies. The fields of Marathon and Platea have been re-enacted in the New World, without the beneficent results which flowed from those battle-fields of freedom, and our country lies prostrate at the feet of the conqueror. But dearer to me is she in this hour of her humiliation than she was in the day and hour of her pride and her power. Each blood-stained battle-field, each desolated home, each new-made grave of her sons fallen in her defence, each mutilated form of the Confederate soldier, her widow's tears, her orphan's cry, are but so many cords which bind me to her in her desolation, and draw my affections closer around my stricken country. When I raise my voice, or lift my hand against her, may the thunders rive me where I stand. Though I will be false to all else, I will be true to her. Though all others may prove faithless, I will be faithful still. And when, in obedience to the great summons, 'Dust to dust,' my heart shall return to that earth from which it sprung, it shall sink into her bosom with the proud consciousness that it never knew one beat not in unison with the honor, the interests, the glory of my country.''

After the war he advocated with zeal the reconstruction policy of President Johnson, and was a leading member of the Convention which assembled at Selma in June, 1866, to send delegates to the National Union Convention appointed to be held in Philadelphia on the 4th of July. In the Selma council he submitted resolutions which he had prepared. He asked permission to read; and, leave granted, he gave them all the power and charm of his effective elocution. They were bold and defiant, and amongst other things declared that "Alabama had hung her banner on the outer wall, and would defend it to the last." The reading of these resolutions by their eloquent author came near firing the Convention, and their lofty tone, under a consciousness of right, reminded one of former days when the process of "firing the Southern heart" was going on; but they were not passed. (The substance of the foregoing is from Garrett's "Public Men of Alabama.")

In 1868 Mr. White supported Seymour for the Presidency. In that canvass he made many speeches which were regarded as able attacks on the Radical party.

I wish I could close this sketch *just here*, but I can not do so with proper regard to truth and propriety.

In 1869 Mr. White changed his party relations, and soon became a conspicuous member of the Radical party.

His former political friends strongly censured his course as a politician from that time to the date of his departure for Texas. In 1872 Mr. White was placed on the Radical ticket for Congress at large, and was declared elected. The next memorable event in his congressional career was the introduction and support by him of the *Force Bill*. Fortunately, under the fair ruling of Mr. Blaine and the vigorous opposition of the Democrats in the House of Representatives, led on by Mr. Randall, of Pennsylvania, it was defeated, as it passed the House too late for consideration in the Senate before adjournment *sine die*.

I have attempted to present fairly the material facts in the remarkable career of this highly-gifted man. I wish I could account for his inconsistencies on some principle which would be conservative of his fair fame, but with real anxiety to do it I find myself unable to accomplish it.

Sidney, the elder daughter of Judge White, was married to a gentleman of distinction. This was Joseph G. Baldwin, the lawyer, the legislator, the author and the judge; and yet, with all his attainments, his wife was a fit companion for him. She was beautiful, discreet, highly educated, and accomplished. Mr. Baldwin was a Virginian of rare gifts and culture. He settled in Gainesville, Ala., and soon obtained a good practice. He was a decided Whig in politics, and yet, in the Democratic county of Sumter, was elected to the House of Representatives, 1843. He at once proved himself one of the ablest and most skilful debators in the House. He was courteous, and always confined himself to parliamentary rules in his efforts on the floor. A man of great firmness, he never blustered. He respected the personal rights and feelings of others in discussion and demanded the like civilities for himself. In 1849 he was a candidate for Congress in opposition to the Hon. S. W. Inge, in the Tuscaloosa district; but his Democratic rival had the advantage of having knocked down an abolitionist on the floor of Congress, and this gave him decided prestige. This district was ably canvassed by both gentlemen, and Mr. Baldwin was defeated by a small majority.

Mr. Baldwin was the author of two works of considerable merit. One was "Flush Times of Alabama and Mississippi." It was designed to show the evil effects of an inflation of paper currency, and covered, in time, a period of about seven years, from 1833 to 1840, when paper money was so abundant and great speculations were carried on upon a small money basis, and when a series of financial experiments were made in loans to debtors, and the formation of real estate banks. The work was quite dramatic and described many transactions and scenes in and out of court, of wonderful originality and humor. It had an extensive sale. The other work was "Party Leaders," in which Jefferson, Hamilton, Adams, Randolph and Clay were introduced as representative men, with contrasts and parallels well delineated, showing a great fund of information, and remarkable power of analysis in the writer.

Not satisfied in remaining in Alabama, where the political majority precluded his hopes of preferment, Mr. Baldwin, not long after his defeat for Congress, removed to California, where his distinguished talents and legal capacity, soon obtained for him a seat on the bench of the Supreme Court of that State, an office which he held until his death, which occurred a few years after the close of the late war (*Garrett's Public Men of Alabama*).

I learn from a letter received from a judicious friend that "the widow of Mr. Baldwin still lives in great splendor and in fine health, retaining much of her youthful beauty and vivacity. She lives with her daughter, Mrs. J. of Oakland, California, who has the finest residence in that pleasant city. Judge Felton died about two years ago, in 1878. He was one of the best lawyers in that State, and his practice, at one time, was said to amount to one hundred thousand dollars per annum.

Ann Catherine, the second daughter of Judge White, was thought to be more beautiful than Sidney. She was married to Mr. William Dixon, a merchant, of Talladega. I am not, at present, well informed as to this branch of the family. I shall have to notice Judge White again incidentally, and when I do, I hope to tell something of his youngest daughter.

There were but two of the Circuit Judges which belonged to Early Times, and we have now disposed of them.

The clerks of the Circuit Courts, including all who have held the office for the past sixty-two years, were twelve in number. These were all old settlers, or descendants of them; I shall therefore speak of them consecutively.

1. George Foote, when the county seat was Melton's Bluff, on the Tennessee river. The lapse of time has been so great that I am not able to give a connected account of our first Circuit Clerk. It seems that he had a son, John, who married and died a few miles east of Moulton. Another son who was once a candidate in our county for the Legislature. George Foote himself moved to Limestone county, near Mooresville. His brother, Philip A. Foote, died in Huntsville many years ago. His daughter Ann married LeRoy Pope, Jr., and with her mother moved to Memphis, where she still lives—a widow (1880).

2. Jonathan Burford, the second clerk, was a good physician, who had an extensive practice in and around Moulton. He was a man of talent and popularity. He did not perform the duties of the office in person, but by a very competent deputy, whom we will notice presently. The Doctor had come from Giles county, Tenn., to which place he returned before his term of office expired. He had a brother, Daniel Burford, who came with him from Tennessee. He was a tall, spare man, with blue eyes, and high

narrow forehead. He had a strong clear mind, and was a fine talker. When he was a boy, in Tennessee new-ground, a dead limb had fallen across his neck and partially broken it, but he finally recovered from the serious injury, and ever afterward carried his head at *half mast*, which gave him a peculiar expression of countenance. Daniel was an old man when I first knew him; lived a few miles east of Moulton, and ginned cotton for toll, extensively, for his poor neighbors. Moreover, he hired a number of white men; and had a great many lawsuits, on a small scale, with his numerous customers. In these, for a long time, he was uniformly victorious. The old man in the preparation of his cases left nothing to chance. He knew what every one of his witnesses (who were his retainers) would say before court; and if the recollection of any one of them seemed to be dim, he would refresh it by recital of concurrent facts so clear that the witness could then see the thing as plain as day. When one of his cases was called Old Daniel seemed to grow taller, his form to expand, and even his head become more erect. He loomed up like a gallant general in the opening of a battle. At first I supposed that the desire of gain was the motive which influenced him, but long observation convinced me that though it was in part, yet that the main motive was a love of the excitement of litigation. But in process of time, the old man, very unexpectedly to himself, was defeated in one of his cases. For his life he could not divine the cause of his disaster. He had prepared the case well, and no one of his veteran witnesses had gone back on him. He concluded that it must have been owing to the young lawyer who hackled and dissected his witnesses, so he employed him on his side for his next case. But all this failed to show up what was the matter. The truth was that the public had tired of the old man and his witnesses. They had been before it too often. The Gunpowder plot had exploded. One by one his cases went off the docket in the same way until the sheriff was no longer heard to sing out of the court house window: "Dan-iel Bur-ford!" The man who is fond of going to law—who is successful for a season, and thinks full surely "his greatness is a ripening," will certainly meet the same fate. A witty fellow, after these defeats, offered to bet any man $20 that the old man could not recover on a plain note of hand. He had one child, a daughter, who married her cousin L. P. C. Burford, who moved to West Tennessee and became very rich.

Dr. Burford's deputy was Gilbert C. K. Mitchell, one of the handsomest men we ever had in the county. He was tall and well-proportioned, and had a light complexion, hazel eyes and light red hair. He studied law whilst he was performing his clerkly duties satisfactorily. He was the son of Nat Mitchell, who was a hatter in Moulton, when there were three on the south side of the mountain—Hansford Fears. John McDowell and himself. The Mitchells were Catholics. The old man and his son moved to Courtland about 1828. The former was appointed postmaster and young Gilbert commenced the practice of law. After living at Courtland a few years father and son moved to the Northwest, where Gilbert became distinguished as a lawyer, and died just before or during the war.

3. John Gallagher, the third clerk, has been already noticed.

4. John M. Jackson, the fourth clerk, when I first knew him, was a small farmer near Moulton, and a bachelor. He was a little under the usual height, but strongly built. His temper was one of the meekest and calmest I ever knew. He was then, and continued until his death, a consistent member of the Methodist Church. But his Christian sympathies were not confined to that branch. Jackson's manner of speech was very slow, and his words fell very softly and lazily from his mouth. So much so that a stranger would not be apt to wait to hear the conclusion of the sentence; but any who knew him would be patient that they might hear "something full of good sense." He continued in office, first, some seven or eight years—made an excellent officer—and then, several years afterward, when Mr. Cummings died before his term of office, as clerk, expired, Jackson filled out his term and handed over the emoluments to the family of the deceased, who were in need of them, thus "proving his faith by his works." I consider it one of the fortunate events of my early life that I enjoyed the

friendship of this good man. It was at our house, in Moulton, that he received his friends after his marriage, more than fifty years ago. I had forgotten it until Mr. William Harris reminded me of it, remarking: "I can't think of any person present on that occasion who is now living except yourself and wife, Mrs. L. N. Owen and myself" (1880). Of Jackson's children one son, William, became a dentist and went to the far West; one daughter married Dr. John M. Clarke, and another Col. John H. Hansell.

5. John McBride was the son of Hugh McBride, who came to the county when quite an old man, and settled about seven miles northeast of Moulton. John had a brother, named Hugh, who lived a few miles north of Moulton. J. K. McBride, who was tax collector a few years ago, was the son of John. He lost an arm during the late war between the States, at Gettysburg, Pa.

6. C. J. M. Cummings lived east of Moulton when I first knew him. He then was a militia Major, and had great fondness for Regimental musters. After that, he became an able Missionary Baptist Preacher. His oldest son was very promising, but died before his father—another married a Miss Deskins, and moved to Morgan county—he had a very pretty, intelligent daughter, who married my neighbor, Paul King, they are both dead.

7. David J. Goodlett, clerk 1864, served as clerk for four different terms, and made an excellent officer. He was born in South Carolina, in 1804; and married a sister of Col. John H. Hansell. For many years after Mr. Goodlett came to the county, he was a farmer and a merchant. In 1872 he was thrown from his horse and lamed for life. His wife died in 1874, and he in 1878.

They reared a large family of children.

a. John S., who died of small-pox, while attending medical lectures at Memphis.

b. William D. went to Texas, was editor of a newspaper in Marshall county, and died.

c. Dr. M. L. resides in this county.

d. David Crockett also lives in this county.

e. W. T., killed at the battle of Shiloh, in 1862.

j. O. E. married J. G. McAlister, and lives in this county.

g. Robert Y. Goodlett, now clerk (1880).

h. A. J. lives in Lawrence county.

8. John M. McGhee was elected in 1860. He was the son of Judge Henry A. McGhee. He married Miss Wear, who lived near Mt. Hope, and they now live in Waco, Texas. He was First Lieutenant in Captain Hodges' company, Sixteenth Alabama Regiment. He had a brother named Silas, who died at "Fishing Creek."

I have, for some time, seen the need of a history of the Sixteenth and Thirty-fifth Alabama Regiments, and would be much obliged to officers, and gentlemen who bore a part in the many conflicts in which these regiments (largely composed of young men from Lawrence) were concerned, for contributions. Let these be written in reference to what the writers themselves knew and saw. If I had a dozen or two letters written freely, carelessly, rapidly, as you please, but full of facts, I could digest a history within convenient compass which would rescue many a gallant deed from oblivion, and be a matter of cherished interest to generations of people yet to come. The members of the Thirty-fifth Regiment ought specially to aid me in this matter; for when the order was issued at Corinth to abolish that regiment and use its young men in filling up other regiments, I spent a large part of the night in laboring with the commander-in-chief and his adjutant general for a reversal of the order, which I succeeded in obtaining.*

9. Christopher C. Harris was elected clerk in 1866. I will notice him more particularly when I come to speak of his father's family, and of his brother who fell by his side on the bloody field of "Perryville."

---

*This patriotic appeal evoked response, and a graphic epic of these noble regiments is published further on.

10. **Asa M. Hodges.** I will notice him when I come to speak of the Hodges family. He was elected in 1868, but declined to accept the office.

11. **D. C. Goodlett** was appointed clerk in his stead—accepted, served several years, and resigned in 1872. I will speak of him in connection with his father's family.

12. **Robert Y. Goodlett** has been clerk since the resignation of his brother (1872), and is now the incumbent. He joined Roddy's escort (Captain Jarman) when he was but a youth, and served on it up to the closing scene, at Selma. Here twenty-three of this gallant company, surrounded by the enemy, but disdaining to yield, cut their way to a swollen stream, plunged in, and so escaped pursuit. Robert Y. was one of the twenty-three.

Judges of the County Court.

While Alabama was a territory five justices of the peace were appointed by the Governor to preside over the county court; one of which was designated as chairman and who was charged with the duties of probate judge. 1. Peter Taylor was the first judge elected by the Legislature after Alabama became a State. He came from Kentucky about 1820, had some experience in the practice of law, and was perhaps between twenty-five and thirty years of age. He was fully six feet high and was well formed. He had black eyes and hair, and was grave and dignified in his demeanor. He was not a bright man, but studious and attentive to business. He was honest and independent, and although slow in the transaction of business, gave reasonable satisfaction to the bar and the people. He practised law in the Circuit Court, but being a dull, heavy speaker was not very successful in getting practice.

He was elected several times to the Legislature, when, one day, in a crowd, he became suddenly a violent maniac. This was without any premonition. He commenced this melancholy career by attacking with a large stick James B. Wallace, Esq., who was one of his intimate friends. It is said that lunatics are apt to take up an aversion to their best friends (hence the necessity of asylums for the insane to restrain them from injuring those who have been most fondly loved before). He was carried to Kentucky by his relatives, and in the course of a year or two he died in a lunatic asylum. It is fortunate he was not married.

2. **James B. Wallace** was the second judge. He came from Middle Tennessee with his wife (whom we have already mentioned), and they were a great accession to the society of Moulton—which was already very good; for there were in the place ten lawyers, four or five physicians, a number of merchants, nearly all of whom were married men, and also many families residing in the town who owned plantations in the neighborhood. Mrs. Wallace was a graceful, refined lady, and one of the best pianists of that age. Judge Wallace was a man of fine presence, about five feet ten inches high, and hazel eyes, auburn hair and Roman nose. He was a gentleman of elegant manners and sound principles. I think he was then better versed in the polite literature than in the law, though he was not deficient in legal attainments. In the outset he was timid, nervous and backward in speaking in public. Because he was not as fluent as some of his competitors, he almost despaired of success as a public speaker. He was not then aware of the fact that a man who speaks good sense in a modest and becoming manner is always listened to patiently by his hearers, whether he has the trappings of an orator or not. He did, however, realize this truth—learned by practice, to think while he was upon his feet, and gradually became a dignified, self-possessed and forcible speaker; but, at his best, he never commanded any opulence of language. In the place of it he had that which was of far more value to a public man, and that was a refined courtesy, a candor in his statement of facts, and a generosity in his bearing toward political opponents; which secured for him a high position in the great brotherhood of cultured gentlemen far beyond that which his talents, respectable as they were, would have won for him.

When Judge Taylor was carried to Kentucky he became County Judge in his stead, and performed the duties of the office very satisfactorily.

In 1833, he commenced his political career, and was elected senator from Lawrence county, which position he retained until 1838 ; his personal popularity steadily increasing at home, while he became a distinguished leader of the Whig party of the State Rights school.

In 1838, he was appointed clerk of the Supreme Court in the place of Judge Henry Minor, deceased. This was one of the most lucrative offices in the State, and the judge removed his family to Tuscaloosa, and held the office ten years.

During this time he became well known to the people of Tuscaloosa county, and in 1851 became a member of the House of Representatives from that county. Having more experience and information, he occupied a still higher position than he had ever done before. In 1853 he was again a candidate, but, before the election, died suddenly of apoplexy.

Mrs. Wallace, who was always of a delicate constitution, died long before her husband. The judge raised six children to be grown, all of whom are dead, except one son, who is living at Caldwell, Texas. His oldest son, John, died in California; Edward, in Mississippi ; James, in Richmond, Va.—Harriet, his oldest daughter, in Tuscaloosa—and his youngest child, and daughter, in Pine Bluff, Ark.

3. James Gallagher, third judge of our county, was a younger brother of John Gallagher, of whom we have already given a full account. James was of very small stature and a lawyer. He started life under favorable auspices, obtained the above office and married a daughter of Rev. ——— Cunningham living near Rogersville, Ala. Judge Gallagher lived but a short time, his constitution having been injured by the too free use of intoxicating liquors.

4. Bolling C. Baker was our fourth judge. He was the descendant of the distinguished family of Bakers which lived at Richmond, Va. His father died while he was a boy, and his eldest brother, Gen. Wayles Baker (of whom we shall speak in full hereafter), assumed the care of him. He studied law, commenced the practice and was made judge. He was tall, spare, and delicate. He married Elizabeth, youngest daughter of Mr. William Banks, of Courtland, and moved to Florida.

5. John B. Sale was the fifth judge of our County Court. We shall notice him in our next number.

6. David P. Lewis was the sixth judge of our County Court. He has filled many of the high offices of the State, and is a man of decided ability, but his history belongs to more modern times. (He was Governor of Alabama in " Reconstruction " times.)

7. Richard O. Pickett was the seventh judge. He came into the county at a late date. I shall, however, have to speak of him as one of the colonels in the brigade of General Roddy, when I come to treat of him.

8. William M. Gallaway, the eighth judge, we have already mentioned as the son of Wiley, and the brother of Col. Matthew C. Gallaway. When his term of service expired, he was elected with Dr. Frank Sykes, a member of the House of Representatives. In 1859 he emigrated to Pine Bluff, Ark., and with two other young men (Owen and Harris) engaged in the practice of the law. Judge Gallaway was twice elected to the Arkansas Legislature, and died in 1873. He was a man of strong mind and popular manners, and had he been less convivial, and more persistent in his efforts, he might have obtained a much higher position.

9. William C. Graham was the ninth judge of the county court, and held the office until 1850, when the civil jurisdiction of the county court was taken away, and it was left merely as a court of probate. It had subsisted under the former organization for thirty years. The father of Judge Graham was named John. He lived near Franklin town, in Tennessee, upon a small farm. I knew him there very well sixty years ago. The leisure part of the year he occupied in hauling tobacco to Nashville, and goods back to Franklin. The two places were eighteen miles apart as the road then ran. It was before the construction of turnpikes and railroads. At some seasons of the year, one living now can not conceive of the miry condition of the roads. Graham used to

encounter them, and with his Scotch tenacity of purpose, always made his trips in good time—and I have heard my father (who was a merchant) say the goods were uniformly delivered according to manifest. Graham was very much respected, and married Miss Ladio Cherry, who belonged to a good family. They moved into this county in 1816. He settled first on the east side of Big Nance, and, after the land sales, moved to the west side, and occupied the place he had just purchased, and on which his son Thomas now lives. They planted the first orchard I had any knowledge of; the boys all worked on the farm, obtained a good English education, and it was one of the happiest families in our county. The old people, however, in the course of time, had some heart-rending sorrows. In the first place their oldest son, Tidant L., who was a house carpenter, was stricken by lightning and killed. Then, after an interval of many years, the war between the States broke out. Their two youngest sons had just grown up. John C., the elder, had gone to Texas, and volunteered in one of her regiments; while Noel C., the younger, entered the Ninth Alabama, the first regiment to which Lawrence contributed volunteers. Nearly three years of hard service transpired, and I know not if these two brothers ever happened to meet during all that time. But when the memorable battle of Gettysburg was fought, both these regiments were in that gallant but disastrous charge under Longstreet, on the 3d of July, 1863, and both of these brave brothers fell on the same field. In their once happy home they had, when boys, knelt for prayers at the knee of the same pious Methodist mother, and slept in the same bed. Then, after years of separation, they had met at the same carnival of blood, and sank, together, into a soldier's grave. The Ninth Alabama had passed through many a hard-fought field ere then. It had been at Williamsburg, the battles before Richmond, the Second Manassas, at Harper's Ferry, at Sharpsburg, at Fredericksburg, at Salem Church, and its members had become veterans. By what route the Texas regiment had reached that fatal field I know not, but I am satisfied it was a "fiery" one, for it is the lot of gallant soldiers always to occupy posts of danger.

Before the expiration of that year (1864) John Graham was in his grave. His good wife still lives at the advanced age of 83 years. Instead of her being a burden to her children, she is yet straight, active, industrious, and has a mind still clear as it ever was. Why was the strong man broken down by this heavy grief, and the feeble woman left. It is the old story of the oak and the reed in a storm. And, it may be, women look higher than men, in the day of calamity, and trust more to Him "who is an anchor to the soul, both sure and steadfast."

William C. Graham, when grown up, learned the tanner's trade under Mr. McLung, who owned the tanyard at Whitesburg, which Graham afterward purchased. During all the time he owned it he devoted every spare moment to study, rising in winter long before day. He commenced the practice of the law, and it was not long before he was elected judge. Then he was elected to the House of Representatives.

After this he returned to the practice of law. The commencement of his career was full of promise and his advancement rapid. But he did not continue to advance. He met an enemy in his path and succumbed to him; that same enemy which has destroyed so many of our professional men in the South.

John Graham and wife had eleven children. We have already noticed four of them. The others were Malvina, who married Joseph Love; he is dead and she still lives a widow; Malcolm S., who married first Eliza, daughter of Jerry Holland, and secondly Mrs. Pittman. He died in 1876. Thomas J., who married another daughter of Jerry Holland; James went to Texas and there died; Mary, who married Rev. L. B. Sanderson; Sarah, who married Thomas, son of Jerry Holland; Louisa, who married J. V. Love; she is dead and he living (in 1880).

John B. Sale,

fifth judge of our county court, was born in Amherst county, Va., in 1818. His father's family moved to Lawrence in 1821;* was descended from Capt. John Sale, who was an officer in the revolutionary army, and served for seven years. His father, Alexander Sale, was an able minister of the Methodist Church, of sound judgment, but deficient in imagination; and his mother was a Burruss, gifted with genius, imagination and wit. Young John was entered at La Grange College (Bishop Paine, Pres.) in 1835, and being well advanced in his studies, graduated with the highest honors in 1837. He then studied law in Courtland, and commenced practice in Moulton early in the year 1839, and, near the expiration of 1840, was elected judge. He had the confidence of the bar and the people. His practice in other courts rapidly increased, but he was seized by a desire to try a new country, and removed to Aberdeen, Miss. My brother, Col. William H. Saunders was reared near Judge Sale—was his college mate—lived near him at Aberdeen—helped him to raise his company in the late war—was his messmate until he was transferred to Richmond—succeeded him as military judge of Bragg's corps, and, at my request, has furnished me with the sketch of his career from the time he left Alabama.

Judge Sale moved to Aberdeen, Miss., in 1848, and immediately formed a partnership with John Goodwin, which lasted until Mr. Goodwin's death, 1854. In 1852 or 53 Jas. Phelan joined them, under firm name of "Goodwin, Sale & Phelan;" this firm did a very large business from the very beginning. After the war, W. F. Dowd was added to the partnership. This firm, probably combining more talent than any other in the State, did an immense business during the lawyer's "harvest" after the war, which lasted to about 1874. Some years after Judge Phelan removed to Memphis; Sale & Dowd continuing partners up to a few months before Sale's death, in 1876. After this dissolution, Sale and E. H. Bristow (a talented young lawyer) became partners.

As a lawyer, Colonel Sale ranked with the very best in the State, and this is very high praise. In his profession, as well as in the conduct of his private and domestic affairs, he was always methodical and systematic. Throughout the economy of his life, anything, from his biggest case at the bar down to the very stationery on his office table, was the subject of perfect order. Some of his friends thought that this invariable devotion to method in matters of detail and minutiæ might interfere with graver matters. Sale contended that nothing paid so well, both in money and comfort. These particular habits became more and more confirmed as he grew older, and might have interfered, to

---

* With this colony of Virginians came the Butler, Booth, Littlebury Jones, Norment and Fitzgerald families, and all settled in the same neighborhood, Judge Sale, etc.

Guilliam Booth, of Dinwiddie county, Va., died 1810. Had sons: (1) Guilliam, and (2) William F. Booth, who married Mary Ann Fitzgerald, and moved to Botetourt county, Va., 1817, and from thence to Alabama, 1826, and finally removed to Quincy, Fla. (William Booth, Sr., and Dr. Booth lived near Courtland, Ala., until they removed to Florida in the 30's.)

(1) William F. Booth married Sarah Guilliam Coe, daughter of Jesse and Celia (Guilliam) Coe, of Virginia.

(2) Mary Ann Fitzgerald Booth, born in Notthig county, 10th April, 1810, died 2d May, 1892, Quincy, Fla.; married A. J. Forman, of Baltimore, Md., and had (1) William Booth Forman, (2) Annie Forman, who married —— Dismukes, Columbus, Ga., and (3) Ellen Forman, who married Du Pont.

George Booth, first mentioned, in Surrey county, 1714. His son, George, 1140 acres on Sappony Creek, 1746. There was also a son (or brother), Thomas Booth, who married Dorcas—, and had Amy, born 1726 (*Bristol Pa. Register*).

George, Sr., died 14th August, 1765, aged 84 years (born 1679), so certified "his *grandson*," George Booth, in the old *Albemarle Pa. Register*. George Booth was of the Committee of Safety for Sussex, 1775. Mary Booth died 1762.

There was also John, Arthur, Beverly, Burwell, Shelley and Gilliam Booth, in 1765. George and Ann Booth had sons: Robert (b. 1770), and Thomas (b. 1773), with Gilliam and Mary Booth as god-parents (*Albemarle Pa. Register*). John Booth married Hollan—, before 1764. George Booth, lands in Prince George, in 1723, and also 1737; Charles, lands in Prince George, 1737.

In Sussex county, in 1804, were Beverly, Robert, Matthew and Peter Booth.

some extent, with a large miscellaneous business. Colonel Dowd, once speaking of Sale, likened him to a great steamboat—slow to go about and start, but when once under way irresistible and fast.

When the war was imminent, but many still hoped it might be averted, Sale with several of his middle-aged friends determined that they (when war was inevitable) would go into the service. The military events in the spring of 1861 removed all doubt as to coming events; the married muscle of the country was needed in the field. He assisted in raising a splendid company of infantry, 111 men, and was elected captain. This company and others were mustered into service separately, and afterward constituted the Fifth Mississippi Battalion of Infantry; went first to Mobile and thence to Pensacola. Before the reorganisation of the army, in the spring of 1862, it was discovered that battalions and small bodies less then a regiment were very useful in the army for all sorts of odd jobs only; in short that your crack battalions were a mistake. As a general rule, ten companies would organize and be mustered in as a regiment. Sale's company, however, and a number of others had been mustered in each as a company, relinquishing under military law the very thing they were aiming at, viz.: the right to choose their associates and regimental officers. General Bragg, who knew the army regulations, but "didn't know any man after the flesh," consolidated these companies into the Twenty-seventh Mississippi Infantry, asking no questions; Sale's command was one of the eleven companies of this splendid regiment of over 1100. Bragg appointed the "field and staff," against which alleged tyranny there was great dissatisfaction and almost mutiny. The "old man," however, took them specially in hand and soon "licked them into shape." After this instance of strict discipline coupled with justice, Bragg became, and continued ever after, exceedingly popular in this regiment, and the regiment was high in *his* esteem, as evidenced by its being chosen as one of the five for Walthall's brigade which played so conspicuous a part in the Army of Tennessee.

Sale's connection with the Twenty-seventh ceased shortly after the Kentucky campaign; about the time Bragg was in great need of some one at the head of the Department of Military Justice (Judge Advocate General, I believe, is the title of this official). He selected Sale, and "had no further trouble in that department," as he told me years after the war.

About the time that Bragg was removed from the Army of the Tennessee, the new military court was adopted by the Confederate Government; in view of the removal of General Bragg, and not caring for a place on Johnson's personal staff, Sale applied for a judgeship on the military court of Hood's Corps, and was appointed. In that office he served for several months, and until President Davis selected Bragg as his military adviser at Richmond. I am not certain that there was any regular official title for this particular service; suppose he was the President's adjutant or chief of staff practically. In this position, Bragg needed (more than ever) an accomplished chief of staff, and urged Sale to accept the position; resigning his judgeship, he accepted Bragg's offer, retaining his rank of colonel of cavalry. He remained with Bragg "to the bitter end."

It was during the time that Bragg held this place near the President that he was sent (I suppose) to assist in the operations against General Sherman, then marching toward Goldsboro. Whether General Johnson detailed troops for General Bragg of his own free will, or by orders, I do not know. At any rate Bragg, with about 6000 troops, by rapid movements placed himself in front of Sherman's right column under Schofield, at Kingston, N. C. The result was, Schofield was surprised and cut to pieces, losing nearly all his transportation, captured or destroyed. Bragg then, by forced marches, returned to Johnson near Bentonville, in time to meet Sherman's left column, commanded by himself. The enemy was attacked about the middle of the afternoon, and driven out of a part of his works, when night put a stop to the battle. Had the attack been made at dawn, or before, the result might have been as complete a success as that at Kingston. The following morning Sherman's middle column, under Gen. Jeff Davis, was at hand; Johnson "fell back," and Sherman went his way to Goldsboro. Colonel Sale accompanied General Bragg in the short campaign in North Caro lina, and they both returned to Richmond (after the battle of Bentonville), where they remained until the evacuation of that city. I regret that Sale did not, as he intended, write an account of this part of the history of the war.

Colonel Sale was married four times. First, to S. Turner Sykes, daughter of Dr. Wm. Sykes, then of North Alabama. Dr. Paul Sale was the issue of this marriage. Second time, to Miss Nannie Mills of Aberdeen; Archie and Susan Turner are the children of this marriage. Third time, to Miss Lou Leigh of Columbus. Fourth time, to Miss Annie Cornelius, who survives him; the children of this marriage are Braxton and Sallie.

Sale was anything than a negative character; he was capable of the strongest attachments, and indefatigable in his services to his friends. He was outspoken as to the foibles of those who claimed his attention, and sometimes impatient with those who differed from him. As for his enemies—well, they didn't love *him*. His intellect was massive, and of the order analytical. Few men could unravel a complication so successfully, or use the reconstructed material so powerfully. His devotion to method and system, as applied to the business of his life, was without change. Nothing could hurry him into disorder. All matters of professional business, domestic business, his arguments at the bar, and his books of account, were the subjects of careful arrangement. Notwithstanding these strong traits and habits, he was sentimental. No one enjoyed romance more than he, and he loved poetry, if it was of the emotional kind; his theory on this subject was that the mission of poetry was to make us feel; that to write of commonplace things, or demonstrate mathematics in verse, was a thundering humbug! Can do it far more pleasantly in prose. He delighted in humor, broad or narrow, and was himself a considerable wit, and was (sorry to say it) much given to "punning." Utterly without policy, he couldn't help rasping his best friends sometimes, when they "stood fair."

Sale's knowledge of the English language, and his use of it, was remarkable; as a letter writer, he was unexcelled; his friendly correspondence combined the force and point of a man's with the ease and gossip of a woman's pen. As a draftsman of business or legal papers, he was considered a model; had great talent for making difficult and complicated subjects read smoothly, in spite of the cant and rugged technicalities which seem indispensable to such writing. A friend (not a lawyer) once suggested that his papers were just a little prolix; he contended, however, that as ink and paper were cheap you had better bear the tautology than run the risk of obscurity.

Before the war Sale had accumulated an ample fortune, but nearly all of it consisted of promises-to-pay and uncollected fees; of course, like others, he lost nearly all, and when the war was over had but little beside his residence and law office. He, however, left his family independent, if not rich, at his death.

His careful forethought was not less remarkable than his uniformly methodical habits. In speaking of these, I might have mentioned many amusing incidents; instance his purchase of the alarm clock for arousing Gus, a sleepy-headed servant, at a certain time in the morning. He was then single, and occupied a room adjoining his office. Gus slept in this office, and usually made his bed under a large table in front of the fire. The clock was started, duly explained, and the alarm set for day break next morning. Now, in order that Gus should have a proper sense of this clock, Sale got up a few minutes before alarm time, and stood ready with a long red cowhide; sharp to the minute, "she went off," but in spite of bells, rattles and smashing crockery, Gus slept well for half a second, when the cowhide joined in the reveille. Gus, tremendously stampeded, bounced up with the big table right on top of his head; the table fell first on one corner, and after one or two ricochets, landed bottom upward at the back door. Such a scatteration of briefs, private correspondence, inks (red, black and copying), postage stamps and kerosene lamps! Augustus thereafter, about daybreak, slept like the mink, with one eye open.

One of Sale's maxims was, that a soldier should always be prepared and ready for *victory* as well as for *defeat*, especially for those sudden emergencies, when there is no time to pack up your things. True to his principles, at the beginning, he had a very large pair of saddle-bags made (the biggest in the army) and in them he kept a complete soldier's outfit; these bags were never used, or even opened, except for the purpose of better arrangement of the outfit, which he kept ready at hand during the entire war. Fortunately, there was no occasion to test the true value of the saddle-bags.

My brother, Col. William H. Saunders, of Mississippi, his life-long friend, who also served with him in the Military Court of Hood's army, in transmitting this sketch, says: " You will of course use it as so much raw material for making up your article for pub- lication." I have taken the liberty of inserting it, just as he wrote it.

From a long and intimate personal acquaintance with Judge Sale, I consider this delineation of him a very successful one. For some years before his death, the Judge was a consistent and pious Methodist; and his Christian duties were performed with as much method and earnestness, as his professional ones. He was an active and efficient member of the church to which he belonged; and his death was deeply mourned by its best members.

In taking a general review of the career of Judge Sale, of the prominent position he held at the bar, as a civil judge, as a military judge, as the trusted Adjutant of General Bragg, in organizing the armies of the Confederacy, and directing their general move- ments; of his ardent patriotism; of his unsullied honor, and his sincere, modest and consistent piety, I think we are authorized in pronouncing him, one of the ablest and best men emanating from our county. One or two others may have excelled him in a single department; but his mind was one of great versatility, and proved to be fully equal to the demands made upon it, in the various positions referred to, requiring different attributes of the intellect.

The Clerks of the County Court,

for thirty-two years, from 1818 to 1850, when the office was abolished, were five in number.

1. Daniel W. Wright was the first. His father settled in Courtland at an early day, and kept a boarding house. His son, Daniel, was very sprightly and studied; and obtained the office of clerk. By this means he became favorably known to the people, and in 1819 was elected, with Arthur F. Hopkins, a delegate from Lawrence county to the Constitutional Convention.

Shortly afterward Mr. Wright moved to the State of Mississippi, where he was elected judge of the Circuit Court, and, I believe, died before he arrived at middle age.

2. John Gallagher was the second clerk. His history we have already given.

3. John Gregg was the third clerk. His father had been a Revolutionary soldier. He came to Lawrence in early times, and died near Moulton. He had, besides John, three sons, Henry, Samuel, and Ellis.

John married Sarah, daughter of Samuel Bigham, Esq., who first settled, before the land sales, at Bigham's Spring—called afterward Hickman's Spring—and now "Pond Spring." There was quite a colony of squatters around this spring, who were over-bid at the sales, and scattered in various directions. Esquire Bigham was a large, and good-looking man, and was elected to the Legislature in 1819 and 1820. He was a poor speaker, and not well versed in public affairs; but he was honest and respectable, and had all the influence of the earliest settlers in his behalf. This constituted a large proportion of the voters then, but the influx of population gave the majority to the new comers, and the old gentleman had to subside into private life.

John Gregg succeeded Bolling B. Burnett as sheriff, and his deputy was his brother Ellis. He was a modest, quiet man in general, but being powerful when roused he was formidable for he acted very promptly. I recollect an amusing incident which happened while he was sheriff. On the McMahon corner, at Moulton, a ring of wild drinking fel- lows had, for several days, caused great annoyance to the court by their noise and clamor, sometimes bellowing like bulls. At length they became so bold that they came into the court house. One of them caused a disturbance, and the judge ordered him to jail. John started with him, when one of his friends attempted a rescue. John knocked the interloper down and he fell at full length on the hard brick floor, and then, turning to the judge, John coolly said: "If your honor please, here is a man interfering." It caused a great laugh, and the "bull" ring was broken up. In John's court the execution had preceded the judgment.

As county clerk (although he was not so expert as some of the others) he was attentive to business, and gave fair satisfaction.

In 1835, during the revolution in Texas, John Gregg, in company with W. D. Thomason, John Wren, James Ellis, James McDaniel, Humphrey Montgomery, Farney Smith and young Kaiser, engaged in that cause. They all entered the same company, except James Ellis, who, hearing of the arrival of the "Red Rovers" from Courtland, joined them, and was amongst those murdered at Goliad.

After the Texan war, John returned to Lawrence for his family, and on his way back to Texas was attacked by the Indians; his wife and one son were killed, and another son, Henry, was carried off a prisoner and detained in captivity for several years. I have tried, in vain, to learn the particulars of this mournful tragedy. John Gregg died not many years after this in Texas. His brothers moved to Arkansas.

5. Wiley Gallaway was the fifth clerk, and held the office for fifteen years—from 1835 to 1850. Lawrence county never had a better clerk than he. We have already related his family history.

Probate Judges of Lawrence County.

In 1850 the civil jurisdiction having been taken away from the county courts, and the office of clerk abolished all the duties were performed by the probate judges.

Henry A. McGhee was the first of these, and his career was in a wonderful degree marked by success and good fortune. I have (as is my habit in such cases) inquired particularly into the history of his early life. His grandfather was Joseph McGhee, who lived in Wake county, North Carolina, and was a soldier of the Revolution.

His father was Merryman McGhee, and his mother Elizabeth Harvill, who was born in Virginia. Henry was born in Wake County, North Carolina, in 1810. The family moved to Blount county, East Tennessee, in 1818. Henry was now eight years old, the period at which education should commence in earnest, but his father was poor, and the chances for education, in that new country, very slim. He managed, however, by going to school two or three months every year, after the crops were made, to get an average education for the times, and enough to enable him, by careful study, to attend to any business which came before him during his different terms of office. The truth is, that nature had endowed him with quick perception and good judgment.

When the family moved to Lawrence, Henry and his elder brother, Silas, performed manual labor with great industry. The first time I ever saw them they were using their pole axes with considerable activity; and then commenced my acquaintance with the judge, which has continued for nearly a half century.

In 1835 the judge married Jane Warren, who was reared near Fayetteville, Tenn. After this, the two brothers purchased the saw-mill near the Chalybeate Spring on the Tuscaloosa road, which they managed with great industry, until Henry was elected constable in 1840; and now commenced a career of success not surpassed by any man who has ever lived in this county.

He was constable until 1843; he was then elected tax collector, and again elected in 1844 and 1845, and in 1846 he was candidate for sheriff against five opponents, and was elected by a vote larger than that of all the others put together; and in 1850, his term of service as sheriff having expired, he was elected Probate Judge. His term of office expired in 1856; in 1857 he was elected to the Legislature over one of the ablest men in the county; in 1858 he was again elected sheriff, and in 1860 he was census enumerator.

What was the secret of this uniform success? It was. that, in every office of trust, he acted honestly; in politics he was true to his principles, and he moreover had very pleasing manners and great tact in electioneering. "All the while the wonder grew" how he could love so many people as warmly as he did. I suppose it was on the principle that a muscle grows in size and increases in power from exercise, the heart being no exception to the general law.

When the war between the States broke out, Judge McGhee, although over fifty years of age, raised a company for twelve months, and went out as captain. It was included in the Twenty-seventh Alabama Regiment. At Fort Donelson the regiment was captured, but the judge was at home on leave of absence at the time.

The judge removed to Texas after the war, and his wife died at Bremond in 1872. His children were: 1. Elizabeth, who married Jere Gibson, who established a newspaper called the *Democratic Standard*. 2. John M., whom we have noticed as clerk, and will have occasion to do so again when I come to the history of the Sixteenth Alabama Regiment. 3. Mattie, who married Ben Talliaferro and died in 1873. 4. Silas, who belonged to Captain Bankhead's company in the Sixteenth Alabama, and died on the morning of the battle of Fishing creek. 5. Mollie, who married J. T. Strain, who was captain in Col. Johnson's Regiment in Roddy's Brigade. They live in Waco. 6. William, living in McLennan county, teaching school. 7. Henry is in Mason county, Texas, as deputy sheriff. The judge has married, for his second wife, Mrs. Green who is a native of Texas. He is her fourth husband.

Crockett McDonald was the second probate judge of our county and like his predecessor was very successful in his aspirations. His character of mind, however, was very different. He was rather a taciturn man, with strong common sense, and strict application to business; and on this foundation he built successfully. I first knew him in 1826, [when he came to Moulton, although he had come to the county two years before from Kentucky. At that time he used to preach, not very fluent, but very sensible, discourses in the court house, as a minister of the Christian (or Campbellite) church. In less than four years, his industry and fine business capacity, sustained by his known integrity, were fully appreciated by the people of Moulton; for he combined in his own person, and at the same time, the offices of justice of the peace, postmaster, treasurer of the county, mayor of Moulton, and preacher, and it seems to me, I have omitted one or two more of his pursuits. He had a good clear head for arranging business, and I never heard that any suffered from the pluralities combined in one hand. A strong proof of this is to be found in the fact that he was elected probate judge, and held the office until his death.

One of his sons, James H., is now (1880) probate judge, and we will notice him in regular order. Another, William S., is postmaster in Moulton. He married a Miss Alexander. A third, Edward C., married Sarah C., daughter of Judge Ligon, and is clerk in the office of the probate judge. Another son, David C., was clerk of the Circuit Court, resigned the office; and has moved away.

Rev. Andrew O. Horn was the third clerk of the County Court, and his name was passed over by accident. Previous to his election he had been a very acceptable preacher in the Cumberland Presbyterian Church, and to the influence of the large membership of that sect he was indebted for his success in obtaining the office. He made a pretty good officer. After his term had expired he had some difficulty with his church; left it and joined the Christian (or Campbellite) Church, and moved away, first to Missouri and thence to Texas. I had not heard of him for over thirty years, when my friend, Major Owen, met him in Austin, where he was visiting his son, Dr. James Horn, who was very promising, and was getting into a good practice. Mr. Horn himself was teaching a school some eighteen miles distant.

Christopher C. Gewin, the third Probate Judge, succeeded Crockett McDonald. During the term for which Mr. Valiant was sheriff, Mr. Gewin was one of his deputies, and formed an extensive acquaintance with the people. In 1840 he was elected sheriff, and made an active, faithful officer; but, within the limits of his duty, performed its functions in so considerate and forbearing a manner, that he increased the number of his friends. In 1844 he was elected to the House of Representatives, and afterward, Probate Judge. Mr. Gewin was a man of but little education, but of a strong, clear, natural mind and energetic character. He was decided in his opinions and movements, and had warm friends and bitter enemies. He was twice married; first to a daughter of William Boyd, and the second time to her sister. Some years ago he moved to Madison county, in this State, where he still lives.

Charles Gibson was our fourth Probate Judge. He was the son of John Gibson, who had moved his family from Georgia and settled them in Lawrence county, near Oakville, in 1818. Charles was then about 17 years of age. He had been reared to work on a farm, with only such opportunities for an education as were afforded by the common schools of Georgia, which he attended at intervals when he could be spared from the business of the farm. In 1823 he married Clarissa, a daughter of John McDowell, an Irishman, and Revolutionary soldier, whom we have noticed in a former article. Their married life was a very happy and busy one, and continued about forty years, during which they made a good estate, and, moreover, reared (to be grown) six sons and four daughters. During the first years of his married life he amused himself with military affairs. He was captain, then adjutant, then major and colonel. I very well remember all this, for I was young, too, then, and I do not recollect in all my travels ever having seen so many long white plumes floating in the air; as many scarlet sashes, and war-horses so richly caparisoned, as I used to see at the brigade musters in Moulton in early times. The taste of the present age has changed in this respect entirely, and the floating plume has degenerated into the pompon, not much longer than your finger, and tufted with colored wool, and all the appointments seem to be designed for the purpose of rendering the officer *inconspicuous* in battle.

Colonel Gibson, whilst busily engaged on his farm, was constantly improving his mind, and kept well posted as to public affairs. Those who knew best his sterling honesty and excellent common sense, at length urged him forward as a candidate for office, but his first efforts were unsuccessful. He was too independent a character to succeed well in this line. His temper was not supple enough, and he was too firm and tenacious of his opinions; in short, he lacked tact in electioneering. But when the people were fully informed in regard to his just claims he became a decided favorite. He was frequently a member of the Commissioners' Court, and has served in all, on that bench, twenty years. Here his experience in practical matters, and his independence in guarding the county treasury from pillage, made him very useful. In 1858 he was elected Probate Judge. As in every other trust, he was faithful, and had but fairly begun to reap benefit from the emoluments of the office when the war occurred, and put a stop to all paying business. His labors, however, did not cease. Our soldiers were in the field gallantly doing their duty, and their wives and children began to suffer. The labor was then imposed on the judge of taking charge of all donations made for soldiers' families, and making distribution of them. As difficult as this was, being deeply devoted to the Southern cause, he performed it with energy, pride and pleasure. Those were scarce and difficult times; the country was becoming bare of everything, and as the facts of the case will shortly fade from memory I will here specify a few of them. The judge had frequently to go to Montgomery to draw the funds for the purpose, and then to scour the country to purchase articles of necessity at fabulous prices. He found a fine lot of molasses in Russellville, sent there for fear of falling into the hands of the enemy, bought it, and hauled it to Moulton for the soldiers' families. There were 100 sacks of salt in Gadsden, sent there for the use of this county; he procured ten wagons and went for it. . Riding ahead, he found many of the sacks in so bad a condition that there would have been great waste of this substance, whose crystals were worth more to our women than diamonds, and he repaired them with his own hands before his teams came up. When this supply was exhausted he bought four barrels which had been hauled from Tuscaloosa, at *one hundred dollars per barrel*. The tax corn and meat of the county had been going into the hands of the army commissaries, and he managed to get it all for the use of the soldiers' families. He had his agents to help him, and had it distributed all over the county. He had several boxes of cotton cards brought in, and it was a timely relief, for the clothing of the poor had become scanty. But, with all this effort, the pressure became heavier every month until the close of the war. At the darkest hour he received a note from a noble-hearted man, donating 100 bushels of wheat, and saying, further, that no soldier's wife should starve as long as he had a bushel of meal. That man has gone from us, but "his works do follow him." I shall have occasion to speak of him again. Many a soldier from our county, when he heard that Charles Gibson was charged with the duty of providing for his dear ones at home, slept soundly by the camp fire, even while the earth was shaken with the thunder of artillery. He was re-elected Probate Judge in 1864, and was disfranchised before two years of this term had expired.

The war closed, and in 1875 he was elected a member of the Constitutional Convention, and then retired from public life. He was a farmer for fifty years, and was very successful. He boasts that, in all that time, he never bought a bushel of meal, or a pound of meat or lard, but, on the contrary, has sold a good deal.

When the judge was about sixty-five years of age he married a second time. And here again he showed his good common sense; for, instead of marrying a young girl, he chose an elderly lady, a Mrs. McCulloch. who has made him a good wife.

Many of my readers will notice that in speaking of Judge Gibson I have departed from the rule adopted in the outset, of saying but little in commendation of the living; but, in this case, they should keep in mind that the judge is over seventy-eight years old, and by this time he has gotten a "set," and will not change much. Don't imagine that I consider him near the end, and am writing his obituary. By no means! The judge is still robust in mind and body, and is now a better *life*, as the underwriters call it, than many men of but half his age. But were I writing his obituary I would not omit the excellent Christian character he has always sustained in the Baptist church.

Judge Gibson's children were: 1. John C., who is now a wealthy farmer in Ellis county, Texas. He is a gentleman, in every sense of the word, and is one of the best managers on a plantation I ever knew in this county. He has been married four times, and has one child by his first wife, two by his third, and one by his fourth. 4. William, who was killed at the battle of Murfreesboro, and belonged to the Sixteenth Alabama Regiment. 3. Sylvanus, who died at 21 years of age. 5. James S., who was in the Sixth Arkansas Regiment, and at the battle of Shiloh was wounded in the head three times, but not severely. He is a Baptist preacher and merchant at Landersville. 2. J. J. (commonly called Mack), who is farming near Moulton. 6. Charles, the youngest, who studied law, went to Texas and married a Miss Ellis. He was clerk of the District Court in Ellis county, and a member of the Legislature in 1878. He was a member of the Sixteenth Alabama Regiment at Shiloh; had a bone in his leg broken at the battle of Murfreesboro, and afterward, at the battle of Chickamauga, was wounded in the same place.

Of Judge Gibson's daughters, one married Darius Lynch, Esq., of Moulton, and has been dead many years; another married J. T. Adair, of Trinity, and never had any children; the third married Robert Prewit, brother of J. W., who now lives east of Moulton. They are both dead, but have left a son named Talbot; the fourth daughter married W. L. Kirk, of Texas.

5. James H. McDonald, the fifth probate judge, is now the incumbent. In the last number we gave a sketch of his father and the McDonald family. He was elected in 1866, and has been judge nearly fourteen years, and from his youth his habits were well fitted for office work. He is thoroughly acquainted with the duties of his office, and performs them with great assiduity. He is supposed to be better acquainted with the minutiæ of the statute laws of Alabama than any man in this section of our State, except Milton McLanaham, of Morgan, who was celebrated in this respect. The judge has but little to do with politics, and has very quiet and polite manners.

Judge McDonald first married Mary Ann, daughter of Wiley Gallaway. By this marriage he has two young daughters of much promise. His wife died in 1874. He has since married a Mrs. Duke, of Memphis, a most estimable lady.

Sheriffs of Lawrence County.

From the year 1818 to the late war, a period of sixty-two years, there were thirteen sheriffs, and every one of them was an early settler. This important and lucrative office was never committed to any man who had not enjoyed the confidence of the people for a long time. What a commentary is this upon the habit of our people of breaking all the ties which bind them to their early homes and friends, and seeking new homes, where it requires a large part of a lifetime to give them the same social position they once had.

Hance M. Cunningham was the first sheriff of this county. His name is mentioned in several of the early Acts for the organization of the county and for the establishment of turnpike roads. His mother was sister to John and Moses McWhorter, a very respectable family of old times, into which Dr. Robert M. Clark married. The McWhorters and Cunninghams moved into the county in 1817. Hance married Mary Tiggs. He was elected sheriff, and Esquire Hogan was his deputy, and this is as much as I have been able to learn concerning him.

William Reneau, the second sheriff, I knew very well. The Reneau family came from East Tennessee; and John (the father of William) died many years afterward, at the house of his son. William was not a man of much education, but of energy and a very kindly disposition, almost too much so for a sheriff. The consequence was that he became very popular, and at the expiration of his term of office he was elected to the House of Representatives of the General Assembly, in which he served during the sessions of 1835 and 1836. His deputies were Asa Hodges and Hugh M. Warren.

Hugh M. Warren, our third sheriff, lived first in Madison, where he was sheriff of that county. He married for his first wife, a Miss Hart, and settled near Leighton. Being well known to our citizens who came from Madison county (and we had a great many of them) he was elected, by their influence, sheriff of the county. I knew him well, for I was then practising law in Moulton. He was a man of energy and method. All his official business was closed up promptly. In this he was assisted by Andrew Kaiser and Levi F. Warren.

By his first marriage he had four sons: William H. Warren, who was major in the Confederate service, and lives in Colbert county. He married first Miss Cassidy, of Florence, and secondly, a daughter of John Dial, near La Grange. He was a fearless officer, but not always temperate. The second son, Robert, married a daughter of Dr. Clark, and also lives in Colbert county. The third son, Thomas, married a Miss Webb, of Madison county, and lives near Moulton. The youngest son, Hugh, married a daughter of John L. Murray, and moved to Texas years ago.

Hugh M. Warren, for his second wife, married Nancy Emily, daughter of John (Pond) Smith. This old gentleman was much respected, and was the head of a pious Baptist family. The issue of this marriage was two daughters, Martha and Mary. Martha married Robert King, son of Oswald King, in 1856; and Mary married Burchett C. King, brother of Robert, in 1858. Each has many children.

Andrew Kaiser, one of Mr. Warren's deputies, studied medicine, found some mineral springs (called Kaiser's Springs), settled and I think died there. Levi F. Warren lived near Moulton, amassed a very large fortune and died a few years ago.

Bolling B. Burnett, the fourth sheriff, was a very sociable, talkative man, made a good officer, and was a Methodist and a man of consistent moral character. He married Mary, the daughter of a stout, lame blacksmith, living near Town Creek Bridge, commonly called Judge Hall; and moved to the State of Mississippi, near Aberdeen, in 1837. Deputies not known.

John Gregg was the fifth sheriff, and had for his deputy his brother Ellis. Of John (who was a clerk of the county court) we have already spoken.

Matthew Roberts, the sixth sheriff, is now living; with physical and mental powers very good for an old man, and although he is about 86 years of age, and deaf, he is as fond of *hearing* the news as any man in the county. Major Roberts is one of a generation, the individuals of which were born and reared when the county was new and wild, and the chances of an education poor, who have, notwithstanding, made a good estate, occupied positions of honor and profit, and raised large families.

His father and mother were both descendants of revolutionary soldiers, and lived in Roane county, North Carolina. In 1809 they moved to Giles county, Tenn., and in 1817, to this county. At the land sales, in the Spring of 1818, they were overbid, lost their improvement, and moved to a place on the southeast branch of Town Creek, where they lived for many years and died. When they moved into this county they brought with them a family consisting of seven children, of whom three are dead, and four living, viz: Matthew (the subject of this sketch), Howard, William (who lives in Texas) and Mary.

Major Roberts, when I first knew him, was a constable, with a very large collecting practice. After a while he became so generally and favorably known that he was elected sheriff, and gave satisfaction to the people in that office, His deputies were Samuel Henderson, who succeeded him, and Boling C. Burnett, who had been sheriff before. The Major was a patriotic man, and was captain of one of the companies raised so promptly for the Florida war, which marched from Moulton to Tuscaloosa in forty-eight hours, of which I will speak more especially hereafter.

Major Roberts was married in 1819, to Susan Wells, who was an orphan, and reared by her grandfather, John Chilcoat. They settled, during that year, in Robert's Cove, southwest of Moulton, where the family still live. This couple reared thirteen children, to be men and women, in comfort and respectability. Ye rolling stones! What think you of a family home sixty-one years old? Of children, the oldest, John C., was in the Confederate service, along with his son John, and both were Baptist preachers, living in Franklin county. Thomas and Absalom both died in the Confederate service (under General Roddy) of typhoid fever. Houston served for two years in Captain Hodge's company, in the Sixteenth Alabama Regiment, and was wounded in the head at Shiloh. To be with his two brothers, he obtained a transfer into Captain Threlkeld's company, Fourth Alabama Cavalry, under General Roddy, and in falling back from Dodge's command from Tuscumbia, he was struck on the head with a fragment of a bomb, and fell apparently dead, but his comrades carried him to the rear, and he finally recovered. One of the daughters married a Masterson, another an Armor, and a third a Milam. One of the sons, James, has practised medicine for many years in Kentucky. This is but an imperfect account of this patriotic family, but it is the best that I can offer.

Samuel Henderson was the seventh sheriff. He had for his deputies Denton H. Valiant and Robert Henderson. The administration of the office, I presume, was satisfactory to the people, for they elected him to the Legislature in 1838. He married his cousin Rebecca, daughter of John Henderson. The family moved to Texas many years ago.

Denton H. Valiant was the eighth sheriff. I am not advised from what State he came. When I moved to Moulton he was industriously carrying on the trade of a cabinet maker. He was a man of good natural mind and embraced every opportunity of improving a very defective education. He was honest and very tenacious of his opinions and was much respected. After being deputy he was elected sheriff and made an efficient and popular officer; so much so that he was elected to the Legislature in 1841 and also in 1842. He married a Miss Kilpatrick, and so did Mr. Branch, who lived in the grove at the Moulton Spring. They were ladies of some culture and sisters to Dr. Kilpatrick, who was a successful practitioner on the lower Mississippi river. I knew him when he came to visit his sisters. I have been told that Mr. Valiant, who with his wife has been dead for many years, left two sons, who have become lawyers of distinction, to-wit, Frank, of Greenville, Mississippi, and LeRoy, of St. Louis. If this be so, it is probable that the direction of the boys' minds was given by the mother. Denton

H. Valiant was Lieutenant in the company of Volunteers for the Florida war, to which I have alluded.

Mr. John C. Burruss, son of Richard Burruss, is said to have been one of the best officers Lawrence county ever had. He was elected in 1851 and served a full term very acceptably to the people, and honorably and profitably to himself. He married Kate, a sister of Samuel D. and John H. Houston. She was a most excellent lady, highly endowed by nature and education, and a great favorite among her acquaintances. When I come to speak of the Burruss and Houston families I shall give an account of the ancestry of Mr. Burruss and his wife.

Wm. Eubank succeeded Mr. Burruss and made a correct, painstaking officer. He was a popular gentleman and much respected by all the people. He moved to Texas before the war and died years ago.

Joseph H. Shrygley succeeded Mr. Eubank, and gave satisfaction as high sheriff of old Lawrence.

C. C. Gewin was the twelfth and Henry A. McGhee was the thirteenth, and we have already spoken of them. We will now give an account of the Burleson family, including Gen. Edward Burleson.

The Burleson Family

emigrated at an early day from North Carolina to East Tennessee. At that time there was open war with the Cherokees, for a sister of Joe and James Burleson (who afterward lived in Lawrence county) was scalped by these Indians. But belonging to a race possessing a great deal of vital energy, she recovered, and was the grandmother of Gen. John H. Morgan, one of the most renowned of the cavalry commanders in the late war (Dr. Burleson, president of Waco University).

These two brothers moved from East to Middle Tennessee. When the Creek war occurred James Burleson became a volunteer, and was made captain of a company. He was uneducated and took his son Edward (afterward General Burleson) along to keep the muster roll of the company. He thus received his first taste of military life under Gen. Andrew Jackson.

Joseph Burleson and his brother James came into this county some time before the Indians were removed. When Moulton was established Joe kept the best public house in it. He moved to Brazos, Texas. He had a son, named Aaron, who had considerable reputation as an Indian fighter; but, as far as I know, never held public office. His daughter married George Jones, of Lawrence county, Ala. Hon. G. W. Jones, the member of Congress from the Austin district, is a grandson of Joe Burleson.

James Burleson settled with his family on the north side of the mountain, on Fox creek. Here, near an Indian village called Moncetown, the family became involved in a feud in consequence of the imprudence of a son-in-law named Martin, and the consequence was that James Burleson and his son, Edward, killed three Cherokees and fled to Missouri. Of course, the circumstances attending the killing can not now be recalled. It is probable, however, that after the scalping, which occurred in East Tennessee in their own family, they had no love for Cherokees, and that it did not require much provocation to bring on a conflict.

From Missouri the family moved to Texas, about the year 1831, to Bastrop county. By this time, his father having become an old man, no longer took part in public affairs, but the career of Edward Burleson continued for twenty years, and steadily became more distinguished until his death. Of course, I will not attempt to give a detailed account of it, for this would be like writing the history of Texas over again; but I will touch on the salient points for the purpose of illustrating his character. For several years, after he became a colonist, his home was on the extreme frontier, and he was frequently called upon to repel parties of marauding Indians. His courage and ability soon inspired confidence, and the people learned to repose in security when Burleson was between them and the hostile Comanches

But matters soon assumed a more serious aspect. The perfidious tyrant, Santa Anna, had reduced every State in Mexico into subserviency to his views except two, one of which was Zacatecas. This was a wealthy mining district, devoted from the first to the cause of the Patriots, and the spirit of liberty had here taken deep root. The people of Zacatecas met Santa Anna with his army upon a plain near that city on the 10th of May, 1835, and after an obstinate contest of two hours the Dictator triumphed, and the Zacatecans were completely routed. Two thousand of them were killed and twenty-seven hundred of them taken prisoners. Santa Anna and his troops marched into the capital of that State, where for two days they engaged in the butchery of its inhabitants, and the plunder of their city. The fugitives who escaped fled to Texas, and spread the news of their bloody catastrophe. The effect of it was depressing even on the bravest hearts, for Texas alone, with a meagre population scattered over a large area of country, was left to battle with this conqueror, who had subdued all the other States of that wide Republic. But " there were giants in those days," and the people, led by their choice spirits, began to rise up against this invasion of their rights. On the 17th of May the people of Bastrop met, and had the name of Edward Burleson added to the Committee of Safety. This was the first movement made toward an organization for protection; and Colonel Burleson's regiment was the first which organized for the reduction of San Antonio, into which General Cos (the brother-in-law of Santa Anna) had thrown his forces. When the Texas volunteers concentrated they elected Austin their General. In a few days the General was appointed Commissioner to the United States, resigned his command, and Burleson was elected to fill his place.

The first affair which occurred after Burleson became general was the " Grass fight." About one hundred Mexicans slipped out on one side of the town to cut grass for their horses. About the same number of Texans, under Col. James Bowie, set out to intercept them. The movement was seen from the town and the besieged marched out with two pieces of artillery to defend the foraging party. Colonel Bowie had to meet both nearly at the same time and the battle was pretty well sustained until the main body of the Texans coming up, charged the Mexicans, who retreating rapidly, they fell back into the town, leaving about fifty killed and several wounded on the field. The Texans lost very few.

A few days after General Burleson was considering a plan of assaulting the town at three different points, under guides familiar with the location, and a certain morning was set for the attack and volunteers were called for, and the army was in a state of great excitement. But the attack was postponed on account of the absence of one of the guides. The burst of indignation and disappointment which followed was indescribable. The next day a curious episode occurred. A rough looking customer appeared in the crowd, with his rifle raised above his head, and cried out: " Who will go with old Ben Milam into San Antonio?" There was a shout of approval on the part of the me and the officers, and the most curious part of this whole proceeding was that the men were ordered to form into line, and Milam promptly elected to the command, and—that all this transpired in the presence of General Burleson and with his approbation. A that time there was no government, and a Texan army was a little republic. General Burleson was waited on and requested to hold his position until the result of the attack should be known, which he is said to have cheerfully consented to do. Milam's attack was ultimately successful, but on the third day he himself was instantly killed by a rifle shot through the head. When the enemy surrendered the terms of capitulation were concluded with General Burleson, who during the whole seige gave all the aid e could to Milam's party. In a few days a garrison was left in the town under an officer of their own selection, and Burleson, his officers and men retired to their homes, and the troops were discharged until they should come together on some future emergency of their own free will.

The victory obtained under circumstances of so much insubordination, proved, in the end, to be almost fatal to the cause of Texan independence. Even after the institution of a provisional government, it encouraged the selfish, ambitious, and reckless Fannin to plot against the commander-in-chief, Houston, to destroy all discipline in the army, and bring about a state of the things which led to the massacre of the volunteers from the United States; and when, the next spring, the army of Santa Anna hung like a dark cloud over the confines of the State, removed every barrier from before, so that it swept in its desolation like a tidal wave even to the waters of Galveston Bay.

When the fatal invasion came rolling on to San Antonio, Burleson and Neill made the most earnest and patriotic efforts to raise a force for the relief of Travis, and to unite the forces of Fannin and Neill for that purpose, as General Houston had ordered, but he failed in all his efforts. After that instead of abandoning a cause which seemed to be hopeless, he quietly went on to raise a regiment, which was no easy matter, when the whole population was flying before an enemy, whose hands were stained with blood even to the elbows. But he did raise it, and ranged himself under the banner of his chief. The morning of the battle of San Jacinto dawned in brightness, and as the sun rose, gradually the waves of the bay were seen to ripple in the sea breeze, over the heads of the enemy. The positions of the parties had been reversed, for Santa Anna was *before* and Houston was *behind*. The latter made his arrangements for battle. Why was Burleson placed in the post of honor? For fifteen years in Texas he had watched his career, and had witnessed his unselfish devotion to his adopted country, and the steady valor which he had shown in battle, tempered by a caution which was sometimes excessive, as it proved at San Antonio. But this was not all; the general in chief was born and spent his boyhood in the same East Tennessee mountains; by tradition he had known that the elders of the Burleson tribe were men, who, like the Beans, the Russells and the Campbells, were " without fear or reproach," who, with heavy hands, had taught the Cherokees to fear them, and thus secured their infant settlement from destruction. And again, he had known General Burleson, when a boy of fifteen, doing his duty as if it were mere sport in the bloody conflicts with the Creeks. He was the cynosure of all eyes, as a gallant boy soldier always is in an army. It is not probable that Houston had forgotten the features of the field, on which he himself (as Lieutenant of Regulars) did his *devoir*, and tasted the first delicious sip of military glory. No wonder then that Houston should have implicit confidence in him. It was not misplaced, for, in fifteen minutes after the charge was sounded, Burleson's Regiment and Millard's Infantry had stormed the breastwork, taken the enemy's artillery, and were driving them back.

After this decisive action Texas had considerable quiet for many years, although Mexico withheld any acknowledgment of her independence. In 1839 Burleson defeated Cordova and his Indians on the Colorado. During the next year he assisted in repelling an attack of Indians above Bastrop. He was afterward in the battle in which the Cherokees were punished for their hostility to the whites. He participated also in the battle with the Indians at Plum Creek.

In 1841 he was elected vice president, but in 1842 he was again at the head of the army, and asked permission of the president to cross the Rio Grande and retaliate upon the enemy his oft-repeated outrages, thereby inflicting a chastisement upon him which would result in honorable peace. President Houston did not favor the idea and the troops were disbanded. In the next presidential election General Burleso was put forward as a candidate on account of the views expressed above, but he was defeated by Dr. Anson Jones, who was an advocate for the peace policy.

The publications respecting General Burleson are singularly bare of information in regard to his qualities as a civilian. He was elected to the Senate of Texas, and then made president of that body. From this fact I infer that he was a man of ready abilities. and some culture, otherwise it would have been very unkind in his admirers to place him in such a position. He is represented as one of the most honorable men, and purest patriots, that Texas ever had. His home was in San Marcos, Hays county, but he died while sojourning at Austin, in 1851.

His son, Edward, was also a brave and patriotic soldier on the frontier, upon which he was raised, won distinction as an Indian fighter, and was a highly distinguished citizen. He represented Hays county in the Constitutional Convention, and died in 1877.

The old Indian fighters to whom our people are so much indebted have nearly all sunk into the grave. Their achievements in future times will be treasured up as the romance of family history; just as English families preserve the memory of the deeds of their ancestors, and hang up in their magnificent halls their old rusty armor and antique swords. The times which demanded such men have passed away, and in this very Burleson family may be found men highly cultivated, such as that excellent Christian divine, and ripe scholar, Dr. Burleson, president of the Waco University, to whom I am indebted for information as to the early history of his family.

Moulton Newspapers and Editors.

The first newspaper established in Moulton was by Alexander A. McCartney, in 1832, and was called the *Moulton Whig*. He was born in Pennsylvania and was a printer by trade. He married, either at Mooreville or Athens, a Miss Beatty, cousin to the Hills, of Athens. He was never engaged in a newspaper after the *Moulton Whig* was sold out; and acquired considerable property, which he left to his wife, who died about the close of the late war, at Decatur, leaving her property to relations, who have long since squandered it. McCartney and his wife had for many years before his death kept the principal hotel at that place, which she continued successfully. She was an excellent lady and was noted for her deeds of kindness to the unfortunate, without regard to the side they espoused, and had the prudence to be silent in politics, so that living on the debatable ground during the war, first in possession of one army and then of the other, she could more efficiently perform her deeds of mercy. Many of those whom she succored will remember her gratefully to the last hour of their being, and the writer among them; for. when in a Federal camp prison, during a cold and wet season in winter, he had nowhere to lay his head except a muddy floor, she sent him bedding, which saved him from great suffering, and perhaps from death.

In 1836, Thomas M. Peters, Esq., then a young lawyer in Moulton, purchased the *Moulton Whig*, and changed the name to *The Moulton News*. Mr. Peters owned the paper but a short time, and as this was a mere episode in the career of a gentleman who, for thirty-five years, was distinguished as a lawyer and a public man, we shall defer a sketch of him until we give an account of the Peters family.

The Moulton News was purchased by Wiley Gallaway, Esq., then clerk of the County Court of Lawrence, and presented to Matthew C. Gallaway, his oldest son, who was then a practical printer in the office of that paper. Lawrence has contributed to the legal, medical and ministerial departments, a number of young men, far beyond what I supposed before I commenced collecting data on the subject. But she has sent out very few journalists. The most distinguished of these is Colonel Gallaway, and we shall give to the several stages of his career special notice. His paternal ancestry came from Scotland and Ireland, and located in Maryland, North Carolina and Georgia. His maternal grandfather was John McDowell. He emigrated from Ireland to America in 1774, and was in the revolutionary war from the beginning to the close. He died near Oakville in 1841, and was a pensioner at his death. He was a hatter by trade, and there are citizens still living in Lawrence who purchased his hats for years. Indeed, for the first ten years of the settlement he made most of the hats worn in that part of the county and Morgan. He made the old-fashioned fur hats, and carried on an extensive trade with the negroes and boys of North Alabama for raccoon skins. He had twelve children; all of them left Lawrence county but Mary (who married Wiley Gallaway, father of the Colonel), and Clarissa, who married Hon. Charles Gibson. Mary Gallaway died at Moulton in 1855, and Clarissa Gibson some time during the war.

Wiley Gallaway and his brothers, Levi, Anderson, Brittain, Nathan J. and sister Sallie, were all born in Oglethorpe county, Georgia. In 1816, the family commenced moving to North Alabama, and in 1819, nearly every member of the family were

NOTE.—The *Moulton Whig* was first owned and edited by a Presbyterian minister, W. G. Mc-Pherson, and McCartney was his printer, to whom he sold out in a very short time.

located in Lawrence county. I shall be compelled to notice these brothers, for they are so connected with the political history of the county, it can not be avoided—, the Gallaways are a buoyant family, and have a knack of coming to the top—but I will defer it for the present.

Wiley Gallaway was a very competent and successful school teacher. He taught in Huntsville, from 1820 to 1823. He then taught at Houston's Store, in Morgan county. In 1824, he removed to Oakville, in this county, and taught two sessions. He then removed to Kittakaska, in the northern end of the county, where he conducted a flourishing school until 1830. He removed to Moulton in 1831, and was engaged in teaching until 1835, when he was elected county court clerk, which place he held until 1850. He was born in 1792, and died in Texas in 1864; very much respected in the many places where he lived, and the head of a family which were well raised, all useful and some distinguished men.

Matthew C. Gallaway, his eldest son, was born in Huntsville, Ala., on the fifth day of March, 1820. In his youth, with such a father, he must have been well instructed. His connection with the newspaper business commenced in 1836, when he made a contract with Mr. Peters (whom we have mentioned as editor of the *Moulton News*) to work twelve months for one hundred dollars. He is fond of telling his friends that the first work he performed, after entering the office, was to aid in printing off the presidential tickets. That Van Buren and White were the candidates and the young foreman pinned a newspaper in front of him to keep the ink from his clothes, and that he stood all day rolling off tickets, and that at night he was tired down with his hands blistered, but that he still determined to stick. In three months he could set up as much matter as any man in the office. After the *News* was printed he folded each paper, carried them to the sixty subscribers in town, and then made up the mails. I conclude that his proficency and energy were uncommon for a youth of his years, for his father was so well satisfied with his progress that he purchased the *News*, gave it to him, and his name appeared as editor, in 1838, before he was eighteen years of age. In September, 1840, he removed to Tuscumbia, and in connection with John H. Tice (now the great weather prophet) started the first Democratic paper ever published in that county. In 1842 he removed to Decatur, and married the niece of Col. L. S. Banks, Miss Fannie B. Barker, a lovely girl who proved herself, in after years, a heroic wife. His connection with the paper, at Decatur, did not continue long.

He permanently located at Florence, in January, 1844; and owned, and edited, the *Gazette*. He was now twenty-four years of age only; but he had more experience than many journalists of thirty. He had been wielding his pen for six years. At first his efforts were crude, but lively and aggressive. It was his habit to strike, directly, at the gist of a subject, and he never failed to make a hit. As his information increased, he became more effective, and by the time he settled at Florence, he had an unusual reputation for so young a man. During the whole twelve years he conducted the *Gazette*, his income, and reputation, gradually increased. Allured by the prospects presented by a new and prosperous country, he established the *Sunny South*, in Aberdeen, Miss., in 1856, and infused such a warm life into it, that in 1857, when he concluded to seek a wider field of action, he sold it for nearly three times its cost.

At length we find him in the city of Memphis, where he started the *Avalanche*. Its editor was a Provincial, it is true, but he brought with him a varied experience. In many a hot campaign he had received countless blows, but they had fallen harmless on his battered shield, whilst he had learned to hurl his lance with such force, that there was no defence against it but "tripple steel." The paper was a success from the start, and he edited it for twelve years.

In 1859, President Buchanan appointed Colonel Gallaway postmaster of Memphis—an office which he held until 1862. This was strong proof of his merits as an editor. It has always been a wonder to me, that high offices are not oftener conferred on journalists who have distinguished themselves by their fearlessness and ability in the fiery political campaigns which prevail in this country. It has been my observation for many years, that they are generally subordinated to men of far less merit—to mere carpet knights, who have done but little during those contests, without which a republic could not long endure. Why is this so? A half dozen young lawyers, educated together at the same State institutions, and residing in different localities, do more to advance the claims of each other to office than fifty editors. There seems to be very little or no fraternity amongst them. They seem to acquiesce in the notion that they are a subordinate class, and designed to be ridden by a highly refined race of politicians, who are "booted and spurred" for that special purpose. It is not so bad as it used to be, before the institution of typographical unions; and I sincerely hope that the beneficent efforts of these institutions may not only be extended to the correction of this injustice, but of all infractions of professional etiquette, so that discussions by journalists of different parties may be conducted without vulgar abuse and personal detraction. After all, may it not be this which is keeping the profession at a discount?

For more than two years, before the close of the late war, Colonel Gallaway was on General Forrest's staff. He was on confidential terms with this commander, who was the greatest military genius this country ever produced. General Forrest spent several weeks with me, at "Rocky Hill, "just before his death, and conversation often turned upon his comrades in arms. He regarded Colonel Gallaway, as one of the ablest and bravest of them. And well he might, so regard him. Gallaway had been a member of his mess, and written most of his letters, reports and addresses. He had been at his side, in nearly all the battles. during that time. With some Generals, a staff officer would have but little use for any weapon except his portfolio, but it was not so with Forrest. It was his habit whenever an engagement was protracted to charge on the flank of the enemy, with the members of his staff at his side, and his escort at his back, with such tremendous impetuosity as to carry everything before him.

It was the good fortune of Colonel Gallaway to save the life of his chief in one of the last affairs of the war—but let Forrest's historian tell the story which could only come from the lips of the general himself: "By this time (5 P. M 1st of April, 1865), General Forrest, his staff and escort, were engaged in a hand-to-hand melee with the enemy, and the general became involved in one of those personal encounters that have marked his life, and his escapes which appear incredible. He was set upon by four troopers, in the road at the same moment. Shooting one, the others dashed down upon him with uplifted sabres, which he attempted to parry with his revolver, but received several slight wounds and bruises, both on his head and arm. The others came up, meanwhile, and took part, so that as many as six troopers were either attempting to sabre or shoot him. By this time the hammer of his pistol had been hacked away, so that the weapon was useless, and his right arm had been sorely weakened by the many blows which had fallen upon it. His staff and escort could not help him, for all (at that moment) were strenuously engaged in like personal combats. On either hand the roadway was hedged in by a dense, impenetrable thicket, and rearward was choked by a two-horse wagon, which barred his escape in that direction, while his enemies filled the road frontward, fiercely cutting and shooting at him. Escape now seemed hopeless, for his horse was severely wounded by a pistol ball in his thigh. But it was not the habit of the man to look upon aught as hopeless. Wheeling his horse toward the wagon, giving him the spur fiercely, and lifting him with the bridle, the brave animal rose in the air and surmounted the obstacle at the bound, going some thirty steps before he was halted, and Forrest turned to survey the field. Scarcely had he done so, when he was charged by a Federal officer who lunged at him with his sabre, but Forrest parried the thrust with his other pistol, which he had been able to draw, and firing, killed his resolute adversary (*Captain Taylor, see Andrews, page 350*). By this time those whom he had eluded, by his desperate leap over the wagon, had contrived to pass it, and were upon him, but Col. M. C. Gallaway, of Memphis, and Dr. Jones of his staff, by this time had come to the aid of their imperiled chief, and, firing, each put an adversary *hors de combat.* Forrest killed yet another, and Gallaway wounding still another, took him prisoner. Meanwhile, the escort fighting with their usual fearless prowess, had first checked and then driven their enemy back; leaving Forrest and his friends masters of the field. The enemy had used the sabre almost exclusively. Forrest and his staff were each armed with two navy revolvers, and the escort with Spencer rifles, as well as pistols. It was a contest of sabres with firearms, in a thick wood with the odds of four to one against the Confederates. Forrest, Lieutenant Boon, and five of the men only, were wounded, while thirty of the enemy were killed, and as many as sixty were left in the hospital near by wounded. (*See General Jordan's Life of Forrest, 668*).

We have noticed Colonel Gallaway as a soldier, fighting by the side of the " bravest of the brave;" but now we have to follow him through a struggle for the liberty of the press, which required moral as well as physical courage of the highest order. We allude to the memorable contest with the Criminal Court, of Memphis, in what was called the Contempt Cases. In the winter of 1867, when the solid, taxpaying citizens were disfranchised, Colonel Gallaway, editor of the *Avalanche*, was arrested and brought before William Hunter, judge of that court, for a contempt, which consisted of an editorial in that paper. The colonel gave bond and security, and the next morning another of a more caustic nature appeared, for which he was again arrested, fined and ordered to be imprisoned, and this process went on day after day, until the fines amounted to a large sum and the terms of imprisonment aggregated fifty years. At length he was thrown into the county prison, and still every morning a fearless, caustic editorial appeared in the *Avalanche*. A profound sensation was produced in the community by this prosecution, and the judge, without any good ground for it, became afraid of personal violence and when Gallaway was brought out one morning by the sheriff the court room was guarded by Federal soldiers with fixed bayonets, and no one suffered to enter the room without special license. But, in spite of all this, a new editorial appeared every morning which denounced the tyrant. At length, in his desperation, the judge determined to seal up Gallaway's prison and ordered that he should have no communication with the outer world. He flattered himself that he could now rest in peace. But next morning a sweet feminine voice was heard from the sanctum of the *Avalanche*, which though "still as the breeze was dreadful as the storm." No one of Gallaway's thunderbolts hurt Judge Hunter so severe as this, which was the inaugural address of his excellent wife, who had assumed the conduct of the paper. It was graceful, it was fit (in view of all the circumstances), it was full of calm heroism—but you shall, presently, read it. The contempt cases were before the court, either every day or at intervals, from the 10th December to the 25th March. Finally, the Supreme Court put an end to them by deciding that the whole proceeding was unconstitutional, and that no court could punish as a contempt anything which was not done in its presence to hinder its process.

These proceedings before the Criminal Court, and the editorials of Gallaway, were published in 1868, in a large pamphlet from which I shall make copious extracts for the benefit of the young men of Lawrence.

The editorial for which the first arrest was made was as follows: " Tuesday, December 19. Saturday, in the Criminal Court, the case of John Henry came up on application for a new trial. It will be recollected that this black desperado some time since, broke into Lyon, Fies & Co.'s dry goods store, corner of Main and Jefferson streets, and stole from thence a quantity of dry goods. An application was made on Saturday for a new trial, and the judge concluded to grant it provided he could give bail in the sum of two thousand dollars for his appearance. This Henry said he could do, and produced as his bondsmen two negroes, named, respectively, George Washington and Tom Smith, who signed the requisite bond. Now, it was well known to dozens in the court that neither of these men, if both were shook up together, was worth twenty-five dollars. Immediately after they had signed the bond an order was issued for his release, and his friends started to convey him the glad tidings. But on the Metropolitan police we happen to have some simple minded and honest officers, who pay more attention to doing their duty than cultivating the negro for the purpose of securing their votes. Knowing these facts, Sergeant Brown arrested one of these bondsmen on a charge of perjury, and asked him where the other was, when he pointed across the street to him.

The negro noticed the motion, and knowing his guilt, immediately broke and ran. The officer placed his prisoner in safe hands and gave chase. The negro ran down the alley between Second and Third, and for an amateur made good time, but the law was at his heels and he was finally brought to bay, snugly ensconced beneath a bed. He was taken out and conveyed to the station.

"This is but one sample in a thousand of the manner in which Hunter turns negroes loose, after they have been arrested for the perpetration of crimes under the Code of Tennessee. It has become almost impossible to convict and punish a negro in this court, as Hunter would sooner allow a dozen crimes to go unpunished than one vote should be lost to his party. This is so, and it always will be, so long as a judge is a partisan, and weighs, as he does, his every judicial action in the scale of politics."

The judge having entered a rule excluding Mr. Campbell, the local editor, from the court room, and prohibiting any publication being made in the various papers of the city of the proceedings of the contempt cases then pending before him, Gallaway comments thus: "In all the annals of American jurisprudence we defy the citation of another rule as arbitrary as this, or one which has struck more evenly and squarely at the foundation of the individual liberty of the American citizen. * * * The friend and boon companion of negro gamblers, he prates of morality, and speaks Puritanical lying words to cover up the festering putrefaction of his acts; this creature, William Hunter, visits gambling houses, feeds on their keno lunches, drinks their liquors, and becomes hail fellow well met with men beside whom Pratt and Horton are respectable. * * * How long will the liberties of the people survive if this shameless Judas, this infamous trafficker on the infamy of the times, this base sycophant to the passions of a negro mob, scarce one degree more brutal or more licentious than himself, is allowed thus to lord it in our fair city?"

In the *Avalanche* of the 24th December: "On Saturday Judge Hunter ordered the arrest of the proprietors of this paper, on three additional charges of contempt for his august majesty. We have expressed no contempt for the *tribunal* over which this infamous poacher upon the rights of the people and the liberty of a free press erects his hang-dog countenance. But if William Hunter imprisons us in proportion to the contempt we entertain for him, as a corrupt man, our imprisonment will be as long as that which made the life of John Bunyan immortal; and if he fines us in proportion to the contempt we feel for him as a stupid Judge, devoid of knowledge, truth, decency and honor, we will soon owe his Court an amount as large as that out of which he swindled his honest creditors in Illinois. The old whangdoodle may play upon his harp of a thousand strings, to the full content of his rotten heart without moving us from our purpose. The principles involved are of too much magnitude for us to shirk the issue, although our devotion to principle and the maintenance of our own rights, may entail upon ourselves personal inconveniences. The Constitution of the United States guarantees the freedom of the Press. The Constitution of Tennessee, in language broad, emphatic and unequivocal, says the Press shall be as free and illimitable as the winds—free to praise—free to censure—free to lash with just severity, corruption in high places—and free to defend the beggar in his hovel. We had "rather be a dog and bay the moon," a toad feeding on the vapors of a dungeon, than to publish a paper over which William Hunter is to be the censor. He is not yet a triumphal conqueror, nor are we captives chained to his chariot. Despotism has made fearful strides, of late, in the South, but it remains to be seen if mankind is to be stripped of every prerogative, and robbed of every right. If a contemptible Judge, a worthless vagabond on society, dressed in a little brief authority, is permitted to override Constitutional law, and to muzzle a free and unshackled press, we are fast drifting back into the dark ages, when to worship God was to mount from the funeral pile, through the flames of martyrdom, to Heaven. Our soul is still our own! * * * In the conduct of this petty judge, we see fully illustrated the truth of the old proverb: 'Put a beggar on horseback and he will ride to the devil.' By some strange accident, a bankrupt swindler, a mountebank musician, who with bleared eyes and inflated cheeks has for twenty years been trying to blow away his worthless life through the mouth of a trombone, has found a seat upon the bench like a snail upon the top of an obelisk; and it is not surprising that the giddy fool should attempt to trample upon justice, and ride to the devil over the laws and Constitution of his country.

Speaking of the trial on December 21, he says: "These gentlemen (E. M. Yerger and others) pled for our cause—the cause of free speech, and the rights of the citizens, with a power and eloquence, we never heard surpassed. When despotic and intolerant hands arrested the parsons for preaching the Gospel of the Son of God, Henry appeared in their behalf, and the minions of despotism bent before the blast of his irresistible eloquence like the frail reed bends before the rushing tornado. So powerful was Henry's defence, so withering his exposure of the enormity of arresting men for preaching the Gospel, that the prosecuting attorney fled in dismay, and the judge, with cheeks burning with shame, trembling hands and faltering tongue, drawled out through his chattering teeth, 'Sheriff, discharge these men.'" But the contemptible whangdoodle who presides over the criminal court at Memphis, is actuated by no such magnanimity, conceptions of justice or appeals to conviction. * * * * This bigoted fool who has undertaken to gag an independent press, will live to learn that he might as well attempt to dam up the Mississippi with the bulrush which grows upon its banks. The rushing tide of water can not be confined by the puny arm of man, and free thought and free utterance can not be confined by an *ipse dixit*, whether emanating from a swindling vagabond, who wishes to hide his corruptions, the leader of a brass band, or a debased judge on a desecrated bench. Such a creature shall be held accursed when the bloody mandates and cruel despotism, of the Jacobins, shall have been forgotten.

> "The common damned will shun his society
> And look upon themselves as fiends less foul."

FRIDAY, January 3.—"But if Hunter expects to keep posted, he must subscribe for the *Avalanche*, instead of borrowing, or stealing it, as he has done heretofore. We give him notice, now, that for the balance of our natural lives he is ours, wholly and in part, in general and in particular. We will take it as a particular affront for anybody to kick or cuff him. This is a luxury for which we have a patent right, and nobody shall infringe upon our letters without being arrested for "contempt" of our prerogatives. When small matters alone remain for editorial comment we intend to impale him on the point of our pen, and dissect him as the entomologist examines rare bugs and curious insects. Occasionally, we may be tempted to pull off his epidermis, as a butcher does the hide of a fat kid. Then again, we may be forced to drop him into a big mortar, and with our editorial pestle pound him into mince meat. One thing they may rely on, that William Hunter will be served up to them, most every morning. We intend to cook him in every conceivable way; first stew him, then bake him, then fry him, and next toast him upon coals of burning fire."

January 26. Gallaway's apology to the ladies for calling Judge Hunter "an old woman": "Had we been Adam, when tempted by Eve, we would have eaten that apple, rich, ripe and luscious as it was, if it had been as large as a cimbling and as sour as a crab-apple. Woman is a great institution. Her faculties, her graces, her heart, her gentleness, her capacity for endurance, her firmness, her submission, her virtue, her character, all indicate her superiority, and her right to tempt poor frail men whenever she pleases. Indeed, woman in this world is a Peri at the gate of Paradise. It is true, her name has been the theme of many a keen reproach, many a ribald jest. 'Woe of the world,' it is said, because she was first in transgression. Woe—of—man, it is alleged, because she is the prime cause, and active agent in the woes which fill the world with sin, and sorrow, and desolation. We sympathize not with the temper, or the injustice of the pen. If first in the disobedience, she has been the chief sufferer. Her history has been one of long-drawn agony, pain and suffering, patience and affliction. The keenest edge of the avenging sword has pierced her soul. Her cup of sorrow has been deepest and bitterest. And it is as true as it is poetic and beautiful,

"Without the smile from partial beauty won,
Oh! What were man?—a world without a sun.

"Entertaining these exalted views of a woman, it is with deep pain that we should ever offend her. It is with profound regret that we learn the ladies of the city felt outraged and indignant at our calling Hunter a *woman*. We understand that this feeling is intense and that our own office is to be attacked with broomsticks, and that we are to be manacled with apron strings. We here make the most unqualified and unconditional apology to the fair sex for the insult we have offered them. When a man or a woman unsex themselves, they always become the subject of ridicule and contempt. A masculine woman, however, is much more endurable than an effeminate man, for both are abandoning their proper sphere, the former seeks to rise above, and the other to sink beneath, it. Be assured, dear lovely woman, we shall not again degrade your sex, by calling Hunter a *woman*. But what shall we do? Men are still more offended by calling the thing a *man*. To dignify Hunter with such an appellation is a libel upon man, sufficient cause for us to be flogged at every street corner. It will not do for us to call him a *hermaphrodite*, for that would be an insult to Francis Thompson, the miserable nondescript, who swore to nearly as many lies, before the congressional committee investigating the Memphis riots, as did Hunter himself."

January 28. "The *Avalanche's* editorial rooms, in a few days, will be temporarily removed to the county jail, on Adams street, where we shall be happy to see our friends. A swindling vagabond, an unprincipled judge, dressed in a little brief authority, may trample upon laws, usurp authority, and incarcerate us in loathsome dungeons; but thank God! he can not chain the mind, the immortal mind, which scorns fetters, soars above despotism, and since our right arm is not manacled or palsied we intend with our editorial pincers to make the putrid flesh, which covers the rotten bones of our prosecutor, quiver like a worm in hot ashes. No amount of imprisonment can change our opinion of William Hunter. We repeat here all we have said about him. We accused him of taking straw-bail, of receiving as security negroes who had been arrested for vagrancy. We *repeat* the charge, and what is more, we can *prove* it. * * * The *Avalanche* for two long years of bitter toil and strife has warred against the plunderers who came into our midst to rob and steal, and to claim rights which they deny to men born and raised on this soil. We have shown that these vagabonds pay no taxes; that they never gave a dollar to advance the interests of the State, and yet they fatten on the hard earnings of the taxpaying people, making them 'hewers of wood and drawers of water' for their greedy avarice. It is not surprising that such a gang of thieves should hate the *Avalanche!* Hunter is made the contemptible instrument—the puny cats-paw either to muzzle or crush out this paper. Had he power he would imitate the olden custom by putting a ring into our nose and a bridle into our mouth, and drive us like a wild beast through the streets. Tyrants always hate a free and independent press, but honest men invite its severest and most rigid investigation. The Southern people have no armies to defend them, and voiceless as they are in the councils of the nation, the press is the last bulwark of the people, and while they impart to it the strength to be free, outspoken and brave, there is no need to despair of ultimate redemption."

January 29.—Judge Hunter having gone to the Nashville Convention, and been absent for ten days. Oh! Hunter, where are you! Eureka! the lost Pleiad has been found. The Knoxville *Press and Herald* gives the following account of him:

"Three distinguished individuals arrived in town yesterday, and put up at the Bell House. Their names are William Hunter, D. P. Beecher and Ed. Shaw, the last named being a citizen of African descent. The two white persons insisted on having a first-class room for their negro friend, and that he should sit at the first table with them. The affable Story politely informed them that they might go to a place where no overcoats were needed, even in winter, and the advocates of negro equality left in disgust.

"The people of East Tennessee must be savages, or they would not thus deprive a Memphis judge of the luxury of eating and sleeping with a negro," etc.

March 11.—The last voice from prison: "We learn that Hunter, whose mean heart is festering in malice and uncharitableness, declared that he—yes, he, a poor old bankrupt thief, had sworn in his heart that the *Avalanche* should be crushed out. We are equally resolved that the *Avalanche* shall NOT be crushed out by so small a despot as William Hunter."

March 12, inaugural of Mrs. Gallaway: "Twenty-six years ago I gave my girlish heart to the husband whose name I proudly own. We have lived through prosperity and adversity, but in whatever condition our lots have been cast, calumny has never dared to assail my husband's name. Notwithstanding this fact he was yesterday torn from his little family, and is now a prisoner in the county jail, but thank God he is a prisoner without a crime. He has been torn from his home for the offence of exercising the rights which are his by the laws of the land. To a free country, a free press is as indispensable as light is to day. It is in fact the sun of the social and political system from which emanates the healthy influences which produce vitality, strength and fertility. For exercising rights which the Constitution guarantees my husband has been incarcerated in jail. Not only my prayers, but the prayers of all good people of both sexes will follow him in his prison cell. I shall not speak unkindly of the man who has sought to degrade my husband, and who has brought unhappiness upon two families. But as the principal editor and the local editor have both been arrested and no free man is allowed to speak through the columns of the *Avalanche*, there is no other alternative left but for me to assume the position forced upon me by the prosecution and misfortunes which despotism always brings on the noble and brave. A preconcerted arrangement has been made to crush out this paper. During the incarceration of my husband and Mr. Campbell I am constrained to take charge of the paper, and can be found at the editorial rooms of the *Avalanche*, and if men are not brave enough to defend their liberties, I trust the paper, for the next ten days, will prove that there is one woman ready to defend the rights which weak and timid men seem to yield.

                                                              FANNY B. GALLAWAY.

We have given copious extracts from the editorials of the *Avalanche* during the contempt cases. You ask me if the style of Colonel Gallaway in these is not amenable to criticism? I answer as Mr. Webster did: "There are no Sabbaths in a revolution." The ordinary rules of rhetoric are lost sight of in such contests as he was engaged in. To judge rightly you must realise the state of things in Memphis at that time; that a negro mob, intoxicated by their newly-gotten liberty and led by a few designing white men, were bringing the whole body of whites into peril, and that the mob had eventually to be subdued by a United States force in a regular battle. In such a contest the ordinary rules of rhetoric *do not prevail*. After all, there was not such an infraction of these rules as one might at first blush suppose. When Gallaway uses a mean metaphor he has a mean subject; when a disgusting one, his intention is to render the object of it disgusting; and when his theme rises in dignity so do his words, until he finally becomes morally sublime. He passes with great versatility from one passion to another. In turn he is humorous, and even playful; uses bitter sarcasm, terrible invective and withering denunciation. These philippics do not, however, present a fair sample of his ordinary style. The contempt cases were a violent episode in his life, in which his bold and manly heart was stirred to its very foundation. In that frame he was not choice in selecting his words, but like the artillerist, when his fixed ammunition is all shot away and there is danger of losing his piece by a charge of whooping savages, he gathers up the iron clippings of the smith's forge, long and short, ragged and jagged, rams them down his gun, and at close quarters sends terror and dismay, consternation and death into their ranks.

To him the battle of life has been fierce, stormy and tempestuous. He has had many rencounters with knives, pistols and sticks. In one of these he was shot through the hand and his thumb paralyzed. This occurred during the fierce war he was carrying on against Radicalism in Memphis. From the commencement of his editorial life he has held himself personally responsible for whatever he wrote. He kept no *fighting* editor. He advocates dueling in the interest of peace—because it saves human life— contends that it is more decent than street encounters and not so fatal—that it makes the man physically weak, the equal of the muscular bully—and says that men punctilious in observing the code seldom give or receive insults. In justice to Colonel Gallaway, I must say that Memphis has long been a battle-field for duelists who have flocked there from Alabama, Mississippi, Arkansas and Kentucky, and from all parts of Tennessee; and that the Colonel has often been selected as arbitrator or second; and has settled more impending duels than any gentleman in that State. There were two cases, however, so impracticable that he failed to settle them. The parties for whom he was second were both North Alabamians and victorious; but as those duels are frequently spoken of, and never twice in the same way, I will here give a brief account of them.

The first duel was between William A. Lake and Henry C. Chambers, a son of Dr. Chambers, who was one of the first United States Senators from Alabama. They resided in Mississippi and were candidates for Congress in 1863. While making the canvass they had a personal difficulty and came to Memphis to adjust it. Chambers selected Gallaway as his friend. The weapons fought with were rifles, and although awkward at first, Chambers became, in three days, quite a proficient marksman. Chamber's party chartered a boat, and were on the ground about sunrise. Lake with his second, Walter Brooks, United States Senator, and his friends, came afterward. Lots were cast for the word, and Gallaway won it. The word was given, and Chambers' ball went whizzing by Lake's head and Lake's ball passed through Chambers' goatee. Neither party was satisfied and there was a second exchange of shots. After which Gallaway made an earnest effort to adjust the difficulty. He presented several propositions as to how the matter could be settled, all of which Lake's friends declined to accept. In about two hours after the second fire, the rifles were again loaded; the hostile parties took their position, and at the word three, Lake fell dead, Chambers' ball having gone crashing through his brain.

Colonel Gallaway was also second for George T. Phelan, son of Judge James Phelan, a native of Huntsville, Ala., in a duel with James Brissolari. At the second fire Phelan's ball passed through the arm and body of his adversary, who had already fired three shots without effect. The parties fought with Colts six shooters, and were to fire until all the barrels were emptied, or one of the parties fell.

About ten years ago (1870) Colonel Gallaway purchased a half interest in the Memphis *Appeal* for thirty thousand dollars. Since then the paper has greatly extended its reputation and its subscription list, and has taken its place abreast of the few Southern papers which are leading public opinion. I doubt now whether the paper could be purchased for one hundred thousand dollars.

Colonel Gallaway, during his career, has written volume after volume of matter— and is now the oldest editor in the Southern States. His success, which was not sodden or accidental, but had a steady increase during a long and varied provincial career, is the best commentary on his ability.

Colonel Gallaway has never been a candidate for office, and was not even an applicant when Mr. Buchanan appointed him postmaster of Memphis. But during this season there were so many manifestations of a desire to have him nominated for the office of Governor of Tennessee, in opposition to the incumbent, Governor Marks, that he was forced to answer, and he did so in a letter so graceful and so indicative of his generous and magnanimous nature, that we shall quote a few lines of it: " My manhood has been active, sometimes tempestuous; but its day-dream throughout has been for quiet serenity in the evening of life. In my younger days, when the future was painted in the colors of hope, which youth always inspires, I had no aspirations; and now when the shadows are lengthened and reversed, and the mind turns retrospective, I can not be induced, under any circumstances, to become a candidate. * * * I served two years as a soldier, in General Forrest's command, by the side of A. S. Marks; was with him in the camp, the march, the battle and had ample opportunities of sounding the man, in all his height, his length, his breadth and depth, and learned to love him for the noble attributes of his generous heart, and to admire his great abilities, his genius, his honesty, his manhood and his heroic patriotism. At Murfreesboro the frosty earth was crimsoned with the blood he shed for the people of Tennessee, and if there he left a leg to tell the story of his fidelity to the soil he was defending, he brought in triumph from the field of battle an unsullied honor and a devotion to the cause which never faltered."

The Moulton Advertiser

was established in 1841, by Levi Gallaway, who purchased the printing materials owned by Wiley Conner, at Courtland, and which had been used for the Courtland *Herald*. The first *Advertiser* was printed on this old Ramage wooden press, the bed of which was stone and could only print one page at a time. Levi J. was a cousin of Matthew C. Gallaway. I don't know how many years he published the *Advertiser*. Perhaps its present editors may supply this information. Levi J. Gallaway removed to Mississippi, and died in Florida in 1867.

The brothers and sisters of Matthew C. Gallaway were William M., Elisabeth C., Harriet, Mary Ann and Levi T. William M. was made judge of the county court, and will be noticed when we come to dispose of that list. Elisabeth C. married James Wise, an old citizen of Morgan and Lawrence counties. She died in Arkansas in 1868, and her husband died near Trinity, Alabama, in 1871. Their children being orphans, two of them were adopted by Col. Matt Gallaway and his wife, they having no children of their own. I am reliably informed that they have raised more than thirty of other people's. Harriet married James Townsend, an old citizen of Lawrence, died in Pine Bluff, Arkansas, on her way home from Texas. Mr. Townsend still lives near Hillsboro, in this county. Mary Ann married Judge James H. McDonald, of Moulton. She died in 1874. Levi T. died in Memphis of the yellow fever, in 1878. Colonel Matthew Gallaway is now the only living member of his father's family.

The brothers and sisters of Wiley Gallaway remain now to be disposed of. They were Levi, Anderson, Brittian, Nathan J. and Sallie. Of these there is not a single one living. The descendants of Levi Gallaway are all in Mississippi. Anderson Gallaway has children still living in this county. Amos P., who was elected sheriff of this county in 1843, was his son. He married a sister of Christopher C. Gowin, moved away in 1847, and was elected to the Texas Legislature in 1852. Levi J., who started the Moulton *Advertiser*, was another son of Anderson Gallaway. Nathan J. Gallaway was a very good saddler. He settled in Courtland and married Hersylia, daughter of Westwood W. James. He was much respected, became postmaster and died before his term expired. From this marriage the only child now living is Clement. He resides in Kildie, Texas, and is a prominent and prosperous citizen.

Melton's Bluff

was the seat of justice for the county whilst Alabama was a Territory. It was the first and largest town, and located at the head of Elk river shoals, on the south bank of the Tennessee river. It was laid out by Gen. Andrew Jackson and his associates. The General thought a town above the shoals must succeed, whilst his relative, John Donelson, my father, and others, thought that Bainbridge, at the foot of the shoals, was the very site for a large town, and they cut a broad canal through the river bottom, for a mile, to the foot of the prospective town. Neither Melton's Bluff or Bainbridge was a success. There are no remains of a town at either place. The former is now included in the cotton plantation of Mr. Thomas Jones, and the latter in that of Mrs. Kernahan. Decatur far above, and Florence below, have become flourishing towns. Sixty years ago, railroads were unknown, and their introduction overturned all calculations based on pre-existing facts. How the completion of the great canal, now being constructed around the shoals, may affect the trade of existing towns, or the location of new ones, remains to be seen. It is probable that the effect of the canal, like that of railroads, may be to diffuse trade, and make, instead of a large city, a number of small towns, at points on the river, which have good landings, and good roads, extending into the back country. Melton's Bluff was settled rapidly, and the houses were built on a line parallel to the bluff. The most prominent citizen in the place then, and for many years after, was Isaac Brownlow, who died at Lamb's Ferry, in 1828, a brother of Hon. W. G. Brownlow, late United States Senator from Tennessee. They were alike in many respects. They were men of considerable natural ability, and were polite and hospitable. Isaac was the brighter, and had more wit, but William G. was the more earnest character, and when he undertook an enterprise he pursued it "with an eye that never winked, and a wing that never tired." In other respects they were unlike. Isaac floated down the stream of existence, caring only to cull the flowers of sensual gratification which overhung its banks, and never married. He had lost (as he said) by the use of calomel, the bones of his fingers and toes, and some from his face, and was awfully profane. On the other hand, William G. had married, and had reared and educated a respectable family. It is true that as a polemic and politician his controversies were marred by rude vindictiveness, and he had scattered from his quiver poisoned arrows; yet as a private citizen he was gentle, kind and charitable; so much so that he was the idol of the poor people around him. His violence was so excessive that many considered him a great sinner; but his moral conduct was so free from blame that no grounds could be found to cut him off from the communion of the church to which he belonged, although thousands "sought for it, carefully and with tears." I have said nothing of his *politics*, and I beg my readers to keep in mind, that these articles are not political: but mere narratives of things which occurred in old times.

The Inn-keepers

of Moulton have been numerous, and they have followed each other in quick succession like scenes in a panorama. One reason of this incessant change was that each found, in spite of the closest economy, that no money could be made in the business. The rush for the dinner table, in old times, was disgraceful when the signal was given. In an adjoining county the crowd, in such a rush, pressed a young lawyer against a door-post until he was for some moments speechless, but he was of very small stature. It was reserved for two noble ladies of Moulton, in modern times, to discover a complete remedy for all this disorder, and that is to provide plenty to eat, and that of the *best* quality. I shall not attempt to give a full account of the Inn-keepers, but merely notice such as occur to my mind.

John L. Stone was in this line. He was of middle age when he came from Tennessee, and becoming discontented, he moved back, and there died.

William L. Wilson was quite an old man when he came from Tennessee and occupied the inn afterward kept by McKelvy. He had several large boys, gave but little satisfaction, and eventually moved to Memphis. Then he went to Randolph, and there died.

George McMahon occupied a large old house on the northwest corner of the square. It was from this quarter that all disorder seemed to proceed. From here the "*Bulls of Bashan*" started to storm the court house, when John Gregg knocked the leader down. When old McMahon was brought to account for these disorders, he would declare, with the most innocent face, that "he couldn't imagine what made the boys act so, and that it was 'diametrically agin' his will." Many people believed the old man was sincere, and that the uproar was owing to the *meanness of his whiskey*.

After all, there may have been another cause. He had a nephew, named Martin McMahon, who was fond of a rowdy crowd, and had more reputation as a bully than any man then around Moulton. It is true he was of medium stature only, but he was built both for activity and strength, and "wore the belt." He had been some time without a fight, and seemed to be "spiling" for one, and I will tell you how he was cured. There came a circus to Moulton. Not a paltry imitation, but a real live circus, with fine horses well trained, splendid actors, and all the requisite furniture. I am a pretty good judge of a circus, for during my life I have frequently attended them; not that I cared anything for them myself, you know, but simply to give the *young ones* a chance to see them. Well, such an excitement as this circus stirred up was never witnessed before. It was kept up from day to day, for the convenience of the country people, and from night to night, for the pleasure of the city people. At length Mr. Wise, the manager, who was a man of experience in his business, saw signs of falling off, and was preparing to wind up, when Martin McMahon proposed to rent his circus for so many days, paying all expenses, and so many dollars per day. The enterprise failed to meet the expectations of Martin, and it became evident that he had no idea of paying the money, but intended to pay off the debt by giving Wise a whipping. The play-actor seemed very reluctant to close the account in that way; but Martin forced it upon him, and a ring was formed. Martin put in a blow, but somehow it glanced off on Wise's left arm, and Wise answered by one which knocked Martin down. The same thing occurred twelve or fifteen times, except that his friends closed around and made the ring smaller, so that Martin might not fall on the pavement but against his friends. At last his proud heart gave way, and "he spoke to the bystanders." When Wise was examined it was found he had not been hit a single blow. I never heard of Martin being engaged in another fight. Wise seemed to have "taken all the starch out of him." The McMahon family moved to the rich lands of Texas, and did very well. Many of them are said to have joined the Methodists, and if Martin was among them it may be that he owed his salvation to the play-actor. To the young men who may read this article I have this advice to give: Never fight an athlete, play cards with a professional gambler, or get into a newspaper controversy with its editor—in short, never play with a man at his *own game*. If he offers to bet that he can swallow his own head don't you take him up!

A man named Boggs also kept a hotel, but this was before my time. He sold out to Mr. Moses K. Thomason, who had been living two miles west of Moulton, on a place which he purchased from Aaron Burleson. Thomason tired of the business in a few years, and moved back to his farm, where he lived until his death. He had come originally from North Carolina. We all know his son, Maj. W. D. (Donnel) Thomason, who served so efficiently during the late civil war as quarter and paymaster in General Roddy's command. But few know that he was a *veteran* when he came into this command. I have already mentioned his going out to Texas in the fall of 1835 to aid in the revolution with eight of our countrymen, all of whom are now dead, except J. McDaniel (who married Miss Wear) and lives near Moulton, and Thomason himself. The latter, during the Texas war, rose to the rank of major, and was commissioned as such by General Houston. He was then appointed district surveyor, and held the office until 1843, Major Thomason then moved to Mississippi, with an elder brother, who had become dissatisfied with Texas. Here he remained until the war between the States, when he volunteered in the brigade of General Reuben Davis, and was marched to Bowling Green. Gen. Albert Sidney Johnston (who himself had served in Texas for many years) had Major Thomason appointed quartermaster and commissary for the post of Russellville, Ky. When Johnston's army fell back to Corinth, he was then sent to bag corn, and pen it up on the Mobile & Ohio road, and send it up, as it was wanted by the army. After General Johnston was killed, and the army fell back, he was made post quartermaster at Meridian, Miss., where an immense amount of stores had been forwarded from New Orleans. After this, upon his request, he was transferred to General Roddy's command, and when we give an account of its services we shall have to speak of him again.

Robert B. Cary also kept a hotel in Moulton, and a very good one. He had the same in Courtland, and was one of the five commissioners when the town was incorporated in 1819. He descended from one of the best families in Virginia, and unfortunately (good man as he was) he thought in his poverty too often of the wealth and splendor of his ancestors. After going to Moulton a serious misfortune happened to the family, and that was a rumor that some man in England of the family, having millions of money, had died without heirs in that country; the money was in bank, and that his heirs *in America* had nothing to do but to prove their relation, and draw a check for the money. It is needless to say that this rumor turned out to be an *ignus fatuus*, as have so many in late years, that Mr. Benjamin (the able American lawyer, now living in London) has issued a general letter, warning his countrymen against such deceptions. After this, however, a more serious and real calamity fell on the family. He had a very pretty and accomplished daughter named Martha, and a tall, solemn, gaunt, sorrel man, named Talmage (who was a partner of Major Hubbard, and supposed to be well off), paid his addresses to her, and was favored by her. He was so jealous in his disposition that he was deeply offended if she spoke a courteous word to any of the other young men who boarded in the house. She, poor thing, construed this as a proof of the *strength* of his affection (many a girl has been deceived in the same way). When she married him, she found out that she was the wife of a cold, selfish, and jealous ogre. In the end, they separated, and he became a wreck. I am not informed as to the other members of this family, except Prof. Cary, a very clever gentleman, who was in the Granger's Academy at Trinity.

There were also in this line of inn-keepers McIntosh, Devan, McCord, McKelvy and others. McIntosh was a tailor, kept the hotel west of the court-house, for many years, moved to Richmond, Texas, and may still be living.

Joseph and James McCord were brothers who came to the county in very early times. They were very good men, and much respected. Joseph was honored by the people with a seat in the Legislature in 1824, and James, in 1834. Sam'l W. McCord, who kept a hotel for a while, was, I believe, a son of his.

William McKelvy married a daughter of Randolph Wren, a fine old man who lived in the Courtland Valley. The descendants of this marriage I will notice in part, when I give an account of the military services of a certain regiment.

The Misses DeGraffenreid will be noticed in connection with their father's family.

LAWYERS OF NORTH ALABAMA.—Hon. Arthur Francis Hopkins

settled in our county before the State Constitution was formed. Here he established his professional reputation and commenced his political career, and it affords me real pleasure to sketch the history of a gentleman so distinguished as a jurist and a statesman and so much respected and beloved for the purity of his private life, and the genial affability of his manners.

He was born 1794 in Virginia, near Danville, in Pittsylvania county. He was well educated, for, after leaving the common school, he went to the Academy at New London, Va., then to one in Caswell county, N. C., and finished his education at the University of Chapel Hill (then one of the best in the Southern States).

He was a descendant of Arthur Hopkins, an Englishman, and a physician of very high standing, who settled in the early part of the eighteenth century, in the Colony of Virginia. His grandmother was a Miss Jefferson, a relative of President Jefferson. His father, James Hopkins, was a volunteer soldier at the age of fifteen; was in the severe battle of Guilford Courthouse, and died at his residence in Pittsylvania county, Va., in 1844.

In obtaining his education for the bar he was also fortunate. There happened to live n the adjoining county of Halifax, the Hon. William Leigh, who was a distinguished jurist, and brother of the celebrated Benjamin Watkins Leigh. In Halifax he was a student with Judge Leigh for some time. He was married before he was twenty-two years old, to Pamelia Mosely (sister of Judge John Mosely); and their families, with his friends, Matthew and Joseph Clay, removed in 1816 to Madison county, Ala. Here these friends improved plantations, but Mr. Hopkins had also a home in the town of Huntsville, where he commenced the practice of law. In January, 1819, the little colony of intimate friends (with the exception of Joseph Clay), moved to Lawrence county. Matt Clay settling upon the place now occupied by Captain Swoope, and Mr. Hopkins and Judge Mosely on adjoining plantations, opposite Clay. The county seat was then at Melton's Bluff. In May, 1819, he was selected a member of the Constitutional Convention, and on the

5th of July took his seat in that body. Its number was about forty only, but there was in it a large proportion of men of handsome abilities, and not a few who became distinguished statesmen and honored members of the U. S. Senate, to-wit: C. C. Clay, Henry Chambers, John W. Walker, and Wm. R. King. Mr. Hopkins, then only twenty-five years of age, was classed with such men as these. Legislation may be regarded as .he "eminent domain" of the law, and he had read so extensively, and reflected so profoundly, that he was familiar with this region of thought. The Convention in less than a month made an excellent Constitution, with the exception of the authority given to the General Assembly to establish State banks—which provision was not approved by Mr. Hopkins. When the public buildings at Moulton were completed Mr. Hopkins removed to that place.

He was elected to the State Senate, and served during the sessions of 1822, 1823 and 1824. It was during this term, that the law was introduced for the establishment of a State Bank, in which the State should own the stock exclusively, and the capital should consist of the various funds which the State held as trustee; in other words, the debts due by the State. It was contended very speciously by the friends of the measure, that, as individuals had no interest in the profits of the institution, there would be a pure management on the part of the directors, who would be entirely disinterested, and being upon the "faith and credit" of the State, its notes would have more character than those of private Banks. Mr. Hopkins made several able speeches against the connection of Bank and State, in which he predicted with remarkable accuracy (considering that no such experiment had ever been made) the consequences which would result from that measure. His views, however, were overruled, and when the final vote in the Senate was taken, he was left in the lean minority of thirteen, amongst whom was Hon. Joshua L. Martin, who, when the eyes of the people were opened, became Governor of Alabama. This bank bubble did not burst as soon as its opponents supposed. Accidental circumstances carried the balloon higher and higher, until all taxes were forgiven to the people, and the annual expenses of the State Government were paid out of the supposed profits of the bank. Many very sensible and wealthy citizens who had adopted Mr. Hopkins' views on the subject, discarded them because this proof of the success of the scheme was decisive, for they actually felt their pockets heavier by the amount of taxes which the State had remitted, and this argument of the increase of the weight of the pocket, which they could see and feel, was too strong to be resisted. Just at this juncture, the opponents of this beneficent system of banking were the most unpopular men, politically, that had ever lived in the State. But at length the bubble burst, the banks became insolvent. To save the State from loss there was instituted a rigorous system of collections, under which thousands of her citizens were ruined, and eventually a debt of millions of dollars was left upon the shoulders of the State—which, however, was materially lightened by the compromise made by that sensible and faithful public servant, Governor Houston.

It is not alone for the purpose of showing the prescience of Mr. Hopkins, that I have at such length reproduced the features of this bank project. The people need to be reminded of this part of our history, for there are many sensible men amongst us now who are too young to have known, (or else have forgotten, it) whom may hear advocating the plan of the United States Government furnishing exclusively a circulation for the people.

When Mr. Hopkins was elected to the Convention and the Senate, there were no political parties; for it was in the halcyon days of Monroe's administration, when parties had subsided. But as the election of 1824 approached, and Clay, Jackson and Crawford were brought forward as candidates, men began to array themselves under one or the other, according to their prepossessions. It was in the Spring of this year that I met Mr. Hopkins at the house of my brother-in-law, Mr. Matt Clay, and formed his acquaintance. Clay, though nearly allied by blood to Henry Clay, the Presidential candidate, was opposed to him; because he (Matt Clay) was a Jeffersonian, as his father (long a member of Congress from Virginia) had been, before him. Mr. Hopkins was a great admirer of Henry Clay. This seems to have been the first time they had met for the purpose of shaping their course for the future. I was then quite young, but eighteen, and understood Latin and Greek much better than politics; but the questions discussed by them were so novel, so interesting, and made so deep an impression upon my mind, that I have never forgotten that interview. The two men had been bosom friends from their boyhood, had moved to new homes, together, twice, and, in county politics, their party was called the "Hopkins and Clay party," and the opposing one the "Anderson and Bingham party." There was evidently great personal anxiety to remain together, but the effort was useless, and they went, in politics, different ways. Mr. Hopkins became one of the most earnest and ablest advocates of Henry Clay to be found in the Southern States.

Some time in the year 1825 he removed from Moulton to Huntsville for the purpose of having a wider field for the practice of his profession, and better facilities for the education of his family. And here, before we follow him to his new home, we will give an account of him personally, socially and professionally. At that period of his life he was a very handsome man, about the average height, compactly built (but not yet corpulent), with clear blue eyes and light hair; he was indeed a fine specimen of physical manhood. His countanance was unusually responsive in its expression to every emotion which he felt. If he was about to try an important case, and had an adversary who was "worthy of his steel," there was a corrugation of the muscles of his forehead, and an expression of deep anxiety pervaded his face; but this would pass off as soon as he found everything ready for the conflict. The general expression of his face was that of great good nature and kindness. It was in the earnest argument when he was thoroughly roused that his form seemed to expand, his eye would flash and his whole face to glow with intellectual light.

Socially he was a great favorite, not only with members of the bar and men of culture, but with plain farmers, who greatly admired him for his genial, unaffected manners. In his intercourse with them he forgot his cases, his books and his conflicts in the court house, and was really interested in learning everything that was transpiring in the country of any interest. He had the power (unusual amongst studious men) of concentrating his mind upon whatever he happened to be engaged in at the moment. This power constitutes the very foundation of success in life. His intercourse with his family was beautiful. When he went from his office to home, instead of carrying some law case in his head and looking as wise as an old owl, he seems to have adopted the rule of Sir Thomas Moore, one of the ablest Lord Chancellors England ever had, "of giving the remainder of the day to my family at home. I must gossip with my wife, chat with my children and find something to say to my servants; for all these things I reckon to be a part of my business, unless I were to become a stranger to my own house." Mr. Hopkins became a great favorite with our people. Mrs. Hopkins was as much so as her husband. She was a lady of fine person, graceful and unaffected manners, and very kind and charitable to the poor. She was very fond of young people, and was idolised by them. Some professional men have hindrances in their wives, but he had a helpmate, indeed, both in private and public life. I knew this excellent Christian lady throughout her life, and she never changed; always genial, kind and hospitable, the sunshine of cheefulness resting on her path. Lawyers' wives have great influence on their lives, and therefore should not be omitted in their biographies.

At the time of his removal to Huntsville he had won the reputation of being one of the best lawyers in North Alabama; clear and learned in his argument of law questions before the court, and of almost resistless force in his appeal to the jury. In fact, there were but few who could contend, successfully, with him. His mind naturally was of the first order, and his memory wonderfully tenacious. He had been a voracious reader. I was present once in a knot of lawyers, when there was a discussion as to the best mode of studying law. A fine lawyer remarked that a student should read no more law at a time than he could digest, and, moreover, when he met with any matter he could not comprehend, he should halt until the difficulty was solved by some competent friend.

Mr. Hopkins, when the matter was referred to him, remarked "that this course seemed reasonable, but it had been *his* habit to read law from twelve to fourteen hours a day, and what he could not understand was made plain as he read on, and the subject was unfolded." I am inclined to think that the quantity of matter which Mr. Hopkin's mind could digest, and his memory retain, was exceptionally large. This accounts for his wonderful success as a lawyer. His mind was well stored with elementary principles, and in preparing his cases he had nothing to do but to examine the adjudicated cases in point, in the reports which were then of authority.

The immense accumulation of them at this day must be very discouraging to the profession, especially, as the profits are in inverse ratio to the required labor. His style was more remarkable for force than beauty; his imagination was not prolific, and moreover was kept under the control of a severe taste, but, occasionally, when deeply excited, he would deliver passages of such rare beauty and force as to cause every nerve in your body to quiver, and which would linger in your memory for years. He had great influence on juries in consequence of the confidence men had in his candor and integrity. Indeed, he was "the very soul of honor." Young men do not realize how *indispensable* integrity is to the constitution of a great and successful man. Men without it sometimes "flourish like the green bay tree" for many years, but my observation, through a long life, is that distrust is sure to cause "their leaf to wither," long before the end of their lives.

There was an amusing defect in Mr. Hopkins' mind, and that was a want of mechanical genius. After severe drilling he would still call mortises *holes.* He was never able to make a pen that would write. When one was furnished to him he was unable to write the lines straight across the paper, which then had no ruled lines. *His* all pointed to the northeast corner of the paper, like the leaves of a fan. His handwriting though legible was rugged. In spite of all this, however, the old clerk, Gallagher, who wrote, himself, a fine engrossing hand, used to say that he had rather write Hopkins' hand than any he had ever seen. The secret of this was that he admired the man and everything he did. Mr. Hopkins treated all the officers of the court with courtesy and kindness, and if he had accidentally omitted anything, so that a case was not ready for trial, the blame was not laid upon the clerk, but, like General Lee, he bravely assumed the responsibility himself. In the smallest matters, the native grandeur of his character was unconsciously shown. Mr. Hopkins from the time of his removal from Moulton to Huntsville, to his election to a seat on the Supreme Court Bench devoted himself to the practice of his profession. He had attained so much distinction that he was enabled to confine his practice to cases of importance where the fees were large, and the drudgery was performed by junior counsel. He practiced in the Supreme Court, in the Federal and Circuit courts at Huntsville, attended the circuit courts of Lawrence and went to other courts in special cases. This phase of professional business, the most pleasant, profitable and least laborious, it is the privilege of but few to enjoy. There was no interruption to the "even tenor of his way," except that the people of Madison county elected him to the General Assembly in 1833. An ugly controversy had sprung up between Governor Gayle and President Jackson, as to the proper jurisdiction over Indian lands within the boundaries of Alabama, for which there seemed to be no solution but force. Governor Gayle showed a good deal of "pluck," and there was an "iron" man on the other side of the controversy. Serious apprehensions of a conflict of arms were entertained; but the difficulty was avoided by the independent course pursued by Mr. Hopkins, and his old friend and rival Mr. John J. Ormond. These two men, nurtured into intellectual strength on the soil of Lawrence, where countless "passages at arms" had occurred between them, had mental visions of such power as enabled them to see far beyond the limits of their State; and, although decided Whigs in politics, took the side of General Jackson, and by their able speeches carried the Legislature with them, in despite of the sectional excitement, which extended their reputation greatly as constitutional lawyers.

In January, 1836, Mr. Hopkins, without ever having sat on a county or circuit bench, was elected a judge of the Supreme Court, and that, too, by a Legislature overwhelmingly Democratic. This tribute to his public character and private worth was almost universally approved amongst the members of the profession. There were very sensible men, however, who feared that Mr. Hopkins, who had shown so much zeal as an advocate, would not add much to his reputation on the bench. They mistook the general principle and its application. A cold neutral man never makes a judge of high order. Decision and fearlessness are requisite, and he who possesses these in mature life must have been zealous and determined as a rising advocate. The veteran who has a steady valor must have had a fiery gallantry when a young soldier. The independence of the bench can not be sustained by timid, neutral men. In this country, that Hydra "vox populi" dares sometimes to rear his horrid front before a court to sway its decisions, and it is indispensable to have incumbents of brave hearts to cut off his heads one after another. He had not been long on the Supreme Bench before his colleagues elected him Chief Justice, and they of all others were best qualified to judge of his merits. In 1837 Judge Hopkins resigned his judgeship and resumed the practice of the law. In regard to his judicial character, I beg leave to refer to the following estimate made of it by that accomplished scholar and lawyer, H. M. Sommerville, Esq., Professor of Law in the University of Alabama. "Judge Arthur F. Hopkins was, in many respects, a conspicuous judge. His decisions may be found in the third, fourth and fifth volumes of Porter's Reports. They are distinguished for quickness of perception, terseness of style, accuracy of logical deduction, and that self-poised consciousness of intellectual power which has always characterized great judicial minds like those of Marshall, Mansfield, Kent and Eldon. He goes at once to the vitals of the question under consideration, and eviscerates its complexities, as it were, by a skilful touch of a surgeon's scalpel. Ignorant or unlearned judges bolster their conclusions by unnecessary citations of authorities to support the simplest assertions of the elementary principles of law. Not so with Judge Hopkins. He never cites an authority unless appropriate and necessary. Chancellor Kent's opinions in Johnson's (New York) Reports, and Lord Eldon's in Versey Jr. are models of the judicial style. Judge Hopkins, I believe, has more nearly approximated their excellencies than any other judge who has occupied our Supreme Court Bench, except Chief Justices Ormond and Rice. Note, per example, what a flood of light is thrown in Vandegraff vs. Medlock (3 Porter, 389) within the short compass of two pages, upon the novel and interesting question as to whether the Chancery Court has power to decree to the mortgagee the proceeds of a policy of insurance effected by the mortgageor on the mortgaged property where the property has been destroyed by fire, there being no covenant to insure. And again in Clark and Lindsay vs. Simmons (4 Porter, 14) it is refreshing to see how, in a few brief lines, he succinctly disposes of a less important question, in the adjudication of which many judges of the present day would obstinately expend vast treasures of legal lore. A judicious regard for the style of this eminent jurist would correct a vast and growing evil of the present day—the rapid and burdensome multiplication of our law reports, for the correction of which there is going forth an earnest cry of protest from the whole American Bar."

Judge Hopkins again resumed his practice and nothing unusual occurred in his career until the Presidential election of 1840. During this campaign he was an elector and the acknowledged leader of the Whig party in the State. This was a high honor, for that party was distinguished by the great number of eloquent and talented men in its ranks; such men as Gayle, Jackson, Davis, Thornton, Langdon, Hillard and others. An able address was issued by a committee of the Whig convention, to the people of Alabama, advocating the claims of General Harrison, and arraigning the administration of President Van Buren. The authorship of it was attributed to Judge Hopkins. He made able argumentive speeches at large mass meetings over the State. These speeches were the magazines from which the stump-speakers of the party drew their arguments and inspirations. As a campaign speaker he used the same style which, at the bar, had raised him to distinction. He had too much good sense to attempt the flippant humorous role so common with popular orators. If he had made the attempt and failed, it would have rendered him ridiculous, and if he had been successful it would have tended to lower his reputation as a man of first-class ability. Had the Whigs come into power in this State, in 1840, Judge Hopkins would certainly have been elected United States Senator. His name was put in nomination by the minority, in opposition to Senator King, as it had been in 1836 against Mr. McKinly, and as it continued to be in every Senatorial election, for many terms afterward. Had he become a member of the Senate, he would, in my opinion, have assumed a position amongst the great, patriotic and conservative Senators, who distinguished that body in ante-bellum times, of which Alabama would have been justly proud.

In 1842 Judge Hopkins removed to St. Louis. Before his departure he partook of a complimentary public dinner given to him by the members of the North Alabama Bar, at Florence. The newspaper reports of it have perished, but a few facts of interest are remembered. The dinner was served in the Florence Hotel, a large brick building which was destroyed by fire during the late war by the Federals. The president was James Irvine, Esq., the senior of the Florence bar, an able lawyer, profoundly versed in its principles, an accurate special pleader, with all his law papers drawn up in a neat hand and with great method, not an eloquent, but a chaste and logical speaker, and one who had made a fortune by the practice of his profession. He delivered a very graceful speech of welcome, and the response of Judge Hopkins exhibited so much taste, such deep feeling, and such devotion to the noble profession to which he belonged that it produced a lasting impression upon his brethren. In the evening a reception was given at the house of Mr. Irvine; the members of the bar and the elite of the town and country attended, and Judge Hopkins moving amongst highly cultured men and beautiful and accomplished ladies, proved that his social qualities were not inferior to his professional. It is melancholy to think how few of the honored guests at this dinner still survive. He in whose honor it was given has passed away. Its president departed in 1867. Out of the nine lawyers who constituted the committee of arrangements only Mr. Robinson of Huntsville, Mr. Cooper of Tuscumbia, and General O'Neal of Florence, remain! (1881).

After residing about one year in St. Louis, Judge Hopkins returned to Alabama. He found the climate of Missouri rugged and unconditonal to his constitution, and that it would be a tedious process to secure so desirable a practice there as he had left behind him. Lawyers of middle age who remove to distant States generally meet with disappointment. They are surrounded by strangers, who may have heard of their reputation but as the faint sound of distant artillery. They are not conversant with the State's laws, and the cases of litigation which arise upon these are more numerous than those which rest on the general principles of law. Therefore, such removals are like transplanting full-grown trees, which require long years of imperfect growth to regain the full vigor of root and leaf; if they ever do. Indeed, I have known of but one case of this kind which was a complete success, and that was the the removal of Judge John A. Campbell, from Mobile to New Orleans; but his reputation for great ability was almost as well known in one city as the other; and, moreover, the civil law was the basis of the statute laws of Louisiana, and as a civilian, Judge Campbell had as much reputation as any lawyer in the South, and it was thought when he resigned his seat on the bench of the United States Supreme Court, he left no judge behind him who was his equal in this branch of the law.

On Judge Hopkins' return to this State, he settled in Mobile; and for several years acted as president of the Mobile & Ohio Railroad, occasionally appearing in court, in important cases. At this season of his life, he was surrounded by every circumstance calculated to render life happy. He had a competent fortune; was surrounded by a numerous family of dutiful children, mostly daughters, happily married; his house was a centre of wide hospitality; he had "troops of friends," and, to crown the whole, he was an humble and consistent Christian. Many years before, when they resided in Huntsville, he and his wife became pious members of the Presbyterian Church, and ever afterward their lives were consistent with the rules of this evangelic body.

Many years passed away in this manner. At length he had a great sorrow in the death of his excellent wife, whose character I have already portrayed. Some years afterward he married Mrs. Ogden, of Staten Island, widow of Colonel Ogden, of the United States army, who, " when the late war broke out, took an active part in the management of the Confederate hospitals at Richmond, and by her intelligence, her sympathizing, and personal attention to the sick and wounded, gained an enviable reputation. In all these efforts and sacrifices she was nobly sustained by her patriotic husband, who, well stricken in years, did what he could to alleviate suffering, and to aid the cause of his native South. The anxieties and results of the war undermined the vigorous health of the judge, whose large and manly form sank under the effects of disease thus produced, and, at the age of 72 years, he died in 1866."

His children by his first wife (he had none by his second) were: 1, Maria, who married Mr. John J. Walker, son of U. S- Senator John W. Walker, of Huntsville. 2. Cornelia, who married an English merchant named Lowe. 3. Louisa, who died early. 4. Mosely, who married Eliza, daughter of Gov. Thomas Bibb. 5. Augusta, who married Mr. Rice, formerly of Talladega. 6. Mary, who married Mr. Barnwell. 7. Kate, who married Mr. Starke Oliver. 8. And a young son, Leigh, named for Judge Leigh, his law preceptor. (See *Bibb* and *Oliver*.)

Joseph Young,

a young lawyer, came from Kentucky, and I judge from the " Blue Grass " region, for he was well grown, about six feet high, and well formed. He had read law sparingly, but he was " death " on Shakespeare, and the staple of his speeches was composed, in great part, of quotations from that author. I think he was a man of uniform courtesy, for I never heard of his refusing to drink with a man when invited. He was of weak judgment, and great vanity. He had heard Henry Clay speak several times, and it seemed " to come so natural and easy-like to *him*," he imagined that *he*, too, was born an orator. He knew it, for he felt it in him. On all occasions, in season and out of season, he would play the orator, and would rise boldly in his flight, yet as certainly as he rose would " his wings be melted," and he would fall heavily to the ground. But no amount of falling would ever convince him that he was not to succeed as an eagle orator. He was like the confident Yankee who tried his flying machine from the top of the barn. As he lay upon the ground in a heap, he was asked how he liked flying. " Wal, I like flyin' well enough," he said, " but the' ain't sich a thunderin' sight o' fun in it when you come to light." The people came to know this tumbling habit of Joe's, and sometimes took unfair advantage of him. On one occasion the question before the Commissioners' Court was where the road to Tuscaloosa should rise the Sand Mountain ; whether at Sutton's Gap, or run through the valley many miles beyond and ascend at Martin's Gap. Joe was the advocate of the valley route. He commenced by saying : " If the court please, suppose you were offered the choice of two routes to Heaven, one like this by Sutton's Gap—sterile, rough, rocky and steep ; and another through a rich and verdant valley, canopied with flowers and—" " Stop, Mr. Young," said a member of the court, " the question is not which is the best road to Heaven, but to Tuscaloosa." Joe's balloon collapsed ; it was " a lost ball," and he never could recover it. Joe was fond of " Old Bourbon," but whether he brought this fondness from Kentucky with him is uncertain, as I did not know him until some years after he came.

It is said the people *now* take a man at his own valuation of himself, but this adage was not true in Joe's case. The people elected him to the Legislature, not only in 1822, but in 1823. He was the colleague of Judge Hopkins. I have wondered what use Judge Hopkins had for him, but I suppose in the canvass Joe did his drinking for him with the people as a proxy, and in the Legislature he made the same use of him which dextrous men now make of the negro—he " voted him." But why did the people of Lawrence elect him? There, you are too hard for me. It was not for want of good material, for I have shown in my early numbers that there was plenty of that. I have been conning over the list of legislators from the commencement (all of whom I knew personally until 1865), and the conclusion I draw is, that the people of Lawrence have a "weakness" for *weak* men—a magnanimity which inclines, in witnessing a fight, to favor the "small" man. It is true that our county has been represented by a number of solid prudent men of experience, and a few able men, but, with them, a large proportion of men who did not comprehend the first principles of legislation. Is there no remedy for this state of things? We have Normal schools for those that wish to be teachers; how would it do to have a Normal school for those who aspire to be legislators? Or is a man born a legislator, as Mr. Grundy said, factiously of himself, he was born a "veteran?"

As Joe Young's professional and political prospects declined, he became fonder of old Bourbon, and gradually seedy in his dress, until he declined finally into a wreck, and died while yet a young man.

William E. Anderson, Esq., was the brother of Hugh A. Anderson, who lived east of Courtland, and was leader of a party in early times. William E. had been Secretary of State in Kentucky, and had practised law there, before he came to Moulton, in 1822. In less than a year he died from sitting in his office one day with his feet wet. I never knew him. Col. Isaac Owen described him as a tall, fine-looking man, a graceful and strong speaker, and said that many persons thought he would, had he lived, become a rival of Judge Hopkins.

Ellison A. Daniel, Esq., came early to Moulton. He was a lawyer of slender abilities, but modest and industrious. He had the good fortune to be elected to the House of Representatives in 1827.

Argyle Campbell, Esq., came from Tennessee. He was a nephew of Hon. George W. Campbell, of Nashville, once Minister to Russia, and he was brother-in-law of Hon. David Hubbard. Mr. Campbell had been pretty well educated for that day; had a fine person, and was a graceful speaker. But, with all these advantages, he had only moderate success in his profession. In his case there seemed to be no lack of intellect, but a want of force of character. He moved to Columbus, Miss., where he died many years ago.

Rufus K. Anderson, Esq., came to Moulton about 1825 from Tennessee. He was a handsome man, dressed well, and had genteel but distant manners. Our people somehow didn't give him much encouragement, and after a year or two he left Lawrence and went into Pickens. His tragic history is told by Colonel Garrett in his "*History of the Public Men of Alabama:*" "Rufus K. Anderson, formerly of Tennessee, resided in Pickens, and was a Senator in the State Legislature from 1829 to 1833. He had previously killed his brother-in-law, Thomas P. Taul, of Franklin county, Tennessee, and was arraigned for murder. He was on trial eighteen days, during which he was defended by Hon. Felix Grundy, the eminent advocate, who succeeded in procuring his acquittal by the jury.

"Mr. Anderson was said to be an overbearing, reckless man, who insulted whom he pleased, and was generally regarded as a dangerous man. Peaceable men avoided difficulties with him, and would often submit to exactions rather than enter into a deadly conflict. To oppose him in any way, or to incur his resentment, brought life into jeopardy. It was reported that he had beaten one of his slaves to death in his barn, and had left him hanging from a beam. Several persons happened to pass near the barn and peep through the cracks to see if the negro was there. Among those who looked in for discovery was Mr. Gideon B. Frierson. It appears that Mr. Anderson was then away from home. In the meantime Mr. Frierson made a journey to Mississippi. When Mr. Anderson was informed of the liberty that had been taken at his barn he declared vengeance, and set out in pursuit of Mr. Frierson to take his life. At one place he dined where his intended victim had stayed the night before, and on learning that the latter had left a bundle for which he would probably return the next day, Mr. Anderson said he would remain, as he wished to see him. Providentially the bundle was sent for by the person to whom it was addressed, and Mr. Frierson went in another direction. Anderson kept on his track, from Mississippi to Pickensville, and arrived in a few hours after Mr. Frierson reached home, April, 1834. The latter was in his office when he was informed of the threats of Anderson to take his life, and was advised by his friends to be prepared. He loaded a double-barreled gun and awaited the attack. Anderson appeared before the office and called out in a loud, angry voice: " Come forth, Gideon, like a man. I am after your blood, and am determined to have it. Face the thing at once, and let it be over."

" In the meantime Mr. Frierson had retired from his office through the back door, and came facing the street where Anderson stood. On the latter perceiving him he advanced with his pistol drawn, swearing that the time had come, and he would make sure work. Mr. Frierson discharged one load without effect, and as Anderson still came on, he emptied the other barrel with better aim. A number of shots entered the breast and shoulder of Anderson, who in the meantime had fired one pistol, and drawn another. Mr. Frierson held his ground, and was about to club his gun. To ward it off, Anderson picked up a chair which he held before him as a shield, when Mr. Frierson struck a blow with his gun which shivered the chair into fragments, and came down on the head of Anderson with such force, that the cock penetrated his brain; he fell to the ground, and died in a few minutes. Thus the bloody encounter terminated fatally to the aggressor, and much to the relief of the community. Mr. Frierson was not even prosecuted."

Hon. David Hubbard,

for thirty-five years, was a man of note in our county. No man ever had more uniform success in elections before the people. He had considerable ability, but was eccentric in mind, person, and manners; and at all times there was great contrariety of opinion respecting him amongst the people. He had warm friends and bitter enemies. I can hardly flatter myself that the account I shall give of him will be satisfactory to all; but it shall be based entirely on facts, and the comments made conceived in a spirit of fairness and charity.

David Hubbard was the son of Major Hubbard, who was an officer in the Revolutionary War, and a very intelligent and respectable gentleman.[*] He moved from Virginia to Rutherford county, Tenn., in early times. Young David had been taught in the country schools, and had just entered an academy, and begun to lay a foundation for a classical education, when during the war with Great Britain, the enemy sent the expedition against New Orleans. Youth, as he was, he became a volunteer under General Jackson, and in the midnight attack on the British, of the 23d of December, 1814, he was wounded in the hip, and left upon the field, when our forces were withdrawn. During the fifteen days which intervened between that time and the battle on the 8th of January, he was a prisoner in the hands of the enemy, suffering from this severe wound. The morning of that battle (so memorable too, in our history) dawned, and when the forces of the enemy, with their scarlet uniforms, gorgeous banners, and perfect dicipline, marched to the attack of our raw recruits, the heart of young Hubbard sank within him. His deep anxiety during the battle was unrelieved until the wreck of the British army fell back on the camp. The spirits of young Hubbard then reacted so powerfully that he flapped his wings and crowed (all the boys in Tennessee could crow in the days of "Old Hickory"). One of the guard was so infuriated that he assaulted him with the bayonet, but his officer arrested the movement and protected him.

This interruption to the course of young Hubbard's education occurring at the " seed time " of life, was never recovered, and he had to enter upon the study, and practice of law with an imperfect preparation, which he felt during his life. Early in his professional career he moved to Florence, Ala., and was fortunate in being elected Solicitor in 1823. I say fortunate because in that position, a lawyer of good natural talent improves rapidly. A Solicitor is engaged in incessant conflict with men of every calibre

---

[*] NOTE.—Thomas Hubbard is the only officer from Virginia, of that name, mentioned in *Heitman's Historical Register of the Officers of the Continental Army.* He was Regimental Quartermaster, First Virginia, 1777 to May 1778.

of mind. There is no sympathy for him either amongst the members of the Bar, or the spectators. He is an Ishmaelite indeed; for "his hand is against every man, and every man's hand against him." What better arena on which a young lawyer can obtain self-reliance, and develop his power of argumentation? A few years in this position will improve a lawyer more than any law school in the United States, as has been demonstrated in the cases of a large number of lawyers, who in our State have become Senators, and members of Congress, Governors, judges of the Supreme, and other courts, and men of distinction. It was in this practical school that Hitchcock, Henry Goldthwaite, Richard W. Walker, Hubbard, Houston, Fitzpatrick, Percy Walker, Shorter, Sampson W. Harris, O'Neal, and many others, were taught the science of "thrust and parry" in mental gladiation. This school, too, was that man who cultivated a masterly style of elocution, who fired the Northern mind almost solitary and alone, set the abolition ball in motion *politically*, was the first candidate of that party for the Presidency, and, by these means, largely contributed to deluge this land in blood. That man was James G. Birney, once Solicitor for the Huntsville circuit!

Major Hubbard held his office four years; and during that time he moved his family to Moulton, in this county. His income had been good, and in 1827 he commenced a mercantile business. During the same year he engaged in politics, and was elected to the State Senate; so he had law, merchandise. and politics, all in full blast, at the same time. A very important question had presented itself, and that was the disposition of the 400,000 acres of land given to the State, as trustee, for the purpose of the cutting a canal around the Muscle Shoals. As this is a very interesting chapter in the History of the Early Settlers, I will give an account of it: When the public lands were first sold in North Alabama, the United States sold them at public auction, and on credit.

Cotton was very high, the rush of immigrants wonderful; and, consequently, lands were bid off at fabulous prices. First-class lands, I think, went off at an average of $20 per acre; and I know of two quarters which were knocked down at more than $100. The purchasers, of course, were not able to pay these rates, and as the instalments fell due, they applied their money to a part of what they had bid off at the sales, leaving the rest of their purchases to be relinquished or forfeited. They applied to Congress for relief, and an act was passed, permitting them to apply the money they had paid on the relinquished lands, to the completion of the payments on the land retained. What to do with these relinquished lands became an embarrassing question to Congress, as the purchasers then insisted, that they ought to have the privilege of entering these at their actual value. The Gordian knot was cut by Congress granting these lands to the State, as trustee, for the purpose of constructing a canal around the Muscle Shoals; leaving it to the State to decide as to the mode of disposing of them. These lands had been, more or less, improved by clearing and fencing.

When the subsequent election for members occurred, there was great excitement, for the planters had a large pecuniary interest in the measures to be adopted. Major Hubbard assumed the ground that poor men, who had no land, ought to have pre-emption of these lands, divided into small tracts, and at a cash valuation; and that, where more than one person applied for the same tract, it should be drawn for. He depicted, very graphically, the trials and hardships of the poor man, and used to say that "poor land was like skimmed milk, for it would not fatten" and he wanted these hard-working men to have a chance for a small tract of rich land. His speeches were models of that kind; and, of course, he was triumphantly elected. If George Washington had been alive, and his competitor, he would have been disgracefully beaten as the advocate of the rights of the planters.

When the General Assembly met, Major Hubbard was at the head of the party favoring his views; and he marshaled his forces, as usual, with great skill. Hon. C. C. Clay, of Madison county, led the members who thought that, in equity, the planters should have the first right to enter those lands at their cash value upon which they had expended their labor, especially as they had paid to the United States for the adjoining lands twice as much as they were worth. The Legislature finally enacted that the lands should all be valued by commissioners, the planters should have the privilege of entering each two quarter sections of the land they had relinquished, and the balance of them should be subject to entry in small tracts as proposed.

In 1829 he moved to Courtland, in our county. His mind was developing rapidly, not so much from the study of books, as from contact with men of broad information. He became deeply interested in the subject of the Tariff, and one of the most powerful opponents of the protection system in our State. He belonged to what was called the *State's Rights School*, in politics. So decided was he, that he denounced the Force Bill, and the proclamation of General Jackson, against South Carolina, as a departure from the Constitution.

He was a member of the House of Representatives in 1831-32, and then followed an interval of some years, during which he was engaged in buying and selling Chickasaw Indian land; and obtained that intermediate knowledge of Indian character, which rendered him, twenty-five years afterward, so useful to the Confederate government.

In 1839 he was elected to Congress, and as a member of the committee of Ways and Means he soon established a high character for his clear comprehension of the great political questions then before the country. In 1841, in his canvass for Congress, his competitor, at the outset, was Col. Francis H. Jones, of our county, an educated man, and a fine speaker. They were both decided Democrats, and the chances for some time seemed to be equal. As Colonel Jones, however, in a previous election, had given some offence to the Whig party, who had the power of deciding the election, between the advice of friends Colonel Jones was withdrawn, and George S. Houston, Esq., brought out in his stead. In Houston Major Hubbard met " his evil genius." Houston was well known to the people of the district, for he had acted as Solicitor for the State for many years. Houston naturally had less genius and grasp of intellect than Hubbard; but he was better educated, and was more logical and systematic in his arguments. In their love for the "dear people" they stood on an equal footing, except that Hubbard had made enemies of the planters and their friends, by the course he pursued on the land question I have mentioned, and the *warm affection* of Houston embraced all classes, rich and poor.

But in one respect Houston had, in this canvass, a decided advantage; he had no political record; for he had never been in political life but once, and that, as a member of the State Legislature from Lauderdale county, some ten years before. As might have been expected, Houston was elected, and was afterward never beaten.

The next year (1842), Major Hubbard was elected member of the House in the General Assembly, and served in 1843 and also in 1845. The engrossing question before the Legislature in 1842 was the " White Basis." Major Hubbard introduced a resolution providing, that in laying off the congressional districts, the committee should report a bill "having regard only to the white population as the basis of congressional representation." It was opposed by the Representatives of the large slave-holding counties in South Alabama, on the ground that the basis of representation should be mixed, vis.: the whole of the white population and three-fifths of the slaves. There was a third phase of opinion on this question, expressed by Hon. John A. Campbell in his protest, which was: That although it was clear to his mind that the basis of representation was the white population, yet he believed that the committee could have laid off the districts in a manner to harmonize both opinions without public discussion, which he considered mischievous. That this last opinion was the wisest, I think subsequent events in the State have clearly shown.

In the session of 1843 there was a good deal of skirmishing preparatory to the Presidential election next year, in which Major Hubbard bore a prominent part. He was chairman of the committee on Federal Relations, and made an able report on which these discussions were founded. In these, in which such eminent men as Calhoun, Erwin, Joseph G. Baldwin, Morrisette, C. C. Clay, Jr., McClung, Howard and Campbell participated, it is just to Major Hubbard to say, that in defending the propositions set forth in his report, he exhibited a familiar understanding of the subject, and powers of debate not surpassed by any.

In 1849 Major Hubbard was again elected, and served during the Thirty-first Congress, when the compromise of 1850 was made (memorable on account of its being the last ever effected before the abolition of slavery). Major Hubbard opposed the compromise, and was classed with the section of the Democratic party called *Fire Eaters;* and on this issue he was beaten by Hon. George S. Houston, who was a conservative, and had retired for awhile from politics. During that Congress the pre-emption question engaged their attention, and Major Hubbard always took an active and influential part in providing homes on the public lands for poor men.

Afterward in 1853, Major Hubbard was elected to the House of Representatives of the State Legislature. During this session the main subject of interest was the liquidation of the State banks, and the amendment of the new Code of 1851, passed without proper examination.

In 1859 Major Hubbard again became a member of this body. It was a time of great excitement on the slavery question.

In April, 1859, he was appointed by the Governor a State delegate to the Southern Commercial Convention. The members of that delegation were amongst the ablest men of the State. It was called a commercial convention, but it had great political significance. In the summer he was elected a member of the House in the General Assembly. The engrossing topic at this session was the slavery question. Major Hubbard made a speech, in closing the debate, on a resolution he had offered for the postponement of the election for Senator, from which I will make copious extracts for the purpose of showing the nature of the crisis and his style of speaking.

"When I made the motion to postpone the election of Senator I stated my object fairly, which was to leave the election to the next Legislature. I intended to speak to no other point, but the debate has been allowed to take so wide a range that the main question has been lost sight of amidst the noise and confusion arising from the discussion of the qualification of candidates (not for Senator) but President; the best means of electing and how we can preserve our institutions amidst this clamor for spoils and office. This makes it my duty, in closing the debate, to go into subjects which I did not expect to arise, and to answer some strange positions which have been assumed by members who have preceded me. All agree the Southern States have lost influence and strength in the Union, up to this date. The South, as a section, has lost her foreign trade, as well as her political standing.

"Something has caused this—what is it? Is it the Union, or is it her system of domestic labor? The Northern man will tell you it is working the land with slave labor. To this I answer, that we had slave labor before the Union was formed, and yet Virginia, alone, had more foreign trade than all the Northern States put together. Then it could not be domestic slavery which has dried up the fountains of her prosperity. Her disease is deeper seated than any supposed deficiency in her industrial pursuits. May it not be found in the perversion of the uses for which the Union was formed, by a dominant majority, seeking to make government an instrument in the distribution of wealth, on the one part, and the giving up of the material interests of the South, compromising away her territorial possessions, and yielding the proper fiscal arrangements for popularity, that her vanity might be gratified by the promotion of her sons to places of distinction, on the other. The same suicidal policy we are now engaged in, where statesmanship has no higher aim than to fool national conventions with double meaning platforms, with which 'voters' are to be fooled afterward. It is to these matters I am now required to speak, for nearly all those who have spoken, in this debate, advise conciliation, and compromise in 'President-making,' in some form or other, through national conventions, as a cure for our political disorders. Before we give our assent to this remedy, suppose we examine our past efforts in this business, and see what success has attended them.

"We were conciliating Northern sentiment when Virginia ceded to anti-slavery all that vast territory of unsurpassed fertility between the great Mississippi and Ohio rivers, whereon five powerful anti-slavery States have grown up.   •   •   •

'Aggression assumed a new form for a time, and our section is next assailed by Protective Tariffs, 'judiciously' or 'injudiciously' framed to conciliate Northern sentiment (Northern *interests*, perhaps, better expresses the idea), and we got a few more Southern Presidents by yielding to these demands. • • • When in the war with Mexico we acquired a country larger than all the Atlantic States put together, did we find the Northern States mindful of their earlier obligations of friendship? Did they keep any portion of the covenant of Union, as set forth in the Constitution? Did they even keep any part of the compromise of 1820? Not a bit of it. They demanded all—every foot; and our Southern men yielded the territory away south, to about the latitude of Vicksburg, Miss., a point in my earlier days deemed almost too hot for a white man to reside upon, even were he able to keep in the shade. • • • Seeing, therefore, that all future acquisitions are intended for the Northern section, and that we are expected to pay and fight our share, and get no part of the spoils, which is directly against the Lord's direction to Gideon, it becomes our duty to examine well our condition in the Union, and to ask how long we are to flee before the enemy for this transgression and disobedience of the Divine commands? .

"How long shall we rely on President-making? is now the question. When I was a boy our fathers did not know of more than two or three men in the broad 'Sunny South' fit to make a President of—and I have shown you the sacrifices to get them elected. Now, sir, we all know, at least, two men in every county who are in every way fit for President, and how is it possible we can give up—compromise—and concede enough of principle and interest to get them all in? It is impossible, sir, and I am almost tempted to say 'we are fools for trying,' but that I suppose would not be proper. Would any of us who had a young friend or son, who at the gambling table had lost four-fifths of his estate, advise him to go back and risk the remnant which is left, amongst gamblers who had swindled him, and divided the spoils—and to play at the *same* game—with the *same* old stocked cards, and the *same* hands to stock them? • • Nothing but a fair share of lands, and jurisdiction, in proportion to population, will answer. I am for trying an election by Congress, which is constitutional. We can, before a vote is taken, insist on the exclusion of those States from voting, or refusing to vote with such as have violated the covenants of union by nullifying acts of Congress made for our benefit; and passed in pursuance of the Constitution. If they give proper pledges, then I would again consider them as brothers, and do a brother's part by them. If however, they refuse such reasonable and just demands, we will be free to seek an association with such States only as will keep and perform what they bind themselves to do, and no longer associate with the perjurer, and covenant-breaker, who glories in his shame."

This speech, delivered a year before the election of President Lincoln, was far in advance of even his section of the party, and the Major spoke under deep excitement. It is easy to account for this, for circumstances of great aggravation had occurred but a short time before. Seward had announced the irrepressible conflict. Some of the large Northern States had nullified the fugitive slave law. A slave owner from Alabama crossing the line to reclaim his property, had been greatly abused. Another, on the same errand, had been seized by a mob headed by his own runaway-slave, stripped of his clothing, which was transferred to the runaway, while the owner was compelled to dress himself in the cast-off clothing of the negro, pay fifty dollars as the expense of this novel process, and leave the State instanter. Old John Brown, with his broad pikes, had incited a negro insurrection at Harper's Ferry, been conquered in a battle and hung, by authority of the United States Court. And yet a few days before the speech was made, bells were tolled all through the Northern States, wails of sorrow were heard throughout the land, and high wrought eulogiums were pronounced from the pulpit, rostrum, and the press upon a cold-blooded murderer, who not only deserved hanging, but should have been drawn and quartered, and his head fixed on a pole. Mr. Ingersoll, once Minister to Russia, declared in a public speech, "I have lived through two wars in which many gallant and patriotic officers fell, but I have never known one, though wrapped in his country's flag as a winding sheet, receive such extravagant praises as pulpit, press and lecture room have lavished upon the leader of the Harper's Ferry Massacre." And, moreover, sixty-seven northern members of Congress had endorsed a most mischievous book by Helper, called "The Impending Crisis," and contributed a large sum of money to defray the expenses of its secret circulation throughout the South. Was it at all remarkable, then, that Southern speakers who were capable of profound emotions should express them in their speeches! The irritation produced by such measures continued to increase, and when the Democratic party was severed, Major Hubbard was one of the electors for Breckenridge, and made effective speeches in various parts of the State.

When the Confederate Government was formed Major Hubbard was appointed "Commissioner of Indian Affairs," which was a most judicious appointment. The object for which this appointment was made was of the utmost importance to the Confederacy. The large tribes which once encompassed Alabama, and many others, were located on the western border of these States, and they were capable (if hostile) of bringing an army of warriors upon our flank, and it was very important to detach them from the Union. In accomplishing his purpose Major Hubbard did not call a convention of these tribes together for a grand pow-wow. He had too much sagacity for that. His work was done quietly and secretly, and was accomplished before the United States could frustrate his plans. His appointment as Commissioner occurred on the 12th of April, 1861, and on the 25th of the succeeding month the Cherokees seceded from the Union and declared themselves an independent nation, and nearly all the other tribes followed in quick succession. The Confederacy was not only relieved of all apprehension from this source, but they raised a large force of Indian volunteers from these tribes, which a Northern historian (*Draper 1, Vol. 239*) estimated at the battle of Elkhorn alone at four to five thousand warriors. But the extent of the services of the Commissioner will never be known until the Confederate archives are brought to light and published.

While these operations were progressing, he made his home at Nashville. His losses by the war were considerable. He lived at Spring Hill, Tenn., near General Ewell (who was a relative), some six or eight years, and died at the house of his son Duncan, in Louisiana, at the age of 82 years.

His mind, by nature, was of a high order, but eccentric. He was original and independent in his habits of thought, and studied human nature more than books. He was not very capable of solving abstract propositions, but where they were concrete, and human nature one of the factors, he rarely failed in working out correct results. On this account, in every deliberative body, of which he was a member, he was dreaded as an adversary. One peculiarity in his mind was a deficiency in the faculty of clear explication. When in Congress he became quite famous for his knowledge of the Pre-emption Laws, and was about to introduce a new bill on that subject; a Northern lawyer of distinction, who was a new member, and very anxious to understand all about pre-emption, tipped across the floor, and took a seat near the speaker. When the explanation was finished he whispered to a friend, "The matter is more obscure to me than it was before." But when the main debate took place, and the major warmed to his work, he got the information he desired, but it came "by instalments."

In person Major Hubbard was very tall, spare, somewhat stoop-shouldered, and his arms seemed disproportionately long. His head and brain were much over the average of men of his stature. His eye was gray and restless. In later years he fattened up, and became a stout man. He was homely, but striking in his person, and in any circle would have arrested the attention of a stranger.

His manners were not graceful, but he was cheerful and interesting; and in his old age he was genial and charming, for he had been a close observer of men and things as he passed along, and his recollections were told in a very original manner interspersed with amusing anecdotes.

NOTE.—At the same time, the author was elector for Stephen A. Douglas, and president of the convention which met at Montgomery.

As a lawyer, he was not profound in his learning, as he had no patience for persistent study. But before a jury, he was always formidable. His experience as solicitor, enabled him to clear many a culprit on technical grounds. His ablest speech, perhaps, was made in defence of Preston Bowling, for murder. I will rehearse the leading facts of the case (which occurred in this county) to show what an achievement the acquittal was. Pres. (as he was always called) had threatened the life of his father (Alexander Bowling), and on this account was kept in prison, for some time. After the old man's death, his great spite seemed to be against his brother James. He had him arrested for the murder of an unknown trader; and brought before a justice's court, where he (Pres.) swore that his brother had confessed to him, that he had killed the trader, by which he got three or four thousand dollars; and that he had hidden the body in a cave in the mountain; and advised Pres. to do the same, and not to be a poor man all his life. There were thirty or forty witnesses examined on the trial, several of whom swore that the bones in the cave alluded to, were there before the Bowlings came to the county; and all of them swore that they would not believe Pres. Bowling on his oath. Of course, James Bowling was acquitted. After this James was found dead; and Pres was arraigned for his murder. Pres was poor, and James, under the will of his father, managed the plantation. The theory of the prosecution was, that Pres. had taken a big bore rifle, and gone to a certain gate, by which he knew James would pass, and stood behind the post. That when James got within thirty or forty feet, he saw Pres., halted, and wheeled; and that Pres. shot him in the back, while his horse was in a gallop. I have talked with several of the old men who were at the trial, who thought that this theory was sustained by the circumstances proven by the witnesses. There was a mountain of prejudice therefore against the prisoner, when Major Hubbard commenced his speech. He made a great effort, and not only removed this mountain, but made so deep an impression on his hearers, that when the jury brought in a verdict of acquittal, the spectators received it with cheers and shouts.

He had the art (when he chose) of mystifying a matter. An anecdote used to be told amongst the lawyers to this effect: Major Hubbard was assisted once in the defence of a case by the late Judge Ormond. Upon the testimony the case proved to be a very bad one. Ormond whispered, "Hubbard, what shall we do with it?" The answer was, "Ormond, you go ahead and make the best speech you can; and when I come on, I'll puzzle the case so that they will never be able to unravel it." And so he did. Oliver Cromwell could not have beaten him in this line, and the consequence was a mis-trial.

But it was in politics that he was most distinguished. He had from his superior knowledge of human nature, great art in planning a campaign. As a speaker he was excelled by many of his competitors. His voice was harsh, but could be heard distinctly in a large crowd; for he generally spoke on a high key. He had no harmony in his style, but a great deal of good sense, and an instinctive knowledge of the most effective arguments to use with a promiscuous crowd. He believed strongly in the depravity of human nature; and he appealed oftener to men's prejudices than to their better sentiments. His speeches were not of the routine order; he was like the captain who had cleared his vessel for any port where he could sell his cargo to the best advantage. He would first try one topic and then another, keeping his eyes intently fixed upon the upturned faces of the people; and when he found that he had made a successful hit, he would enlarge upon it, and illustrate it with one of his good anecdotes. I once heard him demonstrate how far men, having a common interest, would go in sustaining each other by a case which he said occurred in the "Upper-rooting" (the name of a Circuit) where he commenced the practice of law. "A man was indicted for stealing a cow, and the proof of the fact was positive. Nevertheless, his lawyer (one of the old Tennessee stagers) made a labored defence, furiously attacking the witnesses for the State, and almost coming to a fight with the solicitor. When he sat down and was wiping the sweat from his forehead, he asked him in a whisper, "Is it possible you have any idea of clearing your client?" The answer was, "Certainly I will clear him, Hubbard, for eleven of the men on that jury helped to *eat that cow.*"

At this stage of his life he had but crude ideas of the science of government, and was a mere politician, plotting for his own advancement. But, before many years elapsed, he made great measures, such as the Tariff, the slavery question and the land laws, his study; and then, in a section of the State where some of his opinions were not popular, boldly advocated them, regardless of consequences. Instead of the mere politician, he had become a statesman. I do not mean that he was always right; that is not essential to the character of a statesman. Webster and Calhoun were both statesmen, and yet they differed in their theories *toto cœlo*. At this stage of his life, the character of Major Hubbard assumed a dignity and elevation it had not before, which continued to the end of his career.

Colonel Garrett, author of the " Public Men of Alabama," says: "Alabama has had but few men in her councils who understood the framework of her government better, or guarded her interests more faithfully and with more ability than David Hubbard."

Major Hubbard was twice married—first to Miss Campbell, a niece of Hon. G. W. Campbell, of Nashville, Tenn., once minister to Russia. She was of fine person and intellect, and co-operated faithfully with her husband in rearing a family of sons and daughters, who were unusually well educated.

Major Hubbard's second wife was an elderly maiden lady, named Stoddard, who was sister of the Mr. Campbell referred to above. It was a most judicious marriage. The Major occupied a very healthy home in the mountains called "Kinloch" until he moved to Tennessee. His second wife died near Springfield.

The children of Major Hubbard were: (1) Mary, who married Dr. John Tucker, of Virginia. (2) Duncan, who lived in Okalona, Miss., until the close of the war and then moved to Louisiana. He died of yellow fever in 1878. His first wife was Miss Chambers, of Virginia, and his second, Miss Edmondson, of Holly Springs, Miss. (3) David lived near Okalona, until the close of war, and then moved to Louisiana with his brother Duncan. He was twice married; first to a Miss Wiley, of Holly Springs, Miss., a niece of Hon. Jacob Thompson, and secondly to Miss Holt, of New Orleans. (4) Caledonia, who married Gaston Henderson, and lived at Okalona, Miss., until the close of the war and then moved to Mississippi City. (5) Emma, who married Jas. Young, son of Col. G. H. Young, of "Waverly," Miss. (6) George C., the youngest child, lived in Alabama, with his father—was married to Miss Margaret King, daughter of Mr. Oswald King. George was killed at the battle of Baker's Creek, in Mississippi. His widow lives with her father in this county, and has only one child—George C.—a youth of great promise about fifteen years of age, and the only descendant of the Hon. David Hubbard, now living in Lawrence county.

The Physicians of Moulton

whom I knew in early times were Drs. George A. Glover, Edward Gantt, Campbell, J. S. Ringo, Elijah Koons and Tandy W. Walker. Of the history of some of these I have learned so little that it will not be necessary to write separate notices of them. Dr. Campbell, who was well versed in medicine, moved to the West, I think. Dr. Ringo, who was a brother-in-law of E. A. Daniel, I think died in Moulton. Dr. Koons was a young physician of much promise, and a cousin of Judge Taylor, and carried the latter back to Kentucky (when he became insane), and never returned.

Dr. Glover was very much esteemed as a man and physician. He had married a sister of Bishop Robert Paine, and lived in the house now occupied by Judge Gibson, which he (Glover) built. He had the misfortune to lose his wife, and moved back to Giles county, Tenn., where he died. I never knew any of his children except Darthula, who was well reared and educated by Bishop Paine, and married in Aberdeen, Miss.

Dr. Edward Gantt was an old man when he came to Moulton. He was descended from a distinguished Catholic family, and was born and reared in the State of Maryland. He had grown up in polished society—had received one of the best collegiate educations—and as a physician had taken his diploma at the Medical College of Edinburgh; then one of the most celebrated in the world. He was married twice. His second wife was living when he moved from Missouri to Moulton. She was reared in Baltimore, and was a lady of fine person and culture, and a strict member of the Catholic Church. They had a large family of young children. He died in Moulton about the year 1848. After his death she returned to Missouri with her children. I have heard of none of them since, except two sons who became physicians; William, some years ago in Galveston, Texas, and a professor in the medical college at that place; and John, who had settled in Arkansas, and Robert, who also settled in Arkansas, and became distinguished as a lawyer.

Dr. Gantt was quite tall, and had blue eyes and a light complexion. He was an excellent physician, and his manner in a sick room was marked by delicacy and dignity. In his general intercourse he showed the perfect gentleman. His conversation was very interesting; for he had traveled over Europe, and had been a close observer of whatever was worthy of note. I can even now remember distinctly some of the conversations with him in which he would describe the quaint old city of Edinburgh, one street of which was built on a hill-side so steep that you could step out of the first story upon a street on the south, and from the sixth story on the street upon the north side. The vineyards of France, with their heavy clusters of grapes, reminding one of Eshcol, and the cities of Europe, where can be seen such wonderful illustratrations of architecture and art. It was mournful to think that a gentleman who, in youth, was favored by such opportunities of refined enjoyment, should have made the mistake, in his old age, of marrying a wife too young for him, and subjecting himself thereby to the annoyance of young children, and the burden and expense of rearing and educating larger ones, at the season of a man's life when quiet and competence, and the absence of solicitude, are requisite for his happiness.

Dr. Gantt was well informed also in politics. He was the first "Federalist of the John Adams school" I had ever met, and having very strong prejudices against that way of thinking, it was with curious interest that I led him on to explain himself fully. I found that the foundation of the political creed of that party was a strong doubt of the capacity of the people for self-government. The triumph of Mr. Jefferson had been so complete, that at this time there were very few survivors left of that dignified old party, strongly tinctured with aristocratic notions, but with hands unpolluted by bribes. They demanded a strong Federal government. I expected that when these venerable relics of that party passed away it would never be revived. But, strange as it may appear, the demand for a strong government has been renewed by a large party in the country; and, stranger still, that this should have occurred just after a civil war which tested the powers of our general government, and demonstrated that it was capable of bearing a greater strain than any which ever ruled in Europe.

Dr. Tandy W. Walker commenced the practice of medicine at Oakville, a flourishing village nine miles east of Moulton, now abandoned. The doctor was a gentleman of genius, and well educated. He had a genial temper, and became a great favorite with the people. He was elected five times by our county to the House, and for three years to the Senate, and was a very efficient member. Before the people he made good speeches, and understood, well, how to ingratiate himself with them. On one occasion he was defending himself from some small charges, and concluded by saying: " And now, gentlemen, although I am entirely innocent of what was alleged against me, I have often done wrong, and made great mistakes. I don't claim to be any better than other men, but just about as clever as the common run of you, no better and no worse. I am no angel in any respect, but would be greatly obliged to you for your votes." This announcement was received with great plaudits, and the doctor became more popular than he had ever been before—because he admitted that he was *no angel*, and no better than the "common run" of the voters. This declaration, made forty years ago, and the manner in which it was received, I have often thought of since. It showed the truth of the proposition that a representative will generally resemble his constituency. And here a mournful reflection forces itself on my mind. The South has been jubilant for some years over a new and large element which has been added to its voting strength, and consequently its representation in Congress. In the end, however, *it will prove to be a curse.* When this new element shall cease to vote on the color line, it will become a weapon in the hands of unprincipled and ignorant demagogues for their own advancement over the heads of those learned, eloquent and chivalrous men, who, as a class, have shed so much lustre on the South.

When Oakville was abandoned, Dr. Walker came to Moulton, practised medicine for years and died about 1851, very much respected and beloved. To show the impression produced by the doctor at the seat of government for the State, I introduce the following notice of him from "The Public Men of Alabama," by Col. Garrett: "Tandy W. Walker came to the House in 1838, and continued to serve in that body, and in the Senate, until 1845. He was quite convivial, and loved the society of boon companions. No gentleman was regarded with more favor. His heart was formed for friendship, and the more its emotions were indulged, the stronger the tie became. He frequently shared in the debates with a vigor of mind and a degree of culture which did him credit. When passing his winters in Tuscaloosa, he was much in society, and being a widower in the zenith of life, he was quite attentive to the ladies, who seemed to be fond of his company. Among the tender associations which connect the mind with the old Capitol, and with the pleasant scenes of other days, nothing is more natural, nothing more prominent, than the genial face, and merry laugh, of Dr. Tandy Walker. He was a genial favorite, even with the Whigs, when party spirit ran highest in 1840 and in 1844. The social enjoyments afforded by such a man, can never be forgotten by old friends. And yet, after all, it is much to be lamented that the days of Dr. Tandy (as we used to call him, and as he liked to be called) were shortened by the same deceptive, fatal agent which deprived Scotland of her idol poet, Burns, at the age of thirty-seven years. Let the warning be heard by the young in time to resist the temptation, which has brought so much ruin on the world."

Mechanics of Moulton.

Wm. D. C. Jones was the eldest brother of the Hon. Geo. W. Jones, of Fayetteville, Tenn., from whom I have the following account of him:

In the latter part of December, 1820, he left Giles county, Tennessee, and went to Moulton, Ala., and found employment with a Mr. Henderson, a cabinet maker, with whom he had served his apprenticeship in Elkton, Tenn. Joseph Burleson was living in Moulton at that time, and Wm. Jones made the acquaintance of Rachel Burleson. Her father moved out upon the Byler road. Wm. Jones soon followed, and there married Rachel. Their son, George W. Jones, the present Representative in Congress, from the Austin district, in Texas, was born September 5, 1828. His father moved to Tipton county, Tennessee, a few years after the birth of his son, and in the winter of 1848 to Bastrop county, Texas, where he and his son have resided ever since. George W. Jones is a lawyer. He is a Democrat, and supported S. A. Douglas for President in 1860. When the war came on, he volunteered in the Confederate service, and was a colonel in one of the Texas regiments. After the war was over, he returned to Bastrop; was a member of the Constitutional Convention of 1866, and on the adoption of the Constitution formed by that convention, he was elected Lieutenant Governor of the State. He and others were removed by General Sheridan, "as an impediment to reconstruction." He was elected to the Forty-sixth Congress, and is now a candidate for re-election.

Nathaniel Alman, in old times, was a carpenter in Moulton. He was an industrious man, of a social disposition, and very much respected; but like the mechanics, generally, of that day, whenever he finished one job of work, he gave himself an interval for recreation, before he commenced another. It was in one of those intervals that my acquaintance with him first commenced, and which ripened into a friendship which continued during his life. At this time the county prisoners were confined under a temporary shelter, in the corner of the public square, and strongly guarded, during the removal of the county jail from the public square to the site where it now stands. Alman happened to be taking what chancery clerks call "a rest in his account;" and although a peaceable man, got into a quarrel with a member of the guard. This resulted in an affray, during which there was a great uproar, and a large crowd collected around the combatants. When the police put a stop to it, Alman, surrounded by his friends, came to my office. I put them out, and had Alman tell me all about the fight. He did so circumstantially, and mentioned, in conclusion, that his adversary made a furious assault on him with a knife. Says I, "Did he cut you?" "No, but his knife grazed my shirt." I opened his shirt bosom, and found (what in his excitement he had not been conscious of before) a scratch across his breast, at least six inches long, with a drop of blood here and there exuding from it. I advised him to say nothing about it; and in a short time the trial commenced, before two justices of the peace. *This was the first time I had ever appeared in a law case.* Mr. Argyle Campbell conducted the prosecution, and he proceeded to show that this was not an ordinary case, but a very serious assault upon the majesty of the State, in the person of the guard. I began to fear that instead of a simple affray, my client would be convicted of treason. A feeling of embarrassment crept over me when I commenced my speech, and partial blindness, so that the members of the court seemed to be in a mist a great way off. I judge I *said* but little, for I *spoke* very fast; but just as I felt sensible of being out of breath and out of ideas, it occurred to me to play my trump card; and I laid open the bosom of my client before the court. This "brought down the house," and Alman was escorted from the court house by his friends in triumph. I have had a purpose in mentioning my embarrassment in this, my first effort. Young men, when listening to practised speakers, imagine that they never have passed through this climacteric of the profession. But all must experience it, and in every calling. It is said that a carpenter must cut his foot badly with the adze before he ever becomes skilful in using the trade, and I have never known a hunter kill a deer until he had passed through what is called the "buck-ague!"

After this Nat. Alman married, made a modest competence by his trade, and settled in the country, not far from town, where he reared his children. When he began to be an old man he had the misfortune to lose his good wife. After awhile he became more attentive to his dress, and also looked around at the good dames for another wife. His objection to those around him was that he knew them too well. So he went out to fish in strange waters, and "caught a tartar." There was, at that time, in the neighboring town of Courtland a widow Harley, who was quite buxom, was always well dressed and had buried two husbands. She, too, seemed to be looking out for a partner. Her husbands had been tailors, and she was just as skilful as either of them. She could set the buckram in the rolling collars of the coats, they wore in early times, as well as either. Whenever there was a press of business in the shop she came to the rescue, and was like a tailor in every respect, except that she did not seat herself like a Turk on the tailor's board. Instead of that she seated herself in a chair and "drove things ahead," as General Forrest did. Her life had been a stormy one, for she not only strove to do her whole duty herself, but tried to *compel* her husbands to do theirs; the consequence was constant intestine war. When our civil war took place there were some public men who advocated the plan of carrying on the war *within* the Union. Governor Wise, of Virginia, belonged to this class; and in his explanation he made the thing "as clear as mud." But this is what Mrs. Harley understood perfectly. In every *union* she formed, so imperious was her temper, war was carried on incessantly. But when she would lose a husband there ensued a time of profound peace. Mrs. Harley was not fond "of the smooth surface of a summer sea, but loved to hear, amid the rending tackle's roar, the spirit of the equinoctial gale."

At length Alman appeared as a wooer. Things were eligible on both sides. Alman had gained a competence, and so had the widow. She not only owned town lots, but a family of slaves and the head of this family was a large negro woman as black as tar. Capt. Sam Shackelford called her "Snow-ball," and a friend of hers often seen on the street with her who was very large and black, was called "The Big Black," after a certain river, in a sister State. What the baptismal name of "Snow-ball" was is not known, since it was so completely superseded by the new one, that it was supposed to be forgotten, even by her mistress. Well, Nat Alman and Mrs. Harley formed a union, and the war commenced. He stood up manfully at first, but she was in her native element and he was not, and the final consequence was: separation and divorce—on what grounds I never ascertained. Some years afterward, when Mrs. Harley was about sixty years of age, but always so neatly dressed she appeared to be much younger, she hung out her banner again "upon the outer wall." She had become tired of looking upon wrinkled faces, and cast her eyes with favor on a young man, named Doyle, about twenty-seven years of age, who worked in Henry Thorne's gin shop—and they were married. Some time later she removed her young husband and her property to Corinth, and here occurred to her the catastrophe of her life. Hitherto she had gotten along with "Snow-ball" much better than one would suppose. They had their collisions, but whenever Snow-ball saw that a fierce storm was brewing, she would "reef all sails" and "lie to," until it passed over. She had borne much, but at length the vials of wrath which had been bottled up so long, were poured out on the head of her mistress, and she rose up in open rebellion. Her mistress threatened to sell her and all her family. Doyle was much in favor of this course, and sustained it by many plausible reasons. She instructed him to set about it, which he did with great alacrity. He consulted her in all the preliminary steps, but when he closed the sale and received the money, he put it in his own pocket, disappeared, and has never been heard of since. At what time the *devil entered into Doyle* will never be known.

To return to my old friend Alman; in the Courtland campaign he had passed "through great tribulation," and he became a wiser and a better man. His last days were passed tranquilly with his children, who are highly respectable. One of his grandsons is a promising young lawyer.

John Simmons was an excellent saddler, and a man of slight but fine person. He uniformly dressed well, and had very genteel manners. He and the Dewoodys, into which family he married more than sixty years since, descended the Tennessee river in a flatboat. The Dewoodys landed at a place called Cotton-Gin Port, in Limestone county, and he, with his family, consisting then of only his wife and one child (our worthy postmaster) floated on to Lawrence county, and went out to their new home at Moulton. The Dewoodys were a very respectable family, and descended from William Dewoody, who emigrated from Ireland when eighteen years of age. His wife was Hannah Alexander, a Pennsylvanian by birth. They had a large family of children. One of them, John, was a Cumberland Presbyterian preacher (and of the descendants of that family there is one, or perhaps more, Methodist preachers). One daughter, Eliza, married James Hubbard, brother of Hon. David Hubbard. And another daughter, Agnes G., married John Simmons. He was born at Petersville, Va., January 1, 1789, and married at Greenville, East Tennessee. He died at Moulton in 1838, and his wife at the same place, in 1841. They had five children, of whom two died young, and three are now living. The eldest, Alfred D. Simmons, has been acting postmaster in Courtland for thirty years, and is so much respected that he has been, at all times, the choice of both parties for that office.

He married Martha Jane Woolard. She was an orphan, bereft in childhood of her father and her mother, who both died in one day in a subterranean spring from the damps. She was reared by her uncle, Mr. Odel, of Athens, and during a long life, most faithfully performed her duty as a wife, mother, neighbor and a Christian. In her late affliction this notable woman has had the sympathy of the whole community. I am not in the habit of speaking in commendation of the living, but she has nearly "run her course." For a generation past she has been the impersonation of active benevolence. She has aided the poor, comforted the broken-hearted by infusing the spirit of her wonderful fortitude, and the minister who found himself amongst strangers, ready to faint from discouragement, has always been welcomed to the "Prophet's chamber" in her house, and had his heart strengthened by communion with this excellent Methodist lady. They have a number of children: (1) John A. S., was in the late war in Captain Warren's company of the Ninth Alabama regiment, was wounded in the battle of Fredericksburg, recovered and remained with the army to the end. He married Laura McLemore at Petersburg, Va., in 1865; and died at his father's house in Courtland in 1878. His widow is living with her mother in Petersburg. (2) Thomas W., was in the same company—wounded at the battle of Williamsburg, and taken prisoner, exchanged in a short time, and remained with the army until the close of the war. He married Jennie M. Watkins, daughter of James C. Watkins. He died in 1870. (3) Nancy Lou died in 1868. She was postmistress at the time of her death. (4) Edwin J. was in the same company with John and Thomas, and is still living in Courtland. He married Emma Merrill in 1867. (5) Mary V. married Charles J. Gray, lived in Memphis until her husband's death, and died in Courtland in 1874. (6) Alice C. married Henry Jacques in 1876. (7) Alfred D. married his cousin, Nannie Rainey, resides in Courtland, and has been favorably known as a merchant for many years. (8) Josephine and Mattie are young girls. (9) Willie is a youth and living at home.

William T., second child of John Simmons and Agnes his wife, is and has been for many years, an enterprising citizen of Courtland and has served as sheriff of the county, during a term. He married Nancy, daughter of Hiram Campbell. They have two children: Walter W., who married Ida, daughter of Henry Thorn, and Frederick A., who is now at school.

Lucy E., third child of John Simmons and Agnes his wife, married James L. Rainey, of Athens, Alabama. One of their daughters—Nannie—married Alfred D. Simmons, Jr., and now lives in Courtland. John H., was in the army of Gen. Joe Johnston.

Rev. Robert M. Cunningham, D.D.

When I commenced the collection of facts respecting the life of this distinguished minister I made very slow progress. This was not strange, for he was called by the Presbyterian Church, in Moulton, nearly sixty years ago, was eighty years old when he died, and had been dead more than forty years, so that the space of time to be investigated extended as far back as 120 years. I had known Dr. Cunningham, personally, for about a year; admired him as a man and a preacher, and felt satisfied that he had a history of much interest, provided it could be brought to light. I first applied for information to the Alabama State Historical Society, at Tuscaloosa, and obtained valuable items as to the latter part of his life, which closed near this place. From Maj. H. B. McLellan, president of Sayre Female Institute, I received important information as to his long pastorate at Lexington, Ky. Rev. F. B. Converse, of Louisville, editor of the *Christian Observer*, was written to. He promptly supplied what he could, remarking "that it was too long ago for us to furnish any information respecting him from *personal* knowledge," and suggested that, possibly, the Presbyterian Historical Society, at Philadelphia, might contribute some items. I felt discouraged, but nearly fifty years of his valuable life remained unaccounted for, and I addressed an inquiry to that society, who referred it to Rev. Henry E. Dwight, D.D., of Philadelphia. The doctor promptly sent an account of Dr. Cunningham from his birth, covering fully and circumstantially the blank in his history, and shedding much light on the subsequent part of his career. The authorities cited by Dr. Dwight were Revs. J. D. Shane, Nathan S. Beman and S. McCulloch. This forms the staple of the following sketch of the life of Dr. Cunningham. I have interwoven, in their order, such facts as I have ascertained, so as to present at one view the principal events of a long and useful life. I have made this preliminary explanation for the purpose of showing how it happened that I am able to present so circumstantial an account of events of so ancient a date, the reliable sources from which they were derived, and the importance of historical societies.

Robt. M. Cunningham, a son of Roger and Mary Cunningham, was born in York county, Pa., September 10, 1760. In his fifteenth year, his father removed his family to North Carolina, where he bought a plantation, and reared his children. While quite a youth he served as a soldier in the revolutionary war. At the close of the war, he entered a Latin school, taught by the Rev. Robert Finley, in the neighborhood of Rocky River, N. C. He remained here a year, and then went to Bethel settlement, York county, N. C., to be a pupil of Mr. Robert McCulloch, for two years. Then he removed, to an academy on Bullock's creek, taught by Rev. Jos. Alexander. In 1787 (being 26 years of age) he entered the junior class in Dickinson College, Carlisle; and graduated in 1789.

On leaving college, he returned to his parents. While studying theology he taught school for a support. He soon joined the First Presbytery of South Carolina, by which he was licensed to preach, in 1792. Here he married his first wife, Elizabeth, daughter of Charles and Mary Moore, of Spartanburg District. She died on November 3, 1794; issue, a daughter who died early.

In the autumn of 1792 he went to Georgia and organized a church in a part of Green county, now called Hancock; and ordained elders to a church called Ebenezer. He settled in the neighborhood, opened a school, and preached alternately at Ebenezer and Bethany and subsequently removed to Bethany, where he remained until he left the State. On October 15, 1795, he married Betsy Ann, daughter of Joseph Parks, of Prince Edward county, Va. By this marriage he had five sons. In 1796, he, with four other ministers, were sent off from the Presbytery of South Carolina, to form one in Georgia, called Hopewell, which was constituted the March following. On October 14, 1805, he married, as a third wife, Emily, daughter of Col. Byrd, of Augusta, Ga., who survived him. Hers was a family of distinction. Her sister, Caroline, married Benj. C. Yancy, a lawyer of great promise in South Carolina, who died in the morning of life. Wm. L. Yancy, the great Southern orator was her son, by this marriage. She married a second time, Rev. Nathan S. Beman, a Presbyterian minister, who occupied the pulpit in Augusta for many years; and had great reputation for learning and eloquence. A strong proof of this was given in the fact that his Northern anti-slavery opinions were tolerated. Another sister of this family married Jesse Beene, of Cahaba, Ala., a distinguished lawyer and politician. At the time of this marriage, we judge that Mr. Cunningham had won distinction in a ministerial and social respect.

In 1807, Mr. Cunningham removed to Lexington, Ky., and was installed pastor of the First Presbyterian Church, succeeding Rev. Dr. Blythe, who was the first preacher of that church. Lexington was the oldest town in the State of Kentucky, and in the centre of a beautiful and fertile country. Its society was even then celebrated for its wealth and intellectual culture. Of all the pulpits west of the mountains, none required a minister of learning and eloquence more than the one occupied by Mr. Cunningham. Here were the homes of the Clays, Breckinridges, and other families which have since been famous in the history of the country. One would be apt to conclude, that at this early period, the grade of the Presbyterian preachers was much below what it is at the present day, but it is not so. From the progress of the Arts and Sciences the modern preachers may have a broader culture, but I much doubt if any one of them is the equal, in eloquence, of Dr. Samuel Davies, who died a hundred years ago. His fervid, rich, imaginative style, flowing as ample as the current of a great river, was the model for ministers who succeeded him in the early part of this century. Mr. Cunningham's pastorate there was a long one. The records of the board of trustees show that he was called in 1807 and continued until 1821, inclusive. He became a member of the Synod of Kentucky as early as 1803, and was one of the founders of the Kentucky Bible Society in 1817. The early sessional records of this church can not be found; and therefore we are unable to present as full an account of him as is desirable at this period of his life, when he was in full mental and bodily vigor.

He remained in Lexington until 1822, when he resigned and removed to Moulton, a small town in North Alabama. He was now an old man and had been laboring as a minister for thirty years. He became a farmer, preaching constantly in Moulton and surrounding villages. In the fall of 1826 he removed to the South and bought a farm eleven miles from Tuscaloosa, on the Greensboro road. In Tuscaloosa, and at the neighboring town of Carthage, near his plantation, he built up churches. Here he alternated, occasionally preaching at Greensboro, of which church his son Joseph was pastor. For eight years he preached a free gospel at Tuscaloosa, and then resigned in favor of Rev. Wm. Williams. For several years afterward he supplied the pulpit at Carthage, and preached his last sermon in the summer of 1838. From this time his mental and bodily powers began to decline.

He was honored with the degree of Doctor of Divinity from Franklin College, Georgia, in 1827, when Dr. Waddell was President, and Dr. Church, and James and Henry Jackson, were members of the Faculty. In 1836 he removed to Tuscaloosa for the sake of schools for his youngest daughter, and several orphan grandchildren, and partly to provide a comfortable home for his family, in view of his approaching departure; but he still passed the greater part of his time at his retreat near his plantation. Here his favorite authors were Milton, President Edwards and Dr. Thomas Dick. In June, 1839, he attended the meeting of the Presbytery at Tuscaloosa, and was enabled to address that body—his last effort in public. After an illness of a week, he died. His monument stands in the city cemetery of Tuscaloosa, with an inscription on each of its four sides in the Latin language, showing, among other things, that he had been a soldier of the Revolution; that he had been Pastor of Presbyterian churches in Georgia, and in Lexington, Ky., for many years, and that he died on the 11th day of July, A. D. 1839, 80 years of age.

Rev. Joseph Cunningham (above referred to) was one of five sons by his father's second marriage, and a minister of ability. By his last marriage, he had a son, Robert, a physician, who died in Sumter county, Alabama, and three daughters, viz.: Mrs. Maltby. Mrs. Wilson and Miss Louisa, who it is believed was never married.

Dr. Dwight says : ' '' The exterior of Dr. Cunningham was impressive. His stature at fifty-three years of age was more than six feet, and his form was full and well developed. His face was good, his eye mild but expressive, and his utterances in private conversation, in the pulpit and in social meetings were eloquent. In his preaching he was less doctrinal than experimental, aiming ever to bring sinners to Christ, and Christians to higher attainments in holiness. He was on the best terms with all evangelical Christians, and rejoiced in the progress of Christ's kingdom under any form, and the glory of God in all events. He greatly rejoiced in revivals of religion, which, in his time, were wonderful in Kentucky, and extended farther South, till they reached Georgia. Here was the hiding of his power, which tinged and colored all his subsequent ministry. His great tenderness in preaching opened many hearts, whilst God's spirit sealed their souls.

The Presbyterian Church in Moulton had no settled minister for many years after Dr. Cunningham moved away. Early records of the Presbytery have been mislaid, and I therefore can not speak with certainty on this point. I remember that the Rev. —— Morrison filled this pulpit for several years. He was a young man of great dignity, and propriety of deportment, and an earnest, sensible preacher. After him came Rev. —— McMillan, who taught a classical school at the Chalybeate Springs, seven miles northeast of Moulton, and supplied the pulpit in Moulton. He was a good theologian, and a pious, good preacher. I shall have more to say of these ministers in connection with other churches. For several years, also previous to 1830, a young minister of Tuscumbia, named Ashbridge, occasionally preached in Moulton. He was a man of fine intellect, of high culture, and of a rich imagination. He died early, and his death was very much lamented by people of all denominations. Had he lived to middle life he would have been an orator of the first class.

Capt. William Leetch

was born in the northern part of Ireland, of Scottish parentage, in 1766, removed to Mecklenburg county, North Carolina, and married Naomi Knox, daughter of Capt. James Knox, in 1795. He came to Lawrence county in 1818; first lived on his plantation, near Moulton, and then removed his family into Moulton, where he died in 1837. The captain was a tall man, of strangely marked features, and of very decided cast of character. He was one of our best citizens, very much respected in the community for his integrity, and was devoted to his family and his church, which was Presbyterian. Indeed, he was

its main pillar. He believed in its doctrines, and, what is more, his conduct was uniformly consistent with them. He considered " The Westminster Confession of Faith "
as the Bible in epitome, and he received the articles pure and unadulterated, according
to the Scotch interpretation. He performed his secular work as a duty to his family, but
his functions as an Elder in the church seemed to be a luxury to him. He appeared to
strangers to be rather stern; but those of us who had familiar intercourse with him,
knew him to be a man of genuine feeling and principle.

Mrs. Naomi K. Leetch was one of the worthy women of the olden times. In her
youth she had been beautiful, and when old she was well favored and graceful in her
manners. She came of one of the best revolutionary families. She was the aunt of
President James (Knox) Polk, and the first time I ever saw him he was on a visit to her
in Moulton. He was then a young man, and had served only one session in Congress.
He spent a week in Moulton, and was so affable and well informed he became quite
a favorite with our people. My acquaintance with him commenced then, and ripened
into a friendship which continued during his life. The next time he visited Lawrence was
following his election as Governor of Tennessee, after a fierce contest, during which he
had added greatly to his reputation as a popular speaker. At a public dinner given to
him in Courtland, he made a speech so able, so dignified and patriotic, that it made a
deep impression on the public mind. It did not astonish those who knew him, that he
was elevated to the Presidency. The gentleman who made the speech of welcome, at
the public dinner, predicted that this would be the case; and it was, even at this early
stage of his life, a very general impression. Mrs. Leetch died in Moulton in 1854.
Her daughter Maria married David Hunter, whom we have already noticed, and died
in Mississippi. James K., a son, died in Moulton. He was a young man of fine person
and promise. Naomi S., her youngest, married the Hon. Thomas M. Peters, and here
I will give an account of

The Peters Family.

Mr. Lemuel Peters (the father of the Judge) was born in Kean, New Hampshire, in
1772. His nationality was Welsh and his father's family were Quakers. They were,
I understood, a people of great stoutness and resolution. I knew Mr. Peters very well. He
used to say that his father could lift a weight of a thousand pounds. Lemuel Peters married
Sarah Minott, who was born in Dummerston, Vermont, in 1770. In religion she was a
Puritan and Presbyterian, and French and Irish in blood and nationality. The families of Mr. Peters and wife were amongst the earliest settlers of New England. She was
unusually well educated, and intelligent, and very fond of reading. She greatly admired
the *Spectator* and Scott's Novels, which appeared, one after another, about the time our
county was settled. In their house were books and papers for their children to
read, and this accounts for the fact that every son in the family was well educated, and
belonged to a profession. Their home was one of hospitality where ministers, of all
denominations, especially the Presbyterian, were welcomed. Mr. Peters was an ardent
Clay Whig. He came South, after his marriage in 1808, and settled at Clarksville, Tennessee, and from that place he removed to Lawrence county in 1820 or 1821, and settled
near Leighton where he reared a large family of children. Mrs. Peters died here in
1834, and is buried in the "Leigh Graveyard." He removed to Bowie county, Texas; but
sold out his possessions there in 1836, and on his way to visit New England, died,
1837, at the house of Dr. Gideon Williams, on Town creek, and was buried by the
side of his deceased wife.

Of their children Charles became a lawyer, resided in the adjoining county of Mor-
gan, and was for many years the judge of the County Court there. Another son,
John, became a physician, lived for some years in Courtland, and removed to Texas.
Samuel, another son, became a lawyer, settled first in La Grange, then in Tuscumbia.

Hon. Thomas M. Peters, who lives now in Moulton, is a son of this family. He
had good opportunities of acquiring an education, and availed himself of them. He
graduated at the University of Alabama, in 1834, in the same class with Hon. C. C. Clay
and Walter H. Crenshaw, and also Wm. S. Parham and John McI. Smith, of our

county. He studied law and settled in the town of Moulton, where, as we have already stated, he owned and edited a newspaper, which he sold out after a few years. About this time he married Naomi Sophia Leetch, a young lady of much beauty, very modest and amiable, and a great favorite with all her acquaintances. This elegant woman died only a few months ago. Mr. Peters devoted himself to his profession, and not only became a good lawyer, but a man of general literary and scientific culture. He was a decided Clay Whig, and entered into politics in 1845, when, in spite of opposition, he was elected to the House of Representatives, of the General Assembly, with Hon. David Hubbard and Dr. Tandy Walker, both strong Democrats. Here when he took his seat, he proved himself to be a self-possessed, sensible and ready debater. In 1847 he was elected to the Senate, and in this body he maintained the character he had formed for intelligence and ability. After serving through his term in the Senate, he retired to private life, and continued the practice of his profession.

At length the great crisis of 1861 approached, and Mr. Peters (like every other man of information and influence) was called upon to give his counsel in regard to the momentous question then presented to the people of the South for their decision. This he did, in the most emphatic manner, in favor of the preservation of the Union. Whilst the Convention was in session, he published in the Moulton *Democrat* a strong article in which he denied the right of secession; contended that the Convention having been called by virtue of "Joint Resolutions" passed by the General Assembly nine months before the Presidential election of 1860, was not based upon the sovereignty of the people, and that its ordinances would be of no validity unless they were submitted to a vote of the people; and he prophesied that they would not be in the following terms:

"It is to be feared that the 'Joint Resolutions' Convention will be pretty much a secession affair, chiefly owned and worked by Col. Bill Yancey on the plan and platform of his 'Slaughter' letter. He can put the concern nicely into his breeches-pocket—Tom Watts and all—with 'The Union, the Constitution and the enforcement of the Laws.' What he decrees, it will graciously consent to decree also; but these decrees will never be submitted to the ratification of the people if he can help it. The secessionists repudiate the people. They acknowledge no sovereignty but themselves. Their watchwords are: 'Resistance! resistance! Let us overthrow this rotten government! Let us act at once, and not wait to hear from the crossroads and groceries.' So they designate the people. They have no love for majorities unless they can control them. This, most generally, they are unable to do without the most demoralizing confusion, and when this takes place their great remedy is secession. Can it be possible that such utter folly can get forgiveness in this life or in the life to come? Certainly not, unless folly covers a multitude of sins."

When the Ordinance of Secession was finally passed Mr. Peters, with those among us who agreed with him in sentiment, acquiesced, as a want of harmony in action among us would have produced the most deplorable consequences. He remained in private life until the close of the war, when in the marshaling of parties, under the reconstruction policy of Congress he allied himself with the Republican party, and was elected a delegate to form a new State Constitution. He was the nominee of the same party for a seat on the Bench of the Supreme Court, was elected, and served a term as one of its judges. His becoming a member of that party, at the time when the strata of society was turned topsy-turvy—when the solid men of the South were disfranchised, and when the State was virtually under bayonet rule, was very distasteful to his friends; and his motives were frequently attacked. But from my experience for a half century I have become very slow in ascribing to men who have shown integrity in their private lives improper motives in their public conduct. A political question is often a polygon—a figure of many sides and angles. Every man must decide it according to his own tastes and conscience—and the proper test of his freedom from all improper motives is not so much the acceptance of the office as the uprightness and impartiality with which he discharges its functions.

Since Judge Peters left the bench he has devoted himself to the practice of his profession, and training of his children, who are said, by those who are judges, to have been well educated. He has been uniformly a patron of education, and has served for many years as president of the Board of Trustees of the Female Academy at Moulton. On account of some botanic discoveries he has been elected a member of the American Scientific Association.

Southeastern Part of the County.

I have been detained in Moulton much longer than I expected when I set out on this journey, which promises to be a long one. We will, however, jog along at easy stages. In the Southeastern part of the county there settled a great many worthy citizens. Some of them were very wealthy, but the greater part in moderate circumstances. I knew nearly all these old men, heads of families, very well—some of them intimately. Very few of them are now alive, and many of their families have disappeared by death or emigration. I shall be able to notice, especially, some of those who were prominent in the history of the county fifty years ago, and many others will be incidentally mentioned in connection with the gallant deeds of their sons and grandsons during the late war, when I shall write the military articles which I have promised.

The Smith Family.

The head of this family, Andrew Smith, came from North Carolina, about 1818, and settled four miles north of Moulton, on the road to Courtland. His family then consisted of himself, his wife, and his eldest child, George W. His place was not rich, for it was situated on the margin of "The Little Mountain," but he managed by selecting productive spots, here and there, to get arable land enough for the support of his family. He built on the Eastern branch of Big Nance creek a little mill, to help in the struggle of raising his family, and to give them such an education as the neighborhood then afforded. Andy Smith was a man of good person, and was quite intelligent; and the impression he made upon my mind was that he had seen better days. He read the papers, was an ardent Clay Whig, and very strenuous in maintaining his opinions; and impatient of contradiction. His wife having died, he married the sister of Argyle and Archibald Campbell. We have in another place mentioned his second son, Farrar, who emigrated to Texas, in company with John Gregg and Major Thomason, and died there. His oldest son,

George W. Smith,

obtained distinction in spite of the limited means of his family, during his boyhood. As he grew up, he alternately assisted in the labors of the little farm and mill, and attended neighborhood schools until Mr. McMillan (a Presbyterian minister) opened a classical school at the Chalybeate Springs. He became one of his scholars, and being nearly grown and quite ambitious, he profited greatly from his tuition. When a young man he emigrated to Texas. A sketch of his career there is thus given by Thrall, in his history of that State: "George W. Smith was a native of North Carolina, came to Texas during Colonial times, and was commissioner in Jasper county in that State, was one of the signers of the Declaration of Independence, in the Convention of 1836. In 1837 president of the Board of Land Commissioners; in 1845, he was a member of the Annexation Convention; and in 1853-54-55 he was a member of the United States House of Representatives; in 1866 he was a member of the Reconstruction Convention, and died in Austin during the session of that convention." May Thomason was his schoolmate and has frequently heard him speak, while he was in Congress. He says he was very much esteemed; not so much for his proficiency as a public speaker, as for the integrity of his character, and his financial abilities. His descendants live about Jefferson in Texas. He has a son in Beaumont. I have, in reflecting on the slender opportunities which Mr. Smith had in his early days, traced a strong resemblance between his fortunes and those of Hon. M. F. Maury, once Superintendent of the National Observatory. When a boy he was my schoolmate; at least he attended Dr. Blackburn's academy, at such seasons as he could be spared from the labors of the farm and the mill.

His father, Dick Maury, had a little old mill on a small branch of Harpeth creek in Tennessee, and so had Andy Smyth, the father of George W., on a branch of Big Nance. Both of these little old mills were built of unhewn logs. They looked as much alike as two black-eyed peas, and they performed alike; for they ground very well as long as it rained, but as soon as the weather became fair, "the grinding became low." This little old mill stood for a generation, as a monument to show the boys of old Lawrence how little of Fortune's gifts it takes to rear one to eminence, provided he is made of the proper metal, and has sufficient energy; but unluckily the present owner has pulled down the little mill, and built in its stead a new framed one. All its romance has been destroyed. Esquire Masterson, how could you have the heart to commit such a Vandal deed!

I am indebted for the materials of the sketch of George W. Smyth to Dr. Thomas A. Watkins, J. C. Stevenson, Esq., and Major G. D. Thomason, who was his schoolmate in Alabama, and a resident of his congressional district in Texas.

After the death of Andrew Smyth and his wife, the children by the second wife were cared for by Constantine, a son of the first. He was a merchant of Mooresville for many years, but has removed to Texas.

The Priest Family

came to Lawrence in early times from Madison county. They were not rich, but all I ever knew had clear heads, and were persevering in carrying out their plans. Micajah Priest, considering the poor chance he had in early life, has made a good record as a professional man. His parents died when he was in his infancy. He was then taken care of by his grandparents, who also died when he was a small boy, leaving him "to paddle his own canoe" unaided. He had several uncles, but they were poor. From this small beginning he so embraced every interval of leisure (when he was not working for bread, to improve his mind), that without the help of influential family, or friends, he was elected three times, by the people of the county, a member of the House of Representatives, viz. : for the years 1836-37-38. He then studied law, and removed to Rusk, in Texas, where he practised his profession and became a member of the Constitutional Convention of 1869; was elected to the Senate in 1870, and made chairman of the Judiciary Committee, which is everywhere esteemed a high compliment to a lawyer for his legal attainments. Mr Priest was then elected judge of his district, and removed from office by "address." This removal, I am assured by a judicious friend in Texas, was not on account of any personal charges against Judge Priest, but simply on political grounds. When the people of Texas were enfranchised, they elected Mr. Coke Governor by a majority of 100,000 votes. The Republican Governor and Legislature refused to give place to those elected by the people. Governor Coke appointed Gen. Henry McCulloch commander (who was from Lawrence county) and had them removed from the State capitol by force. Moreover, he had every Republican officer in the State, good and bad, removed. Mr. Priest belonged to that party, and went overboard with the rest. He is now an old man practising law in Rusk, and is respected as a man and a lawyer; for, not long since, when the judge of that district was unable to attend a session of the court from serious illness, Judge Priest was appointed to preside in his stead, at the solicitation of members of the bar of both parties.

Rev. Elliott Jones

was a local preacher of the Methodist Church, and occupied a small farm in the neighborhood of Moulton, from a very early day. He was an old-fashioned Methodist preacher, and firmly believed in the doctrines and usages of the church; wore a round-breasted coat, believed in the witness of the Spirit, delighted in camp-meetings and revivals, and when any of his neighbors were sick, he was sure to be there, giving all the aid he could to their bodies and comfort to their souls. There was no sham in the man, from the crown of his head to the sole of his foot, and the consequence was, everybody respected him, whether they agreed in opinion or not. He was a fair preacher, and "held fast the form of sound doctrine" he had received from John Wesley.

Somehow he married more young people than any preacher in that section of the country. Why was it so I never could tell; but I will mention some points in which he differed from other ministers in tying the marriage knot. He always, before he commenced the ceremony proper, took occasion to remind the "man and the woman" of the obligations they were about to assume in a set speech. He reminded them that the woman, in the beginning, was not taken from the man's head to rule over him, or from his foot to be trodden upon, but from his side to be fondly cherished. His address would consume nearly a quarter of an hour. I do not think he would be popular with the girls of the present day, for I have often heard them beg the minister to abbreviate the ceremony. But it was not so in early times. The girls then wanted the marriage knot well tied, if tied at all. They were slow to make engagements, and when made, they considered it a solemn duty to perform them; whilst, in this age, they break one and make another, with as much indifference as changing a pair of gloves.

Parson Jones and his wife reared their children remarkably well. Their son William was one of five children, and gave his name to Jonesboro. Since that name was taken from it, it has had none; for "Town Creek" is a very poor name for a town, unless you annex "City" to it. William Jones was a man of great integrity and much esteemed. He moved to Warrenton, on the Tennessee river. Col. John Jones, who has for many years been a most popular railroad agent at Decatur, is a son of the old gentleman. I think, too, Judge Elliott P. Jones of Fayette county, Ala., was another son. Colonel Garrett, in his history, says that Judge Jones "was born in Lawrence county in 1819, and was elected Judge of Fayette county in 1847. His first service in the Senate was in 1850, to fill a vacancy. He was re-elected in 1853, 1855 and 1857. In 1861 he was a member of the Convention which passed the Ordinance of Secession; and in 1865 he was a member of the Constitutional Convention to reorganize the State. He was re-elected in 1865 to the Senate, from the district composed of Fayette and Marion counties, and served through the sessions of 1865 and 1866. Judge Jones was honored by the Legislature of 1866 by having his name given to a new county; but on the coming in of other political influences, the name of the county was changed to Sanford. He was a Democrat, and a useful, industrious member of the Senate, bringing to the discharge of his duties a large experience in public affairs, and an honest purpose. In the last two sessions I served with him (Colonel Garrett was then President of the Senate), he was often called to the Chair, and displayed intelligence and promptness in the administration of parliamentary law, giving entire satisfaction to the Senate. He resides in Fayette among a people who have long honored him with their confidence, and whose interests he has faithfully served."

The Cowans.

Samuel Cowan, the head of this family, lived four miles northeast of Moulton. He was a man of fine person, of uncommonly cheerful and amiable disposition, and much esteemed by his neighbors. He was born and reared in Virginia, married Mary Dixon, November 25, 1880, near Lexington, Ky., and moved to Alabama in early times. He was a Cumberland Presbyterian. His oldest son, Houston, married the daughter of Wade Cooper, in Courtland. It was a run-a-way match. He accumulated a good deal of property, and died in 1879, near Landersville. B. Cowan, another son, went somewhere to the West. A daughter, Ann, married William McCord, and another, Esther Caroline, Michael Wert.

The Werts.

Michael was the son of an old revolutionary soldier, who was born, reared and died in Pennsylvania. His mother was a native of Virginia, and an intelligent Christian lady of the Presbyterian church. His father died when he was less than a year old, and his estate passed into the hands of an administrator who squandered it. Principal and sureties both proved insolvent; and so, his mother was left with small means, to rear six children, four daughters and two sons, of whom Michael was the youngest. His sisters married very good men, are all living (1880), and in affluent circumstances. His brother died in Ohio, after accumulating a large fortune. Michael obtained permission from his mother, when he was fifteen years of age, to learn the tailor's trade—landed at Louisville at the age of twenty, and worked there one year—moved to Courtland in 1836, and in the fall of 1838 went to Moulton. He had saved $200; and opened a tailor's shop. He worked hard, and obtained a good custom, and made some money. These interesting facts, in reference to his early history, I learned from Mr. Wert himself.

I well remember him when he first came into our county. He was a modest, well behaved young man, and had evidently been well reared. He was never seen in drinking houses, but most assiduously applied himself to his business and seemed to have in his own mind a fixed purpose to succeed in life. With men who do succeed my observation has convinced me that this purpose is formed, much earlier in life, than is generally supposed. At the age of 23 he seriously considered the subject of marriage. In modern times public opinion is averse to the formation of the matrimonial connection until a husband can maintain a wife in luxury and idleness. But it was not so with the "early settlers." Then a young man prepared to marry, without delay, the girl whom he loved, and enjoy with her the property they jointly achieved. Mr. Wert was most fortunate in his selection. In Esther Caroline Cowan he found beauty, good common sense, industry equal to his own, and a strong constitution. She has been to him truly a help-mate in economy and the moral training of his children. In 1840 he commenced merchandising, and did a successful business until the war came on, when, near its close, the Tories burned his storehouse, goods, books, etc. This calamity left him in point of means near where he commenced in 1840, except a debt of $4000, and nothing to pay it with. But he always had good credit and good friends, so he bought more goods, and in a few years he paid his debts; and, moreover, reinstated his fortune. During all this time he had a large and expensive family. This worthy couple have, now living, twelve children—six sons and six daughters. They have been liberally educated, and several of them have graduated. All these occupy a high position in society, are members of the church of their father and mother, and are doing well in the world. To use the words of Major Owen, " few men have been more successful in business, or with his family, in consequence of his strict integrity in his dealings and his example to his family." His success both in these particulars has been so signal that I inquired of him how he had accomplished so much with such small means, and whether in rearing his boys they were made to do any labor. His answer was this : "Soon after we married in 1839, wife and I joined the Methodist Church, and on the same day erected a family altar to the Lord; where we have worshipped night and morning from that day to this, and where we received grace day by day to train our children in the way they should go. We lived on the edge of the town and have a small farm. When my boys were not at school they worked on the farm. Their nights were always spent at home, if not at church. Our great object has been to make home so attractive that they would love home more than any other place; not only at night, but at all leisure times ; hence we had no trouble on that account. My children are very obedient and affectionate. But whatever success we may have had in training our children we give all honor and glory to a kind Providence." These are golden words. I commend them to the fathers and mothers of our country.

Their children were: (1) Mary F., who married W. D. McDaniel, son of P. A. McDaniel, near Moulton (Baptist); (2) Martha W., who married Rev. W. P. Owen, a Methodist preacher, who had charge of Decatur District High School and the station at Moulton; (3) Clara E., who married E. A. Farley, a merchant at Moulton; (4) Julia C., who married C. C. Harris, Esq., lawyer, of Decatur, Ala.; (5) Jacob B. Wert, merchant, Chattanooga, Tenn., who married Augusta Kirby, of Columbia, Tenn.; (6) Michael C., merchant, of Weatherford, Tex., who married Maggie Saunders, daughter of Wm. Saunders, of Jackson county, Ala.; (7) Annie A., who married J. J. Gillespie, then of Nashville, but moved to his farm in Lincoln county, Tenn.; (8) Tennis S. Wert, lawyer, of Decatur, of the firm of Wert & Wert, who married Eliza Gibbs; (9)

Nannie L., who married Dr. W. L. Dinsmore, of Laudersville; (10) B. S. Wert, M. D., who a physician at Moulton; (11) F. O. Wert, lawyer, of the firm of Wert & Wert, of Decatur; (12) Arthur B. Wert, 18 years old, student.

The McCords.

Two brothers of this name, Joseph and James, lived Northeast of Moulton. They must have come very early, for Joseph was a member of the Legislature in 1824, and his brother James ten years after, in 1834. They were men of excellent character, and very much respected. Their descendants have, I believe, nearly all emigrated. William (as I have mentioned) married Ann Cowan, and Samuel W., for some years after 1829, kept the Moulton Inn; but I think all are gone, except a granddaughter of James McCord, who now lives in Courtland.

The Hodges

were prominent in the first settlement of the county. Fleming was the eldest of two brothers who came together. He first married Miss Johnson of Madison, and secondly, Miss Loony of the same county. Col. Fleming Hodges was a member of the General Assembly (Senate) in 1819, 1820, 1821. He died about 1828. His wife survived him. Col. Wm. Hodges was the younger brother and was a member of the House of Representatives in 1828-29. His eldest son, Fleming, had considerable talent for trade, and moved to Mississippi. Wm. (Buck) Hodges of the Sixteenth Alabama Regiment, who made so much reputation in the late war, was his son. Another, Asa, was a lawyer, he moved to Arkansas. Two sons, Moses and James, moved to Mississippi. A sister of Fleming and William Hodges married Samuel W. Wallace in Shelby county, where she happened to be on a visit. They resided in to Dallas county, and were there when the State was organized and then removed to Shelby county again. Thence to Oakville, in Lawrence county, and, in 1840, to Wolf Spring. The old gentleman is now in his 85th year; but is vigorous in mind, and, having been a school teacher, can still write a fine hand.

The Prewitts.

Three members of this family were among the earliest settlers of our county. The eldest of the Prewitts, of whom I have any knowledge, came from Clinch river in East Tennessee. He settled his family in Madison county, Alabama, and lived to the advanced age of 112 years, and his wife to 116 years. I never knew them, but I have known their descendants, and they have been distinguished by fine persons, strong constitutions, vigorous minds, and uncommon energy. His sons, James and Jacob, came to Lawrence, and settled on the Byler Road as soon as it was cut out. James improved the place since occupied by the De Graffenrieds, but after some years removed to another State. Jacob purchased a place (further South) from John McKinney, on the drift (or what our State geologist calls the "Orange-sand"), and having a force of some twenty-five hands, and the soil being fresh and productive, he was quite prosperous. The large old field still seen there attests his industry. His house was on the Pebbly branch, where a bold spring runs over a bed of round, water-worn pebbles, very beautiful and variegated in color. Here he kept a noted stand, where there was an abundant supply of provender for "man and beast." In those days, when the larger proportion of hogs and mules, for the planters of Middle Alabama, was driven down this road, such stands were very profitable. The old gentleman had arrived at the age of 77 years, hale, hearty and active, when in chasing a bear, his horse fell in a pinehole and threw him on the pomel of his saddle, which caused his death.

His son William came from Madison county at the same time with his father, and improved a place Southeast of Moulton about five miles. He, too, was born in Tennessee. He was a prosperous planter, and purchased the plantation belonging to the Price estate, which was one of the finest in the Southern end of the county. His first wife was Nancy Cavit, of Madison county. By this marriage he had two sons, Jacob and Richard. Jacob moved to Texas; Richard lives near Leighton, and carries with him all the bold characteristics I have mentioned as belonging to his race. When I first knew him he lived on a plantation five miles Northeast of Moulton, well stocked with slaves and mules, and it had the highest fence I ever saw. Moreover, there was a splendid pack of hounds, showing that he wisely understood the art of mingling labor and amusement. But he was seized with the ambition of being the largest planter in the county, and I think he became so, for he had some 1500 acres in cotton when, unluckily, the war broke out, and he was crippled in his estate; but he still has enough, and I judge he is a happier man than he was before. He first married a daughter of Senator Fleming Hodges. The name of his second wife I am not advised of.

William Prewit married for his second wife the widow of Fleming Hodges, Sr., and died at the age of 56 years. Mrs. Prewit had three children by Senator Hodges, who are all dead, and four by her second husband. The eldest, Robert, married a daughter of Judge Gibson. They are both dead. They left one son named Talbot. Two others married, and are long since dead. The remaining son is John W. Prewit, who lives on the Price place, where his father died. He is a first-rate planter, and is now the largest taxpayer in Lawrence county. Mrs. Prewit, when her husband died, was in the prime of life, and full of energy. She was indeed a "notable" woman; for when Mr. Prewit died she took the guardianship of her children, bought all the land at the sale, hired an overseer, kept the property together, and made a fortune for herself, and the children.

Col. Nicholas Johnson

was the son of Thomas Johnson, of Louisa county, Virginia, and Ann, daughter of Thomas Merriwether, of Albemarle county, Virginia. He had married in Georgia, Mary, daughter of James Marks, of Broad river. She died in 1815, and in 1819 he immigrated to Lawrence county, and settled on one of the branches of Flint river, some five miles Southeast of Moulton. He was an old man when he came in. His career in Georgia was a remarkable one, as will be shown you in the sequel. We will first speak of that part of it which transpired in this county.

Colonel Johnson was the wealthiest man who came into our county, having brought about seventy-five negroes with him (*Richard Prewit*). No planter, either North or South of the Little Mountain, had brought so many. Col. Ben Sherrod asked him why he did not purchase richer land in the Courtland valley. His answer was, that he intended to raise stock exclusively, and get rich off the cotton planters in that valley, by selling them supplies which they could raise, if they would. I first saw him in 1827. I was riding with a friend, to hear a debate at Oakville, between Hon. C. C. Clay, and Gabriel Moore, when he prevailed on me to call on Colonel Johnson. We passed through a very large plantation, and entered a plain but large log house. The Colonel was in his cotton field, which we had passed on the way, and observed that although it was the month of June, it had not been worked, and the hog weeds were knee high. At length he came in from the field, dressed in a straw hat, cotton shirt, and pants, and coarse shoes, without any socks. Nevertheless, he received us with the civility of a friend. He excused himself until he could reform his dress, and when he came in, engaged in pleasant talk, and showed remarkable conversational powers. I alluded playfully to the foul condition of his cotton field. He said, "Call it *patch*, sir. I plant but few acres for my force; so few that I have never built a gin house, and I never work my cotton until everything else is put in complete order. The fact is, I have a great aversion for cotton." When he heard that I had married a wife from Broad river, in Georgia, he insisted on our paying him a visit, which we did.

It was midsummer when we went. We passed first, large peach orchards (always fifty acres in extent) and approached the dwelling through an avenue of 200 nectarine trees loaded with their rich, ripe, delicious fruit. I thought that the "*utile et dulce*" were as well mingled here as could be. His place was a world of abundance. We spent a delightful day, during which he spoke freely of his peculiar mode of management; and to make a quaint illustration of how successful it had been. He proposed to show us a mirror which had cost him $4000; and when we entered the room he pointed out a small one, perhaps 12 by 18, with a frame of veneered mahogony, and when we looked on him with astonishment, he explained by recounting all the articles he owned when he married, how much his estate had increased, and if the looking glass had increased in value at the *same ratio*, it would now have been worth $4000. I have often thought of this view of the subject, which he kindly intended for our good, as we were young people.

He talked freely of his system of management. His horses were of the Arabian and Medley breeds combined. They were allowed to eat little or no corn until they were put to work. They were small, but of fine wind, and great endurance. I purchased three of them at a sale, where 100 horses were sold, and they proved to be remarkably serviceable. His hogs were raised on an excellent plan; they gleaned on his wheat fields; then consumed the oat fields; then the peaches in his enormous orchards; passed through fields of green corn, and were then fat and ready to have their flesh hardened by a short feeding on hard corn. His cows in summer were turned into the range, but brought home and penned, every night, on some poor spot. He had a very large herd. Some of his notions were strange. He never upset a fence by putting new rails at the bottom, but laid them always on top. When holes occurred by rails rotting at the bottom, he stuck others into the hole, and this he called "darning." His reason for this was that when the fence was moved the row would be very rich. When a Scotch schoolmaster married his daughter, Barbara, he said to him that no man should own a farm until he knew how to do any work required upon it; and proposed that if Frazier would clear up five acres on a very good tract, he would give it to him. The old man used to tell, with great glee, how F. started out next day by sunrise, and had his breakfast sent to him. That he heard his axe ringing very merrily all the morning, but that when he went to see how he was coming on, he had not brought a single tree to the ground, but had seven tall red oaks lodged one against another!

As to his system, I can not pass an opinion unless I were better acquainted with his antecedents. He certainly had a large estate—after his death the sale of his property lasted a week. He claimed to have made it from a small beginning. But, from long experience in this climate, I consider it best for a farmer to make all the "home supplies" he can on the place, and have cotton for his "money" crop. He, however, was very successful, was entirely out of debt, and had considerable money capital at interest; this I know, as I was his collecting attorney. One thing was apparent, his hogs, sheep, cattle, horses and negroes, were *all* fat.

After coming to this county he married, for his second wife, an elderly widow named Bied. Colonel Johnson died about 1832 from cancer in the stomach, as it was supposed.

I am indebted to my friend, Dr. Thos. A. Watkins, formerly of Courtland, but now of Austin, Tex., for the means of giving a full account of Colonel Johnson while he lived in Georgia. Dr. Watkins, when young, was frequently at his house; and, moreover is an antiquary, and has many curious old books, from one of which, Governor Gilmer's "*History of the Early Settlers of Upper Georgia*," he has furnished me with the following extracts:

Nicholas Johnson, when he first visited Georgia, appeared in more dashing style than had ever been seen in that hard, economical and simple frontier community. He was attended by a well-dressed servant, rode a fine blooded horse, his servant another, and a third followed for the relief of the other two. His dress was a blue coat, red waistcoat, and buff pantaloons. His person was stout, his features full and round, his complexion fair and florid, his voice well modulated and his address exceedingly civil. He united grand scheming with successful doing, in a very unusual manner. When he went to any public place, crowds might generally be seen gathered around him, listening to his fervid account of some danger which threatened the nation, or some new fashion of planting corn, tobacco or cotton. His land was very poor, and his plantation very large, with granite rocks scattered about over it. He described to some acquaintances, in Augusta, the beauty of the native flowers and shrubs, and the wild scenery of the rocky hills around him, in such glowing terms that they planned a special visit to enjoy the pleasure of the sight. Colonel Johnson lived in log-cabins, for twenty years after his marriage, in the plainest style.

The public road ran through his plantation, and not far from his residence. He fell in one day with a pompous fellow traveling along his lane, who inquired where he could get his breakfast, and descanted largely upon the unfitness of the accommodation upon the road, for a gentleman. The Colonel told him he could be accommodated at his house. The fellow said he would turn in and see if he could get anything to suit his taste. The Colonel accompanied him, held his stirrup while he alighted, ordered the best to be got for him, waited upon him at the table, and never ceased to press him to eat until he could eat no more. When the fellow asked for his bill he was made to pay a dollar, when he opened his eyes in astonishment. Colonel Johnson then advised him to be more modest when he went amongst strangers.

Whenever a monkey show, or any other, passed through the country, he sent for his negroes, and treated them to the exhibition. His eldest children were daughters, and when his eldest son, Frank, was born, he was so pleased, that he planted in the fence corners of his extensive fields, a hundred thousand walnuts. According to his account, by the time the infant arrived at manhood, each of the walnuts would be grown to a tree, and worth a dollar, which would make a fortune worth talking about.

He used to "shirtee" his fields along the public roads with cowpeas, so as to make the corn which was seen in passing by, exhibit a very luxuriant appearance, and so create the opinion in the lookers-on that his land was very productive. His orders to the cow-boy were that his cattle must never leave the pen in the morning without adding to its fertility. Some lawyers passing on to Court found the boy chasing a cow and crying as if his heart would break. A kind gentleman stopped and inquired what was the matter, and received for an answer that "Brownie would not do what master ordered." Major Oliver H. Prince, and Hon. Augustin S. Clayton, rival wits at the Georgia bar, expressed the opinion in a social assemblage of lawyers, when Scott's poetry was spouted by everybody, that the rhyme was doggerel, and could be written by any versifier. The conversation excited interest, and opposition to the assertions of the wits. To prove the correctness of the criticism, Mr. Prince wrote off, at once, a string of lines ending in words of similar sound, to which Judge Clayton adding a note, after Scott's fashion. The subject was "Brownie, and the little negro boy" aforesaid. The rhyme and note appeared soon after in a newspaper published by David A. Hillhouse, in Columbia, S. C. Colonel Johnson when he heard of the satire, only laughed when he understood why it was written. Not so, Mrs. Johnson was furious, and asked a kinsman, who was a lawyer, to induce Mr. Prince in passing by to the Court to call, that she might teach him a lesson on good behavior.

When a daughter married he gave to her husband five hundred dollars (in addition to what he would have given otherwise) if he removed to a new country, where fertile lands were to be had. Mrs. Johnson inherited her father's wit, and her mother's clear understanding. Though she read but little, and her intercourse with general society was limited, her conversation was very agreeable, and her knowledge accurate. She and her husband, too, were great talkers. Her table was the most profuse of home productions of any I ever set down to. She had seven houses for chickens. A bushel of corn was usually scattered around the yard every morning. They kept forty cows, 500 sheep, and countless hogs.

Their children (there were none by the second marriage) were: (1) Nancy, who married Reuben Jordan. (2) Martha, who married Geo. O. Gilmer. (3) Lucy, who married John Gilmer. (4) Barbara, who married —— Frazer. (5) Betsy, who married Lewis B. Taliaferro. (6) Rebecca, who married Charles Jordan. (7) Sarah, who married Jordan Smith. (8) Frank and James both died young. (9) Edward, the youngest child, who was accidentally killed in a deer hunt.

The Prices.

Charles Price, the ancestor, in the latter part of the last century, lived near Richmond, Va. He had only two sons. The eldest, Robert, came to Alabama, and William, went to Missouri.

Gen. Sterling Price, of that State, was the son of this William. He attained a reputation during the late war, as a soldier and a man, which was truly enviable. He early took the field with the "State Guards" of Missouri, before there was any Confederate organization in the State. Each division was commanded by a brigadier, with General Price as Commander-in-Chief. His command was composed of the best young men of the State, many of whom had been enured to war in the Kansas troubles. The old General was the centre of attraction in this volunteer army, whose cohesion seemed to depend mainly on his wonderful personal magnetism. He marched, fought, advanced and retreated, in turn, until (having no quartermaster and commissary department) these intrepid young men became "ragged" and "bare-footed." When the battle of Wilson's Creek was at the highest, a tall, red-headed fellow, from the central part of the State, advanced beyond the line to get free from the smoke, and to see how to make a better shot. He aimed with deliberation at a particular man, similarly advanced, and when he saw his man fall, he cried out with great glee, "Them's my shoes!" Ever after that, this was the battle cry of the Missouri soldiers. In despite of want and nakedness, they were brave fighters, always rallying around the flag in battle; but, under a lax discipline, were somewhat given to straggling during the intervals. The authorities at Washington were so much amazed by the movements of this army that after sending first one commander and then another, the Secretary of War dispatched General Halleck to the scene of action. Strong Federal reinforcements were thrown into the State, and General Price was compelled to retreat, first into Arkansas, and then to the Eastern side of the Mississippi river. The following tribute was paid to General Price by a Northern historian: "Price had displayed no small skill in his movements, and it was believed in Richmond that if he had been properly supported he would have secured Missouri to the Confederacy." But it was when his soldiers were "exiles" from their homes that General Price exhibited those high qualities of soul which made him their idol. The solicitude he showed to secure their comfort, or alleviate their sufferings, was so great as to call forth the highest admiration. They entertained the most grateful feelings toward him for his tender sympathy for them in their "orphaned" condition, and called him "Pap." He was a fine illustration of

"The bravest are the tenderest."

These high qualities possessed by this descendant of William Price, of Missouri, were found in the descendants of Robert Price, of Alabama. Every one of his grandsons, who were of sufficient age, were volunteers, except one, who was paralyzed. Every name in the list I shall give below is a record of gallant service in the field.

Robert Price was married in 1806, in Charlotte county, Virginia, to Frances S., daughter of Rev. John Campbell, a local preacher of the Methodist Church. The ceremony was performed by Rev. Alexander Sale, who removed to this county afterward— one of the best of men, and one of the best friends I ever had.

Robert Price sent out some of his hands to Lawrence county in 1819, and he followed with his family in 1820. He and his wife were much beloved by his neighbors, and were pious members of the Methodist Church. He purchased the valuable tract of land, already mentioned, improved his estate very much, and died in 1824. He brought with him from Virginia six children; another was born in Alabama, but lived only a few years.

1. Edwin S., his oldest son, married Mildred, daughter of Robert Wood, of West Tennessee. By this marriage there were five children who lived to be grown, viz.: Robert N., Edwin W., William H., Darthula, and Lucilla. (1) Robert was paralyzed while quite young, and never recovered. (2) Edwin belonged to the Fourth Tennessee Regiment of infantry (*Col. R. P. Neely*). He was in the battle of Shiloh. His health became bad, and he was sent home, to Whiteville, Tennessee. He was captured and sent to prison, where he was confined eight months. When exchanged, he returned to

his regiment, and remained until the close of the war. (3) William, of the Ninth Tennessee Regiment of infantry (Col. Henry Douglass), was taken ill from exposure, and died in March, 1862. Edwin S., the father of these boys, was married a second time to Mrs. Jane Redd, of Brownsville, Tennessee, in 1845, and died in 1853.

William H. (second son of Robert Price and Frances S. Chappell), was married to Elizabeth, daughter of William Dixon, near Florence, Ala., in 1831, and moved to Franklin county, and died in 1866. They had six children who lived to be grown. (1) William H., who became captain of the "Florence Guards," after the promotion of Gen. Sterling Wood, and was killed at the battle of Perryville, Ky. I may notice the career of this gallant officer more specially hereafter. (2) Charles S. W. was a surgeon in the army, and was at Columbus, Miss., for a long time. (3) John R. was attending a military school somewhere in the North when the war broke out. He went to Richmond and joined an Alabama regiment. H₃ was detached and sent to Florida as a drillmaster and thence to North Carolina. Here he joined a company which was sent out to Scotland, to bring a vessel which was being built for the Confederacy. The British Admiralty forbade the sailing of the vessel, and the company had to return home. (4) Edwin was only twelve years old when the war commenced. William H., the father of these sons, was married a second time to Mrs. Catharine Peters (of Texas), whilst she was on a visit to friends in Florence.

Robert J. (the third son of Robert Price and Frances Chappell), was first married to Martha A., daughter of Maj. James Moore, near Aberdeen, Miss. He moved to Fayette and thence to Lawrence county, Ala., where he died in 1841. By this marriage he had four children who lived to be grown, viz.: Robert J., Mary E., Abegail, and Martha A. Robert belonged to the Eighth Texas Cavalry Company called the "Texas Rangers." This regiment achieved a high reputation. Commanded first by Colonel Terry, who was killed, and then by Col. John A. Wharton, and then by Col. Thos. Harrison. It was its fortune to be under fire oftener, during the war, than any regiment I knew of. The history of this regiment (if ever written) will be virtually a history of the war south of the Carolinas. The privates were fine horsemen, and there was a great deal of individual gallantry amongst them. At the capture of Murfreesboro, by General Forrest, Colonel Wharton (afterward General) when one arm was broken, placed the reins between his teeth, and plied his revolver with the other, until the enemy surrendered. This feat has been equaled by many of the same kind, amongst the privates. Price still lives in Texas. His father, Robert, was married a second time to Mrs. Elizabeth Douglas, sister of Hon. Luke Pryor.

John C. (fourth son of Robert Price and Frances Chappell) married Margaret, daughter of Col. William Hodges. They had six children, viz.: William, Fleming, John, James, Mary F., and Eudocia Ann. (1) William belonged to General Wheeler's command in Colonel Sharpe's regiment, which went from Columbus, Miss., where his father then lived. Fleming belonged to Forrest's command, under Colonel Boon. His brothers, John and James, were too young for service. The father of these boys was married a second time to Miss McCarty of Columbus, Miss., and died two months afterward.

Dr. Charles W. (the fifth son of Robert Price and Frances S. Chappell), and the only one now living, resides in Morgan county, Ala. He married Mary F. Moore, a sister of his brother Robert's wife, who is still living. They have had the goodly number of nine children, to-wit: James E., Wm. F., John W., Charles L., Fannie A., Martha A., Mary A., Emma V. and Lissie D. (1) Of these James E. had the honor of being a member of the Ninth Alabama Regiment, whose record includes a great many of the bloodiest battles of the war. The last battle in which he took part with this regiment was that of Sharpsburg. The company to which he belonged had been so reduced by casualties that only three men entered the fight, and they were James E. Price, W. Harper and Willis. In that bloody conflict Willis was killed. Price and Harper were elected Lieutenants in Col. James Malone's Regiment of cavalry, and were transferred to it by proper authority. Thomas Malone, Esq. (now Professor in the Law

Department of Vanderbilt University), was their captain. Lieutenant Price was frequently on scouting expeditions within the enemy's lines, near Nashville, which, to one so long confined to the monotonous routine of the infantry, was very exciting. Here an incident occurred which was quite amusing. It somehow became known to the commanding officer that Colonel Brownlow, of the Federal Army (who was a very enterprising young officer and had been troublesome to our side), frequently visited a young lady (whom he afterward married) who was a member of a Union family. As her home was within the Federal lines, the young colonel used no precaution, against capture, in making his visits. Lieutenant Price attempted his capture, and the first effort he made was nearly successful; for the colonel barely escaped the trap. Not long after, he made a second attempt, and approaching the house he left his squad not far off. Finding that his man had not arrived, he entered the house, and commenced a conversation with the young lady. Very soon he heard the steps of several men approaching the door, and seeing no means of escape he slipt under the bed, which was in the room. In a few moments, Colonel Brownlow, and several others entered. The young lady did not betray him; for although she had Union opinions, she had Southern feelings. For two long hours (the longest of any other two in his life) the conversation continued, and at length the colonel and his comrades left without discovering him. He participated in all the battles with his regiment, until his company was captured at Shelbyville, while attempting to defend a battery, which was covering the crossing of our troops. They were taken to Johnson's Island, and were imprisoned there twenty months, before they were exchanged. They arrived at home three or four weeks before the surrender. (2) William F., the second son of Charles W., joined Colonel Scott's Louisiana Regiment, while in this valley; was in several battles; and whilst near Charleston, Tenn., the regiment moved one night to meet the enemy. He was in the advance; and as he passed a comrade who had his gun lying across his lap, it went off and the ball passed through his thigh, injuring the artery; and he lived only a few days. He was buried in Charleston. (3) and (4)—John W., and Charles L.—only thirteen and seven years of age, respectively, when the war commenced.

Rev. Thos. A. Strain.

We have already mentioned the death of Robt. Price, Sr., in 1824. His widow (who was Frances S. Chappell) married Rev. Thomas A. Strain. Where there are children, second marriages rarely do well, but this one was fortunate, for Mrs. Price and her children. I knew all the parties intimately. Mr. Strain was a gentleman in his person, dress, manners and principles. The large family estate was wound up and divided equitably. Mr. Strain and wife afterward moved to Morgan county. He was so much esteemed that he was (although no politician) elected a member of the Legislature. He and his wife died in that county, leaving four children. He had the confidence of that branch of the church to which he belonged. Dr. McFerrin, in his " History of Methodism," a work of high authority, and to which I have frequent occasion to refer, says of Mr. Strain: " Thos A. Strain traveled several years, located and settled in North Alabama, where he lived for many years, and devoted much time to the preaching of the gospel. He was a man of slender constitution, but of ardent piety and burning zeal for the cause of Christ. He was highly endowed by nature, and sanctified by grace, so that he was a popular and useful preacher. He rests from his labors."

Lindseys and Speaks.

Mark Lindsey was a tall, spare, old gentleman, who lived on a branch of Flint river when I first knew him. He wore the round-breasted Methodist coat, and had a most excellant reputation. He was also noted for his industry and good morals. The venerable Mr. McFerrin rode this circuit when quite a youth, and still remembers and speaks of the kindness and hospitality he received from the Lindseys. Mark Lindsey was raised in South Carolina. He went to Kentucky when young, and lived there a long time. In 1827 he and his son, Dennis (who was a second edition of his father, in person and character), came to Lawrence county, and settled in the place I have mentioned. J. B. Speak married Sarah, the eldest daughter of Dennis Lindsey, on the 4th of June, 1833. She was the first child born in that community. Mr. Speak had also emigrated from Kentucky in 1830; and was a school teacher of fine natural sense, great dignity of deportment and good acquirements. Judge Gibson who raised his family there, says that " he taught nearly all the children of that community for nearly a generation." His usefulness was great, as he performed his duties not only with a view to his own interest, but to the future well being of his pupils. His services were duly appreciated. He was county Superintendent of Education for many years before the late war, and was elected a delegate, after the war, to the State Convention and was also elected a member of the House of Representatives, in 1870, and several times since. Our county never was represented by a man who performed his duties with more industry or a more honest purpose than J. B. Speak.

He named his two sons Henry Clay and Daniel Webster. This saves me the trouble of telling what party he belonged to, in old times. Although decided in his opinions, he was always temperate and conservative. His son, Henry Clay, served with distinction throughout the war, in the cavalry arm of the service. He was in the Fourth Alabama Regiment, and was promoted to the rank of adjutant, which post he held at the surrender. He has risen rapidly in the profession of the law. In 1874 he was elected Chancellor of the Northern division of Alabama, and has filled the office with much ability, and very acceptably to the bar, and the people. His term of office having expired, he has been recently elected judge of this circuit. Daniel Webster, his younger brother, is a highly educated young gentleman, having graduated from the State University in June, 1879, with the highest honors and is now practising law in Moulton, with the promise of a bright future.

Major Richard Puckett was a merchant of Oakville during the " Flush Times of Alabama." He was a man of good person and of fair average mind, and made a pretty good speech, for he became a politician. He was elected by the Whig party a member of the House of Representatives both in 1836-37 and was also the leading man in Oakville, which grew up like a mushroom, on loans obtained from the State Bank. He thought, no doubt, he was rapidly getting rich, but when the " crash " of 1837 occurred it broke him, and every merchant in the place. Not only so, but many of the most solvent farmers around were involved as sureties for Major Puckett and other merchants, and broken up. The town itself had been built up on a school section, and was sold by an act of the Legislature, and every building afterward rotted down, so that no vestige of the place is left. Major Puckett afterward moved to Memphis, became a commission merchant, and died there.

The Thomases

were a family of very industrious, moral, and respectable people. The eldest of the family was Esekial; he died in this county. It seems to me that he was involved in the general calamity which prostrated Oakville. His son Jesse became a partner of Patrick O'Neill (formerly of Moulton), in the commission business, in the city of Mobile. The style of the firm was O'Neill, Michaux & Thomas. They failed in business, and Jesse Thomas moved to Burleson county, Tex., where he became a Baptist preacher. Another son, Jerry, moved to the same place. A third son, William E., became a Baptist preacher, but whether he moved to Texas or not, I am uncertain.

Hamptons.

The " Poplar Log Cove " in early times was a narrow but fertile valley, abounding in springs of the purest water. The one which entered the head of the valley had a peculiar and pleasing feature in it. About fifty yards before it emerged from the rock, nature had furnished an upright square door in which you could stand, and dip the cold, limpid element as it passed by. There were a number of families, in this lovely but secluded valley, who were making a good living, took the county papers, were pretty well informed in public affairs, and were the firmest kind of Jackson Democrats. I have not visited the valley for forty years, but have been told things there have very much altered. The hillsides once so productive, have been washed into unsightly gullies, the people no more take the county paper, and there exists a good deal of confusion in their minds as to the progress of political events.

Of the Hamptons (who were cousins to the Shaws in the Northern part of the county), there was a large family, but the principal man in the Cove was Ephraim Hampton. He was justice of the peace, owned a cotton gin, was well informed in politics, and had considerable influence. I think he, as well as Sam Livingston, Elijah Stover, and many others in that part of the county, were soldiers under General Jackson, during the Creek war. This gave him (as it should) great ascendancy over his neighbors and as Ephraim Hampton went, the Cove was sure to go, Ephraim had many an encounter at Oakville, with Puckett, and other Whig champions, but he remained as firm as a rock to his party. At length, an occurrence took place, which gave them (as they supposed) a great advantage over Ephraim. As he drove his wagon to market loaded with cotton (before our railroad was built), in the neighborhood of Tuscumbia, where the mud was very deep, he met a gentleman's carriage. Unfortunately, the wheel of Hampton's wagon locked in that of the carriage. A gentleman from its window, who proved to be Mr. W. Winter Payne, in a furious passion, threatened to give him his cane for running against his carriage; and Hampton raising his wagon whip replied that he would cut his broadcloth into ribbons, if he didn't apologize for that insult. The result was that they mutually descended from their vehicles to the ground, for a pitched battle. Mrs. Payne implored them to desist, but her words were unheeded. There they stood confronting each other, both in the prime of their strength and activity. Payne was fully six feet high, and well developed; Hampton about the same height, but more spare; Payne was wealthy, irascible and brave, for he had Winston blood in his veins; Hampton was just as fearless, for he had heard bullets whistle before, and just as proud, for he was a "Highland Chief" at the head of his clan. Payne was well muscled and in splendid condition, from a habit of deer hunting. Hampton had undergone severe training, not only of manual labor, but he often climbed the steep mountains before the sun touched their summits, in pursuit of wild game. There they stood like two game cocks of the finest feather, with crests proudly arched, and ready for the encounter. When the shock did come it was dreadful. Blows resounded. Mrs. Payne screamed, the combatants maintained the conflict for a long time, when both, bruised and bleeding, fell to the ground side by side, and were so completely exhausted that they were only able to claw each other in the face, with their finger-nails. Then Mrs. Payne successfully interfered, and parted them. Scowling darkly at each other, they rose from the ground and each went his way. It happened afterward that Mr. Winter Payne was nominated by the Democratic party as their candidate for Congress. When the news reached Oakville, Hampton's Whig friends prepared themselves for a good laugh at his expense. When he visited the place, they gathered around him and informed him of the nomination of his personal enemy, and inquired if he would vote for him. Hampton paused a while and reasoned with himself and then replied: "Winter Payne is the best man I ever fought with, in my life, and he is not afraid of anybody. Now is the time we need fearless men in Congress; therefore, I will not only vote for him myself, but will give him all the help I can." The consequence was that Payne lost no Democratic votes in that beat.

I have now closed my article on the Southeast Part of the County. I will now commence the Military articles, and finish them on my way to Courtland.

The War Between the States.

This conflict, in its dimensions, equals any which has ever occurred on the continent of Europe. The soldiers who took part in it, from both sections of the United States, without respect to the flag under which they fought, deserve to be remembered with respect and admiration, by this and succeeding generations; not only for their gallantry, but for the reason, that they shed their blood for an opinion—for an idea—for (what they respectively considered) their rights; and not like the followers of noble chiefs in past ages, who were mere machines in their hands, for the advancement of their personal ambition.

Some people think that this bloody war should be ignored. Could English historians ignore the wars of the houses of York and Lancaster, which desolated England for nearly a century? No! Such are the events which constitute the experience of nations; and from them may be deduced lessons of wisdom for their future conduct. The most useful one taught by our late civil war, is that of non-interference with the domestic institutions of each State, so far as they are consistent with the Constitution of the United States. This has been a most costly lesson. Hundreds of thousands of our young men have been cut down in the bloom of their youth, and a national debt contracted, which may never be paid. There is a fearful responsibility resting on the public men who were instrumental in bringing it about. It is too soon for its history to be written (1880). When, however, the public mind shall have become calm enough to pronounce it, a correct verdict will be given on this matter. When the future historian, free from any bias, shall consider the question philosophically, he will discard all uncertain sources of information, and build his conclusion on public acts of record, State papers, and the allegations *pro* and *con*, of contemporaneous historians. His attention will be arrested by the last message of President Buchanan (himself a Northern man), which immediately preceded the war. In this, the President said that " he imputed the threatened destruction of the Union, to the long continued and intemperate interference of the Northern people, with the question of slavery in the Southern States." He said that " in consequence of this agitation, a sense of security no longer existed around the family altar; it had been displaced by a dread of servile insurrection." He declared that " many a matron retired at night, in dread of what might befall herself and children before the morning. Should this apprehension pervade the masses of the Southern people, then disunion would become inevitable; since ' self-preservation is the first law of Nature.' That, even then, it was the easiest thing for the people to settle the slavery question forever; and restore peace and harmony to the country. All that was necessary to accomplish that object, and all for which the slave States had ever contended, was—to be let alone." This is a simple and true statement of the cause of the war, announced by a temperate, and disinterested statesman, and no sophistry can evade it. That there were serious mistakes made by our public men will now be admitted; but, in the main, we contend that in this unfortunate business, there is nothing of which the people of the South need be ashamed.

In despite, however, of all that has occurred, of the immense loss of our property, of the torrents of blood which have flowed, and the desolation of our country, there is no reason why our nation may not regain its former prosperity. Nations soon forget the past; and it is well it is so. In a few generations after the Norman conquered England, and the lands of her people were forfeited, and divided amongst his followers, the outrages of the past were forgotten, and she became a united, strong and prosperous kingdom. So it will be in this nation, if the same excellent constitution which our fathers made is spared to us. With these preliminary remarks, which self-respect prompts me to make, I will proceed to my subject.

The list of companies of Ninth Alabama Regiment:. Company A, Mobile; Company B, Jackson; Company C, Lawrence; Company D (Howlan's), Lauderdale; Company E, Morgan; Company G, Limestone; Company H, Greene (Hill's); Company I, Lauderdale (O'Neal); Company K, Marshall.

The Invincibles.

The first volunteers for the late war, in our county, were about a dozen young men, mostly under 21 years of age, who commenced raising a company to be called " *The Invincibles*," in March, 1861. Hearing that the " *Florence Guards* " had completed their organization and were about to march, they abandoned the idea of completing their company, and in the latter part of the month they bid adieu to their friends and joined the " *Florence Guards*."

Previous to the act of secession, the people of our county were divided in opinion in regard to secession. One class were in favor of immediate and separate action; a second favored a call for a convention of the Southern States, and a third did not consider the election of Mr. Lincoln a sufficient cause for a dissolution of the Union. But *after* the act was passed, the very air became hot with excitement. People of all shades of opinion became united in a determination to maintain the position assumed by the State. A subscription was raised for the equipment of these chivalrous young men, and the Garths, the Sykes and the Mastersons, representatives of all these opinions, poured out their money like water.

The "*Florence Guards*," into which "*The Invincibles*" were merged, was a large company, composed of the finest young men in and about Florence, and many of the college students, and their captain was Sterling A. M. Wood. It became a part of the Seventh Alabama Regiment, which was organized at Pensacola as a twelve months regiment, and Captain Wood was elected its colonel. In his stead Wm. H. Price was elected captain. The Seventh Alabama, during most of the year, remained at Pensacola, and spent their time in drilling, making fortifications and carrying sand bags. While at Pensacola the regiment was in Bushrod Johnson's Brigade, and in Walker's Division. The regiment, in the autumn of 1861, was ordered to Bowling Green, Ky., to join the army of Gen. Albert Sidney Johnston. After the regiment reached that place, Colonel Wood was appointed Brigadier General, and the regiment continued in his brigade. Hardee's Division, and was commanded by Colonel Coltart. They retreated with him to Corinth. Their term of service having expired, they were discharged about the 1st of April, 1862, just before the battle of Shiloh, but they all joined other commands and nearly all Captain Hodges' company of the Sixteenth Alabama Regiment, and the most of them were in that battle. As they occupied the post of honor amongst the volunteers of our county, I shall, one by one, give such an account of them as my information will enable me.

1. Peter White was the first volunteer in the county. His father, Nelson H. White, came to this county from Virginia in 1819, in company with Alex. Sale and Jack Burruss. He taught a classical school at or near Courtland in 1820-21. In 1823, in company with Capt. Thomas Ashford, his intimate personal and political friend, he visited Natchez, Miss. While there he bought the Natchez Hotel, and conducted it very successfully for two years. In 1825 he bought a farm on Cedar creek, Franklin county, and in 1826 married Mary B., eldest daughter of Major Thomas S. Pope. The issue of this union was 14 children—8 boys and 6 girls. Mrs. White, the mother, still survives, is 75 years old, and remarkably healthy and lively. Mr. White again came into Lawrence county in 1832, where he finished his useful career, alternately following the occupations of farmer, merchant, teacher and hotel keeper. For many years he kept hotel in Moulton, and in 1854, as his son, Major D. C. White, was proprietor of the Moulton *Democrat*, he learned the trade first of a practical printer, and then conducted the paper as its editor until his death. He was a man of good person, of expressive face, of strong convictions, and of much independence. He was a clear and nervous writer, held the views of the extreme party in the South, which he sustained with ability. But he was an editor of integrity, had a great love for the truth, and the columns of his paper were open for articles, from Judge Peters and others, who differed from him in opinion. The paper of the 17th of April, 1863, contains a notice of his funeral sermon, to be preached by Rev. John S. Davis. The paper, which two years before was large for a village paper, was reduced to a sheet not larger than one of letter paper. Small, however, as it was, that number was full of woes. In addition to the funeral of its editor, there was an obituary of William W., son of Judge Gibson, written by his comrade, Edward Stephenson, and also a list of eighteen young men of Moulton and vicinity, who had already fallen in battle, although the carnage of war had but fairly commenced. Their names were John T. White, John Dinsmore, Thomas B. Boyd, Wm. W. Gibson, Goring Crittenden, John W. Irwin, James Gailey, Newton Parker, Jimmie Dick Moore, John W. McDonald, John W. Byler, Waddy T. Goodlett, James N.

McDaniel, Lover Moore, Jack Warren, R. Gailey, M. B. Cox and T. M. Heflin. I know that I am opening many a wound which has long since ceased to bleed, but they will heal again with a healthier action, when it is seen that the patriotic gallantry of our fallen is not forgotten. It is not my purpose in what I write to invade the province of general history, but to fill the chasm about which history is silent. Mine is the humble task of gathering from the neglected battle-fields of the South, the ashes of our soldiers, who, uninfluenced by emoluments and the hope of distinction have given themselves disinterestedly to their country, and to deposit these ashes, with reverence, in the Urn of Memory, over which those who loved them may shed tears, softened by the reflection that their devotion to the country is gratefully remembered.

Maj. D. C. White, now the senior editor of the *Moulton Advertiser*, is the oldest son of Nelson H. White. He became a printer first, and then taught his father and four brothers to set type. He purchased the Moulton paper, then called the *Advertiser*, from Samuel W. McCord and his son, Luther, in 1851, and changed its name to that of the *Moulton Democrat*. He has run the paper from that time, with the exception of one year (1854), when he and Col. W. H. H. Tyson published a paper at Eastport, Miss. When the war closed the name of the paper was changed back to that of the *Moulton Advertiser*. When Captain Hodges raised his company he entered it as a private, but was made second sergeant. In the battle of Shiloh he acted with such steady courage that a few days afterward he was promoted to the post of regimental ordnance sergeant in the Sixteenth Alabama, to which his company belonged. He was wounded at Shiloh, but not so severely as to prevent him from atteding to his duty. General Beauregard's army retreated to Tupelo. In reviewing the state of the conflict the authorities determined to organize the Home Guards for an emergency. Major White was appointed to command them in Lawrence county, with the rank of major. Nine companies were organized, and when Selma was threatened, they were ordered to that point; but they could not be armed and gotten ready in time, and in a short time afterwards the war closed.

Another son of Nelson H. White, John Thomas, belonged to the Fifteenth Arkansas regiment. He was killed at Shiloh, in the van of his regiment, in a charge on Monday. He was esteemed by his officers and comrades as among the truest and bravest.

Peter White, of the *"Invincibles,"* was a son of Nelson H. White. When the Seventh Alabama Regiment was disbanded, he was at home very ill with pneumonia. As soon as he was able he joined Captain Hodge's company of the Sixteenth Alabama Regiment, where he filled the place vacated by his brother, D. C., most faithfully. He was in the battle of Perryville, was shot through the right arm at Murfreesboro, was at Missionary Ridge, Chickamauga, and all the fights from Chattanooga to Atlanta. At the latter place he was so severely wounded that he was afterward unfit for active duty, and was placed in the quartermaster's department at Augusta, Ga., where he remained until the surrender. He is now editing a paper called the *News*, in Belgreen, Franklin county, Ala.

Leonidas, a young son of Nelson H. White, entered the Sixteenth Alabama at the tender age of fifteen years. Those who knew him say that he was gentle and kind as a woman, but as bold as a lion in battle. He might have enjoyed ease and idleness at home, but when the South was bleeding at every pore, he was too chivalrous to do so. On the day his brother Peter was shot down at Atlanta, he was captured by the enemy, taken to Camp Chase, and died with erysipelas, engendered by an attack of the measles. A lovelier boy or a braver soldier never donned the Confederate gray.

2. John Collier came from Morgan county. He studied law with Hon. D. P. Lewis. He was a nephew of Governor Collier. When the Seventh Alabama Regiment was disbanded, I presume he joined the Sixteenth Alabama Regiment, but I have no certain information. He moved to Texas, and is doing well as a lawyer.

3. S. H. Brown was a son of Jenkins W. Brown, was born near Moulton, and now lives in Texas.

4. J. C. Nipper came to Moulton a short time before he became a volunteer. It is not known what has become of him.

5. John C. Chitwood. His father's name was Stephen C. Chitwood. He came from Lincoln county, Tennessee. He was once a man of wealth, but he indorsed for his friends to a very large amount, and his estate was sold to pay these security debts. His mother was a daughter of Parker Campbell and a niece of Archer Campbell, now dead, but formerly of this county. I think he was elected twice a member of the Legislature. She was born in Virginia. Her father moved first to Madison county, Alabama, and thence to Lincoln county, Tennessee, where she was married. Stephen C. Chitwood died in 1875, and his widow in 1877. They had first settled three miles south of Moulton, and afterward moved nearer town, where they died.

The oldest son, William P., received his primary tuition in the schools in Moulton, and finished his education at Irving College in Warren county, Tennessee. He read law with Judge Lewis in Moulton, and got license to practice in 1859. The war came on, and suspended all business. He served in Roddy's cavalry, and at the close of the war resumed his practice at Moulton, where he is much esteemed as a gentleman, and is respected as a sound and learned lawyer.

John C. Chitwood above mentioned was the second son. After the Seventh Alabama was disbanded he became a member of General Roddy's cavalry. When the war closed he practised law for several years in Decatur, and is now living near Moulton, engaged in farming.

Richard Chitwood, the third son and youngest child in this family, belonged to General Roddy's escort; was captured by the enemy, on a scout near Paint Rock, in Jackson county, Ala., and died in prison, at Camp Chase. There were two sisters in this family. One—Virginia—dead; and the other, Camilla, lives in Moulton.

6. Thomas L. Daugherty, son of Noble Daugherty, was born near Moulton; and died of yellow fever in Memphis in 1878.

7. R. S. Milwee was born near New Burg, Franklin county, and is a farmer near Landersville.

8. Elijah B. Stowe, who was a brother-in-law of the Rev. Josephus Shackelford, was born in Edenton, Ga., in 1841. His father, Elijah B. Stowe, was born in Milford, Conn. The Stowes were quite an old family in that State. His mother was Susan Underwood, and was born in Putnam county, Ga. Her maternal grandfather was James Tinsley, a Baptist minister of Virginia. Young Stowe was educated partly at Mercer University and partly at the Georgia University, at Athens. I have learned that he was a sprightly young man, very fond of music, and a fine performer on the flute. He died in Forrest City, Ark., in 1877. He was living at the time with Mr. Shackelford.

9. E. T. Johnson was born in Morgan county, and was going to school at Moulton when he volunteered. He is now a citizen of Mississippi.

10. James N. McDaniel was a son of Jefferson McDaniel, and was born in the vicinity of Moulton. When the Seventh Alabama left Fort Morgan for Pensacola young Daniel was very sick and eventually died. He was the only one of these ten noble young men and true soldiers who failed to visit his home. I much regret that I can not give a circumstantial account of each one of them.

The Ninth Alabama Regiment.

The history of this noble regiment is as eventful as any which served during the late war. Arriving at Manassas only one day after the first battle at that place, they served under Gen. Joe Johnston until he was wounded, and then under General Lee until the surrender, except when they were detached for some bold enterprise under " Stonewall " Jackson. It was Napoleon Bonaparte's habit to emblazon on the flags of his veteran regiments in large letters, the names of the great battles in which they had taken part. But the battle flag of the Ninth Alabama could not have contained the names of the engagements in which they gathered laurels and shed their blood. The material of the regiment, both men and officers, was of the very best, which North Alabama could furnish.

The companies which were to compose the regiment left home early in June, 1861, and were organized in Richmond, Va., in July. Calmus W. Wilcox was the colonel, Samuel Henry the lieutenant colonel, Edward A. O'Neal, also General, afterward Governor of Alabama, was the major, and Jeremiah Williams the second major.

In October, 1861, when Colonel Wilcox was promoted to Brigadier General, Lieutenant Colonel Henry was promoted to Colonel. Eventually he resigned, and Captain Horace King was made Colonel, at the special request of General Wilcox—continued with the regiment until the close of the war, and died a few years after, in Decatur.

When Lieutenant Colonel Henry resigned, Capt. G. C. Smith, of a Limestone company, was appointed in his stead, and served until the close of the war.

When Major O'Neal was transferred to the command of the Twenty-eighth Alabama Regiment, in March, 1862, Lieut. J. M. Crow, of —— Company, was promoted to major.

Dr. John M. Hayes was surgeon of the Ninth Alabama, but was transferred at the same time with Major O'Neal.[*] Dr. Minor, of Mississippi, succeeded him. Dr. J. R. Edwards was assistant surgeon, and served until the surrender in that capacity.

Company A, was from Mobile, Ala. Capt. T. H. Ripley (a half brother of our neighbor, Captain Comegys) was an accomplished officer, of great bravery. He resigned and raised a regiment, and was killed in some engagement in South Alabama. Captain —— Murphy, of Mobile, succeeded him. He was a descendant of Governor Murphry, of Alabama. A gentleman of culture and a brave officer. He was badly wounded at the battle of Second Manassas, and not well fitted for active service afterward, but held his rank until the surrender.

Company B, was from Jackson county, and was commanded by Captain Jere Williams, who is spoken of above. He was a brave man, and resigned because an officer below him was promoted to colonel.

Company C, from Lawrence county, was commanded by Capt. James M. Warren. He was the son of Levi F. Warren, who lived near Moulton. He resigned, and became colonel of a cavalry regiment in General Roddy's command. This was, from its number, the color company. Donley, an Irishman, was first color bearer. He was recklessly brave, and was killed in the bloody battle of Cold Harbor. Shelton was the next one, of the same fearless stamp, and was killed four days afterward. The post was not so much sought for after these casualties, and the men frequently changed until 1863, when the flag bearer was invested with the rank of first lieutenant, when Ed. R. Till, now of Waterloo, Ala., was appointed. He was of the right stamp for such a hazardous place, and although he lost an arm at Burgess' Mills, near the close of the war, returned to his duty, and served until the surrender. It was an honor to be the flag company, but the post was a dangerous one, and not to be sought for.

Company D, was from Lauderdale county, and commanded by Capt. J. B. Houston, a nephew of Governor Houston, of Alabama. Dr. Edwards, who has lived in Courtland since the war, was a member of this company until he became a surgeon.

Company E, from Morgan county, was commanded by Capt. Horace King. He was a very efficient officer, and was promoted, at one step, to the command of the regiment.

Company G, from Limestone county, was commanded by that excellent and brave gentleman, Thomas H. Hobbs (son of Ira Hobbs and Rebecca Macklin) till he was severely wounded at Cold Harbor, and died at Lynchburg. He was succeeded by Capt. John C. Featherston, who is a brother of Mrs. Tweedy, wife of Dr. Tweedy, of Courtland. He was a fine looking gentleman and a good officer.

Company G, was commanded by Captain Hill, and was from Greene county. I am sorry my information is so meagre of this company.

---

[*] NOTE.—The battle flag of the Twenty-sixth Alabama hangs on the wall at "Rocky Hill," the family home of Mrs. Hayes. Faded, and riddled with bullets, it yet proudly displays the names of "Gettysburg," "Chancellorsville," "Mechanicsville."

Company H, was from Limestone county, and was commanded by Capt. G. C. Smith, who was promoted to lieutenant colonel, after the resignation of his predecessor, Williams. He served efficiently until the surrender.

Company I, was raised and commanded by Capt. Ed. A. O'Neal, of Florence, son of General O'Neal. He was transferred before active operations commenced to the command of the Twenty-fifth Alabama Regiment, and thus getting beyond my jurisdiction, I am deprived of the pleasure of sketching the career of this eloquent, impressive and chivalrous officer. He was succeeded in the command of the company by Capt. D. W. Gillett, a splendid fellow, who was wounded at Williamsburg, and died at Richmond This was his first battle. He was wounded in the fleshy part of the arm, marched with his company on foot to Richmond, and died from this slight wound.

Company K, was from Marshall county, and was commanded by Capt. Samuel Henry, who served as colonel of the regiment for some time. In the command of the company he was succeeded by Captain Sheffield, a good officer, who was transferred to the command of the Forty-seventh Alabama (I think). Col. S. has been frequently in our Legislature since the war, and is a politician of some note. The Lawrence company, as first organized, stood thus:

Captain, James M. Warren; first lieutenant, M. G. May; second lieutenant, G. W. Garth; third lieutenant, W. T. Couch; first sergeant, R. E. Davis; second sergeant, H. V. Whitehead; third sergeant, H. H. Bibb; fourth sergeant, A. Livingston; first corporal, Charles F. Davis, second corporal, J. R. Warren; third corporal, W. P. Farley; fourth corporal, D. C. Harrison. Lieut. G. W. Garth having been transferred to another command, those officers who were below him were promoted and J. K. McBride added to the list. Changes in the officers will be noted from time to time.

Privates,

Jeffrey Beck, G. S. Crittenden, R. Ables, J. L. McDowell, J. T. Cooper, James Daniel, Dennis Cullen, B. F. Gray, William Jennings, James Donahue, P. H. Morris. S. C. Clark, J. A. Isham, N. Eddy, E. W. Berry, J. E. Alexander, D. W. Glenn, J. T. Rover, J. M. Wright, J. H. House, J. E. Chilcoat, J. K. McBride, J. L. Harvey, James T. Carter, W. P. Holmes, S. M. Horton, J. B. Windham, J. W. Martin, E. W. Sale, L. P. Jones, Jeff Lindsay, A. F. Johnson, E. H. Coleman, A. L. Johnson, A. J. Wade, T. H. Riddle, A. J. Watkins, J. K. Whitlow, R. A. Hunter, Wm. Foote, John Washer, T. J. Austin, W. W. Alexander, M. B. Castleberry, J. W. Norwood, A. A. Sullivan, S. W. Crittenden, A. P. Montgomery, J. H. Odom, A. N. Thorn, J. R. Free, M. B. Crownover. T. W. Wilson, J. A. Simmons, W. H. Thorn, Thomas J. Simmons, J. A. Bynum, Edwin Simmons, J. J. Whitlow, Noel C. Graham.

In reading over this list of volunteers, my readers will recognize the names of many of the worthy early settlers of the county.

This company on the day of their departure had a beautiful flag presented to them by Miss Mary Elliott, in terms so elegant and patriotic, they must have rung in their ears for many a day. The old men of this county, by a common impulse, opened their purses for the benefit of the volunteers, and the wives of the needy; Mr. John H. Harris heading the list, with the sum of five hundred dollars.

When the Ninth Alabama reached Richmond they were organized at once, and after an address by President Davis, on the 12th of July, 1861, were sent to Strasburg, in the Valley of Virginia. After a few days they were ordered, by forced marches, to Manassas. They arrived at Piedmont, and on 20th July failed to get transportation on the train—and so were prevented taking part in the battle on the next day—officers and men chafed with disappointment. If the curtain of the future had been lifted, and these fiery spirits had been permitted to see, in one grand panorama, the long and "winding way" they were destined to pursue, leading through every one of those bloody fields which marked the career of General Lee—the broad Potomac, which, with bleeding feet, they were to wade four times in one campaign—if they could have felt, in advance, that burning thirst, known only to the wounded soldier, whose blood was gushing from his veins, they would have been well content to have bathed their gallant feet in the cold stream which flowed from the summit of the Blue Ridge, and rested their weary bodies on the green grass, upon its foot hills. It is fortunate that He who does all things well, had hidden these things from their view. The day after the battle, they reached Manass and were encamped there for many months.

In the month of March, the Ninth Alabama was sent to Yorktown, to form a part of General Magruder's small army of some 8000 men The Federals had recovered from the depression produced by their defeat at Manassas. They were organizing a great army at Washington. All was bustle and activity. " The streets resounded with the wheels of artillery, and the tramp of cavalry. The best officers were engaged in drilling the raw troops, and every field around it was alive with regiments, being carried through their evolutions." The command of this great army was committed " to a young officer of rising reputation—Gen. George B. McClellan—who achieved success in Western Virginia. He was not forty, but had impressed the authorities with a high opinion of his abilities. A soldier, by profession, and enjoying the distinction of having served with credit in the Mexican war, he had been sent as United States Commissioner to the Crimea, and on his return had written a book of marked ability, on the military organizations of the nations of Europe. From that time he became famous."—*John Esten Cooke.*

"The route adopted by General McClellan for his advance upon Richmond, was by Fortress Monroe, and up the Peninsula. 113 steamers, 188 schooners, and 88 barges, were employed for thirty-seven days, in transporting his army with the animals, wagons, batteries, and equipage required. When he got ready for an advance, Gen. Jos. E. Johnston, in command of the Confederates, made a masterly retreat from Manassas, and suddenly appeared on the Peninsula with his army. He withdrew General Magruder from Yorktown, who was pursued by General McClellan's army. Gen Jos. E. Johnston was a Virginian by birth. He had held General Patterson in check in the Shenandoah Valley, deceived him and hastened to the assistance of General Beauregard, at Manassas. He, in face, figure, and character, was thoroughly the soldier. Above the medium height, with an erect figure in a closely fitting uniform buttoned to the chin, with a ruddy face; reserved in manner, brief of speech, without impulses of any description, it seemed that his appearance and bearing were military even to stiffness. As a soldier his reputation was deservedly high; to unshrinking personal courage, he added a far-reaching capacity for the conduct of large operations"—(*Cooke*). The enemy having overtaken him at Williamsburg, he turned with his rear guard upon his pursuers and gave them a bloody check, which will ever exact the applause of military critics. The first collision was late in the afternoon of a drizzly and dark day. " There was great confusion in the Federal ranks. The men marched forward over leaves slippery with rain. over fallen trees. and across ravines, so that it was impossible to preserve an alignment of a company, much more of a brigade. The night came on pitch dark; and the Forty-third New York fired, by mischance, into a Pennsylvania regiment. They were so much demoralized that the former had to be withdrawn next day"—(*Northern historian, Draper*).

The next day General Hooker led the Federals to the attack, and he declared that he was " under a hot fire for nine hours." No doubt it seemed to be a long time to the General, when, in point of fact, it lasted from 1 to 4:30 P. M. But, in that short time. the Federals lost 2228 men in killed and wounded, according to their own report. In this fight the Ninth Alabama occupied the extreme right of the infantry, in a grove of pines, which were large enough to shelter the men, so that their loss was small. Not so with their neighbor, the Nineteenth Mississippi, who happened to be posted in a small open field, for their loss was severe, and here fell their commander, Colonel Mott, a gentleman of culture, and an officer of much merit. The next morning General Johnston resumed his march to Richmond. Thomas J. Simmons, son of our worthy postmaster at Courtland, was left behind, having been wounded in the thigh. He was kept a prisoner about five months. It is worthy of remark, that after this battle our surgeons made a hospital of the venerable halls of William and Mary College, which was the oldest in the United States except Harvard. The former had educated, for nearly two hundred years, the sons of the Cavaliers, and Harvard, the sons of the Puritans. Thomas Jefferson was the representative man amongst the alumni of William and Mary, and Samuel Adams amongst those of Harvard. In the struggle for independence, the two stood side by side, and were both jealous of delegated power, and champions of the rights of States. Only a century had elapsed (a short time in the life of a nation) and, lo! the sons of the Puritans, forgetful of their principles, attack the domestic institutions of their sister States, and "like reapers descend to the harvest of death," even under the moss-covered walls of this time-honored institution of learning.

The Federal army did not resume their march until two days had elapsed; for they had dead to bury, and wounded to care for. On the 24th of May, General McClellan arrived at Chickahominy creek, which flows through a flat country, liable to overflow when freshets occur. The Confederates had destroyed all the bridges, after crossing, General McClellan had the lower bridge repaired, and crossed two of his corps; one encamped at Fair Oaks and Seven Pines; and the other behind it. The rest of his army occupied the north bank of the stream, and his headquarters were in plain view of the spires of Richmond. "The Federal sword had nearly pierced the heart of Virginia." His army, however, was in a dangerous position, for it was divided into two parts by the large creek. From the head of the column on the south side, counting by the bridge, to that on the north side, it was twelve miles; although from one to the other, directly across, it was only a few miles. In view of this state of things, General Johnston determined to attack that portion of the Federal army, which was encamped on the south bank. Nature favored this plan. It had rained heavily on the 29th, and on the night of the 30th of May, a deluge of rain fell. On the next day the battle occurred; and it was one of the most desperate and bloody of the war. The Confederate attack was fierce and sudden, and drove the first corps of the enemy back for a mile, took two camps and six guns; and made an unsuccessful attempt to turn the enemy's left, which rested on a swamp. General Johnston then in turn, made a determined attack on the Federal right by passing down between it and the creek, when an event occurred which changed the whole aspect of the battle. It had been going on for three and a half hours, when General McClellan ordered General Sumner to cross the swollen stream, which was rising rapidly, to relieve their comrades, on the south side, who were sorely pressed. Sedgwick's division of 15,000 men crossed the swollen stream over a tottering bridge, which had been constructed nearly opposite the battle-field, and he had dragged over by hand a battery of twenty-four Napoleon guns. It was well he moved rapidly, for it was not long afterward before the bridge was submerged by the angry flood. Sumner urged his men on, and guided them through the woods, by the roar of the battle. In the meantime the Confederates steadily forced their way." The evening was coming on dark and gloomy, and dark and gloomy was the prospect of the two corps who had been separated from the Federal army. But Sumner planted his guns in a clearing of the woods. The Confederate column pressing on victoriously for Bottom's bridge must show its flank to this battery. The flanker was out-flanked—(Draper).

About sunset General Johnston was severely wounded by the fragment of a shell whilst superintending this attack; and the nature of the wound rendered it impossible for him to retain command of the army. Night fell on a field where neither side could claim a victory. The Confederates, however, had given a severe check to the enemy. In this battle the Ninth Alabama Regiment of Wilcox's Brigade was actively engaged, but again suffered a very small loss. An interesting incident occurred during the battle. A good young man named Vaughn, of Hobbs' company, was shot down, and sent for Dr. Edwards. When asked how he was hurt, he answered, laying his hand upon his heart, "Doctor, I am shot plumb through and through." When the doctor examined he found that a large ball had struck him just over his heart, and buried itself in his pocket Bible, which he uniformly carried in his breast-pocket. The effect on the boys in camp was very decided. A great many carried Bibles in their breast pockets. Not long afterward, however, young ——— was saved from death in a similar way, except that the shield this time was a pack of cards. So between the card-player and Bible readers " honors were easy."

> "A steed comes at morning, no rider is there—
> But the bridle is stained with the sign of despair."

In the battle already recounted, this regiment was fortunate in having sustained but little loss; but sorrow came to many a family in North Alabama from the carnage in the engagements which I am about to sketch.

On the 3d of June, 1862, Robert E. Lee was appointed Commander of the Army in the place of General Johnston. Robert E. was descended from illustrious ancestors. The most remote of these, Launcelot Lee, came from France to England with William the Conqueror. A later one, Lionel Lee, went with Richard, the lion hearted, on his third crusade; and displayed great gallantry at the siege of Acre. His father was Gen. Henry Lee (Light Horse Harry of Revolutionary fame). Robert was uniformly a steady, good boy, and during the whole time he was at West Point did not receive a single demerit. Three years after graduating, he married Mary Custis, daughter of Mr. George Washington Custis—the adopted son of General Washington. He entered the army, in 1846, and was a captain and assigned to duty as Chief Engineer of the Central Army of Mexico. He made a great reputation in this position. In 1855, when the Second Cavalry (corps d'elite) of the United States Army was organized he was made one of its officers. The Colonel was Albert Sidney Johnston—the Lieut. Col., Robert E. Lee—Senior Major, William J. Hardee—Senior Captain, Earl Van Dorn—the next ranking Captain, Kirby Smith—Lieutenants Hood, Fields, Cosby; Majors, Fitz-Hugh Lee, Johnston, Palmer and Stevenson—all of whom became general officers on the Southern side, except George H. Thomas (who was the Junior Major) and the three last mentioned, who became generals in the Northern Army. What a constellation of military genius for a single regiment!

When Virginia passed the Act of Secession Lieutenant Colonel Lee resigned his position in the army and took the part of his native State. In a private letter to a friend he said: "The whole South is in a state of revolution, into which Virginia, after a long struggle, has been drawn, and though I recognize no necessity for such a state of things, and would have forborne and pleaded to the end, for redress of grievances, real or supposed, yet in my own person I had to meet the question, whether I should take part against my native State."

McClellan's army, then before Richmond, when it landed on the peninsula had 159,000 men, and, on the day of General Lee's appointment, 115,000 men present and ready for duty. Besides these there were about 60,000 more under McDowell, and other commanders, for which he had been anxiously looking. But Gen. (Stonewall) Jackson was in the Shenandoah valley, with orders to threaten Washington, and to embarrass the movements of McClellan in his attack on Richmond. The manner in which he performed this duty constitutes a brilliant portion of the military annals of the Confederacy. To sum it up in few words, " He had been pursued by three major generals, and turning upon his pursuers, at every opportunity, had made good his retreat. He had diverted large reinforcements from McClellan, had neutralized a National force of 60,000 men, and given to the Southern armies the prestige of victory. He was now ready to join the army in front of Richmond, opposing McClellan's advance " (*Draper*). So great was the consternation produced at Washington by his rapid blows that the Secretary of War issued a circular to each of the Governors of the Northern States " To organize and send forward *all* volunteer and militia force in your State," and the President seized upon all the railroads for the purpose of transporting them. These acts were founded on the belief (which General Lee caused by a *ruse*) that Jackson had been reinforced, and was marching on to Washington, when, at that very time, he was making forced marches toward Richmond, to aid General Lee in crushing McClellan before Federal reinforcements could arrive.

When General Lee assumed command, McClellan had advanced his left wing within four or five miles of the city, and was protected by the strongest defences which bristled with artillery. The right wing of this army still lay north of the Chickahominy, but they were connected by a number of solid bridges. General Lee was satisfied that it would be very hazardous to attack in front, and with a view of ascertaining the defences of the enemy on the right flank and rear, he organized

STUART'S RIDE AROUND McCLELLAN.

Gen. J. E. B, Stuart was a Virginian by birth, and not yet thirty years of age. When the war commenced he was lieutenant in the United States cavalry; he joined Johnston in the valley, and impressed him with a high opinion of his abilities. At Manassas he charged and broke a regiment of zouave infantry, protected the rear of the army when Johnston retreated, and, at Williamsburg, protected our right (the Ninth Alabama) from being turned, marching, and countermarching, in such a way as to make the impression that the cavalry was twice as many as they really were. In person, he was of medium height: his frame was broad and powerful; he wore a heavy brown beard flowing upon his breast, a huge moustache of the same color, with ends curling upward, and the blue eyes flashing beneath a "piled up" forehead, had at times the dazzling brilliancy attributed to the eyes of the eagle. Fond of movement, adventure, bright colors, and all the pomp and pageantry of war, Stuart had entered on the struggle with ardor, and enjoyed it as the huntsman does the chase. Young, ardent, ambitious, as brave as steel, ready with jest or laughter, with his banjo player following him, going into the hottest battle humming a song, this young Virginian was in truth, an original character, and impressed powerfully all who approached him. One who knew him well wrote: "Everything striking, brilliant and picturesque, seemed to centre in him."

The war seemed to be, to Stuart, a splendid and exciting game, in which his blood coursed joyously in his veins, and his immensely strong physical organization found an arena for the display of its faculties. The affluent life of the man craved those perils and hardships which flush the pulses, and make the heart beat fast. He swung himself into the saddle at the sound of the bugle, as the hunter springs on horseback and at such movements his cheeks glowed and his huge moustache curled with enjoyment. The romance and poetry of the hard trade of arms seemed first to be inaugurated when this joyous cavalier, with his floating plume and splendid laughter, appeared upon the great arena of the war in Virginia. Precise people shook their heads and called him frivolous, undervaluing his great abilities. Those best acquainted with him were of a different opinion. Johnston wrote to him from the West: "How can I eat or sleep without you on my outpost?" Jackson said when he fell, "Go back to General Stuart and act upon his own judgment, and do what he thinks best I have implicit confidence in him." Lee said, when he was killed at Yellow Tavern: "I can scarcely think of him without weeping." And the brave General Sedgwick of the U. S. Army, said: "Stuart is the best cavalry officer ever foaled in North America"—(*John Esten Cooke*).

With a picked force of 1500 men, officered by the two Lees and others, he drove the outposts of the enemy from Hanover Courthouse, broke two squadrons of cavalry near Old Church, pushed on to York River Railroad which he crossed burning or capturing all Federal stores met with, including enormous wagon camps; and then finding the way back barred against him, and the Federal army on the alert, he continued his march with rapidity, passed entirely around General McClellan's army, and building a bridge over the Chickahominy, safely re-entered the Confederate lines, just as a force appeared on his rear. He reported to General Lee that the right and rear of the enemy were unprotected by works of any strength.

Jackson marched and countermarched with a pretence of advancing down the valley. At last one morning he disappeared and marched rapidly to join General Lee. Not even his own soldiers knew what direction they were taking. They were forbidden by general order to intimate even the names of the towns they passed through; directed to reply to every question "I don't know," and it is said that when Jackson demanded the name and regiment of a soldier robbing a cherry tree, he could extract from the man no reply but "I don't know." When Jackson reached Ashland, forty-six miles from Richmond, he, with a relay of horses, rode rapidly to General Lee's camp. A council of war was held at once. While the corps of commanders was being convened, General Lee asked General Jackson to take some refreshments, but he answered that he "was not hungry." He then invited him to rest on his bed, and he said he "was not tired." In this council was determined the mode in which the enemy was to be attacked and when it closed General Jackson mounted his horse and rode back to his army as rapidly, as he came. This was the first interview which had taken place between these great commanders since the commencement of the war.

General Lee's plan was to send a force under Gen. A. P. Hill to cross the Chicka-hominy, ten miles above the right of the enemy, which was at Mechanicsville, and when they were driven back, Gen. A. B. Longstreet, who was stationed opposite, was to cross the bridge at that place. "General Hill, a Virginian by birth, was the representative of the spirit and dash of the army. Under forty years of age, with a slender figure, a heavily-bearded face, dark eyes, a composed and unassuming bearing, he was personally popular with all, and greatly beloved as a man and commander. His chief merit, as a soldier, was his dash and impetus in the charge. A braver heart never beat in human breast; throughout the war he retained the admiration and respect of the army and country; and a strange fact in relation to this eminent soldier is, that his name was uttered by both Jackson and Lee, as they expired."—(*Cooke.*) He made the attack in his usual dashing style and he was joined by Longstreet, who crossed the bridge imme-diately, and so the first act in this bloody drama was accomplished. "Gen. A. B. Long-street was able and resolute—an officer of low and powerful stature, with a heavy brown beard reaching to his breast, a manner marked by unalterable composure and a counte-nance, whose expression, phlegmatic tranquillity, never varied in the hottest hours of battle. Longstreet was as famous for his bull-dog obstinacy, as Hill was for his dash and enthusiasm. General Lee styled him his ' old war horse,' and depended upon him in some of the most critical operations of the war."—(*Cooke.*)

General Lee's plan succeeded in all respects except that General Jackson had been delayed in his march and he found himself in front of the Federal army, who occupied a strong position, and as time was precious, he was compelled to make the attack without him. John Esten Cooke, who was on the staff of General Lee, and was an eye-witness, one of the most graphic writers in America. I will here quote his account of this momentous battle—Cold Harbor:

"The memorable 27th of June had dawned clear and cloudless, and the brilliant sun-shine gave promise of a day on which the elements would not check the bloody work to be performed. Hill advanced steadily on the track of the retiring Federal forces, and about noon came in front of the very powerful position of the main body near Cold Har-bor. General McClellan had drawn up his force on the ridge, the left of which was pro-tected by a deep ravine, and his right rested on elevated ground. His whole line was protected by difficult approaches; the ground was swampy or covered with tangled undergrowth, or both. The ridge had been fortified by breastworks of felled trees and earth, behind which the long lines of infantry supported by numerous artillery, awaited the attack.

"The Federal force was commanded by the brave and able Gen. Fitz John Porter. The moment had come. A. P. Hill pressing forward rapidly, with Longstreet's divi-sion, on the right, reached Cold Harbor in front of the enemy, about noon. Hill im-mediately attacked and an engagement of the most sanguinary character ensued. Gen-eral Lee, accompanied by General Longstreet, had ridden from his headquarters to the scene of action, and now witnessed in person the fighting of the troops, who charged under his eye, closing in a nearly hand-to-hand conflict with the enemy. This was the first occasion on which a considerable portion of the men had seen him, and that air of supreme calmness which always characterized him in action, must have made a deep impression upon them. He was clad simply, and wore scarcely any badges of rank. A felt hat drooped low over the broad forehead, and the eyes beneath were calm and unclouded. Add a view of measured calmness, the air of immovable composure which marked the erect military figure, evidently at home in the saddle, and the reader will have a just conception of General Lee's personal appearance in the first of the great battles in his career.

"Hill attacked with that dash and obstinacy which, from this time forward, characterized him; but succeeded in making no impression on the Federal line. In every assault he was repulsed with heavy loss. The Federal artillery, which was handled with skill and coolness, did great execution upon his column as it rushed forward, and the infantry behind their works stood firm, in spite of the most determined efforts to drive them from the ridge. Three of Hill's regiments reached the crest and fought hand to hand over the breastworks, but they were speedily repulsed, and driven from the crest, and after two hours hard fighting Hill found that he had lost heavily, and effected nothing.

"It was now half-past two o'clock in the afternoon, and General Lee listened with anxiety for the sound of guns from the left, which would herald the approach of General Jackson. Nothing was heard from that quarter, however, and affairs were growing critical. The Confederate attack had been repulsed—the Federal position seemed impregnable—and, said General Lee, 'it became apparent that the enemy were gradually gaining ground.' * * It became necessary to act without delay, without awaiting the approach of General Jackson. General Lee directed General Longstreet to make a feint movement against the enemy's left, and thus relieve the pressure on Hill. Longstreet proceeded with promptness to obey the order; advanced in the face of a heavy fire, and with a cross-fire of artillery raking his right over the Chickahominy, and made the feint which had been ordered by General Lee. It effected nothing, and to attain the desired result, it was found necessary to turn the feint into a real attack. This Longstreet proceeded to do, first dispersing with a single volley a force of cavalry, which had the temerity to charge his infantry. As he advanced, and attacked the powerful position before him, the roar of guns was heard on the left of Lee's line. General Jackson had arrived and thrown his troops into action without delay. He then rode forward to Cold Harbor, where General Lee awaited him, and the two soldiers shook hands in the midst of tumultuous cheering from the troops. The contrast between the two men was extremely striking. We have presented a sketch of the grave commander-in-chief, with his erect and graceful seat in the saddle, his imposing dignity of demeanor, and his calm and deliberate tones, as deliberate as though he were in a drawing-room. Jackson was a very different personage. He was in a dingy old coat, wore a discolored cadet cap, tilted almost upon his nose, and rode a raw-boned horse, with short stirrups, which raised his knees in a very ungraceful manner. Neither in his face nor figure was there the least indication of the great faculties of the man, and a more awkward-looking personage it would be impossible to imagine. In his hand he held a lemon, which he sucked from time to time, and his demeanor was abstracted and silent.

As Jackson approached Lee rode toward him and greeted him with a cordial pressure of the hand.

"Ah, general, I am very glad to see you. I hoped to be with you before."

Jackson made a twitching movement of the hand, and replied in a few words, rather jerked from the lips than deliberately uttered. Lee had paused, and now listened to the long roll of musketry from the woods, where Hill and Longstreet were engaged; then to the still more incessant and angry roar from the direction of Jackson's own troops, who had closed in upon the Federal forces.

"That fire is very heavy," said Lee. "Do you think your men can stand it?"

Jackson listened for a moment, with his head bent toward one shoulder, as was customary with him, for he was deaf, he said, in one ear, and could not hear very well out of the other, and replied briefly: "They can stand almost anything! They can stand that!"

He then, after receiving General Lee's instructions, immediately saluted him and returned to his corps—Lee remaining still at Cold Harbor, which was opposite the Federal centre.

"The arrival of Jackson changed, in a moment, the aspect of affairs in every part of the field. Whitney's division of his command took position on Longstreet's left; the command of D. H. Hill on the extreme right of the whole line, and Ewell's division, with part of Jackson's old division, supported A. P. Hill. No sooner had these dispositions been made, than General Lee ordered an attack along the whole line. It was now five or six o'clock, and the sun was sinking. From that moment until night came, the battle raged with a fury unsurpassed in any subsequent engagement of the war. The Texas troops under General Hood especially distinguished themselves. These, followed by their comrades, charged the Federal left on the bluff, and in spite of a desperate resistance, carried the position.

"The enemy were driven," says General Lee, "from the ravine to the first line of breastworks, over which one impetuous column dashed, up to the intrenchments on the crest." Here the Federal artillery was captured, their line driven from the hill, and in other parts of the field a similar success followed the attack. As night fell, their line gave way in all parts, and the remnants of General Porter's command returned to the bridges on the Chickahominy.

In this engagement the Ninth Alabama, in Wilcox's brigade, and Longstreet's division, was actively engaged on the right of our army. Here the contest was in a wood on each side of a ravine which ran parallel to the Federal line and entered into the Chickahominy. The bottom of the ravine was a washed channel, with perpendicular sides, in many places too high to be scaled; and our men were repulsed with heavy loss, until the final charge was made all along the line. The death roll of Lawrence volunteers during the war was very great, and only a remnant of them now survive. It is pretty well known which of them died in battle, but there is much uncertainty as to the battles in which they fell, or were wounded. With most of the survivors with whom I have conversed there is a want of distinctness as to the recollection of the circumstances. The events of the war seem to float before their mental vision like a horrid phantasmagoria. I have therefore concluded to make no special report of casualties after each battle, except in cases well attested, but to append a death roll to the last number I will write on this regiment. As already mentioned, here fell Capt. Thos. H. Hobbs, so severely wounded that he died shortly afterward, also Donley, the brave Irishman, the color-bearer of the regiment, and of Warren's company; Alexander Isham was killed, and J. B. Windham and Gray Whitehead wounded, with many others.

The Retreat of McClellan.

After this bloody victory, for which the Confederates paid very dearly, General McClellan determined to retreat to James river, and the next morning started his supply train of 5000 wagons, his siege train, and 2500 oxen. He had, for some time, contemplated a change of base from York to James river; but he did not expect to execute this plan "upon compulsion." He anticipated the arrival of General McDowell, with a large force, to occupy his right, while, with the remainder of his army, he would move by his left, and rest it on James river. However, his retreat was conducted with the ability of the great commander he was. Lee sent Magruder to attack the Federal rear, at Savage's Station. They were destroying all the material they could not carry away, and as the Confederates approached they set fire to a train heavily loaded with supplies and shells, and turned it loose under a full head of steam. It thundered along with the shells exploding as it went, and was sent headlong over the broken bridge into the Chickahominy.

Their line in retreat was over eight miles long. General Jackson hung upon their rear; but Franklin was there, and he was kept at bay. The Federals had to pass through a swamp four miles wide, and Lee had a strong force under Hill and Longstreet to attack them beyond it in flank; but there they met Keys, who had taken a strong position, and were repulsed. In this action at "Frazier's Farm" it was McCall's Federal division which was attacked. McCall, in his report, says, "Randall's battery was charged by the Confederates in great force, and with a reckless impetuosity, I never saw equaled. They advanced at a run over six hundred yards of open ground. The guns of the battery mowed them down, yet they never paused. A volley of musketry was poured into them by the Fourth Infantry in support of this battery, but it did not check them for a moment. They dashed on, and pistoled and bayoneted the cannoniers."

In this conflict General McCall reported that one-fourth of his division had been killed or wounded. He himself was taken prisoner, and General Meade severely wounded On the part of the Confederates who were repulsed, the losses were great. General Pryor, who commanded the fifth brigade of Longstreet's corps, speaking of the Fourteenth Alabama, says it was nearly annihilated.

Here the Ninth Alabama lost another gallant color-bearer—Shelton. And, amongst the Lawrence volunteers, R. A. Hunter and A. Livingston were killed, and Gray Whitfield and many others wounded. Livingston was a gray-haired man, who was sergeant in his company. I think he was the son of Samuel Livingston already mentioned as having served under General Jackson in the Creek war.

All night the Federal column pursued its weary way, and before day arrived at Malvern Hill. This was an elevated plateau, cleared of timber, about a mile and a half long, by three-fourths of a mile wide. It was a very strong position. Tier after tier of batteries were seen on the slope of the hill which rose in the form of an amphitheatre. The first line of batteries could be reached only by passing over an open field of three hundred yards. exposed to grape and canister from cannon, and musketry from the infantry. Brigade after brigade forming in the woods, was started in a run over the open field to capture the batteries; but the heavy fire of the volleys of the Federal infantry in every instance sent them reeling back, and covered the ground with the dead and wounded. Until dark, General Lee persisted in his efforts to carry the position, but every charge was fearfully repulsed.

This battle was followed by a dark and stormy night, hiding the agony of thousands who lay on the blood-stained slopes of Malvern Hill. The next morning, the enemy was nowhere to be seen. They had retreated to Harrison's landing.

Thus ended the campaign of Lee and McClellan. The most accomplished officer of the Federal army had been beaten—the siege of Richmond had been raised—more than 10,000 prisoners had been captured, including officers, and fifty-two pieces of artillery, and 35,000 stand of small arms. The losses on both sides, in killed and wounded, were very heavy, but it is believed that the losses of the Federals were much the greater.

After these engagements terminated, the Ninth Alabama, in line, counted only sixty-three muskets, so many had been lost by death, by wounds, by details, and by the exhaustion of the men from the extreme heat of the weather.

The campaign was over. Richmond, for this time, was saved. McClellan lay on the James river below, with his army badly shattered and despondent. The army of Lee returned to their quarters before Richmond, for rest. The Ninth Alabama went into their old camp, where their slightly wounded had been collected in a hospital, from the battle-fields of Cold Harbor, Frazier's Farm, and Malvern Hill, under charge of Surgeons Minor and Edwards; while those hurt more seriously were in the hospital at Richmond. For awhile the shadow of battle and death rested darkly over the men; but it was not long before a healthy reaction took place, they regained their wonted cheerfulness, and the camp again became a scene of thoughtless gayety and mirth. In a few weeks the regiment became strong in numbers again.

But the commander-in-chief knew that nothing decisive had yet occurred. McClellan lay thirty miles below the city, with an army of 90,000 men. He was in a position most dangerous to the Confederate capital, and from which General Grant, finally, effected its downfall.

McClellan insisted, in an interview with General Halleck, upon advancing upon the Petersburg side, but his advice was not taken. In the meantime a new Federal commander appeared at Culpeper Court House, and threatened the capital from that side. General Pope had been called from the West, to take command of the forces which operated in the valley of Virginia, with large reinforcements. For some time it was uncertain from which side the real attack would come. But the secret was discovered by Col. John S. Mosby, then a private, who on his return from prison in Washington, saw that Burnside's flotilla from the south, instead of ascending James river, were on their way to reinforce General Pope, and communicated the fact at once to Mr. Davis at Richmond.

In a few hours the army was under marching orders, and General Lee determined to fight General Pope before he became too strong. General Jackson had been sent several weeks before to confront the Federal army, and had checked General Pope's advance by a sharp action at Cedar Mountain. The bulk of the army was moved by General Lee in that direction, and on the 19th of August, 1862, he issued his orders for an immediate attack, but General Pope fell back behind the Rappahannock and guarded all the fords.

General Stuart had been sent to the rear of the Federals, and at Catlett's Station he captured the headquarters of General Pope, and carried away a box of official documents. These papers which Stewart hastened—marching day and night—through storm and flood—to convey to General Lee, presented the clearest evidence of the enemy's movements and designs. Troops were hastening in every direction to reinforce General Pope, and the entire force on James river was to be added to his army. The case admitted of no delay. He decided to send General Jackson, by a route near the Mountain, to fall on the rear of the enemy at Manassas. Jackson crossed the Rappahannock, by an old ford, high up and out of sight of the enemy, marched day and night, passed through Thoroughfare Gap, west of Manassas, and completely destroyed the immense mass of supplies in the depot at that place. The whole movement had been so rapid, and General Stuart had so fully guarded the flank of the advancing column from observation, that Manassas was a mass of smoking ruins, before General Pope suspected the danger. He hastily broke up his camp, and hurried to attack Jackson. General Lee, who had been confronting the Federal army with Longstreet's bare corps, by forced marches, hastened to the support of Jackson, by the same route on which that General had marched. It was a trial of speed, and Lee feared that his friend would be crushed by the great numbers of the enemy before he could relieve him. The Ninth Alabama was still in Wilcox' brigade, Anderson's division, and Longstreet's corps; and shared in his forced march. It is a coincidence somewhat strange, that the year before they were in a march for Manassas which strained every nerve, but missed the first battle at that place by one day—and now, with blistered feet, they were aiming to reach the same place. This time, however, they arrived at the field of conflict in time. Jackson had burned the stores at Manassas on the 29th, and on the next day Pope hurried to attack him. Jackson having accomplished his object fell back to Sadley, and awaited the coming of Lee, with his back to the mountain. Lee reached the western end of Thoroughfare Gap on the 28th, at sunset, and heard the sound of artillery. He had great fear that the gap was strongly guarded, and that he would not be able to reach Jackson. It proved to be occupied by a division under command of General King (*Draper, 2d Vol., p. 439*); but Lee assaulted it at once, sending a flanking column around the north side; and the division fell back, leaving the gap open for Longstreet's corps, which formed next day on the right of Jackson, upon the same field on which the first battle of Manassas was fought; but this time the Confederates occupied the ground which the Federals did then.

The second battle of Manassas was fought on the twenty-ninth and thirtieth days of August. Lee's army was formed in the shape of a V, with the open side next to the enemy; General Jackson's corps being the left, and Longstreet's the right. On the last day after noon, the Federal right attacked Jackson's left, under A. P. Hill. "An obstinate conflict ensued; the opposing lines fighting almost bayonet to bayonet, delivering their volleys into each other at the distance of ten paces." At one time Jackson's line was penetrated in A. P. Hill's division, but the injury was repaired. The Federal troops returned, again and again to the encounter; and General Hill reported six differerent assaults made upon him. (*Life of Lee.*)

On the second day of the battle the armies remained in the face of each other until 3 o'clock in the afternoon. "General Pope then resumed the attack upon Jackson's left with his best troops. The charge was furious, and a bloody struggle ensued; but Jackson succeeded in repulsing the force. It fell back in disorder, but was succeeded by a second and third line, which rushed forward at the 'double quick,' in a desperate attempt to break the Southern line. These new attacks were met with greater obstinacy than at first; and just as the opponents had closed in, a heavy fire was directed against the Federal column by Col. S. D. Lee, commanding the artillery at Lee's centre. (Our readers will remember Gen. Stephen D. Lee, who, with a large cavalry force, once defended our homes in North Alabama from 'war's desolation,' at a time when the night march of Federal armies was illuminated by dwellings in flames. This modest, unpretending, learned, and gallant gentleman is now presiding over an agricultural college at Starkville, Miss., with the same calm energy which he displayed at Manassas.) This fire, which was of the most rapid and destructive character, struck the enemy in front and flank, at once, and seemed to sweep back the charging brigades as they came. The fire of the cannon was then redoubled, and Jackson's line advanced with cheers. Before this charge the Federal line broke, and Jackson pressed forward, allowing them no respite. General Lee then threw forward Longstreet, who pressed them in front and flank; as Lee intended in forming this peculiar line. The Federal forces were driven from position to position; and at 10 at night the darkness put an end to the battle and pursuit. General Pope was retreating with his forces toward Washington."

In this engagement the Ninth Alabama occupied a place near the right of Longstreet's corps, and although they were engaged but a short time, the conflict was stubborn and they lost many in killed and wounded. The latter, as soon as their wounds were dressed, went back at once to the hospital at Richmond (an indication that some unusual movement was contemplated by General Lee), and this proved to be the march into Maryland.

On the 3d of September, General Lee put his army in motion and crossed the Potomac at Leesburg, the infantry wading the river. The troops had not recovered from the fatigue of the heavy marching and fighting they had undergone of late. Moreover, the men were ragged, and with scarcely shoes upon their feet, and in a poor condition to undertake an invasion; the consequence was that there were a great many stragglers from the ranks. At Frederick, Anderson's division was detached to aid General Jackson in the reduction of Harper's Ferry.

In the meantime General Pope reached Washington and resigned his command; and General McClellan was again appointed to command the Federal army. The invasion caused an immense excitement in the North, and in a few days McClellan was able to collect an army and to march in pursuit of General Lee, who was marching leisurely in the direction of Hagerstown, to allow Jackson time for the capture of Harper's Ferry. That officer displayed his usual energy. He occupied the heights around the place with artillery, and after an attack of two hours the garrison surrendered about 8 o'clock on the morning of the 15th of September. Fast riding couriers brought the welcome news to General Lee, as he was approaching Sharpsburg; and soon official information was received that more than eleven thousand prisoners, thirteen thousand small arms and seventy-three cannons had been captured. General McClellan was in pursuit of General Lee; and all along his march he fired signal guns to inform the officer at Harper's Ferry of his approach. General Lee had drawn up his forces on the west of Antietam creek, and waited the coming of Jackson. Longstreet's corps was on the right resting on the creek; D. H. Hill's command was on his left, and next, two brigades under General Hood, and when Jackson arrived he was directed to form on the left of Hood—while Stuart, with his cavalry and horse artillery, occupied the remainder of the ground to the Potomac river. General McClellan formed his army on the ridge east of the creek numbering eighty thousand, according to his report, while that of General Lee numbered less than forty thousand men according to his report.

General Jackson arrived on the field in the evening of the 16th of September, with 4000 of his men, Ewell's division of 2400, and his old division of 1600 men. The last was held back as a reserve. I insert an account of the first act in this bloody drama from a Northern historian. "As soon as he could see, Hooker with his corps (there were 18,000 men—*Swinton*) made so furious an attack on Jackson's brigades that they could not retain their hold, but were expelled with severe loss, across the cornfield of the battle-area, and into the woods, where were their reserves. These issuing forth, after an infuriated struggle, succeeded in checking Hooker's advance. The antagonists fighting in a cloud of sulphurous smoke, almost annihilated each other. It was necessary to withdraw the wreck of Jackson's regiments to the rear, and replace them by Hood's division. On the other side, Hooker's corps was nearly destroyed."

In this first struggle, the roar of which was heard by the Ninth Alabama, as they waded the Potomac at Shepherdstown, a few miles off—Ewell's division had sustained the shock, and it was truly a wreck. In one hour after dawn, General Lawton, division commander, was wounded and carried from the field; Colonel Douglas, division commander, was killed; Lawton's brigade lost 554 killed and wounded, out of 1150, and five or six regimental commanders. Hayes' brigade lost 323 out of 550, and all the regimental commanders. Walker's brigade lost 228 out of less than 700; and three out of four regimental commanders; and out of the staff officers of the division, scarcely one remained. "Mansfield's corps had now reached the field, and made its way down to the Hagerstown road, where it was met by the division of D. H. Hill, which had come out of the woods at the Dunker church. Another furious encounter ensued, and the valley was filled with smoke. Out of the battle's din, the yells of the Confederates, and the cheers of the national troops—down in the cornfield, came forth a ghastly procession of wounded men. Mansfield's troops were driven back to the woods, from which they had emerged. Mansfield was killed and Hooker wounded."—(Draper.) The Ninth Alabama arrived just in time to take part in the second struggle, and lost severely in killed and wounded.

The third act of this drama opened the appearance of a third corps of the Federals under General Sumner (an officer of great dash and courage), which made a vigorous charge. General Lee had sent to the rear the brigades of Colquit, Ripley, and McRea, and with these and the forces he had before, Jackson presented a stubborn front; but his loss was heavy. General Starke, of his old division, was killed; the brigade, regimental, and company officers fell almost without an exception, and the brigades dwindled to mere handfuls. Under the great pressure, Jackson was at length forced back. Sedgwick's division followed the retiring Confederates. This was the turning point of the battle. General Lee witnessed the conflict on his left, with great anxiety, but he was unable to send more troops. Fortunately, however, General McLaws, who had been delayed in his march from Harper's Ferry, arrived, and was hurried to the left. Jackson was holding his ground with difficulty, when McLaws and Walker were sent to him. As soon as they arrived they were thrown into action—the onward rush of the Federal line was checked, Jackson's weary men took heart—the enemy were driven back by the advance of Lee's whole force; and he reoccupied the line from which General Sumner had forced him to retire. The great struggle on the left was over—(*Life of Lee*).

Later in the day, owing to a mistake of orders, a gap had been left in the centre, where D. H. Hill commanded. The enemy saw it, and a sudden rush was made to pierce the line. D. H. Hill, with the help of a few officers of promptness and courage (amongst them Lieut. Col. Ben. Taylor. then commanding O'Neal's old company), rallied a few hundred men (amongst them about seventy of the Ninth Alabama), and filled the gap. With a single gun, Hill opened upon the enemy, and Colonel Cooke faced them with his regiment, as General Lee reported, "standing boldly in line without a cartridge." The bold action by this small force saved the army from serious disaster. In this conflict Lieutenant Taylor was shot through the leg, the ball passing between the bones. Nevertheless, that bold gentleman marched off with the army on its retreat, preferring the torture of his wound to a Federal prison. Many of the volunteers from Lawrence fell in this battle, but we lack specific information, and must refer our readers to the final list   It is known, however, that R. H. Coleman, now of Leighton, was wounded, and T. J. Austin was so severely wounded that he was sent home and died in a few months.

On the next day the two armies remained confronting each other, both being too much exhausted to renew the struggle; and that night General Lee retreated across the Potomac, into the Valley of Virginia, for rest and refreshment. "In this region, so famous for its salubrity and the beauty of its scenery, these gallant men passed the brilliant days of autumn. This section is known as the "Garden of Virginia," and the benign influence of their surroundings was soon seen in the faces of the troops. In their camps along the banks of the picturesque little stream, called the Opequan, the troops laughed, jested, sang rude ballads, and exhibited a joyous indifference to their privations and hardships, which said much for their courage and endurance."

The troops had admired General Lee for his great military capacity, but in this camp, and during this long rest, the awe with which they once regarded him wore off, and they began to love him for the sterling qualities of his heart. It was here that he penned his *eloquent appeal to the people of the South* for the relief of the army.

Said he, alluding to the late campaign, "During all this time, covering the space of a month, the troops rested but four days. And let it always be remembered to their honor that of the men who performed this wonderful feat, one-fifth were bare-footed, one-half in rags and the whole half famished. * * * But great as have been the trials to which the army has been subjected, they are hardly worthy to be named in comparison with the sufferings in store for it this winter, unless the people of the Confederate States, everywhere, come to their relief   The men must have clothing and shoes this winter. They must have something to cover them when sleeping and to protect them from the driving sleet and snow storms when on duty. This *must* be done though our friends at home should have to wear cotton and sit by the fire. The army of Virginia stands guard this day, as it will stand guard this winter, over every hearthstone *throughout the South*. The ragged sentinel who may pace his weary rounds this winter on the bleak spurs of the Blue Ridge, or along the frozen valleys of the Shenandoah, or Rappahannock, will be your sentinel, my friends, at home. It will be for you, and your household, that he encounters the wrath of the tempest, and the dangers of the night. He suffers, and toils, and fights, for you too, brave, true-hearted women of the South. Will you not put shoes and stockings on his feet! Is it not enough that he has written down his patriotism, in crimson characters, from the Rappannock to the Potomac! And must his bleeding feet, too, impress the mark of fidelity on the snows of the coming winter!"

I quote from this appeal, not only to show the deep sympathy of General Lee for his men, but the sufferings endured by our soldiers during the late war. I am satisfied that it requires less real heroism and fortitude to meet the dangers of the battle-field, where the blood is stirred by the deep-toned cannon and the bursting bomb, than to bear the sufferings of the camp.

On the Federal side, General McClellan was steadily engaged in the complete equipment of his army. General Halleck urged him to advance, but he delayed his movement until about the first of November, when, with an army of 150,000 men (see Draper, 2d Vol., 467), he crossed the Potomac on the east side of Blue Ridge, and marched south. General Lee broke up his camp at Opequan, and marched abreast of him on the west side. On the 7th of November winter set in with a heavy snowstorm. How the poor ragged Confederates must have suffered! President Lincoln, vexed that his commander should have wasted (as he thought) the fine autumn weather, removed General McClellan from the command, which act removed also a great weight from the mind of General Lee.

General Burnside was placed in command of the Federal army. At the first battle of Manassas he had commanded a brigade in the centre of the advancing force, and driven the Confederates before him until his men had exhausted every cartridge. He had been at the head of an expedition against Roanoke Island, which commanded the seaboard from Oregon Inlet to Cape Henry, and carried the works and captured the garrison. Having been made a Major General, he drove the rear of Lee's army from Turner's Gap, three days before the battle of Sharpsburg, and, at the latter, he had commanded a corps. He was a modest and honorable gentleman, the bosom friend of McClellan, and was very unwilling to supersede him. His plan was to march directly toward Richmond. On the 20th of November the Federal army, encamped on the heights north of Fredericksburg, "saw on the highlands, south of the city, the red flags and gray lines of their old adversaries." His base was Acquia Creek, and his supplies were brought on the railroad from that place.

General Lee had about 50,000 men, and General Burnside six corps, variously estimated from 80,000 (Draper) to 110,000 (Cooke). Lee, in view of his inferiority in numbers, took a strong position and determined to await an attack. On the morning of the 11th of December, Burnside commenced crossing his troops. Lee had placed Barksdale, with two regiments of Mississippians, along the bank of the river, in the city, to impede construction of pontoon bridges. These sharpshooters did their duty so well that the Federals discontinued the attempt. It was renewed again and again without success, so that General Burnside was provoked and opened a furious fire of artillery upon the city. "One hundred and forty-seven pieces of artillery were employed, which fired more than 7000 rounds of ammunition, and frequently 100 guns in a minute. The town was soon fired, and a dense cloud of smoke enveloped its roofs and steeples. Men, women and children were driven from the town, and hundreds of ladies and children were seen wandering homeless and without shelter over the frozen highway. in thin clothing, knowing not where to find a place of refuge."—(Life of Lee.) The sharpshooters were withdrawn and the crossing continued the whole of the next day.

General Burnside formed his line of battle with General Sumner's grand division on his right, and opposite Lee's left under Longstreet, and General Franklin's on his left, opposite Lee's right under Jackson. The line was four miles long. The plan of attack was for Franklin to march by his left on the river road to attack Jackson's right; then for Sumner to attack Longstreet, and then for Hooker with a corps to attack the centre. A heavy fog covered the river bottom until 10 o'clock. As it began to disperse "Gen. Lee rode along his line to the right, amid the cheers of his men." He was clad in his plain, well-worn uniform, with felt hat, cavalry boots and short cape, without sword, and almost without any distinctions of his rank. In these outward details he differed very much from Generals Jackson and Stuart, who rode with him. Stuart, as usual, wore a fully decorated uniform, sash, black plume, sabre and handsome gauntlets. General Jackson also, on this day, chanced to have exchanged his dingy old coat and sun-scorched cadet cap for a new coat (the gift of Stuart), covered with dazzling buttons, and a cap brilliant with a broad band of gold lace, in which (for him) extraordinary disguise his men scarcely knew him. Lee saw that Franklin was moving a body of men (under Meade) down the river road, when a single gun began to fire rapidly upon it. It was commanded by Major Pelham, of Alabama—almost a boy in years—who continued to hold his exposed position, with great gallantry, until a number of his gunners were killed. Pelham continued the cannonade for about two hours, only retiring when he received a peremptory order from Jackson to do so.

General Lee exclaimed, "It is glorious to see such courage in one so young!" Before the flowers of spring had appeared he fell, in a cavalry fight, at Kelly's Ford. Pelham was, in spite of his youth, an artillerist of the first order of excellence, and his death was greatly lamented. This single gun of his was worked so rapidly that the Federals mistook it for a battery (Swinton). As soon as this impediment was removed, General Meade advanced upon Jackson's right, with his division supported by two others in his rear. Jackson had his men drawn up in three lines to receive him, for he had been expecting the attack for two hours. "The Confederate General Longstreet had personally come so near the Federals under the cloudy veil of the fog, that he could hear their officer's commands. He found that an attack was to be made on Jackson, and notified him of it" (Draper). The Federals were suffered to come within a few hundred yards, when a sudden and furious fire of artillery was opened upon them. In spite of it, they charged bravely up the hill, and encountered the front lines under A. P. Hill. There was a fierce and bloody struggle. But a gap was left in the line by some accident, and they pierced it. They then fell on General Gregg's brigade of reserves, threw it into confusion, and seemed as if they would carry the position. Gregg's brigade, however, was quickly rallied, by its brave commander, who soon afterward fell mortally wounded (this was not General Gregg of Texas). The enemy was checked, and Jackson's second line rapidly advancing, they were met and forced back, step by step, until they were driven down the slope again. Here they were attacked by the brigades of Hoke and Atkinson, and driven beyond the railroad. In this attack, Draper says, Meade lost more than one-third of his troops.

It was now the turn of Lee's left, under Longstreet, to receive an attack, which proved to be far more bloody still. His corps contained the Ninth Alabama, whose steps we are following. The strongest position in this part of the line was Marye's hill. Longstreet's corps was in heavy line of battle behind it and its crest bristled with artillery. The inequalities in the plain beneath were all commanded by guns placed in the right and left, for Lee was accounted the best military engineer that West Point had ever educated, and to his skill in that line much of his success, in pitched battles, may be attributed.

Sumner made ready to storm this hill. He had selected the corps of French and Hancock for that duty, and had Howard's division in readiness to support them. A little before noon, French's corps, preceded by skirmishers, was seen as a long black line, deploying in the rear of the city and advancing to the assault. Behind it followed another black line. It was Hancock's corps. The Confederate batteries were silent until their enemy was half-way across the plain, when, in an instant, they poured forth a tempest of fire. Longstreet said that the gaps made by the artillery could be seen a half-mile off. The thin line moved through the focus of death, quivering but still advancing. The line became thinner and thinner, and becoming too weak to hold together, it halted, and was dispersed. Another attack was made. The line moved through the rain of grape and canister, and closing the gaps torn through it, it seemed as if Fortune, unable to resist such daring, was about to smile on it. Two-thirds of the plain was passed, a few steps more, and the flaming hill itself would give some protection—one moment for taking breath, then a bayonet charge up the heights, and the Confederates would be hurled out of their fortifications. In front was a stone wall. In an instant it was fringed with fire, and hidden in smoke. Enfiladed by the batteries, confronted by a mile of rifles, which were securely discharged behind the fortifications, the surviving assailants were forced back to the shelter of a ravine, within musket shot of the enemy. Here a line of assault was once more formed, and a bayonet charge made on the artillery. Thrice was that attack made—thrice vainly. The storming party, almost annihilated, was compelled to retire."—(Draper.)

General Burnside, when this frightful scene was being enacted, having alighted from his horse, was walking up and down in great agitation. In spite of these murderous assaults, he determined on another. He ordered Hooker to make it. The old soldier protested against it, but sullenly obeyed and opened with artillery upon the stone wall, in order to make a breach in it. This fire was continued until sunset, when the men were formed for the charge. They were ordered to throw aside their knapsacks, overcoats, and haversacks, and not to load their guns. The head of the division charged headlong over the ground already covered with the dead, advanced within fifteen or twenty yards of the stone wall, when they were turned back as quickly as they had advanced. The advance and retreat did not occupy fifteen minutes. Out of 4000 men 1760 were left behind. This great army fell back to the banks of the river, pursued by Stuart with thirty pieces of flying artillery.

The official report made their loss in this battle 13,771, while General Lee reported that of the Confederates at less than 1800. Never was such a victory so cheaply bought, over such gallant foes. General Burnside shortly afterward relinquished the command of the Army of the Potomac, which he could gracefully do as it had been thrust upon him. He was first assigned to the Department of the Ohio—captured Knoxville, repulsed Longstreet, marched his corps thirty miles in one night, to reach "The Wilderness"—and ultimately fell into disfavor, by failing to advance with 50,000 men when the mine at Petersburg was sprung. He was a good corps commander.

During the winter which succeeded the battle of Fredericksburg, the Southern army lay mainly in the woods south of the city, watching the Northern army, which still continued to occupy the country north of it. But Wilcox' brigade (which included the Ninth Alabama) was encamped about four miles above the city, charged with the special duty of watching Bank's Ford and Scott's Dam.

On the 26th of January, 1863, Gen. Joseph Hooker was appointed to command the Army of the Potomac. He had achieved a high reputation, in many battles, as a stubborn fighter and a good subordinate officer. His division had borne the brunt of the battle at Williamsburg. When Pope was retreating, it was Hooker's column which drove Ewell's force from the field, with considerable loss. At South Mountain, Hooker had carried the mountain sides on the right of the gap, while Reno was killed in carrying those on the left. At Sharpsburg he had stood before Stonewall Jackson until his corps was nearly demolished, and he was borne wounded from the field; and at Fredericksburg he commanded the corps, which, after two bloody charges had failed, constituted the "forlorn hope," which made the last fruitless charge, with guns unloaded, and relying entirely on the bayonet.

He reorganized the Federal army. Its strength with infantry and artillery was 120,000, his cavalry 13,000 and he had 400 guns. He determined to attack the Southern army, and his plan was considered very good by military critics. He sent Sedgwick across the Rappahannock below Fredericksburg, to make the impression that his army was to attack on Lee's right, dispatched Stoneman's cavalry in the rear, to cut off communication with Richmond, while the bulk of his great army was rapidly thrown across the upper fords of the river, upon the Confederate left. The great battle of Chancellorsville then occurred; the details of which I shall not relate. as it is not connected with the movements of the Ninth Alabama directly. Stonewall Jackson stormed Hooker's western flank on Saturday evening, the second day of May, 1863—routed the enemy, and then "fell in the arms of victory." Next morning (Sunday) the main battle was fought, and Hooker's army had been driven back in great confusion. Lee was preparing to crush it by a concentrated charge, when news was brought from his right flank which arrested his movements. Sedgwick with a large corps, estimated by the Northern historian, Draper, at 30,000 (see pages 111 and 118 in Vol. 3) was in motion to attack the right flank of Lee. When on Saturday night Jackson had routed Howard's corps, a swift courier was sent to Sedgwick by Hooker, directing him to advance at once. The messenger arrived at midnight, and in half an hour his corps was in motion. A thick fog settled upon the river bottom, and you could not see fifty feet ahead. Generals Early and Barksdale, with 6000 men, occupied Marye's Hill, and the stone wall, which had been made memorable, in the great battle of Fredericksburg; and Sedgwick had first to remove these from his path. Early in the morning an attempt was made in the fog to run over the stone wall. The men moved silently until they came within forty feet, when the Confederates opened with artillery and musketry; and the attacking force retreated in the fog. At 10 A. M., Sedgwick made a combined attack on three different points. "Shaler's column (in the centre) was almost blown away by the heavy artillery fire. The attacking force reeled and staggered—large gaps were made in it, and when it reached the enemy's works it had apparently dwindled into a mere skirmishing line. About 1000 men were lost in ten minutes, but the object was accomplished." (Draper.)

The same morning, General Wilcox, excited by the sound of artillery above and below him, marched his Alabama brigade from Scott's dam, out to an old field on the plank road, near the "Yellow House," and there awaited orders. He was instructed by Lee to meet Sedgwick, and delay his march as long as possible, until he could send reinforcements to him. A messenger also came from Barksdale, asking for immediate assistance. Wilcox marched his brigade at "double-quick," and reached the top of the hill near the Stansburg House, in Fredericksburg, just in time to see the Federals go over the works on Marye's Heights, and the National flag unfurled. As he advanced down the hill he was met by a rapid fire from their sharpshooters. The general formed line of battle; but it was evident that he could not withstand the triumphant foe. The enemy had possession of the nearest road to Salem Heights, and for fear they might reach that point, he marched rapidly to seize it, and protect General Lee's flank. On reaching Salem Church a line of battle was formed across the plank road, with two regiments to the right, and the rest of the brigade on the left of it. After the line was formed, four brigades arrived, under command of General McLaws, which were formed on the right and left of the line. He was the ranking officer, but no change was made in the plan of Wilcox. The two generals took position in the rear of the right of the Ninth Alabama, which was placed directly in rear of the Tenth Alabama, about thirty yards. The generals were surprised that Sedgwick delayed his coming. But his command had been boggling about in the fog during the night, had fought a hard battle, and he had given them rest until 1 P. M. His command was formed in line of battle between 3 and 4 o'clock, and charged upon ours. The whole weight of the assaulting column was directed against the centre of our line at the plank road. They advanced within ninety yards before firing, and the discharge was so deadly that it scattered the Tenth Alabama. It was a critical moment, and Major Williams gave the command, " Forward, Ninth Alabama." Just as the regiment rose to obey this order, a destructive volley was fired into them, at a distance of not more than forty yards, by the Sixth Maine, and the One Hundred and Twenty-third New York regiments, which did great damage. Eleven men of Company K, from Marshall county—Captain Sheffield—fell dead in their tracks, without firing a gun, and almost twice that number wounded. Companies C, from Lawrence, Captain Couch; O'Neal's old Company D, from Lauderdale, Captain Houston, and H from Limestone and Hobb's old Company (commanded now by Capt. G. C. Smith), were next to K in their losses. Company A from Mobile, commanded first by Captain Ripley, and then by Captain Murphy, stationed in a school house forty yards in advance of our line, after firing a volley at the advancing enemy, were prisoners in their hands for a while, and this company did not suffer as did the rest. In Company D, Charles Sharp, and Josiah Whitten were killed, and amongst the wounded are remembered, Thomas Harman, of Florence, and Dr. J. R. Edwards, of Courtland. Of C, the Lawrence company, E. W. Sale was killed, and N. Garrett wounded, and many others not yet ascertained. (I am indebted to Hon. E. P. Patterson, of Savannah, Tenn., who was a member of Company D, for most of the foregoing account of this battle. He thinks Captain Murphy, of Mobile, was killed in this engagement, with the wounds he received at Williamsburg still unhealed.) This first collision was also fatal to the Federals, for 150 dead bodies were picked up on the ground where the Sixth Maine, and One Hundred and Twenty-third New York stood.

With a wild yell the brigade moved forward, right and left at the same time, and the Federals were driven back. The battle, however, continued until night fell on the combatants without any decisive result. In this conflict the losses of the enemy are estimated at 3000 men. It is admitted that Sedgwick while on the south side of the river lost 5000 men. (Draper.) Of these 1000 fell at Marye's Heights, and a few on the evening of the 4th, so we conclude that fully 3000 must have fallen at Salem Church This battle, which was equal in magnitude to that of the 8th January, 1815, was so overshadowed by the terrible conflict which occurred on the same day at Chancellorsville, that no details of it are given in history. For this reason I have labored to ascertain the facts, and record them. The above account, however, is quite partial, and if some competent military man who witnessed it, would forward a full account, it will afford me pleasure to have it published, as a supplement to this article.

On Monday morning General Lee went in person with three of Anderson's brigades to Salem Church, and formed line of battle with the whole force there. For some cause, the attack was not begun until late in the afternoon. Then the whole line advanced upon Sedgwick, Lee's object being to cut him off from Bank's Ford. He failed in this, the stubborn resistance of the Federal forces enabling them to hold their ground until darkness put an end to the conflict. That night Sedgwick retreated rapidly across the river on a pontoon which had been previously laid, Southern cannon firing constantly upon the retreating column. The next morning General Lee returned to Chancellorsville, and spent the day in making preparations for a decisive attack on General Hooker. When, however, the advance was about to commence, it was found that the works were entirely deserted, and that General Hooker had recrossed the river, spreading pine boughs on the pontoon bridge, to muffle the sound of his artillery wheels. Thus ended one of the most remarkable campaigns on record, of only nine days' duration, during which four battles had occurred, and a Federal force of 120,000 men had crossed the Rappahannock "with all the pomp and circumstance of war," and had been defeated by 47,000 Confederates of all arms (for Longstreet with two divisions was south of the Potomac), and the Federals had sought safety by recrossing the river during the dark hours of the night.

The elation of the Southern people was excessive. The hope of having the Southern Confederacy acknowledged by the Washington Government became strong. The occasion was embraced by Mr. Stephens, Vice President, to propose negotiations. He wrote to President Davis, offering to go in person to Washington, and confer with the authorities. He was summoned to Richmond by telegraph; but by that time Lee's vanguard was entering Maryland, and Gettysburg speedily followed; and with this repulse ended all hopes of peace.

We will resume the thread of our narrative. After the defeat of General Hooker, General Lee reorganized his army. Longstreet's two divisions were recalled, and the army, which had been increased by new levies, was divided into three corps, of three divisions each. Ewell succeeded Jackson in command of Jackson's old corps, Longstreet retained in command of his old corps, and A. P. Hill was assigned to the command of a third corps (made up portions of two others). In this new arrangement, Wilcox' brigade was assigned to Hill. The artillery of the army was made a distinct command, and placed under General Pendleton, who had been Lee's Chief of Artillery. General Lee was then in command of a fine army of eighty thousand men, of all arms, composed of veterans, who had followed him on many a hard-fought field, through fire and blood. He was now ready for the

Invasion of Pennsylvania.

Longstreet moving first into the Shenandoah valley, burst upon the force of General Milroy (who had ruled the people with a rod of iron), and defeated him. Ewell's corps followed, and as soon as Hill, who had been left behind to watch Hooker, found that he was moving northward, marched on the same route traveled by Longstreet and Ewell. The cavalry had been brought up to a high state of efficiency. On the 8th of June a brilliant pageant, succeeded by a dramatic and stirring incident, was now to prelude the march of Lee. A review of Stuart's cavalry took place in the presence of General Lee, who was sitting on his horse, motionless, on a slight knoll, while above him, from a lofty staff, waved a large Confederate flag. The long column of about 8000 men was first drawn up in line, and afterward passed in front of Lee, at a gallop, Stuart and his staff officers leading the charge, with sabres at tierce point. There was a sham fight with the "Horse Artillery," who received the cavalry with a thunderous discharge of blank ammunition, which rolled like the roar of battle, among the surrounding hills. This sham fight was kept up for some time, and puzzled the enemy on the opposite side of the Rappahannock. On the next morning, to ascertain what this discharge of artillery meant, two divisions of Federal cavalry, supported by two brigades of "picked infantry," were sent across the river, to beat up the quarters of

Stuart, and find out what was going on. The most extensive cavalry fight of the whole war followed. (*Life of Lee.*) Stuart was attacked in front and rear at the same time. He went to the front in a gallop, brought his artillery to bear on the advancing columns. The enemy's artillery was captured, and recaptured, several times, and finally remained with Stuart. The contest was mainly with the sabre, and was distinguished by numerous instances of great personal valor, and continued nearly the whole day, when the enemy which were computed at 15,000 men, were pursued across the river. This battle of Fleetwood Hill was never surpassed by any cavalry fight in America or Europe.

Lee's columns were in full march for the plentiful fields of Pennsylvania. One object was to find subsistence for his half-starved men. A heavy requisition which he had made on the Commissary Department, at Richmond was returned with this endorsement: " You must seek for your supplies in Pennsylvania." His several corps crossed the Potomac on pontoons at Shepherdstown and Williamsport, and united at Hagerstown, Md.

The Ninth Alabama; Gettysburg Campaign.

General Hill's corps was the last to leave Fredericksburg. On the 5th of May the Ninth Alabama was watching the enemy along the Plank road, in a torrent of rain, when the lightning struck a tree near the head of the regiment, knocking down quite a number of men, three of whom had to be removed in an ambulance; and every one in the regiment felt the shock. From this time, until the 13th of June, when the march commenced, the men were very much exposed on picket, not being allowed to have any fire. I have before me an account of the daily marches of Wilcox' brigade into Pennsylvania, written by a distinguished lawyer of Tennessee, then a gallant young soldier of the Ninth Alabama, from which I will make a few extracts: " The 18th of June was one of the hottest days I ever remember, and, I think, as many as a dozen men in the regiment suffered from sunstroke during the day. We were marching through long dusty lanes, beneath a burning sun, with the dust choking us, and the suffering was fearful. On the morning of the 19th we marched to Front Royal, where we remained until 4 o'clock in the afternoon, as it was said, for the pontoons to be laid across the Shenandoah. But when the head of the column commenced crossing just at dark, we found the pontoons still upon the wagons. When the Ninth Alabama reached the river, the rain was pouring in torrents, and it was dark as pitch. The opposite bank was very steep and slippery, and we had to climb it " on all fours." Some of the men would nearly reach the top, when an unlucky slip would send them back again into the river. After getting across, we fell into gullies and waded through briar patches, until we ran against a fence, which we converted into beds, by laying the rails upon the ground and lying upon them, to keep out of the mud and water, and where we slept, with the darkness and rain for a covering." (Here, reader, you are permitted to go behind the curtain, and see something of the hard life of the common soldier.) " On the 24th we crossed the Potomac at Mill Ford, near Shepherdstown, the water being from three to four feet deep, but we waded it, and kept in good order. As the Ninth Alabama was wading the river, they struck up the song ' Maryland, my Maryland,' and woke the echoes of the hills, far and wide. On the 25th we reached the rendezvous of Hagerstown.

Here the three corps of General Lee's army had concentrated. All arms of the service were here except one. Where was Stuart and his cavalry? Where was the force which, heretofore, in every previous invasion, had hung like a curtain between Lee and the enemy, veiling the movements of his own army, but imparting to him exact information as to theirs. Stuart had been ordered by General Lee to observe the enemy, to obstruct his march, and if he crossed the Potomac, to cross his cavalry and take position on the right of Lee's army as it advanced. Circumstances occurred which rendered it impossible to comply with his orders. General Hooker was very tardy in following Lee. He remained in his camp until Lee's army (with the front marching and the rear stationary) was stretched out for one hundred miles. Hooker, with one eye on Richmond and the other on Washington, remained for ten days after Lee had commenced his march. During all this time Stuart was constantly on the alert, to cover the movements of our army. When Hooker did move, Stuart harassed his rear. It became absolutely necessary that Stuart's cavalry should be driven back. This was undertaken in a deliberate manner. Three corps of cavalry with a division of infantry, and a full supply of artillery, were sent from Manassas to drive him back. A fierce struggle ensued, in which Stuart fought the great force opposed to him, from every hill and knoll. But he was forced back steadily, in spite of a determined resistance, and at Upperville, a hand to hand sabre fight wound up the movement, in which the Federal cavalry was checked, when Stuart fell back toward Paris, crowded the mountain side with his cannon, and awaited the final attack. This was not made. The Federal force fell back; and the next mórning Stuart followed them on the same road over which he had so rapidly retreated. When the Federal army crossed the Potomac near Leesburg, Stuart was at Middleburg. For twenty-three days his men had been almost constantly in the saddle, his horses were worn down with service, and a poor supply of provender. He was in the confidence of Lee and from his plan he concluded that he could not possibly overtake him on the route he had traveled; but could join him by making a straight cut across the country, for Harrisburg. Accordingly he passed through Maryland between Hooker and Washington, stopped to capture a large train of Federal wagons at Rockville, was delayed by combats with Federal cavalry at Westminster and Hanovertown, and was at Carlisle, when he was called by his chief to the field of Gettysburg, where he arrived on the second day of the battle.

The battle of Gettysburg was fought on the first three days of July, 1863. When it commenced Lee's forcés happened to be scattered. A part was approaching Harrisburg and another had captured York, but the Federal army, reorganized, and filled up, and under a new commander, General Meade, was rapidly concentrating near Gettysburg. General Lee intended to march toward Harrisburg, but on the night of the 29th of June he was informed by his scouts of the advance of the Federal army. He sent immediate orders for the concentration of his troops, and on the next day commenced his march toward Gettysburg with Hill's corps in front. The first of July his troops were crossing South Mountain on the Cashtown road. " It was a beautiful day and a beautiful season of the year. The fields were green with grass, or golden with ripening grain, over which passed a gentle breeze, raising waves upon the brilliant surface. The landscape was broken, here and there, by woods; in the south rose the blue range of the South Mountains; the sun was shining through showery clouds, and in the east the sky was spanned by a rainbow. This peaceful scene was now disturbed by the thunders of artillery and the rattle of musketry." The head of Hill's column had descended the mountain side, traversed the valley and began to ascend the western acclivity of Seminary ridge, when it came into collision with Buford's Federal Cavalry. At that moment Wilcox' Brigade, which was marching in the rear of the column, was halted as a reserve on the top of the mountain, from which they could see all the shifting scenes of the battle as they transpired below them. The cavalry fell back before the infantry to the top of the ridge. When they disappeared behind it a long line of Federal infantry, commanded by General Reynolds, appeared. When the two infantry lines first met, the leading Federal brigade was driven back by one from Mississippi. In their turn the Federals nearly surrounded Archer's brigade and took several hundred prisoners, including their general. The affair had become a hot engagement, Reynolds ordered forward Howard's corps, and shortly afterward fell mortally wounded by a shot in the neck. About this time General Lee passed Wilcox' brigade on the way to the scene of the conflict. By this time the sky was darkened, here and there, by clouds of smoke rising from barns and dwelling houses set on fire by shells. Lee ordered Hill's corps to be closed up, and reinforcements to be sent forward rapidly to the point of action. The field was contested stubbornly by both parties, and the action became a regular battle. Hill was hard pressed —when fortunately, from the heights north of the battle-field, was seen a long gray line. Their march was rapid, they had but few wagons, but the ammunition trains were all up, and the red battle flags were waving over their heads. This gray serpent, winding in and out, among the distant hills, was Rhodes, coming, with his Alabamians, to decide the day. Rhodes went promptly into action on the enemy's flank, without "waiting for an invitation." Howard extended his line, bending it to meet the new danger and attacked furiously. Rhodes returned it with interest. It was a bloody affair—when Early, in turn, made his appearance from the north. When he came into the meleé, Rhodes made an impetuous attack on the Federal centre, and Early on its right, with General Gordon's brigade in front (Gordon, who was said " never to be so happy as when the air was full of bullets "), and, under this combined attack, the Federals gave way and retreated in great disorder to Cemetery Hill, where General Howard, as he advanced in the morning had left one of his divisions with three batteries of artillery. It was a decided Southern victory. The enemy lost 10,000 men and sixteen pieces of artillery. The brigade of Wilcox was ordered forward, but before they reached the field the enemy were in full retreat.

General Meade, who had been only two days in command, was that day fourteen miles south of Gettysburg, where he was arranging a defensive line on Pipe creek, when he received news of a battle having been fought, and of Reynolds having been killed. He was one of his most trusted and able generals. He sent General Hancock forward to take command, and he himself arrived at midnight, under a full moon, at the Cemetery. It is a poor index to the Christian civilization of the age, that the council of war, which was a prelude to a battle in which more than 50,000 human beings fell, was held by one commander amidst the glistening sepulchral monuments of a burial ground, and by the other in the quiet grove of a seminary, which was dedicated to the study of theology.

Second Day of the Battle.

The Northern army was posted on Cemetery Ridge, running north and south, with the town of Gettysburg nestling in the valley at the northern end. The Southern army occupied a parallel ridge (Seminary), with a valley of a half mile wide, dotted with farm houses, barns, orchards, pastures and wheat fields between them. The advantage of position was in favor of Meade, for the ridge on which he had drawn out his line of battle was higher—it commanded the other—its front was convex and its extremities tending together, the reserve was in thirty minutes' march of any part of the line; signal flags set on points over-looking the scene could be seen from one to another in the rear; moreover, the rocky ledges (with a little improvement) made substantial breastworks. General Lee pre-ferred to await an attack, but he was in an enemy's country, and lacked provisions, while General Meade was on his own soil, and had abundant supplies. Meade could wait, but Lee could not. Both commanders prepared most carefully for a contest, which proved to be the turning point of the war. The whole forenoon was passed in prepara-tion. "There was scarcely a sound to disturb the silence, and it was difficult to believe that nearly 200,000 men were watching each other across this narrow valley, ready at the word to advance and tear each other to pieces." Down in the valley were fields of ripening wheat, and here and there, unconscious of the impending tempest, cattle quietly grazing.

General Lee, in forming his line of battle, had placed Longstreet's corps on his right, Hill's in his centre, and Ewell's on his left. Wilcox' brigade occupied the ex-treme right of Hill's corps, and stood next to Barksdale's Mississippians, who were on the left in Longstreet's corps. Lee was not ready until 4 o'clock in the afternoon, when the signal was given, and Longstreet suddenly opened a heavy artillery fire on the position opposite to him. the guns of Hill opened from the ridge on the left, and those of Ewell from the extreme left. Then occurred the charge of Hood, to seize "Little Round-Top," 280 feet above the valley, so well known to history. General Vincent had been sent from the Federal side to occupy it, while Hood came up on the other with a like purpose. A violent struggle ensued, in which Vincent lost his life and Hood a leg. Then, too, occurred Longstreet's charge, in which the enemy were driven back to the ridge. To show the part borne by Wilcox' Alabama brigade in this day's fight, I here insert an account of it, written by Hon. E. D. Patterson, at my special request:

" Early in the morning of the 2d our line of battle was formed, with the Tenth and Eleventh Alabama a little in advance of the rest of the brigade. These regiments were much annoyed by the enemy's sharpshooters, who were posted behind a stone wall. They were soon dislodged, and our brigade formed a line of battle along the stone wall. Quite a number were wounded in this skirmish, among whom was Major Fletcher, of the Eleventh Alabama. As soon as the Ninth got into position Company D, of Landerdale, was ordered forward as skirmishers, Capt. J. M. Crow being in command, Lieut. W. J. Cannon leading the first platoon, and I the second. I joined the skirmishers of the Second Florida, on my left, with my right at a large barn, which afforded a good protection, and a good point from which to watch the movements of the enemy.

We held possession of this barn for several hours, and until the Federals brought a battery to play upon it, when I withdrew my men, placing them on a line with the rest of the company. The line of skirmishers were then withdrawn, and we took our places in line with the regiment. It soon became evident that the Federals were moving up men to take possession of the barn (where they could have annoyed us greatly), when Lieut. Rufus Jones, of Company G, of Limestone county, ran through a shower of bullets to the barn, set fire to it and ran back without getting hurt. He was noted for his gallantry. About 3 o'clock in the afternoon, brigade after brigade, and battery after battery of the enemy were moved rapidly toward our right, and we knew the time for action had come. We were not in suspense, for, at a signal, our artillery opened on them with a deadly fire, and then we heard upon our right a cheer, or rather a yell, such as Southern soldiers only can give, followed by a terrible crash of musketry that told us that Longstreet was hurling his forces against the enemy's left, but they were too strong to give way easily. In half an hour they were retreating, followed closely by Longstreet. They were falling back right down the front of our line, and were unable to reform their shattered lines unless fresh troops were sent out to relieve them. But, just at this time, we saw solid masses moving up in our immediate front, and coming between us and victory. The spirit of the troops was never better, and as General Wilcox rode along down our line, giving the order to charge, cheer after cheer filled the air, almost drowning the sound of the shells which were bursting above and around us. The old battle-scarred banner of the Ninth, which had waved amid the wild tempests of battle at Williamsburg, Cold Harbor, Fraser's Farm, Sharpsburg and Salem Church, never rose more proudly than that day, as we moved forward in a storm of shot, shell and canister, and felt confident of victory.

The battle raged furiously, but our line moved onward, straight onward. Grape and canister came plunging through our ranks; bullets, thick as hail-storms in winter, were falling on every side. It was terrible, yet our men faltered not; and we succeeded in breaking their first and second line of battle, capturing many prisoners, artillery and colors. Here, for the first time since the war began, we met the famous Irish brigade. The troops upon their immediate right and left had given way, leaving them exposed not only to a fire in front, but an oblique fire from both flanks. Yet, under this terrible ordeal they did not run, but retreated slowly and in good order—returning our fire, but leaving the ground literally covered with their dead. One regiment of this brigade formed a hollow square around a piece of artillery and carried it some distance by hand, loading and firing it very rapidly, the square opening to allow them to fire, but at last they had to abandon it. We drove them to the foot of the ridge on which was posted their reserve artillery; but there receiving reinforcements, and seeing our terribly thinned ranks, they made another stand. Wilcox, excited by the valor of his troops, moved among them, and before them, as if " courting death " by his own daring intrepidity. The fight still goes on—blood flows like water—but few were left unhurt, and, with ranks torn and bleeding, we felt that capture or death was inevitable if we remained longer. Some one gives the order to fall back—no one knows from whence it came—some fall back and some do not—there were no longer organized regiments or companies —Barksdale's brigade had completely overlapped ours, and we were mingled in inextricable confusion—the air was hot, and filled with sticks, stones, dust and black smoke

—almost suffocating us, when I, with a few Mississippians, and a number of other officers of the Ninth Alabama (in all about fifty men), attempted to make our way to where the Confederate line was re-forming. After getting back about a hundred yards we found ourselves confronted by a line of Federal soldiers. A line of guns was leveled at us, and an officer cried out, "Surrender, you d—n gray-backs!"—and our part in the battle was over. The officers of the Ninth taken prisoners that day were Capt. G. C. Smith (afterward Lieutenant Colonel); Captain John Chisholm, of Company I (O'Neal's old company), and Lieutenants Cartwright, Chisholm, Sharp, Gamble, Nicholson, and myself. The loss of the Ninth on that day was very heavy. Amongst them were Joseph McMurray, of Lauderdale county, who lost a leg, and of the Lawrence volunteers, Lieut. J. K. McBride, who lost an arm; and privates Noel C. Graham, and Jeff. Lindsey, who were killed. Many of our surgeons and chaplains, when General Lee retreated, were left behind to attend to the severely wounded, and these were sent to Federal prisons—most of them to Fort McHenry, and detained about a year. Amongst these were Dr. Minor, of the Ninth, Dr. John M. Hayes, of the Thirty-ninth, and Rev. M. L. Whitten. No distinction was made between them and soldiers in the ranks.

Thus ended the second day of the battle, which had lasted about four hours, when night, in mercy, cast a veil of darkness over the scene,

The Federals acknowledged a loss of 10,000. Ours was fully that much. General Lee had on his right driven the enemy back a half-mile, and on his left Ewell had carried Culp's Hill.

The morning of the third day of this battle dawned with broken clouds, and the sun shining fitfully through them. The attack on Ewell's position, which he had gained on Cemetery Ridge, was made at early dawn by a combined force, and after four hours hard fighting that stubborn soldier was driven from the ridge. Generals Lee, Hill and Longstreet rode along the lines, forming some new combinations. The decision was to attack the Federal centre under Hancock, with a column of 15,000 men under command of Pickett. At 1 P. M. the clouds broke away, and it became still and sultry. Suddenly a cannonade was commenced, with 145 guns, by General Lee and continued for two hours. General Hancock pronounced it "the most terrific one I ever witnessed—one hardly ever paralleled." At 3 P. M. Pickett's line was arranged behind Seminary Ridge. It was a mile in length. Kemper's and Garnett's brigades were in front and Armistead's brigade in the rear. Two or three hundred yards in the rear, on the left, was Pettigrew's division, and, on the right, Wilcox' brigade. Pickett's troops were fresh, having only joined the main army, with Stuart's cavalry, the evening before. Pettigrew's division were new recruits, never having been in action before, and Wilcox' brigade of Alabamians were veterans, but had taken an active part in the struggle under Longstreet the evening before, and their ranks were thinned considerably and the men were jaded. To Pickett was assigned the main duty of breaking the enemy's centre, and to Wilcox and Pettigrew to cover the right and left of the advancing column, and protect it from a flank attack.

Pickett's division was Virginia veterans, and the manner in which they moved in this charge, challenged the admiration of both armies. The opposing ridges at this point were about one mile asunder; and across the space Pickett's force moved at the word, and advanced slowly, and perfectly dressed, with its red battle-flags flying, and the sunshine darting from their gun-barrels and bayonets. The two armies were silent, concentrating their whole attention upon the slow and ominous advance of men, who seemed to be in no haste, and resolved to allow nothing to arrest them. When the column had reached a point about midway between the opposing heights, the Federal artillery suddenly opened a furious fire upon them, which inflicted considerable loss. This however, had no effect upon the troops, who continued to advance slowly in the same excellent order, without exhibiting any desire to return the fire. Where shell tore gaps in the ranks, the men quietly closed up, and the hostile front advanced in the same ominous silence toward the slope, where the real struggle all felt would really begin. They were within a few hundred yards of the hill, when suddenly a rapid cannon fire thundered on their right, and shell and canister from nearly fifty pieces of artillery, swept the southern line, enfiladed it, and threw the right into disorder; which however soon disappeared. The column closed up and continued to advance unmoved toward the heights. At last the moment came. The steady "common-time" step become "quick-time;" this had changed to "double-quick," then the column rushed headlong on the enemy's works." (*Life of Lee.*)

At this juncture, Pettigrew's division, which was composed of new recruits, began to waver. Perceiving that the Federals were moving around their flanks strong parties, they became panic stricken, their lines dissolved, and they doubled up into knots. They then fled in confusion to the rear. All but one of their field officers had been killed, and they fell back under command of a Major. "Pettigrew's division had mustered 2800 strong; at roll-call next morning 835 men answered to their names; many, however, of the lost had been taken prisoners." Perhaps during the whole war raw troops had never been subjected to so fiery an ordeal, or had endured it longer.

Pickett's column, though unsupported on the left, still rushed forward, only pausing to return the fire of the Federals. The smoke soon enveloped the combatants. There was a hurricane of musketry. As they emerged from the cloud, they were led by Armistead, and reached the Stone Wall occupied by Webb. His two regiments fell back on the forces in the rear. The Virginians rushed over the first line of breastworks and charged on the second. This was defended by a strong line, for reinforcements had been coming from all sides. A desperate hand-to-hand conflict now ensued. Men and officers were all fighting together. The attempt to carry this strong line was a desperate one. They were driven back with a frightful loss. Ot fifteen field officers only one was unhurt. Of the brigade officers Garnett was killed; Armistead fell mortally wounded, as he leaped on the breastworks, cheering and waving his hat, and Kemper fell severely wounded. From the first rush of this column to its repulse, was but a few minutes. As Wilcox brought up his brigade from its position, some distance in the rear, Pickett was falling back discomfited. Nevertheless he moved forward to the assault; but the musketry fire being concentrated by the Federals on his brigade, it was literally hurled back. His loss was frightful, but we will speak of that hereafter.

"Seeing from his place on Seminary Ridge the unfortunate results of the attack, Lee mounted his horse and rode forward to meet and encourage the retreating troops. He spoke in a kindly voice to the men. 'All this will come right in the end. We want all good and true men to rally here.' To the badly wounded he uttered words of sympathy and kindness; to those but slightly wounded he said, 'Come, bind up your wound, and take a musket, my friend.' Meanwhile the men continued to stream back, pursued by the triumphant roar of the enemy's artillery, which swept the whole valley and slope of the Seminary ridge with shot and shell. As he was riding about the fringe of the woods General Wilcox, who had advanced about the time of Pickett's repulse, and was speedily thrown back with loss, rode up and said, almost sobbing as he spoke, that 'his brigade was nearly destroyed.' Lee held out his hand to him as he was speaking, and grasping that of his subordinate in a friendly manner, replied with great gentleness and kindness: 'Never mind, General, all this has been my fault. It is I who have lost this fight, and you must help me out of it the best way you can.' The supreme composure of the commander-in-chief communicated itself to the troops, who soon got together again, and lay down quietly in the line of battle, along the crest of the ridge, where Lee placed them as they came up. In front of them the guns used in the great cannonade were still in position, and Lee was making every preparation in his power for the probable event of an instant assault upon him, in his disordered condition, by the enemy. It was obvious that the situation of affairs at the moment was such as to render such an attack highly perilous to the Southern troops. Thus ended the last great conflict on Federal soil."

The Federal loss in killed and wounded amounted to 23,190. The Confederate loss must have been larger. Federal historians estimate it at 36,000 men. This was the grand climacteric of the war. At the very moment (4 o'clock) that Pickett's charge was repulsed at Gettysburg, 700 miles to the southwest at Vicksburg, Pemberton, reduced to the direst straits, was sitting with Grant under an oak tree, surrendering his fortunes and army.

After the repulse, Lee withdrew Ewell's corps from the extreme right of the enemy, and forming a compact line of battle on Seminary ridge, awaited the assault of General Meade. No attack was made. On the 4th of July he buried his dead, and on that night retreated toward Williamsport on the Potomac, forty miles distant. His amunition had been nearly exhausted by the three days fight, and provisions could not be procured. It was dreadful weather, but he continued his retreat for fear the Potomac might rise in his rear, and cut off his retreat. He reached the river on the 7th, to find that the enemy's cavalry had destroyed the pontoon, which had been laid for his army, and to his dismay, that the Potomac was so swollen that it was unfordable. On the 12th of July Meade appeared before Lee, who occupied a strong position, and was in line of battle. Meade hesitated in attacking during that day and the next. In the meantime Lee collected a portion of the pontoon which the enemy had destroyed, built some new boats, and had a bridge constructed in his rear by the evening of the 13th, when the river had fallen and was fordable, so that he was able to cross his army safely into Virginia, and so ended the invasion of Pennsylvania.

General Lee repaired to his old camp on the banks of the Opequan, where he rested his weary troops a short time. His own iron frame also needed relaxation. Colonel Freemantle, of the British Army, who had been with him during this arduous campaign, has described his person and habits at this time; and a short extract may not be out of place here: " General Lee is, almost without exception, the handsomest man of his age I ever saw. He is tall, broad-shouldered, very well made, a thorough soldier in appearance, and his manners are most courteous and full of dignity. He is a perfect gentleman in every respect. I can imagine no man who has so few enemies, or is so universally esteemed. He has none of the small vices, such as smoking, drinking, chewing, and swearing; and his bitterest enemy never accused him of any of the greater ones." The portrait is very attractive to the eye and remains in many memories now, when the sound of battle is hushed, and the great leader, in turn, has finished his life-battle, and lain down in peace.

As soon as General Meade marched South on the east side of the Blue Ridge, General Lee kept *pari passu* with him on the west side, and at length the two armies were found again confronting each other on the Rappahannock. Here Longstreet with his corps was detached to reinforce General Bragg, and on the other side, Hooker with the Eleventh and Twelfth corps, to strengthen the army of Chattanooga. On the 9th of October, General Lee commenced a flank movement on General Meade, with a view of bringing on a battle in some good position, for which the latter was equally anxious, provided he could select his own battle-field. This campaign was remarkable for skilful manœuvres and romantic incidents. The fighting (except in one instance) was done by the cavalry. General Stuart, in the Gettysburg campaign, where he was constantly in combats, had lost one-third of his force; but his white plume floated as high in the breeze, and his spirit was as joyous when he drew his sabre, as ever. Hill, who was raised up in that section of country, led the advance " by circuitous and concealed roads," and Stuart moved between the two armies in such a manner as to conceal the movements of his friends. General Meade was so much in doubt, that he moved his forces first north and then south, and then again marched rapidly toward Manassas, with Stuart and his cavalry in his front, " when, on the night of the 12th, he met with one of the incidents which were thickly strewn throughout his romantic career. He was near Auburn, just at nightfall, when as the rear guard closed up, information reached him from that quarter that the Federal army was passing directly in his rear. Nearly, at the same moment, intelligence arrived, that another column of the enemy, consisting like the first, of infantry, cavalry and artillery, was moving across his front. Stuart was now in an actual trap, and his situation was perilous in the extreme. He was enclosed between two moving walls of enemies, and if discovered his fate seemed sealed. He ordered his troopers to remain silent and motionless in their saddles during the night, ready at any instant to move, at the order; and thus passed the long hours of darkness—the Southern horsemen as silent as phantoms—the Federal columns passing rapidly, with the roll of artillery wheels, the tramp of cavalry horses, and the shuffling sound of feet, on both sides of his command—the column moving in rear of Stuart being distant but two or three hundred yards. The opportunity for escape came at dawn. The Federal rear, under General Caldwell, had bivouacked near, and had just kindled fires to cook their breakfast, when Stuart suddenly opened upon them with his horse artillery, and as he said in his report, knocked over coffee pots, and other utensils for the moment, when the men least expected it. He directed a rapid fire on the disordered troops, and under cover of it, wheeled to the left, and emerged safely" (Life of Lee).

Hill's infantry, with Cook's and Wilcox' brigades in front, overtook the rear of Meade's army under General Warren. Seeing the Federal column hastening along the railroad to pass Broad Run, Hill ordered a prompt attack, and Cook's brigade led the charge. General Warren promptly place his men behind the railroad embankment, who poured a destructive fire into the ranks as they came down the slope, which killed and wounded a considerable number of them. General Cook himself fell wounded. General Warren carried off five captured Napoleon guns. General Wilcox' brigade made an attempt to recover them, but failed with some loss. In the Ninth Alabama there were none killed, but two wounded, Before he could be arrested, Warren had crossed and joined the main army on its retreat. General Lee sent Stuart to follow the enemy, and returned to his camp in Culpeper.

General Stuart had the boldness to flank the Federal army; and attack the second corps. This caused great excitement, for at first it was supposed to be Lee's army. But as soon as they ascertained that they had only dismounted troopers before them, the infantry charged, and Stuart retired toward Warrenton. This audacious assault upon the infantry so excited the Federal commander that he sent a considerable body of cavalry, under Kilpatrick, to overtake and destroy him. Stuart was at Buckland when he heard that he was pursued. Gen. Fitz Lee was his second in command. He proposed that Stuart would return toward Warrenton with Hampton's division, while with his own he should remain hidden from sight, on the enemy's left flank. Then at a given signal, Stuart was to face about, and he, Gen. Fitz Lee, would attack them in flank. This plan was carried out strictly. When the sudden boom of a gun from Fitz Lee gave the signal, Stuart wheeled and made a furious charge upon his pursuers. Fitz Lee in turn fell upon his flank; and Kilpatrick's whole force was routed, and pursued back to Buckland at full speed.

Nothing of much interest occurred until the spring of 1864, when General Grant made his appearance.

Amongst the numerous casualties at Gettysburg in the Ninth Alabama are remembered the following: In Company C—Lieut. J. K. McBride, who lost an arm and was taken prisoner; Privates Jeff. Lindsay and Noel C. Graham, who were killed. Company D—J. M. Crow, commanding; Lieut. E. D. Patterson, made prisoner; Jos. McMurray, lost a leg, and Ashbury Williams, wounded, and both made prisoners. Company E—Lieut. J. H. Sharpe was made prisoner. Company F—Lieut. J. H. Cartwright was made prisoner. Company H—Capt. G. C. Smith and Lieut. R. C. Jones were both made prisoners. Company I—Capt. John L. Chisholm and Lieut. Alexander C. Chisholm, prisoners; Sergt. S. J. Matthews, right leg shot off; John G. Durbin, grape shot through the hip, from which he died some years afterward, and E. C. Holden—all these were captured. Company K—Lieut. Edward Nicholson, a prisoner.

There is in the minds of the few survivors of this regiment a clear recollection of their comrades who fell, but they can not specify "where."

The Ninth Alabama—Grant and Lee.

On the 9th of March, 1864, Gen. Ulysses S. Grant was commissioned Lieutenant

General, and assigned by President Lincoln "to the command of all the armies of the United States." He had distinguished himself in the southwest, as a commander, at Belmont, Fort Henry, Fort Donelson, Shiloh; he had fought five battles around Vicksburg and captured it; and had defeated General Bragg before Chattanooga. General Meade he still retained at the head of the Army of the Potomac, but he came in person to superintend its operations. For the first time, Grant, who had shown his superiority over all opponents in the South, and Lee, who occupied the same relative position in the northern section of the theatre of war, encountered each other. The fortifications made by both these generals, wherever they camped for one night, until the close of the war, attest the caution with which every movement was made, and the respect they had for each other as commanders. That respect with General Lee became a personal one when, after the surrender, there was a threat of a prosecution for treason against him, and General Grant indignantly declared that he would resign his commission if the faith he had plighted to General Lee was broken by the United States Government. The new policy adopted by General Grant, for the prosecution of the war, was instead of having the Federal armies to act separately and independently (as they had done) to have union and vigorous and continuous operations of all the troops, regardless of the season and the weather, to bring about a speedy termination of the war. Consequently, on the same day (4th of May, 1864,) on which the Army of the Potomac crossed the Rapidan, every other Federal army commenced an aggressive march leading to a common centre.

This army was divided into three corps, commanded by Generals Hancock, Warren and Sedgwick, respectively. The strength of the army, as agreed on both sides, was 140,000 men, and they were veterans. The strength of Lee's army was 52,926 as computed by Southern, and 60,000 by Northern historians. Longstreet with his force had been brought back from the West. The army was divided into three corps, and commanded by Ewell, Hill and Longstreet.

By the evening of the 5th of May the Federal army had all crossed the Rapidan. General Grant had determined "to fight General Lee provided he would stand," somewhere on the road to Richmond. He was now marching through the "Wilderness" with a train of 4000 wagons. "It is a region of worn-out tobacco fields, covered with scraggy oaks, sassafras, hazel, pine, intersected by narrow roads and deep ravines." Grant had no idea of fighting in this thicket, for Hancock's corps was ten miles ahead, and emerged from the jungle into the open country, when his flank was suddenly struck by Ewell's corps. There was no choice now, and ordering Hancock to return, he made his preparations to fight where artillery and cavalry could not be used, and superior numbers could be of no benefit. For some time there was a sharp conflict between Warren's and Ewell's corps, until 4 P. M., when both parties fell back and began to fortify. "They were but a hundred or two yards apart, and though the ring of axes to form breastworks and abatis filled the air, not a man on either side could be discerned by the other." On the other flank, Hill pressed the enemy until Hancock returned, about 3 P. M., without any decisive results.

Second Day of the Wilderness.

At dawn on the 6th of May the main battle commenced. Longstreet's corps had not arrived on the field, but delay was impracticable. Both sides were ready, and Ewell attacked first on the left. Hill had been joined by his absent brigades, and formed his line of battle with Wilcox' old brigade as guide centre. General Wilcox had been promoted to the command of a division, and Gen. E. Perrin had been promoted to the command of the brigade in his stead. It was formed in a small old field to the left of the plank road. When Hill advanced his line nearly to the Brock road, he met Hancock, who was also advancing. A most obstinate conflict ensued. On the Federal side the roar of battle became suddenly louder. It was Burnside, who had marched his 20,000 men thirty miles since late in the afternoon before, and thrown them at once into action. Hill's corps began at first steadily to fall back; but Wadsworth, who had lain all night upon his flank, at a given signal, made a furious attack, and Hill's corps were forced back in great disorder to the ground on which they had originally formed. Here he had ample time to reform his line; for Hancock's men, in their rapid advance through the thicket, had fallen into great disorder also, and it took him from 7 to 9 A. M. to restore his line.

In the meantime Longstreet fortunately appeared. His corps consolidated in a line with Hill's, so that when Hancock again advanced he was unexpectedly met by fresh troops; and after a bloody contest, in which General Wadsworth was killed, was forced back to his original position, which was fortified. Here General Longstreet was disabled by a musket ball, which passed through the side of his neck and came out at his shoulder. At first it was thought to be mortal. General Lee took personal command of his corps, and as soon as order was restored ordered the line to be advanced. "The most bloody and determined struggle of the day ensued. The thicket filled the valleys, and a new horror was added to the horror of battle. A fire broke out in the thicket, and soon wrapped the adversaries in flame and smoke. They fought on, however, amid the crackling flames. Night put an end to the conflict, and the struggle had not been decisive of any important results.

"These battles were fought in a jungle, where men could not see each other twenty yards off. Science had but little to do with it, for officers were seen guiding their men by the compass. Death came unseen; regiments stumbled upon each other, and sent swift destruction into each other's ranks, guided by the rustling of the bushes. In this mournful and desolate thicket did the campaign of 1864 begin. Here in blind wrestle, as at midnight, did nearly 200,000 men, in blue and gray, clutch each other—bloodiest and weirdest of encounters. The Genius of Destruction, tired of the old commonplace mode of killing, had invented the unseen death." (Life of Lee.)

In the two battles in the Wilderness Federal accounts make their loss 20,000 men, of whom 5000 were prisoners, and our loss 10,000, of whom very few were prisoners.

The day after the battle both armies remained quiet. That night General Grant moved his army toward Richmond; and General Lee sent Anderson's division forward to intercept him. All through the night, Grant encountered barricades erected by Stuart's dismounted men, who from behind them received his troops with galling fire; and as soon as the infantry was brought up in force, they would mount their horses and ride rapidly forward to erect another, and so on. Warren, who commanded the advance, was delayed in his march four hours. When he arrived in sight of Spottsylvania Court House he encountered Anderson's division behind a breastwork. He endeavored to force his way, and there was a desperate struggle with severe loss on both sides. The First Michigan, which was in advance, went in with 200 men and fell back with only twenty-three. Unluckily, General Perrin made a charge with his brigade (Wilcox' old men) in which he was killed. He was an accomplished officer, and much lamented. In this skirmish Colonel Horace King, once captain of the Company of Morgan Volunteers, and now commanding the Ninth Alabama, was slightly wounded. The next day (9th of May), a similar misfortune happened to the Federals. General Sedgwick was superintending the placing of a battery, where the men were exposed to a sharp fire from the sharpshooters who were up in the trees busy picking off the officers. "Pooh! they could not hit an elephant at this distance," said he. At that moment he was struck with a rifle-ball, in the face, and instantly fell dead. He was an officer of ability and courage, and had risen rapidly in public estimation from the battle of Sharpsburg.

On the morning of the 10th of May, Grant's line stretched for six miles on the north bank of the Po river, confronting Lee's line on the southern side of that stream. There was heavy fighting that day, during which the Federals sustained considerable loss, but the

Battle of the 12th of May

was one of wonderful interest. At early dawn, Grant, with his best troops, advanced with a heavy column, against a salient in the work on Lee's right centre. Hancock was in command. He passed silently over the Confederate skirmishers, scarcely firing a shot, and just as the first streak of daylight touched the eastern woods, burst upon the salient, which they stormed at the point of the bayonet. The attack was a complete surprise, and carried everything before it. The Southern troops, asleep in the trenches, woke to have the bayonet thrust into them, to be felled with clubbed muskets, and to find the works in secure possession of the enemy, before they could fire a shot. Such was the excellent success of the Federal movement, and the Southern line seemed to be hopelessly disrupted. Nearly the whole of Johnson's division were taken prisoners—the number amounting to more than three thousand—and eighteen pieces of artillery fell into the hands of the assaulting column. The position of affairs now with Lee was exceedingly critical. The Federal army had broken his line, was pouring into the opening, and to prevent him from concentrating at this point to regain his works, heavy attacks were begun by the enemy on his right and left wings. At no time during the war was the Southern army in greater danger of a bloody and decisive disaster. At this critical moment General Lee acted with the nerve and coolness of a soldier, whom no adverse event can shake. Line of battle was formed a short distance in the rear of the salient then in the enemy's possession, and a fierce charge was made by the Southerners to regain it. It was on this occasion that, on fire with the ardor of battle, Lee went forward in front of the line, and taking his station beside the colors of one of his Virginia regiments, he took off his hat, and turning to the men, pointed to the enemy. General Gordon spurred to his side, and seized his rein. His men, too, cried out, " Lee to the rear! Lee to the rear!" and they seemed determined not to charge unless he retired. He accordingly did so, and the line advanced under General Gordon. (Life of Lee.)

Notwithstanding the pressure on the wings, reinforcements were sent to the centre, from both of them. Wilcox' old brigade, now under command of Col. J. C. C. Saunders, formerly the Colonel of the Eleventh Alabama, were all sent, with the exception of the Ninth Alabama regiment, which in a thin line defended the works before occupied by the whole brigade, from sunrise until sunset. Burnside's corps was assaulting this wing of the Southern army.

To return to the main conflict in the centre: Ewell having fallen back to an interior line, and been reinforced from both flanks, and his adversary, Hancock, having had Sedgwick's old corps (now commanded by Wright) sent to his aid, a fight took place as severe as any during the war. Five different assaults were made by the Confederates, in heavy force, to recover the works. The fight was desperate and unyielding. A Northern writer thus describes it: " It is to be doubted if musketry firing was ever kept up so incessantly as it was by the contending troops, near the captured salient. The whole forest in range was blighted by it. One tree, eighteen inches in diameter, was actually cut in two by the leaden bullets, and a part of it is now to be seen in Washington City. From dawn to dusk, the roar of the guns was ceaseless; and a tempest of shells shrieked through the forest and ploughed the field. When night came, the angle of those works where the fire had been hottest, and from which the enemy had been finally driven, had a spectacle for whoever cared to look that would never have enticed his gaze again. Men in hundreds, killed and wounded together, were piled in hideous heaps. The writhing of the wounded, beneath the dead, moved these masses at times; at times a lifted arm or a quivering limb told of agony not quenched by the Lethe of Death around. Bitter fruit this! a dear price, it seemed, to pay for the capture of a salient angle of an enemy's entrenched work, even though the enemy's loss was terrible."

The Federal loss on the Po was from 8000 to 10,000, and the Confederate perhaps as much, including prisoners. The loss of the Ninth Alabama was small, as they fought under cover of the works.

The Federal army remained until the 19th of May. It was from this camp that General Grant announced to the President his intention to " fight it out on this line, if it takes all summer." Here he waited for " reinforcements from Washington, and the number he received made up for all his losses." (Draper, Vol. 3, p. 381.) On the other hand, General Lee expected none, and with an army reduced to 40,000, boldly confronted an army of 140,000 men. Not a man could President Davis spare to him, for the Confederacy was assailed at the most vulnerable points; and with its territory circumscribed, its reduced armies stood, as it were, back to back, defending themselves against overwhelming numbers.

Battle of North Anna.

On the 19th of May, at midnight, General Grant moved his army for the purpose of seising Hanover Junction; but when on the 23d he reached the banks of the North Anna General Lee was there ready to oppose his crossing. As Lee, since his arrival, had no time to erect fortifications, Grant crossed over a strong force both above and below his adversary. While Lee was resisting the advance of these most obstinately, he was fortifying in a novel manner to prevent their junction. From a salient on the bank of the stream he extended the wings back in an obtuse angle, forming a broad V with the point in front. It answered its purpose, and Grant becoming satisfied that he could not attack to advantage, marched again on the night of the 26th May toward Richmond. In the conflict at North Anna the whole of Wilcox' old brigade was engaged in repelling the enemy, but as they fought behind breastworks their loss was small.

It was while General Lee was at North Anna that he was plunged into the deepest grief by the intelligence of the death of General Stuart. General Sheridan had been detached from the Federal army to operate in the rear of the Confederates with a large force. General Stuart had been sent to pursue him, and had intercepted his column at a place called "Yellow Tavern." Here an obstinate engagement occurred in which this great Cavalry Chief was mortally wounded, and soon afterward expired. His death was a grievous blow to the South, at this time, when its fortunes were on the wane.

Second Battle of Cold Harbor.

On the 3d of June General Grant determined to attack the small army of General Lee strongly intrenched at this place, which was the scene of his first great battle two years before. On this occasion there were no brilliant manœuvres, but it was an attempt on the part of Grant to carry the position by mere force of numbers—by throwing his army in one great mass upon his adversary. The action did not last half an hour, and in that time the Federal loss was 15,000 men as computed by the Confederates, and 7000 as claimed by the Federals. "Later in the day orders were issued to renew the assault; but the whole army, correctly appreciating what the result would be, silently disobeyed." (*Draper, 3d Vol., 397.*) After this bloody repulse General Grant approached James River for the purpose of crossing and besieging Richmond from the south side of that stream.

The Ninth Alabama—The Siege of Richmond.

(In a former page was a mistake in stating that General Hood lost his leg at Gettysburg. He was wounded there, but lost his limb at Chickamauga. Again, I omitted to mention a reinforcement of 9000 men received by General Lee at Hanover Junction from General Beauregard's Richmond Army.)

In a cloud of dust the head of General Grant's columns came down to the pontoon bridge laid across the James river, at City Point, at daylight on the 15th of June, 1864. It was 1200 yards long and wide enough for twelve men or five horses to pass abreast. On this bridge mainly, but partly on ferry-boats, this great army was crossing in procession for three days. General Butler was already upon the ground and had been for for many days with his 30,000 men, in the fork between James and Appomattox rivers; so completely enclosed by Beauregard's strong works, across his front and from river to river, that General Grant wrote: "His army was as completely shut off as if it had been in a bottle completely corked." The approach of his chief released him from his imprisonment.

General Lee divined that the object of General Grant was to seize on Petersburg and the railroads which supplied Richmond. He put his army in motion, and none too soon. He crossed James river above Drewry's Bluff and appeared before his adversary, at Petersburg, on the morning of the 16th of June. Here, for three days, there was stubborn fighting, in which, however, Wilcox' old brigade bore no part. Commanded now by General Saunders, it left the field of Cold Harbor on the 15th, and camped near Chafin's Bluff. On the morning of the 18th, the brigade was marched, in double-quick time, to Petersburg, and arrived there about dark. Shortly afterward it was placed in General Mahone's division. There were only a few days of quiet, ere this brigade was fated to participate in the most formidable struggle of any which had yet occurred south of the James river. On the evening of 21st of June, General Grant moved a strong force out of his entrenchments, to seize upon the Weldon railroad. Night coming on, they took their position for an attack next morning. General Hill perceived in their movements that a gap had been left between Hancock's and Wright's corps, and threw into the opening a strong column. Both corps were struck on the flank, and thrown into great confusion. The Federal attack was repulsed, and Hill carried off 3000 prisoners. The first attempt to seize the road was attended with great loss on the part of the Federals, who fell back into their trenches, and remained quiet for several weeks. The troops employed by Hill on this occasion were mainly Anderson's division and a brigade of Heath's division. Wilcox' old brigade, in this fight, faced the troops of Barlow and Gibbon on the Union side.

About the time of this engagement, Generals Wilson and Kautz, with two divisions of cavalry, were sent out to destroy the three railroads south and west of Richmond. They were at work, busily, for a week occupied in their destruction, when they commenced their return to the main army. Wilcox' old brigade, and Finnegan's Florida brigade, with Anderson's battery, were marched from Petersburg, to intercept this cavalry force, during a whole night, and did not stop for rest or sleep. They arrived at Ream's station about sunrise and soon afterward saw clouds of dust in their front, which signaled the approach of the enemy. They came on with much confidence, because they fully expected that General Grant was in possession of the Station. When within range, our artillery was opened upon them, and did effective work. A charge of infantry took place, and General Fitz Lee with his cavalry attacked them in their rear, when a complete route of the entire force ensued. All their artillery was captured, and quite a number of prisoners; also about 1000 negroes and a large number of carriages and buggies, which had been stolen by the Yankees for their idols to ride in. The brigade returned to Petersburg the next day, and occupied the same position on the line to the right of Petersburg.

Six weeks had passed. Repeated attempts were made by General Grant to break through the lines without success, when a conflict occurred of so novel a character that we shall give the facts somewhat in detail. The opposing works to the right of Petersburg approximated so near to each other that the idea was suggested by some men who had been Pennsylvania miners, to run a mine under a portion of the Confederate lines. It was approved by General Grant, and commenced on the 25th of June and finished on the 23d of July. The gallery was over 500 feet long, four or five feet across, and when it reached the desired point it had lateral galleries run each way for forty feet. Extensive arrangements were made by the commander to take advantage of the panic to be produced by its explosion, and with a force of 50,000 men to charge through and seize a crest called Cemetery Hill, which commanded the city of Petersburg. To weaken General Lee's defence he sent on the 25th of July a force north of the James river to threaten Richmond, which had the effect of drawing after them a strong force from the Confederate army. Everything so far worked well, and the time fixed for the explosion of the mine was at 3:30 o'clock on the morning of the 30th of July. It was charged with 8000 pounds of powder, the immense body of troops were placed in column, and when the moment arrived the fuse was ignited, but without effect. After waiting till daylight two bold men, Lieutenant Douty and Sergeant Reese, crept into the mine and found that the fuse was broken within fifty feet of the magazine. They set fire to it and barely had time to escape before the explosion occurred. It was indeed a terrible one, and was heard for thirty miles. The effect was frightful. Captain Comegys (a neighbor of mine) who was in full view when the explosion took place, describes the column of flame, mingled with smoke, timbers, the wreck of gun carriages, and the bodies of men, as ascending half a mile high, apparently. As soon as the wreck fell to the ground, and the smoke and dust subsided, he looked across and beheld the largest body of Federals in readiness to charge that he ever saw during the war, on the same space of ground; although he had served from the commencement, and had taken part in many a great battle. The advance of the Federal army charged, but instead of crossing the breastworks they took refuge from a sharp fire in them, and the "crater" which had been heaved up by the tremendous explosion, thirty feet deep, sixty feet wide and two hundred feet long. Here the first division entered, followed by several regiments of negroes, and for hours waited for the advance of General Burnside, who commanded the large army set apart for that purpose. General Lee, whose headquarters were not far off, was soon on the field, accompanied by General Beauregard. General Mahone charged the enemy and dislodged them from a portion of the works they had captured on the side of the crater; while General Wright, who charged them on the other side, failed with much loss. Things remained in this state for hours, during which the Federals in the crater were shelled. The troops brought up by General Lee were sheltered by ditches and ridges where they lay in the hot sun until many suffered from sunstroke—in the Ninth Alabama alone, there were four cases.

At length Wilcox's brigade (then commanded by General Saunders) advanced. Captain Comegys describes their charge as being very rapid. They soon reached the margin and disappeared in the crater. Here a hand-to-hand fight occurred, which, the captain thinks, must have lasted fifteen or twenty minutes. At length the Federals yielded, with a loss of 4000 men, of which 1300 were prisoners. The appearances inside the crater, after the fight, were remarkable. Here was seen bodies torn to pieces by the shells, and the whole cavity of the crater covered by the killed and wounded, and in some places in heaps three or four feet deep, of whites and negroes. They lost an excellent opportunity of breaking General Lee's lines, and General Burnside was much censured for not advancing according to the plan.

About the 25th of August, Hancock's corps and Gregg's division of cavalry, while at Ream's station destroying the railroad, were attacked by the Confederates, and after desperate fighting, the Federals gave way. Here General Hancock lost 2400 men out of 8000. Wilcox's old brigade, whose commander, General Saunders, had been killed some days before, was led to the charge by General Wilcox himself, who having failed to repulse the Federals with other troops, put himself at the head of his old brigade, the men of which received him with cheers. They never failed to follow him wherever he led, and speedily broke the enemy's line.

In our last we gave a brief account of a number of engagements which succeeded the investment of Richmond and Petersburg by the Federal army. But let not my readers suppose that the intervals of time between these were quiet. Far from it. Lee's small, scantily fed force confronted Grant's large one, which had an abundance of supplies of every kind, in parallel lines of fortifications from before Richmond, around Petersburg, and to the west of it, until they finally reached the enormous length of forty miles. These approached each other until in some places they were not one hundred yards apart. "It was one long battle, day and night, week after week, and month after month, during the heats of summer, the sad hours of autumn, and the days and nights of winter." One-third of the army of Lee was, for more than nine months, constantly in the trenches, night and day, ready to meet an assault of the enemy at any place in this long line. During all hours of the night the heavens were lighted up by bombs curving through the air and exploding in these trenches, in which the men had to shelter themselves. This siege was the most arduous campaign of the whole war.

Reference has been made to the conflict, at Ream's Station, on the 25th August. Late in September General Grant intending a heavy attack on General Lee's right, and to conceal his purpose, sent a strong force north of James river on the night of the twenty-eighth of that month. Next morning they advanced suddenly, and carried the strong fortifications called Fort Harrison. Elated with their success, they made an assault on Fort Gilmer, which was repulsed with heavy loss to the Federal troops. There was sharp fighting for several days, in which Wilcox's old brigade (now commanded by General Forney) took an active part. They were in the fight on the 7th of October, in which General John Gregg, of Texas, fell. He was a native of our county, and a gentlemen of high culture and great gallantry. In the proper place we shall give a sketch of his career.

Again on the 27th of October, General Grant made a heavy attack on the Confederate right. The force was very large; for "only men enough were left to hold their fortified line." Generals Grant and Meade superintended this movement in person. They threw their forces across Hatcher's Run, near Burgess' Mill: and an obstinate attack was made on Lee's lines. The cavalry under Generals Hampton and W. H. F. Lee attacked them in front and rear—and infantry was hastened to the point. Here General Hampton lost his son, Preston. When the infantry arrived, the struggle was obstinate, but the Federals were driven back into their works. The next day General Lee reported that "the attack was made by three brigades, under General Mahone, and General Hampton in the rear. Mahone captured 400 prisoners, three stands of colors, and six pieces of artillery. In the attack subsequently made by the enemy, Mahone broke three lines of battle." Forney's brigade (Wilcox' old one) was in this celebrated charge, and the Ninth Alabama sustained a heavy loss.

From this time active operations in the field closed until the opening of the spring of 1865; but the same constant, worrying, wearying conflict, continued in the trenches. The gay livery of spring brought no corresponding cheerfulness into the hearts of the Confederates. Events had occurred of a very depressing nature. Early, in the valley of Virginia, had been overpowered by numbers—Sherman had borne down all opposition, marched through Georgia, and had reached Goldsboro, in North Carolina, on his way to unite with the Army of the Potomac—and Grant with an army of 150,000 men confronted Lee, whose forces were reduced to less than 40,000. The physical condition of the men too was deplorable. "It was the mere phantom of an army. Shoeless, in rags, with just sufficient coarse food to sustain life, but never enough to keep the gnawing fiend, Hunger, at arm's length, Lee's old veterans remained firm." Their morale may be well illustrated by the case of the noble Till (the color bearer of the Ninth Alabama), who in the last battle lost an arm, and in the first battle of the spring led the regiment, holding the battle flag with his remaining arm. This force, purged of its dross, by years of fiery conflict, was all pure gold, and fully equal to the "old guard of Napoleon."

In the attack by Gordon on Fort Steadman, Forney's brigade bore no part, but in the decisive attack of Grant of the 29th of March, they participated. It was stationed near Howlett's battery on the extreme right. The enemy charged but were repulsed with loss, but numbers (as all know) prevailed, and our forces on that wing were routed, and made their way across the Appomattox to join General Lee, who had crossed the remnant of his army far below. There were a number of the men of the Ninth Alabama wounded in these conflicts. They had been collected and were in charge of that faithful surgeon, and warm-hearted gentleman, Dr. Jas. R. Edwards, and were all taken prisoners.

I shall cast a veil over the closing scenes of the surrender, in which one noble looking personage was the centre of attraction to both armies, he who during his wonderful career was guided by the principle that "duty was the sublimest word in our language. You can not do more, and you should never wish to do less." And when the gloom and darkness of that last eclipse, filled every heart in his small army, and in the broad South, with hopeless sadness, his declaration that "human fortitude should be equal to human calamity," calmed the agitation of the country, while his steady application to the duties he assumed in civil life, his strict observance of the laws, and absence from all intrigues against the Federal Government, had much to do with the tranquillity which has prevailed in the country since the cessation of hostilities.

In treating of the personal annals, which it has been my humble task to record, I have drawn from the pages of military history just enough to render my narrative intelligible and interesting. I have not been writing history, but extracting from it. I am satisfied that the histories that have been issued from the press, in reference to Lee's campaign, are quite imperfect and incorrect, in numerous instances. Such a subject deserves a historian of a high order of talent, extensive learning (especially in military history), great perseverance, the taste of an antiquary, and a judicial fairness, which would invite men of all parties to consult his pages for the truth. An officer of considerable ability has remarked, "I can cite no army, either in ancient or modern times, that will figure more prominently in history, than that of the Army of Northern Virginia. Its distinguished commander in all the higher elements of the soldier, will rank with the most renowned captains of the past, and will be regarded as the first in the war which closed so disastrously to the South. The infantry of that army fought more triumphal battles than any other which I have knowledge of, and sustained fewer defeats. Their spirit and organization were maintained to the last, although for two years they were virtually without pay, miserably clothed, and poorly fed."

A complete history of these campaigns would be a text-book in which the student of military science could learn the higher elements of his profession; but such a history could not be well written without having first from officers of talent and learning (who still survive), subsidiary histories of the brigades which they commanded. For instance, how valuable and deeply interesting a complete history of Wilcox's brigade would be from the pen of General Wilcox himself, who still survives in full vigor of mind and body! It is said that he has never forgotten anything. He was greatly respected and admired by the officers and men of the Alabama brigades under his command. He was the first colonel of the Ninth Alabama, then made a brigadier general, and his command was made up exclusively of Alabamians.

This will close the narrative part of the sketch of the Ninth Alabama. I will next give a roll of the Lawrence volunteers, with the fate of each man, as far as it could be ascertained. Rolls of other companies will be published with pleasure if sent to me.

The Ninth Alabama—Fate of the Lawrence County Volunteers.

The roll of Captain Warren's company as published in the Moulton *Democrat* of 31st May, 1861, will be the foundation of the matters of personal history which follow. But this does not, by any means, contain the full number of names which afterward were enrolled. I am credibly informed that, at one time, this company mustered as many as 120 men. I have added as many names as I could ascertain, but still there is a large number wanting. At one time, when Captain May visited home, he brought 17 recruits (mostly from Winston county) and on the way to the army they contracted measles, of a malignant type, and nearly all died. I am not certain that there is a single one of these names on my list. It is due to their memories that they should be there; and I should be pleased to receive information which will enable me not only to complete the list, but to give some account of each person added to it.

The members of this company, with few exceptions, were poor young men and many of them quite illiterate. Indeed, some of them could not write their names, but, like General Morgan of revolutionary fame," they could make their marks" on the enemy. A gentleman who had much to do with the issuance of rations to the several companies of the Ninth Alabama told me that his company, when the signal for battle was given, brought more men into line, in proportion to the number of rations which they drew than any in the regiment. Many of them had been raised up in mountain homes where they had indulged in the chase of wild animals, and had become experts in the use of the rifle. No wonder then that with these habits of early life they were able in the dark days which preceded the end of the war, to march as far bare-foot, could live on as small ration and be as cheerful in their rags as any men of the regiment. They went into the service to "stay," and some of these poor fellows did "stay" on every battle-field which was made memorable by the skill of their great commander.

Capt. J. M. Warren. Of his family and military career I have already spoken.

First Lieut. M. G. May was from South Alabama. (Captain Warren had married his sister, and this accounts for his being an officer in the company). He made a fair captain when he was promoted in the place of Captain Warren, who resigned. Toward the close of the war he resigned and raised some independent cavalry.

Second Lieut. William T. Couch. His father was Washington Couch, who came from Limestone to Lawrence some thirty years ago. The old man was poor, but he and his sons worked industriously. William was the oldest and married a sister of Dr. J. H. Odom. Marion Couch married a widow, Wright. Robert, the youngest son, married a daughter of Rev. Hamilton Moore, a Campbellite minister. When May became captain Couch was promoted to his place, and when May resigned Couch became captain. He was much esteemed by his men and a good captain. He was wounded at Frasier's Farm, but served until the end of the war, and still lives near Hillsboro in this county, and has no enemies that I know of except himself.

George W. Garth's name was on the original muster roll of the company as second lieutenant, but he was never mustered in. He became first lieutenant in Captain Bankhead's company of the Sixteenth Alabama, in which connection I will speak of him.

First Sergeant R. E. Davis was probably an orphan, for he was raised up in the family of Thomas Holland, Esq., of Mallard's creek, of whom he was a relative, but in what degree I do not know. His uncle, a one-legged man, named Davis, married a daughter of Esquire Holland, and she was his cousin. R. E. Davis was killed in some battle in Virginia.

Second Sergeant H. Van Whitehead came from Limestone county before the war. He was a quiet man, but a good soldier, was wounded once or twice, and finally killed, in some battle near Petersburg.

Third Sergeant H. H. Bibb was from Winston county. He was a good soldier and survived the war. When the Winston men returned to their homes, they found the country in great fear of a band of tories, who had been robbing and murdering the people. The soldier boys made short work of them. Some were disposed of "without shriving," and the rest becoming alarmed, "stood not on the order of their going." My old friend, Doctor Andrew Kaiser, had been killed by them, and I think his house burned, and his widow fled from her home. When Bibb returned he carried Mrs. Kaiser to her home, and assisted in rebuilding her house. He has gone out west somewhere.

J. K. McBride was a private when he first went out. When Garth left the company he became third Lieutenant; and at the end of the war was second in command. He was a fearless soldier, and in the company had warm friends and bitter enemies. He lost an arm at Gettysburg, and is at Hillsboro, in this county. I have spoken elsewhere of his family.

Sergeant A. Livingston: (I first spoke of him as the son of Sam Livingston, who was one of Jackson's old soldiers, and celebrated the 8th of January as long as he lived; but I was mistaken) was the son of William Livingston, the brother of Sam, who lived in the near corner of Blount county. He was a brave soldier, and was killed in the charge at Frazer's Farm, when about the centre of the open field. A shell carried away all his head except the hinder part of the skull. In this battle more young men of this company fell than in any other.

Corporal D. C. Harrison: He was a man of gay disposition, fond of whiskey and pleasure, and of much wit; but was always in his place when a battle was on hand. He was wounded in the seven days fight around Richmond, but survived the war. He married a daughter of Wm. Foote, near Oakville. He had a quarrel with a neighbor originating in a bad partition fence, attacked him with a shotgun and was killed by one of the same kind.

William Foote, Jr., was a son of the same William Foote, and grandson of the first clerk of our Circuit Court, at Melton's Bluff. He was quite cheerful, and had all the qualities to make a soldier popular around the camp-fire; but he had consumption, was unable to bear fatigue, was discharged and died before the end of the war.

J. T. Cooper: His father was one of the old settlers, and related to the Couch family; but I have not learned his christian name. J. T. was a brave soldier, and was killed at Cold Harbor, in the second year of the war.

R. Ables was a tanner when he enlisted. He fell out of the ranks complaining of being sick, in the first march into Maryland, after the capture of Harper's Ferry, and was never heard of afterward.

Jeffrey Beck was an old man when he entered the service, and was discharged on account of age,

Dennis Cullen was a brave Irishman who was killed in some battle. There were several of them, all in the same mess; but some of their names are not on my list. They were always cheerful and witty, regardless of discomfort or danger; and when they could get a little whiskey, refused not to sing their native songs, even "in a strange land."

William A. Jenkins, son of Dr. W. Jenkins, and grandson of Dr. Hickey, made a good soldier, survives the war and is living in Mississippi.

John H. Morris, son of Rev. Moses Morris, of Trinity, was never mustered into this company, although his name was on the original roll. He was a well educated young man, and went into Captain Hobb's company of the same regiment. He too was killed at Frasier's Farm. His body was not found until next morning. But for this it was thought that his life might have been saved.

J. Alexander Isham came from Fayetteville, Tenn. Mr. Grant, near Brown's Ferry, had married his sister, and he and his brother Charles came to Lawrence a few years before the war. For some time he was attached to the wagon train. He was a faithful man, wherever he was. The commissary officer under whom he served informed me that he had a presentiment, that he would be killed in his first battle. This happened in fact in the battle of Cold Harbor. But the melancholy impression caused no abatement of his courage. He fell in the stubborn conflict, on the right, on the top of the ridge, after three lines of breastworks had been carried, the most glorious part of the field for a gallant soldier to yield up his life.

Charles Isham, brother of the above, was badly wounded in the thigh at Salem Church. The ball had passed near the artery, and in the hospital erosion took place and he died.

G. W. Berry, son of an old settler west of Town creek, survived the war, and has since died.

D. W. Glen, Irish soldier, survived the war. and lives somewhere in this county.

J. M. Wright died in the service.

J. E. Chilcoat. His name was on the roll, but he was never mustered in. He made a fine soldier in the Sixteenth Alabama.

J. L. Harvey was discharged on account of age.

W. H. Holmes had killed a man named Gibson, near Courtland. Under a Confederate regulation, a nol. pros. was entered in court upon his enlistment; but he was seriously diseased, and unfit for service. He died last year in Moulton.

J. B. Windham was the son of Hardy Windham, an old settler. He was a good soldier, badly wounded at Cold Harbor, survived the war, and has removed to Texas.

E. W. Sale was the son of Lewis Sale, who was the nephew of Rev. Alexander Sale. E. W. was a man of some education, and was mortally wounded at Salem Church. The ball passed through both cheeks far back and crushed the bones of his mouth. The comrade who nursed him told me that he lingered many days before he died.

Jeff. Lindsay was the son of Jack Lindsay, an old settler on Flint, in our county. He was a brave soldier, and fell on the second day of the battle of Gettysburg. A gentleman, who was by his side, told me that he was shot through the breast and fell dead in the bloody conflict with the Irish brigade.

Robert H. Coleman was a man of fine intellect and pretty good education. He was of the Virginia family of Colemans, and a relative of Judge Coleman of the Supreme Court, formerly of our county. His father was named Richard, and married Miss Adair, sister of John Adair, of Trinity, who married a daughter of Judge Charles Gibson. The Colemans had lived in Prince William county, Virginia, near Manassas; moved to Christiansburg, thence to Kentucky, and about fifty years ago came into our county. At the time Mr. Coleman volunteered he was a surveyor, and carried on a steam mill a few miles southeast of Hillsboro. His only brother, William, died in 1855. His only living sister is the wife of Dr. Wm. Cochrane, of Tuscaloosa. Coleman was commissary sergeant of the Ninth, and generally employed in the commissary and quartermaster departments; but when a battle occurred, he was in line. At Cold Harbor, Donell, the color bearer, was killed before they crossed the deep gulley; another man seized the flag and at the second line he was shot down—Coleman raised it, and before he reached the top of the hill he was shot three times without having any bones broken, and from weakness had to resign it to another man, who, amidst the cheers of the men on the top of the ridge, waved it in triumph as the routed Federals went down the slope to the Chickahominy. At the battle of Sharpsburg Coleman was wounded severely, his arm being shattered from wrist to elbow. He recovered slowly, but was in time to take a part in the battle of Gettysburg, where he was taken prisoner, and with some sixty or seventy others of the Ninth Alabama was carried to Fort Delaware, about sixty miles below Philadelphia. The Fort was on an island in the middle of the river, which here became a broad estuary.

On the night of the 12th of August, 1863, some twenty of these prisoners escaped from the island. It was a daring feat and I have been curious to learn the particulars, but I have only succeeded in two instances—that of Coleman and William Patton of O'Neal's old company. Coleman had provided himself, for a buoy, with a seasoned plank about eight feet long, and Patton had a lot of empty canteens tied around his armpits, under his blouse. The night was pitch dark; it was a dead calm, and the tide was running up with great velocity. As the sentinel turned his back to them, they slipped silently in the river behind him and swam out silently into the current. When about a hundred yards out, he blew a low whistle for Patton but received no answer. This was repeated several times, and without success. After floating several miles above the Fort, he was struck by a squall of wind, and was often completely submerged; but he stuck to his plank and the squall was soon over. He found himself now, a hundred and fifty yards from the desired shore, and his escape seemed assured. He passed under the stern of a schooner lying at anchor, and just then, a short distance ahead of him, he heard a cry and a gurgling sound as if some person was drowning. He hurried to his assistance, and found it to be a Mr. Young, of South Carolina. But unluckily, the cry of distress had been heard also on board the schooner; and the two men were picked up, and carried aboard. The Captain was kind, but refused to put them on land. On arriving at Philadelphia he gave each of them a new suit of citizen's clothes and handed them over to the Provost Marshal. The next day Coleman's left was handcuffed to Young's right hand; and they were sent to the Fort on a magnificent bay steamer bound for Cape May, and filled with ladies and gentlemen. Their bracelets being of an unusual style for such company, attracted a great deal of attention, especially from the ladies (God bless them!) who admired courage and are always magnanimous enough to sympathize with the unfortunate.

Before they left the steamer the prisoners had received donations from them to the amount of more than $200 apiece. But what became of Patton? Why, he not only escaped, but he rode into camp one day just as General Lee arrived in Culpeper, with two fine cavalry horses completely equipped. "But how did he get them?" I must first tell you something of his history. He was a printer in Pulaski, and when the Ninth Alabama was being raised he came down to Florence and became a member (as I have said) of O'Neal's company. He was a small man, of not more than ninety pounds weight; but he had a big head and a large heart, and had resources at hand for every emergency. He was expert at the game of cards, and always had money; but he shared liberally with his comrades. He was cheerful and witty, and a great favorite around the camp fire. When floating on the tide he and Coleman were separated. He was smart enough to be in no hurry to leave the river near the fort. In the squall his empty canteens floated like bottles. When he had gotten about fourteen miles above he made a landing, and, trusting to his histrionic talents, he reached safely the neighborhood of Winchester, where an adventure of uncommon interest happened to him. He was trudging along a little after dark, when a large force of Federal cavalry overtook him. He stepped aside in the bushes to let them pass, when the order was given to encamp. The troopers scattered over the woods, and he heard one ask another to take his horse to water. When the request was refused, Patton stepped forward and said: "I'll take your horse to water, sir." The rein was handed to him, and he had just mounted when another asked him to take *his* horse, too. In this way he came into possession of two fine horses in the dark. He was as good as his word, for he did take them to water, but he never brought them back. Patton was again taken prisoner in some affair around Petersburg, but within four days he escaped and was with his company again. He should have joined the cavalry and become a scout. He would have been as skillful and useful as McGuire (now of Memphis), who belonged to the First Kentucky Cavalry. But to return to Coleman. After the war he was appointed county surveyor of our county, and served for many years. He was detained a prisoner until November, 1864, when he was carried to Savannah and released. He was so disabled, and the way was so obstructed by the enemy, that it was January before he reached Tuscaloosa, and much later when he reached home. He married the Widow Mullins, and now lives several miles south of Leighton. His wife is a sister of Rufus Milwee, who was one of ten young men who first volunteered and marched from our county. Mr. Milwee has lately married a daughter of Irwin Smith, near Newburg, and now lives in view of Landersville.

A. J. Wade was the son of one of the old settlers, who lived near Smith's mill. He served through the war, and has since died.

G. S. Crittenden (son of George W., who was a tailor of Courtland, Ala.), was taken ill on the march to Williamsburg, and died in Richmond.

J. L. McDowell was the grandson of John McDowell, the Irish hatter and Revolutionary soldier, whose history I have previously given. He was grandfather of Col. M. C. Gallaway and the father of Judge Gibson's first wife. J. L. McDowell was a good soldier, but was of a delicate constitution. At one time, in camp, he lost his speech entirely. He survived the war, married a daughter of Silas Garrison, and now lives in Borden's Cove.

James Daniel survives the war, and lives near Oakville.

Benj. F. Gray came of good fighting stock. His father was Jonathan Gray, who was captain in the Creek war and at the battle of New Orleans. He was wounded, but served through the war, and now lives near Palarm, Ark.

James Donohoe had his throat cut by a bullet at Williamsburg.

S. C. Clark—his name was on the roll, but he was never mustered in. His mother was sister to Dr. Irwin, and he was a daring, brave man in Roddy's cavalry.

Nicholas Eddy was the son of a man of the same name, who was one of the early settlers in the Poplar Log Cove. Nick was a larger man than his father, and weighed 200 pounds. He was over fifty years of age when he enlisted, and his heart was in the work. At that awful battle of Sharpsburg, Nick was behind the ledge of rocks, which with the addition of fence rails, made a pretty good breastwork, and very busy plying his musket on the advancing Federals, when a long conical bullet tore through a rail, scattered the splinters in the face of a comrade who sat on his right, and striking Nick, who cried out that he was a dead man. As soon as his friend could brush away the splinters from his face he saw Nick with one hand held up bleeding, with lacerated fingers, the other held to his breast and his countenance pale as ashes. On examination the bullet had penetrated the cartilage of the breast-bone, and there it stuck. The hollow end was still above the surface, and by this with the forefinger and thumb it was drawn out, and the healthy color returned again to his face—and none too soon, for now they were forced back by the enemy across the cornfield. It was in this retrograde movement that the brave Lieut. John Rayburn, Adjutant of the Ninth Alabama, was killed. A few days before the Federals on the north side of the Tennessee river had been wantonly firing into the little town of Guntersville, and his mother had been killed by the fragment of a shell. The news had just reached him and he was very sad. Nick Eddy after this battle was honorably discharged from the service.

J. Ephraim Alexander and W. W. Alexander were good soldiers and much respected in the company. They belonged to the Alexanders, a family who settled around Pin Hook, over fifty years ago. The name of their father was George W. Alexander, a substantial citizen, who died a year or two ago. Ephraim was wounded, and perhaps his brother. They survived the war, and now live not far from Moulton.

J. T. Royer was a son of Jeff. Royer (who was a lunatic) and lived about nine miles east of Moulton. A cloud seemed to be over the family, for his son, who was a fearless man, was killed at Frazier's Farm in the charge—and this was the first season of active operations.

A. H. House drifted down from Ohio to Courtland before the war. He was employed for some time (if I mistake not) by the father of Dr. McMahon. When the war broke out, he caught the contagion and went out with the company. He was quite a useful soldier indirectly, for General Wilcox made him an orderly, and he kept his horses in fine order. After the war he lived some time in Nashville, but the last we heard of him he was in Cincinnati in a candy shop.

Jacob Verner was raised in the Warrior mountains, on the Cheatham road to Tuscaloosa, in a small smoky cabin. I am not certain that he could write his name, and yet he proved to be one of the very best soldiers in the regiment. He was quite droll in manners, and had a good store, not of *Attic*, but of *camp* wit. A battle always excited him, and he was in high humor. He bore his full share of the fighting, and survived the war, and lives somewhere in our county. When he first came, he was quite fresh, and the boys were very much amused at his simplicity. They tell the story on him to this day (but I don't guarantee the truth of it) that at the battle of Williamsburg, which was the first he was in, he was astonished when the firing ceased; for he said he supposed that the battle would continue until, on one side or the other, the last man was killed. He acquired the most reputation, however, by accidentally falling into a gulley. You want to know how that was. Well, I'll tell you. On the evening of the day after the battle of Salem Church you remember General Wilcox tells us that he made a night attack on the enemy. The Ninth was moving cautiously around the Federal right when the click of hundreds of musket-locks was heard in rapid succession. "Down," was the word, and flat they fell on the ground. The volley fired by the enemy showed where their line was, and it was returned with interest. The Federals were thrown into great confusion, and the Ninth advanced. In the dark, Jake Verner, J. T. Carter, Lieutenant Sparks of the Morgan volunteers, and a fourth (whose name I have forgotten) rolled into a deep gulley. As soon as they struck the bottom they knew where they were, and that it was a gulch which had once been dug for gold, and washed out very deep, and that there was no way to escape from it except some steps which the boys who had been camped on the spot all the winter had cut in one side. They were approaching this, when they were halted by Federal soldiers and taken prisoners. Presently a battery which Wilcox had masked for some months behind a clump of pine bushes, to guard the crossing of Bank's ford, began to play upon the Federals, and the shot and shell passed right over the heads of those who were in the gulley. The Federals hunted for a place to escape but could find none, for the sides were too steep, and the termination of it on the river-side was a perpendicular rock. The upshot of the affair was, that sixty Federals who had tumbled into the gulley first, surrendered to four of our men who rolled in last.

J. T. Carter, who had a part in the adventure above mentioned, was the son of a shoemaker, who worked for a long time at Ashford's tanyard, and who was lame. J.

T. was a good soldier, served through the war, married afterward and went to West Tennessee, where I am told he is doing well.

J. M. Horton, in 1862, had a severe spell of sickness, was sent home, and when he recovered joined Roddy's cavalry. He now lives southwest of Courtland.

J. W. Martin is said to have survived the war, but I have no certain information in regard to him.

Luke P. Jones, son of Alexander Jones and nephew of Rev. Alexander Sale, was a worthy young man and a good soldier. After the termination of the war, he went to Texas, where he was assassinated.

A. F. Johnson was from Winston county. He died from sickness at Culpeper Courthouse.

A. L. Johnson was the son of Richard Johnson, who resides in the edge of Morgan county. He, also, died in the service.

T. H. Riddle served through the war and lives, I am told, near Pin Hook.

Albert J. Watkins was the son of Albert Watkins and was a good soldier. He survived the war and moved West.

R. A. Hunter was the son of Matthew Hunter of the Poplar Long Cove. He was killed in the charge across the open field, at Frazier's Farm, soon after it commenced.

John Washer's father has been dead many years; his mother died last year. He survived the war, and lives in Illinois. His brother Richard was in Roddy's cavalry, and was sent by the general to guard his family to Tuscaloosa, and was murdered, on the way, by the Tories.

S. W. Crittenden was the son of George W., of Courtland. He survived the war, moved to Arkansas and was murdered.

J. H. Odom, whose name stands on the roll, was never mustered in, but belonged to the Twenty-seventh Alabama. The doctor lives in Tennessee.

J. R. Free was a good soldier, and was wounded in the seven days' fight. He survived the war, and now lives near Landersville.

Tandy W. Wilson was wounded in the same fight. (Mr. Thorn thinks that he was afterward killed; Dr. Irwin thinks that he lives in the county).

J. K. Whitlow was an old man when he went out. He was discharged on account of age, and lives near Hillsboro.

J. J. Whitlow, his son, died in the Richmond hospital.

T. J. Austin was the son of William Austin, of Fox's creek, and was a fine soldier. He was severely wounded at the battle of Sharpsburg, sent home by the surgeon, lingered awhile, and died.

M. B. Castlebury was a good soldier and was shot in the head at Williamsburg. He was from Borden's Cove. His widow still lives there.

A. A. Sullivan, son of Judge James Sullivan, of Winston county, was severely wounded, and came home.

A. P. Montgomery was killed at Cold Harbor.

A. N. Thorne, son of Joseph W. Thorne, a machinist of great skill, who once lived in Courtland, was a good soldier. He was wounded in the knee at Malvern Hill, also wounded in the hand at Chancellorsville—survived the war, and now lives in Arkansas.

W. H. Thorne, a brother of the above, was killed at Williamsburg.

John A. Simmons, Thomas W. Simmons and Edwin J. Simmons, all sons of A. D. Simmons, our late postmaster, who was respected by every one, have already been fully noticed.

Junius A. Bynum, son of Junius Bynum and Josephine Taylor, was a spirited, reckless young man, and a fearless soldier. At Williamsburg, the first battle in which the Ninth Alabama was engaged, he was wounded in the arm. With many others, wounded in a similar way, he marched with the army to Richmond and his wound put on an unhealthy action. He was sent home, and when he recovered he joined another command, in which he shot one of his comrades somewhere north of the Tennessee river. He fled to his home and a provost-gaurd of men, not personally known in

Courtland, arrested him and carried him away—and that was the last that was ever heard of him. Some believed that to screen himself from punishment, he had made his escape from the guard and gone into the Northern army; and others that he had been murdered and his body sunk into the Tennessee river. His mother lived and died in this state of horrible uncertainty. She was a lady of culture and exquisite sensibility, and from a book of poems composed by her, I make a few extracts to show how acute were her sufferings:

> One year has passed—changes have swept
> Across thy mother's home;
> But raised in prayer, her eyes oft weep
> For him who can not come.
> Oh, Thou, who dwellest in heaven above,
> Protect my absent boy;
> Watch o'er him, with a father's love,
> And bless each day's employ.
>
> *   *   *   *   *
>
> O! gently, gently strike those notes—
> Breathe softly the familiar strain;
> It takes me to the blissful past—
> I'm with my "wanderer" again.
> O! lady, sing that song once more,
> It falls upon my frozen breast
> Like sunbeams upon the fallen snow,
> When weeping clouds have sunk to rest.
>
> *   *   *   *   *
>
> He is gone from me, forever gone!
> Gone from his early boyhood's home,
> To plod life's weary paths alone
> Or fills an exile's nameless tomb.
> I often think I hear the tread
> Of his quick footsteps at the door,
> And quickly turn myself around,
> To fold him in my arms once more.
>
> Ah! months have ripened into years—
> A broken circle still we are;
> Hope's wooing stay our falling tears,
> With whisperings sweet "He'll come again;"
> O! quickly haste, long seems the time—
> Absence has smit our hearts with fear;
> Come, bless us with thy happy smile,
> And fill again thy vacant chair.

Gray Whitehead joined in Virginia and was wounded at Frazier's Farm.

Noel C. Graham was killed at Gettysburg. (We have previously published a notice of his family).

M. D. Allen was not of the early settlers of the county. He was accidentally wounded in the hand, survived the war, and now lives in this county near Leighton.

Newton Garnett was a plasterer. (Bailey Hill was his step-father, and he married a daughter of William Borum). He is still living, although at Salem Church battle he was apparently shot through the heart. The bullet must have run around on a rib.

J. Kitchens, I think, came from Tennessee a few years before the war. He was wounded in the "Seven Days Fight," and now lives near Trinity.

A Mr. Bailey, Ewing, Jackson Turner, John Turner, and Melton were from Kentucky. When that State was invaded each one procured his discharge, except Jackson Turner, who remained until the surrender. Melton had been elected third lieutenant.

Mr. Graham, of Hobb's Company, received a remarkable wound. He had a bullet to pass through both lobes of his brain from temple to temple. The brains were escaping from the wound, on each side, for some time, but he still lives—is an industrious man, and although his intellect is somewhat impaired, he still has enough to guide him very well in his work.

I have now noticed the Lawrence Volunteers of the Ninth Alabama, individually (except a few who deserted). In view of the fact that it is a " lost cause;" that in many instances the distress was so great, that sympathy was felt for deserters, and expressed even by that magnanimous commander-in-chief—General Lee—I will not publish their names, but " bury them out of my sight," without a public funeral.

The Sixteenth Alabama Regiment.

In tracing the career of the Ninth Alabama, we were led to refer briefly to the history of every battle fought by the Army of Northern Virginia, under the personal command of General Lee. With the Sixteenth Alabama we have been brought nearer home, to the movements of our army in the Department of the Mississippi, under the command, for a little while, of Gen. A. Sidney Johnston, who fell at Shiloh, just as the sun was emerging, gloriously, from an eclipse; and then under Generals Beauregard, Joseph E. Johnston and Bragg, who were changed from time to time, in obedience to popular whims.

In this number we shall introduce to our readers the regimental officers of the Sixteenth Alabama in general terms, deferring the circumstantial account of them to be given in connection with the regiment as it passed through sunshine and storm, from Fishing Creek to the battle of Nashville, where its organization was virtually broken up. Many of these officers I have known from boyhood; but I shall not give my personal estimate of their characters. I prefer that of their comrades-in-arms. In the ordeal of the camp and the battle-field, if there be any selfishness, meanness or cowardice, it will be seen, while the nobler qualities of the man will be exhibited in a clear light. In many cases I shall give quotations, and if in some cases they seem to the reader to be extravagant, he must keep in mind that nothing but the pure gold will bear this " trial by fire."

The Sixteenth was organized in Courtland on the 8th of August, 1861, about seventeen days after the battle of First Manassas. William B. Wood, Esq., was elected colonel. He was a lawyer of ability, residing in Florence, Ala., and at the same time a local preacher in the Methodist Church, who was very acceptable to his people. His father's name was Alexander Hamilton Wood—so named because his father was an officer in the Revolutionary war who was the intimate friend and comrade of the soldier statesman, Alexander Hamilton. The mother of Colonel Wood was an English woman, Mary E. Evans, daughter of Colonel Evans, of the British army. She came to America in 1816. Colonel Wood was born in Nashville, Tenn., in 1820, and in 1821 he came with his father to Florence, Ala., and has lived there ever since. He married Sarah B., daughter of Major Jesse Leftwitch, who came from Virginia to Columbia, Tenn., and thence to Florence. Colonel Wood was judge of the County Court of Lauderdale county from 1844 to 1850; elector for the State at large on the Bell and Everett ticket in 1860; was elected Circuit Judge in 1863, but remained in the army until the close of the war. In that awful retreat from Fishing creek, he, with many members of the regiment, contracted serious disease. (" This was typhoid fever, which so prostrated him that he was granted sick leave, and was not able to rejoin the regiment until the succeeding November at Estell's Springs."—Surgeon McMahon.) At the battles of Triune and Murfreesboro he led his regiment gallantly, as he had done at Fishing creek, as will be recorded in full in the progress of our narrative. In May, 1863, having been appointed presiding judge of Longstreet's corps, he was transferred to the Army of Northern Virginia. During the time of his service with the Sixteenth he often preached in the camps, and at War Trace he, Colonel Lowry and Colonel Reid assisted the chaplain of the regiment in a revival, in which several hundred were converted. It was here, in June, 1863, the night before he left them, he delivered his farewell sermon to the men of his regiment. I am told that it was a parting in which sorrow was shown on both sides, for the colonel was much loved by his men.

At the conclusion of the war the Colonel was about to assume the office of Judge, to which he had been elected by the people, when, in 1865, he was removed by Governor

Parsons. He was re-elected by the people in 1866, put out by the reconstruction acts of 1868—elected again in 1874, and served until 1880. At the expiration of his term he was not again a candidate for circuit judge, as his friends were urging his claims to a seat on the Supreme Court bench, for which he held a very strong hold, and may now be considered the "heir apparent" whenever a vacancy shall occur.

Judge Wood is rather over the medium size, broad-shouldered and portly, and with frank social manners. His mind is not metaphysical, but masculine; and there is nothing neutral in his character. He is a man of great earnestness and strong convictions—remarkably so, and like most men of that character, he is somewhat impatient of contradiction, and sometimes imperious in his manner. Take him in the aggregate as a man, a minister, a judge, and a soldier, the community in which he has lived so long have reason to be proud of him.

John W. Harris, Jr., raised Company H, was the first captain of it; and was, on the organization of the Sixteenth, elected lieutenant colonel. Colonel Harris was born in Russell's Valley in 1831, and this has always been his permanent home. His father, John W. Harris, Sr., came from Virginia in 1823, settled in the same valley, and although he, at intervals, taught school at La Grange and Tuscumbia, the valley, also, has been his permanent home. His life work has been in the school-room. He was at the head of a classical institution of high character for more than forty years, from which went out an intellectual and Christian influence, the value of which can not be estimated. He is now living with his son, and at the age of eighty years, patiently and hopefully waiting for his Master. He is no kin of Colonel Ben Harris, of Franklin, or Mr. Nehemiah Harris, of Lawrence county, but his father was of English descent, lived in Hanover county, Virginia, and married Margaret Wyatt, a descendant of Sir Francis Wyatt. one of the Colonial Governors. Col. JohnW, Harris' mother was a daughter of Henry Cox, one of the early settlers of the valley, and her name was Judith. One of her sisters was the wife of Capt. Wm. S. Jones.

The comrades of Colonel Harris give a most flattering account of him, as a man and an officer. One says, "He was a most capable, brave and promising officer. Colonel Wood being absent from sickness, he commanded the regiment in the battle at Shiloh, and acted most gallantly, when he was sick from disease contracted at Fishing creek, and scarcely able to sit on his horse. After the battle he went home and suffered from a severe spell of typhoid fever." Another officer says, "He is one of the most cultivated and accomplished gentlemen in North Alabama. His profession is that of teacher, but he has been pretty largely engaged in farming. He is an excellent Christian gentleman. In the army he was brave, true and generous." In August, 1862, finding his constitution shattered, upon the advice of his surgeon he resigned, and for twelve months afterward was so feeble that he was unable to resume business of any kind.

Colonel Harris was educated in his father's school, and in the Centenary College of Louisiana, under Drs. Longstreet and Rivers. The degree of A. M., was conferred upon him by the State Agricultural and Mechanical College at Auburn. The Colonel has been married twice. His wives were sisters, and they were daughters of Mrs. P. Gibson, now the wife of Hon. Charles Gibson of Moulton. The Colonel is a member of the M. E. Church South, and one who performs his duties faithfully. His house is the home of the preachers, and although after a service of many years, he might devolve the duties of Steward upon younger shoulders, he still performs them faithfully. His church has a due appreciation of his worth, for he was sent by the Tennessee Conference as a delegate to the general conference—esteemed a high honor for a private member.

Alexander H. Helveston was captain of Company G, from Marion county, and in the organization was elected major of the Sixteenth Alabama. He had recently come from South Carolina, and had received a military education at the Georgia Military Institute. He was a man of unflinching courage, a good officer and a tried disciplinarian. He was austere and imperious; the men thought him overbearing, and were not fond of him. He was wounded several times. An officer said that it seemed to him that Helveston was wounded every time he went into battle. When Colonel Wood resigned he was promoted Colonel in his place, in May, 1863, having been Lieutenant Colonel since the resignation of John W. Harris, in August, 1862. Colonel Helveston, owing to an injury to his spine caused by the fall of his horse, and to disability from the wounds he received, resigned in December, 1863. I believe he is living, near Gainesville, Ala.

John H. McGaughey was captain of Company A, of the Sixteenth: was the son of Eli A. McGaughey, who resided west of Mt. Hope, in Lawrence county, and a practitioner at Barton, west of Tuscumbia, when the company was organized. When Major Helveston was made lieutenant colonel, he was promoted in his stead. He was a genial companion, an honorable man and a good officer, and like Helveston, he was wounded in nearly every engagement in which he participated. He received a fearful wound at Shiloh on the first volley which the enemy fired. When Helveston was made colonel, he was promoted to lieutenant colonel, and at Chickamauga he was mortally hurt and died of his wounds. Colonel McGaughey was well educated, a gentleman, and an honor to the large family of that name formerly in the southwestern part of our county, of which scarcely one remains bearing the family name.

Frederick A. Ashford was captain of Company B, in the Sixteenth, which he raised and organized. When McGaughey was promoted to lieutenant colonel he became major of the regiment in his stead, and when Colonel McGaughey was killed he was promoted lieutenant colonel. Colonel Ashford was an officer of very fine person and polished manners, was a splendid officer, and was always at the post of danger. His gallantry on many occasions will be recorded as we proceed with the history of the regiment. His brilliant career was closed at the bloody battle of Franklin, where he fell leading a charge of his regiment.

The father of Colonel Ashford was Thomas Ashford, one of the earliest settlers near Courtland. In his youth he, too, had experience in war, was in the regiment of Col. Wm. R. Johnson, of Kentucky, and was near his command in the battle of Tippecanoe, when he killed the Chief Tecumseh. He was a leading member of the Baptist Church, and was very zealous in the performance of his church duties, and much respected. He married, many years before he came from Kentucky, a Miss Elgin, a lady of superior mind, and good education. All their children have had liberal educations. Thomas, the oldest, married Miss Caroline Tate, and died some years ago, leaving a widow and two sons, Thomas and Frederick A. Col. Alva E. Ashford married Miss Caroline Fletcher, and occupies the old mansion. The Colonel commanded the Thirty-fifth Alabama, and his services will be considered in connection with that regiment. Dr. Edward C. Ashford is a good physician, a genial companion, and a man of the kindest heart; but he is not yet married. There was one daughter, Lucilla, who married Rev. D. Bridenthall, of Texas. They have several children.

When Major Fred. A. Ashford was promoted to Lieutenant Colonel, Capt. J. J. May became Major; and when Ashford became Colonel of the regiment, May became Lieutenant Colonel. Nine of the companies composing the regiment were from four neighboring counties on the elevated region of the waters of the Tennessee river, but the tenth was from the extreme southern boundary of Alabama, on the tidewater streams of the Gulf of Mexico. This company was raised and commanded by Capt. J. J. May, and was from Conecuh county. At first they were strangers, but they were commanded by one who proved himself to be a gentleman and a good officer, and following his lead in the many severe engagements which followed each other in quick succession, they were soon received in full brotherhood. Lieutenant Colonel May was wounded in the leg at the battle of the 22d of July, 1864, near Atlanta, and was not able to return to his regiment. I hope to be able to give a fuller account of him as we proceed with our narrative.

On the organization of the Sixteenth, Henry C. Wood became its first Adjutant. He had been a private and a Lieutenant in the Florence Guards, the first company which went out from Lauderdale county. Was at Fort Morgan and Pensacola, and transferred to the Sixteenth. When this regiment was made a part of Wood's brigade, General Wood made him his Aide, and on the return from the Kentucky campaign he succeeded (as Brigade Quartermaster, with the rank of Major) the gallant Gailor, who fell at the battle of Perryville. When the Sixteenth was transferred to Lowry's brigade, he was continued, by General Lowry, in this office. His steady rise in the army shows that he was a faithful officer; and a comrade living near me tells me that " he is one of the best and cleverest men in the world." He is a younger brother of Gen. S. A. M. Wood and Judge W. B. Wood.

Oliver S. Kennedy was the next adjutant of the regiment. He is a nephew of John S. and Elias Kennedy, Esqs., who were lawyers of Florence. Adjutant Kennedy, in the battle of Shiloh, which was contested from morning till night, "acted his part well." He was left sick at Carthage, and was absent on sick leave for some months, when he resigned.

Bryce Wilson was the last adjutant of the regiment. He was the son of Bryce Wilson, Sr., of Russellville. Had been in the Ninth Mississippi. He was transferred to the Sixteenth at Tupelo in the summer of 1863. "Bryce was a fine adjutant and very rigid." He was killed at the battle of Franklin, simultaneously with Col. Fred. Ashford. "There was no braver man in the army. A student of Bethany College, Va., he had begun the practice of law at Hernando, Miss. At the close of the war his father had his remains and those of his brother William (private in the Twenty-seventh Alabama, who died in prison at Camp Douglas) brought home and interred, side by side, beneath the sod of their native valley."—(Col. J. W. Harris.)

The first quartermaster of the regiment was John Gracey, who soon resigned. The next was J. J. Bailey, son of the proprietor of Bailey's Springs. He was a good officer, and continued to the bitter end, "and in the last act of the drama, in North Carolina, he was ready to go into the ranks with his musket." He now lives in Opelousas, La.

The quartermaster sergeant was W. O. Harris, commonly called Buck. He is a brother of Lieutenant Colonel Harris, and continued to serve faithfully through the war, and came home from North Carolina with his furlough in his pocket. His comrades regarded him as "an efficient officer," and as "a good and brave man." He now resides at New Market, in Madison county.

The first commissary was Mr. Hughes, of Franklin county, who was elected colonel of the Thirty-seventh Alabama, and who will be noticed again in that connection. His successor as commissary was Capt. F. O. White, of Russellville. He was a cousin of Col. Harris, "a nice gentleman and a good officer."

The commissary sergeant was Hiram White, of Tuscumbia, a brave man whose history is a melancholy one. "He and his brother were the bravest men I ever saw," says a comrade who was a gallant man himself. Hiram's mother was in a distressed condition, and wrote to him to come home, and a furlough having been refused, he went any how and staid until he provided for his mother. He returned, was reduced to the ranks, and was killed at Chickamauga. "He was first wounded in one or both legs, so badly that he could neither stand or walk. Any ordinary man would have had the infirmary corps to carry him to the hospital. Instead of that, Hiram having exhausted his ammunition, crawled to the body of a dead Federal, and filling his cartridge box from his he fired round after round, until wounded mortally in the spine, his arms became paralyzed, and he was unable to use his rifle. He told Surgeon McMahon, when carried to the hospital, ' that his only regret was that he could not have died fighting on the battle-field.' "

Wm. C. Cross, of Cherokee, Colbert county, was appointed surgeon of the Sixteenth in October, 1861, and was promoted to senior surgeon of the brigade in the spring of 1862 while at Corinth. He remained with the wounded at Perryville; was transferred to hospital duty in the spring of 1863, and remained on duty at Newnan, Ga., until near the close of the war. A brother surgeon who knew him in service, intimately says, " he is a fine physician, a devoted friend, a true patriot, and an elegant gentleman." He lives at Cherokee.

Fortunatus S. McMahon, M. D., of Courtland, was a private in Company I—(Bankhead's)—was commissioned as assistant surgeon in September, 1861, and on the promotion of Dr. Cross became full surgeon of the regiment and continued such until the end of the war. He was the grandson of Dr. Jack Shackelford and inherited the noble qualities of that gentleman, whose memory is very dear to all who knew him. Dr. McMahon had excellent early advantages as learned, in and outside, his profession; and is much esteemed by his old comrades in arms; and has a devotion to them, which I have never known surpassed; and for the brave who fell in "the lost cause" his heart is a mausoleum, on which is inscribed their virtues and their glorious deeds. He never seems to tire of writing or speaking about them; and I am indebted to him for more information respecting the Sixteenth Alabama than to any other person. Since the termination of the war this community is much indebted to Dr. McMahon for quelling a large negro mob which would have assumed huge proportions but for him. It was the second which had taken place within a few months. He still lives in Courtland (1880). He never married. (Died in 1889.)

Dr. William M. Mayes, son of Drury Mayes of our county, served awhile as Assistant Surgeon of the regiment; but was transferred to hospital duty. He will be noticed with his family. Dr. W. J. McMahon—brother of Dr. F. S. McMahon—succeeded him. Dr. W. J. was quite young when the war broke out. He joined his brother at Corinth soon after the battle of Shiloh. He was then assigned to duty as Assistant Surgeon in the hospital at Gainesville, about May 1862, and remained there until January, 1863, when he was assigned to duty with his brother in the Sixteenth, and served with it until wounded on the morning of the 23d of July, 1864, near Atlanta. The day before, a bloody battle had been fought, and on the field we had taken from the enemy, many of their wounded were making piteous appeals for aid. General Cleburne ordered his Assistant Surgeon to go upon the field and dress their wounded. In the discharge of that duty, the medical officers with their infirmary corps, went out, and the enemy in the fog (not being able to see their little flags), fired upon them. Dr. Jack McMahon was seriously wounded in the ankle. He was carried to the hospital and several bones taken out. The wound might have healed, but after the war his horse fell upon the wounded limb, and since then his body has become a perfect wreck; but his heart is still warm and magnanimous, as it ever was.

The first hospital steward was a Dr. Eames, from Cleveland, O. There were in the Confederate army, many gallant soldiers from Illinois, Indiana, and other Northern States. For instance, in the Fifteenth Tennessee regiment, there was an entire company raised in Illinois, General Strahl commanding the brigade. These volunteers believed that the cause of the South was right, and as it was the weaker party they magnanimously espoused their cause, and left their homes to engage in the unequal conflict. Some of them came on General Roddy's steamboat to Eastport, and joined as privates Company A, which was then being raised by Dr. McGaughy. This is the appropriate place to notice a few of these noble men, of whom we happen to have special information.

Dr. Eames was a druggist from Cleveland, Ohio, as I have said, and became steward for the regimental hospital. His capacity was such that he was transferred to Post Hospital duty, and was a long time at Newnan, in Georgia. He had visited some friends in North Alabama, and started over Sand Mountain with the view of settling up his business in Newnan and returning to his family in Ohio, but was never heard of afterward. It is supposed that as he had money and several watches about his person, which friends had sent to be repaired at Newnan, that he had been robbed and murdered by the Tories. Such was the fate of a young gentleman who might have remained at home in safety and affluence, but impelled by lofty motives he, with others, came to our aid in the day of our extremity, and we therefore record the facts, and offer to their memories the tribute of our grateful remembrance. Another of these gentlemen was a young lawyer from Cincinnati named Hassen (or Hassel). After serving in the ranks for a long time, he was made commissary sergeant of the brigade by Major H. C. Wood; and was serving in that capacity at the battle of Chickamauga (although he had just been elected Lieutenant in his old company), when on the third day, while victory was perching on the Confederate banner, and the enemy in full retreat, came to a sad end. While urging a train of provisions to the hungry men of the brigade, was shot by one of our men. His excuse for it was, that he had on a Federal overcoat. It was an act of great folly considering that Lieutenant Hassen was alone in that dress and coming up from the rear. Still another case which I am glad to say had a happy conclusion. Amongst the privates of Company A was a young gentleman of genteel manners and good education, named Almon Brooks. He was left in the hospital with opacity of the cornea of the eye, when General Bragg marched in his Kentucky campaign. He attracted the attention of Dr. Frank Ramsey, Medical Director of the Department of East Tennessee and Virginia. He first made him hospital steward, and afterward transferred him to hospital service at the University of Virginia, where he graduated in medicine, and this unpretending but chivalrous private of Company A is now the learned, wealthy and celebrated Dr. Almon Brooks of Hot Springs, Ark. I am indebted to Dr. F. S. McMahon for a report of these three cases.

Dr. Eames was succeeded as hospital steward by Dr. W. M. Cravens, who was born in Courtland and died in Gainesville; of whom we shall speak in connection with the McMahon family.

There was no ordnance sergeant at first, but at the battle of Fishing creek, Buck Harris, who was in the Quartermaster's Department, acted in that capacity. Orderly Sergeant A. J. Rice, of Florence, was the first regular appointed. He once lived in Texas, I believe. He was then made ordnance officer of the brigade with the rank of first lieutenant. He acted in that capacity at the battle of Shiloh, and at length was transferred to General Roddy's command. "He was outspoken, brave, and irascible," and I judge from his promotion that he was an efficient officer. When he was promoted, DeWitt C. White was appointed ordnance sergeant for the Sixteenth. When Mr. White withdrew from the regiment, Columbus C. Harris was appointed ordnance sergeant of the Sixteenth in his place; and again when Captain Rice was transferred, he was made ordnance officer of the brigade, with the rank of first lieutenant. He was a fearless soldier and was wounded several times during the war.

At the battle of Franklin he was wounded in five places; and perhaps his leg would have been amputated, but for the protest of that skilful surgeon McMahon, who saved the limb by a resection of the bones. Lieutenant Harris is the son of William Harris, one of the early settlers, and is a lawyer of Decatur. A comrade of whom I inquired respecting his character in the army, writes "he was indeed a good soldier. You know him in private life, how quiet and yet how true in the discharge of duty. He was such in the army." I shall give an account of the Harris family should I live to get to the southwest part of the country.

The first chaplain of the regiment was Rev. A. Hamilton, of the Methodist Church. He had been at the head of a female academy before, and had about him that nameless something which you so often find in men who have followed his calling; which at first created a prejudice against him amongst the soldiers. But time corrects all things. He was fastidious in his uniform, but under it was a heart warm with solicitude for the spiritual good of the men, and also full of martial ardor. He proved to be a man at all points. "In the awful retreat from Fishing creek, the quartermaster being absent and the men suffering immensely, Dr. Hamilton was assigned to this duty and performed it so well that he was afterward regularly commissioned. He was fastidious in his dress, but he was a good preacher, a pleasant messmate, a genial gentleman, and when transferred made one of the best quartermasters in the army. He had a good deal of military ardor up to the time that his horse ran away at Perryville, and knocked down a panel of fence and seriously bruised him. Then for awhile he acted as aide for Gen. S. A. M. Wood, the members of whose staff were nearly all killed, and who was himself wounded. He was on duty as quartermaster at Huntsville, Kingston, Ga., and Tuscaloosa. His church had a high appreciation of his ability, and the degree of D. D. was conferred upon him. After the war he was president of a female academy at Cuthbert, Georgia. Understanding that he had kept a diary of the movements of the Sixteenth, I addressed a letter to him not many days since, and was shocked to read in the Nashville *Christian Advocate*, on the next day, an announcement of the death of this fine officer and able minister.

Rev. Frank Kimball, of the Kimballs of Morgan county, was the successor of Major Hamilton as chaplain of the regiment. He was a good, plain, earnest preacher, and was popular with the men. He followed his avocation, alike on the field of battle as in the hospital. A comrade said he truly belonged to the "Church Militant." He, too, died in Georgia. We shall refer to him again in connection with the battle of Murfreesboro. Having disposed of the regimental officers of the Sixteenth, we will now treat of the commissioned officers of the several companies. Charles E. Gibson was sergeant major of the regiment. He was the youngest son of Judge Charles Gibson, and was in this office at the battle of Shiloh—had a bone in his leg broken at the battle of Murfreesboro, when his brother William was mortally wounded—and was, strangely, wounded in the same place, on his leg, at the battle of Chickamauga. He served bravely and faithfully during the war, studied law and emigrated to Waxahatchie, Texas, where he married a Miss Ellis. For some time he was clerk of the District Court of Ellis county, and since a member of the Legislature, to which he has been twice elected, and is now a member.

COMPANY A.—Had for its first captain John H. McGaughey, an account of whom we have given in our last. The first lieutenant was Barton Dixon. He was the son of one of the most useful and honored citizens which Franklin (now Colbert) county ever had. His father was an old man when the war broke out, and might have sat quietly down in the chimney corner until the storm blew over; but William Dixon was not made of that kind of stuff. At a time when great numbers of volunteers were discharged for want of arms, he went into the interior of Georgia and established a large factory for the manufacture of them. He not only devoted his large wealth, but all the faculties of his active and strong mind to the successful prosecution of this patriotic enterprise. When Captain McGaughey was promoted, Lieut. Barton Dixon became captain in his place, about August, 1863. He was wounded severely in the hip at the battle of Jonesboro, Ga., just before Hood's expedition into Tennessee. He was esteemed by his comrades a perfect gentleman and a brave and intelligent officer. He married Miss Nellie Mayes, daughter of Drury Mayes, Esq., near Courtland. Second Lieut. Goodloe Pride, too, was of a good stock, and was, like Dixon, gentlemanly, brave and efficient. They had been reared together, and were warm friends. The day after Dixon was wounded, Pride (who had become first lieutenant) was seriously wounded by the explosion of a shell. The clothes were nearly torn from his body and he bled from his ears. He is still living. John Calhoun was third lieutenant, and was killed at the battle of Franklin, at which he commanded the company. I hope some comrade will give me information respecting him. I omitted to mention that the company was raised in Franklin county.

COMPANY B.—We have given a sketch of Captain Frederick A. Ashford (who became colonel). First Lieutenant Isaac C. Madden became captain in his stead. Capt. M. lived near Leighton in Lawrence county, where the company was raised. "He was no disciplinarian; he was easy with his men; took little authority over them, and yet had unbounded influence over them. He seemed truly to rule by the '*Suaviter in modo*,' rather than by harsh and preemptory command. The men of his company were devoted to him, as they had been to their first captain—the noble and true Fred. Ashford, who never ordered his men to go forward, but to follow him: so it was with Captain Madden. No men were more beloved." This is the utterance of a comrade: he is noble and gallant. The history of the Madden family is one of deep and melancholy interest to me, personally. More than sixty-five years ago, when a boy, I knew in

Williamson county, Tenn., the head of this family, Elisha Madden, well. He was a young man of very fine person, good manners and great energy. He afterward came to this county, as the agent of Hinchea Pettway, a very wealthy merchant of Franklin, and cleared and improved a large plantation west of Town creek. He accumulated a handsome fortune for himself, and married a daughter of Dr. Croom, one of three or four brothers who were wealthy, and came from North Carolina nearly sixty years ago. They moved eventually to South Alabama. Captain Elisha Madden was a man of fine sense, had four sons and two daughters, and gave them all liberal educations. When the war of the States came, every one of these sons engaged actively in the service, and three out of the four gave up their lives for the "lost cause." Richard, the eldest, a private in Captain Fred. Ashford's company, had his thigh broken at the battle of Shiloh, and was laid by Surgeon McMahon in a tent of a captured Federal camp. His brother Isaac was called back from the front, and as the enemy was shelling that part of the field, furiously, they removed Richard from the tent. They had carried him but a short distance when a shell exploded in the tent and tore it to atoms. But this escape availed nothing, for this brave soldier afterward died at Corinth, after the amputation of his limb. Isaac C. was killed at the battle of Chickamauga. "He had studied law before the war, but had not commenced the practice. He was well educated, brave and high-minded, and in person eminently handsome."

Dr. Frank Madden graduated in medicine at the University of Louisiana. He was assistant surgeon of some Alabama regiment, and was killed in the trenches near Atlanta by a shot from a Federal sharpshooter. The fourth son, Capt. James Madden, served gallantly in the Thirty-fifth Alabama (as we will show when we come to speak of that regiment), survived the war, and unfortunately died from fever last autumn. The eldest daughter married Augustus Toney, Esq., and they have a very interesting family. The younger daughter, Camilla, grew up with much beauty and a queenly person—a discreet, sweet-tempered, graceful and cultivated woman. She has been married twice—first to Dr. James T. Jones, of Lawrence, and then to Capt. Alexander D. Coffee, of Lauderdale county. The father of the family, Elisha Madden, died some years ago, much respected by all who knew him for his integrity and many virtues. The "mother of the Gracchi," who gave all her sons to her country, still lives—the same unpretending, kind, true-hearted Christian woman she ever was, performing faithfully her duties in the private circle, as they nobly theirs before the world on the battle-field.

Frederick A. M. Sherrod was second lieutenant of Company B, and when Captain Madden was killed, he succeeded him in command. Captain Sherrod was a cultivated and kind-hearted gentleman, excitable and brave, and proved to be a good officer. He was wounded both at Murfreesboro and Chickamauga, after which he was absent from his command for some time on leave. He still lives, and is highly respected for his Christian and social virtues. He is the grandson of Col. Benjamin Sherrod, of Lawrence, who was the head of a large and influential family, and will be noticed again in that connection.

Chesley Davis was third lieutenant of Company B, and was promoted by steps to first lieutenant. He commanded the company after Captain Sherrod was wounded, and was regarded by his comrades as a brave, good officer. He was the son of Orrin Davis then of Winston county, whose family history we will notice hereafter. Captain Davis was wounded by the fragment of a shell at Atlanta, in the battle of which General McPherson was killed.

A. M. Hill, of Jasper, in Walker county, son of Senator Hill, then of this district, was a good soldier; and was promoted to second, when Davis became first lieutenant.

COMPANY C.—From Lauderdale county, had for its first captain, Alexander D. Coffee. He was the son of Gen. John Coffee, who was a brigadier under General Jackson and acquired considerable reputation in the Creek and New Orleans campaigns. Captain Coffee was a good officer, and had the confidence of his men. "After the battle of Shiloh his health became bad. He had severe bronchitis, and at least one hemorrhage from the lungs; and was apprehensive of pulmonary disease. He was sent back by the surgeon of the Sixteenth Alabama to the hospital at Corinth, and by the post surgeon at that place to the hospital at Columbus, Miss.; from which place, in a few weeks, he sent in his resignation."

William Patton was the first lieutenant of Company G, a brave and most promising young officer, of a fine person, and of a popular turn. In the battle of Shiloh the Sixteenth Alabama had charged so rapidly forward that a strong force of the enemy, with a battery of guns, were playing upon their left. The regiment was reformed, nearly at right angles to its first course, and charged rapidly on the battery. When within twenty feet of it, this splendid young officer was shot in the forehead, and fell dead. He was the son of Governor Patton, and had the blood of the Weakleys and Brahams in his veins. We shall speak of the family hereafter.

Oliver S. Kennedy was the second lieutenant of Company C, and we have given an account of him.

Calvin Carson, who was third, was promoted second, then first lieutenant, and became captain of Company C in December, 1863. He was an efficient officer, and served until the end of the war. He is still living, and has turned his attention to commercial affairs. When he was promoted J. J. Stubbs became first lieutenant. Of him I have no information.

COMPANY D.—We have already spoken of this company, which was from Conecuh county, and of its first captain, J. J, May, who became lieutenant colonel of the Sixteenth. Mr. Stallsworth was first lieutenant, but on the death of his father, Hon. James Stallsworth (who was Congressman from our State), he resigned and returned home. He was succeeded by Lieutenant Jackson, a very promising young officer, who was sick at the battle of Fishing creek, and fell into the hands of the enemy. When he recovered he managed to escape, and rejoined the company at Shelbyville, Tenn. He was killed at the battle of Murfreesboro. Frank Walker was promoted captain, and commanded in the Georgia campaign. I hope to obtain, as we go on, more special information as to the members of Company D.

COMPANY E.—Was from Franklin county. Its first captain was W. W. Weatherford, a son of John Weatherford, a former sheriff of Franklin county. Captain Weatherford was practising medicine in Frankfort when the war commenced. He served faithfully for about two years, and then resigned. He did not have a liberal education, but was a man of extensive reading and good memory. "He was very tall and ungainly, even awkward, and from the peculiar attitude he assumed when standing, the boys nicknamed him 'Parade Rest.' He was a kind-hearted, generous man, esteemed by the people, and elected a member of the Legislature in 1876." He has been dead for several years. Israel P. Guy, First Lieutenant of Company E, is the son of Albert Guy, near Tuscumbia, and is still living at that place. He was a student at LaGrange, a military college, and was well drilled. Although quite young when he volunteered, he was large and fat. He made a good officer. He was severely wounded at the battle of Chickamauga, by a grape shot, and it took a long crucial incision to remove it. There was a Lieutenant Russell in the company, who was killed at the battle of Murfreesboro, about 10 o'clock in the forenoon, while charging a battery.

COMPANY F.—Was from Lawrence county. Its first captain, William Hodges, the son of Col. Flemming Hodges, who was born in this county, although when the war commenced he was practising law at Okolona, Miss. Captain Hodges raised a large company of excellent material. He had belonged to Mott's Nineteenth Mississippi regiment. During the war Captain Hodges was highly esteemed as a gentleman and a brave officer; wounded several times, and was terribly mangled at the battle of Chickamauga, and afterward placed upon the retired list. Since the war he has been a member of the Mississippi Legislature, and now resides in Aberdeen. John M. McGhee was first lieutenant of the company. He was a son of Judge Henry A. McGhee, and a brave and very popular officer. He served until the spring of 1863. Having been elected clerk of the Circuit Court, he was transferred to General Roddy's command. He now lives in Waco, Texas. Second Lieutenant David W. Alexander survived the war, and now lives in Shelbyville, Tenn. D. O. Warren was third lieutenant of this company. And lost an arm at Chickamauga. He is a son of William Warren, and has lived near Moulton until recently, when he moved to Texas.

COMPANY G.—From Marion county, had for its first captain A. H. Helveston, of whom we gave an account in our last. G. W. Archer was first lieutenant and captain in 1861. He remained a long time with the company. W. T. Bishop was also first lieutenant, John Hamilton, second lieutenant, and Robert Roback, third lieutenant. David Bentley, a lieutenant of Company I, was transferred and appointed to the command of Company G by the colonel commanding. Such a measure, no matter how strong the necessity may be, is always hazardous. It was greatly to the mortification of the subordinates, and to the chagrin of the company. The men after twelve or eighteen months, got to respecting their new officer, for he was an excellent man of the finest business capacity and a high-toned gentleman, but he never relished his position. At the battle of Murfreesboro he was an invalid, and unable to walk, but after it commenced he mounted the horse of a friend, rode to the front and took command of his company; in one hour he was brought back to the hospital mortally wounded. Thos. Stanley, lieutenant, in Company——, from Lawrence county, was then transferred and placed in command of the company, and may have continued in command, but of this we have no certain information.

COMPANY H.—From Franklin county, was raised by Lieutenant Colonel John W. Harris, Jr., who was its first captain. Of him we have already given an account. He was succeeded as captain by First Lieutenant James Smith, who after the battle of Perryville, was seriously injured in a railroad collision at Cleveland, Tenn., and resigned. Lieutenant John Bean, son of Col. Dillion Bean, of Lawrence county, succeeded him as captain. Indeed, there were many Lawrence men in Company H. Captain Bean commanded the company to the end of the war. The captain was a brave officer, and did not disgrace his descent from the early Indian fighters of East Tennessee. John Hurst was a lieutenant and a good officer. He was terribly wounded at Chickamauga, but recovered and returned to his duty. John White became a lieutenant in 1863. We have already spoken of him in connection with Hiram White, his brother.

COMPANY I.—From Lawrence county, of which William S. Bankhead was first captain. Captain B. was a lineal descendant of President Thomas Jefferson. We shall speak of him again in connection with the families into which he married. "Captian B. joined General Zollicoffer, at Cumberland Gap, in a bitterly cold spell, and contracted inflammatory rheumatism; and returned home on sick leave, and when the regiment passed through Courtland on its way to Corinth, he resigned his commission. He had in a very short space of time, obtained extraordinary proficiency in drilling and disciplining his men; and but that he almost lost the use of a leg from rheumatism, a distinguished career was before him." First Lieutenant George M. Garth, of Courtland, was promoted to the captaincy, then being in bad health. He resigned in April, 1862, and died a few weeks afterward. "Lieutenant McDonald, too, succumbed to the rigor of the climate, and offered his resignation. He was a perfect gentleman, but of so weak and delicate a frame he ought never have thought of joining a marching regiment. He died recently in Courtland." "I remember," says his surgeon, "when Lieutenant McDonald, who had been on sick leave, joined us on the retreat from Fishing Creek, how pale and exhausted he looked—a better subject for a sick bed than a march." The Third Lieutenant, La Fayette Swoope, M. D., first from Virginia, but more recently from De Soto, Miss., was promoted to the captaincy. He had commanded the company at the battle of Shiloh, and was wounded in the shoulder. In January, 1863, he resigned, and Lieutenant Robert McGregor was promoted to the captaincy. Captain M. was a descendant of a

North Carolina family, which settled near Courtland more than half a century ago, and of which I shall hereafter give an account. He, like Col. Fred. Ashford, was quite a young man, and of splendid person. They fell at the battle of Franklin, near each other, and close to the interior works of the enemy. Their loss was deeply felt in our neighborhood. Lieutenant Thomas S. Pointer, then and now of Courtland, succeeded to the captaincy of the company, and commanded it to the end of the war. Robert H. Cherry was a splendid soldier; he was a good mechanic, and worked in Thorn's gin shop at Courtland; he married a daughter of Noah Cooper, of our county; was a brave man, became second lieutenant of the company and was killed at the battle of Chickamauga—a field upon which fell so many of the best young men of the Sixteenth Alabama. The widow of Lieutenant Cherry is now the wife of Robert Miller of our county, who was also a faithful soldier. Overton Eggleston became second lieutenant in his place, and was the last in the company.

COMPANY K.—From Marion county, had for its first captain, the Rev. William Powers. He was a good officer, much respected by his men, but resigned in 1863. J. N. Watson was first lieutenant when first organized, but I have not learned what became of him. Second Lieutenant John H. Bankhead* succeeded Captain Powers in the captaincy. He was a good officer, has been in our Legislature since the war, and is now warden of our State penitentiary. Third Lieutenant W. S. Humphries became first, and was killed somewhere in Georgia. Captain Powers had a son, a minister of the gospel, who became lieutenant, served through the war, and has since joined the conference again.

I have now introduced to our readers, in general terms, the officers of the Sixteenth Alabama. The actors in the tragedy which was enacted for nearly four long years, in bloody acts, commencing with the battle of Fishing creek and passing through those of Shiloh, Perryville, Murfreesboro, Decatur, Chickamauga, Atlanta and Franklin, virtually closing with that of Nashville.

The survivors of the regiment have it in their power to enrich its history, by communicating to the writer, as we proceed, facts of interest connected with these battles. It is especially the duty of the officers of all the companies to do so. While these campaigns were in progress, they were bound to provide for the comfort of their men, and now when oblivion is fast settling over these transactions, it is their duty to perpetuate the fame of their gallant privates, "for the night cometh in which no man can work."

*John Hollis Bankhead, born in Moscow, Marion (now Lamar) county, Alabama, September 13, 1842, has had a distinguished career. His war service was conspicuous. After the war he had various business interests. His public service for Alabama comprises Representative in the General Assembly from Marion county, for the sessions 1865-66, and 1866-67, member of the State Senate 1876-77, Representative from Lamar county, 1880-81; and Warden of the Alabama Penitentiary 1881-85. He has been successively a member of the Fiftieth, Fifty-first, Fifty-second, Fifty-third, Fifty-fourth, Fifty-fifth and Fifty-sixth Congress from the Sixth Alabama District. He is one of the political leaders of the State, wise and fearless, but with conservative views on all great public questions. He belongs to that sturdy Scotch-Irish stock, to which America owes so much. His parents were James Greer and Susan Fleming (Hollis) Bankhead, who lived and died in Marion county. She was a daughter of Col. John Hollis, who was the son of Capt John Hollis, a Revolutionary soldier in Marion's command, who died in Fairfield District, South Carolina. His grandfather, George Bankhead, and wife, Jane Greer, came to Marion county about 1830, and here they reared a large family. They were from Union District, South Carolina. Here his parents, James and Elizabeth (Black) Bankhead, lived on Broad river, their lands lying on this and Pacolet river. James Bankhead was at one time principal owner of the town of Pinckneyville, the county seat of old Camden District. He and wife lie side by side in the old burying ground at Bullock Creek Presbyterian Church, York District, South Carolina, with tombstones over their graves.

Mr. Bankhead's wife is Tallulah James Brockman, daughter of James and Elizabeth (Shirley) Brockman, of Greenville District, South Carolina. They have five children, viz: (1) Louise Bankhead, married Col. William Hayne Perry, of Greenville, South Carolina; (2) Marie Susan, married Thomas McAdory Owen, a practising attorney and author, of Carrollton, Alabama; (3) John Hollis, Jr., married Musa Harkins, and is practising law at Jasper, Alabama; (4) William Brockman, a lawyer, residing at Huntsville, Alabama; and (5) Henry McAuley, Captain in the Fifth United States Volunteers, Infantry, Cuban War.

I contemplate, as soon as I can collect the material, publishing a number in "conclusion" of the history of the Ninth Alabama, giving sketches of General Wilcox and Surgeon Minor.

The Sixteenth Alabama—Its Departure.

This, like all the regiments which volunteered early in the war, was taken from the cream of the fighting material of the country, and they were volunteers indeed. On the 20th August, 1861, they left their rendezvous at Courtland, cheered by the hospitality of its citizens, and by the enthusiasm which gushed from the patriotic hearts of the people assembled to witness their departure. "From Courtland to Knoxville the trip was one grand ovation. Confederate flags hung from almost every house top; at every cross-roads and town they were greeted with loud huzzas." At Knoxville they were thrown into camps of instruction, where they had to learn the "goose-step" and pass through the "measles" before they were thought worthy to encounter a campaign. These were halcyon days for the boys. They were viewing the sunny side of war. The Confederate army had been so far triumphant, and a spirit of overweening confidence prevailed among those in the field ready to battle for the cause; but, unfortunately, to a greater extent among those who stayed at home, that others might do what little fighting was necessary, for them. The camp was a scene of great merriment. The music of rude camp ballads filled the air. One, which Elijah Stover of the brass band of Oakville, had the honor of composing, or introducing, ran thus:

> "We'll pray for the Doctor, whom I like to have forgot,
> I believe he's the meanest of the whole flock;
> He'll tell you that he'll cure you, for half you possess,
> And when you are dead, he'll take all the rest."

One ingenious fellow ventured to make a change in the laws of war, and to promulgate it in verse:

> "And if we find about our tents,
> A chicken over his owner's fence.
> We take him prisoner, and then he is tied
> Till 12 o'clock, when he is tried."

It is somewhat uncertain whether the last word should not have been "*fried*." Horses had always been contraband of war, but the chickens were now placed in the same category.

The soldiers could be seen in knots talking of the various phases of the great victory at Manassas. Here a lot of very young ones, gravely discoursing about the case of a boy from Florence, who captured a Zouave Colonel with his war horse, sword and pistols, and brought him to General Beauregard—and there a crowd of older ones, enjoying with loud burst of laughter, the account that Asa Hartz gave of what occurred in Washington before, during and after this battle. The reader will remember that Asa was a second Sam Slick and pretended to be on intimate terms with General Scott, who would read to him the dispatches of General McDowell as they came in. At first, they were very encouraging, and the old Guard took the oath (a dram) once; then they were not so good, and he took the oath twice; but when the dispatch came, "the enemy is running, but we are before them. My division is making splendid time, and long tracks," the old hero took the oath three times, and overturned the chairs and tables generally. How fortunate it is that a thick curtain hangs before the future. Could these brave fellows have foreseen, that in the first battle, they were to witness the rout of their army—a retreat at midnight from a fortified camp—leaving all their stores behind them—and that in their march the suffering from cold and hunger would be so great that some of them would beg their comrades for the privilege of lying down by the side of the road to die; it would have unfitted them entirely for the conflict through which they were to pass.

The Sixteenth Alabama was placed in the brigade of Gen. Felix K. Zollicoffer. "He was of a Swiss family of knightly rank, settled in North Carolina before the Revolutionary war, in which his grandfather was a captain. His father was a prosperous farmer in Maury county, Tenn., where Zollicoffer was born May 19, 1812. He began life as a printer, and in 1835 was elected printer for the State. After several essays on journalism he became editor of the *Republican Banner* in 1842, and was noted as the champion of the Whig party. He was then elected comptroller of the State, which position he held until 1847. 1848 he was elected a State Senator, and in 1852 a Representative in the United States Congress, to which position he was re-elected. When the war seemed inevitable he was elected by the General Assembly of Tennessee as a commissioner to the Peace Congress, from which he returned dejected by its failure to accomplish any useful purpose. Governor Harris offered to appoint him a major general, but he would only accept the place of brigadier on account of his inexperience." This account is by Gen. Marcus J. Wright, and copied from the life of Gen. A. S. Johnston written by his son, Col. William Preston Johnston. This is a work of great worth, and abounds in facts. In the case of General Zollicoffer, however, he has done his memory great injustice by launching out into the region of opinions; as I shall show in the progress of this narrative. What he says in this history carries more force from the supposition that he reflected his father's opinions, but had no better opportunity than others to know them, for he tells us he never saw his father after parting from him at Nashville, the day on which he assumed the command of the army.

General Zollicoffer had risen very rapidly in the estimation of the people of Tennessee. In Congress from the commencement of his service, he was placed on important committees, and on the floor his speeches were luminous and strong, and his opinions respected by statesmen of experience, even on abstruse subjects, which could only be accounted for by the fact that he had been a journalist, and while conducting a paper of large circulation for many years, he had stored a mind naturally of the first order with information on all great political questions. He was sober, industrious, honorable, and his reputation was spotless. He was a tall, thin man, of distinguished personal appearance and thoughtful mien. "He was more than a mere popular leader; he was a patriot full of noble and generous qualities. He was the idol of Tennessee, and the people felt his death as a personal bereavement, and still cherish his memory with tender and reverent regret." He was sent in command of a brigade to East Tennessee at a critical moment. Hon. Andy Johnson and other civic leaders were planning a revolt in that region, which, sustained by a Federal invasion, should break the Confederate line of railroad communication between Virginia and the Southwest. Already two regiments of East Tennesseeans had been organized; but as soon as General Zollicoffer assumed command, these regiments (with their Union leaders) crossed the mountains and joined the Federal army in front, commanded by General Schoeff; but by unfrequented paths they still kept up communication with the disaffected at home.

About the 13th of September, 1861, General Albert Sydney Johnston arrived at Knoxville, on his way from Richmond, where he had been invested with the command of the Department of the Mississippi. He came with a reputation, personal and military, inferior to none. He had received a complete education in his profession, at West Point, and was a gallant and experienced soldier. He had served in the Black Hawk war—in the Texan Revolution—in the Mexican war—and had conducted a difficult expedition into Utah. Amongst military men it was a question, who was the ablest, he or Robert E. Lee. When Jefferson Davis was Secretary of War—and he was the ablest we have ever had—he gave the first place in the celebrated Second Cavalry to Johnston as colonel, and the second to Lee as lieutenant-colonel. General Scott thought the appointments should have been reversed. The two men were esteemed the first in the United States Army and were devoted personal friends.

General Johnston remained at Knoxville long enough to have a full conference on the military situation with General Zollicoffer, to approve the plans already made by him (with the advice of Governor Harris, of Tennessee), to advance into Kentucky and seize Cumberland Gap, and to put General Zollicoffer into full possession of his general policy as to the conduct of the campaign, "which was, from the beginning, to keep up such an aspect of menace as would deter the enemy from an advance. A crushing blow delivered by Sherman on any part of his line would discover his weakness, and his wish was to parry rather than to meet such a blow. It could only be averted by inspiring the enemy with an exaggerated notion of the Confederate strength, and with such expectation of immediate attack as would put him on the defensive." (*Life of Johnston, page 362.*)

In pursuance of this policy, General Zollicoffer seized Cumberland Gap 15th of September, and while fortifying it, he sent Colonel Battle, who broke up a camp of Union men at Barbourville—another encampment at Laurel Bridge was broken up, and a supply of salt and ammunition obtained, and a camp near Alburry was attacked, routed and a good many muskets captured—all these before the end of September. During October he advanced to Wild Cat, where he expected to find General Schoeff, with two regiments. "He felt of him," and found him in strong force (six regiments), and fell back, for his orders were not to fight pitched battles.

In pursuance of orders from General Johnston, he was encamped with his force at Mill Spring on the 30th of November.

The regiment had been greatly afflicted with measles. So many were on the sick list, that General Zollicoffer when he moved to Cumberland Gap, took only a Battalion of it with him; leaving the sick with 150 effective men and three cavalry companies, under Col. W. B. Wood, who was in command of the post. The enemy had made extensive arrangements for a revolt in East Tennessee, which was to be sustained by an advance of the Federal army; but it was foiled by General Johnston, who ordered a combined movement up the Cumberland, under Cleburne, and down that river, under Zollicoffer. His information of their designs was so accurate, and the movement was so well timed, "that the Federal army, under Schoeff, fell back to Crab Orchard, with so much precipitation as to resemble a rout. The weather was bad and the roads were deep; and tons of ammunition, and vast quantities of stores, were thrown away."— (*Life of Johnston 363.*) This was on the 11th of November. It put an end to the great revolt; but the arrangement for it on a day fixed had gone so far that it could not be entirely arrested. All the railroad bridges would have been burned, but for prompt measures on the part of Colonel Wood. Captain McGaughey and Lieutenant Sherrod with twenty men, held about 500 of the Union men at bay for two days, at Strawberry Plains; but they barely arrived in time, for sixteen incendiaries, at midnight, had attacked John Keelan, the keeper of the bridge. He defended, it and killed the leader in the act of setting fire to it. He received three bullet-wounds, and many cuts and gashes, and his hand was nearly severed from his wrist; but he fought his assailants so fiercely they fled. Captain May and Lieutenant McGhee, with a like force, protected the bridge near Midway, although surrounded on every side by tories, who were infuriated. Captain Fred. Ashford, with ten men, went up to Lick creek and brought down six of the bridge burners, although the whole country was filled with the disaffected, who could have captured him, had they dared the enterprise. The notorious Colonel Cliff, too, had collected in a camp on Sale creek, 500 to 1000 Union men, which Col. W. B. Wood dispersed by a concerted movement of 100 of his men, and two of Powell's companies from Knoxville, and the Seventh Alabama regiment, under Col. S. A. M. Wood, from Chattanooga. They enclosed Cliff's camp about daylight; but he by some means heard of the movement at three a. m., and fled to the mountains.

When General Carroll arrived in Knoxville from Memphis, with his brigade, Col. W. B. Wood, with the rest of his regiment, marched to Mill Springs. On the 24th of November Gen. Geo. B. Crittenden arrived at Knoxville, and by order of the War Department took command of that district. I presume this was a political appointment. His father, Senator Crittenden, was sitting on the fence of "neutrality," his brother, Thomas L., had gotten down on the Federal side, and been appointed Major General, and Geo. B. taking the Confederate side, was appointed to the same grade for the purpose of countervailing the family influence in Kentucky. His district included the brigade of General Zollicoffer, but for some reason he reported directly to, and received his orders directly from General Johnston, until Major General Crittenden arrived at Mill Springs on the last day of 1861.

A few days after General Zollicoffer arrived at this camp (30th November) he received a communication from General Johnston approving of all his movements up to that time, and suggesting "that Mill Springs was a point from which you may be able to observe the river, without crossing it as far as Burksville, which is desirable." General Zollicoffer answered that he had crossed the river before he had received his information from him, and then described his camp thus: "This camp is immediately opposite the Mill Springs, one and a quarter miles distant. The river protects our rear and flanks. We have about 1200 yards fighting front to defend, which we are intrenching as fast as our few tools will allow. * * *

The position I occupy, north of the river, is a fine base for operation in front. It is a much stronger natural position for defence than that on the south bank. I think it should be held at all hazards. General J. saw at once that the position was a good one for defence and for menacing the enemy in front; and he telegraphed to General Crittenden "to dispatch without delay the supplies and intrenching tools sent there for General Zollicoffer; and to send at once a regiment and a battery to his support; stating also that he has crossed the Cumberland at Mill Springs, has the enemy in front and the river behind and is securing his front." (*Life of Johnston*, pages 398, 400.) If this language means anything, it was that Gen. Z. should be sustained in his position by the most vigorous measures, and not by a withdrawal of the forces. The camp too was plentiful in wood and water, and had a grist and saw-mill at hand.

"While constructing his ferries he sent some troops on the 2d of December and shelled a small force of the enemy posted on the north bank, and compelled it to move. On the 4th he threw over a small cavalry picket, which drove back the Federal horse, and caused a precipitate retreat of the Seventeenth Ohio, which was advancing on a reconnoisance. Next day the pickets wounded and captured Major Helveston and Captain Prime, engineer officers, and along with them a corporal. Then the cavalry crossed Fishing creek (which falls into the river five miles above the camp), and reconnoitred the Federal camp at Somerset. On the 8th they had a skirmish with Wolford's Cavalry and the Thirty-fifth Ohio Infantry, killing 10 and capturing 16, and having only 1 Confederate wounded. On the 11th he sent an expedition to attack a small body of Federals, thirty miles distant toward Columbia, in which they were completely routed. In the meantime, Schoeff, overawed and put upon his guard, retired three miles behind Somerset, intrenched himself in a strong position and called loudly, in every direction, for re-enforcements." (*See Life of Johnston, page 397.*)

These minor movements were carrying out the policy of his great commander-in-chief in a skilful manner. He gained time to intrench and construct a strong camp by making an exaggerated impression of his strength and setting his antagonist to "digging." And these close all the active operations for which General Zollicoffer was responsible. From the time he marched out of Knoxville three short months had expired, and during that short term he had fortified the gaps in the Cumberland Mountains; he had beat up the Union encampments in Kentucky in such a lively manner that Schoeff was completely deceived as to his strength; he had moved in conjunction with Cleburne in so bold a manner that even Sherman was startled and ordered both Thomas and Schoeff to retreat rapidly to central Kentucky (*see his Memoirs, Vol. 1, 199*), and at length Zollicoffer crosses the Cumberland in the face of the enemy, and by a series of quick, bold movements gained time to fortify himself in a chosen camp, where General Crittenden found him on the last day of the year, and superseded him in command.

General Crittenden brought with him the brigade of Gen. Wm. H. Carroll.

On the 31st of December, 1861, General Thomas started from Lebanon to attack the Confederates at Mill Springs. George H. Thomas was an officer of fine abilities and much experience. When Johnston was appointed colonel of the Second Cavalry, and Lee next in rank, Thomas was made major. He was a Virginian by birth, and a West Pointer. "His command consisted of eight and a half regiments and three batteries of artillery. Rains, high water and bad roads impeded their progress, so that it was the 17th of January before they reached Logan's Cross Roads, ten miles from Zollicoffer's intrenched camp. Here Thomas took position to await four of his regiments that had not come up. To secure himself he communicated with Schoeff, and obtained from him a reinforcement of three regiments and a battery. This gave him eleven regiments and a battalion, besides artillery. The remainder of Schoeff's force must have been near by, as they joined in the pursuit" (*Life of Johnston, p. 398*). This left that officer four regiments and some cavalry, and made the amount of the Federal forces, when combined, fifteen regiments and one battalion.

Gen. Crittenden called a council of war, the evening before the battle of Fishing creek, the following account of which has been given me by Col. Wm. B. Wood "He laid before the generals and colonels such information as he had received from his scouts, and citizens who had come into our camp, in reference to the number and position of the army of General Thomas; and the opinion of each one was asked, as to whether it was best to go out and attack him, or remain in our fortifications and await his attack. General Zollicoffer did not vote. All the rest favored going out and attacking him but myself. After the council was over and we had received our instructions, as I went out of the house I met General Zollicoffer on the porch, and he remarked that he very much doubted the propriety of the movement, and believed it to be contrary to the wishes and policy of the commander-in-chief, General Johnston.*

General Zollicoffer and myself rode back together to his quarters, which were not far from mine. On the way we talked of General Crittenden's condition, and his unfitness to go into a fight. The fatal march commenced at midnight.

Why this council of war was called is a mystery. Was it because General Zollicoffer, when consulted, doubted the policy of offering battle to the enemy, outside of intrenchments, which had been projected by a competent engineer, and on which he had labored diligently, for six weeks? I infer from all the facts stated, that this *was* the case.

The force of General Crittenden, according to a weekly report made by him, on the 7th of January, 1862, amounted to an aggregate, present and absent, of 9417 men, but numbering effectives (present for duty) of 333 officers and 6111 rank and file" (*Life of Johnston*).

The day after the council, three regiments which had been encamped on the south of the Cumberland river were carried to the north side, on a stern-wheel steamboat under command of Captain Spiller, and the ferry-boats. The river was then very high. Captain Montsurratt's splendid battery of six brass guns from Memphis was left on the south bank of the river. It would seem that the object of General Crittenden in leaving it on the south side (which was much higher than the camp on the north side) was, in case of a defeat, to secure a safe and deliberate crossing of the river, under the protection of its guns. If that was his design, it was forgotten in the confusion of his retreat.

The Thirty-seventh Tennessee Regiment (Colonel Moses White, which was part of Carroll's brigade) was left as camp guard. "The men who had been standing all day in the trenches, exposed to a constant and pelting rain, and having been suddenly called to arms, and hourly expecting an attack, had neither time nor opportunity to prepare food. They were hurriedly put in motion. At midnight on the 18th of January the

---

*NOTE.—J. W. Harris, then colonel of the Sixteenth Alabama, comments (1881) that he thinks General Zollicoffer's hesitation was due solely to his knowledge of General Crittenden's condition, and that Brigadier General Carroll was seldom in any better plight. General Zollicoffer was "ever anxious for forward and aggressive movements. Brave as a lion, daring and intrepid, nothing delighted him more than a hand-to-hand conflict in an open field."

Confederate army marched against the enemy in this order: First, with Bledsoe's and Saunders' independent cavalry companies as a vanguard; Zollicoffer's brigade; Walthall's (it was Statham's) Fifteenth Mississippi regiment in advance, followed by Rutledge's battery (this had two twelve-pound Howitzers and four rifled guns), Cummings' Nineteenth, Battle's Twentieth, and Stanton's twenty-fifth Tennessee regiments. Then came Carroll's brigade, as follows: Newman's Seventh, Murray's Twenty-eighth, and Powell's Twenty-ninth, with two guns (there were four) of Captain McClung's battery; and Colonel Wood's Sixteenth Alabama held in reserve. Branner's and McClellan's battalions of cavalry were placed on the flanks and rear" (*Life of Johnston*). Besides the cavalry here mentioned, was a company under command of Captain Frank McNairy, of Nashville, and another under command of Capt. Henry A. Ashby, and another under Captain Shelby Coffee. There were in all seventeen cavalry companies, according to the report above mentioned.

"A cold rain continued to fall on the thinly-clad Confederates, chilling them to the marrow, but they toiled painfully along. The road was rough and very heavy with the long rain, following severe freezes. Even unencumbered with artillery, the infantry would have made poor progress in the darkness, rain and mud, but as the guns, from the first, began to mire down the soldier were called on to help them along. Hence it was 6 o'clock or daylight before the advance guard struck the enemy's pickets, two miles in front of the enemy's camps. It had been six hours in getting over eight miles, and the rear was fully three miles behind." (*See the same, 401.*) Now certainly after the effort to surprise the enemy had signally failed, General Crittenden should either have abandoned the enterprise and fallen back on his intrenchments, or he should have called a halt and closed up his lines so as to have made a strong, combined attack. He knew that his antagonist, General Thomas, was an able, wary and experienced officer, and should have exercised ordinary prudence. But so far from this, we are told, " When the Mississippians, under Walthall, followed by Battle's Tennessee Regiment, encountered no resistance, and pressing rapidly forward, in obedience to orders, they increased the interval between themselves and the next regiment in the column to about one mile. It was thus that Walthall's and Battle's regiments came upon the first line Thomas had thrown forward to receive them. General Thomas' troops were encamped on each side of the road, with a wood in the front from one-fourth to a half mile through. In front of the wood were fields about 300 yards across, and beyond this again a low ridge parallel with the wood. The Confederates promptly crossed the ridge and fields and found a force in the edge of the wood in their front. This consisted of the Fourth Kentucky and Fourth Indiana regiments. General Crittenden had warned them, in the Council of War, of the danger of firing into their friends, especially as many of the Southern troops wore blue uniforms, and to avoid the risk they had adopted as a password—" Kentucky."

The morning was dark and misty, and nothing could be seen of the opposing force, except a line of armed men. The skirmishers reported to Walthall that this was Battle's command. Walthall made his regiment lie down behind a slight elevation, and going forward to some ground, hailed the troops in his front, " What troops are those?" The answer was " Kentucky." He called again, " Who are you?" and the answer came as before, " Kentucky." He then went back and got his colors, and, returning once more, asked the same question, and received the same answer. He then unfurled his flag, and the Federal line opened upon him with a volley. He turned to order forward his regiment, and found that Lieutenant Harrington, who had followed him without his knowledge, was lying dead by him, pierced by more than twenty balls. The flag was riddled, and the staff was cut, but Colonel Walthall was untouched. The Mississippians drove this regiment from its cover, and after a severe struggle, it fell back fighting. In the meantime, the Tenth Indiana, coming to the aid of the Fourth Kentucky, was met by Walthall's and Battle's regiments, which had formed on their right. A strenuous combat ensued at the forks of the road, Wolford's Cavalry supporting the Federal troops. The Ninth Ohio also became engaged; but after a desperate conflict the whole Federal line was driven back. Just then the Second Minnesota came up, and held the ground until the beaten regiments could rally upon it; which they did with spirit. In the meantime, the Nineteenth Tennessee (Colonel Cummings) had come upon the left, and found itself opposed in the woods to the Fourth Kentucky, which had returned to the conflict. In the darkness of the morning, it was difficult to distinguish between Federals and Confederates, many of the latter still wearing blue uniforms. General Zollicoffer was convinced that the regiment in his front was Confederates, and preemptorily ordered the Nineteenth Tennessee to cease firing, as they were firing upon their own troops. He then rode across to the Federal line to put a stop to the firing there. Just as he entered the road, he met a Federal officer, Colonel Speed S. Fry, of the Fourth Kentucky, and said to him quietly, "We must not shoot our own men." Gen. Zollicoffer wore a white gum overcoat which concealed his uniform, and Colonel Fry supposing him to be a Federal officer replied, "I would not of course do so intentionally." Zollicoffer, then pointing to the Nineteenth Tennessee said, "Those are our men." Colonel Fry then started toward his regiment to stop their firing, when Major Fogg (Zollicoffer's aide) coming out of the road, at this instant, and clearly perceiving that Fry was a Federal, fired upon him, wounding his horse. Fry riding off, obliquely, saw his action, and turning, discharged his revolver. The ball passed through General Zollicoffer's heart, and he fell exactly where he stood. Zollicoffer was near-sighted, and never knew that Fry was an enemy. Major Fogg was also wounded (mortally).

"The Nineteenth Tennessee now stood waiting for orders, until it was flanked and broken." (Same 402.) But why continue the recital of a combat so humiliating to Southern pride. It is sufficient that regiment after regiment came up and was beaten in detail. "Rutledge's fine battery from Nashville retired under orders, it is said, of General Crittenden, without firing a gun." At length the whole line fell back in disorder, and was followed by the victorious Federals, nearly to their entrenchments at Beech Grove. Fortunately "they were checked repeatedly by the rear-guard." This consisted of the reserve of the Sixteenth Alabama, under Colonel Wood. He had been ordered by one of General Crittenden's staff to form line of battle in an old field, advance to the woods, and there await further orders. During the battle it was with difficulty his men could be restrained from going forward, and taking part in it. In about two hours our army was driven back, and as it passed in disorder, some of the Sixteenth began to follow, but "Colonel Wood advanced to the front of the regiment, and ordered the men to face the enemy, to remember that they were Alabamians, and declared that if they retreated, he would advance on the enemy, single and alone." This inspired the men, who having been joined by Colonel Stanton (who had been wounded in the arm) and a portion of his regiment, and some of Colonel Powell's, met the onset of the enemy, who were twice driven back. When in danger of being flanked on both sides, Colonel Wood fell back over the hill and took position again. Here he remained about an hour and until all our army had passed. Colonel Wood then retreated about two miles to a good position—and continued to do so until they arrived at the fortifications, late in the afternoon.

The men were completely exhausted when they took their places again in the trenches, and were soon in a profound slumber—from which they were aroused at midnight to commence the most disastrous retreat of the war.

The loss of the Confederates in this battle may be fairly estimated in killed and wounded at 390. It fell mostly on the Fifteenth Mississippi and Twentieth Tennessee, who had borne the brunt of the day. There were but few casualties in the Sixteenth Alabama. Amongst them was John W. McDonald, a son of Hon. Crockett McDonald, born in Moulton, who was mortally wounded, and died a prisoner over at Somerset, Ky. Joseph Elkins, also of Company F (Captain Hodges), was wounded and left behind, was exchanged at Vicksburg in the summer of 1882, rejoined his command, and was terribly wounded in Georgia, so much so as to be placed on the retired list; came home and was afterward elected sheriff of our county. Dr. Wm. M. Mayes was captured here, and though paroled in a short time, was not exchanged until August.

The result of this battle was more humiliating to Southern pride than any which occurred during the war; and on the part of the major general in command of our troops there was a succession of blunders from first to last.

The information laid before the council of war was defective and erroneous, although his cavalry (the eyes of an army) was double in number and fully equal in quality to that of the enemy, and well officered. Ned Saunders was a daring partisan officer; Capt. Frank McNairy, a man of splendid person, and descended from one of the best pioneer families of the Cumberland, was afterward a gallant officer under Forrest and killed in battle; and Major McClelland, a man past middle age, cool, practical and brave, was not much given to drilling his battalion, which was mainly from the mountains of East Tennessee, but when the old man would lead they would follow, "even to the cannon's mouth." These officers were personally known to the writer. The rest of the officers who had commands in the seventeen cavalry companies had equally as much reputation as those I have mentioned; and yet when this council was held General C. was ignorant of General Thomas having been reinforced by General Schoeff with three regiments of infantry and a battery on the 17th of January, the day of his arrival; and from the same cause, on the 18th, our men were kept in the trenches under a cold rain, expecting the enemy, when Thomas had his troops twelve miles distant under shelter in their camps. Again, it was absurd to expect that he could surprise an officer with the ability and experience of Thomas, especially with such heavy and deep roads, after he had been in camp thirty-six hours before the night march commenced. But the most astonishing feature of the whole affair was that, after having brought off his army back into the fortified camp, instead of making a vigorous defence, he should have stolen away at midnight, and crossed his troops on his steamboat, barges and ferry-boats—leaving behind him 1200 horses and mules, all his wagons, quartermaster, commissary and hospital stores; after having tumbled eight guns into the river, which was all he ever had on the north bank of it, except two of McCungs, which were left buried in the mud on the battle-field.

The excuses made by General Crittenden for his defeat were numerous, and very remarkable. One was that he had not transportation enough to carry his army and army material across the river, and therefore he fought the battle. This is strange logic. If he had considered it desirable to interpose the river between him and the enemy, he had ample time and to spare; and there were six of his guns already on the south bank (which was higher than his camp) which would have covered his retreat, even if the enemy had been on his heels.

He alleged that there was no range for artillery in front. Here the surface was level for a mile and a half or two miles, and there was no obstruction to cannon except the timber, and that would have been equally in the way of his adversary. It has been alleged also, that there was a point up the river (distance uncertain) higher than the camp, from which cannon could have thrown balls into the camp. If that was the case (of which I have my doubts), such a point would have been dominated by Confederate guns on the south, which was still higher, and where there was already a fine battery of six guns. The feature in the camp which General Crittenden mainly condemned was, that it was on the north side of the river. It was that feature of the camp, strange to say, which the Federals most disliked, also. When the combined movement against Bowling Green and Forts Henry and Donalson was projected, there is good ground to believe that they were annoyed by the fact that Beech Grove, with an army not to be despised, would be on their flank as they advanced to Bowling Green, and General Buell sent Thomas "to deal them a severe blow, or cause a hasty flight across the river." As soon as the Confederates did cross to the south bank, they were no longer in their way, and General Thomas was immediately ordered back, and the combined attack occurred.

General Crittenden's excuse for abandoning the fortified camp was that " the Confederate army was so demoralized that it could not have resisted the combined attack of Thomas and Schoeff." Let us look at the condition on both sides. The Federals had fifteen regiments and a half, and the Confederates, including their cavalry, eleven. The Confederates, in artillery, still had fourteen guns; the Federals, four batteries, of how many guns each we are not told; if four, the sum would have been sixteen. The loss in the battle had not been heavy, and was nearly equal on both sides. With these forces opposing each other, the advantage would have been greatly in favor of the Con federates, in the trenches, which were only 1200 yards long, and the flanks protected perfectly by a swollen river, which the enemy had no means of crossing. I consider it an aspersion upon the officers and men, that they were too much demoralised to have held the trenches, for the order to run away at midnight was heard by them with aston- ishment. White's and Wood's regiments, and parts of Powell's and Stanton's were intact and ready for action, and so would have been the remaining regiments, as soon as the physical strength of the men had been restored by rest and sleep.

This little army was one of the finest the South ever had. It was made up of vol- unteers raised mostly before the battle of first Manassas, and was a selection from the chivalry of Tennessee (Middle, East and West), Middle Mississippi and Northwestern Alabama. It had a great number of excellent officers in it, many of whom were men of ability. One of them (Walthall) became a major general, and had a reputation unsur- passed by any of that rank; and when the army of Hood was shattered to pieces at Nashville, and the indomitable Forrest was ordered to take command of the cavalry and infantry for the defence of the rear in that arduous retreat, with his characteristic bluntness he said he would do so, if he were permitted to name his colleague to com- mand the infantry. His demand (irregular though it was) was granted, and Walthall was his choice. Marshal Ney gained his crowning laurels when commanding the rear guard on the retreat from Russia; and when Forrest and Walthall, fighting step by step, and crowning every hill-top with a canopy of fire and smoke, to give time for the crippled army to escape, at length stood on Anthony's hill, with torn uniforms and faces blackened with powder, and hurled back the forces of Thomas, and put an end to the pursuit, nothing more could have been added to their fame. In that little army, too, there were four other officers—Statham, Battle, Dibrell and Brantley—who be- came brigadiers, but I have no space to speak of them individually. Of the regiments which composed it, I can trace five and one battery through the battle of Shiloh. The Sixteenth Alabama was one of them; and in the regular course of my narrative I shall speak of its conduct with pride and pleasure. Colonel Statham there commanded a large brigade of six regiments, in which were included the four others, Walthall's, Cummings' Battle's and Murray's, and Rutledge's battery. This brigade came into the field as a part of Breckenridge's reserve, about midday on Sunday, after the Federals had been driven back from ridge to ridge, until Hurlbut had collected some of the best fighting men of the Federal army on a ridge, and, after repeated charges, they could be driven no further.

General Johnston regarded this stubborn angle, from which Chalmers on the right had folded back the Federal left, as the key of the enemy's position. Statham's brigade was sent in about noon, and it was their fortune to be placed opposite this angle The Federals were lying down in double lines, and firing, while the opposite ridge occupied by this brigade was commanded and raked by this deadly ambuscade. They stood delivering and receiving a fire as heavy as any during the war.—(Life of Johnston, 609.) General Johnston saw that a crisis had arrived. The afternoon was upon him. The final blow must be struck. He prepared the line for the use of the bayonet, and although the troops had to descend one slope, and ascend another swept by this withering fire, he placed himself at the head of the regiments, "who had known nothing of war except that miserable defeat at Mill Springs." Isham G. Harris, Governor of Tennessee (who had carried away the archives of the State to a place of safety, and might have deposited his person there, too), put himself at the head of the two raw regiments on the right. and the brigade advanced. A sheet of flame burst from the Federal stronghold, and blazed along the crest of the ridge. The Confederate line wavered, and the dead and dying strewed the dark valley. But there was not an instant's pause. Right up the steep they went. The crest was gained. The enemy were in flight—a few scattering shots reply-ing to the ringing cheers of the Confederates.—(*Life of Johnston, 612.*) General John-ston seeing that a Federal battery was enfilading his line sent an order by Governor Har-ris to Colonel Statham to take that battery, so fortune ordered that the troops (who, without any fault of theirs) had been disgraced at Fishing creek, should break the key of the enemy's position at Shiloh, and have the melancholy honor of receiving and exe-cuting the last military order which ever issued from the lips of that illustrious com-mander, whose life blood was then fast ebbing away.—(*Same, 614.*)

On the second day of the battle, "Bowen and Statham, and what was left of the commands of Hindman and Cleburne, formed the nucleus of the defence. The Federal army was held at bay by the Southern troops with obstinate valor. It is a strange coincidence, that some of the regiments of McCook, who conquered at Fishing creek, encountered some of them whom they conquered—and in the words of General Sherman —' in the severest musketry fire I ever saw,' the victors were driven back.

At the conclusion of this day's battle, "General Breckenridge stationed Statham's brigade about a mile and a half in the rear of Shiloh Church; and this brigade and the Kentucky brigade, and the cavalry, formed the rear guard of the retiring army, which retired like a lion, wounded but dauntless"—(*Same, 652.*)

I have gone to a distant field for facts to show that the little army at Beech Grove would have held the trenches. On whom then does the responsibility for this disaster rest? Certainly on the major general who commanded this army. His antecedents were all favorable. A graduate at West Point of the class of 1832, he had, as an officer, of the United States army, been brevetted for gallantry in the Mexican War. In 1856, he was lieutenant colonel. He was a Kentuckian, and was known as a brave and fearless officer. But his fine intellect was under a cloud. His intemperate habits were well known in the army. One reliable officer informed me "I saw him but few times while he was in command. He was either in a debauch, or just getting over one, whenever I saw him.'' I am not responsible for thrusting this subject before the public. Colonel Johnston, in his "*Life of A. S. Johnston*" (a history of great merit, and which covers only about six months, and has more matter official and documentary, than any I have read treating of the whole war), says: "Crittenden had a lot still harder for a brave soldier, than that of his dead colleague. Skulking slanderers were charging him up and down the country with cowardice and treasonable correspondence with the enemy. He was charged with drunkenness also; but the writer has the evidence of impartial witnesses, who saw him on the day, that he was sober.'' It is due to the officers and soldiers who were sacrificed by him, that the author in the next edition of his book should correct the error into which he honestly fell. and notice the proceedings of the court martial which suspended him from office. The truth, especially in a matter like this, which involves the reputation of so many, had better appear on the page of history. General Critten-den was deeply mortified at his suspension; and afterward served gallantly on the staff of Gen. R. E. Lee, in Virginia.

I have less repugnance in discussing this matter because General Crittenden, in making his defence, depreciated the ability of his " dead colleague.'' Colonel Johnston in writing his history was evidently under the influence of it. He seems to hold Zolli-coffer responsible, as chief in command, even after he was superseded. He says, speaking of General Crittenden having been appointed major general: "It was hoped that his long service would *supplement* the inexperience of General Zollicoffer.'' The historian intimates that General Zollicoffer was rash in the manner in which he exposed himself in the battle. Then so was Walthall, and for the same reason. I carefully considered all the facts connected with the short military career of this able man, and I was astonished at the false estimate which, by some, was placed upon his abilities, and wrote to an officer, in whose judgment I had great confidence. His answer was this: "My opinion of General Zollicoffer, from an intimate acquaintance and association of several months, was that if he had lived he would have been in the army of Tennessee what Stonewall Jackson was in the army of Virginia.'' This opinion may seem to be extravagant, but it is certain that those who knew him best appreciated him most.

When after dark, the order was given to prepare for retreat across the Cumberland, at midnight, "it was received by the men who had manned the trenches two or three deep, with the utmost astonishment. At that stage of the war, it had not been known that a Federal force had ever succeeded in storming fortifications with a sufficient garrison; although later, they became as steady soldiers in a charge as the world ever saw. But when the order was given to the commanders of the batteries on the north bank, to sink their guns in the river, it was received with deep mortification. Over the large battery was Captain Arthur Middleton Rutledge, from Nashville, a gentleman of culture and gallantry; (descended from two of the statesmen of South Carolina. who were signers of the Declaration of Independence) supported by his Lieutenants, Falconet and Cockrill, and a company of choice young men from Nashville, the "Rock City." Over the other battery was Hugh McClung, descended from the distinguished Hugh L. White of East Tennessee, with his Lieutenants, McClung and Allison, and a company of young men, who were the pride of Knoxville. With soldiers of this branch of the service, it is a point of honor to save their guns, or to lose them after a bloody struggle; but here they were commanded to throw them away without firing, and flee before the enemy!

The retreat of General Crittenden's army was most disastrous. At my special request, Colonel W. B. Wood has given a graphic and interesting account of it, which I here lay before my readers: "About 12 o'clock that night, I was ordered to move with what rations my men could take in their haversacks to the river bank, and cross over without delay. When I arrived at the river, I found the whole army there before me, being transported across the river by a little steamboat, the river being very high. It was nearly day before I crossed, being in the rear. We left all our baggage, wagons, horses, tents and everything but what we had on. When I found that we were retreating, I went back to the river, and crossed over again to try to recover my papers, which were in my wagon, but before I could find them, Captain Spiller, who had command of the boat, called to me to come on, as the enemy were then on the brow of the hill, and advancing. We had just time to cut loose and get across, before they opened with their cannon upon us. Captain Spiller set fire to the boat, and we hurried on to join the army, which was then several miles on the road to Monticello. We passed through Monticello, and bivouacked a few miles this side.

Here we found ourselves without tents, provisions, with but few wagons, and a hundred miles from our base of supplies. We expected the enemy would be in full pursuit of us the next day. The men were completely exhausted and had nothing to eat, Colonel Battle, Colonel Cummings and myself went to the house where General Crittenden was, to ascertain what could be done for the men and what he proposed to do It was after midnight, the snow was falling, the men were lying around upon the cold, wet ground, and the prospect before us gloomy. We found the general lying across a bed, very drunk. One of his staff tried to arouse him, but could not. We consulted together, and informed the adjutant general that unless the general should sleep off his drunkenness so as to be able to take command and direct the retreat, we would march on our own responsibility early in the morning, toward the nearest point where we could obtain supplies. Just before leaving, I went to the general, and shaking him, succeeded in arousing him so that he asked what I wanted. I told him we wanted to know where we were going, and when he expected to get supplies. He told us "to go where we —— pleased, and let him alone." We left. The colonels told me that they had been to see General Carroll, who commanded their brigade, before they came to me, and he was in the same condition. They proposed that I, being the senior colonel, should take command and bring off the army. I told them I would do so, but would depend on them to lead the way into Tennessee, where we could obtain provisions. I issued an order for the army to move at daylight, Colonel Statham in advance, and moved in the direction of Livingston. It is impossible at this late day, and in the short space of a communication intended for a newspaper, to give the incidents of that disastrous retreat. The roads were over high mountains, and very muddy; the creeks and rivers were full, and had to be waded; the weather was cold, and sometimes the snow falling, and the country as a general thing was uninhabited, at least along the road. Sometimes we would come to a small valley, where there were some good farms, but the cavalry had been along before us, and stripped them of all their supplies. We marched four days without anything to eat, except one night. I had about one hundred dollars in gold, which I gave to Colonel Helveston, Captain Hodges, and one or two others, who went on in advance, and leaving the road, found some farmers from whom they succeeded in buying some bacon and corn bread. They brought it into camp, and it was divided equally, every man receiving a slice of bread and meat. I heard many of them say it was the sweetest supper they had ever enjoyed.

The first day or two the men stood up bravely under the privations. We had three wagons in which our sick and wounded were packed. Every horse and mule in the wagons had a rider in some sick or broken-down man. The third morning of the retreat was one of extreme sadness and gloom. The men could not sleep because of the hunger gnawing at their vitals. They were cold and hungry, tired and sick. Their eyes began to glare, their skins became dry and tight, so as to have the appearance of a man who had been for weeks sick with a fever; the joke and laugh and wit, in which the soldier indulges so much on the march, was gone. The army, as it stretched along the road, looked like a great funeral procession, and indeed it was, for many a poor fellow, exhausted and crazed, fell by the wayside and perished. During this march I was most of the time in the rear of my command. It was the most trying and afflicting time of my experience as a soldier. My men were giving out and falling by the way-side, declaring that they could not go another step, and begging to be allowed to die where they were. To leave them was certain death, no habitation near, and no one to care for them; indeed, it was an enemy's country, for most of the people along that road were opposed to the Confederates, and were glad of our misfortunes. It looked like heartless cruelty to drive a poor, weak, tottering man along, or to make others, nearly as weak, drag him up the steep hills and over rough places; but it was the only way to save him. I knew that in another day or two we would arrive where we would find hospitable homes and abundance of provisions. No one can fully comprehend the horrors of a starving army who has not seen it. One night it rained nearly all night, and the ground was covered with water. The men sat up under the trees and bushes, and tried to sleep, with their clothes wet, and the cold wind cutting like a razor.

They arose next morning completely exhausted; haggard, weak, cold, wet and hungry. They set out on another day's dreary march, through mud and water. Of course, many were left along the road to perish. I brought off nearly all of my regiment. They behaved with remarkable courage and endurance. The officers did all that men could do for their companies, and set examples of fortitude and self-denial which were truly heroic. The men would eat the twigs off the bushes, and everything that had the least nutriment in it. I remember coming to a house abandoned by the family. Some of the men went in and found an old barrel, with bones and scraps of meat, used in making soap; I never saw men enjoy a meal more at a first-class hotel, than these starving soldiers did the contents of that stinking barrel. On the fourth morning one of my officers had been hunting through a garden, which seemed to have been thoroughly robbed, of every sprig of vegetation that had been in it. He succeeded however in finding two onions. He ate one, and put the other in his haversack for his dinner. Coming along where I was sitting on a log, he said: "Colonel, what will you have for your breakfast this morning?" I replied, "Hot coffee, beefsteak and onions." He put his hand into his haversack and brought forth his onion and said: "I can furnish the onion." Another officer near by stepped up, and presented me with a piece of poor beef, that had been burned to a crisp on the coals, without salt, and said: "I will furnish the steak." I never enjoyed a breakfast more, but my noble and generous officers went dinnerless. A more devoted set of officers and men never lived or died, for their country. I mustered into service when I organized my regiment 1088 men, besides officers. In the Fishing creek fight the killed and wounded were 54, at Shiloh 162, at Murfreesboro 164, at Chickamauga 234. The regiment was in other battles and skirmishes, where their loss was heavy. I was not with it then, and do not know the exact casualties. I am satisfied that there were not two hundred who came out of the war that had not been wounded."

I also present below, an extract of a letter from Lieut. John M. McGhee, now of Waco, Texas, on the same subject: "I wish to make a few remarks about our field officers. Colonel Wood was not a strict disciplinarian, and did not believe in bringing volunteers down to regular army rules; but I know that there was not a colonel in the army, who was more beloved by his men, and that he could lead them anywhere. He was very cool in the battle-field, and was very kind to the sick and wounded. When we were on the retreat from Fishing creek, the weather was very cold and we were destitute of blankets, and had nothing but a little parched corn to eat; and we would urge him to go to a house and remain all night; but he would always refuse and remain with us, saying that he had volunteered with us, and intended to stand by us. On the retreat we had some of the sick with us, who had crawled out of the hospital when they saw the Yankees coming; and who were mere shadows. He suffered them to ride his horse, and he walked until he wore his feet into solid blisters; but he stuck to it until he got sick, and afterward came near dying. Such conduct as this *will* attach a command to an officer."

When the command joined the army of Gen. A. S. Johnston, at Murfreesboro, Tenn., the Sixteenth Alabama was placed in the brigade of Gen. S. A. M. Wood. After the battle of Chickamauga, Brigadier General Wood resigned, and Colonel M. P. Lowry, of the Thirty-second Mississippi was appointed in his stead, and in this brigade the regiment remained until the end of the war.

I have made an effort to obtain the names of the officers who composed the staff of General Crittenden's army; but have only partially succeeded. Capt. Charles Morgan, brother of Gen. John H. Morgan, was on his staff. On General Zollicoffer's, Major Pollock B. Lee was Adjutant General, and Major Hall R. Fogg (son of Hon. Francis B. Fogg) was his aide; and on General Carroll's staff, Major F. M. Gailor was brigade quartermaster, and Major (Rev.) John M. Holland was brigade commissary, and the general's son his aide.

On the route to Corinth, the Sixteenth marched through Fayetteville, Athens and Decatur.

Courtland and Its First White Inhabitant.

One of the Dillahunty family was the first man who settled at Courtland, Ala. This family emigrated from Nancy (France) to North Carolina. They were well educated, and had a habit of recording everything important. Their descent for five generations could have been procured. Thomas Dillahunty moved from Jones county, North Carolina, in December, 1773, and purchased land four miles from a then small village, called Nashville, in Davidson county, Tennessee. It must have been very small, for ten years afterward it had a population of only four hundred. He had four sons, Edmund, Lewis, Harvey and John. Edmund studied law, lived in Columbia, was a chancellor, and also a common law judge. Judge Foster, now of our county, once practised in his court, and says that he had a spotless character as a man. and was eminent as a judge. He never came to Lawrence county, but all his brothers and his father did.

Lewis Dillahunty was born in North Carolina, 18th of July, 1793, a few months before his father's removal to Tennessee. These were perilous times. During that year about fifty whites were killed by the Indians, and amongst them some of the best citizens. This state of things continued for several years afterward. In 1813 the Creek war broke out, and young Lewis (then nineteen years old) volunteered, and was elected lieutenant in Capt. Andrew Hyne's company. He made a good soldier, for he came back a captain with the army, which returned in May, 1814. They were received by the people with great enthusiasm; a speech of welcome was made by Mr. Grundy and responded to by General Jackson.

The gallant young men of Tennessee had only a few months for rest, and the enjoyment of the society of their friends and the smiles of the fair ones. Gen. Wm. Carroll made a sudden call for 3000 volunteer infantry for the defence of New Orleans, to rendezvous at Nashville on the 13th of November, 1814. Captain Dillahunty not only was on the ground at the appointed time, but had a full company completely organised, raised in Davidson and Williamson counties. Daniel Bradford, so well known since at Huntsville as General Bradford, was his first lieutenant. The captain kept a blank book in which he recorded all General Carroll's general orders, and such special ones as related to his company, also muster-rolls, requisitions for supplies of provisions and ammunition, a list of casualties, etc., from that day until the return of the army to Nashville. With its paper yellowed and its ink faded with the ravages of time for seventy years, the venerable record lies before me, and will enable me to give (along with the personal facts I have learned from his very intelligent daughter, Mrs. Merritt, of Franklin, Tenn.) a continuous and faithful memoir of a gentleman who was the first white settler of Courtland, and a public man highly respected by our people in his day. I judge that young as he was his company was composed of the best material, for General Carroll, by a special order written by himself, without the intervention of an aide, directed Captain D. to select a sergeant and five men from his company to take charge of the ammunition boat, and by another, ordered Captain D. to send a certain man from his company to superintend the putting up of the beef for the whole command. General Carroll, probably, attached more importance to this than to any other order made before he sailed; since for want of precaution and experience on the part of the officers he and his men were subjected, in the Creek campaign, to protracted and severe starvation.

The voyage of this army down to the Mississippi in a very short time, is a matter of history. When the memorable twenty-third day of December, 1814, dawned they had just landed at the levee in New Orleans. At half-past one P. M. on that day, two French gentlemen who lived on the river below the city, rode up the street with great speed, and suddenly stopped at the headquarters of General Jackson, who with an able staff, including Governor Claiborne the eloquent Grimes and others, had just risen from dinner. The French gentlemen, who were well known as patriots to Governor Claiborne, announced that the British army had landed twelve miles below the city. Question and answer followed each other in quick succession. General Jackson was more a listener than talker during this colloquy. At its conclusion he rested his head upon his hand for a short time, then rose to his feet and said: "Gentlemen, we will fight them before midnight!" Then followed orders to the members of his staff for the concentration of his troops. A part of them was three miles above the city; the regulars were encamped in it, and Carroll's men were still in their boats. That his conclusion to attack was thus made is shown in recent authentic articles published in the New Orleans *Democrat*.

We now return to our company, whose captain, Dillahunty, is composedly writing out a list of his men for the purpose of recording the issuance of arms. It now lies before me, in handwriting which shows no excitement and no tremor, and that each of his men had drawn one musket, one bayonet and one flint. Before night, General Jackson mounted his horse and posted himself at the foot of the street, and remained there until every soldier of his army had defiled before him. The battle occurred in the darkness of the night; companies and regiments of our men and the enemy were intermingled in great confusion, and the British marched down the levee, and our men back to Chalmette, which Jackson afterward fortified. The battle was indecisive, but General Jackson had gained his object, which was time to fortify. In answer to the question why he did not fortify before, the proper reply is that General Jackson had made himself acquainted, by personal inspection, with all the localities around New Orlean as far down as the Belize, and had found so many water approaches to the city, that he could not divine where the enemy would land.

In the battle of the 8th of January, Captain D. gave so much satisfaction to his commander that he was promoted to the rank of major, and Lieutenant Bradford made captain in his place. The only entry in his diary in respect to the battle itself, is that he had one man in the company wounded, and that "James Kirkpatrick was killed while helping a wounded British prisoner over the works." In reading this entry I felt deep regret that so fearless and tender-hearted a soldier should have met such a fate. In burying the dead, a letter was found on the body of T. Wilkerson, major in the brigade of General Gibbs, written the day before the battle, to his brother Robert, who was in the British War Department. Major D. copied it into his diary. This letter shows that the British commander had assiduously sought some route through the swamp by which he might turn the flank of General Jackson's position, without success, and had determined on the next day, to storm the works. He says " the Americans are highly favored by their natural situation, but I hope to-morrow will show that they have trusted to a broken reed by resting their defence on a line. I have no doubt it will be like other lines, when one point is forced the whole will take to their heels." The result is known to the world. This accomplished young officer, Generals Gibbs, Packenham and many others, were killed in a vain attempt to rally their men, when their ranks were broken by the steady and terrific fire of the men who were expected "to take to their heels" as soon as they came to close quarters.

A season of quiet followed this battle. At length the time arrived for the return of the army to their homes. It was cheerful for those who were able to march, but great apprehensions were felt by the sick and wounded, that they would be left in the "low country" to linger and die in the hospitals. But the Tennessee generals had received from the fathers and mothers of these young men a sacred trust, and most faithfully did they perform it.

As to Carroll's division, the sick and wounded were placed under the command of young Major Dillahunty. This was the highest compliment ever paid him during the war. By an order of the 13th of March, General Carroll ordered the sick and wounded to be placed by Major Dillahunty on board of the steamer Vesuvius, and transported to Natchez, and to be placed in camp furnished with everything necessary for their comfort. A report was made by the major, of every man who died on the way, and a copy of it preserved in his book. At length, on the 21st of March, Major Dillahunty was ordered to procure the necessary transportation, provisions, etc., and to move on with such of the sick and wounded as were able, toward Tennessee.

Poor fellows! How many a heart beat with apprehension for fear of being left behind.

An incident I heard when a boy well depicts the state of feeling which prevailed among them. As Dr. Hogg passed along the aisle of the hospital to decide who could go, a poor emaciated soldier claimed the privilege. Says the doctor, "You can't march." Says the man, "Yes I can." The doctor replied, "Why, you can't even stand alone." Then the poor soldier in his agony begged them "to stand him up, and if he fell, let him fall toward Tennessee."

By Major Dillahunty's orders, which are still preserved, it is plain that he was deeply moved by this state of things. Assisted by the surgeon he made two classes of them; such as could march and carry their knapsacks, and such as could march without them.

Transportation was very scarce, and he ordered the private baggage of the officers to be left behind, so that there might be room in the wagons for the exhausted men to ride. Occasionally, some of them from necessity would have to be left behind. In such cases a surgeon was left in charge, and provisions (which were very scarce) provided for them; and the officer directed to report to General Jackson (who was marching in the rear) for further orders.

General Carroll with the able-bodied men in front, arrived at home, and was welcomed with public rejoicing long before Major Dillahunty appeared at the head of his pale procession.

The public appreciated his services, and many a mother remembered him in her prayers for having brought her disabled boy back safely to her arms. But there was one ovation awaiting him which was dearer to his heart than all others besides. One of Tennessee's lovely daughters (Miss Lucinda C., daughter of Mr. John Johnson) had promised before he sailed for New Orleans to marry him on his return home, and they were united on the 18th of April, 1815, just three days after his arrival.

No doubt her heart swelled with pride when, at the altar, she gave her hand to a gentleman not twenty-two years old, who had not only gathered laurels in two wars, but had displayed the wisdom and discretion which belonged to more mature years.

Our people were then rapidly settling up the lands in North Alabama, on the North bank of the Tennessee river, and much anxiety was felt by the United States Government to procure a cession from the Cherokees of the lands on the south side: On the recommendation of General Jackson, Major Dillahunty was sent by President Monroe as an agent to prepare the minds of the Indians for this cession.

Early in 1816 he and his young wife located in the place called Courtland. Whether he was an Indian agent or a confidential emissary of the government, I have not been able to ascertain. A constant correspondence passed between Mr. Monroe and him. He made himself very popular with the Indians, and in 1817, when his patron, General Jackson, attempted to purchase all the Cherokee lands, he succeeded in getting that part occupied by the Indians (Morgan, Lawrence and Franklin counties), through the personal influence of Major Dillahunty.

In 1817 Major Dillahunty was elected to the House of Representatives in the Territorial Legislature, and Green K. Hubbard was his colleague. This was the first election ever held in our county.

The next year Alabama became a State, and Major Dillahunty was again elected a member of the House of Representatives. Samuel Bigham was his colleague, and Fleming Hodges was senator.

Major Dillahunty lived three years at Courtland, and then moved to the neighborhood of Mount Pleasant church. He purchased lands for his father, Thomas Dillahunty, and for his father-in-law, John Johnson. When his father died in 1829 his place was sold to Vincler Jones, and Mr. Johnson's place was the one now occupied by Stewart Hennigan. While Major Dillahunty lived at Mt. Pleasant occurred the first Masonic burial that ever took place in the county, and Major Dillahunty, who was then the highest Mason, performed the ceremony. It was that of Jack Ethridge. He had been married one day to Martha Beavers and the next day he rode to Bainbridge with a friend, and on returning they concluded to try the speed of their horses, and Ethridge was thrown against a tree and killed. I judge she earlier became a widow than any wife ever in our county.

In 1825 Major Dillahunty moved to Hardeman county, Tennessee, where he died in 1826. He left three sons, and one daughter; Mrs. Sallie Merritt, whom we have already mentioned. Two of his sons died early. William Carroll (the remaining son of Major Dillahunty) and his mother moved near South Florence in 1844. He and his son, William Rufus, are thought to be the only male descendants of Thomas Dillahunty living.

Harvey D , brother of Lewis, was by no means equal to him in ability, but was very much respected, and was elected to the House of Representatives in this county in 1830. He married Hetty, daughter of Colonel Savage, of Lauderdale county, Alabama, and removed to Memphis, Tenn., and from there to Mount Pleasant, Titus county, Texas, in 1859, and died there in 1878. He was Circuit Judge there for eight years. His wife died in 1880. Issue: (1) Charles C., of Mt. Pleasant; (2) Harvey died at Mt. Pleasant; (3) Mildred married Major Batte, of Titus county, Texas, a cotton planter of large means. She died in 1859.

John B. Dillahunty, the remaining brother of Lewis D., married (1) Sallie Savage, daughter of the same Colonel Savage mentioned above, and had a son, Samuel S., who died in Sevier county, Ark., 1883. He married (2) Martha N. Littlepage, of Madison county, Alabama, near Huntsville, and had two children—(1) Eliza S., who married W. C. McDougal, of Aberdeen, Miss.; (2) John B., of Nashville, Tenn., married, in 1874, Julia R. Banks, sister of Hon. Robt. Webb Banks, of Columbus, Miss.

The town of Courtland was laid out on the site of a Cherokee town, and was surrounded by old fields, on which Indian cabins were still standing when I first saw it, in 1821. The mound builders had been there before the Cherokees, and left on the west side of the creek one of their largest monuments. Courtland was incorporated on the 13th of December, 1819; and Robert B. Cary, Thomas Wooldridge, Ira Carlton, Benjamin Thomas, and Dr. Gideon G. Williams were the Commissioners.

Robert B. Cary had emigrated from Virginia—was descended from a wealthy family; but was reduced in his circumstances. He was a small man, very much esteemed, and quite industrious in maintaining his family; when news came to him, across the Atlantic, that he was one of the heirs to an estate of millions. He was a nervous man, and it seemed to change his whole nature; and had an unhappy effect upon him and his family. Of course it ended in disappointment, as such claims have always done. In Mobile, many years ago, I was counsel for a gentleman who had such a claim. I investigated the facts; and found there was really a fortune left by a wealthy iron-master, nearly a hundred years before; but came to the conclusion that the lapse of time had been too great, and that there was no prospect of success. When I announced it to my client he first appeared astonished—then he grew very angry—and then became as pale as ashes and came near fainting. But it was too late; and the man was never able to addict himself to regular work afterward. A few years ago, our Minister to England published a circular warning Americans not to be excited by such delusive hopes; but it has not had much effect.

Thomas Wooldridge came from South Carolina, where he had killed a man named Moffit, and seemed to be unhappy. It had this effect—he became intemperate, and moved first to Mississippi, and then to Texas, where he died.

Ira Carlton did a moderate but safe business as a merchant—moved to Green county, where he became a cotton planter.

Dr. Gideon G. Williams was from Tennessee in 1819—was a lagre man of fine *personnel*—of genial nature, and sometimes convivial; but he was a good physician, and very popular. He married Jane Lane, of La Grange, and moved to the plantation since occupied by Robert King. Here he did an extensive country practice for a few years, then removed to Texas, where he died.

I can not remember the other commissioner—B. Thomas.

Within five years after its incorporation Courtland attained its full dimensions; its mechanics were skilful, and of a higher order than I have seen anywhere—its lawyers and doctors eminent and its merchants prosperous, selling from three to four hundred thousand dollars worth of goods annually.

There lived in Courtland in 1825, a man of very amiable disposition, named James A. Francisco. He was powerfully made, and was the son of the celebrated Peter Francisco, a Portugese, of Cumberland county, Virginia, who was noted as the strongest man in America, and was, during the Revolutionary war, every inch a Whig. He killed three Tories, in hand-to-hand fight, who attacked him at the same time. This is verified by history. There are many stories of his great strength. One to this effect: a celebrated bully, who lived in another county, hearing of the wonderful strength of Peter Francisco, rode over to Cumberland to have a fight with him. He rode into the yard and told him his business. Francisco told him he was no fighting man, and asked him to get down, and take some dinner. The bully refused, and said he had come for a fight and a fight he *would have*, and approaching Peter, he was caught and thrown over the fence. The bully was dumfounded, and in a subdued tone, said: "Now, Mr. Francisco, as you have thrown me over the fence, throw my pony over too, and I will go home satisfied," which Peter did. History does not verify this story, but it was believed by thousands of Virginians, and this proves what was thought of his wonderful strength. James Francisco moved from Courtland to Cottongin, Miss., where he died.

A Mr. Hines settled early in Courtland, was a merchant for a short time, and died. He was a brother of Colonel Andrew Hines, who was a distinguished man of Nashville. He left but little for his two daughters, who never married, and were notable for their industry and charity. I mention them here, because they were the first of those "*sisters of charity*" who, for the last sixty years, have distinguished the noble women of Courtland, in their aid to the indigent, and sympathy for the unfortunate.

Noble R. Ladd was amongst the first merchants of Courtland; and his history is connected with the first *excitement* in the town. Mr. Ladd had the misfortune to kill Dr. Mitchell, in a rencounter in the square. The place was divided into two parties. The friends of the deceased were determined on the conviction of Ladd, raised a heavy purse, and employed Felix Grundy, the renowned criminal lawyer, of Nashville, to prosecute him. Mr. Grundy had defended 160 men for capital offences, and succeeded in clearing all except one, Bennet, of Rutherford county. In this case, however, Mr. G. signally failed in convicting; but his speech was so eloquent that many children in the county were named for him (amongst the rest, my friend Captain McGregor.) Mr. Ladd removed to Russellville, where he died a few years ago.

One of the early merchants in Courtland was Charles McClung from Knoxville. Tenn. He had married a daughter of Judge Pleasant M. Miller, of West Tennessee, was the brother of James W. McClung, of Huntsville, and the nephew of the Hon. Hugh L. White of Tennessee, who was so long an able Senator from that State, and once a prominent candidate for the Presidency. Mr. Charles McClung did not remain long in Courtland; but returned to Knoxville in 1825; and in this movement society in Courtland sustained a great loss.

William H. Whitaker was another of the merchants of Courtland. He came from Nashville, where he had married a daughter of Judge Williams White. After many years he removed to Grenada, Miss., where he and his wife both died.

Another merchant, Joseph Trotter, married Miss Flournoy, of Pulaski, Tenn., and came to Courtland; and, on the death of his first wife, married Miss Mayor, of Franklin county. He moved to Caddo parish, Louisiana, and opened a commission house in New Orleans under the style of Trotter & Pearsall. His second wife having died in Caddo, he married the Widow Rivers, of Pulaski, Tenn. He returned to that place, where he died.

Andrew Beirne, Esq., of Western Virginia, a man of large wealth and an accomplished merchant, sent a young man to Courtland, at an early day, named John Anderson, and established a large mercantile business under the style of "Beirne & Anderson," which proved to be so profitable that, in a few years, John Anderson's part of the profits enabled him to retire from business and purchase a large plantation near Montgomery, where he died in 1837. He was a brother of Richard N. Anderson, but a man of more sagacity. He was born in Maryland, but reared in Madison county, Alabama, and left his fortune to his sisters. An amusing story is told of John Anderson getting early news of a sudden rise of two cents per pound in cotton. He concluded then to go hunting for a "stray horse." Took a bridle in hand, and rode into the country. He came to the house of Charles Anderson (no kin to him, however) and inquired, very particularly, about the stray horse, but said nothing at all about *cotton*. As he turned off and bid Mr. Charles a good morning, the latter detained him with a proposition to sell him his cotton crop, which, after some chaffering, John bought at the old price. Charles was a keen man himself, and was greatly vexed. He used to declare afterward that he would never sell his cotton again to a merchant "hunting for a stray horse," even if he offered twenty-five cents per pound.

Jeremiah Pearsall moved his family to this county about 1821. His house stood about one hundred yards south of the large mansion since erected by the late John H. Harris. The Pearsalls were good Presbyterian people, cultivated, refined and hospitable. The head of this family not only squared his conduct by the law, but by the golden rule.

I remember that a horse trader, one spring, offered him a plow horse for one hundred dollars; extolling his good qualities. Mr Pearsall had doubts as to his value, and offered ninety dollars for him, payable in the fall, and bought him. When the drover came for his money the old gentleman paid him the full price of one hundred dollars, saying that the horse was found, on trial, to be everything the trader said he was. One of his sons, Edward, moved to the adjoining county of Colbert, where his descendants live. Another, James M. Pearsall, married a Miss Mayor, of Colbert, and for a long time was a commission merchant of New Orleans, first of the firm of Trotter & Pearsall and then of McMahon & Pearsall. Metcalfe De Graffenried married Dolly Pearsall, and a gentleman from Tennessee, named Bronson, married Catherine. The Pearsalls were all well favored; but a daughter of Jeremiah Pearsall was especially beautiful in person, and lovely in character. She, as a young widow, Mrs. Camp, was sought in marriage by many suitors, and at length married Nathan Gregg.

The Greggs came from East Tennessee, and opened a store in Courtland (amongst the first) under the style of N. & W. Gregg. Their business was prosperous until the revulsion in 1836, when they became embarrassed. Nathan Gregg and his excellent wife, having sons old enough for collegiate instruction, moved to La Grange, Ala., where was then a flourishing institution. They wisely concluded that if they could not leave a fortune to their boys, they would give them an opportunity to get a good education. Here they kept the Steward's Hall for several years. Their son, of whom we shall speak, particularly, in this number, was

Gen. John Gregg.

Born in Lawrence county, Ala., on September 28, 1828, and graduated with such distinction in 1847, that he was selected by Prof. Henry Tutwiler, then principal of a high school in Green county, Ala., as teacher of the languages and mathematics. Mr. Tutwiler had been a professor both in La Grange College, and the University of Alabama, and was known to be a remarkable scholar; and if any professor in college was ill, he could supply his place, no matter what the study in the curriculum. The endorsement from such a scientist was the strongest proof of the genius and scholarship of young Gregg. He remained with Mr. Tutwiler four years, and returned to North Alabama, and studied law with Judge Townes, of Tuscumbia. In 1852 he went to Texas, and settled in Fairfield, Freestone county, just then laid out. His reputation as a lawyer grew so rapidly that in four years he was elected judge of the district over an old Texan, who had held the office for several years.

He had mounted the first step on the ladder of distinction, when he returned to North Alabama and married Miss Mollie Garth, daughter of Gen. Jesse Garth, and sister of Hon. W. W. Garth. Miss Garth was in every respect worthy to be the companion of one whose life commenced so auspiciously, and promised so brilliant a career.

Secession found him still a judge. He was its warm advocate. When Governor Houston refused to call a convention to know the wishes of the people on this subject, one was called over his head; Judge Gregg was a member of it; and represented Freestone and Navarro counties. The acts of the convention were ratified,—in some counties almost unanimously. He was one of the representatives sent to Montgomery. After the seat of government was removed to Richmond he served one term. The battles of Bull Run and Manassas proved that a bloody war was before us. He resigned his place amongst the law-makers, for more desperate work. He asked and obtained, from the War Department, authority to raise a regiment; returned to Texas; and brought to Corinth the Seventh Texas Infantry in an incredibly short time. They were ordered to Hopkinsville, Ky., to Gen. A. S. Johnston. The *Judge* was elected *Colonel*, and the command was surrendered by General Buckner, at Fort Donalson, the 16th of February, 1862. They were incarcerated in Northern prisons until the seven days' fight around Richmond. A general exchange was then effected. Colonel Gregg was promoted to Brigadier General, and assigned duty at Vicksburg, Miss., in command of a brigade composed of Tennesseeans and old Texas regiments. The defence against

Sherman was successful, and the command sent to Port Hudson; and, with Bledsoe's battery of Missourians, did excellent service in repelling the fleet under Farragut, and the land forces under Banks. On the 1st of May orders were sent to General Gregg to bring his command to Jackson in all haste. General Loring's had been scattered along the Big Black; and rumors were coming in of a large force of Federals approaching the place. The afternoon witnessed the welcome arrival of General Joseph E. Johnston from Georgia, who soon brought system out of chaos. While doing so, he sent General Gregg to *feel* of the enemy, and if possible to ascertain their force. He attacked them at Raymond with such vim, as to impress them with the idea that they were confronted by a large force; and he learned from the prisoners he had taken that they belonged to the different army corps, and that he had been fighting 30,000 men with *2500*. After the fall of Vicksburg, General Johnston fell back on Jackson, where there was a week's fighting, when the Confederates were repulsed, and retreated into the interior.

General Gregg's command was then sent to Georgia, and arrived in time to participate in the battle of Chickamauga. A member of the brigade says (*Annals of Tennessee*, 1878) that "he was on the skirmish line when they found the Federals lying down, in line of battle. It was reported back, and in a few minutes he heard General Gregg's stentorian "Forward!" and a wild *yell*, as the boys came on at a charge. The enemy fled, throwing down their guns and knapsacks. The charge was kept up for half a mile, when we heard that our gallant General Gregg, in advance of the line, had been severely, if not mortally, wounded." He fell temporarily into the hands of the enemy. When he became conscious, two Federal soldiers were robbing him, and disputing over a division of the spoils. Suddenly they ran off, and he saw the cause of their flight was the advance of our forces. To escape being crushed, he dragged himself out of the road; and here remained until found by the hospital corps. He was carried to the nearest hospital, and his wound dressed by Doctor Gilmer, who became eminent afterward in Mobile. At the General's request he was taken to Marietta, Georgia, to be attended by his old friend, Dr. Dudley D. Saunders, Director of Hospital in that city. (*Mrs. Gregg.*)

During his long confinement, the army was reorganized, and the brigades formed of regiments from the same State. General Gregg was assigned to Hood's old Texan brigade, Longstreet's corps, wintering in East Tennessee. In the spring of 1864, this command was ordered to reinforce General Lee; and General Gregg participated in all the battles of that memorable campaign, from the Wilderness to the fatal field on the James; where he closed his earthly career. We shall only sketch the two battles.

When General Grant was appointed commander-in-chief, of the Federal forces, and, in Virginia, was pitted against Lee, there was conviction in the minds of all men, North and South, that a decisive campaign was coming. Lee had been in winter quarters on the Rapidan. Grant confronted him, and on the night of the 4th of May he moved his army across the lower fords of the Rapidan, with 121,116 men (according to the report of the War Department). Lee had in his camp 42,000 men only. Grant intended to flank Lee and drive him back before Richmond, where he expected to fight a decisive battle. Lee having perfect knowledge of Grant's movements, on the very next day boldly struck Grant on his flank, in the Wilderness, trusting to the dense thickets to cover the paucity of his numbers. On the 5th of May the conflict commenced on Lee's right. Heth's and Wilcox's divisions received the shock of an immense Federal force. The ammunition of Heth's men gave out, and they fell to the rear, leaving Wilcox's division to bear the brunt of the battle. His line was becoming irregular and much broken, but the musketry died out at 8 P. M., and General Wilcox repaired to General Lee's camp, some 300 yards behind, and was informed that General Longstreet with his corps would relieve him before daylight. This corps had occupied the extreme left of the line on the Rapidan, and had been delayed by having to march a greater distance than any other.

General Wilcox visited his outposts that night. "All was quiet; and it seemed impossible to realize that a fierce battle had been fought only a few hours before; and that so many armed men lay almost within reach, ready to spring forward at early dawn to renew the bloody work. A line had been designated for Longstreet; but 12, 2 and 3 o'clock arrived and he came not. Clear daylight had come, and the tree tops were tinged with the early rays of the rising sun; but the enemy lay quiet. At length the sun rose above the trees, and the Confederates, eager to catch at straws in their unprepared state, began to have hopes that the Federals would not advance; but these were soon dispelled. A few shots were heard on the right which soon extended along the line. The badly formed line of Wilcox received, unaided, this powerful column, which soon enveloped its flank. The fighting was severe, and lasted an hour." (*From a letter of Wilcox published in the Philadelphia Times.*)

It was at this critical moment that the head of Longstreet's column arrived. As Gen- Gregg passed, General Lee asked, "What brigade is that?" and when told it was the Texas brigade, General Lee rejoined: "General, when you go in, give them the cold steel, the *Texans* always move them." (*Major Campbell of Gregg's staff.*) Wilcox was still fighting in front. While the Texans were deploying, Colonel Folsom, of the Four- teenth Georgia, was borne to the rear on a stretcher. In a few minutes Colonel Avery, of the Thirty-third North Carolina, was borne from the field mortally wounded. The brilliant charge then made by Longstreet's corps belongs to history. A captain of the Pennsylvania Artillery says: "It was the charge of the war, and was led by Longstreet in person. Our men stood it like heroes. The guns were double-shotted with canister, and fired at short range; but still the column moved on. We wounded Longstreet, and killed Jenkins. We had repulsed the enemy, but they held their original ground, besides securing their wounded, and thousands of ours. They had lost heavily, and we counted our dead and wounded by thousands. Grant is said to have declared that his previous battles were but skirmishes compared to this." (*Captain Brockoray in the Philadelphia Times.*) That to Gregg's brigade, under his leading, is mainly due the credit of checking the enemy, is generally believed; and the fact that he left half their numbers dead or wounded on the field, is proof of it. In these two days the Federals lost in killed, wounded and missing, 37,000 men, according to *official* reports; and the Confederates as many in proportion to the number of their forces.

But the crowning glory of General Gregg's military career, extending through every department, from the Mississippi to the Rappahannock, was his defence of Rich- mond, on the 29th of September, 1864, with a force of about 2000 men. General Grant had extended his lines far to the west of Petersburg, when he conceived the idea of secretly throwing around on the north side of James river a force sufficient to capture Richmond by a surprise. It might have succeeded but for the gallantry of General Gregg. During a hard day's fight he held in check two corps of the Federals (Orel's and Burney's) until General Lee could reinforce him. Here his horse was killed under him. He resisted nine different assaults, made by a force which outnumbered him eight to one.

On the morning of the 7th of October, General Lee determined to attack the enemy on the north side of the James, with a strong force, and dislodge them from their breastworks. General Gregg fell, while leading a charge, near these works. He was pierced through the neck and died without speaking. In the pride of his manhood and usefulness, at the early age of 36, this patriot, soldier and hero, fell a martyr to the cause so dear to his heart.

I conclude this notice with a tribute to his memory by Dr. Saunders, of Memphis. "Gen. John Gregg was wounded at the battle of Chickamauga. After his wounds were dressed, at his special request, he was sent to Marietta, Ga., to be attended by me, then in charge of this hospital post. General Gregg was a splendid specimen of man- hood, upon whose face and physique the impress of greatness and nobility of soul was plainly stamped. Large, tall, handsome, and well proportioned—massive head—splen- did eye, which set a halo over finely cut features—a face indicative, at a glance, of position, character; and yet a manner so entirely frank and guileless as to impress one with the idea that he was entirely unconscious of his latent powers.

During this long and painful suffering at Marietta, never a murmur of complaint at fate or Providence was uttered; and the first questions when visited in the morning were: "What news have you from the army? What are they doing at the front?" His suffering was alleviated by the company of his wife, whose gentle tenderness and cheerfulness assisted him greatly to bear the long weary hours of confinement in bed. The recollection of my intercourse with General Gregg, at Marietta, has always been to me a pleasant thought, and the news of his death while gallantly leading his command in a charge upon the enemy's works was a source of poignant grief. "The reaper, Death, with his sickle keen," had laid low this fair flower of Southern chivalry, and no brighter gem ever decked his coronet than the brave and noble General John Gregg."

The Swoopes.

Jacob Swoope came from Germany to Virginia. He had been well educated, and was an accomplished merchant, and in view of his coming to the United States, had learned to read and speak the English language fluently.

The first authentic account we have of him is in Governor Gilmer's old book on the Georgians. He says: "While in Rockingham county, Va., I witnessed an electioneering scene, equally interesting with the one I had seen in Charlottesville. David Holmes, who had, for twenty years, immediately preceding, represented in Congress the district of which the county of Rockingham formed a part, had been appointed Governor of Mississippi Territory by President Jefferson. A new member had to be elected, and the Republicans and Federalists were very equally divided in the district. Mr. Smith (now Judge Smith) became the candidate of the Republicans, and Jacob Swoope the candidate of the Federalists. The Virginians vote "*viva voce*." The candidates seat themselves during the day of election on the judge's bench in the court house, and as each voter names the person for whom he votes he is bowed to and thanked by the candidate voted for. I was in Harrisonburg, the county town of Rockingham, on the day of election, and saw Mr. Smith and Mr. Swoope thus seated and occupied. Smith was of an "old Virginia family," Swoope was German and could speak the German language. The farmers of the county were mostly German; the lawyers, doctors, merchants, sheriffs, clerks, etc., were Virginians. Mr. Smith and Mr. Swoope addressed the people on the party topics of the day. British orders in council, Napoleon's edicts restraining commerce, the embargo and anti-commercial system of President Jefferson. After both candidates had spoken, Mr. Swoope commenced addressing the people in German in reply to Mr. Smith. A huge old German rose and in broken English said Mr. Swoope should not talk German, because Mr. Smith could not talk it, and stopped Swoope. Mr. Swoope was a merchant, a handsome man, and usually well dressed. He resided in Staunton, Augusta county. He came to Rockingham dressed in German fashion. The German succeeded, though the Republicans had the majority in the district, and Mr. Smith was the equal, if not the superior of Mr. Swoope in qualifications for congressional service." Mr. Swoope served in Congress from 1809 to 1811, and then very wisely returned to his merchandising, in which he was very successful.

He was the father of three of the best merchants Courtland ever had—John M., Jacob K., and Edgar M. Swoope. They brought to the place a substantial cash capital, and did business under the style of "J. & J. Swoope," and in a few years reaped large profits. The planters then cultivated fresh, productive lands, made large cotton crops, and sold for high prices. No wonder then that the merchants of that day grew rich. We shall now notice each of the merchants in detail.

John M. Swoope, the oldest of these brothers, was one of the best judges of goods in the place, and for several years spent a large part of his time in New York and Philadelphia in making purchases for the firm. Everything he did was well done. He was always neatly and richly dressed; never appeared on the street without having his clothes well brushed and his hat as slick as when it came from the block of the hatter. Indeed, he was fastidiously neat in everything. His house and garden were kept in complete order, and before he became a cotton planter he was often heard to say that his fence corners should always be kept as clean as any other part of the field; but after he became a member of that slovenly crowd I never heard anything more of *that*.

He married Cynthia M., daughter of Governor Peter Early, of Georgia, and sister of Mrs. Richard S. Jones. Mr. Swoope died in ——, and his widow in 1886. Mary, their first born, died when a young lady in 1852. Emma married Dr. Andrew Jackson Sykes, whose family history we shall notice hereafter. The doctor came to Lawrence over forty years ago and soon became one of our most successful physicians. He had a good person, fine manners, a cultured mind and withal so good a temper that he soon had " troops of friends." For several years past he has been afflicted, and is now confined to his bed and has the sympathy of the whole community.

The children of Dr. Sykes are: Lucy Early, who married Watkins Phinizy, son of John T. Phinizy, Esq.; James married Susie, daughter of Mr. Oakley Bynum, and died young; Anna married Mr. Crenshaw, and Emma, the youngest.

Virginia, third child of John M. Swoope and wife, married Hon. E. C. Betts, now Commissioner of Agriculture for the State of Alabama. He was judge of the Probate Court of Madison county, and also represented that county in the State Senate for a number of years. They have a number of children. Of these Rostan is a lawyer of Huntsville, and married a daughter of Minor Merriwether, Esq., of Memphis, and Tancred, a clerk in one of the departments in Washington City, married a daughter of Dr. Wm. L. Brown, president of A. and M. College, Auburn, Ala.

Jacob K. Swoope, the next oldest brother in the Courtland firm was also a very handsome man, with black hair and eyes, whereas his two brothers had blue. He had social manners and a good deal of humor, and was very popular. He was the partner who conducted all matters of contract with customers, while his brother John had more to do with the machinery of the large concern, and felt little interest in association, except with his personal friends. At length the members dissolved partnership. He married first Antoinette, a daughter of Col. Benjamin Sherrod, by whom he had one child, William, who died before he attained his majority. She lived but a short time, and he married for his second wife Mrs. Clay, widow of Hon. Matthew Clay, and daughter of the Rev. Turner Saunders. Mr. Swoope retired from business, and settled on the plantation now occupied by his son, Capt. C. C. Swoope. In winding up his mercantile business he took in payment of his debts a good deal of cotton, and having confidence in the article, he bought largely in addition, and in the end made about $20,000 profit. He was never known to buy any cotton afterward; a remarkable fact, for it is generally the case that when men make in this way, they never rest until they lose it all at the same game. Mr. Swoope proved to be a most excellent planter. His business was conducted with much method, and with the best tools, and the most perfect machinery. In this respect his son, Captain Swoope, who now occupies the same place, has trodden in his footsteps.

Mr. Jacob Swoope after retiring from the counting-room, to which he had been so closely confined for many years, enjoyed his release very much, and was fond of joining his friends in hunting, and other country amusements. There was amongst them a man who owned a small farm near the Big Spring (then called Hickman's), whose cotton field became very foul. Swoope, feeling that he was somewhat to blame for decoying his neighbor from his work, and with his natural love of fun, collected secretly a large number of hands, and had his little cotton field hoed over one morning before the owner waked up. When he did, he pretended to become very angry at the liberty his friends had taken with him; but his anger soon subsided, and the first time the horn blew he joined the hunt again. The issue of this marriage was Jacob K., Charles C. and Frances (commonly called Fannie) Swoope.

Jacob K. married Elizabeth Haley, of Florence, Ala. The issue of this marriage was only two children. The eldest, young Jacob, was fishing on the bank of the Tennessee river with a son of Dr. Alfred Jones, of Florence. Jacob fell into the river, and young Jones bravely sprang into the water to rescue his friend, when, unfortunately, both were drowned. These boys were of uncommon promise. The daughter,

Tempie, married Mr. Darrow, of Virginia. Elizabeth Haley has survived her husband, Jacob Swoope, many years. She was the heir of Jack Peters, one of the wealthiest men of Lauderdale county, and inherited a half dozen plantations.

The second child of Jacob K. Swoope by this marriage was Charles C. He passed through the late war as a captain, and since then has been a very enlightened and successful farmer. There seems to be something in the German blood which predisposes a man to be a good farmer. He married Miss Fannie Hutchins, and has reared a large family in habits of industry and thrift; contrary to the usual custom of parents having ample fortune. Their children are Edgar, William, Susan, Charles, Jacob, Saunders and Clay. Of these, two are married; William, who married a Miss Carter, of Como, Miss., and Susan, who married Thomas Ashford, of Birmingham, Ala., who is a grandson of Captain Thomas Ashford, who emigrated from Kentucky, and whose family will be noticed. Fannie, third child of Jacob K. Swoope, married Edward Moore, of Columbus, Miss. Their children are: Edward, who married Miss Houston; Jacob, who is unmarried, and Fannie, who married James Harrison (son of James T. Harrison, Esq., a distinguished lawyer, of that city).

Edgar M. Swoope

was the youngest of the three brothers, and when he came to Courtland, was under age. He was then a very steady youth. When the firm of "J. & J. Swoope" was dissolved, he came into possession of his estate, and formed a partnership with Richard Trotter, under the style of "Swoope & Trotter." He married Elmira, daughter of Samuel Watkins, a wealthy planter who lived a few miles east of Courtland. After some years the firm of Swoope & Trotter was dissolved, and while the business was being wound up by a clerk, who kept the strong box in the brick house, called Swoope's corner, a remarkable episode occurred in his history, one which had a material effect on his life. That strong box was robbed, and money and bills of exchange to a large amount taken from it. A mystery which seemed impenetrable rested on the theft, until a letter was received by Mr. Swoope, from Mr. Owen, cashier of the Bank of Mobile, informing him that these bills of exchange had been offered for discount by Dr. Phares, of Courtland; and as there were some suspicious features in the case, he wished to know about it. This led to the arrest of Dr. Phares. If a bomb of the largest dimensions had bursted suddenly over the little town, it would not have caused such amazement. Dr. Phares guilty of theft! It was not possible! He was a man of a nice little fortune, was doing a good business as druggist, was always neatly dressed, was a Free Mason, had a fine face, pale and spirituelle, and as the negro would say had " a 'ligous walk." When brought to trial Phares employed every lawyer in Courtland, and Mr. Wm. Cooper, of Tuscumbia, to lead them. Although I had been for some years out of practice, it devolved on me to prosecute the case, as some of the money stolen from the strong box belonged to my sister, Mrs. Swoope. The trial resulted in Phares being bound over, and on his way to jail he took laudanum, but the dose was too large and it failed to kill him. During the trial it was noticed that not a single Free Mason denounced the accused, and they were criticised severely for it. They kept a profound silence, but they listened to the statements of the witnesses with the closest attention, and that night Courtland Lodge convened, and excommunicated Phares. How often have I thought since, that church members would do well to follow the example of these Masons; and instead of taking up a reproach against an accused brother, wait until he was tried, and all the proof given, before they formed an opinion. After the trial, Fergus Phares, a brother of the accused, attacked Mr. Swoope and shot at him with a pistol, then used the pistol by striking him on the head with such violence that he felled him to his knees, and Mr. Swoope, as he rose shot him through the breast. Phares made no effort to evade the shot; and it is believed that he courted death. He was very much esteemed by the young men of Courtland. Dr. Phares mortgaged his property, obtained bail on a bond of $4000, left the country, and was never heard of afterward.

This unfortunate affair had an unhappy effect upon Mr. Swoope. He acted in that encounter with Fergus Phares in self-defence, yet the act seemed to prey on his mind, and he became wonderfully intemperate. How long this habit continued I do not remember, but in process of time he underwent poignant *conviction* for the course he was pursuing, and determined to lead a better life. It was at the conclusion of a long spell of drunkenness, when his nervous system was shattered, that he saw the *Devil in person* rise up before him. However this may have been, he firmly believed it, and used to tell it in the pulpit, as a part of his Christian experience, until the day of his death. He was in consequence of this vision as firm a believer in the *personality* of the Devil as the reformer Luther himself. When Mr. Swoope's conversion was announced very many people believed his reformation was merely temporary, and prophesied that he would soon return to his old ways; but, year in and year out he persevered in a career of zealous usefulness, and consistency of Christian character, which eventually made calumny ashamed, and it retired from the contest. Mr. Swoope became a local preacher of the Methodist Church South. He purchased one of the best historical and theological libraries, studied diligently, and having a strong mind, he was able to discuss thoroughly every subject on which he preached; but this generally took him two hours. On one occasion I had a humorous friend from Mississippi visiting me, and we went to hear him preach, at Courtland. On returning home, the visitor was asked "how he liked the sermon;" he answered that it showed much learning and ability, but he added, "I would not have abused a dog as Mr. Swoope abused the Devil. He seemed to have a special spite against him!" Most of his preaching, however, was among the poor people, who seldom heard service, and were therefore more tolerant of the great length of his sermons. Here he would preach the *terrors* of the Law, and shake them over hell-fire most terribly. He was a firm believer in what the scriptures teach on this subject, and would contend that with any person who believed in the resurrection of the *body* there should be no difficulty in accepting the doctrine of *hell-fire*.

In making these excursions to preach, Mr. Swoope rode in a *fine* buggy, drawn by a *fine*, sleek horse, and was driven by a *fine looking* mulatto servant, named Jim Lewis. Some may suppose that being a rich man, and moving in such style, he would have but little access to these plain people; but they are mistaken. It is not a *rich* man people hate, but a *mean, stingy* rich man. Common opinion expects a man to move in a style suited to his estate; as much as for a poor man to abstain from wearing a costly coat—not paid for. Such is the law too, as you will find if you enter the Probate Court, and witness the settlement of estates. The people knew that Mr. Swoope had a big heart, and had witnessed his many charities. Suffer me to give one instance. At the darkest hour of the civil war, when the men were all in the field—when the Tennessee Valley was a debatable ground, first occupied by the Federals and then by the Confederates, until its resources for food were nearly exhausted—when the southern part of the country, depleted of its efficient laboring men, was reduced to nearly the same condition of scarcity—when that noble old man, Charles Gibson, then Judge of our county court, was devoting his whole time to collecting food for the women and children who were beginning to suffer—and when (as he wrote me) he was at his wit's end to know what to do next, he received a note from Edgar M. Swoope, who had a steam mill in the centre of the county, authorizing him to draw upon him for a hundred bushels of wheat and a quantity of meal, and when that was exhausted to draw on him for more, as long as it was needed; for the women and children should not starve while the men were fighting our battles, as long as he had a bushel of wheat, or a dust of meal. No wonder that as a preacher he had access to their souls, when he was so kindly caring for their bodies.

His style of preaching was direct, earnest and logical. He had no imagination or poetic taste, and when he used a metaphor it was often so quaint as to derogate from the force of the position he was maintaining. Naturally he was a man of strong antipathies, and warm friendships—had nothing neutral about him. He was original and independent, and honest in all he did; and somewhat eccentric. He had some faults, but great virtues; and it would be a boon to this Christian community, if, in every age, the Lord

would send just one man like the Rev. Edgar M. Swoope to break the stereotyped mono-
tony of the pulpit.

He had one son, Samuel, a young man of much promise, who died unmarried,
and one daughter, Mary, who married James Ballentine, of Pulaski, Tenn. These
are both dead, and their children are Edgar C., Orlean V., James H., William H.
and Sadie E. These are now the only descendants of Edgar M. and Elmira Swoope.
She has survived him, and lives in Courtland, with her estate much diminished by litigation.

Jim Lewis,

The servant of Mr. Swoope alluded to above, had a very kind master, who taught him
the ordinary branches of an English education, and in their constant intercourse imbued
his mind with far more learning than usually falls to the lot of men of his race. He
lent him books and at his death gave him a good library, which he read to great profit.
He is a man naturally of fine mind and excellent judgment, and in his manners a real
gentleman, if he be "somewhat off color." He had become a Methodist preacher, and
uses a chaste style of speaking, and though he is earnest and zealous, he has neither rant
nor cant; so you can see at once that he has great influence in repressing the fanaticism of
his people. This assumed, in former years, various forms. I will give you an illustration: A long time ago, one Saturday, when Father Kilpatrick, missionary to the blacks,
had come in, ready for service next day, there was a great rumpus on "the street," or
quarters, and it seemed like a fight. I sent for the fighters, and presently Aunt Violet
and Edy, a young girl, were brought before me; Edy looking very guilty, with a
knot on her forehead as large as a hen-egg. "What does all this mean?" Aunt Violet:
"Mars Jeemes, you know you put Edy in my house for me to make her behave?
Well, sir, Edy cusses, and sometime ago, she cussed, and I tol' her, up and down, dat
if she don' so any mo', I would knock her down. Well, dis mornin' while we was wuckin'
Edy cussed, and I just took a board and knock her down. You see dat knot on
Edy's head? Does you think it was de streak of my poor arm dat made dat knot?
No, sir, it was de streak of my Jesus!" This was too much for my dignity, and I called
the missionary to lecture the parties, and retired for a good laugh. What he said to
them I never knew; but I am satisfied that Aunt Violet was never convinced that she
had done wrong; and as Edy reformed after that, she always thought she had mauled
religion into her with that board.

But I do not wish to be misunderstood. It is the habit of many persons to sneer
at the religion of the colored people. For myself, I have a profound respect for it.
They hold to the doctrine of the witness of the spirit as laid down in the Bible. They
have ultraisms, I admit, but as their teachers become better educated, these are gradually disappearing. But you often hear it said that the negro is apt to back-slide very
often. Well, that is so, but they are good repenters, and when they apply for
pardon they are orthodox, too, for they kneel not before altars made with hands, but
before "the great white throne." I can see a steady improvement in the religious
exercises of the race, and their fanaticism is being toned down, but it is to be hoped
that this will not be carried so far as to make the religion of the emotional negro as
cold as that of the philosophical white man. I have begun to preach, and remember
that I have no license.

Dr. Jack Shackelford

was born in Richmond, Va., March 20, 1790. His father, Richard Shackelford, was
married three times. His last wife, Johanna Lawson, was the mother of Jack Shackelford, and died when he was an infant. Catharine Allgood (a sister of one of the first
wives) took the little orphan Jack (for that was his baptismal name) and reared him
with all the love of a devoted mother. When grown, he left Virginia to seek a new
home, and went to Winnsboro, S. C., where he married Maria Yongue, daughter of a
Presbyterian minister; a lady of small person and much beauty, with most estimable
qualities. He served in the British war of 1812, and, in a skirmish near Charleston,

was cut in the face by an officer's sword. In 1818 he moved to Shelby county, Alabama, where he became a cotton planter, and practised medicine very successfully. In 1820 he was elected member of the House of Representatives of the State Legislature, and served in the State Senate from the district composed of Shelby and Bibb counties for the years 1822-23-24. I knew of his great popularity in this district from our Senator—Matt Clay—long before I saw him. In one election, when his opponent lived in Bibb county, he carried every vote, save one, in his own county, and nearly a majority in Bibb.

At this period of his life, Dr. Shackelford had all the elements that constitute happiness. He had been promoted, politically, and had numerous friends in South Alabama, and such men as Matt Clay, Nicholas Davis and James Jackson as his bosom friends in North Alabama. When the Legislature adjourned, they usually visited the doctor at his home in Shelby, where he lived like a baron of the middle ages, with profuse hospitality, and where guests, escaping from the *short rations* of Cahaba, would revel in the luxury of venison from the woods, and fish from the Coosa. He had a good practice and an ample fortune, and, moreover, a wife whose chief enjoyment was to make him and his friends happy. But he had a *cousin*. This cousin had conceived the idea of making a fortune as a merchant, without capital or previous training. Dr. Shackelford, in the generosity of his nature, became surety for him to a large amount. In the sequel the cousin failed, and to pay *his* debts, Dr. Shackelford had to sell his lands and slaves, except a few old men, women and children.

His friends were as true as steel, and had him elected to the office of receiver of the land office at Courtland, whither he brought his family, and the wreck of his fortune, fifty-eight years ago (1829). The land given to the State for the Muscle Shoals canal was soon disposed of, and afterward he applied himself to the practice of his profession with wonderful success. This was owing, in some degree, to his very popular manners, but more to his merit as a physician. He had the good sense to embrace the mild practice of Broussais, in an age when calomel, jalap, gamboge and the lancet were heroically used. He cured his patients with gentle remedies, and topical applications, while his competitors *killed them scientifically.* He was especially successful in nervous disorders, but his remedies were not always laid down in medical books. In one case a lady of family, living in the neighborhood of Courtland, imagined that she had swallowed a frog. When she mentioned it to him, he first attempted to remove the impression from her mind, but finding it useless, he said sympathetically, "But if it be as you suppose, I can kill the frog in your stomach, and then remove it by an emetic." She acquiesced joyfully. He colored red some effervescing powders, and directed her to take them at regular intervals, until he returned. He had much trouble in securing a tree frog, but a prize of a quarter offered to the boys, at length brought one, and he hastened to see his patient, who was in a state of anxious expectancy. The emetic was administered, and after the first spell of vomiting, she inquired, "Doctor, has the frog come?" He answered. "No, madam." A second dose was given, and she had a severe spell of vomiting, and he threw the frog into the bowl, saying joyfully, "Here it is, madam." She wiped her eyes, and when she saw it exclaimed, "I knew I could not be mistaken." Then she fell back on her pillows and was completely cured.

When the concentrated power of Mexico was invoked to crush the people of Texas after a long course of oppression, the citizens of the United States sympathized profoundly with their friends who had emigrated to that country. Company after company was raised and hurriedly marched forward to the scene of conflict. Among others Dr. Jack Shackelford raised a company of young men, in a few days, called the "Red Rovers," from the color of their jeans uniforms. A meeting of citizens was called for the purpose of raising money to purchase an outfit and supplies for the company. A friend, after making a few remarks, laid a hundred dollar bill on the table, and it was covered at once by eleven others; then followed donations of less amount until the expenses of the expedition were fully provided for. No time was lost on the way. The company sailed from New Orleans on a schooner, and landed at Copano, thence they marched at once to Goliad, about the time the Mexicans marched on the Alamo. The company was incorporated with a regiment commanded by Col. J. W. Fannin of Georgia, on the 10th of March, 1836.

General Sam Houston, commander-in-chief, sent orders to Colonel Fannin, on the 11th, to retreat on Victoria. These did not reach him until the 14th of March. He waited for Captain King, who had been sent out to help in some settlers, and after whom Major Ward had been sent with 100 men. This resulted in the loss of the whole command. Not having found his missing men, Colonel Fannin started on the morning of the 19th, and after marching about eight miles called a halt, to rest his oxen and refresh his men. He had, all along, entertained too great a contempt for the enemy. Captain Shackelford remonstrated against the halt, until they should reach the Coleta, then five miles distant; but he was overruled. Col. F. could not be made to believe that the Mexicans would dare follow him. Here they halted an hour, and Col. A. C. Horton, who had come in with twenty-seven men the day before, was dispatched to examine the crossing of the Coleta. On resuming the march the enemy began to appear in sight, and then Fannan attempted to reach the timber a mile or two in front, but it was too late, and he was compelled to form for battle in a depression in the plain, six or seven feet below the surrounding surface. The Texans in number only 275, were surrounded by the enemy, about ten or twelve hundred infantry (the celebrated Tampico regiment) and 700 cavalry. Here one of the most remarkable contests occurred ever recorded in military history. With the disadvantage of being cut off from timber and water, and hemmed in a depression, this small force stoutly repelled many charges of the Mexicans. After the first heavy charge, for want of water the cannon of the Texans became too hot for use, and they were forced to rely wholly on their small arms, and with these they continued the fight from one o'clock until night. To show the determined spirit of the Texans in this struggle I will mention a single instance. Among the wounded was Henry Ripley, a youth of eighteen years, a son of General Ripley, of Louisiana. He had his thigh broken. Mrs. Cash (who was with the army) at his request helped him into a cart, fixed a prop for him to lean on, and a rest for his rifle. Thus he continued to fight, until another shot broke his right arm. At length the scene became too dreadful to behold. Killed and wounded men, and horses, were strewn over the plain: the wounded were rending the air with their distressing moans, while a great many horses were rushing to and fro back upon the enemy's lines, increasing the confusion among them: they thus became so entangled, one with another, that their retreat after the last charge, resembled the headlong flight of a herd of buffaloes, rather than the retreat of a well drilled regular army as they were.

Night suspended the contest. After dark the Texans, by leaving their wounded, might perhaps have cut their way through the enemy's line, but, after the massacres which had occurred at the Alamo and other places, they felt that it would be dishonorable to leave their comrades in the hands of a savage foe. How different from the state of things in our civil war. No matter in whose hands the wounded fell at the conclusion of a bloody battle, they were secure from violence. As soon as the sound of artillery died away "grim visaged war smoothed his wrinkled front," and the humane surgeon with his torniquet stopped the flow of life blood from the arteries of the wounded; no matter under what flag and tender-hearted women, under the Red Cross ensign, held the cup of water to parched lips to assuage the raging thirst which none but a wounded soldier who feels his life-blood ebbing away can ever know.

Early next morning General Urrea received a reinforcement of 500 men, under Colonel Morales, with three pieces of artillery. The Mexicans fired a few rounds and then hoisted a white flag, but it was soon taken down. The Texan wounded had suffered agonies for want of water, and the officers having held a consultation raised a white flag, which was promptly answered by the enemy. Colonel Fannin then went to meet Urrea, and arranged the terms of capitulation, which were: The Texans should be received and treated as prisoners of war, according to the usage of the most civilized nations. 2. That private property should be respected. 3. That they should be sent to

Copano, and in eight days to the United States, or so soon thereafter as vessels could be procured to take them. 4. That the officers should be paroled, and return to the United States in like manner. Colonel Holsinger, a German engineer, together with several other Mexican officers, came into our lines to consummate the agreement. The first words Colonel Holsinger uttered, after a polite bow, were: "Well, gentlemen, in eight days, liberty and home." The terms of the capitulation were then written in both languages, English and Mexican, and the instruments were signed and exchanged in the most formal manner.

The prisoners were carried back to Goliad. On the 23d Colonel Holsinger and Colonel Fannin proceeded to Copano to ascertain if a vessel could be had to convey the Texans to the United States, but the vessel they expected to obtain had already left that port. The evening of the 26th passed off pleasantly, Colonel Fannin entertaining his friends with the prospect of returning to the United States, and some of the young men who could perform well on the flute were playing "Home, Sweet Home." How fortunate it is that the veil of the future is suspended before us! At 7 o'clock, that night, an order by an extraordinary courier from the Commander-in-chief, Santa Anna, required the prisoners to be shot. Detailed instructions were sent as to the mode of executing this cold-blooded and atrocious order. Colonel Portilla, the commandant of the post, did not long hesitate in its execution. He had four hundred and forty-five prisoners under his charge. But eighty of these (Captain Miller's company) having just landed, without arms, was considered not being within the scope of the order, and were for the time spared. The truth is, that they owed their lives to Senora Alines, whose name ought to be perpetuated to the remotest times for her virtues, and whose actions contrasting so strangely with those of her countrymen, deserve to be recorded in the annals of this country, and treasured in the heart of every Texan. When she arrived at Copano with her husband, who was one of Urrea's officers, Miller and his men had just been taken prisoners. They were tied tightly with cords so as to check completely the flow of the blood in their arms, and in this way they had been left for several hours before she saw them. Her heart was touched by the sight, and she immediately ordered the cords to be taken off, and refreshments given them. She treated them with great kindness, and when, the night before the massacre, she learned that the prisoners were to be shot, she so efficiently pleaded with General Guerrier (whose humane feelings revolted against the barbarous order) that with great personal responsibility on himself, and at great hazard in so doing, counter to the orders of the then powerful Santa Anna, he resolved to save all he could; and a few of us are left to tell of this bloody day." (*This statement is from Regimental Surgeon Barnard.*) The services of four of the physicians—that is, Drs. Barnard, Field, Hall and Shackelford—were needed to take care of the Mexican wounded, and their lives were spared.

At dawn of day, on Palm Sunday, March 27, the Texans were awakened by a Mexican officer, who said he wished them to form a line, that they might be counted. The men were marched out in separate divisions, under different pretext. Drs. Shackelford and Barnard had been invited by Colonel Guerrier to his tent, about one hundred yards from the fort, to remove them further from the scene shortly to be enacted. Soon they heard four distinct volleys, fired in as many directions, accompanied by yells and shouts. The hellish work was going on. Many attempted to escape, but the most of those who survived the first fire were cut down by the pursuing cavalry. As the different divisions were brought to the place of execution, they were ordered to sit down with their backs to the guard. In this last sad hour there were many instances of heroic courage. Young Fenner exclaimed: "Boys, they are going to kill us, die with your faces to them, like men." Others waving their hats sent forth their death cries, "Hurrah for Texas!" Dr. Barnard in an article he wrote on this massacre, said: "Our situation and feelings during this time, is not in the power of language to describe. The sound of every gun which rang in my ears told but too terribly the fate of our brave companions. Dr. Shackelford, who sat by my side, suffered the severest anguish the human heart could feel. His company of "Red Rovers," which he brought out and commanded, were young men of the first families in his neighborhood—his particular and especial friends. Besides two of his nephews, his oldest son, a talented boy, the pride of his father's heart, and the beloved of his company, was here, and included in this butchery." But the end was not yet. In about an hour the wounded were dragged out and butchered. Colonel Fannin was the last to suffer. When informed of his fate he met it like a soldier. He handed his watch to the officer whose business it was to murder him, and requested him to have him shot in the breast and not in the head, and have him decently buried. With the perfidy of his race he did neither.

The foregoing account of the battle of Coleta, and the massacre of Goliad, has been compiled from Yoakum's history of Texas (which the author says was founded on notes furnished by Dr. Shackelford himself), an article published by Dr. Barnard, and many conversations held by me with Dr. Shackelford after his return home. Santa Anna justified his action upon the ground that he did not know of the capitulation; and that there was a law of the Mexican Congress requiring the summary execution of every volunteer from the United States. The answer of General Houston to this excuse, when Santa Anna was captured and brought before him was, " You are a dictator, and responsible for this infamous law;" and it was one which completely silenced him.

But there is no doubt whatever of a capitulation. The detachment of Major Ward, when brought in as prisoners, stated that they surrendered upon the same terms that were granted to Colonel Fannin's command. The whole body of prisoners during the few days they were permitted to live, relied confidently on the promises made by the Mexicans. Colonel Portilla, commandant at Goliad, and a full-blooded Indian, on the evening of the massacre writes to General Urrea thus: " I feel much distressed at what has occurred here, a scene enacted in cold blood having passed before my eyes, which has filled me with horror." And General Urrea in his journal, which has been published, says: " Every soldier in my command was confounded at the news; all was amazement and consternation. They certainly surrendered in the full confidence that Mexican generosity would not be sterile on their behalf. They assuredly did so, or otherwise they would have resisted to the last, and sold their lives as dearly as possible."

Dr. Shackelford and the other surgeons were transferred to San Antonio, where they were detained for months. During this imprisonment, momentous events were occurring. The settlers were so alarmed at the atrocities of the enemy they fled from their homes, leaving nearly all their effects behind them. The Mexican armies covered the country. Texas was fortunate in having such a military commander as General Houston in this crisis. For myself, I confess I was surprised at the wisdom he displayed. I had known him when he was a young man in Franklin, Tenn., parading the streets of a summer evening on a fine horse, dressed with barbaric splendor, courting notoriety, and showing every symptom of a frivolous nature. In sparing the life of Santa Anna he exhibited great self-control and discretion, looking calmly on the question as one of public policy, while a tornado of popular indignation was sweeping over Texas.

At length, Drs. Shackelford and Barnard managed to procure arms and horses and make their escape. They traveled all night and secreted themselves during the day; next night they did the same, and considering themselves safe from pursuit, they approached a deserted house, and entering it, found everything just as if the family had left the moment before. The Bible was on the table, there was bedding, and meal in the barrel. They shot a fat heifer, and during that day and night ate and slept and recovered from their fatigue. On his return, Dr. Shackelford wrote from New Orleans to inform his family that he was still alive and on his way home.

Short as was the notice, Courtland was full of friends, come to welcome the gallant man to his home. A lady who was present, informed me that his excellent wife, who had suffered so long and so acutely, received him (on her knees, with tears streaming down her face and with outstretched arms,) as one raised from the dead. Some time before, solemn funeral services had been held over the dead of the " Red Rovers." and he was numbered amongst them, and a wooden cenotaph erected intended to preserve the names of the massacred until a durable monument was raised. This has mouldered into dust, but I will here insert a roll of these heroic young men who perished in defence of Texan liberty:

Captain Shackelford's Company of Alabama Volunteers.

OFFICERS—Jack Shackelford, captain; Wm. Horton Francis, lieutenant; Fortunatus G. Shackelford. orderly; J, D. Hamilton, A. J. Foley and C. M. Short, sergeants; H. H. Bentley, J. H. Barclay, D. Moore and A. Winters, corporals.

PRIVATES—T. H. Anderson, J. N. Burnhill, —— Cantwell, Seth Clark, D. Gamble, Samuel Farley, John H. Miller, H. W. Jones, E. Burbridge, James Vaughan, G. L. Davis, Harvey Cox, M. C. Garner, J. E. Ellis, Charles McKinley, John Jackson, Wm. Quinn, F. W. Savage, W. C. Douglas, L. M. Brooks, J. W. Duncan, Alfred Dorsey, J. E. Grimes, Joseph Fenner, J. N. Seaton, John Kelly, A. Dickson, Joseph Blackwell, Wm. Gunter, J. G. Coe, Wm. Simpson, Robert Fenner, James Wilder, John N. Jackson, D. Cooper, W. E. Vaughan, John Hyser, F. T. Burts, B. Strunk, H. D. Day, J. W. Cain, E. B. Franklin, R. T. Davidson, Daniel A. Murdock, Wm. Hemphill, G. W. Brooks, Wm. S. Shackelford, J. G. Ferguson, H. L. Douglas, Robert Wilson.

Of these all were massacred but eight—Dr. Shackelford, because he was a physician; L. M. Brooks, G. W. Brooks, W. Simpson, D. Cooper and Isaac D. Hamilton, who escaped after the first volley by swimming the river (Isaac Hamilton had a deep flesh wound in the thigh and yet saved his life), and W. H. Francis and Joseph Fenner, who were detailed on Colonel Horton's advance guard and cut off from the main body by Urrea's army.

There were persons in our community who, after the tragic conclusion of this expedition to Texas, severely criticised it as unjustifiable and fruitless. Suffer me to make a few sober comments on each branch of this proposition in vindication of the memory of one of the dearest and best friends I ever had. When our people began to colonize Texas, Mexico was independent of Spanish domination, and enjoyed freedom under the Constitution of 1824, modeled after that of the United States. Texas was united to Coahuila, because not strong enough to form a State, but the promise in the law was that she should be made a separate State as soon as she had the elements for it. Even in our country, our State or local government has always been regarded as the best security for personal rights; and here we have a homogeneous people; how much more, then, was it required in Mexico, where the masses differed from our colonists in race, language and religion. The stronger Texas became in the attributes required, the more persistently did Mexico deny her the privilege of separate local government. Wrong after wrong was perpetrated upon them. At first, land grants were made to Austin Edwards and many others with the purpose of having these settled with Americans. In a few years they prohibited, by law, the settlement of emigrants from the United States. Then large grants to Americans were demanded, by executive decree, without a resort to the courts of the country—then there was a law for virtually disarming the population; then a commander-general was sent into the State invested with civil and military power, and to complete the list of outrages, on the 3d of October, 1835, the destruction of the Federal Constitution of Mexico was consummated by the abolition of the State Legislature; and that which was a republic when settled by the Americans, became a consolidated despotism. We think we had wrongs when our independence was declared in 1776; but those of Texas exceeded them, as much as the Mexican exceeded the British people in tyranny and barbarity. No wonder that a people who had breathed the air of freedom from infancy should have declared their independence. The flag of the Lone Star was a tacit appeal to their friends in our republic for aid in this emergency. The appeal met with a prompt response in the hearts of many of our noblest men. The United States was at peace with Mexico, and according to the laws of nations could not properly interfere in the contest then looming up. But individuals were free to give their aid to the Texas cause, as Lafayette, DeKalb and others did to us in our Revolutionary struggle; and the opinion of the civilised world not only justifies it, but in such cases invests the act with a higher degree of chivalry than when one defends his own country, because it is disinterested, and a sacrifice offered upon the altar of Liberty for its own sake.

But was the expedition to Texas fruitless? As unfortunate as it was, it bore fruits which contributed more to the Texas cause than any other during the war. These massacres when first announced, caused a feeling of sorrow in all civilised people. But the reaction was tremendous: and such was the indignation, that volunteers rushed to the aid of Texas so fast, that the number had to be limited by requiring passports from the territorial agent at New Orleans. General Jackson, then President, whose bosom was as full of wrath as the crater of a volcano about to blaze up is of melted lava, issued an equivocal order to General Gaines, then commanding on our western border, who instanter, marched fourteen companies of regulars to the Sabine, and sent a messenger to the Indians (who were about to march to Texas), who prevailed on them to remain at home. They accomplished the recognition of Texan Independence by the United States, long before they actually achieved it, and the tidal wave of indignation, crossing the Atlantic, caused the example to be followed by England and France.

Doctor Shackelford, after his return from Texas, resumed the practice of his profession. His estimable wife died in Courtland in 1842. After some years he married Mrs. Martha Chardavoyne, the widow of Wm. V. Chardavoyne, and the mother of Major Wm. V. Chardavoyne. Cheered by the society of this accomplished and excellent lady, the doctor lived until January 27, 1857. His wife survived him many years.

Dr. Shackelford, was natural and unaffected in his manners. He was a charming companion. He had a strong mind, well stored with information, and a large fund of anecdotes (and, having histrionic powers which would have made his fortune in one profession) he told them better than any man who ever was in the State, except Baldwin, author of "Flush Times in Alabama." He was a member of the Methodist church, and a sincere and humble Christian. It is true, he never carried a long, sanctimonious face. These are the mere shells of piety. But, judged by his fruits, he was one of the best men I ever knew. With a most sympathetic heart he relieved suffering wherever he found it, without distinction of color, to the best of his personal ability, and the extent of his fortune. He had unbounded hospitality. To the young disciple who had pursued his weary way until he was oppressed with home sickness, he not only "gave a cup of cold water" but every comfort of his house, and made him feel completely at home; so that he took fresh courage and went on his way reinvigorated. I never knew a man in my long pilgrimage, more beloved, than Dr. Jack Shackelford.

By his first marriage, Dr. Shackelford had four children, to-wit: Fortunatus S., who was massacreed at Goliad. 2. Samuel W., who married first Margaret McMahon, who lived but a short time. He then married Addie, daughter of Colonel Benjamin Sherrod. They have two children—Jack, a young man of much energy, and May, a young lady of many accomplishments. 3. Harriett C., married John J. McMahon. They have four children: Fortunatus S. S., a physician of eminence in Courtland. He followed the fortunes of the Confederate cause, during the civil war, from the disaster at Fishing Creek to the surrender; as will be seen in our previous numbers; Dr. W. Jack, surgeon C. S. A. married Miss Cutter, of New Orleans, and has several children, His army career has already been noticed. Robert, who was a brave soldier also; and Lillie, a young lady of beauty and merit living with her mother, who is a widow (her husband having died in 1857). The fourth child of Dr. Shackelford was Edward P., a skilful man of business in Courtland who died some years ago. He married Caroline Watkins, and their children are Frank W., Harriet C., and Elizabeth, all young.

McMahon Family.

In 1828, John J. McMahon was sent to Courtland by Andrew Bierne to supply the place in his mercantile concern there of a son who became a lunatic, and had been sent to a hospital in Philadelphia. The new firm was called "Bierne & McMahon," and continued prosperously for many years. During this time he married Harriet C. Shakelford (as we have mentioned above). Some ten years after he came to Courtland, Wm. McMahon, his father, moved his family from Harrisonburg, Va., to a plantation north of Courtland. He and his wife were then quite old, but they lived long enough to be known as most estimable people; indeed, the family of McMahons were distinguished for courtesy, amiability and integrity. They had numerous progeny, to-wit: John J., above mentioned; became a commission merchant in New Orleans, and enjoyed the confidence of his customers to a remarkable degree. Charles, who never married, died in Gainesville, Ala. William P., who married Laura Chaffee, and practised law in Courtland for many years. Their children (after their death), moved to South Carolina and Mississippi. Mary, who married Oscar Cravens, a physician of culture, in Courtland for many years. Robert G., who moved to Gainesville and married the widow of L. Branch Fawcett (who once lived in Courtland as book-keeper for Bierne & McMahon). They are both dead. She was born Elizabeth R. C. Scott, daughter of Gen. John Baytop Scott, who died in Virginia in 1813. (See Scott family.) Mrs. McMahon's first husband was Dr. T. D. Bell, by whom were several children, and also three daughters by McMahon's marriage (none living by the Fawcett marriage). C. Waterman, who married Jane, daughter of Prof. James Jackson, of Franklin College, Georgia; Margaret, first wife of Samuel W. Shackelford, above mentioned; Ethelbert S. (Bert), a bachelor, still living, and Paxton, who died in Gainesville in his youth.

Among the physicians of Courtland were Dr. Booth, Dr. Young A. Grey, Dr. George L. Brousseau, 1825; Dr. Thomas A. Watkins, who formed partnership with Dr. Jack Shakelford in 1832. Drs. Booth and Rousseau moved away. After that, Dr. James E. Wyche, 1825; Dr. Robert Martin, Dr. Hayne (1827), of Virginia, friend of Andrew Bierne; Dr. Milligen, 1832; Dr. Baxter, about 1836; Dr. Harper, and Dr. King, about 1840—(Dr. Watkins.).

Dr. Thomas A. Watkins,

born a descendant of Thomas Watkins, of Chickahominy, came to Courtland in 1825. He had graduated at the University of Georgia, and had his diploma as a physician from a school at Philadelphia. He had a good person, hazel eyes and a dark complexion. His manners were dignified and rather cold, and not calculated to ingratiate him with the people; therefore, it was some time before he achieved a good practice. In the meantime, he had a drugstore in which he had invested his slender patrimony which sustained him during the first years of practice. But as he became better known his practice increased until he occupied a place in the front rank of our physicians. He agreed with Dr. Shackelford in his medical theories, and they practised together as partners fo many years.

At length Dr. Watkins finding himself in a condition which justified it, married into the family of Wm. Fitzgerald. He had come from Botetourt county, Va., with a small colony of friends; his brother, Freeman Fitzgerald. who lived at Rocky Hill, (which has been the home of the writer for the last fifty years); Littleberry Jones, who married a sister of the Fitzgeralds, and built the brick house now occupied by Harvey Gilchrist, and Wm. Booth, Sr., the first occupant of the place where Geo. Garth now lives. After the lapse of some ten or twelve years, they were struck by a Florida boom and moved away, except Wm. Fitzgerald. He had married in Virginia long since his cousin, Letty Williams, and when he came to Alabama he was past middle age, but still very fond of young people. In the deer hunts, so common at that day, he was an efficient hand, but as he was fat he was always indulged with a stand, and he was a dead shot. Moreover he would keep his stand until he was called off, as faithfully as a soldier would keep his watch. He would find a log to sit upon, and the deer might be driven by the hounds into the Tennessee river, and hours might transpire, yet when relieved he would be found in the same position. Like a centaur he had grown to his log. He and his wife had no ambition, except to entertain their friends and to make them happy. It was an old Virginia home transplanted from the foot hills of the Blue

Ridge to the valley of the Tennessee. The young people were always welcome, and would not hesitate to make up parties to invade this hospitable dwelling whose doors were always wide open, and here without any restraint, they would divide up into committees of two, in which momentous questions as to the future would be determined. How well I remember "Aunt Letty," with a cap on her head (not a mere pretence no longer than your hand, set on the back of it), a real cap, as white as snow, fitting closely around her face, and furnishing a lovely frame for a countenance once beautiful, still sweet, and wonderfully expressive of the kindness and sympathy of her disposition.

The home of the two old people is now called "Ingleside." It was to this home, years after, that Orrin Davis brought from Providence, R. I., his bride, Hannah Chaffee, of queenly beauty and with a voice unsurpassed in sweetness and compass. And here reside now J. J. Barclay and his wife, once Decima Campbell. If they only belonged to "old times," it would delight me to tell in detail how his ancestor, Robert Barclay, consul-general to the Barbary States, in the days of Washington, by his indignant protests was the inspiration which sent our navy to teach these "pirates," who had thousands of our people in slavery, a wholesome respect for an American citizen; and I should like also to give the reasons why, irrespective of sects, every Protestant Christian should revere the name of her father, Dr. Alexander Campbell. During these three generations of owners and occupants, "Ingleside," in its quiet beauty, has been a favorite seat of the genius of hospitality.

William Fitzgerald and his wife were childless, and they adopted an orphan nephew, William Fitzgerald who married a Miss Bledsoe, and his sister, Sarah Epes Fitzgerald, who married Dr. Watkins, the subject of this sketch. He remained in the county until he had accumulated sufficient capital, and then moved to the State of Mississippi, where he amassed a large fortune. Here he lost his excellent wife, and met the inflictions of the civil war, which made wreck of his estate. His last years were spent in Austin, Texas, to which he moved in 1867, and died there in 1884.

In the Austin *Daily Statesman* there is a truthful notice of him, from which I will quote a paragraph. "No ordinary man passed from the stage of action when Dr. Watkins died. He had played a prominent and useful part in the drama of life, and died at the ripe age of eighty-two, beloved and respected by a host of friends. He was a man of the most varied and accurate scholarship—possessing a fund of knowledge on almost every subject. He was kind, generous and hospitable, and ever the first to seek out and welcome strangers."

One quality of his heart was gratitude. When I commenced these memoirs he wrote me the names of two friends who had aided him financially when he became embarrassed in carrying on his drug business, and requested me to notice them particularly in my articles. More than fifty years had elapsed, and yet the remembrance of the favors was as vivid as if " graven with the point of a diamond."

He was born in Georgia, and his attachment to his native State, her people, her traditions and her politics was wonderful. He had lived in Alabama, Mississippi and Texas, and loved them all, but he *adored* Georgia, and knew every fact of her history by heart. He was the most striking illustration of the English doctrine of "perpetual allegiance" I ever saw. He dressed neatly but plainly, and seemed to have no personal pride, but he was a born aristocrat, and proud of his family descent and connections, and when I shall have briefly sketched them, you will see that he had reason.

On the paternal side, his father, George, was a lawyer of good standing, for he, and his brother, Robert Watkins, were selected to make the first digest of the laws of Georgia, His father married a daughter of Joel Early, and sister of Gov. Peter Early—Charles Matthews, a son of Gen. George Matthews, married also a sister of Gov. Peter Early—George Matthews, a son of Charles Matthews, married a sister of Dr. Watkins—Judge Junius Hiller married another sister—and a Mr. Todd, yet another sister, Thomas Watkins, grandfather of Dr. Watkins, married a sister of Gov. George Walton, one of the signers of the Declaration of Independence, and so on. My readers can see by glancing over this network of marriages that the doctor was closely allied to three of the most distinguished families of Georgia: the Earlys, Matthews and Waltons.

216 EARLY SETTLERS OF ALABAMA.

Dr. Thomas A. Watkins, had but two children, Letitia A., born 1835, and Mary Early.

Major W. M. Walton married (1854) Letitia A. He was a grandson (his father, Samuel) of Mr. George Walton, who came from Georgia, at an early day, and settled in this county near Town creek. Major Walton, now lives near Austin, Tex., and is a distinguished lawyer in full practice. He was a brave soldier and served during the civil war in such a way as to command the favor of the Texans who elected him Attorney General. But this was in the days of the "captivity," and Reynolds, the military Governor, removed Major Walton; a strong proof of his merit and his devotion to his people. Their children are: (1) Newton S., born in 1855, and now a partner with his father in the practice of the law. He married Annie Hicks, of Jackson, Tenn. They have two children, both quite young: Ethel Early, and Wm. Hicks. (2) Early Watkins Walton, M. D., unmarried. (3) George Longstreet Walton, one of the most prominent young men of his day, who was shot in 1836 by a pistol ball, fired at random, by an intoxicated young man at a Christmas tree, which caused his death; and (4) Sarah Walton, who is unmarried.

The other daughter of Dr. Watkins was Mary Early, born 1844, who married, in 1863, Jefferson H. McLemore, who now lives near Waco, Tex. They never had any children.

Dr. Watkins died, 1884. He also wrote a manuscript of the old settlers of Georgia, of his own day, says Major Walton.

Of the Early family I shall speak in the next number, in connection with that of Col. Richard Jones. The family of Matthews in Georgia, descended from Gen. George Matthews, who was born near Staunton, Va., a brave officer of the Revolutionary war, a member of Congress from Georgia, and also Governor of that State. He fought the Indians from his boyhood up. "In 1761, a family not far from his father's residence was massacred. He and two or three youths, supposing from the firing that there was a shooting match at the place, went to join in the sport. Upon riding up they saw the dead bodies lying in the yard. Perceiving at once their mistake, they turned their horses and fled. The Indians rose from their concealment and fired their rifles at them, as they passed in full speed. A ball grazed the head of George Matthews, so as to cut off his cue. Stimulated by the danger he had escaped, and the murder of his neighbors, he collected a party, put himself at their head, pursued the Indians, overtook them and killed nine." In 1774, in the great battle with the Indians under Logan, "he commanded a company and contributed much by his bravery and military skill to the victory gained by the Virginians. The fighting commenced at sunrise, and had continued without any decided advantage, until evening, when Captain Matthews, Captain Shelby, and Captain Stewart withdrew, with their companies from the fighting, out of sight, got into the bed of Crooked creek, then low in water, and concealed by the banks, gained the rear of the Indians, and attacking them unexpectedly, drove them across the Ohio river."

Colonel Matthews did good service under Washington at Brandywine. At the battle of Germantown he attacked the British troops opposite to him, pursued them triumphantly, and had just captured them, when he and his command became so embarrassed in a dense fog that in the confusion which followed he was attacked, knocked down, and a bayonet driven through his body. He was made prisoner, sent to the British prison ship in the harbor of New York, where he suffered many cruelties, and was not exchanged until near the end of the war. Colonel Matthews then joined the army under General Green, in command of the Third Virginia regiment.

He removed to Georgia in 1784, and settled on Broad river. General Matthews was a short thick man; his features were full and bluff, his hair light red, and his complexion fair and florid. His looks spoke out that he would not fear the Devil should he meet him face to face. He talked often of himself and of his services to his country, and admitted no superior but General Washington. His dress was in unison with his looks and conversation. He wore a three-cornered cocked hat, fair-top boots, a full ruffled shirt at bosom and wrists, and occasionally a long sword at his side. He was unlearned, but his memory was unequaled. While he was a member of Congress, an important document which had been read once was lost, and he was able to repeat its contents verbatim. He knew all the officers of the Revolutionary army entitled to land, and he acquired a very large estate principally by trafficking in bounty lands.

His youngest son, Charles, as I have said, married Lucy Early, and moved to South Alabama. His four sons, Joel, George, Thomas and Peter, were all men of great respectability and wealth. Joel was my college mate, and I knew him intimately. He was a man of superior intellect and extensive information. He was the only Southern planter I ever knew who was a practical astronomer, and studied the heavens through a telescope. He had one of considerable power, selected for him by the great scientist, Maury when he was in charge of the U. S. Observatory. The advance of this nation in the last one hundred years in scholastic acquirements could be well illustrated by two pictures, one of Joel Early Matthews at work with his telescope, and another of his successor, Gen. George Matthews, with his pen laboriously writing "coffee" "Kaughphy." But he was great without *schooling*, perhaps a greater man than any of his descendants. For the information respecting him I am indebted to that rare old book, "*Governor Gilmer's Georgians.*" Lucy, daughter of Joel E. Matthews, married Col. David S. Troy of Montgomery, and lived only a few months. (He married (II) Florence L., daughter of Gov. Thos. H. Watts, of Montgomery.)

Of the family in Georgia, the Honorable George Walton was head. Born in Frederick county, Va., 1740, and died in Augusta, Ga., 1804, Governor of Georgia, 1779, fought in Revolution. He was one of the signers of the Declaration of Independence, a member of the United States Senate. Mrs. Levert, of Mobile, was his granddaughter. She was an authoress, and in the firmament of society, shone as a star of the first magnitude. In the city of Paris, on one occasion, the American minister presented a celebrated French statesman to Mrs. Levert. After they resumed their seats, the Frenchman was informed that Mrs. Levert was a granddaughter of one of the signers of American Independence; he rose from his seat, with signs of deep emotion, made her a profound bow, and resumed his seat without a word. This silent bow was an eloquent tribute to her ancestor. She was unaffectedly kind and affectionate in her intercourse with her neighbors. One always left her company feeling better and thinking more of himself than he did before. She was an optimist, always looked on the bright side of things, and never spoke evil of other women. If this was not that charity spoken of in the good book, it was " one floweret of Eden left since the fall," and should be cultivated by every one. I am not traveling "out of the record " in saying so much of Mrs. Levert, for her husband, Dr. Henry S. Levert, was a resident of Lawrence county for several years, while a student of medicine. He made his home with an uncle of mine within sight of where I pen these lines, and taught a classical school that he might perfect his professional education—and he left many dear friends behind him. After more than twenty years I found him in the city of Mobile, in the front rank of physicians, contending for supremacy with such men as Dr. Nott and others; and I was gratified to learn that he cherished a lively remembrance of the friends of his early days. Mrs. Levert, once Octavia Walton, must have had a substratum of good common sense, to have selected so solid a man as Dr. Levert from a crowd of such frivolous suitors as contended for the hand of the Pensacola belle.

Col. Richard Jones

was born in Cumberland county, Va., on the 29th of June, 1773. His father was Harrison Jones, who after being engaged to be married to Anne Ligon of the same State, joined the army as a soldier of the Revolution, and lost a leg at the battle of Guilford C. H. On his return home she did not refuse to perform her part of the contract, although there had been a "partial failure of consideration." He was true to his country, and she was true to her loyer, and I consider it good sound stock to start with. Colonel Jones was the youngest of seven children, all sons, and they have all passed from earth. The Hon. Jacob Thompson, of Mississippi, a member of the Confederate Cabinet of Mr. Davis, married a daughter of Peyton, the elder brother of Colonel Jones.

Colonel Jones graduated at the University of Georgia, in 1812, with the first honors. The war with Great Britain commenced the same year, and young Jones volunteered and served as a soldier, and on his return home he began the study of law in the office of Gov. Peter Early. He married Lucy Early (born in Washington, Wilkes county, Ga., 18th October, 1799), daughter of the governor, and without a sketch of this gentleman, the family history would be incomplete.

It is furnished in the most authentic form in "*The Bench and Bar of Georgia*," a book written by Stephen F. Miller, Esq., the last twenty years of whose life was spent in Tuscaloosa, where he was the able editor of the independent Monitor. He says: "Peter Early was born in June, 1773, in Madison county, Virginia, and migrated with his father, Joel Early and family, about the year 1795 to the county of Green, State of Georgia. After the usual preparation, he entered Nassau Hall, at Princeton, N. J., and in due time received its academic honors, as a regular graduate. From this institution he passed into the office of Mr. Ingersoll, an eminent counsellor of the Philadelphia bar, where he had the benefit of a protracted apprenticeship as a student of law. With the advantages of such a course of study, it cannot be a matter of wonder, that Mr. Early's first appearance in the courts of Georgia, should have made a most favorable impression. His voice and elocution were admirable, and his manners at once dignified and gentle, secured the esteem and favor (not less of the multitude) than of his associates of the bar."

"Though he entered on his professional career with such bright prospects, in pursuit of fame and fortune, he had to encounter competitors who put his great resources to frequent and severe trials. Among these were Carnes, Dooley, Griffin and William H. Crawford of the Western, and Robert Watkins, George Walker and John E. Anderson of the Middle circuit. The three gentlemen last mentioned, were eminently distinguished, for genius and eloquence."

"He had not been many years at the bar before popular opinion began to point him out for the public service. His election to Congress was carried by a majority of votes seldom equalled in this or any other State."

"Amongst the notable transactions in which he bore a leading part was the impeachment of Samuel Chase, one of the judges of the Supreme Court of the United States. "He was an ultra Federalist, and in presiding at the trial of more than one case of breaches of the Alien and Sedition laws, he incurred the suspicion of gross and vindictive bias against the prisoners. Public indignation rose to such a pitch that nothing could satisfy it but the impeachment of the judge. The House of Representatives had appointed a committee to conduct the prosecution—one of which was Mr. Early. John Randolph, of Roanoke, and four or five members of high rank, were on the committee, and took part in the discussion before the court. It has been said, however, that in force and true forensic eloquence, the argument delivered by Mr. Early was decidedly the best. Aaron Burr, then Vice President of the United States, presided, with austere dignity peculiar to the man." The foregoing account of Governor Early, to be found in *Vol. 1, page 345*, was furnished by Hon. Joel Crawford.

Judge Strong, the "Nestor of the Georgia bar," furnishes another. "Mr. Early was present at the great congressional debate on the reception of Jay's treaty, and heard that wonderful and last speech of the great orator, Fisher Ames, and saw him fall and borne from the Hall of the House of Representatives. Never shall I forget his bright tearful eyes, as he portrayed that overwhelming scene. That unsurpassed speech of Mr. Ames so completely overwhelmed the whole house and audience, that Mr. Giles, of Virginia, rose, and said it was easy to see that the members were too much excited and agitated to vote considerately, and therefore he moved an adjournment. Having finished his legal course of study, Mr. Early came to the bar fully prepared. To all these advantages was added a clear, strong, discriminating mind, wonderfully endowed with the power of analysis and condensation. He seldom spoke more than twenty or thirty minutes. To all these was added a fine form. He had square shoulders and well proportioned, fair and healthful complexion, light brown hair, and penetrating blue eyes, of deportment, voice and manner, which proclaimed to all who saw him, that he was a man. His voice was full and somewhat anthoritative. No wonder then, that in one year he was in the front rank of the bar; and in two years at the head. He was truly a noble, honest man, warm friend, and always inflexible in the cause of truth, virtue and justice" (*Vol. 2, page 285*).

Mr. Early, when he retired from Congress, was elected judge of the Ocmulgee Circuit, the boundaries of which were extended to include the county of Greene, in which was his residence; and he had no opposition. He continued to discharge the duties with distinguished ability for some years. In Georgia, then, there was no Supreme Court, and the decisions of a circuit judge were final. For this reason a judge rarely retired from the bench without being very unpopular. But Judge Early had the gratification to know that he possessed the confidence of all classes up to the day of his retirement.

One very peculiar case arose in his court. A woman was indicted as "*a common scold*" under the Common Law, which affixes the penalty of *ducking* to the offence. Her counsel contended that the law was obsolete. The prosecuting attorney insisted that it was still the law of Georgia, unless they could show an act repealing it. The members of the bar knowing the inflexibility of Judge Early were curious to know how he could escape from the dilemma, but he made no attempt. He pronounced judgment against the woman, and after he adjourned this court, and was on his way to the next one, it was executed. On the day fixed there was an immense crowd of witnesses. The sheriff took the culprit in a sulky into a deep hole in a creek and ducked her three times. Two of these duckings were said to be extra-judicial, but the whole country-side was against the woman, and as long as she came up out of the water scolding he was persuaded to duck her, on the ground that the punishment should be inflicted "*pro re nata.*" This is the last time this law was enforced in Georgia. It may have been repealed, or as it became known, in two days, in every log cabin in Georgia, the rigorous punishment may have put an end to the practice of *scolding* amongst the Georgia woman. The latter is the most probable, for I believe the Georgia women *never* scold. I have had one of them for sixty-two years, and she does not even know *how* to scold!

In 1813 Judge Early was elected Governor of Georgia. The country was engaged in a war with Great Britain, and every requisition made by the United States government on the State was promptly filled. He died 1819.

When quite a young man, Governor Early married Miss Smith, of Wilkes county, sister of Colonel—afterward General—Thomas A. Smith, of the United States army. This General Smith married Cynthia Barry White, a sister of Hugh Lawson White, the great Tennessee statesman, who was a candidate for the Presidency.

Governor Early's children were, Lucy, wife of Colonel Richard Jones, Cynthia, wife of Mr. John M. Swoope, and several sons.

Colonel Jones practiced law in Georgia for about seven years with much success; but when the great exodus to North Alabama occurred, he moved to this county in 1822, and settled a cotton plantation west of Town creek. In 1829 he sold this place and purchased a much larger one, east of Courtland. He conducted his cotton planting with such judgment and force that his estate, from a moderate beginning, grew very great, and he was one of the three men in our county who accumulated the largest landed estates. Colonel Jones, with his talents and industry, would certainly have risen to distinction at the bar.

He died on the 3d of February, 1883, having attained the age of 89 years and 6 months. His wife had departed a few years before him, on the 31st of October, 1869. He not only loved his wife, but admired her; to use his own language in a letter received from him, "she was a superior woman in every respect." Up to the time of his death his fine form was unbent by age, for he mounted his horse every morning and exercised it; his mind seemed as bright as when I first saw him more than sixty years ago, as he never suffered it to rust, and his affections kept warm by the sympathies of his children, grandchildren, friends and neighbors, made him welcome to every company he entered.

He had but two children, Thomas and Ella. Thomas was educated for the bar, but his large landed estate has monopolized his attention. He has always been distinguished for his devotion to his family, his father, mother, sister and her interesting family of children. In his early life there was a romance, and he remained single until he arrived at middle age—he then married its object, Mrs. Sarah Pointer, who lived but a short time.

Ella Jones had superior advantages not only in school, but in the society of a mother who, inheriting a mind of uncommon strength, and being an invalid and confined to her room nearly all the days of her married life, found her chief amusement in books. Ella was greatly indulged by her father. He and his neighbor, Robert King, visited Huntsville once when their daughters were there at school, and boarding with Colonel Bradford. King had been making some money arrangements for his daughter, when Bradford turned to Colonel Jones and said: "And now, Colonel, what can I do for Miss Ella? His answer was, "Anything she wishes. If she requires you to have the *court house* moved, have it done and draw on me for the expense." It is a wonder she was not spoiled beyond redemption, but she was no parvenu; belonged to a family which had been rich for generations; and had been taught by an intellectual mother to value other things more than diamonds and ball dresses. Ella Jones, when very young, married Benjamin Sherrod, grandson of Col. Benjamin Sherrod, the wealthiest man in our county, but he died in a short time, and she was left a blooming young widow.

And, now, indulge me in an episode, which happened at the house of Colonel Jones during the late war, and which has not been recorded in history. When Rosencrans, with a large Federal army occupied Chattanooga, Major General Joseph Wheeler made a raid in his rear, to cut off his supplies, which had to be hauled in wagons across the mountains. This was a raid, indeed. General Stuart's raid around McClellan's army has been immortalized by the genius of J. Esten Cooke, but that was nothing compared to Wheeler's. That was for only two days, Wheeler's continued for forty. That was only to gain information; Wheeler's, for material destruction. Stuart had only the narrow Chickahominy behind him; Wheeler had the broad Tennessee between his force and the Confederate army. Stuart's was barren of material results, but Wheeler's cut off the supplies of the Federals, until, in the language of their great historian, Draper, "distress began to reign in their camps—the animals of the trains starved—until there were not artillery horses enough to take a battery into action—and it became doubtful whether the National army could hold Chattanooga much longer." Stuart had one initial skirmish; Wheeler had repeated conflicts with the Federal cavalry, and when in number about 13,000 they pressed upon his small force in his retreat, for some days he had to repulse them from nearly every hilltop until he forded the Tennessee river. But he effected the crossing safely, and made his headquarters in the house of Colonel Jones; and it was here the event happened to which I have alluded, and that was: General Wheeler being *taken prisoner*, not by the enemy, but by the charming young widow I have mentioned.

This capture resulted in the marriage of General Wheeler to Mrs. Ella Sherrod. He was born in Augusta, Ga., on September 10, 1836. Graduated at West Point Military Academy in 1859. When his native State seceded he resigned his commission in the United States army, and served during the war, and from a lieutenantcy rose to the rank of lieutenant general, and that before he reached the age of twenty-eight years. To attempt merely a sketch of his military career would trench on the domain of public history, and consume more space than could be spared in these unpretending articles. He has for some years represented this Eighth Congressional District in Congress, and, to use a term from the cavalry, "he is firmly seated in the saddle."

Their children are Lucy Louise, Annie Early, Julia Knox, Joseph, Carrie Peyton, and Tom Fenwicke.*

Hon. David G. Ligon

came to Courtland from Virginia in 1823. He and Rev. John L. Townes were near of kin, being sons of two sisters of the Leigh family; and this gave him a passport at once into the best society. He had a fine person, was about six feet high, had dark hair and deep blue eyes. In manners he was remarkably social and popular, and soon had many friends. He had been thoroughly educated, and was master of the English language; indeed, in pronunciation and style, he was fastidious. He made a fair start in his profession, considering the fact that Arthur F. Hopkins and John J. Ormand, the two great leaders at the bar, had monopolised the best business. But young Ligon was so distinguished by the splendor of his imagination that he forced himself into public notice. He was more brilliant than Henry S. Foote (who then lived in Courtland, but after two years residence, despaired of success, and removed to Mississippi, where he came to the front as a popular speaker and a politician).

Mr. Ligon had fine colloquial powers, and no matter where he was, in a select company or in a crowd, in a store or on the pavement, his language was choice, and the finest gems of thought were lavishly expended, without reference to the capacity of his auditors. I have seen him surrounded by men who had never advanced farther than "crucifix" in Webster's spelling book, who seemed to be delighted—I suppose by the jingle of his conversation. He was noted for good nature; had fine powers of repartee, and they were not exercised sarcastically but humorously. I never knew him silenced and left without an answer, but once. He was defending a horse thief who was found guilty by the jury, and sentenced by the judge to receive thirty-nine lashes on his bare back, the next day at 10 o'clock A. M. Mr. Ligon entered a motion for a new trial, and next morning, on the opening of court, he commenced his argument. He had gotten to the most cogent part of it, when he observed a titter run around the court room. He paused, and heard the sheriff whipping his client, and then sat down without saying a word, completely silenced, amidst the laughter of court, bar and spectators.

Mr. Ligon's first effort for political advancement was in 1828 when he was a candidate for the House of Representatives in the State Legislature. I was then living in Moulton, and the night of the election, while the returns were coming in from the precincts, I happened to be in the court house. When it became certain that Mr. Ligon had been beaten, some person in the crowd called on him for a speech. I never heard anything from him, before or after, so well conceived, in such graceful, faultless language, so flattering to his friends and so disarming to his enemies. I think this speech elected him in 1829.

And now follows a barren stretch of nearly ten years in the history of Mr. Ligon. He became intemperate, and no wonder; the social qualities of this spoilt child of genius were so great, that he was welcome in every company, and sometimes even dragged from home to give life to a little party of friends. The consequence was he lost his practice and became very poor. He imagined that the fault was in the *place*, and moved to Moulton and staid there awhile; he returned to Courtland and remained there awhile; thence to Decatur where he ran a newspaper; and then finding that the fault was not in the *place* but in *himself*, he returned to Moulton and reformed his habits, a year or two before the great Harrison campaign of 1840. His body and mind soon recovered their strength and elasticity; and during this contest, which lasted for months, he delivered some of the ablest and most brilliant speeches of his life. He was always a decided Whig.

In 1842 he became a member of the Christian (commonly called Campbellite) Church, and after a few years commenced preaching. This confirmed his reformation. Before he became a member of the church he was somewhat unstable; often he attempted to reform, but afterward, with its restraints and friendly bands thrown around him, he

---

NOTE.—Mrs. Wheeler died in 1895, and the young son, Thomas Fenwicke, was drowned in 1898, while his father was the hero of the Cuban war.

advanced rapidly in reputation. He practised law for several years in partnership with Judge Thomas M. Peters. In 1845 he was elected Chancellor of the Northern Division over his competitors, Alexander Bowie and T. W. Woodward.

In 1848 he published a book entitled "Digested Index of the Supreme Court of Alabama, in Chancery Cases, from 1820 to 1847." It was found useful to the profession, and a second edition was soon called for.—(*Brewer's Alabama.*)

Chancellor Ligon was a candidate for Congress in opposition to Mr. Hubbard in 1849. Ligon was beaten, but Hubbard found him a troublesome antagonist. It was a lively canvass, and it was then that Ligon much disconcerted Hubbard with one of his repartees. Hubbard took occasion in his speech to answer the charge of speculating in lands, and being sharp thereat. He confessed it, and said it was the bad laws which enabled him to do it, but that he knew their defects and wished to go to Congress to correct them. In reply Ligon said it was the first time he had ever heard it suggested that the "bell cow" should be sent to put up the fence.

In 1851 Chancellor Ligon was elected Associate Judge of the Supreme Court, beating John D. Phelan, a Democrat of ability and popularity, before a Democratic Legislature. Garrett, in his "*Public Men of Alabama,*" says: "Upon the reörganization of the court in 1853 he declined a re-election. He sustained himself pretty well as a Chancellor, but it was doubted by many whether his legal learning and early training had been equal to the task and responsibilities of a Supreme Court Judge. Be this as it may, his declension of a continuance upon the bench, after a trial of two years was generally appreciated as an act of good taste." The criticism was just, but who can tell how it would have been if so many years of Judge Ligon's life had not been wasted? If through life, he had steadily persevered in a course of temperance and industry, with his fine constitution unimpaired and his mind "going on from strength to strength," I think he might have lived to extreme old age, and been well fitted for any department of service in the State.

In 1854 he was elected trustee of the State University; and on the 21st of January, 1855, departed this life. While preaching in the Christian Church, at Moulton, he was seized with appoplexy, and died almost immediately.

His father was William Ligon, who was born in 1765, and married a Miss Leigh, in Prince Edward county, Va.

Judge Ligon married a Miss Greenhill, his cousin, in this county, in 1825. She was the daughter of Mrs. Greenhill, who married secondly a Rice, and again became a widow. I knew her and Mrs. Ligon well. They were ladies of great modesty, industry and worth. The mother died in 1851, and the daughter in 1868.

Judge Ligon's descendants were: 1. Dr. Charles W. Ligon, born in Courtland in 1825, and married Susan Follis in 1857. He was a physician in good standing, living near Moulton, and died about three years ago. 2. Pascal L. Ligon, born in Moulton in 1828, and married Martha P. Lee about the year 1853. He had a good practice at the law and became Senator in the state legislature of Arkansas, from Powhatan county, before his death, which occurred in 1867. 3. David G. Ligon, Jr., born in Courtland in 1832. Never married, but died in our army, near Shannon, in 1862. 4. John H. Ligon, born December, 1835. He has not married, and lives near Moulton. 5. Sarah C. Ligon, born in Moulton in 1840; was married to E. C. McDonald, a son of the late Crockett McDonald, Esq. She is still living. (1887).

REV. HUGH BARR

was the first Presbyterian minister I ever knew in Courtland. When his church was small he supplemented his salary by teaching a school. He was an excellent man, of unblemished reputation, and a good pastor, but a dull preacher. Alexander Linn married his daughter.

David Smith was then a lawyer of respectable standing at the bar. He had married first his cousin, Miss Smith, of Charlotte C. H., Va., and secondly a daughter of Dr. J. W. Allen, Presbyterian minister at Huntsville.

Mr. Barr, Mr. Lynn, and Lawyer Smith became conscientious on the propriety of holding slaves, and moved to Illinois, manumitting their slaves. Here Mr. Smith made a good fortune, and died during the war. Of the others I have no reliable information after they left Courtland.

Thomas Smith was the father of David Smith, above mentioned, and accumulated a snug living. When the railroad was approaching Courtland he invested his ready money (some five thousand dollars), in stock. As soon as it reached Courtland his hotel made money rapidly, and was crowded with guests. When, however, it passed on to Decatur, his was no longer an eating house, but the breakfast place was Tuscumbia and the dining place was Decatur. One day, shortly after the change, a friend walked into his hotel and found him in tears—for he always cried when vexed. "What's the matter, Mr. Smith?" He answered: "Here I was such a fool as to lay out all my money on this road, and now the passengers, who breakfast at Tuscumbia, pass by my hotel picking their teeth, and I am left in a worse condition than I was before." He was a heavy, fat man of short stature, and his son David was smaller, but of the same form.

The Courtland Herald

was published by Willie Connor, and continued for many years. Connor was a practical printer, and got the advice of young Ormond in giving shape to his paper, who promised to write a leader occasionally. Ormand selected as a motto for his paper:

"Here comes the Herald of a noisy world.
News from all nations lumbering at his back."

Ormand wrote some excellent articles for the paper in the outset, but Connor couldn't comprehend them, and they soon drifted apart. Connor undertook to run the whole machine, mental and mechanical, and did so for many years "after a sort." He was a short, fat man, and Jones called him the "Yam Potato;" and the name stuck to him, for it was appropriate. On week days, Conner used to sit in his sanctum with the hairs on the side of his head drawn up, and tied over the crown of his bald pate with a cotton string—this, on Sundays, was substituted by a blue ribbon.

Rumors began to circulate as to the wonderful capacity of the editor as an eater. One of the most striking proofs of his power in this line was given at Gourdtown Spring, on Spring creek. It was not at a public barbecue, where half done shoat was served up, but a social one, such as we used to have in early times. Hubbard, a red headed man of Courtland, had charge of the cooking department, and had wonderful skill in barbecuing. *It is now a lost art.* All other *industries except this* have improved. For the benefit of posterity I will explain Hubbard's method. When he once put down his pigs and buffalo fishes, flesh side down, over the pit of coals, they were never turned until the drying of the skin showed that they were nearly done, and then when turned the flesh was nicely browned and cracked open in deep fissures, so that when the hot gravy of sweet butter, vinegar and black pepper, was poured on, it penetrated to the bone—a far superior mode to frequently turning and basting. It was to such a luscious feast that the editor of the *Herald* sat down, with the hindquarter of a pig on his right, a half of a stout buffalo fish on his left, and a bottle of whiskey in front. He moved steadily to the attack, frequently washing down the viands with grog. Orrin Davis, always full of fun, watched his eye glisten with pleasure; but at last perceiving that he was wavering in the attack, he rigged a lever in the fork of a sapling, which happened to stand just behind his seat, and passing a cord under his arms, he would raise him and then let him fall suddenly in his seat, so as to settle his food. This was equal to a cotton compress, and the editor, in the best humor, would renew the attack, until all had vanished, except the bones. This was not at all wonderful, for he was the author of the saying that " a turkey was of a very inconvenient size, for it was rather too much for one man, and not quite enough for two."

But the sketch of Willie Connor would be incomplete without informing you that he was the author of the first book written and published in Lawrence county. It was entitled "*The Lost Virgin of the South*," and was a story of a young girl captured by the Indians. While it was in manuscript he would detain his friends, almost by force, to hear him read portions of it, when tears would be profusely shed—by the author. A second edition was never called for, and the work unfortunately has been *lost*. How do we know but that the "Lost Virgin," if found at some future time, may cause as great a revolution in that kind of literature as the Institutes of Justinian (after being lost a thousand years) did in jurisprudence.

At length the editor discontinued the *Courtland Herald* and removed to Mississippi. I never had any authentic account of his subsequent career. We had some rumors, one of which was that he had become a traveling preacher. If this was really so, I judge that on his circuit chickens became very scarce, and turkeys roosted very high!

Courtland Mechanics.

In early times North Alabama was an El Dorado, and our mechanics, as well as our planters, were men of a high order. The absence of railroads afforded them a prosperity which is not known in modern times, when nearly every article we use is made by machinery in large and distant factories. This gave our home workmen an opportunity to educate their children, many of whom are now successful members of the learned professions.

Mr. Kouck,

house builder, came from Philadelphia with Dr. Clopper. He and the doctor had married sisters, who were notable women, ever ready to aid their neighbors in time of sickness and death. Dr. Clopper, who was a very nice man, and respectable physician, soon died. Mr. Kouck died, and his widow married that modest, gentlemanly carpenter, Maurice Morris, who had lived and worked with Mr. Kouck for many years, and who made her a good husband; he died first and his widow before the war. Mrs. Clopper died only a short time ago. Her husband, George, a man of excellent character, went before her. A sister of Mrs. Clopper married Schuyler Parshall, of Tuscumbia.

James Mudd

was an excellent saddler. He was a small man with clear cut features, indicating great intelligence. Mudd was a Clay Whig, at a time when there were but few in Courtland, and the Jackson men, being in great majority, were naturally imperious. But woe be to the Jackson man who attacked the Whig saddler, for Mudd was so witty that he was very apt to come out second best, and somewhat scarified. Mr. Mudd moved to Elyton in 1831, and among his children was William S. Mudd, who became a man of distinction in our State. He was licensed to practice law in 1839. In 1843 he was elected a member of the House, and was re-elected in 1844 and again in 1845. In 1847 he was elected solicitor, and filled the office efficiently for eight years. When you consider the fact that he was a decided Whig, and a majority of his constituents Democrats, he must have been of unblemished reputation and of first rate talents. But he was never extreme in his politics, and in 1851 he was the candidate for Congress of the compromise party, and came very near defeating Sampson W. Harris, one of the most graceful orators Alabama ever had. In 1855 he was selected judge of the Third Circuit, and I believe continued on the bench up to within a year of his death, which occurred in 1883. Mr. Brewer, in his History of Alabama, says of him: "His temperament is dispassionate and his views are practical. As a jurist, he is much disposed to disregard the technicalities of the law, in order to reach equity. As a citizen his exemplary deportment and amiable disposition are the basis of an esteem, which time has only served to build up." He married the daughter of Dr. S. S. Earle.

One of Judge Mudd's daughters married Dr. Jordan, who was at the head of his profession in Birmingham, but his health failing, he accepted a professorship in the Medical College of Mobile. Another married Dr. Cochrane, of Birmingham, a young and very promising physician; and Miss Susie Mudd is an accomplished young lady.

Robert Williamson

was a skilful gun-smith, who had plenty of profitable work in early times, and he was careful in educating his children. One of them, Richard is a lawyer in good practice in the city of Montgomery. He moved to Gainesville, about 1838, where he died.

The James Family

descended from Westwood W. James, who was born in Virginia on the third day of September, 1795, and married to Catherine Conway Owens on the 17th of May, 1821. This family with its connections now constitute, a large proportion of the population of Courtland. They are intelligent and respectable, and are pillars in the Presbyterian Church. W. W. James came to Courtland a year or two after his marriage. He and his wife were well favored in person and reared a family of daughters who were all beautiful. Mr. James and his wife came from Richmond, Va., and were people of refinement. He was a cabinet maker and very skilful. From his shop were turned out samples which would be esteemed respectable, even now, after so many improvements in that line; and owing to the fact that in this section, at that day, there was no transportation, except in wagons, and for a great distance, prices for heavy commodities, like furniture, were wonderfully high. He enlarged his shop and employed more workmen, for the planters were rich, and the demand was great, and he made in a few years money enought to endow his daughters snugly—if he had gotten it. I happened to know how he failed to get it. He had a partner who " spoke trippingly on the tongue," who had a good address and wore a ruffled shirt, whom Mr. James (who was a modest man) thought more competent than himself, and installed as salesman and bookkeeper. The more furniture the concern sold, the less money it got; and at length Mr. James became suspicious, and consulted the writer, then a young lawyer. A suit in chancery was commenced and a decree obtained for a considerable amount—and the decree was all that was ever gotten. The money had been won from the partner with the ruffled shirt at an " underground exchange." (I hope there are none of the kind now in Courtland.)

The two old people, who were highly respected, have departed this life. Ten of their children lived to be grown, all of whom married except Dr. Edward C., Westwood W. and Robert P.

F. A. James married Miss S. E. Davis, of Cornersville, Tenn. They had no children. Miss H. A. James married Nathan J. Gallaway, a brother of Judge Wiley Gallaway, and was left a widow with one child—a son. The widow then married W. G. Campbell. E. O. Campbell (of Campbell & Brown), is a son from this marriage. Miss A. A. James married Jos. C. Baker, Esq., a lawyer of very respectable talents and a very useful man. One of the sons of this marriage is Dr. Woody Baker, who lives in Arkansas. W. W. Baker married Miss Ida Watts, daughter of Dr. Edward Watts, of Gainesville, Ala., and a daughter, Miss E. K. Baker married S. F. Drake first, and secondly E. O. Campbell. Miss M. W. James married William W. Steel, an Episcopal minister. She died, leaving one child—a son. Miss K. F. James married D. B. Campbell, North Carolina. They are the parents of three living children. Miss M. E. James married Thomas E. Cannon, of Columbus, Miss., they had no children. Miss V. V. James married B. B. Hawkins. She was left a widow with one son, and has since married S. T. Torian.

Daniel Wade

was a very decent man, with a fine person, and came with the Booths and Fitzgeralds and Benj. Ward from Virginia. He was a house builder, who employed many carpenters, and was doing a good business. He was wrecked as I will relate. He had married Martha, a lovely daughter of William Booth, Sr., a planter living south of Courtland, and being anxious to own a home, contracted for a small plantation, and borrowed from a Shylock in Huntsville, four thousand dollars, at twenty per cent. per month. His friend, Littleberry Jones, kindly became responsible for the debt, and succeeded in lowering the interest, but it eventually broke Wade and bent Jones, and Wade went to Florida with the small colony I have mentioned on a former page. It may seem strange that any sane man should have borrowed, as Wade did, a large sum of money at such a bloody rate of interest; but he was very sanguine, and having several houses going up, felt certain that he could meet the payment. The debt was sued upon; the case went up to the Supreme Court, and the decision made there was afterward one of the grounds of impeaching three of the Supreme Court judges. "Behold! what a great fire a little matter kindleth."

LEONARD H. SIMS

was a man of remarkable mechanical genius. I think he came from Georgia; for in Athens, when a college boy, I boarded with his brother, Zachariah Sims, who had a like inventive talent.*

Leonard H. came to Courtland in 1822 and erected a huge shop for the manufacture of cotton gins. He was continually improving these until he finally turned out a gin with an iron frame, which was very generally approved by the planters. When at leisure, he was a genial and welcome companion among the young men. He spun long yarns, mostly about himself, very seriously, and came to believe them, until, one day, young Ligon, involved him in a very great dilemma. Says Ligon, taking out his pencil, "Sims, you say when you grew up you taught school so many years—you were deputy sheriff so many years—you practised medicine so many years—you were an apothecary so many years—you were a traveling machinist for repairs, and you have been a settled machinist so many years. Now I have added up carefully and find that you are just 217 years old." This raised a great laugh at Sims' expense, and he was afterwards called Dr. Sims. Even with this foible, he was a useful citizen and much esteemed, and being very prosperous, he married the widow Washington, a handsome and well educated woman, and provided for her very generously. By this, her third marriage, she had two daughters —Elizabeth and Prudence—and after the death of her husband, she returned to Pulaski, Tenn., (where she had lived before marriage).

The Puryears.

Of these there were three brothers. Peter, was a carpenter, and owned and kept the hotel, when Smith moved away. I have heard of one living child of his—a daughter, who married James Mays and moved to Texas. John, the second brother, was first a farmer, and then lived with his brother at the hotel. He was never married, but came very near it once. The marriage was to have taken place at the hotel, and the wedding supper was prepared, when, the same night, Simon Jeffreys came from Pontotoc, Miss., and married his intended bride, "and he was left lamenting." William, the third brother, was a brick-mason Had three children. The first was Major William, well known as one of the best salesmen Courtland ever had. He is now a traveling commercial agent. He has been married twice; the first time to Anna Thorn. Ernest and Addie were chidren of this marriage. His second wife was Alice Harris, who died leaving one child. The second child of William Puryear, Sr., was Anna, who married John Powers, of Tuscumbia, and the third was Susie, who lives with her sister in Tuscumbia.

Thomas Dunnevant

was a skilful smith, and a verygood local Methodist preacher, and had the confidence of the planters who engaged him as missionary to their colored people, to whom he was very acceptable. By his first marriage he had two sons, James B. and John, who moved to Texas. The second time he married a Miss Leiper, and their children were William, who lives in Indiana, Thomas, Albert and Pauline.

---

* NOTE.—Zachariah Sims had married a Miss Saunders, and they were the grand-parents of the Hon. William H. Sims, of Mississippi, Assistant Secretary of the Interior, in Cleveland's second administration.

The Gilchrist Family

is the largest I believe, in the county. It is very intelligent and substantial and is numerous, from the fact that they have never emigrated. Here they were born, here they have grown up; and here they constitute an unbroken connection. It is one feature of American character, that if a prospect of gain is presented by removal to a new country, it is followed, without respect to social or religious ties, which are wontonly broken without compunction. But the houses of the members of this family are dotted over our lovely valley, from the mountain to the Tennessee river. They are, generally, progressive farmers, using improved implements, and impressed with the cardinal idea that "you must feed the land, if you wish the land to feed you." They have, in my opinion, acted wisely. When a family is settled in a good climate and on a good soil they should rest contented. (But perhaps you may ask me, what is a good climate for our staple? For wheat and corn, the heaviest crop is seen near the northern limit of their production. And for cotton, if you take a series of years, the same rule prevails: provided the quality of soil be the same. Observent men admit that in north Alabama, in north Mississippi, and in north Georgia, there are fewer enemies and fewer disasters to the cotton crop, than in climates farther South.) The Gilchrists have inherited the best and most enduring traits of their Scotch and Welsh progenitors; and are noted for their fidelity to their church (Presbyterian), their friends, and to their kith and kin.

As far back as I have authentic information, of the paternal ancestry of this family, Malcolm Gilchrist was born in Cantire, Scotland, settled first in North Carolina, where he married Catherine Buie (or Bowie,) and moved to Maury county, Tennessee, in 1809. Their sons, Malcolm and Daniel, moved to this country at an early day and settled near Melton's Bluff. Malcolm was a surveyor and a land dealer, as all surveyors have been since the days of Washington. He did a good deal in this line in Tennessee before he left it. There the country was a cane brake when his father came to Maury county, and the mode of proceeding was to purchase land warrants, and then survey tracts on which to locate them. In Alabama the mode was a very different one. So much confusion had resulted from each holder surveying for himself, that the general Government employed public surveyors, who first divided the land into townships and then subdivided it into sections, which were sold at auction, the minimum price being fixed at $1.25 per acre. Then a new manœuvre was invented by the land buyers. A mammoth company (we would call it now a syndicate) was formed, and every acre of Uncle Sam's land offered for sale was purchased at the minimum price. Then the company would sell it at public auction, and energetic men, like Malcolm Gilchrist, who had been carefully examining the lands for weeks before the sales, would reap large profits by reselling the lands they would purchase to planters.

In addition to this pursuit he was a cotton-freighter. Before our railroad was built the mode of transporting our cotton crop was in flatboats, through the tortuous and dangerous channel over the Muscle Shoals, down the Tennessee, Ohio and Mississippi rivers to New Orleans. A few men like Malcolm Gilchrist, who had the confidence of the planters and capital enough, would purchase a goodly number of boats and would employ for each one a steersman, and commonly four more to work the oars, when necessary. As fast as the boats were loaded, they were one by one passed under the care of a pilot through the Shoals, the pilot returning from Bainbridge for another trip. The first pilot was an Indian named Melton, after whom Melton's Bluff was named. But as soon as he showed the white man the channel, he could handle a boat so much better than the Indian, that "Othello's occupation was gone," and he went east to join his tribe. The price of freight to New Orleans was $1 per 100 pounds, and the cotton-freighter reaped a rich harvest. Gilchrist would require his steersmen to write to him at several points on the Mississippi river. and when his last boat was loaded he would take passage on it to New Orleans to collect his freights from the commission merchants, and return by steamer to Memphis, and thence home by stage coach. One would suppose that, from the number of boat hands required, the profits of the common carrier would be small; but the wages of these hands (except the steersman) were very low, for these places were eagerly sought for by hundreds of young men in sequestered neighborhoods, who were dying with a desire of seeing the outside world. These after doing New Orleans, and spending nearly all their wages, would have to walk all the way back home, through the Choctaw and Chickasaw nations. They were compensated, however, by eager audiences, who gathered around them to hear of the wonders they had seen; and many of the best looking fellows were "loved" for the "dangers they had passed."

Malcolm Gilchrist, in this way, left a large inheritance, chiefly in lands, to the family of his brother Daniel. He had never married.

Daniel Gilchrist, I think, was endowed with the same attributes of character which belonged to his brother, viz: strong intellect and wonderful perseverance. He became a married man, and these qualities showed themselves in a different channel. His life was therefore less eventful. Daniel was born December 22, 1788; and in 1819 married Nancy Philips, near Nashville, Tenn. She was born 21st January, 1793.

The Philips Family

was descended from Philip Philips, who was born in Wales. He settled first in Pennsylvania, then Kentucky, and thence to Davidson county, Tenn., near Nashville, about 1795. I have information of four of his children—Nancy, the wife of Daniel Gilchrist. Her brother, Judge Joseph Philips and his wife, I knew well in Nashville sixty years ago, when I was a raw young student of law. I boarded opposite their dwelling, and well remember the kindness shown me by this family. The judge was a man of varied experience and extensive learning for that day, and of pleasing manners. I returned to Alabama, and a term of thirty-six years passed away, during which, Judge Philips had departed this life; but his wife survived him. Their daughter had married Major John W. Childress, of Murfreesboro. I was prostrate, in 1863, at that place, from a wound supposed to be mortal, when Mrs. Philips paid me a visit of sympathy. She brought her whole family several times afterward, consisting of her daughter, Mrs. Childress, Major Childress (who was a brother of Mrs. President Polk), and their lovely daughter, Miss Bettie, who afterward married John C. Brown, a major general of distinction during the civil war, and afterward, Governor of Tennessee. I understand they have several living children—all daughters. My readers will pardon me for extending the notice of this branch of the Gilchrist family so far, for their kindness to me in the condition, prisoner in the midst of a hostile camp, has made a deep impression on my memory, and on my heart.

My friend, Dr. James Wendel, of Murfreesboro, informs me that "Major John W. Childress first married the daughter of Elisha Williams, whose wife was a Philips, sister to Judge Joseph Philips. She died leaving six children, four sons and two daughters. The elder one married J. M. Avent, a lawyer of Murfreesboro. The other (as you state) married Gen. John C. Brown; both are living. Three of the sons are dead. His second wife is a daughter of Judge Philips; of course, cousin to the first. Major Childress died in October, 1884, leaving six children by the second wife; three sons and three daughters. Judge Philips died in 1856 or 1857. His widow at the advanced age of ninety, or more, died in November, 1881. Gen. Robert Purdy and wife I knew in my boyhood days. They died in this place, she some years before him.,'

The sisters of Mrs. Daniel Gilchrist were Eleanor, Elizabeth and Mary. Eleanor married Major James Neely, and Rev. Philip Philips Neely, D. D., a Methodist minister of celebrity, was their son. In the latest history of Alabama, by Brewer, a sketch of his life is given. The author after mentioning a number of representative men who have lived in Mobile, and of the learned professions, such as John A. Campbell, of the Bar; Josiah C. Nott, of Medicine; John Forsyth, of the Press; Jones M. Withers, of the Army; and Raphael Semme, of the Navy, selects Dr. P. P. Neely as the representative man of the pulpit, in a city always noted for the ability of its ministers. In concluding his sketch he introduced the following estimate of him as an orator, furnished at the request of the author, by Bishop Payne: "As a preacher Dr. Neely had few equals. He was keenly alive to the beautiful and sublime, and his rare powers of description enabled him to portray his vivid conceptions with thrilling effect."

He was always attractive and instructive, and sometimes was almost overwhelming. His pleasing and impressive person, his tall and erect form, his easy and graceful manners, and his clear and musical voice, like a fine toned instrument in the hands of a skilful musician, gave him great advantages. The writer's acquaintance with him commenced in his youth, and he is familiar with the incidents of his life. On one occasion, when Mr. Neely was young, Bishop Bascom made his home at the house of the writer while presiding over a Conference at Mobile. One night, when Mr. Neely was to preach, the bishop went in late and took a back seat, but in time to hear his whole sermon. On our return home the bishop was asked what he thought of the preacher. He answered, emphatically: "That man has eloquence enough, as a popular speaker in a disturbed country, to produce a revolution." One volume of his sermons was published in his life time, and another, for the benefit of his widow, since his death, and they are worthy a place in any collection. Another sister of Mrs. Daniel Gilchrist, was Elizabeth, who married Gen. Robert Purdy, and still another, Mary, who married Mr. Elisha Williams.

Daniel Gilchrist and Nancy Philips reared a family of four children, and reared them well, and they, in their turn, have reared children, and although the connection is so large, I know of no failure among them. The old gentleman died 24th July, 1850, and the old lady in May, 1863. I will notice their children in regular order.

1. Malcolm Joseph (Malcolm the Third) was born 5th February, 1821. He has always been a cotton planter, cultivating plantations both in this valley and the Mississippi bottom. In November, 1847, he married Frances Foster, daughter of James H. Foster, and his wife, Narcissa (who was the daughter of the Rev. Turner Saunders, and sister of the writer, and who was born in 1825 and died in 1856). Their children were (1) James Harvey, who was born in 1850, and married Nannie Bankhead in 1874. They have only one child, who married (in 1896) Lawson Sykes, grandson of Mr. Oakley Bynum, Sr., of Courtland, Ala. (The father of Mr. Bynum, Drew S. Bynum, came from North Carolina). (2) Malcolm (the Fourth), who was born in 1853, and married Mary F. Burkhead, who soon died, leaving one child. (3) Philip, who was born in 1854, and died, unmarried, in Mississippi.

2. Philip Philips was born 20th November, 1825. He too has always been a cotton planter, but sometimes in public life, and has represented this county in the House of Representatives. He was married three times. First to Sarah E. Moore in 1847, who died in 1849. Had one child, Daniel. Secondly, married to Ellen Philips in December, 1851. They had one child, Joseph P., now a young man. Thirdly married Alice Garth, of Virginia, in 1860. By this marriage there were the following children: Philip P., who married Mattie Carter; Ellen A., who married D. L. Martin; George G., Malcolm F., Alice Armine, William G., and Daniel.

3. John A., the third child of Daniel Gilchrist and his wife, Nancy Philips, married first Texanna Jones. The only child by this marriage is William, who married Agnes Darrell. They have one little daughter. The second marriage of John A. was with Addie Michie, of Charlottesville, Va. Their children are James B., Annie K., and Agnes E. John A. has always been a cotton planter.

4. The fourth child of Daniel Gilchrist and his wife was Katherine, who was born 4th of June, 1830. She married (first) George W. Garth, in 1851. Of his military services, we spoke in former pages. By this marriage the only living children are; Kate, who married Rev. Robert Means DuBose, who was descended from a South Carolina family, and George W., who married Kate W. Burt. They have several children.

Her second marriage was to Capt. Wm. S. Bankhead, a Virginian. He was a lineal descendant of President Thomas Jefferson, and in this way: Thos. Man Randolph, of one of the most distinguished and wealthy families of Virginia, married Martha Jefferson, eldest daughter of the President. Anne Cary Randolph was a daughter of this marriage and married Charles L. Bankhead, and our worthy neighbor, Capt. W. S. Bankhead was a son of this marriage. Thomas Jefferson Randolph was a brother of Capt. Bankhead's mother, and to this grandson Mr. Jefferson in his will bequeathed all his *manu-script papers*, which were published in four volumes under the title of "Writings of Thomas Jefferson." These volumes are the repository not only of his State papers, but of hundreds of his letters. Good judges have pronounced these letters to be written in the finest epistolary syle of any extant in America or Europe.

Capt. Wm. S. Bankhead married (first) Martha J. Watkins, daughter of Paul J. Watkins. There was no issue of this marriage. (Secondly), Lizzie Garth. Nannie Bankhead, wife of James Harvey Gilchrist above mentioned; and Lizzie Bankhead, wife of —— Hotchkiss, are daughters of this marriage. And his third marriage was with Mrs. Kate Garth, as we have said above. One son, John Stuart Bankhead, was born of this marriage, but he is not now living. Capt. Bankhead's military services, during the late war, have been spoken of.

The Points Family.

Four members of it came to Courtland. Joseph Points, their paternal grandfather, was of English extraction. He was mortally wounded in the first year of the revolutionary war, in the unsuccessful assault on Quebec, when General Montgomery was killed.

His son, Joseph Points, was born in Philadelphia in 1760. When the British marched on that city in 1777, although a youth, he joined the Continental army, was wounded, and recovering he rejoined the army, and continued to serve until the surrender of the British at Yorktown. His mother died when he was quite young, leaving four children. After peace he entered the service of Wm. Rose, of Philadelphia, who was considered at that day a large manufacturer of hoes, plows, guns, swords, all kinds of farming utensils and in fact of almost everything made of iron. After serving out his time he remained several years with Mr. Rose, and hearing so much of the beautiful valley of Virginia he concluded to leave Philadelphia and go to Staunton, then a mere village. He opened business on the same plan, though not on so large a scale. It was productive from the start, and it was not long before there were six furnaces, in which the workmen turned out a great variety of articles. Mr. Points was very prosperous, for this was before machinery had cheapened every thing. At first he employed white workmen, but as his means increased he replaced them with black men, until he had two of them at every forge, superintended by a white fireman and a book-keeper. In time he bought a good farm, worked by his own slaves under a white overseer.

In the meantime there came to Staunton a merchant of means and a gentleman of education, and polished manners, David Greiner. He was from Frankfort on the Main. There came also another family, in good circumstances, from Strasburg, and purchased a farm near Staunton. Mr. Greiner married their daughter, Katherine Siler, and had a fine residence in the centre of the town. Joseph Points married in 1778, a daughter of this couple, Katherine Greiner, (who was born in 1779,) and erected a good house on Gospel Hill. No doubt many thought the match between the prosperous mechanic, and the daughter of the polished merchant, a *mesalliance*. But the infusion of vigorous blood from the working classes, is of great benefit to the physical and mental condition of the rich. Before the invention of gunpowder, when war was carried on in hand to hand conflicts, the sons of distinguished families were inured to labor, by a vigorous course of daily martial exercises, which kept the body and mind in vigor; and history exhibits cases where families maintained their ascendency for ages. But it is not so now. Men as old as I, have lived to see many a rich family go down to obscurity under the influence of luxury and idleness.

But the fortunes of Joseph Points were fated to suffer a great reverse. By becoming surety for friends, he failed in business, but managed, in winding up his affairs, to secure a competency, including the house I have mentioned, where his wife lived until her death. Mr. Points in 1837, traveled on horse-back from Staunton to Courtland to visit his children there, and died a few months afterward. He was a man of great energy and force of character, and he and his family were very much respected. I know a great deal of him and his descendants, as my readers will see in the sequel, and I am satisfied that they were uncommonly well reared by their parents, for they have been noted for their industry, integrity and courtesy, and some of them have been distinguished. I will mention them in order.

1. James Points, the eldest son, was a prosperous and popular man. He, and his father, and all his brothers, were unswerving Democrats, in a county which had a large whig majority; and he was appointed marshal of the Northern District of Virginia by General Jackson during his first presidential term, and was continued in office by Mr Filmore until his death, for he was a first rate, officer and numbered amongst his friends many of the most prominent Whigs in the State. He married Eliza Stevenson, of Maryland. Several of his sons were at the University of Virginia and graduated with honors. One of them (John) obtained his diploma in a shorter time than any student ever before. My cousin, Judge Thomas S. Gholson, of Petersburg, Va., was at the university at that time. John became an Episcopal minister, and was called to St. John Church, Richmond. He married a Miss Tyler, a niece of President Tyler. His sons and daughters married well generally. Mr. James Points was trustee in several public institutions, amongst them the Virginia Female Institute. In his death the Masonic fraternity lost its brightest jewel. He was Grand Master and Grand High Priest, and as such laid the corner stone of the Washington Monument.

2. Joseph Points was a man of probity and sound reputation, and was appointed, with his brother James, manager of a lottery to raise money to build a road across the mountains. The means were raised and the road completed, but a great opposition sprung up amongst the Methodists against this *mode* of raising money, and the consequence was that James, Joseph and David withdrew from that church, of which they were all members, without, however, joining another. Their homes were still homes of the preachers, as in former days.

3. David, of whom we have spoken, married Sydney Taylor, and died in 1847.

4. Jacob Points was the first of the family who came to Courtland; he was prosperous in his vocation, which was that of a tinner. He was hospitable in his house, genial amongst his friends, and was remarkable for his good temper. This, however, gave way on one occasion. Young Sale, the clerk of Thos. B. Jones, a merchant, one morning ordered a full load of tin of all sorts and sizes to be sent to the store. In due time Jacob, with his sales wagon, drove up, and began to put the goods into the store. Jones asked for an explanation. Young Sale was called for, but was nowhere to be found. Jones, who was very fiery, kicked the tin out as fast as Points put it in. In a few minutes there would have been a fight, when a friend passing by reminded them that perhaps somebody was trying to make *April fool* of them. Jones quit kicking out, and Points putting in, and they retired from the field under a great laugh. This joke, however, was the making of young Sale. He lost his place, and his father concluded as he was unfit for a merchant, he might make a lawyer of him—and he did make one of the first class. You will find a full account of him amongst our county judges.

Jacob Points first married Eliza Allen, daughter of Robert Allen, by whom he had two sons and a daughter; and several years after her death, he married Mary Ann Allen. About 1843 he moved to Aberdeen, Miss. When the California gold fever broke out, his two sons joined Captain Farris' company and went overland to that country. One of them, was Jacob J., and the other, William Franklin, who after writing home to his father for several years, ceased to write altogether. His daughter, Logan, married Dr. Lawson, of Talladega, Ala., and lives there. Jacob Points died at the home of his brother, George W., in New Orleans, in 1857.

5. Benjamin F. Points married Mary Jane Grove, of Staunton, daughter of a large building contractor. He died in 1875.

6. Catharine Points married James M. Beemer in Virginia, and moved to

Courtland, where they died. James Beemer is a son. I hardly know what is the special calling of my versatile friend Beemer. He can build a house, cover it with tin, and then paint it from top to bottom; in fact he can do anything but plead law, and in a magistrate's court, he could make a pretty good showing even at that.

7. William R. Points was one of the sons who came to Courtland. He had the good qualities which made all of this family respectable, but differed from the rest in having more vitality and curiosity. I can better illustrate this by detailing the adventures of a day in his company and that of John Glass, many years ago. We rode to Moulton one summer's day, and on arriving at the hotel scattered, each one attending to his own special affairs. I remember I was in the clerk's office, busily engaged. After dinner we mounted, and started home. Points asked me if I had heard of the death of a friend, and on my answering in the negative, he told me all about it, and how much property he had left. Then followed news of another death, and all about the family. In a few minutes he turned on the case of a man in jail charged with murder, and seemed to be familiar with all the facts, especially those in his favor. I said to him, "Points, how on earth did you find out all this?" He answered, "Why, I talked with many friends, and then went to the *jail* and conversed with every prisoner in it." It has occurred to me that such a man should never have wasted his talents in the country, but lived in a city, where he certainly would have risen to eminence as a detective. He might have lacked the genius to rival a Fouche, but with his turn for finding out all that was going on, he would have become his right arm and made a good fortune.

8. Felicia Points married William Kyle, a merchant of Staunton, and died in 1873.

9. George Washington Points was the youngest child of Joseph Points. I knew him far better than any of the family. He was quite young, and a sales clerk in Courtland, when he proposed to me to take a place as clerk in my commission house in Mobile. He wrote a fine hand, and had a good reputation for steadiness, and I engaged him for a small salary—which was increased from year to year, until it reached $1200 per year. He was intelligent, industrious, affable and polite to customers, and always in place. He had, at all times the full confidence of his employers, and was intrusted with large sums of money in their absence, for months. Cotton brokers pronounced him one of the best, and promptest, cotton clerks in the city, for their invoices were always ready in time, and at the banks he was regarded by the officers as one of the most reliable men in town. Young Points was a fair judge of human nature, but in *one instance* he was wofully mistaken. One morning when he was alone, an old gentleman came into the office, and inquired for my partner, General Bradford. He was invited to a seat, and told that the gentleman would be in presently. The old gentleman was modest, but affable, and began to tell of all that part of Mobile near the river front being in salt marsh, when he first came to live there. "What business did you follow then?" inquired Points. "I was a commission merchant," he answered. "And what business do you follow *now*?" He answered, "No regular business; I don't do much of anything." Points, looking at his clothes, which were decent but somewhat worn, and the leather strings in his shoes, concluded he had quit work *too soon*, and gave him a sound lecture on *idleness*, which the old gentleman took very meekly. Mr. Bradford came in, and after some conversation the old gentleman left. "Who is that man?" inquired Points. The answer was, "That is William Jones, Jr., by far the richest man in the city." Points *never* (judged a man) after that by his clothes, and some witty man, after he got a money capital of his own to lend out, said that Points would always lend more readily to a man who had *leather strings* in his shoes.

His worth became so widely known that he was offered $1800 a year in New Orleans, and I very reluctantly relinquished him. He saved his money and kept it out at good interest, compounded every year, until his capital overwent $25,000. Then the war came on, his debtors became insolvent, and he was left where he began.

Before the war Mr. Points married Delphine Stuart, a young woman of remarkable beauty. He is now the father of four boys, Richard (who is an invalid), Robert L., George

Ward and Joseph F., and seven daughters, Marguerite, Rosa, Willie, Augusta, Delphine, Eugenie, Marie Louise * and Josephine. The boys and girls have been well educated, and those old enough are clerks, or teachers, and earn, in the aggregate, a comfortable living.

Sherrod.

In "*The Memories of Fifty Years*," by Colonel Sparks, he speaks of the exodus from Georgia to Alabama, as threatening the former State with the loss of her best population, and amongst the families emigrating mentions "the Sherrods and Watkinses men of substance and character," and in this, and other numbers, we shall find them closely connected.

Col. Benj. Sherrod, was born in Halifax, North Carolina, 20th January, 1776. His father was Isaac Sherrod, and his mother's maiden name was Mary Ricks. She was the sister of Abram Ricks (who once lived near La Grange, moved to Mississippi and became one of the richest men in that State). She was married twice. First, to Mr. Copeland, who died leaving only one child, a daughter, who married Mr. Long. Sherrod Long, and William Long, were the children of this marriage. Isaac Sherrod married the widow Copeland, and by this marriage they had only one child, Benjamin Sherrod, the subject of this sketch. His father died before his birth and his mother shortly after, and he was reared by the father of Abram Ricks.

Colonel Sherrod was educated at Chapel Hill, and migrated, when a young man to Washington, Wilkes county, Ga. In the war of 1812, he was an army contractor, with the commissary department, and brought into the service the administrative ability which distinguished his subsequent life. The Georgians, whenever they pitched their camps, if only for a few days, were furnished with good bread from bakers' ovens speedily erected. Promoting the comfort of the troops, he added to their efficiency, as much or more, than would a whole additional company.

His first wife was Eliza Watkins, daughter of Mr. Samuel Watkins, who was a merchant of Petersburg, Va., and a large planter on Broad river. After the death of his wife, in 1821, he removed to this county, and settled a large plantation called " Cotton Garden," on Spring creek.

In 1822 he married his second wife, Mrs. Tabitha (Goode) Watkins, the widow of Coleman Watkins. It was in this year I first saw Colonel Sherrod. He had dark-blue eyes, Roman nose, and a very expressive face. His colloquial powers were great. His conversation was not only enriched by ample stores of experience and observation, but varied by flashes of humor and racy anecdote, which made it very interesting. He was an ardent Whig, and very strong in political argument. I never knew him overcome but once. On the pavement in Courtland, he was seated in a crowd of men and gave General Jackson strong denunciation. When he came to a pause, no one answered him. " Uncle " Woodson May, an humble shingle maker from the mountain, had been listening intently, while he sat on the curbstone. Colonel Sherrod put his hand on the old man's shoulder and asked him what he thought of it. He answered: " Colonel, I don't understand much of what you have been saying, but one thing I know; when the war came to an end, and the boys had all marched toward home, except such as were in the hospital, we were started under an officer, who was riding on a horse, and I was very weak and staggered as I walked. General Jackson and his staff overtook us, and seeing my condition he said roughly to the officer: "Why don't you get down and put that man for awhile on your horse? Dont you see he can hardly drag himself along? By the Eternal! You ought to be cashiered!" This plain talk saved my life, and enabled me to see my wife and child once more, and if I ever forget General Jackson, may God Almighty forget me! " This burst of gratitude was duly appreciated by the Colonel, who was a man of generous feeling, and he said afterward that it was the most eloquent speech he ever heard.

---

* Miss Points has been for years the able writer and correspondent for the New Orleans Picayune.

As a planter, Colonel Sherrod was very skilful. His management was marked by system more than that of any man I ever knew. His plows moved abreast like a company of cavalry in a charge. The foreman with a mule of average speed set the gait, the fast mules being held back, and the slow ones hurried up a little. He was one of the few men who used clover in this valley as a renovator. He wasted nothing which would maintain the fertility of the soil. And here I will mention an operation I witnessed on his plantation of a novel character. He had cleared up a large field, and in the hurry of getting it into cultivation the long worm-fence around it (he had no short ones) had been constructed of poles. When it became rotten and a new permanent fence had to be made, instead of being burned, these poles were buried in deep furrows, and ridges for cotton thrown up over them, and for years afterward you could see how far the fertilizer went. Now, the Yankee would make the world believe that the Southern planter does nothing but sit on the fence and whittle. I repel this charge by asking triumphantly if there be any record in their farming paper of *any Northern man having buried a fence a mile long for a fertilizer!*

The success which followed Colonel Sherrod's farming operations demonstrated the skilfulness of his management. He added plantation to plantation in quick succession. But in justice to the planters of the present day, who are moving so slowly under the drawback of low prices and a worn soil, we should state that *then* it was the reverse, for it was high prices and a rich soil. The first year's crop of cotton on the "Hard Bargain" place *amounted to the price he gave for it.* He purchased the plantation now occupied by General Wheeler, and then a large plantation (still held by the family) near Tuscumbia, and then a large body of land in the Chickasaw session, west of Tuscumbia, and then his means were diverted into a new channel.

Colonel Sherrod was one of the chief promoters of the Tuscumbia, Courtland and Decatur Railroad. He was named as president of the board of directors, composed of himself, Jos. Trotter, Wm. H. Whittaker, P. G. Godley, Micajah Turner, David Deshler, James Davis, Peter W. Taylor, James B. Wallace, David Coopwood, Wm. Leab, Henry W. Rhodes and Jesse W. Garth, in the charter of said company, dated on the 13th of January, 1832. A short road of two miles, from Tuscumbia to the river, had been finished just before this time, and called the attention of the public to this mode of transportation. Colonel, Sherrod, with his fine practical mind, saw at once that it was destined to work a wonderful revolution in the business of the world. The object of this road from Tuscumbia to Decatur was to avoid the obstructions in the Tennessee river, caused by the Muscle Shoals. It was contemplated that produce and goods would be transferred from steamboats to the road, and reshipped on the boats, both in ascending and descending. But there was a mistake made in the descending part of it. The transportation down the river was still continued, yet at reduced freights; but freights up the road were offered in such quantity that it was difficult for the road to do the work with the defective and light locomotives constructed in that day. Moreover the road was built on a primitive plan, unsuited to bear the weight of heavy trains, having string pieces of wood scantlings on which flat bars of iron, a half inch by two-and-a-half inches were laid. On the whole, the road was a failure financially. It has since become a link in the "Memphis and Charleston Railroad," and a part of a system of roads extending to New York. Colonel Sherrod, who had thrown all the force of his strong mind, ardent spirit, and long purse, into the enterprise, was saddled with the debt of the corporation, to the amount of *three hundred thousand dollars*—he having endorsed all its papers. He managed to discharge this debt, and at his death to bequeath to each of his children a plantation stocked with slaves.

The descendants of Colonel Sherrod have been, generally, men of great respectability and intelligence. By his first wife, Eliza Watkins, he had six children—four sons and two daughters, to-wit: Felix M., Federick O., Samuel W., George, Antoinette and Eliza. Of these George and Eliza died quite young. The rest, with their descendants, we will mention in regular order:

1. Felix M. married (first) Margaret McGraw, of Augusta, Ga., and then Sarah Ann

Parrish, daughter of Sophia, eldest daughter of Rev. Turner Saunders. We shall speak especially of the lineage of these families hereafter. The children of the last marriage (except two who died young): (1) Benjamin, who married Ella Jones, who married (second) Gen. Joseph Wheeler, C. S. A.; (2) Frank, who married Mary Harris, daughter of the late Mr. John H. Harris. Frank died many years ago, leaving a widow and two sons, Frank and Harris, now young men. (3) Alice, who married Capt. Robert W. Banks, of Columbus, Miss. He is United States Internal Revenue Collector for that State. They have five living children—Sarah Felix, Lucile, Robert Webb, James Oliver and Alice Sherrod. (2) Antoinette Sherrod married, as we have already stated, Jacob K. Swoope; they had one son, William, who died before he attained his majority.

(3) Frederick O, third child of Colonel Sherrod, married Ann Bolton. They had four sons, John Bolton, Frederick, Felix and Benjamin, and two daughters, who died young. (A) John Bolton of Montgomery, married Judith Winston and has five children, John B., William W., Judith, Edward and an infant. (B) Frederick, who married Mittie Davis, and has four children: Mary, Frederick, Mittie and Annie; (C) Felix who died, unmarried, since the war; (D) Benjamin, who married —— Alexander, and they have four children, Frederick, Bolton, Felix and May.

(4) Samuel W., fourth child of Colonel Sherrod, married Frances Parrish, sister of the wife of Felix. They had two children, Henry, who died before marriage, and Walter, who married Laura Davis. Henry the only living child of this marriage, married Ella, daughter of James Irvine of Florence, Ala.

Colonel Sherrod, as we have already said, married a second time, Tabitha (Goode) Watkins, widow of Coleman Watkins. She had two sons, Willis Watkins, and Goode Watkins, by her first marriage, which we will speak of in connection with Mr. William Watkins, Sr. Colonel Sherrod, by this second marriage, had four children: A. Eliza, who died young; B. Adelaide, who married Samuel W. Shackelford. They have two living children, Jack and May; C. Charles Fox of Columbus, Mississippi, married Susan, daughter of Col. Thos. Billups, of Columbus. Children: Thomas B. who married —— Pope; Charles F., who married Mary Harrison; Benjamin M.; Joseph B.; William C.; Sarah; Ella; Lily; Antoinette; Irene and Loleta. Mr. Sherrod and sons Benj. and Joseph are dead.

(4) William C. (last child by the second marriage,) married Amanda Morgan, daughter of Mr. Samuel Morgan, an eminent merchant of Nashville. Col. Wm. Sherrod has been a member of Congress from this district. His wife is a cousin of Gen. John Morgan, the celebrated calvary chief. Their children are Charles M., William C., St. Clair, Benjamin, Eugene, Lillian and Lucile.

The Watkins Family.

Our readers will remember that in connection with Dr. Thos. A. Watkins, we gave an account of a branch of this family which settled about Augusta, Ga. These descended from "*Thomas Watkins, of Chickahominy.*" I will now speak of another from Prince Edward county, Va., which came mostly to Elbert county, Ga., in the latter part of the last century. There are good reasons for believing that both these branches have descended from a common ancestor, but I have not been able to make out the connection.

William was the first of the latter branch whose name appears in the family records. His son James (I will call him the first) was born 5th of February, 1728, was married to Martha Thompson 20th of November, 1755, and died 21st December, 1780. His wife, Martha, was born 10th December, 1737, and died the 20th October, 1803. This Martha was daughter of Robert Thompson, who was a goldsmith, and had money to lend. Mrs. Harris (the mother of the late Stephen W. Harris, of Huntsville) and their granddaughter, in a long written account she gave me, thirty years ago said she remembered her grandparents, James and Martha Watkins, very well; that he was of ordinary stature, well set, of light complexion and blue eyes, and her grandmother was a handsome woman of medium size, and black eyes. This union produced in nineteen

years nine children; all of whom grew up, all of whom married, all of whom had a
family of children (except one), and all of whom lived to a good old age. The names
of the children were: William, James, Sarah, Robert, Samuel, John, Thompson, Joseph
and Isham. Of these: William, Samuel and John first moved to Georgia 1783, for they
were all born in Prince Edward county, Va. After awhile about 1796 (*Mrs. Harris*) the
rest of the family moved also, and the old people now " well stricken in years " with
them. They were devoted members of the Baptist Church. I will speak of their eight
sons and one daughter in order especially of those who came to Lawrence county,
and generally of those who migrated to Madison and Montgomery counties in Alabama,
or remained in Georgia.

1. **William Watkins**, the eldest son of James the First and Martha, was born 20th
October, 1756. He was married to Susan Clark Coleman about 1789, in Elbert county,
Georgia. She was born 25th February, 1769. He was a stalwart, finely formed man,
with black eyes and dark complexion; and she was a beautiful and very charming young
woman of the same complexion, and a notable housekeeper (*Mrs. Harris.*) After some
years of prosperity, his imagination was inflamed by accounts of the great fertility of
Maury county, Tennessee; and he moved to that county, and, at length, when his relatives began to settle in North Alabama, he removed to Madison county, about 1819; a
poorer man than when he left Georgia. He had been worsted in his encounter with the
tall thick heavy timber of Tennessee. The farmers had not learned to girdle the
timber, let it die, cut down the cane, and then at some dry time set fire to it, and when
everything is as hot as an oven, the burning is complete. Such a conflagration where
thousands of canes heated by the fire are exploding every minute, resembles a battle of
musketry. The settlers either didn't know, or had not time to wait for this process. William Watkins encountered the forest in the " green tree," and not in the " dry," and
was badly defeated.

In Madison county he had begun to retrieve his fortunes when I saw him for the
first time; and although sixty years ago, I shall never forget what occurred. I was
sitting in the back parlor at Dr. James Mannings, when his niece and the young ladies
in the front room exclaimed: " Why! Uncle Billy, how *are* you!" He was then 70
years old; but he sprang up and struck his heels together *twice*, and said: " *That's* how
I am." They asked him why people could not do that " now-a-days." He answered
emphatically that it was owing to "*calomel, coffee* and *Prunella shoes.*" There was something quite original in his manner, and a great deal of droll humor. I have known
three of this old Watkins family who were born (all of them) before the revolution,
and who had the same cast of character; and all men of solid judgment and keen judges
of human nature. Some years afterward Mr. William Watkins moved to Lawrence
county and died near Courtland on the 28th May, 1832, 76 years of age. His wife lived
until 20th April, 1843. These old people were much revered, and good members of
the Baptist Church.

1. **Coleman Watkins** was the eldest of their children (except three who died in infancy). He married Tabitha Goode, who was born near Cambridge, S. C., 25th April,
1792. They lived in Madison county. They had two children; William Willis and
Samuel Goode, both of whom are living. William Willis has been married twice. His
first wife was Susan Burt. Their children were John Coleman, who married a Miss
McWeaver, of Louisiana, and died, leaving two children, Jennie and Coleman. 2 Adelaide, 3 Caroline and 4 Frank. Of Caroline, the widow of Edward P. Shackelford, we
have already spoken. Adelaide married a Mr. Guitor, and lives in Bibb county. The
second wife of William Willis was Mrs. Martha Whiting, of Tuscaloosa, and by this
marriage there were four children, Good, Thomas, Leigh and Tabitha. Samuel Goode,
second son of Coleman and Tabitha Watkins, has been married three times. First to
Caroline Oliver, secondly to Martha Jane Foster, and thirdly to Elizabeth Daniel.
There were no children of the two first marriages. Those from the third are Sandy H.,
John W., Elizabeth D. and Goode. Coleman Watkins died in a few years, and his

widow, as we have said, married Col. Benjamin Sherrod, who reared her two boys as if they were his own, and gave them handsome legacies in his will.

2. Milton died unmarried.

3. James Coleman, the third son of William Watkins, was a merchant of Courtland. He was married three times, first to Isabella M. Moore. The issue was Milton, Samuel and Sarah I. Milton and Samuel were members of the celebrated Eighth Texas Cavalry in the late war; and I happen to know that Colonel Wharton detailed them for dangerous service, and heard him say they were amongst the bravest soldiers he had. I understand that Milton died in 1885. Susan I. married Arthur A. Acklen, who conducted a drug business in Courtland, and died there, and who had been reared in Huntsville, of a fine old family. Their daughter, Blanche, married Mr. Macke, of San Marcos, Texas. They have six children. For his second wife Mr. Watkins married Lottie Williams. The children were: William (who joined the Eighth Texas, and died early in the war), Paul James, Jane M., and Martha. Jane M. married Thos. Simmons, and when she became a widow married a Mr. Woods; had a son by the first and a daughter by the second, marriage. They live in Texas.

James C. married for his third wife Mary Calvert, in Moulton, Ala. Her sister, Susan, married Jack Hays, the celebrated Indian fighter of Texas. By this third marriage the issue was Calvert, Mary, Hettie and Bettie.

4. William, the fourth son of William and Susan, lived in Madison county. He married Harriet Anderson, sister of John and Richard Anderson. Their children were Mary, Susan, Ann, John William, Martha, Harriet, and Cobert. Ann married Henry C. Bradford. John William married Lydia Hayes, and Martha married Wm. Spotswood, a descendant of Alex. Spotswood, who was governor of Virginia in colonial times (1714).

5. Martha, the youngest child of William and Susan, was born in 1810. Being the only daughter she was reared, and educated, with great care. For many years she was under the special supervision of Mrs. De Vandel, who by her graceful manner had such *eclat*, then in Huntsville, and, years afterward, in Mobile. She was also a woman of genius, and transmitted it to her daughters; one of whom wrote " Mrs. John Johnson Jones," a satire which had quite a "*rus*" in that day. And well did young Martha repay the care bestowed on her by a mother of excellent mind and great discretion, and that gifted instructress, Mrs. De Vandel. She married a young commission merchant of New Orleans who was reared in New York—William Vermylie Chardavoyne. It was a marriage of affection, ratified by judgment. The husband was descended from a Huguenot family, which fled from France from Roman Catholic persecution, on the fall of the Protestant stronghold of La Rochelle. Elise Chardavoyne was the founder of the family in New York and his direct descendant. William Chardavoyne married Susanna Vermylie of an old Knickerbocker family of New York (*see* Baird's "*History of the Huguenots of New York*," and "*The Huguenot Colony of New York*," in which these families have honorable mention). The head of the family was knighted in France on account of valorous conduct, and raised to the peerage by the title of "Count de Chardavoyne" and came into possession of the Lordship of *Crescouer et Valse*, by marriage and descent (*see* "*History of French Kings and their Retainers*," in which their coat of arms is minutely described). Such a descent is not to be despised; but dearer by far to this family should be the remembrance of that heroic virtue, which sustained their ancestors in the surrender of everything for conscience sake.

On the marriage of William V. Chardavoyne and Martha Watkins she accompanied him to New Orleans, but after a few months the state of her health required her to return to North Alabama. I was in New Orleans afterward, and business detained me for several weeks. I spent much of my time in the office of the young husband. The city was threatened with cholera, and I returned home. In a few days news was received of his death by that fell disease. A son had been born to her, and she wrote the pathetic entry in her diary: "Wife, mother and widow in less than one year!"

Maj. William V. Chardavoyne is that son. He married Lavinia Harris, daughter of Mr. Daniel Harris, of Madison county, who married Eliza Bentley, both from Virginia.

The children of Major Chardavoyne are Martha, who married Major Thoms, Civil Engineer on the Muscle Shoals Canal, and Edward, who is a young man (has since married Miss Annie Pippin, of Courtland, Ala.).

Sarah Watkins.

In a family of nine, was the only daughter of James Watkins and Martha Thompson, and was born 20th of June, 1760. I have heard the old people say that in her youth she was very beautiful. She married, in Georgia, Capt. Robert Thompson, who for distinction where there were so many of the same name, was called "Old Blue." His father, Robert, was the son of Robert Thompson, the immigrant (from England) and the brother of Martha Thompson; and so Captain Thompson and his wife, Sarah Watkins, were cousins. The captain was a man of uncommon sagacity, and like his grandfather, the goldsmith, "he always had money to lend." He was a merchant of Petersburg, Ga., and moved with his sons-in-law, at an early day, to Huntsville, Madison county, Ala., where both he and his wife died.

They had three children; Sophia, Pamelia and Eliza. Sophia married Dr. James Manning, a man of great worth and modesty. Their eldest daughter married Gen. Bartley M. Lowe; Dr. Felix Manning, their son, married Sarah Millwater, and settled in Aberdeen. Peyton married Sarah Weedon, James married Indiana Thompson, William married Frances Weedon, and Robert married Louisiana Thompson.

Pamelia married Thomas Bibb, who was a brother of Gov. William W. Bibb, and on his death succeeded him in that office by virtue of being President of the Senate. Their children were numerous, and the Bibbs, Bradleys and Pleasants are scattered, like the descendants of Dr. Manning, over several States. It does not comport with the plan of my brief articles, to give a detailed account of these families, but simply to fix a few links from which those who live after me can finish the family chain.

Samuel Watkins,

Was the son of James Watkins (the first) and Martha Thompson. He was born in Prince Edward county, 17th of May, 1765, more than 120 years ago; removed to Elbert county, Georgia, about 1783, and there married Eleanor Thompson, daughter of Robert Thompson above mentioned, and sister of "Old Blue." She had been born also in Virginia, in the same county, and was a woman of great beauty, a notable housekeeper. Mr. Samuel Watkins was not only a large cotton planter on Broad river, but a merchant doing a large business in the town of Petersburg, Ga. For twenty years or more this place was noted for the intelligence and wealth of its inhabitants. Its importance, however, was far greater than its population. Here lived at one time, the Bibbs, the Olivers, the Watkinses, the Stokes, the Popes, the Walkers, the Remberts and a number of other aristocratic families. It was here that the wealthy young Benjamin Sherrod found his beautiful and wealthy bride, Eliza Watkins, the eldest child of Mr. Samuel Watkins. This city in epitome, was sustained by the lucrative trade of the Broad river planters on the Georgia, and the Calhoun settlement on the South Carolina, side—and academic facilities for education were furnished for the young men at an academy under the charge of Dr. Moses Waddel, a distinguished educator, near the house of Patrick Calhoun, the father of John C. Calhoun. Dr. Waddel married his sister. He was afterward president of the Georgia University, where the writer was a student. But this little city began to wane. Its wealthy and talented citizens emigrated, one by one, mostly to Alabama, and it was literally *depopulated*. A sentimental descendant of one of these families, seeking to find "where the home of his forefathers stood," would have to employ a guide to show him the *site* of the ruined town.

Mr. Samuel Watkins purchased a large tract of land in this county, extending from the head of Spring creek southward to the Brown's ferry road, and his eldest son. Paul J. Watkins, moved out, and prepared the lands for cultivation, and built the houses, so that his father, when he came to his new home, had but to hang up his hat. At this time, although an old man, he was very fine looking, with brown eyes, and a dark but rich complexion. He seemed to enjoy his release from mercantile life, and the society of his old Georgia friends by whom he was surrounded. He was very polite and graceful, and like most retired merchants, dressed very neatly. Now, in warm weather you often see cotton planters of his age in their broad halls, going slip-shod; but I never saw him under these circumstances when his feet were not cased in fine pumps.

Like all of his name, he was full of humor. Colonel Sherrod's young sons, during a vacation, were visiting the old gentleman, with a large pack of dogs. Says he, "Boys, why don't you go to work? Why do you idle your time in this way!" "Why, grandpa, we have no work to do, and we don't know where we can get any." He relieved them of the difficulty by accepting their proposition to burn brush in his new ground at a quarter of a dollar a day. Well, next Monday morning, bright and early, the boys came over and brought all their dogs with them. To tell the truth, they worked pretty well, except when the dogs would jump a rabbit. Then they would break ranks, for the temptation was too strong to be resisted. At the end of the week the boys proposed a settlement. The old gentleman required each one to make out his account, and then he made out his. Upon charging them and their dogs a very moderate amount for board, he brought them a little in his debt. The boys looked amazed, and cried out, "*Grandpa!*" all in one breath. But he insisted that there was no stipulation for him to furnish board *gratis*. Col. William Sherrod, who furnished me with this amusing incident, says that this lesson from the old gentleman was worth more to him than any he ever learned at school, and that he never signed an agreement after he grew up without the "burning brush" contract coming into his mind, and without having every material stipulation inserted before he signed it.

Mr. Samuel Watkins and his wife were members of the Methodist Church. They had a family of five children. Eliza, the first wife of Colonel Sherrod, who died (as we have already said) in Georgia, Paul J., Edgar, and Elmira, who married Rev. Edgar M. Swoope, and whose family has already been spoken of.

Mr. Paul J. Watkins after clearing up the Spring Creek place for his father moved to a large tract he had purchased on the Tennessee river below Brown's Ferry. This place, also, he reduced to cultivation and founded a home still called "Flower Hill." He had married Elizabeth Watt, a young lady of sweet face, great vitality and remarkable love of flowers. She was not a botanist who filled her garden with ugly blossoms on account merely of their rarity, but cultivated varieties for their beauty and fragrance, hence the name of this family seat, which was dedicated to hospitality. She was a woman of energy and an excellent manager. His days were assiduously devoted to business. But when night came he was unlike most of our farmers who are still thinking over their business, and laying plans for to-morrow. No, a general cheerfulness pervaded the mansion. On his violin he would accompany one of his daughters who were excellent performers on the piano, with the most enlivening music. The tunes were popular, and the effect was delightful. If farmers were more studious to render their homes happy, their sons would not be so anxious to abandon them for the excitement of cities where they are so often wrecked both in body and soul.

Eliza, daughter of Paul J. Watkins, married John Phinizy. Their daughter, Lizzie, married Samuel Pointer; Maggie married James Strong; Watkins married Lucy Sykes, and Maud, Ferdinand and James are still single.

Susan A., daughter of Paul J. Watkins, married Ephraim H. Foster. Their son, James H., married Ida Speaks; Bettie married Thomas Pointer; Harry C. married Laura Dove; Fannie C. married William Wallace, and Narcissa H., Susie A. and Ephraim H. are single.

Amelia, a daughter of Paul J. Watkins, married Edward Munford. They had but one child, Paul, and he died unmarried.

Martha J., as we have stated, married William S. Bankhead. No issue.

Mary E., youngest child of Paul J. Watkins, married James Branch. Their children are James H., who married Cornelia Bail. Their children are Joseph C., Susan S. and Robert W.

Eleanor, daughter of Mr. Samuel Watkins, married Jesse Thompson, and died in a short time after her marriage, without issue. A 476

Edgar, a son of Mr. Samuel Watkins, died recently, never having married.

James Watkins My 473

was the second of that name. Like his brothers William and Samuel he was born before the revolution and on the 20th October, 1758. In person he differed from them, for he had blue eyes and light complexion. He was of ordinary stature, but well set and of fine judgment and great industry.

On the 27th February, 1779, he married Jane Thompson, daughter of Isham Thompson and Mary Ann Oliver, his wife. Jane Thompson was a pretty woman with black eyes and a notable housekeeper (*Mrs. Harris*).

Their home was a few miles above Petersburg, Ga., on the bank of the Savannah river. They were not wealthy, but independent. The plantation, however, was fertile, for it comprised an island in the river and rich creek lands, and there was a mill on it. Although foreign luxuries were not to be had then, the family abounded in domestic comforts. One who sits near me while I write, has been telling of the home of her grand parents where she spent so many Saturdays when a child—of the hill, on which the mansion stood shaded by forest trees with wide spreading branches—of the cool spring at the foot of the hill, and the gourd which hung upon a nail driven into a tree near by—of throwing off her shoes and stockings and wading in the branch—of the large watermelons brought from the island—of the apples and peaches, and cherries, and the cherry pies made in *deep plates* and *full of juice to the brim*. I give a side glance at her. She is looking through the window in the distance. She is a child again, and her black eyes alternately sparkle, or are dimmed by tears as scenes of other days flit across the landscape of her memory. She sees a light,

> "That ne'er shall shine again
> On life's dull stream."

The daughters of the family were black-eyed, and noted for their beauty; not that kind of beauty which disappears like the morning dew, but a quality founded on a good constitution, which retains the bloom on the cheek long after youth has departed. I have seen four of these ladies, and even in old age "they were fair to look upon." These daughters were trained to habits of industry. There were no sewing machines, mantuamakers or milliners in that day, and each girl had to win her diploma with her own fingers, and the exercise of her individual taste. Of course having to rely exclusively on the needle for the fabrication of their dresses, there were no superfluous flounces or "fubelows" as now. And perhaps there was another reason: the figures of the girls, in that day, were most perfect, and such illusions in dresses as are now common were not required to hide personal defects.

The sons were brought up to labor, and habits of business. There was one exception. The youngest was most indulged, "wore soft clothing," and in the sequel we shall see the effect.

In this family there were not only physical influences which gave force to the character of the young, but a spirit of pure and simple piety imbued members generally. Their Methodism was earnest and pronounced, and sprang from the pure seed planted by John Wesley himself, while he was in Georgia. This country home was the resort of many of the rising young men of Georgia, and its sons and daughters formed worthy alliances, and families of great respectability in Georgia, Alabama, Mississippi and Texas trace their origin to it. Two of the sons died before marriage. Garland T. served during the war of 1812, returned home, and being a man of great sprightliness, he studied law, but died before he commenced the practice. Another son, Theophilus, died at the age of 15 years. The other children of James and Jane Watkins we shall notice briefly in succession.

Major Robert H. Watkins was born 1st October, 1782. In person he was over six

ROBERT H. WATKINS
As a Youth.
Born 1782, Died 1855.

Mrs. Prudence Oliver Watkins.
Born 1788, died 1867.

feet in height, and had a finely proportioned person. His eyes were black and his nose acquilline. He was noted for a perseverance which never flagged, and great sagacity in practical business, and for an unselfish devotion to the welfare of his children, which is gratefully remembered.

On the 25th April, 1805, he married Prudence T. Oliver, who was born 22d October, 1788. She was the daughter of Mr. John Oliver, a merchant and planter of great worth and purity of character. The late Dr. Samuel C. Oliver, so long State Senator from Montgomery, and Rev. Christopher D. Oliver, D. D., of the Methodist Church, South, descended from the same stock. Major Watkins was the neighbor and intimate friend of Colonel Sherrod, of whom we have spoken in a previous number; but they were rivals in cotton planting. In their rapid accumulation of wealth (which was only equaled by one planter in Madison county), they advanced " *pari passee.*" Major Watkins owned all the land from the first hill north of Courtland to the Tennessee river; and when Colonel Sherrod, for want of room, took his flight to the Chickasaw cession, Major Watkins passed the Tennessee river and made large purchases on Elk river. As managers, however, they differed very much in their modes of action. Major Watkins, a man of wonderful physical strength and endurance, superintended his overseers as closely as they did the hands—and he moved business on with great energy. While Colonel Sherrod, whose health would not bear exposure, accomplished about as much by systematic management; but to do this he had to employ overseers of a higher grade and at greater costs.

But there was a principle of action which was common to both of those great managers, and that was never to expend labor on poor land. If this was correct policy *then* when the labor was owned, how much more is it *now*, when it is dear. On the plantations I cultivate, it requires double the number of laborers it did before the emancipation, to work the same land; and it is therefore very costly. No matter on what contract you work, labor must be paid in some form—labor must have food and clothing, and houses and fuel, in winter; therefore you should work (as the eminent planters did) none but rich lands. But how are we to make them so? I answer: study your farming papers, as an essay on that subject would be out of place here.

In their old age Major Watkins and his excellent wife moved to Pulaski, and after some years they died. She had been a most exemplary and humble Christian from her youth. When quite old he also was brought into the Methodist Episcopal Church, South.

Their eldest child, Mary Frances, married James E. Saunders, the writer of these reminiscences. Of their children (1887), Robert Turner has not married. Elizabeth D. married Dr. Bruno Poellnitz, of Marengo county, and died young, 1852. Mary Louisa married Henry D. Blair, of Mobile, and died young, 1859, leaving one child, Elizabeth Saunders, who married Prof. Wm. C. Stubbs (who is in charge of the experiment stations of Louisiana). Dr. Dudley Dunn Saunders lives in Memphis. He married (first) Kate Wheatley. They had two children, Mary Louisa, who maried Samuel Gordon Brent, a lawyer of Alexandria, Va., and died leaving a little boy named Samuel Gordon; and Kate Wheatley, her sister. The doctor married (secondly) Mary Wheatley, and they have two children, Dudley Dunn, and Elizabeth Wheatley. Sarah Jane Saunders married Dr. John M. Hayes, formerly of Florence. They now live in Birmingham (1887). Prudence Oliver Saunders, who died soon after completing her education (1864), Lawrence Watkins Saunders, who entered the army during the late war, when quite a youth. and died from hardships endured during his imprisonment at Camp Chase; and Ellen Virginia, who married L. B. McFarland, Esq., lawyer. They reside in Memphis.

Sarah Independence Watkins, daughter of Major Watkins, married Geo. W. Foster. We shall say more of him under the head of "The Foster Family." Their daughter, Mary Ann, married James Simpson. She died early, leaving one child, Margaret M., who married Thomas McDonald, of Limestone county. Dr. Watkins Foster commenced life with promise, but was wrecked on the rock of intemperance. He died in 1885. Virginia, who married James Irvine, a lawyer of Florence. He died several years ago.

Their children are Mary, who married William Houston; James, who married a daughter of Dr. McAlexander; Ella, who married Henry Sherrod; and Emma, and Virginia, and Washington, who are not married. Geeorge W. Foster, C. S. A., married Emma McKiernon, She died several years ago, leaving several children. Andrew J. Foster, C. S. A., married Mrs. Hellen Potter, of Tunica county, Miss. He died leaving one son. Louisa Foster married Charles Fant, of North Mississippi. She died several years ago, leaving several children. Sallie Foster married Sterling McDonald. They live in Florence, and have a half dozen young children.

Major James Lawrence, eldest son of Major Robert H. Watkins, married Eliza Patton, daughter of Mr. William Patton, one of the early merchants of Huntsville, who had been very successful in life. He was father also to Gov. Robt. Patton, of Alabama. Major James Lawrence Watkins was one of General Forrest's staff officer when he captured Murfreesboro, and was sent during the battle on a special mission. In returning, the fire of a whole company of Federals was drawn upon him, and two others. He escaped unhurt, but had his boot heel shot off. He has only one surviving child, Virginia, who married Charles Robinson (a merchant of Mississippi. They now live in Louisville, Ky.). They have one youngd aughter, married Mr. Glazebrook. Major Lawrence also had one son, William, who took his diploma as a physician with great honor in New York, and was about to sail for Europe to complete his medicinal education when he died suddenly in 1882 at his home in Huntsville.

Virginia P. Watkins, another daughter of Major Watkins, married to Hon. Thomas J. Foster, who will be noticed fully in another number. She died soon after marriage and left no living issue.

Robert H. Watkins (son of Major R. H. Watkins), married Mary Margaret Carter, daughter of Dr. Benjamin Carter, of Pulaski, Tenn. They died in Huntsville. Their daughter, Mary M., married Yancey Newman, and they reside in Birmingham, Ala. They have several children. James Lawrence Watkins and Robert H. Watkins, their sons, edit the "*Birmingham Age.*" James Lawrence married Bettie Matthews, daughter of the late Luke Matthews, of Huntsville. They have two sons, Lucius and Lawrence. Robert H. married Mamie Lindsay, daughter of ex-Governor Lindsay. They have one daughter. Lizzie Watkins married Col. Guilford Buford, of Giles county, Tenn. She is a widow with several children. Sallie Watkins married James Patton, of Huntsville, and has three children. Frank Watkins married Minnie Murray, and has lived in Oregon for several years. They have several children. And Dr. Lindsay Watkins, of Nashville, Tenn., has recently married a Miss Connolly. He is in good practice for a young physician.

Mary (Polly) Thompson, daughter of James Watkins (the second) and sister of Major Robert H. Watkins, was born 5th of March, 1784, and married Dr. Asa Thompson 15th January, 1801, in Elbert county, Ga. The doctor lived a few miles from Petersburg, and was a practising physician, and cotton planter. They moved to Madison county, Ala., and settled in Mullins' Flat. He died about fifty-five years ago. She was left to rear and educate the younger children, and well did she perform that duty. She was a good manager of property as well as children.

Her eldest child, Louisiana, married Robert Manning, as we have already said, Watkins married Nancy Lewis, whose sister had married Hon. Amos Reeder Manning, of Mobile. Watkins Thompson was killed accidentally in a deer hunt in Marengo county. His widow moved to Matagorda, Texas. They had two sons, Watkins and Wells. Some years ago a copy of an Austin newspaper was sent to me, speaking in high terms of the latter on the occasion of his being elected President of the Senate. It gave a sketch of his history; of his being a member of the Constitutional Convention of 1866; of his election as District Attorney, and of his removal by the Military Governor; of his being the only Democrat in the field for a State position in 1869; of his canvass for Lieutenant Governor; and of his removal by the same authority, and of the earnestness with which he contended for the rights of the people. In 1873 he made another contest, the only fruit of which was to show the malpractices of the opposite. He was a gallant soldier in the war between the States, and bears on his body five honorable wounds received in defence of the lost cause. The third son of Dr. Thompson was Wells who married Louisa Harrison (sister of the wife of Dr. Matt Clay). They moved to Waco, Texas, and had no children. Indiana Thompson married James Manning, as already stated. Isaphena Thompson married Dr. John Bassett, a physician and surgeon of high standing in Huntsville. Their children were, Dr. Henry Willis, who inherited the genius of his father, married Carrie Neal; Alice, married Mr. Young, and Laura, Leonora, John and William—Darwin, another son of Dr. Thompson, died unmarried—and Elbert married Anne Taliaferro, and had Louisiana, Martha and Elberta (*See Thompson family*).

I am sorry I can not bring the annals of the family down to a late date.

Judge Stephen Willis Harris married Sarah Herndon, daughter of Jas. Watkins (the second) on the 19th January, 1806. She was born 12th February, 1786. Judge Harris came of a very worthy family, some of whom have won distinction, and many of whom have been successful in life. I have known and esteemed members of it for three generations. I have had in my possession for thirty years their "family tree," carefully gotten up, and I see no necessity for it to perish. I, therefore, set it out in full below:

"John Washington (who was the father of Lawrence Washington, who was the father of George Washington) had a daughter Elizabeth Washington who married Thomas Lanier. Their children were Richard, Thomas, James, Elizabeth who married a Craft, and Sampson who married Elizabeth Chamberlain. Sampson Lanier and his wife Elizabeth had children; Lewis Lanier, of Scriven county, Ga.; Burwell Lanier, Winifred Lanier, grandmother of Judge Nicholson, of Savannah, Ga.; Nancy Lanier, wife of Major Vaughn, of Roanoke, N. C., and Rebecca Lanier. Rebecca Lanier married Walton Harris, and they had the following children: Buckner Harris, "Sampson," Joel, Edwin, Augustine (who was the father of Iverson Harris), Nathan, Simeon, David, Walton, Elizabeth, Littleton and Jeptha. Sampson Harris married Susannah Willis (daughter of Stephen Willis), and their children were Stephen Willis Harris, Thomas W., Ptolemy T., Rebecca, Susan, Elizabeth and Catherine.

The Stephen Willis Harris mentioned in this family-tree is the Judge Harris who married Sarah H. Watkins. He was a man of marked ability. Judge Eli S. Shorter was his brother-in-law, and Colonel Sparks in "*The Memories of Fifty Years,*" speaks of them as compared with other distinguished men, of the Crawford and Clarke parties, thus: "Among the most prominent and talented of those was John Forsyth, Peter Early, Geo. M. Troup, the man *sans peur et sans reproche*, Thomas W. Cobb, Stephen Upson, Duncan G. Campbell, the brother-in-law of Clark, and personally and politically his friend, and who from the purity of his character and elevated bearing was respected, trusted and beloved by all who knew him; Freeman Walker, John M. Dooly, Augustus Clayton, Stephen W. Harris and Eli S. Shorter, perhaps mentally equal to any son of Georgia." What a constellation of genius and patriotism!

Judges Harris and Shorter were perhaps the youngest in this array of prominent men. They lived in Eaton, Ga. They were not partners, because it was not their interest—being leaders on the circuit—but they were closely united in business otherwise. They purchased jointly and stocked with labor the plantation now occupied by Malcolm Gilchrist, Jr., in Lawrence county, and visited it in 1822, having then the intention of leaving Georgia and settling in North Alabama. But during the same year (1822) Judge Harris, at the early age of 36 years, died, leaving a family of nine children, most of whom were of an age to require educational facilities. His widow was equal to the emergency. She removed from Eatonton to the town of Athens, and their gave personal attention, day and night, to their education, and was richly rewarded for her pains.

1. Their eldest son, Sampson W. Harris, was born 1814; graduated at the University with the first honors; read law with his uncle, Judge Shorter, and was partner of Col. Wm. L. Yancey at Wetumpka. He married Pauline, daughter of Stevens Thomas, of Athens, Ga., and removed to Wetumpka, Ala. His capacity as a lawyer was considerable, and he rose rapidly at the bar. But he was drawn into public life,

and after a service of sixteen consecutive years, in the State Senate and in Congress, he died in Washington, D. C., in 1857. "Mr. Harris was one of the most accomplished men whose talents Alabama has fostered. He was handsome in person, decorous in deportment and genial in companionship. His elocution was graceful and flowing. Catholic in his views and generous in his friendships, he was exceedingly popular." —(*Brewer's History of Alabama.*) His widow and family after his death returned to Athens, Ga. Their children were Sampson W., HughN., Frances, Isabella and Sallie.

2. Mary W. Harris married Hugh W. Nesbitt in Georgia. She was a beautiful and accomplished young lady. He was educated at the University of Georgia. I knew them very well. At an early day they moved to the Big Creek settlement, near Memphis, Tenn., where was fine society. His health failed and they returned to Georgia. He died of consumption, at Pensacola, in 1839, and she during the last year. They had no children.

3. James Watkins Harris lives at Cartersville, Ga. He is gifted with a person and genius of the same order of his brother Sampson. He is planter and local minister of the Methodist Episcopal Church, South. He has the reputation of being an orator of high grade. He married Anne Eliza Hamilton, daughter of Thomas N. Hamilton, of Augusta, Ga. She died in 1856, leaving children, viz.: Sarah Virginia, Anne and James Watkins. He has, I understand, married a second time, but I have no late account of his family.

4. Jane Victoria Harris had auburn hair, bright hazel eyes, and is an accomplished woman, and married James M. Smith, who about thirty years ago was postmaster at Augusta, Ga. Many years ago their children were Mary Frances, Samuel, Brenda, William and Susan.

5. Anne Maria Harris was a rosy-cheeked, dark eyed girl, and married Hon Robert B. Alexander, who was judge of the Superior Court of Georgia, and died in 1852. Of their children, Arabella married Rev. Thomas Boykin, a Baptist minister; and Mary married Mr. Harris Toney, and lives near Triana, Madison county, Ala. He is a planter and merchant. They have several young children.

6. Arabella Rebecca Harris was tall, and blue eyed; very graceful and sweet-tempered, and of a highly cultivated intellect: She was married to Col. Benjamin F. Hardeman, of Oglethorpe county, Georgia, and died in 1845, leaving a son, Sampon, and daughter, Arabella.

7. Stephen Willis Harris was educated with great care, graduated with the first honors at the University of Georgia, and had made (when I first formed his acquaintance in 1840) unusual acquirements in literature for a man of 22 years of age. He married, in 1841, Louisa M., daughter of Major Robert H. Watkins, and came to live in this county. He was a lawyer of fine abilities and would have succeeded well in his profession, but his estate was too large for success in the legal profession. Lord Campbell wrote the lives of the lawyers who had, successively, for a thousand years, filled the office of Lord Chancelor; and on taking a review of that long term, remarks that there was no instance of a lawyer attaining this eminence who had large possessions when he commenced his career, but one. In this case, the young lawyer had inherited a large estate, which was covered with mortgages to the full amount of its value; and he had the laudable ambition of succeeding in his profession that he might clear it of incumbrances. By the time he did so, the habit of work was so fixed that he reached ultimately the highest rank in the profession. Then let not parents who are in moderate circumstances, and have studious sons, despond; for it is out of such families that the great lawyers come. Mr. Harris eventually moved to Huntsville, Ala. He was a member of the House of Representatives from Madison county just before the war between the States. He died a calm, peaceful death, in the year 1867, as an humble Christian and member of the Methodist Church, South. His widow. who is a most estimable and intelligent lady, survives him. They had two children, Watkins and Stephen Willis. Watkins, before he came of age, volunteered in a company of the Fourth Alabama, participated in the first battle of Manassas, and many other engagements, and was pro-

moted to the Captaincy of his company. The hardships of the camp were too wearing for his young frame, and he went into the hospital in Virginia, with a serious spinal affection. When the war closed, he made his way slowly back towards his home; but never reached it. He died at his grandmother's at Athens, Ga., greatly lamented by all his friends. Never was an offering laid upon the altar of the "Lost Cause" more precious than the life of the pure, Christian, highly educated and gallant young Captain Harris. The surviving son, Stephen Willis Harris, married Mary S. Darwin, of Huntsville.

8. Susan M. Harris, when young, was a beautiful girl of blond complexion, chestnut hair and dark blue eyes, and was distinguished in music. She married William T. Baldwin, son of Dr. Baldwin, of Lexington, Ga. They live in Columbus, Mississippi, and have a number of children.

9. Thomas Eli Robert was a planter and married Emily Bowling, of Oglethorpe county, Ga. He died in 1885. (*See Watkins Geneology.*)

Judge Eli S. Shorter

has been spoken of, incidentally, in connection with Judge Harris. We shall now give an account of him more in detail. "Amongst the proudest intellects of Georgia, at any period of her history, none was more commanding, none more transparent, none more vigorous and subtle in analysis, than that of the Hon. Eli S. Shorter. He was indeed a man of a century."

He and his brother, Gen. Reuben C. Shorter, were left orphans, losing both their parents when the former was five, and the latter was eleven years of age. The General, by hard work and close study, obtained his medical diploma at Philadelphia in 1809, and commenced practice. Being successful, he was able to send his brother Eli to school, and by this means he acquired a pretty good academic education. In 1811 he commenced reading law. He lost no time, and possessing uncommon powers of mind, after seven months study, he obtained license to practice law. He went first to Dublin, and thence to Eatonton, Ga.

From a letter he wrote to a young lawyer many years after, we learn that during the first year he got but one fee, and that was $6, but he finally succeeded in getting into a good practice, all over the circuit. After a few years there was a great pressure in money matters, and numerous suits were brought. Within one month he brought four hundred and twenty cases for the collection of money, and his fees amounted to more than $7000.

He married on the 17th of June, 1817, Sophia Herndon Watkins, sister of Maj. Robert H. Watkins. She was born the 12th day of May, 1797. She had black eyes, auburn hair, and a fine personal appearance. Judge Shorter was also distinguished in person. "A forehead round, projecting and expanded, with that beautiful arch so expressive of genius. Perfectly black, keen, flashing eyes, luminous with intellect, and capable of that intensity of gaze which riveted court and jury to his arguments.

He was elected to the House of Representatives from Putnam county, a post which he continued to occupy as long as he wished. In 1822 he was elected judge of the Superior Court of Flint Circuit, and presided over the first court held in Macon, Ga., which was in 1823. In 1825 he resumed the practice of the law. But in this short sketch I will not attempt to follow him through his luminous career. The most exciting contest he was ever engaged in, was in 1828, when the Hon. Thomas W. Cobb, who had resigned his seat in the United States Senate for the purpose of obtaining the judgeship of the Ocmulgee Circuit, was opposed by him for that office. "No instance can be mentioned where intellect and address in competitors were so nearly equal. It was indeed a contest between giants. Judge Cobb, too, was a man of extraordinary powers, and a most delightful companion." And yet Shorter beat Cobb before the Legislature, two to one.

In 1832 Judge Shorter moved to Columbus, Ga., where he engaged in mercantile pursuits, and died in 1836, in his forty-fourth year.

I am indebted mainly for the foregoing facts to "*The Bench and Bar of Georgia*," written by Mr. Miller. He makes an extraordinary remark about Judge Shorter; saying that in the conflicts in which he was engaged, he seemed never to be pressed to the exhibition of all his powers, and he believed he died without a knowledge of all his gifts. This opinion he had formed, not from his reputation, but from trials of strength with the ablest men of his State, which he had witnessed himself.

Judge Shorter, however, he says, was a man of blemishes and attractions, but that his good qualities far outweighed all his defects. That he possessed great vivacity of spirits on all occasions, and was fond of good jokes; and even took them kindly at his own expense; and bestowed his wit and humor with no parsimony. He relates a joke, played off in Putnam Superior Court. "Judge Shorter and his brother-in-law, Hon. Stephen W. Harris, were arrayed against each other in a very important action of eject- ment, and as the court adjourned for the day, the presiding judge announced the case as first in order next morning. Shorter knew his danger, and made his best preparation. The next morning Harris was called, but did not appear. The court waited for him a half hour or more, when at last he came hurriedly into court. Judge Strong said, "The Court, Mr. Harris, regrets that you have kept it so long waiting; and hopes that you will at once proceed with the case." Shorter with a mischievous gravity appealed to the court in behalf of his rival brother to this effect: "Mr. Harris ought to be excused as it was evident that he has used all possible expedition; for the Court will perceive that in his hurry to complete his toilet he has put on his shirt wrong end up- ward," alluding to his enormous shirt collar, which was only a full-grown specimen of the prevailing fashion. Being very sensitive, and the roar of laughter which filled the Court House, deeply mortifying to him, Mr. Harris lost his self-possession, and with all his acknowledged ability, managed the case so badly that he lost it for no other reason. So much for a joke, as cruel as it was artfully applied. Harris found it difficult to forgive it."

Judge Shorter's wife survived him many years. She was a woman of very decided character, and died in 1856 an enthusiastic Methodist (*Mrs. Harris*). "They left three children: Reuben Shorter, a clever, intelligent man, of small stature and blue eyes. Married Miss Kate Ward, daughter of a U. S. Army officer. They reside in Colum- bus, Ga.; Mary Jane, a woman of pleasant manners, fine personal appearance and strong intellect. Married Dr. John A. Urquhart, of Columbus; Virginia, who married a Mr. Oliver, of Florida," (*Mrs. Harris*). It has been many years since she gave me these notes. I have written for more recent information, which will appear in a subsequent number.

[From a letter of the Hon. Henry S. Shorter, 1887.]

"I think that the notes furnished you by the widow of Judge S. W. Harris are sub- stantially correct; and it is my recollection that the widow of my uncle, Judge Eli S. Shorter, of Georgia, was dead at the time those notes were furnished by Mrs. Harris.

You have correctly stated the names and residences of the children of my uncle, Judge Shorter; and I am not sure that I can furnish you much additional information.

(1) Reuben C. Shorter (now dead), the son of Judge Eli S. Shorter, had four children by his first marriage, as follows: Eli S. Shorter, who died a few months ago, being a practicing physician in the city of New York. I think he leaves two or three little children surviving him. He married a Pennsylvania lady, I think residing in the city of Philadelphia. Dr. Eli S. Shorter was quite a distinguished physician, a very intelligent and cultured man.

(2) John U. Shorter, the second son is now a lawyer of distinction, residing in the city of Brooklyn; he has made a good reputation, and is succeeding well in a business way. He has fine habits, is very popular, and enjoys a lucrative practice. He married a Massachusetts lady, and I believe has several children.

(3) Mollie Shorter, the eldest daughter, married Mr. Thomas S. Fry, of Mobile, Ala., where she and her husband now reside, and they have six children. One of their sons is now a cadet in our State University. Mr. Fry is engaged in the cotton business, in Mobile.

(4) Katie Shorter, the next eldest daughter, married a Mr. Geo. Brown, the proprietor of the Brown House, at Macon, Ga., and they have several children—four I believe. Mr. Brown died a few months ago, and his widow still resides at Macon, Ga.

(5) Sophy Shorter is the youngest daughter, and is the off-spring of her father's second marriage. She is now the wife of Mr. John Aldridge, of Atlanta, Ga., who is engaged in conducting a family grocery business. They have several children, but I do not know how many.

You are correct in the statement that Mary Jane, the eldest daughter of Judge Eli S. Shorter, married Dr. John A. Urquhart, of Columbus, Ga. They had no children, and have both departed this life.

Virginia Shorter, the second daughter of Judge Eli S. Shorter, married a Mr. Oliver* of Florida. I am not able to give you, for the want of information, any report whatever of this family, beyond the fact that Mrs. Oliver died quite a number of years ago, leaving several children surviving her. (*See Oliver family.*)

With my kindest and affectionate regards to yourself, wife, and children, I remain
Very sincerely yours,
HENRY R. SHORTER.

In answer to a second letter asking Colonel Shorter to inform me specially of his father's history, and also that of his descendants, he said:

MONTGOMERY, Ala., August 1, 1887.

Col. James E. Saunders:

DEAR COLONEL—Now at the earliest possible moment I send you some hasty notes of family history, in compliance with your request contained in your letter of the 14th ult.

Reuben Clarke Shorter, my father, departed this life in Eufala, Ala., July 14, 1853, being then 66 years of age. I presume he was born about the year 1784, but I have no record of his age; this statement is simply calculation. He was a native of Culpeper county, Va., and was left an orphan, when a mere boy. I have heard him say that he lived and worked among his kin people in Virginia, and with his work, labor and economy he saved enough money to receive a common, fair, old school education. After his school days had ended, he worked for several years, saving his money, and then went to the Medical University of Pennsylvania at Philadelphia, where he graduated as a physician. He then settled in Eatonton, Putnam county, Ga., and engaged in the practice of his profession. He was a man of uncommon energy, great decision of purpose, strong will power, and I might, with propriety, add of great ambition. He quickly succeeded in his profession and made and accumulated money and property quite rapidly. I have heard him say that he was about 30 years of age when he married Miss Mary Gill, daughter of Mr. John Gill, who lived somewhere in that neighborhood, and a short while after his marriage he moved to Monticello, in Jasper county, Ga., where his prosperous conditions seemed to follow him up, for he here began to accumulate a good and handsome property, as a reward of industry and economy, Getting himself and family in a comfortable condition his next anxiety seemed to go out after his kin people. At that time, the late Col. Alfred Shorter of Rome, Ga., who was his first cousin, was in very poor condition, clerking in a little country grocery store, on Beaver Dam creek, in Wilkes county, Ga., and my father sent for him and had him come to Monticello and live with him in his own home, and with his own family. He secured for him a position as a merchant clerk in the town of Monticello. Alfred Shorter developed habits of great industry and economy, and here he formed the basis and habits of

---

* She married Berrien Oliver, of Georgia, and removed to Florida.

character, on which he successfully built his good repute and great fortune, for he died in July, 1882, at Rome, Ga., honored and respected, leaving an estate estimated to be worth nearly seven hundred thousand dollars. He never had any children, but during his lifetime he erected his own monument in Shorter College, standing on a high hill near the centre of the city, which he built and endowed at an expense of one hundred and fifty thousand dollars or more.

My father next directed his attention to completing the education of his only brother and sister, which was done, to the best of his ability, by sending them to the best schools within reach. His brother was the Hon. Eli S. Shorter, whose character is well known to every Georgian, and by none better than yourself and estimable wife.

His only sister, Elizabeth Shorter, married Mr. William Stroxter. They both lived and died without any children at Cusseta, in Chambers county, Alabama. I do not remember with certainty the year of their death, but it was, I think, in 1850 or 1851.

My father was successful as a profession and business man at Monticello, and several times during his residence there he represented Jasper county in the Legislature. In the fall of 1836 he purchased and settled up a large cotton plantation on the Chattahoochie river, in then Randolph, now Quitman, county, Georgia; and in the fall of 1837 he moved with his family to the town of Irwinton, in Barbour county, Ala. The name of the town was changed from Irwinton to Eufaula by an act of the Legislature in 1844. Here he lived with his family until the time of his death, on July 14, 1853, as above stated. My father and mother had twelve children, and all of them were born in Jasper county, Georgia; and now I will endeavor to give you a brief and detailed report of them:

(1) Emily, who married Mr. David C. Kolb, a cotton factor and commission merchant at Apalachicola, Fla. Both of them departed this life about one year after marriage, one about a week or ten days after the other. They left surviving them one son, Capt. Reuben F. Kolb, who was reared in my father's house, graduated at the University of North Carolina, and who greatly distinguished himself as the captain commanding Kolb's Battery of Artillery in General Bragg's Tennessee Army. He is now the Commissioner of Agriculture for the State of Alabama.

John Gill Shorter graduated in the University of Georgia, at Athens, and married, in Eufaula, Mary J. Battle, daughter of Dr. Cullen Battle. Here he commenced his successful practice of the law, and subsequently represented Barbour county in the Alabama State Senate, and was afterward appointed by Governor Collier, Judge of the Circuit Court; and on the expiration of his term of service he was elected by the people to the same office. Subsequently he was a member of the Confederate States Congress, and his last official position was Governor of the State of Alabama. John Gill Shorter and his wife both died in Eufaula, Alabama, leaving surviving them but one child, who is now Mrs. Mary J. Perkins, a widow, living in Eufaula.

3. Sarah married Mr. James L. Hunter, a son of Gen. John L. Hunter, who moved from South Carolina and settled on the Chattahoochie river, in the edge of Irwinton, about the same time that my father went there. Hon. James L. Pugh, now United States Senator from Alabama, married a daughter of General Hunter's. Mrs. Pugh is now living with her husband in Washington City, one of the most accomplished and magnificent women in the land. Gen. H. D. Clayton, who is now the president of the State University, also married a daughter of General Hunter's, and Mrs. Clayton is now living with her husband at Tuscaloosa, and is, like Mrs. Pugh, a most splendid and magnificent woman.

James L. Hunter departed this life, leaving surviving him two children, Sallie and Mary. Sallie married Junius K. Battle, and they have both died, leaving surviving them only one child, Dr. J. K. Battle, now a practicing physician in Eufaula. Mary, the other daughter married the Hon. John D. Roquemore, now of Montgomery, and a few years ago she departed this life, leaving surviving her five children, three sons and two daughters. My sister Sarah is now living in Eufaula, quite advanced in age, and in very feeble health.

(4) Martha, married Mr. William H. McKleroy, a merchant at La Grange, Ga.,

who subsequently moved to Wetumpka, Ala., where they lived for many years, and then settled in the city of New Orleans, where Mr. McKleroy engaged in business as a cotton factor and commission merchant. They are both dead and but three of their children are now living. One of them a married lady in Florida, and another a married lady in Eufaula, and the third is the Hon. John M. McKleroy, now President of the Anniston Land and Improvement Company.

(5) Eli S. Shorter, who graduated at Yale College, in Connecticut, and married Miss Marietta Fanin, of La Grange, Ga., andlived at Eufaula. My brother Eli S. Shorter practiced law at Eufaula, and twice represented that congressional district in the United States Congress. He died leaving surviving him his widow and two sons and one daughter. My brother had four children, and the first one, Wm. A. Shorter, died a few years ago, unmarried, in Rome, Ga. The daughter, Annie, married Col. A. H. Leftwich, of Lynchburg, Va. The next son in point of age is Clement Clay Shorter, who has, for the last three successive sessions, represented Barbour county in the House of Representatives. He was named for Hon. Clement C. Clay, formerly United States Senator from Alabama, and who was the intimate and confidential friend of his father. The last and youngest son, Eli S. Shorter, who married the daughter of Col. Henry J. Lamar, at Macon, Ga., but now lives in Eufaula; is engaged in the commercial business.

(6) Reuben Clarke Shorter, Jr., graduated at the University of North Carolina, and married Miss Carrie Billingalea, of Clinton, Jones county, Ga. He settled in the city of Montgomery, and died May, 1853, leaving surviving him two sons, both of whom are now living here—one in the country engaged in farming, whose name is James B. Shorter; and the other in the city of Montgomery, a lawyer, and bears his father's name.

(7) Mary married Dr. William H. Thornton, a practicing physician at Eufaula, and one of the best men God ever made. He died a few years ago, leaving surviving him four daughters, viz: Anna, who married Mr. George H. Estes, and they now live at Talbotton, Ga. Sallie married Hon. Edward A. Graham, of Montgomery, who represented the county of Montgomery during the last session of the Legislature in the State Senate. Laura married Hon. G. L. Comer, who is now the mayor of the city of Eufaula. He is an able and successful lawyer. Marietta, the youngest daughter, married Mr. Thos. G. Berry, of Eufaula, who recently died, leaving surviving him his widow and one child.

(8) Sophia married Col. Tennant Lomax, and, died quite early after her marriage without issue. Subsequently my brother-in-law, Colonel Lomax, married the widow of my brother, Reuben C. Shorter. Colonel Lomax was killed at the battle of Seven Pines, in Virginia, leaving surviving him only one child, the present Tennent Lomax, of the city of Montgomery, who is the State solicitor for Montgomery county.

(9) William Shorter died at Eufaula at about nine years of age.

(10) Henry Russel Shorter, your humble servant married Addie Keitt, from Orangeburg District, S. C. We have four children, three daughters and one son. My oldest daughter Adele, is unmarried. Alice, my second daughter is the wife of W. D. Jelks, who has just moved to Birmingham as business manager of the "Herald Publishing Co." of the city.

Henry R. Shorter Jr. my only son, is now a member of the Junior Class in the University of Alabama. My youngest daughter, Louisa, is now 13 years of age.

I graduated at the University of North Carolina in June 1853, and practiced law in Eufaula until the commencement of the war between the States, when I went to Pensacola, Fla., and served 12 months as a private in Company A of the First Alabama Regiment. I subsequently went to Virginia as 1st Lieutenant Aid de Camp to Brigadier General C. A. Battle, and later on was his Adjutant General. I continued in the army until the close of the war, and was wounded only once, by a slight flesh wound across the left breast in the battle of the Wilderness. After the war I resumed the practice of my profession, and engaged also in cotton planting until 1870. I then abandoned it, not find-

ing it very profitable to me. I commenced to give my entire time, talent and energy to
the practice of law, and I think with a very fair success.

I was a factor, in some way, in every political struggle in my section, and all of my
efforts were directed to party success, for I never was a candidate in my life. The only
office I ever had, I now hold, and without my knowledge I was nominated by Governor
O'Neal with two others, viz.: the Hon. James W. Lapsley, of Autauga, and Hon. W.
B. Modawell, of Perry, and our names were sent to the Alabama Senate, for the office of
president of the Railroad Commission of Alabama. The law required the Governor to
name three competent persons, and the Senate to select the president. I had the honor
to be elected by a two-thirds vote on the first ballot. I have been reappointed by Governor Seay to the same office, the law having been changed, giving the Governor the
power of appointment, to be confirmed by the Senate. I have nothing further to add
concerning myself, except (between you and me) I will say that I am "on deck,"
and intend to do the best I can for myself in the future, and I hope at some future time
to receive from the people of Alabama a still higher position of honor.

(11) Samuel Shorter died in Eufaula, Ala., when about 6 years of age.

(12) Laura, the last daughter, my youngest sister, married Capt. Thos. W. Cowles,
and died in Atlanta, Ga., November, 1886, leaving surviving her a husband and three
sons, all of whom are now living in Atlanta, Ga. Yours very truly,

                                                                HENRY R. SHORTER.

Major Benjamin Taliaferro

married Martha, daughter of James Watkins (the second), and sister of Maj. Robert H.
Watkins. She was born August 22, 1787, and was married on October 10, 1807. She
had a fine personal appearance, and black eyes. The Taliaferros, in Virginia, are
described by Mr. Jefferson as being wealthy and respectable, Chancellor Wythe, who
signed the Declaration of Independence, and was a great Virginian, married one of
them.

Gen. Benjamin Taliaferro, of Amherst county, Virginia, was the father of the gentleman who married Martha Watkins. He was a captain in the continental line under
General Washington, during the hard service in the Jerseys. At the battle of Princeton
with his company he captured a British Captain with his command; but when that
officer approached, in his splendid regimentals, to surrender his sword, Captain Taliaferro being bare-footed, was too proud to meet him, and sent his lieutenant forward to
receive it. Late in the war he served with that dashing partisan officer, Colonel Lee, in
many of his most successful exploits until he was taken prisoner at Charleston, and permitted to return home on parole. He was then in the full vigor of young manhood.
His person was six feet high, his features handsome, and his understanding good.

He married Martha Meriwether, the only daughter of David M. and his wife
Mary Harvie. She was one of a family of nine brothers and sisters, whose aggregate
weight exceeded 2700 pounds. When Mrs. Meriwether became old, she weighed
between 300 and 400 pounds. The four daughters in this family were all well favored
and all made good wives. General Taliaferro, in 1784. moved his family to Broad
river in Georgia. He became one of the leading men in the State. He was President
of the Senate, a member of Congress, and filled many other high offices. He was made a
judge of the Superior Court, although he was no lawyer; and there was then no Supreme
Court to correct his decisions. I am indebted for the foregoing facts to Governor
Gilmer's book on the "Georgians."

Major Benjamin Taliaferro married Martha Watkins, in Georgia; moved to Alabama and lived in Marengo county. He was low in stature, but very squarely built, and
in old age weighed largely over 300 pounds. He inherited the fattening tendency from
his grandmother. Major Benjamin T. was of sprightly mind, and sharp wit; and he
had a fund of the best Georgia anecdotes, which made him the life of every company he
entered. His rippling, guttural laugh, much resembled that of the renowned English
actor—Hackett, when he personated Falstaff. He never "took much thought of the

morrow," and was like the man spoken of by one of the Prophets, who put his earnings "in a bag full of holes." The consequence was, that at his death, his widow was left with a large family, and with slender means.

There was much beauty with the daughters; and they were taught by their thrifty mother all the domestic arts. The plainest of the family was Martha. She had blue eyes and was short of stature like her father, but in industry, piety and unselfishness she was a prodigy. She sewed and frilled and tucked to make her sisters more beautiful. She seemed to live for them; and I at one time concluded that marriage had never been thought of, but it is very hard to tell what is in a woman's mind. When she arrived at forty years of age she married a very worthy gentleman, Mr. Blackshear, who was richer than any man married by her sisters. Her sister, Elizabeth, married Mr. Drummond, and had several children, one of whom married Mr. J. F. Yeldell; Emily, married Mr. Donald in Alabama, and moved to Georgia; Theophilus went to California, and married a Spanish lady of great beauty and wealth; Benjamin Taliaferro was one of the "Red Rovers" (under Dr. Shackleford), and was massacred at Goliad; David, is a lawyer, a man of genius, remarkable for his wit and pleasantry, and married Mary Neal; his twin sister, Anne, married Elbert Thompson, and has since his death married Mr. Chinn, a lawyer; Amanda, married Mr. Bradley, a fine business man of Marengo county. One of their daughters married Porter Bibb, Esq., of Limestone county, Alabama; and another Rev. —. Ellington. Elmira, the youngest daughter of Major Talliaferro, married another Mr. Blackshear. (*See Thompson Family.*)

Jane Watkins,

daughter of James Watkins, the second, was born 13th November, 1789. She resembled her sister (already noticed) in person, and was remarkably graceful and active. She was married on the 10th July, 1810, to James Minor Tait, Esq. He belonged to a family of distinction in the early history of Georgia. His brother, Judge Charles Tait, was a man of a high order of talents, but he is now remembered mainly by an amusing incident which happened on a dueling ground. He had challenged Judge Dooly, one of the wittiest men that State ever produced, and the parties promptly met with their seconds. Judge Dooly coolly took his seat on a stump, and his second went down into the woods. Some time elapsed and the second of Tait approached Dooley, and inquired where his second was. Dooly answered that he had gone to hunt for a hollow log to stand one of his legs in, while he fought Tait (who had lost a leg). "Then you don't intend to fight," says the second of Tait. Dooley responded, "Certainly not, unless you agree to this," said Dooly, and of course this ended the fight.

Mr. James Minor Tait lost his wife, Jane Watkins, in a few years after marriage. He moved his family to North Mississippi where the descendants of this marriage are to be found. They had three children, Louisa, who married Lemuel Banks; Antoinette, who married Andrew Sims, who was accidentally killed in a deer hunt. She married a second time a Mr. Smith; and George, a physician, of Panola. He married a Miss McGehee (*Mrs. Harris*).

Susan Watkins was born March 17, 1791. She became the second wife of Major John Oliver, of Petersburg, the father of Mrs. Robert H. Watkins. Major Oliver died a few years after this marriage and his widow married Dr. William N. Richardson, a distinguished physician of the same town. They moved to Barbour county, Ala. Their children were, 1. Mary, who was married to Gabriel Toombs, of Wilks county, Ga. He was a brother of Gen. Robert Toombs, the great orator. 2. Sarah Willis, who married Mr. Thompson, a civil engineer, of Barbour county, Ala. 3. Louisa, who married Mr. Thompson, a brother of the former. 4. Walker, who married Miss Sanford, of Barbour county, Ala. 5. William. 6. James, and 7. Martha (*Mrs. Harris*).

Eliza, another daughter of James Watkins (the second), was born February 5, 1793, and was married to William McGehee, the fifth son of Micajah McGehee, of Broad river. He was a merchant, and instead of prospering like his brothers, Abner, of Montgomery, and Edmund, of Louisiana, he lost his property. He died, and his widow lived with her brother, Major Robert Watkins, near Courtland, until her death. She had five children, Robert, James and three daughters, who are somewhere in South Alabama.

James Watkins, the son of James Watkins (the second), was born September 20, 1795. His youth gave much promise, which his manhood did not fulfil. He was educated for a lawyer; had a fine person, and married Miss Jane Urquhart, of Augusta. He became intemperate and died about 1825, with no issue.

This concludes our account of the descendants of James Watkins (the second,) and we will now briefly furnish the notice of his brothers who were sons of James (the first.)

Robert Watkins

was born June 7, 1762. He married Jane Thompson, and lived and died in Georgia. I am not informed as to his descendants.

Mr. John Watkins

was born 12th February, 1768. He lived and died in Georgia. He married Susan Daniel, of Virginia; who had blue eyes and a delicate constitution; and he survived her many years. Whilst I was a student at Athens he, with his two daughters, Lucy and Sarah, spent a summer at the house where I boarded. He was in person and manners much like his brothers, of whom I have already spoken. He was a man of fine judgment and despised all dandyism in manners and dress. During the "Reign of Terror" in France, many Frenchmen of distinction and refinement sought refuge in America. Our people felt much commisseration for them (for they were generally destitute), and freely received them into their houses. One of those gentlemen was offered a home in his house. Whenever Mr. Watkins entered he would rise and bow most politely, and hand him a chair. This amused him at first, but after awhile it became annoying. One morning in June, when it was showering nearly every day, and the grass growing fearfully, and things were going wrong generally, Mr. Watkins, after several hours of turmoil, entered the house, heated and vexed. The Frenchman rose, as usual, and said; "Mr. Watkins! do take a chair," and was more profuse in his attention than usual. Mr. Watkins waved the Frenchman imperiously away, and said: "Do sit down, and don't be such a fool." The Frenchman could understand but little English, but he could read "manner," and did not parlezvous around so much, and after that restrained his politeness.

Mr. Watkins was fortunate in the alliances formed by his children. His daughter Lucy was married to George H. Young, of Lexington, Ga. He graduated at the University of Georgia with the first honors, and had a reputation even then as an orator. I saw him first at the commencement at which he graduated. I remember that Governor Troup (who was an honorary member) was introduced into the hall of the Phi-Kappa Society, and Mr. Young, who was in the chair as president, made an impromtu speech of welcome, which was responded to by the Governor. The speech of Mr. Young was one of the best I ever heard on such an occasion, and we college boys thought he laid the Governor completely in the shade. He had an illustrious career before him. But shortly after his marriage, the Indian lands in Mississippi were offered for sale. In the treaty, each Chicasaw buck was given a section of land, and every Chief, a principality. The buck uniformly held his mile square at $1.25 per acre, in silver, and cared for no more, for $800 was as much as he could tie up in the corner of his hunting shirt. Many of these lands were very valuable. With Mr. Young there was a conflict between fame and fortune, but the decision was in favor of fortune. He dealt largely in lands, and became very wealthy. In eastern Mississippi, Colonel Young, of Waverly, in his old age, was widely known for his wealth, intelligence, and hospitality. Of their children, Watkins, died unmarried. Susan, married first Colonel Johnson, of Georgia. and secondly, Colonel Henry Chambers, of Mississippi. Josephine, married Sandy Hamilton, Esq. Thomas, married Miss Butt, of Georgia. Beverly, was killed in battle during the late war. George Valle, is unmarried. James, married Emma, daughter of Hon. David Hub.

bard, of Alabama. Sallie, married Hon. Reuben O. Reynolds, of Aberdeen, Miss. Lucy, (Lou) married Col. James O. Banks, of Columbus.

Daniel Watkins, son of Mr. John Watkins, was (as were all his daughters) educated with every advantage. He finished his course in Schenectady, N. Y., and married the daughter of Governor Yates of that State. An amusing incident occurred when Daniel brought his wife to his paternal mansion. His father went out to meet them, and a neatly dressed, well favored woman descended from the carriage first. The old gentleman caught her and gave her a rousing kiss before he was informed that this was the white maid. When the real daughter-in-law appeared, of course he had to go through the same salutation. His son-in-law, Judge Daugherty, who was an irrepressible joker, used to describe the scene amusingly. He said the first salute was the tragedy, and the second, the farce. I am not informed as to the descendants of Daniel Watkins.

Sarah, daughter of Mr. John Watkins, married John Banks. There were twelve children reared to mature years under the parental roof. Three of their sons were killed in battle during the war between the United and Confederate States. Lieut. Eugene Banks at Resaca, Ga., and Captain Willis and private Watkins Banks in the battles of Atlanta. Their loss was a sore grief to their parents the remainder of their lives. Gilmer R. (Talassee, Ala.) represented his district in the State Senate a few years ago. Two brothers live at, and near, Columbus, Ga. Josephine A. V. married Gideon J. Peacock, and they with their family reside in the old family home at Wyanton, a suburb of Columbus, Ga. Susan (unmarried) lives with her. Sarah Lucy married Edward E. Yongue, and they live near them. Dr. Elbert lives in New York City.

Martha, daughter of Mr. John Watkins, married James Harris, son of Gen. Jeptha Harris, and has a number of children; one of whom married Dr. Lanier (see Watkins family).

Susan, daughter of Mr. John Watkins, was married to Judge Robert Daugherty (brother of Judge Charles and William Daugherty, of Georgia). One of their daughters, Susan, married William D. Humphries, Esq., of Columbus, Miss., and another, Sarah, married Robert Leonard.

Thompson Watkins

son of James Watkins (the first) was born on 17th August, 1770. "He married Nancy Taliaferro, a very industrious, economical woman. They lived near Broad river. They had but two children: Zachariah, the eldest, married Edna Bibb, daughter of Peyton Bibb. James Franklin married Martha Marks, daughter of Mr. Merriwether Marks" (Governor Gilmer.) The only child of this marriage was Rebecca, who married Samuel Matthews. She was very wealthy but remained a widow for many years. I understand she has married again.

Joseph Watkins,

another son of James Watkins (the first), was born May 17, 1772, and lived in Elbert county, Ga. He married, first, Mary Sayre, and after her death, her sister Delia. He never had any children.

Dr. Elbert A. Banks, of New York City, reminds me that I had made but a slight reference to Joseph Watkins (son of James Watkins, the first). That I did not mention the fact of the connection of his name with the mention of the cotton gin, and he sends me an article on the subject published in the Montgomery *Advertiser* several years since. The following is an extract from that article: "The cotton gin was invented and patented by Joseph Watkins, of Elbert county, Ga. At the death of Mr. Joseph Watkins, his papers, with this patent, fell into the hands of John Watkins, his brother, and at the death of Mrs. John Watkins, née Richardson, who married (11) Mr. Harris, who survived her husband many years, it came into the possession of Mrs. Martha P. Jones, formerly of Wilks county, Ga., and was unfortunately burned, immediately after the late war between the States. Mrs. Jones was the sister of the second wife of John Watkins, and the sister of the writer of this article. A short time before Mr. Watkins' invention (the exact date of which the writer does not recollect), two bags of cotton had been shipped to Chaeleston, S. C., in the seed; but it was thought it could never become an article of commerce, on account of the difficulty of separating the seed from the lint. Great excitement prevailed on the subject, and the invention of a machine for that purpose was much talked of and discussed.

Mr. Whitney, a school teacher from Connecticut, was then spending his time with Mrs. Green, on her estate in the neighborhood of Savannah. As he was from the land of inventions, he was earnestly applied to, to invent a cotton gin. He immediately became deeply interested in the subject. Mr. Watkins was living at old Petersburg, on the Savannah river, fifty miles above Augusta, where he had his cotton gin in successful operation.

Mr. Whitney hearing of this, determined to make him a visit. Mr. Watkins received Mr. Whitney with the liberal hospitality of a Southern planter, and during the day he showed him his cotton gin. Mr. Whitney returned home, and made such alterations, or perhaps improvements, on his machine, as to obtain a patent on his cotton gin also. We have heard this subject repeatedly discussed in the Watkins family, and Mr. Watkins was always blamed for not indicting Mr. Whitney for a breach of his patent right. He was constantly urged to do so, but being a wealthy Southern planter and amateur mechanic, who pursued his inventions more for his amusement and the gratification of his tastes, than for the purpose of money making, never did it. Mr. Whitney, however, never realized anything from his invention, so called. Not content with the sale of his patent rights, he claimed a part or the profits of each separate gin. This the planters stoutly resisted. He was therefore constantly involved in a series of expensive and ruinous law suits, each one of which was a never failing source of enjoyment to the Watkins family (Joseph Jones, M. D.).

Isham Watkins,

the youngest son of James Watkins (the first), was born February 28, 1774. He married Emily Talliaferro. She was the daughter of Gen. Benjamin Taliaferro, of Georgia,

The Scotts and Jamiesons.

Their home, sixty years ago, was on a lofty hill overlooking the Tennessee river, opposite *Watkins' Island*, called "*Tick Island*" on the map. From its summit could be seen some of the finest scenery on the Muscle Shoals, and on its western slope a spring of pure, cool water, embowered by beech trees, bubbled up from the pebbles. Here had settled Mr. Jamieson and his wife, whose maiden name was Nancy Wyatt Scott. The wife died and (as well as I remember) the husband also, for I have no recollection of him. Then her mother, Mrs. Scott, the widow of Major Frank Scott, of Virginia, came to live with her grandchildren and to take care of them, assisted by Thomas Jamieson, the eldest. This family, living in this sequestered but romantic home, was allied by blood and marriage with many of the most respectable and wealthy families of Virginia, Georgia and Alabama, amongst them the Bibbs, Colliers and the McGehees.

The sister of Mrs. Scott, was Sally Wyatt, who married William Bibb, and was the mother of the Bibbs of Alabama (scattered from Huntsville, by way of Montgomery, to Mobile); of William Wyatt Bibb, who was Governor of Alabama Territory and State —— of Thomas Bibb who was also Governor of the State, —— of Peyton Bibb, who was an enthusiastic Methodist preacher —— of John Dandridge Bibb, who was State Senator from Montgomery county —— - of Joseph Bibb, who was a skilful physician, —— of Benajah S. Bibb, who was judge of the county court of Montgomery for many years —— of Dolly Bibb, who married Alexander Pope, of Mobile, —— and Martha Bibb, who married Fleming Freeman. Mrs. Bibb, in her old age, imagined that she needed a husband, and Col. William Barnett, an old gentleman of Georgia, thought he needed a wife. She was a widow in high position, and he had been frequently in Congress; and each of them had an independent estate, and lots of children, and grandchildren. Well! they married; but they soon found that they had made a mistake. They had been living separately when I first saw her; but I never heard of any disagreement. They simply "drifted apart," and she was then performing her duty to her own descendants, which should never have been abandoned. She would pay long visits to her sister, Mrs. Scott; and whilst here they frequently visited the famly of my father-in-law, Major Robert H. Watkins, with whom Mrs. Barnett was connected; for her son, John Dandridge Bibb, had married Mary X. Oliver, sister of Mrs. Watkins. I had been a room-mate of Mrs. Barnett's grandson, C. Milton Pope, and also college mate of Alfred Scott, of Montgomery, who married her grand-daughter. These connections brought the families closely together; and I was enabled to form a correct estimate of these two gentle women. They were by no means of a common stamp of character.

They were cheerful, sensible and bright, and I am satisfied in my mind that the Bibb family owed its brilliancy, and much of its force, to the infusion of Wyatt blood. In ethnology it would be called potent; but it always controlled others for their good. Joseph Wyatt, the brother of these ladies, represented in the Senate of Virginia, for more than twenty years, a part of John Randolph's congressional district, showing that he, too, was a man of great force of character. During the visits of these ladies I heard much of early times, and I will relate an incident which will present an inside view of a Georgia school house. A very pretty girl of eight years, full of life and spirit, had incurred, by some act of childish mischief, the penalty of the switch—the only and universal means of correction in the country schools. She was the favorite of a lad of twelve, who sat looking on, and listening to the questions propounded to his sweetheart, and learning the decision of the teacher, which was announced thus, "Well, Mary, I must punish you," William laid down his book and, stepping quickly up to the teacher, said respectfully: "Don't strike her; whip me; I'll take it for her," as he arrested with his hand the uplifted switch. Every eye in that little log school house brightened with approbation, and in a moment after filled with tears, as the teacher laid down his rod and said: "William, you are a noble boy, and for your sake I will excuse Mary." Ten years after Mary was the wife—the dutiful, loving and happy wife—of William; and William, twenty years after, was a member of Congress, United States Senator from Georgia; and subsequently was Governor of Alabama. This pleasant story was of William W. Bibb and Mary Freeman. Many years after I head it, it was published in Colonel Sparks's book, and I have adopted his version of it.

John Dandridge Bibb was born in Prince Edward county, Virginia, March 10, 1788. Mary Xenia Oliver was born in Peters Virginia, 18 September, 1799. They were married May 6, 1812. He died on the Yazoo river in Carrol county, Mississippi, May 9, 1848; and she in the same county October 13, 1846. They had 14 children, but only 5 lived to be grown up, and of these only will we speak.——1, Elvira Antoinette who was born in Madison county, (then Mississippi Territory,) 6 September 1814, married Dr. Samuel Booth Malone (a surgeon on board the Vincennes, when she sailed around the world), April 2, 1833, and died February 24, 1839. They lived in Columbus, Miss., and had 3 children. ——Ellen, who married William Gibson and died in Matagorda, Texas, about 1864. ——Selwyn B., who was killed at the second battle of Manassas. ——and Antoinette B., who married Alfred Glover, of Alabama. They had several children.

2. William Crawford, son of John Dandridge, was born in Montgomery county, Ala., 1st January, 1820, and married Priscilla A. Sims, of Tuscaloosa, Ala., 11th May, 1842. Their children were: Cornelia D., who married Vernon H. Vaughn 4th October, 1860, and have (1876) four children. Vernon H., Mary P., Joseph and Anna. They reside in San Francisco. John Dandridge, who married Eusebia Foreman, and Mary Frances, who married Charles H. Leffler, in 1867; and has two children, Charles D. and Mary. His first wife having died in 1842, Mr. William C. Bibb, in 1853, married Rebecca Lanier Harris, daughter of Gen. Jeptha Harris. The issue of this second marriage was William C. Bibb, Jr., born in Montgomery county, Ala., 27th February, 1854—and Sallie Hunt Bibb, who married Oscar Thomason in 1876, and 2st of August, 1886, Dr. Cornelius Hardy, of Columbus, Miss. William C. Bibb and family live at Montgomery, Ala.

3. Dandridge Asbury, doctor of medicine, son of John Dandridge Bibb, was born in Morgan county, Ala., 10th November, 1827, and died in 1861; leaving two children, Laura E. and Dandridge A.

4. Algernon Sidney, son of John Dandridge Bibb, was born in Morgan county, 4th January, 1829, and married Mary E. Carraway in 1841, by whom he had two children; Mary Katharine who married Mr. Van Lyttle, and Charles C. Bibb. The wife of Algernon Sidney, having died, he married Miss Hoad, of Murfreesboro, Tenn., in 1876, and lived in Phillips county, Ark. They had two children, Thomas and Anna.

5. Laura Angerona, daughter of John Dandridge, was born at Columbus, Miss., 19th October, 1833; married Henry L. Rogers in 1852, and died in Tuskegee, Ala., in 1866, leaving several children. Wife and husband are both dead.

The Wyatts and Scotts and Colliers were related to each other in several ways. Cornelius Collier (the grandfather of the distinguished Alabamian, the late Henry Watkins Collier, who was judge of the Supreme Court and Governor of the State), married Elizabeth Wyatt. He was a wealthy planter of Lunenburg county, Va., and his family seat was "Porto Bello" in York county, Va. The Colliers were orginally from England, but all of them who settled in America were Whigs during the Revolution. It was a mournful illustration of the way family ties are ruptured by civil war, that at the time young Wyatt (son of Cornelius) was pouring out his life blood at the battle of Eutaw Springs in the cause of American Independence, his English cousin, Sir George Collier, a rear admiral of the Red, was ravaging with his fleet the coast of Rhode Island. About the same time Tarleton with his dragoons was trampling the crops at Porto Bello into the ground; proudly unconscious of the fate which awaited him at Yorktown. The father of Governor Collier was James Collier, who married Elizabeth Bouldin.

There were three brothers of the Scotts of English origin, in the county of Gloucester, Va., Frank, James and Thomas. 1. Frank Scott married and remained in Gloucester. 2. James Scott, married Francis Collier, sister of Cornelius Collier, of "Porto Bello." 3. Thomas Scott married Catherine Tomkites. Their son Frank married Nancy Wyatt, the Mrs. Scott, of Lawrence county, of whom we have been speaking. (*See Scott Family.*)

And now a little in regard to the relation of the McGehees to the Scott family. To show this, I will quote a paragraph from Governor Gilmer's old book, because it has gone for an age out of print. "Micajah McGehee was a native of Virginia, and descended from a Scotch family. He was broad-shouldered, short-necked, and was a tobacco planter of the right sort. He knew nothing about books, and spoke out what he thought directly, and in the plainest way. Soon after he became his own man, he was employed by Mr. Scott (Mr. Thomas Scott above mentioned, I suppose) to do some plantation business for him. According to Virginia fashion intercourse between employers and employed was without restraint. Nancy Collier Scott soon saw that, in the looks of young McGehee, which suited her fancy. It is not in woman's heart to be unmoved by admiration. She looked in return at the hearty, hale, strong-built, rosy-cheeked youth, until his image became so impressed upon her imagination, that saw others very indifferently. When two such people have wills under such influences, they are very apt to find a way to do as they want. The gentility of the Scotts induced them to look down upon the working Micajah, and oppose the union. The young people, nevertheless, got married. Not choosing to belong to the society of those who thought themselves above them, they removed to Georgia. Though Micajah was wanting in polish, his father-in-law understood his worth, and gave him liberally of his property. He made good use of it by purchasing a large body of the best land in Georgia, particularly suited to the production of tobacco, which was then the staple of the State. He was an adept at cultivating and putting it up in the best way. Though he was without book learning, he had the instinctive capacity of the Scotch people, for making and keeping money. Mrs. McGehee was kind and hospitable. She added to the genteel habits of her own family the industry of her husband's. She never tired in working for her husband and children. She performed a feat of industry which was hard to beat. She spun, wove, cut out and made up a petticoat in one day, and wore it on the next. Industrious as she was, she continued to have the quality taste of her family for display. She induced her husband to buy a carriage when nobody else on Broad River had one."

Having disposed of the collateral branches of her family, but very briefly, we will return to Mrs. Scott, the mother of Mrs. Jamieson. Mrs. Scott died in 1836, at the house of Mrs. Unity Moseley, near Wheeler, this county, a relative; and the family then scattered in all directions. The plantation was sold first to Major Watkins, then became the property of his son, James L. Watkins, and is now owned by Mr. Hayes Matthews.

Mrs. Scott (Nancy Wyatt) had thirteen children. I have received a list of them from Mrs. Benagh, daughter of Governor Collier.

1, Joe Wyatt Scott, who married Polly Carrington, daughter of Gen. George Carrington; 2, Kathrine Tompkies Scott, who married Dr. Gorden, of Charlotte county, Virginia; 3, Sallie Scott, who married Dr. Young, of Missouri; 4, Nancy Wyatt Scott, who married Mr. Jamieson, of Charlotte county, Virginia (and moved to Lawrence county, Alabama); 5, Frank Scott, who married a Miss Price, of Charlotte county, Va.; 6, Judge Thomas Scott, of Louisiana, who married a French lady; 7, Charles Scott, a lawyer in Louisiana; 8, Robert Scott, who was a lawyer in Louisiana, and died there; 9, Elizabeth Scott, who married a Mr. Williams, of Virginia; 10, Polly Scott who married Thomas Bowldin Spencer, of Charlotte county, Va.; 11, Martha, who died young 12, John B. Scott, who married a French lady in Louisiana; 13, William Scott, who died in Texas—he left two sons, Frank and Tom, who moved to Alabama.

THE SYKES FAMILY.

In early times there came a colony of them from Greenville county, Va., and settled in North Alabama. They were ten in number, and settled in Morgan and Lawrence counties, but mostly in Morgan, and around Decatur. They were nearly all in affluent circumstances. They were industrious, honest, thrifty; and were endowed with good solid minds; more distinguished by judgment than imagination. The Sykes family became a power in this section, and Dr. Henry W. Rhodes was connected with them by marriage, as he married Miss Dancy, sister of the wife of Colonel James T. Sykes. He owned the land where the town was laid off, and the ferry which crossed the Tennessee river there. He was a man of genius, of enterprise and of unflagging industry. When in 1832 a branch of the State Bank was to be located (though not a politician) he was selected, and sent to the legislature to secure the location for Decatur, which was the youngest of all the neighboring towns by fifteen or twenty years. But then the Tuscumbia, Courtland and Decatur railroad was partly finished, and the canal around the Muscle Shoals under construction; and the Doctor by urging the central position of Decatur, and the convenience of approach, succeeded in securing the bank. There was a great scramble for it, and the defeated towns were so much disgusted that a correspondent of one of our leading papers wrote home, that the bank had been located at "Rhodes' Ferry Landing." Decatur was indeed very small then, and I am not certain that it had been incorporated, but from this time it grew rapidly, until the great crash in money matters, and the failure of the State Banks. The canal also failed. It was whispered that the U. S. Engineer had made a mistake in the level of the lowest lock, and boats could not ascend. I trust that this may not be the case with the new canal now being completed. But another very material cause of the suspension of the growth of Decatur was that the Chickasaw lands in Mississippi, fresh and fertile, were opened for settlement; and the Sykes family, almost in a body, (with many other planters) moved away.

These early friends of Decatur, in its first effort for success, are all gone. Could they have lived to see this renascent town, it would have given them exquisite pleasure. Will this new effort succeed? It certainly has been made upon a correct principle, and this is a foundation of industrial pursuits. If its manufactures are confined to heavy articles, and the provisions of the late railroad law are enforced, so that distant factories can not flood the South with their products; if in the inception of these enterprises, the projectors of the town can secure banking capital enough to enable manufacturers to hold heavy stocks until outlets can be found, and if real property does not rise so high as to forbid the purchase of homes by laboring men, I can see no reason whatever why it can not be made a complete success.

The common ancestor of the Sykes' was Benjamin Sykes, an Englishman, who married Alice Wren, in the county of Greenville, in the State of Virginia. One of his sons was Benjamin Sykes, of Virginia, who married Mary Rives. His sons were Richard, William, James and John. Another son of Benjamin Sykes and Alice Wren, was Dr. William Sykes, of Virginia, who married Birchett L. Turner. His sons were James Turner, Joseph, Dr. William A., Benjamin, Simon Turner, and Dr. George Augustus. Of all these, William and James only, settled in the eastern part of Lawrence county, and the rest in the county of Morgan. In this brief article we will make no attempt to give a full account, or even a list of this numerous family, but furnish brief sketches only of the members of it mentioned above. Of these:

1. Richard Sykes, son of Benjamin Sykes and Mary Rives, was father of Augustus A. Sykes, who was so long a commission merchant in Mobile. He married Georgia, oldest daughter of Dr. George Augustus Sykes, of Aberdeen. She is now a widow with a number of children, amongst them the eldest son, named Clifton, who is a very promising young man and fine farmer.

2. William Sykes, son of Benjamin Sykes and Mary Rives, moved from Lawrence to Columbus, Miss., I am not informed as to his descendants.

3. James Sykes, son of Benjamin Sykes and Mary Rives, married Martha W. Lanier, daughter of Robert and Elizabeth Lanier, of Greenville county, Virginia, and related to the Harris-Lanier line. He moved from Lawrence county to Columbus, Miss. His son, James William, married his cousin, Marcella, daughter of Dr. William A. Sykes, of Aberdeen. The issue of this marriage was two daughters: Wildie, who married James Saunders Billups, son of Col. Thomas C. Billups by his second marriage with Mrs. Frances A. Swoope, who was a daughter of Reverend Turner Saunders; and another daughter, Ida Sykes, who married T. Carlton Billups, son of Col. Thomas C. Billups (by his first marriage) with Sallie Moore, daughter of Judge Moore. (See Saunders family).

4. John Sykes, youngest son of Benjamin Sykes and Mary Rives, died about the age of twenty-six, unmarried.

And now we will sketch the sons of Dr. William Sykes, the other son of the common ancestor, who married Birchett L. Turner, and lived in Greenville county, Virginia.

1. James Turner Sykes lived about six miles west of Decatur—was a tall, handsome man; commanded a regiment in the war of 1812, and was stationed at Norfolk. He married Sallie Dancy. He was a member of the Legislature in 1828, was president of the Branch Bank at Decatur for many years, and was, generally, a leading citizen. He had three sons—Dr. Frank W., Dr. Andrew Jackson and James Turner. Dr. Frank W. Sykes was born April 19, 1819. He graduated at the Nashville University, and took his diploma as a physician in the Transylvania University. He located in Courtland, in this county, in 1840, and such was his skill, confidence and perseverance that he soon enjoyed a full practice. After a few years, he married Elizabeth, a daughter of Gen. Jesse W. Garth, who lived near Decatur. The General was senator from Morgan county for many years, and a man of note and influence. He was a practising lawyer when a young man, and used to attend the Morgan county court, but he soon retired from the bar and became a very successful planter. Dr. Frank Sykes purchased the plantation owned by Mr. George W. Foster, and retired from the practice. He was several times elected to the House of Representatives of the State, and in 1865 as State senator. During the reconstruction period he was fairly elected United States senator, but he was unjustly excluded from his seat. In public life, Dr. Sykes was an honest and efficient representative of the people. His mind was of a robust order, and he was an earnest and forcible debater, always respected and feared by his adversaries.

Afterward he directed his attention to the cultivation of the soil, and carried it to more perfection than had before been reached in this country. Labor saving machines of the very best kinds were used on his plantation; and with a full supply of mules he greatly economized human labor. He used the Hughes plow on wheels for breaking up his ground, heavy harrows for leveling it, the best planters for seeding it, and buggy cultivators for its subsequent cultivation. In a field which had been fallowed during the winter, I have seen cotton ground laid off and the ridges made, and the cotton planted with three furrows, viz.: one furrow of a bull-tongue to lay off the rows, a second with a cultivator on which was hung four little turning plows to make the ridge complete, and then the third furrow with the Harrison cotton planter to finish the planting. But here I must say, that though Dr. Sykes, with his labor saving machines, was the most economical and efficient cultivator we had, he ignored virtually the improvement of the soil. Fertilization and cultivation should proceed by equal step, on any upland soil, to insure success. Our soil should have a regular rotation of manurial crops, such as clover and peas, and all the domestic manure which can be made, and in addition such a proportion of commercial fertilizers as has been sanctioned by experiment, before you can evoke full crops. In former times the difficulty was in disposing of the surplus of sundry crops constituting a rotation; but now towns are springing up all around us, and this difficulty will disappear. Towns and farms will act and react favorably on each other. I was a neighbor to Dr. Sykes about forty years, and never had a better one. He was a very interesting man socially, but not because he would always agree with you in your opinions. He was positive in his opinions, and very combative, and always fresh and full of vitality. He had a great sorrow many years ago in the death of his only son, John, who gave promise of being an influential and useful citizen. The doctor and his very bright and intelligent wife have both gone from earth. They left two daughters, Eunice, who married Captain Michie, of Charlottesville, Va., and Molly, who married Mr. Groesbeck, and is now a widow.

Dr. Andrew Jackson Sykes, the second son of Col. James T., has already been spoken of in connection with his father-in-law, Mr. John M. Swoope. He, like his brother Frank, had an intellect of a high order. Dr. Frank was more rapid in coming to his conclusions and stubborn in maintaining them; Dr. Jack more deliberate and philosophical in forming his, but always ready to open the opinion for re-examination at any time. There was a marked difference in their theories on agriculture. Dr. Jack was a strong believer in the "intensive system," and before his health failed he achieved a great success in market gardening. But for the failure in health, I think he would have carried this plan of high manuring to the field as well as to the market garden.

James T. was the third son of Col. James T. Sykes. He moved to Mississippi and married Sallie Lundy. Their daughter, Sallie Lundy, married Robert, son of the lat Bishop Paine, of Aberdeen. The issue of this marriage is Sallie Lundy Paine.

2. Joseph Sykes, son of Dr. William Sykes, of Virginia, and his wife, Birchett L. Turner, moved from Alabama to Columbus, Miss. He is the father of Major William Joseph Sykes, of Nashville, the journalist, who writes and speaks with great fluency. His daughters live in Columbus. He died in 1878.

3. Dr. William A. Sykes, son of Dr. William Sykes of Virginia, and his wife, Birchett L. Turner, married Rebecca Barrett. He moved from Alabama to Aberdeen, Miss. His eldest daughter, Susan Turner, married Judge John B. Sale. The issue of this marriage was Dr. Paul Sale, of Aberdeen, who is distinguished in his profession, and married Molly, the daughter of Dr. George Augustus Sykes. Another daughter, Marcella (as we have stated) married James Sykes. Josephine another daughter of Dr. William A., married Dr. Evans, and is now a widow.*

Captain Thomas, a son of Dr. William A., married a Georgia lady and has several children. Another son, Dr. Granville Sykes, married a Miss Clopton, and another (a physician) married a daughter of my old friend John A. Walker, and was killed by lightning. And the youngest son (I think) Captain Eugene Sykes, one of the leaders of the Bar in Aberdeen, Miss., married Miss Rogers, daughter of Judge Rogers.

4. Benjamin Sykes moved from Alabama to Columbus, Miss., where his descendants are to be found.

5. Rev. Simon Turner Sykes, when his brothers came to North Alabama, was stationed in the city of Richmond; the best station in the Virginia Conference; which proved the high estimate which was formed of his abilities as a preacher. He came a little later. His daughter, Indiana, married Judge Rogers, and his only son, Capt. Turner Sykes, married Mary Bynum, of Courtland, Ala. They have one son, Lawson (married to the daughter of Harvey Gilchrist.)

6. Dr. George Augustus Sykes, son of Dr. William Sykes, and his wife, Birchett L. Turner, removed from Alabama to Aberdeen, Miss. His daughter, Georgia, married Major Augustus A. Sykes, long a commission merchant in Mobile; and his daughter, Mollie, (as we have said above) married Dr. Sale.

Dr. Henry W. Rhodes, of whom we have spoken above, married Miss Dancy, sister of the wife of Col. James T. Sykes, was quite wealthy and full of enterprise. He conceived the idea that the cotton planters should make their own bagging and rope, and actually commenced the business, raising the hemp on the river bottom just below Decatur, and erecting his factory and rope walk on the hill opposite. But he soon abandoned the business, as cotton bore a full price, and Kentucky could undersell him in bagging and rope. He moved to Mississippi about the same time with the Sykes'. They had been cautious and left with estates unimpaired by the crash of 1837. But the doctor was embarrassed, although he had a large estate. He obtained large acceptances from E. L. Andrews, a Jew merchant of Mobile, and in return lent the merchant his name for a large amount, on accommodation paper. In consequence of the failure of a branch house in New Orleans, the house of E. L. Andrews went down also. Poor Andrews! when he heard of the failure he was so mortified at the loss of commercial honor, that he filled his pockets with the paper weights which lay on his office table, and went out on the wharf and drowned himself. I deeply lamented his tragic end. I knew him well, having been a member of the Directory of the Bank of Mobile with him for some years, and learned to respect him as a gentleman and an accomplished merchant. I never learned how Dr. Rhodes' estate wound up.

Hon. John James Ormond,

Who reflected so much honor on the bench and bar of the State of Alabama, was born in England of respectable and well educated parents, who came to America in 1773, when he was about one year old. After living awhile in New York, they came to Virginia and made Richmond their home. While he was still a child his father died, leaving his children, John James, Annie and Margaret, to the care of their widowed mother. Mrs. Ormond was a woman of superior intelligence and fine culture. She devoted herself to the improvement of her children, who grew up well educated and very comely. The daughters married early and died young, leaving no living issue.

After having completed his education, John James Ormand studied law in Staunton, Va., and, being fond of books, he derived great benefit from having access to the extensive library of Dabney Carr, Esq. I suppose he never was a graduate of any college; but I never could detect any want of knowledge in living or dead languages, or in any department of learning. Any defect in his early education had been supplied by severe and constant study.

After practising law for a short time in Charlottesville, Va., he came in 1820 to Courtland, Ala. I first saw him in 1822. He was tall, spare, with a thin visage, pale from study, and countenance expressive of great intellectuality. He would have been distinguished in any assembly. His manners were dignified and reserved, especially with strangers, but when well known, he was a charming companion. He came among entire strangers, but he was neither truckling to the rich, nor courting the favor of the populace. He rested his professional success on his merit alone. He was modest in his personal demeanor, but in the legal tournament he boldly struck the shield of his antagonist with the very point of his lance. The field was full of them. There were fifteen lawyers then in our county, and many more (learned and eloquent) attended our Circuit Court. A rival, *par excellence*, was Arthur F. Hopkins, of Lawrence. But this rivalry was between as noble spirited men as Alabama ever produced—there was no bitterness in their conflicts—and they were warm personal friends until their death. In these conflicts I never could see that one gained any advantage over the other, except when he had the stronger case. They were both able men, but quite dissimilar. Mr. Ormond had studied the English classics with great care. His style was polished, and perspicuous. It was not florid, but chaste and beautiful. He had gotten clear of "the *hell* of learning," but its odor pervaded his style. His mind was orderly and logical, and he founded every argument on principle. In his speeches there was no repetition, and if a listener by inattention lost a link he was unable to comprehend them fully. On the other hand, Mr. Hopkins, as a learned lawyer as he was, had very little style, but he was persistent in urging his points in various aspects, until he forced them upon the comprehension of the most ignorant jury. They never knew how much they owed to each other, for like thoroughbred coursers by emulation each was put at the top of his speed.

He formed a partnership soon after he came to Courtland] with John White, Esq., which terminated in 1825, by the election of the latter to a Judgeship. By this partnership he had been brought sooner before the public and had secured a lucrative practice. He was in a condition to justify it, and, in 1826 married Minerva J., daughter of Mr. William Banks. She was a young lady of much beauty of person and well educated, and was an industrious and managing wife, who discreetly relieved her husband as well as she could from family cares. In a few years more, his means increased so that he was able to purchase a cotton plantation, adjoining Courtland on the south. His morning rides to his place improved his health, which had been somewhat impaired by sedentary habits. One morning in a rainy season, we met in the office rather later than usual, for we were partners, and both cotton planters, and had been riding around our cotton crops. He was in high spirits, but I was dejected; and having been on a plantation, saw plainly that we were to have a battle with the grass. He said in surprise, "Why! have you any grass in your crop?" Says I, "Yes! lots of it. Have you any?" He answered with some hesitation, "No!"—and added, measuring his finger, "thousands of it this length, but I don't regard *that*."

In a short time his corn field looked like a green pasture. The old planters around had become very fond of Mr. Ormond, and came to his rescue. One morning a long line of negro men filed into Courtland armed with hoes. Some thought there was going to be an insurrection. An old planter when asked what was the matter, with great glee measured a half inch on his forefinger, answered that they were marching to weed out the "Ormond grass', *unbeknown* to him—and this small grass was so called for years, and long after Mr. Ormond had become a better planter than any of these "old codgers," and understood not only the theory better, but used more improved tools and better methods every way. Commend me to an educated man for administrative ability in any department of industry.

Mr. Ormond was noted for strict personal and, professional integrity. After he had attained eminence, an incident occurred which illustrated this. A cotton freighter (who was a rich cotton planter) received 400 bales of cotton on a flatboat for shipment to New Orleans, which never reached their destination, and it was reported that the boat and cargo were lost by fire. He was sued for the value, and came to Mr. Ormond to defend his case. In stating it he said that the hands on the boat one night tied up on the bank and covered up the fire carefully, but by some accident the cotton took fire and all was burnt. Mr. Ormond told him that this defence was not good, and that a common carrier was liable for loss of a cargo by fire, unless it occurred from the act of God, as in case of lightning. The freighter was profoundly astonished and retired. In a few days he came back and informed Mr. Ormond that on re-examining his boat hands he found he was mistaken. That on the night of the accident they had put out every spark of fire on the boat, but that the night was stormy, with terrific thunder and lightning, which no doubt had consumed boat and cargo. Mr. Ormond, believing that a conspiracy existed between the freighter and his hands to defraud the owners, declined to defend his case, although the fee would have amounted to thousands. The case was carried to another lawyer who, of course, knew only the "lightning" theory of the case, and the defence was successful. So you perceive in his ethics he differed essentially from a distinguished Boston lawyer who, in a recent lecture, contends virtually that the worse the case, the stronger is the obligation on a lawyer to defend it.

We now approach an event in the life of Mr. Ormond which brought him for the first time prominently before the people of the whole State, and this was " *The Trial of the Judges.*" In this case he made an able and eloquent speech in their defence. His learned and accomplished daughter, Mrs. Mallett, told me some years ago that her father considered this the best speech he ever made. Our State historians have, very properly, recorded every conflict of arms which has occurred on Alabama soil, from the canoe fight of Sam Dale to the fearful naval combat in Mobile Bay, near the conclusion of the late war; but they have strangely failed to mention the great battle for the independence of the judicial department of the State. Be it mine to preserve the memory of it! and I shall speak at some length of the case—the prosecutor and the counsel for the defence.

The case was this: On the 13th of February, 1818, a law was passed by the Alabama Territory providing that "any rate of interest or premium for the loan or use of money, wares, merchandise or other commodity, agreed upon by the parties to a contract, expressed in writing and signed by the party to be charged therewith, shall be legal and recoverable; and no contract shall be vacated by reason of *any* rate of interest so stipulated." This law placed money on the same basis with land or other property. It removed all restraints from the rate of interest, and expunged the offense of usury from the statute book. The advocates of this hazardous experiment cited Smith, Say's Political Economy and other political economists to show that money (like other property) ought to bring whatever price in the market it would.

But it was a very unlucky time for such a novel change. Our staple, *cotton*, was very high. So was land; the annual rent of which was then ten dollars per acre, and had been for several years. And in every kind of property there was a great inflation in prices. The consequence was, that money was raked together from this, and the surrounding States, for the purpose of being loaned at exorbitant rates. Five per cent per month was the market rate of interest, and in one instance twenty per cent. per month was contracted for in our town of Courtland. This case of Thompson vs. Jones was prominent in the Supreme Court, and the Impeachment of the Judges. After awhile it became plain to all, that this law was causing ruin to the people of the State—and it was repealed by the General Assembly on 22nd of November, 1819; having been in operation less than two years. In that short time it was a cause of untold misery to our people; but a rich carnival for the money-lenders. The banks were under a limit of six per cent, and while the carnival lasted, they had no money to lend, except "in the family"—to their directors and stockholders.

They ran little banks in their offices, and retailed what they borrowed from the banks at 6 per cent. and conveyed "through a hole in the wall," to people outside at excessive rates. The borrowers for some years paid as much as they were able, and many of them were ruined or much embarrassed; but the validity of the law was not questioned, for its intention and language were without ambiguity. At length a lawyer of reputation filed a bill in chancery to recover back the interest which had been paid. Numerous suits of the same kind were commenced, and held in the lower courts, by agreement of counsel, to await the decision of the test cases. In the meantime the question became a political one. Previous to this time parties had been put to sleep by Mr. Monroe, but they were revived (wonderful to tell!) on a question merely judicial. The most bitter personalities were indulged in. Those who favored, on principle, the sustaining of the contracts made under the act of 1818, while it was in operation, were called the "Royal Party." In Huntsville the organ of the agitators used the most offensive language respecting its opponents, and even singled them out personally. The mansion on the Acropolis was called "The Palace," and one lower down, "The Sub-Palace." I remember that the editor of this organ (who was a Methodist) was called upon by Rev. Wm. McMahon, who was the most eloquent and influential of the Methodist ministers of that day, who gave him a severe reprimand for violence of language. He said, "Oh, brother Mack, you are making too serious a matter of this. What I said in the paper was as an editor." Mr. McMahon, who was a man of ready wit, replied, "Tell me, brother, if the Devil gets the *editor*, what will become of the *man!*" This agitation pervaded the State. It was not altogether spontaneous; but was directed by a master in politics. The wind blew at first very strong—then it became a gale—at length a hurricane, and able men, in high places, bent before it. To the honor of our State, however, three judges of our Supreme Court, John White, of Lawrence; Reuben Saffold, of Dallas, and Anderson Crenshaw, of Butler county, had the independence to sustain the act of 1818, as odious as it had become. When the General Assembly met in the fall of 1829, coming fresh from an excited populace, the House of Representatives voted for the impeachment of those judges and sent it to the Senate for trial. And what was the offence charged? "The head and front of their offending" was their decision to sustain the contracts under the act of 1818. Other matters were spoken of in the memorial of the prosecutor, but he failed to prove them, and they were abandoned.

The Prosecutor in the celebrated trial, William Kelly, was born and reared to manhood in the northeastern part of South Carolina. His family was very respectable and well connected, and he well educated. When a young man he settled in Tennessee and became judge; hence was always called Judge Kelly. He was the first member of Congress from Alabama, and then United States Senator. In person he was well set, and had blue eyes and light hair, and wonderfully resembled my old friend, Thaddeus Sandford, of the Mobile *Register*, whose *portrait* hangs on the wall before me.*

He was a man of fine genius and an able lawyer. There was nothing sophomorean in his style. It was always conversational in its tone. When addressing a jury he often left the bar, and leaning on a chair, he *talked* to them very effectually. He was no optimist, for he appealed to the worst passions, and evidently believed in the fall of man. He was their great champion, and loved the dear people; but I never observed that he was fond of their society. I have often seen him retire from crowds and amuse himself with a pocket edition of Horace, which he generally carried, and could read with facility. I judge that much of his cynical style had been imbibed from that Roman satirist.

The counsel in defence of the judges were John J. Ormond and Arthur F. Hopkins, Esquires; both nurtured into greatness on the soil of Lawrence county. I have given a sketch of the latter, amd therefore shall have less to say of him. Mr. Ormond commenced his argument by giving a clear exposition of the functions of the several departments of the State government. He argued with great force that it was not the prerogative of the Legislature to judge of the decisions of the Judges, for if it was, they could at all times control the action of the court by impeachment, which would effectually destroy the independence of the judicial department. He was severe on the prosecutor for introducing a bill to take away from the defendants the right to plead the statute of limitations in a batch of cases in which Judge Kelly had a fortune in fees involved—but I find I will lack space to follow him in his argument. In conclusion he said that the prosecutor had staked everything, which was dear to a man, on the issue of the impeachment. It seems that Judge Kelly thought so too, for when the Judges were vindicated by the Senate, he removed from the State, settled in New Orleans, and died from yellow fever the next year, 1837.

Thus ended the trial of the judges in an acquittal, and the independence of the judiciary was vindicated. So great was the public excitement that the result might have been different, but for the fact that the members of the Senate had been elected

*NOTE—This *portrait* Colonel Saunders afterwards presented to the city of Mobile, Ala.

for the longer terms than those of the House, and the influence of lawyers in and out of the Senate. This class of men, who from their profession, learn the philosophy of constitutions, prove themselves to be the special guardians of the judicial department of the State. As to interest on the loan of money, the State returned to its plan of placing a limit upon it. But the economists still contended that money, like other property, should be governed by the law of demand and supply. Their arguments have not been satisfactorily answered; but experience has proven them to be delusive, and every State and Territory in this broad Union has placed a limit upon interest and affixes a penalty for usury.

In 1832 and 1833 Mr. Ormond reluctantly consented to serve in the House of Representatives of the General Assembly. In the latter year an ugly controversy had sprung up which was the second edition of the one in Georgia in which the fiery Governor Troup threatened, in a letter to President Adams, to send his Commander-in-chief, Gaines, back to him in irons. The controversy in Alabama was between Governor Gayle and President Jackson over the Indian lands within the boundaries of Alabama, for which there seemed to be no solution but force. Governor Gayle showed a good deal of pluck and there was an iron man on the other side of the controversy. Serious apprehensions of a conflict of arms were entertained, but Mr. Hopkins who had moved to Madison and was a member from that county, co-operated with Mr. Ormond, and the difficulty was avoided by their independent course. They were both decided Whigs in politics, but took the side of General Jackson, and by their able speeches carried the Legislature with them in spite of the sectional excitement, which extended their reputation greatly as constitutional lawyers.

As the result of this discussion an event happened, which was entirely unexpected, but had a material effect on the private fortune of Mr. Ormond. Mr. John Morrisette was then a member of the House, and a man of decided ability and much practical sense; and he was charmed with the oratory of Mr. Ormond. At that time the "Canebrake" in Marengo county was but little known. The water falling upon its surface was impeded in its flow by the cane and leaves and limbs which had fallen, and it was believed to be too wet for cotton. Mr. Morrisette knew better, and, as it was open for entry, he was quietly, without any public proclamation, investing every dollar he could raise in these lands. When the Legislature was about to adjourn, he took Mr. Ormond aside, and proposed (if he had money with him) he would enter some of the lands for him. Mr. Ormond handed him $800, with which he entered 640 acres of land for him, the nucleus of his splendid Marengo plantation, which was worth fully $50 per acre before the civil war. This was like Morrisette. There was no tinsel about him. He could have parted from his friend with a well-rounded compliment, but he didn't understand these "incorporeal hereditaments," and wished to confer a substantial favor, and he did it.

In 1837, Mr. Ormond was elected a judge of the Supreme Court, notwithstanding his politics, for by this time the purity of his character, and his learning as a lawyer, had become known to the people of the State. Mr. Brewer, in his History of Alabama says: "The great achievement of Judge Ormond's life is embodied in the jurisprudential services he rendered to his age. A compeer in all respects of that illustrious triumvirate of jurists, Messrs. Goldthwaite, Collier and Ormond, he occupies a page in the Alabama law reports, which will pass down to future time and be cited as authority in the adjudication of human rights, as long as the common law maintains a footing among civilized nations. For purity and elegance of style, I do not believe his reported opinions have been surpassed by anything which has appeared in the history of Alabama jurisprudence."

In 1841 he was called upon, as Judge, to exercise that virtue and independence which as counsel, he had so eloquently commended in the Judges who were impeached; and it was in the celebrated "Bank case." On the fifteenth of July, 1841, immediately after delivering an elaborate opinion in the case, he wrote to me, and from this letter I quote: "The court, which is over, has been a most arduous one, both for the amount and importance of the cases. The bank cases, as they were called, were decided in favor of the bank (Goldthwaite dissenting), the amount involved about $300,000. You perhaps know that the suits were brought by the bank on a contract by which they advanced money and received cotton, or rather took the control of it, to refund the advance by the proceeds of the sale. Cotton fell, and those suits were brought for the deficit, or *reclamations*, as they were somewhat pompously called by the merchants. The defence, that it was "a dealing in goods, wares and merchandise," and prohibited by the 20th section of the charter of the State Bank. I thought the contract, though highly impolitic, yet entirely legitimate. The cases have made a great noise. When the opinion is published I will send you a copy." Mr. John M. Bates, one of the defendants, published a pamphlet of seventy pages, the design of which was to injure Judges Ormond and Collier and get public revenge against his defeat. This pamphlet disclosed some curious commercial facts, which it may be well for planters to remember. The season preceding these contracts had been unpropitious and it was known that the crop coming forward would be greatly deficient. Although the price was 19 cents per pound, the planters wanted more, and accepted advances from the bank of $600,000 to enable them to hold for four months in Liverpool, and the bank wanted sterling exchange to resume specie payments. But in consequence of the high price many cotton mills stopped, and all curtailed their operations, and the price of cotton fell down to 12 cents! The deficit due the bank was great. The author of the pamphlet himself owed more than $30,000, from the payment of which he wished to be released upon a technical plea. Many men who are too honest to cheat their neighbors, will not hesitate to cheat the State. This opposition to Chief Justice Collier and Justice Ormond but caused their opinions in this case to be widely known, and highly approved; and acted as the mordant of the manufacturer which stamps the highest colors indelibly on his fabrics. Garrett in his "*Public Men of Alabama*," in reference to it, says: "In the succeeding year they were both re-elected to their high offices, without opposition or complaint. Chief Justice Collier was afterwards elected Governor of the State almost by acclamation, and Judge Ormond continued in office until he resigned, about January 1, 1848. He then resumed the practice of law in Tuscaloosa, where he died March 4, 1866. Now that his presence is no more seen among men, and he is alike insensible to flattery or censure, in the grave, truth and justice to an excellent citizen, and a pure and upright member of the highest tribunal known to the State, requires that Judge Ormond should be ranked with the very foremost in all the qualities which constitute a lofty and dignified nature. He was modest and somewhat retiring in his disposition, and never made any parade of his extensive learning and refined literary taste. It required a close acquaintance with him, even for years, to find out his sterling qualities. The more one saw of him, the more esteem did he inspire. He was truly a Christian gentleman in the highest sense of the term, and was for many years, and up to his death, an exemplary member of the Methodist Episcopal Church—always ready with his purse, and example, to support the ministry, and to aid in all benevolent enterprises. His memory, without a blemish, is dear to the hearts of his friends, and to the people of Alabama, whom he faithfully served in the halls of legislation, and on the bench of the Supreme Court for a long period."

In the *Southern Law Journal* of February, 1879, the Hon. John Mason Martin, the Professor of Law in the University of Alabama, and since then a member of Congress from the Tuscaloosa district, published a brief but well written sketch of Judge Ormond, from which I have drawn freely in the preparation of this article. As to his character as a Judge, Mr. Martin said: "It was but natural that he should be called to high judicial position, and the citizen of our day owes a debt of gratitude to the men of that era, for throwing aside the shackles of political partizanship, and for giving us a judge, who was the worthy colleague on the bench of Henry W. Collier, and Henry Goldthwaite. It was this court which first placed Alabama decisions on a level with those of the older states of the Union. The writer will not undertake a criticism of Judge Ormond's opinions as a Justice of our Court of Appeals, for in the reported decisions, they will remain as monuments of his great industry, integrity and legal learning. Of the style in which they are expressed, it may be said that they are models in point of purity, terseness and perspicuity. No Southern Justice has surpassed Judge Ormond in this respect; and no one of his own times, or before that period, in the South, ever equalled him, except the great Gaston of North Carolina."

From my correspondence with the Hon. John A. Campbell, during this year, I submit the following extracts:

"I was pleased to receive a token to show that you were living, and engaged in the pious work of clearing the moss from the gravestones of those who have gone before us. * * * I am obliged by the transmission of your county paper, and if the sixty-four articles ever become a book please let me have it." * * * My acquaintance with Judge Ormond commenced about the time of his appointment to the bench of the Supreme Court. He removed not long after to Tuscaloosa. His culture was liberal and comprehended much outside of his profession. His garden and grounds were highly improved, and were favorite resorts for members of the bar. I was a regular visitor, and have a very pleasant memory of his family and the intercourse I had with them. At his election, in 1837, Major David Hubbard proposed to refer the selection of a judge to a party caucus. I objected, and declared that I would not attend one if called. The court was composed of H. W. Collier, Chief Justice; H. Goldthwaite, and Ormond. It was as well constituted as it could have been; all industrious, faithful in the performance of duty, and had attained a high grade in the ranks of the profession.

"The Chief Justice had seen service in the Circuit Court. He was prompt, with a good deal of self-reliance, and prosecuted his inquiries in the examination of cases with care and diligence. He was habitually urbane and kind in his intercourse.

"Judge Goldthwaite had a very powerful mind; was confident and self-reliant, and indefatigable when interested in the case. His judgment was strong, his mind very subtle, and sometimes he deceived himself thereby. But this was not long or often.

"Judge Ormond was an able judge. His mind was well balanced, and there was a solidity about him, and a capacity of estimating the weight of evidence, and the finest of arguments. He was laborious, conscientious and fully impressed with the importance of his duties, and what was becoming in his office.

"The Supreme Court thus constituted was at its zenith. I remember it with cordiality and affection. There was no incident, during its existence, which disturbed its order or diminished the respect of the bar. The reports of this court have been often cited before the British Courts; and in one instance an eminent judge in a difficult case referred to a decision made by it, as the most satisfactory he had seen on the subject. I have regarded the reports of the court during this period as quite on a level with any of the same number of volumes in any of the States. This court I have always esteemed as the best court we ever had in Alabama. The judges were in the prime of life. They were conscientious, scrupulous men, under the guidance of personal honor and a noble ambition to do their duty." Judge Campell had a large practice in our Supreme Court, and is in every way competent to form a correct opinion of the matters spoken of above.

The members of the Supreme Court in 1840 digested a Criminal Code, which has removed much uncertainty from the administration of this branch of the law. I can speak with some confidence as to its merits; for it was before the Judiciary Committee of which I was chairman for weeks, and examined carefully, section by section, before it was reported to the House. The Code cost the judges much study and labor.

Judge Ormond was a Whig in politics and he was one upon principle. He believed that the Government of the United States, if ever it was put to the test, would prove to be too weak. But he lived to see the day when this weak Government exhibited a strength unequalled by any power on earth, of the same population.

As the conflict between the North and South approached, he was deeply moved, and in a letter he wrote me, of four pages, on the 30th of January, 1860, he ably reviewed the controversy. He said the "irrepressible conflict is upon us." He reviewed the Territorial question, and condemned the position of Mr. Douglas. He said the South should require fresh guarantees, or prepare for the worst by arming her people. He did "not consider the right of secession, so called, Constitutional. What I would recommend in plain words is Revolution. Not that I desire a dissolution of the Union, but that I am satisfied nothing short of it will secure our rights."

In 1861 he was an elector for President in the Tuscaloosa District. I do not remember on which ticket, but judge, from the complexion of his sentiments, that it was on one for Breckenridge.*

Judge Ormond was like all learned public spirited men, a patron of education, and was several times elected Trustee of the State University.

Judge Ormond lost his wife many years before his death. Their children were:

1. Mary Elizabeth, the eldest, educated with great care, and under the tutilage of her father, took an extensive course of reading, and was learned far beyond her sex. She married Professor J. W. Mallet, then of the University of Alabama. The professor is of a highly respectable family. His father was a civil engineer and died in London, England, in 1881. His father was from North Tawton, in the northeastern part of Devonshire. The professor is now Professor of Analytical Chemistry in the University of Virginia. His reputation in his profession is so great, that his services were lately sought at the old and distinguished Jefferson School of Medicine, in Philadelphia, at a large salary; but the trustees of the university advanced his salary, and have been able to retain him. He had the misfortune to lose his wife in August, 1886. They had three children. The eldest was John Ormond M., finely educated, and taught for some time in the "Academy of Augusta," Ga., but had to give up its work from the appearance of consumption in its earlier stages. His father sent him to Nebraska, and afterward to southern California, with the hope of benefit to his health, and finally took him to Austin, Texas, where he died from the fell disease.

2. Robert William M., their second son, after completing his education and studying law at the Virginia University, is beginning life as a young practising lawyer in Norfolk, Va., with good prospects of success. The one daughter, Mary Constance, is living with her father.

3. John James Ormond, M. D., who has practiced medicine to some extent, but who for many years farmed a plantation given him by his father, is now residing at Birmingham, Ala.

4. William Banks Ormond, who died while a student at the University of Alabama.

5. Margaret Cornelia, who married Major Charles Hayes, who was a member of Congress. His widow lives on her plantation in South Alabama.

6. Catherine Amanda Ormond, who married Colonel Crews, of Arlington, Tennessee.

7. Thomas W. Ormond, who has been farming, but when I heard from him last was about to make some change in his plans.

The following letter from Hon. R. C. Brickell (who lately resigned his seat on the bench of the Supreme Court of Alabama) was received too late for publication in our last number, of which it is essentially a part.

"HUNTSVILLE, Ala., August 29, 1887.

DEAR SIR—I regret that your favor of the sixth inst., has not been earlier answered. It came when I was absent, and by some oversight did not come to my observation until yesterday.

The Penal Code of 1841 passed in view of the establishment of the penitentiary and a change in the mode of punishment of crime from that provided by the common law, which remained, or was imported into our legislation was the work of the three judges of our Supreme Court—Collier, Goldthwaite and Ormond. As I have always heard, it was, especially, the work of Judge Ormond. For clearness, certainty and precession of expression it has not been equalled in our legislation. In its general principles and features it remains to-day the criminal law of the State. There have been additions

---

*Colonel Saunders was himself elector for Stephen A. Douglas, and president of the convention which met at Montgomery.

to it; there have been changes in the mode of procedure; there have been amendments to adapt it to the changed and changing conditions and circumstances of the State, but it is the foundation of the whole body of our criminal law.   It bears internal evidence of large learning, patient study and profound thought.

Yours respectfully and truly,

R. C. BRICKELL.

The Banks Family.

To this Mrs. Ormond belonged, and the Judge was always very respectful and kind to all who were akin to his wife.   This is the most delicate compliment a husband can pay, and is always appreciated by his wife.   Some husbands are so dull they never learn the importance of it.

John Banks was an accomplished merchant.   His life, until he was forty years of age, had been spent as a commercial agent.   In the early part of this century, before the era of steamships, international mails and telegraph lines, when ships crossed the ocean, it was the custom to send on each ship an agent to sell the cargo and purchase another for the return voyage, and this agent was called a *supercargo.* I have not heard the word spoken for an age, for commercial habits have entirely changed and resident commission merchants are employed now at every port to which a vessel sails.   Mr. John Banks, who had been well educated as a merchant, sailed to foreign ports as a supercargo year by year.   He had been frequently to England and visited their cotton factories, and became familiar with the different kinds of cotton.   He had been often up the Mediterranean and knew the commercial wants of her larger ports, and his voyages had extended even to China, and when he did go there it was a triangular voyage, viz: first a cargo carried to China, then another taken to England, and lastly a third brought from England home. In short he was the best informed merchant of that day.   He and David Mason, who had resided in Lawrence county for several years, founded the great cotton commission house of Mason & Banks in New Orleans, which had a great run until the death of David Mason. John Banks never married.

William Banks, his brother (who was the father-in-law of Judge Ormond), was a very handsome man, of medium size, with black eyes, dark skin, and very fine manners. He married, in Virginia, a Miss Jenkins, daughter of Dr. Jenkins, who received his medical education at Edinboro, Scotland, and was a surgeon in the army of the Revolution.   She was a very pretty woman, with blue eyes and fair complexion.   They moved from Brunswick county, Virginia, to Franklin, Tenn., about the same time with my father (1808), and lived near us.   They moved again to Courtland, Lawrence county, Ala., with a little colony, composed of John White (who became Supreme Court judge), Dr. Young A. Gray, an eminent physician, my father, and others.   Mr. Wm. Banks was in good circumstances, and a dry goods merchant.   He reared his children with great care, and educated them well.   They were—

1. Minerva J., who became the wife of Judge Ormond, and of whom we have already given an account.

2. Cassandra, who was more highly educated than any of the family.   She married Watkins Leigh Harris, a young lawyer of taste and erudition, who was a nephew of the celebrated lawyer, Benjamin Watkins Leigh, of Virginia.   Cassandra Harris died in Courtland a few years after her marriage.   Mr. Harris, for some reason, did not succeed in his profession very well. and moved to North Mississippi, where he died a few years after.

3. Mary Banks, who married a Mr. Robinson, and, after his death, a brother of his.   She has three children living—William, a physician, and two daughters, Florence and Mary.

4. Amanda Banks, who married Richard N. Harris, Sr.   They both died in Tuscaloosa, and left several sons and daughters.   One of them, Cornelia, married the Hon. H. M Somerville, one of the judges of our Supreme Court, who, though young, has already achieved a high judicial reputation.   Another daughter, Amanda, married a

physician of high standing of Tuscaloosa, Dr. John Little. John Harris married Maggie Fitts; Richard married Miss Nevil, and Norfleet married Miss Bettie Blocker.

5. Elisabeth Banks married Judge Bowling C. Baker. They are both dead. They left two daughters, Mary and Lizzie, who live in Florida (1887).

6. Dr. William Banks married a Miss O'Conor, of Chicago, where he practiced medicine, and died while visiting relations in Tuscaloosa, a few years ago. He left no child.

7. Cornelia Banks, the youngest, married Andrew S. Nicholson, Esq., who was reared in Middlesex county, Va., educated at William and Mary College, and finished at the law school at Fredericksburg, Va. He was a law partner of Judge Ormond, after the latter resigned his office. At the time of Mr. Nicholson's death, he was Register in Chancery. His widow lives in Tuscaloosa. Their oldest living son, Ormond, is a lieutenant in the navy; another son, Richard, and daughter, Mary Gray, are living with their mother.

The Harris Family

belonged to Scotland-Neck, a fertile bend in the Roanoke river, in North Hampton county, North Carolina. They were respectable, well off, and highly connected. The Norfleets and Harrises were blended by intermarriages. It was a Miss Ruth Norfleet whom Brigadier General Hogan married in South Hampton, North Carolina (3d October, 1751). He commanded a brigade of regulars in the Continental line. They had one son, Lemuel Hogan. He was father to John, Smith, Arthur and James Hogan. These four all lived in Franklin county, Alabama, near Tuscumbia. Col. R. S. McReynolds married a daughter of John Hogan.

Norfleet Harris, the ancestor of the Harrises about Courtland, married Mary Hunter in North Carolina, and after the birth of their four children, he died. Several years afterward Mrs. Harris married a Mr. Boykin, who lived but a short time. About 1822, Mrs. Boykin brought her children, and her slaves, and cultivated a cotton plantation, near Courtland. She was a small woman, of great cheerfulness and intelligence, and managed her plantation as skilfully as any man in the valley. She was the first advocate of "Woman's Rights" I ever heard of; and I will tell you how I happened to know of it. The first year I became a planter I had an overseer named Murphey, who had lived with Mrs. Boykin the year before. During a long rainy spell, Murphey came to me to know what work I would have the negro men to do. I was really at a loss to say, when he suggested that Mrs. Boykin, in such weather, put them to spinning thread, and required them to turn off as many cuts as the women. And she declared that a set of great, fat, lazy men, should not be suffered on her plantation, to be dozing by the fire, while the women were hard at work. I never knew her first husband, Mr. Harris; but he had the reputation of being of the same class with herself in industry—and this accounts for the energy and persistence which characterize their descendants, male and female, to this day. I will now speak of their children.

Lacy Norfleet Harris married Richard A. Turner, a farmer in North Carolina. She was a very small and beautiful woman, with graceful manners, and there is very little change in her to-day. She had moved with her mother in a carriage over the roughest kind of roads, and proposed to her young husband to return to North Carolina on horseback; which they did, as she told me, with great comfort. A racing man said the horse had a good time too, for he only carried a "ketch." After some years Mrs. Turner, then a widow, married Dr. James Perrine, of Courtland. The Doctor was from Wheeling, Va. He had first gone to Hamilton, Miss., near Aberdeen, where he practiced medicine two years. Thence he came to Courtland, where he married Mrs. Turner. After some years he moved to Mobile. The Doctor was a tall, spare man of very genteel manners, and fine, colloquial powers. I don't mean that he was fluent, but that he used choice language to convey his ideas. Although he was a good physician, he was too indolent to do a large practice, but preferred politics to medicine. He became quite influential, and was appointed Collector of Customs at Mobile, by President Harrison. I was his successor in this office, and yet although of opposing political faith, we remained personal friends, as long as he lived. This was owing to the fact that he had learned that I (who had the friendship and confidence of President Polk) had advised him to move slowly, in turning out good men, on account of their politics, as it was a practice corrupting to the public conscience; and I will here say, that I myself acted on this principle, during my term of office. Dr. Perrine died in Mobile many years ago.

John H. Harris, son of Norfleet Harris and Mary Hunter, married Susan Smith, daughter of Gabriel and Mary Smith, of Limestone county. Mrs. Mary Smith was sister of William Banks, above mentioned. Mr. Harris was one of our most respectable and successful planters, and would have left a large estate to his children but for the results of the war. He and his wife both died acceptable members of the Methodist Church, South. Their children are:

1. Mary Harris, who married Frank Sherrod, son of Felix Sherrod, and grandson of Colonel Benjamin Sherrod. Her husband died many years ago, and she is a widow and has two grown sons, Frank and Harris, who are cotton planters.

2. Elizabeth, who is unmarried.

3. Susan, who married Capt. E. F. Comegys, son of E. F. Comegys, who for many years was cashier of the State Bank at Tuscaloosa. The captain commanded a battery in the Confederate army during the late war, and was quite near when the mine exploded near Petersburg, destroying a battery and a large part of a Confederate regiment, and opening a crater 200 feet long and 30 feet deep. The captain is finely educated and now has supervision of a school of several hundred pupils in Denton, Texas. They have six children.

4. Ida Harris, who married Colonel Alexander Allison, of Knoxville, also a gallant officer of artillery during the late war; commencing with the disaster at Fishing creek. They have three small children.

5. John H. Harris, a cotton planter, who married Susan, daughter of Mr. William Jackson, of Florence, son of Hon. James Jackson, who was so long State Senator from Lauderdale county. They have seven children.

6. Richard N., a planter and merchant, who married Miss Lizzie Hood,* daughter of John and Caroline Hood, of Lauderdale county. They have four children.

7. Lucy Harris, who was recently married to Mr. Joseph Brewer, of New Orleans.

The third child of Norfleet Harris and Mary Hunter, was Richard N. Harris, of whom we have given an account with the Banks family.

The fourth child of Norfleet Harris and Mary Hunter married James Cotton, in North Carolina, moved to Memphis, and after a few years moved to Louisiana. Their children were James, Joseph, Mary and Lucy. Mrs. Cotton is dead.

The Clay Family

in America, seem to be all akin, and have (as far as I know) acknowledged their relationship to one another. It has produced a number of our able and distinguished men, and a little space is due to their descent. I have before me the *"family record"* of General Green Clay, of Kentucky; the *"Family Tree"* of the *Clays, of Huntsville, Ala.;* the first volume of the *"Memoirs of Hon. Cassius M. Clay,"* and a number of letters from members of the family, to guide me in my conclusions. I find no difficulty in the last two hundred years; for the line of descent for that period is plain, and well supported by family records, but beyond that there are two traditions. One came from Porter Clay, a brother of Henry Clay, the Kentucky orator, who said that "in the reign of Queen Elizabeth, Sir Walter Raleigh brought over to the Virginia plantations, among others, three brothers, sons of Sir John Clay, of Wales, England. He gave them each £10,000. They were named Charles, Thomas and Henry. They settled on James river, near Jamestown. Charles and Thomas had large families, but Henry had none. Cassius M. Clay is a descendant of Charles Clay; Henry and myself from Thomas Clay." The other tradition is "that John Clay, the original stock from whom the numerous families

---

* NOTE.—The gallant Lieutenant Hood, of the U. S. Navy, in the Cuban war, is her brother.

of the Clays descended, was born in England, and came over to America in the King's service, a British grenadier, in Bacon's rebellion. That he had a son named John, and a daughter named Hannah, and John had two sons, named Henry and Charles, and that Henry was grandfather of General Green Clay, of Kentucky, and Matthew Clay, of Virginia, by his son Charles, and grandfather of Henry Clay, the orator, by his son John."

I have examined carefully the proofs and reject the tradition of noble descent, and have adopted that from the "British Grenadier" as the true history. General Green Clay in his family record, and the Clays of Huntsville, assume it to be true, and trace their descent step by step from him. There are some discrepancies, but I think they can be reconciled, and present the following genealogy as being the true one.

1. John Clay was the common ancestor of the Clays of America, but he must have come to America long before Bacon's rebellion, which was in 1676 (*Campbell's History of Virginia*), whereas his great grandson (as you will see below) was born in 1672.

2. John, son of the Grenadier, had several sons, but we only know the names of two, Henry and Charles, of Amelia county, Virginia.

3. Charles, who was the son of John Clay the II., married Hannah ——. He had several sons, whose names are not mentioned in the record before me, entitled "*A Table of Consanguinity of the Ascending Line of Green Clay's Family*," but the eldest was Henry Clay.

It was from this Charles, numbered 3 in this line, that Senator Clement Comer Clay, of Huntsville, descended.

4. This Henry was born in 1672, and died suddenly at supper, at the mature age of 92 years, on the third day of August, 1764. General Green Clay says that this "Henry was my grandfather, and married Mary Mitchell (daughter of William and Elizabeth Mitchell). They lived and died in Chesterfield county, Virginia, at the old place on the west side of Swift Creek. They had four sons, William, Henry, Charles our father, and John, the grandfather of Henry Clay, late member of Congress, and negotiator of the treaty of Ghent, and several daughters." This record was sent many years ago by Mr. Brutus Clay, son of General Green Clay, to my nephew, Dr. Matthew Clay. Mary Mitchell, wife of Henry Clay, who is numbered 4 in this line, was born in July, 1693, and died 7th August, 1777, aged 84 years.

5. Charles Clay (the second of the name), mentioned above, the fourth and last son of Henry Clay, was born 31st January, 1716, and died 25th February, 1789. He married Martha Green November 11, 1741. She was born 25th November, 1719, and died 6th September, 1793. She was the daughter of Thomas Green and Eliza Marston, and their line on the family tree is extended away back in the past for generations, including the Filmors and Marvells; and Mr. Brutus Clay has extended this family for two generations in the descending line, through the Greens, Williamsons, Moseleys, Condons and Bookers. From all this I infer that the Greens were people of wealth and position; for people who are poor, and have no pride in the past, or hope in the future, seldom keep their family records carefully. In the earlier steps of the Clay family I find no family records, and this was one reason why I was inclined to believe in the tradition of their descending from the poor Grenadier. Had there been a *coronet* in the family, and ten thousand pounds sterling inherited by each of three brothers, there would have been plenty of family records—but, perhaps, a scarcity of *great men* among their descendants.

Bishop Meade, in his "*Churches and Families of Virginia*," has given the following account of Charles Clay. He says: "The Rev. Charles Clay was a near relative—probably first cousin—of our statesman, Henry Clay; and inherited no little of his talents and decision of character. He was ordained by the bishop of London in 1769, and on the 22d October, of same year, was received as minister of St. Anne's parish. The vestry-book opens in 1772 and closes in 1785: all which time, as well as the three preceding years, he was the minister. He preached in Amhurst and Chesterfield occasionally. The places of his preaching I ascertain from the notes on a number of his

sermons which have been submitted to my inspection. The sermons are sound, energetic and evangelical, beyond the character of the times. One of them on the New
Birth, is most expressive and experimental. Another, on the Atonement, for Christmas
day, is very excellent as to doctrine, and concludes with a faithful warning against
profanation of that day by "fiddling, dancing, drinking, and such like things," which
he said were so common among them. In the year 1777, on public fast day, he preached
a sermon to the minute-men, at Charlottesville, in which his patriotic spirit was displayed. He said in the course of his sermon, "Cursed be he who keepeth his sword
from blood in this war." He declared that "the cause of liberty was the cause of God,"
and calls upon them to "plead the cause of their country before the Lord *with their
blood*." And yet he said "there might be persons present, who would rather bow the
neck in abject slavery than face a man at arms."

It was at this time, and under these circumstances, that he became acquainted with
Mr. Jefferson, who, having removed into this parish, was now elected to the vestry of
St. Anne's, though it does not appear that he ever acted. This intimacy was kept up
until his death. During the latter years of his ministry in St. Anne's parish, the connection of Mr. Clay with the vestry was very unhappy. The salary of one year was the
occasion of it. There appears to be some division in the vestry about it. The majority,
however, was against Mr. Clay, and a lawsuit was the result. The decision was not
satisfactory to Mr. Clay, and he refused to receive the amount offered, and told the
vestry that if they would not pay him what he considered right, he would receive none.
Mr. Clay must have left St Anne's in 1784, for we find him representing the church in
Chesterfield in 1785, at the Episcopal Convention at Richmond, but never afterward.
The church was daily sinking, and his mind being soured perhaps by his controversy
with the vestry, and discouraged by his prospects as a minister, he removed to Bedford
county, where he had a plantation, and betook himself to a farmer's life, only officiat-
ing at marriages and funerals to the few Episcopalians in that region.

There was something peculiar in the structure of Mr. Clay's mind, in proof of which,
it is mentioned, that by his will he enjoined, what has been strictly observed, that on the
spot where he was buried, and which he had marked out, there should be raised a huge
pile of stones for his sepulchre. It is about twenty feet in diameter and twelve feet
high, and, being first covered with earth and then with turf, presents the appearance of
one of those Indian mounds to be be seen in our Western States.

Charles Clay and his wife (Martha Green) had eleven children, to-wit: Mary
Lockett, born 2d September, 1742; Eliza, born 4th August, 1744; Charles, born 24th
December, 1745; Henry, born 5th March, 1748; Thomas, born 31st July, 1750; Eliza
Marvell, born 21st April, 1752; Lucy Thaxton and Matthew (twins), born 25th March,
1754; Green, born 14th August, 1757; Priscilla, born 30th April, 1759, and Martha Lewis,
born 3d July, 1761.

The above, showing, I believe, the descent of the Clay family from their common
ancestor, is merely preliminary to the descent of the families of Matthew Clay, of Virginia; of Green Clay (his brother), of Kentucky; of Henry Clay, the Senator, and
Senator Clement Comer Clay, of Alabama.

Family of Matthew Clay, of Virginia (Born 1754).

As we stated in our last, he was the son of Charles and the brother of Green Clay,
of Kentucky. Matthew Clay lived in Pittsylvania county, Va. He was a man of talent
and distinction. He was first lieutenant of the First Virginia Regulars in the Revolution, and represented in Congress a district in Virginia, comprising Pittsylvania, Halifax and Henry counties, from 1797 to 1813. This was an eventful time in the political
history of the country, when Mr. Jefferson resisted the invasion of the liberty of the
press, by the Sedition law, and of personal liberty, by the Alien law, and conquered
anew the freedom we thought we had secured in the war of the Revolution. During this
struggle, Mr. Clay was the firm supporter of Mr. Jefferson, and is so spoken of in the
third volume of his writings. This was by no means an ordinary conflict between par-

ties then called "*Republican*" on one side, and "*Federalist*" on the other. The ablest Republican journalists were heavily fined and imprisoned for criticisms on the conduct of President Adams, which, if made in England on the King, would have passed without a prosecution. The proceedings under the Alien law were still more tyrannical. The President was empowered by the bill to imprison at discretion any alien, resident in the United States, and the privilege of the writ of *habeas corpus* was denied him. There was a great panic amongst the French residents, against whom the bill was mainly directed, and many French gentlemen purchased a vessel and embarked secretly for their native country. But I will mention, especially, one case to illustrate the operation of this monstrous measure. ' Gen. Thaddeus Kosciusko, who had served under Washington, in the American Revolution, had to flee, in June, 1797, from a country which he had helped to liberate, by a passport obtained for him under an assumed name by Mr. Jefferson, and so suddenly, he had to leave his personal effects behind him. In the spring of 1799, Mr. Jefferson addressed the following lines to this renowned hero: "May heaven have in store for your country a restoration of these blessings, and you be destined as the instrument it will use for that purpose. But if this be forbidden by fate, I hope I shall be able to preserve for you here an asylum, where your love of liberty and disinterested patriotism will be forever protected and honored, and where you will find in the hearts of the American people, a good portion of that esteem and affection which glow in the bosom of the friend who writes this." *See Jefferson's writings, 3d volume, pp. 395 and 402.* But this fervent wish was never realized. Kosciusko became the commander-in-chief of the Poles, and '' Warsaw's last champion," in the final struggle for national independence; "the bloodiest chapter in the book of time."

Jefferson, from his opposition to these laws, his advocacy of the liberty of the press, and personal liberty, and his opposition to the right of primo-geniture and to an established church, has been called the "Apostle of liberty," and we feel proud in seeing the name of Matthew Clay, of Virgiana (the father of the Clays of Lawrence county, Ala.,) inscribed on the list of his supporters. Mr. Clay had several times as his opponent, Rev. John Kerr, the most gifted Baptist preacher of his day, but he prevailed over all opponents, and finally, in 1815 died suddenly while making a speech at Halifax Court House, Va.

His person is said to have been an imposing one. His eyes and hair were very dark. He married a Miss Williams, who was the mother of all his children. She died in 1798, and he afterward married a widow Saunders.

In 1811 he had to bear the infliction of a great sorrow; he had a daughter, Mary, of great beauty and promise, who was one of the victims in the fire which consumed the Richmond Theatre. Some of the wealthiest and most distinguished citizens of Virginia were in this sad list. Governor Smith, of Virginia, had married a niece of the wife of Dr. Benjamin Franklin, (the identical Miss Reed who saw the Doctor when a youth walking down the street munching his roll of bakers bread) and had carried his wife, and another lady, to the Theatre that night. On the alarm of fire, he hurried out the two ladies he was escorting, and dashed back into the body of the burning building to rescue other ladies, and that was the last of this noble man. Mary Clay, (as I have been told by a venerable lady who married her brother), was soon to have been a bride, and the last time she was seen, she was standing at a window, with her arm resting in that of her lover, waiting for a rescue—which never came.

Amanda, another daughter of Matthew Clay, of Virginia, was an invalid, and had epileptic fits every two weeks. Her father supposing she would never marry, gave her a much larger portion of his estate, in his will, than any other child. But nevertheless she found a husband in George P. Kezee, a man of great sagacity. I saw him but once, and that was when he came to this county to get "his belongings" from the Executor. She lived but a few years, and had several children. I don't know whether he is living or not.

Joseph Clay was the eldest son of Matthew Clay of Virginia, and had blue eyes and light hair. His father was boring for salt, near Sparta, in middle Tennessee, and young

Joseph was sent to superintend the work. There he came across a sprightly blooming girl (thirteen or fourteen years old), the daughter of a respectable farmer of that vicinity, Margaret Bowen, and married her against the consent of her parents. She made him an excellent wife, and since his death in West Tennessee she has reared his children well, for she is a woman of intellect, and much decision of character. When over eighty years old she became blind from cataract, and not only consented to a surgical operation, but refused to be held when under the knife. Now over ninety years of age (1887) she is living with her grand-daughter, Mrs. Stevenson, in San Francisco, and has uncommon activity, and can see well to read.

The children of Joseph Clay and Margaret Bowen (except two who died unmarried) were Amanda and Clement C. Amanda married Norment Cherry, and they are both dead. Their daughter Hetty married a Mr. Stevenson, and is now a widow living in San Francisco with three children.

Major Clement C.. son of Joseph Clay, was a gallant soldier during the civil war—settled in Memphis, after it as a commission merchant, and afterwards removed to San Francisco, Cal., where he has amassed a large fortune. He has a high character in business circles, and also in the Methodist Church, South, to which he belongs (having been a lay-delegate to the last General Conference). He married the only daughter of Rev. Phillip Tuggle, of the same church. and has two children not yet grown.

Matthew Clay, of Alabama,

second son of Matthew Clay, of Virginia, migrated from Virginia (1816)to Madison county, Alabama, in company with his intimate friends, Arthur F. Hopkins, and John Moseley. Clay soon after, being young and fiery, engaged in a fight with pistols, during a heated election, missed his antagonist, Rice, and the ball broke the jaw-bone of Major William Fleming, who was then, and continued through life, one of his best friends.

In January, 1819, he removed to Lawrence county, Alabama, with the same friends, Hopkins and Moseley, who settled on adjoining places. Clay possessed himself of the magnificent plantation, now owned by Capt. C. C. Swoope. He soon established a comfortable home, where a generous hospitality was dispensed to his young friends. He built, at once, a double log house, with two stories, hewn neatly, with a broad hall below; and at that early day such a house was considered a badge of gentility. On the walls of this hall, hung the antlers of many a buck who had been killed in the chase, and each one had a story. But there was one pair not broad, but crumpled, that had more points than any other in this hunting gallery, and which had a peculiar history, which he was fond of relating.

The Chase at Melton's Bluff.

Early one Monday morning, a man belonging to Clay came home from his wife's house (which was in the valley to the north) and informed him that he had seen the largest and fattest buck his eyes had ever beheld, leap from a field of corn and peas. Clay felt sure it was the "big buck" which had been so often hunted unsuccessfully. Instead of sending the man to the field, he mounted him on his mule and sent him round to summon his friends to the hunt. Horses were fed, guns were cleaned and loaded and breakfast was dispatched, and the signal horn was blown. It was long, scraped very thin, and blown by Clay (whose lungs were strong), and who knew how to modulate the notes of the instrument, from its loudest blast to its lowest flute-like notes. The music rose first above the trees, and then on the lower stratum of the clouds, until it was lost in the distance. Presently it was answered by one at Hickman's Spring (now Wheeler), and then by another, far away. The cavalcade then started, Horace in front. But I must tell you who Horace was. In those days, when a planter could live like a gentleman and entertain his friends, there was one great drawback on his personal comfort, and that was, that he had to ride with the hounds and drive the deer from his lair amidst briars and thickets. Now, Horace was a mulatto boy, very smart, very light for his years, fond of dogs and a bold rider; and he was gradually inducted into the office of " driver." Mounted on "Long Hungry," a long, lean horse, of good blood, it was rarely the case that he failed to come to the stand with the hounds. He used a ram's horn, whose shrill, penetrating notes could be distinguished over every other in a hunt. On this particular morning, Horace led out his hounds and put them on the track of the deer. At first the "old buck" rose and hoisted his white flag, and bounded contemptuously before the hounds, like a high-mettled charger just turned out to pasture, in large circles. The ramshorn interpreted every movement as plainly as if you had seen it. But pack after pack came to the help of the Clay hounds, and the clamor behind him sounded louder and louder. Moreover, he was fat and began to be thirsty, as, in the autumn, the surface streams are dried up, and he took a straight course for the Tennessee river. The ramshorn now gave no uncertain sound, the hounds no longer baffled on the track, the hunters closed in with shouts behind the noble animal. He mounts the ridge from which he can see the azure gleam on the surface of the broad river, which had been so often his refuge. He plunges down the long slope, in sight of the whole field of hunters and hounds. He nears the bank and his hopes revive, when, just in front, he is met by a shot from a gun heavily loaded, but aimed badly by a raw hunter who had the " buck ague." In his desperation, he turns back through the hounds and huntsmen, and seeing no other opening, he dashes into the main and only street of Melton's bluff. Clay, now on a fine horse, was on his right, and a towering perpendicular bluff on the left, and the hounds snapping at his heels. Every man, woman and child in the place, stand witnessing the unwonted spectacle. Clay fires his short rifle as it lay across his saddle, but the bullet passes over the buck, and quick as lightning, he turned squarely to the left and leaped over the bluff, while three of Clay's best hounds leaped after him. They were all four found dead at the foot of the bluff, and so ended the hunt of the " Big Buck." His horns are still kept in the family, as a trophy of this chase.

We have noted Matthew Clay's qualities as a citizen and a neighbor, and we will now notice him as a public man. His first services were in the House of Representatives of our State Legislature, of which he was member in 1820, 1821 and 1822. His natural abilities were great, but, up to this time, he had not profited by the opportunities afforded him of obtaining a complete education. But when stung by ambition, he gained information rapidly not only by reading, but by association. He and Mr. Hopkins were intimate friends, although Hopkins was a wonderful student, and he was warm hearted and social to a fault. They were quite dissimilar; but, as in chemistry with two substances of a different nature, so there was affinity between them. Clay, in the intervals of time he could spare from his friends, his hunts and his canvasses, gained much knowledge in his intercourse with Hopkins, by absorption.

Clay was the embodiment of independence and fearlessness. There was no policy in his movements, and he was sometimes reckless; but like all the Clays I have known, he was incapable of doing a mean thing. He had warm friends, and vindictive enemies; and when he was engaged in a canvass, it was a whipping race, from the drum beat to the moment the candidates passed " under the string." He was a strong public speaker, and very efficient as a member of the Legislature. His influence was increased by his gaiety, affability and love of fun. At Cahaba during the session mentioned, he and Dr. Shackelford, of Texas fame, met for the first time, and they soon found they were congenial spirits. At that early day, Cahaba was dependent for its supplies entirely on Mobile, and steam navigation. During one very dry season, steamboats could not run, and members were put upon short rations. Clay had bought a ham, and had been filling up the cavities of himself and friends by night suppers of broiled ham. But the bone had been polished clean. One night, at bed time, when the wood-fire had burned down to coals, as he and Dr. Shackelford were sitting alone, a rollicking member came in, and Clay proposed to bet him an oyster supper for twelve, and champagne, that he could have a dozen members in his room in fifteen minutes, without saying a word. The bet was made, and Clay laid the ham bone on the live coals. The delightful flavor soon permeated the hotel, and the members filled the room, before the expiration of the time. When the first steamboat arrived the oyster supper came off, and they had a high time. One incident I remember: A gentleman who presided over one of the houses, of fine abilities, but whose form was crooked from rheumatism, after being thoroughly relaxed by the champagne, rose up, flourished his arm over his head, and cried out, "By George, Matt! I am as straight as a shingle." This was too much, and the party adjourned with a good laugh.

Year by year, without losing the cheerfulness and animation which made him the life of every company, he seemed abler, as a politician. When John Quincy Adams became President, he opposed his administration. This was painful to him, because it was sustained by Henry Clay, the statesman of Kentucky, who was a kinsman, and who when a young man was the protege and favorite of his father—as will be seen in a subsequent number. But Clay, of Lawrence, as much as he admired his Kentucky relative, could not forget the Jeffersonian creed he had inherited. If some young reader should inquire, what that creed was, I answer that it is to be found in the tenth amendment to the constitution of the United States, which provides that "the powers not delegated to the United States by the constitution, nor prohibited by it to the States, are reserved to the States respectively, or to the people." This doctrine secures home rule to the States, prevents collision between the general and State Governments, and faithfully observed, will "invoke the music of the spheres." But you sometimes hear it said that the Civil War *altered the constitution.* War cannot alter a constitution, unless it overturns the government founded upon it.

Mr. Clay was elected State Senator in 1825, and made a very efficient member, until his career was suddenly arrested by death. Early in February, 1827, he left the Capital, and traveled home by stage, across the mountain, during a very cold spell. He was seized with pneumonia, and fell its victim at the early age of thirty-two years.

Mr. Clay had married May, 1824, Frances Anne, daughter of Rev. Turner Saunders, and sister of the writer, and she is still living and in full possession of all her faculties (1887).

The children of Matthew Clay and his wife Frances A., were Thomas F. and Matthew.

1. Thomas F. was born in 1825 and was, in person and character, much like his father. His home was the abode of hospitality, and he was nearly always surrounded by friends. His life was short, and he died in 1856, after having been in feeble health for several years. Thomas F. Clay, in 1845, married Caledonia Anne Oliver. She was the daughter of John Oliver, who married Ruth Ann Weedon. They once lived on the place, now owned by Malcolm Gilchrist, Jr., in this county, and moved afterwards to Columbus, Miss. John Oliver was born in Petersburg, Ga., and was the son of John Oliver of that place, and the brother of Mrs. Robert H. Watkins. Mrs. Caledonia Clay is still living, and is amongst the excellent of the earth. Their children are (besides one who died in infancy), three in number: (1) Alice Clay, who married in 1871, Wheeler Watson, who entered the C. S. Army at the age of sixteen, and served to the bitter end, making a splendid soldier, and since the war an energetic planter. They have five young children living: Asa W., Caledonia C., Alice, Fanny B. and Thomas C. (2) John Oliver Clay, who married in 1884, Fannie Wilson Lawler. He is a young energetic planter, living in the Mississippi bottom. They have one young son, Thomas F. (4) Fannie Lou Clay, who married Henry D. Watson, in 1881. He is a progressive planter living near Columbus, Miss. They have one young child.

2, Matthew Clay, second son of Matthew and Frances A. Clay, was born in February, 1827, two weeks after the death of his father, and is still living. In person he differs from his father, for, like his mother, he has blue eyes and a light complexion; but has a disposition much like his father. He married Mary, the youngest child of Mr. Isham Harrison, and, as the Harrison family were well worthy of union with the Clays, I will here give a brief account of them.

Mr. Isham Harrison was born in the northeastern part of South Carolina. He was a near relative of President Harrison, a cousin of Benjamin Harrison, of Brunswick county, Virginia, and father of Mrs. David Moore, of Huntsville, and his mother was a sister of Gen. Wade Hampton of Revolutionary fame. His brother, Thomas Harrison, was father of James J. Harrison, the distinguished lawyer of Columbus, Miss., whose daughter, Regina, married Gen. Stephen D. Lee. Isham Harrison married in South Carolina, Harriet Kelley, who was a sister of Senator William Kelley, of Alabama, already spoken of. She was a woman of commanding appearance, of superior intellect, and great force of character. They moved to Jones' Valley, near Birmingham, Ala. Here he represented Jefferson county in the Legislature of Alabama, in 1823. When he moved to Eastern Mississippi, he owned a large body of land here, which has since become immensely valuable for its minerals. I much doubt if any man who owns land in North Alabama is doing justice to his heirs to sell it, before a hole is bored down into the earth, at least 2000 feet deep. The children of Isham Harrison and Harriet Kelley were thirteen in number. No. 1. Eliza Harrison, who married, before the family moved from Alabama, Dr. B. W. Earle, a son of General Earle, of South Carolina. 2, Laura Harrison, who married (also in Alabama) the late William H. Jack, an eminent lawyer of Texas. 3. James E. Harrison, who raised a regiment in Texas, where he lived, and, during the war, rose to the rank of brigadier general; he is dead, and his family live in Waco; he married, first, Mary Evans, daughter of J. Evans, and. secondly, Mrs. Carter. 4. Louisa Harrison, who married Dr. Wells A. Thompson, who died in Waco, Texas. 5. John Hampton Harrison, who died at the age of twenty-two; graduate in medicine in the University of Pennsylvania. 6. Isham Harrison, who made a great reputation during the civil war, and gave up his life for the cause he so well loved, in the bloody battle of Harrisburg. Here (the left wing of Sherman's army) nearly 13,000 infantry and 3000 cavalry, with twenty-four pieces of artillery, on 14th of July, 1864, was confronted by the combination cavalry of Lee and Forrest (*see campaigns of Forrest by Jordan*) with about 8000 men.

The Federal movement was to pierce the Confederacy as far as Selma; the right. under Sherman, passing through Meridian (*see Draper's history, on the Federal side*). The Confederate commanders, in consultation. determined to arrest so fatal a march at all hazards. The Federal general, assaulted on every side, and at every step, entrenched himself at Harrisburg. In the morning an attack was made all along his line of two miles in length. "As stoutly as ever men confronted death, did the Southerners face the terrific torrent of fire thus let loose upon their thin and exposed lines, and no battle-field was ever illustrated by more general or shining courage than was displayed in this onset. The charge was renewed from time to time, until the Federal commander commenced a retreat, which almost became a route before he reached Holly Springs. The Confederates defeated this gigantic enterprise, but at a great cost. Buford's division, which included Colonel Isham Harrison's regiment, lost 22 officers killed and 104 wounded, and 825 men killed and wounded—and here the gallant Isham Harrison was killed." He had married Julia, daughter of Governor Whitfield. (7) Dr. Richard Harrison (twin brother of Isham) raised a regiment, and became a prisoner on the fall of Vicksburg. He is dead. He married Mary Ragsdale, daughter of Daniel Ragsdale, of Aberdeen, Miss. (8) General Thomas Harrison was "first major of the celebrated *Eighth Texas Cavalry*, and subsequently became a most valuable and conspicuous brigadier general of cavalry" (*see Campaigns of Forrest*). I made his acquaintance during the forced march for the capture of Murfreesboro. He was a well educated lawyer, and then major of the Eighth. Strange! Its colonel, Wharton, its lieutenant colonel, Walker, and its major Harrison, were all distinguished lawyers! The regiment included a large number of the wealthiest and best educated young men of Texas. The career of the regiment has been one of the most brilliant during the war. I wonder that its history has not been written by some competent survivor who witnessed its magnificent charges.

General Harrison married Sallie McDonald and still lives, after so many hairbreadth escapes. His home is in Waco. (9) William Kelly Harrison was an eminent lawyer and died before the war. (10) Harriet Kelly Harrison married William B. Evans, son of Jas. Evans, of Aberdeen, Miss. (11) Dr. Moses Kelly Harrison was surgeon during the civil war, either in the field or hospital. He married Mary Bradford, and his family will again be spoken of in connection with her father, General B. M. Bradford. (12) Elisabeth Hampton Harrison married Dr. Thomas Barron, of Marion, Ala., where her descendants are to be found. She has been dead for many years. (13) Mary Harrison (the youngest child of Isham and Harriet Harrison) became the wife of Dr. Matthew Clay, as we have said above. She was black-eyed and noted for beauty, in a family of sisters who were famous for attraction. She had fine judgment, and, like her mother, great force of character. She loved her husband and children and the Baptist Church; was neutral in nothing, and yet her manner was so sweet that her decision of purpose never gave offence. It was a sad misfortune when she died a few years ago.

Green Clay, of Kentucky,

was the son of Charles Clay, of Virginia, and his wife, Martha Green. He was born 14th August, 1757, and received as good an education as was common for the sons of wealthy men at that day. When he was quite young he went to Kentucky and possessed himself of fertile lands in the Blue Grass region, many of which, to this day, belong to his descendants. In the last war with Great Britain he was a general, and commanded the Kentucky volunteers. He went to the relief of General Harrison, who, in 1813, was beseiged in Fort Meigs by Generals Proctor and Tecumseh, with a combined force of British regulars and Indians. Instead of forcing his way through the besieging force, at great loss, he hastily built flat boats above, on the river Raisin, with high side planks, which were bullet proof, and thus dropping down the river, he scarcely lost a man. (*Memoirs of Cassius M. Clay.*) General Harrison, the day after the siege, left General Clay in command of all the department forts, showing the confidence placed in his courage and ability.

General Clay was of commanding person, and wonderfully like his older brother, Matthew (who has been spoken of already), judging from family portraits. He married a Miss Sallie Lewis, and died October 31, 1826.

His daughter, Mrs. Elizabeth Clay Smith, has recently died (October, 1887,) at Richmond, Ky., aged ninety-nine years.

Their children living are (1) Matthew Clay, an energetic young planter of Noxubee county, Mississippi, who married Hattie P. Casey, of Virginia. They have several children. Bettie Clay has inherited her mother's gifts, physical and mental (and deserves more than a passing notice). Some years ago her father, like many other Southern planters, became embarrassed in circumstances, and she formed the purpose of supporting herself by teaching music. By uncommon assiduity, she became proficient in that science; and is a teacher of music in the State Female Institute at Columbus, Mississippi, with a large salary. All honor to her, and the Southern women who have become self-supporting teachers; for since the war they have conquered back the territory which the men lost. Formerly, not a teacher could be found in our schools who was not from the North. If they were old and *ugly* they were *noting everything against our people, ready for publication when they got home*. But if young and good looking, they gave us no trouble on that score, for they soon became as fond of the help of the dusky-waiting maids as the Southern girls. In the soft clime of the orange and magnolia, they bloomed out and became fairer; and some of our dames said maliciously, their manners were much improved. However this was, one thing is certain; they were death on old widowers—especially if they had large plantations. Thanks to the energy and independence of our Southern girls, this foreign invasion of Southern women's rights has ceased. (3) Harrison Clay, and (4) Thomas Clay, both young men of much promise; (5) Charles, if he takes his departure (as the surveyors say) in the right direction, will do well; but he is a mere boy, and there is no telling anything about it yet. (6) Nina is a young child. I have never seen her.

Brutus J. Clay

was the son of General Clay. He was perhaps the most successful farmer in the Blue Grass region of Kentucky, and was, for many years, president of the State Agricultural

Society. He died three years ago. His sons, Christopher, Green. Esekiel, Field and Cassius M. Clay, and one daughter, Martha Davenport, are all alive. Green Clay was secretary of legation to his uncle, Cassius M. Clay, when he was minister at the court of St. Petersburg. He lived for awhile in Bolivar county, Mississippi, and removed to Missouri. He is a man of strong intellect and polished manners. His brother, Cassius M., is State Senator.

Cassius M. Clay,

the younger brother of Brutus J. Clay, and son of Gen. Green Clay, was born in Kentucky, October 19, 1810. He finished his education at Yale College, and under the influence of that region and the teachings of W. Loyd Garrison, he came home much opposed to the institution of slavery. He thinks he was so when he left Kentucky. His career has been a remarkable one, and has been interwoven with the history of our country during the stormiest period of its existence. In giving a mere newspaper sketch of him we feel embarrassed by superabundance of material. We shall. therefore, give a general outline of his public life, and then illustrate his motives by extracts from his " *Memoirs*," the first volume of which appeared a few months since (1887).

In these memoirs he handles all subjects and personages, dead or alive, with a fearlessness that will sometimes make you cringe. He holds that the maxim " *De mortuis nisi bonum* " is a false one, and truth, in all cases, should be spoken. And he dashes off crayon sketches of a great number of the public characters who have, for the last fifty years, played their parts on the stage, with a freedom unequalled by any writer since Columbus discovered America. His work is very similar, in some respects, to '' The Letters of Horace Walpole," and will last as long.

In 1835 and 1837 he was member of the Kentucky Legislature, when his views against slavery began to develope, and where he had to meet the most violent opposition. He made emancipation speeches all over Kentucky; and wherever the threats were loudest he would go first, and maintain his right to address the people with pistol and bowie knife. He became the most odious living man to the South, and finally sided with the Republicans in carrying on the war against the South. Perhaps he had more influence in prevailing on President Lincoln to issue the Emancipation Proclamation than any other man. He was sent as Minister to the Court of Russia, and it was a most fortunate selection for the Federals. The Czar against the will of his Nobles, had emancipated twenty-three millions of serfs, and Clay, fresh from his conflicts in favor of emancipation in the United States, was received with open arms; and his speeches and newspaper accounts of his bloody personal conflicts, were translated into Russian, and circulated all over that country. The Russian Bear gave him a warm hug of friendship, and his ministers at every court in Europe announced that formidable power as the friend of the government at Washington. France and Great Britian wavered with regard to the blockade, but the attitude of Russia deterred them from interference. Every well informed man knows that it was the "blockade" which conquered the South. When Mr. Clay returned from Russia, the Republican party "had put every enemy under its feet," and, under the guise of Reconstruction, was tyranizing over the Southern States. He, then, fearlessly espoused the cause of the down-trodden South, and showed the same zeal for the Democratic party he had done on the other side, with no prospect before him of political advancement. Here he was carrying out in practice what he announced before, that "no honest man who was guided by *principle* could remain for any length of time, a member of a *party*."

I will now give you some quotations from his memoirs, and first, to show you the nature of some of his personal conflicts. In a canvass with Robert Wickliffe, Jr., he says, "I challenged him. Colonel Wm. R. McKee, who fell at Buena Vista, was my second, and Albert Sidney Johnston, who fell at Shiloh (when Grant had retired for security to his gunboats, and the Union cause was saved by Buell and Nelson) was Wickliffe's. We fired at ten paces, at the word, and both missed. Raising my pistol, perpendicularly, I demanded a second fire, but the good sense of our seconds prevailed."

He says on another page, "Grant's whole political and civil career, ending in the unfortunate affair on Wall street, only needed his account of the battle of Shiloh, as told by himself, to convice the world that my estimate of him was true to life. It was a misnomer of the highest type to call Grant's army at Pittsburg Landing "an army." It seems that he knew not where Johnston or his forces were, or at least where he was himself. And the farce was about to be completed, had not Albert Sidney Johnston, the greatest of Confederate generals, been killed in battle."

Again in the canvass between Wickliffe and Garret Davis, Mr. Clay was the active friend of Davis, and when a personal conflict seemed inevitable, the Wickliffe party sent for Samuel W. Brown, the traveling agent under Charles Wickliffe, Postmaster General. He was a political bully, and, by pre-concert, brought on the fight. "Brown gave me the 'damned lie,' and, at the same time, struck me with his umbrella. I knew the man, and that it meant a death struggle. I drew my Bowie knife, but before I could use it, I was seized from behind and borne some fifteen feet from Brown, who being now armed with a Colt's revolver, cried out, 'clear the way! and let me kill the damned rascal.' The way was soon cleared, and I stood isolated from the crowd. Now as Brown had his pistol bearing upon me, I had to run or advance. So turning my left side toward him, and with my left arm protecting it to that extent, I advanced rapidly upon him, knife in hand. He saw that I was coming, and knew very well that nothing could save him but a fatal and sudden shot held his fire and taking deliberate aim, just as I was in arm's length he fired at my heart. I came down upon his head with a tremendous blow, which would have split open an ordinary skull, but Brown's was as thick as that of an African. This blow laid his skull open about three inches to the brain, indenting it but not breaking the tissues; but it stunned him so that he was no more able to fire. * * * Brown had one ear nearly cut off, his nose split, one eye cut out, and many other wounds. I was indicted and Henry Clay was my counsel. Brown was put on the witness stand, and admitted that he had entered into a conspiracy with four others, and was to bring on the attack—and I was acquitted. Of all the men I ever encountered in mortal combat, Brown was the bravest."

In a canvass for the convention in 1849, after a discussion of the slavery question, with a lawyer named Turner, "as I stepped down from the table on which I stood, Cyrus Turner, his son, gave me the lie, and struck me. I was immediately surrounded by about twenty of the conspirators, my arms seized and my knife wrested from me. I was struck with sticks and finally stabbed in the right side, just above the lower rib, the knife entering my lungs and cutting apart my breastbone, which has not united to this day. Seeing that I was to be murdered I seized my Bowie knife, catching it by the handle and the blade, cutting two of my fingers to the bone, I wrested it from my opponent and held it firmly for use. The blood now gushed violently from my side, and I felt the utmost indignation. I flourished my knife, clearing the crowd nearest me, and looked out for Turner, determined to kill him. The way was opened; and I advanced upon him and thrust the knife into his abdomen, which meant death. At this time my eldest son procured a pistol and handed it to me. It was too late. I was borne to my bed in the hotel by my friends. Turner was also taken into another room. He died and I lived. Before his death I proposed a reconciliation. This he accepted, and returned me a friendly answer of forgiveness."

Cassius M. Clay after a long and stormy life of 77 years is still living, and is in possession of his faculties of mind and body.

He married a Miss Warfield, but the marriage was an unhappy one, and they have separated. Of their sons, Brutus Junius is the only one alive. He married Patti Field, and has four children: Buell Lyman Clay, Field Clay, Orville Clay, and Mary B. Clay. Green Clay, the eldest, married Cornelia Walker. He was a major in the Federal army, was aide to General Nelson in the battle of Richmond, and carried him, when wounded, through the lines to Jessamine county. Green Clay died in 1883. Of their living daughters, Mary B. Clay is a widow with three sons, Green, Clay, and Frank. Mrs. Sallie Lewis Burnett has four children. Laura Clay, another daughter of Cassius M. Clay, is single, and Ann Crenshaw, of Richmond, Va., still living.

Henry Clay of Kentucky,

the orator, the criminal advocate, the diplomat and statesman! So much has been written of him as a public man, that in this short article I shall mainly confine my remarks to incidents which will illustrate his character, in private life.

He was born 15th of April, 1777, in Hanover county, Virginia. His father was John Clay, a Baptist preacher. His family united with the Clays of America, in Henry (marked number four in the family chart), so says General Green Clay, in his record, and the Huntsville Clays, on their family tree. But there is a difference, for General Clay makes Henry Clay of Kentucky the great grandson of Henry numbered four, and the latter the grandson. I am not able to reconcile the two opinions.

When young Henry was only five years old, his father, who was of slender means, died, leaving him, with a large family of brothers and sisters, to the care of an excellent mother. The only education he had was obtained in a country school. At the age of fourteen he was put as a clerk in a retail store, in the city of Richmond. The next year he obtained a subordinate place in the Clerk's office, where the bright-eyed boy was fortunate to attract the attention of Chancellor Wythe, one of the signers of the Declaration of Independence, and he became his patron.

When qualified for practice as a lawyer, he was desirous of going to the West. His outfit for this purpose was kindly furnished to him by his relation, Matthew Clay, of Virginia. Clay, of Kentucky, never forgot this favor. More than forty years had passed away, and he had filled every great office in the nation except the presidency, when at Nashville, he was introduced, by Joseph Clay, to Thomas Clay, a mere youth. He inquired eagerly who he was, and when he learned that he was the grandson of Matthew Clay, of Virginia, he said with deep feeling: "I do not know what condition the young man is in, but as long as I have a dollar, I am willing to divide it with him, for his grandfather was the first man who ever did me a great favor."

In North Carolina, when in 1844 Henry Clay was making a tour of the United States, he was, in some town, received by the ladies in the parlor of the hotel; and when presented to them he was kissing some of the young "buds," when a lady who was a leader in society, playfully said to him, "Mr. Clay, I understand you kiss none but the pretty women." A shadow passed over his face, and with deep feeling he replied, "You are mistaken Madam! for the sweetest kiss I ever had, was from the ugliest woman I ever saw." The ladies crowded around him, and in his own inimitable way, he told the story of which I can only give you the outlines. How that when he first went to Kentucky, young, poor, and a stranger, he boarded with an aged widow lady, who became a friend (indeed, a mother) to him, when he needed one. How that this widow had a son, who was generous hearted, but somewhat dissipated; and who had the misfortune to kill a man in a sudden broil. How that it fell to his lot to defend the young man against the charge of murder. "Ladies (said he) my feelings were deeply moved by my sympathy for the mother, and friendship for the young man. If ever I made a great speech, it was on that case. The jury were gone but a short time, when they returned with a verdict of 'not guilty.' She was sitting behind the box, by the side of her son. When I turned I saw by the expression on her face, that she did not understand what had occurred, and I said to her plainly, "your son is cleared, and you can take him home with you." She caught me by both arms, drew me down and kissed me, with the tears of gratitude streaming down her face; and so it happened that the sweetest kiss I ever had was from the ugliest woman I ever saw." These incidents show that Mr. Clay had a warm, grateful and sympathetic heart. No wonder that when he went to the Bank to pay one of his notes (when he had a heavy load of debt upon him) and was told by the cashier that all his notes had been paid by his friends, unable to control the emotions of his grateful soul, he bursted into tears, in the midst of a crowd.

So great has been the fame of Mr. Clay as a statesman, that the fact has been overlooked, that in early life he was a great criminal advocate. The Hon. Cassius M. Clay, in his "*Memoirs*" says that he never lost a case. That generally he stood as near his audience as possible, especially if it was a jury. That he generally stood still, gesticulating with one or both hands; and when in the most intense force, advancing a few steps only. His great rival in early life was Felix Grundy, who moved to Tennessee; and although opposed in politics they always admired and respected each other. On one occasion Mr. Clay making a speech in Tennessee, inquired where his friend Mr. Grundy was. The answer was that he was absent making speeches for Mr. VanBuren. "Ah! ah! (says Mr. Clay payfully) still at his old tricks of defending criminals." The first time Mr. Grundy spoke after hearing of this witticism of Mr. Clay was at Murfreesboro, when he replied in the same vein, that if he were employed to defend Mr. Clay from his political sins, he feared it would be a second Bennett case. This was the first criminal out of 165 that Mr. Grundy lost. The people of Murfreesboro understood the allusion very well; for Bennett was a farmer in that vicinity, and the only rich man I ever knew to be hung.

As a popular speaker he has never been surpassed. Judge Guild (*The Old Times of Tennessee*) tells of a speech he made in Hopkinsville, Ky., in 1825. "He began his address with pleasing reminiscences of a former visit to that part of the State; the tone of his voice was soft and gentle, his language smooth and flowing, his manner graceful and elegant, his countenance radiant with smiles, charming and facinating every beholder, in that vast audience. After having completely mesmerized his hearers, taking captive all their feelings and sympathies, he launched out in defense of himself against the charge of bargain, intrigue and corruption. His clarion voice rang out like the notes of a war trumpet; his vehemence resembled a storm rushing through the forest, prostrating everything in its path. Mr. Clay had the rare gift of infusing his own feelings, emotions and passions into his hearers; he swayed them at his will; a popular audience was absorbed by his magnetism, and borne along with him as if they had been a part of himself." * * * "We Tennesseeans forgot all about Old Hickory, whilst under the magic influence of Mr. Clay's speaking, and did not recover our judgments for some time after our return home."

It is not generally known that Mr. Clay was offered by President Madison the leadership of our arms in the war of 1812, which he declined. Mr. Cassius Clay thinks he and General Jackson were wonderfully alike, in boldness and independence; and that the Kentuckian would have won glory in the military line.

And now I come to speak of the crowning quality of Mr. Clay's character, and that was his love of country, and before I close I will give two proofs of it. The Missouri question had become a very serious matter, so much so, that excitable Southern men like John Randolph, and philosophical men like Mr. Crawford, alike declared for a separation. The sage of Monticello was roused in retirement by the news from Washington, and declared that "it startled him like the sound of a fire bell in the dead hour of the night." In this crisis Mr. Clay was forgetful of himself, and boldly came to the rescue by the introduction of the Missouri Compromise Bill. When he made his able speech on the measure "there was oil on the waters, and turbulent waves went down." Colonel Sparks in his "*Memoirs of Fifty Years*" gives a glowing account of it. The conclusion was in these words: "In the measure there is security; there is peace and fraternal union. Thus we may say, we shall cover this entire continent with prosperous States, and a contented, self-governed, and happy people. To their unrestrained energies, the mountains shall yield their mineral tribute, the valleys their cereals and fruits, and a million of millions of contented and happy people, shall demonstrate to an admiring world, the great problem, that man is capable of self-government."

The second great proof of Mr. Clay's patriotism occurred when nullification threatened the peace of the country. South Carolina, "solitary and alone," had in a convention passed the ordinance and fixed an early day when all collections of revenue by the United States was to cease, and was levying troops and collecting munitions of war, and in fact had given herself "no place of repentance." On the other hand President Jackson had declared "By the Eternal! the Union shall not be dissolved," and issued his famous proclamation. A collision now seemed inevitable when Mr. Clay offered his compromise bill of 1833, which provided for the gradual reduction of duties down to the revenue standard, and a provision that after that time "duties should only be laid for raising such revenue as might be necessary for an economical administration of the Government." This was a complete surrender of his protective system on which he had staked all the hopes he had of political preferment. He had laid all these upon the altar of his country. He had not even consulted Mr. Webster, who was the main pillar in upholding protection—(Mr. Benton in his "*Thirty Years in the Senate*") Fortunately from either party patriotic men came to the support of Mr. Clay's Bill, and the frame-work of the Government was saved for a second time from a test of its capacity to sustain a conflict of arms.

The great pacificator died in 1852, and it was perhaps fortunate for his peace of mind that he did not live to witness the secession of 1861. Doubtless he would have made a third attempt to have prevented it, which would have been fruitless.

As to Mr. Clay's descendants, I find the following statement in a late St. Louis *Republican:* "The recent death of John Clay removes the last member of the immediate family of the illustrious statesman, Henry Clay. The eldest son died in the Lunatic Asylum, near Lexington, where he had been confined for many years. The next eldest, Henry Clay, Jr., a bright and promising young man, was killed in battle during the Mexican war. He was a friend and comrade of the sprightly and gallant O'Hara, whose poem, "The Bivouac of the Dead," is so familiar to American readers. Another son, James B. Clay, at one time owned a large stock farm on the Bellefontaine road, near St. Louis. but removed back to Lexington on the death of his father, and was sent to Congress from the Ashland district.

The Clays of Huntsville, Ala.,

were united to the line of the Clays of whom I have written; in Charles Clay. who is numbered 3 in the Family Chart, but for the sake of clearness I will give the descent from the common ancestor.

1. John Clay.

2. John Clay, his son.

3. Charles Clay, the son of John the second. His eldest son, Henry, was the ancestor of the families of Henry Clay, of Kentucky, and Matthew and Green Clay, of Virginia, but a younger son.

4. James Clay was the ancestor of the Clays, of Huntsville. Their family tree lies before me. He married Margaret Muse, and died about 1790.

5. William Clay, the son of James, was born 11th August, 1760. He was, young as he was, a soldier of the Revolution. He married Rebecca Comer in 1787. Her mother was a Claiborne. He removed his family from Virginia to Granger county, East Tennessee, about 1800; and died 5th August, 1841.

6. Hon. Clement Comer Clay, who was Supreme Court Judge, Congressman, Senator, and Governor, was born in Halifax county, Va., on the 17 of December, 1789. His early education was directed by Mr. Muse, a relation, who was very stern, and his recollection of him had more of fear than love in it. He was a small boy when his father removed to East Tennessee. His education was completed at the University of East Tennessee at Knoxville. He studied law under the Hon. Hugh L. White, of that city. He was licensed to practice in December, 1809, and in 1811 he settled in Huntsville, Ala., about the time its name was changed from Twickenham. The town was then small, for the population of the whole county of Madison was only 4000 people. Here he had his home for fifty-five years, one of the most useful and honored citizens.

Soon after he settled here he had a difficulty with Dr. Waddy Tate, which resulted in a duel, in which both parties were wounded.

In 1813, when the Creek war broke out, he enlisted as a private in a battalion of volunteers, raised in Madison county, of which he became adjutant. On reporting to General Jackson, he kept the battalion on the south bank of the Tennessee river, to secure his communications with the State of Tennessee, for Madison was surrounded then on all sides but the north, by Indians, who, thus far, had continued friendly.

In 1815 Mr. Clay married Susannah Claiborne Withers, daughter of Mr. John

Withers, and sister of General Jones M. Withers; a woman of brilliant family, good person, and strong mind, who lived with her husband most affectionately for fifty years, and assisted him in rearing one of the best educated families in North Alabama (see *Withers family*).

He was elected a member of the Territorial Legislature in 1817, and also in 1818. He was also a member of the convention which formed the State Constitution in 1819.

He was afterward elected judge of the Fifth Judicial District, and, as the Supreme Court was then held by the circuit judes, as soon as they met they elected him chief justice of the court, although he was the youngest man in the body. In this position he remained for four years, with great satisfaction to the members of the legal profession and the public, until 1823, when he resigned his judgeship with a view of devoting himself to his profession.

Then closely and successfully did he devote himself to his profession for several years. Of imposing person, about medium stature, with dark hazel eyes, bright and restless, an earnest manner, a good voice, a very distinct enunciation, with a style which had more of logic than ornament, with a self-reliance which sustained him under all difficulties, he would have been distinguished at any bar in the State. But he had more than all these. He had been for years on the circuit and supreme bench, and had assisted in making the laws of the State from the very first germ; was familiar with their construction, and was always thoroughly prepared in his cases. This gave him great prestige, and he was employed in the most important cases, with the ablest lawyers in North Alabama.

In 1827 he ran for Congress against the Hon. Gabriel Moore, who was the incumbent. Both had settled in Huntsville about the same time. They had been together in the Territorial Legislature, and in the Convention which framed the Constitution of the State. When Moore went to Congress, Clay went on the bench, and a few years later they contested for the seat in Congress. They were both men of ability, but their methods were entirely different. Clay was bold and independent, and based his claims on substantial grounds; but Moore was a skilful electioneerer, and courted the lower stratum of society. I was a young lawyer in Moulton when they had their first meeting in Lawrence, at Oakville. Moore was early on the ground, and treating the boys in the groceries. When asked what sort of a man his opponent was, he would answer that he was a smart man, but very proud. "Now," says he, "when he comes you will not see him keeping company with the poor people, but you will find him with the rich ones, and he will be very apt to go home with Col. Nich. Johnson." When Clay came upon the ground with his dignified, erect carriage, he had a very cold reception from the crowd, but was welcomed by the rich planters, and actually went home (as Moore predicted), with that noble old gentleman, Colonel Johnson. By such arts as these Judge Clay was defeated.

United States Land Sales.

This canvass however, made Judge Clay much better known, as a man of ability, to the people of this section of the State, and they looked to him for help in an emergency which occurred in 1828. As all know the lands in the Tennessee valley were sold by the United States, on credit (payable by installments) at enormous prices, for cotton was very high also. But the staple fell, and the purchasers found themselves unable to make the payments on them. Relying, however, upon the Government for relief, the planters continued to clear, fence and improve them. Congress, under the influence of our able senators, Walker and King, passed an act permitting the purchasers to relinquish to the Government a portion of their purchase, and to transfer the amount paid on that part, so as to make complete payment on the part retained. This was some measure of relief, but our members in Congress obtained a cession of 400,000 acres of this relinquished land to the State of Alabama, for the purpose of constructing a canal around the Muscle Shoals. This was done with the belief that the men who were the original purchasers, and had cleared and improved them, would certainly be given a pre-emption of them, at their assessed value. But it was not long before it was claimed that the land should after being valued, be divided, and drawn for by the people at large. So you see there were prototypes of Henry George in the land at that early day. The planters became very uneasy, and brought out their best men for the next session of the Legislature. Madison, amongst others, sent Judge Clay. To show the high appreciation of his abilities by the people of the State, he was elected Speaker of the House without opposition.

The question of the relinquished land was the prominent one of the session. The danger had not been exaggerated. The Communists mustered in force, and all that the friends of the planters, led by Judge Clay, could obtain, was a pre-emption of two quarter sections of improved land. This, however, relieved all except the largest planters, and was a great boon to the people generally.

In 1829 Judge Clay was elected to Congress over Col. Nicholas Davis, by a majority of 10,000 votes. He was re-elected in 1831. and co-operated with the members from the South and West in procuring "land relief" for their people.

Judge Clay was re-elected again in 1833, and bore a part in a question (Nullification) which came near ending in a conflict of arms. We have given a general account of this matter on a previous page. Judge Clay was in favor of a revenue tariff, and *ad valorem* duties, disapproved of the course pursued by South Carolina in nullifying an act of Congress, but he was opposed to the "*Force Bill.*" The truth is, there never was such a bill; its opponents gave this name to the "*Revenue Collection Bill*" of General Jackson. It is difficult, at this day, when we calmly review the events of that crucial period, to understand how one opposed to Nullification could consistently oppose the Revenue Collection Bill. Its solution will be found in the fact that the Southern members had a great repugnancy to drive South Carolina to the wall, and believed in the words of Mr. Tyler: "That we can never be too tardy in commencing the work of blood." The country was relieved from this awful perplexity by the introduction by Henry Clay of his Compromise Bill of which we have given an account.

Judge Clay was elected Governor in 1836 by the largest majority ever given to any one man before. It was during his administration that the "Creek Indian Troubles" occurred. Governor Clay with great promptitude issued an order to Major General Patterson, to bring down a force from North Alabama, hasten to the seat of war, and take command of all the troops. He ordered Brigadier General Moore, of the Mobile Division, to send troops to Eufaula and made requisition on the Commandant at Mt. Vernon for arms, ammunition and tents, and went immediately to Montgomery, where he established his headquarters. Knowing that the Hon. John A. Campbell had acted as the Aide-de-Camp of Governor Clay during the campaign, I asked him for an account of it. From his answer, which is very interesting, but too long for insertion here, I will make a sufficient number of extracts, to show the true history of the case. The Judge says "My first connection with the world of politics was in connection with your inquiries about the Creek war. The Indian Territory lay adjoining to Montgomery, the place of my residence then. The trouble came from the intrusion of the whites, upon the Indians. The treaty of 1832 provided for a reservation of land to every Indian who was of age, or the head of a family, with a right to the Indian to sell his land, under the supervision of a Government agent. Judge Campbell then details the mode by which the speculators "stole the land" of the Indians, by getting another Indian to falsely impersonate the real owner before the agent. He says: "Col. J. B. Hogan was appointed to examine into this matter and found it to be true, shockingly true. Men of respectable standing were incriminated, but none doubted the truth of his report. The Indians, thus cheated, were expelled from their lands. The privations, poverty and persecutions of intruders and squatters drove the Indians to despair. They were famished and miserable, and so became pillagers and thieves—they burned houses—robbed the mails—and became disorderly, unruly and injurious."

Judge Campbell had the confidence of the Creek Chiefs, for, ten years before, his father had treated with them as U. S. Commissioner; and Duncan C. Campbell had impressed them (as he did everybody) with the idea of his ability and probity. The mantle of the father had fallen upon his son. In 1835, Opothela-yo-ho-la had sent his son to Montgomery for him; and he remained in the Nation three weeks, trying to adjust the difficulties between the Indians and whites.

When Governor Clay established his headquarters at Montgomery, he made Judge Campbell a member of his staff by special order, and arranged for an Indian Council of a dozen chiefs at Montgomery. Here the principal chief, Opothela yo-ho-la, "with great energy described the wrongs of his tribe, and said they were in despair—that the tribe was friendly, and wanted no war—and that he would join his men with ours to put down the war." In this wise step Governor Clay laid the foundation for the peace with the hostiles, which was afterward secured.

General Jessup arrived and took command of all the State troops, and the Governor returned to his regular duties. Before doing so, he transferred Judge Campbell to the staff of Major General Patterson, as his Adjutant General. Judge Campbell says that "in all these operations, Governor Clay was courageous, intelligent, considerate, and (although sick with fever) entirely competent to every duty.

General Jessup promptly faced the hostile Indians, who were in Barbour and Russell counties; along two streams swollen by rains, and difficult of passage. The general was here joined by Opothela-yo-ho-la with 1600 friendly Indians; thus proving the sincerity of his promises to Governor Clay.

Judge Campbell says that " the same night Opothela-yo-ho-la, Captain Walker, an Indian countryman, Barent Dubose, the son-in-law of Thelucoo the big warrior, with others, white and red, crossed the stream, and interviewed the hostiles; and promised that if they would come to us quietly, where a warrior had an old gun, a new one should be given him, and that calico dresses should be furnished the squaws, etc. The next day I was deputied to receive them. They were led by the Blind King, riding on a pony. Shrivelled and blind, I enquired of him his age. His answer was four generations of persons had been born, grown up and died, and he was here yet. In the arms of some of the squaws were picaninnies who had been born the day before. The war was ended. General Jessup was amazed to find when we reported to him, that all questions were settled."

The great white chief, General Scott, had been all the time, listening, with his ear to the ground, for the sound of cannon, and becoming impatient, he sent a peremptory order to General Jessup to report to him in person, at Columbus, at once. General Jessup was much enraged at the order. He had, however, before that time, arranged the troubles with the fraudulent purchasers from the Indians, and the titles to these lands now repose on that settlement. The speculators made great efforts in Congress to have it cancelled, but J. Q. Adams read it, and said that if there ever was an honest contract, that was one, and that put down all opposition."

Thus by the wisdom of Governor Clay, and the tact of his Adjutant General, young John A. Campbell, a formidable Indian insurrection was quelled without bloodshed, followed by the removal of the Indians to the West.

In June, 1837, Governor Clay was elected to the Senate of the United States, without opposition. He took his seat at the session of Congress in September, called to provide some remedy for the failure of the State banks, in which the public money had been deposited. It would, no doubt, have been restored to the United States Bank again, but that idol of the Whigs, like Dagon of old, had fallen on its face—and its assets were in the hands of a receiver. In this emergency, President Van Buren recommended the Sub-treasury plan. This passed the Senate at the same session, but, although founded on the simple principle "that the government should collect its own money, keep its own money, and disburse its own money," it did not become a law until 1840. Senator Clay supported this measure, and Democratic measures generally, whilst he was in Congress. One occurrence gave him great pain, and it was his friend and preceptor Hugh L. White abandoning the Democratic party. Senator Clay, however, promptly, but reluctantly, parted company with him, knowing that a public man who joins a party with whom he has no community of principle, is shorn of influence and dignity.

Senator Clay remained in the Senate until the termination of the called session of 1841, when he resigned his seat on account of the health of his family.

After this he was appointed to make a new digest of the laws of Alabama, which was reported to the General Assembly in 1842. He sat, by special appointment, to fill a vacancy on the bench of the Supreme Court in 1843—and again was elected one of the commissioners to wind up the affairs of the State banks, and then he retired to his home in Huntsville to enjoy that quiet which he so well merited after a long life of arduous and faithful public service.

But this enjoyment was denied him. " North Alabama was invaded by Federal troops; his home was seized and himself put under military arrest. Indignities were *heaped* upon this venerable public servant and Christian gentleman." (*Garrett's Public Men of Alabama.*)

Sherman's Infamous Order.

It transpired that the atrocities committed at Huntsville were prompted by Maj.-Gen. W. T. Sherman. His order as to the treatment of the people was first published in the Nashville Times, and a copy of it will be found in Mr. Garrett's book, page 486. Too long for insertion here, I will make a few extracts to show the import of the document: "In Europe the law of war was and is that wars are confined to the armies and should not visit the homes of families or private interests. * * * But that which prevails in our land is essentially a war of races. * * * The people of the South have appealed to war and must abide by its rules and laws. The United States as a belligerent party, claiming right in the soil as the ultimate sovereign, have a right to change the population, and it may be, and is both politic and best, that we should do so in certain districts. The United States have, in North Alabama, all the rights which they choose to enforce in war—to take their lives, their homes, their lands, their everything, because they can not deny that war exists here, and war is simply power unrestrained by constitution or compact. I know thousands of people who, at simple notice, would come to North Alabama and accept of the elegant houses and plantations there. * * * To those who submit to the rightful law, and authority all gentleness and forbearance, but to the petulant and persistent, secessionists why death is mercy, and the quicker he or *she* is disposed of the better. Satan and the rebellious spirits of heaven were allowed a continuance of existence in heaven merely to swell their just punishment in hell."

This military order is unequalled for its ferocity, even if you go back a thousand years for a precedent. *It affords strong corroborative proof that he was the incendiary who burned the capital city of South Carolina.* I judge that the warm-hearted gentlemen of Louisiana, who, before the war, nursed this frozen viper into life, were amazed at his venomous hissing.

That southern lands would be confiscated is plainly foreshadowed in the above military order. Then, when the South was finally subdued, why was it not done? I will tell you. It was owing to a proviso in the Constitution of the United States, not as wide as my finger, which provided that " no *attainder of treason shall work corruption of blood, or forfeiture, except during the life of the person attainted.*" But the lands could have been forfeited during the life of the owner? Yes! but that kind of a title might not have been a very peaceable one for a discharged Federal soldier. The wisdom of the framers of the Federal Constitution, appears in this proviso. In the history of England, for several generations, they say that civil wars had been carried on, mainly for the possession of lands and cattles; and they purposed that in any conflict of the kind in this country, avarice should not be added to the rancor which characterises such wars.

What must have been the sad feelings of Governor Clay, on perusing this manifesto, setting forth doctrines and ideas repugnant to humanity, to be enforced by the bayonet, may be imagined, but cannot be expressed. No wonder that his strong spirit and his feeble body, bent by age, could not survive the shock of subjugation!" He had no sanctuary but that of religion, in which to take refuge from the storm, and that sheltered him in his last moments. Governor Clay died on September 7, 1886 (*Garrett.*)

The encomiums bestowed on him by this historian were well merited. I knew him well for forty years of his life. Alabama never had a more efficient or more faithful public servant. He never pandered to the prejudices of the ignorant. The promotion to the many high offices which he held was honestly earned by the ability, and integrity, and energy which he devoted to the performance of every trust committed to him. As he was without fear in his public career, so he was without reproach in his private life. A half century ago a large portion of the members of the bar were dissipated (there has been a great change since then in this respect), but Governor Clay had the moral courage to erect a high standard of deportment for himself. He was a gentleman, not only in his dress and manners, but of scrupulous honor in his dealings with all the world. He was an affectionate and courtly husband to a refined, beautiful and excellent wife, who departed this life a few months before him. As a father, as many and onerous as were his public duties, he found time for the training of his children. According to my observation, as a rule, the sons of men of distinction have been failures, but Huntsville has the honor of producing two exceptions—the Clays and the Walkers.

Hon. Clement Claiborne Clay.

the eldest son of the Hon. Clement Comer Clay, was a statesman, and had attained a national reputation while yet a young man. He was born in Huntsville, December, 1817, and graduated at the University of Alabama, taking the degree of Master of Arts. He studied law at the University of Virginia, and was licensed to practice in 1840. He soon showed a proclivity for politics, I suppose from the influence of his father, who had obtained so many honors in this department of life.

In 1842 he was elected to the House of Representatives of the General Assembly. He was then only twenty-five years of age, and his colleagues, some of them, were old members, and able ones; but he seems at once to have been admitted, by common consent, to the ranks of influential members. I happened to be at the seat of government for some days during the session, and was struck by his extensive learning, his readiness in debate, as if he had been for years in the harness; his chaste and classic style, and more than all, the maturity of his intellect. He must have been a great student in his youth. He introduced the resolution instructing our members in Congress to vote for the bill to refund to General Jackson the amount of the fine inflicted upon him by Judge Hall, in New Orleans, in 1815, and made a speech which was by a competent judge pronounced "a brilliant effort in style and execution."

Mr. Garrett speaks of Mr. Clay's marriage very felicitously. "An event in the life of Mr. Clay took place at this session, which may be mentioned as contributing much to his future happiness; and no doubt to his great popularity and success. In February, 1843, his marriage with Miss Virginia Tunstall was celebrated by a wedding party, and by preparations at the residence of Chief Justice Collier, in Tuscaloosa, which had never been equalled on any similar occasion in that city. The Rev. Thomas H. Capers officiated in the nuptial ceremony. Most of the members of the Legislature and many citizens were invited guests. The bride was a daughter of Dr. Peyton Tunstall, formerly of Virginia, and a near relative of Mrs. Collier. At another point of this narrative I shall refer again to the *bride* as a moral heroine after she had been more than twenty years a *wife*." (*Public Men of Alabama*). Another historian speaks of her as "a lady of fascinating attributes of mind, and elevated qualities of heart. While her husband was in Washington, Mrs. Clay was one of the brightest ornaments of society." (*Brewer's Alabama*.) Mrs. Clay gave early promise of her success in society, for she had beauty, a quick perception, tact, great kindness of disposition, was entirely unaffected, and I observed that she was not only a fine conversationalist, but an *eloquent listener*, which is rather uncommon with the female sex!

Mr. Clay was re-elected to the General Assembly both in 1844 and 1845, and was then elected Judge of the County Court of Madison county. Judge Clay gave great satisfaction in his office to the bar and to the people; but after two years he resigned and retired to the practice of law.

In 1853 he became a candidate for Congress against H. R. W. Cobb. Mr. Cobb was the incumbent, who was very popular with his constituents, especially the ignorant portion of them. He had been a clock-peddler and many believed he was a Yankee; but that was a mistake, for he was a native of Madison county, uneducated, but a man of uncommon shrewdness and very popular manners. In this canvass Judge Clay was beaten, but was elected by the General Assembly, during the ensuing year, Senator in the United States Congress, to succeed Hon. Jeremiah Clemens. Strange! that Mr. Clemens had been beaten by Mr. Cobb and elected Senator at the very next session. Verily! this man Cobb was a Warwick, except that he made *Senators* instead of *Kings!*

Senator Clay served in the Senate with ability for nine years, having been re-elected at the end of his first term without opposition. The questions during that time discussed in the Senate, although thought to be important then, have paled into insignificance compared to the one upon which he made his farewell speech to that body on the twelfth day of January, 1861, and that was the controversy between the North and the South.

It is the province of history, in recounting the acts of a public man, to set forth plainly the motives and counsels by which he, and those who acted with him, were guided. I can do this best by inserting here the body of Senator Clay's farewell speech, which was considered one of the ablest delivered on the momentous question. He said: "I rise to announce in behalf of my colleagues and myself, that the people of Alabama, assembled at their capitol, in convention, have withdrawn from the Union. In taking this momentous step, they have not acted hastily or unadvisedly. It is not the eruption of sudden, violent and spasmodic action. It is the conclusion they have reached after years of bitter experience, of enmity, injustice and injury, at the hands of their Northern brethren, after long and painful reflection, after anxious debate, and solemn deliberation, and after argument, persuasion and entreaty have failed to secure them their constitutional rights.

"It is now nearly forty-two years since Alabama was admitted into the Union. She entered it as she goes out of it, whilst it was in convulsions caused by the enmity of the North to the domestic slavery of the South. Not a decade, nor scarce a lustrum, has passed since her birth, that has not been strongly marked by the growth of this anti-slavery spirit of the Northern people, which seeks the overthrow of that domestic institution of the South, and had on the secession of Alabama, Mississippi, Florida and South Carolina, severed most of the Union. It denied us Christian communion because it could not endure what it styles the moral leprosy of slave holding; it refused us the permission to sojourn, or even to pass through, the North with our property; it proclaimed freedom for the slave if brought by his master into a Northern State; it violated the Constitution and treaties and laws of Congress designed to protect that property; it refused us any share of lands acquired by our diplomacy and blood and treasure; it refused our property any shelter or protection beneath the flag of a common government; it robbed us of our property and refused to restore it; it refused to deliver criminals against our laws who fled to the North with our property and blood upon their hands; it threatened us by solemn legislative acts with ignominious punishment if we pursued our property, and the thief, into a Northern State; it murdered Southern men when seeking recovery of their property on Northern soil; it invaded the borders of Southern States, burnt their dwellings and murdered their people; it had denounced us by resolves of popular meetings, of party conventions, of religious and legislative assemblies, as habitual violators of the laws of God and the rights of humanity; it had exerted all the moral and physical agencies that human ingenuity can devise, to make us a by-word of hissing and reproach throughout the civilized world; yet we bore these wrongs for many years under the assurance that these were the acts of a *minority* party; but the fallacy of these promises has been clearly shown. The platforms of the Republican party of 1856 and 1860 we regard as a declaration of war against the lives and property of the Southern people.

"To cap the climax of insult to our feelings and menace to our rights, this party nominated for the presidency a man who indorses their platform. A large majority of the Northern people have, at the ballot box, thus declared their approval of this platform, and the candidates selected thereon, and by their solemn verdict the people of the South have been outlawed, branded with ignominy, and consigned to execration and ultimate destruction.

" Have we no pride of honor, no sense of shame, no reverence for our ancestors, no regard for our posterity, no love of home, or family or friends? Must we confess our baseness, discredit the name of our sires, dishonor ourselves, degrade our posterity, abandon our homes, and flee from the country, all for the sake of the Union? Must we agree to live under the ban of such a government? Must we acquiesce in the inauguration of a president chosen by confederate but hostile States, whose political faith constrains him, for his conscience and country's sake, to deny us our constitutional rights, because elected under the forms of the Constitution? Must we consent to live under a government which we believe will henceforth be controlled and administered by those who not only deny us justice and equality and brand us as inferiors, but whose avowed principles and policy must destroy our domestic tranquility, imperil the lives of our wives and children, and degrade and dwarf, and ultimately destroy our State? Must we live, by choice or compulsion, under the rule of those who present us the dire alternative of an irrepressible conflict with the Northern people in defence of our altars and firesides, or the manumission of our slaves, and the admission of them to social and political equality? No, sir; no! The freemen of Alabama have proclaimed to the world that they will not, and have proved their sincerity, by seceding from the Union, and hazarding the dangers and difficulties of a separate and independent station amongst the nations of the earth."

When the Confederate government was organized he was elected a Senator to Congress and served until 1863, when he was superseded by Hon. R. W. Walker. In April, 1864, Mr. Clay (with another gentleman) went upon a secret and confidential mission to the British provinces, and did not return until January, 1865.

After President Lincoln was assassinated by that lunatic, Booth, President Johnson issued a proclamation offering a reward of one hundred thousand dollars for the apprehension of President Jefferson Davis, and twenty-five thousand dollars each for the arrest of Senator Clay and several other gentlemen on a charge of complicity in the murder. When Mr. Clay heard of the proclamation he was on his way to Texas, but he turned back and rode one hundred miles on horseback to deliver himself and meet the charge boldly. But though he demanded it, he was never brought to trial. In very feeble health he was imprisoned at Fortress Monroe. He was dying by inches. "After toils and buffetings which would have crushed a less heroic woman, and after interviews with the President and Secretary of War, Mrs. Clay succeeded, after months of imprisonment in a dark cell, which nearly cost him his life, in having her husband placed at the disposal of his angelic wife. The scene was morally grand. Romance can furnish nothing superior to it, in firmness, consistency and devotion." (Public men of Alabama.)

Scott, in his "Marmion" has immortalized the name of Tunstall, "the stainless knight, whose banner white" was seen all over Flodden Field, where he was slain. But knight of chivalry never performed a nobler emprise, than the Tunstall of America, who persevered in the face of obstacles that seemed insurmountable, until the husband to whom she had pledged the loyalty of her young heart was surrendered to her entreaties.

She carried him to their home at " Wildwood " in Alabama. Here he lingered a few years, before his death, in great debility. He attempted to write the life of the great Southern orator, William L. Yancey, (he wrote me) but he was not strong enough to finish it.

The two younger sons of Senator Clement Comer Clay are both well educated, and talented, but have not been in political life. John Withers Clay has conducted the "Huntsville Democrat" for forty years. Since he has been paralyzed it has been in the charge of his daughters Jennie and Sue; very competent journalists. John Withers married Mary Lewis, and his children are Willie, Mary, Sue, Withers, Jennie and Elodie. Hugh Lawson Clay, the youngest son of Senator Clement Comer Clay, is a lawyer of ability. and had a bright future until he was paralyzed. When I saw him during the war, he was on the staff of General E. Kirby Smith. He married Celeste Comer, and has no living children.

A number of families who settled in this county sixty-five years ago were descendants of the Fontaines and Maurys, who were driven from France by persecution; or Swiss Protestants, who came voluntarily to America. We will first notice

The DeGraffenried Family.

Judge C. B. Strong, of Georgia, who was distinguished as lawyer and judge for fifty years, was descended from this family, and collected with great pains, the history of their Swiss ancestors, and set it forth in " *The Bench and Bar of Georgia* " as follows:

" In the latter part of the seventeenth century, the English government invited the persecuted Protestant Palatines on the continent of Europe, to take refuge in their dominions. This induced them to emigrate to England in such numbers that they soon became burdensome as objects of charity. Queen Anne, in 1711, proposed to Emanuel de Graffenried, a wealthy and leading citizen of Switzerland, then on a visit to England, to colonize these Palatines in some of her American dominions, as he could speak most of the languages of Europe, and his wealth would justify the enterprise. The Baron agreed to the proposition. The Queen, by letters patent, conferred upon him and his heirs male, the right and title of a Baron of Great Britain; and they entered into a written agreement that when he should have settled a certain number of Palatines in the unappropriated territory lying in what is called North Carolina, the government should convey to him and his heirs, by grant, fifty miles square of such tract as he might select, lying in said province.

" The contract was fulfilled on both sides. His colony on the Neuse river, was the permanent beginning of the State of North Carolina; and the city of Newbern, founded by him, was the first town in the State, south of Albemarle Sound. He himself settled a plantation in the more civilized colony of Virginia, where he left his son Tscharnar (pronounced Tischainar); but he returned to Europe, and died there in 1735, leaving an estate in Europe valued at half a million. On the death of Baron de Graffenried, the government and the representative (abbaye) took charge of his estate—his only child being in America. By his will he conveyed his money and personalty to his son in America; together with all his American possessions. His castle and lands adjoining, near Berne, he conveyed for life to some one in Switzerland, in satisfaction of some indebtment, incurred in the removal of the Palatines; remainder to his son in America, and the heirs male of his body.

"The great wealth possessed by his son in America and afterward by his family, in connection with the discomforts and perils of a voyage across the Atlantic, and the unsettled state of Europe, prevented the heirs in America from either claiming or inquiring into their rights in Switzerland, until the French took possession of Berne in 1778, when they were informed that Bonaparte and the Directory had confiscated their property, or had robbed them as they did the citizens of Berne, when their officers sent off sixty wagon loads of specie and plate, plundered from the public and private treasuries of Berne. My investigations on the spot in 1839, enabled me to prove by the most authentic records, political and judicial, that the charge against Napoleon and the French, of having plundered the Orphan's Treasury, was untrue. The records and the testimony of the de Graffenried family in Berne, proved that when the French took possession of Berne, and commenced their plundering, the keeper of the Orphan's Treasury conspired with one Boligney, a French nobleman living in Berne, to rob the Orphan's Treasury. The plan was this: Boligney was to demand, at the head of an armed force, the key of the treasury, and threaten Graff, the treasurer, with instant military execution in case of refusal.

"After thus perpetrating the robbery, Boligney wrote to the heirs in America, that the French were robbers. This tale is the more likely to be believed, from the fact that a de Graffenried commanded that division of the Swiss army, which in a pitched battle routed the French under General Brune, covering the field with their dead and wounded, and taking from them great part of their artillery, only the day before Shauenburg defeated Erlach, and captured Berne.   After the restoration of the Swiss government they instituted a strict investigation touching the affair, and learning the truth, promptly commenced legal proceedings against Boligney and Graff.   The latter at once did justice on himself by suicide.   Boligney died soon after.   The suits prevailed against the heirs for sixteen years, when both estates proved insolvent, so that only one thousand dollars was obtained.

"The heirs of the first taker of the castle and real estate, contested the legality of the devise ; and after the government had litigated the question with them on behalf of the American heirs, for thirty years, the highest court of resort decided, that by the law of Switzerland, real estate could not be thus entailed—whereby the defendants gained their suit.   The castle, called Worb, six miles from Berne, is still in excellent perservation ; and was valued in 1735 at twenty thousand pounds sterling.   It was founded in the middle ages by a de Graffenried, one of the followers of Berchthold the Fifth.

"Such is the brief narrative of how the large estate left by Judge Strong's ancestor in Europe was purloined from his descendants in America.

   •   •   •   •   •   •   •   •   •

"In the beginning of this century the heirs of this vast estate in North Carolina employed Wm. Johnson, Esq., of Charleston (afterward one of the Judges of the Supreme Court of the United States) to investigate their title to this property, and if not barred to bring suit.   After looking into the whole affair he gave it as his opinion that the statute of limitations barred them.

"The baron borrowed money of one Pollock, of North Carolina, before leaving for Europe, to enable him to support his colonists, and gave him a mortgage upon his grant to secure payment; but dying, before returning to America, it had never been redeemed or foreclosed.   One of the descendants, George Pollock, Esq., was the wealthiest man in the South.   He owned several large estates in North Carolina, and worked 2000 slaves.   The town of Newbern, planted by the Baron de Graffenried, was his immediate residence."

Col. Wm. L. Saunders (my relative) who has been Secretary of State in North Carolina for many years, has been collecting material for the Colonial Records of the State, in Europe and America, and published the first volume last winter.   Nearly 200 pages of it are taken up with a history of his colony, written by the Baron de Graffenried, and deposited in the public library of Yverdon, Switzerland.   Here the manuscript had lain dormant for 150 years, until it was brought to light by the agent of Colonel Saunders.   This manuscript will correct several errors in the account set forth above, and will present a faint idea of the difficulties of settling a colony in America at that early day.

The Baron was a Protestant, and no doubt felt great sympathy for the Palatines (Germans), but had also conceived " the hope of making a more considerable fortune in those far off countries of English America."   His first shipment of emigrants was from England in January, 1710, and as there was war with France, it was under the convoy of Rear Admiral Norris.   The weather was wretched, and thirteen weeks were consumed in the voyage.   One of the vessels, loaded with valuable goods, and the better class of emigrants, was captured by a French cruiser, on its arrival in Chesapeake Bay, in sight of an English man-of-war, which, unluckily, had its mast down for repairs, and could not pursue the Frenchman.

The Baron did not accompany this expedition but waited until June, and went in company with the second, which was loaded with Swiss ; and when he arrived in North Carolina, he found the Palatines in a destitute condition, discouraged and demoralized.

He remained with his emigrants a little over two years; and if there is any work of fiction, which has crowded into that short space, more wars, battles, adventures, accidents and troubles, I have never seen it.   I have only space to catalogue a few of them.   In the first place there was Cary's' rebellion ; and as he felt bound to take the part of the

Governor of North Carolina, he was leader in a battle in which small cannon was used—the rebels driven off—and Cary finally captured and sent to England in chains.

For his emigrants the Baron was compelled to bring provisions from a great distance and at fabulous prices. Then he and the Surveyor General Lawson went up the river Neuse on a prospecting tour. They were taken prisoners by the Tuscarora Indians and condemned to death. His account of the Indian orgies when he expected to die was fearful. "In the centre of the great square the Surveyor General and myself were bound and undressed, with bare heads and in front of a great fire. In front of us was the conjurer performing his incantations—a wolf skin—by which an Indian savage of hideous aspect stood motionless, with a knife in one hand and an axe in the other—he was the executioner. Further on, upon the other side of the fire, was a great mob who danced with fearful contortions." The sun was about to set, when the Baron, knowing that there was one Indian, who understood English pretty well, made a short discourse, saying that if they took his life the Queen of England would avenge it. Moreover, he asked them if according to their laws they could put to death a King (or Governor), and that he was "King of the Palatines." The sequel was that he was spared and they executed Lawson—the same who had published "A Diary and Description of North Carolina."

The Baron was kept a prisoner for six weeks, during which time they made war on his colony, and over sixty of his Palatines were killed, and many women and children were taken prisoners. At length, he made a treaty of peace with them. The war prevented the colonists from making crops during 1711, and he busied himself and emptied his purse in supplying them with food. After awhile, his brigantine was wrecked. He sent his larger vessel to Pennsylvania and had her loaded with flour, leaf-tobacco and some powder. On the way to the colony fire got into the leaves of tobacco, and communicated to the powder, and the vessel was blown to atoms, but not before the crew had escaped.

During this season of scarcity he had run up a large account with Mr. Pollock mentioned above, and one of the bills of exchange he had drawn on the Swiss Society of Emigration was returned protested, and he was in danger of imprisonment for debt. In this emergency he consulted his excellent friend, Governor Spotswood, of Virginia, who advised him to return to Europe and arrange his financial matters. Before leaving he wrote to Mr. Pollock and "requested him to take a legal inventory, by sworn commissioners, of all things belonging to the colony as well as himself." We infer that it was under this document that Mr. Pollock succeeded to this immense landed estate. One of the Baron's descendants intermarried with a lady who was a direct descendant of the Fontaines and Maurys, and they, and several other families who came of the same lineage, were settlers in our county. We shall trace this line down from John de la Fontaine, of France, before we give an account of the families separately. Our readers will find the history of interest, at every step.

The Fontaines and Maurys.

Who has not heard of the gallantry of the French Protestants (or Huguenots) who in the sixteenth century were so persecuted by the Roman Catholics, that, although only a tenth of the French population, they took up arms and for nearly 100 years, performed feats of valor which were renowned in history and fiction? They succeeded in placing upon the throne, Henry the Fourth, who by the "Edict of Nantes" granted them religious toleration. This was revoked in 1685 by his successor, and a cruel persecution, for many years, followed, in which it is computed, that 300,000 Protestants were lost to France by emigration. How many fell martyrs to the cause has never been known, for "their blood flowed like water." Some idea may be formed, by the fact that in the one massacre of St. Bartholomew, 50,000 perished. These horrid assassinations, under the name of *Christianity*, caused men to regard religion as a sham; made France a nation of infidels, and fostered that recklessness of temper which brought on the "Reign of Terror."

The Huguenot refugees who came to America were uniformly patriots, and the war of the Revolution made famous some of the noblest names; such as Chief Justice Jay, Boudinot, the Bayards, Legare, the Lawrences, Marion, Rutledge, and others. Many of these refugees became ministers of the Episcopal church in Virginia, at a time, "when it was so greatly depressed that there was danger of its total ruin." It is a melancholy fact, that many of the clergy were addicted to the race-field, the card-table, the ball-room, and the theatre—nay more, to the drunken revel. One of them about this period was, and had been for years, the president of a Jockey-club." (Bishop Meade, in his "*Old Churches and Families of Virginia.*") And when this evangelic Bishop was reforming this branch of our Christian church, he was ably sustained by the Huguenot element in it. This was pure gold which had been refined by the fires of persecution. And, as we proceed with our sketch, it will be seen that the decendants of the Huguenots, have not degenerated, either in the field, the forum, or the pulpit.

John de la Fontaine, the common ancestor of these two families, was born nearly 400 years ago, and, though his descendants, James, the first of the name, James Fontaine the second; James Fontaine the third; Mary Ann Fontaine, who married Matthew Maury, and their son Abraham Maury, six generations were comprised, inclusive of the ancestor—and this may be regarded as the *trunk* of the Fontaine and Maury families; from which, at different times, proceed branches of their various descendants in the United States. Although so long a time has elapsed, the lineage of the persons above mentioned can be verified, for various things have conspired to render the task an easy one. The early history of these families was connected with public times, which sheds a flood of light upon the matter. They were highly educated, and left papers and numerous letters. James, (the Third) in 1722, wrote a history of the Fontaine family, and John kept a diary for many years of his experience in the army, and his travels in Virginia—the vestry books of the old churches in Virginia were collected by Bishop Meade and published—and from all these, Miss Ann Maury, (daughter of the Maury who was, for twenty-five years, Consul to Liverpool) assisted by Dr. Hawks compiled a book called "*The Memoirs of a Huguenot Family*," which is a veritable history, and a great aid to the devotions of a true Protestant. Moreover Miss Maury (assisted by Gen. Dabney H. Maury) has constructed a chart of the Fontaine and Maury families, for nine generations. It is in circular form—has the names of 25 families, and hundreds of their descendants—a work which required great labor, and was performed with great ingenuity.

1. John de la Fontaine (the common ancestor) was born in the province of Maine, France, and as soon as he was old enough to bear arms his father procured him a commission in the household of Francis First. It was in the tenth year of that monarch's reign that he entered his service, and he conducted himself with such uniform honor and uprightness that he retained his command, not only to the end of the reign of Francis First, but during the reigns of Henry Second, Francis Second and until the second year of Charles the Ninth, when he voluntarily resigned. He and his father had become converts to Protestantism about the year 1535. He had married, and had four sons born to him, during his residence at the court. He wished to retire to private life at an earlier period; but being in the King's service was a sort of safe-guard from persecution, and gave him the means of shielding his Protestant brethren from oppression. He was much beloved by his brother officers and by the men under his command, which made the Roman Catholic party afraid to disturb him. In January, 1561, there was an edict of pacification, he resigned his commission and retired to his paternal estate in Maine, where he hoped to end his days peacefully in the bosom of his family, worshiping God according to the dictates of his conscience. In the year 1563 a number of ruffians were dispatched from the city of Le Mans to attack his house at night. He was taken by surprise, dragged out of doors and his throat cut. His poor wife, who was in a few weeks of her confinement, rushed after him in the hope of softening the hearts of these midnight assassins; but, so far from it, they murdered her also, and a faithful servant shared the same fate. His eldest son was never heard of afterward, but was supposed to have been massacred

also. God spared the lives of the three younger ones, and guided them to a place of safety. Of the three, James was the eldest, Abraham twelve, and the youngest about nine, years old.

2. James Fontaine, the first of that name, and the one mentioned above, found his way to Rochelle, a fortified city and the stronghold of Protestanism. These poor boys were at one blow deprived of parents and property. A shoemaker, in easy circumstances, received him in his house, taught him his own trade, but without binding him to it as an apprentice. This was no time for pride of birth, or titles of nobility to be thought of. It was not long before he was in receipt of sufficient wages to support his young brothers, but they all lived poorly enough, until James reached manhood. He then engaged in commerce, and his after career was comparatively prosperous.

He married, and had two daughters and one son. Like the Fontaines, generally, he was a very handsome man, as we shall see by the following incident. Having married a second wife, who was a very wicked woman, she tried to poison him, though she did not succeed, for medical aid was promptly obtained; she was taken to prison, tried, and condemned to death. It so happened that Henry IV was then at Rochelle, and application was made to him for pardon. He replied that, before making an answer, he would like to see the man she was so anxious to get rid of, to judge for himself whether there was any excuse for her. When James Fontaine appeared before him, he called out, "Let her be hanged! *Ventre Saint Gris!* He is the handsomest man in my kingdom."

3. James Fontaine (the second of that name), and the one son mentioned above, became a minister. He married first a Miss Thompson, and had five children, and the second time Miss Marie Clallon, and by her he had same number. His daughter married Rev. Mr. Santreau. His church was condemned. He left the Kingdom, sailed for America with his wife and five children, and the vessel was shipwrecked in sight of Boston, and all the family perished. I have no space to notice the members of the family in detail.

4. James Fontaine (the third of that name), and the youngest son of the foregoing family, was born in 1603, and died in 1666. He had a life full of adventure. He, too, was a Protestant minister, was imprisoned for a long time, and at length escaped from France. In England he married a French lady, Anne Elizabeth Boursiquot, also a refugee. Although he was lame from a fall in childhood, yet he was active and energetic, and used many ingenious devices to support himself and family. He received Holy orders from the Protestant Synod, assembled at Taunton. Here his first child, Mary Ann Fontaine, was born 12th April, 1690. He moved to Cork, Ireland, in 1694, and supported his family by having baize manufactured on *hand looms*, for power looms had not yet come into use in England. He preached to a congregation, but they were so poor he declined to receive any compensation. On the day of a baptism of a son, he made a great supper, as though he intended to feast the wealthiest of the French refugees in Cork; but instead of that, he invited the poor of his flock, and after they had eaten and drank abundantly of the best, he gave each a shilling to take home.

Mr. Fontaine then concluded, as his family was becoming large, to find a country home, and he rented a farm on Bear Haven Bay. His plan was to eke out his income by a fishery. But here he encountered trouble entirely unexpected. One morning in June a French privateer hove in sight. She floated gently toward his house in a perfect calm. She had a force of eighty men on board, besides four of his Irish neighbors who acted as guides. She mounted ten guns. He made a feint which deceived the enemy as to his numbers. The privateer entered the mouth of the creek and anchored a long musket shot from the house, presently the lieutenant landed with twenty men and marched directly toward the house, Mr. Fontaine had seven men with him in addition to his wife and children. He placed them at different windows and he posted himself in one of the towers over the door, and as the lieutenant was advancing with every appearance of confidence he fired at him with a bluderbns loaded with large shot, some of which entered his neck and the rest his side. His men took him up, crossed the ditch and carried him to the vessel.

The captain was furious at this unexpected resistance from a minister; and sent another officer on shore with twenty more men and two small cannon, which were discharged against the house; but the position of the battery was oblique, and the balls glanced from the heavy stone walls. The conflict became a hot one. During the time there were several hundred Irishmen collected on a neighboring height, rejoicing in the anticipation of the defeat of the Fontaines. The Frenchman who was pointing the cannon was killed, and an incessant fire was kept up, and as soon as a musket was emptied it was handed down to one of the children to reload, and he was given another. Mrs. Fontaine was here and there and everywhere, carrying ammunition and giving encouragement to all, as well by what she said as by her own calm deportment. She was praying incessantly, but she took care "to keep the powder dry," and in good supply. Claude Bonnet, a French soldier, received a ball in the fleshy part of the arm, and she applied the first dressing to it with her own hands. The engagement lasted from 8 o'clock in the morning until 4 o'clock in the afternoon, and during the whole time there had been no cessation of firing. The enemy then retired with three men killed and seven wounded.

The name of James Fontaine, and his wife, too, became known throughout Europe by means of the newspapers giving the history of this defence. The government furnished him with ammunition in abundance, and he bought several six pounders which had been fished up from a wreck, and he raised a fortification and planted his guns upon it so as to command the mouth of the inlet. Mr. Fontaine then went to Dublin to wait on the Council and concert measures for the better defence of the coast. During his absence a privateer approached the house. Mrs. Fontaine was on the alert, had all the cannons loaded, and one of them fired off to show that all was in readiness for defence, and when they saw this they veered about and sailed away. Then and there the coat-of-arms of the Fontaine family ought to have been changed, and instead of the mysterious emblems known only to a herald's office, should have been substituted the picture of a lady bravely applying the fuse to a cannon, the smoke rolling in volumes from its mouth, and the ball flying through the air in the direction of a vessel in the offing. No blood ever mingled with the Fontaines and Maurys, more noble than that of Anna Elizabeth Bouraiquot.

But a French privateer attacked his house for a third time, in the night, and sent eighty men in three boats on shore. Although taken by surprise, Mr. Fontaine prepared for defence. The enemy set all the outhouses on fire, and in a half hour the defender was enveloped in smoke, so that he was unable to see his enemies. He had to fire haphazard; and overloading his piece it burst and he was thrown down with such violence that three of his ribs and his collar-bone were broken, and the flesh of his right hand much torn. After he was prostrated, Mrs. Fontaine assumed the command; she had an eye to everything; she went round to furnish ammunition as it was required; and she gave courage as well by her exhortations as her example. But such heroic efforts were of no avail and they were conquered, and Mr. Fontaine and two of his sons were carried away prisoners; the Captain announcing that he would release them on the payment of £100. Did the lady sit down and weep? Nothing of the kind! She flew around to borrow the money. She succeeded only partly, and seeing the vessel under sail, she determined to follow by land, and keep the vessel in sight as long as she could. She ran to a promontory, and made a signal to the pirate with her apron tied to a stick. A boat was dispatched to hear what she had to say. After a great deal of bargaining the Captain agreed to release her husband upon a cash payment of £30, and retained her son Peter as hostage for the payment of the balance of the money. Peter was subsequently released. Mr. Fontaine left this inhospitable coast, and removed to Dublin.

James Fontaine (third) and his wife had a large family of children. Of them the Rev. Peter Fontaine removed to America. He was rector of Westover parish, in Virginia, and his daughter, Mary Ann, married Isaac Winston, who had " a good fortune and a spotless reputation." He is the ancestor of a large family of wealthy and respectable citizens of Alabama, which gave a governor to that State in the person of John Anthony Winston.* A daughter of James Fontaine, Mary Ann Fontaine, married Matthew Maury, in Ireland, on the 20th of October, 1716. She had been born in England, in 1690. He was of Castle Mauron, in Gascony, France. He had lived in Dublin about two years, having come hither as a refugee, on account of his religion. He was *not* a minister, as some have supposed ; was " a very honest man, a good economist, but without property." There is no doubt of his having been well educated, as we shall show when we come to speak of his sons. His wife (who lived until she was sixty-five) had a checkered exist- ence. She was a girl of fourteen when she had to assist her father in defending his home against the French privateers ; and, after the family came to Virginia, although the public wars with the Indians had ceased, yet the frontiers were frequently visited by their incursions, and fire, and sword, and perpetual alarms, surrounded them all the latter days of her life. The effect was to form one of the most perfect characters in the whole list of men and women belonging to her descendants (who have never been want- ing in nerve or intellect). Matthew Maury and his wife came to Virginia in 1719, and settled in King William county, on the Pamunkey. They had three children—James, Mary and Abraham.

Rev. James Maury was born in 1717. He was ordained a minister in 1742, and spent one year in a parish of King William county. He then removed to Louisa county, where he became the minister of the Fredericksville parish. Here he married Mary, the niece of Dr. Thomas Walker, of Albemarle county, Virginia. " Dr. Thomas Walker is

---

*Fontaine, of Columbus, Ga.

1. Thomas Fontaine married Mary Brutas. Their son,
2. John Fontaine (died 1867) married Mary Stewart. Children : Henrietta married James T. Flewellen, one died ; Mary married Dr. W. P. Copeland, Eufaula, Ala.
2. John Fontaine.
3. Mary married Dr. F. A. Stanford.
4. Benjamin Fontaine married Mary E. Shorter, now a widow, 1887, with two daughters, viz. : Mary and Benjamin B.
5. Theophilus S. Fontaine, Columbus, Ga., married Mary E. Young.
6. Francis Fontaine, Atlanta, Ga., married (1) Mary Flournoy and (2) Nathalie Hamilton. Children : Francis, Henry and Mary.
7. George Hargraves Fontaine, Columbus, Ga., Student University, Va., 1866.
Mr. T. S. Fontaine wrote in 1887 that his brothers and sisters were all dead, except Francis and George Fontaine, and that they were related to the families of Stewart, Hargraves and Shorter. (*Theophilus S. Fontaine in 1887.*)

Fontaine, of Mississippi.

833 NORTH STATE STREET. JACKSON, Miss., December 29, 1887.

James E. Saunders, Esq., Courtland, Ala.:

DEAR SIR—Your favor of the 26th inst. was handed me last night and took me somewhat by sur- prise, as I thought that all the Fontaines of the South knew that I was the oldest Fontaine of the numerous branches, geneologically speaking, now extant since the death of my father, Edward Fon- taine, L. L. D. and D. D. & C. I am one of the Fontaines set down on the Fontaine chart. On the Ameri- can chart descended as follows : John Fontaine X Martha Henry, eldest daughter of Patrick Henry, of Virginia ; Patrick H. Fontaine (eldest son of John Fontaine and Martha Henry) X Nancy Dabney Miller, Edward Fontaine (eldest son of Patrick Henry Fontaine and Nancy Dabney Miller) X Ann Swisher (nee Mary), eldest son is myself ; and I was born in Texas (10th October, 1839, one of the first male births in Stephen F. Austin's colony in that State) before it was a republic. I married Lemnella S. Brickell, of Yazoo county, Miss. My eldest child is Henry Bourguoine Brickell F. ; second, Jeanie Wilson ; third, Edward L. ; fourth, Mary Agnes ; fifth, James Francis ; sixth, Annie Gale ; seventh, Lemoella Moore ; eighth, Lamar, Jr. My youngest is now six years old and my eldest will soon reach his majority. I am a surveyor and civil engineer by profession.

During the war I served under Lee, Jackson, Beauregard, Bragg and Joseph E. Johnston. My last commander was P. D. Roddy, of North Alabama, and I was once in command of Tuscumbia, Ala.

Very respectfully yours,

LAMAR FONTAINE.

NOTE.—Author of "All Quiet Along the Potomac To-night." and "Charge of Rodes Brigade at Seven Pines" and celebrated poems of the civil war.

believed to have been the first discoverer of Kentucky in 1750. In 1755 he was with Washington at Braddock's defeat. In 1775 he was one of the committee of safety appointed by the convention of 1775 on the breaking out of the troubles with England. He was repeatedly a member of the General Assembly. Col. John Walker, his eldest son, was for a short time aide to General Washington during the war. He was also for a time a member of the Senate of the United States. Col Francis Walker, the youngest son, was repeatedly a member of the State Legislature, and represented the counties of Albemarle and Orange in Congress, from 1791 to 1795." (Bishop Meade's *Old Churches and Families of Virginia.*) Mary Peachy Walker (a sister of Dr. Thomas Walker) married Dr. George Gilmer, who was sent from London to Williamsburg as manager of the affairs of the London Land Company. She became the great-grand-mother of Gov. Geo. R. Gilmer, of Georgia. (*See Gilmer's, Georgians.*) Whether the Walkers, who have been so conspicuous in public affairs in Alabama for sixty years, descended from the family into which Rev. James Maury married, I have not been able to ascertain. John W. Walker, the ancestor, was certainly a Virginian by birth.

" After the death of his father, Thomas Jefferson (then fourteen years of age) was put under the charge of Rev. Jas. Maury (of Huguenot descent), a good classical scholar, and a thorough teacher, where he continued two years, until he entered William and Mary College."—*Campbell's History of Virginia*. Mr. Maury, I presume, had graduated at the same college as his uncle, Rev. Francis Fontaine, was professor of Oriental languages there, and no doubt Matthew Maury had prepared his son James for college.

We now approach an interesting chapter in the history of Rev. James Maury, in which he became plaintiff in the " Parson's Case," where he sued for his salary, which was payable in tobacco. The law of the case had been determined in Mr. Maury's favor at a previous term of the court, and a special jury had been summoned, simply to assess the damages for the non-delivery of the tobacco. The defendants, as a *dernier resort*, employed Patrick Henry, then a young lawyer. He took a wide range, arraigning King and clergy. Mr. Maury was very much disgusted with the young attorney, for his illogical argument, especially when the jury brought in a verdict for the plaintiff of only one penny damages, and there was a breach between these two gifted men; but time can heal all things. Years rolled on, and a near relation of Mr. Maury, John Fontaine, married Martha, a daughter of Patrick Henry, and, moreover, Maury and Henry stood shoulder to shoulder against the " Stamp Act" when passed. The former, in a letter to a friend in England, makes an argument against the right of England to tax the colonies, which is equal to any I have ever read. He was certainly a man of great ability. He died in 1770. Had he lived until the Revolutionary struggle commenced, I judge that, like his brother, Muhlenburg, he would have exchanged the garb of a priest for the uniform of a general. We shall not attempt to mention the names of the descendants of the old patriarch, Rev. James Maury, for we have no space, but we shall notice a few of them who happen to be *best known to me.*

James, who was born in 1746, became consul of the United States at Liverpool, and as proof of the high estimation in which he was held, he was kept in that office forty-five years—(*Campbell's History of Virginia*), and so just and enlightened had been his administration, that the corporation of that commercial city conferred upon him " the freedom of the city." I judge he was a man of much ability. I was in a position for some years in which I had much to do with consuls, and learned that their duties were heavy and multifarious. A consul must have a knowledge of international law, and subsisting treaties. He acts as a judge in deciding all controversies between captains and their crews in a foreign port. And then their sympathies are kept in full exercise, for they are required to have destitute sailors cared for and sent home. I have not time to hint at their numerous duties. It requires as much talent to manage the consulship at Liverpool, as the embassy at London. But, you may reply, the questions at London are of more importance? Yes, that is so; but when that is the case, instructions are sent out which are so plain that there need be no mistake. I have lived a long time, and I have learned that the higher a man rises the less work he has to do. The rail-splitter, at the foot of the ladder, does fifty times as much work; but the ambassador, at the top of it, gets fifty times as much pay. Let the boys who read this article note this, that "*knowledge is power*"—and *money*, too. Miss Ann Maury, the author of "*The Memoirs of a Huguenot Family*," was the daughter of the consul, and has been dead about twelve years.

Henry Maury (we called him "*Harry*" at Mobile) was descended from the Rev. James Maury, through his son Abraham, and *his* son, Butler Maury,. Colonel Maury was the most fiery and impulsive Maury I have ever known. He fought a duel with Count de Reviere at Mobile, and, hitting him in the mouth, broke his jaw. It was not Maury's quarrel, but he was somewhat of a knight-errant, and espoused the cause of a lady, and said he struck the Frenchmen just where he aimed—to "*punish the offending member*." The colonel commanded a regiment during the war, leading it with a bravery bordering often on recklessness. He died in Mobile some years after the war.

Dr. Richard B. Maury, of Memphis, Tenn., was born and reared in Fredericksburg, Va., and educated at the University of Virginia. His father, Richard B. Maury, was twice married. The doctor is a son of his second wife, Ellen Magruder. His grandfather, Fontaine Maury, married E. Brooke, and his great-grandfather was the Rev. James Maury. Dr. Maury is a physician learned in his profession and with an extensive practice, and a man of scientific and literary attainments, and of unsullied reputation.

Maj. Gen. Dabney H. Maury is also a descendant of Rev. James Maury. His father was John Minor Maury, who married E. Maury; his grandfather was Richard Maury, who was born in 1776, and married Diana Minor. This Richard Maury (the father of Commodore Matthew F. Maury) was the son of Rev. James Maury, above mentioned.

Dabney H. Maury had a remarkable military career. When the battle of Elkhorn was fought, in March, 1862, he was simply a staff officer of General Van Dorn, but when the last battles around Mobile were fought, which ended the war between the States, he was Major General, and in command of the Department of the Gulf. During these four eventful years, thousands had started in the race for promotion, and but few succeeded. Some failed for want of physical courage (but the number was small, for this is a very common quality), many more failed, not for want of bravery, but they were so nervous and excitable that they could not *think* in a moment of danger, and of course were unfit for commanders; and a much larger number failed because they had no military knowledge. This is indispensable for an important command. I knew but one man who was a *born* soldier. He was endowed with an estimate of the value of time (equal to Napoleon's), and if he committed blunders, his enemy was so dazed by the celerity of his movements, that he failed to perceive them (*Forrest*).

As my space is small, I will only notice the beginning and close of his military career. At Elkhorn, the plan of battle was for the wing under the command of Generals McCulloch and McDonald to attack the enemy in front, and General Price's wing on the flank. The battle had but fairly begun, "when a staff officer, Colonel Dillon, galloped up, with disaster on his face. Riding close up to Van Dorn, he said, in a low tone, 'McCulloch is killed. McIntosh is killed, Herbert is killed, and the attack on the front has ceased.'" These fatalities imposed a heavy burden on Van Dorn's staff. How Colonel Maury performed *his* part in this sudden emergency, can be seen by the report of the commanding General: "Colonel Maury was of invaluable service to me, both in preparing for, and during, the battle. Here, and on other fields, where I have served with him, he proved to be a zealous patriot and true soldier—cool and calm under all circumstances, he was always ready, either with his sword or pen."—*Southern Historical Papers*.

Preparations to reduce Mobile were commenced soon after the battle of Nashville, and the command of the Department of the Gulf was entrusted to Dabney H. Maury, now Major General. General Canby had 60,000 men, and the fleet of Farragut, (which had recovered from the consternation produced by the audacious attack of the ram—Tennessee). To oppose these, there were, of all arms, only 9,000 Confederates. Of these, there was a brigade of Alabama "*boy reserves,*" under General Thomas. It has been remembered, for two thousand years, that the women of Carthage gave their *tresses* for bow-strings, in a great emergency; but the *women of Alabama did more,* for they gave their tender beloved sons, "the dew of their youth," for the rough service and perils of the camp. The base of the enemy was at the mouth of Fish river, twenty miles distant from Spanish Fort. General Maury had erected defensive works here, and at Blakely. The enemy, in marching the twenty miles before them, consumed nine days, and entrenched every night. What a compliment to General Maury and his bold little army! He offered battle to them on the way, with his small force, reduced by a garrison of 300 men left in Mobile, but they declined, and sat down before Spanish Fort for a regular siege by parallel approaches. General Maury had used every resource known to science to meet the impending blow. He had plenty of heavy guns.

Federal historians say that he had Parrott guns. The General, himself, in his account of the siege (*Southern Historical Papers*) says "the only Parrott gun we had, at that time, was the 'Lady Washington,' captured by my division at Corinth. But we had cannon better than any Parrott ever made. These guns were cast at Selma, of the iron about Briarfield, in North Alabama. It must be the best gun metal in the world. Some of our Brooke guns were subjected to extraordinarily severe tests, yet not one of them burst, or was in any degree injured during the fourteen days siege, at the same time they outranged the enemy's best and heaviest Parrotts, which not unfrequently burst by overcharging and over elevation." General Maury also used torpedoes. He says "every avenue of approach was guarded by submarine torpedoes. No vessels drawing three feet water could get within effective cannon range of any part of our defences. Had we understood their power in the beginning of the war, as at the end, we could effectually have defended every harbor, channel, or river, in the Confederate States, against all sorts of naval attacks. During the siege a number of armed vessels and transports were sunk. But the obstinacy of the defence was of no avail. The last gun in the war between the States was fired in this siege, on the Eastern shore. The Federals lost 7000 in killed and wounded here. On the fall of Mobile, General Maury marched its garrison to Meridian, where, hearing of the surrender of General Lee, and the capture of President Davis, he surrendered his forces. He is now U. S. Minister to Columbia, South America (1888).

In his Report of the defence of Mobile he says that the last gun of the war was fired on the eastern shore of the bay on the 12th of April, 1865. But from a number of letters I have received since that statement was published, I am satisfied that the General was mistaken, and that the last conflict of the civil war was a bloody affair, which occurred at *West Point, Ga.,* under the leadership of

Gen. R. C. Tyler.

Capt. L. B. McFarland, of Memphis, gives this account of him:

"He was born and reared in Baltimore, Maryland. He was in the Nicaraguan Expedition with Walker. Came to Memphis in 1859 or 1860. Joined as a volunteer private, company D, 15th Tennessee regiment, Colonel Carroll, commanding. Was made Quartermaster of a Regiment at Union City, Tennessee. Was elected Lieutenant Colonel of the Regiment after the battle of Belmont, in which (though Quartermaster), he took command of the Regiment, and gallantly led it into the thickest of the fight. He was badly wounded at Shiloh, and, at the reorganization at Corinth, was made Colonel of the Regiment. He was made Provost Marshal of the army by General Bragg after the battle of Perryville. He was then placed in command of Tyler's Brigade, and was badly wounded at Missionary Ridge (in the leg); so badly that excision of the bone for four inches, was necessary; and he had to go on crutches afterwards. He was in command of West Point, at the time of Wilson's raid. It was of the greatest importance that the enemy should be delayed at this point. The hospital, and hospital stores, from Auburn and Montgomery, were being moved out, and had just crossed the river. For their protection, and to enable organization for resistance east of this point, it was necessary, at any sacrifice, to delay the enemy. General Tyler organized a force of about 125 men. including a small battery commanded by Lieutenant Waddell, and a section of Capt. C B. Ferrill's battery. The force was largely composed of volunteer convalescents from hospitals (which were passing through), and some citizens; and, with these, he went into a small fort, situated on an eminence near the town. The writer had received a few days furlough after the Tennessee campaign, and was returning to his command (Cheatham's Division) and was just ahead of Wilson's raid. When he arrived at West Point, he called on General Tyler, who told him he intended to hold the fort, and invited him to act as his Adjutant. They were captured, and taken to Macon, Ga., where they heard of the surrender and were paroled."

Captain McFarland enclosed, in his statement of the battle, an article from the Eufaula *Daily News* of August, 1865: "On Sunday morning, 16th April, about 10 o'clock, the enemy came in sight, and General Tyler with his artillery opened upon them. The firing on both sides continued slowly until about 2 o'clock in the afternoon, when the enemy galloped into town under a heavy fire from his fort. Dismounting, they prepared to charge the fort, in the meantime taking possession of the bridge. Firing continuously, with cannon and rifles, they slowly and cautiously approached the little band of heroes until within about twenty steps of them, then with loud yells they attempted to scale the works, but were repulsed and held at bay until all the ammunition in the fort had been exhausted; and then, when the Yankees were in the ditch and around the fort, the brave and gallant men inside of it hurled stones, ignited shells and even their guns upon them. The Confederate flag was *never* hauled down, until by the Yanks; nor any white flag hoisted until the enemy had leaped the parapet. Thus did 125 men hold a fort for about two hours against a force of about *two thousand* of the enemy, well armed with Spencer rifles. A more gallant instance has never been known since the time of Charles, King of Sweden, when he with his body guard and a few servants, in the heart of the enemy's country, defended himself against an entire army of Turks, until his place of retreat was burned to the ground by lighted arrows from the assaulting party.

"The particulars of the taking of Fort Tyler, with the name of every man in that noble little squad of "rebels," should be printed in *letters of gold* and handed down to posterity, that it might ever be known what men can do when actuated by a sense of duty.

"Nine of the garrison were killed, including General Tyler, of Memphis, and Captain Gonzales, of Pensacola, and about fifteen wounded."

"I am informed by a reliable party, living in West Point, that the Federals lost eighty men in this affair, and that after the battle the town was sacked and burned." (*Mrs. Florida M. Reed.*)

Among the killed of the Confederates were two men of the battery of Capt. C. B. Ferrill, who served so skilfully and faithfully on the "debatable ground" of the Tennessee valley, and among the wounded was Charles Locke, of Memphis, who lost an arm, and a gentleman who was editor of a newspaper in Winchester, Tenn.

General LaGrange, who commanded the Federals in this affair, in his official report paid a high compliment to the garrison, and said it was composed of "desperate men."

Commodore Matthew Fontaine Maury

was born in Spotsylvania county, Virginia, January 16th, 1806. His father was Richard Maury, who was the son of the James Maury (above mentioned). Mr. Richard Maury moved from Virginia to Williamson county, Tennessee, when his son Matthew was but a child. The country was then mostly a canebrake, but the soil wonderfully fertile. His farm was not large, and he had only a few slaves, but he was a solid, sensible and industrious man, and managed to rear and educate a family of ten children; commanding, however, whenever the crop required it, the labor of his sons. He made his home on Harpeth river, four miles below Franklin. His only amusement was a grist mill, which he erected on a small tributary of that stream, and which was a great convenience to the Perkinses, the Childress' and the Maurys. He rode this hobby very hard, little dreaming that his son "*Matt*" would mount one which he would ride around the admiring world, in the presence of Kings, Princes and peoples, and "take the purse" from all competitors—the renowned Humboldt being the judge.

I never knew young Matthew Fontaine Maury until he entered Harpeth Academy—then under the presidency of Rev. Gideon Blackburn, D. D. He was fortunate in having such a teacher and guide. Dr. Blackburn was an eminent minister of the Presbyterian church. He was of commanding person, graceful manners, and a scholar of extensive learning—for an age in which science did not constitute so large an element as now. As an orator, I think he was the equal of Dr. Samuel Davies of Nassau Hall. He never *wrote* his sermons, but spoke extemporaneously, sometimes for more than two hours. Judge Guild (who was an orator himself) says of him, in his "*Old Times in Tennessee:*" "Dr. Blackburn's eloquence as General Jackson's chaplain, inflamed the hearts and nerved the arms of the Tennessee volunteers, who carried the victorious flag of our country through the great campaigns of Jackson. He was the most eloquent and powerful minister I ever heard. I have heard many of the pulpit orators that have arisen since then, and my first impression has not been diminished, but deepened by the accumulation of years. Few American orators have shown themselves his equal, and none his superior." About his pupil, young Maury, there was a striking feature, and that was an undivided concentration of mind upon whatever he was doing. He was no dreamer. On the play-ground he was active, strong and cheery, and a favorite with his fellows; and when "books were called" he devoted his attention, as singly and earnestly, to his lesson; and so gained the approbation of his teachers. He was a fine example of "a *sound mind in a sound body.*" We were school-fellows for some years. At length my father moved to Alabama, and I went to a college in another State, and he went into the Navy.

About 1826 we happened to meet at Franklin, *our old home.* He wore the glazed cap, and the uniform, of a midshipman. There was quite a crowd of schoolmates around him, and a happy reunion took place. At length the young men began to look at their watches, for a *quarter race* was to come off. In a short time we were left alone, and had a most interesting conversation. He had been on a cruise in the Pacific Ocean—and talked, mostly, of the currents of the sea. I remember to this day, that he told me of a *broad current of cold water* which ran from South to North, up the Western coast of South America, and with so strong a current that a sail vessel to double Cape Horn would have to make an offing of one or two hundred miles from the coast to escape the resistance of the current. I mention this fact to show, that young as he was, he was a close observer of what he saw, and the tenacity with which his mind held on to a subject, and revolved it over and over again. It is this quality which distinguishes a great man from an ordinary one.

Mr. Maury became Lieutenant in the Navy in 1837. "He had a leg broken and many other injuries (I think from the overturning of a stage) and during his convalescence he spent several years in Fredericksburg in study, and preparing a series of articles ("*The Lucky Bag,*" by *Harry Bluff*), for the *Southern Literary Messenger* which wrought a revolution in the Navy Department, and led to the establishment of the Naval Academy. (*Mr. R. A. Brock, in Vol. 5, New Series of Virginia Historical Collections*).

In 1842 he was made Superintendent of the Depot of the Charts and Instruments in Washington, which under his inspiration became the National Observatory. Here he made his renowned Current Charts and Sailing Directions, and wrote his "*Geography of the Sea,*" which was pronounced by Humboldt "a new science." Conscious that his new system of navigation would not be perfected without accurate observations everywhere, he suggested a Congress of Maratime Nations at Brussels, where sailors on every sea were instructed to report to their governments—and in their turn these reports were sent to the National Observatory at Washington. What a triumph this was for the scientist at the head of it, who had barely attained to middle age! In recognition of his services in the cause of science, the leading powers of Europe showered honors and decorations upon him. The University of Cambridge, England, conferred upon him the degree of LL. D. President Tyler wanted him (though only a lieutenant) at the head of the Navy Department, and the position of the Hydrographer of the Southern Exploring Exposition was offered him. The Academies of Science of Paris, Berlin, Brussels and St. Petersburg conferred membership upon him.

But he was not only honored by the great and learned, but as well by the common sailors of every nation. At first they were incredulous. They had never heard of "sailing by great circles." They thought the proper course from port to port was "plumb straight." These old tars had often crossed the ocean and had never seen any current in it, and did not believe there was any. But when the sailing master would spread out the new chart on the binnacle, lay his course as if sailing to a different port than the desired one—when after a while they would fall into a current which would waft them along without an adverse wind, and the voyage would be a short and easy one, they would begin to see the riddle. But then again when on the return voyage the sailing master, instead of laying his course on the same track on which they had come, so smoothly from home, would take a route entirely different, they would be again mystified. After a while, however, they would feel a steady wind at the backs—the sails when once set would not need trimming for days—and when they would reach the home port, in shorter time, and with less labor, than ever before, they would frankly acknowledge their mistake. In this way, the name of Columbus, when he discovered a New World, was not more universally known than that of "Maury," and had these mariners lived in ancient Rome, a new God would have been added to the Mythology, and his image would have been the figure-head for good luck on every vessel which floated on the ocean.

When, in the war between the States, Virginia seceded from the Union, he resigned his commission in the Navy, and the charge of the National Observatory. When this became known, France and Russia invited him to become their guest, with every provision for his comfort and studies. He replied that his first duty was to Virginia, his birth place, and his home, since his marriage. His vindication of the South (to be found in Southern Historical Papers 1, Vol. 49) is a dispassionate and very able paper. In that contest we lost everything "but honor"—let us always keep that untarnished, by keeping in mind the grounds which justified our action. He was promoted to a Captaincy and a member of the Advisory Committee; the first act of which body was to recommend R. E. Lee as commander of the Virginia army. He gave much attention to torpedoes, believing in their efficiency as much as his cousin, Gen. Dabney H. Maury.

In 1862 he was sent on a special mission to England, and remained there until 1865. On the downfall of the Confederacy Maximilian persuaded him to make his home in Mexico; and he was appointed Honorary Counsellor of State, a member of the Cabinet, and an Imperial Commissioner of Immigration, and was sent on special mission to Europe. Shortly afterward Maximilian fell, and he remained there until 1868. He was elected to the Presidency of the University of Alabama, which he declined; (President Clayton). He was elected Professor of Physics of the Virginia Military Institute, which he accepted, and have never risen above text-books; he returned to Virginia. After a most useful life he died at Lexington, Va., February 1, 1873. He was a sincere, humble Christian. Whilst some men, who have had no original ideas, and have never risen above text-books, have become skeptics from an exaggerated idea of their learning, he wrote text-books—books for the advancement of science into unexplored fields, and yet held fast to the faith which sustained his ancestors, the pious Huguenots in their afflictions—and the last words he spoke were " all is well."

Commodore Maury married Anne, daughter of Dabney and Elizabeth Herndon. Her father was for many years President of the Virginia Bank at Fredericksburg, Va. A number of her brothers were men of distinction. William Lewis Herndon, when a Lieutenant in company with a friend of the same grade, explored the Amazon, the largest river in the world, from its head springs, in the Andes, which overlook the Pacific on the west for 4000 miles, to the Atlantic on the East, where through a mouth 100 miles wide, it pours out its immense accumulation of waters.

It was a feat equal to the navigation of the Congo River by Stanley, with this difference: Stanley, in his first expedition to the interior of Africa, projected his plan, and when he did attempt the descent of the Congo, he had provided a vessel made in segments, which were carried across the *portage* on the backs of Indians to the great river; whereas, Herndon, from a U. S. vessel lying in port on the Pacific, took thirty-five or forty men (I speak from memory), and without any boat, but with a few tools to construct canoes, and depending on his gun and fishing tackle to save his company from starvation, he boldly embarked on an unknown stream, where for 2000 miles he never saw a human face except that of a savage. He became a captain and heroically went down with the ill-fated steamer "Central America," of which he was the commander, September 12, 1857, after having seen every passenger transferred from the decks of the sinking ship, and saved it. It was from such blood, mingled with that of the Fontaines and Maurys, that the children of Commodore Maury sprang. From long observation I feel authorised to say that the children of distinguished men, especially the sons are, in a majority of cases, failures, because the fathers let their light shine outside, instead of inside their families; but this was not the case in the family of Commodore Maury. He made his children his companions. He elevated their minds to the plane of his own great thoughts. Mr. Brook says that his four youngest children assisted him in preparing his charts and geography of the sea for the press. From no other source except free intercourse with their father could they have acquired the knowledge requisite, to give him help in so novel a work. I will now notice each of his children in their order

1. Elizabeth Herndon married, in 1857, her cousin, Wm. A. Maury. He is a man of extensive learning; was a Professor of Law in Columbia College; had the degree of L.L. D. conferred upon him; is now Assistant Attorney General of the United States, and I am informed by one of the ablest lawyers of the bar of the United States Supreme Court, is a man of decided ability. 2. Diana Fontaine, in 1858, married Spotswood W. Corbin. 3. Richard Launcelot married, in 1862, Susan Gatewood Crutchfield. He enlisted as a private in the Confederate army, in April, 1861. He was promoted, grade by grade, for his gallantry to a coloneley; was badly wounded at the battle of Seven Pines, and again badly wounded through the hips at the battle of Drewry's Bluff, which permanently disabled him; but he rejoined the army on the evacuation of Richmond, and surrendered at Appomattox Court House. He is now a prominent member of the Richmond, Va., bar. 4. John Herndon, born in 1842. "He was a lieutenant in the Confederate States Navy. Going out alone from camp, opposite Vicksburg, January 27, 1863, to reconnoitre the enemy, his horse returned without its rider, who is supposed to have been murdered by an ambushed foe. He lies in an unknown grave." 5. Mary Herndon was married in 1877 to James R. Worth. 6. Eliza Hall, married in 1878 to Thomas Withers. She was the author of a paper on the State Debt. She died in 1881. 7. Matthew Fontaine, born in 1849; married Rose, daughter of Capt. John A. Robinson. He is a civil engineer. 8. Lucy Minor married, in 1877, Meverill Locke Van Doren of "Blenheim," Albemarle county, Va.

I am indebted to R. A. Brook, Esq., the indefatigable secretary of the Virginia Historical Society, for most of the statistics on which this article is founded.

Colonel Abraham Maury

was the younger son of Mr. Matthew Maury, who married Mary Anne Fontaine. He was born in King William county, Va., in 1731. His widowed mother said of him: "He is a youth of happy temper, very dutiful, chaste, and hearkening to good counsel." His uncle, Peter Fontaine, gave the same account of him. This was a happy presage of his success in life. I know that with many the impression prevails that these dare-devil boys are the boys that make their mark in life, especially in the military line. This is a grand mistake. General Henry Lee said of his son when he was a youth: "Robert was *always* a good boy." When he was at West Point he never received a demerit. The good boy was a good young officer; and became in due time the good commander-in-chief.—(*Cook's Life of General R. E. Lee*). A dashing, rude boy may become an effective sub-altern, but for high office a man must not only be brave, but thoughtful. He must have "*mens æqua in arduis.*" Arduous indeed were the duties which devolved on Colonel Maury, and well did he perform them.

A summary of his life is given in the Danville (Va.) *Times*, consisting of extracts of a letter, and headed, "*Who Colonel Maury of the Old Trunk Was.*"

EVERHOPE, NEAR GREENSBORO, N. C., December 25, 1871.

MR. P. BOULDIN—DEAR SIR: I have received your letter making inquiries as to who Colonel Maury was, mentioned in a letter found in *your old trunk*, dated 18th April, 1758, and addressed to Captain (afterward) Colonel Bouldin, from Clement Reid.

I can think of but two children Mr. Matthew Maury had, besides the Rev. James Maury, rector of Fredericksville. One was a daughter, Mary, who married Daniel Claiborne, of an old and honorable family of Tidewater, Va.—the other a son, Abraham, born in 1731. He was a man of good character, great decision of mind, and possessed of excellent education. He was a graduate of William and Mary College; for it was a cardinal principle of the Fontaines and Maurys, of those days, to educate their children thoroughly. Abraham had the confidence of John Blair, "President and Commander-in-Chief of this Dominion," as he is called in the Acts of the General Assembly of that period. You may observe that Clement Reid in his postscript says to Captain Bouldin: "You must cause your lieutenant to keep an exact journal of your marches, and of the different routes you take, and of all your transactions relating thereto; that it may be returned to the president at Williamsburg, according to order."

John Blair was that president. Abraham Maury had formed his acquaintance whilst a student of William and Mary, and that great and virtuous man had full confidence in the intellectual, but modest and retiring student, and probably it was owing to this that Abraham Maury obtained the high and honorable distinction, in those days, of being made Colonel of Halifax county, at so youthful an age, for he is the "Colonel Maury of the old trunk." In 1758 he was but 27 years of age, but he had been appointed colonel at least two years previously! In 1752 Halifax was formed from Lunenburg. Peter Fontaine and Clement Reid were appointed receivers of the county debt. After that, Peter Fontaine was appointed Surveyor of Halifax county, being a frontier county; Abraham, who had a military turn, was made Colonel, and was very active in resisting all attacks from the various tribes of Indians, beyond the mountains, and in North Carolina. History (or at least none that I recollect to have seen), has not recorded his humble yet useful efforts; yet I remember, when a child, seeing aged men in the county of Henry who used to speak of Colonel Maury, and the way he used to keep the Indians down. * * * Very truly yours, WM. S. FONTAINE."

The period during which young Maury was Colonel of Halifax county was the most disastrous of our colonial times. General Braddock had been defeated. The French and Indians had encroached on our frontiers until the settlers were driven back in some places 150 miles. Colonel Washington was thoroughly discouraged. In the agony of his great soul, in one of his dispatches to the Governor, he exclaims: "The supplicating tears of the women and the moving petitions of the men melt me into such a deadly sorrow that I solemnly declare, if I know my own mind, I could offer myself a willing sacrifice to the butchering enemy, provided that would contribute to the peoples' ease!" In the central counties of Virginia the incursions of the savages had become alarming. In the county of Louisa alone sixty persons were massacred. When the people were called together to form volunteer regiments, the drum and fife excited no military fervor, for every man felt a reluctance to leave his home, when on his return he might find it a heap of ruins and his wife and daughters captives in the hands of the a ruthless enemy. It required the sanctions of religion to rouse the people to the performance of their duty. The eloquent and patriotic Dr. Davis when there was an effort to be made was nearly always in requisition. In one of his appeals he concludes by saying: "In short our frontiers have been drenched with the blood of our fellow-subjects through the length of a thousand miles, and new wounds are still opening. Now while I am still speaking, perhaps the savage shouts and whoops of Indians, and the screams and groans of some butchered family may be mingling their horrors and circulating their tremendous echoes among the rocks and mountains.

But it was all of no avail; a defensive policy was adopted of dividing a small appropriation amongst the frontier counties to purchase arms and ammunition, and leaving it to the colonels of each frontier county to repel the sudden incursions of the savages —and Washington, worn out with his fruitless efforts to unite the people, retired in disgust to Mount Vernon.

My readers, after this retrospect of the history of that gloomy period, can form some idea of what was then meant by being a colonel of a frontier county. Many of these colonels, in attempting to rescue the captives, were shot down by the savage in his ambush and scalped, and left where he fell, for his bones to decay, "unbūried, unhonored and unsung." Others, in scouting by day and unceasing vigil by night, were broken in constitution. This was the case, I presume, with Colonel Maury, for he died before he became an old man. Mr. Fontaine says he has seen no history which records the deeds of these colonels of the frontier counties. No! the genius of history, horror-struck, in profound gloom, sought the deepest shade, and "hung her harp upon the willows." What sorrows did our ancestors incur in winning this fair domain for us from the wilderness and the savage! In the far East there is a nation of people who *worship* their ancestors; and if in view of all which *ours* have suffered and achieved for us, we should drop into this heresy, it is hoped that "the recording angel while he writes it down, may let fall a tear and blot it out forever."

Col. Abraham Maury married Susanna Poindexter, a blood relation of Senator Poindexter of Mississippi. He was a prosperous merchant but built some county flouring mills, which were washed away by a freshet and this broke him. When he went again to Baltimore he frankly told his merchant his condition; but, knowing his integrity, the goods were sold him. On his return home he was attacked with small-pox contracted on the streets of Baltimore. Knowing that he must die, he ordered the *return* of the goods. The October preceding, his eldest son, Matthew Fontaine, had died from the effect of· wounds received at the battle of Guilford Court House. (*Dr. W. S. Ried.*)

Col. Abraham Maury died on the 22nd January, 1784. He had seven children. 1. Matthew Fontaine, above mentioned, who married W. Tabb. 2. Elizabeth, who married W. Dowsing. 3. Susan, who married Joel Parish, Sr. 4. Abram T., who married M. Worsham. 5. Mary, who married Metcalf DeGraffenried. 6. Philip, who married C. Cunningham. 7. Martha, who married Chapman White. Except Elizabeth and her husband, W. Dowsing, (who moved to Columbus, Miss.,) all moved to Williamson county, Tenn. Richard Maury (the father of the Commodore) went with them; and, together, they formed a large colony of the best people that ever crossed the border of that State. I knew them *personally*, and was reared among them. Many of their descendants were among the early settlers of our county of Lawrence, in Alabama.

1. Matthew Fontaine Maury, the eldest child, was born in 1760; entered the army when a mere youth, was wounded at Guilford, C. H., and died in 1783 from the effect of his wound. He left two sons—Thomas and Abram. Their mother married a second time a man of property, named Stewart, who (the sons thought) mistreated them. They ran away, and sought the protection of their uncle, Major Abram Maury, and came with him to Tennessee. The two boys were prosperous, but died of consumption, unmarried. Col. Thomas Maury was a man of ability, and represented Williamson county (when quite young) in the Legislature.

2. Elizabeth Maury, born in 1762, who married W. Dowsing. They moved first from Virginia to Georgia, and thence to Columbus, Miss. He was the Registrar of the Land Office—a good officer and a good man. His descendants bear the names of Dowsing, Thompson, Bassey, Ware and Turner.

3. Susan Maury was born in 1764, and married Joel Parrish, Sr. He died before

my recollection, but I knew her very well. She was a kind, indulgent mother. Her boys were old enough (Matthew Fontaine and Joel) to make fine soldiers under Jackson. Her eldest child, Caroline (the only daughter), was of queenly beauty, and married Hinchea Petway, one of the wealthiest merchants of Franklin. A man of fine sense and very genial disposition. He had a mortal aversion to onions, and when some friend would slip one into his coat pocket, as soon as he detected the nauseous scent he would take out his pen-knife, cut off his pocket and throw both away together. He was a man of great sagacity, and I don't know of his being mistaken but once, and that was when Bennett was hung for murder. An ambitious young physician conceived the idea of resuscitating him, and as he was cut down, he was taken and placed in a carry-all and carried away rapidly. Hundreds of people crowded around the office. When the young doctor found all efforts to bring the body to life futile, he fixed his galvanic points, and when everything was ready called in Petway and another merchant, and applied the points. The dead body opened its eyes, gave a ghastly stare at the two merchants, and stuck out one leg—and the merchants broke and ran, and reported that "Bennett was alive." In a short time it was reported that Sheriff Hunt had been bribed, and Bennett had been hung in stirrups, and there was great excitement, until his body was exhumed from its secret grave, in the woods, and exposed openly in the court house.

I am mistaken; for there was another instance in which Petway's sagacity was at fault. He built a costly brick house right across the south end of main street in Franklin, which had to be torn down. A man can not make a greater mistake than to fix *limits* to a young American town, located in a fertile country. When cotton rose to 25 cents per pound, and the county of Lawrence in Alabama was settled, Mr. Petway bought and opened up, a large plantation on the west bank of Town creek, where the brick house now stands. After residing there for a while, he sold out and bought a home in the vicinity of Nashville, where he died. He had one son, Ferdinand Petway, who was an itinerant Methodist preacher. He was a man of education and taste, and a good speaker, and a singer of unusually fine voice. He died in the Memphis Conference. The descendants of Mr. Petway are to be found in Davidson county, Tennessee. See *Fontaine Chart.* Col. Joel Parrish (a son of Susan Maury, who married Joel Parrish, Sr.,) married Sophia Saunders, eldest daughter of Rev. Turner Saunders (and sister of the writer.) Colonel Parrish and his wife lived in Nashville, and both died there before they attained middle age, leaving a family of young children who were brought to Lawrence county, Alabama, and reared by members of her family. Two daughters of this family married sons of Col. Benjamin Sherrod, and are mentioned *ante.* A son, Joel Parrish, married a Miss Bodie, and died in Lauderdale county without issue. A daughter, Sophie, married Mr. Alfred Gibson. She is a widow living in Mississippi, and has one daughter, Mary, and two sons, Joel and Willis.

The youngest son of the Parrish family in Tennessee was David Winston. He was about my age, and we were schoolmates. Our path to the Academy led through his mother's orchard, where the mellow Father Abraham apples lay, in profusion, on beds of Nimble Will grass. It then wound along through the shadiest places of the beech and poplar grove, and along side of Mr. McKey's orchard; and we had to do some *skilful engineering* to make it hit *both* orchards. David Winston Parrish, when grown, moved to Mississippi, and married Mary, daughter of Solomon Clark, of Pontotoc, one of the best men I ever knew. They had two children. One of them, Susan, married Judge Locke Houston, of Aberdeen, "a first-rate man, and one of the best lawyers in the State." They have four or five children, one of whom is a young lawyer, and another, Mrs. Mary Gillespie, a wonderful singer, and, now (1888) postmistress at Aberdeen. The second daughter of David Winston Parrish, is Sallie. unmarried. His widow married Judge Stephen Adams, then Circuit Judge, an excellent man of fair ability, who served two terms in Congress. They had two children, Edward, a very intellectual young man, who is connected with the cotton business in Mobile, and Belle Adams (Mrs. Professor Wills) principal of the Aberdeen Female College. "Belle was one of the prettiest and sweetest girls we ever had at Aberdeen (says my informant).

Mrs. Wills is a wonderful woman (for her size) as teacher, mother, and domestic manager. She has several children, all bigger than herself," and now lives in Auburn, Ala. (1896).

4. Major Abram Maury, son of Colonel Abraham Maury, whose history we sketched in our last, was born in 1766 in Lunenbury County, Virginia, and married M. Worsham, and his two oldest children were born in Virginia. At a very early time he emigrated to Williamson County, Tenn., with all his brothers and sisters, except Mrs. Dowsing. He had fortunately become the owner of a fine tract of land. He laid off the town of Franklin on one end, and was mainly instrumental in having Harpeth Academy erected on the other. When the latter was built I can not ascertain, but from the fact that the shingles were put on with wooden nails, I infer that it was before General William Carroll erected his nail factory at Nashville, and Mr. Clem another at Franklin. He was a man of fine person, good manners and of fair education and a leader in his county. All the Maurys were very much respected, but he was the wealthiest and had the means to foster public enterprises and of dispensing wide hospitality. Major John Reid, who married his eldest daughter, had been a member of General Jackson's staff and his confidential secretary through all his campaigns. This brought about an intimacy between the General and Major Maury, which (as you will see), had much to do with the fortunes of the Maury family. After the war with England closed I have often seen the General on his way to Major Maury's house with a small staff, all in neat undress uniform and with bear skin holsters.

This was while he was Major-General in the United States army, charged with the special duty of making treaties with the Indians for the cession of their lands. The red man when defeated by the general conceived a high respect for him; but when he beat the British at New Orleans it ripened into awe, and when "Captain Jackson" (as they called him) insisted on a cession of their lands they were very apt to comply. It was General Jackson who procured a commission for young Matthew F. Maury in the navy. If this had not occurred, what would have been the consequences? Would the "Geography of the Sea" have been as little understood now as it was early in the century? After General Jackson's election to the presidency, Cary A. Harris, a son-in-law of Major Maury, was invested with the lucrative office of Public Printer at Washington City. And now we will briefly notice the descendants of Maj. Abram Maury:

(A) Elisabeth Branch married Major John Reid, above mentioned. He was of remarkably clear intellect, of much decision, and strong nerve. He dispatched business, under all circumstances, promptly, and enjoyed the confidence and friendship of General Jackson to such a degree that he requested him to write his life. He had written the first four chapters, when he sickened and died. The papers Major Reid had collected were then handed over, at General Jackson's request, to Major John H. Eaton, who finished the book. Dr. William J. Reid is a son of this marriage. His wife is Sarah Claiborne Maury. They live at the old homestead of Major Abram Maury. Their eldest daughter, Mary Maury, married Andrew J. Puryear, who died about four years ago. She has four children, two sons and two daughters. A son of Dr. Reid, John William, married Maud C. Perkins, and the younger son of Dr. Reid, is Maury Thorpe, a youth of fifteen years.

(B) Matthew Fontaine, who died at twelve years of age.

(C) Daniel Worsham, when grown, made a venture in the mercantile line in Courtland, in this county. He did not succeed well, and I think went back to Tennessee. He never married.

(D) Hon. Abraham Poindexter Maury had a brilliant career. He was born at Franklin 26th December, 1801, and early showed a decided literary taste. He was taught grammar by that accurate teacher, Rev. Lewis Garrett, and was for some time at Harpeth Academy under Dr. Blackburn. At about the age of seventeen years he was invited by the citizens of Franklin to deliver a Fourth of July speech. When quite young, at the instance of Hon. Thomas H. Benton, who had lived at Franklin and known him well, he went to St. Louis to edit a newspaper. After a year's stay he returned to Tennessee and went as a cadet to West Point. As he had more taste for literature and politics than mathematics, he returned to Tennessee, settled in Nashville and edited a paper entitled the *Nashville Republican*. Here he made a reputation as a journalist. He married Mary Eliza Tennessee Claiborne (a lady of great beauty and fine fortune), the daughter of Dr. Thomas Augustine Claiborne, and his wife, Sally Lewis, the daughter of William T. Lewis, of Nashville. Dr. Claiborne was a brother of Wm. C. C. Claiborne, first Territorial Governor of Louisiana, and subsequently elected to the office by the people for thirteen years. Dr. Claiborne, father of Mrs. Maury, after the death of his wife, became a surgeon in the United States Navy and died young.

Hon. Abram P. Maury, after his marriage, bought out the interests of his brothers and sisters in his father's farm at Franklin. Served in both branches of the Legislature, and then in Congress for two terms, commencing with 1835. He was the father of nine children: (1) His eldest daughter, Martha Thomas, is still living, the widow of Nicholas Edwin Perkins, whose father, Nicholas T. Perkins, captured the famous Aaron Burr. She had three children—Edwin Maury, unmarried; Leighla Octavia, married to Dr. Harden T. Cochrane, of Birmingham, Ala., and Maud Claiborne, married to John William Reid, above mentioned. (2) The second daughter of Hon. Abram P. Maury. Sarah Claiborne, was married to Dr. Wm. S. Reid, as we have mentioned above. The third, fourth and fifth died unmarried. (6) Abram P. married, before he was of age, the daughter of Wm. O'Neal Perkins, of Franklin, and died quite a young man, leaving a son, Wm. Perkins Maury, now superintendent of the public schools at Fort Smith, Ark., and a daughter, James Slaughter, who is married to Mr. Benjamin Mann, of Haywood county, Tennessee. (7) Septima died at the age of twenty-six. (8) Octavia died early. (9) Ferdinand Claiborne, the youngest member of the family, is a lawyer in Nashville, and was married some years since to Mrs. Ida Rains, the widow of General Rains of the Confederate service, who was killed at the battle of Murfreesboro.

(E) James Philip, another son of Maj. Abram Maury, was an excellent man. Never married.

(F) William Henry, lived and died in Fayette county. His descendants are to be found there.

(G) Martha Fontaine, married Cary A. Harris. He was made Public Printer by General Jackson as stated above. They had several children set down in the Fontaine chart.

(H) The youngest of Maj. Abram Maury's children was Zebulon M. Pike. He married Virginia Ashlen, a lady of Williamson county and died while being unjustly detained as a prisoner at Sandusky, Ohio, during the late war. His youngest son was drowned a few years ago, and one of his sons, James Henry, married Helen Deas Ross, daughter of Mr. Wm. H. Ross, of Mobile, and is a prosperous merchant in the city of Paris, France. (1887.) He afterwards returned to the United States, and to New Orleans, to live.

The DeGraffenrieds—Second Part.

Our readers will remember that we gave an account of Baron DeGraffenried, and suspended it until we could bring down the history of the Maurys to the point where the two families were united in marriage. This was the union of—

(5) Mary Maury, fifth child of Col. Abraham Maury (who was born in 1768) to Metcalfe DeGraffenried. On the authority of Judge Strong (in the "*Bench and Bar of Georgia*") it was stated that Tscharnar was the son of the Baron D. Since that number was published I have found this to be a mistake. In my correspondence I have learned that the eldest son of the Baron was named Christopher, and Tscharnar was *his* son. Mrs. Mary H. DeGraffenried, a widow lady of much intelligence, residing in Washington City, has in her possession the old family bible of Cristopher DeGraffenried, son of the Baron. It has been somewhat mutilated, but contains entries important to the history of the man who established the first colony in North Carolina. Some of them I will set forth before I proceed with the regular narrative. "Baron Christopher De-

Graffenried was born 21st November, 1661; Regina Tscharnar, his wife, was born 7th December, 1665. They were married 25th April, 1684." The wife of Christopher De-Graffenried, Jr., was Barbara Tempest Needham. "She was born in Hertfordshire, England, and they were married in Charleston, S. C., February 22, 1714." Their son "Tscharnar was born in Williamsburg, Va., 28th November, 1722, and was baptized by Commissary Blair. His godfathers were the Hon. Nathaniel Harrison, Hon. Cole Diggs, Hon. Philip Ludwell and Lady Harrison." Metcalfe (Mac) was one of Tscharnar D.'s sons, and of course the great-grandson of the Baron.

He married Mary, daughter of Col. Abraham Maury, and died in Williamson county, Tenn., and we will notice his children in order.

(1) Abram Maury DeGraffenried (commonly called by his middle name) first married Mary, daughter of Col. Green Hill, of that county. He had commanded a regiment during the Revolutionary War, and was a man of large influence and property. From the fact that Dr. McFerrin, in his sketch of Colonel Hill (in his *History of Methodism in Tennessee*), does not mention the name of this daughter, I had my doubts, until I was assured by Judge Wm. Hill, her nephew, that it was an omission. She lived but a few years, and had but one child, Abram, who moved away to Louisiana, and died many years ago.

The second wife of Abram Maury D. was Maria White. She was a daughter of a Mr. White, who was born and reared in Scotland, migrated to America, and married a Miss Tabb in Charlottsville, Va. After her death he moved with his family to Williamson county, Tennessee, where his youngest daughter, Maria, married Mr. De Graffenried.

Abram Maury D. and his brothers, Metcalfe and Matthew F., were in the war of 1812, under General Jackson, and the latter was shot through the hand. Soon after the land sales of 1819, Abram Maury D. was amongst the first of a colony of more than a dozen families which moved from the vicinity of Franklin, Tenn., to this county. A half dozen of these belonged to the Maury tribe, and the remainder included my father, William Banks, Judge White, William Manning, Cordial Faircloth, John Graham, and others. Abram Maury D. was in his proper element in a new country; was an excellent neighbor; and as his friends came in, one by one, he extended the right hand—not only by way of courtesy, but such help as a man needs when he pitches his tent in the wild woods, on the site of his future home. In old communities, where charity is performed by proxy and visiting is done with cards, people have no adequate idea of what it is to be a good neighbor; but when population is sparse, and houses are few and far between, one feels the true value of a *neighbor*, especially when sickness or death invades a family. He had a sturdy self-reliance which was a relief to the distressed. He did not "weep with those who wept," but he extended a helping hand, and a strong arm, for them to lean upon, in their hour of desolation.

His home was in sight of *Rocky Hill* (where I pen these lines). His was the first orchard planted, and in his house the first sermon was preached, before there were any churches. He was the first Justice of the Peace and he was a terror to evil doers. He had three kinds of testimony. In addition to the positive and circumstantial, he had a third kind, which he called *persuasive testimony*. This he described as a kind of electrical influence which pervaded his whole system, and could be felt to the tips of his fingers. This last could not be found in *Starkie* (which was the standard work on evidence in my day), but perhaps the student of law might find it in *Greenleaf*, which I understand is the work now in vogue! Woe be to the felon that was brought before him, especially if he was a horse thief, for if he was not caught on one of the two first hooks, he was very apt to be hung on the last. From all of which, you would infer that the squire was a man of originality and individuality? Exactly so. His ideas sprang directly from his own brain, which was a large one. He had less respect for *books* than either of his brothers. His reading was in the *great book of nature*. He was quaint in his language. I met him one day in the road and told him our friend, Parson Burruss, had been married for the fourth time. He inquired who the lady was, and when told that she was a beautiful girl of eighteen, whom he knew very well, after holding his head down, he thoughtfully exclaimed, "Well, he has a nag now that is shod all round, and I think she will carry him to his journey's end!"

Mr. Maury was a warm politician of the *Henry Clay Whig* order, in a community where there was a vast majority of *Jackson Democrats*. He was decided in his opinions, and if there had not been a man in the county voting on his side, it would not have shaken his confidence in the least. He seriously entertained the belief that the majority were generally right and would fight, too, for his party against all odds. At a barbecue at Bynum's Spring once, in a political altercation, Murdock, the silversmith, struck the Squire in the face. Now having more of the Swiss Baron, than the French Huguenot in him, he drew a spear which he always carried in his walking cane, and in the fury of his passion ran Murdock through and through three times in the region of his abdomen. Everybody was looking for him to die, but in a short time he was out again hurrahing for Jackson, and about as good as new. His escape from death was owing to the spear being round on the point. It was sharp enough to penetrate the walls of the chest, but not sufficiently keen to cut the intestines.

The Squire was immoderately fond of hunting, and was an expert in the art. Cooper's *"Leather-stocking"* was an apprentice compared with him, for he was a mere deer stalker (a still hunter), while the Squire was a chevalier in "wood-craft." He not only hunted the deer with horses and hounds, and with standers, in the usual way, but in a manner so unusual that it is worthy of remark here. He would go out on horseback alone, and when he would find a herd of deer standing he would ride around them as if he meant no harm. As they would run off he would pursue them at full speed until they would give signs of stopping, by waving their tails from right to left. He would then turn his horse and circle around them. Every time this movement was repeated, they would become gentler, until he could get near enough to shoot down the leader (the oldest and largest buck). When he could succeed in doing this the herd would become completely demoralized and he would sometimes kill half of them. This novel mode of hunting, however, could only be successfully followed as long as the woods were open and clear of undergrowth, and the deer unaccustomed to the sight of man.

But, as I remarked, his usual mode of hunting the deer was to drive for them. When a big hunt was coming off the Squire would invite the young men of the neighborhood to spend the night with him, and the next morning, before day, they were breakfasting around an ample repast, with his gentle wife at the head of the table "as calm as a summer morning." I shall never forget an off-hand compliment he paid her once in the woods. Our stands were near each other on a low ridge, and the hounds were running a deer in the thicket in front of us. I heard the crack of the Squire's rifle, and in a little while I heard it again. I ran down to see what was up, and when I got there he was ramming a bullet down his fine silver-mounted rifle, and had two large round holes cut out of the corners of his hunting shirt, for he had left his patching at home, and had used his garment to supply the deficiency. Says I, "your wife will give you thunder when you get home." "No, young man, my wife never scolds. She'll just take her shears, round off the corners and hem 'em, and the thing will look better than it ever did."

The Squire entertained his friends and hunted, and his negroes played. While others were accumulating every year, he was losing. At length there came a storm and a ship-wreck—and his property all went overboard. Unfortunately his health failed, and he was attacked with cancer of the stomach. In this dilemma he fell upon a feasible expedient for the support of his family, and that was to settle them upon the Byler road, and open a house for the entertainment of travelers. This road running south across Sand Mountain to Tuscaloosa, (then the seat of Government), before the construction of railroads, was a great thoroughfare of travel, thronged with carriages, buggies, horsemen, wagons and droves of stock (horses, mules and hogs). The stands (or public houses) of Baker, DeGraffenried, Davis, Underwood, Mallard, Strong, and others were greatly crowded with company, and the fare was excellent at many of them. The family of Squire DeGraffenried was not fairly settled at their new home, when visiting the valley on business, he suddenly died at the house of Dr. Frank Sykes. His excellent wife never recovered from the shock, and died in less than two years thereafter. The morning of their married life was auspicious, the meridian too, was bright, but the evening was dark. They had severe physical sufferings, but bore them with Christian resignation, and died in peace. The burden of the family then fell on two young girls, who heroically performed their parts, and educated their younger sisters and brothers, sending one of them, Metcalfe, (Mac) to a school of high grade, to be educated in medicine. But fortune frowned upon them, for the war came on, and in their new and prosperous home they were broken up. They had a brother who was a practising physician to aid them, when a most untoward event happened. The Doctor was visiting a patient one day where lived a man named Briggs, who had once been in a lunatic asylum, and had been sent home as cured. While the Doctor was stooping to arrange the fire, Briggs struck him across the back of the neck, with the iron poker, and killed him.

Of the children of Abraham Maury DeGraffenried, Thomas married a Miss Guthrie; of Columbus, Miss., and died in 1842, leaving a widow and one son, Thomas, who entered the army at sixteen years of age, and was killed at Atlanta, Ga. Fontaine never married. He died in Decatur in 1879. Tscharnar served in the Sixteenth Alabama Regiment during the war and afterward married the widow White and moved to Texas. Matthew Maury married S. W. Patrick, a daughter of Edward Patrick. She died in 1871, leaving two children, Mary F., who married Dr. E. T. Simms, of Hillsboro, and Maury who married Lula, a daughter of Col. O. D. Gibson of this county. His second wife was the Widow Dandridge, near Courtland. She lived only a short time, and he is now living in Moulton with his third wife, the Widow McDaniel. Freeman F. never married. He served during the war in Roddy's command, went to Arkansas and died in 1869. Susan M. married Capt. J. W. Allen. He died in 1880, leaving three children of whom Lizzie M. married Dr. John H. Farley; Mary C. who married J. C. Kumpe, Probate Judge of this county, and the other daughter is living with her mother on the Byler road. Sallie C., the youngest child of Abraham Maury D., married Rev. W. E. Mabry, a preacher of the first class in the Alabama Conference. The two daughters upon whom the burden of rearing and educating the sons and daughters of this family fell, when they were left orphans, were Mary Ann and Elizabeth. Fortunately they were naturally intelligent and had been well educated. They have been keeping a hotel for some years in Moulton, that is so well conducted as to receive a liberal patronage. But few of those who have observed the modest and graceful manner in which they have performed their duty as hostesses are aware of the fact that their ancestors, both on the paternal and maternal side, were noble, and that they had bluer blood in their veins than any ladies in our county.

Beverley Reese lives with his sisters and has aided them in rearing the family. He has never married.

2. The second child of Metcalfe DeGraffenried, whose wife was Mary Maury, was Metcalfe DeGraffenried. His first wife was the beautiful Dorothy (Dolly) Pearsall, daughter of Mr. Jeremiah Pearsall, of whom we have spoken. He lived near Courtland, Ala., near where the Harris mansion now stands. His wife died, I think, two years after the marriage—and he moved to Tennessee and married Candace Pope—and after her death, Lucy Gee. By all three marriages he had but two children : Catherine, by his first marriage, and Benjamin, by his last. The latter died unmarried.

Catherine married Powhatan Perkins, son of old Mr. James Perkins, a wealthy gentleman of Williamson county, Tenn. By this marriage there was a son, Metcalfe Perkins, who was killed during the late war; and two or three daughters; amongst them Mrs. Benjamin Allen and Mrs. Edmund Baxter of Nashville. Mrs. Perkins became a widow, and then married John H. Ewing, a prominent druggist of Nashville, by whom she had a number of sons and daughters. One of her daughters married Martin Baldwin of Montgomery. Her granddaughter, Eliza, married a Mr. Hutchinson, also of Montgomery.

3. Sarah, third child of Metcalfe de Graffenried and Mary Maury, married the Rev. Lewis Garrett, a man of note in the Methodist Church, both in Kentucky and Tennessee, as an itinerant minister. "He was born in Pennsylvania, 24th April, 1772. His father, Lewis Garrett, in a few years after moved to Botetourt county, Virginia, and in 1779 removed to Kentucky, then very thinly settled, for very few ventured to settle any other way than in forts and stations—being perpetually exposed to the hostile attacks of the savage Indians. He, however, died before reaching the place of his destination, and left a widow and eight children (the eldest about sixteen) in the wilderness, who were obliged to live in tents until log cabins could be built. The winter was very cold. It was long remembered in Kentucky as the *hard winter*. This was a trying scene to a woman who had been educated and spent her early life near Philadelphia, and had seen better days. The Indians stole her horses; her funds were in Continental money, which became depreciated; breadstuffs were hardly to be procured at any price, and many ate no bread till it grew and matured the next season—having to sustain life with wild meat without salt. She did sometimes procure a little corn at the rate of seventy dollars a bushel (depreciated currency), but it was a scanty supply.

"In the Spring of 1780, a son about eleven years of age, went out to catch a horse, and never returned. It was supposed that he was taken by the Indians; but no trace of him could ever be discovered About 1783, her eldest son, about fifteen or sixteen years of age, went on a hunting excursion with two men; both the men were killed, and he taken prisoner by the Shawnee Indians. Their dogs returned home, and the bones of the men were found sometime afterward; but she was compelled to remain, for full eighteen months, in a state of painful suspense, respecting his destiny, until all unexpectedly, like one raised from the dead, he arrived at home to cheer the almost broken heart of a widowed mother. His account of his captivity was a tale of interest. After having been dragged on through the wild wood with little or no nourishment, to the Shawnee's towns, he was adopted into an Indian family, where he remained about six months. He was then taken to Detroit on a trading expedition, and while he was left to keep a camp on the river, was taken in a canoe by a white man, and conveyed to the house of a Frenchman. The savages sought him diligently for some time, and threatened to burn if they found him. The Frenchman carried him to the house of his brother, several miles distant, where he was hospitably treated, and remained nearly a year, when there was an exchange of prisoners, and he was permitted to return home." The above account was written by Rev. Lewis Garrett himself, and published by Doctor McFerrin, in his work, "*Methodism in Tennessee.*"

Young Lewis, when a boy had not the advantage of good schools, but was fortunate in having a mother, who was well educated, and under whose instruction he became a very accurate scholar in all branches of learning, then taught, except the dead languages. Young Lewis was converted during a revival carried on by the Baptist, who were the religious pioneers of Kentucky; but became a member of the Methodist church.

In 1794 there was a conference held at a private house, for there were but seven traveling preachers. At this conference he was admitted on trial and appointed to Green Circuit, in what is now termed East Tennessee. The wilderness had to be passed through, and they waited until sixty men all around were collected, and passed through in safety. When he reached the circuit there was not yet an end of the danger. It mostly was a frontier, and the Cherokees were in a state of hostility. The presiding elder rode up to a cabin one day and saw the family lying bleeding, just butchered by the savages. Mr. Garrett in passing around his circuit frequently saw dreary tenements from which the occupants had fled in fear, and passed on, alone and unattended, to preach to the inhabitants of the forts. The creeks were without bridges, and the paths were dim, and the fare of the coarsest kind. Under circumstances like this, men brought up in luxurious habits would have taken a furlough until more peaceful times.

In 1804 Mr. Garrett was made presiding Elder of the Cumberland District, which included several circuits in Middle Tennessee, Natchez, Miss., and lower Illinois. The lower end could only be reached on horseback, through the Chickasaw and Choctaw nations. He started to reach his work in Illinois with a companion, but the season being wet, the Ohio had overflowed its banks, and obstructed their passage so they could not proceed. They however turned up the Ohio, swam their horses across the streams, and beyond Green river they formed a new circuit, where there was only one member of their church. Here they had a camp-meeting the next summer. The people gathered from twenty to forty miles around; and they formed a society of thirty or forty members.

After such a life of hardship and exposure the health of Mr. Garrett failed, and he asked for a location. But he had lain up nothing for his family. In that day the preachers had little ease, and spent no idle time. The good people sometimes gave them a suit of home spun clothes, but their pockets were penniless. He opened a grammar school in the town of Franklin, Tenn., and never had a teacher better success in that line. He had at least forty pupils (of whom I was one), and perfect discipline. He believed in Solomon's doctrine; and on two pegs above the fire-place he kept a bundle of rods seasoning. When they were laid on an unruly boy, it was done in such an honest manner as to make a lasting impression. Modern schools are said to be governed by "moral suasion," but this could not be done in early times in Tennessee, where not only boys, but steers and horses were all wild. He was an autocrat in his school, and when there came a revolt in the way of a "barring out," never was one so mortified as he at his defeat. Fortunately this relic of the Roman Saturnalia has disappeared from our schools.

When his brother-in-law, Abram Maury DeGraffenried removed to Lawrence County, Ala., he removed with him and fixed his home just above Redbanks, where he had the misfortune to lose his good wife. He then re-entered the traveling connection, and in virtue of his ability, occupied Nashville and other important stations in the conference.

Many years afterwards, when the renowned John Newland Maffit, the great orator and revivalist, was at the acme of his fame, friends effected a union between them for the purpose of publishing a religious newspaper called the *Western Methodist*, which was the forerunner of the *Christian Advocate* at Nashville. Their paper was a very good one. Mr. Garrett, a writer of great cleverness and force, furnished the logic, and Mr. Maffit (who was highly cultured in that line), furnished the rhetoric, but it was financially a failure, and soon abandoned.

Rev. Lewis Garrett died at the house of his son, Abram Maury Garrett, in Mississippi, April 28, 1857, having labored as a Methodist preacher for sixty-three years. In person he was rather under the usual size, had hazel eyes, a nose slightly Roman and fine features. With a clear, full voice and slow delivery, he could be heard in the open air by large congregations. His style was didactic, and the substance of his sermons doctrinal; just such sermons as produced the wonderful effects witnessed in the revivals which occurred early in this century, when (to use his language) "it was difficult to discriminate between a Presbyterian and a Methodist, for they preached together and shouted together." In our day *doctrinal* sermons are not in favor. Orthodoxy and Heterodoxy (like the lion and the lamb) have lain down together, and in another age it may be difficult to distinguish one from the other.

In addition to his son, Abram M., spoken of above, he had two sons, Phineas and James, and one daughter, Anne. I have not been able to get any satisfactory account of their families.

4. Susan (the fourth child of Metcalfe DeGraffenreid and Mary Maury) married Beverly Reese. He was the son of a wealthy man and pious Methodist, who lived a few miles South of Franklin. Near him was Reese's chapel, where, in early times, a conference had been held over which Bishop McKendree presided. The old gentleman died first, and then his saintly wife. Of all men I have known in early life, Beverly Reese was the most genial, cheerful, and beloved. His father had secured (when it was cheap) an ample fortune in land, and Beverly purchasing the hill which commands so fine a view of Franklin from the Southeast, there made his home for many years. Whilst

living there an amusing incident occurred between him and a Universalist preacher, named Streeter, who had made quite an impression on the young people of Franklin. He was a polished, bland speaker, and spoke charmingly of the "mercy of God," but said not a word about a "hell." Why it was that Beverly was so wonderfully taken with this new doctrine I can not tell. Perhaps it was owing to the fact that in early life the old people had drawn the Methodist curb upon him too tightly. When Mr. Streeter was about to leave the town, Beverly started a subscription paper to raise a salary to induce him to remain as their permanent preacher, and headed the list with two hundred dollars. Whilst the names were being set down, he was informed by a friend that Mr. Streeter *did* believe in *a hell*. Beverly, in his off hand style, stepped over to Mr. Streeter, who was with a number of gentlemen, and asked him if this was so. He answered in the affirmative, and explaining that a man would only be kept there until his sins were purged away. "And how long would that generally take," inquired Beverly. "A thousand years, or so," humorously replied the Universalist. Beverly indignantly exclaimed, "I would be a *confounded poor crackling* to go to Heaven after being burned in hell for a thousand years;" and as he walked off he tore the subscription paper to pieces. His niece informs me that he returned to the faith of his fathers, and died a class-leader in the Methodist church.

When so many of his kin moved to Lawrence county, Ala., his family was amongst the number. He made his home on Town Creek, and his wife's mother, Mary Maury, resided mostly in his house, where she died. Mr. Reese, and indeed all of this connection, except the family of Abram Maury DeGraffenried, moved back to Tennessee, having become dissatisfied, on account of the sickness with the country. Thousands and thousands of acres of woods had been deadened, and the decomposition of the timber was the cause of great mortality amongst the people for several years.

Beverly Reese died many years ago, and his wife soon after. Their daughter Sallie, married Mordecai Puryear. They are both dead. Their daughter, an only child, married Thomas Watson, and is now a widow with two sons and five daughters. "She is wealthy and a woman (says my informant) of superior gifts and accomplishments." Another daughter of Beverly Reese, Elizabeth, married John Currin, nephew of Robert P. Currin, who was one of the leading merchants of Franklin when I was a boy. By this marriage there were two daughters, Sallie P. Currin, now of Franklin, and Evelyn Metcalfe, widow of Dr. Bellville Temple, of Mt. Meigs, Ala. She has a son and a daughter. My informant says she is beautiful.

5. Matthew Fontaine was the fifth child of Metcalfe and Mary (Maury) DeGraffenried. He was called General both in Tennessee and in Mississippi. In the latter State he married Miss Stewart, a wealthy lady. Of thirteen children by this marriage, only three arrived to maturity, and are living near Eddyville, Ky. (A) Mary Ann, who married Mr. Pritchell, and is a widow with children. (B) Matthew Fontaine, twice married, first to a daughter of old Mr. Stith, of Franklin, who died without issue, and a second time to Henrietta Williams, of Tuscaloosa, Ala. (C) Duncan, who married twice also; first, to a Miss Pope, of Williamson county, Tenn., who dying, left a son, Matthew F., who is married and has two children; and, secondly, to Sallie Kennedy, of Oxford, Miss. They have a number of children.

General DeGraffenried, was married secondly to Miss McLemore, of Williamson county, Tenn. By this marriage he had a number of children. Of those who lived to maturity, John and Thomas, live in Tennessee, and have children; Jefferson and Reese live in Texas; a daughter, Minor, is married to William Daniels, a distinguished gentleman, of Clarksville, Tenn.; Penelope, Flora and Dixie, are well married in, or near, the same place, and Susan is unmarried.

6. Benjamin D., sixth child of Metcalfe and Mary (Maury) DeGraffenried, removed with his brother, Abram Maury, to Lawrence county, Ala. He made his home with his brother and was a young man of merit and much esteemed. In the summer of 1824, when so many died of a violent fever, he, who was unremitting in his attendance on the sick, took the fever and died.

6. Philip P. Maury, sixth child of Col. Abram Maury, was born in Virginia in 1770. He married Miss C. Cunningham, moved to Tennessee with his relatives, and settled within a mile or two of Franklin, Tenn., on the Southwest side of it. He was an industrious good citizen, and raised a large family on a small estate. Like others of the same name, he was more solicitous to give his children a good education, than to amass a fortune for them.

His children succeeded well in life. None of them are settlers in this county. Four or five of his sons (I believe) had no descendants. He had only one daughter, Elizabeth C. Maury, who in 1827 married Franklin L. Owen, and moved to Mobile, Ala. He was a man of business, and of unblemished reputation, and served for many years as cashier of the Bank of Mobile. Mrs. Owen is still living there. Their son, Richard B, is Mayor, and Dr. ——— Owen is an eminent physician of that city. Their daughter, Bettie Owen, married her cousin, James F. Maury, and is now a widow living also in Mobile. James H. Maury, who married Lucinda Smith, and John Michaux Maury, who married Caroline Sessions, sons of Mr. Philip P. Maury, were lawyers, and moving to Mississippi, they became eminent in their profession.

7. Martha Maury, seventh child of Col. Abraham Maury, was born in Virginia in 1772, and married Chapman White. He was a man of property; but his estate was impaired by the profuse hospitality then so common in old Virginia. He moved also to Tennessee, and lived near Franklin in great comfort.

Here we bring the account of the Maury's and DeGraffenried's to a conclusion, and perhaps some of my readers have thought that too much space has been given to it. But they should keep in mind the plan on which I first set out; which was to say but little of those now on the stage of action, but to trace families into the past, as far as I could go with authenticated facts to sustain me. In this case the account was so strangely blended with the persecution of the Protestants in France, the early history of Virginia and North Carolina, the war of the Revolution, and the war between the States, that to have written less would have been an essential departure from our plan. In guarding from mistakes, I have carefully consulted with many authorities, and have had very many intelligent correspondents, but from none of them have I received as much aid as from Dr. William S. Reid, of Franklin, Tennessee, whose clear head and retentive memory have enabled him to thread the genealogical labyrinths encountered, without confusion.

I have learned from Mrs. Berkley (a very intelligent Maury), several facts of much interest, in reference to the family, which I will here transcribe: "Dr. Thomas Walker, of Castle Hill, Albermarle County, Va., was married twice, his wives being double first cousins. The first wife, Mildred Thornton, was the mother of his large family, and the other was Elizabeth Thornton, both of them being granddaughters of Mildred Washington, the aunt of George Washington, and sister of his father, Augustine."

The Rev. James Maury, after graduating at William and Mary College, went to England for Ordination. He married Mary Walker, daughter of Mr. John Walker, a brother of Dr. Thomas Walker. He served as rector of Walker's church for thirty years without compensation. His children, being numerous, he taught a family school and received in addition a few sons of his personal friends. At one time he had under his tuition Thomas Jefferson, James Monroe and light-horse Harry Lee.

Rev. Matthew Maury (eldest son of Rev. James Maury), married Elizabeth, the daughter of Dr. Thomas Walker, and succeeded his father in the rectorship of Walker's church.

John Minor Maury.

The following is a very interesting sketch of the career of John Minor Maury, eldest brother of Commodore M. F. Maury, and father of General Dabney H. Maury, which was written by a member of the family, who knows all about his history.

"John Minor Maury, eldest son of the marriage of Richard Maury and Dinah Minor, entered the United States Navy as Midshipman when thirteen years old.

"Just before the war of 1812 with Great Britain, Captain William Lewis, United States Navy, procured a furlough for young Maury and himself, and sailed on a trading voyage to China. At the island of Nukaheeva, Captain Lewis left Maury and six men to procure sandal wood, and other articles of commerce, for which he would touch on his return to the States.

"Lewis, with his ship, was blockaded in China, by a British force, and no relief came to Maury and his men for two years. The island was divided by a mountain ridge, into two independent and hostile tribes. The Americans were befriended by the chief of the tribe in which they had been left, but all of them save Maury and a sailor named Baker, were killed by raiders from the other side of the mountain.

"The two survivors made a home for themselves on the tops of four cocoa-nut trees, where they built a palace of concealment about as large as the maintop of a frigate, a rope ladder serving as a means of access to it.

"One day, just two years after they had landed, they saw a large ship standing in for anchorage, displaying the American flag. They at once took their canoe and hastened toward the ship; but the fate of Captain Cook was recent enough then to make our sailors cautious in receiving the crowds of natives who swarmed around their vessel. So the sentry warned all canoes to keep off. Maury and Baker were as naked as any of them, and they were included in their order to keep away. They went back to their perch, and soon a launch came ashore from the ship, and among the officers Maury recognized and hailed an old shipmate, McKnight, who was passing under his trees. With much astonishment McKnight cordially greeted his old friend, who with Baker came down the ladder, arrayed like Adam before his fall. They were at once taken aboard the frigate Essex, Capt. David Porter commander, and enrolled in the crew.

"Porter had with him a recent prize, a very fast sailer, which he named the 'Essex Junior,' and armed as a consort. Lieutenant Downs was appointed captain and Maury first lieutenant. And after refitting his ship Porter resumed his famous cruise, until he reached Val Paraiso. Here shortly came the English frigates, Cherub and Phœbe, with orders to capture the Essex whenever they might find her. Porter at once prepared for action, and his two ships stood out to sea in order to regain the marine league required by the laws of nations. The United States was not then like England powerful enough to disregard the laws of nations when dealing with a feeble power. Therefore the American ships stood out to sea to gain the marine league. The Essex Junior having gained it, could not for twenty-four hours return to the neutral port, and after the old Essex was captured the younger ship could not venture an encounter with the Englishman. The Essex Junior was the better sailer and well handled, got well away, but the Great Essex was dismantled by a squall, and Hillyard, the gallant English captain, not having the law of nations in respect when it interfered with his orders, fell aboard the disabled Essex, and after a long and bloody battle destroyed her. Porter, when unable to manœuvre his ship, warped her up to the shore, and fought one broadside as long as it was possible, and then brought the survivors of his crew away in safety.

"The 'Essex Junior,' unable to take any part in the battle, stood away for the States, where young Maury was in time to take his part in McDonough's victory on Lake Champlaine. In 1815 he wrote from the deck of the Saratoga to a friend in Fredericksburg, Va.: 'We have won a glorious victory. I hope the first great result of this will be to confirm the wavering allegiance of New York and Vermont to the Union. They have been threatening to secede unless peace be made with England on any terms.' The pirates of the West Indies had become bold and destructive, and in 1823–24 Porter was ordered to fit out a fleet against them.

"He was authorised to select his officers for this service, and his first choice was John Minor Maury, to be his flag captain. The service was desperate; no quarter was given. The pirates were scattered or destroyed. And young Maury was sent home with dispatches announcing the result of the expedition. He died of yellow fever on board the United States storeship 'Decoy,' and was buried at sea off the Capes of Norfolk. Admiral Tatnall and Admiral Buchannan declared him to be the cleverest officer of his day in the United States service. I have heard Admiral Buchannan say that when Maury was first lieutenant of the Macedonian, in a foreign port, all the other men of war would look with admiration on the manner in which 'little Maury handled his ship.' He died at the age of twenty-eight years. Next year his younger brother, Matthew Fontaine Maury, was made a midshipman. This was done at the request of Gen. Sam Houston, then Congressman from the Franklin district of Tennessee. But the memories of his elder brother's services and the influence of his uncle, Fontaine Maury, then high in favor with the government, and of his near kinsman Richard Brooke Maury, Register of the Navy Department, gave force to General Houston's recommendation, and secured to the world the service of the greatest philosopher America has ever produced. From the time I was five years old he was to me as a father. It is from him, and from my mother, I have these facts of the history of his elder brother, also from our kinsman, Captain Lewis Herndon, and many others, officers of the old United States navy.

"DABNEY H. MAURY."

The Saunders Family,

according to its tradition, is of English descent. Edward Saunders was its progenitor in America, and its first settlement was in the Northern Neck of Virginia, in Northumberland county, near the Lancaster county line, not far from a place known as Fairfield, and the Rappahannock river. After some years, the Saunders homestead was across the county line in Lancaster, but only some eight or ten miles from Fairfield.

Precisely when Edward Saunders came from England to Virginia, tradition does not say. He had, however, a son named Ebenezer, born 1661, in Virginia, who left a son named Edward.

The date of Edward Saunder's birth has not come down to us (*it was 1688*) but as in 1718 he was married and had at least one child; and as in 1720 he was a vestryman in St. Stephen's parish, in Northumberland county, and was a "Captain," (see Meade's *Old Churches and Families of Virginia*, page 468) it is safe to say that he was born some time before the year 1700.

The date of Edward Saunder's death is uncertain. He was, however, alive in the year 1744, as in that year he executed a deed of gift now of record in Lancaster county.

Edward Saunders left three sons—William, Edward and Thomas. Edward moved to Brunswick county, Virginia. His will (1783) mentions wife, Sinah, and sons, Eben and Edward, and daughters, Judy Freeman, Lucy Peebles, Sinah, Peggy, Sally and Celia Saunders.

Thomas (third son of Edward) married in Lancaster county, moved to the lower part of the State of Maryland and had several children who bore themselves with credit in the Revolutionary war.

William Saunders, the eldest son of Edward, and with whom, as the lineal ancestor of our family, we have most to do, was born in the year 1718, in the county of Lancaster, at the homestead above mentioned. His youngest son, James Saunders, for whom I was named, wrote (1824) a memoir of the Saunders family of fifteen pages, which his grandson, Col. Wm. L. Saunders, of North Carolina, had printed many years ago, and distributed among his relatives. When the author wrote this memoir he was sixty years old, and his memory extended far back. Moreover, he lived with, and survived, his parents, and fell heir to all the family records. This will account for the specialty in dates which I am able to give for 170 years past. This "*Family Memoir*" describes William Saunders, above mentioned, as being about five feet eight inches in height, well made, of light complexion and blue eyes, from 150 to 160 pounds in weight, very active and fleet, possessed of agreeable manners, and "a good education for the times."

"On the 18th of May, 1738, he married Betsy Hubbard, of his own neighborhood, daughter of Thomas Hubbard, of Scotch descent. She was born 22d of February, 1721, and had two brothers, Joseph and Ephraim Hubbard, (ancestors of the Fosters of Nashville, Tenn). Unlike her husband, she had dark complexion, black hair and black eyes. She was of common stature and good make, religious and intelligent. She did perhaps come as nigh performing all the duties intended by her Maker for her to do, as any woman of my knowledge." (*Family Memoir*). Her memory is honored and cherished by her descendants in a remarkable degree.

The issue of this marriage: (1) Thomas, born 18th June, 1739; (2) Mary, born 6th May, 1741; (3) Jesse, born 21st July, 1743; (4) Winifred, born 24th February, 1746; (5) Frances, born 5th August, 1748; (6) Edward, born 5th May, 1751; (7) Presley, born 19th October, 1753; (8) Joseph, born 7th June, 1757; (9) Ephraim, born 14th March, 1760; (10 and 11) William and James, (twins), born 25th April, 1765.

Of the above, our ancestor, Thomas, was the eldest, but we will find it most convenient first to give a brief account of his brothers and sisters.

Mary lived to advanced age, without being married, with her brother Joseph, in Brunswick, where she died.

Jesse Saunders "traveled while young to Granville county, North Carolina, and married Ann, daughter of Colonel Yancey of that county; had many children; moved to Georgia, near Augusta, then to the new purchase in that State, where he died. He was an excellent partisan officer, harassing the British on their way to Yorktown. He had several skirmishes with the enemy, some of them sharp. This brother was in the battle with the Regulators, as it was called many years before the Revolution and had a horse shot under him, ran several hair-breadth escapes after the battle, while taking up the straggling Regulators; was waylaid and shot, yet, out of them all, Providence delivered him. He appeared never to regard risking his person or his life in performing duties of any kind. There are several of his children I have seen, and I will try and name them: William, Yancey, James (and perhaps Lewis), Betsy, Jesse, and others I can not think of."—(*Family Memoir*.)

Winifred Saunders "married pretty early in life Mr. Thos. Elliott; had several children, but one of whom (John) is now living, in Brunswick county. Those who died (as far as I know) had no descendants."—(*Family Memoir*.)

Frances Saunders " married Mr. Abraham White in the county of Lancaster, Va., and had several children, none of whom are living. She married a second husband, Mr. George Davis, and had two children, Holland and Ephraim. The first lives in Tennessee, and the latter in Brunswick county, Va. She died in advanced age in the county of Brunswick, Va."! (*Family Memoir*).

Edward Saunders "traveled when young to Granville county, North Carolina, married Jane, daughter of Colonel Yancey, and sister to the aforesaid Ann, and had three children, I think, Peggy, Nancy and Elizabeth. The first two married Johnstons and have moved to some other part of the world, I know not where. This brother, Edward, during the Revolutionary War, was called on by his brother Jesse, of Granville, to go with him in pursuit of some deserters, who had likewise been stealing horses in that county. This was done under authority of military law. They, with several others, pursued and took the deserters. While on their way to jail, one of the prisoners said to Jesse Saunders, who had the command, that if he would go by his mother's he would produce his discharge. Whereupon he complied, and while in the house looking for the discharge, another of the deserters out at the door, snatched a gun from one of the soldiers and attempted to shoot Jesse who was in the house, at which Edward interfered and received the whole discharge in his bowels, and fell dead on the spot. Jesse hearing the disturbance out of doors, sprang out and was able to shoot the murderer as he was making off, and brought him to the ground. Jesse gave himself up and was acquitted with great triumph, not being allowed to stand in the place common for such trials. Thus died Edward as noble and worthy a man as any private character of his day." (*Family Memoir*).

Presley Saunders " entered early in the Revolutionary War and remained therein for several years, chiefly to the northward. He belonged to the Second Virginia Regiment. He was in the battles of Brandywine, Monmouth, the storming of Stoney Point, and several others which I do not now recollect, and finally at the capture of Lord Cornwallis at Little York. After the capture of Cornwallis he returned to the place of his nativity and to private life, married Winifred, daughter of Mr. William Kent, near him, had several children, and moved in advanced life to the county of Chowan, State of North Carolina, and died in 1816. He embraced religion in advanced age, though he had at all times been moral, upright and steady. His children were William, Betsy, Edward, Presley and Nancy." (*Family Memoir*). The writer knew Betsy Saunders well. She first married a Mr. Wilder, a thrifty planter on the Chowan river, who at his death left her with a fertile farm, and one child—James Wilder. After some years she was married a second time to Mr. Henry Hubbel, a man of sprightly talents but with no turn for getting or keeping money. After a while they were forced to sell their delightful home, abounding in all the comforts of land and sea. They moved to Alabama and settled in Courtland, in Lawrence county, where several families of their relations had already preceded them. Here they made a good living by keeping a hotel. Her son by her first husband, James Wilder, was one of the "Red Rovers" who went out to the aid of Texas under the lead of Dr. Jack Shackelford, and was massacred at Goliad. The sympathy in this community for Mrs. Hubbel was profound, for she was a woman of strong mind and a sweet temper, was welcome in every family in times of prosperity, for she was a genial companion; and more than welcome to a family when overshadowed by a cloud of sorrow or the pall of death, for she had a heart which could sympathize with and the discretion and tact to administer consolation to them.

Mrs. Hubbel has been dead for many years. By her second marriage she had one child, Sarah, who, like her mother, was gifted with fine intellect, and has been favored with a higher degree of culture. Sarah Hubbel married General Lewis Garrett, of Huntsville and Tuscumbia. He became rich and purchased a valuable plantation on the Arkansas river, where he made his home. He died a few years ago, and his widow owns and still resides on the fine estate. She has no children.

Joseph Saunders

was the eighth child of Thomas and Betsy (Hubbard) Saunders. He was born in Lancaster county, Va. He entered, when quite young, the Revolutionary Navy, in which he gained distinction (see *Family Memoir* written sixty-five years ago by my great uncle, James Saunders); the particulars of his services will be given before we close.

After the war he married Margaret Shackelford, of Richmond county, Va. She was the daughter of Colonel Frederick Shackelford, and the half sister of the late Dr. Jack Shackelford, of Courtland, Ala. He moved in the year 1789 to the county of Brunswick, Va., and having lost his first wife, married Martha, daughter of Colonel Frederick Mecklin, of that county.

He purchased bounty land warrants and located them on the frontiers, and made great profit. President Adams appointed him to a lucrative office in the excise; conferred upon him, solely, on account of his services in the Revolution. His condition became very comfortable. He had a good plantation and a spacious house, and a heart full of hospitality. He was an ardent Baptist, and became much attached to a promising young Baptist, to whom he gave a home for several years, during which he prepared himself by a course of diligent study for great usefulness in the church. This was the famous preacher Jesse Mercer, who compiled a book of hymns which was generally in use in the Baptist Churches eighty years ago, called "*Mercer's Cluster*." This Mr. Mercer moved to Georgia and became famous, and his name was conferred upon the Baptist University of that State.

In 1822 Mr. Joseph Saunders moved to Giles county, Tenn., and the next year he moved to Lawrence county, Ala., and purchased a home adjoining to that of my father. I had heard a great deal of this great uncle, and was prepared to reverence and love him. He was about five feet eight inches high, remarkably well made, fair complexion and blue eyes. He was then about 65 years old, and his head was white, and his countenance noble and prepossessing. I gave him my full confidence, and when, a few years afterwards, I had the opportunity to do him a great favor, all my powers were exerted to make his old age happy.

When the War of the Revolution was fairly opened, the State of Virginia solemnly promised the officers and sailors of her small Navy to give every one of them half-pay for life, if they would serve faithfully *during the War*; and when this small Navy was transferred to the Confederation of States, a promise was made to perform all the promises made to these officers and sailors by the State of Virginia. It was fifty years before this promise was redeemed. A majority of them were in their graves. I brought the case before the Pension Office, and Lieutenant Joseph Saunders was allowed a pension, the first payment on the same (including back pay) amounting to thirteen thousand dollars. That excellent officer, Gen. J. C. Black, at my request, hunted up the old record of the case, and has sent me the following abstract of it from the Pension Office:

The Declaration.

"In March, 1777, Joseph Saunders enlisted in the navy of the State of Virginia for three years, going on board of the ship 'Dragon,' then on the stocks at Fredericksburg, in charge of the provisions and issue of rations, but his rank is not specified. He assisted in rigging the ship, and after the guns were mounted, he was temporarily placed in charge of the magazine until a gunner was appointed.

"A squadron rendezvoned at a station near the capes of Virginia, consisting of the ships 'Tartar,' Capt. John Taylor, who was also in command of the squadron; the 'Tempest,' Capt. Celey Saunders; the 'Dragon,' Capt. Eleazer Callender; the brig 'Home Forgot,' commanded by John Leister, previously a lieutenant of the ship 'Dragon;' and a tender. Orders were soon received from the Navy Board to sail on a cruise, and in two or three days after leaving the station they were pursued by a 74-gun ship, which compelled them to separate and escape to their former station While the 'Dragon' was in that vicinity, under loose sail, she was approached by a British privateer, and after exchanging two or three broadsides, the privateer discovering its mistake in the character of her opponent, hauled off to escape: but the cannonade was heard by Captain Taylor, of the 'Tartar,' who pursued, and in an engagement he received a dangerous wound, and his lieutenant permitted the enemy to escape. Soon Captain Taylor resigned, and was succeeded by Captain William Saunders, with Capt. James Barron in command of the squadron. Captain Callender also resigned, and was succeeded by Capt. Edward Travis, in command of the ship 'Dragon.' Just before his term of service expired, Saunders was promoted to the post of Master's Mate, and being pleased with his station, continued in the service. At the time the British fleet came into Hampton Roads, the ships 'Tartar' and 'Dragon' were at the mouth of James river, and retreated up that river. Saunders, in connection with Lieutenant Chandler, obtained permission to man one of the State galleys, with which they sailed down the river to its mouth, where they attacked a Letter of Marque, carrying 12 or 14 guns, and continued the fight until their ammunition was exhausted, without losing a man. Under date of 20th March, 1781, Saunders received orders as Lieutenant to prepare and man the 'Lewis' galley for the purpose of going down the river to watch the enemy's fleet and report the same to General Lafayette, who was in the vicinity, and follow his instructions. After the British army occupied Petersburg their fleet moved higher up the river, and soon sent gunboats to destroy the ship yards on the river and the public stores. Lieutenant Saunders had filled his galley with naval stores to transport them further up the river, but the wind and tide being against him, he discharged his guns at the hostile gunboats, and sank his vessel previous to retreating in safety.

"This was his last active service in the navy. By the orders of Capt. Edward Travis, he procured some smaller vessels, with which he rendered service at the mouth of York river in conveying forces and provisions for the army that was prosecuting the seige of Lord Cornwallis at Yorktown, until a signal from the French admiral informed him of the surrender of the British army (17th October, 1781)."

You will notice that Joseph Saunders when he went aboard the ship Dragon, was not twenty years old, and yet, young as he was, he occupied positions of trust from the first. As a proof of his fearlessness and enterprise, he sought, and obtained, a separate command twice in the darkest period of our struggle for independence, before the French fleet appeared to shut up the British fleet in the Chesapeake. In the Virginia squadron of four war vessels, two of them had captains and a third a lieutenant, who bore the name of Saunders. They were no doubt reared on the sea coast, probably all in the northern neck of Virginia, and, although I can not assert it with any confidence, I judge that Captains Celey and William Saunders were brothers, and sons of the Thomas Saunders who married in Lancaster county, and moved to Maryland, and, therefore, cousins of Lieutenant Joseph Saunders.

The latter lived for some years in Lawrence county, universally respected and beloved and in great favor with his Baptist brethern. His piety was deep and entirely unaffected. But few persons, unacquainted with his history, having seen his benevolent face, all bathed in tears, under the ministry of his beloved Townes, would have dreamed that in our contest for liberty, amidst the smoke and roar of battle, and on the bloody deck, he had sustained the flag of his country with stern resolution. He was well educated for the times, and was fond of books, and when his feelings became interested in any matter, he wrote very sweet poetry, even when he was eighty years old. His death was a sad one. He had started to Tuscaloosa in a sulky, to draw his pension, when during the first day's drive his horse became frightened and ran away, and that excellent old gentleman was instantly killed.

We will now briefly notice his children. By his first wife he had only one child, Margaret, who became the wife of Mr. Robert Taylor, of North Carolina, who moved to Alabama, and lived for some years in Courtland. Their children were first, Mary Eliza, who was married to the Hon. Samuel W. Mardis, a member of Congress, from Alabama. Their children, were State Rights, a merchant of Louisiana; Eugenia, who married Dr. A. Hester, a famous New Orleans physician; and Samuella, who married a Mr. Cohen, a merchant of New Orleans; Matilda, who married Isaac N. Glidewell, a hotel keeper of Memphis and New Orleans; Josephine, who married Junius A. Bynum. Like her grandfather and mother, she had literary taste, and wrote many poems, which were published in a small volume under the assumed name of "Dixie." The poetry was very sweet, and many of the stanzas were beautiful; but all was tinged with a deep melancholy. Her husband had been killed in a street fight; and her son Junius, who was a Confederate soldier, disappeared mysteriously, and was never heard of afterward; and her life was full of sorrows. Her daughter Margaret, married Philip Pointer; She had also a son Burt, and a daughter Laura, who married a Dr. Jones of Tennessee.

The children of Mr. Joseph Saunders by his second marriage were: 1. Lucy, married Robert Fenner, who belonged to a wealthy family of Halifax, North Carolina. Mr. Fenner was a man of handsome talents, had been in the army in early life, was fond of company, and had luxurious habits. It was generally believed that he inherited five fortunes, and spent them all. I think this was a mistake, for with a good opportunity of knowing, I never could count more than three. Their children were: 1. Robert, who was a member of the "Red Rovers" in the war for Texas liberty, and was one of those massacred at Goliad. 2. Mary, who married Dr. Julius Johnson. Their children are Fenner, who was a soldier in Forrest's command, and a daughter named Margaret. The family live in Jackson, Tenn. 3. Joseph, who also was in the company of the "Red Rovers," but on the morning of the battle of Copano, was sent forward on a reconnoitering party, under Col. A. C. Horton, which was cut off from Fannin's army, and so he was saved from the massacre. 4. Richard. 5. Margaret. 6. Ann; and 7. Lucy.

8. Martha, another child of Mr. Joseph Saunders, by the second marriage, was married first to a Scotch merchant named Finley, and secondly to a Baptist preacher named Holcombe. She had no children.

Ephraim Saunders

"was the ninth child of William and Betsy (Hubbard) Saunders. He was born on the 14th of March, 1760. He moved early to the county of Frederick, married a Miss Edmonds had several children, three of whom I have seen, to-wit: Ephraim, Elias and Eppa." (*Family Memoir.*)

William Saunders

and his twin brother James (the historian of the family) were the last children of William and Betsy (Hubbard) Saunders. "He was considerably deaf from his infancy, rather of a noisy turn, and a little fractious. He has never married that I know of, and has lived for several years past in the State of Georgia." (*Family Memoir*).

James Saunders, born in 1765, was the ancestor of the North Carolina branch of the family. He describes himself as having dark hair and blue eyes. He remained with his mother (after the death of his father, which took place when he was quite young) until her death, which occurred when he was about twenty-five years of age. He had determined to remove to the distant West, but his elder brothers persuaded him to remain in Brunswick county three years longer; "when he turned down into the district of Edenton, North Carolina, where he 'peregrinated' (a favorite word with him) until he was about thirty years of age, when he, on the 7th of January, 1796, intermarried with Hannah, widow of Jacob Simons, in the county of Chowan, about seven miles below the town of Edenton. She was the daughter of James Sitterson, of Perquimans county. She was a large, portly, handsome woman, and an excellent manager of her domestic concerns. She died 12th of May, 1819, leaving only one child.

Joseph Hubbard Saunders

" who was born on the 26th of December, 1800. He was educated in the country until he was fourteen, when he studied for awhile in the academy at Edenton; was transferred to the academy at Raleigh for about forty months, when he was, on the first of January, 1819, placed in the University of North Carolina, at Chapel Hill; joined the sophomore class, half advanced, and remained until June 7, 1821, when he graduated with much applause and credit to himself and preceptors. He remains a tutor in the college and a student of the law. He is about six feet high, weighs about 200 pounds, and of a dark complexion, with dark hair and eyes" (*Family Memoir*). And here we must leave these simple, graphic annals which have given us so much satisfaction. He completed his *Memoir* in 1824, and on June 22 of the same year died—a reminder to all old men that if they have anything to record which may be of interest in the distant future, they should do it " before the night cometh, when no man can work."

His son Joseph, after the death of his father, resigned his professorship at the University and commenced the study of the law under Judge Francis Nash, but soon abandoned it for the study of theology with a view of entering the church.

He taught school in Edenton for several years, the insolvent condition of his father's estate requiring his presence and necessitating immediate exertion on his part. He appropriated the proceeds of his own labor to the payment of his father's debts. On the 6th of February, 1831, in Richmond, Va., he was ordained a deacon by Bishop Moore, and on the 18th of March, 1832, at Warrenton, North Carolina, he was made a priest by Bishop Ives, of the Episcopal Church. On the 28th of April, 1833, he married Laura Locinda, daughter of Dr. Simmons J. Baker, of Martin County, North Carolina. In the fall of 1836 he moved to Pensacola, Florida, having received a call to the parish church there. In the autumn of 1839 the yellow fever became an epidemic in that place. He did not seek safety in flight, but heroically sustained his parishioners in meeting the grim foe, and became one of its victims. He was buried under the vestry room of his church. His noble qualities (as we shall see below), were transmitted to his sons. I never knew him personally, but I carried on, for years, a correspondence with him which was a source of great pleasure, for he was a ripe scholar and a man of the most cheerful temper. I have often met with members of his congregation, and they had a wonderful appreciation of him. After his death his widow returned to the protection of her father, Dr. Baker, who, in the spring of 1840, carried them from his place in Jackson County, Florida, to Raleigh, North Carolina. Her sons having advanced far enough, Mrs. Saunders, in 1850, removed to Chapel Hill to give them the benefit of a collegiate education. We will notice each one of them in their order.

Richard Benbury Saunders was born in Raleigh, 12th April, 1834. He was taught first in the Raleigh Academy, under the charge of Mr. J. M. Lovejoy, and entered the freshman class in 1850. He graduated in 1854, and after a course in chemistry established himself at Chapel Hill as a druggist. On the 26th November, 1856, in Natchez, Miss., he married Mary Stanton, daughter of the late Girard Brandon, formerly governor of that State. In response to a call of the governor of North Carolina he volunteered as a member of the Orange Light Infantry, Capt. R. J. Ashe; was elected second lieutenant, and went with his company to Raleigh in 1861, when it became a part of the First Regiment of North Carolina Volunteers, Col. D. H. Hill commanding—known in latter days as the Bethel Regiment. He was at the battle of Bethel. Upon the recommendation of Col. C. C. Lee (who succeeded to the command of the regiment after the promotion of General Hill), he was commissioned captain and A. Q. M. of the regiment. He did not re-enter the service afterward; his brothers insisting that some member of the family should remain at home, and that his occupation, his health, and the fact of his having a wife and children, plainly pointed him out as the one to remain. He reluctantly assented. He is still living, actively engaged in the manufacture of fertilizers, for which his chemical education has especially fitted him. He has eleven living children.

William Lawrence Saunders, the second son of Rev. Joseph Hubbard Saunders, was born in Raleigh 30th July, 1835. He was also taught in the Academy af Raleigh, and when he removed to Chapel Hill he entered the Freshman class at the university, and graduated in 1854. He studied law under Judge W. H. Battle, of the Supreme Court, and obtained license to practice in 1856. In October, 1857, he removed to Salisbury, and resided there until the beginning of the war. In April, 1861, he volunteered as a member of the Rowan Rifle Guards, Capt. Frank McNeely, and was ordered to Fort Johnston, below Wilmington. In June, 1861, he was appointed a lieutenant in the "Rowan Artillery" (better known as Reilly's Battery) then in camp of instruction near Weldon. The battery went with the Fourth Regiment of North Carolina troops, Col. G. B. Anderson commanding, to Manassas Junction; arriving there a few days after the battle, and remained until its equipment was somewhat perfected, and then having been detached from the regiment, it was assigned to the artillery corps bf Colonel Pendleton. Having received an appointment as captain from Governor Clark, of North Carolina, he resigned his lieutenancy in January, 1862, and returned to Salisbury, and enlisted a company of infantry for the war, and carried it to Raleigh for instruction at camp Mangum, where it became a part of the Forty-sixth Regiment of North Carolina troops, Col. E. D. Hall commanding. It was then ordered to Richmond, thence to Drewry's Bluff, where it became a part of Gen. J. G. Walker's Brigade. It was better known afterward as Cook's Brigade, Heth's Division, A. P. Hill's Corps, Army of Northern Virginia. He (Colonel Saunders) was promoted in 1862 to be major, in 1863 to be lieutenant-colonel, and on January 1, 1864, to be colonel of his regiment. He was twice wounded—once on the declivity of Marye's heights, at the battle of Fredericksburg, by a bullet which entered near his mouth and passed through his right cheek—and again in the Wilderness, in May, 1864, very severly; the ball entering the left corner of the mouth, breaking his jaw-bone, taking off some of the bone of one of the vertebrae, and lodging in the ganglion of nerves at the back of his neck, from which it was cut out.

Since the war Colonel Saunders has been a great sufferer from neuralgia, rheumatism and partial paralysis—but he is one of the most cheerful men in North Carolina. His faculties are unimpaired, and perhaps he has performed as much public work as any citizen of that State. When the State University, his "alma mater," was in a state of decadence, from the baneful influence of Federal reconstruction, he was made a trustee and fearlessly contended for its rights, until it was rescued from its degradation and became more prosperous than it ever had been. He has been all the time a

REV. TURNER SAUNDERS.
Born in Virginia 1782, died 1853.

trustee, and is now the treasurer of that institution. He is also a very efficient advocate for the public works of his State. He writes with great clearness and force, and his articles have greatly contributed to the consummation of those works.

But perhaps the most noteworthy achievement accomplished by Colonel Saunders, has been his success in bringing to light, from the archives of Europe and America, documents in reference to the Colonial History of North Carolina, since he became her Secretary of State. Although not required by law, he has applied all the force of his strong mind to these researches; for which he was so well fitted by his antiquarian taste. The State has published already four heavy tomes, of about 1000 pages each, and there is matter for several more. These volumes have opened up a mine of material for history of great richness and extent, of which writers in future will not fail to avail themselves.

On the 3d day of February, 1864, at the residence of Mr. Thos. Barnes, of Marianna, Florida, he married Florida Call, third daughter of the late John W. Cotton, of North Carolina. They had one child, who lived but an hour. His wife died July, 1865. The gentleness, purity and integrity of her character, were such as to win the love and esteem of all who had the happiness to know her.

Anne Saunders, the only daughter of this family, studied at Dr. Smede's school, at Raleigh, for some time; then under the tuition of Mr. Lovely, and finally completed her education at Mr. Archer's, in Baltimore. She never married, and died in 1887.

Joseph Hubbard Saunders, Jr., third son of Rev. Joseph Hubbard Saunders, was born in Pensacola, 23d October, 1839. He entered the freshman class at the University in 1856, and graduated in June, 1860. In April, 1861, he joined the Orange Light Infantry, and served until the company was mustered out. In December, 1861, he was appointed by Governor Clark a lieutenant in Company A, Thirty-third regiment of North Carolina troops, Col. L. O'B. Branch commanding.

The regiment was, in January, 1862, ordered to Newbern, and after the promotion of General Branch, assigned to his brigade. After the engagement at Newbern, the brigade was ordered to Virginia, and assigned to the command of General A. P. Hill; it was better known as the Light Division, Hill's Corps. After General Branch's death, General Lane succeeded to the command of the brigade, and Generals Pender and Wilcox, successively, to the command of the division. Joseph Hubbard Saunders, in 1862, was promoted to a Captaincy—in 1863 he was made Major—and in 1864 made Lieutenant Colonel of his regiment—he then being under twenty-five years of age. He was twice wounded—once at second Manasses, in the right shoulder—and again very severely at Gettysburg, in July, 1863, the ball entering the left nostril and passing out behind the left ear. He was supposed to be dead and left on the field, captured by the enemy and carried to Chester Hospital, Pennsylvania, from whence after some months he was sent to Johnson's Island, where he was confined until March, 1865, when paroled for exchange and returned home. The war ending before his exchange was effected, he did not again perform military duty.

He was married to Fannie Neal and died in 1885. His widow and four living children reside in Pitt county, North Carolina.

Thomas Saunders.

Although we notice him last, he was the eldest child of William and Betsy (Hubbard) Saunders; and was born 18th June, 1739. "He traveled while young to the county of Sussex, Va., where he married Ann Harper, a widow, whose maiden name was Turner. They settled in Brunswick county. He was an officer of militia, and was in service during the Revolutionary War. He was a pious man, dressed neatly and had a pretty good English education." (*Family Memoir.*)

Rev. Turner Saunders

was a son of Thomas and Ann (Harper) Saunders. He was born on the 3rd of January, 1782, in Brunswick county, Va. He was well educated in the English branches and in the sciences, as they were then taught, and became an accurate surveyor. He was my father, and to avoid the errors into which sons so often fall, I will speak of the simple facts of his history, leaving any estimate of his intellectual and moral qualities to be made by abler and more disinterested persons. On the 24th July, 1799, (before he reached the age of 18) he was married to Frances Dunn of the same county. Before he was 25 years of age he taught a high school with much success, at the Court House of that county.

In the year 1808 he removed from Virginia and settled upon a tract of land six miles southwest of Franklin in Williamson county, Tennessee. The country was then covered with cane; but strange to say, society was refined and intelligent. Here were the Bentons, parents of Thomas H. Benton, then a young lawyer of Franklin, and afterward the distinguished Senator from Missouri; Mrs. Dudley, a cousin of John Randolph, of Roanoke, and with as much natural ability. She had a husband, but he was so modest and so much overshadowed by his wife, that few, except the neighbors knew it. And Col. Matthias B. Murfree, oldest son of Col. Hardy Murfree, after whom Murfreesboro was named, and brother of William H. Murfree, Esq., a talented lawyer of Franklin, who was the grandfather of the lady, who has electrified the literary world lately, by her weird tales of the lonely mountains of Tennessee. And then there was Dr. James Manny, ancestor of the Mannys, of Rutherford county. And Major David Dunn, brother of my mother. This little colony submitted cheerfully to the deprivations of this new country. Everything really necessary was made at home, and the luxury of sugar was furnished from the maple tree. The earthquakes however, of 1812, disturbed their tranquility greatly, and during the disturbances, when the foundation of the earth seemed to be upheaved, Reelfoot Lake on the western border of the State was formed; thirty miles long, from one to two miles wide, and its depth so great that in some places no bottom could be found.

This little colony very soon had plantations cleared up, and were making large crops, when they were confronted with a great difficulty—they could find no market for their products. They made corn until it fell to ten cents a bushel; they turned on tobacco, until it became a drug; and then on hemp, until it would not pay for the cost of breaking and hackling. This was before the day of railroads and steamboats, and they had no transportation to the outside world.

Under these discouragements the colony was broken up, and dispersed in various directions. Dr. Manny and Colonel Murfree moved to Rutherford county; Major Dunn, who was a widower, married in Davidson county, and went there to live. Colonel Dudley had died, and Mrs. Dudley went to live with a married daughter; and old Mr. Benton also died, and his widow went to live with one of her sons.

My father rented out his plantation, and moved his family into the town of Franklin. He engaged in merchandise, and in a very short time his business was greatly expanded. By a course of liberal and just dealing, he almost monopolized the trade in furs and peltries of the Cherokee and Chickasaw Indians, who lived on the Tennessee river. The rest of his history may be deduced from the following extracts:

Dr. McFerrin, in his *History of Methodism in Tennessee* (p. 415, Vol. 3), says: "The Rev. Turner Saunders, a native of Virginia, was a local preacher, and a most refined and cultured Christian gentleman, and an excellent preacher. He exerted a fine influence on the public mind, and did much in giving Methodism a prominent and permanent position in Franklin, his adopted town. Mr. Saunders afterward removed to the neighborhood of Courtland, North Alabama, where he lived an ornament to society. He finally settled in Aberdeen, Miss., where he died at a good old age, honored and respected by all who knew him."

Rev. Richard H. Rivers, D. D., in No. 1 of his series of articles on *Methodist Educators*, says: "At an early period in the history of Alabama the Rev. Turner Saunders removed from Tennessee and settled near Courtland. He became a planter on a large scale. He carried the system which made him so successful a teacher to the plantation. His intelligence was directed to the scientific culture of the soil. He was eminently prosperous, and became the owner of large wealth. His home was the abode of elegance, and an enlarged and generous hospitality. All his surroundings exhibited a taste of exquisite refinement. He was elected the first president of the board of trustees of La Grange College. For a quarter of a century he presided with dignity and honor over a board whose benevolence and wisdom have rarely been surpassed. He was *primis inter pares*. He faltered at no opposition; and his energies received a new impulse from increased difficulties. As a presiding officer, he was dignified, just and impartial. As a promoter of education, he was among the first and most efficient. As a man of purity of character, without spot and blameless; his praise was in all the churches. His manly countenance, his perfectly white hair, his erect and noble form, well proportioned and of medium size, gave him a commanding presence. For sound, solid, practical sense he had few equals, and no superiors. He was a clear, logical preacher. He had a full appreciation of the gospel ministry, and often exhibited deep emotion while preaching the Word. Had he devoted himself to politics, he would have ranked with our ablest statesmen. Such a man as Turner Saunders ought not to die! He may pass away, but he ought to live in his influence, he ought still to speak in his noble philanthropy, and tell by his exalted worth upon the destinies of his race, long after all that was mortal was sleeping in the grave. Let amaranthine flowers adorn the tomb of the noble old man."

From his obituary written by Bishop Paine, we make an extract: "Rev. Turner Saunders, our deceased friend, was in the proper sense of the word, a gentleman—a Christian gentleman. Without claiming for him remarkably brilliant intellectual parts, he certainly possessed, in a rare degree, a clear, sound, and a well balanced intellect, a judgment singularly correct, a mind so practical and logical as to be seldom misled by speculations, or puzzled by sophisms, and what is of still higher moment, he had a heart alive to all the interests of humanity.

"Few men were more extensively or favorably known in our community. His capabilities and business habits were a guarantee of success. Industry, method, neatness and punctuality were his characteristics. He has left an ample fortune for his family, but the great aim of his life was higher and nobler than the mere acquisition of wealth, and his consistent, pious and useful life is the richest legacy he has left behind him. For about forty years he was a local preacher, and was devoted to the doctrines, institutions and usages of the church. He was an old fashioned class-meeting Methodist, and when he became too old to preach effectually, he gladly became the leader of a female class, and continued so until his death, which occurred at 72 years of age."

In the government of his family my father, with all his cares, was uniformly successful. Every night after supper there was a family reunion, in which my father, with much tact, drew out from each child, no matter how young, what he had been doing and what he had seen, and some of the most amusing incidents would be recounted. Then the young ones were sent to bed, and those going to school were sent to the study to prepare their lessons for the next day. His experience had taught him that no teacher could do full justice to a pupil unless the parents at home sustained him in his efforts.

My mother, whenever family government is spoken of, should always be mentioned conjointly with my father. She was a woman of great beauty—whoever knew a very young man to marry a plain woman! She had been reared just after the Revolutionary War, when people were poor, and had learned habits of industry and economy, which well fitted her to be the head of a large family. One rule she had for her boys that I shall never forget: every fellow had to be in his seat at each meal, no matter how engrossing his projects might be. This was her roll call, by which she maintained the discipline of her young soldiers. But it was in the management of her daughters that she was pre-eminent. She refused to pay any mantua-maker's, or milliners' bills, for them, and they became expert in both lines. There were certain days for work, and my mother would head the coterie in the sewing-room, and it was the most cheerful one in the family. Occasionally she would weave into the warp of their idle conversation a silver thread of wisdom which they would remember for life.

In the autumn of 1824 a most virulent fever pervaded the valley of the Tennessee, and a great many people died. Thousands upon thousands of acres of timber had been deadened, and left standing to taint the air with malaria. In less than one month I lost my mother, my eldest brother, then a young man, named Thomas, and a brother about fifteen years of age, Franklin.

I will now speak of the other children of my father by his first marriage:

Sophie Dunn Saunders, married Colonel Joel Parrish, in Franklin, Tenn., 28th November, 1816. The children (with the exception of those who died in infancy) were Sarah Anne, Frances, Joel, and Sophia. (1) Sarah Anne Parrish married Felix A. O. Sherrod, son of Colonel Benjamin Sherrod; and their children were Benjamin, Frank, and Alice. (1) Benjamin Sherrod, married Daniella Jones; no living issue. (2) Frank, married Mary Harris, daughter of Mr. John Harris. He died young. His widow is still living and his two sons, Frank and Harris, who are young men. (3) Alice, married Maj. Robt. W. Banks, and they have five children—Sarah Felix, Lucile W., Robert W., James O., and Alice S. Frances Parrish, married Samuel W. Sherrod, also a son of Colonel Sherrod. Their children were Henry and Walter. Henry died unmarried. Walter married Laura Davis, and died young. Their only child is Henry Sherrod, who married Ellen Irvine, daughter of James B. Irvine, Esq., of Florence, Ala. Joel Parrish married Mary Boddie, of Lauderdale county, Ala. He died young, without issue. Sophia Parrish, married Alfred Gibson. He died young. His children—Mary, Joel, and Willis —are unmarried.

Louisa Turner Saunders, daughter of Turner and Frances (Dunn) Saunders, married Robert C. Foster. An account of their descendants will be given in an article on the "Foster Family."

Narcissa Hubbard, daughter of Turner and Frances (Dunn) Saunders, married James H. Foster. (*Foster Family.*)

Frances Anne Saunders has already been fully spoken of in connection with her three husbands Clay, Swoope and Billups.

Martha Maria Saunders, daughter of Turner and Frances (Dunn) Saunders, married Benjamin M. Bradford. He was then Register of the Land Office at Courtland. They had a large family: Robert M. married Medora, daughter of Dr. D. F. Alexander, and granddaughter of Major William Dowsing, who was Register of the Land Office at Columbus for so many years. They had a large family. Mary McFarland married Dr. Moses K. Harrison, of Noxubee county, Miss. They have a number of children. Louisa Jane, died a young lady, and so did Antoinette Malone. James Saunders, and John D. have not married. Benjamin M. married a Miss Hatch. She soon died and left three children. Henry Blanton, died of wounds received in the Civil War. Frances Saunders, married Latimore Dupree, and has several children. Rosaline Narcissa, married John Jefferson. They have one child. Martha, the youngest, married James Harris, and they have two children.

Eliza Jane, daughter of Turner and Frances (Dunn) Saunders, married William Hancock, son of William Hancock of Madison county, and his mother was sister of Rev. Sterling C. and Hartwell H. Brown of Tennessee. My sister, and two sons, died of yellow fever in Texas in 1858. Turner on 13th of September, Sterling Brown on 14th of October, and she on the 24th of the same month. Of the other children, Frances E. married Thaddeus C. Armstrong, and they now have only one child. Bradford married Fannie Parish and has five daughters. He was city clerk in Galveston a few years ago. William James married Nellie Bagby of Houston, Texas, and has two children. Martha Jane married Sterling Fisher of San Marcos, Texas, and has seven children. Robert lived in Galveston when I last heard from him, and was not married. Mary Louisa, the youngest, is not married.

William H., son of Turner and Frances (Dunn) Saunders, married Susan Goodwin, daughter of John Goodwin, Esq., a lawyer of distinction in Aberdeen, Miss. William H. is a planter in Mississippi. His wife has been dead for many years. He had one child, James Edward, who is unmarried.

Rev. Turner Saunders married his second wife in 1826. She was a widow; a Mrs. Millwater. Her maiden name was Henrietta M. Weeden, and she had been born and reared in the city of Baltimore. She had two young daughters when she married my father—Sarah and Mary Eliza Millwater, in whom my father took great interest. The eldest, Sarah, married the late Dr. Felix Manning, a son of Dr. James Manning, of Huntsville, and the younger, Mary Eliza, married the late Bishop Robert Paine. They moved to Aberdeen, Miss., about the same time my father did, and their society contributed much to the happiness of his declining years.

The children of my father by his second marriage were four sons: Turner, Thomas, Franklin and Hubbard. 1. Turner was married first to Marie Victoria McRae, and by this marriage there were six children, John McRae, who married Sallie E. Keys, Norman, Henry Gholson, Adele Josephine, Marie Victoria, and Corinne Eloise. His wife died in 1869, and in 1877 he married Kate Downing Garrett. By his second marriage there are two young children, Helen and Edith Turner. He died of apoplexy in October, 1882. 2. Thomas, married Anna Hullum. They had a son, Eugene Thomas, and a daughter Eva, both young and unmarried. The father has been dead for many years. 3. Franklin, third son, married Sarah Herndon, and they have two sons, Edward and Franklin, who have married twin daughters of Mr. Robert Whitefield. 4. Hubbard, the fourth son, married Clara Cunningham, and they had five children: William C., Henrietta, Turner, Franklin and Clara. Losing his wife he was married a second time to a Miss Eager, and had several children. He has been dead for a number of years. His widow married H. S. Hyatt, of Mississippi City.

Rev. Hubbard Saunders

was born in Brunswick county, Va., in 1765. He was the son of Thomas Saunders and Mrs. Ann Harper (whose maiden name was Ann Turner), and said Hubbard was brother of the Rev. Turner Saunders, an account of whom we have given in our last number. Rev. Hubbard Saunders was married to Chloe Russell on the 2nd of December, 1792, daughter of General William Russell of the Revolution, and his first wife, Miss Adams.

We have devoted several chapters to the family of the husband in this marriage, and now we will give an account of that of the wife: General Russell's second wife was Elizabeth Henry, daughter of Colonel John Henry, who was the progenitor of the Henry family which became so distinguished in Virginia. He was a native of Aberdeen, Scotland. He emigrated to America previous to 1730, and enjoyed the friendship and patronage of Governor Dinwiddie, who introduced him to the acquaintance of Colonel John Syme, in whose family he became domesticated. In a few years Colonel Syme died, and Mr. Henry married his widow. Her maiden name was Sarah Winston, and she was of a good family. Her father, Isaac Winston, had five children. One of the daughters, who married a Mr. Cole, was the grandmother of Dorothea (Dolly) Payne, who married James Madison, President of the United States.—(*Campbell's History of Virginia*.)

Colonel Byrd, in the same book, has given a graphic delineation of Sarah Winston, when she became the Widow Syme: "She was a portly, handsome dame, of a lively, cheerful disposition, and with much less reserve than most of her country women. It becomes her very well, and sets off her other agreeable qualities to advantage. The courteous widow invited me to rest myself there that good day, and to go to church with her; but I excused myself by telling her that she would certainly spoil my devotions. (See how nicely gentlemen of 150 years ago could turn a compliment.) She possessed a mild and benevolent disposition, undeviating probity, correct understanding, and easy elocution."—(*The Same.*)

Col. John Henry and his wife raised a family of nine children at their family seat, "Studley," in Hanover county. I have been able to find only the names of six of them in history, Wm. Henry, the merchant; Patrick Henry, the orator and statesman; Elizabeth Henry, wife of both General Campbell and General Russell; Lucy, who married Valentine Wood, and Jane, who married Col. Samuel Meridith. "The dwelling house at Studley is no longer standing; antique hedges of box, and an avenue of aged trees recall recollections of the past." From the fact of Patrick Henry having been so often called "the forest-born Demosthenes," many persons have supposed that his family was illiterate and poor, but this was a mistake. Mr. Campbell says that the family was "in moderate but easy circumstances," and that "Col. John Henry enjoyed the advantages of a liberal education; that his understanding was plain but solid, and that he was a member of the Established Church, but supposed to be more conversant with Livy and Horace than with the Bible, and moreover he made a very good map of Virginia." It has been a question which side of the house Patrick Henry's genius came from, and Mr. Campbell says it came from his mother, and mentions that her eldest brother was an officer of volunteers soon after Braddock's defeat; that the men, poorly clad and without tents, were clamorous to return to their homes. At this juncture Wm. Winston mounted a stump and made to them an appeal so patriotic and overpowering, that when he concluded the cry was, " Let us march on; lead us against the enemy."

The Elisabeth Henry spoken of above, married for her first husband Capt. Wm. Campbell; who afterward became a Brigadier General, and led the patriot forces at King's mountain battle. She lived at the head of tide-water in eastern Virginia, and he beyond the mountains near Abingdon in the same State; and as there was some romance connected with their courtship, I will refer to it. In 1776 the first regiment of volunteers in Virginia was ordered to be raised, and Patrick Henry was appointed to command it. It was strange that the first company of this regiment which arrived at Williamsburg, the rendezvous, had marched hundreds of miles across the mountains and was commanded by this Captain Campbell. The regiment shared in dislodging Lord Dunmore from Gwynn's Island, and then marched back to their rendezvous; when a long interval of inactivity prevailed. John Bull was dazed with astonishment at the Declaration of Independence; and it was some time before the giant became fully awake. He said to himself: "I will go out and stretch myself," and when he became fully aroused, there was the broad Atlantic between him and his victims, and no transportation for troops except on slow sailing vessels. During this interval of security, Williamsburg, which in Virginia, was the seat of Government, the seat of learning and the seat of fashion, was visited by all the belles of eastern Virginia, and became the seat of unceasing gaieties. Amongst others came Elisabeth Henry, Juno-like with her queenly step.

Her brother, Patrick, with a heart full of enthusiasm, greatly admired young Campbell, for he was of the same type, and in her country home she had heard frequent commendations of him; but when she met this young officer and saw with her own eyes " his imposing personal appearance, the beau ideal of a military chieftain," she said in her heart " Eureka," but she locked up the secret there. At length the news came that the Cherokee Indians had attacked the frontiers, and he was not a little uneasy about the unprotected situation of his mother and sisters. He resigned his commission, but before he left for his distant home he called on Miss Henry, explained to her all the embarrassments of his situation, and offered her his hand in marriage. She laid her delicate one on his broad palm regardless of danger, and he made a splendid soldier and she as good a soldier's wife. This union lasted only five years, during which he performed much service and received many public honors. He died in 1781. A son, a daughter and his widow survived him. The son died young; the daughter, Sarah, became the wife of Gen. Francis Preston and mother of Hon. William C. Preston, Gen. John S. Preston and Col. Thomas L. Preston. General Campbell's widow, after a few years, united in marriage with Gen. William Russell. For many of the facts stated in this article I am indebted to " King's Mountain and Its Heroes," by Lyman C. Draper, LL. D. The author of this book was collecting authentic materials for it for forty years before he published it. It is a charming union of Biography and History. The family descent of every officer in that battle is given by the learned author.

General Russell and his wife lived in Southwestern Virginia, at the saltworks on the North Fork of the Holston. The members of the Henry family, ever since Patrick Henry in the famous " Parson's Cause " had abused the clergy and the king so unmercifully, were alienated from the establishment, and became Dissenters. At a conference held on the Holston, in 1788, over which Bishop Asbury presided, the General and his wife joined the Methodist Church. In 1792 Rev. Hubbard Saunders (as we have said) married the General's daughter, Chloe Russell. He was an itinerant preacher of this church, until the increase of his family rendered it proper for him to locate. In 1810 he removed his family to a fine farm in Sumner county, Tenn. The place is now called Saundersville. Dr. McFerrin knew him intimately for many years and says that "he lived to an advanced age laboring all the while as a local preacher. Mr. Saunders was of a good family, and had a fine reputation as a citizen and a minister. He was a man of wealth for those times; and brought up a large and respectable family." ("History of Methodism in Tennessee.")

The children of this family were indeed numerous. On 1st of April, 1876, I requested Hubbard Saunders (the youngest of fourteen children) to send me an account of them. I here transcribe it for the benefit of the Saunders tribe.

(NOTE: Colonel Saunders here appended a list of the descendants of the Rev. Hubbard Saunders and Chloe Russell, which has since been greatly added to, and incorporated, in its proper place, in the genealogy of the Saunders family, in Part II of this Volume, which see):

Elizabeth Saunders,

daughter of Thomas Saunders and Ann (Turner) Harper and sister of Turner and Hubbard Saunders, (who have already been noticed) "married Mr. Samuel Edmonds of Southampton, Virginia, a very wealthy, amiable and religious man. She died without issue." (Family Record.)

Martha Saunders

married Lewis Saunders (her cousin) son of Jesse Saunders, already mentioned, who lived in Georgia. This family moved to lower Mississippi, and I have been unable to get any reliable information as to their descendants.

Nancy Saunders

married Mr. John Bass, of Brunswick. He belonged to a good family, and having a competent estate, he started life with good prospects. His habits were not bad for those times, when sideboards were covered with wine and ardent spirits. It is true that occasionally he got "gentlemanly merry;" but the habit of drinking grew on him, until he became the worst drunkard in all Virginia. Liquor in its effect on some men elicits all their good humor; and on others it provokes every bad passion. To this latter class Bass belonged; and his ill nature increased until he not only abused her personally, but drove her from her home, and as she went off, shot at her. She separated from him, and found a home for herself and children with my father (Turner Saunders) and moved with him from Virginia to Tennessee, and thence, after some years, to Alabama.

She had two children: Mary ("Polly") and Thomas (for Thomas Bass, see Saunders Genealogy). Polly Bass was a young woman of much beauty and great natural vivacity. In defiance of the clouds that lowered over her childhood, she grew up one of the most cheerful girls I ever knew, and married Thomas B. Jones, a young Virginian of fine estate. They never had any children, but still their estate decreased, until when they moved to Alabama and settled in Courtland, he invested his last instalment in a stock of goods. He was an excitable, patriotic man, and took part in every war which occurred in his day. He was apt to get into the most serious difficulties, but, somehow, he always came out of them without serious hurt; as will be seen from the following incidents:

At the battle of Talladega, when 1000 Indian warriors were surrounded, they found a small gap in the line, where the infantry and mounted men should have united. Through this gap, after discharging their rifles, the warriors, in a strong body, tomahawks in hand, and with terrific yells, attempted to make their escape. Jones' horse broke away, and he was left in a position of great peril, when in the retreat he jumped on a log, motioned to another mounted man to approach, and vaulted up behind him, and so he saved his life. As soon as the troops were ordered to re-form, he dismounted without finding out the name of the man from whom he had received this great favor. Many years after, Jones, who was attending court in Moulton, was one night at a hotel relating the circumstances, in a large circle, and when he had finished, remarked that he would give anything to find out who it was that had saved his life. A gentleman present exclaimed, "There he is, Captain Jones, leaning against that post, Capt. Joseph G. Evetts. I have heard him tell of it often." And so these two men were united with a bond of friendship ever afterward. Another narrow escape that Captain Jones had, was in the war with Great Britain, on the night of the 23d of December. The light was very dim, and there was great confusion. The Captain was advancing at the head of his company, when a British captain near him ordered his company to fall into line. Jones stepped forward and ordered him to surrender. The Briton was not prepared to do this, and immediately crossed swords with him, and being an expert fencer, after a pass or two he disarmed Jones, and turned the point of his sword to his breast, when one of his men ran his bayonet through the Briton. He and his wife moved to Louisiana, where they both died.

Thomas Bass, her second child, was married, in Alabama, to Sarah Weeden, a sister of my father's second wife. They also moved to Caddo parish, La., where they died, leaving three or four children.

But we are not done with the history of Nancy Bass, the outset of whose life was so disastrous. She had been a widow for many years, and was now an old lady, when unexpectedly to all her friends, she conceived the idea of a second marriage. She had crossed the matrimonial sea once in a vessel commanded by a drunken captain, and she had a curiosity to cross it again under a sober one, and this she found in a very worthy old widower,

Mr. William Manning.

The Mannings came from Brunswick county, Va. About the time Mr. William M. moved to Tennessee his brother, Joseph Manning, went to Edenton, North Carolina. William married his cousin, daughter of Caleb Manning (whom I knew very well when I was a boy at Franklin). Mr. William Manning reared a large and respectable family of children, who settled in Tennessee. He was among the earliest settlers in this county, and lived on a small plantation about six miles northwest of Courtland, where he lost his wife, in 1824. His sons who were old enough, were all through Jackson's bloody Indian war. He brought only one child to Alabama: Elizabeth, who was married to one of our best early settlers:

Mr. John Scruggs.

The Scruggs family emigrated from Powhatan county, Va., and settled on the place afterward called Nashville, Tennessee, about 1804. The progenitor of the Tennessee branch of the family was Mr. Finch Scruggs. He had married Nancy Thomas of Cumberland county, Virginia, in November. 1773. Subsequently they removed to Williamson County, Tennessee, a few miles from the town of Franklin, where I was reared, and where I first knew this family. My father had a high opinion of Mr. John Scruggs when he was a mere youth. and established him in business. He was remarkably successful, moved to this county of Lawrence, married here, and raised a numerous and respectable family of children. He had a large brain and was distinguished for his good sense, modesty and industry. And yet I do not remember to have seen him in a hurry. His steps were so well considered in advance that he made no useless ones. He and his excellent wife were noted for their affection for each other, and the harmony with which they devoted themselves to the welfare of their descendants. A few years since this exemplary christian calmly breathed his last, and four days afterward his good wife followed him to the "better land." They had twelve children.

Of these (1) William reached manhood and died unmarried. (2) Nathan married Ellen Rutland in Franklin county, Ala. He now resides in Memphis and is engaged in commercial business. His only child, Frank, lives there also, and is a druggist. (3) Jane died young. (4) Mary married John W. Hall, who was amongst our most intelligent and enterprising citizens. His death, which occurred some years ago, was a great loss to our community, socially and economically; for he devoted himself to experiments for the purpose of testing the fitness of our section for the stock business. Their children were Elizabeth, who married George Potter; Annie; John; Ella, who married William May of Pulaski, Tenn.; and Mary. (5) Narcissa Scruggs married James Neely. She has been a widow for many years and has three children: Elizabeth, who married William Dinsmore, M. D.; James, who lives in Birmingham, Ala.; and Frank, who resides in Texas. (6) John Scruggs, who married Miss Douglas, of Landerdale county, Ala., and has four young children. (7) Lacy, died young. (8) Virginia Scruggs, who married William Moore, of Columbia, Tenn., and has four young children. (9) Joseph Scruggs, who married a daughter of Philip King and died several years ago. She survives him with only one child living. (10) Thomas Scruggs, who is an itinerant preacher of the Methodist Church, South, and married a lady of the State of Illinois, and has a large family of children. The sons of Mr. John Scruggs, Sr., did their duty as soldiers during the civil war, and Thomas was severely wounded. (11) Sallie Scruggs married Prof. J. W. Smith, of Lynnville, Tennessee. They have no children. (12) Walter W., of Nashville.

NOTE.—The continuance of the "Early Settlers" was abruptly abandoned after this last number.

Governor Gilmer's Map of the BROAD RIVER SETTLEMENT, GEORGIA, enlarged to include *Elbert County*, after 1780, and also some other settlers.

NOTES AND GENEALOGIES

MORE OR LESS COMPLETE, OF FAMILIES OF

Banks, Bankhead, Bibb, Billups, Blair, Cantzon, Clay, Coleman, Cox,
Du Bose, Dudley, Dunn, Elliott, Flint, Foster, Fry, Gholson, Goode,
Gray, Harris, Hill, Hopkins, Lanier, Ligon, Lowe, Manning,
Maclin, McGehee, Maury, Moore, Oliver, O'Neal, Phelan,
Poellnitz, Ray, Richardson, Saunders, Shelton, Sherrod,
Shorter, Speed, Swoope, Tait, Taliaferro, Thompson,
Tillman, Urquhart, Walthall, Watkins, Webb,
Weeden, Wells, White, Withers, Wyatt,
Yates, Young, and others.

BY

MRS. ELIZABETH SAUNDERS BLAIR STUBBS.

NEW ORLEANS,

1899.

PART II.

INTRODUCTION.

" Let's talk of graves, of worms, and epitaphs."—*Richard II.*

Descent from honorable ancestry is to be desired, and is something of which to be proud indeed—the transmission, link by link, of a bright chain, of which the inheritor, while adding to it *his own link*, should feel that *this one*, must have the unsullied strength of the others—" *noblesse oblige.*"

The Chinese similarly explain their worship of ancestry ; "The mortal body of each," say they, "having conversed with his father, the communication with the first-created man is thus unbroken"—a kind of *apostolic succession* of ancestry.

Since each bears the stamp of his own lineage—the aggregated characteristics of many generations—it is the highest service one can do his family to chronicle and hand down these acquired and transmitted qualities. But, for the proper genius and patience perfectly to accomplish this, he must have the "*God-within enthusiasm*," that aptitude for the mission which falls, an Elijah's mantle, only upon the one consecrated to this work, of which he finally becomes also the victim !

The "*Notes and Genealogies*" were begun lightly—unwitting the great *onus* of work entailed—as supplementary to Colonel Saunders' "*Early Settlers*," and while yet the venerable author was alive to approve and counsel. The plan was to compile all the valuable data, hitherto unused, relating to the within families, as well as to conduct an extensive correspondence with members of the same—valuable aid from some of whom is gratefully acknowledged under proper heads.

Despite every precaution, error, the *mocking-demon* of compilers will sometimes unaccountably slip in, and dates and localities become perverted. Again ; if one finds himself left out on his *family roll*, and is, therefore, sorrowfully indignant, his disappointment can not be greater than that of the compiler, who has often waited long and patiently for the "*answer* that never came," and which might, perhaps, have contained the name of the one so chagrined. The *letter of inquiry* is often laborious work in itself, as the transcribing of *whole lines* of descent, for the enlightenment of the person appealed to for information, is perhaps necessary.

Preliminary to several of the within genealogies are lists of persons of the same name, who could not be identified with the immediate line to which he or she belonged, but the dates and localities are given, as a *clue* only, for future investigation, since the material collected is far too valuable to omit. Of some of the within families, it is but natural that most information is given of those of whom most data happened to be in the author's possession. Others are added to show the Alabama continuation of important Virginia families, and to link the whole. It is regretted that outlines only of some could be obtained without longer delay. But what is given is at least a good nucleus for future genealogists. And so it was thought best, to publish now, in dread of the "thief of time," else the work might never be done. By all means publish what you can of your family history, before it is lost !

The usual authorities have been consulted for this work, *viz.*: *Land Grants, Court Records, Vestry Books, Parish Registers, Henning's Statutes, Meade's Old Families, Early Histories, Hotten's Emigrants, Heitman, Saffell, Virginia Almanacs, The Critic,* the two *Historical and Genealogic Magazines of Virginia, Brown's Genesis of the United States, Hayden's Genealogies, Goode's Virginia Cousins, Keith, Burke's Landed Gentry, Peerage and Baronetage,* and also *Genealogies* of many families not mentioned here; *Colonial Records of North Carolina,* by William L. Saunders, *old Records in South Carolina, Gilmer's Georgians,* and other sources, known only to the writer, who, dominated by the accumulated force of all this material, felt impelled to give to others interested, the labyrinthian thread which conducted her through such bewildering mazes of research, and admitted herself no longer a free agent, but wrote because she *must*—the humble medium through which this message of all the ages, "falling upon a drop of ink," is handed down to kinsmen and others, thus surging out to meet its own in every land. Would it were more perfect ! That the Oracles are sometimes *dumb* is not always the fault of one who consults them.

Patents and Court Records of Edward Saunders (or Sanders), of Northumberland County, Va., 1688.

28th August, 1660—2000 acres, South side of Wicomico, 4 headrights (*Book 6, page 164*).

February 10, 1662—In an old court order book Edward Saunders made his right appear to 300 acres of land for the transportation of six persons into the colony. (*Northumberland Records.*)

5th May, 1662—A grant from Sir Wm. Berkeley, Governor, 3737 acres between the counties of Northumberland and Lancaster, beginning on a branch of Dameron's creek, next to John Hopper, on to the head of a branch of Corotoman river (*Book 6, 270*).

5th March, 1662—2900 acres between the two counties of Lancaster and Northumberland (*Northumberland, Book 27, Entry 597, page 168*).

August 28, 1668—207 acres South side Great Wicomico river, on North side of a branch dividing the lands of Thos. Salisbury (*Northumberland Land Book*).

"Thos. Salisbury's land (September, 1666) at the head of Dennis' creek, beginning on the North side of a swamp which divides this land from the land of *Dr. Edward Sanders*" (*Entry No 210*), and again, 540 acres joining Dr. Sanders, (*No. 381*). This was Dr. Saunders' home place, upon which was the ferry.

December 14, 1669—Certificate is granted Mr. Edward Sanders for 600 acres for the importation of twelve persons, viz.: John Reynolds, John Brooks, Sus. Whitsett, Ed. Jacobs, Alvin Cratshaw, Wm. Potts, James Allen and son and Eliz. Jermine. (*Northumberland Records at Heathsville*).

September 18, 1660—At a court held at the house of Capt. Peter Ashton, upon petition of Edward Sanders, who married the widow and administratrix of John Hudnall, deceased, attachments were obtained against the estates of—— Jones, and ——Pierce.

1662—"Whereas Mr. Edward Sanders, *Chirurgeon*, has petitioned the court for 1940 pounds of tobacco and *3000 4 p. nayles* out of the estate of Mr. George Colelough, his administratrix, Mrs. Eliz. Colclough, is ordered to pay the same" (*Court Order Book*).

1664—"Whereas Dr. Edward Sanders hath undertaken to keep a ferry both for horse and foot that shall have occasion to pass over Great Wicomico river *from his house to the point above against it on ye other side of the river*, the court ordered the same," etc. (This is now "Ferry Farm," or Blackwell's wharf, 1899.) (*Order Book*, beginning in 1652.)

1669—Order of court, permitting Edward Sanders to employ Indians.

May 20, 1670—Edward Saunders made complaint that his servant John Richards had demeaned himself rudely towards him and his family, and an order of court was entered that said John Richards be punished with "twenty stripes on his bare back until the blood comes."

1670—One John Jones ordered by the court to be taken in safe custody by the sheriff until he hath given bond and security for "scandalizing and abusing Mary Hudnall, daughter-in-law of Edward Sanders."

1671—It was ordered that Edward Sanders' servant, John Richards, serve his master "for one full year according to act" for default.

May 20, 1671—Edward Sanders, in a deposition, states his age to be fifty years, or thereabouts.

August 25, 1672—An order of court contains these words: Mrs. Mary Sanders "freed from the bond wherein her deceased husband, Mr. Edward Sanders, stood," etc., (hence he died 1672).

1710—On the motion of Samuel Downing and his wife, Elizabeth, daughter of Ebenezer Sanders, deceased, certain parties are appointed by the court to divide the land of said Ebenezer Sanders, according to his will (*dated 28th February, 1692-3*) between his daughter Elizabeth Sanders, his son Edward Sanders, and his brother Edward Sanders. The report of the division was made to the court April 2, 1711.

April 16, 1711—A deed from Edward Sanders (the brother) to Alex. Love for 100 acres, within the parish of Great Wicomico—"the said 100 acres of land being part of 365 acres bequeathed to the said Edward Sanders, by the last will and testament of my brother Ebenezer Sanders, deceased, dated *28th February, Anno 1692-3*," and the said 365 acres "being part of a tract bequeathed to said Ebenezer Sanders, deceased, by the last will and testament of his father Edward Sanders, deceased, *dated 4th October, 1669*—the same being part of a tract (3747 acres) granted to the said last named Edward Sanders, deceased, *by patent* dated 5th March, 1662." On 17th May, 1711, Elizabeth Sanders, wife of Edward Sanders, grantor in above deed, gives power of attorney to Thomas Hobson to relinquish her right of dower in the land to Alex. Love (Thos. Hobson was clerk of the court in 1669).

July 13, 1711—Deed from Edward Sanders to Edwin Conway, for 200 acres, partly in Northumberland, and partly in Lancaster.

1712—Deed from Edward Sanders, of St. Stephens parish, to Edwin Conway.

11th November, 1721—Edward Sanders, of St. Stephens parish, 70 acres, to Elis. Robinson, on the North side of Great Wicomico river, for 3600 pounds tobacco.

1725—Edward Sanders, of St. Stephens parish, Northumberland, *planter*, a deed to Thomas Gill (Thomas Gill was Justice in 1725).

1736—*Will* of Edward Sanders, proved by his wife, Elizabeth, and by the oaths of John Colton and Thos. Gill.

1st August, 1712—Deed from Edward Sanders, Junior, to John Ingram, for 100 acres of land beginning from a stream out of Colonel Carter's mill-dam, being part of a tract belonging to the said Edward Sanders, Jr., commonly called *Sanders' Quarter*, and formerly *granted by patent, dated 5th March, Anno, 1662*, to Mr. Edward Sanders, *Chirurgeon*, deceased, and by him devised by his last will and testament, bearing date *4th October, 1669*, as follows: "A part to his youngest son, Edward Sanders," who is uncle to the said Edward Sanders, Jr.—and the rest he gave to "his son Ebenezer Sanders, *son and heir* to the first-mentioned Edward Sanders, and by the said Ebenezer Sanders, by his last will and testament, *dated 28th February, 1692*, devised to his son Edward Sanders, *son and heir* of the said Ebenezer Sanders, by which devise, as also by descent from his father Ebenezer Sanders, and, likewise, from his grandfather Edward Sanders, *Chirurgeon*, the *first patentee*, the said Edward Sanders, Jr., became, and now stands seized," etc. (This deed was admitted to record (1712) with Wm. Bledsoe and William Ingram as witnesses.) (*Northumberland Records, Volume dated 1710-1713*.)

20th May, 1712—Deed from Edward Sanders to Hugh Edwards, for "a tract of land."

16th January, 1719—Deed from Edward Saunders to Elis. Paskquett for 50 acres, and *Winifred*, wife of said Edward, came into court and relinquished her right of dower. (Admitted to record 20th July, 1720.)

"*Captain Edward Sanders*," in the list (1720) of the Vestry of St. Stephens parish (*Bishop Meade, Vol. II.*)

19th May, 1724—Deed from Edward Saunders to John Blundle, for 60 acres.

17th October, 1725—Deed from Edward Saunders to Thomas Gill, for 70 acres on Great Wicomico river, "which was formerly the land of *Edward Phillips, grandfather* of said Edward-Saunders" (This deed recorded 20th July, 1726.)

Edward Sanders, Jr., had lands on St. John's creek, Green swamp and Cold Spring swamp (*Northumberland Records at Heathsville*).

Lancaster County Records Begin 1652.

Will of Philip Sanders (29th March, 1697) names children, Thomas, John, Duke, Robert and Margaret. (These are *not* of the Edward Saunders line.)

May, 1710—Edward Sanders, gent, disagreeing with Edward Taylor as to "the lines of a former *patent of 2900* acres in Morratico parish. certified to by Ebenezer Sanders to John Seaman in March 1683," these lines were settled by John Copedge and Edwin Conway, gent, who was "well skilled in ye art of surveying"—to the satisfaction of Ed. Taylor and Edward Sanders (*Book 9-339, at the C. H.*).

1736-37-39—Edward Sanders "constable in the public service for viewing tobacco succors."

1741—Deed of gift from Edward Sanders to his son William, of Lancaster, 250 acres, "the place on which they live," reserving a life-estate for himself and wife.

1742-1743—Deed of gift from Edward Sanders to his sons, Thomas and Edward, of 400 acres. Witness, William Sanders.

March, 1744—Edward Sanders, deed of gift to his son Thomas, of Lancaster, "100 acres of Pasquet's land."

1744—William Sanders, *"of the county of Lancaster, planter,"* acknowledgment to Thomas Sanders. Witnessed by Edward Sanders in 1748 (*Lancaster Book, 14-205*).

1751—Wm. Sanders, *"school-master* of Wicomico parish, in both counties, of Northumberland and Lancaster." An acknowledgement. Witness, Edwin Conway.

1749—Deed to Wm. Sanders of Great Wicomico parish, Lancaster, from Thomas Sanders, and Judith, his wife (*Book 15-76*).

1755—Thomas Sanders, of Lancaster, appoints his worthy and beloved friend, Wm. Sanders, his attorney for a tobacco debt due him. (He is about to leave for his new home, in the lower part of Maryland).

1751—Deed from Peter Conway, to Wm. Sanders.

1758—John Carter and Mary, his wife, make a deed of 150 acres in Wicomico parish, Lancaster, to Edward Carter, being purchased of Thomas Sanders, to whom they were given by his father in two deeds of March, 1742-3 and March, 1744, and sold by Thomas Sanders to Hunton, November, 1755. This deed witnessed by Dale Carter, Thomas Sanders and Ann Warwick.

1760—William Sanders sells to Harvey, lands formerly bought of Maj. Peter Conway and bounded by the lands of Edward Sanders and Harry Carter.

Saunders.

EDWARD SAUNDERS, JUSTICE AND 'CHIRURGEON,' 1660.

"At a Court held for Northumberland co ye 23d of June 1669
Anno f E E Caroli i 21 Co.
P'sent, Col Peter Ashton   Mr William Presley
Capt John Rogers   Capt Corn. Lyster
This day by order from ye right Honrble ye Governour Mr Edward Saunders & Mr Ambrose Fielding were sworn Justices of ye Peace for this county "

(The other Justices were Capt. John Mottrom and Mr. Nicholas Owen. In the next five years the additional Justices were Col. St. Leger Codd (1671), Thomas Matthews, the "T. M." of the MS. (1672), Mr. Francis Lee (1673), Nicholas Green (1675), Philip Sharpleigh and Edward Porteus (1676), (grandfather of Bishop Porteus, of London).

At this same court (1669) "Thomas Holbrook was appointed constable for the court; George Clark for ye north side of Great Wicomico, John Nicholls for ye *Dividing Creek*, William Jallon for *Cherry Poynt*, Wm. Sheares for *Matapony*."

Edward Saunders, of Northumberland county, Chirurgeon, 1660, was probably he whom Hotten mentions as coming to Virginia in 1635 in the ship "*Safety*," aged 9, with his father, Thomas, aged 40, and brother Thomas, aged 13. Others of this family may also have come to Virginia. Until 1634 all immigrants were landed at James City, and the commander at " Poynt Comfort " was required to administer the oath of "*Allegiance and Supremacy*" (*Hen. 1, 166*). Before 1660, Edward Saunders removed from James river to Northumberland county—named for the noble Percy, but called "*Chicacone,*" until after 1645, when it was represented in the Assembly by Capt. John Mottrom, who died in 1655. *Act of 1649:* "All south of the Potomac shall be accounted within the county of Northumberland," * * and, after 1st of September, 1649, "from that day, and not before, it shall be lawful for any of the inhabitants to remove themselves to the north side of Charles (York) river and Rapp river." This, because of the massacre by the Indians in 1644, when the whites had fled. The Northumberland patents began 1648, with Capt. Francis Poythress to collect the assessments. At first, commanders of plantations held monthly courts, with right of appeal to the Quarter Court held by the Governor and Council. These were succeeded by Commissioners of Monthly courts, later called County Courts, when commissioners were first called *Justices*, in

1645. Edward Saunders, or Sanders (as it is variously spelled in the old records) was born in England 1625. His *will*, written in Northumberland county, 4th October, 1669, was not proved until 1672. He evidently had much intercourse with Isle of Wight county, and in 1660 he stated in a court "held that month at Capt. Peter Ashton's house," that he had married Mary, widow of John Hudnall,[*] who had removed to Northumberland in 1655 from Isle of Wight county, and died 1658, and whose plantation was on the south side of Wicomico river, near "the Island." (His descendant, James Saunders, of North Carolina, wrote in Edenton, N. C. (1824), a "*Pamphlet of the Saunders Family*," which gives an unbroken line from the immigrant; and *his* son, Rev. Joseph Saunders continued the chapters, and *his* son, Col. Wm. L. Saunders, Secretary of State, and compiler of its "*Colonial Records*," added more to the pamphlet, which is greatly valued in the family.)

Edward Saunders was physician to Col. George Colclough (former Justice) at his death in 1662—and the *bill* for his services not being paid by the estate, he presented it in court, and Elizabeth Colclough, widow and executrix was ordered to pay it. His land *patents* are given on another page—(also see *Virginia Magazine of History, I–456*) His wife was born Elizabeth Webb (and probably of Isle of Wight county). (*See Webb.*) She married (3) Mr. William Thomas,[†] and was granted a commission of administration on his estate, 1678. The appraisers were William Downing, Sr., and Samuel Webb. She died 1683-4, and Ebenezer Saunders and Edward Saunders, her sons, were granted letters of administration on her estate, and gave bond of 30,000 pounds of tobacco. The appraisers were Thomas Webb, John Cocke, William Horem and others. (*Northumberland Records.*) It is best to conclude with Edward[²] Saunders, the second son, before going on with the line of Ebenezer, the eldest. He was born in 1663, and died

---

[*]John Hudnall (1655) "of Isle of Wight county"—lands on Wicomico river.
　　John Hudnall, August 24, 1658, 250 acres south side of Great Wicomico, near the Island.
　　John Hudnall (1665) 250 acres on Dennis Creek. These lands were formerly granted to John Hudnall, deceased, by *patent* August, 24, 1658. His residence, on the river.
　　Hudnall Partian (1695) 150 acres in Northumberland.
　　Hudnall Partian, son to Harry Hudnall, baptized 1686.
　　Hudnall Joseph, son to Thomas Hudnall, baptized 1679.
　　Hudnall Richard, son to Thomas Hudnall, baptized 1689.
　　Hudnall Thomas, was of the vestry of Upper and Lower St. Stephens parish, 1781.
　　Hudnall Joseph was of the vestry of Upper and Lower St. Stephens parish, 1784.
　　Hudnall Richard, of the vestry of Wicomico parish, Northumberland, 1784 with George and David Ball (*St. Steph'n's Parish Register*).
　　Hudnall Ezekiel, and Thomas, of Lancaster county, in 1763 and 1776.
　　Hudnall Richard, 1751,—land in Northumberland county deeded to him by Col. Peter Conway. (*Hayden's Virginia Genealogies.*)

[†]Hon. R. S. Thomas, attorney at law, Smithfield, Isle of Wight county, Va., has furnished much valuable matter to the two *Historical and Genealogical Magazines* of Virginia. He kindly sends the following:

"In 1681, an Elizabeth Thomas made deed to Robert Saunders, of Nansemond, of part of a former patent to John Saunders, of Isle of Wight. There was a William Thomas with his wife Grace, in 1668.

"The usual emigration was from here (Isle of Wight) to Nansemond and to North Carolina. The last William Thomas died in this county a few years ago. Jordan Thomas went to North Carolina about 1760, and he had a son William (which was a family name). The loss of our records earlier than 1660 prevents our going back as far as you desire.

"At first there was a great deal of intercourse between the Isle of Wight and the Northern neck of Virginia."

In Vol. VII, 268, of *William and Mary Quarterly* Mr. Thomas has this entry of his family—(of which Gen. George H. Thomas is also a descendant). "Captain Robert Thomas—Justice, 1688—with Arthur Smith, George Moon, and James Day."

Will of Richard Thomas, 1687—son John, daughters Phoebe, Elizabeth and Sarah. Richard Thomas had a patent issued him (April, 1681), with Jonathan Robinson and John *Saunders*, for 1680 acres.

1756. When 14 years of age (1677) he chose his mother, Mrs. Mary Thomas, for guardian. He was coroner in 1702. Mr. John Webb, in his will (1709), appointed "my cousin (nephew) Edward Saunders, executor, with Thomas Webb, and my loving sister Mrs. Dickenson." Of his marriage, or descendants, nothing is known. His wife's name was Elizabeth, with whom he made a deed, 1711, to Alexander Love. He and his brother seemed often to have had dealings with Edwin Conway, with whom there was probably some connection.

EBENEZER² SAUNDERS, of Northumberland county, (born 1661, died 1693) *will* February, *Anno* 1692-3. He was put in possession (1678) of a "seat of land" left him by his father, on the south side of Great Wicomico river. That he was of a literary turn, is instanced by a suit brought against his mother, Mrs. Mary Thomas, 1683, for three books of his father's, "*Sonatus at Large*," "*The English Xtian*," "*Ambrose Parvey*." He was foreman of the grand jury in 1686, and that year was sued by Philip Ladwell, but the latter "not appearing, the suit was discharged—Ladwell to pay the cost." In 1689, he acted as attorney for Capt. Peter Wright in a suit vs. —— White, and again, 1687, he sued Mr. A. Thomas. His will was probated in 1693 by Elizabeth his wife and executrix, and proven by the oath of Mr. Peter Presley, and Mr. William Tilhagan. He married Elizabeth, daughter of Mr. Edward Phillips, Issue: (*See Philips note p. 363.*) Edward² and Elizabeth,² between whom, and his brother Edward², he divided his estate.

ELIZABETH³ SAUNDERS (b. 1686), married about 1702, Samuel Downing, son of Captain William Downing, Sr., who in 1657-64-67, patented lands "adjoining Mrs. Jane Claiborne on Great Wicomico River." Captain Wm. Downing (also son perhaps) much land in Stafford after 1692. There were also George, Thomas and John Down‚ng in Northumberland in 1704-11. Edward, a son to John Downing, baptised 1679 ; i Elis, daughter to William, baptised 1679. (*Records.*) Wm. Downing, Sr., was Justice in 1698 (*Virginia Magazine of History I, 217*). Nothing known of any descendants.

EDWARD³ SAUNDERS (born 1686, and living in 1744). Bishop Meade mentions him as of the vestry of St. Stephen's Parish 1720. He was living at the time of his death in Wicomico Parish, which then extended on either side of the river, in both Northumberland and Lancaster counties. His descendants all lived in Lancaster county. He married (1717) Winifred,⁰ who was probably of Presley, Conway, and Ball, connection, as in the

---

*NOTE.—Wm. Presley (1649), patented 1150 acres in Northumberland county. He was justice 1652; Burgess, 1663.—(*Land Grants; Hening*, Vol. II; and *Virginia Historical Magazine*, Vol. I, 456.)

Mr. Peter Presley, Justice, 800 acres (formerly belonging to Geo. Colclough), patented 1664, and 500 acres on Chickacone river, 1670.—(*Land Grants, and Virginia Historical Magazine*, Vol. I, 456.)

William and Peter Presley (1666) patented 2700 acres in Northumberland county (Land Grants). They were civil officers after 1680 for Northumberland county, with Mr. Wm. Downing, John Motirom and Capt. Thos. Mathews, the "T. M." of history.—(*Virginia Historical Magazine*, Vol. I, 391.

Col. Peter Presley, of "Northumberland House" (will, p. 1750), seems not to have been old enough for the Justice of 1663, and must have been his son, and grandson of William Presley, of the patent of 1649 (which is the second patent in the Northumberland Book at Land Office in Richmond, Va.) He married Winifred, daughter of Col. Leroy Griffin (will, 1701), and his wife, Winifred Corbin. Their only daughter and heiress, Winifred, married Anthony Thornton, and was mother of Col. Presley Thornton (born 1710) of Northumberland House, Councillor, 1760. John Edwards patented Northumberland House in 1662, and it passed from him to the Presleys.—(*DeBow's Review*, XXVI, 126.) William and the first Peter Presley, doubtless, had other descendants.

JOHN³ and DENNIS³ CONWAY, of Northumberland county, were brothers. John died in 1739, leaving a son, George² (will, 1746), who married Ann, sister of Presley Thornton.

Dennis³ died in 1729 (will, 1730). Children: John³ (will, 1754), George,³ Dennis,³ Elis.³ Winifred,³ Judith³ and Nancy³. Of these; John³ had, among others, Winifred, who married—Coles. Dennis³ (the constable, 1744) had a son, Thomas⁴ Conway, whose orphans, George,⁴ Chloe⁴ and Betty⁴, were under the guardianship of Joseph Hubbard (and Joseph's sister, Betty, was the wife of Wm. Sanders).

MR. PETER⁴ CONWAY (Edwin,³ Edwin,² Edwin¹) Burgess 1748, died in 1758; married (I), Betty Span (whose sister, Frances Sinah Span, married John Conway), and married (II) Betty, daughter of Richard Lee. He deeded a bequest of land (1751) to Richard Hudnall. He had a son, Peter, and a daughter, Agatha, who married (1765) Jesse Ball.

Col. Edwin Conway, administrator of Wm. Sanders' will, was born in 1742, and was county lieutenant for Lancaster. 1781, and fifth of his name.—(*Hayden*, 361.)

line of her eldest son, William (whom we follow), are transmitted such names as Sinah, Jesse, Winifred and Presley; common to those families. Deeper search in the Lancaster Records might reveal her parentage. Issue: William[4], Thomas[4] and Edward.[4] Of these, we will dispose, first, of Thomas and Edward; THOMAS[4], Saunders (or Sanders) of Maryland (born 1720), married (about 1742), Judith _____, with whom he made a deed in 1755 of lands given him by his father in 1744. (*Records.*) He then moved to the lower part of Maryland where, says the family chronicler (James Saunders, his nephew), " he reared many children, some of whom served with credit to themselves and country in the Revolution." It is greatly desired to learn more of them.

EDWARD[4] SAUNDERS (third son), of Wicomico Par., Lancaster county (born 1723), married (1743) Sinah _____, who was reared in his own neighborhood. Her surname, and that of Thomas Saunders' wife, would throw much additional light on the family connection, and might yet be obtained from the Records of Lancaster county. They moved, about 1760, to Brunswick county, Va., where his will was dated September 27, 1783. It is still on record, and mentions "wife, Sinah, and children: 1. Ebenezer. 2. Edward. 3. Judith, who married — Freeman. 4. Lucy married — Peebles. 5. Sinah. 6. Margaret. 7. Sarah. 8. Celia." It was witnessed by James Mason, James Bass, Enoch George, and proved by his son, Eben Sanders. (*This line has not been followed.*)

WILLIAM[4] SAUNDERS† of Wicomico Par., Lancaster county, planter (born 1718, died 22d November, 1779), married, May 18, 1738, Elizabeth or Betty (born 22d February, 1721, died 14th November, 1889), daughter of Thomas Hubbard of Lancaster county, and of Scotch descent. (*See Hubbard.*) He is mentioned in *Hayden's Va.*, *Genealogies*

---

†I, William Sanders, of the county of Lancaster, being sick, and weak of body, but of sound mind and memory, thanks be to God, do make this my last will and testament in manner following, viz.: I resign my soul to God my Creator, and my body to the earth, its original, being fully assured that the sacrifice of Christ is a worthy expiation for all the sins of the faithful, and therefore hope that my soul and body will have a joyful meeting at the resurrection of the just, by the merits, mediation and intercession of our complete Redeemer, the Lord Jesus Christ, Amen.

Imprimis.—I give the use of all my estate now in my possession, or that shall be in my actual possession at the time of my death, to my loving wife, Betty Sanders, during her widowhood, for her comfortable subsistence, and for the support of my children that shall be living with my said loving wife at my death, and for bringing up in a Christian manner my two young sons, William and James Sanders, and that it is my will and desire that my said two sons, William and James, shall be under the management and control of their said mother, Betty Sanders, until they shall arrive at the age of 21 years ; and also it is my wife's and my desire that, either at the marriage or death of my said wife, all my estate, both real and personal, and of what nature soever, shall be sold by my executors hereafter named, and the money arising from the sale of my said estate to be equally divided among all my children, or their representatives, after deducting, or including, the sums out of those of my children, or their representatives' part of my estate, of what they, my children, had received in my lifetime, which is as followeth :

Item.—I give and bequeath to my son, Thomas Sanders, to him and his heirs, etc., an equal part of the money arising from the sale of my estate, including one bed and furniture, value £7 current money, already received.

Item.—I give, etc., to my son, Jesse Sanders, his heirs, etc., equal part of the money arising from the sale of my estate, including £50 which I paid to the estate of Mr. John Mitchell, deceased, which I was the said Jesse's security for ; also the sum of £13 17s 2d, the whole amounting to £63 17s 2d.

Item.—To the children of my daughter, Winny Elliott, deceased, an equal part of the money arising from the sale of my estate, including £11 12s, value on sundry articles to be equally divided among them.

Item.—To my daughter Franky (deceased), her children, an equal part of the money arising from the sale of my estate, to be equally divided among the children she had by her husband, Mr. Abraham White, deceased, including £11 2s 8d value in sundry articles which my said daughter did receive in my lifetime.

Item.—To the children of my son, Edward Sanders, deceased, one equal part of the money arising from the sale of my estate, including £7 for one bed and furniture, which the said Edward received in my lifetime, etc.

Item.—To the following children (to-wit) Mary, Presley, Joseph, Ephraim, William and James Sanders, equal parts, etc. (like the above).

Lastly.—I do appoint my said *dear wife, Betty Sanders*, and my friend, *Col. Edwin Conway*, and my son, *Thos. Sanders*, executors of this my last will and testament, revoking all former wills. In (page 247), as commissioner with Thomas Brent, to divide the estate of George Conway, 1764 (son of Colonel Edwin Conway), between his children George, Walker and Ann Conway. Colonel Conway was his, and his father's, friend, and was "well skilled in ye art of surveying," and was also administrator of his will (dated 26th June, 1779.) (*See below.*) He had also been his surety in several business transactions. For a while William Sanders conducted a school for the youth of both Lancaster and Northumberland. (*Records.*) He, fair, with light hair and blue eyes; she, dark eyes and hair; issue, 11 children, born when their mother was in her 45th year: 1. Thomas[1]. 2. Mary[2]. 3. Jesse[3]. 4. Winifred[4]. 5. Frances[5]. 6. Edward[6]. 7. Presley[6]. 8. Joseph[6]. 9. Ephraim[6]. 10. William[6]. 11. James[6] (twins).

1. THOMAS[1] SAUNDERS, of the Revolution (b. 18th June, 1739; died before 1808); married (1764) Ann Turner, widow of Edward Harper, of Sussex county Va. (who died 1764) and whom he met when visiting his uncle in Brunswick county. She had sons; Wilkins Harper* and William Harper (b. 22d April, 1763). Thomas Saunders then settled in Brunswick county, Va., near his uncle Edward. He served occasionally in the Revolutionary War as a militia officer (*Pamphlet*). Issue: (1) Rev. Hubbard Saunders, (2) Betty, (3) Nancy, (4) Thomas, (5) Polly, (6),Patsy and (7) Rev. Turner (*see further on*).

2. MARY[2] SAUNDERS (b. 6th May, 1741), never married; lived with her brother, Joseph Saunders, while in Brunswick county.

3. CAPT. JESSE[3] SAUNDERS, of the Revolution (b. July 21, 1743), was captain in the Sixth North Carolina (*Heitman*). But first, in the battles with the Regulators, before the Revolution. Married Ann, daughter of Colonel Yancey, of Granville county, N. C. " Had many children, and moved to Georgia, and some of his children probably to Tennessee. Issue: (1) William, (2) Yancey, (3) James, (4) Lewis, (5) Betty, (6) Polly, and others.

witness whereof I have hereunto set my hand and seal, this 26th day of June, A. D. one thousand seven hundred and seventy-nine.   WM. SANDERS.
    Witness : JOSEPH TAYLOR.
             JOHN BEAN.
             THOMAS GARNER.
    At a court held for Lancaster county, 20th day of April, 1780, this last will and testament of Wm. Sanders, deceased, was presented in court by Betty Sanders, the widow of the said deceased, and executrix therein named, who made oath thereto according to law, and being proved by the oath of John Bean and Thos. Garner was admitted to record, and on the motion of said executrix giving security, a certificate is granted her for obtaining a probate thereof in due form.
                    Test.: THADDEUS MCCARTY,
                                       Cl. C.
His inventory of cattle and household goods follow, footing up £4633 10s, 18th May, 1780.
Recorded.   THOS. GARNER.
                                JOHN BEAN.
                              STEPHEN LOCK.
                          (*Lancaster C. H. Book 20.*)

    * Edward and Anne Harper, godparents (1758) to Goodwyn, "son of Thomas and Frances Ann Hunt, deceased" (*Albemarle Parish Register*).
    Wilkins Harper married Lucy Tucker, and removed to Lawrence county, Alabama, near his half-brother, Rev. Turner Saunders, and had children: Wilkins, Robert, Richard and Berryman Harper.
    [1] Wilkins Harper, son of Wilkins Harper, removed to Greenwood, Caddo parish, La. Among his children are Dr. Harper, of Jefferson, Tex., and Mrs. Ragan, of Columbia, Mo., whose first husband was Colonel Winans. a gallant officer of the Confederate army, by whom she had four daughters. One daughter by the last marriage (Ragan). Mr. Harper died at the home of his daughter in Columbia, Mo.
    [2] Robert Harper, also son of Wilkins. removed to Tennessee and married (1816) his cousin, Ann A. (b. 1795), daughter of Rev. Hubbard and Chloe (Russell) Saunders (*vide*).
    [3] Berryman* Harper never married. Assisted Rev. Turner Saunders in managing his estate in North Alabama. His father's plantation, in Lawrence county, Ala., was bought by the Rev. John C. Burruss (when he removed to Louisiana), and was afterward sold to the McGregor family, and joined the old "*Parson Sale place*," which was afterward owned by Hon. Wm. O. Sherrod.
    [4] Richard Harper moved to Hinds county Miss., where he died, a physician.

    *Alexander Berryman, living in York county. 1702.
    John Berryman, Vestry of St. Paul, King George county, after 1720.—*Meade.*
    John Berryman, Vestry Christ Church, Lancaster, 1776, signed protest 1765, against Stamp Act.

4. WINIFRED[4] SAUNDERS (b. Lancaster county, Va., 24th Feb., 1746; died 22d Feb., 1797), married in Lancaster county (*circa* 1764) Thomas Elliott, of Lancaster. (*See Elliott.*) Issue, an only son: John[5] Elliott, of Brunswick county, Va. (b. *circa* 1765), married Mildred Maclin, of Brunswick county (Colonel Frederick Maclin of Brunswick, was member House of Delegates (1781), with Wm. Stith). (Joseph Saunders, brother of Winifred, and lieutenant in the Navy of the Revolution, also had married Martha, daughter of Colonel Maclin, his second wife). Issue:

1. *George*[7] *Elliott* (b. *circa* 1792), *m.* his cousin Patsy Walker, and removed to Tennessee; several children; only one living in 1897, an aged daughter.
2. *Nancy*[7] (1794), *m.* Samuel Bolling, of Brunswick. Issue, among others: (1) Henriette, "a belle and beauty in Brunswick, seventy years ago," *m.* Dr. Field, and had several children. (2) John Bolling, of Petersburg, "an eventful life," several children; a son living in Texas.
3. *Robert*[7] (*circa* 1796), *m.* Minerva G. Hill (b. *circa* 1804, d. 1878), daughter of Richard and Anne (Dunn) Hill, of Brunswick county (*see Dunn family*). They moved to Mississippi. Issue: (1) Robert, *m.* ——, and had an only daughter, who *m.* (1) her cousin, Carter Hill, and (II) ——; (2) Frances. Mrs. Elliott, *m.* (2) Judge Mills, of New Orleans, and had David and Andrew. (*See Dunn Family.*)
4. *Martha*[7] (1798), *m.* Nathaniel Mabry; children, and grandchildren, living near Clarksville, Tenn.
5. *Thomas*[7] (1800), *m.* Miss Clark.
6. *John*[7] (1802), *m.* (I), Henrietta Barker, and (II), Mary Slaughter.
7. *Mildred*[7], died young.
8. *William*[7] *Henry* (b. Brunswick county, Va., 13th May, 1805; d. 2d January, 1895, in New Providence, Tenn.) *m.* (14th Aug. 1832), in West Tennessee, Frances Eliz. (b. Brunswick county, Va., 12th Dec. 1812; d. in Christian county, Ky., 11th March, 1896) daughter of Richard and Anne (Dunn) Hill, of Brunswick county, Va. (sister of Minerva Hill, above). (For descendants of their eight children, see *Dunn Family*.)
9. *Mary*[7] (b. 1812; died in Clarksville, Tenn., 1896), *m.* Joseph Sturdivant. Her last days were spent with her niece, Mrs. Buckner, at whose home she died.

5. FRANCES[5] SAUNDERS (b. 5th August, 1748); *m.* (I) Abraham White, no surviving issue; *m.* (II) George Davis. Issue: (1) Holland*, of Tennessee, several children; (2) Ephraim, of Brunswick: several children (*their lines are not followed*).

6. EDWARD[5] SAUNDERS of the Rev. (b. 5th May, 1751), killed defending his brother Jesse in the Rev. war. He married Jane, daughter, also, of Colonel Yancey, of Granville, N. C. Issue: three daughters (1) Margaret*, *m.* —— Johnston; (2) Anne*, *m.* —— Johnston, brother of above; (3) Eliz*.

7. PRESLEY[5], SAUNDERS of the Rev. (b. 19th October, 1753, d. September, 1816); sergeant 7th Co., 2d Va. Reg., Col. Alex. Spotswood; received, in 1783, land warrants for 200 acres, as sergeant, for three years' service in the Rev. (*Saffell*); *m.* in Lancaster (after the Rev.), Winifred, daughter of William Kent, and had several children; moved late in life to Chowan county, N. C. Issue:

1. William*, married and moved to Alabama.
2. Betty*, *m.* (I), Mr. Wilder, of North Carolina. Issue: James Wilder, massacred at Goliad, in Texan war; *m.* (II), Henry Hubbell,* and moved to Alabama; issue: Sarah, *m.* Lewis Garrett, and moved to Arkansas.
3. Edward*, *m.* and lived in Camden county, North Carolina.
4. Presley, went to sea, and was never heard of after.

8. JOSEPH[5] SAUNDERS, of the Rev. (b. 7th June, 1757), Lt. of the ship "Dragon," and Lt. Commander of the galley "Lewis" in 1781. In 1783, he received land warrants for 2666⅔ acres as Lieutenant in Rev. Navy, and pension in 1832. Moved from Lancaster to Brunswick, in 1789; *m.* (I). 1788, Margaret, daughter of Richard Shackelford, of Richmond county, Va. In 1822 he moved to Giles county, Tenn; in 1823, to Lawrence county, Ala. Issue:

---

* Browning's "*Americans of Royal Descent*" give the Hubbell family as descended. through the Stuarts. from Robert II.

1. *Margaret*[6], m. Robert Taylor, of North Carolina. Issue:
  1. Mary Eliza[7], m. Samuel Mardis, lawyer, Shelby county, Ala., and member of Congress, and had (1) States Rights[8]; (2) Eugenia[8], m. Dr. Hester, of New Orleans; (3) Samuella[8], m. Mr. Cohn, merchant of New Orleans.
  2. Matilda[7], m. Isaac Glidewell; one son; died in U. S. A., 1870.
  3. Josephine[7], m., 1837, Junius A. Bynum, of Courtland, Ala., and had (1) Junius[8], C. S. A., and never returned from the war; (2) Margaret[8], m. Philip Pointer; (3) Burt[8]; (4) Laura[8], m. Bolling Tabb, and had Ross, Laura and Lippie. Lt. Joseph Saunders, m. (II), Martha, daughter of Col. Frederick Maclin, of Brunswick county, Va. (*see Maclin note to Dunn Family*). Issue:
2. *Lucy*[6], (d. 1862), m. Major Robert Fenner (d. 1848), of Halifax, N. C. Issue:
  1. Robert[7]. Lt. in Capt. Shackelford's Company of Red Rovers in the Texan war; massacred at Goliad, Tex.
  2. Mary H.[7], m. Dr. Julius Johnson; issue: Fenner[8], in C. S. A., with General Forrest; and Margaret[8], (of Jackson, Tenn).
  3. Thomas B[7].
  4. Joseph T[7]., m. Miss Gossett, of Ripley, Miss., and was also in Texan war.
  5. Richard H[7].
  6. Margaret E.[7] (d. 1861).
  7. Ann M[6]. (d. 1876).
  8. Lucy[7], m. Mr. Walton.
3. *Martha*[6], m. (I), —— Finlay, a Scotchman; (II), Rev. Parker Holcomb. No issue.
  9. EPHRAIM[5] SAUNDERS of the Revolution, (b. 14th March, 1760), Lancaster county; m. Ann, daughter of Colonel McCarty, of Richmond county, Va., and settled in Columbia county, Ga., where he died in 1799. Issue: Three daughters—not known—"but there must have been one *Bet.* and one *Nan.* among them, for he was another mother's child indeed."
  10. WILLIAM[5] SAUNDERS (b. 25th April, 1765, twin), moved to Georgia, and never married.
  11. JAMES[5] SAUNDERS, twin with William, and author of the old "*Family Pamphlet*" (1824). In 1790, after the death of his mother, he left Lancaster, "the old castle, the place of his nativity, childhood and youth," the last of his family there; he also turned Southward, and settled in Edenton, North Carolina, where he married (1793), Hannah, daughter of James Sitterson (b. 1759, d. 1819). He died 22d June, 1824. Issue:
  1. Rev. Joseph Hubbard Saunders[6] (b. 26th Dec., 1800), only child, ordained in Richmond 1831, by Bishop Moore. m. (25th April, 1833), Laura Lucinda, daughter of Dr. Simmons Baker, of Martin county, North Carolina, and moved to Pensacola, 1826. (He died 24th October, 1839) of yellow fever, in Pensacola, Florida, while performing his duty, and was buried under the Vestry room of his church. Issue:
    (1.) Dr. Richard Benbury[7a] of Churchill, N. C. (b. Raleigh, N. C., 12th April, 1834, died Durham, N. C., 6th Sept. 1890) Second Lieutenant First Regiment, Cramp's Light Infantry, North Carolina Volunteers, C. S. A., Col. D. H. Hill. Married at Natchez (1856), Mary Stanton, daughter of Gov. Girard Brandon, of Mississippi. Issue:
      (I) Frederick Stanton (b. 1857); (II) Wm. Lawrence (b. 1859, d. 1863); (III) Laura Baker (b. 1861); (IV) Bessie Brandon (b. 1863); (V) Mary Varina (b. 1865).

(2) *Col. William Lawrence Saunders*[7] (b. Raleigh, N. C., 30th July, 1835; d. 1891), Secretary of State of North Carolina and compiler of that great work, "*Colonial Records of North Carolina.*" Gallant colonel of the Forty-sixth Regiment North Carolina troops in the Civil War, and was wounded several times. Married (1864) Florida Call, daughter of John W. Cotton, of North Carolina; she died 9th July, 1865.

(3) *Anne*[7] (b. Pensacola, Fla., 1837; d. ——).

(4) Joseph Hubbard[7] (b. Pensacola, 23d October, 1839; d. ——); Lieutenant Colonel Thirty-third Regiment North Carolina in 1864; wounded twice severely at Second Manassas and at Gettysburg; married ——. Issue:

   1. Norfleet, d. (See old *Pamphlet of Saunders Family.*)

Returning to Thos[6]. Saunders, of the Revolution, and of Brunswick county, Va.; his eldest son was—

Rev. HUBBARD[6] SAUNDERS, M. E. Ch. South, of Davidson county, Tenn., born in Brunswick county, Va., September 3, and christened in P. E. Church, October 19, 1766; Thos. Hunt, one of the godfathers (*Old Sussex and Surrey county, Albemarle, Pa. Register*). He died 1828. Married (2d December, 1792) Chloe (b. on Clinch river, 1776), youngest child of Gen. Wm. Russell, of the Rev., and Tabitha Adams, his first wife. The General's second wife (1783) was Sarah Henry, widow of Gen. Wm. Campbell, of the Rev., and sister of the great orator, Patrick Henry. General Russell was born 1735, and was eldest son of Wm. Russell, of Orange Co., Va., who came to Virginia 1710, with Gov. Spotswood, and patented 40,000 acres in and around Spotsylvania Co.. His home was at *North Garden Salt Works*, Washington Co., Va., where he died 1797. His wife and Rev. Hubbard Saunders, were his administrators. The latter made a final settlement of his account, 1816. The Rev. Hubbard Saunders married his wife about six weeks before her father's death, and at that time was deeply engaged with his celebrated mother-in-law, in her great work of *religious revival* among her family and community. In 1798 he removed from Virginia to Sumner county, Tenn., and there reared a large family. By his contributions and influence, a brick church was built at *Turner's Springs*, and called "*Saunders' Chapel*," for its venerable founder, who died about that time. Since then a thriving little village, called *Saundersville*, also perpetuates his revered memory. His widow died 1850, aged 74, and their tombs, and those of a number of their descendants, may be found at the old homestead. The large house still stands; upon the wall of its old parlor hang the portraits of this remarkable couple—he, a splendid looking man, and she, quite lovely. (See *Russell Family*, by Mrs. Anna Russell des Cognets, also *Methodism in Tennessee*, and *Life of Mrs. General Russell*). Issue of above Saunders' marriage, fourteen children, as follows:

1. Nancy A.[7] (b. 18th September, 1773, m. (1816) her cousin, Robert, son of Wilkins Harper, of Alabama and Virginia, and had nine children, viz.:

   1. Lucy[8] S. Harper (b. 1818, d. Caddo parish, La., 1864), m. James B. Vinson, of Louisiana (b. 1814).

      I. R. Walker[9] Vinson, of Texas, C. S. A., Fourth Louisiana Regiment (b. 1838), *m.* Sophia Saunders Gibbs, of Mansfield, La. Issue: Mary G.[10], Douglass[10], Lucy S.[10], Harper[10], and John M.[10] Vinson.

      II. Richard Tucker[9] Vinson, Shreveport, La., C. S. A. (b. 1842) Fifth Company of Washington Artillery; Mayor of Shreveport, and one of its most prominent and useful citizens, married (1864) Sallie, daughter of Allen Hill, and granddaughter of Colonel Peace, of Wilson county, Tenn. Issue: Ada[10], a bright and charming daughter; and Allen[10] Vinson (b. 1872).

      III. Alice B. Vinson[9], *m.* John T. Green, of Nashville, Tenn. Issue: 1. Minnie Lon.; 2. Vinson; 3. Marvin (b. 1878).

      IV. Lillie Vinson[9], *m.* John McKee Harper, son of Dr. Wm. Harper, of Jefferson, Texas. Issue: 1. Charles Robert (b. 1882); 2. Lucy Vinson; 3. Addie.

2. Chloe Russell[3] Harper *m.* John Duncan, of Russellville, Ky., and removed to Texas. Issue:
    I. Robert Harper[6] Duncan, of Trinity Mills, Texas.
    II. Eugene[6] Duncan, *m.* Maggie Dixon, and has Mary, Emma and Eugene.
    III. Ella[6] Duncan, *m.* Asa Dupre Dickinson, and has Robert C. and Asa Dupre.
    IV. Daniel Dunscomb[6] Duncan.
    V. Hubbard Saunders[6] Duncan.
3. Sally[3] Harper, died in infancy.
4. Maria[3] Harper, *m.* Capt. W. T. Sample, of Trinity Mills, Texas.
5. Anne[3] Harper, *m.* James Duncan, of Russellville, Ky., and had one son, Wilkins[6], who died.
6. Clara[3] Russell Harper *m.* Professor C. W. Callender, of Hendersonville, Tenn. Children: William[6] and Ewing[6].
7. Col. Robt. Goodloe Harper[3] d. 1863, *m.* (I), 1855, Sophie Valentine, of Louisiana, and (II) Thomasella Hardeman, of Franklin, Tenn. Issue by first marriage: Sophie H.[6], who *m.* Robt. E. Cowart, of Dallas, Tex., son of Judge R. J. Cowart, Atlanta, Ga.; son, Robert Erwin[6].
8. Dr. Hubbard Saunders[3] Harper, died *unm.* aged twenty-five.
9. Adeline[3] Harper *m.* Col. T. T. Turner, C. S. A., of Gallatin, Tenn., lawyer, who served with distinction in late war. Issue: Robert Harper[6], Adeline[6], Clarabel[6], Anna[6] (dead), James[6] (dead).
2. Elizabeth Henry[7] Saunders (b. 8th September, 1795) *m.* (1816) Capt. John A. Walker, of Davidson county, Tenn. Issue:
    1. Mary[3] Walker *m.* Benjamin Hamlin—no issue.
    2. Chloe[3] Walker *m.* Wm. Pierce, Davidson county, Tenn. Issue:
        I. Mary E.[9] *m.* Wm. Allen, Nashville, Tenn.
        II. William H.[9] of Texas.
    3. Catherine[3] Walker *m.* Wm. Chambers, Erwin City, Tenn. Issue:
        I. Charles A[9]. Chambers, of Nashville.
        II. Mary H.[9] Chambers.
        III. Sallie E [9] Chambers *m.* John R. George, of Union City, Tenn.
        IV. William C.[9] Chambers.
3. Maria Roberts Saunders (b. 15th June, 1797, d. 1838) *m.* Dr. James L. Gray, of Tennessee; (d. 1886 in Mississippi). Issue:
    I. Hubbard G[3]. of Texas (d. 1888); II. William[3] of Texas (dead); III. Leonidas[3], of Tippah county, Miss., C. S. A. (d. 1862); IV. James[3] (dead); V. Cornelia[3] (dead); VI. Chloe[3] (b. 1838) married Mr. Bratton, and has four daughters, and a son (born 1882.)
4. Sally Edmonds[7] Saunders (b. 13th September, 1799) *m.* (I), Peter Byson, of Sumner, county, Tenn., and (II), Hugh Joyner. *Issue first marriage:*
    I. Chloe Russell[3] Byson *m.* (1839) Benj. W. Mills, of Sumner county, and had:
        1. Sally A.[9] Mills *m.* (1859) Dr. H. J. Wells, of Nashville, Tenn.
        2. Dero F.[9] Mills, of Hendersonville. Tenn., *m.* (1867) Annie E. Shute. Issue: Maggie[10], Willie[10], Annie[10], Lee S.[10], Bessie[10] and Mary D.[10]
        3. John P.[9] Mills, Sherman, Texas, *m.* (1872) Ellie W. Wilson. Issue: Haydie[10], J. Rowan[10], Ethel[10], Lawrence[10], and Mary[10].
        4. Minnie[9] Mills *m.* R. S. Murray, of Sumner county. Issue: Samuel B.[10], Mary[10], and John Dee[10] Murray.
        5. Bettie[9] Mills, unmarried. *Issue of second marriage:*
        6. Thomas[3] H. Joyner, Huntsville, Tenn., *m.* (1881) Sue Anthony.
5. Minerva[7] Saunders (b. 29th September, 1801; d. 1844); unmarried.
6. Clara[7] Saunders (b. 23d October, 1803); *m.* Samuel D. Read, Davidson county. Issue:
    1. John[3] Read, d. young.

2. Mildred Ann⁶ Read, *m.* Madison Martin, Sewanee county, Tenn. Issue:
    I. Samuel A.⁷ Martin, Atchison, Kas.; *m.* (I), Eunice Crenshaw, of Gallatin, Tenn., and had a daughter, Mary L.⁸; *m.* (II), Bettie Crenshaw, of Gallatin.
    II. Emma⁷ Martin, *m.* Lorenzo Stowe, of Rome, Tenn.
    III. Clara L.⁷ Martin, Gallatin, Tenn.
    IV. Mattie⁷ Martin, *m.* Russell Word, of Arkansas.
3. Chloe Russell⁶ Read, *m.* John Drake, of Nashville, Tenn. Issue:
    I. Wm. H.⁷ Drake, Nashville, *m.* Laura Brodie. Issue: Medora⁸ and John⁸ Brodie.
    II. Clara L.⁷ Drake, *m.* Wm. Wilkinson, Nashville, Tenn.
    III. Sarah A.⁷ Drake, married Belfield Bratton. Issue: Clarence Russell⁸ and Hattie⁸.
    IV. Mary⁷ D. V. Maud M⁷. VI. Joseph Hubbard⁷. VII. John Warfield⁷ Drake.
4. Sarah E.⁶ Read; *m.* Rev. James Warfield, of Baltimore, Md., and removed to Lexington, Ark. Issue:
    I. Samuel D.⁷ II. Eliza⁷ III. Robert Paine.⁷ IV. Clara Gertrude.⁷ V. George Hanson⁷. VI. Charles Marion⁷ Warfield.
5. Hubbard Saunders⁶ Read, Davidson county, Tenn.; *unm.*
7. Addie⁷ Saunders (b. 8th August, 1805, d. in infancy).
8. Chloe⁷ Russell Saunders (b. 14th January, 1807, d. 1839); *m.* (1825) Alex. Ewing, of Davidson county, Tenn. Issue:
    1. Sarah Ann⁸ Ewing, *m.* (I) Boyd McNairy Simms, of Franklin; (II) Joseph W. Carter, lawyer, of Winchester, Tenn, and (III) Judge John C. Gant, of Nashville, Tenn. *Issue (first marriage):*
        I. Annie⁹ Simms, *m.* J. W. McFadden, of Nashville, and has a daughter, Sallie⁸ McFadden.
        II. Marianne B.⁹ Simms, m. R. N. Richardson, of Franklin. *Issue (second marriage):*
        III. William E.⁹ Carter.
        IV. Joseph W.⁹ Carter, *m.* Kate R. French, of Nashville; one son, Joseph W.¹⁰ Carter.
    2. Alexander⁸ Ewing (b. 1830, d. 1850).
    3. Hubbard Saunders⁸ Ewing, living at the old *Ewing Homestead*, near Franklin, Tenn.; *m.* (1859) Sallie Hughes, daughter of Dr. Brice Hughes. Issue:
        I. Susie Lee⁹ Ewing, married (1883) Winder McGavock, only son of Col, John McGavock; daughter, Hattie¹⁰.
        II. Alexander⁹ Ewing, Birmingham, Ala.
        III. Sallie⁹ Ewing.
        IV. Malvina⁹ Ewing, *m.* Mr. Titcomb: a son, Alexander¹⁰ Titcomb, of Columbia, Tenn., m. Miss Smiser, and has one son, Alex. Titcomb, Jr.
        V. William, R.⁹ Ewing, *m.* Miss Brown; one son, Wheless Brown¹⁰ Ewing, Franklin, Tenn.
9. ¶William Russell⁷ Saunders, lawyer (b. 8th June, 1811, d. at Salt Works St. Stephens, Washinton county, Ala., 20th August, 1864), *m.* Ann. H. Mills, of Sumter county, Tenn. They removed to Lexington, Miss., 1844, and then to Carroll county. He graduated at University Nashville when sixteen years of age. His influence, morally and intellectually was great in his community. Issue:
    1. Hubert⁸ Saunders, of Starkville, Miss., *m.* Ella W. Rogers and has issue. I. Hubert T.⁹; II. Eliz. McMillan⁹; III. Robert Percival⁹.
    2. Caroline Ann⁸ Saunders, *m.* C. B. Turnipseed, of Vaiden, Miss. Issue: I. Annie Lola⁹; II. Maggie May⁹; III. Nettie Alma⁹; IV. Hubert Homer⁹; V. Grosie Ella⁹ Turnipseed.
    3. William Russell⁸ Saunders, of Winona, Miss., *m.* Fannie E. Allen: a son, Wm. Russell⁹ Saunders.

4. Thomas Mills[5] Saunders, Cleburne, Texas, m. Alice de Mumbre. Children: I. Dero de Mumbre[6]; II. Annie Mills[6]; III. William Russell[6].
5. Chloe Bennetts[5] Saunders, m. Dr. T. L. Wilburn, Winona, Miss: a son, William Russell Saunders[6] Wilburn, of Kilmichael, Miss.
6. Dero A.[5] Saunders, Starkville, Miss., m. Grosie Ames. Issue: 1. Madison Ames; 2. Grosie.
7. John Spotswood[5] Saunders, Starkville, m. Pattie Curry. Issue: 1. Virginia; 2. Annie May.
10. Tabitha Turner[3] Saunders (b. 6th April, 1812), m. W. H. Moore, Nashville, Tenn. Issue:
    1. Frances[4] Moore, m. William Lelyette, Nashville: a son, John Lelyette, of Nashville, with two children.
    2. Eliz.[4] Moore, m. Mr. Stewart, Williamson county.
    3. Catherine[4] Moore, m. Edward Jones, of Virginia (and now of Nashville); has six children.
    4. Turner[4] Moore, Davidson county, m. Miss Whitsell, of Nashville; has two children.
    5. Wm. H.[4] Moore, Tullahoma, Tenn., m. Ethel Porter, daughter of Capt. John Porter, of Kentucky. Issue: I. Margaret Amelia[5]; II. Kate Beatrice[5]; III. Frank Moore[5].
    6. Anna[4] Moore, m. John Whitesell, Davidson county, Tenn.
    7. James[4]; 8, John[4]; 9, Alice,[4] and 10, Benjamin[4] Moore, all of Nashville.
II. Catherine M. J.[3] Saunders (b. 26th December, 1814, d. Coushatta, La., May, 1836), m. Peyton Randolph Bosley, of Davidson county, Tenn. They removed to Red River, La. Issue:
    I. John Randolph[4] Bosley, Bossier parish, La. (born 22d September, 1832), m. 1st, (15th May, 1851) Mary Jane, daughter of Henry F. Jones. His Plantation is between Lakes Swan and Bistineaux, La. Issue:
        I. John Randolph[5] Bosley, Grandview, Tex. (b. 18th February, 1852), m. (1880) Ida Clarendon Smith, of Dallas. Son, John Houston[6] (born 1881).
        II. Katharine Saunders[5] Bosley (b. 2d December, 1853), m. (2d December, 1873) Orrin S. Penny, Coushatta, La. Children: Orrin Saunders[6] (b. 1874), Monte Leon[6] (1876), Harvey Robertson[6] (1879), Arthur Stephenson[6] (1881), Spiser Mailheux[6] (1883). Mr. Bosley m. (II), (28th May, 1861) Josephine Letitia, daughter of James and Elizabeth (Carter) Houston, of Red River. Issue:
        III. Joseph Houston[5] Bosley, Bossier parish, La. (b. 1862). IV. Wilhimena[5] Bosley (b. 1864). V. Ora Eugenia[5] Bosley (b. 1869). VI. Susie Saunders[5] Bosley (b. 1871). VII. Eva Leonie[5] Bosley (b. 1874). Henry Russell[5] Bosley (b. 1878).
    2. Hubbard Saunders[4] Bosley, Coushatta, La., m. (1856) Mary Powell (d. 1883). Their children:
        I. Thomas Randolph[5] (b. 1858, d. 1881). II. Marion Powell[5] (b. 1863). III. Anna[5] (1865). IV. Milton H.[5] (1868). V. Hubbard Saunders[5] (1871). VI. Percival Leigh[5] (1875). VII. Walter Warren[5] (1878).
12. Thomas Turner[3] Saunders (b. 16th December, 1816, twin with Adeline Celia) m. his cousin, E. Letitia, daughter of William Trigg Breckenridge, of Kentucky. They removed to Nashville, Tenn.; and had thirteen children, of whom only two survive, viz.: 1. William[4] Saunders, m. Miss Bondurant. 2. Rosa[4] Saunders.
13. Adeline Celia[3] Saunders (twin, b. 16th December, 1816), m. Dr. Alexander Graham, Sumner county, Tenn., who d. 1857. They lived near Hendersonville, Tenn. Issue:
    1. Chloe Frances[4] Graham (b. 31st December, 1857), m. George Whitfield Sumner, son of Duke W. Sumner, of Davidson county, Tenn. Issue:
        I. Lou Carter[5] Sumner, m. (1881); Samuel J. Bloodworth and has son Samuel.[10]

II. Hattie[2]. III. George Graham[2]. IV. Charles Douglas[2]. V. Hubbard Saunders[2]. VI. Adeline Mary[2]. VII. Jay Gould[2] Sumner.

2. Susan Alexander[6] Graham (b. 31st December, 1845), m. Prof. C. S. Douglass, Gallatin, Tenn. Issue: I. Ada[7] Douglass. II. Clare[7] Douglass.

14. Hubbard Henley[7] Saunders (b. 5th May, 1819; d. 23d October, 1879). He inherited the old *Saunders homestead*, where he lived and died; m. (22d June, 1848) Eliza Bondurant. Issue: 1. William[8] Saunders, of *Saundersville*, Tenn. 2. Jacob T.[8] Saunders, of *Saundersville*; m. Miss Weaver, of Stewart county. Issue: 1. Hubbard Thomas[9] Saunders. 2. Jefferson Weaver[9] Saunders. 3. Edward[8] Saunders, Sumner county, Tenn. 4. Joseph[8] Saunders, Sumner county, Tenn. 5. Elizabeth[8] Saunders, Sumner county, Tenn.[6]

(II) ELIZABETH[4] SAUNDERS (baptized 23d December, 1768 (*Old Sussex and Surrey Albemarle Parish Church Register*); m. (27th April, 1794) at Lawrenceville, Brunswick county, Samuel Edmonds, of Southampton county, Va. No issue (*William and Mary Quarterly, Vol. VII, p. 36*).

(III) ANNE[4] SAUNDERS (b. 1770, Brunswick county; d. Lawrence county Ala.); m. (I) in Virginia, John Bass, of Brunswick, officer in the Revolution; removed to Courtland, Ala.; after his death she lived with her brother, Rev. Turner Saunders, until her second marriage with Mr. William Manning. Issue by the first marriage (none by the second):
1. Mary[5] m. Thomas B. Jones, of Virginia. They removed to Caddo parish, La. Her beauty was of a striking type. He was for awhile postmaster at Courtland, Ala., in the early times and also merchant.
2. Thomas Bass m. Sarah Weeden, sister of the second wife of the Rev. Turner Saunders, and moved to Shreveport, Caddo parish, La. Issue:
    1. Thomas, of Texas, lawyer, General Confederate States Army. 2. Turner, of Texas, lawyer. 3. William, of Texas, lawyer. 4. Henrietta; 5. Sarah; 6. Mary Eliza, lovely and accomplished lady, died in Shreveport, La. Two others died in infancy (*Mrs. Bishop Robert Paine*).

(IV) MARY[4] SAUNDERS (b. Brunswick county, 1776); m. (1805) Major William Gholson (b. 1775), d. 24th March, 1831), brother of Thomas Gholson, M. C. 1808–16. Issue: 1. James Hubbard[7]. 2. Thomas Saunders[7]. 3. Ann Eliza[7]. 4. Robert A[7]. 5. Mary[7]. 6. William[8]. 7. Martha E[7]. (*See Gholson Family.*)

(V) MARTHA SAUNDERS, b. 1779, m. her cousin Lewis, son of Jesse Saunders. Issue: Several children, who removed to Alabama (*this line not followed*).

(VI) REV. TURNER[4] SAUNDERS, sixth child of Thomas[4] (b. Brunswick county, Virginia, 3d January, 1782; d. Aberdeen, Miss., 9th March, 1853), married (I) 24th July, 1799, Frances (b. Brunswick county, 24th June, 1779; d. Lawrence county, Alabama, August, 1824), daughter of Ishmael and Mildred (Dudley) Dunn (see *Dunn Family*). He married (II), 1826, Mrs. Millwater (née Henrietta Weeden), born in Baltimore, 1793. Rev. Turner Saunders was reared in Brunswick county, Virginia. His father's plantation was the site of the present town of Lawrenceville. Within two and one-half miles was the old home of his relatives, the Gholson family (afterward of Petersburg, Va.). In 1808 he removed to Franklin, Tenn., and with him his brother-in-law, Maj. David Dunn. In 1821 he again removed, to Lawrence county, Alabama. His worldly success was great. He was the first President of board of trustees of La Grange College. In 1834 removed to Aberdeen, Miss. Wherever he went his home was the nucleus of pious and intellectual gatherings. (See *Methodism in Tennessee; Articles on Methodist Educators*, by Rev. R. J. H. Rivers; *Methodism in Alabama; Obituary* by Bishop Paine, etc.). Issue, first marriage (*Dunn*):
    I. THOMAS[7] SAUNDERS, b. Brunswick county, 1800; d. Lawrence county, Alabama, 1824,

---

of a malignant malarial fever, which decimated this neighborhood that fall, caused by the decay of vast bodies of deadened timber. Within a month, his mother and young brother, Franklin, had also died of this fatal fever.

II. SOPHIA DUNN[1] SAUNDERS, (b. Brunswick county, Virginia, 1802, m. 28th November, 1816, in Franklin, Tenn., Col. Joel Parrish,[2] son of Joel and Susan (Maury) Parrish. She was daughter of Abraham Maury, b. 1731, and granddaughter of Matthew Maury, the immigrant(see *Maury Family*). Colonel Parrish was captain in Gen. Andrew Jackson's Indian wars, 1813, and they were personal friends. Issue:
1. Sarah Ann[3] Parrish, b. 1817, m. Felix A. Sherrod, son of Col. Benj. and Eliza (Watkins) Sherrod, of Alabama. Issue:
    I. Benj.[4] Sherrod, m. Daniella, daughter of Col. Richard Jones, of Lawrence county, Alabama (*Early Settlers*), and had two sons who died infants. She married (II) Gen. Joseph Wheeler, of Alabama, C. S. A., M. C. for Alabama and United States General in Cuban war (for issue see *Early Settlers*). They own the old Felix Sherrod home, "Pond Spring," now called "Wheeler."
    II. Francis[4] Sherrod, d. 1864, m. Mary, daughter of John Harris, Lawrence county. Issue: Frank,[5] b. 1862, merchant and planter of Courtland, Ala., and John Harris,[5] b. 1864, planting with his brother.
    III. Alice Clay[4] Sherrod, only daughter, born at "*Pond Spring*," Lawrence county, Alabama, the Sherrod home; married 18th November, 1869, Robert Webb Banks, born Columbus, Mississippi, 1843, son of Col. Dunstan Banks. He was a cadet in University of Alabama, in beginning of the civil war joining Company B, Forty-third Mississippi, Capt. John M. Billups, Stirling Price's Division, General Van Dorn; transferred to Thirty-seventh Infantry, after battle of Corinth, as Sergeant Major, Col. O. S. Holland; and at the siege of Vicksburg, which surrendered 4th July, 1863; Adjutant of Twenty-ninth Alabama, in 1864. At the battle of Franklin, Tennessee, 30th November, 1864, in the superb charge of General Walthall's Division, he planted the colors of his regiment on the enemy's fortified line; next day promoted to General Walthall's staff, and served in battles around Nashville, December 15 and 16, and other engagements; was with Hood's army in the famous retreat from Tennessee; with the remnant of which he was ordered to North Carolina in Spring of 1865, under Gen. Jos. E. Johnston, and was in battles of Smithfield and Bentonville (the last battles of importance of the war). Engaged in planting after the war, and also in editorial work in Mississippi. Collector of Internal Revenue in President Cleveland's first administration, and Receiver of Public Moneys in the second. In 1898 appointed by Governor McLaurin, Colonel of Third Mississippi Volunteers, enlisted for the

---

FORT WILLIAMS, SIXTY MILES BELOW FORT STROTHER, April 6, 1814.

Dear Uncle: You have, no doubt, ere this, heard of the engagement we had with the enemy on the 27th ultimo at Tehopeka. I deem it unnecessary to give you the particulars, as you will so soon see the official report of Major General Andrew Jackson (or copy thereof), I shall merely observe that we commenced the attack with the artillery at about 10:30 A. M., and continued firing on the breastworks (which were built in a very strong and compact manner), about two hours, but had not the desired effect. The works were strewed with a good deal of bloodshed, but nothing in comparison to that of the enemy. For particulars refer you to the official report. The loss of my company was eleven wounded, one of whom has since died. The others are recovering. The General will take up the line of march to-morrow; destination the hickory ground, by way of Hothlewaulee, where I hope you will have a good account of us. My determination is never to abandon the cause until I can have it in my power to say that I have seen the last of the hostile Indians, or be buried in their nation. I hope you will approve this determination.

Enclosed you will receive a rough plan of the battle ground and line of battle on the 27th ult., drawn in haste. You can easily perceive from that, the way in which the military skill of our General had fixed the red rascals; no place for their escape but by breaking through the firm phalanx of a determined people. I am in perfect health and hope to remain so during the campaign. You will please remember me to Aunt Maury and family. Present on sight my love to my dear mother and family. In great haste I am sir. very respectfully, your affectionate nephew, JOEL PARRISH, JR.

To Colonel Abram Maury, Franklin, Tenn.

Spanish war. His bright, genial and fun-loving spirit makes him a great favorite with his friends. Issue:

1. Sarah Felix[10] Banks, married Charles David Hill, of Louisville, Ky., and has Charles Banks Hill, b. 1894; 2. Lucile Webb[10] Banks, bright young successor of her father in editorial honors, and also otherwise quite an accomplished woman; 3. Robert Webb[10] Banks; 4. James Oliver[10] Banks; 5. Alice Sherrod[10] Banks (*see Banks Family*).

2. Frances[6] Parrish, b. 182-, *m.* Samuel W. Sherrod, son of Col. Benj. Sherrod (*see Watkins Family*). Issue:

I. Henry[6] died, a young man. II. Walter[6] *m.* Laura, daughter of Mr. Orrin Davis, Lawrence county. Issue: 1, Henry[10] *m.* Ella, daughter of James B. and Virginia (Foster) Irvine, of Florence, Alabama, and had Virginia Sherrod.

3. Joel[5] Parrish, b. 1825, d. Florence, Alabama, 187-, *m.* Mary Boddie, of Florence Alabama. No issue.

4. Sophia[5] Parish, d. July, 1899, *m.* Alfred Gibson. Issue: 1, Mary[6]; 2, Joel[6]; 3, Willis[6].

5. Thaddeus[6] and 6, Leonidas[6] Parrish, died young.

III. LOUISA TURNER[7] SAUNDERS (b. Brunswick county, Virginia, 1803, d. Florence, Ala.; *m.* 8th October, 1819), Judge Robert Coleman Foster, of Nashville, Tenn. (b. 1st November, 1796, d. Florence, Ala., 5th December, 1871); son of Robert C. and Ann (Hubbard) Foster, of Virginia. This couple lived to an honored old age, and died at the home of their daughter, Mrs. Narcissa McAllister, in Florence, Ala. Of great dignity and handsome person, it was remarked that Mrs. Foster preserved in extreme old age the pink and white complexion of her youth. Their home in Nashville was the centre of a most distinguished circle. Issue, 16 children, of whom those who survived were:

1. Ann E.[8] Foster, b. 24th September, 1820, d. 23rd February, 1840; *m.* Dr. Richard R. Hightower. Issue:

I. *Florence Ann[9]* Hightower, b. 4th March, 1841; *m.* 2d June, 1862, Jordan J. Puryear. Issue:

Annie H.[10] b. 7th April, 186-; *m.* 26th February, 1885, James Henry Sims. Issue: a. James Henry,[11] b. 12th October, 1889; b. Florence P.,[11] b. 27th September, 1893; c. Robert P.,[11] b. 21st January, 1896. Marietta,[10] b. 31st December, 186-, d. 20th March, 186-; Florence H.,[10] b. June 24th, 187-. Jordan J., b. 22d July, 187-. Lourena H.,[10] b. 27th September, 187-, *m.* 29th September, 1891, Charles M. Foster, and has issue; Lourena H.[11] Emma[11], b. 1893, and Florence[11], b. 1896.

2. *Richard R.[9]* Hightower, b. 18th October, 1843, *m.* 5th December, 1861, Loula Nichol. Issue:

Robert[10], b. 24th November, 1872, d. y.; Richard[10], b. 26th May, 1874, d. y.; Lizzie[10], b. August 8, 1876, d. y.; Annie[10], b. 12th October, 1878; Martha[10], b. 29th January, 1881; Wilbur Foster[10], b. 12th June, 1883; Clarence Nichol[10], b. 13th December, 1885; Evelina[10], b. 27th February, 1890, d. y.

3. *Loulie[9]* Hightower, b. February, 1845, d. 1872, in beautiful young womanhood.

2. Turner Saunders[8] Foster, of Nashville, Tenn., b. 9th June, 1821, d. 14th June, 1897, Judge of Circuit Court; *m.* (I) 18th February, 1846, Ann Eliza, d. 25th January, 1849, daughter of John S. and Anne Wilson, of Lauderdale county, Alabama. He married (II) 3d June, 1856, Harriet, daughter of James and Margaret (Caldwell) Erwin, Nashville, Tenn. Issue, first marriage (*Wilson*):

1. Randolph Wilson[9] Foster of New Orleans (b. 18th August, 1847, in Lauderdale county, Alabama); unmarried (1899). Served in General Roddy's command, C. S. A., 1864. Member of firm of "*J. U. Payne & Co.*", New Orleans. His aged partner, Mr. Payne, now 96 years of age, one of the oldest and most prominent citizens of this city, is still active in business, and an honor to the great century he has adorned, and at whose residence died President Jefferson Davis, of the Confederate States—his life-long friend. His brother, A. M. Payne, *m.*, 1827, the sister of

Mr. John Wilson, above, hence the family connection. When the Federals and Tories raided Florence, Ala., Randolph Foster, then a mere lad, was three times hung up and let down by them, in order to make him reveal where his grandfather's money and plantation stock were hidden, but, despite the torture, he never told. The old gentleman, reared in ease and elegance, was taken out of bed by them, laid before the fire, and twisted paper and hot coals shoveled upon him, from which he died in great agony. His nephew and grandson, in the room with him, were shot, and the house then set afire. Faithful slaves extinguished the flames, and put their old master in bed, when the enemy had galloped off. It is needless to say the Tory fiends were later exterminated by the enraged citizens.

2. Turner Saunders' Foster, of St. Louis, Mo., b. Lauderdale county, Ala., 11th January, 1849, *m.* 3d November, 1881, Mary Wiggins, of St. Louis, b. 26th February, 1858. He is the wit. and "*merriest man withal*" of the family. Issue: 1, Charles Wiggins¹⁰, b. 28th November, 1883. 2, Mary Foster²⁰, b. 29th May, 1885. 3, Virginia Foster²⁰, b. 11th November, 1893; all in St. Louis. *Issue second marriage (Erwin)* all born in Nashville, Tenn:

3. Annie Erwin' Foster, b. 6th March, 1857, *m.* 18th September, 1877, Nashville, Tenn., Charles Sheppard, son of Alexander S. and Mathilda W. Caldwell, of Nashville, Tenn. Issue: 1, Charles Sheppard¹⁰, Jr., b. 8th June, 1878. 2, Louise Caldwell¹⁰, b. 7th December, 1879. 3, Turner Foster¹⁰, b. 28th January, 1882. 4, John Foster²⁰, b. 7th June, 1884. 5, Erwin²⁰, b. 8th June, 1886. 6, Randolph Foster²⁰, b. 12th June, 1888. 7, Jere Witherspoon¹⁰, b. 26th February, 1890. 8, Leland¹⁰, b. 24th October, 1891, d. 12th March, 1892.

4. Louisa Turner' Foster, b. 25th October, 1858, d. 29th April, 1885, *m.* 28th September, 1882, Irby M. Moore, of Nashville, Tenn. No issue.

5. John McEwin' Foster, M. D., Denver, Colo., b. Nashville, Tenn., 11th January, 1861, *m.* 29th December, 1885, Bessie Perkins, b. 18th December, 1862, daughter of Colonel William Decatur Bethell and Cynthia Pillow, his wife, of Maury county, Tenn. Colonel Bethell and Dr. Foster removed from Memphis, Tenn., to Denver in 1890. Issue: 1, William Bethell¹⁰, b. Denver, Colo., 26th July, 1890. 2, Pinckney Bethell¹⁰, b. 10th August, 1893.

6. Margaret' Foster, b. 18th January, 1863, d. 21st June, 1864.

7. Ellen Craighead' Foster, b .26th April, 1866, d. 23d September, 1866.

8. Alexander Caldwell' Foster, b. Nashville, Tenn., 25th July, 1867, *m.* 28th October, 1897, Alice Eddy, daughter of Lucius G. T. Eddy Fisher, of Chicago.

3. Robert Coleman' Foster, M. D., Nashville, Tenn., b. 10th April, 1824, Franklin, Tenn., d. 11th January, 1879, Nashville, Tenn., *m.* 23d December, 1851, Julia Hannah Woods, b. 23d December, 1830, d. 28th June, 1890, sister of Joseph Woods, who married Fannie Foster. Issue:

1. Sallie Lou', b. July, 1853, d. 3d November, 1856.

2. Joseph Woods', b. 3d November, 1854, *m.* 4th September, 1883, Mary Bartee Edwards. Issue: 1, Julia Woods¹⁰, born 28th July. 1885. 2, Thomas Keenan¹⁰, b. 28th November, 1889. 3, Robina Armistead¹⁰.

3. James Loric', b. 11th February, 1856.

4. Robina Armistead', b. 30th July, 1858, *m.* 20th March, 1888, William Harris Edwards. Issue: Mary Bartee¹⁰, b. 20th March, 1889.

5. Edwin West', b. 30th May, 1860, graduate of Annapolis, *m.* 9th January, 1889, Susie Collingsworth Cockrill of Nashville. Issue: 1, Nellie Cockrill¹⁰, b. 3d November, 1889. 2, Robert Coleman¹⁰, b. 1st September, 1896.

6. Robert Fulton', b. 24th August, 1864.

7. Julia Thora', b. 17th June, 1866, *m.* 1899, Mr. Wallace.

8. Martha Jane', b. 27th August, 1871,Nashville, Tenn.

4. Martha Jane', b. April, 1826, d. 23d September, 1848, *m.* Goode Watkins. No issue.

5. Narcissa', a surviving twin, *m.* John W. McAllister, of Edinburgh, Scotland ; merchant in Florence, Ala. Issue: 1, Charles', d. in early manhood. 2, Robert F'.,

merchant of Florence. 3, Bessie[8], *m.* John McGuirk; issue: John[10] and Narcissa[20]. 4, John[9], merchant, unmarried.

6. Thomas[9], b. ——; d. 1878 of yellow fever, Memphis, Tenn.

7. Frank[9].

8. Fannie Saunders[9], b. 1832; d. 20th November, 1872 in Mississippi; *.m.*, 1855, Joseph L. Woods, of Nashville, Tenn. Issue:

1. Frank[9], b. 17th April, 1856; d. 25th March, 1892; *m.*, 1881, Annie Hancock, of Florence, Ala., who died young, leaving one daughter, Annie Frank Woods, b. 19th January, 1889.

2. Julian L.[9], b. 24th March, 1858; *m.* 3d January, 1883, Mary E. Polling. Issue: a. Fannie Robena[10], b. 1884; b. Josephine Lois[10], b. 1893.

3. Robert L.[9], b. 9th June, 1860; *m.* 21st March, 1883, Carrie D. Gregory. Issue a. Frank G.[10], b. 1884.

9. William H.[9], C. S. A. 10. Benjamin F.[9], b. 25th March, 1834; d. 10th August, 1853. 11. James H.[9], b. June and d. June, 1836. 12. George W.[9], b. May and d. August, 1840. 13. Serena[9], b. November, 1841; d. 1872, in lovely young womanhood, of acute neuralgia. 14. Laura[9], b. February, d. August, 1843. 15. Pauline[9] D., b. March, d. June, 1845. 16. Louisa T.[9] lived but a short while.

IV. NARCISSA HUBBARD[7] SAUNDERS, born 1804, died 17th December, 1845; married, 4th July, 1821, James Harvey, born 1st October, 1798, died 1876, son of Robert C. and Ann (Hubbard) Foster, of Nashville, Tenn. Issue:

1. Robert[8], shot, and killed by an accident; 2. Ann[8] died young; 3. James[8] died young. 4. Ephraim H.[8] Foster, lawyer and planter, of Courtland, Ala., born ——, married Susan, second daughter of Paul J. and Eliza (Watts) Watkins, of Lawrence county. Issue:

I. James H[9], of New Orleans, married Ida Speake. Issue: several children. II. Paul J.[9]; III. Bettie[9] married Thomas Pointer. Issue: several children. IV. George[9]; V. Narcissa[9] died young; VI. Susie[9] married —— Robinson, and now owns the old homestead "*Flower Hill*," in Lawrence county, Ala.; VII. Fannie[9] married Mr. Wallace, of Lawrence county, Ala.; VIII. Ephraim[9].

5. Frances[8] Foster, born 2d August, 1825, married, 17th November, 1847, Malcolm Gilchrist, of Courtland, Ala. Issue:

1. James Harvey[9] Gilchrist, born 8th July, 1850; married, 10th November, 1874, Nannie, daughter of Capt. Wm. Bankhead, of Courtland, Ala., who is great-grandson of Thomas Jefferson, President of the United States. Issue: 1. Kate Garth[10] *m.*, 26th September, 1896, Lawson, son of Capt. Turner Sykes and Mary, daughter of Mr. Oakley Bynum, of Courtland, a descendant of Bernard Moore, of Virginia. (See *Americans of Royal Descent.*) 2. Malcolm J.[9] Gilchrist, born 9th January, 1853, *m.* Miss Burkhead, daughter of the Rev. Mr. Burkhead, Presbyterian minister. Issue: a daughter[10]. 3. Philip Philips[9] Gilchrist, born 20th November, 1854.

6. Narcissa[8] never married, but nobly devoted her life to the last days of a most pure and gentle father.

V. JAMES EDMONDS SAUNDERS, *Author* of "*Early Settlers*," C. S. A., lawyer, planter and commission merchant (born Brunswick county, Virginia. 7th May, 1806, died in Lawrence county, Alabama, at "Rocky Hill," 23d August, 1896); married July 14, 1824, by the Rev. Alexander Sale, Mary Frances (born Petersburg, Ga., 13th November, 1809, died at "*Rocky Hill*," 6th February, 1889), daughter of Robert H. and Prudence (Oliver) Watkins. (*Watkins Family.*) See introduction to this volume for his life. Issue:

1, Frances Amanda[8], 2, Robert Turner[8], 3, Elizabeth Dunn[8], 4, Mary Louisa[8], 5, Dudley Dunn[8], 6, Sarah Jane[8], 7, James Edmonds[8], Jr., 8, Fannie Dunn[8], 9, Prudence Oliver[8], 10, Laurence Watkins[8], 11, Ellen Virginia[8], as follows:

1. Frances Amanda[8], b. "*Spout Spring*," Tenn., 11th June, 1825, d. 6th

August, 1826; died suddenly at 13 months of age, in the absence of her young mother.

2. Robert Turner[2], b. 22d February. 1827, d. at "*Rocky Hill*" 2d October, 1888; never married; of the cotton commission firm of "*Saunders & Son*," Mobile, Ala., served on staff of Gen. Philip St. George Cooke in Civil War, 1861. and after that was engaged for a while in running the Blockade to England; a fine linguist and of a finished address. Nature blessed him with the great gift of humor; went to California in 1849, and engaged in merchandising and gold-digging; member of the Legislature which located the capital at San Francisco, and framed the Constitution.[*]

3. Elizabeth Dunn[3] Saunders, born 18th October, 1829, died at "*Rocky Hill*," 5th October, 1852. Married at Mobile, Ala., 31st July, 1850, by Rev. P. P. Neeley, Dr. Bruno B. Poellnitz[*], of Marengo county, Ala., born 1822, grandson of *Baron Frederic Charles Hans Bruno von Poellnitz,*[*] of Prussia. Their romantic courtship began before

---

---

[*] Baron Wilhelm Christian Gotlieb Von Poellnitz was of a noble Prussian family, whose lineage dates from 1238, according to the records preserved in the family. His son. Baron Frederic Charles Hans Bruno Von Poellnitz, of Prussia, was a prime favorite of Frederick the Great and upon whom he conferred many honors and emoluments. He married Mlle. De Bondelie, of France, and removed finally to Marengo county, Ala., with a French colony of Napoleon's adherents, for whose battle the county was named. In the first volume of Thomas Jefferson's correspondence he mentions, while Minister Plenipotentiary to France, 1795, in a letter from Paris—that "Baron Poellnitz was there, en route for the United States, and he would send State documents to the President by him." He located in the territory of Alabama, 1818, with his four

---

[*] "Frederick the Great, by the by, with his contempt for religion of every kind, actually had the audacity to appoint his chamberlain, Baron Pollnitz, as Roman Catholic prince archbishop of Breslau, after having induced the baron, who was a Lutheran, to become a convert to Judaism just for the purpose of adding to the joke of the appointment."

the days of railroad communication between North and South Alabama, when Colonel Saunders conveyed his family to Mobile in the winter, and to North Alabama in the summer, by his own private train of vehicles. On one of these trips his young daughter, aged 15, was taken ill, in Marengo county, through which their road ran. The white, peaceful home, at whose gates they stopped for the needed remedies, was that of General and Mrs. Poellnitz, who responded with true Southern hospitality, by urging them to remain until her recovery. Their young son, then at home from his medical studies in Philadelphia, was the attending physician, and Love poured the philter, which worked so well that, in a few years, after a short and brilliant social career for her, the young people were married, and a bright future seemed to await them, only to close in two years with the death of the happy young wife. No issue of this marriage. Seven years after, Dr. Poellnitz married his lovely cousin, Mary Rogers, and several children bless his declining age; and one of them is named Elizabeth.

4. **Mary Louisa**⁴ Saunders, born Courtland, Ala., during the great snowfall of 20th December, 1832, died July 24, 1859, at "*Rocky Hill;*" married Mobile, Ala., 22d February, 1852, by Rev. William H. Milburn (the blind chaplain of the United States Senate), Henry Dickenson Blair, born October 3, 1825, at Camden, S. C., died 7th December, 1855, *Spring Hill*, near Mobile, Ala., the residence of his parents, John J., and Martha (Ray) Blair, of South Carolina (*see Blair*). After three years of happiness, Mrs. Blair was left a widow. She continued her home with her parents until her own death four years later; issue one child:

   I. Elizabeth Saunders Blair (*author of these genealogies*) reared by her loving and beloved grandparents until her marriage, 25th July, 1875, to Dr. William Carter Stubbs, son of Jefferson W. and Ann Walker Carter (Baytop) Stubbs, of Gloucester county, Va. In his line are united the families of Robins, New, Boswell, Hansford,

---

children: Wilhelmina, Charles, Alex. and Julius Poellnitz. Of these, Gen. Julius Poellnitz, was the only one who left descendants in America. He married Elizabeth, daughter of Benj. Rogers, of South Carolina, and Miss McAlester of Scotch descent. They lived in a charming home at Minden, Ala., in a pious and beautiful old age. Issue:
1. Gen. Charles A. Poellnitz (b. 1807). Children:
   1, Euphradia, married Gen. George D. Johnston, of C. S. A., son lives in New Orleans; 2, Elizabeth; 3, Ellen; 4, Charles; 5, John D. B.; 6, Julia; 7, Eric; 8, Caroline; 9, Ida; 10, Stella.
2. Dr. Julius Edwin Poellnitz. Children:
   1, Rembert; 2, Edwin, student University Virginia, 1851; 3, Mary; 4, James; 5, Sidney.
3. Elizabeth De Bondelie Poellnitz, married Col. J. M. Rembert, of Marengo county, C. S. A., Captain Twenty-first Alabama. Children:
   1, James; 2, Celeste; 3, Bettie; 4, Caleb; 5, Julius; "all now deceased, except Celeste, who is married, and living in Birmingham, with a large family." "Julius Rembert and his family, except Helen and Rosa, were drowned in a steamboat explosion, near Demopolis, Ala., some years since."
4. Dr. Bruno B. Poellnitz, of Rembert, Ala. (b. 1822, living in 1899), student Philadelphia Medical College 1845, lieutenant in Twenty-first Alabama on its organization, and later, Assistant Surgeon in Twenty-fifth Alabama, Gen. Joseph E. Johnston, in the Dalton-Atlanta Campaign; also with Forrest, in North Mississippi. Gentle and with all the polish of the old nobility, he still survives all the elder members of his family. He m. (1st) in Lawrence county, Ala., 1851, Elizabeth Dunn Saunders—no issue; and (2d) 1858, his cousin Mary, daughter of Col. Robert Rogers, of South Carolina. Children:
   1, Henrietta, lives with her father; 2, Elizabeth, married; 3, Robert; 4, Bruno B., Jr.; 5, Edwin; 6, Margaret De B., married; 7, Walter; 8, Frederic Poellnitz.— *Sketch by Dr. B. B. Poellnitz.*

DR. DUDLEY DUNN SAUNDERS.
Memphis, Tenn.

Carter, Catlett, Buckner, Booth, Cooke, Taliaferro, Walker, Robinson and others of the old Virginia stock. Dr. Stubbs was a student of Randolph Macon College, William and Mary College, and University of Virginia, at which noble institution he graduated in 1868; coming to Alabama in 1869 as professor of Chemistry in the Agricultural and Mechanical College at Auburn, where he remained sixteen years, devoting his efforts to the agricultural progress of the State until 1885, when he removed to New Orleans, Louisiana, to make similar exertions for that State as State chemist, and Director of its three Experiment Stations, and Professor of Agriculture in its State University. Member of Twenty-fourth Virginia Cavalry, Company B, Fitzhugh Lee's division, J. E. B. Stuart's corps in the late civil war. Life member of the Southern Historical Society of Virginia, and of the Administrative Council of the Southern History Association of Washington, D. C.; author of several works on agriculture, and also author of the "*Descendants of Mordecai Cooke, of 'Mordecai's Mound,' Va., 1650;*" lives at Audubon Park, New Orleans, La.

5. Dudley Dunn[2] Saunders*, M. D., of Memphis, Tenn., b. 23d February, 1835, at *Rocky Hill, m.* by Bishop Otey 14th March, 1860 (I) Catherine Stewart, b. 22d December, 1840; d. Marietta, Ga., 29th March, 1864; eldest daughter of Seth and Mary (Cook) Wheatley[†], of Memphis Tenn. Her bright young life closed suddenly amidst the sadness of the civil war, and at the birth of her second child, at the Medical Post, Marietta, Ga.; was married by Bishop Quintard (II) 7th February, 1867, to

---

*CONFEDERATE STATES OF AMERICA,
SURGEON GENERAL'S OFFICE RICHMOND, Va., October 5, 1864. }
SIR—Medical Director Stout, in a report of his inspection of the condition of the Hospitals in the Army of Tennessee, reports that the hospitals under your charge are the most creditable in his department.
Surgeon Saunders, and the corps of medical officers, will please accept the thanks of this office for the creditable manner in which they have performed their duty.
Very respectfully, your obedient servant,
(Signed) S. P. MOORE,
To Surgeon D. D. Saunders, Surgeon General, C. S. A.
Through Medical Director Stout, Columbus, Ga.

† Joseph Cook, Pittsylvania county, Va., married Sarah Edwards, and removed to Davidson county, Tenn., and thence to Nashville. Issue:
1, William A. Cook. of Nashville. Tenn., married Catherine Stewart Brown; 2, Thornton Cook; 3, Thos. Jeff. Cook; 4. Mrs. Hall; 5, Daughter, m. (I) Buchanan, (II) Rutland; 6, Daughter, m. Dr. King. father of Judge T. W. King, of Clarksville, Tenn., and also other sons and daughters.
MORGAN BROWN, Nashville, Tenn. (fourth of his name). born 1758, m. (I) Miss James, and (II) Elizabeth Little, and lived on Pedee river. In 1774 removed to Nashville, Tenn., and in 1794 to Montgomery county, Tenn., and again in 1829, to his plantation, within three miles of Nashville. His grandson, Hon. Wm. L. Brown, of Nashville, has the Family Bible, containing an extensive *Brown family Ancestry.* He had three daughters, by his last wife, as follows:
1. Elizabeth Brown, m. (I) Mr. Vance, father of Colonel William Vance, of Memphis; and m. (II) Mr. Thompson.
2. Sally Brown, m. F. W. Huling, of Pennsylvania, father of Judge Huling, of Louisiana.
3. Catherine Stewart Brown. m, William A. Cook, and had issue:
1, Mary; 2, Elizabeth; 3, William, d. s p.; 4 George, d. s p. Of these—
1. Mary Cook, m. Seth Wheatley, of Virginia, wealthy merchant and planter of Memphis, and had, 1, Kate Stewart (b. 1840), married Dr. D. D. Saunders, of Memphis (first wife); 2. Arthur W. (b. 1845). m. his cousin, Bettie Bowen. of Va., and had Ella, (d. 1866), Pinkney Bethell, and Ada; 3, Mary Elizabeth (b. 1847). m. Dr. D. D. Saunders (second wife).
2. Elizabeth Cook, m. (I) Mr. Ayres, of Memphis, and (II) Dr. Boiling Pope, of New Orleans, and had—
1. William Ayres, M. D., of New Orleans (deceased).
2. Professor Brown Ayres. the brilliant scientist of Tulane University, New Orleans, m. Miss Anderson, of Lexington. Va., and has Mattie, Warren, Elizabeth, and others.
3. Dr. Boiling Pope, of New Orleans.
Mr. Seth Wheatley. m. (II) his cousin, Jane Wheatley, of Va. (d. 1893). a noble ornament to church and society of Memphis. She m. (II) Mr. Weaver, and had Dudley Weaver, of firm of "*Porter, Deming & Co.,*" Memphis; and Lily.

Mary Elizabeth, second daughter of Mr. Seth Wheatley; b. 26th June, 1847, d. June 1893, Memphis, Tenn.; a lovely woman and conscientious wife and mother. Dr. Saunders is now (1899) the only surviving son of his parents, and the head of his house, and has led the useful and unselfish life of the good physician. Professor in Memphis Medical College; and President of the Board of Health in the fearful yellow fever epidemic of 1878, of which he was also a surviving victim. It is hoped he will long continue his useful and honorable career. Issue first marriage:

1. Mary Lou' Saunders, b. 2d April, 1861, d. at Frostburg, Md. 8th August, 1888; m. 6th December, 1882, by Rev. Geo. S. White, Saml. Gordon Brent, of Alexandria, Va.; b. 28th June, 1855; son of Col. George Brent, C. S. A., staff of Gen. G. T. Beauregard (see Goods's Virginia Cousins for descent from Pocahontas). Just eighteen years before, on the Southern Army's march into Tennessee, Col. George Brent with his general, G. T. Beauregard, and brother staff officers, paused for a few hours' rest and consultation with Colonel Saunders while taking breakfast at Rocky Hill. His future daughter-in-law was then toddling about the house a babe; one son, the only issue of this marriage, Samuel Gordon" Brent, Jr., b. Alexandria, Va., 13th August, 1883.

2. Kate Wheatley', Saunders, second daughter of D. D. Saunders, married 7th December, 1893, George W. Agee, of Virginia (second wife) with young sons; Worthen and Hamilton. Superintendent of Southwestern Division of Southern Express Company, and son of Benj. Hooper Agee, and Ann Elizabeth Mitchell, of Virginia. His cool, quick mind and imposing carriage, and the unmistakable stamp of the Virginia gentleman, win him prestige in every circle. The Agees were among the early Huguenot settlers on James river, and are mentioned in Bishop Meade's list. He is also author and writer, and keenly alive to the great questions of his day.

3. Dudley Dunn, Jr.', Saunders, M. D., born 5th March, 1869, (issue of second marriage of Dr. Saunders), Graduate Philadelphia Medical College, m. 6th June, 1895, Florence, Ala., Wylodine, only child of William and Josephine (Thompson) Hardin, of Memphis, Tenn.

Isaac Hardin, of Albemarle county, Va., (related to the Maury family), married Sarah Pine Lewis, daughter of James Martin Lewis, Columbia, Tenn., major in the Revolution, and a cousin of Meriwether Lewis. Issue: Isaac, Benjamin and William Hardin, of Memphis, who married Josephine Thompson.

Lawrence, Joseph, Nicholas, William and Thomas Thompson, of North Carolina, came to Alabama, "Colbert's Reserve," near Florence, in its early settlement. Their parents were Samuel' Thompson, of North Carolina, and Sarah McAlester, daughter of a Presbyterian minister from Ireland. They had sevens sons and four daughters. Of these, Joseph', above, tenth child, married in Alabama Mary Elizabeth Anderson Maverick, widow of Joseph Wyman, daughter of Samuel Maverick, Charleston, S. C., and with several children. Her mother was Sarah, daughter of Gen. Robert Anderson of the Revolution. Issue: Col. Samuel Maverick Thompson; and Josephine, who married (1) Colonel Bryan, of Nashville; no issue; and married (2) 1873, Col. Wm. Hardin, of Memphis. Wylodine Hardin born 10th February, 1875, only child, married Dr. D. D. Saunders, Memphis, Tenn (the Hon. Jacob Thompson, of Jefferson Davis' Cabinet, is also of this family). Issue: (1) Dudley Dunn", born New York, 23d March, 1896; (2) William Hardin" Saunders, born Memphis, Tenn., 20th June, 1898.

4. Elizabeth', youngest child of Dr. D. D. Saunders, Sr., married, 1895, Harry B. Deming, of Providence, R. I., Cotton merchant of firm of "Porter, Deming & Co.," Memphis (second wife).

6. Sarah Jane' Saunders, b. at "Rocky Hill," 1836, d. at "Rocky Hill," 15th October, 1896; m. by Bishop McTyeire, 5th August, 1868, to Dr. John Moore Hayes, of Athens. Ala., son of Col. W. D. Hayes and grandson of the Hon. Thomas K. Harris, M. C, from Tennessee (see Moore), surgeon C. S. A., Twenty-sixth Alabama Regiment. Unselfish wife, and affectionate Christian daughter, she was spared to comfort the old

age of her parents; her own life ending just six weeks after her devoted father had died in her arms. She was of that striking type of women who preserve their youthful figures, and nature, beyond middle age.

7. James Edmonds[8] Saunders, Jr., b. 17th January, 1838, d. when 4 years of age; buried at "Oak Grove."

8. Fannie Dunn[8] Saunders, b. 1840, d. 1842; buried at "Oak Grove," Watkins' home.

9. Prudence Oliver[8] Saunders, b. 21st January, 1842, d. at "Rocky Hill," 2d June, 1864. Unusually thoughtful for one so bright and lovely, she faded during the closing scenes of the Civil War, in which she had taken such patriotic pride.

10. Lawrence Watkins[8] Saunders, C. S. A., b. 12th June, 1846, d. at "Rocky Hill," 20th December, 1867. When 17 years of age joined a company of young scouts, organised for General Roddy's brigade, in the Civil War. Was captured in 1864, and for many months languished amid the cold and privations of Camp Chase prison, Lake Erie; and when released, at the close of the war, came home to die; his young life offered a pure libation to his country.

11. Ellen Virginia[8] Saunders, m. 5th April, 1872, by Bishop Paine, of Methodist Episcopal Church, South, Judge Lewis Birchette McFarland, of Memphis, son of Dr. Felix and Martha (Douglass) McFarland, and for many years of the noted law firm of "Morgan & McFarland." A brave soldier of the Confederacy, in Cheatham's division, and on General Maney's staff. Served as aide on General R. C. Tyler's staff in last battle of the war, at West Point, Ga., 16th June, 1865. He is making a reputation, as a judge, second to none.

VI. FRANCES ANN[7] SAUNDERS (b. Franklin, Tenn., 12th April, 1806; d. Columbus, Miss., 1st June, 1890); m. (I) 4th May, 1824, Matthew, son of Matthew Clay of Virginia (member Congress and friend of Jefferson). He died January, 1827, at his home near Courtland, Ala. She m. (II) 16th November, 1830 (2d wife), Jacob K. Swoope, son of Jacob Swoope, Congressman of Virginia. She m. (III) 13th September, 1847, Col. Thomas C. Billups, of Columbus, Miss. (2d wife). (See Billups.)

ISSUE FIRST MARRIAGE (Clay.)

1. Thomas F.[8] Clay, b. 1825, d. 1836, m. (1845) Caledonia, daughter of John and Ruth (Weeden) Oliver, of Columbus, Miss. (See Oliver Family.) Issue:
   1. Matthew Clay, b. 1847, d. 1849. 2. Alice Clay, b. 1849, m. Wheeler Watson; issue: Asa Watson, b. 1872; Caledonia Watson, m. James N. Pulliam, and had Norman and Thomas Clay Watson. 3. Oliver[9] Clay, born 1852, m. Fannie Lawler; issue: Thomas, b. 1885; John Oliver, b. 1887, and Alice, b. 1890; 4. Fannie Lou. Clay, 1854, m. (1890) Henry D. Watson, brother of Wheeler Watson; issue: Henry D. and Julienne.

2. Matthew[8] Clay, b. 18th February, 1827, m. 23d February, 1854, by Bishop Paine, Mary ("Nina"), 13th child of Isham Harrison, of South Carolina, who was nephew of Gen. Wade Hampton, of the Revolution, and father also of Mrs. David Moore, of Huntsville, Ala., and uncle of James Harrison, a distinguished lawyer of Columbus, Miss. (whose daughter, Regina, married Gen. Stephen D. Lee, of Confederate States Army). Mrs. Clay was a beautiful woman and brilliant conversationalist, and greatly beloved in the connection. Issue:
   1. Matthew[9], b. 1855, m. Hattie P. Casey, of Virginia. Issue: Matthew and Hattie Casey.
   2. Bettie[9] ("Has inherited her mother's rare gifts, physical and mental.") Unmarried, and lives in New York.
   3. Harrison[9], b. 1864. In business with "Sherman & Clay," of Oakland, Cal. m. Nannie Prather, of Oakland, Cal., and had several children. 4. Thomas[9], b. 1867, unm.; 5. Charles, b. 1875, unm.; 6. Nina, unm.

ISSUE SECOND MARRIAGE (*Swoope.*)

3. Jacob K.[8] Swoope, b. 26th July, 1832, d. 4th July, 1871, in Memphis, of hæmaturia, m. Elizabeth Haley (d. 26th November, 1890), of Florence, Ala. Issue:
    1. Jacob K.[9] Jr., drowned in Tennessee river, at 14 years of age, with his play-mate, young Jones, of Florence, Ala., who attempted to save him.
    2. Tempie[9], only surviving child, married (1885) George M. Darrow, of Virginia. They now live in Murfreesboro, Tenn. No issue.
4. Charles Carroll[8] Swoope, of Wheeler, Ala., born 4th February, 1835, m. 13th July, 1858, Frances Hutchins (b. 22d November, 1837), daughter John and Eliza (Hols-man) Hutchins. They live at the old homestead in Lawrence county; he a model planter and fine example to his sons, and she, the model helpmate and housekeeper, whose home is noted for hospitality. Issue:
    1. Edgar[9], b. 4th May, 1859. Of the Illinois Central Railroad.
    2. William[9] C., born 7th October, 1860, m. Mary Carter, of Miss. Issue: 1. William C.; 2. Tempie Darrow, and others.
    3. Charles[9] C., b. 12th May, 1862. In business in Mississippi.
    4. Susie[9], b. 15th May, 1866, m. (December 31, 1885) Thomas Ashford, now of Birmingham, and has one daughter, Etoile.[10]
    5. Jacob K.[9], b. 31st August, 1869, unm.
    6. Saunders Billups[9], b. 21st December, 1872, m. 18 January, 1891, Fannie Pippin, of Courtland. Beloved by all, she died 1894, leaving an infant: Susie[10] Ashford. He married again.
    7. Matthew Clay[9], b. 29th March, 1874, d. 6th May, 1896.
5. Frances Swoope[8], b. 1838, d. February 1, 1880, m. Edward Moore, of Columbus, Miss. Issue:
    1. Frances[9] m. James T. Harrison, State Senator several times, and son of Hon. James T. Harrison, of Columbus, Miss. Issue: Edward, Antoinette, Eugene M., Lee, and several others.
    2. Edward[9], Jr., m. Alice Hairston, descendant of *Montague family*. Issue: Ed-ward, Alice, Mary Montague, Sallie Billups, and several others.
    3. Jacob Swoope Moore[9] m. Sallie Cox.
6. Lou[8] Swoope died young.

ISSUE THIRD MARRIAGE (*Billups*).

7. James Saunders[6] Billups, of Columbus, Miss., b. 1850, Planter, and General of State Militia, married Wildie, daughter of James W. and Marcella Sykes. (His venerable mother lived with him during the last years of her life. A small and stately dame, who made her strong personality felt always, and an humble follower of the Saviour of Mankind. May the spell of her beautiful life fall upon her descendants.) Issue:
    1 Wildie[9], married John Morgan. Issue: Louise Caroline, b. 1894.
    2. Fannie[9], unm.; 3, Ida[9] unm.

VII. Franklin[7] Saunders, b. 1810, d. 1824, of the malignant fever so fatal to his mother and brother in the same year.

VIII. Martha Maria[7] Saunders, b. 6th November, 1812; d., Aberdeen, Miss., 27th January, 1856; m. 28th December, 1830, Gen. Benj. McFarland Bradford, of Tennessee and Mississippi (first wife); Gen. Bradford was partner, in the Forties, in a cotton com-mission firm, Mobile, Ala., with his brother-in-law, James E. Saunders, of Alabama. He was brother to Gen. Alex. Bradford, and descended from Gov. William Bradford, of Colonial Massachusetts. He married (II) Mrs. John Farrington (*née* Pope McGehee, daughter of John McGehee, of Panola, Miss). No issue by this marriage. Issue first marriage (Saunders):
1. Robert Morris[8], b. 15th November, 1834; m. 13th May, 1858, Medora, daughter of Dr. D. F. Alexander. Issue: 1. Medora, born 1859, m. Dr. Henderson. 2. Charles 3. Frank A. 4. Rose, m. Dr. Isham Harrison. 5. Benj. M., died young.

2. Mary McFarland[5], b. 23d June, 1836; m. 27th October, 1859, Dr. Moses Kelly Harrison, graduate of Louisville Medical College, 1855, and Surgeon C. S. A.; b. Birmingham, Ala. (his father's site), 27th May, 1829; d. Deerbrook, Noxubee county, Miss., 30th April, 1894; son of Isham and —— (Kelly) Harrison, who removed from Anderson, S. C., to Alabama, and thence to Mississippi. His grandmother was sister to Gen. Wade Hampton of the war 1812. His uncle, Wm. Kelly, was United States Senator from Alabama 1822, and afterward a distinguished lawyer in New Orleans. He was one of thirteen children; among them Gen. James and Cols. Richard, Isham and Thomas Harrison, all in the late war (all of whom he survived), and also brother of Nina Harrison (Mrs. Matt. Clay), noted for her beauty and intellect. Issue: five children, among them Dr. Isham, m. Rose Bradford; Moses; Nina, who married Charles Sherrod, Jr., deceased, and others.
3. Louisa Jane[5], born 1837, d. 1856.
4. Antoinette Malone[5], b. 1841, d. 1860; a lovely young girl.
5. James Saunders[5], b. 23d May, 1839, C. S. A., Cavalry of Miss., m. ——.
6. John Drake[5], b. 24th December, 1842, never married.
7. Benj. M.[5], b. 29th March, 1842, m. 19th May, 1861, Sallie Hatch. Issue: three children.
8. Henry Blanton[5], b. 1st January, 1845, C. S. A., wounded at battle of Murfreesboro, and d. November 2, 1864.
9. Frances Dunn[5], b. 24th February, 1847, m. Lattimore Dupre, third wife; had two sons. He m. (IV) Mary Pope.
10. Rose Narcissa[5], b. 29th December, 1848; married John Jefferson, of Memphis, Tenn. Issue: Bradford; and Rose.
11. Mattie[5], b. 24th December, 1850, d. ——; m. James, son of Andrew, and nephew of United States Senator Isham G. Harris, of Memphis, Tenn. (who died 1897 while serving in Senate). Senator Harris was born 1818; M. C. 1849. Governor of Tennessee thrice in succession, beginning in 1857. On staff of Gen. Albert Sydney Johnston in late war; also staff officer to Gens. Beauregard and Bragg. He was a native of North Carolina, from which State his father migrated to Tennessee. Issue of James and Mattie Harris: 1. George Harris, lawyer, of Memphis, Tenn.; 2. Daughter.

IX. ELIZA JANE[7] SAUNDERS (b: 1814, d. Galveston, Texas, of yellow fever, 24th October, 1858), youngest daughter of Rev. Turner Saunders; m. William Hancock of Mississippi and Texas, who died at Galveston, a half brother of Bishop Paine, of the M. E. Church South. She was small, and of a lovely Christian character. Issue:
1. Frances E.[5], m. 16th January, 1861, Thaddeus C. Armstrong, of Galveston, Texas; one child, William[5] Armstrong, b. 1866, prominent lawyer of Galveston.
2. Bradford[5]. m. 1869 Frances Farish. Issue: 1. Laura; 2, Fannie; 3, Nellie; 4, Nettie; 5, Mary Shaw.
3. William. James[5], bookseller, Houston, Texas; m. 1878, Nellie Bagby, of Houston. Issue: 1, Eleanor Francis, b. 1879; 2, Elsa Stuart.
4. Martha Jane[5], m., 1868, Stirling Fisher, of San Marcos, Texas. Issue: 1, Anne, b. 1871; 2, Stirling; 3, Asbury; 4 Loula; 5, Robert; 6. Fannie; 7. Oeenith.
5. Robert[5], b. 1852, d. 1895, at Galveston. Never married.
6. Mary Lou[5], living with her sister, Mrs. Armstrong.

X. WILLIAM HUBBARD[7] SAUNDERS (b. Franklin, Tenn., 1816, d. 1895, near Muldon, Miss.); m. 21st July, 1851, Susan, daughter of John Goodwin, a lawyer, of Aberdeen, Miss. She died soon after marriage, leaving one son, James, born November, 1852, who died in 1888, unmarried.
Colonel Saunders was the most quiet and studious of his family, but his keen wit and quaint humor, coupled with an almost infallible judgment, gave him great prestige. This, and his hermit-like simplicity of life, won him earnest friends. In the civil war he was a member of the military court, Army of Tennessee, with the Hon. J. L. M. Curry, Col. William Dowd, Judge John Sale of Mississippi, and others.

Rev. Turner Saunders, m. (II) 1826, Mrs. Millwater, née Henrietta M. Weeden, b. 1793, reared in Baltimore; d. 24th June, 1869. Her brother, Dr. William Weeden, and sister, Mrs. John Oliver, of Columbus, Miss., were also of Baltimore (see *Oliver Family*). Her eldest daughter, Sarah Millwater, m. Dr. Felix Manning, son of James, of Huntsville, Ala. The second, Mary Eliza Millwater, m. Bishop Robert Paine, the devoted friend of Rev. Mr. Saunders. These all removed to Aberdeen with the elder couple in 1844. Mrs. Paine, honored and beloved, alone remains, of the happy group, and lives in the old residence built by the Rev. Turner Saunders. Issue 2nd marriage, four sons; 1, Turner, 2, Thomas, 3, Franklin, and 4, Hubbard, as follows:

XI. TURNER[7] SAUNDERS, Major, C. S. A.; b. 12th August, 1829, d. Demopolis, Ala., 30th October, 1882. Cotton planter in Alabama and Mississippi. On the staff of Gen. William W. Loring in Civil War, and also major in Gen. Featherston's command. Of distinguished bearing, and with a very long, flowing beard. Married first, 1852, Marie Victoria McRae (d. 1868), daughter of Col. John McRae, grandson of the Duke of Athol, Scotland, and an officer in British army, who, in 1830, sold his commission in army, married Josephine Ravisies, of Bordeaux, France, and came to Marengo county, Alabama, and engaged in extensive cotton planting. Turner Saunders m. second, 30th October, 1877, Kate Downing Garrett, of New Orleans. Issue, first marriage (McRae):

     1. John McRae[8], b. 22d August, 1853, m ., 1878, Lillie E. Keyes, of New Orleans. Issue, Pearl, Shelby and Lillie. 2. Norman[8] b. 2d May, 1857; unmarried. 3. Hal Gholson[8], b. 18th August, 1860. 4. Adele Josephine[8], b. August 30, 1863, m., 1879, Jacob Schoultz, of Baldwin county, Alabama. 5. Marie Victoire[8] b. 12th November, 1866, m. John C. Oatman, Austin, Tex. Issue second marriage (Garrett): 6. Helen E.[8], b. 28th October, 1879. 7. Edith Turner[8], b. 11th June, 1881.

XII. THOMAS[7] SAUNDERS, Captain C. S. A., 1831, d. 1868. Organised a company of *Independent Scouts* and joined Gen. Polk's command, and after his death, Gen. Forrest's. Of great daring and coolness, and strikingly handsome person. Married, 1863, Annie Hallam, of Memphis, Tenn., and was a large cotton planter in the Mississippi bottoms. Issue:

     1. Eva[8], fancied the drama, and is now, 1898, on the stage, as the wife of Mr. Tim Murphy, also of the histrionic profession. 2. Eugene, planter; unmarried.

XIII. FRANK[7] SAUNDERS, Captain C. S. A. (b. 8th March, 1833), organized the "*Home Guards*" at Aberdeen in civil war, and afterward joined his brother's company of "*Independent Scouts;*" lives in Aberdeen, Miss. Losing his wealth by the war, he has served several years on the staff of the "*American Artisan*," a scientific paper of New York, attaining eminence as a scientific and mechanical draftsman. His great musical talent has also been turned to business profit. Married (10th July, 1850), when 17 years of age, Sarah J. Herndon of Aberdeen. Issue:

     1. Edward Herndon[8], and 2, Frank Weeden[8]. These brothers married the twin daughters of Mr. Robert Whitfield.

XIV. HUBBARD[7] SAUNDERS, *aide-de-camp* C. S. A. General Loring's staff (b. Lawrence county, Ala., 20th September, 1836; d. Bay St. Louis, August 11, 1879). Served first as special scout for General Price. Wounded at the siege of Vicksburg once, and, again, had six horses killed under him. Located in Hancock county, Miss., after the war, and served in Legislature 1876; also clerk of Circuit and Chancery Courts when he died. He married (I) 25th April, 1854, Clara C., daughter of Mr. Wm. C. Cunningham, banker, of Aberdeen, Miss., and (II) Miss Eager (daughter of Dr. Robert Eager, of Charleston, S. C.). She married (II) Mr. H. S. Hyatt, lawyer, of New Orleans. Issue by first marriage (none by second):

     1. William C.[8]. 2. Turner[8], m. Mary J. Eagar (cousin to Mrs. Saunders). 3. Henrietta[8], m. G. A. Lux, of Birmingham; several children. 4. Frank[8], m. Roberta D. Hager; several children. 5. Clara C.[8] unmarried. (*See Early Settlers for Saunders.*)

Excursus—WEBB—(*See Edward Saunders*).

Stephen Webb, aged twenty-five, came to Virginia, 1620.—*Virginia Carolorum.*

Stephen Webb, 300 acres in James City county, 1635; Burgess, 1642. His sons Robert and William died without issue, and his brother William in England sent a son, William, 1659, to take possession.

Wingfield Webb, Burgess for Gloucester county, 1664, and John Webb in Gloucester, 1745.—*Old Survey Book*

Giles Webb, Burgess from Upper Norfolk (Nansemond), 1659. He married, in Henrico county, Judith, widow of Captain Henry Randolph, the immigrant. In 1689, he was required by Orphans' Court to account for estate of the Randolph orphans.—*Henrico Records.*

Robert Webb's lands processioned in Henrico county, Virginia, 1739.

Henry Webb, 1661, Constable in York county, and John Webb, 1699, mentioned in a suit.—*York Records.*

William Webb, *will* 1708, married, before 1674, in Isle of Wight county, Mary, daughter of Thomas Taberer, Justice, who lived there in 1672, and made his will, 1692, mentioning grandson, Thomas Webb. Taberer's wife "was very loving to the Quakers," and was a legatee under the will of Rd. Bennet, 1674, who, with Colonel Joseph Bridger, were also Quakers (*William and Mary Quarterly, VII, 248*).

William Webb, Jr., at school in 1698. The children of William Webb (*will* 1708), were Richard, William, Mathew, Elizabeth, Susanna, Joseph, Thomas.

Richard Webb witnessed a will, 1726.

One William Webb's will, p. 1700. James Webb, 1713, left legacy by Samuel Bridger (*Isle of Wight*).

One Thomas Webb, came, 1633, to Isle of Wight, with the family of John Arvine and four other persons.

When William Thomas died in Northumberland county, 1678, Samuel Webb was one of the appraisers; and when his wife died, 1683, Thomas Webb was an appraiser. And "Mr. John Webb's" will, in Northumberland, 1709, mentions his "nephew, Edward Saunders." These three were probably brothers of Mrs. Thomas, who was Elizabeth Webb, of Isle of Wight county, before her marriage with John Hudnall.

James Webb, Jr., signer of Association, in Northern Neck of Virginia, against the *Stamp Act*, 1766. He married Mary Smith, of Essex.

There were also Webbs in Middlesex county, Virginia. A book of the *Webb family* has been published by Robert Dickens Webb, M. D., of Yazoo City, Miss., in which *William or Micajah Webb, Isle of Wight county, Virginia,* is the progenitor. It was probably William, of the will of 1706.

John Webb's lands, in Henrico, processioned 1730.—*St. John's Parish Vestry Book.*

John and Lucy Webb, a daughter, Sarah, b. 1760.—*Sussex and Surry County Albemarle Parish Register.*

Robert Webb also mentioned in the Register in 1771, and William Webb, 1773.

George Webb, married in Goochland county, 1756, Hannah Fleming.—*Marriage Bonds.*

Francis Webb, of King and Queen county.—*Virginia Gazette.*

John and Mary Webb, a son, James, b. 1673, and Giles, 1677. From *Register of Farnham parish, Richmond county, Va.*—*Virginia Magazine of History, etc.*

Isaac Webb, m. 1678. Mary Bidwell, and had Isaac, b. 1681.

Giles and Elizabeth Webb, a son, John Span, b. 1703; Isaac, b. 1705; Betty, 1711; Giles, 1714; Mary, 1717; Cuthbert, 1718; Tabitha. 1722.

Isaac and Frances Webb, a son, John, b. 1737; Isaac, 1739; Giles, 1741; James, 1743; Cuthbert, 1745; Amy, 1750; Ann, 1753; Priscilla, 1754; Frances, 1755; Giles, 1756; Isaac, 1758.

James and Barbara Webb, a son, William, b. 1720.

John Span and Sarah Webb, a son, William, b. 1742.

James Webb d. May, 1750; Sarah Webb d. 1754; John Webb d. 1756.

James and Ann Webb, a son, James Hawks, b. November, 1750.

John and Clara Webb, a daughter, Sarah, b. 1761. *All of Farnham parish, Richmond county.*

Colonel John Webb, of the Revolution—Bounty lands paid him, 1784, and also Isaac Webb, the same.—*Saffall.*

Winifred Webb, of Lancaster county, Virginia, m. 1745, Joseph Norris, d. 1747. Of their two sons, William and Joseph, only the latter, b. 1747, lived. Mr. Norris m., second, Sarah, widow of Joshua Phillips, and had Septimus, b. 1763; Thaddeus, b. 1765; Eppa, b. 1767; Sarah, b. 1769; Mary, 1772; William, 1774, who moved to Baltimore, 1793, and was grandfather of S. Henry Norris, now of Philadelphia, lawyer, and Mrs. Evelina Norris Magruder, of Charlottesville, Va.

Joshua and Sarah Philips had a son, William Phillips, b. 1767.

Will of Edward Phillips, recorded, 1710, in York county; witnesses, James Cooke and Orlando and William Jones.—*Records.*

David Phillips, in 1681—800 acres on Dividing creek, Northumberland county.

Will of John Phillips, in Lancaster county, 1655. Wife Sarah, and Moore Fauntleroy, executors. His patent (1651), 400 acres on north side of Rapp.

Will of Thomas Phillips, Lancaster county, 1666, wife Margaret administratrix.

Will of James Phillips, Lancaster county, 1689, wife, Wary; sons, James, George and Samuel.

Lawrence Phillips, 1653, 100 acres in Nansemond county.

Muster of Thomas Phillips, aged twenty-five, 1624, at Basse' Choice, Elizabeth City county. He came, 1618, in the "*William and Thomas.*" Wife, Elizabeth. There were Phillips also in Surry, Prince William, Spottsylvania and James City counties, early in 1700.

HUBBARD FAMILY.—LANCASTER COUNTY, VIRGINIA.

(From County Records, and old Saunders Family Pamphlet, 1834.)

THOMAS (　　　d. after 1684) of "Scotch descent" m. Sarah ———. In Lancaster Records 1671, he bought land of John Seaman, on "East branch of Corotoman river, on the Rapp, next to land of Edward Saunders." In 1684 he sells some of this tract to which deed his wife puts her signature. Issue: Thomas, Joseph, Ephraim, "of White Chappel Parish," and perhaps others. (*Land Books, Vols. 4 and 5*).

I. Thomas[2] (　　　d. 1745.) Inventory of estate, 1745: m, 1717, Mary ———, Issue, among others:

1. Joseph, b. 1718, d. 1776. m. Betty———, lived and died on his father's plantation. His widow "came into Court and renounced benefit of her husband's will." It was ordered that Dale Carter, Richard Selden, Samuel Topp, John Morris and Tobias Brent divide the estate, and possess the widow with her part thereof." She was

---

Matthew Hubbard (Inventory of his property and library, 1667) was a merchant and early Justice of York county. (He married Sibilia, widow of Jerome Ham, also a Justice and Burgess). From him many of the names of Hubbard, Huberd, and Hubberd, in Virginia are descended.—*William and Mary Quarterly, II. 175.*

Hubbard Robert, 1699, Civil Officer for Warwick and J. P. in 1702.—*Historical Magazine 1, 247, 372.*

Hubbard Jesse, 1775, Navy of Revolution.—*Historical Magazine, 247 and 372.*

Hubbard Matthew, 1745, Tobacco drowned in Grey's Creek Warehouse, Surry county.—*Hening, V, 371.*

Hubbard Edward, 1775, Ensign at Fort Cumberland.—*Historical Magazine 1, 287.*

Hubbard John, son of Matthew and Mary, christened in Sussex county, in 1763.

*Ann Hubbard, born 27th April, 1770; m. Robert Coleman Foster of Nashville, Tenn. (born 1769, died 17th November, 1850. (*See Foster, in Saunders Family.*) She had four Hubbard brothers; Ephraim, Eppa, Austin, and Thomas, and two sisters, Sally (Mrs. Slaughter), and Polly (Mrs. Worthern), all of Virginia. It is believed they are of the descendants of Thomas Hubbard (above) and probably of the second Ephraim. The Hon. Ephraim H. Foster, of Tennessee, son of Ann Hubbard, was of this family. (*See Rev. Turner Saunders' descendants.*)

appointed guardian of her three children in 1776. Will probated by John Yerby and William Stamps. Issue: 1, Amos, who moved to Frederick county, and two others, names unknown.

2. Ephraim, b. 1720, m. Miss Edmonds, and moved early to Frederick county, Virginia. Issue:
1, Ephraim; 2, Elias; 3, Eppa and others. "The two Ephraims, father and son, were handsome and active men."[6]

3. Betty Hubbard, b. 22d February, 1721, d. 14th November, 1789. m. 18th May 1783, William[4] Saunders, b. 1718 (Edward,[3] Ebenezer,[2] Edward,[1] 1659). She had dark hair and eyes, and was of remarkable piety. (James Saunders, a twin, and her youngest son, and author of the "Saunders Pamphlet," was the "last to leave the old castle the home of his youth" at his mother's death, when he removed to Edenton, N. C.) Issue:
Thomas, b. 1739; Mary, 1741; Jesse, 1743; Winifred, 1746; Frances,1748; Edward 1751; Presley, 1753: Joseph (1757) Lieutenant in the Rev. Navy; Ephraim 1760, and William and James (twins).—Saunders Family.

4. Thomas Hubbard married Margaret —— in Lancaster. A deed 1753, to Joseph Hubbard, of £500.

II. Joseph Hubbard d. 1770, will 16th October 1765; married Betty ——. Executors of will: William Saunders and William Yerby. Commissioners to divide his estate 1770: Dale Carter, John Meredith and James Kirk. Children: Thomas, Joseph, James, Hannah, William, John, Jesse and " perhaps another—expected."

III. Ephraim, of "St Mary's White Chappel Parish" ( ) Bought a tract, in 1749, of 100 acres, "being lands of Edmund Saunders, deceased" in Wicomico parish, and "adjoining Edmund Saunders the younger."—Lancaster Records, Vol. 14.

The names in the Hubbard family, above, are mostly identical with those in the Ball family.

ELLIOTT.

John Elliott, 1623, James City county, "living over the river."

John Elliott, 1635, came to Virginia in the Constance, aged 36. Hotten.

Lt. Col. Anthony Elliott, of Gloucester county. Patent in Elizabeth City county, 1636, for 400 acres. In the war with the Indian king, Opechancanough, 1645 (Col. Francis Poythress commanding). Burgess for Elizabeth City county, 1647. In the Assembly for Gloucester 1657, with Captain Thomas Ramsey (Hening; and Virginia Carolorum), and of the Council, 1658. Married Frances (d. 1685), daughter of William Armistead of Gloucester, the immigrant, (patent 1636 in Elizabeth City). She married (1) Rev. Justinian Aylmer of York county, b. 1639, and (3) Col. Christopher Wormley of Middlesex, whose step-father was Governor Sir Henry Chicheley. (Lee Family.) Her great-niece, Judith Armistead, daughter of William and granddaughter of John, the Councillor, married Captain George Dudley, of Gloucester. Mrs. Elliott's niece, Judith Armistead, married Robert (" King ") Carter.

Jeremy Elliott, in York county, 1679.

John Elliott, 1699-1714, Justice, Westmoreland county, Virginia.

Robert Elliott, 1677, vestry of Kingston parish, Gloucester, now Mathews. "Elliott's Corner Line," 1735, Old Survey Book of Gloucester.

George Elliott, married, 1732, Patience Colgate (widow of William Buckner, d. 1731, of Gloucester county, Virginia, whom he married, 1724. He moved to Maryland in 1722, and left one daughter, who soon died.) The brothers and sisters of William Buckner, in 1733, sued George Elliott and Patience, his wife. They were: Thomas, Philip, Ann, Elizabeth and Mary Buckner and Charles Debois and Christian, his wife. (William Buckner, Mr. Tyler thinks, was the son of John, who was a son of John and Ann Buckner.) In 1727, John Buckner, of St. Mary's parish, Essex, gave to his son, William, 500 acres in Essex, "part of the tract given me by my mother, Ann Buckner." In Stafford county is an old will of a John Buckner, 1752, wife, Elizabeth, daughter,

Susannah. John Buckner, Sr., died 1695. Inventory in Essex Records.—*Chancery Papers*.

John Elliott, 1786, living at East River, Kingston parish, Mathews county. *Ibid*.

Rev. James Elliott, 1790, minister Petsworth parish, Gloucester county, Va.

James Elliott, married before 1805, Mary Whiting, executrix (with Meacham Boswell,) of Peter Whiting, of Gloucester county.

One of the Elliotts of Gloucester county married Priscilla, daughter of John Robinson, who was deceased in 1791, and whose lands on the Pianketank river were surveyed and divided between "Mrs. Elliott, John, William, Peter, Robert and Christopher Robinson and their sisters: Judith and Mary Robinson, Mrs. Elizabeth Whiting, widow of Mathew Whiting, and who afterward married Major James Baytop, of the Rev. " and Mrs. Thomas Wyatt's children." *She* was Catherine Robinson, and married Thomas Wyatt on July 2, 1785.—*Old Survey and Christ Church Register*.

William Elliott, of Gloucester county, deceased 1822, widow, Dorothy, children, 1, John; 2, Elizabeth, married Benjamin Minor, tobacco inspector; 3, William; 4, Margaret, married Claiborne Kinningham, of the "*Ordinary;*" 5, Richard, and 6, Frances Elliott. Administrator; Joseph Robinson.—*Old Record*.

Thomas Elliott, d. 1716, married in Middlesex county, Sarah ——, and had Mary, b. 1686, m. 1705, John Goodwin.

William Elliott, d. 1716, m. 1708, in Middlesex, Mary Neal, and had Thomas, b. 1714.

Thomas Elliott, m. 1710, Elizabeth Dudley, in Middlesex county, and had Margaret, b. 1712 and Elizabeth, b. 1715.

Robert Elliott, m. 1742 in Middlesex county, Elizabeth, b. 1722, daughter of Capt. Mathew and Mary Kemp, and had Mary, Mathew Kemp, John and Robert, b. 1750. He was clerk of Middlesex county court, 1762-67, when he died. (*Virginia Gazette*.) Mary Elliott, m. 1772, Michael Payne.

Robert Elliott, in French and Indian wars, 1754, with Col. George Washington, Capt. Hogg's company.— *Virginia Historical Magazine, Vol. 1*.

Thomas Elliott, Colonel in Continental line, Revolution.—*Virginia Historical Magazine, Vol. 2*.

Robert Elliott, Lieutenant in Continental line, Revolution.—*Virginia Historical Magazine, Vol. 2*.

Robert Elliott, 1767, living in King William county.

Thomas Elliott, of Lancaster county, b. about 1740, married 1794, Winifred, b. 1746, daughter of William and Betty (Hubbard) Saunders, of Lancaster county, Virginia. Their only son, John Elliott, moved to Brunswick county, Virginia, and there married Mildred Maclin. (*Saunders Family*.)

Richard Elliott, of vestry of St. Andrews, Brunswick county, Virginia, between 1732 and 1786. (*Meade*).

Richard Elliott, of Brunswick, 1775, owner of celebrated horse, "Apollo."— *Virginia Gazette*.

Mary, daughter of Thomas Elliott, born New Kent county, 1686.—*St. Peters Parish Register*.

John and Seaton Elliott, 1756, students William and Mary College.

William Elliott, 1774, committee of safety for Augusta county.— *William and Mary Quarterly*.

FOSTER SKETCH.

Anthony Foster, (born 13th March, 1741, died 3d November, 1816;) married, (29th January, 1760,) Rose Coleman, (born 20th December, 1742, died 5th August, 1816). Issue, five sons and six daughters: 1. Anthony; 2. John; 3. Robert; 4. Thomas; 5. Edmund; 6. Sarah Gray; 7. Hannah Stubblefield; 8. Mrs. Read; 9. Mrs. Ray; 10. Mrs. Compton; 11. Mrs. Long. Of these—

Robert Coleman Foster, (born Fairfax county, Va., 18th July, 1769 ; died 27th September, 1844;) married, (8th March, 1790,) Ann Hubbard,* who had brothers: Ephraim, Eppa, Austin and Thomas Hubbard; and sisters: Sally Slaughter and Polly Worthem. They were among the first settlers of Nashville, Tenn., coming from Danville, Va., 1794, first to Bardstown, Ky., and thence to Nashville, where he was a member of the Legislature, and President of the State Senate, and one of the founders and trustees of the University. Issue, ten children:

1. Anthony, died an infant.
2. Anthony Coleman Foster, born 19th December, 1792; died January, 1816.
3. Ephraim Hubbard Foster, born 17th September, 1794; died 6th September, 1844; married, 24th June, 1817, Jane Dickerson. He was an eminent lawyer, and, as leader of the Whig party, he represented Tennessee in the United States Senate when Clay, Calhoun and Webster were also members of that august body. Issue several children:
4. Robert Coleman Foster, born 1st November, 1796; died December, 1871; married, 8th October, 1819, Louise Turner Saunders. (See *Saunders*.)
5. James Hubbard Foster, born 1st October, 1798; died ——; married, 4th July, 1821, Narcissa Saunders, sister of Louisa. (See *Saunders*.)
6. Addison D. Foster, born 2d December, 1800; died an infant,
7. Benjamin Franklin Foster, born 25th October, 1803; died, Florence, Ala., —— married, July, 1835; Agnes Temple; lived in Florence, Ala.; several children.
8. Mary Ann Eliza, born 13th July, 1805; died an infant.
9. George W. Foster, of Florence, Ala., born 28th November, 1806; died ——; married, 1st October, 1829, Sarah J. Watkins, daughter of Robert H. Watkins. (See *Watkins*.)
10. Thomas J. Foster, Confederate States Congress, born 11th July, 1809; died ——; married (I), 30th October, 1833, Virginia, daughter of Robert H. Watkins. No issue. He married (II), Miss Hood, of Florence, Ala.; and married (III), Mrs. Longshaw. No issue. Issue by second marriage (Hood):
   1. James married Matilda Toney, and had two daughters.
   2. Coleman, unmarried, lives in Lawrence county, Ala.
   3. Annie married Lieutenant Longshaw, of United States Army.

BILLUPS SKETCH.

(*From Dr. Dudley Dunn's Family Bible, and Members of the Family.*)

Bartley and Susan Cox had issue:
1, Jane, b. 4th October, 1784. 2, Swepson, b. 30th June, 1785. 3, Susan, b. 23d May, 1787, d. 27th December, 1818, married —— Thomas. 4, Edward, b. 2d July, 1788. 5, William, b. 11th April, 1792, and, 6, Elisabeth, b. 1790, married Dr. Dudley Dunn, of Memphis, Tennessee. (*See Dunn*.)

Bartley Cox died 27th October, 1792. His widow married (II) Capt. John Billups, of Mecklenburg county, and died 10th January, 1817, leaving Billups children, as follows:

1. Nancy R., b. 4th December, 1799, died 24th October, 1831; married Dr. William Baldwin, of Columbus, Mississippi, son of Major Baldwin†, of Oglethorpe, county, Georgia.
2. John Billups, b. 11th June, 1802.
3. Col. Thomas Carlton Billups, b. 24th April, 1804, married (I) Sarah Moore, sister of Edward Moore, who married Fannie Swoope, and sister, also, of Mrs. James Saunders

---

*This family of Hubbards, from the identity of names, is certainly of the same into which William Saunders, born 1718, of Lancaster county. Va., married, in 1738. They were descended from Thos. Hubbard, the Scotchman.

†Other children of Major Baldwin, of Oglethorpe county, Georgia, were Lemuel Baldwin, of Georgia, and Nancy, who married (I) Marco Phinisy, of Georgia, and married (II) Mr. Nisbet, of Alabama.

Sims, mother of the Hon. William H. Sims, Lieutenant Governor of Mississippi and Assistant Secretary of Interior in Cleveland's first administration. Colonel Billups was most prosperous in life, a firm and consistent member of Methodist Church, and his household, and affairs, were conducted with remarkable system and energy. Children:

1. Major John Marshall Billups, of Columbus, Mississippi, banker and planter; of extensive means and influence, and imposing presence. The leader of his church (Methodist), in that section; married (I) Sarah Phinizy, daughter of Jacob Phinizy,* and (II) Sallie Govan,† daughter of Andrew R. Govan, of South Carolina. *Children, first marriage:*

    1. Anna, m. Willis Banks Harris, and has three living children, Willis C., John Billups and Mary Jeptha.
    2. Jake, m. Jennie Tarleton, of Mobile. Three living children: Melvin, Margaret and Maida.
    3. Sue, m. Richard Fontaine Hudson, d. 1891. Issue: Sue, Cornelia, and Sarah Phinizy.
    4. John Marshall; of New York.
    5. Sallie Govan, unmarried.
    6. Margie, m. R. Patterson, of Memphis, Tennessee; son, John B. *Children, second marriage (Govan):*
    7. Joseph, Traveling Passenger Agent of Southern Railroad.
    8. Mary Jones Govan. 9. Elizabeth Govan.

2. Susan Billups, m. Charles Sherrod, of Columbus. (See *Saunders*.)
3. Joseph Billups, kind, genial, and quite a humorist, died unmarried, and greatly lamented.
4. Thomas Carlton Billups. d. 1898, married Ida Sykes, sister of Mrs. Saunders Billups. Children: Marcella, Elizabeth J, James S, Thomas C.

(For Col. Thomas C. Billups' *second marriage*, see *Saunders family*, in which is mentioned his son, Gen. Saunders Billups).

YATES FAMILY.

Until recently, it was believed that Rev. Robert Yates, who came to Virginia in 1699, and was minister of Christ Church parish, Middlesex county (returning to England in 1704), was father of Rev. Bartholomew Yates, minister of Christ Church, 1703. But it is now proven they were brothers, as Robert was born 1673, and Bartholomew, 1676, and had also a brother, Rev. Francis Yates (b. 1666), ancestor of the Jefferson county family.

William and Mary Quarterly (Vol. IV), published the following from Dr. A. G. Grinnan, of Madison county, Va., who said he received it from Mr. Aiglonby, of England, who was of the Jefferson county family of Yates: "After the death of Waddington, the French statesman, it was discovered he was related to the Yates family in England, from which sprang the Jefferson county, and Tidewater, Yates of Virginia. Waddington was descended from the Penderells of Shropshire, Eng., who had hidden Charles II in the famous oak at Boscobel, two of whom had married Yates. This led to tracing back the family still further, and showed the connection between the Jefferson county family and that of Lower Virginia.

(The present representative of the family in England is Francis William Yates, of Capsollwood, Wolverhampton.)

William Yates (d. 1697), of Shockerly, parish of Donnington, Eng., 1656, had

---

*Jacob Phinizy, was brother to Marco, and married Matilda, daughter of General Stewart, of Virginia.

†Andrew Robinson Govan, born Orangeburg District, South Carolina. Represented that district in Congress in the days of Clay, Calhoun and Webster. He was a son of Donald Govan, of Scotland. He married Mary Pugh Jones, born in New Berne, North Carolina, daughter of Morgan Jones, of Maryland.

issue by Catherine, his wife, who died 1706: John, b. 3d November, 1658; William, b. 1661; Benjamin, b. 1663; Samuel, b. 1665; Francis, b. 1666; Richard, b. 1669; John, b. 1671; *Robert, b. 1673; Bartholomew, b. 1676*; the latter was baptised August 24, *on St. Bartholomew's day.*" Robert returned to England in 1704 and died there.

1. **Rev. Bartholomew Yates**, b. England, 1676, died Middlesex county, Va., 1734. Graduated Brazenose College, Oxford, 1698; licensed for Virginia 1700, by the Lord Bishop of London, and followed his brother Robert to Middlesex county, Va., 2d February, 1700, where he married (1704) Mrs. Sarah (Stanard) Mickleborough.[*] He entered 24,000 acres in Spotsylvania county (south side Rapidan) in 1722, with Edwin Thacker, John and Christopher Robinson, William Stanard,[*] Harry Beverly, Lewis Latane and John Clowder. Was visitor to William and Mary College, 1723, and Professor of Divinity, 1729. Had been minister in 1702, first, of Sittenbourne parish; second, Kingline parish, Rapp. county, and in 1703, of Christ Church parish, Middlesex (*Hayden*). His three sons were all ministers. Issue: 1. Catherine (b. 1706); 2. Sarah (1707); 3. Bartholomew (1713); 4. Robert (1715); 5. Frances, (1718), and 6. William (1720) (*Christ Church Register*) as follows:

I. CATHERINE[2] YATES, born 1706, died 1739, married by Rev. Emanuel Jones, 1733, to John Walker, born 1709, of Middlesex (will, p. 1745), son of James and Clara (Robinson) Walker, of Urbana. The "*Page Book*" calls him a "wealthy Englishman," and so was his father and his uncle, Richard Walker, the merchant of Urbana, who were the immigrants, and sons of John Walker, of England. Issue:

1. Sarah[4] Walker, born 1734, married, 1750, Robert Page, of "*Broadneck,*" Hanover county (son of Mann Page and Judith Carter), born 1722, died 1768. Issue: Mann, born 1750, died infant; Robert, born 1752, married, 1779. Mary Braxton; Judith, born 1756, married, 1774, Jno. Waller; Catherine, born 1758, Married, 1778, Benjamin Carter Waller, of Williamsburg, born 1757 (and had Martha married Geo. M. Holmes; Benjamin Waller married Hetty Catlett, Wm. Waller married Mary Berkely Griffin, Dr. Robert Page Waller married (1), 1815, Eliza C. Griffin, and (II) Julia M. Mercer; and their daughter Louisa Mercer married Joseph Cosnahan, of South Carolina, who were parents of Mrs. T. Jefferson Stubbs, of Williamsburg); John Page, born 1760, married Maria C. Byrd 1784, and lived at "*Pagebrook,*" Clarke county. ; Matthew Page, born 1762; married, 1787, Anne, sister of Bishop Meade. Walker Page, born 1764, d. s. p. Sarah Walker Page, born 1766; married, 1788, Hon. Robt. Page, of Janeville, Clarke county. (See *Page and Waller Families.*)

2. Clara[4] Walker, born 1737; married Colonel Allen, of *Clairmont*, James river, where is said to be her portrait. (*Page Family.*)

II. SARAH[2] YATES, born 1707, may have been first wife of John Robinson, born 1707, son of Christopher Robinson and Judith Wormley. (*Va. Mag. History.*)

III. REV. BARTHOLOMEW[2] YATES, born 1712; died 1767; married, 1741, Elizabeth, daughter of William Stanard,[*] above. He was minister of Christ Church, Middlesex county, 1734-67. Ordained by Bishop of London, 1736; Visitor of William and Mary College, 1766. Issue:

1. Sarah[4] Yates, born 1742; died, 1794; married, 1765. John Chinn, of Middlesex, born 1739, died 1791; vestry, 1769-84. Children:

*NOTE.—Eltonhead, b. 1640. daughter of Edwin Conway, m. (I), 1662, Henry Thacker and m. (II) William Stanard. Daughter. Sarah Stanard. b. 1680, m. (I) Tobias Mickleborough, and (II) Rev. Bartholomew Yates, b. 1677. *Their* son, Rev. Bartholomew Yates, b. 1712, m. Elizabeth, daughter of William Stanard and Elizabeth Beverly.

In an Orderly Book, Williamsburg, Va. (*T. H. Wynne*), is a General Order from Gen. Andrew Lewis " that Bartholomew Yates, John Stubbs, and Tarleton Paine act as ensigns in the first battalion until the pleasure of the Congress" etc.

For *Yates' Family* see Richmond *Standard*, March 20, 1880, article by Mr. Brock. *Virginia Genealogies* (Hayden)—*Christ Church Register*, Middlesex county, Va., and "*Yates Family,*" by Rev. John T. Gholson, in *Southern Churchman*, February 13, 1880.

William Yates, of Gloucester Co., Va., m. Susanna (*nee* Hughes), widow of James Bentley, who died 1791, and, before that, widow of John Throckmorton.

1. Priscilla[2], born 1767; married, 1783, Rawleigh William Downman, of *Belle Isle.*
2. Joseph[5], born 1768; died, 1808; Justice, 1792; married, 1794, Eliz., daughter of Leroy and Judith (Ball) Griffin.
3. Dr. John Yates[5] of Richmond county, born, 1770; died, 1826; Justice, 1799, married Sarah Fairfax, daughter of Councillor Robert Carter, of *"Nomini,"* Westmoreland county.
4. Bartholomew[5], born, 1771; died, 1801; married Olivia Downman, born, 1781; died, 1824; Justice in Lancaster county, 1799.
5. Sarah Yates[5], born 1773.
6. Elizabeth[5], born 1774; married (I) Dr. Nutt, and (II) Capt. Rd. Selden, born, 1760; died, 1823. Eliza[2], daughter of first marriage, married Joseph Addison Carter (parents of Addison Lombard Carter, of Lancaster, and others), and by Selden marriage, one son.
7. William[5], born, 1776; died, 1795.
8. Rawleigh[5], born, 1778; died, 1799,
9. Benjamin[5], born, 1782; died, 1784. (*For issue of all these see Virginia Genealogies, by Rev. Horace Haydm*).

2. Bartholomew[4] Yates, b. 1744, d. 1777, student at William and Mary College, 1762, with his cousin, Edmund Randolph Yates. He was a lieutenant in Revolution. M., 1769, Ann, b. 1750, daughter of Robert and Lucy Daniel, of Middlesex, and had issue: 1. Bartholomew[5] Yates, b. 1770.

Mrs. Ann Yates m. (II) in 1782, Dr. Robert Spratt, and had son, Robert B. Spratt.
3. Mary[4] Yates never married. Her *will* mentions her niece, Elizabeth Montague.
4. Elizabeth[4] Yates, b. 1747, m., 1769. Rev. Samuel Klug, minister, 1770, of Christ Church, Middlesex county.
5. Catharine[4] Yates, m., 1776, Capt. John Montague; a daughter, Elizabeth Stanard Montague, born 1777.
6. Harry Beverly[4] Yates, b. *circa* 1753, d. 1790, married (I) Lucy, daughter of James Murray. M. (II) 1788, Jane, b. 1767, daughter of Col. James Montague, of Middlesex county (see *Montague Family*). Thomas Roane, who married Sarah Murray in 1781, was guardian of his (Yates') orphans in 1790, and administrator of his estate. Issue:
    1. Elizabeth[5], b. 1780, m., 1797, Capt. John Quarles, of King and Queen county.
    2. Rachel Murray Beverly[5], b. 1781, m., 1799, Thomas, son of John and Elizabeth (Lee) Cooke, of Gloucester county (2d wife). (See *Cooke Family*.)
    3. Catharine Klug[5], b. 1784, m., 1807, James, b. 1754, son of James and Sarah (Smith) Baytop, of *"Springfield,"* Gloucester county (his 3d wife); captain in the Revolution. (See *Baytop Family*.)

IV. REV. ROBERT[3] YATES, Petsworth parish, Gloucester county, Virginia, b. 1715, ordained by Lord Bishop of London 1740, minister Petsworth parish 1741, m. Mary, daughter of Edmund Randolph, son of William, the immigrant. Issue:

1. Robert[4] Yates, d. 1806, Executor: Bartholomew Yates, of Williamsburg; and Administrator: Matthew Kemp. He was Justice in Gloucester Co. 1787, with Col. Francis Willis; (*Chancery Papers*) and Guardian, 1803, to Charity Buckner, of Gloucester. Edward Conoley brought suit against him 1794, in King and Queen county; John Buckner paid for him, 1796, some fees due the clerk of Matthews county (*old papers*). He m. Mary Tomkies, daughter of Col. Francis and Eliz. (Cooke) Tomkies, of Gloucester county. Issue:

    I. Bartholomew[5] Yates, of Gloucester, d. 1821, probably lieutenant in Rev.; m. Sally, dead before 1827, daughter of John and Ann Walker (Carter) Catlett, of *"Timberneck,"* Gloucester county, Virginia. Mrs. Catlett was daughter of Charles Carter, of *"Cleve,"* (son of Robert, *"King Carter"*) and Lucy Taliaferro, his third wife, who married (II) Col. Wm. Jones, of *"Marlfield,"* Gloucester county, Virginia. Her son, Col. Catesby Jones, was made guardian to the orphans of Bartholomew Yates, who were:

1 Robert Yates, m. Mary Ann, daughter of John and Mary Ann (Field) Wood; Mrs. Wood was daughter of Stephen Field, Jr., and Ann, daughter of George Booth, of "*Poropotank*," who died 1786. Issue, four daughters, of whom one, Robinette, m. John S. Cooke, and had John, and Lila, m. Robert F. Ross; 2. Charles Ann Yates; she died unmarried.

2. Elisabeth C.[5] Yates m. (I) Matthew Kemp, who died 1822; they made a conveyance, 1822, to sister, Catherine Yates, of 46 acres in Gloucester. Issue:
   1. Amelia, dead in 1822, m. Richard Hoard; 2. Louisa B.; 3. Matthew W.; 4. Peter W.; 5. Leroy H.; 6. Oswald S. Kemp.

3. Catherine[4] Yates, sold "*Locust Grove*" 1820, Gloucester county, to James Dillard.

4. Sarah[4] Yates, d. 1820; m. Thomas M. Henley. Issue:
   Mary, Leonard and Robert Henley.
   2. Daughter[4] m. in England. *Slaughter's Bristol Parish.*
   3. Daughter[4].
   4. Daughter[4].
   5. Katherine[4] Yates, m. September, 1777, John Thornton, Esq., of Stafford county. In publishing the marriage, the Virginia *Gazette* said she was " the *fourth* daughter of the Rev. Robert Yates." She m. (II) Dr. Robert Wellford, of English army, and settled at Fredericksburg; a son, Wm. Wellford.

V. FRANCES[3] YATES, b. 1718, m. 1737, Rev. John Reade, d. 1743, of Christ Church, minister in 1734, son of Thomas and Lucy (Gwyn) Reade; a daughter, Sarah Reade, m. 1760, John Rootes; a son, Thomas Reade, was student at William and Mary College, 1764; a son, John Reade, b. June 19, 1744, d. young.—*William and Mary Quarterly, III.*

VI. REV. WM.[3] YATES, b. December 14, 1720, d. 1764; ordained by Lord Bishop, of London, 1745, minister of James City parish, 1745, and of Abingdon parish, Gloucester county, 1752, and President of William and Mary College 1761; m. Elizabeth Randolph, (sister of wife of his brother Robert), and she married (secondly) Theodorick Bland[*], of Prince George. Issue:

1. Elizabeth[4] Yates married Rev. William Bland, son of Richard Bland of Jordan's and who was minister of James City, Parish, 1742, and had Ann Bland, who married Richard, son of John Pryor,[†] and had nine children: William Bland, Mary Ann, Richard, Samuel, Eliz. Yates, Theodorick Bland and others d. y. Of these:
   1. William Bland Pryor m. Jane Atkinson, and moved to Mississippi.
   2. Mary Ann m. John Atkinson.
   3. Richard Pryor m. Virginia Boyd, and moved to Arkansas.
   4. Samuel Pryor m. Mary Ann Hamlin, of Amelia (mother, Miss Goode,) Col Wm. Pryor, of Lynchburg, is a son.
   5. Elis. Yates Pryor m. Benjamin Jones, of Petersburg.
   6. Rev. Theodorick Bland Pryor, D.D., L.L. D.. m. (1) Lucy Atkinson, and had Lucy, who m. Robert McIlwaine of Petersburg, Va., and Roger Atkinson Pryor, M. C. from Virginia, General in Confederate army, Judge Supreme Court N. Y. Rev. Theodorick B. Pryor m. (II) Frances Epes, by whom: Frances, m. Thomas Campbell, Nanny, m. George Jones, Archibald M., m. Ann Augusta Bannister of Petersburg. (For these, and Pryor family, see *Virginia Magazine History, VII*, 75.

2. Edmond Randolph[4] Yates, student with his cousin Bartholomew, at William and Mary College, 1762; Lt. in Colonel Muhlenburg's company 1779. (*Hayden*). "All persons having demands against the estate of Lt. Bartholomew Yates, are desired

---

[*]Theodorick Bland, Jr., of Prince George county, 1779, advertised in the *Virginia Gazette* 1400 acres on York river, at *Cappahosic*, within eight miles of Williamsburg, which had thereon a dwelling house, a public house and a ferry.
Rev. Wm. Bland's first wife was Miss Wells, of Warwick county, whom he married in 1778.—*Virginia Gazette.*
[†]Richard, son of John Pryor (above) had a brother, Luke Pryor, who emigrated to Alabama; m. first in Virginia, Martha, sister of Gen. Winfield Scott, and second by Mrs. Lane, to whom was born Luke Pryor, U. S. Senator.

to make them known to William Yates Esq." Signed "Edmond R. Yates," 1777. (*Virginia Gazette*.)

3. Colonel William⁴ Yates of the Rev., b. 1750, d. 1789, student at William and Mary College, 1764, from Williamsburg; his home called "*Grampian Hill*." On General Washington's staff; Lt. Colonel in the department of muster-master-general: justice Amelia county, 1793, m. (I) June 22, 1777, Ann Isham Poythress, and (II) Elizabeth, daughter of George Booth.

ISSUE FIRST MARRIAGE (*Poythress*).

I. William⁵ Yates. Delegate (1818-20) for Brunswick county; moved to Wilkinson county, Miss.; member Legislature 1820, and died 1822.

II. Benjamin Poythress⁵ Yates of "Grampian Hill" (b. Petersburg, Va., 7th April, 1780, and died there 1817); married (18th December, 1805), Sophia, daughter of Captain Buckner and Ann (Walker) Stith of, Rock Springs, Va., (and a descendant of the Buckner, Drury, Dade, Townshend, Langhorne, Bathurst and Meade families).

Their son, William Yates, of Springfield, Ill., was born in Petersburg, Va. (18th November, 1806), married (I) 19th April, 1835, F.J. Hinton, widow of Charles Marr Hinton; m. (II) 16th November, 1852, Eliza Ann, daughter of John Randolph and Malinda (Harlin) Murphy of Kentucky; and had David Stith, Mary Ann, Benjamin, Poythress, Frederick Ferdinand, Meade, Walker, Frances Elis. Julia Stith and Grace Eliska Yates. (*See American Ancestry, Vol. XI.*)

ISSUE SECOND MARRIAGE (*Booth*).

III. Ann⁵ Yates (b. *circa*, 1787, died Little Rock, Ark., 1855); married (I) 1806. Hon. Thomas Gholson of Brunswick county, Va. (b. 1782, d. 1816), member Congress 1808-16; on General Porter's staff in war of 1812. From exposures incurred in this war he died at the age of 33. Issue: 1. William Y⁶. 2. Mary Ann⁶, and 3 Thomas Gholson.⁶ (*See Gholson Family*).

Mrs. Thomas Gholson m. (II) George W. Freeman, Bishop of Arkansas P. E. Church. Their children:

4. George Russell⁶ Freeman, m. (1848) Kate, sister of Senator (and General) Walthall of Mississippi, and had 1. Mary Ann, Mrs. Clark, now a widow, with daughter, Kate. 2. George Yates Freeman, died 1896, m. Rosa Belle Hunter, and had Edward Walthall. 3. Edward Russell Freeman, U. S. N. and on Battleship Nashville, in war with Spain. Now Ensign on Battleship Indiana.

5. Rev. Andrew⁶ Freeman, Louisville, Ky., m. 1849, Miss Ashley, who died 1851, leaving a daughter.

THOMAS YATES married, 1679, Rose Stake, in Middlesex county, and had a son, Thomas, born 1689.—*Christ Church Register*. These may have been progenitors also of a Virginia family of that name.

In Culpeper county, Virginia, now Rapp., were three Yates brothers, writes Miss Augusta Yates of Danville, Va., 1897: William, Charles and James Yates, descendants of Rev. Francis Yates, b. 1666 (*ante*), as follows:

1. *William Yates* had a son, Benjamin Gaines Yates, who had a son Lewis Augustus Yates, father of Miss Yates.

2. *Charles Yates*, one of these brothers, was grandfather to the Rev. Charles Yates, living in Sperryville, Va.

3. *James Yates* was grandfather of Mr. Thomas A. Yates, of Washington, D. C. Charles Yates, old merchant of Fredericksburg, b. 1728 and died there in 1809, aged 81.—*American Register, 1802, 260.* See letter to him written during Revolution 1777, from Col. Lewis Willis, in camp at Morristown.—*Virginia Magazine of History, II.*

Rev. Charles Yates, of Virginia, moved to Washington county Pennsylvania, 1781. William Yates married Rebecca Watkins, Overwharton parish.

William Yates married Sarah Harris (who was born 1759, and was aged 18 in 1777), daughter of Benjamin Harris, who died in 1777, leaving issue: 1, Benjamin; 2, William Wager; 3, Mary Spencer; 4, Henson Wager, who married.Edward Moseley; 5, *Sarah, m. William Yates*; 6, Phoebe; 7, Edith, and one other.

Abram Salle, Bernard Markham and Samuel Niven were executors, and Abram Salle was guardian of Mrs. Yates (Sarah).

William Yates, justice of Nottoway 1789.—*Hayden.*

Lieutenant Bartholomew Yates, Continental army, 1776–1783, received, in 1795, 2666 acres.

Lieutenant John Yates, State Line, received in 1786, 2666 acres, for three years' service.

George Yates, surgeon's mate, received in 1787 the same. He was in Continental line during the war.—*Hayden.*

GHOLSON GENEALOGY.

1. ANTHONY GHOLSON[1], b. ——, was perhaps the first of the name who settled in Virginia. In a deed dated July 5, 1725, he is referred to as of Spotsylvania county, and there is a like recital in a deed of February 2, 1739; in 1728 he patented 1000 acres. In June, 1763, he was living in St. Thomas Parish, Orange county, and was the owner of a considerable estate there. Nothing is known as to the date and locality of either his birth or marriage. He died some time prior to December 3, 1764—his widow, Jane, in a deed of that date, referring to his recent death. How long she survived him does not appear. Their children, as their names appear in a deed of gift executed to them by which he disposed of his property, were:

I. William[2], b. ——, d. ——; was living in Spotsylvania in 1749, and of age; a deed executed by him in 1760 is signed by his wife, Susanna.

II. Anthony[2], Jr., b. ——, d. ——; was living in Spotsylvania in 1743. He married and left issue, several children, from whom were descended the Gholsons of Kentucky.

III. Elizabeth[2], who married —— Rice.

IV. Lucy[2], m. —— Step.

V. ——[2], daughter. who m. —— Pollard, probably died prior to 1763.

VI. John[2], b. ——, m. prior to June, 1741, Esther, daughter of Thomas Cooke. In a deed of that date "Thomas Cooke, of St. Thomas parish, in the *county of Orange*, colony of Virginia, planter," conveys certain lands on the north fork of the North Anna river, to "John and Easter Gholson, of same county, parish and colony," in consideration of his love for his said daughter. He continued to reside in Orange until his death. His will was probated July, 26, 1790. Whether or not his wife survived him is not known; she was alive in October, 1786, this being the date of his will in which she is mentioned and provided for. Their children were:

I. Thomas[3], of Brunswick county (*see below*), born in Orange county.

II. John[3], b. in Orange county, ——, m. Frances ——; was executor of his father's will, and qualified as such July 26, 1790; removed from Orange shortly after and settled in the neigborhood of Raleigh, N. C. He probably left issue, as there are, I understand, some of the name still living in North Carolina. (*Edwin Gholson.*)

III. Martha[3], m. —— Vivian.

IV. Lucy[3], m. —— Bunch.

V. Lucy (probably a grand-daughter), m. —— Long.

VI. ——[3], daughter, m. —— Quin; died probably before the execution of her father's will, as his bequests are to my "grandsons, Thomas Quin and John Quin." Of these:

1. Thomas[3] Gholson, (*above*) born ——, in Orange county, Va., moved to Brunswick county before November, 1772, on the Meherrin river, and his name figured often in the county records. Judging from the realty transfers, to and by, him, he was a man of considerable affairs. Married Jane Perry. His will, May 14, 1806, probated

April 24, 1809. His wife died 1829. "*Gholsonville*" named for him. Issue: John, William and Thomas, as follows:

I. John⁴ Gholson died 1802; no issue, or no mention of such in his father's will.

II. William⁴ Gholson, born 1775, died 24th March, 1831; married, 1805, Mary, born 1776, died 1842, daughter of Thomas and Ann (Turner) Saunders, of Brunswick county. (*Saunders Family*.) Major Gholson was justice in Brunswick, and in 1824 he was contractor for that part of the United States mail, from New Orleans to New York, which ran from Petersburg, Va., to Raleigh, N. C. His plantation was two and a half miles from the present town of Lawrenceville, (and is now (1899) owned by descendants of the venerable Turner Saunders, born 1800, who was long a landmark of the county). He owned, also, "New Hope," and "The Springs," plantations, and was a man of much importance. Issue:

    1. James Hubbard. 2. Thomas Saunders. 3. Ann Elizabeth. 4. Dr. Robert A. 5. Mary. 6. William T. 7. Martha E., as follows:

I. Hon. James Hubbard⁵ Gholson, Brunswick county born 1807, died 2d July. 1848, member Convention 1829; Legislature, 1824-32; member of Congress, 1833-35, and judge of Circuit Court. Graduated at Princeton 1820. Married. 1826, Charlotte Louisa, died 9th March, 1852, daughter of Col. Miles Cary, born 1757, died 1808, and Mrs. Elizabeth (Booth) Yates, widow of Col. William Yates of the Revolution. He formed a law partnership with his brother in Petersburg, 1840. His wife was of frail and nervous physique. She was sister to Hon. George Booth Cary, M. C. of Southampton county, and also half-sister to wife of her husband's uncle, Hon. Thomas Gholson. Issue: Two daughters, both died young, and buried, with their parents, at old Blandford church, Petersburg.

II. Hon. Thomas Saunders⁵ Gholson, born at Gholsonville, 9th December, 1808, died, Savannah, Ga., returning from England, 12th December, 1868; educated at Oxford, N. C., and University of Virginia. Removed to Petersburg 1840. Visitor of William and Mary College 1844; President of bank of Petersburg; founder of the Library, Petersburg; formed a partnership after this brother's death, 1848, with Judge James Alfred Jones, of Mecklenburg county and of Richmond, Va.; Judge of Circuit Court 1858; Member of Confederate States Congress with Thomas S. Bocock. Formed a cotton and tobacco commission house in Liverpool, Eng., after the war, with his son-in-law, Col. Norman G. Walker; died suddenly of heart failure, and is buried at old Blandford church. Married, 14th May, 1829, Cary Ann, (born 1806; died Staten Island, N. Y., 10th December, 1896,) daughter of his uncle, Hon. Thomas Gholson. A most pious and cultivated woman. Issue:

    1. Rev. John Yates⁶ Gholson, born Petersburg, 1828; died on his plantation in Marengo county, Ala., 7th August, 1886; minister of St. Bartholomew P. E. Church, Baltimore, for ten years, when, his health failing, he removed to Oxford, N. C., and thence to Alabama, where closed his promising career. Great scholarly attainments and personal charm were his. He wrote an article in the *Southern Churchman* on "*Yates Family*." Married, 1858, Alphese de Courval Oswald, in New Orleans; no issue.

    2. Georgiana F.⁶ Gholson, born 1832, married, 17th November, 1852, Col. Norman Stuart Walker, b. 1831, of Richmond, Virginia, staff officer C. S. A. Of him President Jefferson Davis, of the Confederate States, wrote the Hon. James E. Saunders, of Alabama: "Col. Norman S. Walker, after gallant service in Virginia, was selected for the very important and responsible position of Commercial Agent for the Confederate States at Bermuda. His services in that position were, in a high degree, valuable to the Confederate States, and the address with which they were performed under the embarrassment of blockade, both of the Island and of our forts, was such as fully justified his selection for the duty. His dear wife is the intimate, beloved and trusted friend of my wife and myself. I held the widow and children of Judge Thomas S. Gholson, as well as himself, in most affectionate regard." After the war Colonel Walker and family lived

awhile in Liverpool, Eng., becoming in 1865 English subjects, but now reside in New Brighton, Staten Island. Issue:

1. Cary Gholson[7], b. 1854; 2, Lillie[7]; 3, Norman Stuart[7]; 4, Georgia Gholson[7]. m. 18th January, 1891, Capt. Bruce Stuart, of English Army; 5, Randolph St. George[7]; 6, John Yates[7], b. 1870; 7, Kenneth[7], b. 1872, and one other.

3. Cary Ann[6] Gholson, lived to lovely young womanhood and died in Hastings, Eng.," where she lies buried in the most romantic spot, of that ancient churchyard," wrote her mother.

4. Pauline[6], died young.

III. ANN ELIZA[4] GHOLSON, married Dr. Richard Hill, son of Richard and Ann (Dunn) Hill, of Brunswick county, Va. They moved to Tennessee and Mississippi, had four beautiful daughters, who died upon reaching maturity. One, Ann Eliz., married 1861, Mr. Briscoe, of New Orleans, and soon died. No issue.

IV. DR. ROBERT A.[4] GHOLSON, of Petersburg, Va., married Eliz. Turner, of Southampton county, Va., and removed (1869), to Griffin, Ga., Meriwether county, where he died, leaving three sons and two daughters.

V. MARY[4] GHOLSON, witnessed probate of her mother's will in 1842; married Samuel Blount. No issue.

VI. WILLIAM T.[4] GHOLSON lawyer, of Tennessee; married Miss Hart: was killed in a duel at Hopefield, Ark., 1837, while defending some trivial remark made of a lady friend—a useless sacrifice of a useful life.

VII. MARTHA E.[4] GHOLSON, married Thomas S. Martin, of Petersburg, Va. ;. and had a daughter, born 1852, died 1862, and son Thomas S. Martin, Jr., b. 1854, engineer, removed to Sanford, Fla. His mother lived with him.

III. Thomas[4] Gholson, member of Congress. (See below.)

IV. Patsy[4] Gholson, b. ——; m. —— Hartwell.

V. Elizabeth[4] Gholson b. ——, married —— Fox.

VI. Daughter[4], died before her father wrote his will; married James Powell, and left one son, Addison Powell.

III. THOMAS[4] GHOLSON (above), third son of Thomas and Jane (Parry) Gholson, b. in Orange county, Va., 1780, died 14th July, 1816; Member Congress 1808-16. Died from effect of a wound, received while serving several years previously as volunteer aide on the staff of General Porter, war of 1812, at the time of the threatened attack of the British on Washington. He married 28th July, 1806, Ann (b. 2d May, 1787, d. Little Rock, Ark, 18th June, 1855), daughter of Col. Wm. Yates, of the Revolution, and Elizabeth (b. circa, 1760), daughter of George Booth. [Mrs. Yates married (II) Col. Miles Cary (b. 1757, d. 1808), and had issue: Hon. George Booth Cary, M. C. from Southampton county; and Charlotte Louisa Cary, who married the Hon. James Hubbard[3] Gholson (Ante)]. Issue: 1, Judge William Yates[4] Gholson, of Mississippi and Ohio; 2, Cary Ann[4] Gholson, (b. 1808, d. 1896), married her cousin, Hon. Thomas Saunders Gholson (Ante); 3, Thomas[5] Gholson, M. D. Of these:

I. WILLIAM YATES[4] GHOLSON, eldest son of Thomas and Anne (Yates) Gholson, was born in Southampton county, Virginia, December 25, 1807. He married, December 25, 1827, Ann Jane (b. November 12, 1805, d. December 20, 1831), niece of Chancellor Creed Taylor, and daughter of Samuel and Martha (Woodson) Taylor. In 1834 Judge Gholson moved to Pontotoc, Miss., where he speedily became prominent at the bar. He married secondly, May 21, 1839, Elvira, only child of Judge Daniel W. and Martha (Patrick) Wright. In 1844 he freed his slaves and removed to Cincinnati, Ohio. From 1854 to 1859 he was judge of the Superior Court of Cincinnati, and from 1859 to 1863 was a justice of the Supreme Court of Ohio. His partner at one time was Hon. James P. Holcomb, Professor of Law, University Virginia, and member of Confederate Congress. He died September 21, 1870. His wife, Elvira (Wright) Gholson, died October 19, 1885. He is said to have had few equals at the Ohio bar. (See Appleton's American Encyclopedia.) The children of William Yates and Anne Jane (Taylor) Gholson, were:

I. Samuel Creed[6] Gholson, b. at Farmville, Va., September 23, 1828. Physician residing at Holly Springs, Miss. Surgeon of Ninth Mississippi Regiment, C. S. A., and later Brigade Surgeon with Gen. James R. Chalmers' command. He m. (June 12, 1855), Mary, daughter of Dr. Samuel C. and Annie (Backus) Caruthers. Eight children were born of this union, viz. :
  1. William Yates[7], b. July 2, 1856, m. July 24, 1886, Edith Kempe, and has three children, Edith, Yates and Catherine. Lives at Aberdeen, Miss.
  2. Sam Caruthers[7], b. January 1, 1859, d. October 5, 1893. Was a physician at Holly Springs, Miss.; m., June 6, 1886, Kate W., daughter of Col. Thomas W. and Sue (Watson) Harris. Children : Harris and Winifred.
  3. Edwin[7], born May 3, 1863, practising law in Cincinnati, Ohio ("Gholson & Cabell"), m., September 24, 1890, Eleanor L., daughter of Elbridge L. and Isabella (Isham) Thomas. His wife died November 25, 1891, leaving one child, Eleanor Lawrence, b. July 26, 1891. Mr. Gholson has furnished much of the above record of the early Gholson ancestors.
  4. Arthur[7], b. March 3, 1867, m. Lizzie B. Clark, July, 1893. She died July 2, 1897, leaving two children, Mary and Sam.
  5. Cary Freeman[7], b. January 12, 1870; died, s. p., 1898.
  6. Anna Jane[7], b. January 3, 1873, m. (January, 1892), Dan. I. Howard, of Aberdeen, Miss. Three children, Dan, Mary and Cary.
  7. Norman Glasgow[7], b. September 21, 1875.
  8. Mary Virginia[7], b. September 4, 1879.
II. Anne Jane[6] Gholson, b. at Needham, near Farmville, Virginia, December 9, 1831. Married Frank T. Glasgow, of Richmond, Virginia, July 14, 1853, and died October 27, 1893. Their children were:
  1. Emily Taylor[7], b. ——.
  2. Annie Gholson[7], b. ——, m. Frank T. Clark, of Norfolk. Has one child, Josephine Glasgow Clark.
  3. Joseph Reice[7], b. ——, died at age of 16.
  4. Cary Gholson[7], b. ——, m. Geo. W. McCormack, of Charleston, South Carolina. No issue.
  5. Arthur Graham[7], b. ——, living in London, England. Unmarried.
  6. Francis Thomas[7], Jr., b. ——, lives in Richmond, Virginia.
  7. Kate Anderson[7], died in infancy.
  8. Ellen Anderson[7], b. ——. Author of "The Descendant," and "Phases of an Inferior Planet." Lives in Richmond.
  9. Rebe Gordon[7], b.——, Richmond. Issue second marriage, (Wright:)
III. Virginia Elizabeth[6], b. July 24, 1840. Died January 26, 1880. She married February 20, 1866, Edward W. Kittredge, Lawyer, of Cincinnati, Ohio. Their children are:
  1. Elvira W.[7].
  2. Anna G.[7]
  3. William G.,[7] m. Katharine Leaman.
  4. Edmund[7].
  5. Bernard S[7].

NOTE: Francis Gholson, of Virginia, went to Scott county, Kentucky, after the Revolution, and there married Mary Craig. Afterward removed to Maury county, Tennessee, and later to Hamilton county, Illinois. Fought in Revolution and Indian wars; in latter, 1794, with Colonel Washington. Company H. (Virginia Magazine History, Volume 1). His three brothers, James, John and William, all moved to Scott county, Kentucky, and thence near Nashville. Tennessee. James was Major in some of the old wars, and died at Jackson, Tennessee.

John Gholson (son of Francis) of General Jackson's Tennessee Militia; and fought in battle of the Horse-Shoe Bend, Alabama, in Indian war. (From a letter of his grandson, John G. Gholson, to Col. James E. Saunders, of Alabama, in 1899. He is author of a 'New Physics,' 'The Grammar System,' and 'The Participle.' Lives in Broughton, Hamilton county, Illinois. He added, "many Gholsons are in Kentucky and Tennessee, but he did not know their lineage.")

6. Daniel W[7].
7. Benjamin[7].
IV. William Yates Gholson, Jr., b. at Pontatoc, Mississippi, March 11, 1842. Graduated from Harvard in 1861. Commissioned Lieutenant in One Hundred and Sixth Ohio Regiment, July 16, 1862; Senior Captain, July 24; killed at Hartsville, Tennessee, December 7, 1862. Unmarried.
3. THOMAS[5] GHOLSON, M. D., b. 1810, d. 1st November, 1856. Moved to Memphis and practised there awhile. Married Kate McLemore, of Nashville, Tennessee, and removed to Mississippi, where he died, one child surviving him: Josephine[6] Gholson, married Mr. Hays, of Memphis, Tennessee.

DUNN (OF VIRGINIA).

Sir Daniel and William Dunn, members of the Virginia Company 1620, sons of Robert Dunn, citizen and draper, of London. (*Brown's Genesis of the United States.*)
Dr. Donne, Dean of St. Paul, member of London county for Virginia, 1622 (*Hotten*). George Donne, probably his son, member of the Virginia Council, 1637, and Muster Master-General of the colony. Died in office, 1642; was succeeded by John West. He visited England in 1640 in behalf of the colony, and addressed a letter to the King styled "*Virginia Reviewed.*" His father, Dr. Donne, married a daughter of Sir George Moore. (*Genesis United States.*)
Arthur Dunn, of Lancaster county, Virginia (*will 1655*). Legacy to Bertram Obert, of Middlesex county.
Joseph Dunn, 1653, witnessed *will* of Joseph Cobbs, in Isle of Wight county, Virginia.
Thomas Dunn, 1620, came to Virginia in the "Temperance," aged 74, and was in Sir George Yeardley's muster, in James City. (*Hotten.*)
Thomas Dunn, 1666, living on the north side of the Rapp. river, on a path leading from Rapp. to Pope's creek, on the Potomac river, Westmoreland county, "where is a marked oak, at the corner of Major John Ware's and Mr. Thomas Dunn's lands," mentioned in a grant to Philip Waddy, and also copied in the "*Quisenberry Family.*"
William Dunn, Westmoreland county, Virginia, 1718. Sons: Samuel and Charles, whose births are registered in *St. Stephen's Parish Register*, Northumberland county.
Peter Dunn, 1623, alive on Hogg Island, James City, after the massacre.
Clement Dunn, 1635, came in the "*Primrose*," aged 22, and was an early patentee.
John Dunn, 1635, came in the "*Bonaventure*," aged 26.
Henry Dunn, 1635, came in the "*Assurance*," aged 23. (*Hotten.*)
Mr. Henry Dunn, 1677, in Henrico county; and John Wortham testified to the vestry that he had been "drunk, on his *own* confession."
Dunns were numerous in Essex county, Virginia, which was a part of old Rapp. county, and they founded there the village of *Dunnsville*, on the Rapp. river.
Also *Dunn's Creek*, mentioned in the *Accomac patents* of 1635. (*Critic.*)
Dunn's Branch, in Surrey county, 1724, on the south side of Nottoway river. (*Land Book.*)
James Dunn, 1739, married, in Spottsylvania county, Elinor Savage. (*Marriage Licenses.*)
Mrs. Eleanor Purcell Dunn, married (II.) 1739, Rev. James Marye, in Spottsylvania.
Eleanor Dunn married Robert Green (who came to Virginia 1717, aged 22), parents of Col. John Green, b. 1730, of Culpepper, of the Sixth Virginia in the Revolution, whose son, Robert, was also in Revolution. Col. John Green had also a son, Moses Green, of Culpepper county, whose son, William Green, married Mary, *daughter* of Commander John Saunders, of Norfolk, and *granddaughter* of Capt. Ceeley Saunders, of the Revolutionary navy, ship Tartar.
Charles Dunn, born in Kentucky, 1799, and Judge of the Supreme Court.
John Dunn m., 1782, Anne Cawthorn, Middlesex county, Va.

Hannah Dunn m., 1784, Ralph Watts, Middlesex county, Va.

Elizabeth Dunn m., 1786, George Goodwin, Middlesex county, Va.
—*Christ Church Register.*

Charles Dunn, 1754, French and Indian Wars, with Colonel Washington.

Peter Dunn, Captain in Revolution (Continental line).—*Virginia Historical Magazine,* II, 246.

Waters Dunn, of Halifax militia, 1765, and Indian Wars (*Hening,* VIII, 181), and also of Henry county, in 1780.

Morris Dunn, in Sussex county, 1761.

Andrew Dunn, 1781, lands in Princess Anne county.

Andrew Dunn, 1781, lands in Prince Edward county, on Sawny's creek. (*Records.*)

Charles Dunn, b. 1640, d., York county, 1678, came to York county, 1658, as *head-right* of John Hansford, who died 1661. He married (I) Elizabeth, relict of Mr. Thomas Harwood, who died 1656. He was constable, 1661. He married (II) Temperance ——, and had an only child, Mary Dunn, to whom he left his estate, with reversion to Thomas Harwood, and remainder to Robert Calvert. John and Ann Wisdom witnessed his will, 1678. Mrs. Dunn married (II) Samuel Tiplady, d. 1702. The daughter, Mary Dunn, married Robert Shield. Dunn Shield d. 1732; son, Francis Shield, whose guardian was Robert Shield.—(*York Records.*)

Samuel Dunn, 1678, going on a visit to England, made John Hyde his attorney in Virginia.—(*York Records.*)

Pascho Dunn, justice in York county, 1682.—(*Records.*) He married, in Elizabeth City county, 1695, Hannah, widow (I) of Thomas Hinde, and (II) of John Power. Her daughter, Hannah Hinde, b. 1673, married, before 1696, Maj. Wm. Armistead, of Elizabeth City county, Justice and Burgess, *will 1715*. Major Armistead married (II) Rebecca, *will 1755*, daughter of Edward Moss, of York county, *will 1716*, who married (II), 1719, John King. Major Armistead had son, John Armistead, m. Miss Gill, of New Kent county, and in 1769 conveyed lands which descended to him by death of his brother, Hinde. Major Armistead had also son, William Armistead, *will 1727*, who had, among others, a son, Dunn Armistead.—(*Keith's Harrison Ancestry.*)

Henry Dunn, 1702, a suit in York county, Va.—(*York Records.*)

Abel Dunn, 1709, a suit, York County vs. Arthur Law, for fifth part of six messuages, six outhouses, etc., in Charles parish, which Henry Heywood, Jr., and Elizabeth, his wife, devised to the plaintiff. Abel Dunn had lands in Gloucester county, also, near Poropotank creek. He sued, in 1710, Wm. Trotter and Edward Curtis, for the fifth part of six messuages and 2000 acres in Charles parish, York county, left him by Henry and Elizabeth Heywood, for a term not yet expired. The verdict of the jury on the case was: "We found the will of *Armiger Wade,* dated 15th January, 1676, and that he died seized of the lands, and left only five daughters, viz.: Ann, Elizabeth, Dorothy, Mary, and Frances; and Henry Heywood, Jr., m. Elizabeth and, if upon the whole matter, the plaintiff hath title, we find for the plaintiff."—*York Records.* Abel Dunn leased from Thos. Chisman lands which his brother Edward Chisman, had patented, 1670, and forfeited, when he became one of Bacon's rebels, 1676. An only child, John, had died, and the widow of Edward, Lydia Chisman (née Bushrod) m., 1678, Thomas Harwood, and d. 1694; and Thos. Harwood m. (II) Elizabeth ——, and d. 1699, and his widow married John Wills. Thomas Harwood patented this land, 1699, as having lapsed from Edward Chisman, "as he had been in possession thirty-two years." Thomas Chisman, the brother, brought suit as heir in 1699, through his lawyer John Clayton. In 1711, suit was renewed—John Broadnax, lawyer for Thomas Chisman, and Robert Hyde, lawyer, for John Wills and wife, Elizabeth. John Drewry, Sr., was witness for Dunn, in whose favor the suit was decided. Florence MaCartie was one of the jury to decide the case.

1749—Abel Dunn, his land on Poropotank, next to Humphrey McKendree, surveyed, and in 1750 a survey of land between his lands and those of Richard Longest.

1738—Abraham Dunn " deceased, without a will," and William Dunn qualified on his estate, with James Barber and John Timson securities (*York Records*).
1744—Nathaniel Dunn, plaintiff, vs. William Keith (*York Records*).
1735—James Dunn vs. Thomas Hodges (*York Records*).
1737—William Dunn, in York county.

John Dunn, in North Carolina, 1713 (*Colonial Records. Vol. II, 84*).
John Dunn (1754), Judge of the General Court (*V 153*).
John Dunn (1755), clerk of Rowan county, N. C., and Justice 1757–64 (*V 8.28*), met the Regulators, with other citizens, to redress their grievances, 1771.
John Dunn (1762). Assembly from Anson county (*VI 801*).
John Dunn (1769), of Saulsbury Town, Rowan county, on the Com. of Public Claims, in the Assembly, and of the Vestry of Saulsbury, 1770—was a Tory—and remonstrated (1775) with the Committee of Safety—was afterward banished to South Carolina by them, but later permitted to return.
Robert Dunn, 1754, in Bladen county, N. C. (*VII 7.*)
Bartholomew Dunn, 1768, signed petition, with others, against fees (*VII 736.*)
William Dunn, a Regulator, 1771, released from prison. (*Ibid. 522.*)
Simon Dunn, Jr., Regulator, 1771, exempted from pardon by the Governor's proclamation. (*Ibid. 613.*)

The baptismal name of Drewry, or Drury, has been quite popular in families of Dunn. Sir Drew Drewry or Drury, and Sir Robert Drury were both of the Virginia Company, 1609, and the latter, member of the Council for the Virginia Company, 1609. He was also a patron of the celebrated Mr. John Donne, to whom he gave apartments in his own house in Drury Lane, and with whom he traveled on the continent for three years, 1611. His heirs were Sir Henry Drury, and his sisters. *Brown's Genesis of United States.*

DUNN FAMILY, OF SURRY, SUSSEX AND BRUNSWICK COUNTIES, VIRGINIA.

Thomas[1] *Dunn*, b. 1679, d. 1772 (probably son of Thomas Dunn who, in 1666, was living in Westmoreland county Va.), patented lands in Surry county in 1727. Thomas Dunn, Jr., in 1741, owned 350 acres on the "South side of Nottoway river, and North side of Guilliam's Branch." Surry county was formed in 1652 from James City county, and from Surry, was taken Sussex, in 1753, in which county Dunns were living before 1740.

Through these counties the Dunns were scattered, and much data of them is given in the old "*Albemarle Parish Register,*" of Surry and Sussex counties. This old Register contains also the appointments of the Rev. William Willie, at St. Pauls, St. Marks and St. Andrews churches, which last is in Brunswick county, and at their dependent chapels. The quaint chirography of the old parson reveals the births and deaths of many of the name of Dunn. "Thomas, Sr., and Jr., David, Gray, Drury, John, *two* Williams (contemporaneous), Lewis, Nathaniel and Henry, their wives and children." Our genealogy deals, more especially, with the descendants of *David Dunn*, son of Thomas, though all contained in the old *Register* are entered below. It is assumed from their propinquity, and the, similarity of family names, that Thomas was the common ancestor and the two Williams were probably uncle and nephew.

Thomas Dunn, Sr., was aged 93 when he died in 1772, as certified to by *Lewis Dunn*, in the old *Register.* His wife, Elizabeth, died in 1767, as certified by *William Dunn.* It is thought her *family name* was *Gray,** as son and grandsons have borne it, in regular descent, to the present day. Issue:

---

* *Gray Arms* of the Carse-Gray family, county Forfar, descended from Andrew Gray, a younger son of Lord Gray's family. *Gu.*—a lion rampant within a bordure wavy arg. *Crest*—An anchor seaways fastened to a cable, ppr. *Motto—Anchor fast.*

I. Gray Dunn. No other record of him than that of god-father, in 1768, to an infant.

II John ³ Dunn, married Lucy ——. Issue:
1, Isabella, b. 1740, 2, Lucy b. 1743, *God-parents:* William and Ann Dunn,,and Elizabeth Hancock. 3, Drury, b. 1746, *God-father: David Dunn.* 4, William, 1761, *God father: Thomas Dunn.*
  John Dunn recorded birth of slaves in 1763.
  In 1792 William Dunn, of Sussex, and wife Jean, born, a daughter, Mary.

III. Thomas² Dunn, "Jr.," d. 1773. Lands in Sussex county entered in 1764, " *on South side of Nottoway river by 'Tnomas Dunn, Jr.'* " Married Lucy ——. Issue:
1, Gray, b. 1744. 2, Ruth, 1747. 3, Lavinia, 1749, *God-mother:* Mary Dunn. 4, Dorothy, 1751, *God-mother:* Mary Dunn. 5, Allen, b. 1758, *God-mother:* Lucy Dunn. 6, Henry, 1768, *God-mother:* Lavinia Dunn.
  Thomas Dunn, "Jr.," 1743, with Henry Thornton and Elizabeth Shelton, was *God-father* to a Pritchard infant, and, in 1744, to a daughter of John Jones
  In 1763 Ruth and Mary Dunn were God-mothers to Elizabeth Webb, and Mary Dunn *God-parent,* with Burwell Gilliam, 1747, to Ann, daughter of Ralph McGee.

IV. Drury² Dunn,‡ 1740, *God-father* to an infant.

V. Lewis² Dunn, God-father, 1763, to child of Charles Gilliam and to others. *Hening's Statutes of Virginia,* X, 211, records, in 1799, Lewis Dunn of Sussex, emancipating a slave. With John and Thomas Dunn, in 1760, he had slaves christened. Lewis Dunn, of Warwick county, student, 1811, at William and Mary College.

VI. Henry³ Dunn, in 1762, God-father, with George Rives, to Epes Young. Henry Dunn had lands in Frederick county in 1778.

VII. Nathaniel³ Dunn, d. 1749, m. Mary ——, who d. 1749. Issue:
1. Nathaniel³ Dunn, married Rebecca ——. Issue: 1, Henry, b. 1770. 2, Frances, b. 1772. *God-parents:* John Petway, and Rebecca and Sarah Parham. Rebecca Dunn

---

Thomas¹ Gray was an ancient planter of the time of Sir Thomas Dale, 1616, when 100 acres was due him in James City county, 50 for the personal adventure of Annis Gray, his first wife, and 50 for his " now wife," 1635, Rebecca, and 350 for his two sons, William and Thomas, and five servants. His lands were on Gray's creek, in the present Surry county. He had patents also in 1689-42. Issue: William², Thomas², died s.p. before 1677, and Frances² and John³. Francis was Justice and Burgess of Charles City county, now Prince George, 1666. His patents, 1652, for 760 acres.—*Virginia Magazine of History, V, 130.* Thomas² Gray, 800 acres in Surry, 1654; John² Gray, 800 acres, 1678, William² Gray, 800 acres, 1680.—*Land Book.*

William² Gray, of Lawnes Creek Parish, Surry, (will, p. 1719), Justice and Burgess 1718; wife Elizabeth. Issue: William³, Gilbert³, Mary³, Priscilla³, and Judith³ Ruffin. The son William had sons William⁴, Robert⁴, Joseph⁴ and Thomas⁴, in 1719.

Gilbert³ Gray's will, 1758, p. 1764; wife, Margaret. Issue: Joseph⁴, James⁴, John⁴, Sarah⁴, Mary⁴, Lucy⁴ and Elis⁴. Marricott.—*Hening's Statutes, V, 369.*

William³ Gray (will, p. in Surry 1788.) Issue: William⁴, Robert⁴, Joseph⁴, Thomas⁴, Edmond⁴, James⁴ and Lucy⁴ Briggs. He was Burgess 1726-36.

William³ Gray, Burgess in Surry 1744. Col. Joseph Gray, Burgess for Southampton county 1744-61, was his son, and he was believed to be father of Col. Edwin Gray, Burgess 1769-1774; Member convention 1774; State Senate and Congress 1799-1813.—*Virginia Magazine of History, III, 403*

William Gray and others in 1747 had a grant of 5000 acres in Lunenburg county, and by 1748, 30,000 acres in Augusta county.—*Ibid.. V, 176.*

William Gray of Surry married, 1738, Mrs. Ellis. Chamberlain, of New Kent county, widow of William Chamberlain.—*Virginia Gazette.*

Edmond Gray, 1743, a grant, with his brother-in-law, George Carrington, 6000 acres in Amherst county. He married a daughter of Maj. William Mayo, and was Justice 1747. Made a deed to William Gray, of New Kent, 1749.

Rev. John Dunn, 1790, minister of Manchester parish, Chesterfield county, Virginia. He married the daughter of Rev. James Marye, the Huguenot.

‡Drury Dunn's estate sale, 1771, " at his plantation where he lately lived. on Monk's Neck creek, Dinwiddie county, seven miles from Petersburg," fifty-eight slaves, horses and stock. Administrators were William and Henrietta Dunn.—*Virginia Gazette,* 1771.

John Dunn, 1779, Tobacco Inspector at Bowler's warehouse.

§Lewis Burwell, son of Thomas and Lucy Dunn, born 1792.—*Bristol Parish Register.*
William Dunn, of Sussex, m. Jane ——, and had Mary, b. 1792.—*Ibid.*

was God-mother, 1772, to child of Henry and Frances Gee. Nathaniel Dunn represented Sussex county in 1788, with John A. Briggs. In 1771 he recorded christening of slaves.

VIII. William³ Dunn m. Mary ———. Issue:
1, Ambrose, b. 1742; *God-father*, John Dunn. 2, Lewis, 1754; *God-fathers*, William Bird and Thomas Hobbs.
In 1761, William Dunn was God-father, with Sarah and Judith Rives, God-mothers, to Tabitha Mitchell.
In 1757 he was God-father to Nathaniel Mason.
Another William Dunn m. 14th July, 1740, Amy ———, who died of quinsy, 1773. Her physician testified to her great suffering. Issue:
1, Amy, m. Jo. Chambliss, and d. 1772. 2, Elizabeth, b. 1744. 3, William, b. 1750. 4, Drury, b. 1752 and d. 1772, "a most promising youth." 5, Lewis, 1754. 6, Thomas, 1755. 7, Mary, 1758. 8, David, 1760. 9, Thomas, 1763. God-parents: Nathaniel Jones and Ann Hamilton.
William and Amy Dunn, God-parents, 1744, to William, son of Henry and Elizabeth Gee.
William and Elizabeth Dunn, God-parents, 1760, to Mary Bellamy.
William Dunn, Jr., and J. Wyche certified to the death of William Anderson in 1773.

IX. DAVID² DUNN, m., 1746, Frances ———. He was ancestor of Major David and Dr. Dudley Dunn of Tennessee, the Elliott family, of Clarksville, Tenn., DuBose of Memphis, Foster of Nashville, Clay, Bradford and Billups of Mississippi, and Colonel James E. Saunders of Alabama, and others. His wife's *family name* is unfortunately not preserved; neither is it *certain* he was brother to other than Thomas, Gray, William and John Dunn. The others may have been cousins. The birth of only two children is recorded in the old *Albemarle Parish Register*: 1, Ishmael³. 2, Elizabeth³. Of these:
ELIZABETH³, was born 1751. *God-parents:* Edward Epes, Mary Moss and Mary Tomlin. Nothing more is known of her. The son,
ISHMAEL³ DUNN, of Brunswick county, Virginia, b. January 13, and christened March 12, 1748-9, O. S., d. near Town Creek, Lawrence county, Alabama, 1828. His God-parents were William Bird, and Peter and Rebecca Hawthorne. He m., 1772 Mildred Dudley,* of Virginia. They removed when quite aged to Alabama, to live near their children, Dr. Dudley Dunn, and Mrs. Turner Saunders, carrying with them the young orphans of their son, Gray Dunn. They are buried one-half mile north of the little village of Town Creek, on the Tennessee river road. This spot is marked only by a cedar thicket, in a field near the road. (Mrs. Dunn, it is said, had a sister married to Mr. House† of Virginia and they removed to Tennessee.) Issue:
1, David⁴; 2, Dudley⁴; 3, Anne⁴; 4, Frances⁴, and 5, Gray⁴, as follows:
1. MAJOR DAVID⁴ DUNN, of Memphis, Tenn.; born Brunswick county, Va., 1773; died, Memphis, 183—. His first wife died in Brunswick county, Va.; name unknown. He married (II) in Davidson county, Tenn., Mrs. John Deadrick, and married (III) Mrs. Hawkins. He removed to Franklin, Tenn., near his brother-in-law, Rev. Turner Saunders, in 1808. He represented Davidson county in Legislature. Later he removed to

---

*Daughter, probably, of William Dudley, since her grandson bore that name. (See *Dudley Family*.)
One Thomas Dunn married Barbara, daughter of John Bransford, Sr., of Chesterfield county, Va., the immigrant, who came to Richmond City, Va., 1743, and was afterward planter in Chesterfield county, with sons: John and Charles Bransford, and daughters; Ellis., married Francis West; Mary, married, Dr. Lewis Warwick. John² Bransford's daughter, Sarah, married James Agee, and son, James, married Celia Agee.—*American Ancestry, V, 11.*
†Laurence House, lands in Surry county, Meherin river, 1727.
Laurence House, lands in Sussex, 1787.
Laurence House, of Brunswick county, 1775.

Shelby county, Tenn., four miles from Memphis, where he died quite wealthy and full of honors. Issue by his first marriage, only one child (none by the others).

Elizabeth Garland Dunn[4] married John T. Deadrick, son of Mrs. Dunn, her step-mother. Issue:

1. Michael David[5] Deadrick married Jane Park. Issue: 1. Don[7], died young; 2. Jennie[7]; 3, John[7], died young; 4. Garland[7]; 5. Joseph[7]; 6. Park[7]; 7. Anna[7].

2. William Pitt[5] Deadrick, married (I) Rachel Hayes. Issue: Samuel[7], who died young. He married (II) Mattie Park. Issue: 1. Birdie[7], 2. Elise[7], 3 Anna Mai[7].

3. Newton D.[5] Deadrick married Miss Magget. Issue: 1. John[7], married Miss Wilson ; 2. Mary[7], married Mr. Wilson, and had 2 children. 4. Michael[7], died at twenty. 5. Nannie[7].

4. Mary Elizabeth[5] Deadrick, died, 1898 ; married John H. Speed,[*] of Memphis, Tenn., who died 1873, merchant of the firm of "*Speed & Strange,*" and son of Robert Speed, of Henderson, Ky. During the Civil War he established the Confederate Government Works, at Macon, Ga. (Major Strange, his partner, was on Gen. N. B. Forrest's staff, 1862.) Mrs. Speed had great dignity and elegance, a noble example of the superior breeding of the women of the "*Old South.*" She died calmly, and suddenly, while conversing with her daughter. Issue:

1. Robert D.[7] Speed, of Dallas, Texas, married Waldine Putnam, and had Julian H[8], and Robert D[8]. Speed.

2. Aline[7], married Carneal Warfield, of Greenville, Miss., and had Mary S[8], and Carneal Warfield.

3. Lida D.[7]; 4. Belle[7]; 5. John Strange[7] Speed; 6. Mary[7]; married John S. Brown, of St. Louis, and had: 1. John[8], killed when nine years old, on a bicycle; 2. Garland[8]; 3. Aline[8]; 4. Speed[8], and 5. Bertram[8] Brown.

II. DR. DUDLEY[4] DUNN, of Memphis, Tenn., b. Brunswick county, Va., 6th May, 1780 ; died, Memphis, Tenn., February, 1848. He married (I) daughter of Jeffry Early, of Lexington, Ga.; cousin to Gov. Peter Early. He married (II) 11th December, 1814, Elizabeth W. Cox, of Lexington, Ga., b. 27th September, 1790, d. 1st September, 1831, daughter of Bartley and Susan Cox. *(See Cox and Billups' Note.)* He married (III) 1833, Mrs. Perkins, of Memphis, Tenn. He first practised his profession in Lexington, Ga. In 1822 he removed to Lawrence county, Ala., on an adjoining plantation to his brother-in-law, Rev. Turner Saunders. After the death of his aged parents, 1828 (whom he had located near him,) he made Memphis, Tenn., his home. He owned what is *now Estival Park,* buying large tracts of land which, in time, made him quite wealthy. Weighing between two and three hundred pounds, fair complexion, red hair, tall and commanding, witty, and most hospitable, his influence was wide; and many are the humorous sayings handed down by his friends and kindred. "Aunt Betsy," his wife, was ever the friend of the distressed and needy, and always urging him to that activity which his great weight discouraged, especially toward the latter part of his life. Issue by *Cox marriage:* 1, Susan Ann[5]; 2, Camilla Frances[5]; 3, William Dudley[5], and (by *Perkins marriage*) 4, David[5] Dunn, as follows:

1. Susan Ann[5] Dunn, b. 2d October, 1815, died 3d July, 1846; m. 21st March, 1832, Lafayette Jones, b. 7th October, 1806, of Big Creek, Tenn. Issue: 1. Elizabeth Ann[6], b. 25th February, 1833; 2. Chamberlayne[6] Jones, of Memphis, Tenn., married Miss Arthur, and had several children.

---

[*] Descended from the historian John Speed, of England, b. 1552, reign Henry III. His grandson James[2], son of John[1], came to Surry county, Va. 1695, Southwark parish, and died 1719. He there married, 1711, Mary Pulley. Their second son John[4], b. 1714, d. 1782, m., 1737, Mary Mistry and had seven sons and four daughters; of whom, Joseph, b. 1750. lived in Mecklenburg county, and was a member of Virginia Convention 1776, and of his parish vestry. He married Ann Bignall, of North Carolina, 1782. His third son, Robert, b. 1787, married (I) Mary Coleman, and (2) Isabella Towns, and removed to Kentucky after 1800. John H. Speed, of Memphis, was son of the second marriage. John S. Speed, of Memphis, is also of this line, as was James Speed, President Lincoln's Attorney General of the Cabinet.—*Speed Family,* by Thomas Speed.

2. **Camilla Frances⁴ Dunn**, b. 1st June, 1817, married 19th November, 1833, Dr. Alfred Bishop Capels DuBose, of South Carolina and Memphis, b. 20th May, 1804. Her beauty was of the handsome and stately order, with broad smooth brows; she was greatly admired for many fine traits. Issue:

    1. Dudley McIvor⁵ DuBose, b. 28th October, 1834, d. 1888; m., 15th April, 1858, Sarah, only child of Robert Toombs, of Georgia; General, Senator and great orator. Gen. DuBose was, first, on General Toombs' staff, then a Colonel; wounded at Chickamauga; promoted for gallantry at Malvern Hill, and finally Brigadier General in Longstreet's corps. Issue:

        1. Rev. Robert Toombs⁶ DuBose. M. E. Church, m.; several children.
        2. Camilla⁶ DuBose, m. Dr. DuBose, her cousin.
        3. Julie⁶ DuBose, m. a lawyer in Georgia (?)
        4. Judge Dudley⁶ DuBose, Member Congress from Georgia, and Judge in Montana; married, with several children.

    2. Elizabeth Rebecca⁵ DuBose, b. 7th January, 1836, married George Bayne. Issue:
    • 1. George; 2 Catherine, teaching in Staunton Institute, Va.; 3 Bessie, died young.
    3. Alfred⁵ DuBose, born 1838, twin with Sarah, died young.
    4. Pauline Sarah⁵ DuBose. b. 1838, d. 1865, m. Oswald Pope. Issue:
        1 Anna Stevens Pope m. Mr. Nail, of Arkansas. She was born October 17, 1861.
        2. Camilla Sarah Pope, born September 15, 1863, m. Edward, son of Judge William Smith, of Memphis (and formerly Brownsville, Tenn.), and has several children.
    5. Judge Julius Jesse⁵ DuBose, of Memphis, Tenn., b. 13th December, 1839. Lieutenant in Ninth Arkansas Regiment, C. S. A., also Captain of Ordnance and Chief Inspector of Indian Territory; married 29th November, 1870, Mary Murfree Polk, daughter of George W. Polk and Sallie Leah Hilliard, niece of Bishop, (and General,) Polk, andcousin to President Polk. Issue: 1. Tasker Polk⁶, b. 4th January, 1873; 2. Mary Hilliard⁶, b. 26th December, 1876; 3. Alfred Bishop Capels⁶, b. 20th September, 1878; 4. Jessie⁶ McIvor; 5. Sarah Camilla⁶; 6. George Polk⁶; 7. Julius Jesse⁶, Jr.
    6. Amanda Catherine⁵ DuBose, b. 22d April, 1841, m. Gov. Robert Anderson, Lieutenant Governor of California, and son of Nathaniel Anderson, of Memphis, Tenn. (an old resident). No issue.
    7. Harriet Frances⁵ DuBose, b. 17th October, 1842, m. Commodore Hunter, of United States Navy. No issue.
    8. Thomas Carlton⁵ DuBose, b. 16th August, 1844, d. 16th April, 1845;
    9. John Samuel⁵ DuBose, b. 26th June, 1846, d. 25th October, 1846.
    10. Susan Ann⁵ DuBose, b. 25th October, 1847.
    11. Myrtice Mildred⁵ DuBose, b. 7th November, 1849, m. Dr. William DuBose, of Florida, her cousin, and had, 1. Dudley⁶; 2. Eugene⁶, of Alabama, and others.
    12. Camilla⁵ Du Bose, b. 17th of July, 1851.
    13. Swepson Billups⁵ Du Bose, died twenty-four years old.

3. **William Dudley⁴ Dunn**, b. 15th May, 1824, d.1866; married 6th August, 1846, Annie Henry Neal, of Pulaski, Tenn., niece of Col. Thomas Martin, of Pulaski, and cousin of the first Mrs. Enoch Ensley, and of Mrs. Senator Spofford, of Louisiana. They re-

---

* NOTE.—RICHARD HILL, 1000 acres in Accomac county, Va., 1664, "*Hill Farm*." Richard Hill, Jr., 650 acres the same year. Richard Hill married Tabitha Scarsbrough Smart, granddaughter of Lt. Col. Edmund Scarsbrough. Her mother, the widow of Col. William Smart, married (II) Col. Edward Hill, of "*Shirley*," son of Edward Hill, Burgess, 1644, Charles City.
John Hill, 1663, sheriff of James river, Norfolk county (*Hening*).
Richard Hill, 1663, commissioner to the Indian King of Potomac (*Hening*).
Maj. Nicholas Hill, 1666, Burgess for Isle of Wight county (*Ibid.*).
William Hill, deceased, 1686, of Surry county.
Edward, John and Frances Hill, in Amelia county, 1735, 1737-42, and Wm. Hill, 1748.
Richard Hill, 1739, two acres on south side Blackwater Swamp, next his old land, Surry county.
John Hill, 1745, 378 acres south side Nottoway river, Surry county.

moved to Arkansas, where he died, the result of an accident with a mowing machine on his plantation. Issue:

1. Neal[4] Dunn, of Arkansas, unm.; 2 Willie[4] Dunn, of Memphis, m. Miss Mosby.
3. Gray[4] Dunn m. Miss Cooper, and 4 Daughter[4] m. Dr. Porter, of Memphis, and had Edward Porter[5], and others.
4. David[4] Dunn, b. 1836, m. 1858. 5 Annie, sister of Dr. William Nichol, of Nashville, Tenn. An only child, Pauline Dunn, m. Eugene Lewis, of Nashville, Tenn., who was Director-General of the Nashville Exposition, 1897. They have several children. (All of above from *Dr. Dudley Dunn's Family Bible*, now in possession of Judge DuBose, of Memphis, Tenn.)

III. ANNE[4] DUNN, born Brunswick county, Va., 1777; died, Vicksburg, Miss., 1863, at the home of her son, Dr. Herbert Hill; married *circa*, 1798, Richard Hill,[*] of Virginia. Several of his brothers, it is said, went to Georgia. Their children went to Tennessee and Mississippi, and after her husband's death in Virginia, she resided with them, first in Shelby county, Tenn., and later, 1833, in Vicksburg, Miss.; often visiting her brothers in Memphis, where she was known and loved, by her nephews and nieces, as "Aunt Hill." "A splendid woman, of great managerial capacity," comments her nephew, Hon. James E. Saunders. She made the match of her brother, the Dr., to Mrs. Perkins, much to her satisfaction. Issue: 1. Anne[5]; 2. Minerva G[5]; 3. Alfred[5]; 4. Richard[5]; 5. Harriet[5]; 6. Frances Elizabeth[5]; and 7. Herbert[5] Hill, as follows:

1. Annie[5] Hill, born about 1802; married (1) Mr. Jackson, and had one son, Dr. David Jackson, deceased. She married (2) Dr. Halsey, of Greenville, Miss. The only living *issue* of first marriage (none by the second) was Laura[6]Jackson, now Mrs. Russell, of Vicksburg; she has several children.

2. Minerva G.[5] Hill, born about 1804; died, 1878; married (1) Robert Elliott, son of John Elliott, of Brunswick county, Va., whose parents were Thomas and Winifred (Saunders) Elliott, of Lancaster county, Va. (See *Saunders Family*.) She married (2) Judge Mills, of Holly Springs and New Orleans (second wife). Issue, only by second marriage:

     1. David[6] Mills never married, died, with his aged mother, in yellow fever epidemic, 1878.
     2. Andrew[6] Mills, of Galveston, Texas, married Lucy, daughter of Judge Ballinger, of Galveston. Issue: One son, Ballinger[7].

3. Alfred[5] Hill, of Shelby county, Tenn., and Mississippi, born about 1806, married Eliza Maclin, of Brunswick county, Va. Issue:

     1. Henry[6] Hill, died 1865.
     2. Thomas[6] Hill, killed by lightning, 1866, in Mississippi. Married (1) ——, and *his* eldest daughter married her cousin, Henry Maclin, of Petersburg, Va. He married (II) his cousin, Mollie Maclin, of Virginia.
     3. William[6] Hill died 1863. His widow lives in Mississippi (and married again 1866); several children.

Moses Hill, 1757, 340 acres south side Nottoway river. Surry county.
Richard Hill, 1755, lands in Surry.
Herbert Hill, 1787, in Sussex county (once Surry), when his lands joined Richard and Henry Cook. (*Records*.)
The widow of Capt. Thomas Hill, m., 1661. Col. Thomas Bushrod, b. 1604. He was fifty-seven years of age.—(*York Records*.)
Thomas Hill, *will* 1711, York-Hampton parishes. York county; wife, Mary; left son, John Hill, his plantation called " *Essex Lodge*," 900 acres; daughters, Eliz:, Lucy, Mary and Ann Hill.—(*York Records*.)
Saml. Hill, in York, 1712, in which year he died. His wife, Martha, then got license to "keep an ordinary in her house." Children: Mathew, Samuel and Lydia Hill—(*York Records*.)
Thomas Hill, major in Virginia Continental line in revolution.
Baylor Hill, captain in Virginia Continental line in revolution.
Michael Hill, 1670, Charles City county.—(*Land Book*.)

4. Richard[4] Hill, b. 1808, m. Anne Eliza, daughter of Major William and Mary (Saunders) Gholson, of Brunswick county, Virginia. (See *Saunders Family*.) Issue: Four most beautiful daughters, all dying young. One, Ann Eliza, m., 1851, Mr. Briscoe, of New Orleans.

5. Harriet[4] Hill, b. 1810, m. Mr. Edmonds; no issue.

6. Frances Elizabeth[4] Hill, b. Brunswick county, Virginia, 1st December, 1812, d. Christian county, Kentucky, 11th March, 1896, m. 14th August, 1832, in West Tennessee, William Henry Elliott, of Clarksville, Tennessee, son of John Elliott, of Brunswick county (above), whose mother was Winifred Saunders, of the Saunders family, into which Frances, daughter of Ishmael Dunn, had married; (see *Saunders Family*.) William Henry was the youngest of fourteen children. b. Brunswick county, Virginia, 13th May, 1805, d. 2d January, 1895, at New Providence, Tennessee. His mother was Mildred Maclin,* of Virginia. (*See Elliott Note.*) This aged couple lived in Clarksville, Tennessee, greatly beloved by all who knew them. Issue: ten children, of whom six lived to adult age,

    1. Thomas Herbert[5] Elliott, b. Warren county, Miss., August, 1834, m. April, 1855, Elizabeth Maria Tuck, of Lafayette, Kentucky. Issue:
        1. Quintius[6] Atkinson, b. 1856, m. Emma Cooper. No issue.
        2. William Davis[6], b. 4th July, 1861, m., 1889, Carrie Jones. Issue: Thomas Herbert[7], b. 1892; and William Davis[7], b. 1893. 3. Pauline[6], b. 1865, m. Brice Martin, of New York.

    2. William Alfred[5] Elliott, Capt. C. S. A., b. 21st June, 1840, in Montgomery county, Tennessee, d. Nashville, November, 1881, m., 1878, Lizzie Cooley. He was Captain in 1st Kentucky Regiment, General Helm. Brave and gallant soldier, and of handsome and most noble form. Issue: a daughter, Willie Frances[6], b. 1880.

    3. Joseph Sturdivant[5] Elliott, b. 18th February, 1844, unmarried; lives in New York.

    4. Harriet Edmonds[5] Elliott, b. 8th May, 1846, in Montgomery county, Tennessee, m., 12th December, 1867, W. Francis Buckner. (Mrs. Buckner has furnished much of the above information of her family.) Issue:
        1. Elliott[6], b. 1872, m. 17th November, 1891, Maud Drone; 2. Gordon W.[6], b. 1874; 3. Annie Wooldridge[6], b. 1878; 4. Lewis[6], b. 1884; 5. Mildred[6], 1887.

---

*WM. MACLIN, 1723, 500 acres in Surry county. William and John Maclin came from Scotland; and William, in 1736, had large grants in Brunswick county, Va.; surveyor, 1733; sheriff, 1738; justice, 1732–46; Captain of Foot, 1731 Vestry, St. Andrew's Parish, will probated Brunswick county, 1752; Executor, son James[2]; securities, John Maclin and Sampson Lanier. Children: James[2], William[2], John[2], Ann[2] (married to Lanier); Judith[2], married McKnight, and grandson, Thomas[2] Lanier.
    John[2] Maclin. vestry St. Andrews. lieutenant, captain, major and colonel in militia, 1748–74; will probated 1774. Children: Frederick[3]. Thomas[3], John[3], William[3], Amy[3], Eliz.[3], Rebecca[3], Susannah[3] Executors "Frederick and Thomas Maclin, gentlemen;" William[3] Maclin, Jr., married 1754 Sally, daughter of James Clack, in Brunswick county: Colonel Frederick[3] Maclin. married Lucy Rollins of Brunswick county: Vestry St. Andrews; Justice, County Lieutenant. Burgess. 1767–69; member Virginia Convention, 1775; will probated, Brunswick county, December 26, 1808. Children mentioned: James[4], Frederick[4], Nathaniel[4]. Patsy[4] (wife of Joseph Saunders, see Saunders Family), Lucy[4], married John Lewis; Amy[4], married Mr. Clack; Eliz[4]., married. 1788, John Hardaway. Executors: Joseph Saunders and John Hardaway. John Lewis was grandson of John Taylor, who was President Madison's maternal great-grandfather. Robt. H. Hardaway, of Newnan, Ga., a great-grandson of Frederick Maclin. Eliz.[3], sister of Frederick[3] Maclin, married James Maclin, of Greenville county, who died 1794, and had eight children. Her daughter, Susan, widow of Lundie. married (II). 1810. Col. Jesse Read (war 1812), and had five children. Their daughter, Ann Eliz.[3] Read. married (I) Rd. Lewis Starke, and had one daughter, Dionysia; she m. (II) Ebenezer Davis McKinley, cousin to President Wm. McKinley.—(*Miss Jennie McKinley, William and Mary Quarterly, VII, 109.*)
    Leah Maclin m.. 1775, James Wyche; Rebecca Maclin m., 1755, Matthew Parham; Ann Maclin, daughter of John Maclin, m.. 1772, Thomas Clements; Col. John Maclin m., 1773, Anne Cryer; James Maclin m., 1781, Lucy Jones; Joseph Maclin m., 1796, Nancy. daughter of David Walker; Augustus W. Maclin m.. 1799, Patty Jones; John D. Maclin m., 1806, Charlotte Edmonds.—(*Brunswick County Marriage Bonds.*)

5. **Mary Frances[6] Elliott**, b. 16th July, 1848, m. 27th February, 1868, John W. Barker. Issue:
   1. Mary Louise[7], b. 1869, m., 4th October, 1889, George Hendricks, of Waco, Texas; 2. John W.[7], b. 1871; 3. William Elliott[7], 1873; 4. Trump Wray[7], 1875; 5. Joseph Lewis[7], 1877; 6. Kate[7], 1879; 7. Roy[7], 1882; 8. Margarette[7], 1887.
6. **Mildred Lewis[6] Elliott**, b. 6th July, 1850, d. February, 1897, m. (I) 1868, Stephen Pettus, of New York and Tennessee; m. (II) 1891, Dr. John W. Ross, of the U. S. Navy. She was bright, beautiful and very lovable, a witty writer and fond of family genealogy, and of the fact that she bore the sweet old name of a grandmother on either side: Mildred Dudley and Mildred Maclin. Her varied life, of much happiness and some sorrows, closed at her fine old residence in Clarksville, Tennessee. No issue.
7. **Elizabeth Douglas[6] Elliott**, b. 20th December, 1854; m., 1875, Edward Howard Pettus, of Tennessee, brother of Stephen Pettus, above. Issue:
   1. Howard Douglass[7], b. 1875.
8. **Robert Dudley[6] Elliott**, b. 1852, d. 1858.

7. **Dr. Herbert[5] Hill**, of Vicksburg, b. Brunswick county, Va., *circa*, 1814, m. Sarah Jones (Widow Johnson). Issue:
   1. Dr. Carter[6] Hill, m. his cousin, Robert Elliott's only daughter, who, after his death married a second time.
   2. Ann[6], m. ———.
   3. A daughter[6], m. ———.
   4. A daughter[6], m. ———. These unknown.

IV. **Frances[4] Dunn**, b. Brunswick county, Va., January 24, 1779, d. Lawrence county, Ala., 1824; m., 24th July, 1799, in Brunswick county, Va., Rev. Turner Saunders, b. 1782, son of Thomas and Ann (Turner) Saunders, of Lancaster and Brunswick counties. Issue, ten children:
1. Thomas[5], b. 1800, died young.
2. Sophia Dunn, 1802, m. Col. Parish.
3. Louisa Turner[5], 1803, m. Col. Robert C. Foster, of Nashville.
4. Narcissa Hubbard[5], b. 1804, m. James Hubbard Foster.
5. James Edmonds[5], 1806, m. Mary Frances Watkins, Lawrence county, Ala.
6. Frances Anne[5], 1809, m. (I) Matthew Clay, Alabama; (II) Jacob Swoope, Alabama, and (III) Col. Thomas C. Billups, of Columbus, Miss.
7. Martha Maria[5], b. 1811, m. Gen. Benjamin Bradford, of Mississippi.
8. Franklin[5], died young.
9. Eliza Jane[5], b. 1814, m. Mr. William Hancock, of Galveston, Texas.
10. William Hubbard[5], b. 1816, m. Susan Goodwin, of Alabama. (See *"Saunders Family"* for the descendants of the above.)

V. **Gray F.[4] Dunn**, b. Brunswick county, Va., 1782, d. *circa* 1823; m. ———, and after his death his three infant children removed with their grandparents, Ishmael and Mildred Dunn, to Alabama. Issue:
1. Dudley[5] Dunn, died in Alabama when a child, from accident while playing near a cotton-gin.
2. Mary[5] Dunn, m. George W. Smith, lawyer, of Lebanon, Tenn., who died 1864, and had Effie and Frances Smith. both married in Lebanon, Tenn., also a son, Roy Smith.
3. Frances[5] Dunn, married a Mr. Epps, of Virginia.

DUDLEY FAMILY NOTES (OF VIRGINIA, AND THE SOUTH).

Edward[1] Dudley (1651) witnessed a deed in York county, Va. He was of Lancaster county (which then included Middlesex county), and is considered progenitor of most of the name in Virginia and the South. His tithes were rated in Lancaster, 1654, and in that year the Rev. Thomas Sax, of Lancaster county, in his *will*, left a legacy to

"Robert[2], second son of Edward Dudley." His sons, William[3] and Richard[3], were seated in Middlesex and Gloucester counties, with their children, before 1660; and their descendants rapidly spread through King and Queen, New Kent, Warwick, Spotsylvania, North Carolina, Kentucky, and then later, the far South. In 1680, a Rev. Charles Dudley was minister in Farnham and Cittingbourne parishes, Rapp. county. Elisabeth Robinson (widow) a deed, in York county (1660), from Thomas Bootes, for two cows, for the benefit of her two children, Elizabeth and *Robert* Dudley (*York Records*). Richard Dudley, of Elizabeth City county (1646), was fined, with Capt. Christopher Colthorpe, Francis Ceeley, James Harris, Richard Wells, John Hartwell, William Sawyer and Hugh Dowdy, 200 pounds tobacco each, for not rendering their accounts, as *guardians*, to the York court. "This suggests," says Mr. Tyler (in *William and Mary Quarterly, I.*), "that they may have married widows."

1. RICHARD[3] DUDLEY, of Gloucester county (1660), was of the vestry of Kingston parish (now in Mathews county), 1677. His sons were: James, and Col. Ambrose Dudley.

1. James[3] Dudley, married (1679) Mary Welch, in Gloucester county (*Christ Church Register*), Vestry of Petsworth Par., 1682—son, Robert, b. 1707.
   James Dudley was living at Turk's Ferry, Pianketank river, in 1741 (*Old Gloucester Survey Book*).
   A James Dudley married (1773), in York county, Lydia Hill.

2. Col. Ambrose[3] Dudley, vestry Kingston parish. Justice of Gloucester county, 1698, with Mordecai Cooke, Thomas Todd, Thomas Buckner and others (*Va. Mag. Hist. I*). Issue:

   1. Col. George[4] Dudley, vestry Kingston parish, 1720, with Hugh Gwyn, John Hayes and others. Justice in 1743. Lands on East river, west side, mentioned, 1735 and 1748, in old Survey Book (*which begins 1732*), married before 1718, Judith, daughter of William Armistead and Anne Lee (who was daughter of Hancock Lee and Mary Kendall). Her sister, Joyce Armistead, m. Mordecai Booth. Issue:

      I. Capt. George[5] Dudley, Jr., vestry Kingston parish, 1735. In 1773 there was a difference as to division lines between him and William Tabb, "lessee of Major Thomas Peyton." He died in 1776, when his household furniture was advertised in Virginia Gazette. His son, Armistead[6], was a private in Gen. Rogers Clark's Illinois Regiment, 1778. (*Virginia Mag. Hist. I.*)

      II. Capt. Robert[5] Dudley. In 1750 (with John Perrin and William Hayes) defendant in a chancery suit vs. Richard and George Ransom, over a division line. The lands were on North River, Gloucester county, between Broad-Neck and Isle of Wight creeks. Dudley's lands were in Kingston parish, near the head of North river, next to those of Dr. John Symmer (who died in 1767) and Sir John Peyton. (Dr. Symmer was very wealthy, and married Margaret, daughter of Philip Lee. Her sister, Hannah, married —— Bowie. Their brother, John Lee, was clerk of Essex county, 1761, and sold "Paradise," in in Gloucester, for his cousin, John Lee, of Maryland, the owner. These two Johns married Mary and Susannah Smith.) (*Lee Family and Virginia Gazette.*)

Frances Dudley, m. (1758), in Kingston parish, Mr. Peter Bernard.
Betty Dudley, m. (1772) Robert Longest, of Gloucester.
Sarah Dudley m. (1773) William Cary, in York.
Dudley Cary was of the vestry of Kingston parish.
Joanna Dudley, of Gloucester. m. (*14th March, 1787*) James Taylor Horsley.

Phillis Dudley married — Saunders of York county, Virginia (ancestors of the Hyde-Saunders family). She was heiress to a large fortune in England (which her descendants never got, owing to a technicality in law). She was mother, among others, of Jesse Saunders, who married Miss Jovitian (*Huguenot*). His son, Robert Saunders (born 1778), had daughter, Mary Saunders (b. 1806), who married Patrick Booth (b. 1796), ancestor of a York family.
Jesse H. Booth was trustee of University of Alabama, 1868-72.

Rhoda Dudley, of Gloucester, *m.* (*14th March, 1787,*) Christian Rymer (*Christ Church Register*).

Benjamin and George E. Dudley, living in Gloucester county in 1800. Thomas Dudley in Gloucester in 1796 (*old papers*).

William Dudley, deceased, and Cary K. Dudley, his executor, Gloucester county, 1820. (*Records.*)

Edward Cary, of Gloucester county (1740), Inspector of Tobacco. Samuel and Dudley Cary in Gloucester, 1775. Dudley. John and Robert Cary, vestry of Kingston parish. Dudley Cary, justice of Matthews county, 1791, and afterwards left the county. (*Critic.*)

Hening's Statutes of Virginia mentions a ferry, 1702, at *Dudley's plantation*, in Middlesex county, "on the Rapp river, across to Chewning's point, and Matthew Wright's plantation."

2. William² Dudley, of Middlesex county, Virginia, 1660, Justice in 1676, (was perhaps *elder* brother of Richard² of Gloucester). Dame Ann Skipwith and Sir William Skipwith brought suit against him, 1671. (*General Court Records*). His children were John², James², William³, Thomas², Robert², Francis² and Elizabeth² Dudley. (*From Christ Church Register*) as follows:

1. John³ Dudley. living in Middlesex 1676, when he registered death of a servant. He died 1719. Married (I) Elizabeth, and (II) Edyth, who d. 1709. Had by first mar.:
    1. John⁴ Dudley, (b. 1695), married Ann Hill (*see further, for these*). By second mar.;
    2. Edyth⁴ Dudley (b. 1706), *m.* (1727) James (b. 1702), son of Thomas and Eliz Stiff.
    3. Richard⁴ Dudley (b. 1709)
2. James³ Dudley, married (I) Eliz, who d. 1688, and (II) Anne, d. 1722. Issue:
    1. Sarah⁴ (b. 1681).
    2. Elizabeth⁴ (b. 1687), married (1710), Thomas Elliott (ancestors probably of the Elliotts of Lancaster and Brunswick counties).
    3. Mary⁴ (b. 1693), married (1711) John Berry, and had William⁵ Berry (b. 1715), Ann⁵ Berry (b. 1718).
    4. William⁴ (b. 1696), married (1721), Judith Johnson, and had Robert⁴ (b. 1726), who married (1745), Joyce Gayle, of Spotsylvania county, and had Rev. and Captain Ambrose⁶ Dudley, of Lexington, Ky. (b. 1760),, of the Rev. Served with General Wayne (1794), in the Northwest. Married (1773), Ann Parker, and had Robert (b. 1774), and Ambrose, living in Kentucky in 1845, who married Mary Hawkins. (*Va. Mag. Hist. etc II*).
3. William³ Dudley, married Mary——. Issue:
    1, William⁴ (b. 1683); 2, Robert⁴ (b. 1686), and 3, *Thomas⁴* (b. 1688), married (1706), Elizabeth Marchant, and had Peyton⁵ (b. 1710), Thomas⁵ (b. 1717), and John⁵ (b. 1722):
4. Thomas³ Dudley, married Frances——. Issue:
    1, Frances⁴ (b. 1683), married (1708) John Mundy.
    2, William⁴ (b. 1693); 3, Dorothy⁴ (b. 1696).
    One Thomas Dudley signed, 1662, the letter of the Virginia traders, in petition to the King. (*William and Mary Quarterly, Vol. III*).
5. Major Robert³ Dudley, Justice and Burgess, Middlesex, 1698. Associate justices: Henry Thacker, Gawin Corbin, John Smith, Harry Beverly, John Grymes and others. Married Elizabeth Curtis (who died 1706). Robert Green, of Bristol, Eng., (grocer) made his will (1601) in Middlesex county, at Captain Robert Dudley's house, and desired his body "to be buried at the direction of John Bernard, then residing at Captain John Walker's, King and Queen county;" witnesses: Robert Dudley, Sr., and Robert Dudley, jr. and William Reynolds. (*Water's Genealogical Gleanings*). Issue:
    1. George⁴ (d. 1707).
    2. Robert⁴ Dudley (b. 1691) married (1713) Elizabeth Curtis (who died 1739).

Issue:
1, Chichester[4] (b. 1715), Elizabeth (1716), Robert (1718), Ambrose (1719). This Ambrose it was, probably, who married Keziah——, and had Elizabeth Dudley (b. 1755).
3. Averilla[4] (b. 1706).
6. Francis[3] Dudley married——, and had Ambrose[4] (b. 1698).
7. Elizabeth[3] Dudley, married (1678) James Parker. He married (II) 1689, Eleanor Abbott (widow). (*Middlesex Christ Church Register.*)
James Dudley, m. (1727) Jane Stanton. Issue: 1, William (b. 1728), 2, Stanton (b. 1730), m. 1760, (I), Mary Berry, and (II), Judith Jackson; 3, Mary (b. 1732).
James Dudley, m. Jean—— and had Jean Dudley (b. 1735).
Robert[4] Dudley (son of William above) *born* 1686, *m.* (I, 1730) Jane Moulson (d. 1775), and (II, 1738) Jane Segar, of Middlesex. Issue:
1. Lewis[5] (b. 1734) m. (1761) Frances, *daughter* of John Alden, dec'd.
2. Marlow[5], (b. 1738) m. (1763) Maria Ashton. 3. Robert (b. and d. 1740).
Lewis[4] and Frances (Alden) Dudley had issue: Francis (b. 1769), Jane (b. 1771) and Thomas.
Rebecca, widow of William Dudley, *m.* (1762) Richard Iveson.
John Dudley, m. (1783) Elizabeth Moulson of Middlesex county.
Thomas Dudley, m. Joyce——, and had 1, Lucy (b. 1742) *m.* (1762) John Clare, witness John Berry as security. 2, Thomas Dudley (b. 1755).
Robert Dudley (1789) *m.* Ann Blake.
Thomas Dudley m. (1789) Betty Shepard Crittenden, of King and Queen county.
Agnes Dudley, m. (1778) Jeremiah Powell.
Mary Dudley, of King and Queen county, *m.* (1791) Benjamin Walden.
James (son of Benjamin Dudley) born 1788.
——(*All from Middlesex Marriage Bonds, and Christ Church Register.*)
Thomas Dudley (1739) Vestry of Stratton, Major parish, King and Queen county. (*Bishop Meade*).
Robert Dudley, of the Vestry some years later.
William Dudley of King and Queen county, (1772) sold a negro to Stephen Field. Robert B. Dudley, witness——(*Old Family Papers*). He was Sheriff in 1774.
William Dudley, Sr., of King and Queen county, (1780) witness to sale of "*Dragon Swamp*" by Stephen Field, to Francis Scott.—(*Ibid*).
William Dudley, of King and Queen county, had a legacy left him by Lydia Wedderburn; Stephen Field came from Glo. county as witness to the fact in 1790. Mr. Wedderburn, married Ann, daughter of Benj. Grymes of Spottsylvania county, and Miss Rootes—(He was son of John Grymes, of "*Brandon*," Middlesex county). A son, Dr. Alex John Wedderburn, Surgeon United States Navy, was founder of the Medical College of New Orleans. Another daughter of Benjamin Grymes married —— Dudley. (*Bishop Meade*).
Captain Thomas Dudley, of King and Queen county, d. 1779—Executors: Robert B. Dudley and Thomas Dudley. (*Virginia Gazette*). He was of vestry Stratton, Major parish.
Robert Dudley, was also of vestry of Stratton Major parish, with John Livingston and others.
Thomas Dudley, Deputy Sheriff, 1781—Robert B. Dudley, D. S. 1782. (*Glo. Records*).
These were of the family at '*Dudley's Ferry*', King and Queen county, opposite West Point, Va., on York River.

"The Dudleys" says Bishop Meade, were also "among the earliest families in Warwick county." It is probable they went from Middlesex or Gloucester.
Col. Wm. Dudley of Warwick, member of County Committee, 1774.
James, son of Capt. William Dudley, (living in 1776) of Warwick county, Student at *William and Mary College*, 1770.

William Dudley (1741), already married to Jane, a daughter of Robert Ballard, in York county, when Ballard's widow married Matthew Hubbard, with James Clack, of Georgia, as guardian to her children. (*Records.*)

William Dudley m. Sarah Shields, of York county, who was born in 1745. She married (II) William Cary.

Mr. Ambrose Dudley (1736 to 1757—in place of William Chamberlain) was of the Vestry of St. Peter's par. New Kent county Va., with Col. William Macon, Mr. William Hopkins, Mr. John Parke, Mr. Walter Clopton and others, with Rev. David Mossom, minister, who was installed by Robert Carter, Governor, 1727.

John Dudley, of Hanover county, married Ursula (daughter of Robert Beverly and Ursula, daughter of Col. Wm. Byrd, of "Westover"). She was born before 1698. (*Va. Mag. Hist., III, 172.*)

William Dudley removed from Hanover Town to Caroline county, 1766. (*Va. Gazette*).

William Dudley, in 1768, conducted a large lottery of his property at Hanover Court House, to pay his debts and provide for a large family. "The tract I live on called '*New Flanders.*'" Among managers of his lottery were Wm. Aylett, Walker Taliaferro, John Boswell, Col. Edward Pendleton, John Taylor, Duncan Graham, Alex. Donald, Rd. Adams, Thos. Underwood, John and Ed. Pendleton, Jr., "of whom tickets may be had," etc. (*Va. Gazette.*)

William Dudley, in Prince William county (1761). (*Records.*)
Thomas Dudley, of Caroline (1766), a stray mare. (*Va. Gazette.*)
William Dudley, in Caroline county (1773). (*Va. Gazette.*)
William Dudley, of Bedford (1774), a stray mare. (*Va. Gazette.*)
Ambrose Dudley, trustee (1765)) for the improvement of the Chickahominy river, in New Kent county. (*Hening, 8th Vol.*)

Ambrose Dudley, in Spotsylvania county (1783), had 10 slaves, Peter Dudley had 7, and James Dudley had 1. (*Va. Mag. Hist., IV.*)

John Dudley, member of the Williamsburg Lodge of Masons, Captain in Rev. army. His nephew, James Southall, claimed his bounty lands as heir. (*William and Mary Quarterly.*)

Henry Dudley, Captain in Rev. (*Va. Mag. Hist. II.*)
Ambrose Dudley, Captain in Rev. (*Va. Mag. Hist. I.*)
Robert Dudley, Lt. in Rev., Va. Cont. Line.
John Dudley, of Northumberland county, was Lt. in Rev. navy, and died in Elizabeth City county, 1797. (*William and Mary Quarterly, I.*)

Henry and Robert Dudley, Rev. soldiers, received bounty lands prior to 1784.

Ann Dudley married John Ragland, of Goochland, whose father, John Ragland, came from Wales to Hanover county, Va., 1723, and had a 16,000 acres grant. (*Brock's St. John's Vestry Book, Henrico County.*)

To return to the descendants of John[4] Dudley, of Middlesex (b. 1695): John[4], William[3], Edward[1]), who married (June, 1720) Anne Hill (b. 1701). Anne Hill was daughter of William (d. 1720) and Anne Hill (d. 1726). (*Christ Church Register.*)[*]

1. Elizabeth Dudley, born 1723.
2. Ambrose Dudley, born 1727.
3. John Dudley, born 1729.
4. William Dudley, born 1731.
5. Anne Dudley, born 1734.
6. Mary Dudley, born 1737. (*Ante, 388.*)

Of these, it is probable that William Dudley (b. 1731) was father of Mildred Dudley, who married Ishmeal Dunn, of Sussex and Brunswick county (b. 1744), parents of Major David and Dr. Dudley Dunn, of Memphis, Tenn., and this William Dudley may have removed to Sussex county.

---

*Other children of Wm. and Anne Hill were: Isabella (b. 1698), Eliz (1706), John Hill (1710), Mary (1713), Dinah (1715), Priscilla (1718).—*Christ Church Register.*

The earliest Dudleys lived on the south side of Rappahannock river, in Middlesex and Gloucester, and the earliest Dunns lived on either side the Rappahannock, in Westmoreland and Essex. The Hills and Elliotts, who intermarried with them, also lived in Middlesex county. And later, Thomas Elliott, of Lancaster county, married his wife Winifred Saunders (b. 1746), daughter of William and Betty (Hubbard) Saunders, also in Lancaster. These all removed to counties south of the James river, and from thence on, South. In North Carolina were also Dudleys and Hills.

Dudley (from the North Carolina Colonial Records).

Chistopher Dudey, of Chowan county, planter (1712), assaulted the officer, Wm. Jones, and was find ten shillings. Defended by the great lawyer, Edward Moseley. He was sued 1713 by the widow of Gov. Edward Hyde for £8. Was on the Chowan jury 1719 with Wm. Thompson, John Beverly, Samuel Taylor, and John Watkins (all emigrants from Virginia).

Christopher Dudley (1731), Justice in Onslow county, 500 acres, 1735. Thomas Dudley (1744) 300 acres in Onslow county.

Thomas Dudley (1744), 100 acres in Perquimons county.

John Dudley, Justice in Onslow, 1739, 300 acres 1749, and 300 1751.

Wm Dudley, of Onslow (1739), a witness.

Christopher Dudley (1743) 200 acres in Carteret county.

Thos. Dudley (1748), 400 acres in Carteret county.

Bishop Dudley, New Hanover county (1754), petition as to roads, signed also by Christopher Dudley.

Bishop Dudley, of the Committee of Safety for New Hanover county, January, 1773.

Thomas Dudley (1750), Justice in Carteret county.

Christopher Dudley, in Craven county, 1739, 130 acres.

Christopher Dudley, of the vestry of St. James parish, New Hanover county, 1760.

Christopher Dudley, of the Halifax Committee (April, 1776) to collect arms. He was Justice 1776 and keeper of the Magazine, and Tobacco Inspector at Halifax.

Thos. Dudley, of Currituck county, on a jury 1740.

Thomas Dudley (1762) member of Assembly from Currituck county.

James Dudley, 200 acres in Craven county, 1743.

Aaron Dndley (July, 1775), Committee of Safety for Perkins county.

Guilford Dudley, of Halifax county (1776) in charge of polls for electing a member to Congress.

Edward Bishop Dudley, 28th Governor of North Carolina (1837-41), born Onslow county, N. C., 1787, Member of Congress 1829 (d. 1855). His father, a wealthy planter, and also member of Legislature.

Thomas Underwood Dudley (b. Richmond, Va., 1837), major also in Confederate States Army. Son of Thomas Underwood Dudley, merchant.—*American Cyclopedia of Biography.*

THOMAS[1] DUDLEY (b. Northampton, Eng., 1576, died Roxbury, Mass., 1653) came to New England in 1630, and was four times Governor, 1634-51. His son, Joseph[2] Dudley (b. 1647, d. 1740), Governor 1686; also Lieutenant Governor of Isle of Wight, Eng., and M. P. 1701. His son—

William[2] Dudley (d. 1743), Justice and Colonel; another son, Paul[2] Dudley (b. 1675, d. 1731), was Attorney General Massachusetts 1702, Chief Justice 1745 and F. R. S. He had sons: Thomas[4] and Joseph[4].—*American Cyclopedia Biography.*

MOORE.

Mark Moore, living in Northampton county, N. C., 1758, married Sarah Mason. Of his brothers (or perhaps sons) one went to Kentucky and two to South Carolina. It is said he was, probably, an Episcopal minister. His son, Rev. John[2] Moore, of M. E

Church South (b. Northampton county, 1st January, 1758, d. 28th April, 1852), m. in Brunswick county, Va. (to which he finally removed), the widow Lealie (see Rebecca Fletcher), with one son, Capt. William Lealie. Removed 1807 to Davidson county, Tenn., and in 1818 to Limestone county, Ala. Licensed by John Pope, 1784, and ordained by Bishop Asbury. Five children; as follows:

I. JOHN FLETCHER[2] MOORE (d. 1850), m. his cousin, Nancy Fletcher, of an old family. Issue:

1. Dr. Thomas E.[4], Bolivar, Tenn., m. (I) Miss Joy, and had one daughter. He m. (II) Miss Morgan, and had Morgan Moore.
2. Dr. John Richard[4], m. ——. Issue: 1, Dr. Augustus Thomas[5]; 2, Pickens[5]; 3, Mary[5], m. —— Childress.
3. Dr. Mathew[4], of Richmond, Texas.
4. Dr. Robert[4], of Texas.
5. Dr. Albert[4], of Texas.
6. Maria[4], m. her cousin, Milton Moore. No issue.

II. MARY[2] MOORE, married (1809) Thomas Kent Harris (b. in Virginia , member Congress from White county, Tenn. Issue:

1. Algernon Sidney[4] Harris, M. D. (b. Sparta, Tenn., 1811), m. (1836) Musidora Cheatham, of Virginia. Issue:
   1. Virginia (b. near Huntsville, Ala., 1837), m. at Madison, Ala. (1872), Thomas Bibb Hopkins (see Bibb); 2, Thomas Branch, C. S. A. (b. 1839, d. 1868), m. (1859) Hibernia Jones, of Tennessee, and had Musidora (b. 1860). Sidney m. ——, Mary (b. 1862) m. Robert Hopkins (see Bibb); Lewey, 1866, and Wiley (b. 1868); 3, Emmet Harris (b. 1841).

2. Caroline[4] Harris (b. 1813, d. 1853), m. (1833) Col. Wm. Duke Hayes, Athens, Ala., and had: 1, Mary Elizabeth (b. 1833); 2, Dr. John Moore, M. D. (b. 1836) m. Sallie Saunders; 3, Martha Wyatt (b. 1839) m. Dr. L. H. Binford, and had Sarah E. (b. 1860), m. Frank Patterson Turner; William, Thos. M. (1862), Sidney H., Carrie L., Sue Gee Binford, unm., and Mary Charles Swoope; 4, Wm. Hayes died young; 5, Annie Shelton (b. 1845), m. (1872) James Devereux Markham, and had James D. and Jane H., died young; Sadie Henry and Carrie Bernard; 6, Sarah Bass (1847), Mollie (1850), died unm.

3. Mary Ann[4] Harris (b. Winchester, Tenn., 1816, d. 1870), m. Huntsville, Ala. (1836), Judge John Dennis Phelan (d. 1881). Issue: 1, Thomas (b. Huntsville, 1836), killed in battle of Gaines Mill, Va., 1862; 2, Watkins (b. Tuscaloosa 1838), killed in battle at Petersburg, Va., 1865; 3, Dennis (b. 1839, d. 1856); 4, John, Capt. Phelan's Light Artillery, C. S. A., (b. Marion, Ala., 1841, d. Birmingham, 1890), m. (1871) at Moulton, Ala., Anna Owen, daughter of Thomas Sale, and had Owen (b. 1872), Thomas Sale (1874), Watkins died young, Anna Mary, Agnes (b. 1880), died young; John Ellis (1883), and Joseph; 5, Judge Ellis (b. Marion, Ala., 1843,) Capt. 45th Reg. Ala. Volunteers, clerk of House of Representatives, 1870, d. Waterbury, Conn., 1897), m. (I) 1869, Amy Hawkins, and had Mary W. (b. 1872), John Dennis, Natalie and Sarah E. He m. (II) 1888, Mary Frisbie, and had Ellis F., b. Waterbury, Conn., 1892; 6, Priscella, (born 1845), m. (1881) G. A. Williamson, Nashville, Tenn., and had George Robert (b. 1882), Phelan (1884), and Benj. Patterson, d. 1888; 7, Mary (b. Limestone Co., Ala., 1847), m. (1872) Sewanee, Tenn., Robert Leonidas Watt (d. 1886), of Montgomery, and had Mary P. (b. 1872), Robert Watkins (b. 1876, d. 1876), James F., d. infant; Mary P. Watt m. (1896) R. W. Goldthwaite, and has Mary Theresa (b. 1899). Mrs. Watt has furnished these notes of her grandmother's descendants; 8, Anna King, m. (1884) Chattanooga, Tenn., James Chester Derby, and had Chester (b. 1886); 9, Sidney H. Phelan, m. (1877), Montgomery, Ala., Palmer Graham, and had Malcolm G. (b. 1879) Palmer, Mary A., Effie Beale, Sidney H. (b. 1885), Ellen M. and Leman (b. 1891); 10, Caroline Blount, m. (1877) in Birmingham, Ala., Jesse Drew Beale, and had issue: Caroline

Phelan, Phelan (b. 1880), Jesse D. and Sidney H. (twins), 1883; 11, James Lalor (b. 1859) m. (1889) in San Angelo, Tex., Sallie Tankersley, and had Kathleen Lalor (b. 1890), and John Sidney Phelan (b. 1892).

III. DAVID² MOORE m. (I), about 1832, Harriet Haywood, and (II) 1852, Martha Harrison. Issue: 1. David; 2. Harriet⁴ m. (I) Col. Barnard, and had, 1, Mattie, m. —— Caldwell, and 2, Kate Barnard. Mrs. Barnard m. (II) Col. Barnwell Rhett, of Huntsville; one child. 3. Samuel Moore, of Huntsville, born 1843, General of State Militia, (son by the second wife). 4. Kate Moore, m. Nov., 1876, Mr. Grimbrell, of S. C., lawyer, in N. Y.

IV. RICHARD³ MOORE m. Eliza, daughter of Sugars Turner. Issue: Milton, m. —— Fletcher, and had son, Milton Moore.

V. DR. ALFRED³ MOORE m. (I) Eliza, daughter of Rev. Edmund Jones, of Jackson, Tenn. Issue:
1. Judge John Edmund⁴ Moore, member Legislature, 1847; Judge of 4th Judicial Circuit, 1852-58; Col. C. S. A., lived in Florence, Ala., died in military service 1865, m. Letitia Watson, of Richmond, Va. No issue.
2. Sydenham⁴ Moore m. Eliza Hobson, of Greensboro, Ala.; captain in Mexican War and colonel C. S. A. in Civil War. Issue: Mary Quitman⁵, m. Harris Waller; Captain Alfred⁵, killed C. S. A., battle Missionary Ridge; Rittenhouse⁵, of Mobile, m. Miss Randolph; Sydenham⁵, of Birmingham, Ala.; Caroline⁵, m. Smith Bird; Alice⁵ m. —— Smith; Gertrude⁵.
3. Olivia⁴ Moore m. Edward A. O'Neal, Lawyer, of Florence, Ala.; General in C. S. A. and Governor of Alabama, 1882; Prominent citizen of North, Ala. Children:
   1. Capt. Alfred⁵ O'Neal, C. S. A., m. Annie Warren, of Tuscumbia, Ala., and has children, Alfred and Annie.
   2. Rebecca⁵ m. (1866) Reuben L. Shotwell, now of St. Louis, and has O'Neal, Alfred, Rebecca, who m. Samuel Piper, and had James (b. 1897); Kate m. Dr. Roach, of St. Louis.
   3. Edward A⁵. O'Neal, C. S. A., d. y., Lawyer, m. Mary, daughter of Capt. Alexander Coffee, of Florence, and had Edward. Mrs. O'Neal m. (II) William Campbell, of Florence, Pres. of Bank.
   4. Julia⁵, unmarried.
   5. Emmet⁵ O'Neal m. Lizzie, daughter of Capt. Samuel Kirkman, of Florence, and has Lizzie, Kirkman and Olivia.
   6. Georgia⁵ m. Eugene Williams, of Mississippi, now of St. Louis, and has Eugene W. and George Gates.
   7. Syddie⁵ m. George Dudley, and has Olivia and George.
4. Dr. George H⁴. Moore, of Memphis, Tenn. (b. 1822), married (1859) Ann H. Hoskins. He was surgeon C. S. A.; came to Memphis 1867; descended from Moore and Jones, of North Carolina; also Mason, Fletcher and Batte families of Virginia. Issue:
   1. Thomas Clay (b. 1864), of printing house of "Page & Moore," Memphis.
   2. Mary E. married (1897) Daniel Killian, of St. Louis, and had Alfred Daniel Killian (b. 1st June. 1898). 3. George (b. 1869) married Stella Capuro. 4. Dr. Alfred Moore, of Memphis. (b. 1872), Graduate Memphis Medical College, 1895; House Physician of St. Joseph's Hospital; a prominent young physician of Memphis. (See Oliver.)
5. Alfred⁴ Moore (d. y.), also, 6, Erasmus⁴ Moore, d. y.
7. Eliza⁴ Moore (b. 1827. d. 1860), m. Judge James Phelan, of Aberdeen, Miss., law partner of Judge John B. Sale, and brother of Judge John D. Phelan. Issue:
   1. George Richard⁵ Phelan, Lawyer, of Memphis; a brilliant, wayward and lovable genius; Colonel of a Fenian regiment organized in New York after the Civil war; died young; m. (1872) Julia, daughter of Wm. R. Hunt, of Memphis; and had Wm. Hunt, lawyer, George (d. y.), and Julian.
   2. Elizabeth,⁵ m. .... Calloway, of Louisville.

3. Kate[4] m. Wade Hampton, Jr., son of General Hampton, C. S. A.

4. James[5] Phelan (b. 1856, d. 1891), U. S. Congress from Tennessee; m. Mary Early, of Virginia, and had James[6], Mary[6] and Early[6].

Dr. Alfred[3] Moore married (II) 1837, Mary Watson, of Richmond, Va., and had: 8. Leslie (b. 1838, d. 1861.) 9. Fanny, m. Charles Mastin. 10. Sallie. 11. William (d. 1897). 12. Alfred, now mayor of Huntsville. 13. Ella (b. 1847) m. Samuel Donegan, of Huntsville, and had: Leslie, James, Mary, and Alfred Donegan. (*From notes by Mrs. Olivia O'Neal, and Mrs. Dr. George Moore, and Mrs. Mary Watt.*)

John Phelan, the ancestor, and his wife, came to Richmond, Va., from Ireland, and thence to Huntsville, Ala. (see "*Irish in America*"). Children: 1. Judge John D. 2. Rev. Joseph. 3. Mrs. Mary P. Horn, whose son, Phelan, m. Mary Early, widow of his cousin, James Phelan, of Memphis. 4. Judge James.

Wm. Moore, nephew of Rev. John Moore, lived in the Cherokee nation. His son, David, visited Huntsville in 1847.

Dr. Lemuel Moore, of Columbia, S. C., moved to Lincoln county, Georgia. His brother was the celebrated Methodist preacher, Mark W. Moore, who was in New Orleans in 1819, and founder of the Bible Society. Dr. Lemuel had sons: Mark, and Everett Bird Moore, of Nixburg, Ala., and Col. B. B. Moore, of Egypt, Miss. (deceased). (*Mrs. Ann Moore.*)

(Lemuel Mason lived in Virginia, and Sarah Mason, wife of Mark Moore, may have been of this family.)

Cantzon, of South Carolina.

Dr. John Cantzon, of Waxhaw, Lancaster county, S. C. (died 1775), came from La Rochelle, France, and married (1765) Sarah Dickey (b. *circa* 1750, d. 1797), probably of York county, S. C., as the Dickey family lived *there*. His grant in Lancaster county (1767), from Sir Charles Granville, Lord Montague, was for 400 acres in the Waxhaws, and more later on. (Waxhaw was settled in 1751. (*Records*.) His widow m. (II) a relation, Dr. Daniel Harper, a Tory, whom the Regulators banished. He fled to Antrim, Ireland, with his wife, and her young Cantzon children (he had none of his own); but returned, later, to Waxhaw, in spite of repeated warnings. His name was in the *Book of Doom*, kept by Regulators (where it was seen long years after, by Judge Witherspoon), and he was finally killed by them in 1791 (Many Harper tombs are at old Waxhaws). Much of Dr. Cantzon's wealth was thus wasted. He was a prominent physician, and of French education. Issue:

1. *William Cantzon* (b. 1766), ran off to sea, when his mother went to Ireland, and was never afterward heard from; 2. *Moses*, d. s. p., 1817, his mother's dependence on their return to America. Several of their joint deeds are among the old Records at Lancaster; 3. *John Cantzon* (b. 1768, d. 1829), m. (1791) Rachel Foster (b. 1769, d. 1825), and had son, Henry, who was father of Wm. H. Cantzon of New Orleans, and of Eliza, Charles, and Mrs. Rugeley, of Texas; 4. *Mary* (b. 1773) m. James Blair (*below*); 5. *Margaret*, m. Wm. Young (grandparents of Rev. James E. Dunlap, of Williamsburg county, S. C., and others).

* Roger[1] Moore (or More) of Ireland, fled in 1641 - the great rebellion—to Flanders. His son—James[2] came to America and was governor of South Carolina, and married Governor Yeaman's daughter. *His* son—

Roger[3] (*King Roger*) lived near Wilmington. N. C. His son—
George[4] was twice married, and had twenty-eight children. Of these—
George[5] married Mary Walters. His daughter—
Sallie[6] m. (I) Samuel McCulloch, and (II) James Jackson, whose descendants live near Florence, Ala. His daughter—
Elizabeth[7] Jack(on, m. Thomas Kirkman. His son—
Samuel[8] Kirkman, Florence, Ala., m. Lizzie, daughter of James Woods. of Nashville, Tenn., and their daughter—
Lizzie[9] Kirkman m. Judge Emmet O'Neal, Florence, Ala.
(*Sent by Mr. Samuel Kirkman as extract from letter of Mr. George Davis, attorney, of the C. S. A.*)

John and Rachel (Foster) Cantzon (above) had also daughter, Ann Kelsey Cantzon, b. 1795, who married John Foster. These were parents of John, and Dr. Joseph Foster, of Lancaster C. H., S. C. They have a *Matthew Henry Bible*, printed in Chester, Eng., 1706, and owned by Rev. Wm. Richardson. and bought at the sale of Wm. R. Davies' estate, 1772, by Henry Foster, father of Mrs. John Cantzon. The ancestor, Henry Foster, was born 1730, and came from Pennsylvania with Anne, his wife, to Waxhaw. This old Bible contains the Foster-Cantzon Register.*

HENRY FOSTER, the *immigrant*, of Lancaster county, S. C. (b. 1730, d. 19th December, 1797); m. (*Circa* 1754); Anne — (b. 1732, d. 14th January, 1795.) They came with the Scotch-Irish settlers from Pennsylvania, and had issue: 1. Joseph, b. 1756, d. 1789. 2. Catherine, b. 1758, d. 1792; m. John Dunlap. 3. Rachel, b. 1761, d. 1764. 4. John, b. 1762, d. 1812; m. (1) Mary Atkins, and (II) Catherine Collins. 5. Anne, b. 1769, d. 1806; m. William White. 6. William, b. 1767, d. 1802, unm. 7. Rachel, b. 2d July, 1769, was baptized by the William Richardson, died 11th October, 1826; m. 18th July, 1791, John Cantzon (above.)

Blair, of South Carolina.

James[1] Blair, of the "*Waxhaw Settlement*," Catawba River, Lancaster county, S. C., was b. 1768, on his River Mill plantation, where he died 1801, and was buried at Waxhaw Church. An only child. His father (name unknown, but supposed *James*), with a brother, John Blair,† came with the Scotch-Irish immigration from Antrim, Ireland, through Pennsylvania or New Jersey and Virginia (where John settled) to Lancaster county, S. C. "Blair's *Mills*," says Howe, in his *History of Presbyterian Church*, "was used by both armies in the Revolution," 1781. That part of South Carolina was freed from the Indians after 1760, and became rapidly settled, and the first Blair must have come after that date. (William Blair, b. Antrim, Ireland, 1759, d. 1824, came "with his father's family from Antrim when fourteen years of age," says inscription on his tomb at Waxhaw. He was father of Gen. James Blair, of Camden, member of Congress; and the two families claimed kinship.)

James[1] Blair (above) married at Kingstree, Williamsburg District (or county), 15th May, 1792, by Rev. Joseph Lee, Mary Cantzon, b. Kingstree, Black River, Williamsburg District 1773; died Marshall county, Miss., 1843. Daughter of Dr. John and Sarah (Dickey) Cantzon, of Waxhaw, Lancaster county; Williamsburg county was settled 1731 by Scotch Presbyterians. Mrs. Blair m. (II) Thomas McDow, by whom was no issue. Issue *(Blair)*: I. John James[2]. II. Sarah Dickey[2]. III. Mary Harper[2]. IV. Jane Dickey[2], as follows:

*It is probable the Cantzons settled first in Williamsburg district, S. C., or some of the lower counties with other Huguenots. The *Family Bible* has these entries of births of children:
1. William Cantzon. eldest son, supposed to have died at sea. 2. Moses Cantzon, d. 1817. Tomb in old Waxhaw church yard. 3. John Cantzon, b. 1768, d. 1829, m. (1791) Rachel Foster, b. 1769, and had, Daniel Harper, b. 1798, baptized by Rev. James Stephenson; Ann Kelsey, b. 1795, m. John Foster; Henry Foster, b. 1796, m. Miss ———— John Foster, b. 1802, d. 1806; and Rachel, b. 1806, who m. Wm. Royall, and had Annie, Henrietta, Daniel and Henry. 4. Mary Cantzon m. James Blair. 5. Margaret Cantzon m. William Young, and had Margaret, who m. William B. Dunlap of York county, S. C. (Died in Bainbridge, Ga.). Issue: 1. David, m. Miss Albright. 2. Susan, d. y, 3. John, d. unm., 35 years old. 4. Jane, m. Thomas Evans. 5. Rev. James E. Dunlap, m. Miss McIntyre, and had Thornwell, d. y.; Gary, d. y.; Marie, Maud, and perhaps others. 6. Amelia, m. ————, and d. y. 7. William Wilson, d. 18 years of age.

†It is greatly desired to learn if this John Blair left descendants in Virginia. It is believed the family was related to the Princeton College Blairs and the Witherspoons, the latter family in South Carolina, always being their staunch friends and neighbors. In Orange county, Va., (now Augusta,) Alexander Blair, March 24, 1740, entered 360 acres; the fee rent was signed by James Blair; and his family consisted of James, Jane, Mary and John Blair.—(*Land Book 19, p. 938, Richmond, Va.*)
In the militia of Augusta county, Va., 1758, is mentioned William, James and John Blair.— *Hening's Statutes, VII, 185-195*).
Probably a clue to the information sought might be found in this entry.

1. JOHN JAMES[2] BLAIR, of Mobile, Ala. (b. at River Mill plantation, Waxhaw, 12th April, 1793; d. Marshall county, Miss., while visiting Mrs. Kelsey, 13th January, 1844). Tomb at Spring Hill, near Mobile. Moved to Camden. S. C., when a youth, and was Clerk of the Court. The old records kept by him are marvels of penmanship and drawings. He became extensive merchant of the firm of "William Johnson and J. J. Blair;" was also cashier of Camden Bank. Residence (1822) was northeast corner DeKalb and Broad streets. Removed to Mobile, Ala., 1838, where he engaged in extensive grocery business, with James Harrison as partner. His lovely home was at Spring Hill, where, with Mr. McMillan, he founded a Presbyterian church and cemetery on his own lands. Married at Camden by Rev. Samuel S. Davis (5th Nov., 1822) Martha Conturier Ray (b. 8th April, 1802, St. John's parish', Santee, Charleston county; died New Orleans, 29th May, 1869), daughter of Captain Peter and Mary (Flint) Ray, of Charleston county, Santee, and afterward Camden.   She possessed rare firmness, and that Christian strength which should ever prove a grand model for her descendants.   Issue:

1. Mary Eliz[3] (b. 14th Dec., 1823; d. 10th April, 1842). Her twin brother, James Ray, lived but a few hours, and is buried at Camden.

2. Henry Dickenson[3] Blair (b. Camden, 3d October, 1825; d. Spring Hill, Ala., 7th Dec., 1855), continued his father's business firm in Mobile, and lovingly assisted his mother with her affairs, and the rearing of her children, until his early death.   Married Mary Lou, daughter of Col. James E. Saunders, author of the "Early Settlers." Their only child, Elizabeth Saunders, m. Dr. William Carter Stubbs, of Virginia. She is the compiler of these genealogies.   (See Saunders.)

3. Emily Louisa[3] Blair, b. 1827, died a young girl.

4. James Douglass[3] Blair (b. 4th Dec., 1828; d. Caney, Texas, 1874), merchant of New Orleans, and planter; lieutenant colonel of Fourth Louisiana in Civil War, and a brave soldier.   Married Parthenia Rugeley, of South Carolina and Alabama.   Issue: John[4], m. Caroline Rugeley; William[4] (d. young): Rochelle[4] (b. 1867 d. y.); Alfonzo Rugeley[4] (b. 1868, d. 1898). m. Miss Kidd, and left three children; Mary[4], m. her cousin, Mr. Rugeley, of Texas.

5. Martha Shannon[3] Blair (b. Camden, S. C., 1st March, 1831), m. (1858) Charles Farwell, merchant of New Orleans, brother of U. S. Senator Nathan Farwell, of Maine, and Captain in Confederate States Army; killed, leading his company in a charge at Griswoldville, Ga., 1864; a truly noble, generous and upright man, of great popularity.   Issue:

   1. Henry Blair[4] Farwell, b. 1858, sugar broker, of firm of "Murphy & Farwell," New Orleans. Unmarried.

   2. Charles Alfonzo[4] Farwell, b. 1860, firm of "Milliken & Farwell," New Orleans. The senior partner, Mr. Richard Milliken, dying in 1897, the widow (an aunt of Mr. Farwell's, nee Deborah A. Farwell) continues the firm as partner, and has recently erected in New Orleans the noble monument to her dead, "The Richard Milliken Memorial Hospital" for Children.   Mr. Farwell was "Rex" of Mardi Gras of 1898, and is President of the Cane Grower's Association, of Louisiana.

   3. Ellen R.[4] Farwell lives in New Orleans with her mother.

6. Ellen Charlotte[3] Blair, b. Camden, 3d August, 1832; d. 1896, an exalted woman, the guardian angel of her family, and leader in every unselfish act; married at Spring Hill, 2d January, 1856, Alfonzo Irvine Rugeley, of an old South Carolina family which preserves records of its ancestry into remote English history, having also a coat of arms, which may be found on the stained glass windows of the old church of St. Ives, England.   The South Carolina ancestor was colonel in the English army during the Revolution, and mentioned in history.   His descendants remained near Camden.   Mr. Rugeley was also a noble sacrifice to the Civil War, being shot by the Federals while crossing the river in a boat at Baton Rouge, 1864, and dying, a prisoner, of his wounds.   Children:

MRS. MARTHA RAY BLAIR,
Born in South Carolina in 1802.

1. Mary Lou[4] m., February 4, 1880, her cousin, Wm. H. Cantzon,* merchant, of the firm "Smith Bros. & Co.," New Orleans, wholesale grocers; Second company Washington Artillery (Col. John B. Richardson), in Civil War. Children: Henry Foster[5], b. 1881, now a student at University Louisiana; Nellie Ray[5] and Alfonso Rugeley[5].

2. Mattie[4] m., January 8, 1880, Danfel De Sassure Colcock (second wife), Secretary Sugar Exchange, New Orleans, and also a brave soldier in Civil War. (He has a daughter, Augusta, by his first wife, Augusta, daughter of the famous Presbyterian divine, Dr, Benjamin Palmer). Issue: 1. Richard Woodward[5], b. 1880; Mary Rugeley[5], Daniel D.[5] and William Ferguson[5].

3. Alfonso James[4] Rugeley, unm.

7. John James[3] Blair, b. 20th July, 1834; d. 1862, m., 1860, Julia Rowe, of Mobile. Issue: Margaret[4] m. Rev. Robert Woodward Barnwell, of an old South Carolina family, pastor Episcopal Church, Selma, Ala. Issue: Julia[5], Robert[5], Emma[5], Elliott[5], John[5], and two others, names not known.

8. Thomas McMillan[3] Blair, b. Mobile, 3d August, 1839; lieutenant in Fifth Company Washington Artillery'(Capt. Slocomb); killed in battle of Chickamauga, Tenn., in Civil War; name on the Artillery monument, Metairie Cemetery, New Orleans.

9. William Ray[3] Blair, b. 1836; died aged seven. (Dates from a Family Bible which which was presented to John J. Blair, 1832, at Camden, by Rev. J. K. Douglas.)

II. SARAH DICKEY[2] BLAIR (b. River Mill plantation, Waxhaw, 1795; died young).

III. MARY HARPER[2] Blair (b. River Mill plantation, Waxhaw, Lancaster county, S. C., 20th December, 1797), m. (at the home of Thomas McDow) by Rev. James Witherspoon, (1) 1820, John A. Dunlap, of York county, S. C., who died at his Ellison Creek plantation, York county, 1827. She m. (II) Capt. Samuel Kelsey, and removed to Tyrone, Marshall county, Miss. Issue first marriage: 1. Thomas Lafayette[3] Dunlap, m. Miss Arnelt, and moved to Arkansas, Maj. Ark. Regt., C. S. A., d. s. p., and 2. Mary Jane[3] Dunlap. Issue second marriage: 3. Robert[3] Kelsey, b. 1832, killed in the Civil War while leading his regiment as lieutenant colonel of a Miss. Regiment at battle Jonesboro, Ga., 1864. 4. Ann Eliza[3] Kelsey. Of these four:

Mary Jane[3] Dunlap, d. 1875, m. (1) 1840, Albert T. McNeal, Coffeeville, Miss., d. Sept. 1844, m. (II), 1849, Judge Austin Miller, of Bolivar, Tenn., d. 1868. Albert T. McNeal was son of Thomas[4] McNeal, who m. Clarissa[4] Polk, daughter of Ezekiel[4] Polk, who was son of William[3] and Priscilla (Roberts) Polk, ancestors of the celebrated Polk family of North Carolina, of whom were President James K. Polk, and the warrior bishop, General Leonidas Polk, whose daughters, Mrs. Dr. Joseph Jones, Mrs. Huger, Mrs. Blake and Mrs. Chapman, are now such ornaments to New Orleans society. The grandfather of William[3] was Robert Polk, of Ireland, who m. Magdalen Tasker. (Copied from a beautiful "Polk Family Tree," sent the writer by Judge Albert T.[4] McNeal.) Issue McNeal marriage:

1. Judge Albert T.[4] McNeal, of Bolivar, Tenn. (b. 9th December, 1842); prominent lawyer. His culture is commensurate with his large library of 8000 volumes. He is fond of genealogical research, and with his sister, Mrs. Hill, has furnished this list of his grandmother's descendants. He married 24th April, 1867, Kate Fentress, (b. 1st April, 1844, d. 1st August, 1893). Issue eight children : 1, Irené, b 10th September, 1868, m. October, 1890, W. A. Swazey, and has son, Albert McNeal Swazey, and Irene (died); 2, Ezekiel Polk, b. 15th September, 1870; 3, Albert T., Jr., 7th December, 1872; 4, Kate, 17th November, 1874: 5, Sallie Hill, 28th January, 1877; 6, Mary

---

*James Paxton, of the Virginia family, removed to Pennsylvania and was a Rev. officer and member of the "Order of Cincinnatus," the old parchment certificate of which is preserved in the family, dated 1788, and signed by George Washington, and Maj. Gen. John Knox, Secretary. His son, John Addems Paxton, came to New Orleans, and was compiler of its first city directory. He was grandfather of Wm. H. Cantzon, of New Orleans.

Dunlap, 9th December, 1878; 7, Austin Miller, 3rd December, 1880; 8, Una, 4th December, 1882.
2. Irene McNeal, b. Coffeeville, Miss., 1st March, 1845 (after her father's death;) m. (I) 1868, Capt. Lewis Bond, who died of yellow fever, 1879, and had four children. She m. (II) 1893, Col. Jerome Hill,* of Memphis. No issue. Children: 1. McNeal[5] Bond, m. Amelia Foard, and has Irene McNeal. 2. Marie Louise[5]; 3. Kate R[5]., m. R. G. Morrow, and has R. G. Morrow, Jr., and 4. Irene Lewis[5] Bond.
   Issue of Miller marriage:
3. Ann McNeal[4] Miller, b. 1851; d. 1868.
4. Charles A[4]. Miller, lawyer, Bolivar, Tenu.; b. 1853, m. Lizzie Lee Unthank. Issue: Mary, Sallie, Austin, Lizzie Lee and Annie.
5. Austin[4] Miller, of Memphis, general manager of *Memphis Trust Company;* b. 1856, married Fannie Lea Neely, and has Elizabeth Lea and Mary Louise.
6. Mary Dunlap[4] Miller, b. 1858. m. Judge Henry W. Bond, of St. Louis, Judge of Court of Appeals and cousin of Lewis Bond. Issue: Thomas, Irene McNeal, Henry Whitelaw and Mary Miller.
4. Ann Eliza[3] Kelsey (above) b. 1834, married Robert E. Hibbler (d. 1866), and had Robert Kelsey[4] Hibbler, d. 1870, and aMry Hibbler, who was reared by Mrs. McNeal, and married James Knox Polk, of Nashville, Tenn., now Adjutant of First Tennessee Regiment in the Philippine Islands (1899), and has *Issue:* 1. James Knox; 2. Kelsey Hibbler; Albert McNeal; 4. Edward M. and 5. Lawrence.

   IV. JANE DICKEY[2] BLAIR (b. Ellison Creek Plantation 25th October, 1799) married, by Rev. David Hutchinson, 1819, Alexander Brown, b. Ellison Creek Plantation, York county, 1799. Issue: 1. William N.[3], 2. John Blair[3], 3. Mary E[3]. Brown. Of these
1. William N.[3] Brown of Memphis, firm of "*W. N. Brown and N. C. Perkins, Jr.,*" is of immense proportions in body and heart—married Helen I. Allen, step-daughter of Dr. Joseph Todd. Issue: I. William Jr.[4], m. Ida Erb, and has Annie and Helen. II. Sarah[4]. III. Allison[4], M. D. *нвм.* IV. George[4], *ннм.* V. Howard[4], *ннм.*
2. John Blair[3] Brown, of Arkansas. *deceased*, married Lydia Garrett. Surviving issue: Cantzon[4], married; Lydia[4], married; Mary[4], married; and all of Arkansas.
3. Mary E.[3] Brown married Mr. Garrett. Issue: 1. James[4] C. S. A. Killed in battle. William,[4] killed in battle. Benjamin[4], Henry[4], John[4], Mary Jane[4], Louisa[4], Martha[4]. Of these all are married. Mary Jane *m.* Mr. Milam. Louisa *m.* Robert Wilson; and Martha *м.* W. J. Phillips, and has several children.

FLINT, AND RAY FAMILIES OF SOUTH CAROLINA.†

   William Flint, Sr. (b. 1733, d. 1789, at St. Johns, Santee, Charleston county, S. C.), m. Martha (†) Couturier. Issue:
1. Elizabeth (b. St. John's parish, 1763, d. Mobile, Ala., 1836), married Charles Rogers, of South Carolina. No issue.
2. Ann Jane (1766-1785). 3. William, Jr. (1771-1793).
4. Mary Flint (b. 20th December, 1773, at St. Johns parish, Santee, Charleston county, S. C.; d. at Camden, S. C., 11th May, 1834); married, *circa*, 1792, Capt. Peter R. Ray (b. 29th December, 1764, at St. Johns parish, Berkley, Charleston county, S. C.; d. on his plantation, near Camden, 6th May, 1814). He came to Kershaw county from Santee in 1811, and died suddenly of heart affection. His and wife's

---

*Col. Hills father, "a physician, was born in Asheville, N. C., in 1799, and died at Holly Springs, Miss., 1845. His mother was of Houston and Bills descent. John and Samuel Houston settled in the Cumberland Valley. early in the eighteenth century. John was the progenitor. Went from Penn to Iredale county, N. C. Descendants scattered over Tennessee, Missouri and Texas."
   Judge McNeal writes "he has a 'Prayer Book,' given him by his mother,—in which is written that its first owner was Thomas Dunlap, and was bought in Kings street, Charleston. It next belonged to John Dunlap, 1797—and to James Dunlap, in 1830."
† Said to be related to General Francis Marion of the Revolution, the Huguenot patriot of S. C.

tombs are in Camden cemetery. Upon its removal to Camden from his plantation, his body was found to be *petrified*. This family claims relationship with General Marion. Issue five children:

1. Elizabeth Ray, married Joseph Goodman, and had several children.
2. Emily Ray, married Bellfield Starke and had Lizzie, and James.

McMILLAN, OF SOUTH CAROLINA.

3. Louisa Rogers Ray (d. January 1, 1855), *m.* 25th February, 1830, bv Rev. S. S. Davis, Thomas McMillan, of Camden, Merchant; (first wife), he moved to Mobile. Ala., 1834, and made his home at Spring Hill, opposite his brother-in-law, Mr. John J. Blair, where he led a most honorable and useful life. Issue, five sons and six daughters, as follows:

1. Mary Eliza (d. 1856), *m.* Charles E. Bridges, and left one son, Charles Thomas, died a young man, and also Eleanor Louisa, born 1853, died 1860.
2. Thomas James McMillan, merchant, moved to New Orleans 1856, *m.* (1860) Rowena Carey, only daughter of Dr. Orson Carey and Martha Monroe, a grandniece of Thomas Jefferson. Issue: 1. Thomas Jefferson, d. y. 2. Carey Lee, of New Orleans, merchant, *m.* (1885) Etta Richards, of Mobile, Ala., son, Lee Richards (b. 1893). 3. Rowena. 4. Martha, d. y. 5. Emma Ray, d. y. 6. Randolph, d. y. 7. Henry, d. y. 8. Mary. 9. Robert. 10. Louisa Ray. 11. William Mayo.
3. John Blair McMillan, of Mobile, Ala., (died 1885), *m.* Elizabeth Douglass, and had: 1. Thomas Douglass, *m.* Mary Sims, no issue. 2. Henry. 3. Marion, *m.* Fannie Gildes and had John Blair. 4. Emile, *m.* Lola Buchanan and had James Gray. 5. Lizzie Lou, *m.* (1898) James Clanton Haygood, Montgomery, Ala., and has James Douglass. (Five sons died young.)
4. Martha Ray McMillan, *m.* C. Fleetwood Westfeldt, of Fletchers, N. C., and had Jennie Fleetwood, Marie Louise, Dodette Eltonie and Hunt Westfeldt.
5. Louisa Rogers McMillan, unmarried.
6. Robert McMillan, Grain Merchant, of New Orleans, C. S. A., Fifth Company Washington Artillery, *m.*(I) 1866, Nannie A. Mayo, and had Phosie, who *m.* (1898) John David Malone,* of Birmingham, Ala., and has Lilian Mayo. He *m.* (II) Henrietta Miltenberger, of New Orleans, and had Charles Miltenberger, Robert, Jr., and Henrietta Louise.
7. Emma Ray McMillan (d. 1887), *m.* Chauncey Drummond, now of New York (first wife). Issue: Chauncey.
8. Ellen Marion McMillan, *m.* William E., son of Dr. Gordon, of Mobile, Ala. Issue: Thomas McMillan, *m.* (1897) Agnes Rowe, of New York; William Elliott, Ellen Ray, Clarence Henry (d. y.) and Lee Owen Gordon.
9. William Blair McMillan, San Antonio, Texas, *m.* Fannie Howard, and has Robert and a daughter.
10. Henry Blair McMillan, of Mobile, *m.* Clara Richards, elder sister of Mrs. Lee McMillan, and has Orline, Leila and Annetta (twins).
11. Alice Kennedy, died young.

The elder Thomas McMillan, of Mobile, *m.* (II) Elizabeth James, of Scotland, and had Elizabeth, who *m.* Chauncey Drummond (above) of New York (second wife), and had four children (names unknown).

4. Martha Couturier Ray, b. St. John Berkley, Charleston District, S. C., 8th April, 1802, d. New Orleans, 29th May, 1868), married John James Blair (above) (*see Blair*).

---

* Mr. Malone's mother was a Miss Spotswood, of Huntsville, Ala., a descendant of Governor Spotswood (1713), of Virginia.

5. Peter Wm. Ray, b. St. Johns, Berkley, 1809, d. 1826. Tomb in Camden Cemetery, near his parents—"*A mother's last gift to her only son.*"

KENNEDY, OF SOUTH CAROLINA.

David Kennedy, Laird of the Craig, Ayreshire, Scotland, m. Margaret Douglass.
His son. Alexander, m. Elizabeth, daughter of John McMillan, of Pulgowan, and had :
1. David, the present Laird ; 2. Margaret, m. Rev. Wm. McDowell ; 3. John McMillan ;
4. Anthony McMillan ; 5. Sarah ; 6. Robert ; 7. Alexander ; 8. Mary, m. Mr. Carnes ;
9. Agnes ; 10. James Douglass. Of these : John, and Anthony McMillan Kennedy
came to Camden. S. C., in 1832, and remained with their cousin, Thomas McMillan,
followed by their brother, Robert M. Kennedy, in 1842. John settled in the North,
and Anthony and Robert married sisters : Sarah Ann and Margaret Doby, daughters of
John and Ann (Belton) Doby, S. C. Elizabeth McM., the daughter of Anthony, m.
Alfred English Doby, of General Longstreet's staff, who was killed at the battle of
Chancellorsville, leaving Elise, who m. Beverly Means English, Rookland county, S. C.
Anthony Kennedy was also father of Gen. John D. Kennedy, of Camden, C. S. A.,
Lieutenant Governor of South Carolina, and Consul General to China in President
Cleveland's administration. He m. (I) Miss Cunningham, and had several children ; m.
(II) Harriet A., daughter of Burwell Boykin, S. C., and has Flora McKae.

David Kennedy, (above) Laird of the Craig, was of a family of landed proprietors who
had lived for many generations in Ayreshire. Their neighbors, of the same standing, were
the family of John McMillan, of Holm, whose son Robert (d. 1844,) married (1794,)
Elizabeth (d. 1846,), eldest daughter of the elder David Kennedy, and had fourteen
children. Of these, three came to the United States : 1. David, to Wilcox county, Ala.,
leaving a son, Thomas B. McMillan, of Knoxville, Tenn. ; 2. Anthony, family of Boise
City, Idaho ; and 3. *Thomas*, of Camden, and Mobile, (fifth son), born at the homestead
"*Pulgowan*," in Gallowayshire, 19th July, 1804, and came to Camden, S. C., in 1820.
The Kennedy and Doby relatives are yet numerous in South Carolina.

McCARTHY.

Arms of McCarthy, of *Castle Carrignavor*, County Cork, Ireland. (Justin MacCartie (b. 1816),
M. P., the *chief* of the family.) Arg. *a stag trippant* ys., *attired and unguled* or. Crest : *A dexter
arm couped below the elbow erect, cloaked with mail arg.*, *and hand holding a newt, all ppr.*—*Burke's
Landed Gentry.*

Earliest Records of McCarthy in Virginia.

Charles McCartie, aged 27, and Owen McCartie, aged 18, came to Virginia, 1635, in
the *Plain Joan* (*Hotten, p. 78*).

Dennis McCarty (spelled *MacCartie* in the Virginia Land Books) is believed to have
been the *first* in the colony of Virginia, says *Hayden* in his "*Virginia Genealogies.*" It
is probable that others of his connection followed him to America, as will be shown
farther on. In September, 1675, he had a grant of 250 acres on the Eastern Shore,
Lynn Haven, Lower Norfolk (Land Book, VIII, 179), which he sold that year to Adam
Keeling. There was a grant also (in 1691) of 400 acres in Princess Anne county. Mr.
Denis MacCartie, of Rappahannock county, had a grant (1691) of 250 acres in Northumberland county. In 1686 he was "attorney for Mr. John Rice," and died about 1700.
"There was also a Denis McCartie, of Princess Anne, in 1693," says Rev. Horace
Hayden, "who was old, poor and lame." Bishop Meade (Vol. II, 573) says : "It is
an ancient Virginia family, springing from Denis and Daniel McCarty." They were
prominent in York, Richmond, Stafford, Westmoreland and Fairfax counties. Daniel
was *Speaker* of the House of Burgesses, 1715. Rev. Horace Hayden adds, that Capt.
Page McCarty wrote him, in 1884, that Capt. Daniel McCarty was a scion of the Irish
family of McCarty, (or McCarthy,) and that he had some of his silver, "all blazoned
with the shield and crest of that house. Dated, 1620." And, though the tradition was

that he was the earl of Clancarty, it is more likely that he was the son of Mount Cashel (head of the younger branch of the family), as the helmet on his *arms* is a *knight's* and not an *earl's*, and that his people merely considered him the earl, after the *elder branch* became extinct, as represented in Ireland by younger branches of the family than the colonial one in Virginia. Daniel McCarty was King's attorney for Rappahannock in 1692.

The tomb of the Speaker is at Montross, Westmoreland county, Va., and gives the date of his birth 1679, and also his family *coat of arms* (*Virginia Mag. of Hist. and Gen. I. 118*); Burke gives the *arms* of Earl of Clancarty, and Viscount Muskerry (attainted 1690), the same as those on the silver of 1620.

(See old Rapp. Records at Essex Court House, for more of the Virginia McCarthy's.)

Denis married 1668, a daughter of Luke Billington, or Bullington, of Rapp, who died 1672, and had issue: (1) Daniel, (b. 1679—d. 1724), Burgess and Speaker, married (I) Mrs. Payne, (II) Ann Lee, widow of Col. Wm. Fitzhugh, of "Eagle's Nest," who died 1713.

(II) Denis MacCarty.

(III) Florance MacCartie (d. 1717) mentioned in York County Records after 1690, was son (or nephew) to Captain Denis MacCartie, the immigrant, as he named his eldest son Dennis. The baptismal name of Ovid is mutually distributed among their descendants, and his own name of Florance, places him as of the distinguished family of the South of Ireland. The *arms* on the tomb of the Speaker, Daniel McCarty, also located *him* certainly in that family.

The children of Daniel McCarty, the Speaker, were: Denis, d. 1744 (married 1724, Sarah Ball): Daniel, (d. 1744), married Penelope Higgins; Billington m. (1732) Ann Barber, (b. 1709 and died 1771); *Thaddeus* (b. 1712, d. 1732) Ann, married John Fitzhugh—Winifred, Sarah and Lettice (*Hayden* 89).

Thaddeus McCarty was clerk of Lancaster, and of the vestry of Christ Church, Lancaster, in 1770.

"John Macartey" is mentioned in the York Records of 1681 as a small planter, brawling with his neighbors, in the house of Mrs. Elisheba Vaulx (*York R. 1675, 1684*).

"Charles Macarthy" is also mentioned 1682, in friendly transactions with his neighbors. (*Ibid.*)

Another "Charles Mackartie" came in 1688, with Capt. Francis Page, to York county, as a headright, with forty-five others. With every person brought over, a planter was granted 50 acres, and hence his own family, friends, relatives and indentured servants, were all registered together by him on the ship's list, he, paying their fare, and, in return, receiving the 50 acres offered by the Crown, as an inducement to immigration. Often the indentured servant was to serve for a term of years, and for *other* considerations as well. Among those who came on this trip with Captain Page, were some whose families were already land owners, and well-to-do in the young colony, and bore the names of the best of those early settlers (as was often the case). Captain Page's list (1688) included the names of *Dennis Mackartie,* William Seaborne, John Hampton, Joseph Hill, Thomas Gooding, Ralph Danby, William Barker, Benj. Lucas, Robert Case, James Brown, Jane Palmer, Jane Pepper, Alice Cockin, William Cockin, Nath'l Goldin, Phillis Turner, Mary Reade, Mary Lonman, John Jones, Sam'l Ward, Richard Rogers, Robert Berkley, Isabel Makeland, Margaret *Billington,* Ann Philips, Mary Bennett, Elizabeth Lunn, Thomas Wilkinson, Thomas Smith, Henry Clinch, Andrew Moore, Jeremiah Brooks, Mary Chapman, Ellinor Fford, John Knight, Thomas Butler, Elizabeth Watts, Margaret Robinson, Thomas Pratt, Henry Holecraft, Elizabeth Tully, Jane Powell, Richard Ffoulks, James Wharton and Jane Barker. (*York R., 1687-1691, page 139.*)

FLORANCE MACCARTIE, of Bruton Parish, York County, died 15th March, 1717. (*Bruton Register*). Mentioned in York county Records, 1698, where he brought suit *vs.* Mary, widow of William Dyer—(which suit was dismissed the next year, he failing to prosecute.) He bought a tract of land, 101¼ acres, in 1705, from William Jordan; witnessed a power of attorney, 1709, from Mrs. Mary Harrison, and in 1714 bought another tract from John Harrison and wife, Mary. In 1702 he was security with George Hughs for a debt of John Marshall[*] to the estate of Cope Doyley. (*All from York Records*). John Marshall was probably his kinsman, and from Ireland. In 1711 he was on a jury with Walter Shelton, Philip Debuam, William Taylor, Thomas Burnham, Russell Wagstaff and John Hansford (whose brother, Thomas Hausford, Mrs. Bacon's celebrated Rebel), John Brooks, Richard Kendall, Edward Power, Thomas Vines and Aduston Rogers, to "try the issue," in a suit between Abel Dunn, plaintiff, and John and Elizabeth Wills, defendants. Robert Hyde, the celebrated attorney, was for the defendants. (*Wm. and Mary Quarterly*, Vol. 1—95).

He was appointed constable of the upper precinct of Bruton parish to succeed Mr. John Smith, in 1717, in which year he died.

He married (before 1700) Mary, daughter, probably, of Dionysius Wright,[†] Justice of James City county, 1702, and had issue: Dennis, (died 3d October 1705) Florance, Dionysius, John, Eleanor, Margaret, Mary, and Anne McCartie (b. 25 June 1706). (*Bruton Parish Register*.)

There seems little doubt that he was the son of Dennis McCartie, who came early to Virginia. In those days of promogeniture, the eldest son was named either for his father or grandfather.

Will of Florance MacCartie (*17th March, 1717*), *proved* 19th May, 1718, by the oaths of William McCraw, Henry Holdcraft and Richard Kendall; widow, Mary, executrix, John Bates and William Horbush, her securities.

" In the name of God, Amen. I, Florance MacCartie, of Bruton parish, York county, being sick and weak of body, but in sound and perfect memory, praise be to God, and calling to mind the uncertainty of this mortal life, and that all flesh must die when it shall please God to call, do make, ordain, constitute and appoint this my last will and testament in manner and form following: And first and principally I commend my *soul* into the hands of Almighty God, my Maker and Redeemer, hoping through the merits

---

[*]John Wright, Minister in York county, New Poquosin par. 1677.
Anthony Wright. Notary Public in York county, 1698. (*Records*.)
[†]Dionysius Wright sued Lyonell Morris (1648) in Henrico Court. John Woodson his security. (*Henrico Records*.)
Dionysius Wright was Justice in James City county, 1702. Also Philip Lightfoot, Benjamin Harrison, James Bray and others. *Virginia Magazine of History in Vol. I.*
He had also a daughter, Margaret, married to Richard Kendall, who brought suit, 1712, *vs.* Mrs. Rebecca Cobbs, and William Eaton, and Sarah his wife, daughter of William Pinkethman, dec'd, for a legacy left his wife, Margaret Wright, who was a neice of William Pinkethman. Ralph Graves also sued for a legacy left his wife Mary, (William and Timothy Pinkethman, John Kendall and Ralph Graves of the Vestry of Bruton parish after 1689, Prickethman Eaton and William Eaton, in 1769. *Meade*.)
(Robert Wright of James City county, old planter, grant from Yeardly 1637. *Virginia Magazine of History*, Vol. I.)
Dionysius Wright's daughter, Dionysia, married (I) Samuel Ravenscroft, of York, and (II), 1695, Thomas Hadley. With her father, she witnessed (169-) the will of Mrs. Catherine Thorpe, (widow of Thomas Thorpe), who left all her estate to James Whaley—whom she intended to marry.
Mrs. Hadley was sued, in 1708, as widow of Samuel Ravenscroft, by Edward Jaqueline and Mary Whaley, "trustees of ye estate of Captain Samuel Ravenscroft."
Captain Thomas Ravenscroft (1733), in Bristol parish, Henrico, contracted to build the old brick church of *Blandford*, in King George (Petersburg), on an acre of land on " *Wells Hill*," bought of John Lowe—John Ravenscroft offered to build a new church, 1739.
Thomas Ravenscroft, gent, died 1785. John Stark Ravenscroft, Bishop of North Carolina, was born at Blandford, 1772, (son of Dr. John Ravenscroft), Minister Mecklenberg county, St. James parish, 1817. "Of the ancient Virginia family to be found about Williamsburg and Petersburg, according to records of the House of Burgesses and Vestry Books, and related to old Lady Skipwith, of Mecklenburg, says Bishop Meade.

of Jesus Christ to obtain full pardon for all my sins past, and that my soul, with my body, at the last day, shall rise again with joy, and receive that most blessed kingdom, which God has prepared for his *elect* and *chosen*," etc.

" And now for the settling of all my temporal estate, goods and chattels, lands and negroes, debts and other movable and immovable estate, which God has been pleased to endow me withal. I give and dispose the same as follows, viz. :

" And first, I give and bequeath unto my son, Florance MacCartie, my dwelling plantation, 101 acres of land which I purchased of Mr. William Jordan (in 1705), and for want of issue of his body. the land to fall to my son, John MacCartie, and for want of his issue, the said land to fall to the next heir of my blood.

" 2d. To my son Dionysius MacCartie, that plantation, and sixty acres more or less, which I bought of John Harrison," etc.

" 3d. To my son, John MacCartie, £50 current money, to purchase him a seat of land. to be paid by my executors when he attains the age of twenty years.

·' 4th. My will and desire is that my said sons be educated and brought up to schooling—that is that they be taught to read, write, and to cypher as far, until they are able to work the rule of three, all out of the profits of my estate.

"5th. That my loving wife, Mary MacCartie, have the liberty to enjoy and live upon my dwelling plantation during her natural life, she not claiming her dower in my other plantations, but that she may have use and occupation of all my lands and plantations, while she remains a widow, and the profits of the labor of my negroes during the time of her widowhood ; and if she do not marry again, to enjoy all the profits of my estate until my children attain to twenty years, or any of my daughters are *marryed*, and then they to have their estate, etc. That if my wife marry again, she to have an equal part with her children, with all her right of dower in my mansion house during her life.

" 6th. To my daughter *Ellinor*, my negro woman Frank and her future increase, etc.

"7th. To my daughter *Margaret* my negro girl Peggy, to be delivered to her when 20 years of age, or when married, etc.

"Item. To my daughter *Mary*, negro girl Kate, etc.

"Item. To my daughter *Ann*, negro boy Emanuel, when she attains the age of 20, etc.

"Wife, executrix ; with my two friends, Mr. Richard Kendall[*] and Mr. Henry Holdcraft,[†] overseers (or trustees). Flor MACCARTIE." [SEAL]

In a codicil (March 12, 1717), he leaves his horse *"Jockey"* and his *Operdino* and belt, pistols and holster and sword to his son Florance, to be given him when he attains to 20 years, etc., and his wife to have his *"large Bible,"* and after her death it to fall to his daughter Elinor and her disposing forever.

The will was further proved in court (June 16, 1718), by oath of Charles Goss, and ordered to be certified. Inventory amounted to £439-4-2.

Mrs. Mary MacCartie, the widow, married (II) Thomas Larke. The court in 1727 took the estate of the orphans from his control, charging him with mismanagement. At

[*] "Capt. George Kendall went to Virginia in the first expedition, 1606-7, and was executed there in 1607. I believe he was cousin to Sir Edwin Sandys ; a little later Edwin and Miles Kendall, cousins of Sir Edwin Sandys. were born in the Bermudas, and I believe all these Kendalls to belong to the same family. Sir Edwin Lundys, of the Virginia Company, had a first cousin of the same name. whose daughter, Dorothy, married a Mr. Kendall, whose pedigree I have not found, but I believe George Kendall to be of this family."—Brown's *Genesis of the United States*.

William Kendall was Burgess for Northampton county 1657, and Speaker in 1666. His only daughter, Mary. married (1675) Hancock Lee, son of Richard, the immigrant.—*Lee Family*.

*Thomas Marshall died, Westmoreland county, 1702, was the immigrant of the family. He had a son, William Marshall.

[†]Henry Holecraft was attorney in York 1702.

this court Dionysius MacCartie chose James McKindo for guardian, and John MacCartie chose Thomas Holderaft.*

The appraisers of the personal property were William Fraser, Ralph Graves and John Davis.

Florance MacCartie, Jr., died 14th February, 1719 (*Bruton Parish Register*).

James McKindo died 1731, and Dionysius MacCartie chose Patrick Farguson (who d. 1738) as guardian (John Ballard administered the estate of James McKindo).

Mr. William Robinson made motion, September, 1731, that the accounts of Florance MacCartie's estate, which was taken from out of the hands of Thomas Larke, be settled by a committee consisting of John Blair, Samuel Cobbs, William Prentis and Joseph Davenport. Admitted to record. Ordered that John Ballard, administrator of James McKindo, pay to Patrick Farguson, guardian of Dionysius MacCartie, the sum of £59, 7s. 1d.

Dionysius and John McCartie (1740) were reported for attending another parish church, than Bruton.

Dionysius MaCartie, 1741, sued by —— Keen.

Dionysius MaCartie came of age between 1731 and 1740. He married Elizabeth Power (?), had son, James MaCartie, and died February, 1746. Elizabeth, his wife, administratrix; with Folliot Power† and John MacCartie, securities.

Personal estate appraised, £330 and a plantation.

(There was a Dr. James McCarty, in Petersburg, Va., partner of Dr. James Field in drug business, succeeding Alex. Glass Strachan).—*Virginia Gazette.* The widow died before 1757. John MaCartie administrator.

John McCarty (d. 1757), left no issue as far as is known. He was administrator of the estate of Thomas Holderaft, who died 1747, and had been his guardian in 1727. He was probably a near relative. Frederick Bryan, Deputy Sheriff, settled the estate of John MaCartie. He paid taxes on nine tithables and quit rent on 150 acres. There was a settlement of Mrs. Elisabeth McCarty's *estate account* with Mr. John McCarty's estate, £200,18.3 and 14 slaves, delivered to Mr. Benjamin Weldon, guardian to James McCarty. Bruton parish register, records the baptism of negroes of Mrs. Eliz. McCarty and Mr. John Macarty, 1747-8. There was a balance of £250 left in the hands of the sheriff.

Eleanor MacCartie married, probably, Robert Drewry (who d. 1744). She was executrix of his will 1744 (Records): He was son of John Drewry, Jr., (b. 1649), was Commissioner of Records in York county 1702. Capt. Glenham Drewry was in York, 1658.

Anne MacCartie (b. 25th June, 1706) married Thomas, or *Peter,* Oliver (descendants differ as to his name). He was a son of Dionysius MacCartie's neighbor, John Oliver, *planter,* in York Co., Hampton Par, 1647. These were parents of Dionysius Oliver

---

*Capt. Thomas Holcraft, member of the Virginia Company, came to Virginia with Lord De la Warr in 1610, and afterward commanded one of the forts at Kickoughtan, and died there. He was son of Sir Thomas Holcraft, of Vale Royal, Cheshire, who paid ten subscriptions, son and heir of Sir Thomas Holcraft, Knight (receiver of the Duchy of Lancaster to Edward VI), by Julianne, daughter and heir of Nicholas Jennings, Alderman of London.

Capt. Jeffray Holcraft, member Virginia Company, son of Thomas Holcraft, of Battersea, in Surrey.—Alex. Brown's *Genesis of United States.*

One of the Holcrafts was of the Vestry Blisland parish, New Kent county, Va.. between 1721-38.

†Dr. Henry Power, of York Co. (will p. 1692), m. Mary, daughter of Rev. Edward Folliot, (will 1690), of Hampton Par. Issue: 1. Eliz.² m. Col. Cole Digges; 2. Maj. Henry². of James City Co., d. 1738, leaving Molly², m. (1759) Thos. Hall; Susannah² m. Lawrence Taliaferro, and Henry² Power. 3. John³. d. 1720, who had Edward³, Folliot², John³, Rebecca³.—*Wm. and Mary Quarterly, I. and VII. Vols.*

Ellen, daughter of Cormac Dermod MacCartie, Earl of Clancarty and Lord of Muskerry, and granddaughter of the Earl of Ormond, married Crogher O'Callahan, Esq.. of County Cork, and their daughter, Eleanor, married John Gillman, who went to Ireland towards close of the 16th century, owing to religious persecution, and settled in Munster (Co. Cork). He was of the notable Gillman family of England, Ireland and America, and of ancient Welch descent. He died 1644. (*Burke's Landed Gentry.*

who went to Wilks Co., Ga., (now Elbert Co.) during the revolution; and of Thomas, John, James, Peter and others (*see Oliver Family*).

Of the daughters, Margaret and Mary McCartie of the *will*, nothing is known.

James McCarty appears 1768, in a transaction with Joseph Valentine (son of James Valentine, of 1702).

Michael McCarty also in York Records of 1768.

McCARTHY.

(*Brown's Americans of Royal Descent.*)

1. Ceallachan Cashel, forty-second Christian King of Munster in Ireland, had—
2. Doucha, Prince of Desmond, father of
3. Saorbhreathach (brother of Foghartach, forty-third King of Munster) who had—
4. Carthach, Prince of Desmond (d. 1045), who had—
5. Mundach MacCarthach (or McCarthy), who had—
6. Cormach Magh Tauchnach McCarthy, King of Desmond (d. 1138), who had—
7. Desmond, of Cillbachhuime, brother of Fingan Leice Lachtna, King of Cork, 1144–85, who had—
8. Donald *Mor* na Curra MacCarthy, Prince of Desmond 1185–1205, who had—
9. Cormac Fionn MacCarthy, who had—
10. Donald Roe MacCarthy *Mor*, Prince of Desmond, who had—
11. Donald Oge MacCarthy *Mor* (d. 1303), who had—
12. Cormac MacCarthy *Mor* (d. 1359), who had—
13. Dermod MacCarthy *Mor* (created first feudal Lord Muskerry in 1353, and killed by the O'Mahoneys), who had—
14. Cormac MacCarthy, Lord Muskerry (killed 1374), who had—
15. Teige (or Timothy) MacCarthy, Lord Muskerry (d. 1449), who had
16. Cormac (or Charles) Laider MacCarthy, Lord Muskerry, of *Castles Blarney, and Kilcrea* (killed 1494).
17. Cormac Oge MacCarthy, Lord Muskerry (d. 1536), who had—
18. Teige (Timothy) MacCarthy, Lord Muskerry (d. 1569), who had—
19. Dermod MacCarthy, Lord Muskerry (d. 1570), who had—
20. Cormac Mor MacCarthy, Lord Muskerry, of Blarney Castle (d. 1616), who had—
21. Cormac Oge MacCarthy, first Viscount Muskerry, of Blarney Castle (d. 1640), who had—

22. Donach (or Daniel) MacCarthy, *Baron of Blarney*, Viscount Muskerry, and created by Charles II, Earl of Clancarty. He was commander of the Irishmen of Munster for Charles I and II, and the last to lay down his arms, being defeated by General Ludlow in Kerry. Subsequently his estates were restored to him, and he died in London 1665; leaving issue by his wife, Lady Ellen Butler:

    (1) Charles, Lord Muskerry, killed on the "*Royal Charles*" 1665; (2) Justin, Viscount Mount Cashel (died 1694), and

23. Donald MacCarthy, younger son, built *Castle Carrignavar*, county Cork, who had, 24. Donald Cormac MacCarthy, who had, 25. Fingan MacCarthy, of Croom, who had, 26. Fingan Mor MacCarthy, b. 1720, who took an active part in the insurrection of 1798, and died 1818. He had issue by his wife, Margaret O'Connor (Leagh): (*Canada Mac-Carthys*), Margaret MacCarthy, who married Owen O'Connor (Cashel), a "'98" man also, and had—

    I. John O'Connor, who had John O'Connor, of Ottawa, Canada; II. Timothy O'Connor, who had Rev. John S. O'Connor, P. P., of Alexandria, Canada; III. Owen O'Connor, who had—

        1. Eugene O'Connor, of St. Paul, Minn.; 2. Edward O'Connor, of St. Paul, Minn.

27. Capt. Donal Mor MacCarthy, a commander of the Irish forces in the battle of Bal lynoscarthy in the insurrection of '98, who removed to Canada, where he died in 1825; m. Mary Eicheson, and had—

    I. Joanne MacCarthy m. Joseph De Foe, of Toronto, Canada; II. Charles MacCarthy, of St. Paul, Minn. (b. 1808), removed to America 1828, and to St. Paul 1868. He married, in Canada, Ellen O'Connor (Cathal), and had—

        1. Cornelius Mor MacCarthy, of St. Paul; 2. Daniel Francis MacCarthy, of St. Paul; 3. Florance Joseph McCarthy, d. s. p. 1874; John Collins MacCarthy. Of these, Daniel and John Collins both have descendants living in St. Paul, Minn.

Gough, in his edition of *Camden's Britannica*, says: "The Irish antiquarians allow but *eight* families of Royal extraction in Munster, of which they place four in Carbery (or the southwest part of Cork). Of these were MacCarthy, O'Mahon, O'Donovan and O'Driscol" (*Burke*).

O'Hart, in his "Irish Peerage," says Donough, first Earl of Clancarty, had *four sons* (of whom the fourth was Lord *Mount Cashel*, who died (1694) s. p.), as follows:

    1. Donald, the first son, the "Buchaill Ban," or the "fair haired boy," had more than one son, and is represented in America by Cornelius McCarthy, lawyer, St. Paul, Minn.

    2. Cormac, the second son, was Lord Muskerry, now represented (1880) by Justin McCarthy, hereditary earl of Clancarty, in the United States.

    3. Ceallachan, the third son, is not said to have married.

Burke, in his "*Landed Gentry of Great Britain and Ireland*," says: "Few pedigrees in the British Empire can be traced to a more remote or a more exalted source than that of the *Celtic House of McCarthy*. On the arrival of the English, in the 12th century, they were styled *Kings* in Desmond and in Cork.

"From Cormac *Mor* (or Great), who lived in the beginning of the 12th century, sprang two sons: Daniel, the elder (succeeded his father as the McCarthy More), and Diarmid (or Dermod), the younger, who was founder of the powerful house of Muskerry.

"The descendant of Daniel (or Donoch) was created Earl of *Clancare* by Queen Elizabeth, 1565. He died without issue. His last collateral representative was Charles McCarthy Mor, officer in the Guards, who died 1770. The dwindled possessions of this branch became vested in his cousin, Herbert of Muckruss.

"Justin MacCarthy, of 'Carrignavar,' county Cork (b. 1816), is now the chief of his name and representative of the oldest existing branch of the once sovereign '*House of MacCarthy*.'")[*] He is the great Parliamentarian, and author, and anti-Parnellite.)

"The first who bore the name of MacCarthy (or *son of Cartagh*), was the grandfather of Diarmid McCarty More, whom the English found in possession of Cork, and who swore fealty, gave hostage and subjected his kingdom to Henry II. Diarmid was slain by Theobald Butler (founder of the house of Ormond) in 1186. His successors were Donald, Cormac (or Charles) Fionn, Donald Roe, Donald Oge and Cormac, all of whom were distinguished as *McCarty More* (or great) an adjunct which was continued in this senior branch until 1556, when Donald McCarty More, seventh in descent from the

---

Dear Madam: I fear I can not be of much assistance to you as regards the inquiries you are making. There were no collateral branches of my family after the Revolution of 1688 to about the end of the last century, when my grandfather's sister married a Colonel Attryn. There were, however, several other branches of the *old stock* whose properties were confiscated after the Revolution. I may go further back than I have done so far, as I find that there were no collateral branches since my ancestor, a grandson of the then Lord Muskerry, of Blarney Castle, left the *main stock* (about the end of the sixteenth century), which has since become extinct from failure of male issue. I remain, madam,
Yours very faithfully,
JUSTIN MACCARTHY.

eldest son of the last mentioned Cormac, was created Earl of Clancare, in Kerry, on resigning his estates to Queen Elizabeth, from whom he again received the investiture of them, "to hold of the crown of England, in the English manner." This branch is extinct for more than a century. But the above Cormac Mor had second son, Dermod, first feudal lord of Muskerry, and *founder* of that potent house, who was killed by the O'Mahonys in 1367. From him sprang in succession as Lords of Muskerry:

"Teige Cormac, d. 1374, Teige, 1448; Cormac Laidhir (the stout), 1494; Cormac Oge Laidhir, who defeated the Earl of Desmond at the battle of Morne, 1521, d. 1536. Teige d. 1565, Dermod d. 1570. His son, Cormac, Lord of Muskerry, had his residence at Blarney Castle, and died 1616, leaving two sons:

1. Cormac Oge, Lord of Muskerry, the first Viscount (as stated by some writers), died in London, 1640, leaving a son, Donald, first Earl of Clancarty, whose male line is extinct.[*]

2. Daniel (or Donald), second son of Cormac, built the *Castle of Carrignavar*, County Cork, and married Katherine, *dau.* of Stephen Meade. His son, Charles, Esq., of *Carrignavar*, married Katherine, *dau.* of David Roche, Seventh Viscount Fermoy, and was succeeded by his grandson, Charles, son of Daniel and Eliz (Matthews) McCarty. Charles died s. p. 1761, and was succeeded by his nephew—Daniel, son of Daniel and Grace (Fitzgerald) McCarty, who died 1763. His second son, Robert, married (1784) Jane Capel, and died 1823, leaving a son, Justin, born 1786, father of *Justin, now of " Carrignavar"* (b. 1816) and who married (1848) to Louisa, *dau.* of Major Edward Fitzgerald. A brother, Joseph, of "Shrub Hill," County Surrey, vicar of Wilton, County Cork, married Mary Frances, *dau.* of the Ven. William Thompson, Archdeacon of Cork, and has several children, among them: Florence MacCartie. He adopted the old spelling of his name, "*MacCartie,*" and died 1874.

"Equally important in the Muskerry line are the descendants of Florence McCarthy, of *Clodane*, and Donough (or Daniel) McCarthy, of *Drishane*, 1602. (See *Burke's Landed Gentry.*)

"Florence McCarthy, of *Clodane*, had a daughter Jane, who married John Marshall, son of Thomas Marshall, who came to County Kerry in the expedition of Sir Charles Wilmot, 1602, and married Mary, daughter of Maurice Fitzgerald, of *Ballymac Adam Castle*, and settled there. John Marshall was driven out by the Irish in the great rebellion of 1641, but returned as captain in Cromwell's army. These were ancestors of the Markham and Pursell families. (*Burke's Landed Gentry, p. 1340.*) Florence McCarthy was of the family of Donough (or Daniel) McCarthy, of *Drishane*, descended from the noble family of Muskerry. Members of *this line* came to Virginia, as did, also, the Marshalls, Markhams, Pursells and Fitzgeralds."

Florence McFinnen McCarty, of Ardtilly, son of Charles McCarty, of Carrick-nainack, had a daughter, Honora, who married Colonel Owen McSweeny, of Muskerry. Their daughter Mary married Owen O'Sullivan, of Ardia, and had issue: Major Philip O'Sullivan, of Ardia, who married Joanna, daughter of Dermot McCarty *Mor*, of Killoween, County Kerry, descended from the Earl of Clancare, and his wife, a daughter of McCarty Reagh, of Carberry, and his wife Eleanor, daughter of Lord Muskerry. A son, John Sullivan, born in Ardia, 1699, came to Maine in 1723, and was father of Major General John Sullivan, of New Haven (b. 1740, d. 1795), of the Revolutionary army; member of Congress, 1774, and President of New Hampshire, 1786 (see *New Eng. Hist. and Gen. Register for October, 1865*).

---

[*] Peter Flournoy. of France, became naturalized in England, 1682, and obtained the patronage of the Earl of Sunderland, to whose sons he was tutor. Also, in the Patent Rolls, 1715, His Majesty declares "We are graciously pleased to allow for the maintenance of the late Countess of Clancarty's children, and for their education in the Protestant religion, the yearly sum of £1000, and the same shall be paid to our trusty and well beloved Peter Flournoy, Esq.," etc. In his will, 1719, he remembers his "pupils," Lord Muskerry, and his brother, Mr. Justin McCarty. (*Flournoy Rivers, in Va. Mag. of Hist., Vol. II, 82.*)

DATES OF CREATION OF "SOUTH SIDE" COUNTIES, IN VIRGINIA.

Surry (1652) taken from James City county. Brunswick (in 1720), and Sussex (1754), both taken from Surry county. Southampton (1748), from Isle of Wight county. Lunenburg (1746) from Brunswick. Bedford (1853), from Lunenburg.—(*Virginia Magazine of History*, II, 91.)

Amelia (1736), and Dinwiddie (1752), both taken from *Prince George county*, which, itself, was taken (in 1702) from Charles City county. Prince Edward 1753, and Nottoway 1788, both taken from Amelia.

Goochland, in 1727, and Chesterfield, 1748, both taken from *Henrico county*, which, itself was taken in 1677, from Charles City county. Albemarle, 1744, and Cumberland, 1748, both taken from Goochland. Powhatan, 1777, from Cumberland county. Amherst, 1761, from Albemarle.

OLIVER FAMILY.

Arms of Oliver.

SCOTLAND. | Ar. two chevrons gu. betw. three martlets sa. in chief, and a heart crowned in base. ppr.
Crest. A dexter arm. ppr. vested ar., turned up gu. grasping an olive branch fruited ppr.
Motto: Ad fædera cresco.

ENGLAND, KENT Co. | Erm. on a chief gu. three lions ramp. or.
Crest. A lion's head erased gu.
Motto: Non sine.

IRELAND. | Erm. on a chief sa. Three lions ramp. or.
Crest. An heraldic tiger's head erased or. collared sa.

There were in the middle ages families of Oliver in several counties of England, especially Kent, Lincolnshire and Devonshire. "In the south of Scotland," writes Major General J. R. Oliver, C. M. C., R. A., "there is quite an Oliver clan, which probably came from Scandinavia, and derived from 'Olaf,' a common name in the Basque country, and it is also a Norman name."

He adds "the Oliver family owned twenty-four townlands in the borough of Corklea, county Limerick, Ireland, and nineteen in the borough of Clanmorris, county Kerry, and were settled in county Limerick as early as the reign of Elizabeth. The borough of Kilmallock was incorporated by Queen Elizabeth 1584, with power to select a 'soverain,' and the corporation seal, dated 1585, has an inscription around the rim, 'Robert Oliver, Jr., Esq., soverain.' General Oliver's ancestor, of whom he has the first definite record, was Robert Oliver, captain in Cromwell's army for the reduction of Ireland, in 1649. He was ancestor of the 'Cloghanodfoy' line, and possibly came from Kent, Eng. Berry's *Encyclopædia Heraldica* states that the *arms* of the '*Olivers of Ireland*' were Ermine, on a chief sable, three lions rampant or; *crest*, an heraldic tiger's head, erased or. collared azure.

"These arms are identical with those he gives of the Olivers of Exeter, except that the lions of the latter are 'arg.' instead of 'or.'

"There has not been another family of the name of any importance in Ireland," continues General Oliver (in a pamphlet of his family), "except one in the North, and they had quite different *arms*.

"The arms confirmed in 1653 to Capt. Robert Oliver, of 'Cloghanedfoy' (afterward 'Castle Oliver,' county Limerick) were:

"Or. on a chevron between two pellets in chief sable, and one mullett nayant en bas proper, a crescent argent.

"*Crest*, on a helmet and wreath of his colors, a hand holding a branch of olive proper, mantled gules, doubled argent.

"The *crescent* indicates a second son.

"He was M. P. for Limerick in 1661, and he, or his father, was known as *Robin 'Rhu,'* or *'Roux.'* He married Valentina, daughter of Hon. Sir Claude Hamilton, of Castle Toome, County Antrim. Sir Claude Hamilton was son of Claude, Lord Paisley, by Margaret, daughter of Lord Seaton, and was descended from James II of Scotland. A descendant of Robert Oliver's, Lady Colthorpe, lives at *'Blarney Castle,'* Ireland, and has the portraits of her ancient ancestors. (*Letter of General Olivier, 1897.*)

"Olivers were seated at *Oliver Castle*, Peebleshire, Scotland, in 1328. From these were descended Rev. Stephen Oliver, of Jedburg (d. 1740), and also John and Robert Stephen Oliver.

"There were also, in Scotland, the Olivers of *'Dinlebyre,'* county Roxburg. John and William were the names oftenest transmitted from sire to son, and some of their descendants may be traced to Virginia."—(Hayden's *Virginia Genealogies.*)

The Earlier Olivers of Virginia.

Francis Oliver, 1620, of the *Virginia Company of Adventurers and Planters.*

Edward Oliver, 1623, alive, "on the Maine," after the massacre, in James City county.

Edward Oliver, 1636, fifty acres deed of gift to Ann Cordwell, his wife, from Sir John Harvey.—*Virginia Magazine of History, V. 459.*

Edward Oliver, 1639, Tobacco Commissioner, with Christopher Lawson and Robert Hutchinson, in James City county.

Edward Oliver, 1657, bought of Henry Perry 350 acres in Surry county, on upper Chippoaks' creek, on the river (*once James City county*).

Edward Oliver, b. 1661; died, 1695; of Henrico county; his home with John Worsham, "where he lived." In 1694 he was sued by Wm. Byrd for 430 pounds of tobacco; John Worsham, his bail. His estate appraisement was small.

John Oliver, 1647, living in York county. Va., and, later, John and Thomas Oliver, also.

John Oliver was a planter in Hampton parish.—*York Records.*

James Oliver, living in Hanover town, 1788, advertised a stray cow.—*Virginia Gazette.*

Miss Oliver, of Hanover, m. 1789, Mr. Menx, of New Kent county.—*Virginia Gazette.*

William Oliver, will, 1687, in Middlesex county, Va.

Thomas Oliver, 1708, married Sarah Howe, Middlesex county, Va.

Isaac Oliver, died in Middlesex county, 1725.

Thomas Oliver married Susannah ———, and had issue:
William, b. 1722, died infant; Isaac, b. 1725, William, b, 1726 (*Middlesex county*).

Ignatius Oliver, of Northumberland county (*will proved* 1710); wife, Elizabeth.

William Oliver, of White Chapel parish, Lancaster county, 1730 (*will, 1750*); wife Ellison. Children: John Oliver and others; witnesses, Isaac White, Martin Shearman, Hannah, Tomlin and Ann Shearman, wife of Martin Shearman (she was the daughter of Rawleigh Chinn, who was of Christ ch. vestry in 1739. Her mother was Esther Ball).—*Lancaster Records and Lee Family.*

Mrs. Ellison Oliver, of Rapp, "*received a letter, through Hobbs Hole Post Office,*" in 1769.—*Virginia Gazette.*

Nicholas Oliver, m. Elis ———, and had Elis, b. 1701.

William Oliver, m. ———, and had William, b. 1710; Edward, b. 1715; Alex., b. 1722, and Andrew, b. 1734.

John Oliver, m. ———, and had Sarah, b. 1720 (*all from Abingdon Parish Register, Gloucester county, Va.*).

William, Thomas and John Oliver were living in Abingdon parish, Gloucester county, 1786, and each owning slaves.

Thos. Oliver, 1795, was heir to a portion of John Figg's lands in Gloucester, as was, also, Thomas Wiatt, John Johnson's children, Jonathan Lyall's children and John Figg.—*Old Surry Book.*

Graveley Oliver, 1820, conducts a suit in Gloucester, in which year *all the Records were burned.*

James, son of James Oliver, living in Gloucester in 1821.—*Gloucester Records.*

James Oliver, died 1822; Agnes Oliver, administratrix, with will annexed.

John Oliver, died in Gloucester county. Children: Catherine, John and Nancy. Edward Dew was guardian of John, and John Dixon guardian of Nancy Oliver. In 1822 Edward Dew and Catherine, his wife, who was Catherine Oliver, sued John Dixon, guardian. In 1823 Edward Dew, guardian of John Oliver, summoned Susan, widow of William Oliver, to administer on the estate of her husband, William Oliver.

William Oliver (1824) settled estate of Ambrose Oliver, in Gloucester county.

Graveley Oliver (1823) a suit; William K. Perrin, his common bail.

John Oliver, of Isle of Wight county. His grant was on the river (1652) and joined Thomas Greenwood and Major Fawden, also James Pyland. His will, 17th April, 1652, mentioned: Wife, Ellen; son, John Oliver, Jr.; daughters, Eleanor and Mary. *Overseers:* James Pyland and Robert Bird. *Witnesses:* James Pyland, John Burton and John Renney.   Eleanor and Mary Oliver, 100 acres (March, 16.2), joining Major Fawden and Thomas Greenwood, on the river.— *William and Mary Quarterly, VII, 222.*

John Oliver (1714-1727), lands in Princess Anne county, on Blackwater. "*Oliver's Run Creek,*" mentioned 1711, in Nansemond records.

Thos. Oliver, 1740, *God-father* to James, son of Joseph and Mary Wheless.—*Albemarle Parish Register Surry and Sussex counties.*

Thomas Oliver (1741), 175 acres, south side of Nottoway in Surry county. He died in 1760, as certified William Oliver.—*Ibid.*

(*From Bristol Parish Register; Chesterfield Prince George, Amelia, Nottoway and Dinwiddie Counties.*)

William and Elizabeth Oliver, had issue: Drury. b. 12th April, 1685 (first entry in the Register).

Drury and Anne Oliver, had issue: Elizabeth, b. 1718; John, b. 1720; William, b. 1722.

Drury and Amy Oliver, of Bristol parish, had issue: Martha, b. 1725, d. 1726; Martha, b. 1727; Mary, b. 1728.

Drury and Elizabeth Oliver, had issue: Ann, b. 1734.

Thomas and Anne Oliver, of Bristol parish, had issue: John, b. 1728.

Isaac and Elizabeth Oliver, had issue: Mildred (b. 1742), Thomas, (b. 1743).

James and Ann Oliver had issue: Mary (b. 1748).

(Bristol parish then included Chesterfield county (which was taken from Henrico in 1748) Goochland (taken from Henrico in 1727) and parts of Prince George and Amelia (which was taken from Prince George 1734); Cumberland (taken from Goochland, 1747); Prince Edward (taken from Amelia 1753); Nottoway (from Amelia 1788); Dinwiddie (from Prince George 1752).

Thomas and Agnes Oliver Godparents 1741—to neighbor's infant.   (*Albemarle Parish Register.*)

Isaac Oliver, of Surry (1751) had 354 acres on Nottoway river. He married Elizabeth ———, and had issue:

Martha, born 1751. *Godmother;* Mildred Oliver.—(*Ibid.*).

William Oliver, of Surry (1750); married Frances ———, and had Isaac. (b. 1751); Lucy (1758); Ann (1761); Frances (1763); Jane (1765) and Rebecca (1771), who married William Wellborn, and had son, Benjamin O. Wellborn, father of Mrs. Scruggs, of Marion, Ala. *Ibid.*

John Oliver, of Surry (1740). Married Elizabeth ——, and had Elizabeth (b. 1741) *Godparents;* John Pointer, John King and Elizabeth Rogers.—(*All from Albemarle Parish Register.*)

James Oliver (June 1743) 400 acres both sides Great Nottoway river, and both sides Snales Creek.—(*Amelia Land Book No. 376.*)

James Oliver (June, 1749) 75 acres both sides of Deep creek; and in 1751, 400 acres on south side of north fork of Great Nottoway.

Isaac Oliver, (1751), 354 acres in Surry, south side of Nottoway, on county line between Surry and Brunswick. Isaac Oliver's lands in Sussex in 1755, near Richard Cooke.

Drury Oliver (1749), Land in Prince George county, on Maw Whippowack creek and Hatcher's Run.

Drury and William Oliver, Godparents (1769) to Thomas, son of John and Betty Chambliss.—(*Abemarle Parish Register.*)

Drury Oliver of Dinwiddie county (1769) advertised a stray horse (*Virginia Gazette*). His estate near Petersburg (7 miles) administered 1773. Considerable property. (*Ibid.*).

John Oliver, of Dinwiddie county. Inventory 1813. (*Records.*)

JAMES OLIVER, of Amelia county (will 1745). On Nottoway river.

James, Oliver of Amelia county (will 1787) mentions children; James, John, Asa, Isaac, William, Richard, Elizabeth Forest and Sarah Bolton. (*Will Book 4, p. 42.*)

Isaac Oliver of Nottoway (son of James of the above will, 1787), married Sarah, sister of Elisha Betts.[*] When a widow, Mrs. Oliver, with her four younger daughters, removed to Botetourt (now Roanoke county) to be near her brother, who had married a Miss Walton, of the family of Madame Octavia Le Vert, of Mobile, Ala. Mrs. Betts died 1857. Mrs. Oliver, and daughters, lived on their estate called "Huntingdon," in Roanoke county. Issue:

I. William. 2. Carter, m. Sarah E. Mitchell, and had Carter B. and Isaac H. of Glade Springs. 3. Charles, of Roanoke county, b. 1777, d. 1851; m. 1807 Lucy Young Neal, and had Col. Yelverton Neal. b. 1808, d. 1887, only son, who built Metairie race track in New Orleans; and was father, among others, of Lucy Neal Oliver, who m. 1854, Dr. James McGavoc Kent, and had several children. 4. Asa, of Nottoway, d. s. p. 1850. 5. Isaac, m. Mary A. G. Bacon. 6. Nancy, m. Mr. Coleman and had Mary; m. Charles Carter of Nottoway. 7. Sally C., d. s. p. 8. Elizabeth, m., late in life, Thomas Walton, nephew of Mrs. Betts; no issue. 9. Mary, m. Mr. Spraggins and went South. 10. Matilda. M.; d. s p. 11. Rebecca 8. d. s. p.

Of these: No. 5, Isaac Oliver, of Nottoway m. Mary A. G. Bacon, and had issue:

1. Judith, drowned, 8 years of age.
2. Martha C., m. Peter Epes, of Nottoway, who, when he died, was about to move South. Had five children, and among these Richard Epes, father of Professor Horace Epes.
3. Edmund Parks, of Alabama, Student William and Mary College 1830; m. Sarah Ward; three children living.
4. James, d. s. p.
5. Judge Wm. C., of Tuscaloosa, Ala., b. 1817, Eminent lawyer; m. (I) Miss Phillips, and had one son; m. (II) Lizzie Whitehead, and had a son (not known), and also Mrs. D. W. Duncan, of Eutaw, Ala.
6. Mary Booker, m. Alexander White; twelve children, among them a dau. Fanny.

[*] Elisha Betts was of the vestry of Cumberland, Va., Lunenburg county (now Mecklenburg), after 1746; also George Walton and Lyddall Bacon, and later on John Cox, Wm. Watkins, Peter Fontain, John Parrish, Edmund P. Bacon, Thos. Lanier, John Billups, Peter Epes and others.

Lunenburg was taken from Brunswick county. 1746; Mecklenburg and Charlotte taken from Lunenburg after 1764

7. Isaac, of Hendersonville, m. Julia Murphy: three children.
8. Charles Augustus, M. D., of Mississippi, came with his brother from Virginia; married Sarah Spann. Issue: Tyrie Spann, Edward Park, Isaac Epps, Alexander White, Sallie Generosa, William and Rev. Father Charles Augustus Oliver, Catholic priest, of Jackson, Miss., a popular and scholarly man, taking great interest in his lineage, who has furnished these notes of his ancestry, in conjunction with Mrs. Lucy Neal Kent, Mrs. Anna Watkins and Mrs. Lucy J. Tuggle of Nottoway Court House, whose father was John Oliver, son of *Richard*, mentioned in James', his father's, will, 1787.

Thomas Oliver, Trustee, in Charlotte county, 1791, for a Mason's lottery, with Joseph Wyatt, and John B. and Francis Scott, Wm. Hubard, John Coleman and others, (*Hening's Statutes, XIII, 315*).

Isaac Oliver, of Prince George county, m. Sally, daughter of Colonel Peter and Mary Poythress Epes. (*Va. Mag. of Hist. III.*)
Martha C. Oliver, m. Peter Epes, son of Richard, and grandson of Colonel Peter Epes of Nottoway. (See above.)
Captain Benjamin Oliver, Jr., m. Lucy Harrison Tomlin (b. 1792), daughter of Colonel Walker Tomlin, in Hanover county. She m. (II) 1825, Dr. William Randolph Nelson (who d. 1862), of Hanover. No issue. Her daughter, Lucy Oliver, m. (1839) in King William county, Dr. Cary C. Cocke, of Bremo (b. 1814, d. 1888), and had John Hartwell, Nannie Oliver and Lelia Cocke.—(*Hayden*).

James Oliver (1772) private in Colonel Nathaniel Gist's Regiment, 8th Company.
William Oliver (1777) 3d Corporal Company C, in Colonel Alex. Spotswood's Regiment.
William Oliver, Captain Lieutenant in Virginia Continental Troops, State line.—(*Saffell.*)
John and Moses Oliver, privates in the same.
John, Lewis and Turner Oliver, privates (1778) in General George Rogers Clark's Illinois Regiment.

John Oliver of North Carolina, Ensign in Second North Carolina.
Thomas and James Oliver, privates in General Marion's regiment.
William Oliver, Corporal 3d Company, General Marion's regiment.   Killed 1779.
—(*Saffell.*)

Oliver, of North Carolina.

John Oliver (1767) Justice in Orange county, North Carolina.—(*North Carolina Colonial Records.*)
James Oliver (1768) of Orange county, signed petition with other citizens.
Mr. John Oliver (1773) petitioned the Assembly to be relieved of a moiety debt, and the Treasurer of the Southern district was ordered to discharge the same.—(*North Carolina Colonial Records, XIII, 445.*)
George Oliver (1773) of Guildford county, petition, with other citizens, as to Court House. Also John Oliver, the same.—(*IX, 806.*)
John Oliver, of Granville county, North Carolina, member of Provincial Congress which met at Halifax, 13th April, 1776.—(*Wheeler's History North Carolina.*)
Andrew Oliver, of Bertie county (1788) member of convention which met at Hillsborough (1788) to consider the Federal Constitution, which they did not ratify until 1789.
Francis Oliver, of Duplin county, same convention.
—(*Southern Historical Magazine, III, 122.*)

John Oliver and Fleming Pope, Ensigns of First and Second Regiments, North Carolina Continental Line, 8th August, 1775, by order of Congress.

(The Rev. Horace Hayden, of Wilkesbarre, Pa., has published a pamphlet of the descendants of *Pierre Olivier, of Virginia, the Huguenot*. They now live, mostly, in New York, Connecticut and Pennsylvania.)

Oliver, of Kentucky.

Peter Oliver, of Virginia, and of the Revolution, married (1775) Mildred (b. 1761, d. 1848), daughter of John (*will* 1787) and Ann (Osborne) Randolph, of Prince William county, Va.; Mrs. Randolph was the daughter of Thomas Osborne, Burgess of Prince William county, Va., who had daughters: Mary, Margaret, Ann, and Prudence Osborne, "co-heiresses, daughters of Thos. Osborne, deceased, and owning 161 acres in Prince William, 1741."

Mrs. Osborne married (II) Cuthbert Harrison. Peter Oliver removed to Fleming county, Ky., after 1790. Children:

1. William Oliver, Major in war of 1812. Had military land warrant for much of the land on which Toledo, Ohio, was built, and where he resided; also had government position in Cincinnati, 1850, and was an elegant gentleman. Issue:
   1. Mrs. Harriet Hall, of Cincinnati. Her husband built the Oliver Hotel in Toledo—for some time the largest in that city.
   2. Mildred Oliver, married (I) - Patterson, and (II) —— King, of Troy, Ohio.
   3. Margaret Oliver, m. Joseph Hill, Sr., of Ohio. (His first wife.) He married (II) her cousin, Mary Purcell. Issue 1st mar.:
      Sarah Hill (b. 21st November, 1801), m. (7th May, 1821) Calvin Fletcher, and had Stephen Fletcher, father of Mrs. Hodges.

Margaret Randolph, sister of Mrs. Oliver, married George Purcell, ensign in the Revolution from Alexandria, and brother-in-law of Colonel Symes. He removed to Kentucky, 1800, died 1805. His brother-in-law, John Randolph, Jr., witnessed his will. Issue:

Mary Purcell, who married Joseph Hill (above) (second wife). His two mothers-in-law, Mrs. Oliver and Mrs. Purcell, sisters, resided with him, and died at his home and are buried near Urbana, Ohio. Issue:
   1. Joseph Hill, Jr., of St. Louis, m. ——, and has Joseph Hill.
   2. Josie Hill, of St. Louis (*Miss Hill*, who furnished these notes).

Four Oliver brothers also lived in Kentucky about this time, and were probably of the same family as the above—Peter G., Thomas, William, John, and sister, Mildred Oliver—of these:

1. Peter G. Oliver, lived in Fleming county. Ky., m. Mary, daughter of Trueman Day, and his wife, Miss Saunders. Issue:
   1. William Trueman Oliver, of Rayville, Miss. 2. Thomas F. Oliver (dead), and 3, *Saunders Day Oliver* (b. Fleming county, 1826, d. 1887). m. Cornelia Elizabeth Dollerhide (whose father, —— Dollerhide, from Holland, married Miss Smith). Issue: several children—of these, a daughter married Dr. Rollo Knapp, of New Orleans (parents of Miss Emily Knapp, who furnished these notes).
2. William Oliver, of Cincinnati, Ohio, postmaster under Wm. Henry Harrison. Children: 1. Washington Oliver; 2. Mary, m. Mr. Hall.
3. John Oliver, of Indiana. Had many children.
4. Mildred Oliver, m. Mr. Fitch, and lived in Urbana, Ohio.

Oliver, of Georgia.

Mac Oliver, of Virginia, was twice married, and had eight children, all of whom settled in Georgia. 1, Wiley[2]; 2, James[2]; 3, Joseph[2]; 4, John[2]; 5, Ann[2]; 6, Charlotte[2]; 7, William[2]; 8, Mac[2] (by second wife) and killed in civil war. (Mrs. Oliver m. (II) a Mr. Wheeler, of Clayton, Ala.) Of the above, 1, Wiley[2] Oliver, lived in Barbour county, Alabama.

2. James[2] Oliver, m. ———, Issue: 1 Henry[3] Oliver, Macon, Ga., m. ———, and had Kate[4], m. Mr. Cooper. Her son. George[5] Cooper, in U. S. N; Nannie[4], m. Mr. Orr; a son, Oliver Orr. 2. William[3], 3. Frank[3], 4 Sarah[3], 5, Nancy[3].

7. William[2] Oliver, (b. 10th Dec., 1798; died 1836), lived in Twiggs county, Georgia, and removed, 1835, to Randolph (now Quitman) county, married (I) Dorcas Harrison*, (b. 29th Oct., 1802; d. 18th September, 1830) and (II) 1834, Irene Drake, of Americus, Ga. He has relatives in Eufalua, Ala. Issue:

I. Andrew J.[3]Oliver veteran of Mexican war, living near Clyattville, Ga. Born 1825, married, (1862) Sarah Francis Studstill. Issue: 1. William Thaddeus[4] (b. 1862) of Quitman, Ga. 2. Alice Ida[4], (b. 1866), m. Alex Keel. 3. Dora Ann[4] (b. 1870), m. James Lowry. 4. Florida S[4], (b. 1874). 5. Florence E.[4] (b. 1877). Mr. Oliver has 13 grandchildren.

II. Thaddeus[3] Oliver, (b. 25 Dec., 1826), m. Sarah P. Lawson (living in 1899). He is said to be the author of "All Quiet along the Potomac To-night."* Issue:

---

*In the above list only two of the children of Mac Oliver are accounted for. It was copied for this work by Mrs. Marion (Carter) Oliver, who regrets not receiving a list of the other descendants. She sends the following of Dorcas Harrison's lineage:

Benjamin Harrison. drowned in Oconee river, near Dublin, Georgia, m. Charity Williams (d. 1864) and had James, Dorcas, Charlotte and perhaps others. Of these, Dorcas m. Wm. Oliver above. James Harrison (d. 1870), of Twiggs county, and afterward of Randolph county, Georgia, 1880, m. ———, and had 1. Samuel, m. 2, Martha. m. Theodore Guerry, 3, James, m. Miss Rice, and 4. Colonel William, now of the old homestead. Georgetown, Georgia. and member of Legislature, m. Virginia Crawford, and had Crawford and Mittie Harrison. He alone survives of the name. His brothers, their sons, and his own sons all being dead.

*Thaddeus Oliver lawyer, died 20th August, 1864, in the *Soldiers' Relief Hospital*, Charleston, S. C., six weeks after his leg was torn off by a cannon ball. He was Solicitor General of the Chattahoochee Circuit at his death.

"Actuated by a desire of 'rendering unto Cæsar the things that are his,' and to a dead soldier the honor he so justly deserves. I have shown in a previous letter to the 'Sunny South' that the noble poem 'All Quiet Along the Potomac To-night' was unequivocably, and without the solicitation of friends, ascribed by Alexander Stephens, to '*Georgia's gallant and gifted son, Thaddeus Oliver.*' The Great Commoner, having sifted the evidence, made this declaration a few weeks before his death. on the occasion of the *Sesqui-Centennial Celebration*, at Savannah, Ga.

"Other writers male and female, Northern and Southern, have also spasmodically claimed its authorship, but all were refuted a score of years ago by the son, Rev. Hugh F. Oliver, who had gathered his father's fugitive pieces—which, in spite of the author's modest protests, were published from time to time by others, who selected for him *pen names* suggested by the subject or the occasion. He wrote '*All Quiet Along the Potomac To-night*' while in camp at Manassas, 1861, when slightly wounded in the wrist, and it was intended solely for his wife, and,' the two on the low trundle bed. in his cot far away on the mountains,' thus referring to his two young sons."

The article appeared in Harper's Weekly, 30th November, 1861 (many weeks after it was really written), with *Mrs. Beers* as claimant for authorship.

"Her son," continues Mr. Oliver, "brazenly alleges '*she dashed it off in his presence*,' which was an extraordinary *impromptu* feat. But, if she merely *memorized* the poem and committed it to paper in her son's *presence*, and afterward sent it to Harper as an *original* production for which she received *pay*, she did only what any woman of ordinary ability is capable of—always provided, however. she had no scruples as to appropriating 'to her *own* use. benefit or behoof,' as the lawyers express it, the property of another—dead or alive.

"Again the manuscript poem, it is asserted by Mrs. Carol G. Johnston, of Abingdon, Va., was found in the satchel of two Confederate soldiers, but she neither affirms nor denies, and it was evidently copied from the newspapers of that day when editors vied with each other in disclosing the authorship."

The son, Rev. Hugh F. Oliver, republished in the '*Columbia State*," South Carolina, September 7, 1898, letters and corroborative articles, which he had furnished the Southern Historical Society Papers for June and July, 1880, at the earnest request of the editor, Dr. J. Wm. Jones.

Among these is the assertion from Mr. Shaw, of a Texas regiment camped near the Second Georgia when the poem was written, that Mr. Oliver. as its author, showed it to him. Also a letter of John D. Ashton, of Waynesboro, Ga., 1874, to Rev. H. O. Olsen, Madison. Ga., saying he had been a comrade, and also co-member with Thaddeus Oliver of the Milledgeville convention, 1860. Their regiment went to Acquia creek, Virginia, and afterward Centreville, from which weekly detachments of pickets were sent out to the Potomac, and while serving on one of these posts the two men welded their friendship. Mr. Ashton produced some lines he had written "*To Wilson's New York Zouaves*." on one of these occasions, and in return Mr. Oliver showed him the wonderful *War Lyric*, saying he had written it. but he did not want it published, or his authorship known; he heard it then for the

1. Rev. Hugh F., of Florence, S. C., *m.* Bessie Smith; Children: Hugh, Thaddeus, Bessie, Edith, Louise, Esther M., and David. He has written articles in the *Sunny South* and the "*Columbia (S. C.) State*," proving his father's authorship of the celebrated poem.

II. Lieut. James H. Oliver, distinguished officer in the United States Navy, *m.* 1882 Marion, daughter of Robert Carter, of the famous old Virginia family at "*Shirley*," James River, Virginia, who has recently published an enlarged edition of her father's "*Carter Family Tree*"—a most valuable aid to the student of Virginia genealogies.

III. Ann² Oliver, *m.* (I), H. H. Rainey, and had Laura, *m.* Mr. Evans, of Greensboro. She *m.* (II), Charles Darden.

IV. Charlotte² Oliver, *m.* Christopher McRae. Children live in Telfair county, Georgia.

V. Francis² Oliver, d. y.

VI. Dorcas² Oliver. Her mother died at her birth, and the children were reared by their Harrison relatives, as their father died soon after his second marriage. Dorcas *m.* John McLean. Children:

    1. William⁴, lives at *McRae*, Telfair county, Georgia. 2. Thaddeus⁴ and others.

VII. William³ Oliver, solicitor of city court of Albany, Ga., (mother, a Miss Drake), *m.* Sally Collier, of Albany, Georgia. Children: 1. Willie⁴, *m.* S. C. Moore. 2. Irene⁴, *m.* W. T. Cox, and had Oliver⁵, Thomas⁵, Wilmore⁵, and Kathleen⁵. 3. George⁴.

first time, and when his friend drew the picture of the "little trundle bed" his voice trembled and tears came to the eyes of both. Soon after, upon returning, as captain, to Georgia, Mr. Ashton was trusted with a copy of the poem, with a request not to reveal the author, but he, notwithstanding, read it to Dr. Charles Bostick, John H. Hudson, and his brother, Dr. William H. Ashton, of Shreveport, La., and gave it to his wife, by whom it was preserved, and to whom he had written about it on October 3, 1861. Captain Ashton says the poem itself furnishes positive internal proof of being written by a married man, upon whom the sacred memory of wife and children was crowding, and such a man was Thaddeus Oliver, the gifted and cultured, but whose quiet modesty would not suffer him to publish over his own signature. Mr. Ashton's letter to his wife, October 3, 1861, said: "I would like for you to know my girlishly modest friend, for though as diffident and retiring as a gentle girl, he is a man of culture, fine literary tastes and an excellent lawyer."

In a communication to the *Richmond (Virginia) Dispatch*, May 4, 1872, "R. A. B.," of Richmond, said: "In connection with the recently reviewed question as to the authorship of the poem, now so generally discussed in Southern journals, be remembered being in the company of several Mississippi soldiers in 1862, comrades of——(mentioned as author), who asserted positively he did not and could not write the poem, which was supposed by their comrades to have been written by a private soldier in a Georgia regiment."

Judge Alfred Aldrich, of Barnwell, S. C., 1872, also wrote, controverting Lamar Fontaines' claims.

Andrew Young, surgeon of the Second Georgia, Paul J. Semmes, colonel, wrote in the "*Sunny South*," 1885, that Mr. Oliver showed him the poem at the American Hotel in Richmond as his own, in August, 1861, and he was pleased to see that the "*Sunny South*" had awarded it to him; a man who would scorn any act of deceit or dishonor. Some exquisite letters of Thaddeus Oliver to his wife are then given—sad, and worthy a poet. In one he was standing guard in a dark and stormy night, thinking of her and their little boys. The drum tapped the hour of nine. She was on her knees praying for him, and he mingled his prayers with hers, and called down God's blessing upon her and their little ones.

He is camped on Acquia Creek, August 19, 1861. The Yankee gunboats are lying in sight, and the trains on the Maryland side arrive every day, bringing troops. In the midst of such vast military preparations he feels the longing for battle, which he finds hard to reconcile to his desire, above all things in the world, to be a pure and consistent Christian, and his thoughts run to the desolation of home should he fall, and in tender despair he sends loving charges to his two boys. They were his all, and sleeping nightly in their little trundle bed in the home at Buena Vista, Georgia. The "young mother" survives, now seventy years of age, "an unimpeachable witness, and a woman worthy a place in the *Bible Picture Gallery*, besides Anna, the venerable prophetess."—*Hugh F. Oliver*.

The *States'* editorial of the above date comments: We were aware that the authorship of the poem that stirred the heart of humanity, "*All Quiet Along the Potomac To-night*" was long in doubt. It was generally credited to Lamar Fontaine, and we had seen no reason to upset this view, although, as far as known to us, *Lamar Fontaine, himself, never claimed it*. Mr. Hugh F. Oliver makes out a strong case for his father's claim—in fact, it amounts to little less than *proof*. * * * The New York *Sun* is responsible for the statement that the poem had a Northern source, and now owes it to its readers to produce what Mr. Oliver has to say. The man who wrote lines so exquisitely musical, so tender and true, should have *his own*.—(*From papers sent by Mr. A. J. Oliver*).

WILEY OLIVER, of Twiggs county, Ga., moved, in 1833, to Barbour county, Ala. Among his children were:

1. William Oliver, b. Twiggs county, Ga., 24th February, 1829; d. at Wesson, Miss.. July, 1891; married, first (12th October, 1847), Mary Milner Callaway (d. January 10, 1888), and settled in Eufaula, Ala.; moved to Minden, La., 1853, and ten years after to Trenton, La., and formed partnership with Mr. Drake in merchandising; captain in Thirty-first Louisiana Regiment in C. S. A., in quartermaster's department; engaged in cotton business in 1866, in New Orleans, with John T. Hardie. They bought the Wesson (Miss.) Manufacturing Company in 1870, and he moved to Wesson, and took charge of the mills as secretary and treasurer. The plant was then estimated at $100,000; Mills burned in 1873, when Col. Ed. Richardson, the Commercial king of Mississippi, bought the stock, and established a new company, with $344,000 stock and Captain Oliver general manager, and the stock increased, by 1891, to $2,000,000. His daughter, Mary Ella, married John P. Richardson, son of Colonel Richardson, who, after his father's death, became president of the company.

Rilla E. Oliver (eldest daughter) married Dr. R. W. Rea.

John M, Oliver, the only son, is a merchant of Wesson.

Col. Wm. Oliver married (secondly) a niece of his wife: Melissa D. Callaway. He joined Dr. Palmer's church (Presbyterian), in New Orleans, in 1867.

2. A. B. Oliver, of Osyka, Miss.

3. —— Oliver. Has a son, Wiley E. Oliver, merchant, Wesson, Miss. (from whom these notes are obtained).

McDONALD OLIVER, of Twiggs county, Ga., was twice married. By last wife, who was Lurena Holmes, had issue:

1. Augustus L. Oliver m. ——. Issue: eight children.

2. Nancy A. Oliver m. George W. Roberts. Nine children, among them: Clarence P. Roberts, of Eufaula, Ala.

3. McDonald Oliver m. Paine Ricks. Issue: 1. McDonald, d. s. p. 2. Lamar Oliver, of Houston, Texas. Mrs. Oliver m. (II) Captain Hart, and her daughter, Lila Hart, m. Washington Toney Flournoy.

Oliver, of Alabama.

SAMUEL WHITE OLIVER, lawyer; born in Virginia, came to Dallas county, Ala., when quite young, and engaged extensively in cotton planting; married a sister of Judge John Hunter, of Dallas. He was speaker of the House, and Attorney General of Alabama, and ran for Governor in 1836. Died at the age of 36. One of the most popular men ever in the State. Issue:

1. Henry Oliver, d. 1862, at the old home in Dallas county. (Issue not known.)

2. Virginia married Paul Ravisies, of Mobile, Ala. Issue:
   1. Gertrude, now widow of Cecil Fleming, of Alabama. 2. Paul.

3. Betty, a belle and beauty of Mobile, in ante-bellum days, married Geo. James Hagan and died 189—. Issue: James, Oliver, and others.

4. Samuel White Oliver, d. Dallas county 1894; married Pauline, eldest daughter of Samuel W. Allen. Children: 1. Amandine m. —— Clarke; 2. Pauline died young; Samuel W. and Starke H.

5. Frances m. Aristide Bienvenue. (Issue not known.)

6. Starke Hunter Oliver, Mobile, Ala., married Kate Hopkins,* daughter of Judge Hopkins, Supreme Court of Alabama. Isaue:
   1. John Walker Oliver, Thomasville. Ala.

---

*Mrs. Stark Oliver was sister to Mary Hopkins (Mrs. John Walker). (See Hopkins.)

All the above notes of Olivers in the far South are given with a view of linking them with their more remote Virginia ancestry, and in hopes that some future genealogist will follow the threads.

2. Percy Oliver.
3. Katherine Hopkins Oliver, m. 7th June, 1899, Arthur Addison Hall.
4. Henry Oliver.

The widow of Samuel W. Oliver, Sr., m. (II) Colonel Sprague. Issue: 1. Laura Sprague m. (1) Charles Forsyth, (II) Mr. Becker, of Milwaukee. 2. Pauline m. James Lyons, of Mobile, Ala.; no issue; 3. Corinne m. Mr. Weber. and had several children.

JOHN McCARTHY OLIVER, of Wilks county, Ga., married the Widow Edwards. with children, Austin, Edward, James and Betty Edwards, who m. John Hill. Issue:

Jane McCarty Oliver, b. 1783, died 1833; married Marshall Martin, b. 1780, d. 1845, of Edgefield District, S. C., and moved to Meriwether county, Ga. Issue: 1. Abram Martin. 2. Elizabeth m. Col. Alfred Wellborn. 3. Nancy m. (I) James Ogletree and (II) Rev. Thomas McGehee (first wife). 5. Nathaniel. 6. John Oliver died young. 7. John Oliver, the second, died young. 8. Rev. William D. married Martha Johnson. 9. Peter Marshall Martin, b. 1827, of Columbus, Ga., married Jane Ellison Ware.

An Oliver family was in Jefferson county, Ala., in its early settlement. "John Oliver lived on the Cahawba," writes Mr. Thomas M. Owen, and left descendants there.

Oliver Family, of Elbert County, Ga.

JOHN[1] OLIVER, planter, was living in 1647, in the parish of Hampton, York county, Va., when he made an acknowledgment to Dennis Stevens, merchant, of a debt of 1030 pounds tobacco. In 1648, he, with James Besouth, Francis Flood and Thomas Shaw inventoried the estate of John Hartwell, of Queens creek, deceased. In 1659 he sold to Major Joseph Croshaw a tract of land called "*St. Andrews Neck*," signing ''John Oliver, his [seal]."—*York Records.*

JOHN[2] OLIVER, son or grandson of above (1737), a suit vs. John Mundell, for £7 (which he gained), and also a suit vs. John Taylor.

THOMAS[2] OLIVER (1743) had a negro adjudged 12 years old.

In 1719 Richard Oliver and wife, Sarah, of Antigua, son and heir of the Hon. Richard Oliver, of Antigua, appointed an attorney to take charge of their property in Virginia, ''late the estate of Richard Oliver, deceased."—*York Records.*

JOHN[2] Oliver had sons Thomas[3] and Peter[3]; If others, it is not known. Peter[3] Oliver (or, as some of the descendants say, *Thomas[3]* Oliver) married Mary, daughter of Florance McCartie, of Bruton parish, York county, Va., born 25th June, 1706, (*see McCarty Family*).

The unusual masculine name of *Florance* is repeated often in the *Muskerry line* of the great *McCarthy* family, of Ireland (of which was also the Earl of Clancarty, and the Lord of *Mount Cashel*, titles now extinct). Through their intermarriage with the old Munster royal line of O'Donoghues, the name of *Florance* is remotely traced also into that family.—(*Burke.*) Florance McCarty, of the *Clodane*, and *Drishane*, county Cork, line, whose daughter, Joan, married John Marshall (whose father, Thomas Marshall, came to Ireland in the expedition of Sir John Wilmot, 1602) was of this Muskerry line (*Burke*), and some of his *Marshall descendants* are also in America. Justin MacCartie (as *he*, himself, spells it), b. 1816, of *Castle Carrignavar*, county Cork, the great parliamentarian, anti-Parnellite, and author, is now the chief of his name in Ireland, and representative of the oldest existing branch of the once *sovereign* house of MacCartie (as is also claimed for Justin McCarthy, of St. Paul, Minn., in the United States).

NOTE.—So far, we have positive knowledge only of Dionysius, Francis, Mary Ann and Eleanor. Correspondence is being earnestly prosecuted to complete the other lines. It is reasonable to assume that most of these located on the south side of the James river, before scattering in the far South and West.

Many of the names are mentioned in the old county records, and church registers, of these counties.

Dennis, and Daniel, and Thaddeus McCarty, of Westmoreland county, Va. (1691), are also of this family, as their *coat of arms* on the tomb of Daniel, the Speaker, plainly indicates. Justin MacCartie, of Ireland, has a nephew by the name of Florance MacCartie. An accompanying short *genealogy* of the McCarthy family, in Ireland and America (ante), is given in order to trace family *identifying* names, and in this way to place the ancestry of Mrs Oliver of Virginia, as far as we can with the Clodane or Drishane branch of McCarties of Ireland. Olivers of Georgia have always preserved the names of *Mac* and *Thaddeus* in their families—almost certain indications of their McCarty ancestry. "After the Revolution" (1688), writes Justin MacCartie, of Ireland, "many of the Irish fled to America, and the properties of several branches of the *old stock* of MaCarties were *then* confiscated." (See *MaCartie Family*.)

Peter² (or Thomas) Oliver and his wife, Ann McCartie, removed to the neighborhood of Petersburg,Va. ,some time before the Revolution. Of their children, little is known except their names. These were:

1, Peter⁴; 2, John⁴; 3, McCarthy⁴; 4, James⁴; 5, Dionysius⁴; 6, Eleanor⁴; 7, Mary Ann⁴; 8, Francis⁴, and *perhaps*, 9, William⁴, and others. Of these:

6. ELEANOR⁴ OLIVER (b. circa 1738) married Drury², son of Robert² Thompson,"the goldsmith and planter." Issue:

1. Jane Thompson⁵, married Robert H. Watkins (b. 1762) of South Carolina, son of James⁴ Watkins the first, (b. 1728) of Virginia. (*Watkins Family*.)

7. MARY ANN⁴ OLIVER (   ) m. (1758) Isham Thompson, also son of Robert Thompson. (See *Thompson* family.) Issue:

1. Sarah⁵ Thompson (   ) m. Daniel Marshall, of Virginia.

2. Polly⁵ Thompson, died *unm.*

3. Jane⁵ Thompson (b. 1762, d. 1815) m. (1779) James² Watkins the second (b. 1758). They removed from Virginia (with their kindred) to Elbert county, Georgia, after the Revolution, seating on the Savannah river, ten miles above Petersburg. (See *Watkin's family*, for descendants.)

8. FRANCIS⁴ OLIVER, b. ——, married ——; remained in Viginia. Issue: among others.

1. Elizabeth⁶, m. Peter⁴ Oliver, her cousin, and son of Dionysius.

2. Frances⁵, m. Dionysius⁴ Oliver, Jr., also son of Dionysius. Of other descendants of Francis, we have no .record.

5. DIONYSIUS⁴OLIVER, above b. 1735 (in Petersburg, Va., it is said), d. 1808, in Elbert county, Ga.; m. (I) in Virginia, 1758, Mary Ann (born 1740, d. in Elbert county, Ga., 1802), daughter of Valentine Winfrey,* of Virginia, and had ten children. He m. (II)

*The Winfree family originally from New Kent county (see *St. Peter's Parish Register*) and also numerous in Cumberland and Chesterfield counties, Virginia.

There is a variation in the *spelling* of the name, which was, doubtless, once the same.

In *Chesterfield county*, Henry Winfree made his will, 1779; wife, Judith. *Sons:* Henry, Archibald, Matthew and Marable. *Daughters:* Elizabeth, Ann and Sarah.

Will of Elizabeth Turpin, 1767; daughter, Mary Winfree and granddaughter, Sally Winfree. (*Records*.)

Martha Winfree, daughter of William Graves, who made his will in Chesterfield in 1776.

Elizabeth Winfree, was daughter of Sarah Harrison, who made her will, 1781.

Mrs. Ann Winfree, daughter of Walter Scott, Sr. (his will, 1782).

Jacob *Winfrey,* of New Kent county, St. Peters parish, Va., *m.* (1698) Elizabeth Alford who died 1814, and had issue: John (b. 1699), Jane (1701), Jacob (1794), Elinor (1707), Elizabeth (1709), and Henry (1710).

Mary, daughter of John Winfrey (b. 1706).

John and *Frances Winfrey* had issue: Anne (b. 1725), Peter (b. 1726), John (b. 1728).

Susanna. daughter of Charles.Winfrey (b. 1716).

Charles and *Jane Winfrey* had issue: Susanna (b. 1724), Anne (b. 1725), Charles (b. 1727), Richard (1729), Mary (1729). (*St. Peter Parish Register*.)

Charles Winfrey, lands processioned in Henrico county, 1789.

Henry Winfrey, of Dale parish, Chesterfield county, 1780.

Mary, daughter of Ralph Graves and Rachel Croshaw married Isaac Winfree, 1775. (*William and Mary Quarterly,* 1, 51.)

in South Carolina (1805) Susan Jackson (relative of Governor Jackson), and had one son. He removed from Virginia, through South Carolina, to Elbert county, Ga. (then a part of Wilks county), where he served in the Revolution as captain of a *Privateer*, and also with General Lincoln at the sieges of Savannah and Augusta; was in the battles of King's Mountain and Kettle Creek, in Wilks county. It is said he also served with General Marion. He was captured by the British and, many years after, would relate to his grandchildren the hardships he, and his family of young children, then endured. His home place, says his grandson, Dr. James Oliver, was in Elbert county, on Beaver Dam creek, near "Stenchcomb Meeting House," where he died and was buried. Another grandson, Wm. T. O. Cook, of Georgia (yet living, 1898, at the age of 90), says he had a place in Wilks county, on the south side of Broad river, in the flatwoods, about three and a quarter miles above the mouth of Wahatchee creek. These lands were afterward owned by his sons, Peter and Rev. Florance McCarthy Oliver. There was a fort near by, called the "*Block House*" (now *Washington*), to which the people fled when attacked by Tories and Indians. When the men and boys, and their negro slaves, went to their work they carried guns lashed to their backs, even when ploughing. Wilks county began to be settled in 1770, when the Indian line of frontier was thrown farther out. "The young wife," continues her grandson, "was large and handsome, and gifted with great courage, and generally softened the hardships of her little family by playing to them spirited airs on the violin, of which she was the complete mistress, often dancing to its accompaniment, to the no small delight of her youthful audience. Such was the *Nerve* of the *Women of the Revolution.*"

In an old minute book (bound in untanned hog's skin and yet preserved in Wilkes county, Ga.), of the revolutionary proceedings of 1779, in "the proceedings of the court, which met at the house of Jacob McLendon, Sr.," about thirteen miles from *Heards Fort* (now Washington), on the 25th of August, 1779, during which, after a summary trial, nine Tories were declared guilty, and hung in ten days after. Wilks county had neither court house nor jail at the time, and prisoners had to be closely guarded, and all able-bodied men were needed for the common defence, and judges did not feel they could waste the time of men who were anxious to serve their country, in guarding those who had sided with the British, Tories and Indians, in murders, pillage and arson. The nine Tories hung were, John Bennefield, James Mobley, Dread Wilder, Joshua Rials, Clement Yarbrough, Edmond Dormey, John Watkins, Wm. Crutchfield, and John Younge.

At the time, Savannah was in the hands of the British, and raiding parties of Tories and Indians disturbed the interior as far up as Augusta, and the people gave short shrift to the murderers when caught.

The Council had fled from Augusta, and established the State government, for a short time, in Wilks county, about six miles north of the site of Washington, and

---

In Cumberland county, Francis Winfree, daughter of Charles Winfree, m. (October 24, 1786) William Robinson.

John Winfree, m. (1752) Mary Walton.

Israel Winfree, brother-in-law to William Harris, who made his will 1753.

Isaac Winfree, m., (1756) Sarah Brown.

Jacob Winfree, (will 1772). Wife Jane. *Sons:* Isaac, Charles and Jacob. *Daughters:* Ann and Sarah Robinson.

Stephen Winfree, m. (1789) Mary Bailey.

John Winfree, will 1793. Wife Judith. *Sons:* John and Jesse. *Daughters:* Francis Howard and Elizabeth Farris. *(Cumberland Records.)*

NOTE.—Amelia county was taken from Prince George in 1744. Dinwiddie county also taken from Prince George, in 1752. Nottoway was taken from Amelia, in 1788.

In these counties were many Olivers—but the *Dinwiddie Records* were nearly all destroyed by Federal troops in the war between the States.

There is an inventory, however, of the estate of John Oliver (1816) "yet preserved, among a few others," writes Mr. Gilliam, clk. C. (1897).

Stephen Heard (mentioned as foreman of the grand jury) was President of the Executive Council of the State.

This court was held by the Hon. Wm. Downs, Benjamin Catchins and Absolum Bedell, Esqs., assistant judges of the county aforesaid. John Dooly, Esq., was State's attorney. Eight esquires, and eight gentlemen, besides the foreman, were sworn in as grand jurors. The list included, George Walton, Signer of the Declaration, and Stephen Heard, Chief Executive. Here is the list in full:

GRAND JURORS:

Esquires.	Gentlemen.
Stephen Heard, foreman.	Holman Freeman*
George Walton (see Gilmer's "*Georgians*)."	Thomas Strand.
David Burnett.	Micajah Williamson.†
Thomas Carter.	James McLean.
Richard Aycock (see Gilmer's "*Georgians*"	
for his strange life).	Jacob Farrington.
Robert Day.	William Bailey.
John Gotham. (†)	John Gless.
DIONYSIUS OLIVER.	

Charles Jordan, Drury Rogers, Wm. Henderson, Abraham Till, John O'Neal, George Dooly, Robert Morgan, John Leggett and Samuel Lamar, were witnesses against Rials and Mobley. Rials' indictment was as follows: " State of Georgia vs. Joshua Rials for high treason, against the State, and acting in conjunction with Tate and the Creek Indians.

" We, the grand jury for the county of Wilkes, State aforesaid, on our oaths, do present that Joshua Rials is guilty of high treason against this State, and that he did act in conjunction with Tate and the Creek Indians in doing murder on the frontiers of this county last March, it being contrary to all laws and good government of said State, and to the evil example of others.

'' JOHN DOOLY, Attorney General.

" The grand jury say the above is a true bill.

" STEPHEN HEARD, Foreman."

The court met and the following petit jurors were sworn:

Holman Freeman, William Butler, John Burness, William Bonier, Henry Duke, James White, Matthew Moore, William Daniel, Joseph Collins, Jacob McClendon, Jr., Morderai Moore, Robert Hanna, John Scott Riden, Sheriff; William Harper, Deputy Sheriff.

The nine prisoners were sentenced to death. Mr. C. E. Smith, of Washington, Wilkes county, Ga., wrote to the " *Commercial* " of this trial:

" Jacob McLendon's house was in southeastern part of the county, near Fishing creek, and about 6 miles east of Danburg. Washington had not then been settled or laid off, and the populous parts of the county were near Broad and Savannah rivers.

It will be noticed that half of the grand jurors are written by the clerk as "Esquires," and the other half as "gentlemen."

Heavy bonds were required of prisoners who were not ready for trial. John Anderson, not ready on a charge of murder, was required to give bond for £10,000, equal to about $50,000.

---

*Colonel Freeman was one of the first settlers on Broad river and a Whig leader under General Elijah Clark. His son Fleming married Martha, sister of the two Governors Bibb of Alabama. His only daughter, Mary Freeman, was the lovely wife of Governor Wm. Wyatt Bibb. She was the beauty of Broad river.

†His daughter married Gen. John Clark (Governor), son of General Elijah Clark of the revolution. Another daughter married Col. Duncan G. Campbell, parents of the Hon. John A. Campbell of New Orleans. (See Gilmer's "*Georgians*").

JOHN OLIVER, OF PETERSBURG, GA.
Born in Virginia 1765, died, 1816.

John Crutchfield, it seems, lodged a complaint before the grand jury against Colonels Dooly and Pickens for leading him into the British camp as a spy, but John failed to make out his case. On 14th February of that year, Clark, Dooly and Pickens had fought and won the battle of Kettle Creek, and had become so popular that no jury could have been found to question any of their official actions.

The extreme simplicity of the proceedings of this court is striking, and to a reader at this distance of time it seems to have been *organized to convict*. At that date, August, 1779, the outlook for the patriots was not very hopeful, and it is not to be wondered at that this court was ready to visit speedy punishment on all who aided the British.

Altogether the record of this noted trial is something unique in the history of Georgia courts." (See Gilmur's "*Georgians*," 184.)

A curious feature of the proceedings was that the grand jury found as a grievance the "running at large" of certain persons whom they suspected of giving aid and comfort to the British.

(*From an article cut from a newspaper and pasted in the diary of Dr. James S. Oliver of De Soto, Miss.*)

Children of Dionysius Oliver, of Broad River, Ga.

I Peter², II John², III James², IV Dionysius², ,V Thomas Winfrey⁴, VI William², VII Eleanor², VIII Florance McCarthy², IX Martha², X Frances², XI Jackson².

I PETER² (born about 1763) married his cousin Betty⁴, daughter of Francis⁴ Oliver, of Virginia, whom he met while on a visit to Virginia. He lived on Broad river, on the lands of his father, in Wilks county. Issue:

(1) Dionysius⁴, his only child (b. circa 1785), married (I) Lucinda, daughter of Micajah McGehee, of Broad river. He married (II) her elder sister, Sarah McGehee, widow of Thomas Hill (with several children, among them: Thomas and Wiley Hill, who moved to Texas); Mrs. Hill was the beautiful daughter of Micajah McGehee. (*See McGehee family.*) After 1849 Dionysius and his second wife, followed some of their relatives to Mississippi, and settled at Oxford. Issue: by first marriage (none by second)—1 Martha⁷, 2 Peter², 3 Dionysius⁴, 4 Margaret⁷, 5 a daughter⁷:

1 Martha⁷, b. 1810, m. (1) about 1826, her cousin Dr. Thomas Winfrey⁴ Oliver, born 1804, died 1827, son of Rev. Florance McCarthy⁴ Oliver (b. 1775); his son Thomas Winfrey⁷ Oliver, born 1827, and after the death of his father, lived to the age of 26, and died in 1853, at the home of Llewellyn Oliver, Sumter county, Ala., a brilliant young man. He studied law with Judge Watson, of Holly Springs, Miss., and was of a charming and happy nature, spending lavishly the gifts of fortune, in a very short life. His mother married secondly Rev. Isaac Newton Davis, and moved to Mississippi, and had two daughters.

2. Peter⁷, born circa 1812, married ———. Issue: Dionysius⁴.

3. Dionysius⁷, called "Nish D." went to Texas with Tom and Wiley Hill.

4. Margaret⁷, married Mr. Phillips, a merchant of Holly Springs, Miss.

5. A daughter⁷.

(Thomas and Wiley Hill settled in Texas (Bastrop), before 1849, when Major John Oliver, of Columbus, Miss., visited them there. "Tom Hill had married an Oliver.")

II. JOHN⁴ OLIVER, of Petersburg, Ga. (b. January, 1765, near Petersburg, Va., died 24th December, 1816), married (I), 20th December, 1787, Frances (b. 1769 in Virginia; d. Petersburg, Ga., 1806), daughter of William and Mary (Wells) Thompson, of Virginia (see *Thompson family*); married (II), 1811, Susan (b. 1790), daughter of James and Jane (Thompson) Watkins, her cousin, by whom no surviving issue. She married (II) Dr. William N. Richardson, of Georgia (see *Watkins family*). A picture of

John Oliver is yet preserved in the family. Elbert county, Ga., was taken from Wilkes county in 1770. In 1773 the frontier town of *Dartmouth* was laid off at the confluence of the Broad and Savannah rivers, as a land office and trading post.—(*Pickett's History of Alabama.*) Soon after a colony of Southern Virginians swept into Elbert county, and the name of the town was then changed to Petersburg—probably for Petersburg, Va. It acquired a thriving population, and descendants of some of the most refined families in Virginia now arrived. Wealth and its luxuries ensued. Lines of freight wagons soon plied busily to and from Philadelphia, which then, and afterward, had a monopoly of trade with the merchants of Southern towns. Down this historic route came the Scotch-Irish immigrant to Virginia and the Carolinas from Pennsylvania—since there was no port in North Carolina at which they could then enter, and the ship-loads of immigrants from Ireland landed only at Philadelphia or Charleston before that time. Here Major Oliver became an extensive merchant and planter, owning also the point of land from which plied a ferry to both the South Carolina and Georgia side, and his merchandise came from Philadelphia, as did also that of his wife's relatives, the firm of *Watkins & Thompson.* A few settlers had gone on into Western Georgia and its Territories of Mississippi and Alabama, and were living in a state of constant terror, with Indian wars raging in their midst.— *Pickett's Alabama, II, 14*). Augusta and Savannah were the great marts for the surrounding country, and at Augusta, treaties were made with the Indians. It was with such stirring environments that John Oliver began his successful career. He had seen the hardships of the Revolution in a frontier town, and witnessed the sufferings of his parents, and had grown up in the atmosphere of victory, and in the presence of men and women of stern mould; and his faculties were strengthened by that success which made him the admiration of his neighbors. He had six children, three of whom lived to have issue:

1. Prudence Thompson, b. 1788; 2. Caledonia X., b. 1790, d. 1796; 3. Sarah W., b. 1792; 4. Sophia N., b. 1794, d. 1798; 5. Mary Xenia, b. 1797; 6. John. Of these—

    1. Prudence Thompson⁴ Oliver, b. Petersburg, Ga., 22d October, 1788, d. Huntsville, Ala., 19th October, 1868, married, 25th April, 1805, at Petersburg, Ga., her consin, Robert H. Watkins, b. 1st October, 1782, d. Pulaski, Tenn., 1855; son of James and Jane (Thompson) Watkins, of Savannah river, Elbert county, and before that of Virginia.

    The daughters of John Oliver, after a preliminary course in Augusta, were sent to that fine old institution of the *Moravians,* which was founded in Bethlehem, Penn., 1749; carrying out the principles of the Moravian bishop, John Amos Comenius, the great educator of the eighteenth century, and is the oldest female school in America. The Moravian Seminary at Salem, N. C., founded a few years later, was on this plan. In the Bethlehem catalogue for *1803* are these entries:

Oliver, Prudence T., b. October 22, 1788, daughter of John Oliver.
Oliver, Sally W., b. August 6, 1792,   " " " "

It was the most popular of all schools with the daughters of Southern planters. There was no safer stronghold for young innocence than living in cloistered simplicity with those good sisters, who taught the stately and exquisite music of the old masters with other accomplishments. They also wrought most artistic specimens in needle work—birds, flowers and scenery—and yards of sampler embroidery on canvas were brought home as trophies. One very popular representation was a moribund figure, drooping, like the weeping willow at its side, over the tomb of some loved one. This was framed in triumph, and presented to the dear mother at home. Here the young girl was so impressed with the holy mode of living and teaching, that, in after years she prevailed upon her husband to send their own child, Mary Frances, in 1819, to the Salem Institute, N. C., when she was but eleven years of age, and she has told me that the recollection of this exquisite period of her youth colored all her after life. The quaint art-work embroidery of both mother and child accomplished at those two famous Institutions have been long preserved; and the writer made a pilgrimage a few years since, to Salem, to imbibe some of the fragrance of old memories lingering around the ancient pile. At the age of eighty, with soft brown hair of which Time stood in awe, and smiling blue eyes, Prudence Oliver looked out upon the world with the same innocence which those good sisters had fostered, and a tender heart, at peace with God and man, the gentle epitome of her sex and ancestry. Beloved by all, childhood dreamed her a beneficent fairy, while sorrowing men and women knew her to be the saint of Pity, pouring her soul into the offered chalice of sympathy. Plentifully endowed with wealth, her opportunities for good were great. Issue:

1. Mary Frances' Watkins (b. 13th Nov. 1809), married James E. Saunders, of Lawrence county, Ala. (See *Saunders Family*, for their children.)
2. Sarah Independence' Watkins (b. 4th July, 1811), married George W. Foster, of Florence, Ala. (See *Watkins Family*.)
3. James Lawrence' Watkins (b. 10th May, 1814), married Eliza Patton, of Huntsville, Ala. (See *Watkins Family*.)
4. Virginia Prudence' Watkins (b. 22d Oct., 1816), married Thomas S. Foster, Florence, Ala. (*Watkins Family*.)
5. Louisa Matilda' Watkins (b. 29th Dec., 1819), married Stephen W. Harris, of Huntsville, Ala. (*Ibid.*).
6. Robert H.¹ Watkins (b. 10th May, 1824), married Margaret Lindsay Carter, of Pulaski, Tenn. (*Ibid.*).

2. Sarah Wells⁴ Oliver (b. 6th Aug., 1792; died 1812) married (1807) Daniel Bird. of Georgia. No issue. Mr. Bird was living in 1862. He married again, and named his only daughter Sarah Oliver (b. 1841, d. 1859). A son was a brave captain in the Confederate army, wounded, and a prisoner of war in Huntsville, Ala., in 1862.

3. Mary Xenia⁴ Oliver, b. Petersburg, Ga., 18th September, 1797, d., Hancock county, Miss., 6th October, 1846, m., 6th May, 1812, in Petersburg, Ga., John Dandridge Bibb, of Montgomery, Ala., b., Prince Edward county, Va., 10th March, 1788, d. in Carroll county, Miss., 9th May, 1843. He was the son of William, and Sarah (Wyatt) Bibb, of Prince Edward county, Va., who moved to Georgia in 1789, and were parents of the two first governors of Alabama, Dr. William and Thomas Bibb (see Bibb). John D. Bibb and wife located first in Madison county, Miss., in 1813, and thence to Montgomery, county, Ala., 1818, next to Morgan county Ala. (above Decatur), 1826, and to Columbus, Miss., 1832. Their remains are interred at Montgomery, Ala. Issue:

1. Charles Sydney, 2. Elvira Antoinette, 3. Sarah Frances, 4. Mary Dandridge, 5. William Crawford, 6. Edwin Augustus, 7. Lavinia Arabella, 8. John Dandridge, 9. Dandridge Asbury, 10. Algernon Sydney, 11. Mary Cornelia, 12. Laura Angerona. (*For these see Bibb*.)

4. John⁴ Oliver, Columbus, Miss., b. 1800, d., 2d July, 1835, m., 13th July, 1820, Ruth A. Weeden, b. 12th September, 1804, d. 3d October, 1835, daughter of Col. William and Sarah (Sands) Weeden, of Maryland, and sister of Mrs. Turner Saunders and Dr. William Weeden, of Huntsville, Ala. His father dying when he was but sixteen years of age, he removed to Alabama with his guardian and brother-in-law, Maj. Robert H. Watkins, who purchased for him a plantation in Lawrence county, four miles from his own "Oak Grove" place, and stocked it with family slaves brought from Georgia (it is now owned by Malcolm Gilchrist). Dr. William Weeden was colonel of a regiment in 1812, and lived in central Alabama, where he lost his first wife. It was while visiting his sister, Mrs. John Oliver, he met, at the home of their neighbor and kinsman, Maj. Watkins, the very young widow of James Watkins, who was Jane, daughter of Dr. Urquhart, of Georgia (see *Urquhart*). They were married and removed to Huntsville, Ala. (Dr. Weeden had also two brothers in Florida: John and Frederick

Weeden.) Here also the Rev. Turner Saunders married Mrs. Oliver's beautiful widowed sister, Henrietta Weeden, who was Mrs. Millwater, with two young daughters; and disposing of his comfortable home north of "Rocky Hill," he and the Olivers removed to Mississippi, he erecting a handsome home in Aberdeen, (now the Paine residence), and John Oliver parchasing an estate near Columbus, Miss., of the Indian chief, "*Peachtree*," who was selling the "Reservation" to the whites. Here he reared five children (two others died young), 1. Sarah Frances. 2. Caroline. 3. Maria Louisa. 4. Caledonia. 5. John Oliver:

1. **Sarah[7] Frances Oliver** (b. 1823, d. 1852), m. (1637) Edmund Blount Hoskins (b. Edenton N. C., 1811, d. Columbus, Miss., 1852). The Colonial Records of N. C. mention the Blount family from earliest times. Issue:
   1. Ann Eliza[8] Hoskins (b. 1838) m. (1859) Dr. George H. Moore, of Memphis, (b. Huntsville, Ala., 1822). Surgeon C.·S. A. (Fee Moore family for issue.) (Mrs. Moore has furnished this list of her grandfather's descendants.)
   2. Caroline Watkins[8] Hoskins (b. 1840) m. (1865) James Le Noir. Issue: (1) William G.[9] (b. 1866), (2) Sterling Paine[9], (b. 1867), (3) Dr. James[9] Le Noir, (4) Sarah Louisa[9] (b. 1872) m. (1895) James R. Taylor, Memphis, and has Carolyn[10] and James Taylor[10] (b. 11th June, 1897), (5) George[9], (6) Edward[9].
   3. Richard Blount[8] Hoskins, Meridian, Miss., C. S. A., N. C Artillery; (b. 1843), married (1872) Ida Daves. Issue: 1. Ida[9] (b. 1874), 2. Robert Lee[9], 3. Yallie[9], 4. Francis Ol'ver[9].
   4. James W.[8] Hoskins (b. 1845) d. s. p.
   5. John Oliver[8] Hoskins (b. 1851) m. (I), Bettie Harrell, and (II), Mary Ferguson, Ch. 1 Annie Mary[9], and by 2d marriage, 2. Caroline[9], d. y. 3 Carrie[9], 4 Mary Paine[9], 5 John Oliver[9].

2. **Caroline[7] Oliver** (b. 1824, d. y.) m. (1847) Goode Watk'ns (1st wife). No issue. (*See Watkins*.)

3. **Maria Louisa[7] Oliver** (b. 1825, d. 1879) m. (1847) Dr. Stirling Paine half brother of the Methodist Bishop. Issue:
   1. Dr. Frank[8] Paine (b. 1848) m. Onie Brown. Issue: 1. Louisa[9] (b. 1881), 2. Onie[9] (b. 1884), 3. Sterling Paine[9] (b. 1886).
   2. Julia[8] Paine m. (1868) William[9] Le Noir. Issue: 1. Marion Louisa[9] (b. 1869, d. 1874), 2. Mary[9] (b. 1872), 3. William Stirling[9] (b. 1875), 4. Julia Paine[9] (b. 1879), 5. Ruth[9] (b. 1882), 6. Stirling Paine[9] (b. 1887), 7. Whitman[9] (b. 1891).
   3. Caledonia[8] Paine, married (1876) William Wade. Issue: 1. Stirling Paine[9] (b. 1877), 2. Roberta Julia[9] (b. 1884), 3. Caledonia Paine[9] (b. 1886).
   4. Ruth Weeden[8] Paine, married (1882) John L. McMillan. Issue: 1. William Alexander[9] (b. 1883), 2. Stirling Paine[9] (b. 1887), 3. Julia Le Noir[9] (b. 1889).

4. **Caledonia[7] Oliver** (b. 1826), married (1845) Thomas Clay, b. 1825, d. 1856, son of Matthew and Frances (Saunders) Clay. Issue:
   1. Matthew[8], 2. Alice[8], 3. Oliver[8], 4. Fannie Lou[8]. (See *Saunders Family* for these.)

5. **John[7] Oliver**, Brookville, Miss., b. Lawrence county, Ala., 1830, d. February, 24, 1897, married, 1850, Francis Rebecca Conolly, of Jackson, Tenn. He took great interest in the compiling of this record, furnishing much information. Issue:
   1. Francis[8] b. 1852, d. 1855.
   2. Mary[8] b. 1853, m. 1880, Thomas W. Baker. No issue.
   3. Maria Louisa[8], b. 1855, m. 1879, James H. Box. Issue: 1. Oliver[9], 2. Fannie Lou[9], 3. Nina[9], 4. Lily[9], 5. Reuben[9], 6. James[9].

4. John[3], Jr., Columbus, Miss. (b. 1860), m (1892) Laura Sturdevant. Issue:
    1. John[9] (5th in line, b. 1894), and one other.
5. Caledonia Clay[3] (b. 1857, d. 1864).
6. Robert Conolly[9] (b. 1863), m. (1889) Betty Cook, of Heidelburg, Miss.
    Issue: 1. John[9] (b. 1890); Fannie Sue[9] (b. 1892).
7. George Anderson[8] (b. 1868), m. (1889) Estelle Selby, of Heidelburg,
    Miss. Issue: 1. Earle[9] (b. 1892); 2. Mary[9] (b. 1895).
8. Nina Clay[9], named for Mrs. Matthew Clay.

III. JAMES[4] OLIVER, third son of Dionysius, Elbert county, Ga., b. 1767, m. (1) 1795
Mary, b. *circa* 1779, daughter of William and Mary (Wells) Thompson, of Virginia,
and had, only child, Simeon[5] Oliver; he married (II) Lucy, daughter of Christopher
Clark, of Albemarle county, Va., and sister to Mrs. Thomas Winfrey Oliver and also
to Mrs. Florance McCarthy Oliver, all of Elbert county. Issue, eleven children, eight
lived to adult age:
    1. Simeon[5], 2. Shelton[5], 3. Mary Winfrey[5], 4. Mildred[5], 5. Judith[5], 6. James[5],
    7. Washington[5], died young, 8. Alfred[5], 9. Eliza[5], 10. Francis[5], died young,
    11. Lucinda[5], 12. Martha E.[5]. Of these—

1. Simeon[5] Oliver, of Hernando, Miss., b. 6th of August, 1796; died 26th December, 1865, m. 5th September, 1816, Mildred Terrell White, b. 21st March, 1801,
d. 17th July, 1876; daughter of Shelton and Mildred (Clark) White, of Georgia.
Removed from Elbert county, Ga., to Hernando, Miss. Gen. Bedford Forrest,
the great Confederate cavalry leader, was, in his youth, manager of Simeon Oliver's
plantation. (See *White*.) Issue:
    1. James Shelton[7], 2. Asa Thompson[7], 3. Lawrence Mansfield[7], died young,
    4. Mary Mildred[7], d. s. p., 5. Shelton[7], 6. Simeon[7] (twins), 7. Sarah
    Lucinda[7], 8. Lucy Jane[7], d. s. p., 9. Prudence Thompson[7], 10. John
    Thomas[7], 11. David Terrell[7], 12. Ann Eliz.[7], 13. Elbert[7], 14. Georgia[7],
    Of these—

1. James Shelton[7] Oliver, M. D., b. 29th July, 1817, d. 18th October, 1882, m. 5th
    November, 1839. Sarah Ann, b. 29th May, 1818, d. 4th December, 1891; daughter
    of William and Concord Hamilton (Brown) White, of Elbert county, Ga.; Surgeon C. S. A. and prominent physician of De Soto county, Miss; greatly lamented
    at his death. He preserved a record of his line of Olivers, and also of the Shelton, Clark and White families, which was kindly loaned for publication herein,
    by his daughter, Mrs. Dockery. Issue: Six children, all of whom but one, died
    in infancy. The surviving child,
        1. Elizabeth White[8] Oliver, b. 1st July, 1846, married Alfred, son of Gov. Alfred
        Dockery, of N. C., and lives at Lodockery, near Hernando, Miss. She takes
        great interest in her lineage, having the above records, copied from her grandfather, Simeon's family Bible. Issue:
            1. James Oliver[9], married Sallie Withers, 2. David Terrell[9], 3. Alfred[9],
            4. Mary E.[9], 5. Annie[9], 6. Tallulah Brown[9], 7. Lilly Franklin[9], 8.
            Sarah Shelton[9].
2. Asa Thompson[7] Oliver, Colonel C. S. A., b. 14th November, 1819, m. (I) Beatrice
    Eliz. Tait and (II) Drucilla Daniel. Col. Thompson Oliver after the fall of the Confederacy, 1865, moved to Santa Barbara, Province San Paulo, Brazil, with other
    Southerners, where he purchased plantations and slaves, and where he was
    murdered by the latter 28th July, 1873. His widow settled in Jack county, Texas.
    Issue first marriage.
        1. Indiana Tait, dec'd, 2. Mildred White, 3. Zimri Shelton, *Issue second
        marriage:* 4. Catherine Meriwether, 5. Asa.
3. Lawrence Mansfield[7] Oliver (b. 1821, d. 1822).
4. Shelton[7] Oliver (b. 20th December, 1825, d. Texas, 13th August, 1863); m. Eliz.
    Jones Crisp. Issue:

1, John Crisp[2], m. Florence ———; 2, Loula[2], m. William Dickerson, and had William[3] and Walter[3]; 3, Maie[2]. m. W. P. Martin, and had Frank[3] and Shelton Simeon[3] Martin.

5. Simeon[7] Oliver, of Hernando (b. 20th December, 1825, d. 30th July, 1874) twin; m. Martha, dau. of John Scott McGehee. (See McGehee.) Issue:
  1, Malinda Hill[8], m. Wm. Pitt Martin, and had Wm. Pitt[3] and John Oliver[3] Martin, twins; 2, Charles Dandridge[3]; 3, Sarah McGehee[3], m. Shawl Poston, Memphis, Tenn., and has Linda[4], Stuart McGehee[3], Martha[3], Elizabeth[3]; 4, Simeon Shelton[3]; 5, Edward Oliver[3].
6. Mary Mildred[7] Oliver (b. 1827, d. 21st June, 1847).
7. Sarah Lucinda[7] Oliver (b. 16th March, 1828), m. Joseph Simon Boykin B.·one, of Hernando. Issue:
  1. Oliver[3], m. Georgia Gambrell, and had John Herron[3] and Mary Louisa[3].
  2. Joseph S[3]., m. Linny Perkins, and had Kate[3] and Simeon[3] and Lewis[3] (twins).
  3. Mary Lucy[3], m. G. E. Holmes, and had Boone[3], Edward[3] and Ballard[3].
  4. William Boykin[3], unm.
  5. Mildred White[3], m. C. R. Boyce, and had Cramner[3], Bessie[3], Joseph Boone[3].
  6. Mary[3], m. Dr. T. Jones, and had Meta[3], Elviryn[3], Josie[3].
  7. Hattie[3], m. Peter Percy Boyce, and had Lucile[3], Sarah[3], Laura[3], Percy[3] and Boykin[3].
  8. Simeon O.[3], m. Maude Phillips, of Georgia.
  9. Annie Muldrow[3], m. Monroe Smith.
  10. Daniel[3], and 11, Louise[3], Boone (twins); d. y.
  12. Louisa[3], m. R. M. Banks.
8. Lucy Jane[7] Oliver, d. y.
9. Prudence Thompson[7] Oliver (b. 14th March, 1832; d. 18th March, 1892), m. James Minor Tait, of Georgia. Issue:
  1. Charles[3], d. y.; 2, Mary Mildred[3], m. (I) John T. Owens, and (II) Paul Owens, and had by first marriage: Helen Clifford[3], Mary Alexander[3], and John[3]; and by second marriage: Corinne[3], George[3], James[3], Shelton[3], Oliver[3], and Jane Watkins[3], who m. Ruffin Sledge, and had James Brown[10], and Minor Tait[10].
10. John Thomas[7] Oliver, Hernando, Miss., (b. 29th May, 1834), m. Mrs. Mary Blount Williams. He was in Polk's Corps, C. S. A., Chalmers' Old Brigade, Company B, of Browning's 9th Mississippi Battery of Sharp-Shooters. Children:
  1. John Blount[3], 2. Lucy Wyatt[3].
11, David Terrell[7] Oliver, C. S. A. (b. 11th December, 1836; killed at the battle of Franklin, Tenn., 30th November, 1863), Company F, 22d Mississippi Regiment, Brown's Brigade, Cleburn's Division, Hardee's Corp, Army of Tennessee, m. Sarah Concord Fraser. Children:
  1. Eliz. Terrell[3], m. James M. Dockery, and had Corinne[3], Martha[3], Elizabeth[3], and Charles[3]; 2, James Simeon Oliver, unm.
12. Anne Eliz.[7] Oliver (b. 7th February, 1839), m. Robert Muldrow. Issue:
  1. William[3] (dead); 2. Simeon Oliver[3], m. (I) Lida ———, and m. (II) Mary Fly. Children (by second mar. only): William[3], Robert[3] and Annie[3]; 3. Robert[3] m. Elizabeth, and had Louise[3]; 4. Loula[3] m. Allie Montgomery, of Osborn, Miss., and had Aline[3], Robert[3] and Samuel[3]; 5. Henry[3]. Mrs. Muldrow lives with her daughter, Mrs. Montgomery (1898).
13. Elbert[7] Oliver, C. S. A., b. 26th August, 1841, d. Little Rock, Ark., 24th September, 1889, Company A, 18th Mississippi Cavalry, Gen. N. B. Forrest. Part of his foot shot off at battle Spring Hill, Tenn.; married Betty M. Boone. Children:
  1. William Boone[3] m. Lulu Van Trump, and had Helen[3] and Elbert[3], 2. David Terrell[3], 3. Augusta[3], 4. Mildred[3].
14, Georgia[7] Oliver, b. 29th May, 1844, d. 15th March, 1891, m. David Marcus Slocumb. Children:

1. Jessie M[6], 2. Ida T.[6], m. William A. White, and had George[6], 3. Durward M[6], 4. George[6], 5. Mildred[6], 6. James[6], 7. John[6]. *(End of Simeon Oliver's Record, much of which was contributed by Mrs. Shawl Poston.)*

2. Shelton[5] Oliver, of Lexington, Ga., first child of James (b. 1767) and Lucy (Clark) Oliver, of Elbert county, Ga., m. Martha Williams. Children: 1. Cornelia[7], 2. Lucy[7], 3. Elizabeth[7], 4. Emma[7]. It is regretted that their *descendants* are not given.

3. Mary Winfrey[5] Oliver, m. Willis Banks (first wife). One child: Mary Winfrey[6] Banks, who m. Col. Jeptha V Harris, of Columbus, Miss., son of Gen. Jeptha V. and Nancy (Hunt) Harris, Athens, Ga. Issue: 1. Nancy[7], died young. 2. Willis[7], m. Anna, daughter Major John Billups. Issue: Willis[8], John Billups[8] and Mary Jeptha[8]. 3. Lucy Jeptha[7] m. Robert Duncan, and has Mary Lou[8]. *(See Banks and Harris.)*

4. Mildred[5] Oliver m. (I) James A. Banks (cousin to Willis), and (II) Charles S. Meriwether, of Georgia (first wife), who m. (II) Louisa Watkins Tait, widow of Lemuel Banks *(Watkins Family)*. *Issue, first marriage:*
   1. William[7] Banks, of Panola, Miss.; m. ——, several children. (See *Banks*.) *Issue, second marriage,* (Meriwether): 2. Mina Barbara[7] Meriwether, m. Col. Thomas White (d. 1890), of Hernando, Miss. Issue:
      1. Mildred Concord[8], m. John McGehee Farrington, of Memphis, and had Dr. Pope McGehee[9] Farrington, eminent young physician of Memphis, m. Josephine Burford.
      2. Barbara Mina[8], m. Elijah Bell, of North Carolina, and had Mildred W.[9], m. George T. Banks, and Barbara Mina[9], m. Caffery Robinson
      3. Thomas W.[9], m. Marian Carpenter, and had Carrie[9] and Thomas W.[9]. Jr.
      4. Louisa Toombs[8], m. Charles Latham, of Hopkinsville, Ky., and Hernando, Miss., and had Mina W.[9], John[9] and Corinne[9].
      5. Concord Hamilton[8], m. Robert Wilkinson, son of Thomas (below). Issue: Robert, Thomas W., and Barbara Allen.
      6. Nellie[8]. 7. Frederick[8], d. young.
      8. Corinne Meriwether[8], m. Charles Smith, of Tennessee (see *Shelton* and *White* families).

5. Judith[5] Oliver, m. (I) Henry Banks, (brother of Willis Banks), m. (II) William Moore. *Issue, first marriage.*
   1. Sarah Banks, m. Henry Scales, and had Lucy, d. y., and Henry Scales.
   2. Lucy Banks, m. Thomas Wilkinson, of Hernando, Miss. (For issue see *Banks* family.)
   Mrs. Scales has also contributed much of the above list, and now lives with her son at Clarksville, Tenn.

6. James[5] and (7) Washington[5] Oliver, d. y.

8. Alfred[5] Oliver, of Elbert county, Ga., lived fifteen miles up the county from Petersburg, at the old family home. He was killed by a white tenant; married Sarah Pharr, of Newton county, Ga. Issue:
   1. Dr. Alfred[6] Oliver, of Elberton, Ga., still living (only son), married Gertrude Maude, daughter of Col. J. D. Mathews. He has contributed this list of his father's line. Children:
      1. Alfred Shelton[7], Jr.. 2. Ella[7], 3. Samuel Thomas[7], 4. Stanley Mathews[7]. 5. Maude[7], 6. Frank Chappel[7].

9. Eliza S[5]. Oliver, m. Jett Thomas, of Georgia. Children:
   1. James[7] of Montgomery, Ala., m. Miss Banks, of Mississippi, 2. Sue Jett[7], 3. Mary Julia[7], m. D. B. Cade, of Washington, Ga., and has, Gilford[8] Cade, 4. Alfred[7].

---

[6]NOTE.—Willis Banks, m. (II) Mary Gray, and had issue, Col. James Oliver Banks, who married Lucy, daughter of Colonel George and Lucy (Watkins) Young. (See *Watkins family*.)

10. Francis[5] Oliver, d. y.
11. Lucinda[5] Oliver, m. Edmund Taylor, and is still living, at Elgin, Arkansas (1897). Children:
    1. James Oliver[6] Taylor, married ——, and has several children.
    2. Lucy Ann Taylor, unmarried.
12. Martha[5] Oliver, m. Gen. Benjamin Heard, of Wilkes county, Ga., died without issue. (End of James[4] Oliver's, (b. 1767) descendants.)

IV. DIONYSIUS[3] OLIVER of South Carolina (b. 1768, d. Edgefield District, South Carolina) married (I) his cousin, Frances, dau. of Francis Oliver,. of Virginia, and sister to his brother Peter's wife. (Dr. James Oliver, in his diary, says he married also Mary Ann Hancock). He lived near his sister, Mrs. Hancock. Issue:
1. Seaborn[4] Oliver, "died in Jackson's Mexican War, 1717-1718," says W. T. O. Cook.
2. Berrien[4] Oliver, married Mary Royster of North Carolina. Lived near Petersburg, Ga., until 1835, when he removed to Florida. Issue:
    1. Major John Berrien[5] Oliver, lawyer, Tallahassee, Fla. (d. 1881), married Virginia, daughter of Judge Eli and Sophia (Watkins) Shorter, of Georgia. Issue:
        1, Virginia; 2, Mrs. Bird; 3, Mrs. Richardson; 4, Peter M. of Gainsville, Fla.,
        5, Dr. Junius, became blind; 6, James, very prosperous, until in a personal difficulty he killed his opponent.
    2. Matilda[5], 3. Asa B.[5], 4. Malinda[5], 5. Stephen Mann[5], 6. Mary Ann[5], m. (I) Richard Hudson, and (II) Richard Rice.
3. Dionysius[4] Oliver, Edgefield, S. C., died at the age of 40; married Ann, daughter of John and Anne (Freeman) Goode, of Abbeville District, and sister of the second Mrs. Benjamin Sherrod, of Courtland, Ala., who was Talitha Goode, b. 1792, d. 1873. Issue: One son—
    1. Llewellyn[5] Oliver, of Sumter county, Ala., b. 1812, reared by Mrs. Benjamin Sherrod, after the early death of his mother. He married (I) 1831, Eliza Perrin, of Edgefield District, and removed to Sumter county, Ala. He married a second time, but no issue of this marriage. Children:
        1. Ann Goode[6] Oliver, born 1832, m. 1853, Dudley Moore, d. 1872, of Columbus, Miss. She was beautiful and attractive, and is yet living in a charming old age, and gives the following list of her family. Issue:
            I. Lillie[7] Moore, b. 1854, d. 1899, m. 1872 Edward Watson, lawyer, (d. 1887), of Holly Springs, Miss. Issue:
            Dudley Moore[8] Watson, of Times-Democrat, N. O., m. 1899, a daughter of Judge Poché, of New Orleans; Edward[8] Watson; William[8] Watson; Jean[8]; and Annie[8]
            II. Thomas[7] Moore, m. Susan Weston, of Alabama, and had Dudley[8], Robert P.[8], and Weston[8]
            III. Fanny[7] Moore m. Col. W. W. Humphries, lawyer of Columbus, Miss., and had Edward Watson[8], and Fannie Moore, b. 1896.
            IV. Anne Dudley[7] Moore, m. Charles Evans, planter, and had Anne Dudley[8], and Fannie Moore[8].
        2. Dionysius[6] Oliver, of Sherman, Sumter county, Ala., b. 1834, m. Hester Patton. Issue:
            1. Annie[7], m. Charles Wier; 2. Kate[7], m. Dr. McKinley, of Columbus, Miss.; 3. Llewellyn[7], m. Sallie Windham; 4. John Patton[7], m. Mary Holt, of Memphis, Tenn.; 5. Nannie[7], 6. Sarah George[7].
        3. Llewellyn[6] Oliver, of Sherman, Ala., m. Miss Deale, and both died soon after birth of their third child. Issue: 1. Fannie[7], 2. William[7], 3. Dudley[7].
        3. Robert[6] Oliver, Sherman, Ala., m. Nannie Little. Issue: 1. William, m. Sallie Conner; 2. Robert, unm.; 3. Goode, m. Annie Connor; 4. Eliza, m. Dr. Philips; 5. Tempie.

V. THOMAS WINFREY[5] OLIVER, Elberton, Ga., b. circa, 1769, m. Mary, daughter of Christopher Clark. Owned the Tavern at Elberton, and is buried in its yard. Kind-hearted and of a pompous bearing, he was wont to converse in quite high-flown phrases, which the young people of the neighborhood often quoted in great merriment; as, for instance, he would invariably say, of threatening weather, while grandly waving his hand: "The zenith is clear, but the horizon is portentous!" (Mrs. Martha Harris). This, to illustrate his good natured conceit. No issue of this marriage. Mrs. Oliver was sister to Mrs. James Oliver and Mrs. Florence McCarthy Oliver.

VI. WILLIAM[5] OLIVER, b. 1778, was the traveler and adventurer among his brothers, (it is said). After the death of his second wife he went to the Creek Indian wars with General Floyd's troop of Georgians, and was supposed to have been with Col. Samuel Dale and Capt. Jerry Austill and James Smith in the famous "Battle of the Canoes" on the Alabama river, 1813. He afterward disappeared with the Indian tribes, and was seen no more by his family. Dr. James Oliver says, in his diary, he m. (I) Barbara Tait (W. T. O. Cook thinks a Miss Alston). He m. (II) Miss Ragland. Dr. Alfred Oliver of Elberton says one of his wives was a widow, of Wilks county, Ga. Issue: 1. Mathilda[6], m. Osa Brown; 2. Malinda[6], m. Asa Mann; 3. Mary Ann[6], m. William Hudson; and 4. Fanny[6], m. (I) John Chenault[6], of Tenn., and had John, of Danburg, Ga., and the Rev. Dionysius Chenault, who weighed 300 pounds. His cousin, Mrs. Henry J. Long of Florida, sends this incident: "When, in 1865, President Jefferson Davis and his cabinet fled to Washington, Ga., with the accompanying wagons of currency, they disbanded and separated on the plantation of John Chenault, which was near. They were aided in their escape by Dionysius Chenault, some of them being at his house when the treasury wagons were emptied of their contents. The pursuing Federal troops, thinking him accessory to its concealment, hung him up by the thumbs until he fainted. He never recovered from the nervous shock to his system, and his gentle and lovely wife was searched and handled so roughly by the ruffians that her reason fled. Her husband, though a minister, then vowed vengeance on the commanding officer."

VII. ELEANOR[5] OLIVER, m. John Goss of Georgia; she was poisoned by a vindictive slave, soon after the birth of her only child, which also died young.

VIII. MARTHA[5] OLIVER (b., Va., 1773, died Edgefield District, S. C., 1827), married (1792) Thomas Hancock, of Edgefield District, S. C. (b. 1769, d. 1820), her cousin. She rode on horseback with him from Elbert county, Ga., to their home in South Carolina. Their four daughters all married, left issue, and died, in Edgefield District, S. C. Martha[6], Harriet[6], Frances[6] and Sophia[6], as follows:
1. Martha[6] Hancock, married (I), 1813, Thomas Still, and married (II), 1830, John H. Cosby, of Virginia. Issue first marriage:
   1. Harriet[7] Still, married Mr. Dendy, of Laurens county, S. C. Issue second marriage:
   2. Sarah[7] Cosby, married Mr. Simonton, planter. Four children.
   3. Elvira[7] Cosby, married G. I. Denton. Four sons.

NOTE.—1. The Llewellyn and Lewis families were related, and emigrated from Wales to Ireland together.

In 1730, John Lewis, of county Dublin, Ireland, killed the Irish Lord, and fled to Virginia, where the Alexanders, McDowells, Prestons, Pattons, Matthews and others followed him.

His sons were Thomas, Andrew, Charles and William.
—(Gilmer's Georgians.)

* 2. Stephen[1] Chenault and wife came with the Huguenot immigration to Monikin Town, James river, Va., about 1700. Their son, Hugo[2], was father of Felix[3] Chenault, who married Miss Dabney, of Virginia. His son, William[4] (b. 1749), went to Kentucky, 1786, and founded a large family, and was in Revolutionary War, as was also John Chenault, living in Columbia county, Ga., in 1830, whose son John Chenault, born 1805, was ancestor of above family.—(See Quisenbury Family.)

4. Martha' Cosby, d. unmarried.

5. Mary² Cosby, married Robert Hall, and had Roberta Hall, married her cousin, Vernon Denton, of Island Grove, Florida.

6. John Oliver² Cosby, lawyer, Micanopy, Florida. He alone, of all his mother's children, was living in 1897.

2. Harriet⁶ Hancock (d. 1845), married (1813) John Curry. No living children.

3. Frances⁶ Hancock, married (1820) Sampson Sullivan, and had Martha' Sullivan, who married John Adams, of Edgefield county, S. C. Several children.

4. Sophia⁶ Hancock (b. 1808, d. 1876), m. (1828) Benjamin Ryan Tillman, of Edgefield county, S. C. (d. 1849). "No one ever had greater fondness for family history, or was more loyal to her blood than she," writes her distinguished son. "She was the strongest minded, best balanced woman I ever met, and to *her* I owe whatever of ability and judgment I have in life, though my father was also very bright!" He adds that his mother visited Wm. T. O. Cook, her cousin, in Georgia, in 1865, and they went over, together "the whole matter of the family and its history, with many anecdotes of family traits," etc. Issue, eleven children:

1, Thomas F.' Tillman, killed in Mexican war (battle of Cherubusco). 2, George Dionysius' Tillman. 3, Martha A.' Tillman (d. 1883, s. p.). 4, Harriet' Tillman (d. y.). 5, John Miller' Tillman (d. 1860, s. p.). 6, Oliver Hancock' Tillman. 7, Anna Sophia' Tillman. 8, Frances Miller' Tillman. 9, Captain James Adams' Tillman, C. S. A. (d. 1866, s. p.). 10. Henry Cummings' Tillman (d. 1859, s. p.). 11, Benjamin Ryan' Tillman; as follows:

2. George Dionysius' Tillman, of Clark's Hill, S. C., m. (1860) Margaret Jones—seven living children:

1. Lona⁸, m .... Bunch—four boys and two girls.

2. Sophia⁸, m. Judge Osmond Buchanan—two sons and one daughter; James' Buchanan, the eldest son, is a lawyer of Edgefield.

3. James⁸ Tillman, of Edgefield, lawyer, m. Miss Norris.

4. Frances⁸ Tillman.

5. Sallie⁸ Tillman, married ...... Bailey—1 son. 6, Benjamin⁸, Jr., and 7, George D.⁸, Jr., the last two students in the "Citadel," Charleston, S. C.

6. Oliver Hancock' Tillman (d. 1860), m. Martha Roper. Issue: Alice⁸, married G. W Bunch, and has four children.

7. Anna Sophia' Tillman, m. John C. Swearingen. He was killed April, 1895, by Benjamin Jones, in a political difference. Issue: John⁸ (blind by an accident), is a very bright student, despite his affliction; George⁸; and Sophia⁸ (teaching in Johnson's Institute). Mrs. Swearingen has kindly furnished most of the record of the descendants of Martha Oliver Hancock.

8. Frances Miller' Tillman, m. Henry Garlington Simpson, of South Carolina. Issue: 1. Sophia⁸. 2. Margaret⁸. 3. Mae⁸. 4, Nettie⁸. Mrs. Simpson is a widow, and matron of Winthrop College, Rock Hill, S. C.

11. Benjamin Ryan' Tillman, Governor of South Carolina 1893, and member of U. S. Senate (b. 1847); m. (1868) Sallie Starke, of Elbert county, Ga. "As you see," he writes, "I went to old Elbert county, Georgia, for a wife, as did my grandfather Hancock, and we were equally lucky in our choice." Issue:

1. Benjamin Ryan⁸, Jr. 2. Lona⁸. 3. Sophia Oliver⁸. 4. Henry⁸ (b. 1885). 5. Sallie May⁸.

Governor Tillman's long political career, in his State, and in the United States Senate, is now a matter of history, and would take a book in itself to record. He is the friend and champion of his beloved South, now and forever.

His brother George is equally as distinguished as the *model farmer of South Carolina.*

IX. Rev. FLORENCE McCARTY⁴ OLIVER, b. in Virginia, 1775, m. in Elbert county, Georgia, 27th October, 1796, Susanna, born, Virginia, 5th March, 1783, daughter of

Christopher Clark. He was a Wesleyan Methodist Minister of great purity of life, and also a planter. Removed to Chambers county, Alabama, 1840, from Elbert county, Ga. Ten children, names given, as follows, by Maj. Thomas W. Oliver, of Mitylene, Alabama:

1 Dr. Samuel Clark⁴, 2 Polly Mellissa⁴, 3 Thomas Winfrey⁴, 4 Mildred Terrell⁴, 5 Florence McCarthy⁴, 6 James Ovid⁴, 7 John Alfred⁴, 8 Susan Rebecca⁴, 9 Rev. Christopher Dionysius⁴, 10 James Percival⁴.

1. Dr. Samuel Clark⁴ Oliver, b. Elbert county, Georgia, 29th July, 1799, d. March, 1848, m. 10th January, 1826, Mildred Spencer, (b.   , d. May 4, 1887), daughter of Abner McGehee, and in the same year, 1826, moved to Montgomery county, Ala. His practice was extensive. Member of the House and Senate of Alabama for seventeen years and was never defeated. Wrote a political novel, "*Onslow*," and many songs, and fugitive pieces; some novelettes, and an epic, "*The Hindoo Bride*." Issue:

1. Major Thomas Winfrey⁷ Oliver, of Mitylene, Alabama, b. Montgomery county, Alabama, 27th August, 1827, d. 19th February, 1899. C. S. A., Surrendered with General N. B. Forrest on the Warrior river, in 1865, serving from first to last in the Confederate Cavalry. He graduated 1847, at University Alabama, "made a splendid soldier and rendered faithful service to the cause he loved so well." A typical Southern planter, genial and hospitable, with loyalty to friends that knew no bounds, and his devotion to honor was a shining characteristic. Died at his lovely old home, seven miles east of Montgomery, Alabama. Married, December, 1854, Mary Eliza, daughter of Dr. Thomas and Eliza (Hull) Brown. She died 1880. He furnished this list of his grandfather's descendants in 1896, and took great interest in his ancestry, and has himself transmitted much to posterity. His only child, Thomas Winfrey⁶ Oliver, b. 1873, married, 1893, Fannie Ledyard, and has issue: 1 Thomas W⁹., b. 1894, Mary⁶, 1896.

2. Dr. Abner McCarty⁷ Oliver, died young.

3. Dr. Samuel Clark⁷ Oliver, died young.

4. Mary Meteora⁷ Oliver, b. 15th November, 1833, the night of the famous meteoric shower, married, 1850, Dr. McKenzie Johnston, who died 1896. They went to Texas in 1860. Issue: Mildred⁶ and Annie⁶ Johnston, and two sons, (dead).

5. Susannah Jane⁷ Oliver, married, 1st, James Harvey, d. 1888. Issue, two sons⁶ and four daughters, all married. She married (II) 1893, Mr. Stockwell.

2. Mary Melissa⁴ Oliver, b. 20th December, 1801, married, 5th September, 1818, Alexander McDonald. No issue.

3. Thomas Winfrey⁴ Oliver, b. 17th July, 1804, died 1827, married 6th June, 1826, Martha⁷, daughter of Dionysius⁴ Oliver, son of Peter⁴, of Broad River, Georgia. Issue: 1. Thomas Winfrey⁷ Oliver, b. 1827, d. 1853, lawyer, young and witty, died early. 2, a daughter⁷. Mrs. Oliver married (II) Rev. Isaac Newton Davis, and had two daughters, now of Mississippi. (*See Peter line*.)

4. Mildred Terrell⁴ Oliver, b. February, 1807, d. 1892, married, 14th February, 1822, Dr. Samuel Clark Dailey; several sons and daughters. Of these, Rachel⁷ married James McGehee, son of Col. Abner McGehee, of Montgomery, and is the oldest living descendant, in 1896, of Rev. F. McCarthy Oliver. (*See McGehee*.)

5. Florence McCarty⁴ Oliver (b. 10th March, 1809), married (I), Hannah K., daughter of James Banks, and married (II) Sarah, daughter of Rev. Thompson Glenn. *Issue first marriage:*

1, James McCarthy⁷ Oliver, married ——. His son Earnest⁶ Oliver, of Lafayette, Ala., married Nannie Williamson. 2, Samuel Clark⁷ Oliver.

Issue second marriage:

3, Susannah⁷ T. Oliver. 4, Mildred⁷ A. Oliver. 5, Caroline⁷ Oliver. 6, Juniu Percival⁷ Oliver, of Dadeville, Ala. (student East Alabama College, 1860) 7, John Alfred Glenn⁷ Oliver.

6. James Ovid[6] Oliver* (b. 16th August, 1811), married (24th December, 1835) Charity A. Chambers. Two sons and two daughters. Thomas[7] Oliver, a son.

7. Dr. John Alfred[6] Oliver (b. 13th October, 1813, d. 1838), married Susan Dillard. Issue: Three sons, all dead.

8. Susan Rebecca[6] Oliver (b. 27th January, 1816), married (26th September, 1832) Maj. John Harper, of Covington. Five children; a daughter Susan; and a son, Leonidas[7] Harper, is member Legislature of South Carolina. He has a daughter Berenice[8] Harper, and others.

9. Rev. Christopher Dionysius[6] Oliver (b. 30th January, 1819, d. Calera, Alabama, 15th January, 1892), (named for both grandfathers). Prominent Methodist minister, of Alabama, married Laura Reid, of South Carolina. Issue:

   1. Henry L[7]. Oliver (student East Alabama College, 1860), lawyer (d. 1895), married a lady of Hebrew descent and has several children.

   2. Dr. Charlton Christopher[7] Oliver, of Calera, Ala., married Jessie Allen (b. 1852, d. 1896). Several children.

   3. Walter[7] Oliver, lawyer, Calera, married.

10. Junius Percival[6] Oliver (b. 16th January, 1823). Died quite a young man.

The children of Rev. F. McCarthy Oliver, were all baptised by Rev. Hope Hull.—*Family Bible.*

X. FRANCES[5] OLIVER married William T. Cook, of Virginia, son of Benjamin Cook. (An uncle of his, a physician, lived in Philadelphia, and another in North Carolina). They had several children, of whom only two survived:

1. Mary Ann[6] Cook, b. 1803, married Benjamin Burch, of Georgia. Issue:

   1. Capt. John[7] Burch, C. S. A., and Solicitor General, killed in first day's battle around Richmond, Va., 1862.

   2. Mary Ann[7], married —— Johnson, of Atlanta, uncle of Judge Lumpkin, of Atlanta.

   3. Elizabeth[7] married (1876) Dr. Henry J. Long (who died in 1896), of Florida (his second wife). No issue. He was cousin to Dr. Crawford Long, of Athens, Ga., discoverer of anesthesia, and a brother, James Long, married Frances Gholson, of Madison county, Ga., parents of Dr. Nathaniel Gholson Long, of Elberton, Ga. (She gives this line of her family.)

2. William Thomas Oliver[6] Cook (b. 1809, living in 1898), six years younger than his sister, Mrs. Burch, and author of a newspaper article on the "*Oliver Family*" (which, however, was not altogether correct), married Nancy Tennyson Ridgway. Issue, three sons and four daughters:

   1. Thomas[7], C. S. A., married Sarah Herndon. Died from a wound in late war.

   2. Elizabeth[7], married Benjamin T. Higginbotham.

   3. James[7], married Martha Campbell.

   4. Mary[7], married Banks Cunningham.

   5. Frank[7], married (I) Miss Ray, (II) Martha Landis, (III) Tawsie Landis, of Frederick City, Md., and died in Maryland, a physician of some note.

   6. Rebecca[7], married (I) Harrison Ray, and (II) Harrison Agnew.

   7. Effie[7], married John Gary. A daughter, Ella Inez[8], of Royston, Ga., sends this list repeated from her grandfather (1898).

XI. JACKSON[5] OLIVER, died Banks county, Ga., 1869, only child of Dionysius[4] and Jane (Jackson) Oliver, married Mary Maxwell. Issue:

   1. Rev. Dionysius Crandall[6] Oliver, C. S. A., married —— Sanders. Issue:

      1. Mary Elizabeth[7]; 2. Sarah Jane (dead); 3. Dionysius[7] Jackson; 4. Sanders Bar-

---

*Ovid is a name common to the McCartys. Capt. William Downman McCarty, of United States Navy (son of Dennis McCarty) married (1816), Frances Ravenscroft Ball (Mrs. Humphrey Carter), and had, among others, a son, *Ovid* McCarty.

tow[r]; 5. Tallulah Lee[r]; 6. George Pierce[r] (dead); 7. Adisa Ann[r]; 8. Thomas Brittain[r], and, 9. Roberta Estelle[r].

2. William Capers[s] Oliver, C. S. A., married Eva McKie. Issue:
   1. De Witt; 2. Lovick Pierce; 3. Leonora: 4. Denvor; 5. Atticus; 6. William (dead); 7. Nettie; 8. Lelia; 9. John.

3. Thomas Parks[s] Oliver, C. S. A., married (I) Arminda McDonald, (II) Mrs. Fannie Barrett. *Issue first marriage:*
   1. Mittie Beatrice[r]; 2. James Jackson[r]; 3. Victor[r]; 4. Robert Lee[r]. *Issue second marriage:* 5. Thomas Parks Oliver.

4. Jane Ann[s] Oliver, married Charles Allison Lilly. Issue: 1. Egbert[r]; 2. Annie[r]; 3. Roberta[r]; 4. Lucy[r]; 5. Charles[r]; 6. Lilly[r].

From the Oliver record it is seen that four of them: Mary Ann, Eleanor, James and John (sisters and sons of Dionysius[s]) married Thompsons; respectively, Isham, Drury, Mary and Frances. Of these, Isham and Drury were brothers, and Mary and Frances were daughters of another brother, William Thompson—sons of Robert Thompson, Falling creek, Chesterfield county, Va., goldsmith and planter.

BIBB FAMILY.

Family records of Hon. William Crawford Bibb, of Montgomery; Col. Robert A. Hardaway, of Tuscaloosa; Mrs. Eliza Hopkins, Thomas B. Hopkins, and Mrs. Martha Dandridge Bibb.

BENJAMIN[1] BIBB came from Wales to Hanover county, Va. Whom he married is not known. It is said he was a Huguenot who fled to Wales after the revocation of Edict of Nantes, 1685. He had three sons—James[2], William[2] and Thomas[2]. Of these—
   1. WILLIAM[2a] BIBB[2a] had issue: 1. John[2] Bibb; 2. Nancy[2] married Robert Edwards; 3. Mary[2] married Barton Key.—*William and Mary Quarterly, VII, 103.* The son—
   1. JOHN[3] BIBB, of Goochland (*will* 24th May, 1769; *proved* 17th July, 1769). A John Bibb, in 1738, entered 800 acres in Amelia county, on Buffalo river, and in 1745, 1200 acres, and in 1759, 150 acres.—(*Records.*) Married Susannah, daughter of William Bigger.[†] His will mentions: "Sons *Richard*, John, James, *William* and daughters *Susannah*, wife of James Clark, (whom she married 19th May, 1762); *Elizabeth*, wife of William Farrar; my granddaughter, Lucy Clark, my granddaughter, Susannah Elis. Bibb; my father-in-law, William Bigger." "In an affidavit made by Judge Benajah S. Bibb, of Montgomery," says Col. R. A. Hardaway, "he gives the sons of John as above, and mentions Nancy and Lucy Bibb as his two daughters. But, as he states, he does not remember Nancy's marriage, and gives *Lucy* as married to David Clark, *she* was probably the *granddaughter* of the *will*. It was evident he had not seen a copy of his grandfather's will." Of these six children—
   I. RICHARD[4] BIBB married, in Prince Edward county, Lucy Booker, daughter of the wife of his brother William Bibb, and hence half-sister to William's children. He was member of the Assembly (1787) from Prince Edward, with John Clarke; trustee of Hampton Sidney College, Virginia, 1784–1807.—(*Virginia Almanack.*) Removed to

---

[*]William Bibb (1744) 1200 acres in Amelia county, 150 in 1759 and 40 in 1774. William Bibb, trustee (1788) for Warminster, Amherst county.—*Hening and Land Book.*
Robert Bibb entered 180 acres in Amelia county in 1754.—*Amelia Land Book.*
Rev. Richard Bibb, of the Protestant Episcopal Church, South, was an eloquent and eminent minister in Virginia.

[†]Martha, widow of Nathaniel West, and before that, of Gideon Macon; married 3d (1727) Mr. Bigger, a Scotchman. Her daughter, Unity West, married (1719) William Dandridge and had Nathaniel West Dandridge, who married Dorothy Spotswood (b. 1724, d. 1773), parents of Nathaniel West Dandridge (b. 1762, d. 1810), who married Sally, daughter of John Watson and Mary Bigger, daughter of Mr. Bigger above. (See *William and Mary Quarterly, Vol. V, 139.*) Ann, daughter of William and Unity (West) Dandridge, married Mr. Dancy. "Susanna Bibb to James Clark, of Amelia county; daughter of John Bibb. Security, William Bibb. John Bibb's letter of consent. Witnesses· John Bigger, William Bibb and John Bibb, Jr." (*Goochland County Marriage Bonds*).

Kentucky. A Capt. Richard Bibb was of the Goochland militia in the Revolution.
—(*Virginia Magazine History, VI, 402.*) Issue:

1. George M.[5] Bibb, of Kentucky, b. 1772; d. Georgetown, D. C., 14th April, 1859;
student William and Mary College, Va., 1795; graduate of Princeton; distinguished
lawyer and Chief Justice of Kentucky; U. S. Senator (1811), succeeding Henry
Clay, and again; in 1829, with Henry Clay; Secretary of Navy, 1844, under
President Tyler (succeeded by Robert John Walker under James K. Polk);
continued his law practice in Washington, and wrote *Reports of Kentucky*. Married (I) Rebecca Latham Ashton, and (II) Mrs. Horsley, née Scott, of Kentucky. (See *National Encyclopædia*).

2. Major Richard[5] Bibb died Russellville, Ky., 1839. Freed his slaves, leaving his
son, Zach. Bibb, his executor to carry out this provision of his will. One colony
of these was located on his lands near Russellville, and called *Bibbtown*, and consisted, in 1896, of about seventy-five people. He also left them money, stock and
provisions. The other colony located in Liberia, Africa. The son—
Zach. Bibb, born 1798, died Frankfort, Ky., 1893, administered his father's
bequest *to the letter*, even adding to it much of his own wealth in trying to encourage his African colony, of which much has been written in periodicals and
papers.

3. John[5] Bibb, b. 1789; d. Russellville, Ky., when nearly a hundred—loved by all
for his goodness and many charities; no children.

4. Mrs. Burnley[5]; descendants in Frankfort, Ky.

5. Mrs. Slaughter[5], mother of Richard Bibb[6] Slaughter, lawyer, who removed
to Courtland, Ala., in its early settlement—but afterward returned to Kentucky.
Her grandson, Thomas I.[7] Slaughter, lives in New York (1880).
Her daughter, Mary[6] Slaughter, married (1807) Gabriel Jones Lewis, and had
Elizabeth Lewis[7], married Col. Samuel Starling, of Hopkinsville, Ky., and had
Fielding[8], Thomas[8] and Mary[8] Starling.
*It is regretted this list of descendants of Richard Bibb, of Kentucky, is so imperfect.
But there was no reply to letters of inquiry about them.*

II. JOHN[4] BIBB, born in Virginia.

III. JAMES[4] BIBB, born in Virginia. Removed to Elbert county, Ga., with his brother
William, and there "left many descendants, who are scattered," says Governor Gilmer's "*Georgians*."

IV. WILLIAM[4] BIBB, of Prince Edward county, Virginia (b. Hanover county, 1735).
Removed to Prince Edward county in 1774. Member of the Convention in 1774-5;
and of Committee of Safety, Prince Edward county, 1775, Captain in Revolutionary
Army, and Sheriff in 1789. Married in Prince Edward county, (1) Mrs. Booker
(née Clark), and (II) 4th of December, 1779, Sally Wyatt, sister of Col. Joseph
Wyatt, of Charlotte, and relative of Mrs. Washington through the Dandridge family.
"*Marri d*—Captain William Bibb, of Prince Edward county, to Miss Sally Wyatt, of
New Kent, an amiable young lady, with a handsome fortune."—(*Virginia Gazette.*)
They removed to Elbert county, Ga., 1789, where he died, 1796. (His widow married, when elderly, William Barnett[5] of Elbert county, Ga., who was also old, and with
grown children.) Mrs. Bibb was born in 1769, and died 15th August, 1826, at the
home of her son, Governor William Wyatt Bibb, Autanga county, Ala. Issue: 1st
marriage: (*Clark*) 1. Elizabeth[5], 2. Lucy[5], 3. Hannah[5], 4. Sally Booker[5]. Issue: 2d
marriage: (*Wyatt*) 5. William Wyatt[5], (Gov.) 6. Thomas[5], (Gov.) 7. Peyton[5]. 8. John
Dandridge[5], 9. Joseph[5], M. D., 10. Benajah Smith[5]. 11. Delia[5], 12. Martha D.[5] Of
these:

Mrs. Barnett's sister, Nancy Wyatt, married Frank Scott, and lived in her widowhood in Lawrence county, Ala., in its early settlement, with her daughter, Mrs. Jamison. There Mrs. Barnett
came to visit her, after a separation of many years. The aged sisters met at the Mountain Spring
camp meeting, and their pathetic interview affected the audience to tears. (See *Wyatt*.)

1. ELIZABETH[5] BIBB, *m.* (1), Captain John Scott, and moved to Franklin, Tenn. Issue:

    1. William[6] Scott, *m.* ———. Issue: two sons. 2. John[6] Scott. No issue. 3. Lucy[6] Scott married Branch Bibb, son of John Bibb, and died in Todd county, Ky., leaving children: Henry[7], Susan[7] and John[7] Bibb. Mrs. Elizabeth Scott *m.* (II), Mr. Clarke, and had two children.

3. HANNAH[6] BIBB, *m.* (I), Peyton Wyatt, and (II) Major John Titt.e. *Issue:* (*1st Mar.*) 1. William[6] Wyatt. 2. Peter[6] Wyatt. Issue: (*2d Mar.*) 3. John[6] Tittle, 4. Margaret[6], (b. 1809), *m.* Dr. Fowler, of Montgomery, Ala., and died in New York, 1893. 5. Harriet[6], *m.* (I) ——— Darden, and (II) ——— Knox, of Autauga, Ala. No issue.

4. SARAH BOOKER[5] BIBB, *m.* (I) Marable Walker, of Augusta, Ga. No issue; and *m.* (II), Archelaus Jarrett,[*] of Elbert county, Ga. Issue:

    (1) Martha Bibb[6] Jarrett, married Robert S. Hardaway, of Columbus, Ga. The[r] son, Col. Robert A.[7] Hardaway, of Tuscaloosa, Ala., who died in 1899, was a splendid example of the gentleman of the Old South and a brave Confederate officer, and afterward professor in Agricultural and Mechanical College, Auburn, Ala., and later, in the University of Alabama. He was a charming conversationalist and friend. Married Miss Early, of Georgia, the perfect wife and mother. Issue: Early[8] and Benjamin[8] Hardaway. Both married.

    (2) Eliza Dandridge[6] Jarrett, married (I) Llewellyn Hudson, of Patawamba county, Ga., and (II) George W. Ross, of Mobile, Ala. Issue, first marriage (*Hudson*), Sallie[7], Anna[7] and Virginia[7] Hudson; second marriage (*Ross*), Lula[7] and George[7] Ross.

5. WILLIAM WYATT[5] BIBB, M. D., and Governor of Alabama (b. Prince Edward county 1781, d. 10th July, 1820, in Autauga county, Ala., from the effects of a fall from his horse, which became frightened in a violent thunder storm); graduated at Medical College, Philadelphia; member Georgia Legislature, and U. S. Congress from Georgia, 1806, and U. S. Senator from Georgia, 1810; and Territorial and State Governor of Alabama, 1817-20; declined appointment as minister to Russia (on account of health) by President Madison. Practised his profession first, *in* Petersburg, Elbert county, Ga., and there married Mary, daughter of Col. Holman Freeman[†], "*The belle and beauty of Broad river.*" Issue:

    1. George Bailey[6] Bibb, a student of the Pestolozzian School which the Hon. William H. Crawford established in Georgia; married ———. Issue: 1.

---

[*]Robert[1] and Mary Jarrett, of New Kent county, had a son, Robert[2], b. 1696; Robert[2] Jarrett married ———. Issue: Mary (b. 1731, David (1728), Robert (1734) and Susannah (1737).

    Devereux Jarrett, married ———, and had Mary (born 1724), Archelous (b. 1726), Anne (b. 1727), Fanny (b. 1728).—*New Kent County St. Peter's Parish Register.*

    To this family belonged the great preacher, Devereux Jarrett (b. New Kent, 1733, d. 1801), minister Bath parish, Dinwiddie and Brunswick counties, 1763 to 1780, (which was taken from Bristol parish, 1742, and all once in Prince George county, until Dinwiddie was taken from Prince George, 1752). He said he was named for *Robert Devereux,* Earl of Essex, in whose army his grandfather served. His father was a carpenter, who died when he was seven years old, and leaving him to the care of his elder brother, Robert, who inherited the estate. He married a daughter of Mr. Claiborne, of Dinwiddie, or Brunswick.—*Meade, Vol. 1.*

    D. Hardaway, vestry of old Blandford Church, Petersburg, 1788. Daniel Hardaway was of the vestry of Grubhill Church, Amelia county, 1790.

    [†]Lands of Holman Freeman, in Henrico county, processioned 1732, and also his widow, Bridges Freeman, Burgess, 1629 for Pashbyhoy, and (1632) for Chickahominy (*Records and Hening, I Vol.*). Henry Freeman of York county, died 1676.—Henry Freeman's will, 1680, (Records).

George' Bibb, 2. William' Bibb*, of Decatur, Ala., and formerly of Dallas county. (Descendants not obtained.)

2. Mary' Bibb married Alfred Vernon Scott, of Montgomery (b. 5th August, 1808), his *first wife*. Issue: I. Mary Sophia' Scott, died young. II. Eliza Ann' Scott, married James Boykin. Issue. Mary B., Charlotte T., James Burwell, Ernest and Thomas. III. John Randolph' Scott. IV. Ellen' Scott, married Robert D. Boykin. Issue: Catherine, Sarah, and Robert D. V. Thomas James' Scott, C. S. A. Killed in battle of Seven Pines. (*See Scott Family Pamphlet by Mrs. Semple.*)

6. THOMAS⁴ BIBB, Governor of Alabama (b. 1783, d. 20th September, 1839, Huntsville, Alabama) moved from Elbert county, Georgia, to Huntsville, Alabama†, 1816. Succeeded his brother, as the second Governor of Alabama (1820) by virtue of being president of the Senate 1818. Member of Convention to frame Constitution of Alabama, 1819; and also Convention 1825, to amend the same, and, afterward, several times in the Legislature. Of great intellectual force and indomitable energy, and of marked distinction of bearing. Very wealthy. Married Parmelia, daughter of Robert Thompson and Sarah Watkins (who was b. 1760) only daughter of James and Martha (Thompson) Watkins, Virginia. Their home, near Huntsville, Alabama, was '*Belle Mina.*' (*See Watkins and Thompson families.*) Issue: 1. Adaline⁴; 2. Emily⁴; 3. Thomas⁴; 4. William Dandridge⁴; 5. Porter⁴; 6. Elmira⁴; 7. Robert Thompson⁴; 8. Eliza Parmelia⁴; and three who died in infancy. Of these:

1. ADALINE⁴ BIBB (b. 1806, d. 1894), married (1821) Major James Bradley. Issue: I. Susan' Bradley (b. 1823, d. 1893), m. (1839), Thomas W. White. Issue: 1. Adeline (b. 1840.) *Unmarried*. 2. Alexander⁶ (b. 1842) m. (1870) Maria Withers, and has two sons. 3. James Bradley⁶ (b. 1844) m. (1866) Susie Withers, and has three living children. 4. William⁶ (b. 1846) *unmarried*. 5. Ellen⁶ (b. 1848, d. 1870) m. Charles Hunt; no issue. 6. Bessie⁶ (b. 1850) *unmarried*. 7. Jane⁶ (b. 1853) *unmarried*. 8. Thomas⁶ (b. 1854) *unmarried*. 9. Frank⁶ (b. 1856) married. 10. Addison⁶ (b. 1858) unmarried. II. Sarah Ann' Bradley (b. 1824) *unmarried*, and living in 1899. III. Thomas Bibb' Bradley (b. 1826, d. 1854), never married. IV. James Pleasants' Bradley (b. 1828, died young.) V. William' Bradley (b. 1835, d. 1880) married; two children. VI. Adeline' Bradley (b. 1837), married Lucien Weakley; widow, no children. VII. Pattie' Bradley (b. 1840, d. y.) VIII. John' Bradley (b. 1845, d. 1896), *unmarried*. Talented and bright. Prominent in railroad affairs, connected with Memphis and Charleston road in Alabama, and Assistant Manager of Mississippi Valley road, 1887, headquarters at New Orleans.

2. EMILY⁴ BIBB⁴ (b. 1806, d. 1854) m. (1825) James Jay Pleasants.‡ Issue: I. Julia' Pleasants (b. 1826, d. 1871) m. Judge David P. Cresswell. Issue: Two children. II. James Jay' Pleasants (b. 1828, d. 1898), m. (1858) Laura Robinson; several children. III. Adeline' Pleasants d. y. IV. Thomas Bibb Pleasants, d. y. V. Emily' Pleasants, m. W. Keenan Hill. Three sons, all married. VI. Samuel

---

* W. A. Bibb was the recipient last week of a beautiful photographic reproduction of a miniature of his grandmother, the wife of the first Governor of Alabama. The miniature bears the date of 1807, and represents a sweet-faced young matron of perhaps 30 years. The hair is dressed high with a fringe of soft curls on the forehead, and the dress about the neck is low and round; in general style it might be taken for a lady of to-day. The resemblance to Mr. Bibb is quite striking.—*Decatur Advertiser, 1897.*

† In the western suburb of Huntsville, Ala., not far from the M. & C. R. R., are the tombs of the Rev. Charles Bibb, and of Sarah Bibb, who died Aug. 3, 1829, aged 88 (b. 1746), and near the site of an old Methodist church, erected by a first settler, Robert Langford.

‡ John Pleasants came to Virginia from England, and settled in Henrico county, 1665. He had sons: Joseph (d. 1739) and John. He was ancestor of Governor James Pleasants. Mr. Brock, of Virginia, has a tree of this family, unbroken in names, though deficient in dates.

Tarlton[7] Pleasants (b. 1842, d. 1873), *m.* Mary, daughter of Dr. D. D. Shelby, of Madison county, Alabama. Issue: 1. Shelby. 2. Marie. VII. Robert Bibb[7] Pleasants (b. 1848, d. 1884), *unmarried*.

3. THOMAS[5] BIBB (b. 1810, d. November, 1861), *m.* (1859) Anna Pickett. Issue: Sarah (b. 1861, d. 1897).

4. WILLIAM[4] DANDRIDGE BIBB (b. 1710, d. 1880), *m.* Mary Mitchell. No living issue.

5. PORTER[4] BIBB (b. 1814, died 1865), *m.* (1835) Mary Betts. Issue:
   I. Henry Chambers[7] Bibb (b. 1837, d. 1878), *m.* (1863) Ella ——, and had, 1, Fannie, d. y.; 2, Ella, *m.* Moro Farris, of Columbia, Tenn., and has two children.
   II. Porter[7] Bibb (b. 1839), *m.* (1863) Amelia Bradley, of Demopolis, Ala. Issue: 1, Thomas[8]; 2, Porter[8]; 3, Bradley Bibb[8], *m.* Miss Sanders, niece of Mrs. Col. Alva Ashford, of Courtland, Ala. (née Carrie Fletcher); 4, Mary[8] Bibb, twin with Bradley, *unm.*; 5, Gussie[8] Bibb, and others.
   III. Lockhart[7] Bibb (b. 1841), *m.* (1865) Kate Bradley, of Demopolis, Ala. Issue: 1, Porter[8] (b. 1868), *m.* ——, and living; 2, Eliza[8] (b. 1871), *unm.*, and others.
   IV. Thomas[7], d. y.
   V. Mary Chambers[7] Bibb (b. 1842, d. 1874), *m.* Wm. Eggleston. Issue: Eliza[8] and and Pattie[8]. both *unm.*
   VI. Eliza[7] Bibb (b. 1844), *m.* (1774) William Greet; two sons and two daughters, *unm.*
   VII. Robert[7] Bibb (b. 1846, d. 1883), *m.* Virginia Townes; son and three daughters.

6. ELMIRA[4] BIBB (b. 1816, d. 1887), *m.* (1833) Archibald E. Mills. Issue:
   I. Thomas Bibb[7] Mills (b. 1835, d. 1868), *m.* Miss Goodman, of Montgomery, and left a daughter; II. William Bibb[7] Mills (twin with Thomas; d. 1870); *m.* Miss Gilmore, Montgomery, Ala., and left one son; III. Archibald E.[7] Mills (b. 1838, d. 1890; married; IV. Flora[7] Mills (b. 1841, d. 1875), married Samuel Ragland. No living issue. V. Eliza[7] Mills (b. 1843, d. y.); VI. Mary Martin[7] Mills (b. 1845, d. y.); VII. John F.[7] Mills (b. 1847, d. 1880), *unm.*; VIII. Frank Martin[7] Mills (b. 1850), married, and had two children; IX. George Bierne[7] Mills (b. 1852), married; (not given). X. Porter[7] Mills (b. 1854), married, (not given).

7. ROBERT THOMPSON[4] BIBB, of Nashville, Tenn. (b. 1818, d. 1861), married Anne Bradley. No living issue.

8. ELIZA PAMELIA[4] BIBB (b. 1821, d. Birmingham, Ala., 18th January, 1899), youngest child of Governor Bibb. Gifted with the great vitality and individuality of her notable ancestry, and preserving her bright intellect to the last, she survived all her contemporaries. Her just pride of family was great, and she took encouraging interest in the compiling of these records. Married (1836) Arthur Mosely Hopkins[*] (b. 1816, died 1866), son of Judge Arthur Hopkins, of Alabama, of whom is a lengthy notice in the "*Early Settlers*" (*ante*). Issue:
   I. Maria Belle[7] Hopkins (b. 1838, d. y.).
   II. Arthur Francis[7] Hopkins (b. 1840, d. y.).
   III. John Walker[7] Hopkins (b. 1842, d. 1891), married (1866) Anna Cox. Issue: 1. John Walker[8] Hopkins (b. 1867, d. 1886), *unm.* 2. Lizzie May[8] Hopkins (b. 1870), *m.* Duncan Harding, of Nashville, Tenn. Widow with one son. 3. Arthur Moseley[8] Hopkins (b. 1873), *m.* (1895) Fannie Bang, Nashville, Tenn. Two children. 4. Ellie Cole[8] Hopkins (b. 1876, d. 1898), *m.* (1896) Fred. Prescott, of Boston, Mass. No issue. 5. Margaret[8] (b. 1878, d. y.). 6. Charles Thomas[8] (b. 1880, d. y.). 7. Thornton[8] (b. 1883).
   IV. Thomas Bibb[7] Hopkins, of Bowling Green, Ky. (b. 1844). *m.* (1872) Virginia, daughter of Dr. A. Sydney Harris, of Limestone county, Ala. (see *Moore* note). Mr.

---

[*] Arthur Moseley (1776), Committee of Safety, Amherst county, Va.

Bibb is a merchant in high standing, dealing in hardware and house furnishing goods. He takes much interest in his lineage, having greatly aided in perfecting this list of his grandfather's descendants. Children:

1. Fannie[6] Bibb (b. 1874, d. 1898), m. (1896) Vernon D. Leake, of Todd City, Ky., and left one child, Jennie V. Leake. 2. Sydney Harris[6] Bibb (b. 1876, d. 1891).

V. Arthur Moseley[7] Hopkins (b. 1846, d. y.).
VI. Bessie Moseley[7] Hopkins (b. 1849, d. 1882).
VII. Sallie Barnett[7] Hopkins (b. 1851, d. 1877) unm.
VIII. Fannie Carter[7] Hopkins (b. 1852, d. y.).
IX. James Bennett[7] Hopkins (1854), m. (1878) Madeline Sanders, daughter of Dr. Wm. Tell Sanders, of Limestone county, Ala. Issue, three daughters.
X. William Bibb[7] Hopkins (b. 1854, twin with James; d. y.).
XI. Porter Bibb[7] Hopkins (b. 1856, d. y.).
XII. Frank Webb[7] Hopkins, of Birmingham, Ala. (b. 1858), m. (1880) Mary Harris, granddaughter of Dr. A. Sydney Harris, of Limestone county, Ala. Has eight living children. Of these, twin boys, born 1899.
XIII. Robert Thompson[7] Hopkins, of Nashville, Tenn. (b. 1860), m. 1884) Ada Martin, Nashville, Tenn., and has two sons (one Robert[8]) and two daughters.

7. REV. PEYTON[5] BIBB, of M. E. Church, South (b. Prince Edward county, 1785, d. 1841); planter of Autanga county, Ala., educated by Dr. Waddel; married, says Governor Gilmer, "Martha Cobb (niece of old William Cobb, who lived to be 111 years old, and when 110, married a girl of 18)." He also established the line of steamboats running from Montgomery to Mobile, Ala., before the time of railroads. Issue:

1. Nancy[6], m. James Terry; both deceased. One surviving child, Mrs. Sarah F[7] Hardaway. 2. Edna[6], m. Zachariah Watkins, no surviving children. 3. Harriet[6], m. Dr. Albert Goodwyn, nephew of Governor Adams of South Carolina, and had Eliza[7]; m. Samuel Oliver, C. S. A. Caroline[7], Thomas Mills[7], graduate of Annapolis with rank of lieutenant. And officer in the Confederate navy, Julia[7], m. Captain Bailes Taylor, C. S. A., Albert T., m. Priscilla Tyler, granddaughter of President Tyler, Joseph B.[7] m. Sallie McDade, Orline[7], m. Mr. Adams. 4. Peyton Dandridge[6] Bibb, m. Sarah Allen, and had Loula D.[7], Caroline E.[7], unm. Walter[7], m. Miss Spires, Henry Allen[7], unm., Frances[7], m. John Murrey, of Montgomery. 5. Colonel Joseph[6] Bibb, m. his cousin Martha Dandridge Bibb. 6. Caroline[6], m. Walter L. Coleman in 1869, Mayor of Montgomery. No issue. 7. Frances[6], m. Joseph P. Saffold, Judge of Chancery; and had Peyton B.[7], Joseph P.[7], Mary Ellen[7], m. (I) Wm. Joseph, and m. (II) Dr. Walter Jackson, and had issue: Fanny[8], m. Whiting Brown; and Elis[8], m. Austin Pickett, son of the author of "History of Alabama.," Martha[8], m. Charles Joseph; Caroline unm.; Willie[8], m. Jordan Soovel; Sophie Lee[8], m. Dr. Foster of Atlanta. (Mrs. Martha D. Bibb.)

8. JOHN DANDRIDGE[5] BIBB, named for Mrs. Washington's brother, at her request (b. Prince Edward county, Va., 10th March, 1788; d. 9th May, 1848, on plantation on Yazoo river, Carroll parish, Miss.); married (6th February, 1812) Mary Xenia (b. 1797; d. 1846); a lady of beauty and intelligence; daughter of John and Frances (Thompson) Oliver, of Petersburg, Georgia. He studied law under Hon. Wm. H. Crawford, and practised with him as junior partner. (See Oliver family.)

"The wealth acquired by this marriage," says Gov. Gilmer, "enabled him to quit the profession of law for that of planting." They removed to Madison county, Mississippi territory 1814, and to Montgomery City, Alabama Territory, 1818, and was judge of the Territorial Court, and State Senator, and member Constitutional Convention, then moved to Morgan county (above Decatur) 1827, returning finally to Montgomery, Ala. This couple were buried in Mississippi, but remains were finally removed to Montgomery by their devoted son, William Crawford Bibb. Issue: (Family Bible.)

1. Charles Sydney[6], (b. Petersburg, Ga., 2d April, 1813, d. 8th July, 1813); 2. Elvira Antoinette[6] (b. Madison county, Mississippi Territory, 6th September, 1814, d. in

Columbus, Miss., 24th February, 1839); 3. Sarah Frances[a] (b. Madison county 26th September, 1816, d. at Sharon, Montgomery county, Alabama, 19th September, 1821); 4. Mary Dandridge[a] (b. Montgomery, Alabama Territory, 17th March, 1818, d. 14th October, 1821); 5. William Crawford[a] (b. in Montgomery county 1st January, 1820, d. in Montgomery 23d May, 1896); 6. Edwin Augustus[a] (b. 11th January, 1822, d. 28th September, 1835); 7. Lavinia Arabella[a] (b. 20th January, 1824, d. 28th October, 1825); 8. John Dandridge[a] (b. Morgan county, Alabama, 14th November, 1826, d. 27th August, 1827); 9. Dandridge Asbury[a] (b. Morgan county, Alabama, 20th November, 1827, d. Morgan county, 1861); 10. Algernon Sydney[a] (b. Morgan county, Alabama, 4th June, 1829); 11. Mary Cornelia[a] (b. Columbus, Miss., 26th April, 1832, d. 5th September, 1832)—she was twin with a still-born infant; 12. Laura Angerona[a] (b. Columbus, Miss., 19th October, 1833. d. Tuskegee, Ala., July, 1866.) Of these:

2. Elvira Antoinette[1] (b. 1814), married (2d April, 1832) Dr. Samuel Booth Malone, of Columbus, Miss. Issue: 1. Ellen[2] Malone (b. 1834, d. 1864), m. William Gibson; died in Matagorda, Texas. 2. Ulwyn Booth[2] Malone (b. 1836), C. S. A., killed in second battle of Manassas. 3. Antoinette Booth[2] Malone (b. 1838), m. Alfred Glover, of Green county, Ala., and had several children.

5. WILLIAM CRAWFORD[5] Bibb (the fifth child), born 1st January, 1820, Montgomery county; d. Montgomery, 23d May, 1896; was named by his father for the Hon. Wm. H. Crawford, of Georgia (in return for his courtesy in naming a son John Dandridge Bibb Crawford). Married (I), 11th May, 1842, Priscilla E. Sims, of Tuscaloosa, Ala. (b. 1823, died 10th April, 1852, in Montgomery, Ala.). He m. (II), 13th June, 1853, Rebecca Lanier (b. Elbert county, Georgia, 30th April, 1823), daughter of Gen. Jeptha V. and Sarah (Hunt) Harris, of Athens, Ga.

Of much culture, and caring more for research in his family lineage than many of his relatives, his *Record of the Bibb Family* has been mainly followed in these pages. A while after the Civil War he lived in Madison, Ga., but returned finally to his old home, Montgomery, Ala. His humor and wit were very attractive, and his influence in his family and community great.

In the spring of 1865 Mr. Bibb, after a conversation with Governor Watts, of Alabama, undertook a mission to Washington City to interview Mr. Lincoln personally. Armed with letters to General Washburne, he was given passport without being called upon to take the oath of allegiance. In Washington City he met O. H. Browning and Attorney General Speed, who made an appointment for him to meet Mr. Seward; and Admiral John L. Worden (whom he had befriended when a prisoner in Montgomery) sent him a letter to Mr. Lincoln.

Mr. Seward greeted him kindly, and said he once knew his father and uncle, Wm. Bibb, when Senator from Georgia, and that he also once resided in Georgia, "and had he continued to live there might have done much toward preventing the war." General Lee surrendered before his interview with Mr. Lincoln, which then became unnecessary, but he called, nevertheless, hoping thus to serve his people. Mr. Bibb published this interview in the March and April numbers of the "*Gulf Messenger*," 1893. "We arrived at the White House on time, and without the usual formalities I was introduced to Mr. Lincoln; I was struck with astonishment at his homely face and ungainly appearance, but the total absence of all effort to impress one with the fact that he was President of the United States, and the kind and informal manner of his reception excited my admiration; handing me a chair and requesting me to be seated, then drawing his chair a little back from his table, he slid into it, gave his legs a fling over the arm and clasping his hands around his knees, reminded me of some country farmer who had fixed himself for a long comfortable chat with his neighbor. * * *

"The letter from Admiral Worden was presented, and as he read I noticed a change from rather a sad to a more pleasing expression of face, and at its close he extended his hand, and again expressed his pleasure at seeing me, adding that Mr. Browning had mentioned that I was related to the Hon. Geo. M. Bibb, of Kentucky, with whom he was well acquainted. * * * 'Mr. Lincoln, I would be glad to be able to say that your plan of reconstruction will be marked with leniency and liberality.' He asked if I had heard his speech of last night, and his *proclamation of general amnesty*? I then asked him if I could assure the Southern people that that would be the basis of his policy of reconstruction. He answered, 'Yes, if I live, and retain the power to enforce its terms.' I asked if its terms extended to our leaders. 'Yes, to all. It is universal in its application. I consented to withhold it from publication for a few days for special reasons urged, which I regard of little force, but I thought it better to pay that respect to the opinion of others.'

"He continued: 'I love the Southern people more than they love me. My desire is to restore the Union. I do not intend to hurt the hair of the head of a single man in the South if it can possibly be avoided.'

" 'Mr. Lincoln, what will be required of the Southern States to allow their admission into the Union?'

" 'All that I ask is that they shall annul their ordinances of secession, and send their delegates to fill the seats in Congress which are now awaiting their occupation.'

" 'Mr. Lincoln, what do you propose to do in relation to the slave property?'

" 'I am, individually, willing to grant either gradual emancipation, say running through twenty years, or compensated emancipation, at the option of the Southern people. But there are certain amendments to the Constitution now before the people. I have no power to do anything at present, but if it should so happen that I could control it, such would be my policy.'

"I said I believed the Union restored under a liberal policy would become more strongly reunited than ever; that both sections had suffered, and through that suffering, wiser, calmer and greater forbearance would prevail. • • •

"Two hours were thus consumed and I arose. At this he reached out and taking hold of my lapels, requested me to reseat myself, and taking up the letter of introduction, said: 'What can I do for you?' I replied I would be glad to be given a passport to my home. He at once wrote the two following cards: '*Any military commander, in whose way it may fall, will give protection to the bearer, W. C. Bibb, his family and property.*

" '*April 12, 1865.*   A. LINCOLN.'

" '*Allow the bearer, W. C. Bibb, to pass our lines with ordinary baggage, and go South.*

" '*April 12, 1865.*   A. LINCOLN.'

"I said : 'Mr. Lincoln, I feel very grateful for your kindness, and it is due you and myself to tell you I have not taken the oath of allegiance to the Federal Government, and can not, until the surrender of the Confederate armies.' This, with trepidation, which increased, as he cast his eyes down, and I thought I saw a shadow pass over his face, but only momentary; he raised his eyes, and looking at me, said: 'I respect your scruples. Probably under the same surroundings I would do the same.' • • • With a grateful heart, and cordial farewell, I took my departure. In five minutes after meeting him I had felt my prejudices fast melting away, and being supplanted by a high appreciation of the man, and in conclusion, the idea was forced upon me that of all previous men I had ever met, this was "*the noblest Roman of them all.*"

"I was on the train from Baltimore to New York on the fatal night of the 14th, and just before reaching Philadelphia the conductor announced the assassination of Lincoln and Seward as a rumor. • • • The President was dead before he could publish his proclamation. The attack was made upon the two most conservative men, Lincoln and Seward, who, if they had lived, would have prevented, in united action, the horrors of the years that followed Lee's surrender." Mr. Bibb returned to Montgomery to find his home in ruins.

Issue of William Crawford[4] Bibb's first marriage (*Sims*):

1. Cornelia D.[5] Bibb (b. 15th November, 1842), m. (4th October, 1860) Vernon H. Vaughn, of Tuscaloosa, Ala. They removed to San Francisco. Issue: 1, Vernon[6]; 2, Mary[6]; 3, Joseph[6]; 4, Anna[6].

2. John Dandridge[7] Bibb (b. Hancock county, Miss., 29th October, 1846), m. (1868) Eusubia Forman (d. 1871). They lived in Lowndes county, Ala. Issue: Letitia Woodson[8] (b. 1869).

3. Mary Frances[7] Bibb (b. Montgomery, 1st September, 1848), m. (28th November, 1867) Charles H. Leffler, of Sanford, Fla., and had Charles D.[8] (b. 1868). Mary[8] (b. 17th October, 1876)—Issue Mr. Bibb's second marriage: (Harris.)

4. William Crawford[7] Bibb, Jr., of Montgomery (b. 27th February, 1853), married Martha Shepherd. Children: 1, Evelyn[8]; 2, John Dandridge[8];[•] 3, Rebecca Lanier[8].

5. Sarah Hunt[7] Bibb (b. Montgomery, Ala., 28th March, 1855), m. (I) 20th September, 1876, Oscar Thomason (no issue), and (II) Dr. Cornelius Hardy, of Columbus, Miss., (second wife). They entertain with charming hospitality in Columbus, Miss.

9. Dandridge Asbury[4] Bibb, M. D. (b. Morgan county, Ala., 1827, d 1861), m. (1849) Emma Taylor. Children: Elizabeth Sophia[7] (b. 1851); Dandridge A.[7] (b. 1855).

10. Algernon Sydney[4] Bibb, of Arkansas (b. Morgan county, Ala., 4th June, 1829), m. (I) 1848, Mary Carraway, and m. (II) 1856, Miss Hoad, Murfreesboro, Tenn. Issue first marriage: 1, Mary Katherine[7] (b. 1849), m. Mr. Van Lytle, of Tennessee. 2, Charles C.[7] (b. 1852), of New Hope, Ky. Issue second marriage: 3, Thomas[7]. 4, Ada[7], and two others.

12. Laura Angerona[4] Bibb (b. Columbus, Miss., 19th October, 1833, d. Tuskegee, Ala., 1866), m. (1852) Henry L. Rogers, of La Grange, Ga. and Tuskegee, Ala. (d. 1863). Issue: Annie[7], m. McDuff Cain, and had several children, and lived in Montgomery; and others, not known.

9. Joseph[4] Wyatt Bibb, M. D. (b. Prince Edward county, Virginia, 1788, d. 1831). Graduated medical college, Philadelphia, about 1811. Practised in Petersburg, Ga., and with Dr. McDonald, in North Alabama. Removed to Montgomery, 1830. Married (I) Louisa Du Bose, sister of Mrs. Robert Toombs, of Georgia, and m. (II) Martha Dancy, the accomplished belle of North Alabama. (Descendants not given.)

10. Delia[4] Bibb, m. Alex. Pope, of Georgia (grandson of Col. Pope of the Rev., who was also a member of the "Order of Cincinnatus"), secretary to Gov. W. W. Bibb, and held several offices under the U. S. government. Issue: 1. Lawrence[5], m. Ann Fort, of Huntsville, Ala.; 2. Milton[5], m. in Philadelphia; 3. Henry[5], m. Lydia Holcombe; 4. William[5], m. the widow of — Randolph, Confederate States Secretary of War; 5. Maria Jane[5], m. Newton St. John, banker, Mobile, Ala.; son: Pope St. John, of Mobile.

11. Martha[4] Bibb (died February, 1835), m. Fleming, son of Col. Holman Freeman, (of Rev. fame in North Georgia, and Whig leader under Gov. Elijah Clark). Fleming Freeman was grandson of George Walton, the signer. No surviving issue.

12. Judge Benajah Smith[4] Bibb, of Montgomery (b. Elbert county, Ga., 30th September, 1796, d. 17th February, 1884), a posthumous son, and "the companion of his mother." Educated by Dr. Waddel; moved to Alabama 1822; Judge of Montgomery County Court 1825. Went to Morgan county 1827, and represented it in Legislature 1829. Returned to Montgomery 1832. Again Judge and State Senator 1834-36; Legislature 1845-49, Senate 1851. An "old-line Whig," and chairman of the committee to receive Henry Clay 1844, and also President Fillmore and Secretary John P. Kennedy in 1854. Trustee of the A. & M. College, Auburn, Ala., and Judge of the Criminal

Court 1864. The first office holder removed in Alabama by Federal authority, because of his unflinching devotion to the Confederacy. He married (1819) Sophia Lucy Ann Gilmer (d. 9th January, 1887), sister of Gov. Geo. R. Gilmer, author of the "*Georgians.*" Their father was Thomas, grandson of Dr. George Gilmer, of Virginia, who married the daughter of Thomas Lewis—all celebrated Virginians, who settled on Broad river, Georgia. Mrs. Bibb was best known for her love of the Confederacy and its soldiers, for whom she founded a hospital in Montgomery and was its President; she, and her devoted band of co-laborers maintaining it from their own efforts and resources. They then organized the "*Ladies Confederate Memorial Association,*" of which she was President; and erected the towering Monument, to the laying of whose corner-stone President Jefferson Davis came in 1886, when their meeting was very pathetic. She was honored in death with a public demonstration unparalleled in the history of the State. Her mantle seems to have fallen upon her noble daughter, Mrs. Martha D. Bibb. Issue:

1. William Joseph[6], m. Ann Rogers, of LaGrange, Ga.; both deceased, leaving daughter, Sarah G[7].

2. George R.[6], m. Mary E. Lipscomb, sister of Rev. A. A. Lipscomb, Chancellor University of Georgia, and professor English literature, Vanderbilt University (both deceased); a son, B. S.[7] Bibb, of Selma, married Helen Robbins.

3. Louisa S.[6], unmarried.

4. Sarah E.[6], m. (1) Dr. Eldridge; and (II) Mr. John Sears Hutchinson. Issue:
   1. Thos. Gilmer[7] Hutchinson, lawyer, Nashville, Tenn., m. Kate Baxter.
   2. Kate Sears[7] Hutchinson, m. E. P. Morrisette, of Montgomery, and had Sallie Bibb[8], m. Crosland Hare; Frances Gaines[8] and Edmund Pendleton[8] Morrisette.

5. Martha Dandridge[6] (sends this list of her father's descendants), member of Daughters of the Revolution, and Ladies' Memorial Society; married her cousin, Joseph B.[6] Bibb, lawyer; colonel Twenty-third Regiment, Alabama Volunteers, in Civil War. Issue: 1. Wm. G.[7] Bibb, M. D.; m. Susie Dunlap, daughter of Gov. James D. Porter, of Tennessee; 2. Peyton[7] Bibb, graduated United States Naval Academy, Annapolis, 1878, served in Mediterranean and Pacific cruises, and resigned; m. Josephine Martin, of Augusta, Ga.; great-granddaughter of Gen. Elijah Clark[*] of the Revolution and Governor of Georgia.

PARTLY FROM FAMILY REGISTER OF COL. JOSEPH WYATT, OF VIRGINIA. Copied by Mrs. Sion B. Spencer,[†] for her daughter, Miss Ann Spencer, of Keysville, Charlotte county, Va., who gave it to her cousin, Thomas J. Garden, of Prospect, Va. (Prince Edward county), who sent it to Mr. Daniel H. Cram, of Montgomery, Ala., in 1875.—*Mrs. Virginia Semple.*

"THOMAS[1] SCOTT, of Gloucester, county, Va., married Anne Baytop, of Gloucester county. (Note.—She was the daughter of Thomas Baytop[2], of County Kent, England, (b. 1676), (son of Thomas[1]) and was sister of Col. James[2] Baytop (d. 1767), of Gloucester county). They left issue several daughters, and three sons: John[2], Thomas[2], and James[2] Scott. Of these—

I. John[2] remained in Gloucester.

II. Thomas[2] (b. 21st March, 1727, d. 29th November, 1804), married (I) (6th April, 1754) Catherine Tomkies (b. 10th June, 1733, and d. 2d January, 1766). Daughter of

---

[*] The children of Gen. Elijah Clark were: 1. General John (b. North Carolina, 1766, and Governor of Georgia); m. a daughter of Micajah Williamson; 2. Elijah, lawyer; 3. Gibson, lawyer; 4. A daughter, m. —— Thompson; 5. Another, m. Josiah Walton; and 6. Another, Benajah Smith, whose daughter[2] m. Eldrid Simpkins, and *his* daughter[3] m. Hon. Francis Pickens, grandson of General Pickens, the associate in arms of Gen. Elijah Clark.

[†]Son of Sion Spencer (b. 1744), son of Thomas Spencer, of Virginia, and Eliza Julia Flournoy (b. 1751); who was daughter of John James Flournoy, the immigrant, and Eliz. Williams, his wife, who was the daughter of James Williams, the Welsh lawyer, and Eliz. Buckner, his wife.

Dr. Charles Tomkies, of Gloucester, who died 1735. They moved to Prince Edward county, Va. Issue:
1. Thomas² (b. 19th January, 1755, d. 22d February following).
2. Maj. Francis² (b. 16th August, 1756), m. "Nannie Wyatt" (says Judge F. N. Watkins, of Farmville).
3. Mary³ (b. 25th October, 1758), m. Wm. Watts, of Bedford, Va.
4. John³ B. (b. 26th February, 1761) of Halifax county (Gen. John Baytop) married (I) Betsy, daughter of Colonel Coleman, of Halifax, no issue; and m. (II), Patsy Thompson. Issue: Several children
5. Captain Charles³ (b. 21st July, 1763), m. Priscilla Read.
6. Thomas Tomkies³ (b. 6th December, 1765). An old letter of his to Capt. James Baytop, of Gloucester, his cousin, is preserved. He never married. Died at the old homestead in Prince Edward.
(II. Thomas Scott (above), married (II), 1st November, 1768, Mrs. Sarah Barford (widow) (b. 10th July. 1728, d. 7th June, 1788). No issue. He then married (III), Mrs. Ruth Billups (widow) on 16th July, 1790. No issue.)
*2. Maj. Francis² Scott (b. 1756), married (11th January 1777) Nancy Wyatt, eldest daughter of Joseph and Dorothy Wyatt, of New Kent county, Va. Nancy was born 17th November, 1760, and was sister of Col. Joseph Wyatt, of Charlotte county, Va. Issue:
1. Catherine Tomkies⁴ (b. 28th October, 1777), m. John, son of Rev. James Garden, of Scotland. In 1875 she had grandchildren living, and son Thomas J., and grandson Thomas J., Jr.
2. Joseph Wyatt⁴ (b. 19th December, 1780), m. (I) Polly Carrington, and (II) Betsy Wyatt. One child living in 1875.
3. Francis⁴ (b. 8th January, 1872), married Miss Price.
4. Thomas⁴, of Louisiana (b. 25th January, 1784), married Miss Inge.
5. Sarah⁴ (b. 26th February, 1785), m. Mr. Taylor.
6. Nancy⁴ (b. 21st March, 1788), m. Mr. Jamieson. Moved to Lawrence county, Ala.—See Early Settlers.
7. Betsy⁴ (b. 30th July, 1790), m. Capt. Mathew Williams, a school teacher. Two children.
8. Charles Tomkies⁴ (b. 7th October. 1792), went South.
9. Pasty⁴ (b. 9th September, 1794), married; and died in the West. Four children.
10. Mary⁴ (b. 14th November, 1796), m. Sion Spencer, and had five children.
11. Jack⁴ (b. 21st January, 1799), or John Baytop.
12. Robert⁴ (b. 16th June, 1801), went South.
13. William⁴ (b. 7th March, 1807). And all were dead in 1875.
James Scott (third son of Thos. and Ann (Baytop) Scott), married Frances Collier, and lived in Prince Edward county, Va. Issue: 1. Thomas, 2. Jack (or John Baytop), 3. Mrs. Keyes, 4. Mrs. Spencer, 5. Mrs. Micajah McGehee, of Georgia; 6. Francis, father of John, of Gloucester county. (All from letter of Judge F. N. Watkins, of Farmville, Va., to Mr. Cram, of Alabama, in 1875. Also see Mrs. Virginia Semple's *Scott Family Pamphlet*.)

BANKS FAMILY.

Miles and John Banks, members of the Virginia Company 1620 (*William and Mary Quarterly*, V).
Thomas Banks (1623), alive at James City after the Massacre.
Henry Banks came to Virginia 1635, aged 19, in the *Paul*.
James Banks came to Virginia 1635, aged 35, and Thomas Banks, aged 4 years, and Elizabeth, aged nine months, all in same ship.
James Banks, aged 30, came in "*The Thomas and John*," 1635. (*Hottens Emigrants*.)

Thomas Banks (1668), a deed in Lancaster county.

Dr. William Banks, Justice in Stafford county, before 1681, in which year his friend, William Fitzhugh, the immigrant, applied to Lord Culpeper and Secretary Spencer, for the office of High Sheriff for him.

William Banks (1728), 590 acres in Spotsylvania county.

Adam Banks was living in Stafford county in 1674. His son, *Gerrard Banks*, living in 1709. Will proved in Orange county 1768. He married Frances Strother, and had a son, Gerrard[2] Banks. (*William and Mary Quarterly.*)

Gerrard Banks *m.* Frances Bruce, and had *dau.* Agatha Banks, married William Waller Hening. (*See Hayden's Virginia Geneologies.*)

George Banks, of Caroline county, *m.* Judith, *dau.* of Joseph Walker, of York county, who d. 1723. Her sister, Mary Walker, was 1st wife of Charles Carter of "Cleves," to whose children Mrs Judith Banks left legacies in 1778. (*Hening's Statutes, Virginia Gazette, and William and Mary Quarterly.*)

Wm. Banks, of Stafford county, student at William and Mary College in 1795; afterwards Judge in State Court.

George Banks, of Stafford county, student at *William and Mary* 1798.

Linn Banks, of Rapp, student 1806—afterwards Member of Congress.

H. J. Banks, student 1823 (*probably of Georgia*).

Anthony Banks, of Middlesex county, married Isabella ———, and had Elizabeth, b. 1693. (*Christ Church Register.*)

Members of the Banks family were vestrymen in Blissland par., New Kent county, and also the Richardsons, Dandridges, Holderofts, and others. 1721-1786. (*B. Meade.*)

Banks in vestry of Austin pa., Halifax county, after 1752. (*B. Meade.*)

James Banks of the *Northern Neck* of Virginia, signed resolutions against the Stamp Act, with Rodham and Winder S. Kenner, John Berryman and others in 1765—(John Berryman was of vestry St. Paul, King George county in 1771).

The heirs of Commodore James Banks of the Rev. got 5734 acres from Congress 1848 (half pay claim).

WILLIAM BANKS, of King and Queen county, Va. *Will 1709 (Hening's Statutes).*

His son Ralph Banks died 1735, and left among others, 1. William, 2. Tunstall, 3. Baylor, 4. Olivia Banks[3], 5. Elizabeth Thruston.

1. William's will was proved in Albemarle county in 1812, and mentions only his sisters and brothers. He left a legacy to his brother Baylor, and also to William T. Banks. (*Hening V. 214*).

Tunstall Banks, of King and Queen county, of the committee of safety—1774-5.

Tunstall Banks, Justice in Essex county, between 1780-1800. (*B. Meade*).

Tunstall Banks, *m.* in Middlesex county (1793) Polly Murray Curtis.

James and Mary Banks of Bristol pa. had issue: Charles (b. 1716); Mary (b. 1718); Sarah (b. 1721); *Priscilla*, a family name, (b. 1723) and *William Banks* (b. 1725). (*Bristol pa. Register.*)

William Banks (1749), 150 acres in Surry, south side of Nottoway. (*Land Book.*)

William Banks (1755), lands in Essex county. (*Probably same as above.*)

James Banks and Susanna Banks, died, 1758. (*Albemarle parish*, Surrey and Sussex county *Register.*)

William and Sarah Banks had son, *James Banks*, born (1754) in Albemarle parish, with Burwell Banks as godfather. (*Ibid.*)

Burwell and Mary Banks, had daughter, Mary (b. 1768). In 1760 he recorded birth of some slaves. (*Ibid.*)

Alexander Banks (1765) recorded birth of some slaves. (*Ibid.*)

Alexander Banks (1773), living in Manchester, Chesterfield county, Virginia. (*Virginia Gazette*). Trustee (1791) in *Mason's lottery*, in Chesterfield county, with John Baytop Scott, Joseph Scott, Francis Scott, Thomas Oliver, Joseph Wyatt, John Coleman, etc.

Henry and William Banks, after the Revolution, mentioned by Hening also. (*Hening's Statutes.*)

Robert and Peter Banks, in Rowan county, N. C., 1771, signed a petition to divide that county. (*N. C. Colonial Records.*)

Thomas Banks (1750), justice in Johnston county. (*Ibid.*)

William Banks was a juror in Craven county, N. C., 1771. (*Ibid.*)

Thomas Banks, of Craven county, with Memucan Hunt, was of the assembly of 1776, and on a committee to procure arms for that county. (*Ibid.*)

Banks Family, of Elbert County, Ga., and Before that, of North Carolina.

The ancestor, Ralph Banks (b. *circa* 1766), was probably a relative or descendant of William Banks, of King and Queen county, Va., *will 1709*, as the names Ralph, William, James and Thomas were common to the families of both.

In 1780 there had been quite an emigration of *Dissenting* families from Hanover, King and Queen, and New Kent counties, to North Carolina, under the preaching of Samuel Davies. (*See Colonial Records of North Carolina.*) Also families from Isle of Wight, and *South Side* counties generally, were rapidly moving into the Carolinas (which, it must be remembered, were a part of Virginia until 1693).

Ralph[1] Banks married Rachel Alston Jones, of North Carolina. (Her mother was of the celebrated Alston family, famous in North and South Carolina, of whom it was said "*the men all died in their boots.*" Theodosia Alston, wife of Aaron Burr, was her cousin). They removed to the Broad river settlement, Elbert county, Ga., and had ten sons and three daughters:

1. Thomas[2], 2. Willis[2], 3. James A.[2], 4. Ralph[2], 5. John D.[2], 6. Sarah[2], 7. Richard[2], 8. Mary[2], 9. Dunstan[2], 10. Priscilla[2], 11. Henry[2], 12. Lemuel[2], 13. Elbert[2], 14. Marion[2].

I. Thomas[2] Banks m. Miss Triplett. Issue:
1. Ralph[3] Banks m. four times, and had, by last wife, several children.
2. Elbert[3] Banks was blind from youth; m., and had several children.
3. Richard[3] Banks m. Fanny Green and lived in Hancock county, Ga.; several children.
4. Mary Louisa[3] m. John Stevens, of Forsyth, Ga. Issue: Pearl[4], m. ——, and has several children.

II. Willis[2] Banks, m. (I) Mary Winfrey Oliver, daughter of James Oliver, of Elbert county, Ga., and m. (II) Mary Gray. Issue, first marriage:
1. Mary Winfrey[3] Banks, m. Gen. Jeptha V. Harris, of Columbus, Miss. (*See Harris notes in Watkins family*). Issue, second marriage (Gray):
2. Thomas Gray[3] Banks, m. Mary Waldron.
3. James Oliver[3] Banks, Columbus, Miss. (named for the father of Willis Banks' first wife), m. (I) Martha Coleman, and (II) Lucy, daughter of Col. George and Lucy (Watkins) Young, of "*Waverly*," Miss., near Columbus. Issue, first marriage (for the second, see *Watkins*):
1. Mary Gray[4], m. (I) Fernaudis Pope, and had Fernandis Pope; and m. (II) Hampton Osborne (his third wife).
2. Willis[4] m. Jennie Dunlap; one child.
3. James O.[4] m. Julia Coleman, of Eutaw, Ala., and has six children.
4. Francis[3] died young.

III. James Jones[2] Banks m. Hannah Alston (cousin to his mother). Issue:
1. Jabez Jones[3] Banks m. Jane Harvey; several children; of whom, Judge James J. Banks, of Birmingham, Ala., is the youngest. He m. Lee Frazer; and another Wm. Banks m. Lou Rogers, whose daughter, Nona, m. a son of Rev. Allan Andrews, of M. E. Church, South. Another daughter of Jabez J. Banks m. Dr. Franklin, of Union Springs, Ala.
2. Jasper[3], d. s. p.
3. Rachel Jones[3] Banks m. Monroe Tarver. Issue: Several children.

4. Newton Paley[3] Banks, M. D., Opelika, Ala., m. Fanny Jernigan. Issue: Several
children, of whom,
   1. Sarah Hannah[4] m. J. B. Tarver, Columbus, Ga. 2. Pearl[4] m. Warren Watkins,
   Opelika, Ala,.
5. Sarah Eliz.[3] Banks m. *Bishop Oscar Fitzgerald*, M. E. Church, South. Issue:
   1. Genella[4] m. Mr. Nye; several children. 2. Eleanor[4] m. Mr. Robinson, and had
   Sarah[5]. 3. Lilian Banks[4], unm. 4. Oscar Penn[4], unm. 5. William[4], Professor
   of English in Military Institute, Roswell, New Mexico. 6. Lee[4] died a young
   man.
6. Rev. Marion Dunstan[3] Banks, Opelika, Ala.. m. Cordelia Allen; minister M. E.
Church, South, and taught a prosperous school for many years, ably assisted by
his young daughter, Mary. Issue:
   1. John[4] Banks (deceased) m. Martha Cotton; three children. 2. Bettie[4] m. H. C.
   Jenigan, and has six children. 3. Nellie[4] m. Walter Hurt; seven children. 4.
   Mamie[4] m. Albert Barnett, of Opelika, Editor, and Register in chancery; three
   children.

IV. RALPH[2] BANKS, m. "a plain girl," *says Mrs. Georgia Young*, "and was disin-
herited by his proud parents, but reared a family of fine sturdy children, of whom
naught evil was ever said, unless *poverty* be a crime."

V. JOHN D.[2] Banks (b. 1794), lawyer of Columbus, Ga., m. Sarah, *dau.* of John
and Susan (Daniel) Watkins, of Petersburg, Ga. Issue:
1. John Troup[3]; 2, Willis Dunstan[3]; 3, George Young[3]; 4, Daniel Watkins[3]; 5, Edward
Sims[3]; 6, Susan Martha[3]; 7, Rockingham Gilmer[3]; 8, Rd. Eugene[3]; 9. Dr. Elbert
Augustine[3]; 10, Wm. Kelley[3]; 11, Lucy Watkins[3]; 12, Anne Virginia[3]; 13, Mary
Priscilla[3]. (*For these see Watkins.*)
   VI. Sarah[2] Banks m. Edward Sims. Issue:
1. Jerusha[3] Sims, m. —— Reedy, of Wetumpka, Ala.
2. Mary[3] Sims, m. —— Hemphill, of Tuscaloosa, Ala.; daughter m. Prof. Benj. Meek,
   Alabama University.
3. Jane[3] Sims, m. Judge Frank Moody, of Tuscaloosa.
4. Tenett[3] Sims, m. —— Trimble, of Montgomery.
5. Priscilla[3] Sims, m. Hon. Wm. Crawford Bibb, Sr., of Montgomery (1st wife).—(*See*
   Bibb.)

VII. RICHARD[2] BANKS, M. D., m. Martha Butt Dawson (widow); lived and died in
Gainesville, Ga.; an eminent oculist, and for whom Banks county, Ga., was named.
Issue:
1. Joseph Marion[3] Banks.
2. Dunstan[3] Banks.
3. Philoclea[3] Banks, m. Blackshear.
4. Susan[3] Banks, m. (I) —— Brewster; (II) —— Becker; (III) —— Pledger.

VIII. MARY[2] BANKS, m. —— Napier. Issue: Several sons, one of whom
Lemuel[3] Napier, m. Mary Palmer Reedy, and their only daughter, Rachel[4], m. Frank
Siddons.

IX. DUNSTAN[2] BANKS, of Columbus, Miss. (b. 10th December, 1800, d. 10th September, 1881), influential citizen and kind father, and one of the earliest residents of
Columbus, where the fine old home is a land-mark; m. Lucretia Webb (b. 8th December, 1811, d. October, 1873), *dau.* of Thomas and Martha (Dickens) Webb, of N C.
Thomas was son of William, and a gr. son of James Webb (b. 1705), of Essex county,
Va., who m. (1734) Mary Edmonson.—(*See Webb Family Book.*) Issue:
1. Martha[3] Banks, m. Davidson Cross.
2. Henrietta[3] Banks, m. (I) —— Martin; (II) David I. Armstrong (2d wife), and has
   one living child, Mrs. R. W. Carroll, of Beaumont, Tex.
3. Col. Robert Webb[3] Banks, m. (18th November, 1869), Alice Clay Sherrod, *dau.* of
   Col. Felix and Sarah (Parrish) Sherrod, of Lawrence county, Ala. Issue: 1, Sarah

Felix⁴; 2, Lucile⁴; 3, Robert Webb⁴; 4, James O.⁴; 5, Alice⁴.—(*For these see Saunders Family*.)

4. Lucretia³ Banks, *unm.*

5. Julia³ Banks (died 1894), *m.* (1874), John B. Dillahunty.—(*See Dillahunty in Early Settlers*.) Issue: 1, Dunstan Banks⁴; 2, Mattie⁴; 3, Lucy⁴; 4, Julia⁴; 5, John⁴; 6, Lilian Dillahunty⁴.

X. PRISCILLA³ BANKS (b. 1802), *m.* Moses Butt). Issue:

1. John Henry³ Butt, *m.* Johngeline Winter. No issue.

2. Richard Lemuel³ Butt, *m.* (I) Eliz. Leonard, and *m.* (II) Patty Gamewell, and *m.* (III) Mary Henderson. Issue, six children.

3. Sarah Alabama³ Butt, *m.* Dr. Harvey King; three children.

4. Mary Virginia³ Butt, *m.* Daniel Butler Bird, of Florida; two children.

5. GEORGIA PRISCILLA³ BUTT, *m.* Thomas Erskine Young, son of Colonel George and Susan (Watkins) Young, of "Waverly," Columbus, Miss., a bright and lovely woman, who has given many of the above notes of her family. Issue, six daughters (*for these see Watkins*).

6. Rev. Moses Edward³ Butt, of Alabama M. E. Church South, *m.* (I) Henrietta Allen, of Alabama, and had two children. He *m.* (II) Jerusha Reedy, and had four children.

7. Willis Banks³ Butt, *m.* Julia Treutlen. No issue.

8. James Eldridge³ Butt, C. S. A.; killed in battle.

XI. HENRY³ BANKS, of Northwest Mississippi, *m.* Judith Oliver, *dau.* of James and Lucinda (Clark) Oliver, of Elbert county, Ga., and sister to Willis Banks' wife. Of several children, only two daughters lived to adult age, as follows:

1. Sarah³ Banks, *m.* Henry Scales, Clarksville, Tenn., and Mississippi. She is a bright and charming member of her family (of which she has furnished much information for this work); widow, and lives at Clarksville, Tenn., with her only son, Henry⁴ Scales. She had also a daughter, Lucy⁴, who died young.

2. Lucy³ Banks, *m.* Thomas Wilkinson (now deceased), of Hernando, Miss. Issue:
   1. *Thomas⁴*, d. s. p., aged 35; 2. *Henry⁴* (b. 1855), of Memphis, Tenn., *m.* Sallie Johnson, and has Lucy (b. 1883), Rebecca, and Baby; 3. *Robert⁴* (b. 1857), of Memphis, married Connie White, daughter of Colonel Thomas White, of Hernando, and had Robert⁴ (b. 1892), Thomas⁵ (1894), and Barbara⁵ (1896). 4. *Charles⁴*, of Palestine, Ark. (b: 1859), married Kate Taylor, and has several children; 5. *Lucy⁴*, *unm.*; 6. *Edward⁴*, of Hernando, Miss., *m.* and has several children.

XII. LEMUEL³ BANKS, of DeSoto county, Miss., *m.* Louisa A. Tait, *dau.* of Judge James Minor Tait and Jane Watkins (b. 1789), *dau.* of James and Jane (Thompson) Watkins, Elbert county, Ga. (See *Watkins*). Mrs. Banks *m.* (II) Charles Meriwether. Issue:

1. Lemuel³, d. s. p.; 2. Elizabeth³, d. s. p.; 3. Ralph³; 4. George Thomas³; 5. Charles³; 6. Mary³; 7. Richard McPherson³; 8. Henry³. Of these—

3. Ralph³ Banks moved to Lee county, Ark.; was twice married, and had several children, of whom none reached majority. He died a few years since.

4. George Thomas³ Banks, now living at White Haven, Shelby county, Tenn., *m.* (1866) Susan Love, and had:
   1. Lemuel⁴ (b. 1870), law firm of *Myers & Banks*, Memphis, Tenn., *m.* (1892) Lilian Fitzgerald, and lives in Memphis. No children. And has furnished this list of his grandfather's descendants.
   2. William Love⁴, of Becton, Ark. (b. 1872), *m.* (1891) Lucy Hartsell, and had Hartsell³. King⁴ and David⁴.
   3. George Thomas⁴, Jr. (b. 1875) *unm.*
   4. David Goodman⁴, d. y.

5. Charles³ Banks, moved to Marianna, Lee county, Ark., there married and is living.

Children: Myra[4], married James P. Brown, of Mariana, Ark., and has three children. Dolly[4], married Mr. Ache, of Newport, Ark., and has several children. Daisy[4], unm.

6. Mary[3] Banks, m. Jordan Payne, and died soon after, s. p.

7. Richard McPherson[3] Banks, of Hernando, Miss., m. (I), 1867, Betty Campbell, and had Richard McP.[4] (b. 1869), m. Lulie Boone, and has one child[5]. George[4] (b. 1875), m. Millie Bell, and has one child[5]. Nicholas Campbell[4] (b. 1879), m. Betty Berdoe, and all living. Mr. Banks m. (II) Mrs. Ida Campbell, of Oxford, Miss., and had Harvey (b. 1889), and Charles (b. 1893).

8. Henry[3] Banks, now of Memphis, Tenn., m. (1890) Sallie Dockery, and had Lemuel[4], d. infant, Henry[4] (b. 1892), Love[4] (b. 1894).

XIII. ELBERT[2] BANKS, died young.

XIV. MARION[2] BANKS (b. 1810, d. 1884), of Alabama. First trustee of the University. Never married and shunned womankind. Member of the Legislature. The bulk of his estate was left to his nephew, Joseph Marion Banks. He left also much property to his old slaves, who formed a flourishing colony at Vance, on the Alabama & Great Southern Railroad. He gave the family Bible and register to his niece, Susan Martha Banks. [*]

McGehee Family.

†THOMAS[1] MACK GEHEE, the immigrant, was seated in St. John's parish, King William county, Va., before 1727, where his *will* was dated 27th July, 1727.[*] It is not known whom he married. He had nine children:

1. William[2].

---

[*] William[2] Banks (cousin to the above family), nephew of Ralph, Sr., m. Mildred, dau. of James and Lucinda (Clark) Oliver (and sister to Mrs. Willis and Mrs. Henry Banks). His son—
    1. William Banks, m. Rebecca Hunt (cousin to Gen. Jeptha V. Harris) and lived in Southwest Mississippi.

† In the name of God, amen! I, Thomas Mack Gehee, of St. John's Parish, King William county, being sick and weak, but of perfect mind and memory, do call to mind the uncertainty of this life, and here make my last will and testament, etc.

I bequeath as here followeth: Item 1st. I give and bequeath to my son, William Mack Gehee, ten shillings to buy him a mourning ring, being in full of his portion.

Item 2nd. to my daughter Anna Butler, the same, etc.

Item 3rd. to my son-in-law John Lipscomb and my daughter, Dinah, his wife, 20 shillings, the same, etc.

Item 4th. to my son Abraham 96 acres of land being part of the dividend of land I now live on—with the orchards and appurtenances belonging thereunto, to him and his heirs forever.

Item 5th. to my son, Abraham, a negro man named Bristol, and a feather bed and furniture and large chest.

And it is my further will and testament that when my two sons Jacob and Samuel and my daughter Sarah come of age that my said son Abraham do pay them 5 pounds each.

Item 6th. to my son Edward 50 acres of land and a negro man named Peter, and one feather bed and furniture and a chest which was his mother's.

Item 7. to my son Samuel 50 acres, feather bed and furniture and one large chest, and my riding mare, saddle and bridle, etc.

Item 9. to my daughter Sarah a bed filled with feathers, one chest and drawer, and one seal skin trunk, and 5 pounds current money or goods from a store, and etc., and also her mother's horse, saddle and bridle.

Item 10. to my daughter Mary Dickson, one feather bed, a pair of blankets, my desk and all that is in the desk, etc. Cattle, sheep, hogs, etc., equally divided, etc.

My loving sons Abraham, Edward and Samuel my whole and sole executors, etc.

27 July, 1727.

                                  Thomas Mack Gehee.

Robert Bambridge.
W. Craddock.
J. Buckley.

NOTE.—A William McGehee from Duplin county, North Carolina, was member of the Assembly, 1760, with Andrew Thompson.

In 1696, Wm. Mack Gehee, of New Kent county, bought 200 acres in Henrico county, on the river, of Alex. MacKenny, of New Kent, for 3000 pounds of tobacco. Witness, Gideon Macon, of New Kent, and Mary Swan. *(Henrico Records.)*

2. Anna[2] married —— Butler.
3. Dinah[2] married John Lipscomb.
4. Abraham[2].
5. Jacob[2] married a daughter of Benj. Collier, of the Peninsular, who was son of John Collier, of "*Porto Bello.*"
6. Samuel[2].
7. Sarah[2].
8. Edward[2] (father of Micajah), 2830 acres in *Amelia county*, in 1746, and 5798 acres additional in 1748. In the *Amelia Book* his name is spelled *Mack Gehee*. His brother Jacob (name also spelt *Mack Gehee*), 727 acres in 1746, and 400 acres in 1748. He married Miss *De Jarnette*. (Mumford and Daniel De Jarnette, her brothers probably, each entered 400 acres in Amelia county in 1754.) The De Jarnettes were of Huguenot descent, and settled in Prince Edward county.
9. Mary[2] married Dickson.

Children of Edward[2] and —— (De Jarnette) McGehee were seven sons and two daughters, as follows:
1. John[3], of Prince Edward county, married. Issue: Two sons.
2. Micajah[3] (see below), of Broad River, Oglethorpe county, Ga.
3. Daniel[3], of Augusta, Ga., married Jane Hodnett, of Charlottesville, Va. Issue: 1. William; 2. Archibald, of Jackson, Miss.; 3. Nathan, all wealthy and successful; 4. Mrs. Ann Tyler; 5. Catherine Brooks Garthray McGehee, who married David Urquhart, of Augusta, Ga., the Scotchman, and ancestor of the Urquharts of Georgia, and several others.
4. Mumford[3], of Pearson county, N. C., (b. Prince Edward county, Va., 1744; d. Pearson county, N. C., December, 1816); married, ——. Issue; Four sons:
   1. Thomas[4] McGehee m. Eliz. M. Jeffreys. Issue: Montford[5] McGehee, m.——, and had Thomas,[6] George Badger[5], William Polk[5], and Lucius Polk[5]. 2. Thomas[4] McGehee.
   2. William[4] McGehee m. Miss Clay, and moved from Pearson county to Rutherford county, and then to Alabama, 1836; Issue: Martha[5]; Amanda[5]; Sarah[5]; Robert[5]; Frank[5], of Pulaski, Tenn.; Joseph[5]; Gallatin[5]; and Edward[5].
   3. Joseph[4] McGehee m. Miss Wall (?). Issue: Martha[5]; John[5]; Joseph[5]; Sidney[5]; and William [5]. These moved from Coswell county, N. C., to Alabama about 1839.
   4. John[4] McGehee m. Miss Chambers, and moved from Pearson county, N. C., to Alabama 1836. Issue: Eliza[5]; Patsy[5]; John[5]; Joseph[5]; and William[5].
5. William[3], of Milledgeville, Ga.
6. Samuel[3], of Amite county, Miss.; six sons and two daughters; among them, Dr. John, of Gloster, and Pollard McGehee, merchant, Gloster, and Mrs. Macillas.
7. Jacob, of Georgia; fourteen children.
8. Daughter[3], married Charles Womack, of Prince Edward, county, Va.
9. Daughter[3], married Mr. Wright, of Tennessee. Issue: Twenty-one children.

MICAJAH[3] McGEHEE, of Broad River, Ga., (   ), married Anne, daughter of James Scott, of Prince Edward county (son of Thomas and Anne (Baytop Scott), who married Frances[3], daughter of John Collier, of "*Porto Bello.*" Issue: fourteen children, of whom thirteen lived to be grown as follows:
1. JAMES[4] McGEHEE, of Georgia., married Miss Johns. Issue: 5 children.

NOTE.—Katherine *Mack Gehee* married (circa 1715) Mr. Thomas Butts, gentleman of *St. Peter's parish, New Kent county*, and had John (b. 1716), and daughter Frances (b. 1719), and probably others. She was a daughter of one of the sons (above) of Thomas Mack Gehee, the emigrant.

NOTE.—"Her brother Thomas Collier, was ancestor of Hon. Thomas Hardeman, M. C. Georgia, and from their sister, Judith Collier, who married Benjamin Hicks, is descended Col. Robt. A. Hardaway, of Tuscaloosa Ala. (*See Bibb family*).

2. Thomas⁴ McGehee, married Betty, dau. of John Gilmer, of Georgia, and sister to his brother Abner's 2nd wife. Lived on Long Pond Creek, Oglethorpe county, and finally removed to Texas. Issue, twelve children: Thomas, of Atlanta, and George T., of the State Senate of Texas, are among his descendants, for whom see addenda.

3. Elizabeth⁴ McGehee married Abraham Hill, of Georgia. Issue: Dr. Abraham Hill, and Mrs. Blanton Hill, of Athens.

4. Charles⁴ McGehee, killed in a deer chase by the discharge of his gun.

5. Francis⁴ McGehee, d. s. p.

6. Abner⁴ McGehee, (b. Va. 1779 and d. 1855) Montgomery, Ala., (see his life, written by Major Semple, of Montgomery). married (I) Charlotte Spencer* and had eleven children. Married (II) Jane,† daughter of John Gilmer, and widow of Thomas Johnson, (who was nephew of Col. Nicholas Johnson), and had three children, and married (III) Mrs. Graves, (nee Mary Russell). No Issue. *Issue first marriage:*

 1. Ann Scott⁵, married William Taylor. Dana Taylor, Professor in University of Louisiana, a descendant.
 2. Harriet⁵, married Thomas Key Jarrett, and died near Hope Hull Church.
 3. Mildred⁵, (d. 1887), m. Jan. 1826 to Dr. Samuel Clark Oliver. (*See Oliver family*), a grandson: Samuel Clark Oliver, lives at Talladega, Ala.
 4. Spencer, d. y.
 5. Charlotte⁵, married George Bibb, and died young.
 6. Abner⁵, married Elizabeth Smith, died at Hope Hull.
 7. James⁵, married Rachel Susannah Dailey, and died at his homestead, which had been the home of George and Charlotte Bibb. The Rev. Oliver Clark McGehee, M. E. Ch. South, is their son (b. Jan. 1857), married 6th Jan. 1881, Mary Lincoln Henderson, daughter of G. C. Henderson, Auburn, Ala. Graduated at A. and M. College, Auburn, Ala., in 1879, and tutor there for three years. Joined Conference of M. E. Ch. South in 1886, and has been stationed at Greensboro, Mobile, Salem, Opelika and other appointments.

Issue: 2d mar. of Abner McGehee:

 8. Thomas⁵, killed by lightning while riding along the road.
 9. Elizabeth⁵, m. (I) Dr. Briggs, and (II) Col. James Gilchrist of Montgomery county.
 10. Sarah⁵, married Peyton Graves, and lived in New Orleans, and had a daughter Sarah⁶.
 11. Daughter⁵, m. George Tait.

7. William⁴ McGehee (b. ——, d. Montgomery, May 3, 1833), son of Micajah, of Oglethorpe county, Ga., married (I) Martha, daughter of Gen. Benj. Taliaferro, of Virginia, who was captain in Rev. and M. C. from Georgia.—(*See Taliaferro Family.*) He m. (II) 21st February, 1817, Eliza (b. 1783, d. 1844), daughter of James and Jane (Thompson) Watkins, of Savannah River, Elbert county, Ga. (*Watkins Family.*) His home in Georgia was between his father's place and the Goosepond Tract (*see map.*) Governor Gilmer says "he built there the large white house on the Augusta road, and contrary to the cautious habits of his family he entered upon the ocean of trade and was stranded. He was a quiet and gentlemanly man. He finally removed to Montgomery, Ala., where he died." His widow resided with her brother, Major Robert H. Watkins, in Lawrence county, Ala., until her death, when her children then returned to Montgomery, Ala., under the care of their uncle, Abner McGehee. Issue: First mar. (*Taliaferro*):

 1. Martha Ann⁵, died young.

---

*Her brother, Octavius Spencer, lived in Jones Valley, Jefferson county Ala., and served in the legislature in the early forties.

Note—†*Jane Gilmer* was sister of Mrs. Burton Taliaferro, Mrs. Tom McGehee, Mrs. Gabriel Christian, and of Thornton, Nicholas, Frances, George O., and David Gilmer; and Nicholas and David Gilmer married daughters of Micajah Clark. (*Gov. Gilmer's Georgians.*)

2. **David Meriwether⁴ McGehee**, M. D., of Panola, Miss., married Elis. Greenlief Elsberry. He was in Mexican war, Jeff. Davis Rifles. Went to California 1849, and was killed (in a party of nine) by the Indians. Issue:
   I. Martha Taliaferro⁵, died 1895, m. William King Poston, of Memphis.
   II. Benj. Elsberry⁵, of Birmingham, Ala., m. (1879) Mary Belle Callaway, and has: 1, Conrad C.'; 2, David'; 3, Martha E.'; 4, Mary Elis.'; 5, Benj. Elsberry'.

3. **William⁴ McGehee.** Issue: Second mar. (*Watkins*):
4. **Elisa Ann⁴**, died young.
5. **Elisabeth⁴**, died young.
6. **Sarah Elisa⁴** (born 1821), m. Vincent Porter, of Montgomery, Ala. Issue:
   1, Elisa⁵, m. Capt. Tom Stacy; 2, Mildred McGehee⁵; 3, James⁵; 4, Robert⁵; 5 Thomas⁵; all of Montgomery.
7. **Mary Jane⁴** (b. 1823), m. (I) Meriwether Olive, and m. (II) Thomas White Phillips, of Monroe, La. Issue: First mar. (none by second):
   1. Ann Meriwether⁵ Olive (d. aged 25), only child; married John Lawrence Byrne, merchant of New Orleans (first wife.) He was born in Ireland. Issue: 1. Rebecca Hillas⁷ (   ), only child of her mother; married Col. Cyrus King Drew, of New Orleans, of the U. S. Army. No issue.
8. **Lucinda⁴** (b. 1825), m. John B. Callaway, of Montgomery, Ala. Issue:
   1. Edna⁵, m. Mr. Slaughter.
   2. Henry⁵.
   3. Nina⁵.
   4. James⁵.
9. **James Watkins⁴**, of Texas (b. 1826).
10. **Robert⁴** (b. 1828), never married. Killed in Confederate Army, battle of Shiloh.

8. **SARAH⁸ McGEHEE** (   ) m. (I) Thomas Hill, of Georgia, and m. (II) Dionysius, son of Peter Oliver, of Georgia; (second wife) she was very beautiful. Issue by first mar. (none by second), six children, of whom:
   1. Tom⁴ Hill; went to Texas.
   2. Wiley⁴ Hill (also went to Texas.)

9. **EDWARD⁸ McGEHEE** (b. 1786), of Wilkinson county, Miss. (*see below*).

10. **JOHN⁴ (SCOTT⁴) McGEHEE**, of Panola county, Miss., m. Malinda, daughter of Miles and Tabitha Hill. He was a most successful and wealthy cotton planter. Eleven children, of whom are
   1. **Miles Hill⁵ McGehee**, planter of great wealth (b. 26 Nov., 1813; d. 15 Jan., 1865) m. Mrs. Mary (Crouse) Porter. Issue: 1. Ida Blanche⁶ (b. 6 Oct., 1849; d. 12 Aug., 1889) m. James F. Stokes, had several children and died young. 2. Kate Crouse⁶, b. 1852, d. y.
   2. **Edward F.⁵ McGehee**, planter (b. 6 Apri., 1816; d. 10 November, 1879) m. Mrs. Pattie (Williamson) Penn. Issue: 1. Pattie⁶ m. Philip Pointer, of Como. 2. Edward F.⁶ m. Migia Crabtree, of Trenton, Ga.
   3. **Tabitha Ann⁵ McGehee** (b. 10 April, 1818; d. 21 Jan., 1888) m. Charles F. Dandridge. Issue: McGehee⁶, C. S. A.; killed in battle of Shiloh, 7 April, 1862.
   4. **Sarah E.⁵ McGehee** (b. 12 Feb., 1820; d. 17 Sept., 1895) m. her cousin, Edmund McGehee. Issue: 1. Emma⁶, (b. 23 Feb., 1842; d. May, 1677) m. A. S. Yarbrough, of Como. 2. William E.⁶, merchant, of Memphis, Tenn. (b. 6th August, 1858) m. Kate E. Poston. He furnished this list of his grandfather's descendants. 3. John Scott⁶ (b. 21 August, 1861) married Rosa Taylor, of Como, Miss. Also, three who died in infancy.
   5. **Mary Pope⁵ McGehee** (b. 6 Feb. 1822; d. 29 Aug., 1880) m. (1) Gen. Jacob F. Fannington, of Memphis, and had John McGehee⁶ (b. 7 June, 1850); m. Milly White, parents of Dr. Pope McGehee⁶ Fannington, of Memphis. (*See White and*

Oliver.) Mrs. Fannington *m.* (II) Gen. Benj. M. Bradford, of Aberdeen, Miss. (second wife).

6. John Hampton[4] McGehee (b. 20 Aug., 1824; d. 17 Aug., 1827).

7. James Blanton[4] McGehee (b. 18 March, 1826; d. 27 Sept., 1866) *m.* Eugenia Wittich. Issue: 1. John Lucius[4] (b. 22 July, 1850) *m.* Ada Hartridge, of Savannah. 2. Julia Hill[4] (b. 27 Nov., 1854; d. 19 Dec., 1870). 3. James Blanton[4], *m.* Jennie Dalton, of Memphis.

8. Lucinda S.[4] McGehee (b. 3 Feb., 1828; d. 10 March, 1847) *m.* Wm. M. White. Issue: Anna Scott[4] (b. 1 April, 1846; d. in infancy).

9. Nicholas Abner[4] McGehee (b. 6 April, 1830; d. 11 Sept., 1834).

10. Martha Malinda[4] McGehee (b. 7 Nov., 1832; d. 18 Aug., 1872); *m.* Simeon Oliver, of Hernando, Miss. Issue: 1. Linda Hill[4] (b. Feb. 16th, 1854; d. September, 1884) *m.* W. P. Martin. 2. Charles Dandridge[4] (b. 16 March, 1856, *unm.* Sallie McGehee[4] (b. 19 Dec., 1858; *m.* G. S. Poston. 3. Simeon Shelton[4] (b. 20 Dec., 1867, *unm.*; and 4. Edward[4], unmarried. (*See Oliver.*)

11. William Thomas[4] McGehee (b. 16 Dec., 1835); m. (I) Lida Malone[4]; no issue. (II) Pattie Hardeman; no issue.

12. Louisa Terrell[4] McGehee (b. 17 Nov., 1837) m. Malcolm F. Gilchrist, of Miss. Issue: 1. Lula[4] (b. Oct., 1858) m. Elsey Meacham. of Memphis. 2. Annie[4], d. infant. 3. William A.[4] (b. 31 Dec., 1861); m. Mrs. Laura Shields, Nashville, Tenn. 4. Malcolm[4], Jr. (b. 22 July, 1865); m. Julia Kerr, Memphis, Tenn.

13. Ella Hill[4] McGehee (b. 19 April, 1839) m. Thomas H. Hunton, influential citizen of New Orleans, now deceased. Issue: Annie[4] (b. 1858) m. Gilbert Green, prominent merchant of New Orleans. 2 McGehee Dandridge[4], of New York; m. Mary Moss, of Columbia, Mo. 3. Ashley[4] (b. May, 1881).

11. ABRAHAM[4] McGEHEE m. (I) Harriet Hill, and (II) Catherine, daughter of John Peniston, of Richmond, Va., and formerly of England, and Governor of the Bermudas, and (III) Miss Smith, of Alabama, who died without issue. Issue (*first marriage*):

1. James[3], *m.*, and died without issue. 2. Harriet Sophia[4] m. Lawson Porter, of Mississippi, and had Martha Harriet[4], m. J. H. Jarnagan, of Mississippi. Issue (*second marriage*):

3. Ira Edward[4] McGehee m. Betty, daughter of George Ward, of Kentucky. Issue: Ira[4], George[4] and Robert[4], each unm.

4. Marie Josephine[4], m. Aug. W. Jourdan. Issue: Kate[4] and Augusta[4] Jourdan, of New Orleans, unm.

12. HUGH[4] McGEHEE married Sarah, daughter of Shelton White, and had five children, of whom 1, Edmund married his cousin Sallie, daughter of John McGehee. Issue: John McGehee, New Orleans; and Wm., of Memphis.

13. LUCINDA[4] McGEHEE married Dionysius Oliver (first wife). (He married (secondly) her sister Sarah). Issue: Five children. (*See Oliver Family.*)

JUDGE EDWARD[4] McGEHEE (born 1786, in Oglethorpe county, Ga., died 1st October, 1880), ninth child of Micajah McGehee, was one of Mississippi's most remarkable men, as planter, philanthropist and financier. (*See Memories of Mississippi*, Vol. I, p. 1191.) Married (I) 6th June, 1811, Margaret Louisa Crosby, of Wilks county, Ga.; (d. 9th January, 1821). He married (II) 23d December, 1823, Harriet Ann Goodrich (d. 15th October, 1827). He married (III) 15th February, 1829, Mary Hines Burruss (b. 21st March, 1812; d. 30th October, 1873), daughter of Rev. John C. Burruss and Elisabeth Brame, his wife, (Rev. John C. Burruss[a] was a distinguished divine in the Methodist Episcopal Church, South; came from Virginia to Lawrence county, Ala., 1891, and from thence to Louisiana. His fourth wife was Miss Nutting, of Boston, whom he married Tuscumbia, Ala., a most accomplished and lovable woman. She lived to be quite aged; and, honored and lamented by all, died, 1894, at the home of her daughter, Mrs. Claiborne Foster, of Shreveport, La. (Mrs. Bishop Linus Parker, of New Orleans, and Mrs. Harding, of Shreveport, La., noble and intellectual women, are also daughters).

Judge McGehee lived at Woodville, Miss., his lovely home was called " *Bowling Green*," and he had large planting interests. He was also founder of the Carondelet street Methodist Episcopal Church South, New Orleans, and of the Female College at Woodville, named for him; built the first railroad in Mississippi; owned the first cotton factory, the patron of Centenary College, and engaged in every enterprise for the welfare of his State. Issue of first marriage (*Cosby*):

1. Cythia Ann[4] (————), married John S. Walton, of New Orleans; *d. s. p.*
2. James Jack[3], died young.
3. Sarah[3] Houston (————), married John W. Burruss, son of Rev. John C. Burruss,* Issue:
    1. Ann McG.[5] m. Judge John H. Kennard, of Baltimore. Issue: John, Burruss, Thomas and William.
    2. Catherine F.[5] m. Henry Ginder, of " Griswold & Co., New Orleans."
    3. Edward McG.[5], d. unm.
    4. Mary E.[5], d. unm.
    5. Sarah L.[5], m. Judge Robt. Semple, of Point Coupee. Issue: Robert, Sarah, d.; Kate, Mary and John. (Two infants died young.)
4. James Hayes[3], died young.
5. Edward John[4] (b. 1820; d. 1868); married (1841) Ann B. (b. 1825, d. 1879), daughter of George Washington Carter, and Mary B. Wormley, his wife, both of Virginia and Mississippi. The father of G. W. Carter was Charles Carter, who married Betty, daughter of Fielding Lewis and Betty Washington, sister of the President. Issue:
    1. Edward J.[5], C. S. A., Twenty-first Mississippi Regiment, m. Corinne Evans. Six children.
    2. Harry T.[5], C. S. A., m. Margaret Percy. Three children.
    3. A. Merwin[5], m. Kate Towles. Six children. Second marriage (*Goodrich*.)
6. Charles Goodrich[4], of Westwood, Miss. (b. 21st Sept. 1823). His purity of life, and strenth of character is great. Married (I) Stella McNair, of New Orleans (who d. 1859); married (II) Anna G. McNair, her sister (b. 1831, d. 1884), by whom no issue. Children:
    1. Robert M.[5], married Selah Henderson, of Natchez, Miss. Issue: G. G.[7], E. Putnam[7], Anna[7], G. McGehee[7].
    2. Edward[5], M. D., of New Orleans, married Anna, dau. of Col. J. H. Y. Webb (see *Webb Book*). Issue: J. Webb[7], Edward L.[7], L. D.[7], Charles Goodrich[7], Jr., and R. Micajah[7] McGehee. Dr. McGehee has greatly aided in securing family data.
    3. Laura[5], m. Hugo Davis, of Austin, Texas, nephew of President Davis. Issue: Hugo Jefferson[7] Davis.

---

*Rev. John Crenshaw Burruss was secretary, 26th November, 1814, to a Methodist quarterly meeting of the Gloucester (Va.) Circuit. " James Boyd, the presiding elder; John C. Ballew, the assistant preacher, and Mr. Burruss the helper." In May following he was "Allowed $40, quarterage for two quarters, and Sister Burruss, $7.86, as part of her quarterage." Parsons in those days preached *for love* only. The circuit extended through King and Queen and Mathews counties, and the appointments were for Shakelford's Chapel, the old colonial churches of the counties, Cole's Chapel, Sheppard's, Pace's Chapel, Mann's, Olive Branch, Bellamy's, Bethlehem, Abingdon Church, Bethel, Point Comfort, Mathews' Chapel, Tarifts', Mount Zion, Providence, Billups' and New Hope. Later, Rev. Ethelbert Drake was presiding elder, John C. Burruss, assistant, and John Lettimore, helper. In 1816 he was Local Deacon, and Samuel B. White, assistant. He appears for the last time in November of that year at the quarterly conference held at Providence Meeting House, in Mathews county. (Copied from the old Circuit Book of Bellamy's Church, Gloucester county, Va.)

Edward McGehee married in Middlesex county, Va. (1801), Caroline C. Jones; Sarah McGehee married in Middlesex county, Va. (1801), William C. Humphries. Daniel Dejarnette married in Middlesex county, Va. (1775), May Davis; George Dejarnette, married in Middlesex county, Va. (1798), Ann Walker, of Sussex county; Nancy Dejarnette married in Middlesex county, Va. (1801), Berrien Abbot. (*Christ Church Parish Register*, Middlesex county, Va.).

4. Stella[4], married Mr. Adams.
5. Charles[4], d. y.
6. Howard B.[5], m. Hattie, dau. of Bishop Galloway of the M. E. Church South!
   Issue: H. B.[7], Jr., and Stella F. McNair[7].
7. Micajah[5] (b. 1826, d. 1880); had an eventful life; never married. Was in General
   Fremont's expedition in 1848, across the Rockies, and member of the California Legislature (see article in *Century Magazine, March, 1891*).
8. Harriet Ann[5], d. y.   Issue of the the third marriage—(*Burruss*).
9. William[5], d. y.
10. Francis[5], d. y.
11. George Thomas[5], of Woodville, Miss. (b. 1833); A. M. of Yale College; C. S. A.,
    Captain Twenty-first Mississippi, and on General Kershaw's staff. Married Lily
    McNair. No issue. Adopted in 1880 the two young daughters of General Hood, of
    the C. S. A.—Odile and Ida Hood.
12. John Burruss[5], of Laurel Hill, La. (b. 1835); C. S. A., and planter, of Louisiana;
    President West Feliciana Railroad; member of Legislature. Bright and humorous.
    His quaint wit and charming ease endear him to many friends. Married (1839)
    Catherine Elizabeth Stewart. Issue:
       J. Stewart[6] McGehee, of St. Louis, only child, married Miss L. C. Johnson.
13. Caroline Elis.[5], married Duncan Stewart, of Louisiana. Issue: George[6], Mary[6],
    Louise[6], Ida[6], Henry[6], Edward[6], Catherine[6].
14. Wilbur Fisk[5] McGehee (b. 1839, d. 1859).
15. Mary Louisa[5], married S. H. Snowden. Issue: Wilbur Fisk[6], d. y., Mason[6], married
    Eliz., dau. of R. M. McGehee, and had Samuel[7].
16. Scott[5] (   ), of New Orleans, C. S. A., Third Louisiana (Colonel Ogden); mar-
    ried (1872) Louise (b. St. Louis, 31st January, 1850; d. New Orleans, 19th June,
    1896), daughter of Charles W. and Orleanna (Wright) Schaumberg, of St. Louis. A
    charming friend and wife, and a most devoted mother, and a great promoter of social
    good. Issue: 1. Louise[6]; 2. Ethel[6]; 3. Schaumberg[6]; and two d. infants.
17. Abner[5], d. y.; 18. Harriet[5], d. y.; 19. Augusta Eugenia[5], b. 1854, d. 1882, unmar-
    ried, in lovely young womanhood.

Excursus—Urquhart.

Lord Brooks came to Virginia early. His daughter married an Englishman named
Hodnett, and had two sons and two daughters. The sons and father fought in Rev.
War, and lived in Charlottesville, Va.

The youngest daughter, Jane, m. Daniel MacGehee, much to the opposition of her
family, who thought his position not so good as hers. They removed to Columbia
county, Ga., ten miles above Augusta, when the Indians were living among them. Issue:
Eight children; among them—William, Archibald, of Jackson, Miss., Nathan, Mrs.
Ann Tyler and Catherine Brooks Garteray McGehee, who m. David Urquhart, of Augusta, Ga.

The sons, William, Archibald, and Nathan McGehee, were very successful, and
each amassed a large fortune. The descendants of Archibald live in Jackson, Miss.

DAVID URQUHART was the son of John and Katharine Urquhart, of the county of Ross,
Cromarty, Scotland. Their children were David (b. 1779), John, Robert, Charles, William, Hugh, Katherine and Jane. Only one son, David, and the two daughters were married. (The "*Urquharts and MacGehees*" by Mrs. Caroline Lucy Urquhart Downing, of
Columbus, Ga.)

David Urquhart (born in county Ross, Scotland, 1779), m. Catherine Brookes Gar-
tary McGehee, b. in Prince Edward county, Va., 1789. The family of Urquhart once
owned Hilton Castle on the border of Loch Ness, in Cromarty. David Urquhart came
to South Carolina to his maternal uncle, Charles Banks, merchant in Charleston. He
became a merchant in Augusta, Ga. Young Wm. McGehee, who lived in Columbia

county, ten miles above Augusta, on his father's farm, was his book-keeper. David Urquhart accompanied him home on a visit, where he met and wooed the sister, Katherine McGehee, whom he married. They lived in Augusta, and became very wealthy in land and negroes, and built a home above Augusta, which he called "*Hilton.*" Issue:

1. KATHERINE LOUISA BANKS URQUHART m. Jesse Ansley and had thirteen children.
2. JANE ELIZA BROOKS URQUHART m. (1st) James[4] Watkins, of Elbert county, Ga., brother of Robt. H. Watkins, of Lawrence county, Ala. No issue; and (2d) Dr. William Weeden, of Huntsville, Ala., (second wife) brother of the wife of Rev. Turner Saunders. Issue (*Second marriage*):
   1. Jane Weeden m. Mr. Wm. T. Read.
   2. William, died unmarried.
   3. Katherine, unmarried.
   4. Col. John D. Weeden, C. S. A., m. Mattie Patton, of Florence, Ala. Four children.
   5. Dr. Henry Vernon Weeden m. Miss Dunham.
   6. Maria Howard Weeden, "*Miss Howard,*" artist and author, a charming ornament to her sex and family.
3. DR. JOHN AUGUSTUS URQUHART, of Columbus, Ga., m. Mary Jane Shorter, daughter of Judge Eli Shorter, and his wife, Sophia Watkins. No issue. (*See Watkins Family.*)
4. SARAH ANN URQUHART m. Mr. John Garner, of Augusta, Ga. One child, Katherine, married Dr. Stephen Elliott Habersham, of Savannah. Issue: Katherine Virginia, and John G. Habersham.
5. DAVID WM. URQUHART, d. s. p.
6. MARY MATILDA URQUHART m. Mr. W. W. Garrard, of Columbus, Ga. One child, Mary Isabel, m. Dr. W. A. Robertson, of Louisiana.
7. FRANCES ISABELLA GARTERAY URQUHART m. Wm. W. Garrard, Columbus, Ga. Six children: William m. Mary Lawton, of Savannah; Eva m. Humphreys Castleman, of Kentucky; Helen Augusta m. John T. Glenn, of Atlanta; Gertrude Kate m. James W. Harris, of Mississippi; Louis F. m. Anna Leonard; Ada Frances died young.
8. CAROLINA LUCY URQUHART m. (second wife) Lemuel Tyler Downing (born 1814 in Preston, Conn.,) lawyer, who died Columbus, Ga., 24th March, 1882. They had six children: Frances Urquhart, Katherine Tyler m. Francis Hart Mitchell (who died 1885), Carolina Lucy, died young; Helen Mary m. Joseph B. Hill, of Columbus, Ga.; Carolina Lucy, also died young; Hugh Urquhart m. Brenda Gibson, of Newman, Ga. (*From Mrs. Downing's Urquhart Family.*)

Clark.

CHRISTOPHER CLARK, Louisa county, Va., m. Penelope—(Bolling?) Issue:
1. Edward[2]; 2, Bolling[2]; 3, Micajah[2]; 4, Elis.[2], m. Joseph Anthony; 5, Sarah[2], m. Charles Lynch, Burgess for Albermarle, died 1753; parents of Charles (b. 1739), for whom Lynchburg was named (and also "lynch law;") and of Sarah (d. 1773), m. her cousin, Micajah Terrell; 6, Daughter, m. Benj. Johnson. These all joined the Quakers. Christopher Clark patented with Nicholas Meriwether (1722) 972 acres in Hanover; and, again (1742), 4926 in his own name. Louisa county was taken from Hanover 1742, and Hanover (1720) from Kent, which was formed from York 1654. (Hence the earliest Clarks may be found in York Records.) Nicholas Meriwether I is mentioned in York Records. Christopher Clark was one of the first merchants in Louisa. Joined Quakers 1743-9, and from that time on Bolling and Edward Clark were busy with the meetings of the Dissenters. Mrs. Terrell, the Quakeress, freed her slaves, as did also Micajah Terrell and Christopher Johnson in 1774. (*See "Osbells and their Kin."*) MICAJAH[2] CLARK, said to be a cousin to Gen. Rogers Clark (*Va. Mag, Hist. III, 95*), m. Judith, daughter of Robert Adams. Issue: 1, Robert[3] (b. 1738); 2, Christopher[3]; 3, John[3]; 4, Micajah[3]; 5, James[3]; 6, Bolling[3]; 7, William[3], and 8, Elizabeth[3], as follows:

1, Robert[3] (b. Albemarle, then Louisa, county, 1738), m. Susan, daughter of John Henderson (whose will was p. 1786). They removed to Campbell (then Bedford

county), and, in 1779, to Kentucky. Among his sons were: 1, Robert[4], of Clark
county, Ky, who married a daughter of Benj. Shakelford, of King and Queen
county, and of Baytop-Taliaferro descent; 2, Patterson[4], of Clark county, Ky., m.
also daughter of Benj. Shakelford; 3, James (b. 1799), Governor of Kentucky
1836; 4, Bennett, father of the Hon. John T. Clark, of Missouri; 5, *Christopher C.*,
M. C., 1804, from Bedford county, Va., m. daughter of Judge Joseph Hook;
and other sons scattered over the West. 2, Christopher[2] (see below). We have
not the lines of John[2], who m. —— Moore, or of Micajah[2], James[2] and Bolling[2]
Clark (above). 7, William[2] Clark, m. Sarah, daughter of Richard and Ann (Meriwether) Anderson, of Virginia and removed to Kentucky. His sister, Elis.
Anderson, m. Waddy Thompson, and Cicely Anderson, m. William Kerr, of Kentucky (*Gov. Gilmer*). 8, Elizabeth[2] Clark, m. Joseph Anthony. (Two of the
Clark brothers were in the Revolutionary Army.)

2. CHRISTOPHER CLARK[2] (above) married Mildred Terrell. Issue:
1. Micajah[4] Clark (b. *circa*, 1765), m. Ella Gatewood. Their daughter, Amelia[5], m.
Nicholas, son of John, and Mildred (Meriwether) Gilmer, and moved to Kentucky.
Another daughter[5] m. David Gilmer, son also of John, and moved to Arkansas.—
(*See Governor Gilmer's Georgians.*)
2. David[4] Clark m. his cousin, Mary Clark.
3. Mourning[4] Clark married William B. Key.
4. Judith[4] Clark married Peter Wyche.[*]
5. Rachel[4] Clark married (I) John Bowen; (II) John Dailey.
6. Agatha[4] Clark married John Wyche.
7. Mary[4] Clark married Thomas W., son of Dionysius Oliver, of the Revolution, and of
Elbert county, Georgia.
8. Samuel[4] Clark d. s. p.
9. Joshua[4] Clark d. s. p.
10. Mildred[4] Clark married (1794) Shelton White, in Elbert county, Georgia.—(*See
White.*)
11. Susan[4] Clark (b. 1783) married the Rev. F. McCarthy Oliver (brother of Thomas.)
12. Lucy[4] Clark married James Oliver (b. 1767), (also son of Dionysius), (his second
wife). Elbert county, Ga.—(*From Diary of Dr. James Oliver.*)

Christopher Clark mentioned 1758, in a poll, taken for Col. Washington, in Frederick county.—(*Va. Gazette.*)
From York County Records: Will of Nicholas Clark, 1658. His "only son, Nicholas
Clark."
John Clark's widow, Elis., married (1680) Samuel Tompkins, and with Nicholas
Clark, they sold lands to James Forsithe.
Will of John Clark, 1689, wife Jane, son; Nicholas and "other children."
Will of John Clark, 1694, wife, Ann; sons, Robert and John Clark. His goddaughter, *Ann Rogers*, and godson, John Hubard.
Will Nicholas Clark, Sept. 1694, wife Elizabeth. No issue (son of Nicholas).

Ancestry of General George Rogers Clark.

Jonathan[1] Clark, of King and Queen county, Va., m. Elis. Lumkin, and was the
first to go to Albemarle county, 1734, in which year he died, leaving sons: John[2] and
Benj.[2]. His widow m. (II) Mr. Richards.

---

[*]Peter Wyche (1688) 1482 acres, in Charles city county, with John Lanier. (*Records*). George
Wyche (1718), 400 acres in Surry county, on Nottoway river. Henry Wyche (1722), 370 acres (same).
Nathaniel Wyche (1791), in Sussex county.

Nicholas Meriwether was clerk of York county 1644, and Mrs. Elis. Meriwether his executrix,
1679. This county then included New Kent, King and Queen, Hanover and Louisa counties. Meriwether and Clark descendants have frequently intermarried. Richard, William, Edward and John
Clark, revolutionary soldiers, received bounty lands prior to 1784.

JOHN[2] CLARK (b. K. and Q. county, 1725, d. Jefferson, Kentucky, 1799), m. (1749) his cousin, Ann Rogers (b. King and Queen county, 1734), daughter of John and Mary (Bird) Rogers; removed to Caroline county, Va., 1757, and thence to Kentucky. Issue, among others:

1. General Jonathan[3] Clark (b. Albemarle county, 1750, d. Jefferson county, Kentucky, 1811), m. Sarah Hite (b.1758), of Frederick County, Va.; His daughter Ann m. James Pearce.

2. General George Rogers[3] Clark (b. Albemarle county, 1752), of Rev. and French and Indian Wars (1777); never married; lived with his sister near Louisville; paralysed in 1809.

3. Gov. William Clark, of Kentucky (9th son), b. Carolina county, Va., 1770, d. 1838, m. (I) Julia Hancock.

4. Frances, m. (I), James O'Fallon, of Kentucky, and (II), Charles Thurston (b. 1765), (son of the fighting parson, Charles Mynn Thurston, of Va). He was murdered by a slave.—(*Wm. & Mary Quarterly IV, 183.*)

Shelton Notes.

From Middlesex county, Va., Christ Church Register.

Peter and Susannah Shelton, a son, Peter, b. 1687.

Ralph (died 1733) and Mary Shelton, a son Thomas, (b. 1707) Ralph, (1709), Crispin, (1713), Reuben, (1715), Catherine, (1719), John, (1722), Benjamin, (1724), James, (1726), Daniel, (1729).

Thomas (d. 1742), and Mary Shelton, a son, Reuben, (b. 1733), Mary, (1737–d. 1742), Thomas, (b. 1740), Micajah, (1742.)

Ralph Shelton married (1731) Mary Daniel. (In 1745 Ralph Shelton 400 acres on north side Nottoway River, Amelia county.)

Crispin and Letitia Shelton, a son, William (b. 1735).

Crispin, Daniel and Gabriel Shelton were Members of the Pittsylvania county Committee of Safety, 1775. He was also of the vestry of Camden pa. with Abram Shelton.

Elizabeth Shelton, m. (1728) William Davis. Mary Shelton died 1719.

York county Records mention William Shelton on a jury 1706, and executor (1716) with Lawrence Smith of the estate of John Moss

James Shelton and Thomas Cole (1716) sued church wardens of Charles pa., York county, for a debt.

Arms of James Shelton, the immigrant, mentioned in William and Mary Quarterly Vol. 1.

Ralph Shelton, (1703), mentioned as a minor, and his mother about to marry Joseph Bickley, of King and Queen county, Va. (*William and Mary Quarterly, Vol. 124.*)

William Sheldon married Elizabeth, daughter of Robert Rogers, of Goochland county, Va., whose will was p. 1740; and her sister, Ann Rogers, m. before 1740, William Begar.—(*Ibid. VI.*)

William Shelton, of York county, m. Hannah, dau. of Capt. Anthony[2] Anmstead (William[2], Anthony[1]). (*William and Mary Quarterly, VII.*)

Jesse Shelton, lived in Lancaster county (1784), opposite Urbana, on Rapp River. (*Hening.*)

Samuel Shelton, vestry of St. Ann's pa. Albemarle county, after 1775. (*Bishop Meade.*)

Rd. Shelton, vestry of Lexington pa., Amherst county, after 1779—also William Shelton and, later, Ralph C., and later still William and Edwin Shelton. (*Ibid.*)

John Shelton, of Hanover county, married Eleanor Parks, daughter of William Parks, editor of the *Virginia Gazette* (whose will was p. 1750. Executors "wife Eleanor Parks, and son-in-law, John Shelton."

John and William Parks Shelton, his sons, advertised (1771) 2464 acres in Augusta county. These they sold in Hanover county, by subscription. (*Virginia Gazette.*)

John Shelton, of Cumberland county, 1768, advertised a stray horse in *Virginia Gazette.*

Clough Shelton, of Amherst county, was Captain in Rev. and member of *Order of Cincinnatus* 1783.

Sarah Shelton m. Patrick Henry and their daughter Elizabeth (b. 1769), m. Philip Aylett (b. 1761) (*William and Mary Quarterly, III*). She was granddaughter of John and Elenor (Parks) Shelton, of Hanover county.

Thomas Shelton, in Captain Taylor's Company, 2nd Virginia Battalion, 1777.

David Shelton, Captain in Virginia Militia, in the Rev. (*Virginia Magazine of History, VII., 98.*)

SHELTON AND WHITE FAMILY.

Thomas Shelton, (name of wife unknown) had issue:

1. Henry[2] Shelton, married ——— Ray, and had, among others, Sarah[3], (the eldest daughter) who married *Thomas White* (below). 2. Peter[2] Shelton, 3. William[2] Shelton, married ——— Harris. 4. David[2]. 5. Nelly Shelton, married Charles Stratham.

WHITE FAMILY.

Conyers[1] and Mary White, of Leistershire, England, had a son, John[2] White, who came to Virginia, and married Ann Wisdom, of King and Queen county, Va., and had 1, Mary[3], m. Cornelius Rucker; 2, Theodosia[3], m. John Early; 3, John[3], married Miss Grumm; 4, Cornelius[3], m. Rosa Dearing; 5, Frances[3], married Zachariah Philips; 6, Thomas[3], m. Sarah Shelton (see Shelton); 7, Ann[3], m. Epaphroditus Rhodes; 8, Joseph[3], d. s. p.; 9, Elizabeth[3], m. William Davis; 10, Sarah, m. John Leathers. Of these, 6, Thomas[3] and Sarah (Shelton) White had issue:

1. *Shelton[4], m. (11 Dec., 1794), Mildred Clark, of Elbert county, Ga.*; 2, John[4], m. Rachel Carter; 3, Nancy[4], m. Caleb Oliver; 4, Henry[4], m. Mary Starke; 5, Thomas[4], m. Elizabeth Clark; 6, Joseph[4], m. Avarilla Harper, of a Middlesex county, Va., family; 7, William[4], of Elbert county, Ga., m. Concord Hamilton Brown, daughter of Frederick Brown, Columbia county, Georgia. Of these: 7, *William[4] and Concord Hamilton (Brown) White*, of Georgia, had issue:

  1, Eliz. Louisa[5], m. James W. Fraser, of Abbeville, S. C., and had Tallulah, m. Dr. Joseph Presley, of S. C.; Victoria; Sally Concord, m. David T. Oliver.
  2, Victoria Antoinette[5], d. unm.
  3, Sarah Ann[5], m. James S. Oliver (d. 1882), of DeSoto.
  4, Frederick[5], d. s. p.
  5, Col. Thomas William[5] White, of Hernando (d. 1890), m. Mina Barbara Meriwether, and had Mildred Concord[6], Barbara Mina[6], Thomas[6], Louisa Toombs[6], Concord Hamilton[6], Nellie[6], Frederick B.[6] and Corinne Meriwether[6].
(*For these see Oliver and McGehee family.*)

1, Shelton[4] and Mildred (Clark) White, of Elbert county, Ga., (above) had issue:
1, Christopher Clark[5]; 2, Sarah T.[5], m. Hugh, 9th son of Micajah McGehee, of Oglethorpe county, Broad River, Ga. "They lived below Webb's Ferry, in Elbert county," says Gov. Gilmer, "before removing to Mississippi." (*See McGehee.*)
3, Mildred Terrell[5], m. Simeon Oliver, (*see Oliver*). 4, Thomas I.[5], d. s. p.
5, John H.[5], m. Mildred T. Satterwhite. 6, Mary S.[5], m. Welborn A. Herring.
7, David S.[5], m. (I) Catherine C. Rucker, and (II) Mrs. Maria A. Price.
8, Christopher Clark[5], m. (I) Barbara Williams, and (II) Mary Withers.
9, Shelton R.[5], m. Sands Walker. 10, Childs T.[5], died aged 20. 11, William W.[5], married (I) Lucinda S. McGehee, and (II) Ann Pegues.

Capt. Zack[4] White, Tunica county, Miss., is a son of William and Ann (Pegues) White.

John and Thomas White (1756), lands in Surry county, Va., south side of Black-water swamp.—(*Records*.)

SAUNDERS.

The Hyde-Saunders, and Williamsburg lines it is said descend from EDWARD SAUN-DERS, who was father of—

JOHN[1] SAUNDERS, planter (1677) of Hampton Pa., York county, Constable in 1677 (succeeding William Wade). Surveyor of highways, with Henry Lee and John Cosby, 1682; patented land in Goochland, 1690; progenitor of the Hyde-Saunders and Wil-liamsburg-Saunders line; (will *proved 1700*; a large estate). Married Sarah, daughter of Peter Hargreave, who died 1684, and his estate divided (1685) by Robert Booth. Wm. Clopton and John Mihill (prominent men of York) between John Saun-ders (the administrator) and Robert Roberts, who married Mary, the *other* daughter of Peter Hargreave. Robert Roberts d. 1705 (his son, Robert Roberts, was sheriff, 1712. —*Records*.) Children mentioned in above will (1700):

Christabel[2], "now wife of Samuel Waddem"—*John*[2], *Edward*[2], *Robert*[2], *George*[2], *Har-greave*[2], *Peter*[2], *Sarah*[2] and *Susunnah*[2] Saunders.

Of these, John[2] and Edward[2] Saunders made a deed (1707) to William Barber, gent, which John's wife, Mary, also signed: George and Robert Saunders "acknowl-edged" a debt (1711) to William Timson, who was a large merchant; and Hargreave Saunders (with guardian—Henry Atkinson) was *not* of age in 1712. (*Records*.) The son, JOHN[2] SAUNDERS, married (before 1707) Mary, daughter of Robert Hyde (d. 1718), the attorney, who had married (in 1679) Jane Underhill (executrix of Mrs. Mary Clopton, widow of Dr. Isaac Clopton) and had Samuel and Mary Hyde. John Hyde, the pro-genitor came to York Co. after 1650, and married Mary Hansford (of the family of the *rebel*, Thomas Hansford, of *Bacon's Rebellion*). (Note: It is claimed for the Hyde family that they were related to Edward Hyde, first Earl of Clarendon (b. 1609—d. 1674); Lord Chancellor of England 1658, and grandfather of Queens Annie and Mary. Robert Hyde was of the grand jury in York Co. 1692, with Robert Green, Ralph Graves, Seymour Powell, Philip Debnam and Henry Collier. James Hyde, mentioned in 1690. Samuel Hyde and wife Elis., mentioned 1717. (His will 1738.)

Of the brothers and sisters (above) of John[2] Saunders, we have no data beyond the *will* of 1700, and they were born too early for any to have figured in the Revolution.

JOHN[2] and Mary (Hyde) Saunders had issue: 1, John Hyde Saunders; 2, Samuel Hyde[3] Saunders, and *perhaps*, Col. Peter[3] Saunders of Halifax (afterwards Henry) Co. (unless he was son of one of those mentioned in the will above. But the descendants of John and Mary (Hyde) Saunders seem to have preserved the name of Peter among them.) Of these:

1. John Hyde[3] Saunders (b. *circa* 1707) was the one who made deed, 1735, to his uncle, Samuel Hyde, in York county. in which he recites that John Hyde Saunders, was son and heir of John Saunders, who was son and heir of John Saunders, who patented land in Goochland county, 1790, etc. (There seems to have been confusion among the family records as to the identity of this John Hyde Saunders and that of his nephew, the Rev. John Hyde Saunders, of Cumberland county, who was a student at William and Mary College, Virginia, 1762.) And here the name of the son of John Hyde Saun-ders, the ancestor of the Williamsburg line, is uncertain, but it was, probably, also:

1. John[4] Saunders, a planter in James City county. Whatever his name, the follow-ing list of his children was sent by his grandson, Rev. William Turner Saunders, in 1887, to Col. James E. Saunders of Alabama. He wrote: "I have heard my uncle, Robert[3] Saunders (the lawyer of Williamsburg), speak of his father as a most indus-trious planter, of comparatively small means, and a large family, but cannot now recall his *name*. Of his children were 1. Matthew[4], 2. John[4], 3. Lewis[4], 4. Betsy[4], 5. Patsy[4],

and perhaps another not remembered, and of these, all who left descendants were Robert[4] and my father, John[6],'' as follows:

(1) ROBERT[4] SAUNDERS, Sr., lawyer of Williamsburg, born 1762, d. 1840, mentioned while student in William and Mary College, 1776, as "*son of John.*" Left college later, with others, to join the American army—(*Catalogue*). Witnessed a marriage in York county, 1786.

> His only son, Hon. Robert[5] Saunders, died 1869. Eminent scholar. Professor Mathematics William and Mary College, 1833, and President, 1847, and also mayor of Williamsburg. Married, 1828, Lucy Burwell Page (b. 1807), youngest of the twenty children of Gov. John Page, of "*Rosewell.*" After his death she resided in the noble institution, "Louise Home," Washington. (*See Page Family Book.*)
> Children: 1. Barbara[6], 2. Leila[6], 3. Robert[6], now of Baltimore; 4. John[6] d. y., and 5. Page[6] Saunders,- a lovely and talented woman, died unm.; 6. Mary Ann[6], married George T. Williams, of Virginia.

(2) JOHN[4] SAUNDERS (third son) married Lucy Galt, and removed to Norfolk, and was an officer of the customs. Issue: Mary, d. s. p., Sarah, d. s. p., and a son, the Rev. William Turner[6] Saunders (b. in Norfolk, 1817), an Episcopal clergyman (1741), and for twenty years rector at Appalachicola, Fla., (until the Civil War). Spent his last years in Philadelphia with his children: 1, Robert, 2, William Lawrence, civil engineer, New York, and married; 3. Jennie, and 4, Walter B. Saunders, publisher, of Philadelphia (who is very much interested in his family lineage).

In his letter (1887) the Rev. William T. Saunders continued: "I am an old man past 70, and am sometimes fearful the family name will run out and be lost, so I advised my boys to marry. It is *Cousin Robert's* turn first, but he doesn't show any inclination," etc. "When one has made a mark in history we are apt to hope he was our ancestor. So, to excite my boys to good deeds, I have ventured to tell them I rather thought the martyr, Laurence Saunders, buried in Westminster Abbey, was our ancestor. There is no evidence. But it was comforting to indulge the thought when I stood on the famous spot where he is buried. * * * I went to Florida after the death of the Rev. James Saunders at Pensacola, and when Dr. Scott was at Pensacola, as he still is. I should like to know you and hope you are a Christian, and have the blessed hope of everlasting life. Truly yours," etc.

2. SAMUEL[3] HYDE SAUNDERS, married, according to the family record, Phyllis Dudley, heiress to a fortune in England, which her descendants never recovered, it is said, because of the "burning of a marriage record."

Relationship is claimed for her to the great Dudley family of England, of whom were Lord Guilford Dudley, who married Lady Jane Gray, and his brother, Robert Dudley (b. 1832), Earl of Leicester, favorite of Queen Elizabeth. Be that as it may, her descendants all preserve the tradition of the lost fortune, which, like that in the Booth, Jennings, and other influential Virginia families, never materialised. The issue of this marriage is given by Shields Saunders, of Richmond, and Major Robert C. Saunders, of Ewington, and a letter of Mrs. E. A. Turpin (dated "Bremo, 10th November, 1868 "), to her stepmother, Mrs. Eliza Saunders, in which, after giving the following list, she

---

* Robert Hyde (d. 1718), grant in York county, 1697, Laurence Hyde, in York county, 1679. (*Records.*) John Hyde, land in *Lunenberg* county, 1753. (*See Wm. and Mary Quarterly, VI, 1897*)

Edward Hyde, Governor of North Carolina, probably a relative.

Samuel Hyde Saunders (1771), in Cumberland county. Va., advertised stray cow. (*Va. Gazette.*)

Peter Saunders (1775), of the county committee for Pittsylvania county. Pittsylvania county was taken from Halifax, 1766.

†Col. Peter Saunders (1780), specific taxes in Henry county. Henry county was taken from Pittsylvania county, 1776. (*Va. Mag. History, I.*)

Robert Hyde Saunders, ensign Virginia State Regiment, 20th March, 1777; resigned, 1778. (*Heitman.*)

Capt. John Saunders (1789), in Louisa county (?), a stray cow. (*Va. Gazette.*) Louisa was taken from Hanover, 1742; Hanover from New Kent, 1720; and New Kent from York, 1654.

comments: "Our great-grandfather was related to the Lord Chancellor Hyde, and gave the name of Hyde to each of his sons. Our great-grandmother was Phillis Dudley, related to Sir Guilford Dudley, etc. * * * Cornelius Dupree, grandson of Rev. Hyde Saunders, visited me when I lived in Petersburg, Va., and he, as well as the others, thought we were the heirs of a large Dudley estate in England. His grandfather's library was sold to William and Mary College, and among these books was our Family Record—a *tree* with all the different branches of the family. He visited the College hoping to find it, but it was burned when that building took fire."

Children of Samuel[2] and Phyllis (Dudley) Saunders: 1. Peter Hyde[4]; 2. Rev. John Hyde[4]; 3. Chancellor Hyde[4]; 4. Samuel Hyde[4]; 5. Robert Hyde[4]; 6. Mrs. Ligon[4]. Of these, Rev. John Hyde Saunders must have been born before 1748, as he was a student at William and Mary College, 1762. However, the succession of children is copied just as it was sent:

(1) PETER HYDE[4] SAUNDERS (b. 20th September, 1748; d. August 14, 1813); married (October 31, 1767), Mary Sparrell (who d. 1790), ward of Governor Giles, and moved to Franklin county, Va. (Their descendants are the families of Judge Fleming Saunders (b. 1778), Col. Samuel Saunders, The Hales, Gen. Peter Early and a line of the Hairstons.) His home was twice burned. Issue:

Judith (b. 1768), Lethe (1770), Elizabeth (1772), Peter (1776), Fleming (1778), Robert (1781), Samuel (1783), Polly (1788). Of these,

Judge Fleming Saunders (second son), of Franklin county (b. 1778, d. 1858), married (19th May, 1814) Alice, daughter of William and Mary (Scott) Watts, of Flat Creek, Campbell county, Va. Mary was daughter of Francis Scott, of Prince Edward county, Va. (*See Scott Family.*) Issue:

Mary Elis. (b. 1815), Sarah Watts, William Watts, Edward Watts (all died young), Peter (b. 1823), Anna Maria (b. 19th October, 1825), married Thomas L. Preston, of Charlottesville, Va.; Robert Chancellor (b. 26th May, 1827), of Ewington, Campbell county, Fleming (b. 1829), Louisa Morris (b. 1833), married Richard T. Davis. Of these, Major Robert C. Saunders, of Ewington, Va., is father of Eugene David Saunders, Professor of Law in Tulane University; and Walter Saunders, lawyer, of New Orleans. (Mrs. Thomas L. Preston furnished this list of her grandfather's descendants.)

(2) REV. JOHN HYDE[4] SAUNDERS, the "colonial parson," student at William and Mary College, 1762; ordained 1772 in England. (It is probable he was older than Peter Hyde Saunders.)

Peterville church, Southam parish, Powhatan county (formerly Cumberland), built for him: the pastor until 1791, member of committee of safety for Cumberland county, 1775. For some boyish prank of insubordination, while at college, he was expelled 1765. His children:

Horatio[5], John[5], the first Mrs. Payne[5], Hyde[5], Mrs. Eagan[5], and Mrs. Dupree[5], mother of Cornelius[6] Dupree (mentioned above), of South Carolina.

(3) CHANCELLOR HYDE[4] SAUNDERS, of Powhatan county, Va., (will p. 1720). Children: John C. Robert H., Alban G., William C., and Mrs. Jane Mosley.

(4) SAMUEL HYDE[4] SAUNDERS, Powhatan county, Va., m. Miss Jude. Children: John[5], Tarleton[5], Samuel Shields[5] (father of Mrs. E. O.[6] Turpin, of the letter of 1868, above), Edward Archer[5], James[5], and the 2nd Mrs. Payne[5].

(5) ROBERT HYDE[4] SAUNDERS, of the "Short Pump," Henrico county, Va. Reared by his brother, Samuel, and both married sisters, the Misses Jude, of "Jude's Ferry." He married (II) Lucy Mayo. Her daughter, Martha[5] Saunders, married Dr. Joseph Mosby, (their son, Frank[6] Mosby, living in 1898). A son, Robert Mayo[5] Saunders, of Richmond, died 1845, leaving issue: Howard[6], and Margaret Ann[6] Saunders (who d. 1870), married (1863) Lucian S. Lanier, of Baltimore, and had four children.

(6) MRS. LIGON, of Powhatan county (once Cumberland). Descendants: Gen. Ligon, James Ligon, of Petersburg, and Daniel Hatcher, and his sister, Mrs. William Wat-

kins, of Powhatan. James Ligon left three daughters, all in Pulaski county, Va.:
Mrs. McGavock, Mrs. David Kent, and Emma Ligon

3. Of Col. Peter² Saunders, of Henry county, 1780, nothing is known except a mention of him as Collector of Specific Taxes in Henry county, Va. (*Va. Mag. of Hist.,* Vol. I).

YET ANOTHER SAUNDERS LINE claims descent from Phillis Dudley, *the heiress.* It is said she had, also, a son,

Jesse Saunders, who married Mary Jovilian, of French descent, and had Robert Saunders (b. 1778, d. 1857); married (1803) Susan Hoard, and had Mary Smith (b. 1806); married Patrick⁴ Booth, (b. 1796); (John², John³ and Eliz. Cobb, and Thomas⁴ Booth). (From a letter of Mrs. Cyrus A. Branch (1878), of James City county, who was Miss Booth).

Jesse Saunders'¹ name does not occur in the list of Samuel Hyde and Phyllis (Dudley) Saunders children given above, and Mrs. Preston is at a loss to place him.

A JOHN SAUNDERS was from near Norfolk, and was a United Empire loyalist during the Revolution and captain in Simcoe's British Regiment (which contained many *Virginia Tories*). After the Revolution he went to England and was then sent to New Brunswick, Canada, as Chief Justice of that colony, with the title of Sir John Saunders. Gen. Jubal Early, of the late war (1861), related in a most interesting letter to his cousin, Mrs. Thos. Preston, the incident of meeting Sir Johns' grandson at the capital of New Brunswick, just after *our* war. While at the hotel there, a gentleman called for him upon whose card was written "Mr. Peter Saunders." He was then President of the Legislative Council of New Brunswick. "Mr. Saunders, this is a very familiar name to me," said the general, "we have many of that name in Virginia." "My grandfather *was* a native of Virginia, and came somewhere from the vicinity of Norfolk or Richmond," he answered. "Then," said I, "we are related. My *grandmother was a* Saunders, and from that section also." "But," he replied, "my grandfather was a *United Empire loyalist,* and a captain in Simcoe's regiment." (Supposing I would repudiate the relationship when informed that his ancestor was a *Tory*.) "Nevertheless," said I, at once, "Mr. Saunders, I think, we are related, and I am of opinion that your grandfather showed more sense than the balance of the family." He then replied, "Well, he always said that the time would come when the people of Virginia would bitterly regret ever having had anything to do with the Yankees." "And," I then answered, "*that time* has already *come.*" "I mentioned this," continued General Early, "to show that the Saunders' family is quite widely spread over the country."

Mr. Peter Saunders, of New Brunswick, Canada, was doubtless descended from John Saunders, of York county, 1677.

SAUNDERS OF VIRGINIA.

Thomas Saunders, aged 20, came in the "*Transport,*" July, 1635.
John Saunders, aged 22, came in "*Ye Merchant Hope,*" July, 1635.
William Saunders, aged 19, came in "*The Globe,*" August, 1635.
Edward Saunders, aged 40, came in "*The Safety,*" August, 1635.
Thomas Saunders, aged 13, came in "*The Safety,*" August, 1635.
Edward Saunders, aged 9, came in "*The Safety,*" August, 1635.
Edward Saunders, aged 20, came in "*The Thomas,*" August, 1635.
John Saunders, aged 17, came in "*The William and John,*" September, 1635.

(*Hotten's Emigrants.*)

Some Early Patentees of Virginia by the Name of Saunders.

ACCOMAC COUNTY.

Roger Saunders, Burgess, 1632. Grant of land, 1628 (*Records*).
Ustns Saunders, 150 acres, Northampton, 1663 (*Land Book 5*).

JAMES CITY COUNTY.

George Sanders, 1663 (*Book 5*).
Francis Sanders, 1669, at the head of the Chickahominy (*Land Book 6*).
John Sanders. 1669, Mulberry Island, Warwick county (*Book 6*).

ISLE OF WIGHT COUNTY.

John Sanders, 1681 (*Book 7*, at Richmond). He entered 1650 acres with Richard Thomas, and Jonathan Robinson, April 3, 1681.

NANSEMOND COUNTY.

Hugh Sanders, 1664 (*Book 5*).
William Sanders, 1683, in the upper parish (*Land Book 6*).
Francis Sanders, 1683, in the upper parish (*Book 7*).
Thomas Sanders, 1686, in the upper parish (*Book 7*).
William Sanders, 1686, in the upper parish (*Book 7*).
Richard and John Sanders, 1689, in the upper parish (*Book 8*).
Richard and Robert Sanders, 1717 (*Book 10*).

SURRY AND SUSSEX.

Wm. Saunders in Surry (1723), (*Ld Book*), Wm. Saunders in Sussex, 1765, on Blackwater Swamp.
John Saunders in Sussex (1759) with wife Mary; and son William (b. 1759), Charlotte (1775).
Michael Saunders in Sussex, 1738 (*Albemarle Par. Register.*)
Michael Saunders (1768), lands in Southampton county.
Wm. Saunders (1737) 200 acres north side Gravelly Run. (*Pr. George.*)
John and James Saunders (1746), on Stony Creek. (*Book 26.*)
Edward Saunders and Winifred Stephens (1728), 400 acres adjoining John Stephens and Joseph Moreton. (*Book 26, Pr. George.*)
Thomas Saunders (1725), 400 acres in Henrico Co.

Rev. Jonathan Saunders. of Princess Annie Co., had daughter, Mary, who married (July, 1719) Cornelius Calvert, parents of Saunders Calvert (who m. 1757 Frances Tucker of Norfolk). Cornelius Calvert (b. 1723) m. Eliz. Thorowgood 1749. (*Wm. and Mary Quarterly, IV.*)
William Saunders m. (1761) Ann, daughter of Samuel Timson (will 1739), Justice of York Co. She had first married Robert Crawley. (*Wm. and Mary Quarterly, V.*) A Saunders and Crallé family, both lived in Northumberland Co. at that time.
Edward Sanders in Northumberland Co., '*Chyurgeon*,' 1660. (*Records.*)
Wm. Saunders (1715) 75 acres in Westmoreland Co. (*Ibid.*)

Others by the name of SAUNDERS, Northumberland Co., Va.; George Colclough brought over John Sanders as a head-right in 1655. In the Register of *St. Stephens Parish* are these entries:
William Sanders, son to John, baptised Jan. 28th, 1699. Edward Sanders*, son to William, baptised Oct. 11th, 1700. Betsy Sanders, daughter to Zacharias, baptised Sept. 17th, 1717. Judith Sanders, daughter to John, baptised 1727. Elizabeth Sanders, daughter to Edward, baptised 1731. Hannah Sanders, daughter to Edward, baptised 1726.

---

*One Edward Sanders died in Northumberland county, 1739, and George Carter came into court and made oath that Edward Sanders, Jr., died without a will, and on his motion and security he was made administrator. The inventory, May 21, 1739, amounted to £7. 9s. op. Who *this* Edward was, is not known, but the descendants of John Sanders were in Northumberland at that time, and he had a grandson, Edward, b. 1700, son of William, who was born 1699.

From *Christ Church Register*, Middlesex Co., Va.:

Edward Saunders and Frances, his wife, a daughter, Eliz., (b. 1681).

Edward Saunders married (1685) Eliz. Teil. Edward Saunders died 1718.

Edward Saunders (d. 1715) married (1687) Mary Brown. Issue: George (b. 1693), married (1714) Anne Clark. Thomas (b. 1708) married Christian Davis.

John Saunders married (1708) Eliz. Sibley (d. 1727). Issue: Mary (b. 1711), John (1715), Edmund (1718), William 1724).

John Saunders married Mary ———, and had son, John (b. 1742). Mary (1751), William (1759), Amy (1762), Patsy (1767), Charlotte (1775).

Edward Saunders married (1710) Eliz. Austin. Issue: Mary (1711), Sarah (1716), Edward (1721), John (1719).

Edward and Eliz. Saunders, a daughter, Mary (b. 1742).

Edward and Rebecca Saunders, a daughter (b. 1754).

George and Anne (Clark) Saunders (above). Issue: Edmund (b. 1715), George (1716) Judith (1720), William (1723).

Thomas and Christian (Davis) Saunders. Issue: Benjamin (b. 1727, d. 1730), Anne (1735), Nathaniel (1744), Eliz. (1745), Christian m. (1781) George Blake.

Thomas m. Lucretia, and issue, William (b. 1735).

John and Sarah Saunders. Issue: Eliz. (b. 1744), John (1757).

Susannah Saunders married (1733) John Curtis.

Thomas Saunders, Jr., married (1753) Averilla Stiff (b. 1732). Issue: Jacob Stiff Saunders, who married (1780) Lucy Humphries, and Averilla married (1792) John Miller, and Thomas Saunders, who married (1792) Mary Stiff.

Anne Saunders married (1786) Bartholomew Bristow.

George Davis Saunders married (1790) Charlotte Marchant.

Hugh Saunders (1733), 207 acres in Spotsylvania county.

Nathaniel Saunders (1768), land in Spotsylvania county, 2200 acres.

YORK COUNTY.

Thomas Saunders, debtor in York to Thomas Deacon, 1646.—(*Records.*)

William Saunders (1658), deed from William Davis.

John Saunders, one of *Bacon's Rebellion* men (1676), fined 2000 pounds tobacco, by Sir Wm. Berkley, Gov.—(*Hening, II, 548.*)

John Saunders' plantation (1677), of Hampton parish, York county.

Richard Saunders (1683), suit versus Francis Rosser.—(*Records.*)

NEW KENT COUNTY.

William Saunders, of New Kent county, (1686), 165 acres.

Thomas Saunders, of New Kent county (1686), 165 acres next to William.

WILLIAM (died 1717) and Elizabeth Saunders, of New Kent, had issue:

Sarah (1697), Thomas (1700), Susannah (1702), Mary (1705), Major (1708), Frances (1711), Agnes (1714). Of these, Susannah m. (1717) Isles Cooper, of whose desertion she afterwards complained bitterly on behalf of her children, and was granted a separation. (*See Hening's Statutes of Virginia.*)

JAMES (died 1717), and Sarah Saunders had issue:

Thomas (born 1699), John (1701), Alice (1703), Hannah (1708), Sarah (1711), Stephen (1713), Elizabeth (1716).

JOHN and Elizabeth (Waddell) Saunders (married 1709) had issue:

Anne (b. 1710), George (b. 1712), John (b. 1715).

John Saunders had daughter Mary (b. 1700).

JOHN and Judith Saunders had issue:

Frances (b. 1718), Frances (b. 1727), Elizabeth (b. 1730.)

James and Eliz. Saunders, a son, Thomas (b. 1738).

Thomas and Susannah Saunders, a son, William (b. 1774).—(*St. Peter's parish Register*, New Kent county.)

Alexander Saunders, of South Farnham parish, Essex county, Va., (will 1777, p. 1778), mentions wife, Mary (married (II) 1778 James De Jarnette). Children: William, Alexander, John, Edward, Henry, Susanna and Fanny. (*Chancery papers, Williamsburg, Va.*)

Mrs. Anne Swann Saunders, of Petersburg, 1784, warehouse on her land. (*Hening.*)

Celey Saunders' Line.

Celey*, and William†, Saunders, were captains in the Revolutionary Navy of Va. (What connection there was, if any, between them, is not yet known.) Capt. Celey Saunders commanded a packet before the Rev., which ran to, and from, the Potomac river, to Liverpool. It is a tradition in the family that he was the immigrant, and from Scotland. But it is highly probable he was *not*. A bounty was paid to him by the State, and the United States issued, in 1834, 1601 acres additional to Ann B. Taylor, John L. Saunders, and Jane B. Hunter, heirs of John Saunders, *sole heir* of Celey Saunders. 1, John, the son, was major of artillery and engineer in the U. S. A., and commanded Fort Nelson (which is now the parade ground of the Naval Hospital, Norfolk,) where stands his monument. He married Martha B. Selden; 2, Ann B. Saunders married Arthur Taylor, of Norfolk; 3, Mary Saunders, married William[1] Green; 4, Jane B. Saunders married W. W. Hunter, father of Commodore Hunter, of the U. S. and C. S. Navy, who died in New Orleans, 189—.

William Green had son John[2] Green, Col. of the 6th, who was father of Moses Green, father of Mr. W. W. Green, of West Point, Va.

John L. Saunders, only son of John L., was also commander in U. S. Navy, and died 1860. Of his four sons, only one survived: Col. John Selden Saunders, of Baltimore, who has only one living son: William Turner Saunders. Maj. W. V. Taylor, and Mrs. George Newton, represent this family in Norfolk.

EARLY NORTH CAROLINA SANDERS (OR SAUNDERS) FROM THE COLONIAL RECORDS OF NORTH CAROLINA, COMPILED BY COL. WM. L. SAUNDERS.

Joseph Sanders (1719). Petitioned Assembly for grant of 300 acres, lapsed patent (*II. 352*).

James Sanders (1728). Grand jury at Edenton, Chowan county.

James Sanders (1732). 300 acres in Edgecomb county (*IV. 333*), and on jury, 1740.

Benjamin Sanders (1731). Justice, Beaufort and Hyde counties (*III. 251*), and 1200 acres Tyrrel county, 1742.

Nathaniel Saunders (1741). 612 acres, Edgecomb county (*IV. 602*).

John Sanders (1731). Paid for apprehending a criminal (*III. 319*).

Moses Saunders (1743). 600 acres in Onslow county (*IV. 638–641*).

James Sanders (1744). Lands in Bertie county joining Chowan county (*IV. 705*).

John Sanders (1745). 300 acres in Carteret county (*IV. 761*).

Benjamin Sanders (1745). 155 acres in Craven county (*IV. 761*).

Robert Sanders (1743). 640 acres in Edgecomb county (*IV. 642*).

Isaac Sanders (1760). Justice, Perquimons county.

Charles Sanders (1668). Halifax county. Citizens' tax petition (*VII. 867*).

William Sanders (1768). Exempt from taxes in Anson county.

---

*Thomas Ceeley Burgess (1629), in Warwick River Co. (Hening I); Francis Ceeley(1646), of Elizabeth City Co., fined, in York Court, with Richard Dudley, Capt. Colthorpe, Richard Wells and others, for not rendering their accounts, as guardians. (They probably married widows.) Charles Ceeley married (1697) Elizabeth Saunders (of Elizabeth City Co.) Capt. Ceeley Saunders' name indicates another alliance of these families, later.

†Capt. William Saunders, Capt. in State Navy, with rank of Major, besides the State and U. S. bounties paid to him, had 944 acres additional issued, 1834, to his sole heir, Elizabeth Murray. Nothing more is known of this line.

Patrick Sanders (1768). Anson county. Petition, with others, in behalf of the Regulators.

Daniel Sanders (1768). Petition of citizens of Orange county against high fees, etc.

Thomas Alexander Sanders (1768). Petition of citizens of Orange county against high fees.

William Sanders (1768). Petition of citizens of Orange county against high fees.

James Sanders, Sr., and James Sanders, Jr., (1768). On a jury to try the Regulators, Orange county, and both sign petition (1768), with citizens of northern part of Orange county, to divide the county.

William Sanders (1768), of Orange, signed the above, and also Major Thomas Donohoe.

Adams Sanders (1768), of Orange, signed the above.

James Sanders (1772), of Guilford county.

Nathan Sanders (1772), of Granville county.

Alexander Sanders (1772), captain of Wake county militia, Raleigh.

Andrew Solomon Sanders (1773), Rowan county. Petition in behalf of legality of marriage ceremony as performed by Presbyterian ministers (*IX. 625*).

Hardy Saunders (1773), captain of Wake county militia.

Jesse Saunders (April 16, 1776), Orange county, captain in Sixth Regiment of Foot, organized at Hillsborough. Soon resigned.

Robert Saunders (1775). Committee of Safety for Pitt county, and one of the county patrol.

James Sanders (April 4, 1776), of Orange. Member of Provisional Congress which met at Halifax, and colonel of a regiment (organized April 22, 1776) from the northern part of Orange. (*See further.*)

James Sanders, of Hillsborough district, Orange county (April 23, 1776). On committee, as member of the Assembly, to equip the military, and for working the sulphur mines, and also on Committee of Claims, 1776. (*Colonial Records.*)

Brittain Sanders (1788), Wake county. Member of convention which met at Hillsborough to consider the Federal Constitution, which they did not adopt till next year.

Will of James Sanders, of Orange Co., 28th Feb., 1776. p. 12, Nov. 1776. Sons: James, Richard and William. Daughters: Sarah, wife of Wm. Trigg; Fanny, wife of *William Sanders, the elder* (?); Susannah, wife of Robert Terry, and Cassandra. Grandson, Jeremiah Terry. Trustees: James and Rd. Sanders and Wm. Trigg. Witnesses: James Sanders and Robin Terry and Andrew Haddock.

SAUNDERS OF ORANGE CO., (NOW CASWELL CO.,) N. C.

William[1] Saunders (or Sanders) of Orange Co., born *circa* 1700, married (1725) Miss Adams, of Orange Co., and came, it is said, from Bedford Co., Va., to N. C. Issue: 1, Adams[2]· 2, Thomas[2]; 3, Agnes[2]; 4, Richard[2]; 5, William[2]; 6, Betsy[2]; 7, Daughter[2]; 8, James[2]; 9, Kesiah.

I. ADAMS[2] SAUNDERS. represented Caswell Co. in the assembly 1785. (Caswell was taken from Oswego 1777.) Whom he married is unknown. (*Wheeler's Hist.*)

II. THOMAS[2] SAUNDERS m. Miss Mitchell, of the New Bern family, and removed to Sumner Co., Tenn., Cumberland river, 1790, when he and his wife were quite aged. Issue: 1, James[3]; 2, Edward[3]; 3, Frank[3]; 4, Juliet[3]; 5, Martha[3]. Of these;

    1, James[3] Saunders, called "Jimmie Dry" (founder of his family in Tenn.), b. 31 Oct., 1764, Newbern, North Carolina, and there m. (I) Hannah Mitchell (d. 34 years of age), and had 5 children, all of whom removed to Tenn., with their parents, and settled on a tract of 700 acres, at the junction of Drake's Creek with the Cumberland river. He m. (II) 1806, Mary Smith, daughter of Gen'l Daniel Smith of the Rev. and widow of Samuel Donalson (brother of Rachel Donalson, who was wife of Pres. Andrew Jackson). Mrs. Donalson was the mother of Jackson, Daniel and Andrew Jackson

Donalson, Secretary to the Pres., (and also sister to Col. George Smith, whose daughter, Mary, married Judge Lafayette Saunders, of Baton Rouge, La.) Jackson Donalson died a soldier, in Creek war, in Florida. Daniel Donalson (d. 1863), Brig. Geu'l Confederate Army. Andrew J. Donalson's wife became mistress of the White House (as Mrs. Jackson died before the inauguration). Her daughter Mary was the first child born in the White House. James Saunders was one of the legatees of his Uncle James, Sr., of N. C. (Whose will 1825.)

Issue 1st mar. (*Mitchell*): 1. Mary[4], 2. Letitia[4], 3. Harriet[4], 4. Charles Grandison[4], 5. David M[4]. Issue 2d mar. (*Smith-Donalson*): 6. Sarah[4], 7. Elizabeth[4], 8. Martha[4], 9. Mary Ann[4], 10. Ann C.[4], 11. Emily[4], 12. Alethia[4], 13, James[4], 14. Margaret[4], and two others.

Of these: Mary[4] *m*. Dr. Barry, and had *dau.*, Maria J.[5], married Maj. Andrew Price, and had son, James[6] Price, of Jefferson City, Mo. 12. Alethia[4], *m*. Dr. Robert P. Allison, and both were living in 1887, in Lebanon, Tenn.

2. Edward[3] Saunders, of Sumner Co., Tenn., *m*. his cousin Lockie Trigg, of N. C. Issue: Thomas[4], Trigg[4], Sarah Ann[4], and Daniel[4].

3. Frank[3] Saunders, of Davidson Co., Tenn., *m*. his cousin, Alethia, daughter of William Saunders. Issue: Mary[4], Thomas[4], Adaline[4], Leonidas[4], Elizabeth[4], and Frank[4].

4. Juliet[3] Saunders *m*. Peter Moseley, of Sumner Co. Issue: Mary[4], Adaline[4], Lycurgus[4], Socrates[4], and Peter Moseley[4].

5. Martha[3] Saunders *m*. Abram Trigg, and removed to Alabama. Issue not known.

III. AGNES[2] SAUNDERS, m. William Richmond, ancestor of the Richmond families, of Caswell county, N. C., and Atlanta, Georgia. A son, Adams, was father of Calvin Jones Richmond, recently deceased, grandfather of Mrs. Wm. Calvin Jernigan, of Atlanta.

IV. RICHARD[2] SAUNDERS, m. ———. His son, James, Jr., was legatee of his uncle, Col. James Saunders, of Dan River.

V. WILLIAM[2] SAUNDERS, Jr., of the Rev. (Died Sumner county, Tenn., 1808.) Member of 1st Provincial Congress, at Halifax. (*Colonial Records*.) Officer in 6th North Carolina Reg. Original member of the "Cincinnati Society" (1783), which he joined with his brother-in-law, Maj. Donoho, of Orange county. Married (I) Miss Mitchell, and (II), Miss Cunningham, sister of a brother officer of the *6th N. C.*, who was also member of *the Cincinnati*. He removed to Sumner county, Tenn., with his brother Thomas, 1790. His widow m. (II) Richard Alexander, whose descendants live near Dixon Springs, Smith county, Tenn.

Issue 1st mar. (*Mitchell*), as follows :

1. Franklin[3] Saunders. Married late in life a widow of Nashville, Tenn. No issue.

2. Romulus Mitchell[3] Saunders, born in N. C. After the death of his father, 1808, he was adopted by his uncle James, of N. C. Educated at University, N. C. Minister to Spain. M. (I) 1812, Rebecca Pine Carter, Caswell county, and had issue: 1, James[4]; 2, Franklin[4]; 3, Camillus[4]; 4, Anne Pine[4]; 5, Rebecca[4]. He m. (II) May, 1823, while Member of Congress, Anna Hayes, daughter of Judge Wm. Johnson, of the Supreme Court, U. S., (appointed 1804,) and had surviving issue; 6, William Johnson; 7, Margaret Madeline; 8, Jane Claudia; and, 9: Julia A. Of the first children: all died unmarried except Camillus Saunders, who married Harriet Taylor, Newport, R. I. No issue. Of the second children,

6. William Johnson⁴ Saunders, of Raleigh, N. C. Lawyer, familiarly called "*Spanish Bill*." Takes great interest in his lineage, furnishing much information for this branch; *m.* Jacqueline Minnissier, daughter of Peter S. Bacot, of S. C., Huguenot descent. Surviving issue: 1, William Louis, of Montana; 2, Bradley Johnson, m. Marie Sutherland; 3, Anna, m. S. W. Bacot, of Baton Rouge, La. ; 4, Jane Claudia, m. L. A. Denson.

7. Margaret Madeline⁴ Saunders, m. (1855) Wm. L. Eagle, surgeon U. S. A., and lived in Atlanta, and had two sons and one daughter.

8. Jane Claudia⁴ Saunders, m. (1851) Gen. Bradley Tyler Johnson, of Va. and Maryland. Surviving issue: Bradley T.⁵, Jr., m. Nannie Rutherford, and has Bradley T.⁶, the 3rd.

9. Julia A.⁴ Saunders, m., in Italy (1880), Frank Slayton, of New England, and has one son.

It is said William Saunders, who died 1803, had also three daughters; one, Edna.

Issue 2d marriage (*Cunningham*), as follows:

3. Jordan M. Saunders never married. Moved to Warrenton, Va., to a fine country home, where he died, 1886. A. D. Payne, of Warrenton, administrator of his estate.

4. Alethia Saunders.

5. Judge Lafayette³ Saunders, of Baton Rouge, La. (named for Gen. Lafayette), married at the "Hermitage," home of President Jackson, near Nashville, Tenn., Mary, *dau.* of Col. George Smith (above). Issue: 1. Augusta⁴ *m.* Judge King, of Louisiana, and had several children. 2. Tabitha⁴ *m.* Mr. Herron, of Louisiana. Their *dau.*, Mary⁵ Herron, *m.* Mr. Charles Bird, of Baton Rouge, son of Col. Charles Bird, of the C. S. A. in the Civil War, and "Commissioner of Agriculture and Immigration for Louisiana" in 1894.

6. Ethelbert³ Saunders married Dosia Twigg, of Memphis, Tenn., and lived in Selma, Ala. Had four or five children, of whom two daughters lived in Mobile, Ala.

VI. BETSY⁴ SAUNDERS *m.* William Trigg, and removed to Tennessee.

VII. DAUGHTER⁴ (name not known) married Mr. Allen, and removed to Tennessee.

VIII. JAMES⁴ SAUNDERS (will 1825, d. 1826), mentioned last, but probably eldest of his family, lived on Dan river, near Milton, and had large wealth. Never married. Left his property to nephews and nieces. Member of the Assembly and of the two Provisional Congresses at Hillsborough (1788) and Halifax, N. C. Treasurer of Caswell county, and sheriff, 1786. Colonel of Orange county militia, and of the Sixth Regiment of Foot, in which William Saunders and Maj. Thomas Donoho were officers. In 1768 James Sanders, Sr., and James, Jr., William Saunders and Thomas Donoho, all of Orange county, signed petition to divide the county (*Colonial Records*). He took an important part in the Revolution.

Donohoe Line.

IX. KEZIAH⁴ SAUNDERS (b. 1765, d. July 18, 1844) married (1774) Major Thomas Donohoe, of Orange county, North Carolina (b. 1750, d. 1827). The Donoho home is in Caswell county, North Carolina (once Orange), about three miles from Milton, and not far from Yanceyville. Thomas Donohoe was major of the Sixth Regiment North Carolina Foot, organized at Hillsborough, 1776, and was a brave Revolutionary officer. Joined the "*Order of the Cincinnati*," with Col. William Saunders, of Orange (or Caswell), at its inception at Newburg, on the Hudson, in 1783. The Hon. J. F. Donohoe, of Yanceyville, is now the lineal representative of that branch in the family. In 1839 Mrs. Donohoe received a pension from the United States for her husband's Revolutionary services.

A granddaughter of Mrs. Donohoe's is Mrs. David⁴ Johnston, of Madison, Ga. Her son is Mr. A. S.⁴ Johnston, now of Meridian, Miss. She has also a charming daughter in Sallie, the second wife of Mr. James G. Penn*, of Danville, Va., who is much interested in the Saunders lineage. These are descendants, also, of Dr. Hugh McAdam, the Scotch Highlander, who came to Lunenburg county, Virginia, and m. (1762) Catherine Scott, and also removed to Caswell county, North Carolina.

Mildred⁴, daughter of Mrs. Donoho, married ——— Watlington, and their daughter, Kesiah⁴, married Mr. Jeffries. James Saunders, of North Carolina, wrote to them both as his "nieces," and Richard Saunders, who had moved to Tennessee, 1830–40, wrote to Mrs. Jeffries as "dear cousin." James Saunders' letter to his niece, Mrs. Kesiah Jeffries, was addressed to her "at Capt. Terry's, Halifax county." (Probably Robert Terry, above.)

THOMPSON.

Families of Thompson have been numerous in Virginia since its earliest settlement. It is difficult to trace each through the Colonial period to its fountain head. The greatest number were in Henrico county, and what are now its subdivisions, which once included Goochland (1727), Chesterfield (1748), Cumberland (1748), Albemarle (1744), Powhatan (1777) and others. Thus, from one of the eight great shires formed in 1632 we get many counties, and, it would seem, as many distinct Thompson families, which also were not confined to the south-side only.

After much research in Virginia land books, parish registers, county records, the two historical magazines, genealogies and books of reference, and all other available resources, the following data of some of these separate lines is given, with the hopes of inducing further investigation among the descendants:

1623, Roger and Ann Thompson, at *Fleur de Hundred*, after Indian massacre; and also Nicholas, George, William and Paul Thompson.—(*Hotten.*)

1635, William, aged 22, came in "The George," and Edward, aged 24, in "The Transport."

1654, William Thompson, Tithables in Lancaster county.—(*Va. Mag. Hist., etc., V.*)

1649, ROBERT THOMPSON, first patentee of Northumberland county, with William Presley and others. His father, Richard Thompson, married Ursula Bysshe. She m. (II) Col. John Mottrom (d. 1655). She m. (III) Col. George Colelough, of Northumberland, and he at her death, 1658, was guardian to her children, Richard and Sarah Thompson. Sarah m. Thomas Willoughby. In 1634 Rev. Thomas Sax left legacy to Mary, daughter of Robert Thompson.—(*Lancaster Records.*)

1660, William and Robert Thompson, living in Middlesex county.

1674, Edward Thompson, of London, merchant, died in Middlesex county, Va., and was buried at Christ Church, with *coat of arms* on tomb.

1682, John and Thomas Thompson were both married in Middlesex county. Thomas to Elisabeth Hill, and had son, Thomas, b. 1684.—(*Christ Church Register.*)

1680, William Thompson m. Grace Elwood, and had Thomas, b. 1682; Sarah, 1683; William, 1685; Mary, 1689; Samuel, 1699.—(*Ibid.*) William Elwood, mentioned in York county records, 1674.

1684, William Thompson m. Ellen, daughter of Peter Montagne, whose will p. in Lancaster county, 1659.—(*Montagne Book.*)

1695, Elizabeth Thompson m. Edwin Conway, Lancaster county (he was b. 1640), second wife (*Hayden*).

1729, Dr. William Thompson, of Middlesex county, Eng., appointed Dr. Charles Tomkies, of Gloucester county, his "legal attorney."—(*York Records.*)

1699, SAMUEL THOMPSON, Justice Northumberland county.

1699, Matthew Thompson, Justice Stafford county. (*Virginia Magazine of History.*)

1710, Thomas Thompson, living in Northumberland county.

1714, Thomas Thompson, Surveyor in Westmoreland county.—(*Northumberland Records.*)

---

* Mrs. Penn is making arduous research as to the line of Mrs. Donohoe, of whom she may publish more accurate information.

1733, William Thompson, in Stafford county. (*Virginia Gasette.*)

1797, William Thompson, of Culpeper, dec'd. He married Francis Mills. and had William Mills Thompson, (b. 1775), who married (1820) Mildred Thruston Ball, *dau.* of Burges Ball. His son by a former marriage (*Broadus*) was the Hon. Robert W. Thompson, M. C., from Indiana, 1841.

1715, HENRY THOMPSON, of Abingdon pa., Gloucester county. Son John (b. 1714), also sons James and William. *Abingdon pa. Register.*)

1747, Capt. John Thompson, of Gloucester county, administrator with James Balfour, of Patrick Vance, of York county. (*York Records.*)

1686, Will of WILLIAM THOMOSON, Nansemond county. His daughter, Elizabeth, married Capt. Thomas Swann, Burgess of Surry, 1692. (*Hening's Statutes, VI. 446.*) Their son, Thomas Swann, was living in Nansemond, 1740; and his son, Thompson Swann, removed to Cumberland county, and was Clerk of the Court, 1754. Josiah Thompson *m.* 1754, in Cumberland county, Mary Ann Swann, and had sons: William Morris Thompson and John Thompson, who made his will, Cumberland county, October, 1785, and mentioned; "wife, Elizabeth son, John Daniel Thompson; brother, William Morris Thompson, and father, Josiah Thompson."—(*Records.*)

Martha Thompson married (November, 1755), in Cumberland county, Lawrence Smith.

1685, William Thompson, patent in Upper Norfolk county; (*Nansemond county.*)

1751, Sarah, *dau.* of John and Ann Thompson, born—(*Norfolk County Records.*)

1712, Rev. Andrew Thompson, minister, Hampton pa., Elizabeth City county, died 1719. (*Meade.*)

1639, John Thompson, James City county, Commissioner to view tobacco.

1660, REV. WILLIAM THOMPSON was minister of Lawne's Creek Church, Surry county, Va. In 1673 he was reported to the Court as "an orthodox, faithful and painful minister, and then in the 14th year of his ministry in the parish." His son, Samuel Thompson, died in Surry county, 1720-2ò. *Will* named nephew Samuel, brother William, cousin William Moseley, cousin Robert Payne, wife Mary (who was born 1663). William, (son of Rev. William), died 1732; wife Martha. He was minister (1690) in Westmoreland county. His children; 1. Samuel. 2. John. 3. Katharine. 4. Hannah, and grandchildren Samuel and Mary. (Isle of Wight Records.—*William and Mary Quarterly, VII. 261*).

1666, William Thompson, lands in Surry.—(*Land Book.*)

1673, William Thompson, 400 acres in Surry.—(*General Court Records.*)

1682, Rev. William Thompson (" Clerk "), 460 acres in Surry.—(*Land Book.*)

1684, William Thompson, 300 acres in Surry. and, in 1686, 1160 acres.

1689, William Thompson, lands in Surry, next to Samuel Watkins and Nicholas Meriwether (*York Land Book and Surry Land Book.*)

1686, Samuel Thompson, lands joining William Thompson. He was Burgess for Surry 1702.

1694, John Thompson, Burgess for Surry.—(*Va. Mag. Hist., III, 426.*)

1727, Samuel Thompson, 160 acres, escheat lands formerly Elizabeth Thompson's.

1742, William Thompson, 700 acres, Surry, south side Nottoway river.(—*Land Book.*)

1774, Capt. Thompson, records birth of negro slaves in Surry.—(*Albemarle Parish Register.*)

1756, William Thompson, of Sussex county, land on Nottoway river; wife, Hannah; son, Bastian (b. 1745); Susannah (b. 1747).—*Albemarle Parish Register.*)

1768, WELLS THOMPSON in Mecklenburg, a letter for him in Petersburg postoffice, also a letter there for Wm. Wells, of Lunenburg. These counties were taken from Brunswick in 1740; Brunswick from Surry 1720.

1721, James Thompson, witness to will of Peter Jones, Sr., of Bristol parish, Prince George.

1730, Perkins Thompson, 400 acres in Prince George county.

1748, William Thompson, Jr., Prince George, 2000 acres on both sides Burnt Quarter Run, joining the lands of Charles Thompson.

1773, John Thompson, living in Prince George county; son of John Thompson, Sr. (—Va. Gazette.)

1746, Robert Thompson, lands in Amelia county.

1780, William Thompson in Pittsylvania.—(Va. Gazette.).

1646, JOHN THOMPSON, in York county.

1657, Robert Thompson, planter of Chiscake parish, York county. Indenture to his neighbor, Robert Chandler.

1658, Richard Thompson, carried letters from York to the freshes of the Rapp.

1660, George Thompson, witness to will of Thomas Whitehead, York county.

1769, Stephen Thompson, merchant in York county.

Rev. Rowland Jones, of Bruton parish, in his will (Aug. 15, 1687) left legacy 3000 pounds tobacco to his sister, Mary Thompson, and also to his sister, Mrs. Jane Gooch. His son, Orlando, was grandfather to George Washington's wife, Martha Dandridge (Mrs. Custis).

1689, Samuel Thompson, of York county, 200 acres in Surry county next to Mr. Nicholas Meriwether, and William Thompson, who in 1673 patented 400 acres in Surry. Samuel Thompson was Burgess for Surry 1702.

1689, Wm. Thompson, of York county (Clerk) patent in Surry, next to Mr. Nicholas Meriwether, and Samuel Watkins.—(York County Land Book.)

1694, John Thompson, witness to probate of will of Rev. John Wright, by Judith, his wife (York Records).

1690, Bartholomew Thompson, witness to will of William Gill.—(York Records.)

1694, Henry Thompson, Sr. and Jr., witnesses to deed. Henry, Jr., married (before 1680) Mary, daughter of Maurice Hurd (will p. 1683). He became planter in James City county, and in 1690, with wife Mary, sold 140 acres in Bruton parish, York, next to John Daniel, and a part of Dividend of 200 acres, which was divided among Maurice Hurd's orphans in 1690.—(York Records.)

1719, Daniel Thompson, keeper of Ordinary in Williamsburg.

1732, James Thompson, of York Town; will mentions nephew, James Lowe, sister Hannah Thorpe. Legacy to Rev. John Richards, of Ware parish, Gloucester county.—(York Records.)

1792, Francis Thompson, security to the marriage of Elizabeth Manning to John Stokes, in York county.

1674, THOMAS AND ROBERT THOMPSON, in New Kent, 700 acres.

1687, Robert Thompson, of New Kent (died 1702, wife Judith(?) d. 1709). Children: Robert (b. 1687), David (1690), Susannah (1696), Hannah (1698), Martha (1701).

1702, Roger Thompson, Justice New Kent county. (Hayden.)

1708, William Thompson, New Kent, and wife Hannah, son John (born 1708), Susannah (b. 1716), George (1717).

1728, John Thompson, of New Kent, and wife Mary, daughter Sarah (b. 1729).— (St. Peter's Parish Register.)

1783, William Thompson, of Spotsylvania, 13 slaves. (Va. Mag. Hist.)

"Early in the 18th century," writes Dr. Grinnan, "Sir Charles Thompson came to Hanover county from Scotland, where he had married the Lady Joan Douglass. Their

---

In York were families also of the name of Watkins, Oliver, Drewry, Dunn, Daniel.

The p in Thompson is more distinctive of Irish families of that name, Burke mentioning several of prominence in his Landed Gentry, more especially in county Longford and Antrim. Drury, Waddy, Lowe and Manning, Irish familes, occasionally intermarried with Thompson as they have in America.

children were: Charles Garland (of Culpeper county, died 1826), Nelson (died 1808), and David. (Hanover was taken from New Kent, 1720, and New Kent from York, 1654, and Louisa from Hanover, 1742.)

1713, Waddy Thompson* and son, Waddy, Jr., in Louisa county. In 1775 Waddy Thompson was on a committee for the relief of the poor, with George Meriwether, Charles Yancey, William Peters, and others.—(*Va. Gazette.*)

1788, Waddy Thompson, of Louisa county, took deposition, as a commissioner, (with others) as to votes in Louisa county.—(*Virginia Gazette.*)

Waddy Thompson married Jane, daughter of Col. Robert Lewis, of "Belvoir," Albemarle county, Virginia.—(*Hayden.*)

Governor Gilmer says: "Mr. Thompson, of South Carolina, married daughter of John Lewis, of the Revolution, son of William and Ann (Montgomery) Lewis, of Virginia.—(*The Georgians.*)

Waddy Thompson, Chancellor, of South Carolina, was father of Hon. Waddy Thompson, M. C. for many years, and Minister to Mexico under first President Harrison, and also a descendant of Henry Patillo of Colonial and Revolutionary fame. Chancellor Thompson had also a daughter, Maria Swann Thompson, who married Dr. Richard Harrison, son of Maj. Richard Harrison, of the Revolutionary War, who came from James river, Virginia, to South Carolina. Major Richard's brother, James Harrison, married Elizabeth Hampton, sister of General Wade and Colonel Henry Hampton of Revolution.—(*American Ancestry.*)

(These were ancestors of a distinguished family of Columbus, Miss., into which Gen. Stephen D. Lee, of the Confederate army, married, and also Mr. Matthew Clay—i. e. Regina and Nina Harrison, cousins).

A son; Waddy Thompson, lived in Mobile, Ala., before the civil war.

1747, Samuel Thompson, of Hanover, deed to son, William Thompson.

1752. Samuel Thompson, of Hanover, deed of property from John Garland. Dr. Grinnan, of Madison Mills, Va., says there are several Garland Thompsons mentioned in the Louisa County Records.

1756, Robert Thompson, sixty-five acres in Louisa.—(*Land Book.*)

1756, David Thompson, of Hanover, deed to his son, Waddy Thompson, Sr. (whose own will was dated 1801). This deed was for land in Louisa county.—(*Dr. Grinnan.*)

David Thompson, 1756, bought 250 acres in Louisa.—(*Land Book.*)

1769, William Thompson advertised five tracts of land in Louisa and Hanover counties.—(*Virginia Gazette.*)

1771, Nathaniel Thompson, in Hanover.—(*Virginia Gazette.*)

1780, Charles Thompson, in Hanover.—(*Ibid.*)

1788, William Thompson's (above), will (he was son of Samuel, of Hanover) mentions wife, Ann. Children: Rhodes, William, Clifton, Asa, John, David, Ann, Mary, Eunice, Lydia, Sarah. Hening, vol. 13, mentions Rhodes Thompson as trustee (1790) of Georgetown, in Woodford county.

1787, William Thompson, sheriff of Louisa county—R. Yancy, D. S.—(*Virginia Gazette*).

1742, Roger Thompson, Fredricksville par. Vestry, Louisa county and Albemarle county, took the *test oath* against *transubstantiation* in the Sacrament, with T. Meriwether, John Poindexter, Ephraim Clark, John Stark and others. Later vestrymen (until 1787) were John Nicholas and William D. Meriwether, William and Thomas Johnson, John Harvie, John Rodes, James Marks, Dr. George Gilmer and others.—(*Bishop Meade.*)

_____

*Benjamin Waddy lived in Northumberland co. 1704, and Thomas Waddy lived in Westmoreland 1718. Samuel Waddy lived in New Kent, 1689, when his daughter Elizabeth was born, also Anthony Waddy, who had Mary (b. 1711), and Anthony (b. 1714), and John (b. 1726). (*St. Peter's par. Register.*) Mr. Thomas Waddy's wife was left a mourning ring in the will of Bartholomew Shrewe, 1730, of Northumberland co., Va., also Mr. Richard and Charles Lee, and Mr. Thomas Heath.

1790, Roger Thompson, of Louisa county, and "wife Lucy, now dead," leaving children: Joseph, George, Foster, Eliz. and Sarah. Trustees: George and John Thompson, and Wm. Payne, Sr., gents.—(*Hening*.)

1772, Roger and George Thompson, Vestry St. Anne's pa., Albemarle co. Also Wm. Burton, John Harris, Orlando Jones, Sam'l Shelton and others.

1792, Samuel Thompson in Franklin co., trustee for town of Wiesenburg with John Early and Wm. Turnbull and others. (*Hening*.)

1752, William Thompson, Vestry Antrim pa., Halifax co., and Wm. Thompson, Jr., of Halifax, 1789. (*Hening*.)

William Thompson in Augusta co. long before 1792. (*Hening*.)

1775, James and John Thompson, merchants in Petersburg, Dinwiddie co., Va. (Mostly drugs.) (*Va. Gazette*.)

1761, John Thompson, of Petersburg, Va., student at Wm. and Mary College.

1768, John Thompson living in Dinwiddie county.

1813, Robert Thompson, of Brunswick co., student at William and Mary College.

1783, William Thompson, living in Dinwiddie county.

1793, John Thompson, of Petersburg, student at Wm. and Mary College.

1787, George Thompson, House of Delegates from Fluvanna co. with Samuel Richardson.

1773, Benajah Thompson, living in Cumberland co.

1789, Benajah Thompson, living in Buckingham co.

William Thompson, officer in the English Navy, 1678 (and a son of Sir Roger Thompson of Eng.) Had daughter, Martha, who married (1699) Col. James Taylor, of Orange co., son of James Taylor, of Gloucester. They were ancestors of Pres. Madison; she died 1762; aged eighty-three. Her nephew, Sir Roger Thompson, lived at Blackwell's Neck, in Hanover co. This line became quite numerous, extending through Hanover, Louisa, Goochland and Albemarle, and numbers at the present time numerous Thompsons of Ky. (*Hening XII, 118*.)

1740, Rev. John Thompson, of Scotland, minister of St. Mark's, Culpeper co., married the widow of Gov. Spotswood, 1742. His son, William Thompson was student at Wm. and Mary, 1765, married Sarah, daughter of Charles Carter, of "Cleves," King George co. (*Lee Family and Hayden*). A daughter, Ann, mar. Mr. Francis Thornton, of Fredricksburg. He m. (II) 1760, Eliz. Roots, and had Mildred, John, and Philip Roots Thompson, who m. daughter of R. Slaughter. (*Meade*.)

Attorney General Stephens Thompson's line is represented in the descendants of George Mason, who married his daughter Ann. Another daughter, Mary Thompson, married (I) Robert Booth, of York, and (II) Capt. Graves Packe.

Wiley Thompson, Mem. Congress (1829), from Ga.

Drewry Thompson came to Mobile, Ala., about 1840, and was Clerk of the Court. He married Elisa, daughter of Capt. George, and Sarah (Howard) Conway, of Ala. (*Hayden*.)

William Thompson, Capt. of Va. State Regiment, Rev. Army.

John Thompson, 1st Lt. 7th Va.

David Thompson, 1st Lt. 1st Va.

Cornelius Thompson, 1st Lt. 12th Va.

Anderson Thompson, 2d Lt. 3rd Va.

James Thompson, 1st Lt. 12th Va.

John Thompson, 2d Lt. 1st Va.

Leonard Thompson, 2d Lt. 7th Va.

George Thompson, 1st Lt. of Va. State Reg., 1779.

Robert Thompson, Adjutant.

William and George Thompson received bounty lands, 1784, for serving in the Rev. Army. (*Saffell*.)

1689, William Thompson witnessed deed of Col. Byrd, of Westover, and in the year published that he was going abroad on a visit.—(*Henrico Records.*)

1718, William Thompson bought lands in Charles C'ty county, next to Thomas Hardaway, Jeffrey Munford, George Bates and Robert Crewes.—(*Henrico Records.*)

1759, Edward Watkins *m.* in Cumberland county, Rhoda Thompson.—(*Records.*)

1777, William Thompson died in Charles City county; Edward Marable his administrator.—(*Va. Gazette.*)

Thompson, of North Carolina.

(*From N. C. Colonial Records.*)

WILLIAM THOMPSON (1716). Chowan county, on a jury with Christopher Dudley, Lemuel Taylor, John Beverly and others. -(II. 262.)

Dr. James Thompson (1732), Justice for Chowan county, with Capt. John Pratt, Joseph John Alston, Dr. John Bryant, John Hardy, John Pope, Edward Young and others.—(III, 417.)

James Thompson (1732), Justice of Bertie county, with Thomas Bryant, Benj. Hill, John Edwards.—(III, 556.)

Thomas Thompson (1758), of Orange county, claim against the State for provisions furnished the friendly Indians. (Orange county formed that year.)—(V, 979.)

David Thompson (1754), petition for good roads.—(V, 165.)

David Thompson, "Esq." (1759), Justice Duplin county.—(*VI, 80.*)

Lawrence Thompson (1757), Justice Orange county.—(*V, 813.*)—Mentioned three times.

Andrew Thompson (1760), Member of Assembly from Duplin county. with Wm. McGehee.

Job Thompson dec'd 1761.

William Thompson (1766), exempted from taxation in Johnston county, with Elias Crawford and Alex Parker.

Capt. William Thompson (1768), militia Orange county. to "quell the regulators." He was Justice of Orange that year, with John Oliver; and Colonel in 1771 of county militia.—(*V, 707-710.*)

John Thompson (1768), Justice Halifax county.—(VII, 869.)

Thomas Thompson (1768), counterfeit bill, in Orange county.

Elisha Thompson (1769), petition of grievances with other citizens. John Thompson the same.—(VIII, 80.)

William Thompson, "Esq." (1771), grand jury of Carteret county, and Member of the Assembly, from Carteret, with Jacob Shepard.—(*VIII, 106-303.*)

Descendants of Robert Thompson, of Virginia (Chesterfield County).

ROBERT[1] THOMPSON, goldsmith and planter, *patent* from Sir Edmond Andros, Governor of Virginia (April 23, 1688), for 850 acres in Henrico county (now Chesterfield), Varina parish, on *south side* of James river, "near Falling creek, and Mr. Gowers' line, and also near Walter Clotworthy, for the importation of seventeen persons, viz.: Edward Wise, Thomas Stanhope, Ann Howell, Wm. Blast, Simon Ligon, Cornelius More, John Rockford, ffra. Mathews, John Day, Mary Spencer, Eliz. Turner, Vir. Cowell, Edward Hughs, John Alexander, John Magae, Wm. Holly and John Adams."

In 1693 this tract was increased to 1230 acres, and a new patent secured. (*Book 8, Patents 1689–1695, p. 303, Capitol, Richmond.*)

In 1688 he had also another grant of 390 acres on south side of James river, on *Branches creek.* In 1690, "an act for clearing the river" was passed, and he was one of the *surveyors* for Falling creek.

In 1692 he bought, of John and Mary Woodson, a lot in the town, founded "according to an act for ports," joining Capt. Peter Field, on the river, and on "ye east side of ye market place." (The *Woodsons* owned the lands on which the town was located.)

Church vestrys entered largely into the control of a man's household and morals, and that Robert Thompson, and many of his neighbors, were sometimes given to profanity and other lapses, is recorded in *fines* entered against them in the book, and always promptly collected in *tobacco* (then the currency): " Robert Thompson for swearing once, ' *by God*;' Richard Ligon, for swearing once, ' *by God*;' Col. Thomas Chamberlayne, swearing nine times, and drunk, on his own confession, while serving as Justice ;" also Wm. Drewry, and many others.

Robert Thompson died January, 1697. His wife was Elizabeth Stewart, sister of John Stewart. He left sons, Robert[1] and William[2] Thompson. His estate appraised (8th February, 1696–97) by Seth Ward[*], and Thomas, Christopher and Samuel Branch[†], his neighbors. Among the *personal* property is mentioned his goldsmith's tools. Wife, Elizabeth, executrix. (*Henrico Records*, 1688–1697.)

His widow married Philip Tancock. whose will (p. 1703) mentioned wife, Eliz.; daughters, Mary (by first wife) and Eliz. "To sons-in-law (*step-sons*), Robert and William Thompson, each, a mare." Witnesses: Seth Ward, Sr. and Jr., and also John and Richard Ward.

Will of Mrs. Elizabeth Tancock (11th May, 1703, p. 1st June, 1703), mentions "daughter-in-law" (step-daughter), Mary, and her own daughter, Elizabeth Tancock, to whom she left "that part of Philip Tancock's estate which was left to her" (*Henrico R. 1697, 1705*). "My two sons, Robert and William Thompson;" "my brother, John Stewart, sole executor." Witnesses: John Oglesby, Mary Forest, John Stewart, Jr.[‡] Estate inventoried, by William Cocke, Richard Ward and Thomas Bailey, at £230 97 0. Giles Webb was then justice, and James Cocke clerk of the court.

ROBERT[2] THOMPSON, of Chesterfield county (b. *circa* 1687, d. 1754), "son and heir of Robert Thompson, deceased," made a deed in 1708 of 700 acres on Branch's Creek to Richard Wood—' being part of 1236 acres grant, by *patent* of April, 1693, to Robert Thompson, Sr." Witnesses: Thomas Epes, Thomas Eldridge and Arthur

---

[*]NOTE—John Stuart married Dorothy ——, and died 1706; appraisement of his estate by John Farley, Jr., Henry Walthall, Nicholas Dixon and Samuel Newman. In 1692 he was security on the marriage bond of Bart Stovall and Ann Burton. The son, John Stuart sold lands, in 1748, to John Walthall. (*Records*.)

[†] Christopher Branch, Sr., patent in Henrico county, 1634, and Burgess, 1639, lands in Chesterfield county, at Dutch Gap (he came in 1619, with wife, Mary, and son, Ephraim, in the *London Merchants*). Christopher Branch was Justice in Charles City county (1657), with Henry Isham[§] and Francis Epes.

[‡] John Stewart, Jr., married a daughter of Dr. John Bowman; lived in the era of *horse-racing* in Henrico county, of which some curious facts are preserved in the old records. He and his neighbor, Richard Ward, made bets, in 1697, on "*Bonnie*," owned by Thos. Jefferson, Jr. (grandfather of the President), and " *Wat*," owned by John Hardeman. "*Bonnie*" won, and Ward sued Stewart for his wager, £5. His father, Richard Ward, had been Justice, 1686, as was his grandfather, Seth Ward, 1684—(*Mr. Stanard*)—all of Chesterfield. [*]John Ward, at Varina, 1688.

[§] George Isham (1620), member of the Virginia Land Company, paid £27—(*Brown's Genesis U. S.*). Robert Isham (1635) came to Virginia in " *The Globe*."

An Isham had a patent in Northumberland county as early as 1651, with other patentees—*i. e.*, Richard Wells, Nicholas Meriwether, Francis Clay, Richard Flint, Anthony Steavant, etc.

The name *Isham* in the families of Epes, Oliver, Thompson, Wells, Watkins, is presumed to have descended from Henry Isham, of Henrico, one of its earliest settlers.

James Thompson, of Henrico, made his wife, Mary, his attorney (1731). He willed (1746) half his estate to his wife, Mary, and half to his daughter, Anna; and his son-in-law, Isham Randolph, executor—(*Inventory, 1747*.) (*Records*). Anna, widow of Isham Randolph, of "*Dungeness*," Goochland county (son of William, of Turkey Island), married (II) James Pleasants (parents of Governor Pleasants).

Samuel Thompson (1763) witnessed deed in Henrico.

Isham and Richard Randolph owned, respectively, 6000 and 3148 acres in Amelia county, both sides of Falling Creek.

Will of Mary Thompson (Chesterfield county. January, 1758). Daughter, Ann, wife of John Sturdivant. Grandchildren: Thompson and Mary Eppes Sturdivant. Also granddaughters: Mary, Isham Green and Betty Green.

Moseley. It is said he was twice married. He accumulated much wealth, lending out money with great profit. He must also have kept up the goldsmith business of his father, as eye-glasses from his establishment were long exhibited among his descendants. His last wife was Sarah ——. (So far no data has been secured of his brother, William[8] Thompson.) His will *(March, 1751)* was proved in Chesterfield county; and mentions: Wife, Sarah; sons: ¹*Robert*, ²*Peter*, ³*William*, ⁴*Drury*, ⁵*Isham*, ⁶*John Farley*; daughters: ⁷*Sarah*, ⁸*Elisabeth*, ⁹*Mary*, ¹⁰*Martha*. Of these, nothing is recorded of Peter and Elizabeth Thompson in the family annals. Of the rest:

1. ROBERT² THOMPSON (b. Chesterfield county, Va.), removed to Amelia county, Va., and owned lands on Deep Creek in 1746 *(Records)*. Wife not known. Among his children were: Robert Thompson, Jr., Eleanor, and a son, who was father of Jesse Thompson, who m. daughter of Samuel Watkins, of Alabama. Of these:

    1 ROBERT³ THOMPSON, called *"Old Blue"* (b. Amelia county, 1757—died, Belle Mina, Madison county, Ala., 1831), moved to Petersburg, Ga., with his relatives, after Revolution. He engaged in merchandising with his sister's husband, Sam'l Watkins. He kept the *specie* of the firm in *blue denim bags* (made for the purpose), hence his *soubriquet*. He became wealthy, and finally removed with his two sons-in-law to Huntsville, Ala.; married in Virginia (1778) his cousin Sarah, (b. Virginia, 20 June, 1760—   ) *only* daughter of James² (b. 1728) and Martha (Thompson) Watkins. Issue: 1. Sophia⁴, 2. Parmelia⁴, 3. Eliza⁴:

        1. Sophia⁴ Thompson, b. *circa* 1780, living in 1846, m. DR. JAMES MANNING, who came with his brother, DANIEL MANNING*, from New Jersey, to Georgia. Issue:

    1. Sarah Sophia⁵, 2. Robert J.⁵, 3. James⁵, 4. Felix⁵, 5. Peyton⁵, 6. William⁵, as follows:

    (1.) SARAH SOPHIA⁵ MANNING) b. *circa* 1802) m. Gen. Bartley M. Lowe, of Huntsville, Ala., (born in Edgefield District, S. C.), General of militia, 1836, in Indian war; President of Branch Bank of Huntsville until 1844. Head of a commission house in New Orleans. Their lovely old residence in Huntsville, *"The Grove,"* is greatly admired as a representative *Southern home*, both in architecture and hospitality. Issue:

    I. Dr. John Thomas⁶ Lowe, graduate Univ. of Penn., 1857, C. S. A., Surgeon in Chief of General Loring's Division.
    II. Sophie⁶ Lowe, died 1897, a fine social light of Huntsville, and a most attractive woman; married Col. Nicholas Davis, son of Nicholas Davis, of Virginia. Issue:

        1. Lowe⁷ Davis, a sad and tragic fate of dissipation, m. Miss Meriwether, of Memphis.
        2. Nicholas⁷ Davis.
        3. Sophie Lowe⁷ Davis.

    III. Susan⁷ Lowe m. Clinton, brother of Col. Nicholas Davis. No issue.
    IV. Bartley M.⁷ Lowe m. Fannie Jolly, of Huntsville. Several children.
    V. Robert J.⁷ Lowe (d. 1864), C. S. A., 4th Ala. Regiment, 1st Co.; Ala. Legislature 1859; m. Mattie Holden, who m. (II) Capt. Sydney Fletcher. Issue:
        1. Robert⁸ Lowe.
        2. Son⁸. Name not given.
    VI. Col. William M⁷. Lowe (   ), C. S. A. 4th Ala. Regiment, afterward on the staffs of Genls. Clanton and Withers. Captured at battle of Franklin, and imprisoned at Camp Chase on Lake Erie, and at Fort Delaware. Ala. Legislature 1870—U. S. Congress.
    VII. Sarah⁷ Lowe unmarried, lives at the old home, in Huntsville.
    VIII. Lucy⁷ Lowe also unmarried, and at the old home.

---

* Daniel Manning's son, Reeder Manning, m. Martha Lewis (sister to Watkins Thompson's wife). He was a prominent lawyer of Mobile, Ala.

(2) ROBERT.[3] J. MANNING (b. 1804, living in 1846) *m.* Louisiana (his cousin), daughter of Dr. Asa and Mary (Watkins) Thompson. Hers was a refined and perfect beauty, with great piety to support her many sorrows. She was born in Elbert county, Ga., and with her cousin, Mary Frances Watkins (daughter of Robert H. Watkins), attended school in Augusta, Ga. After her marriage lived a while in Texas. With a dissipated husband, her trials were many. In an attack of diphtheria the operation of tracheotomy was performed, and she breathed through a silver tube. The latter years of her life were spent in patient waiting for the end.

(3) JAMES[4] MANNING, of Macon, Ala., (b. 1806, d. 1849), prominent in the Methodist Church, *m.* Indiana, daughter of Dr. Asa Thompson. Issue: Mary Sophia (b. 1832), Louisiana (1834), Josephine (1837), Reeder (1839). (For these see *Asa Thompson*).

(4) DR. FELIX[4] MANNING, of Aberdeen, Miss., (   ) *m.* Sarah Millwater, 2nd daughter of the Rev. Mrs. Turner Saunders (by her first marriage). Mrs. Millwater was born 1793.) Issue:

   I. James[7] Manning (d. 1896) *m.* (I) Mrs. Sims, and (II) (a daughter of Reeder Manning (his cousin) and his wife, Martha Lewis (sister of Mrs. Watkins Thompson). Issue: Mary Manning.
   II. Henrietta[7] Manning d. s. p.
   III. Peyton[7] Manning, *m.* Julia Watson, and d. s. p., and she *m.* (II) Dr. Duncan, of Columbus.
   IV. Thomas[7] Manning, of Mobile, Ala.
   V. Mary Paine[7] Manning, *m.* Maunsel White Chapman, of Clay county, Miss., (and formerly of New Orleans). Issue: Virginia, and a son deceased.
   VI. Virginia[7] Manning, *m.* F. Winston Garth. Issue: 1, Mary. 2, Willis.
   VII. Sophie[7] Manning, *m.* Rev. R. K. Brown, of M. E. Church South. Her loveliness is unexcelled among her relations.

(5) PEYTON[4] MANNING, C. S. A., on staff of General Longstreet (1861), m. Sarah, daughter of Dr. William Weeden, of Huntsville; both dead. Issue:

   I. Felix[7] Manning, M. D., Belton, Texas; married.
   II. Julia[7] Manning, m. (1) John O. Cummings, of Mobile, Ala., and married again in Belton, Texas.
   III. James Manning, married in Mexico, and living in El Paso.
   IV. Ada Manning, m. (I) —— Price, and (II) —— Densel, Abilene, Texas.
   V. Frank Manning.
   VI. John Manning.
   VII. William Manning. All in Texas.

(6) WILLIAM[4] MANNING, of Montgomery county, Ala. (died 1864), m. Elizabeth, daughter of Dr. Wm. Weeden, of Huntsville, Ala. Several children, of whom—
   1. Fannie Manning m. Mr. Peabody, of Georgia.
   2. Elizabeth married Matthew R. Marks.
   3. Sarah, and others, all in Texas.

2. Pamelia[2] Thompson, 2d daughter of Robert and Sarah (Watkins) Thompson (and living in 1847), m. Thomas Bibb (d. Huntsville, Ala., 20 Sept., 1839), of Elbert county, Ga., who as second Governor of Alabama, succeeded his brother, Dr. William Wyatt Bibb. Issue:
   1, Adeline[3]; 2, Emily[3]; 3, Thomas[3]; 4, William Dandridge[3]; 5, Porter[3]; 6, Elmira[3]; 7, Robert Thompson[3]; 8, Eliza P.[3]—See Bibb Family.

3. Eliza[2] Thompson, 3d daughter of Robert and Sarah (Watkins) Thompson, *m.* Dr. Waddy Tate (2d wife). Issue:
   Two sons and two daughters, all now dead.

   2. ELEANOR[4] THOMPSON, sister of "*Old Blue*" (born in Amelia county, Va., 1768), *m.* (*circa* 1787) Samuel (b. 1765), son of James and Martha (Thompson) Watkins, her

cousin. He was merchant and planter of Petersburg, Ga., and a partner of his brother-in-law, Robert Thompson, and removed to Lawrence county, Ala., in 1821. Issue: 1, Eliza[2]; 2, Paul, J.[3] "Don"; 3, Eleanor[3]; 4, Elmira[3]; 5, Edgar[3]. (For these, see *Watkins Family*.)

II. Peter[3] Thompson, nothing known of him.

III. William[3] Thompson, (b. Chesterfield county, Va.), married Mary, daughter of Thomas Wells, of Va.; some say Thomas Wells was from Augusta county, Va. (See *Wells*.) Issue: 1, William[4]; 2, Wells[4]; 3, Robert[4], d. s. p.; 4, Asa[4]; 5, Prudence[4]; 6, Sarah[4]; 7, Mary[4]; 8, Frances[4], as follows:

1. WILLIAM[4] THOMPSON, of Morgan county, Ala., called "*Uncle Billy Kieley*," m. his cousin, Henrietta Williams, and removed from his plantation in Elbert county, Ga., (humorously called by the family "*Kieley Castle*," says Mrs. Martha Harris, in 1896) to Ala., in its early settlement. This hospitable and lovable old couple lived near Huntsville, Ala., and it was the delight of the neighboring young people to visit them. Issue: 1, John[5]; 2, William[5]; 3, Mary[5]; 4, Asa[5]; 5, Elbert[5]; 6, Caroline[5]; 7, Elizabeth[5]; 8, Hartwell[5]; 9, Prudence[5], as follows:

  1. John[5] Thompson (b. Elbert county, Ga.), and m. in Georgia. Issue: 1, Edwin ; 2, George[6]; 3, Joseph[6], and others not known.

  2. William[5] Thompson (b. Elbert county Ga.). Issue not known.

  3. Nancy[5] Thompson (b. Elbert county, Ga.) m. Dr. Frederick Weeden, of Huntsville, Ala.; removed to Florida. Issue not known.

  4. Asa[5] Thompson (b. Elbert county, Ga).

  5. Elbert[5] Thompson (b. Elbert county, Ga).

  6. Caroline[5] Thompson (b. Elbert county, Ga.), m. Wm. Rogers.

  7. Elizabeth[5] Thompson (b. Elbert county, Ga.) m. Walter Troup, of Georgia.

  8. Hartwell[5] Thompson, of Columbus, Miss. (b.Elbert county, Ga.; d. Columbus, Miss., 1843) m. Martha (b. Va.; d. Columbus, Miss. 1843); daughter of Francis and Nancy (Wyatt) Scott. The Scotts were then living in Lawrence county, Ala. Mrs. Scott was sister to Gov. Bibb's mother, (who was also a Wyatt,) and died in Lawrence county at the house of Mrs. Unity Moseley, near Wheeler in 1836.—(See *Bibb and Scott Families*.) Issue, all born in Lawrence county, Ala.:

    1. Francis Scott[6] m. (I) a daughter of Joseph Sykes, and (II) Mrs. Outlaw; several children by first wife (names not known), and Baird[7] and Scott[7] Thompson by the second, and now living in Florida; 2, Thomas Burton d. y. 3, DeWitt[6], m. ——; no issue; 4, Elbert H[6], m.——; no issue; 5, Sarah[6]; 6, Julia Scott[6] (b. Morgan county, Ala.); m. Milton Odeneal, of Columbus, Miss.; no issue.

  9. Prudence[5] Thompson (——) m. Rev. Mr. Williams. Issue (if any) unknown.

2. WELLS[4] THOMPSON, of Georgia, (——) m. Betty Alston. No issue. Left his estate to his nephew, Watkins Thompson, Ala.

3. ROBERT[4], d. s. p.

4. DR. ASA[4] W. THOMPSON, of Georgia and of Huntsville, Ala., (d. 1832) m. (15th January, 1801) Mary, called "Polly" (b. 1784, d. 1835), daughter of James (b. 1758), and Jane (Thompson) Watkins, of Elbert county, Ga. They moved to Madison county, Mullin's Flat, near Huntsville, Ala., and near his brother, William Thompson, and his cousin Robert Thompson, "*Old Blue.*" He died young, and she was left to rear their children alone. Issue:

  1. Louisiana[5], 2. Asa Watkins[5], 3. Wells[5], 4. Indiana, 5. Isaphena[5], 6. Darwin[5], 7. Elbert Asa[5], as follows:

  1. Louisiana[5] Thompson (b. 1806, d. 1862) m. her cousin, Robert Thompson (*ante*).

  2. Asa Watkins[5] Thompson, Sumter county, Ala., (b. 1810, d. 1840); removed to Sumter county from Madison county, Ala., after death of his parents, and engaged in cotton planting; was killed by accidental discharge of his gun in a deer hunt; married Ann (b. 1809, d. 1894), daughter of Davis Lewis, of Hancock

county, Ga. Her sister, Martha Lewis, married Judge A. Reeder Manning, of Mobile, Ala. After the tragic death of her husband, Mrs. Thompson removed to Matagorda county, Texas, and settled near her brother, James Lewis, and her brothers-in-law, Darwin and Elbert Asa Thompson, and lived to the ripe age of 85. Issue:

1. Asa Watkins Thompson.
2. Hon. Wells Thompson, Columbus, Tex. (b. 1840, six months after father's death). Captain in C. S. A.; bears five honorable scars. Member of State Convention of 1868. District Attorney and Member of State Senate. President of the State Senate. Lieutenant-Governor of Texas, and appointed by act of Legislature to Codify and Digest the Laws of Texas. Is District Judge. Now engaged in extensive planting (1898); married Carrie Tait, of Columbus, Tex., great-granddaughter of Judge Charles Tait, U. S. Senator, from Georgia, and afterward U. S. Federal Judge of Alabama. No issue. Judge Thompson is the last male representative of his line.
3. Wells[r] Thompson, M. D., of Monroe county, Miss., and Waco, Tex. (b. 1812, d. 1866), married Louisa, daughter of James Harrison, of Columbus Miss., a distinguished lawyer, who was father also of Col. Isham Harrison, of Columbus, Miss., and of Mrs. Matt. Clay.—(See *Waddy Thompson Line*). No issue.
4. Indiana[s] Thompson (b. 1814, died 1871) married her cousin, James Manning, of Macon, Ala. (b. 1806, d. 1849), who was of great piety. Issue:
   1. Mary Sophia[6] Manning (b. 1832) married (1854) Dr. William F. Drummond, of Petersburg. Va., who claimed ancestry, of many centuries, though the Duke of Perthshire, Scotland, and asserted himself the hereditary Duke in America. Issue: 1, James Manning[7] (d. 1895); 2, John (d. 1868); 3, Eliza Clarke[r] m. William A. Gaines, and has Thomas B.[6], Mary D.[6] and F. Drummond[6] Gaines; 4, Thomas Fletcher[7] Drummond m. (1886), Annie L. Shields, four girls and two boys; 5, Richard[7] Drummond m. (1895) L. Janie Agee, three boys; 6, William Clarke[7] Drummond m. (1895) Mary I. Henderson, two boys; 7, Mary Sophia[7] Drummond m. (1889) James W. Hudgins, Hampden, Ala., five boys; 8, Allen Percy[7] Drummond, unm.; 9. George Douglass Percy, unm.
   2. Lou[s] Manning (b. 1834) married (1858) William W. Harder. Both dead. Issue: 1. Son[7], married in Texas. 2. Son[7], married in Texas. 3. Lila[7], married Asa Skinner—no issue. 4. India[7] married Lee Dandridge and has three boys and two girls. 5. Julian[7], married (1898) Pattie —— (name not known).
   3. Josephine[s] Manning (b. 1837), m. her cousin, Reeder Manning (both dead). Issue: 1. Daughter[7], m. Sidney Mann, of Georgia. 2. Son[7], married in the North, 3. Son[7], unm. All living in New York.
   4. Reeder[s] Manning (b. 1839) m. J. J. Archer, of Marengo county, Ala. No issue.
   5. Indiana[s] Manning m. Alex. H. Archer (brother of above), and is living in Dayton, Marengo county. Ala. Children: two girls and one boy.
5 Isaphena Thompson (b. 1816) m. Dr. John Bassett,* of Huntsville, Ala. (who was

---

*The ancestor was Richard Bassett, signer of Declaration of Independence, and Governor pro tem. of Delaware.

Isaac (born 8th March, 1763, in Delaware, d. in Baltimore 6th July, 1809) m. Nancy Davidson, of Baltimore. Issue: 1, Isaac; 2, Richard; 3, Henry Willis; 4, *Dr. John*, m. Isaphena Thompson, of Huntsville; 5, William; 6, Frank; 7, Marguerite.

Miss Bassett, of Virginia. who married Benjamin Harrison, signer of the Declaration, and Governor of Virginia, was probably nearly related to Richard Bassett, the signer, of Delaware.

Capt. William Bassett was Burgess for New Kent county, Va., 1692.

William Bassett, of New Kent, was student at William and Mary College, 1720. (*See Carter Tree, of Virginia.*)

of a distinguished family of that name, and died young). She was noted for her cheerful spirit and droll sense of humor, the life of every gathering of friends, and withal of great piety and charity. Issue:

(1) Dr. Henry Willis[6] Bassett, a physician of note; inherited his mother's fine genial wit and popularity. Life ended sadly, in an altercation, in which he was killed; married Carrie Neal, of Huntsville, Ala. His widow moved to Texas. Issue: I. Neal[7]. II. Wells Thompson[7]; both now living in Waco, Texas.

(2) Watkins[6] Bassett, d. y. and unmarried.

(3) Alice Lee[6] Bassett m. D. B. Young. Issue: I. Bassett[7]. II. Nannie[7], m. Mr. Boynton (living in Waco, Tex.) III. Henry Willis[7]. IV. Berenice[7]. V. Benj. Lee[7]. VI. Lenore[7]. VII. Laura[7].

(4) Laura[6] has never married—a noble and talented woman.

(5) Lenore[6].

(6) John[6] Bassett, d. y.

(7) William[6] Bassett.

6. Darwin S. P.[5] Thompson (of age in 1846), died s. p. 1874 Matagorda county, Texas; lame, and very talented. In his papers was found a long list of the Thompsons.

7. Elbert Asa[6] Thompson, (b. 1817, d. July 31, 1854), married (May 6, 1846) his cousin Anna (b. 1824), a daughter of Col. Benjamin and Martha (Watkins) Taliaferro, of Demopolis, Ala. They removed to Watagorda county with their relations. Issue: 1, Louisiana[6], m. Harris, W. Bowie, no issue; 2, Martha d. s. p.; 3, Elberta Asa, nsm. Has given much information of her own line, in which she takes great interest. Mrs. Thompson m. (II) 5 Oct., 1856, Dr. Robert H. Chinn, and had Richard I. Chinn; all of Watagorda county, Texas. (See Taliaferro).

5. Prudence[4] Thompson (born in Virginia) came to Georgia with her relatives, and married Walker Richardson. Issue:

1. Dr. William[5] Richardson, of Petersburg, Ga., (b.   , d. 1855), where he practiced his profession with Dr. John Watkins, who was afterwards of Burnt Corn, Monroe county, Ala.; married (1811) Susan (b. 1790), widow of John Oliver, of Petersburg (2nd wife), and daughter of James and Jane (Thompson) Watkins, of Elbert county, Savannah river. Issue:

  1. Mary[6] Richardson married Gabriel Toombs, brother of the great orator, Robert Toombs, of Georgia. 2. Sarah Willis[6] Richardson m. —— Thompson, of Barbour county, Ala. 3. Louisa[6] Richardson m. —— Thompson (brother to above). 4. Walker[6] Richardson, m. Miss Sanford, of Barbour county, Ala. 5. William[6] Richardson. 6. James[6] Richardson. 7. Martha[6] Richardson. Descendants not given.

6. Sarah[4] Thompson (b. in Virginia) m. —— Harper (or Peterson) and died without issue.

7. Mary[4] Thompson (born in Virginia) married James, son of Dionysius Oliver, of Broad River, Elbert county, Ga. (His first wife.) Issue: 1. Simeon[5] Oliver, of Hernando, Miss. (For these See Oliver Family.)

8. Frances Wells[4] Thompson (b. in Virginia, circa, 1769; d. Petersburg, Elbert county, Ga., 1808) m. (1787) John Oliver (b. circa 1765), son of Dionysius Oliver, of Broad River, Elbert county, Ga., (his first wife). (His second wife was Susan Watkins, who married (2nd) Dr. William Richardson). Issue:

  1. Prudence T[5]. (b. 1788). 2. Sarah[5]. 3. Mary Xenia[5]. 4. John[5] (b 1800) and others. (For these, see Watkins, Bibb and Oliver Families.)

IV. DRURY[3] THOMPSON married Eleanor, daughter of Peter (or Thomas), and Anne (MaCartie) Oliver. A daughter, Jane[4] Thompson, married Robert H. Watkins (b.

1762), son of James Watkins (b. 1728), and had several children. No other descendants known.

V. ISHAM[4] THOMPSON[6] (b. Chesterfield co. Va.) married Mary Ann (b. 1742), daughter of Peter (or Thomas), and Ann (MaCartie) Oliver. Issue:

1, JANE[4] THOMPSON (b. 1762, d. 2d August, 1815); m. (27th February, 1779). James Watkins (b. 1758), son of James Watkins (b. 1728), and Martha Thompson (b. 1737.) Issue:

1, Garland Thompson[6]; 2, Robert H[6].; 3 Mary[6]; 4, Sarah[6]; 5, Martha[6]; 6, Jane[6]; 7, Susan[6]; 8, Elizabeth[6]; 9, James[6]; 10, Sophia[6]; 11, Theophilus[6]. (For descendants see Watkins Family.)

2, Sarah[3] Thompson married Daniel Marshall, of Va. Issue not known.

3, Mary[4] Thompson, d. s. p.

VI. JOHN FARLEY[4] THOMPSON, nothing known of him.

VII. SARAH[4] THOMPSON (b. Chesterfield co., Va.) married Thomas Burton†; and nothing further known of her.

VIII. ELIZABETH[6] THOMPSON. Nothing known of her.

IX. MARY[6] THOMPSON (b. Chesterfield county, Va.) married Archibald Farley. Descendants not known. John Farley, mentioned above, is probably related.‡

X. MARTHA[3] THOMPSON (b. Va., 10th December, 1787, d. Elbert county, Ga., 20th October, 1808) m. (20th November, 1755) James (b. 1728), son of William Watkins, of Chesterfield county, Va. Issue:

1. William[4], b. 1756; 2. James[4], b. 1758; 3. Sarah[4], b. 1760 (only daughter, who m. Robert Thompson, above); 4. Robert H[4]., b. 1762; 5. Samuel[4], b. 1765; 6. John[4], b. 1768; 7. Thompson[4], b. 1770; 8. Joseph[4], b. 1772; 9. Isham, b. 1774.

(For these see Watkins Family.)

WELLS FAMILY NOTES.

Thomas Wells (1620), member of "Virginia Company of Adventurers and Planters," (second charter,) and mercer, of London.

Richard Wells (1635), came in the " Globe," aged 26.

Robert Wells (1635), came to Virginia, aged 30, in the "Thomas."—(Hotten.)

William Wells (1636), Eliz. City county, "at the head of Hampton river."

Thomas Wells (1647), 200 acres in upper Norfolk, on Elizabeth river.

Richard Wells (1647), Burgess for upper Norfolk.—(Va. Carolorum).

Richard Wells (1651), 1000 acres in Northumberland county, Va., Annesley's creek.

John Wells (1697), deceased in Northumberland county.

Richard Wells (1658), 100 acres in Westmoreland county. "Wells Point," in Westmoreland.

Richard Wells (1646), summoned to give guardianship account to the Orphans' Court of York county; as well, also, Richard Dudley and Capt. Christopher Colthorpe.

---

*Appraisement and division of estate of Isham Thompson on record in Amelia county; also wills of Samuel, Robert (1783), and Peter Thompson (1785).

NOTE—†Thomas Burton, of Henrico co., died 1685. Susan, his wife, administratrix. Robert Burton, 1666, imported six persons into Va., and was Surveyor of the Highways, with Thomas Jefferson, grandfather of the President. (Henrico Records.)

NOTE—‡Henry Farley (1740). 318 acres in Amelia county, on Flat Creek; and in 1745, William Farley, Sr. and Jr., and Daniel Farley owned, each, 400 acres in Amelia county (Records). The "C-tie" gives "Francis, Thomas, John and Matthew Farley, all born in Bedford" (then Lunenburg county), where they appeared after 1734, and Francis had a son, Drury Farley.

John Farley was a planter in Henrico (now Chesterfield), 1684. James Parke Farley married Elizabeth daughter of Col. Wm. Byrd, of "Westover," and Elizabeth Carter, of " Shirley" (Lee Family) Thomas Farley patented "Archer's Hope," James City county, 1638; wife, Jane, and daughter, Ann.

Richard Wells (1647), deed of gift to children of Eleanor Robinson, of cattle.—
(*York Records, 1633–1794, p. 644.*)

John Wells (1657), witness of will of John Fletcher, in York county.—(*York R.,
1638–1648.*)

Thomas Wells (1661), on a jury in York county.

Emanuel Wells (1690), suit vs. Thomas Montford (*1687–1691.*)

Thomas Wells (1700), suit vs. Capt. Charles Hansford.)—(*York R., 1694–1702.*)

William and Elias Wells (1702), witnesses in York—Elias, administrator of David
Condon.

John and Emanuel Wells (1676), escheat lands, 100 acres, in Warwick county,
Mulberry Island parish, and John (1682), 255 acres west side Warwick river.

Emanuel (1682), 420 acres, west side of Warwick river.

Ancoretta Wells married (1679) Robert Thomas, of Middlesex county, Va.

Thomas Wells (1665), patent in Henrico county for 700 acres.

Thomas Wells (1672), 560 acres, Henrico county, on north side of Appomattox.—
(*Henrico Land Book.*)

THOMAS WELLS (1677) was assessed *Tithables*, in "*Turkey Island Precinct*," to equip
soldiers (during Bacon's Rebellion). He was called "father" (step-father) by William
Harris,* who, with his wife, Mary (b. 1642), made him a deed (1677), in which they
relinquished their title to a deed of gift of land, from Thomas Wells, which he formerly
gave them, "to have and to enjoy in the same manner and form as he gave it to us,
and if Richard Holmes, who is now in possession of one parcel of said house and land,
do leave the said plantation, that the rights and privileges return to my father-in-law,
Thomas Wells." Witnesses: Thomas Cheatham and Thomas Gregory.—(*York R.
Minutes of 1682–1701.*)

Thomas Wells and wife, Grace (1679), of ye plantation of "*Northhampton*," in
Bristol parish, Henrico (now Chesterfield) county, sold to Richard Holmes, of said
parish, "a parcel of land called '*Scurvy Hill*,' (100 acres) next to Maj. Thomas Chamberlayne (being the line formerly had by William Harris), and being 'a part of the land
granted to said Thomas Wells by Sir William Berkley, Knight, Governor, and Captain
General of Virginia, under the hand and seal of this Colony, ye 28th October, 1672, as by
said Pattent appears.' "—(*Records, 1677–1692*).

In 1680, Col. Wm. Byrd, of Henrico county, made him a deed to 100 acres of land,
"now in possession of Richard Holmes," the said lands "being imagined to be a part
of Sir John Zouche's† Pattent, lately escheated and granted to Mr. Abel Gower, and
since assigned to *me*."—(*Recorded in 1690.*)

He was on a jury in 1678. Had Indian slaves, and in 1683, one was taken up and
returned to him by *Tomakin*, a Pamunkey Indian, "living at ye Appomattox Indian

---

*The immigrant of this family was Capt. Thomas Harris, of the Virginia Company (b. 1587);
came with Sir Thos. Dale, 1611, Burgess, Charles City, 1632–33. His children were: Major William,
Justice and Burgess, of Charles City, 1657 (d. 1678), wife Lucy. Thomas, d. 1679, and Mary, b. 1635,
married Col. Thomas Ligon, of Henrico county, justice 1657, and had Richard, b. 1657, and Hugh
Ligon; Major William Harris, Burgess, was father of 1, Thomas, of Henrico (will, p. 1730), 2. John, of
Cumberland (will proved 1751), whose daughter, Eliz. m. (1748), Samuel Flournoy, of Powhatan
county, and 3, William, of Henrico. 1657, Mr. Thomas Ligon. Justice in Charles City county, who
bought a tract of land from Col. Wm. Byrd on James river, 1692. (*See Harris Genealogy by W. G.
Stanght.*)

†Sir John Zouch, of the old Derbyshire family, was a Puritan, and had served in the Netherlands.
In 1627 he was recommended for the governorship of Virginia, and while not appointed, he was one
of the King's commissioners (in 1631) to consider the condition of Virginia. In 1634 he came, with
his son and daughter, to live in Henrico county (then including Chesterfield); daughter Isabel and son
John] ("who lost £350 in the iron works, as well as much more of his father's, because others
neglected to join them in their designs"); (will 1636). His grant is not on record, but Mr. R. A.
Brock says "there is evidence of his having taken up 567 acres, as, in 1681, William Bird, of Westover,
made a deed to 567 acres, lately the property of Sir John Zouch, Kn't, and *escheated*." (*Wm. and
Mary Quarterly, I, 233*).

town." He acknowledged to his Vestry, in 1689, that "he had been drinking," and paid his *fine* in tobacco, as did many of the best of his neighbors.

The court had granted him a separation in 1686 from his wife, Grace, who was, he said, such a termagent he was "afraid to live with her."

Thomas Wells (1690) sold to Hugh Ligon, a part of his plantation "*Northampton*" for 8080 pounds tobacco; next to Maj. Thos. Chamberlayne, on the north side of the *Appomattox River*. His wife, Mary Wells, signed the deed.

In 1691, he and Hugh Ligon, together, made deed to the tract of 100 acres, (called "Scurvy Hill," which they owned in common,) to Richard Holmes, "being a part of a greater dividend granted to Thomas Wells by patent from Sir William Berkley, 1672." Mary, wife of Thomas Wells, and Elizabeth, wife of Hugh Ligon, relinquished their dower. In 1693 he was on the Grand Jury, with Thomas Holmes, Ed Jones, Hugh Jones, Henry Turner and others.

Thomas Wells' will (*1st October, 1696*), mentions "wife, Mary, and daughter, Mary (not yet fifteen). To son, *Thomas Wells, jr.*, all his lands and servants (he also not fifteen)." Thomas Parker married the widow, and in 1697, he and his wife, Mary Parker,* give bond "for the administration of the estate of Mr. Thomas Wells."— (*Henrico Records, 1688-1697.*)

(Thomas Parker, living in Varina parish, Charles City (Henrico), 1632, probably father.)

Thomas Wells, jr., born Bristol parish, Chesterfield county, 1695, *m.*, and had, among others, Mary, b. 17—, *m.* William Thompson, son of Robert, above.

William and Sarah Wells, of Bristol, Pa., has issue: Anne Wells (b. 1724).

William and Frances Wells, of Bristol, Pa., had issue: William (b. 1728), David (b. 1730), Phoebe (b. 1732), Frances (b. 1741), Isham (b. 1743).

Abraham, and Sarah Wells, of Bristol, Pa., had issue: Reuben (b. 1731), Abraham (b. 1733).

Abraham and Amy Wells had issue: Jane (b. 1735).

Adam and Eleanor Wells had issue: Mary (b. 1734), Anne (b. 1735), *Drury* (b. 1741), Sarah (b. 1743), Pattie (b. 1746), Randolph (b. 1749).

Barnabas and JoyceWells had issue: Margaret (b. 1634).

David and Sarah Wells had issue: Jeremiah (b. 1735).

Richard and Hannah Wells had issue: Richard (b. 1747).

Blandford Church. Petersburg, was built (1736) on *Well's Hill*. (*All from Bristol parish Register*).

William Wells (1726), 200 acres in Prince George county, on Picture Branch.

Barnaby Wells (1743) 578 acres, in Amelia county, on Flat and Molloy creeks.

John Wells (1749), 354 acres, in Amelia county, on south side of Lazaretta creek.

Thompson Wells (1765), 605 acres, in Lunenburg county.

William Wells (1795), 580 acres, in Amelia, south side of Nottoway River.

William Wells, of Lunenburg (1768), received a letter through the postoffice at Petersburg, Dinwiddie county, which was then the mailing point for all that part of Virginia. Wells Thompson, of Mecklenburg, had also a letter at that date. (These two counties were taken from Brunswick county 1740, and Brunswick from Surry 1720).

Samuel Wells, private in Armand's corps, Revolutionary war (Saffell).

One of the Wells family owned the Tavern at Nottoway, C. H., and fought the famous duel with John Raudolph, of Roanoke.

Isham Wells, of Charlotte county (1776), advertised a stray horse—on the little Roanoke river.—(*Virginia Gazette, 1776*).

Drury Wells, of Dinwiddie county 1776.—(*Ibid.*)

---

*Mary Parker married William Burton. John Burton's will, 1689, mentions children: Robert, *William*, Rachel, Elizabeth Glover, and grandchildren: Mary, William, and Elizabeth Davis.

John Wells, Major of Second Virginia, released by British from prison 1780.— (*Saffell.*)

John S. Wells (1787), Represented Isle of Wight county, with John Lawrence.— (*Va Almanack* 1787.)

Benj. Wells, of Mulberry, Ireland, 1775, was "much troubled by Lord Dunmore's *banditti.*"

Mrs. Wells, of Warwick county, *m.* (1773) Rev. Wm. Bland, who *m.* (secondly) a daughter of President William Yates, of William Mary College.

* Abraham Wells (1756), 200 acres in Dinwiddie county.

William Wells (1759), also with land in Dinwiddie county.

The old *brick church* was built on "*Well's* Hill," near Petersburg. Dinwiddie county, on land of John Lowe 1736; Col. Thomas Ravenscroft agreeing to build the church for £485. Williams Wells, Jr., with others, helped to run the parish line in 1746. The Wells family is said to be of Welsh descent.

THOMAS WELLS, of Virginia, above, with whose descendants the Thompsons intermarried, had one son and two daughters.

Mrs. Martha (Watkins) Taliaferro wrote in 1859 that his son and a daughter had also been well married among the best families of Virginia, but omitted the names of the two.

Mary Wells, the second daughter, married William Thompson. They were parents of Mrs. John and Mrs. James Oliver, who lived in Elbert county, Ga. (1788).

"COL. GEORGE WELLS, of Amelia county," writes Col. J. P. Fitzgerald, of Farmville, Va., "had two daughters: Hannah and Susannah. One of them married Mr. Foster, and had son, George Wells Foster, who moved to Georgia about 1790. He married Elizabeth Julia, (daughter of Thomas Flournoy,) of Prince Edward county (who was born in 1730). Issue:

1. Ann Martin Foster married Dr. Lovick Pierce, of M. E. Ch. South. (Parents of Bishop George Pierce.)

2. Judge Thomas Flournoy Foster, of Georgia. Born Greensboro, Ga., where he studied law (with Matthew Wells, Esq.), after 1812.

The second daughter of Colonel Wells (above), married Mr. Vance, and was mother of Frederick Vance, of Virginia, great-grandfather of Col. Fitzgerald's wife."

"These Wells, "Colonel Fitzgerald adds: "were from Lunenburg county, Va."

Thomas F. Wells, in 1822, was Attorney General of Georgia.

MARTHA WELLS, married *circa* 1752, Col. Thomas Green. Their 3rd child, Thomas Marston Green, was born in James City county, Va., 1758.

He was Member of Congress from Mississippi, 1802. "Mr. Green traced his lineage through his maternal grandmother to the distinguished English Howard family of which the Earl of Surry, afterwards Duke of Norfolk, was the head, and whose daughter, Catherine Howard, was 5th wife of Henry VIII and Queen of England. He was

---

In 1678 Colonel Ligon, Richard Cooke, Henry Watkins and Gilbert Jones surveyed "Mawburne Hills." Thomas Ligon had patented 800 acres in 1668.

Hugh Ligon m. (1665) Ellis., daughter of Wm. Walthall (who d. 1690). She was sister to William, Richard and Henry Walthall. Richard Ligon (b. 1657) m. Mary Worsham, daughter of Mrs. Eliz. Epes (who d. 1678), her first husband, John Worsham.

William Ligon (will 1689), mentions wife, Mary. Children: William, Thomas, John, Joseph and Mary. Legacy to Thos. Farrar, Jr.; witnesses, John Worsham, Robt. Hancock and Richard Ligon. The widow bought lands on Swift's Creek in 1692.

Wm. Ligon (d. 1694) m. Mary, daughter of Joseph and Mary Tanner. Mrs. Tanner had m. (II 1678 Gilbert Platt, who died 1691. Complaining of bad treatment from his wife and stepson, Joseph Tanner, he left his property to Edward Osborne and wife (brother of Thomas, and son of Thomas Osborne, Sr.), because "they cared for him in his last illness."

Hugh Ligon's mother, Mrs. Mary Ligon, deposed, in 1689, that "Hugh Ligon's sister-in-law, Mrs. Platt, had accused him of taking her corn out of her crib." In 1690 he had a deed from Thomas and Mary Wells of a part of Wells' plantation, called "Northampton," north side Appomattock's river, and with Thos. Wells, he sold, in 1691, the tract called "Scurvy Hill" to Richard Holmes.

also cousin of Gen'l. Green Clay, of Kentucky, the father of the latter having married a sister of Col. Thomas Green." (*Liberty Herald*, Miss. 1897.)

Ralph Green, Patent 1653, of Vestry of Petsworth pa., Gloucester county, Va., after 1677, and later Patent of Oliver Green, 1651.

Thomas Green, Sr. and Jr., 1714. Robert Green's lands, in Kingston pa., near ,the head of North river, 1768, and next to Dr. John Symmers, dec'd. (*Old Survey Book*.)

William Green, 1747. Vestry of St. Marks, Culpeper county, in place of Robert Green, dec'd. (*Meade*.)

In 1775, Maj. John Green entered Continental service, and Richard Yancey was chosen vestryman in his place.

WATKINS GLEANINGS.

Ancient arms of Watkins in England, after the Conquest:
Az., a fesse between 3 leopard's heads jessant de lis or. *crest*.; a Griffin's head gules.—(*Montague Family*.)

The first of the name known in America was James Watkins, who in 1606 accompanied Capt. John Smith in his perilous voyages in Virginia. "WATKINS POINT" was so named as an honor to him from the great commander; nothing more is known of him.

Some Early Watkins.

HENRY WATKINS subscribed with twenty-five other Burgesses means with which to send Mr. Pountis, in 1623, with a petition to the Crown.—(Campbell, 178, and Hening I, 129.)

DAVID WATKINS, cashier for the Virginia Company in 1624.

HENRY WATKINS, alive on the Eastern Shore in 1623, after the great Indian massacre of March 22, 1621.

RICE WATKINS, ditto, in James City county.

DANIEL WATKINS, ditto, in James City county; came in 1621, in the *Charles*.

PERIGRIN WATKINS, came in "the George" 1621, when twenty years old. His *muster* at James City 1624.

RICHARD WATKINS, came in the "Francis Bonaventure." He was 30 years old in 1624, and in the muster of *Mr. Blarney's Plantation* in James City county.

RICHARD WATKINS, on Hogg Island 1623.

RICHARD WATKINS, came in "the Abraham" 1635, aged 20.

THOMAS WATKINS, came in "the Constant" 1635, aged 35; also John Cock and John Hancock, and Rd. Gray.

DAVID, aged 20; Robert, aged 5; and Thomas, aged 10, came in 1680.—(*Hotten*.)

"THE WATKINS' are in the earliest old Warwick county records of its first settlers.'
—(*Bishop Meade, I, 240*.)

THOMAS WATKINS (1636) 50 acres on Elizabeth River, near Norfolk.

An old English work on *Kentish Genealogies* in the Hist. So. Library, Richmond, Va., gives Thomas Wells, of Bambridge, county Southampton, and wife, Mary, parents of Gilbert Wells, 1622, who m. Isabel Seaborne (dau. of John Seaborne, of Hertfordshire), and had Swithin, Thomas, Gilbert, Edmond and others.

Descendants intermarried with families of Robert Watkins, Drew, Lord Zouch and Leigh, with whom they quartered their arms as follows:
Wells Arms: Ar. a chevron vert. charged with five erm. spots of the field, between three martlets, as
Drew Arms: Erm. a lion passant gu.
Watkins Arms; Az. a fesse between three leopards' heads jessant de lis, or.
Leigh Arms: Ar. on a chief embattled sa., three plates.
Zouch, not copied

THOMAS WATKINS (1665), 300 acres on Elizabeth River (Bk. 3-24.)
JOHN WATKINS (1715), 63 acres on Lynhaven River.—(*Lower Norfolk, Bk 96*.)
HENRY WATKINS (1766), in Princesse Anne county.—(*Princesse Anne, Bk.*)
JOHN¹ WATKINS, of Lower Norfolk county, member of a committee that appeared before court to secure the services of the Rev. Mr. Harrison in 1640.
JOHN¹ WATKINS, of Lower Norfolk, married Frances ——, and had, among others John² Watkins. (*Va. Mag. Hist.*, I, 327.) Mrs. Watkins married (II) Edward Lloyd, justice of Norfolk 1645, and Burgess 1646. He and his brother, Cornelius Lloyd, joined the Dissenters and removed with that Puritan colony to Maryland, and he became ancestor of the distinguished family of Lloyd of "*Wye*." Cornelius Lloyd, the brother, was born 1608, Burgess 1642-53, Lt.-Col. of militia, assignee of Edward Lloyd 1651, married Elis ——. and died 1654. A son, Philemon Lloyd, went to Maryland. Edward Lloyd's will is published in "*Waters' Gleanings*," in the *New Eng. Hist. and Gen. Register;* and Harrison's "*Old Kent County, Md.*," contains the genealogy of his descendants.

JOHN WATKINS (1638), 150 acres, in James City county, 3 headrights (*Land Book*).
JOHN WATKINS (1641-8), 1350 acres, Surry county, north side *Gray's Creek*, 27 headrights (*Land Book, II, 144*).
SAMUEL WATKINS (1686), 600 acres, in Surry, next to William Thompson.
WILLIAM WATKINS (1686), 1160 acres, in Surry, on Cypress Swamp.
ELIZABETH, widow of JOHN WATKINS, mentioned in Surry county records as making a marriage contract (April, 1655) with Sackeford Brewster, of *Sackeford Hall*, county of Suffolk, gent., in behalf of present and future children. License signed by Nicholas Meriwether, Cl. C., and Rev. Mr. Lake married them "in the presence of John Corker, that gave her" (*W. & M. Quarterly, IV, 42*). Sackeford Brewster, Rd. Bland. Abra. Weekes and Elias Tennant made a voyage in 1650 up the Appomattox to the Falls.
JOHN WATKINS (1694), 966 acres, in Surry (*Land Book*).
JOHN WATKINS, Southwark par., Surry county, sold (in 1694) 966 acres in Henrico county, 850 of which had been formerly granted to John Watkins, deceased, father of the above John, who was his eldest son and heir (*Henrico Records*).
GEORGE WATKINS (1667), 1400 acres, in Surry (*Land Book*).
JAMES WATKINS (1682), 100 acres, Surry, near head of Upper Chippoaks Creek.
THOMAS WATKINS, JR. (1743), 400 acres in Surry.
THOMAS WATKINS, 400 acres in Amelia Co., Bush river, 1743, and 1200 acres in 1747 on Bush river.
HENRY AND ROBERT WATKINS (1745), tobacco drowned by the overflow in Gray's creek warehouse, Surry co. (*Hening*).
JOHN WATKINS (1755), lands in Surry, north side Nottoway river.
ROBERT WATKINS, of Surry, d. 1767, estate near Swan's bay. No issue.
His sisters, Rebecca, who m. Richard Figures, and Charity, who m. Nathaniel Hicks, were co-heirs, and they, with Thomas and Elis. Bage and Thomas Bailey, the executor, were all sued in Surry (1768), by Wm. Clench. administrator of Philip Clench, James and Hugh Belches, assignees of Benj. Harrison, James Belches, administrator of Wm. Royal, deceased, John Debreaux and John Buchanan. (*Va. Gazette, 1768*).
JOHN WATKINS, SR., and JR., on committee (1776), with John Cocke, Sr. and Jr., and John Hartwell Cocke, in Surry.
JOSEPH WATKINS (1776), committee for Goochland co.
JOHN WATKINS (1785), lands in Sussex co., north side Nottoway river.
WILLIAM WATKINS (1788), represented Dinwiddie co. with Joseph Jones. (*Va. Gazette.*)

Watkins, of York County, Va.

SAMUEL WATKINS (1639), patent lands joined those of John Hartwell on Briery swamp; of these he sold (in 1644) 250 acres to John Bell.—(*York Records, 1638-1648.*)
NICHOLAS WATKINS (1642), 100 acres in York county.—(*Land Book.*)

JOSEPH WATKINS, of York, married (before 1657) Elizabeth (first), widow Xpher Stafford, and widow (secondly) of William Purnell, with son, Humphrey Stafford. Humphrey Watkins, a descendant also.

RICHARD WATKINS, of York, 1662, a commissioner to divide an estate between his neighbors, William Hay and Robert Shields.

MRS. FAITH WATKINS (widow) had sons, RICHARD, THOMAS, HENRY (b. 1660) and *William* Watkins. The son, Richard, unmarried, made his will 1681, proved by Mr. Thomas Watkins, and witnessed by Lawrence and Thomas Platt and Rachel Pescud. Left everything to his "dear mother," with reversion to his brothers, and to each of them a riding mare, and one also to Anne Williams.—(*York Records, 1675–1684.*) THOMAS PLATT went to North Carolina 1704.

THOMAS WATKINS (1671), on a jury.

WILLIAM WATKINS (1672), 470 acres of his lands declared by the General Court "not deserted."

MR. PHILIP WATKINS (1672), witness for Mrs. Letitia Barber in a suit.

WILLIAM WATKINS, dec'd, 1679. Susannah, his widow, relinquished administration and apprenticed her son, James Watkins, to John Marsh, planter, in 1683.—(*York Records.*)

DR. THOMAS WATKINS, physician in York county 1679. He with Henry Watkins appraised the estate of John Platt 1686.—(*Records.*)

HENRY WATKINS, SR. (1681), was born 1657 (*Records*), witness to a deed of gift (with John Wythe), of Mrs. Rebecca Hathersall to her son-in-law, John Tiplady, in 1689.

HENRY WATKINS (b. 1660) mentioned, 1696, as 36 years of age.

WILLIAM and HENRY WATKINS (1695), with Thomas Chisman, inventoried estate of Joseph Stroud.

WILLIAM WATKINS (1695) married Rebecca Hathersall, widow of Capt. John Tiplady, Sr. (1689), whom she married 1687. (Her step-daughters, Rebecca and Eliz. Tiplady, married Peter Goodwin and Seymour Powell. Peter Goodwin *m.* also Mary, daughter of Starkey Robinson). Wm. Watkins' *will* (14th January, 1702) mentioning wife, Rebecca; children, William and Thomas Watkins, and Rebecca and Eliz. (another son expected), leaving everything to wife. *Witnesses* Philip Moody, Ralph Walker and John Wythe (*York Records*). Rebecca Watkins married Nathaniel Hook. She was daughter of Thomas Watkins.

THOMAS WATKINS, de'cd (1716); Nathaniel Hook and John Gibbons, administrators.

WILLIAM WATKINS, a witness, 1717, and appraiser in 1738 of an estate.

WILLIAM WATKINS, of Charles parish (*will* 1739); wife, Sarah. Sons, Thomas, William and John; daughter, Elizabeth Watkins.

EDWARD WATKINS (1695) in York county.

HENRY WATKINS, married (1755), in York county, Mary Freeman.

PHILIP WATKINS, of York county (1672), 650 acres, next to Wm. Goss and John Madison, in New Kent county. His wife, the widow of John Adkins, whose daughter *m.* (I) John Poteet, and (II) John Hathersall, of York, who was sued by Philip Watkins in 1674 (*General Court Records*). John Adkins' mother, Sibella, *m.* Capt. Robert Felgate, of York (will, p. 1655); his sister, Marah Adkins, *m.* Henry Lee (*Wm. and Mary Quarterly, I, 83*).

THOMAS WATKINS (1693), in New Kent county, 1750 acres on the Mattapony.

LEWIS WATKINS, married (1711) Margaret Stone. Issue: John (b. 1712), Edward (b. 1714), Mary (1717), Agnes (1724), Sarah (1730). *(St. Peter's Register, New Kent.)*

JOSEPH WATKINS, of New Kent, was dead in 1771, when his estate on Pamunkey river, 600 acres, was sold by Edward Watkins and Wm. Campbell.

ROBERT WATKINS, of New Kent, married Ann ——, and had son, John, born 1773 *(St. Peter's Parish Register.)*

JOHN WATKINS, and William Dandridge, represented New Kent, 1781

WILLIAM WATKINS (1745) of St. Stephens parish, King and Queen county, witnessed a deed, in Henrico, of Thomas Tanner to Francis Worsham, also of St. Stephens parish. JOHN WATKINS (1776) in King William county.

GEORGE WATKINS (1752) of vestry in Halifax county; also owned a ferry. MICAJAH WATKINS (1774) Burgess, Halifax county.

Watkins, of Henrico County.

HENRY WATKINS, SR. (born 1637), was living in Varina parish, Turkey Island precinct, before 1675. His tithes paid in this parish mentioned 1678 (*Records*). He was a member of the *Society of Friends*, and in 1684 was *fined* by the court for " *continuing in his Quakerisms.*" His fine was remitted. Also, his young daughter, Elizabeth, fifteen years of age, was sentenced to prison for refusing to take the *oath*, but was finally " ' excused ' by the court (1684), by reason of her tender years." (*Henrico Records.*)

Henry Watkins owned " *Mawburne Hills*," of which his grandson, John Watkins, sold 100 acres in 1737 to John Pleasants, joining Stephen Wood. With Richard Cocke Col. Ligon and Gilbert Jones, he had assisted in its survey in 1677.—(*Henrico R.*, 1677-1701.) In a deed of gift (February, 1691) to sons: WILLIAM[4]; 2, JOSEPH[5]; 3, EDWARD[2]; 4, HENRY[1]; 5, THOMAS[3], he gives to the three first 120 acres each of a tract of land on south side of *Chickahominy swamp*, and to the two last " the tract whereon I now live (" *Mawbourne Hills* "). To Thomas he gave 200 acres, additional, in Henrico county.—(*Henrico Records, 1688-1697, p. 267.*)

Henry Watkins, Sr., of Varina parish, planter, 1690; bought lands in that parish of Lyonell Morris, of St. Peters parish, New Kent county.

HENRY WATKINS, Jr., born 1660 (will 1714), mentions wife, Mary. Sons : John, Benjamin, Joseph and Stephen (will of Stephen Watkins in Amelia Records, April, 1754).

Witnesses : Robert Woodson, Jr., Thomas Edwards and Allen Tye.—(*Henrico Records.*)

Edward Watkins, in 1742, made a bond with James Cocke, based upon " an agreement two years since (*i. e.*, 1740) between said Cocke and William and Joseph Watkins for a division line between their respective places on Chickahominy swamp" (*Records*). Edward Watkins, of Cumberland (once a part of Henrico) sold one acre in 1752, in Henrico county, " being a part of the tract that my son, Thomas Watkins, now lives on." Witnesses : Thomas and John Watkins.—(*Henrico Records.*)

Edward Watkins married, April 1759, in Cumberland county, Rhoda Thompson.—(*Records.*)

Henry Watkins, of Henrico parish (1715), made a deed of gift "to Thomas Watkins, son of my son, Thomas Watkins" (furniture, bedding, etc).

Henry Watkins, planter, was dead before 1737, in which year his son, John Watkins, made a deed to John Pleasants, of " that tract of land in county aforesaid, called *Malborn Hills* (*sic*), being the plantation whereon Henry Watkins, the grandfather of John Watkins, and also Henry Watkins, the father of John Watkins, dwelt the last part of their lives," 100 acres. John Watkins made another deed in 1737, " as *eldest son and heir* of Henry Watkins, planter," to Gov. James Cocke of lands on Chickahominy, " which he had as heir of his grandfather, Henry Watkins, and joining Edward Watkins' land."

John Watkins was processioner of lands next to Chickahominy swamp 1739, with Nathaniel Bacon and Peter Patrick.—(*Henrico Records.*)

Thomas Watkins, of Henrico parish (1746), a deed to Valentine Adams, of 100 acres he had bought in 1735 of Richard Childers; his lands processioned in 1730.

Thomas Watkins, *the Elder*, of Southam parish, Cumberland county (once Henrico county), a deed (1752) to Benjamin Jordan, of Henrico parish, lands in Henrico county, north side of James river, 256 acres, named before in an old deed (of 1719, and still another (1729), from Thomas Pleasants to the aforesaid Thomas Watkins.—(*Henrico Records*).

ELIZ., widow of John Watkins, of Henrico parish, married (II) Sackfield Brewer, clerk of the vestry of Curls Church from 1731 to 1743—(*St. John's Parish Register*). *Eliz. Watkins'* lands were processioned in 1747.

THOMAS WATKINS (1715) owned 400 acres on main branch of the Tuckahoe, below the " Devil's Woodyard," in Henrico county—(*Land Book, 10–244*.)

THOS. WATKINS', of Henrico parish, lands joined, in 1735, those of Joseph Woodson, Wm. Porter, Sr., Col. Harrison, Wm. Lewis, Thos. Binford, Edward Mosby and George Freeman, and were on the Chickahominy swamp. In 1768 he, with others, appointed to select a new site for Curl's Church—(*St. John's Register*).

Thos. Watkins sent by vestry of St. John's (1768) with Wm. Randolph, in place of Wm. Lewis and Bowler Cocke (dec'd).

Mrs. Phoebe Watkins, was the daughter of Benj. Horner, whose will was proved in Henrico county, 1784—(*Records*).

Will of John Watkins, Henrico county (23d July, 1743, p. 9th May, 1744), mentions sons: David, Josiah, John and Nathaniel (lands in Goochland, now Cumberland); daughters: Lucy Perkins and Constance Woodson—(*Henrico Records*).

WILL OF EDWARD WATKINS, in Cumberland county, June 2, 1765, p. March 25, 1771 (he was brother of Thomas, of Swift's creek), mentions sons: John and Thomas; daughters: Martha, Mary Anderson and Judith Bass; grandsons: John and Edward Clay, and Edward and Samuel Watkins; son-in-law: Francis Moseley.

John Watkins, of Cumberland county (now Powhatan), (b. 1710), son of Edward, married (*circa* 1735) Phoebe Hancock (b. 1719). Nine children: MARY (b. 1736) m. (4th February, 1755), Wm. Moseley; SARAH (1739), JOHN (1742), RACHEL (1744), EDMUND (b. 1747), m. Miss Walthall, and had Maj. Henry Walthall Watkins, and others. He was great-grandfather also of H. Sallé Watkins, of Richmond, Va. SAMUEL (b. Cumberland county, Va., 1750), moved to Lexington and Versailles, Ky., 1790; PHEBE (1753), ELIZABETH (b. in Cumberland county, Va. 1755), married (May 22, 1774) Edward Wooldridge, and moved to Kentucky (1790) with her brothers, Samuel and Henry Watkins. Her daughter, Phoebe, married Philip (b. 1782), son of her brother, Samuel Watkins, and *their* daughter, Catherine S. Watkins (born Nashville, Tenn., 1812) married Thomas Mount-joy Buck. Both were living in Albemarle county, Va., in 1893 (aged 82 and 80) at their old home, to which they had returned in later years. (They are the parents of Mr. Samuel H. Buck, of New Orleans, who gave these notes (in 1896) from his mother's family record.) And, lastly, HENRY WATKINS (b. 1758), who married the widow Clay, mother of Henry Clay, the great Kentuckian. Samuel and Henry Watkins owned large bodies of land in Kentucky, and were among the pioneers; their descendants still holding parts of their original estate. (See *Addenda*.)

Susannah Watkins m. 1770 (April 23), Thomas Clay—(*Cumberland Records*).

Frances N. Watkins, of Farmville, Va., (author of the *Watkins Pamphlet*) wrote Col. James E. Saunders, of Alabama, in 1859, that John Watkins (b. 1710) was son of Edward Watkins, who was brother of Thomas, of *Swift's Creek* (d. 1760), and *both* of Powhatan (*then Cumberland county*). He added, "I am getting a pretty full history of this Edward and his descendants. John Watkins of Louisiana (a very literary man), and Henry Watkins, who married Henry Clay's mother, are of this family. Mrs. Duggers' mother is the daughter of Samuel Watkins, the son of John" (above).

Will of John Watkins (6th November, 1764, p. April 22, 1765), mentions wife, Phoebe; sons: John, Edward, Samuel and Henry; daughters: Mary Moseley, Sarah Watkins, Rachel, Phoebe and Betty Watkins. "To John and Henry, lands my father purchased of George Ryner Turner"—(*Cumberland Records*).

Samuel Watkins m. Cumberland county (July 26, 1773) Elizabeth Goode.

THOMAS WATKINS, of Henrico (1745), son of Edward Watkins, was *presented for* reflecting upon the established church, saying: "Your churches and chapels are no more than the synagogues of satan!" "This," says Bishop Meade, "was probably the beginning of the defection in that family from the established church." Campbell, the historian, comments: "Watkins had been listening to John Roan, the Presbyterian, who was himself indicted at the same time."

Thomas Watkins dec'd (1787). Lands in Chickahominy swamp, five miles from Richmond, and next to Capt. Joseph Price, to be sold.—(*Virginia Gazette.*)

WATKIN'S CHAPEL, in Prince Edward county, when it left the established church, had the Rev. McRoberts for pastor, in 1799, says Bishop Meade.

Thomas Watkins, the younger (1743-47), 1600 acres in Amelia, on Bush river.—(*Land Book*).

John Watkins (1745-48), 800 acres in Amelia county, Appomattox river.

William Watkins (1746), vestry of Cumberland parish, Lunenburg county.

Joel Watkins (1751), 730 acres in Amelia, both sides of Appomattox.

✘ Benj. Watkins, of Cumberland county, m. (26th December, 1774) Agnes, daughter of Benj. Hatcher.

Eliz., daughter of Edward Watkins, of Powhatan (Cumberland) m. (1796) Henry Flournoy.

Nathan Watkins m. (1768) in Cumberland county, Elizabeth Watkins.—(*Records.*)

Thomas Watkins was cousin to Miles Cary and his sister, Hannah Cary, who made her will, Chesterfield county, Dec., 1781.

Edward Watkins married about 1725 Mary Taylor (who was born 1689 in Gloucester county). She had married (I) (1703) Henry Pendleton (son of Philip, the immigrant 1674). She was ancestress of the Pendleton and Gaines families, and was sister to James Taylor (b. 1670), who m. (1700) in Lancaster, Martha Thompson.—(*Hayden.*)

Lewis Watkins, of Henrico (b. 1640), paid tithes at "*Owls*" 1683. A suit, 1695, vs. Francis Willis. Owned Indian slaves 1683.—(*Henrico Records*). Descendants moved to New Kent county.

Goochland, and Chesterfield, Watkins.

BENJ. WATKINS WILL. Goochland county (27th September, 1752, p. 18th September, 1753), wife, Jane (who was daughter of Thomas Watkins, of "*Swift's Creek*," Cumberland county, who d. 1760), mentions *sons:* Joseph, Benj. and Thomas. *Daughters:* Elizabeth, Mary, Lida, Jane, Edith and Susannah.

This was Benj. Watkins, of "*Jenitos*," Goochland.

MRS. JANE WATKINS' WILL. Goochland (*31st October, 1777, p. March 16, 1778*), mentions: *Sons:* Joseph, Thomas and Benj. *Daughters:* Mary Johnson, Judith Johnson, Lydia Johnson, Edith Riddle, Jane Matthews and Susannah Gray.

THOMAS WATKINS' WILL, of Goochland (*p. January 15, 1776*), wife, Dolly. *Sons:* William, John, Thomas, George, Chisman, Joseph, Benj. and Peter. *Daughters:* Elizabeth, Mary, Sarah, Ann and Mildred.

JOSEPH WATKINS, of Chesterfield (*will July 15, 1783*), wife, Mary; brother, Benjamin Watkins. *Sons:* Francis, Stephen, Joseph and Benjamin. *Daughters:* Judith and Martha.

DAVID WATKINS, of Chesterfield (*will 16th March, 1778*). Brothers: Benjamin and Joseph, and John Watkins: and "my mother."

JOHN WATKINS, of Goochland m. (1763) Sarah Turner.—(*Marriage Bonds.*)

SUSANNA WATKINS, of Goochland m. (1772) John Gray. son of Henry G.—(*Marriage Bonds.*)

JANE WATKINS, of Goochland m. (1772) Edward Matthews; Security, Stephen Sampson.—(*Marriage Bonds.*)

EDITH, dau. of Benj. Watkins, deceased, of Goochland, m. (1773) Thomas Riddle.—(*Marriage Bonds.*)

✘ DAR records that Benj. was b. 7-5-1755 in PA, d. 10-10-1831 ✘

CHARLES WATKINS, of Goochland, m. (1777) Lucy Curd.

JOSEPH WATKINS, of Goochland, a witness (1777) to marriage of John Stephen, Woodson and Ann Woodson.

At " *Watkinsville*," Goochland county, lived many of the name.

WILLIAM WATKINS (1711), 300 acres next to Col. Carter, Pr. William county.

JOHN WATKINS (will proved Essex county, 1747) son; William Watkins. Daughters: Ann Smithers and Barbara Hill, and his five grandchildren.—(*Records*.)

EVAN WATKINS, on Potomac river (1743). A ferry across from his land to Canegochego Crk., Md.—(*Hening*.)

HUMPHREY WATKINS, married, in Middlesex county (1770), Elizabeth Thruston.

HENRY WATKINS (1758), Ensign Militia, Pr. Edward county. '

JOHN WATKINS (1775), Militia, Albemarle.

JAMES WATKINS (1776), Lt. Va. Navy.—(*Hening, Vol. VII, and Va. Mag. Hist. I.*) Captain in the Navy later, and captured by British, and died in prison at Charleston, S. C.—(*Campbell's Hist. Va.*)

JOHN WATKINS, JR., (1776), Captain 4th Va. Reg.

ROBERT WATKINS (1776) Ensign, 5th Va. Reg.

SAMUEL WATKINS, private (1776), Gen. Rogers Clarke's Ill. Reg.

CAPT. THOMAS WATKINS with his company of Pr. Edward Co. Dragoons, fought in battle of Guilford C. H., North Carolina. The hero-giant, Peter Francisco, was in Capt. Watkins' company.

HENRY WATKINS taken prisoner by British.—(*Schenck's Hist. North Carolina*.)

Line of Thomas Watkins (d. 1760), of Swift Creek, Powhatan Co. (once Cumberland.) Children:

Thomas of " *Chickahominy*" (b. 1714, d. 1783); Stephen (1720, d. 1755); Joel (b. 1716) (trustee for Humphrey-Sidney College 1760). (*Hening XI.*) Benjamin (b. 1725), (first clerk of Chesterfield, ancestor of the Leighs); Mary, Mrs. Woodson (b. 1710); Elis., Mrs. Daniel (b. 1712)—of these:

1. Thomas, of *Chickahominy*, married Miss Anderson, of Chesterfield. They lived near Bottom's Bridge, Henrico county. Children:
    1. Henry Watkins m. Temperance Hughes, of Chesterfield, and moved to Prince Edward county.
    2. Francis Watkins, of "Poplar Hill" (d. 1826), came to Prince Edward county 1767, married Agnes Woodson.
    3. Joel Watkins, of Charlotte county, married Agnes Morton.
    4. Thomas Watkins, Swift's Creek, Powhatan (d. before 1783), married (before 1763) Sally ———, his descendants went to Georgia.
    5. Betsy Watkins (d. before 1783), married Nathaniel Massie, of Goochland.
    6. Susannah Watkins m. (1764) Col. Wm. Morton, of Charlotte county, and of the Rev.
    7. Sally Watkins married Capt. John Spencer, of Charlotte county.
    8. Mary Watkins m. Stephen Pankey, of Manchester.
    9. Nancy Watkins m. Smith Blakey, of Henrico.
    10. Jane Watkins m. Charles Hundley.
    11. Prudence Watkins m. William Royster, of Goochland county.

THOMAS WATKINS, of Swift Creek, had a brother, Edward Watkins (wrote Mr. Francis N. Watkins, of Farmville, in 1859), of whose descendants he had gathered much information.

In 1859, when Francis N. Watkins, (of Prince Edward county, Va.), was cataloguing the descendants of his great grand-father, "Thomas, of Chickahominy " (of whom he published a pamphlet), he wrote to Col. James E. Saunders, of Courtland,

Ala., who had married a daughter of Robt. H. Watkins, of Alabama (who was born 1782, in Virginia). The grandfather of this Robert H. Watkins was James the First (born 1728), second son of William Watkins, of Chesterfield county, Va.—(See *Hayden's Virginia Genealogies*, Daniel Family, for this James Watkins). But they could not unite the lines of THOMAS, of "CHICKAHOMINY," and JAMES WATKINS, OF PRINCE EDWARD (though a common ancestor was always assumed by their descendants), scions of whose lines married and intermarried, and moved to the new States, side by side, together. When James Watkins' descendants settled in and around Petersburg, Ga., those of Thomas, of Chickahominy, located in and around Augusta. They also moved to Alabama, *pari passu*. But just which of those ancient *patentees* of Virginia, was their *common ancestor* is yet unknown.

Henry E. Watkins, father of Francis N., said there was a tradition in the family, "that two brothers came from Wales, and one settled near Richmond, and the other on the Rappahanock;" and that M. David Watkins, of Maryland, often visited his father (who was Francis) and called him *cousin*, and very much resembled him, but they could not trace relationship to a certainty. But that several families of Powhatan, Appomatox, Pittsylvania and elsewhere in Virginia, were also supposed to be related. "There were also many of the name in Goochland."

Prince Edward county was taken from Amelia in 1753. Amelia county was taken from Prince George in 1734. Prince George was taken from Charles City in 1702.

THE WATKINS FAMILY (OF ELBERT COUNTY, GA.)

tradition is that two brothers came to James City county, in the early settlement of Virginia. One family seated in the Northern Neck (and we have no record of his descendants), and the other brother remained in the Peninsula, between York and James rivers, and was progenitor of the following line. His widow, two daughters and at least one son survived him. He was scalped by the Indians, but the time and manner of his death (if by war, or massacre) is lost, and unfortunately, also his baptismal name. His son,

WILLIAM[1] WATKINS, was born about 169—, and is cited in an old family paper as being of *Chesterfield county*. Patents of early *Watkins* were numerous on either side of James river, in what was then Henrico county, and also in York county. From Chesterfield, to Prince Edward county, after 1728, may be traced the line of William Watkins. Name of wife not known. A close search of records of Chesterfield and Charlotte might throw some light on the names of his wife and of his children, of whom there were six sons and two daughters. Of these the *Family MS.* preserved the names of but two sons; Richard and James Watkins as follows:

1. RICHARD[2] WATKINS, born Chesterfield county, Va. (*circa* ·1725). Wife's name unknown. Issue, among others:

   (1) Joseph P[d]. Watkins, (b. ———); removed to Petersburg, Ga., and, later, to Rutherford county, Tenn.

   (2) Richard[3] ([1]) Watkins, born in Virginia, married (1st) Miss Walthall (no issue); and married (2d) Ruth Pope, sister of Col. Leroy Pope, of Huntsville, Ala., and had Dr. Richard Leroy[4] Watkins, of Mobile, Ala.; in drug business before the Civil War. He married (1st) ———, in Claiborne county, Ala., and (2d) Miss Cunningham, of Cincinnati. Issue (by first marriage): James[5] and Ruth[6] Watkins, and several by the second.

   (3) Dr. John Watkins, of Burnt Corn, Marengo county, Ala. (born in Virginia 176— died before 1850); educated in Virginia. Formed a medical partnership, in Georgia, with Dr. William N. Richardson (who married Susan, daughter of James Watkins, the second, who was widow of Mr. John Oliver, of Petersburg, Ga.). He removed to Alabama Territory 1813; member of the Convention (1819) which framed the Constitution for the admission of Alabama into the Union. It is not known whom he married. *See Picketts' Hist. of Ala.* for mention of his attendance upon

the wounded in the Creek-Indian war. His descendants have not been reached. It is said a son lives in Texas. (*See Addenda.*)

2. JAMES[2] WATKINS (the first), of Amelia, now Prince Edward, county, Va., born, (probably in Chesterfield county), 5 Feb., 1728; died Wilks county, Ga., 21 Dec., 1800; married (20th Nov., 1755) Martha Thompson (b. Chesterfield county, Va., 10 Dec. 1737, d. Wilks county, Ga., 26 Oct., 1808), daughter of Robert Thompson, of Chesterfield county and Branch's Creek, planter and goldsmith. Her hair and eyes were dark—his light. They were of the Baptist faith, and she quite handsome and notable as a housekeeper. It is said he was sheriff of Chesterfield before removing to Amelia. They came to Georgia 1796, and lived with their eldest sons, who had secured homes in Elbert, Wilks and Lincoln counties; four of their sons were of the fair type, and four with dark eyes and hair, and all born in Virginia. Issue: 1, William[2]; 2, James[2], Jr.; 3, Sarah Herndon[2]; 4, Robert H[2]; 5, Samuel[2]; 6, John[2]; 7, Thompson[2]; 8, Joseph[2]; 9, Isham[2], as follows:

I. WILLIAM[2] WATKINS, second of the name (b. 20th of October, 1756, d. in Lawrence county, Ala., 28th May, 1832), *m.* (1785) Susan Clark Coleman (b. 1769 in Virginia, d. Lawrence county, Ala., 1843), a beautiful and charming woman, ward of the prominent Baptist preacher, Jeremiah Walker. They moved to Georgia 1790, and to Murray county, Tenn., 1808. In that year, accompanied by Col. Leroy Pope and Thomas Bibb (Governor of Alabama in 1820), he rode on horseback to New Orleans through Alabama and Mississippi, returning via Natchez, where they were joined by John W. Walker, first United States Senator of Alabama, (brother of the Rev. Jeremiah). Their route lay through various Indian tribes, and was very interesting. He removed to Madison county, Ala., in 1819, and finally (in 1827) to Lawrence county, Ala. His brother, Samuel, and nephew, Robert H. Watkins, having preceded him 1821. He purchased the *now* " *Widow Bird place*," near Courtland. He was active and cheerful in old age, and much sought by young people for his bright qualities. Issue:

1, Coleman[3]; 2, William[3]; 3, James[3]; 4, Martha[3] (and four died young), as follows: 1. COLEMAN[3] WATKINS (b. 1786, d. 1819) *m.* 1809, Talitha Goode (b. 1792, d. 1874), daughter of John and Ann (Freeman) Goode, of Abbeville District, S. C. (see *Goode's " Virginia Cousins*). (She m. (11) 1821, Col. Benj. Sherrod, of Lawrence county, whose first wife was the daughter of Samuel Watkins). Issue: 1, William Willis[4] and 2, Samuel Goode[4] Watkins, as follows:

1. WILLIAM WILLIS WATKINS[4], of Texarkana, Texas (b. 1810), *m.* (I) Susan Burt, his cousin, and *m.* (II) Mrs. Martha Whiting, of Tuskaloosa (widow with two daughters), *issue first marriage:* John Coleman[4] *m.* Miss McWeaver, and had Jennie[5] and Coleman[5]; 2, Susan Adelaid[5] married Mr. Garber, of Bibb county; no issue; 3, William Willis[5]; 4, Caroline Eliz.[5] *m.* Edward P. Shakelford, son of Dr. Jack Shakelford, Courtland, Ala., and had Frank W.[5], *m.* (1899) Anna Edwards; Harriet Catherine *m.* Rev. Ira F. Hawkins, and Caroline Eliz.[5]; 5, Frank B.[5]. Issue second marriage (WHITING); 6, Goode[5]; 7, Thomas[5]; 8, Leigh[5]; 9, Talitha Goode[5]. 2. SAMUEL GOODE[4] WATKINS, Muldon, Miss. (b. 1816), *m.* (I) Caroline, daughter of John Oliver, of Columbus, Miss., no issue, *m.* (II) Martha Jane, daughter of Robert C. Foster, of Nashville, no issue, *m.* (III), 1855, Lizzie (b. 1828), daughter of Woodson Daniel. Issue: 1, Alex. Hamilton[5]; 2, John Woodson[5]; 3, Elis. Daniel[5]; 4, Goode[5].

2. WILLIAM[3] WATKINS (b. Georgia 1798, d. Huntsville, Ala., 1859) *m.* (1826) Harriet (d. 1856), daughter of John Anderson, of Montgomery county, Md. Issue: 1, John Wm.[4] Watkins, of Nashville, Tenn. (b. Alabama 1827), *m.* (I) Lydia Harris, and *m.* (II) daughter of Wm. Hayes, of Nashville. *Issue first marriage:* 1, Robert[5]; 2, Kate[5] *m.* George Dury, of Nashville.

2. Mary Susan[5] Watkins (b. 1830) m. (1853) Lucien Lorance. Issue: 1, Harriet[6]; 2, Lorena[6].

3. Ann[5] Watkins (b. 1832) m. (1854) Henry C. Bradford, Huntsville, Ala. Issue: 1, Eva[6]; 2,Charles[6]; 3, Annie[6]; 4, Percy Bradford.

4. Martha[5] Watkins (b. 1835) m. (1854) Wm. K. Spotswood, Huntsville, Ala., great-grandson of Gov. Spotswood, of Virginia. Issue: 1, Ella[6] d. infant; 2, Wm.[6] d. infant; 3, Lucy Ann[6] m. Rev. Charles E. Cabiness, now of Lincoln, Ill., and had Robert[7], Mary[7] and Elizabeth; 5, Harriet[5] Watkins m. Wm. Fackler, of Huntsville, Ala.; 6, Robert[5] Watkins, of Pine Bluff, Ark., twice married; issue not known, and 7, Ophelia[5] Watkins.

3 JAMES COLEMAN[4] WATKINS, of Seguin, Texas (b. 1800, d. 1833), m. (1823) Isabella, sister of Wm. Moore, Madison county, Ala. He m. (II) Letty Williams, niece of Mrs. Wm. Fitzgerald, Sr., of Courtland, Ala. He m. (III) Mary Calvert (sister of Mrs. Jack Hays, wife of the noted Indian fighter). Issue first marriage (MOORE):

1, Milton[5] (d. 1885), C. S. A., m. Ann E. L. McGehee, and had nine children (*See Addenda, McGehee.*); 2, Samuel H.[5], of San Marcos, Texas, C. S. A., Eighth Texas Cavalry; Gen. Wheaton; 3, Susan[5] m. Arthur, son of William Acklen, of Huntsville, Ala., and had Blanche[7], m. Mr. McKee, of Texas, and has six children; Mattie[6] d. y., and Corinne[6] d. y. Issue second marriage (WILLIAMS): 4, Thomas[5] d. s. p.; 5, Martha[5] m. Capt. James Peacock, of San Antonio, Texas, and has several children; 6, Jennie[5] m. (I) Thos. Simmons and had two children, and (II) —— Woods, and moved to Texas: Issue third marriage (CALVERT): 7, Calvert[5]; 8, Mary[5]; 9, Hetty[5]; 10, Battle[5].

4. MARTHA[4] WATKINS (b. Murray county, Tenn., 1810, d. Courtland, Ala., 24th October, 1885). All that was exalted in womanhood and in society, family and church, and a gentle teacher of the young in her old age. Her influence will long linger in Courtland. Married (I), 1832, William Vermylie Chardevoyne, son of Wm., who m. (1800) Susanna Vermylie, of an old Knickerbocker family. The Count de Chardevoine et Crévecoar Valué was knighted 1191 at Ascalon, in Palestine, "for ye valorous conduct in ye Crusade," and raised to the peerage on his return. After the fall of La Rochelle the family emigrated to Holland, and thence tothe British colonies in America. "*Crest*, a heart argent with lance shivered against it. *Motto*, "*Le Cœur Duer*." *Arms:* Three chevrons crossed over ye fleur de lys argent on a field azure. The whole surmounted by ye coronet of a count of France." Elias Chordavoyne came to New York 1692.—(*Baird's Hist. of Huguenots of America, and Hist. of the Colony of N. Y.*)

Mr. Chardavoyne died in New Orleans of cholera a year after marriage, and leaving a posthumous son, Maj. William Chardavoyne, of Courtland, Ala. The widow m. (II) 1843 Dr. Jack Shakelford, of the Texan war fame. No issue.— (*Early Settlers.*)

(1) William Vermylie[5] Chadavoyne (b. Courtland, Ala., 1833), merchant Courtland, Ala., and a leading man of the State, Secretary to Governor Lindsay, of Ala., and clerk in the Naval Department at Washington with Secretary Herbert (Cleveland Administration), married (1856) Lavinia Harris, of Huntsville, Ala. Issue:

1. Martha Gay[6], married (1885) Major Thoms, of U. S. Corps of Engineers, then engaged on the Muscle Shoals Canal of the Tennessee River, whose *first* locks, (now too small for modern traffic) were contracted for and built by Rev. Turner Saunders[*]. Major Thoms died 1887, leaving a son, Edward Vermylie[7] (b. 1886).

---

[*] In 1791, there was a Block House, or Log Fort, at the Muscle Shoals.

MAJ. ROBERT H. WATKINS (when aged).
Born in Virginia 1782, died 1855.

2. Edward Vermylie⁴ Chadavoyne, Railroad Agent, since his extreme
youth, of Memphis and Charleston Road, at Courtland, married
(1888) Annie Pippin, of Courtland, Ala., sister of Mrs. Oakley
Bynum, and Mrs. Saunders Swoope. Issue: 1 Eva, 2 Louisa.

[End of descendants of William Watkins].

Descendants of James Watkins the Second.

II. JAMES³ WATKINS, (the 2d) b. Prince Edward county, Virginia, 20th October, 1758,
d. Elbert county, Georgia, Savannah River, ten miles above Petersburg, 10th October,
1824), married, in Virginia, (27 Feb. 1779) Jane, (b. 1762, d. 2d Aug. 1815),
daughter of Isham and Mary Ann (Oliver) Thompson of Virginia. (Isham. was son
of Robert Thompson, goldsmith and banker.) (See *Thompson and Oliver Families*
and also "*Early Settlers.*") Issue:

1, GARLAND THOMPSON; 2, ROBERT H.; 3, MARY THOMPSON; 4, SARAH HERNDON;
5, MARTHA THOMPSON; 6, JANE; 7, SUSAN; 8, ELIZA; 9, JAMES, JR , 10, SOPHIA
HERNDON; 11, THEOPHILUS; as follows:

(1) Garland Thompson⁴ Watkins (born Prince Edward county, Virginia, 30th January, 1780, d. 1816), never married. Educated for the law, served one term in
Georgia Legislature.

(2) ROBERT H.⁴ WATKINS (b. Prince Edward county, Virginia, 1st October, 1782,
d. Pulaski, Tennessee, 10th September, 1855). Successful planter and merchant
of Petersburg, Georgia. Member of Legislature. Followed his uncle, Samuel
Watkins, to Lawrence county, Alabama, in 1821, bringing with him his wife's
brother, John Oliver, of whom he was guardian.

He married, in Petersburg, Ga. (25th April, 1805), Prudence Thompson (b. Petersburg, 22d October, 1788, d. Huntsville, Ala., October, 1868), daughter of John
and Frances (Thompson) Oliver, of Petersburg, Ga. (See *Oliver Family*.) He
settled in Lawrence county, Ala., four miles north of Courtland, and built a large
red brick mansion, called "Oak Grove." In old age he partitioned out his
lands and slaves to his children and removed, in 1849, to Pulaski, Tenn., and
made his home near his youngest child, Robert H. Watkins, Jr. Here they lived
in great content until his death, when his widow, with an ample income, thence-
forth resided alternately with each of her children, driving to their homes with
her own carriage, maid and coachman. Issue:

1. Mary Frances⁵; 2. Sarah Independence⁵; 3. James Lawrence⁵; 4. Virginia
Prudence⁵; 5. Louisa Matilda⁵; 6. Robert H⁵., Jr., as follows:

(1) MARY FRANCES⁵ WATKINS (b. Petersburg. Ga., 13th November, 1809, d. at "Rocky
Hill," Lawrence, Ala., 6th February, 1889), m. (14th July, 1824) by the Rev. Alexander Sale, James Edmonds Saunders (b. Brunswick county, Va., 7th May, 1806. d.
at "Rocky Hill" 23d August, 1896); son of Rev. Turner and Frances (Dunn) Saunders, and author of "*Early Settlers.*" Her earliest teacher in Petersburg was Mr. Reid.
and later on Mr. Nathan Warner (who was afterward a Judge, and married Miss Elis,
Rembert, daughter of Mr. Samuel Rembert, in whose home Mary Watkins boarded
while attending school. (Eliz. Rembert married (II) Mr. Holmes, and lived near
Memphis, Tenn.) Her next school (1819) was the old *Moravian Institute* at Salem,
N. C., remaining there until her thirteenth year. The next was to Mr. Hopkins, in
Augusta, Ga. Accompanied by her cousin, Louisiana Thompson, they boarded with
Mrs. Bacon, sister of the Mayor, Nicholas Ware. Her father moving to Alabama in
1821, she next attended Nashville Female Academy (Principal, Rev. Mr. Hume) with
her cousins, Sarah Manning, and Adeline and Emily Bibb, daughters of Gov. Thomas
Bibb, Huntsville, Ala. Her wedding attendants were: Eliza Towns, Eliza Booth,
Martha Finlay and Minerva Banks; Thomas Saunders, Judge John J. Ormand, Dr.
William Booth, and James Pearsall, all of Courtland, Ala. She has left a *diary* of

much interest, and breathing the deepest piety. Their children were: Frances Amanda[4]; 2, Robert Turner[4]; 3, Elizabeth Dunn[4]; 4, Mary Lou[4]; 5, Dudley Dunn[4]; 6, Sarah Jane[4]; 7, James Saunders[4]; 8, Fanny Dunn[4]; 9, Prudence Oliver[4]; 10, Lawrence Watkins[4]; 11, Ellen Virginia[4]. (See *Saunders Family* for these.)

(2) SARAH INDEPENDENCE[3] WATKINS (b. Petersburg, Ga., 4th July, anniversary *Declaration of Independence*, 1811, d. Florence, Ala., 30th January, 1887) married (1st October, 1829) George Washington Foster, of Florence, Ala. (born Nashville, Tenn., 1806, d. Florence, Ala.), son of Robert and Rose (Coleman) Foster, of Nashville, and formerly of Virginia. (*See Foster:*) Lived in Florence, Ala., where their stately home was long noted for its hospitality, and they, also, for much charity (both being reared by pious parents). Mr. Foster gave $10,000 to the Methodist College established at Florence, and *she* will long be remembered by the poor. Many sorrows tested her Christian fortitude, but her vitality was great, and nature endowed her, from the first, with that irresistible sense of humor, called "dry wit," which kept her noble heart young to the last, and gave a great charm to her presence. All loved her. Issue:

1, Mary Ann[4] Foster, d. 1853; married James Simpson of Florence, Ala. Issue: Margaret[5] Simpson, married Thomas McDonald, of Athens, Ala., and has several children.

2, Dr. Watkins[4] Foster (1835), a promising life ending in sad disappointment, kind and dearly loved son.

3, Virginia[4] Foster, m. James Irvine, of Athens, Ala., and planter of Florence, Ala., of an old and distinguished family. Issue: 1, Mary,[5] m. Wm. Houston. Issue: several children. 2, James[5] m. a daughter of Dr. McAlexander, of Florence. Ella[5] m. Henry, son of Walter Sherrod of Lawrence county, Ala. Issue: Virginia;[5] 3, Emma;[5] 4, Virginia[5]; 5, Washington.[5]

4. Louisa[4] Foster, married Charles Fant, of Mississippi. Issue: Several children.

5. George W.[4] Foster, planter, C. S. A., served with General Roddy; m. Emma McKiernon; both dead. Several children.

6. Andrew J.[4] Foster, planter, Miss., C. S. A., served with General Roddy (dead); m. Mrs. Helen Potter, of Mississippi. Issue: One son.

7. Sallie[4] Foster (b. 1850, d. 1898); m. (1871) Sterling McDonald, brother of Thomas, and lived in the family home at Florence (above). Issue: Several children.

(3) JAMES LAWRENCE WATKINS[3] (b. 10 May, 1814, d. in Huntsville, Ala., 1891), m. (26th April, 1838) Eliza (b. October, 1820), daughter of William Patton, of Huntsville, sister of Gov. Robert Patton, of Alabama. He served awhile in Civil War, on General Forrest's staff in 1862, and was a large planter in Mississippi and Alabama. Issue:

I. Virginia Patton[4] Watkins, (b. 1841,   ), m. Charles Robinson, planter, (near Memphis, Tenn.,) in Mississippi. Removed to Louisivlle, Ky. Mrs. Robinson's aged mother living with her in 1899. Issue: Annie[5] Robinson m. Mr. Glazebrook.

II. Dr. William Watkins (b. 1853, d. 22d July, 1882), a young physician with a brilliant future and the idol of his aged parents, died in Huntsville, Ala., after one week's illness, of peritonitis.

(4) VIRGINIA[3] WATKINS, (b. 22nd October, 1816, d. 12th May, 1837), m. (30th October, 1833) Hon. Thomas J. Foster (b. Nashville, Tenn., 1813, d. Lawrence, Ala., 12th February, 1887), son of Robert and Rose (Coleman) Foster, Nashville, Tenn. He was the youngest of seven sons, a large planter in Alabama. Member of Confederate States Congress in 1861. But first, went as Colonel of a regiment; and aided in locating and constructing Fort Henry, under Governor Tilghman of Tennessee. Was elected to United States Congress in 1865, over General Garth and C. C. Sheats, but prevented by the '*Radicals*,' from taking his seat (like other patriots of that trying period). Of courtly bearing and fine conversational talent, his popularity was great. He married (II) 1844, Ann Hood, of Florence Alabama. (Her nephew is " the gal-

lant Lieutenant Hood, of the U. S. Warship "Maine," which was blown up in Havana Harbor, then serving in the war with Spain.) Children of this marriage were: 1. James, of Lawrence county, Ala., m. Tillie Toney, and had two daughters. 2. Coleman, unmarried, and educated, with his brother, at Edinburgh, Scotland. 3. Annie m. (1872) Lieutenant Longshaw, of U. S. Army.

Colonel Foster m. (III) Mrs. Longshaw. His son, Coleman Foster, is a planter on the Tennessee river, Lawrence county, Ala., 1899.

(5) LOUISA MATILDA[4] WATKINS (b. Petersburg, Ga., 29th December, 1819, d. Huntsville, Ala., 1892); married (1st December, 1841) Stephen Willis Harris, of Huntsville, Ala. (son of Judge Stephen Willis and Sarah (Watkins) Harris, of Athens, Ga., a lawyer with the inherited wit of his celebrated father, and with keen powers of observation and satire. (See "Bench and Bar of Georgia.") She was of noted piety and strength of character. Her earnestness was characterized by the pair of fine, honest eyes which always seemed to look you quite through. Her memory pervades the old town of Huntsville like a consecration. She lived a widow for many years with her only son; and, with her cousin, Mrs. Isaphena Bassett, and Mrs. Frank Mastin (also a woman of grand character), formed a *Christian triumvirate*, who were affectionately called "*pillars of the Methodist Church.*" With such women, passed that grand *ante bellum* type of the old slave-owning class, with whom the title "Mother, and Mistress" were almost the same. The colored race will never again have such friends and guardians.* Mrs. Harris' early married life was saddened with the death, by accident, of her only little daughter. Her sons were:

1. Watkins[6] Harris (b. 1843, d. 17th January, 1865). While serving as Captain in Fourth Regiment, C. S. A., the health of this most pious and talented young officer failed, and he died (a noble offering to his country) at the home of his uncle in Athens, Ga.† (See *Harris*.)

---

* Letter of Mrs. S. Willis Harris to her mother, dated Huntsville, 11th May, 1862: "I don't know when we shall meet again, as the Federal forces are here, probably for the rest of the war. My nephew, Robert T. Saunders, has been a prisoner here two weeks to-day. Is out on parole, and spends his nights with brother Robert H. There are in the African Church forty prisoners taken at Bridgeport; and forty others in the Court House, brought in from this and Jackson counties, said to be accessory to burning bridges, tearing up railroad tracks, firing on pickets. etc., and also Bishop Lay, Mr. Wilson, Mr. Bierne, Mr. Gus Mastin, Mr. Tom McCauley, Wm. Moore, Mr. Withers, Mr. McDowell, Mr. Wm. Acklen, Dr. Fearn, and lastly, my husband. These twelve were arrested on the 2d. They are required by the General to sign an instrument in writing before they can be released. Among some prisoners captured 16th April, on a train coming up from Corinth, Miss., is a Captain Bird, son of your brother-in-law, Mr. Daniel Bird. He is wounded in the thigh, and staying at the College. * * *

"When last we heard from our plantation the negroes were all at work, but the Yankees had been there, broken open smoke-house, and distributed all the salt and meat among them, and fifteen wagon loads of corn.

"We have not heard from my dear son in two months, but I am trusting in God that "all things shall work together for good to them that love Him.""

To Mrs. James E. Saunders: MY DEAR SISTER MARY—My precious, noble boy is gone where he shall bear of wars no more. He died in great triumph at 1 o'clock Tuesday morning. I have been present at the death of several who have passed from earth to heaven, but none have left brighter assurance of happiness *beyond the grave.* It was not until Sunday morning that he showed signs of speedy departure. We had been conversing cheerfully on historical subjects, but when I came back into his room, after a late breakfast, he told me he had great difficulty in breathing. I gave him stimulants, his pulse being very feeble, and he rallied. After church, the Methodist minister, Mr. Parks, came, at his request, and administered the sacrament of baptism to him and to me, and then the Lord's Supper to all the family. His answers to the minister were marked with emphasis and enthusiasm * * * It was no sudden resolution of fear; but I had his own assurance, even months before, that he had experienced a change of heart, and he had all along spoken of his approaching death with perfect composure and resignation, and his mind never shone with more brilliant strength than on the last day of his life. Singularly pure and virtuous as he was, he yet knew it needed more than mere morality to prepare him for another life. He said he had resolved to receive the "declarations of Holy Writ in the spirit of a little child," and that he relied solely on the *atonement* of Christ. His conversations from thence on abounded in the precious promises of the Bible and snatches from the beautiful hymns of Zion. Just before his death he asked Colonel Hardeman for a prayer, and after

II. Stephen Willis' Harris (b. 1849, d. 1895), planter and lawyer; m. Mary S.,
daughter of James L. Darwin, of Huntsville, Ala. He died suddenly while
riding horseback from his plantation to his home in town. He was as quick-
witted and talented as his father. Issue: 1, Mary Lou,; 2, Sidney', d. y. ; 3,
Willis'.

(6) ROBERT H°. WATKINS (b. 10 May, 1824, d. 1866, in Huntsville, Ala.); m. (6
January, 1846) Mary Margaret (b. 29 April, 1827, died 20 June, 1865), daughter of
Dr. Benj. and Eliz. (Lindsay) Carter, of Pulaski, Tenn., where they made their
home also. In 1861 they moved to Huntsville, Ala. Both died soon after the war. His
aged mother, Mrs. Robert H. Watkins, lived at their elegant home awhile, caring
for the young orphans. Issue:

   I. Mary' Watkins (b. 1846) m. (1868) Yancey Newman, of Huntsville; lives in
   Birmingham, Ala., where he conducts a drug business with great success. Issue:
   1, Robert' m. Miss Turner, of Huntsville; 2, Bessie', married Mr. Stone.
   II. Elizabeth' Watkins (b. 1848) m. Guilford Buford, of Giles county, Tennessee.
   Issue: Several children.
   III. James Lawrence' Watkins (b. 2 October, 1851), now of the Government
   Statistical Department at Washington, D. C. (1899); m. Bettie, daughter of
   Luke Matthews, of Huntsville. Ala. Issue:
      1, Lucius M.' (b. 1876), of U. S. Statistical Department, and Sergeant Company
      A. (Capt. Pool), 1st Reg. La. Volunteers, in war with Spain 1898 ; 2, James
      Lawrence' (b. 1879) in Huntsville, Ala., also in same company, U. S.
      Army.
   IV. Frank' Watkins b. 1853) m. Minnie Murray, of Huntsville, Ala. Issue: Sev-
   eral children. He moved West many years ago.
   V. Sallie' Watkins (b. 9th May, 1855) m. (19th May, 1873) James, son of Hon.
   John Patton, of Huntsville, Ala. Lives in Birmingham, Ala. Issue: 1,
   Louise' Patton; 2, Margaret' Patton m. (1895) Mr. King. Issue: a son (b. 1898);
   3, John' Pattou.
   VI. Robert H.' Watkins (b. 6th July, 1857) m. Mary, daughter of Governor Lind-
   say, of Alabama. Issue: 1, Minnie Margaret'; 2, Mamie'.
   VII. Dr. Lindsay' Watkins, of Nashville, Tenn., m. (1886) Miss Annie Connolly,
   niece of Dr. Thos. L. Maddin, of Nashville, Tenn. No issue.
This ends the descendants of Robert H. Watkins, of Pulaski, Tenn.

III. MARY THOMPSON' WATKINS, "Polly" daughter of James and Jane (Thompson) Wat-
kins (b. 7 March, 1784, d———) m. (15 Jan'y., 1801) in Elbert County, Georgia.
Dr. Asa (b.———, d. 1832, in Huntsville, Ala.,) son of William and Mary (Wells)
Thompson. Issue: (1) Louisiana' m. Robt. Manning, no issue: (2) Asa Wat-
kins', m. Mary Lewis, of Hancock County, Ga.; (3) Dr. Wells', of Waco, Texas, m.
Louisa, dau. of James Harrison, Columbia, Miss., no issue: (4) Indiana' m. James
Manning, of Huntsville, Ala., and lived in Macon, county, Ala.; (5) Isaphena' m. Dr.
John Bassett, of Huntsville, Ala.: (6) Darwin', d. s. p. : (7) Elbert' m. his cousin, Ann,
dau. Maj. Benj. and Martha (Watkins) Taliaferro. (See *Thompson family* for these).

---

this he said "Sing." His mother and all of us sang the old chant of the Christian, "On Jordan's
stormy bank's I stand," and when we reached the lines, "No chilling winds, &c.," he exclaimed,
" Glory to God! " and then he asked me to repeat, " I reckon that the sufferings of this present time
are not worthy to be compared with the *glory* that shall be revealed in us." " Don't cry, father; there
is no cause for *grief*." At 12 o'clock, in the midst of great suffering from the oppression in breathing,
he said: " I am going now; good-bye, mother; meet me in heaven! " clasping her hands and kissing
her; and so to all of us. To Allen, his faithful servant, who had accompanied him in all his weary
marches and nursed him so lovingly in his illness, he stretched out his hand and said, " Good-bye, my
good and faithful friend; meet me in heaven! " And when beyond the power of speech, he smiled
and lifted his hand, pointing to Heaven. And so passed away our precious boy. * * *
               Affectionately, your brother,   S. W. HARRIS.

IV. SARAH HERNDON[4] WATKINS, (b. in Prince Edward County, Va., 12 Feb., 1786, d. 1871), m. (19 Jan., 1808): Judge Stephen Willis, (b. 1785, d. 14 Sept., 1827), son of Sampson and Susannah (Willis) Harris of Va. (See *Washington, Lanier, Harris sketch*). Lived in Edenton, Putnam County, Ga. When quite aged she was still handsome and bright. She took great interest in the family genealogy, and in 1856, when visiting the family of James E. Saunders, in Lawrence County, Ala., corroborated much of the above data of the elder members of the family, all of whom she knew personally. She lived in Athens, Ga., after her husband's death. Issue:

    1. Sampson W.[6]; 2, Mary W.[5]; 3, James Watkins[6].
    4. Jane Victoria[6]; 5, Ann Maria[6]; 6, Arabella Rebecca.
    7. Stephen Willis[6]; 8, Susan M.[5]; 9, Thomas Eli[6]. Of these:

(1) SAMPSON W.[5] HARRIS, (b. 1814, d. April 1; 1857), of medium statue, intellectual and agreeable, m. Pauline, daughter of Stevens Thomas, of Athens, Ga. He moved to Wetumpka, Ala., where he served sixteen years in the State Senate, and Congress of United States, dying in Washington, D. C., during his term of office. Issue; I, Sampson W.[6], of Athens, Ga. m. Lucy Todd, of Atlanta, her mother Emily, was sister to Dr. Thos. A. Watkins. of Austin, Texas; II, Hugh N.[6]; III, Francis[6]; IV, Isabella[6]; V, Sallie[6].

(2) MARY W[5]. ———— m. Hugh W. Nesbit. He died 1839. They lived on Big Creek, near Memphis. No issue.

(3) REV. JAMES WATKINS[5] HARRIS, of Cartersville, Ga. Fair complexion, bright and warm-hearted; and much beloved minister of Methodist church, m. (I) Ann Eliza (d. 1856), daughter of Thomas W. Hamilton, of Augusta, Ga. He m. (II) ————. Issue, first marriage: I, Sarah Virginia[6]; II. Annie[6]; III, James Watkins[6]; IV, Thomas Willis Hamilton[6] (b. 1856).

(4) JANE VICTORIA[4] Harris, auburn hair, hazel eyes, m. James M. Smyth, of Augusta, Ga. Issue: I, Mary Frances[6]; II, Samuel[6]; III, Brenda[6]; IV, William[6]; V, Susan[6].

(5) ANNIE MARIA[5] HARRIS (————, d. 1858) m. (1839) Hon. Robt. B. Alexander, Judge of the Superior Court of Georgia, who died at Columbus, Ga., 1852. They both died young, and their children were reared by their uncle, Stephen Willis Harris, of Huntsville, Ala. Issue:

    I. Arabella[6] Alexander (b. 1840 ————), m. (1856) Rev. Thomas Boykin of the Baptist church, of a fine old South Carolina family—noted for beautiful women. (The Rev. Isaac T. Tichenor, a distinguished educator of the South, and Secretary of the Baptist Home Mission in Atlanta, married two of his sisters). Issue: Several children, II, Willis[6] (b. 1843); III, Robert[6] (b. 1851); IV, Mary[6] (b. 1847), m. Harris Toney, of Triana, Ala., merchant and planter. Issue: Several children.

(6) ARABELLA REBECCA[5] HARRIS (————, d. 1845) m. Col. Benjamin F. Hardeman, of Oglethorpe Co., Ga. She had blue eyes and brown hair, was tall with great grace and sweetness of manner, and an accomplished musician. Issue: I, Sampson H.[6] Hardeman; II, Belle[6] Hardeman.

(7) STEPHEN WILLIS[5] HARRIS, lawyer and planter (b. 1818, d. at Huntsville, Ala., 187-), member Legislature in 1856, m. (1841) his cousin, Louisa Matilda Watkins. Issue: I, Watkins[6]; II, Willis[6]. (*For descendants, see Robt. H. Watkins, above.*).

(8). SUSAN MARTHA[5] HARRIS, dark blue eyes, blonde and tall (b. 1820, ————), m. William T. Baldwin, of Columbus, Miss., planter. Issue: I, Harris[6] (————), m. Abbie F. Park, of St. Louis; II, William[6]; III, Susan[6] m. Toby W. Johnston, of Columbus, Miss. Issue: (a) Juniata[7], (b) Harrison[7], (c) Edna[7]; IV, Sarah m. Martin Teasdale (third wife).

(9) THOMAS ELI[5] HARRIS, planter (b. ————, d. 1855), m. Emily Bolling, of Oglethorpe Co., Ga., and lived in Cass Co., Ga.

V. MARTHA[4] WATKINS (b. 23d August, 1787, died March 17th, 1865) m. (15th Oct. 1807) Major Benjamin (b. Elbert county, Ga., 1782; d. Demopolis, 3d June, 1852), son of Gen. Benjamin and Martha (Meriwether) Taliaferro, of Amherst county, Va., and Wilkes county, Ga. Gen. Taliaferro was captain in the Revolution (*see Heitman's Official Register*). He moved to Broad river, Ga., in 1780; member of the Legislature; refused to vote for the "*Yazoo Act.*" Became member of Congress and Judge of the Superior Court (see Gov. Gilmer's "*Georgians*"). He had many children (*See Taliaferro family*). The son, Major Benjamin, moved to Marengo county, Ala. Issue:

(1) Martha⁴ Taliaferro (b. March 12th, 1810, died May 20th, 1883) married Uriah Blacksheer. No issue.

(2) Elizabeth⁴ Taliaferro married (before 1840) Dr. Charles Drummond, of Virginia. Issue:

    I. Mary⁵ m. Mr. Yeldell and had: 1, Edwin⁷; 2, Frank⁷; 3, Fenner⁷; 4, James⁷; 5, Lizzie May⁷, all married (1899) and living in Texas.

    II. Elizabeth⁵ m. Robert Yeldell, Jr., and had: 1, Margaret⁷; and 2, John⁷, married and living in Texas.

    III. William⁵ Drummond, d. s. p.

(3) Emily⁴ (or Sarah Amelia) Taliaferro (b. 1818) married Dr. Donald, of Georgia and died 14th January, 1878] Children: I, Eugenia⁵, and II, Benjamin⁵ (both dead).

(4) Benjamin⁴ Taliaferro (b. 1822). In his young manhood joined the company of "Red Rovers," which was organized (of the flower of the youth of North Alabama) by Dr. Jack Shackelford, of Courtland, Lawrence county, for the Mexican war. He was massacred, with his company, in 1836, by order of General Santa Anna, at Goliad, Texas. Dr. Shackelford's son was also of the victims, and the agonized father, who was spared only to attend the enemy's wounded, was led off to a tent, from whence he heard the shots that ended their young lives. A county in Texas was named for Captain Shackelford. (See *Early Settlers.*)

(5) David⁴ Taliaferro (b. 15th February, 1824), lawyer, of Demopolis and Birmingham, Ala., student of La Grange College, Ala., in 1843. Wit and genius of a fine order are his; of medium height, and fair, with blue eyes. Married Mary Green. (He is living in Birmingham, in 1899.) Issue:

    I. Ida Belle⁵, married Thomas Watson, of New Orleans; 2. Martha, unm.; 3. Benjamin⁵ Taliaferro, clerk of K. C. M. & B. Railroad, unm.

(6) Anna⁴ Taliaferro (b. 15th February, 1824), (twin with David), and died 30th March, 1894). Beautiful, with black eyes and charming person. Married (I) 6th May, 1846, her cousin, Elbert Asa Thompson, and was left a widow with three children. She moved to Matagorda, Texas, near her relatives, and there married (II), 1856, Dr. Robert H. Chinn. Her children:

    I. Louisiana⁵ Thompson, married Harris W. Bowie, merchant and planter of Coultersville, Texas. No issue.

    II. Martha⁵, d. s. p., (III) Elberta Asa⁵ Thompson, unmarried (who has contributed much data of her family), and (IV) Richard J.⁵ Chinn, all of Coultersville, Matagorda county, Texas.

(7) Theophilus Watkins⁴ Taliaferro (b. 1825, d. California 7th December, 1893). Went to California when young, and there married the Spanish Donna, Josepha Ariosa, of beauty and wealth. Issue:

    I. Mary⁵; II. Benjamin⁵; III. Frances⁵; none married, and all living in San Francisco, 1899.

(8) Amanda⁴ Taliaferro, married Nathan Bradley, of Marengo county, Ala. She was, like her sister, very pretty with auburn hair and dark eyes. Issue:

    I, Amelia⁵ m. Porter Bibb, Jr. Issue: Thomas, Porter, Bradley, Mamie, Gussie, and others. II, Annie⁵ (b. 1849) m. Rev. Wm. Ellington, of Texas. Issue: Elmira. III, Watkins⁵, living at Belle Mina, Ala., 1887, m. Margaret Rankin.

BENJAMIN TALIAFERRO.
Demopolis, Ala.

Mrs. Martha Watkins Taliaferro.
Born 1787, died 1865.

Issue: Amanda and Elizabeth. IV, David⁶, *d. s. p.* V, Louis⁶ *m.* Sarah Fletcher. VI, Kate⁶ *m.* Lockhart Bibb. Issue: Watty, Porter and others. VII, Elmira⁶, unmarried. (*See Thompson and Bibb.*)
(9) Elmira⁵ Taliaferro (b. 1828, d. 24th May, 1895), married U. T. Blackshear, Jr., (step-son of her sister, Mrs. Martha Blackshear). Issue:
I, Eugenia; II, Mary Blackshear, married Mr. Evans, and lives at Opelousas, La.

VI. JANE⁴ WATKINS, (b. 13th November, 1789, d. 1837), *m.* (10th July, 1810) Judge James Minor Tait, brother of Judge Charles Tait, of Georgia. Tall, dark-eyed, graceful and active and of a vivacious temperament. Her husband was member of Tariff Convention, that met at Milledgeville, 1832. They removed to North Mississippi. Issue:
    1. Louisa⁵ Tait, married (I), Lemuel Banks, of Panola county, Miss., and had several children. She married (II), Mr. Charles Meriwether. (*See Banks and Oliver.*) 2. Antoinette⁵ Tait, married (I) Andrew Sims. He was killed in a deer hunt. She married (II) Mr. Smith. Several children. 3. Dr. George⁵ Tait, of Panola, Miss., married daughter of Abner McGehee, of Montgomery, Ala. (*See McGehee Family, and also Banks Family.*) 4. Joel⁵ Tait. 5. James⁵ Tait (b. 1827).

VII. SUSAN⁴ WATKINS (b. 17th March, 1791) married (I), (17th February, 1811), Major John Oliver, of Petersburg, Ga., (2nd wife). Their infant, and only child, fell from the arms of its nurse, and died from the effects. She married (II) Dr. William N. Richardson, of Elbert county, Ga. (partner of Dr. John Watkins, who removed to Monroe county, Ala., in 1813). He removed to Barbour county, Ala. At his wife's death he married (II), 'Polly' Moseley, who was the 2nd wife of John Watkins, of Petersburg, Ga. (who was father of Mrs. Young, Mrs. Harris and Mrs. Banks, of Columbus, Miss., and Georgia. His first wife, Susan Daniel.) Issue:
    1. Mary⁵ Richardson, married Gabriel Toombs (brother of the great orator of Georgia, Robert Toombs), and lived in Wilks county, Ga. She was very beautiful; black eyes and hair. Issue: Wm. Henry Toombs *m.* (1875) Julia, *dau.* of Troup Butler. 2. Sarah Willis⁵ Richardson married ——— Thompson, Barbour county, Ala., a civil engineer. 3. Louisa⁵ Richardson married ——— Thompson (brother of above.) who died 1857. 4. Walker⁵ Richardson (b. 1827, d. 1882) married Miss Sanford, of Glennville, Barbour county, Ala., an only daughter. He was tall, with black eyes and hair, and of elegant person, and an interesting talker. 5. William⁵ Richardson. Major in Confederate States Army, Civil War. His mind became unsettled in later years. 6. James⁵ Richardson, married and had several children. 7. Martha⁵ Richardson.

VIII. ELIZA⁴ WATKINS (b. 5th February, 1793, d. 1836), *m.* (21st May, 1817) William (d. 1832, at Tuscaloosa), son of Micajah McGehee, of Ogletharpe county, Ga. (2d wife). She was very handsome, and equally frail and delicate. The McGehees are a distinguished Southern family, and descended, maternally, from Thomas Scott, who married a Miss Baytop, of Gloucester county, Va., early in the eighteenth century. (William had twelve brothers and sisters.) Issue:
    1, Eliza Ann⁵, d. y.; 2, Eliz.⁵, d. y.; 3, Sarah Eliz.⁵; 4, Mary Jane⁵; 5, Lucinda Scott⁵; 6, James Watkins⁵; 7, Robert⁵, as follows:
    3. Sarah Eliz. (b. Tuscaloosa, Ala., 1821); educated with her younger sisters (1834-1838) at the Moravian Institution, Salem, N. C. They were accompanied by their cousin, Sarah Scott, daughter of Dionysius Oliver, of Panola county, Miss., and Bastrop, Tex., and Broad River, Ga.; *m.* (1839) Vincent R. Porter. (*See McGehee.*)
    4. Mary Jane *m.* (I) (1842) Meriwether Oliver, of Georgia, who died in a few months. Issue: Ann Meriwether (b. 1843), educated at Baton Rouge; *m.* (1860) John L. Byrnes, and had Rebecca (Mrs. Drew), and *m.* (II) Thomas W. Phillips, of Wetumpka, Ala., and moved, in 1849, with her brothers, James and John McGehee, to Monroe, La.

5. **Lucinda Scott** m. John B. Callaway, of Montgomery. (*See McGehee.*)

6. **Judge James Watkins,** of Weimer, Tex. (b. Tuscaloosa, Ala., 7th October, 1827.) Educated Athens, Ga., with his cousins, Abner and James McGehee, of Montgomery, going there in 1837, and living for awhile afterward with his uncle, Hugh McGehee, on Broad River, Ga., who, removing to Panola county, Miss., with Dionysius Oliver, in 1839, he lived with John Scott McGehee, in Pontotoc county, Miss., for several years, and then with his own brother, Dr. David McGehee, who removed to DeSoto county, Miss., in 1844. His uncle Abner was his guardian. He removed to Monroe, La., in 1849; m. (19th May, 1857) Ann Sankey, daughter of James Daniel, of Montgomery, and moved to Round Top, Fayette county, Tex., in 1859. Issue: 1, Mary Eliza (b. 2d March, 1859) m. (10th March, 1881) William S. Shaver; 2, Robert Watkins, M. D., of Yokum, Texas (b. 2d February, 1862); 3, Frank Eary (b. 6th August, 1873.)

7. **Robert H.** (b. Tuscaloosa, Ala., February, 1832). With his widowed mother and brother and nurse lived, in 1834 (until her death), with his uncle, Robert H. Watkins, Courtland, Ala. Joined the Company of "*Greys*" from Monroe, La., in Civil War, Capt. Frank P. Stubbs, and was killed in battle of Malvern Hill, Virginia, 1862.

IX. **JAMES[4] WATKINS** (b. 20th September, 1795, d. 15th March. 1826) m. Jane, daughter of Dr. John Urquhart, of Augusta, Ga. No issue. "Educated for the law, and of handsome person, too much prosperity was his ruin." He became dissipated, and died young—no issue. His widow m. Dr. William Weeden, of Huntsville, Ala. (2d wife), and their descendants are numerous. (*See Oliver and Urquhart*).

X. **SOPHIA HERNDON[4] WATKINS** (b. 12th May, 1797, d. 1856) m. (18th June, 1817) Judge Eli Sims Shorter, of Georgia (b. 1792, d. 1836), Judge of the Superior Court in 1822, member Legislature 1829, and of great distinction and remarkably striking personal appearance, (See "*Bench and Bar of Georgia.*") She was of a very bright and lively disposition, and a fine talker—spirited, and a bit eccentric. A devoted member of Methodist Church. Issue:

(1) **REUBEN C.[5]** (b. 1818) Columbus, Ga.; small statue, light hair and blue eyes. Married Kate Ward, daughter of U. S. Army Officer. Issue: I. Dr. Eli Sims[6], of New York (———, d. 1886), m. in Rhode Island. A son, Eli[7] Sims, survives him. II, John U[6]., 'Lawyer, Brooklyn, N. Y. (———), m. Miss Denio, of Massachusetts. Of several children, one daughter survives. The two brothers were bright and genial. III, Mary[6] (———), m. Thomas Fry, of Mobile, Ala. Of nine children, seven are living. IV, Kate[6] (———, m. (1) George C. Brown, of Macon, Ga. Issue: Three children. She m. (2) Mr. Preston; no issue. V, Sophie[6] (———), m. John Aldredge, of Atlanta. Of several children, one survives.

(2) **MARY JANE[4] SHORTER** (p. 1820, ———) m. Dr. John A. Urquhart, of Columbus, Ga., where they lived in great elegance. They had no children. (*See Urquhart Family.*)

(3) **VIRGINIA[4] SHORTER** (b. 1821, ———) m. J. Berrien Oliver, of Columbus, Ga. (who died *circa* 1881). They moved to Florida. She was very delicate. (*See Oliver Family.*)

XI. **THEOPHILUS[4] WATKINS** (b. 1799, d. 1814, fifteen years of age).

(End of descendants of James[3] Watkins, b. 1756.)

DESCENDANTS OF

III. **SARAH HERNDON[3] WATKINS** (b. Prince Edward county, Va., 20th June, 1760; d. Huntsville, Ala.); only daughter of James and Martha (Thompson) Watkins; m. Capt. Robert[3] Thompson ("*Old Blue,*") of Amelia county, Va., son of Robert,[2] who was son of Robert,[1] the "goldsmith and banker." Issue: 1. Sophia[4] (Manning). 2. Pamela[4] (Bibb). 3. Eliz.[4] (Tate). (*For descendants see Thompson and Bibb.*)

DESCENDANTS OF

IV. ROBERT H.[3] WATKINS of South Carolina (b. Pr. Edward co., Va., 7th June. 1762); m. Jane, daughter of Drury and Eleanor (Oliver) Thompson. Issue: Seven sons, most of whom died young. One of these, Leric,[4] the youngest (perhaps), was ward of his uncle, John[2] Watkins. He heired a fortune, and lived a life of pleasure, and died young and unmarried.

DESCENDANTS OF

V. SAMUEL[3] WATKINS (b. Va., 17th May, 1765; d. Lawrence co., Ala., October, 1835), married (1792) Eleanor Thompson. She was a sister of Robert (or "*Blue*") Thompson, of Amelia co., Va., with whom he formed a mercantile partnership in Petersburg, Ga., both removing to North Alabama 1825· Samuel Watkins' plantation in Georgia, was near the Savannah river, Elbert co., and near his brother, James Watkins. He came from Virginia in 1790. "My Aunt Eleanor's home," said, recently, Mrs. Martha (Watkins) Harris, of Columbia, Ga., "was noted for its fine surroundings, even in those early days, and especially its lovely flowers, which were her specialty. The old lady rode in her coach, always attended by her black maid in great state." (*See* "*Early Settlers.*") Issue:

1. Eliza[4]; 2, Paul J.[4]; 3, Elmira[4]; 4, Eleanor[4]; 5, Edgar[4]—as follows:

1. ELIZA[4] WATKINS, (b. 1793, d. 1817,) married (1812) in Petersburg, Ga., Col. Benj. Sherrod, son of Isaac and Mary (Copeland) Sherrod, of North Carolina; (he was born Halifax County, N. C., 1776; d. Lawrence County, Ala., 24th April, 1847): Reared by his Uncle, Abram Ricks,[*] of Halifax. Educated at Williams and Mary College, Virginia, and University, N. C.; removed to his "*Cotton Garden*" plantation, Ala., (with his father-in-law) and amassed great wealth; was principal owner of the railroad from Tuscumbia to Decatur, (one of the first constructed in the South), and part of the great line then projected from Memphis to Charleston, S. C. Railroad engines, and steamboats, often bore his name at that time.

---

[*]Benj. and Isaac Ricks came to North Carolina from Virginia. It is said the family first settled in Salem, Mass., 1630, with the Puritans.

Isaac Ricks married (I) ——, and had two children. He married (II) Olivia Fort and had five daughters and six sons, among them: Benj. Sherrod Ricks and Abram Ricks, who was uncle and guardian of Col. Benj. Sherrod, of Alabama. Descendants of Abram Ricks, live now at Tuscumbia, Ala.

Robert Ricks, of Rocky Mount, N. C., is also of this family, who says that three brothers Ricks, William, Benjamin and Isaac came to Virginia from England about 1780, and Isaac and Benjamin removed to Rocky Mount neighborhood, North Carolina, in 1780. They were followed to North Carolina later by William's son, Isaac, from Virginia. Isaac, Sr., died 1790 and left sons, John and James Ricks. John reared a large family in North Carolina; Benjamin Ricks died 1774 and had sons: Louis, Thomas, Joel, Abram, Benjamin, Josiah, John and William. He was great-grandfather to Robert H. Ricks, of Rocky Mount, N. C. The sons of Isaac, Jr., who came from Virginia and died 1890, were John, Abram, Isaac, Benjamin, Robert, William and Richard. Of these, Benjamin, Isaac and Abram moved South about 1835; Robert P. Ricks, of Spring Valley, Ala., a grandson of Abram, of Alabama.

Benjamin Sherrod, of Edgecombe county, signed petition (1768) in behalf of free negroes that they should not pay taxes on their wives and daughters.—(*N. C. Colonial Records.*)

Benj. Sherrod, 1776, testimony against counterfeiters.—(*Ibid.*)

Thomas Sherrod, of Bute county, member of Provisional Congress at Halifax, 1776, was made first major of his county militia; Thos. Eaton, colonel; Wm. Alston, lieutenant colonel; and Green Hill, second major.

Thomas Sherrod, of Franklin county, N. C. (1788), member of convention which met at Hillsborough, N. C.. to consider the Federal Constitution, which they did not ratify until 1789; Wm. McKinsie, of Moore county, in same convention.—(*Southern Hist. Mag. III, 123.*)

He was twice married. His second wife (1818) was the widow of Coleman[4] Watkins, son of William[3], with several children. She was Talitha Goode (b. 22 April, 1792, d. 14 May, 1873) daughter of John Goode,* of Abbeville District, S. C. Besides her Watkins and Sherrod children, the second Mrs. Sherrod reared, also, Llewellyn Oliver, son of her sister, Ann Goode, and Dionysius Oliver, of Edgefield County, S. C. (See OLIVER; and *"Goode's Virginia Cousins."*)   Issue of ELIZA WATKINS:

1. Marie Antoinette[5]; 2, Felix Alonso McKinzie[5]; 3, Frederick O. A.[5]; 4, Samuel Watkins[5], as follows:

    1. Maria Antoinette[5] Sherrod, (b. 1813,) married Jacob Swoope, (1st wife) and lived only a short while. Issue: WILLIAM[6] SWOOPE, heir to a considerable fortune, died at the age of 20. (His father married (secondly) Frances, daughter of the Rev. Turner and Frances (Dunn) Saunders, and had other children). (See *Saunders family*).

    2. Felix Alonso McKinzie[5] Sherrod m. Sarah Ann Parrish. (*See Saunders, for children*).

    3. Frederick O. A.[5] Sherrod married Anne, daughter of Col. John Bolton, of Baltimore. (She married (II) Dr. Farrar, of Jackson, Miss.). Issue: I, John Bolton[6] Sherrod, of Montgomery, Ala., married Judith, dau. of Col. Winston, Tuscumbia, Ala., several children. II, Frederick O.[6] Sherrod, Birmingham, Ala., m. Mittie, youngest daughter of Orrin Davis, of Lawrence County, Ala., several children; III, Felix A. O.[6] Sherrod, d. y.; IV, Frances, d. y.; V, dau.[6], d. infant; VI, Benj. Watkins[6] Sherrod, married Miss Alexander.

    4. Samuel Watkins[5] Sherrod, married Frances Parrish, sister of his brother Felix's wife. Issue:

---

* John[1] Goode, of Barbadoes (son of Richard Goode, of Cornwall, Eng.), born about 1620, went to Barbadoes about 1643; there married Frances Mackerness and removed to "*Whitby*," James river, four miles from Richmond, Va.. (before 1660,) where his wife soon died, leaving son, Samuel. He married (II) Anne Bennet, who left twelve children.

Samuel[2], the son, born in Barbadoes before 1660, (will 1734,) mentioned in Henrico Records, married Martha Jones, and had seven children. Of these the third son:

Philip[3] (b. 1700-20) went, through Mecklenburg county, to Edgefield, S. C., about 1760; had three sons. Of these:

Samuel[4], of Edgefield district, had son:

John[5], of Abbeville district, S. C. (b. 1760-70); married Ann Freeman, and lived near Cambridge, scarce a vestige of which remains. It is near Ninety-Six. Issue: 1, John; 2, Col. Freeman Goode, of Lawrence county, Ala.; 3, Talitha m. (I) Watkins; (II) Sherrod; 4, Mrs. Larkin Griffin; 5, Ann m. Dionysius Oliver; 6, Elizabeth m. Mr. Burt, of Edgefield district, S. C.; 7, Daughter m. Mr. Burt, of Green county, Ala.; 8, Frances m. —— Brooks; 9, Lucinda m Mr. McLemore, of Edgefield, S. C., and removed to Courtland, Alabama.—(Goode's *Va. Cousins*.)

CHILDREN OF COL. BENJ. AND TALITHA (GOODE) SHERROD:

1. CHARLES FOX SHERROD, of Columbus, Miss. (b. Lawrence county, Ala., 3d November, 1827) m. (1851) Susan, daughter of Col. Thos. C. Billups. He was a student of Lagrange College, Ala. and the University N. C. 56th Ala. Cavalry, C. S. A. Issue: 1, Thomas Billups (died 1898), m. Bettie Hope; three children; 2, Charles F. m. Lena Harrison; 3, Sarah A. m. Mr. Sheffield; 4, Ella. m..; 5, Wm. Henry m. Miss Barksdale; 6, Lily (dead); 7, Antoinette m. Turner Champney; 8, Irene, d. y.; 9, Lolita, m..., and two d. y.

2. SUSAN ADELAIDE SHERROD m. Col. Samuel W. Shackelford, of Lawrence county, (son of Dr. Jack Shackelford, hero of the Mexican War.) The father and son, were, both, Nature's noblemen. Issue:

May Adelaide m..

Jack Shackelford, of Courtland, Ala., and Columbus, Miss., married Lottie Taylor. Issue, two children.

3. HON. WILLIAM CRAWFORD SHERROD, of Alabama and Texas. Legislature Alabama 1859, and member Charleston Convention of Secession; C. S. A., Major Patterson's Brigade. U. S. Congress 1869-71. Planter, Alabama, Mississippi, and Texas. Married (1856) Amanda, dau. of Col. Samuel K. Morgan, of Nashville, Tenn. Issue: 1, Charles M., married —— Redus; several children; 2, William Crawford, Jr.; 3, St. Clair Morgan; 4, Lillian K.; 5, Benjamin; 6, Lucille; 7, Eugene; all now living in Wichita, Texas.

John Goode (or Good), aged 22; Wm. Goode, aged 21; and Henry Goode, aged 19, embarked in the ship "*Expedition*," from Gravesend, Eng., in November, 1635, for Barbadoes, and were "examined by the minister touching their conformity to the Church of England."—(*Hotten's Emigrants, 138.*)

1. Henry[4] Sherrod died when grown; leaving a considerable fortune.
2. Walter[4] Sherrod, of Town Creek, Lawrence County, Ala., married Laura, daughter of Orrin Davis, Lawrence County, and died young. A son, Henry[5] Sherrod (b. 1864,) married Ella, daughter of Mr. James Irvine, of Florence, Ala. and had Virginia, Irvine Sherrod.

II. PAUL J.[4] WATKINS, of Lawrence county, Ala.. called " DON" Watkins (b. Petersburg. Ga., 1795), d. at his home, "*Flower Hill*," Lawrence county, Ala. Married (I), Madison county, Tenn. (1822), Eliz. Watt; married (II) (1857) Mary Morrison, who married (I) Gen. Bartley Lowe, of Huntsville, Ala. He preceded his parents to Alabama in 1820, for whom he purchased a plantation, and also "*Flower Hill*" for himself. Like his mother, Eleanor Thompson, he made his home a floral kingdom, and his exquisite collection was noted throughout North Alabama. He preserved much of his family history, of which he wrote an abstract in 1853 (at the request of his neighbor, Col. James E. Saunders). Issue, all by first marriage: 1, Eliza[5]; 2, Susan[5]; 3, Amelia[5]; 4, Martha J.[5]; 5. Mary E.[5], as follows:

I. Eliza[5] Watkins *m.* John T. Phinizy, of the noted Georgia family. He died Wheeler, Ala., 1887. Issue:
   I. Lizzie[6] Phinizy *m.* Samuel Pointer (second wife).
   II. Maggie[6] Phinizy *m.* James Strong.
   III. Watkins[6] Phinizy *m.* Lucy, daughter of Dr. Jack Sykes, of Courtland, Ala.
   IV. Maud[6] Phinizy.
   V. Ferdinand[6] Phinizy *m.* Miss Barclay, daughter of Dr. Robert Barclay of Virginia, son of Rev. Dr. Robert Barclay, of the Christian Church, Missionary to Jerusalem, and author of the "City of the Great Kings." He was father also of the Hon. J. Judson Barclay, for some time a resident of Lawrence county, Ala., U. S. Consul, in 1861, to Island of Cypress, and Consul, in Cleveland's last administration, to Tangier, and who married Decima, tenth and youngest daughter of the Rev. Alexander Campbell, of Bethany, Va., founder of the *Christian Church*. These two Barclay brothers, with their aged and lovely parents, and the venerable Mrs. Alexander Campbell, made their home for many years in Lawrence county, Alabama.
   VI. James[6] Phinizy.
2. Susan[5] Watkins, married Ephraim H., son of James and Narcissa (Saunders) Foster, of Nashville, Tenn. (See *Saunders Family*.)
3. Amelia[5] Watkins, married Col. Edward Mumford, of Virginia; on Gen. Albert Sidney Johnston's staff in the Civil War, and with Gov. Isham G. Harris, of Tennessee, and other staff officers, lowered the dying General from his horse when mortally wounded at the great battle of Shiloh. One son, (1) Paul Watkins[6] Mumford, died a young man, Memphis, Tenn.
4. Martha T[5]. Watkins, married William S. Bankhead*, of Courtland, Ala., great-grandson of President Thomas Jefferson. (First wife) no living issue. Capt. Bankhead has always been the model planter and Christian gentleman, prominent in Presbyterian Church work, and with all the refinement and culture of his noble race inherent in a descendant of Jefferson (the *born aristocrat*, though the great apostle of Republican Democracy). Capt. Bankhead married (II) Miss Garth, by whom he has a lovely daughter, Nannie, now Mrs. Harvey Gilchrist,† of

---

*Martha, eldest daughter of Thomas Jefferson, married Thomas Mann Randolph, and had, among others, Anne Cary Randolph, who married Charles L. Bankhead (a cousin of Colonel Bankhead, of the United States army, who was father of Smith L. Bankhead, of Mexican war fame).

†The *ancestor*, who came to America, was Malcolm Gilchrist (born Cantire. Scotland) and came first to North Carolina, where he married Catherine Bule, and removed to Maury county, Tennessee, 1809. He was grandfather to Philip, Malcolm, and John Gilchrist, and Mrs. Bankhead, of Courtland, Alabama. The maternal grandfather of this family was Philip Phillips, who came from Wales, first to Pennsylvania, then to Kentucky, and finally, to Davidson county, Tennessee, near Nashville, in 1796.

Courtland, Ala. He married (III) Kate Gilchrist, widow of Capt. George Garth, of Courtland, by whom he has two children, Elizabeth and John Stuart Bankhead.

5. Mary E.[5] Watkins married James Branch, of the Virginia family; a great beauty and the pet of her family. Issue: 1, James[6] Branch, lawyer and member of Legislature, Alabama. Several children. II, Susie[6], unmarried. III, Robert W.[6] Branch.

III. ELMIRA[4] WATKINS, married Rev. Edgar M. Swoope, of Lawrence county, Alabama, brother of Jacob Swoope (above, and son of Jacob Swoope, Congressman from Staunton, Virginia). A very wealthy and charitable member of the great class of planters before the war. Wild and hot tempered in his youth, he became, at last, the humble and unselfish servant of God. He did much good in providing food for the families of soldiers, absent in the Civil War. Issue: 1, Samuel Watkins[5] Swoope, died young. 2, Mary Eleanor[5] Swoope (b. 1848) m. (1867) James Ballentine, of Pulaski, Tenn. Both died young. Issue: I, Edgar; II, James, lawyer;·III, William; IV, Sadie; V, Orlean, adopted by her aunt, Mrs. General Palmer, and married Turner Henderson, of Nashville, Tenn.

IV. ELEANOR[4] WATKINS married her cousin, Jesse Thompson, nephew of "Old Blue." No issue. He removed to Russellville, Ala., it is said, and died in New Orleans.

V. EDGAR[4] WATKINS never married, lived with his sister, Mrs. Swoope, and died after the war.

DESCENDANTS OF

VI. JOHN WATKINS[3], Elbert county, Ga. (b. Prince Edward county, Va., 12th February, 1768, d. 5th March, 1841, Petersburg, Ga.), m. (I) (27th October, 1798) Susan, daughter of Chesley and Judith (Christian) Daniel, of North Carolina. They lived in Petersburg, and had also a plantation five miles above, called "Thorn Hill." He m. (II) Polly Moseley, cousin of John C. Calhoun. (Her sister married Dr. Joseph Jones.) She married (II) Dr. William Richardson, whose first wife was Susan Watkins (widow of Major John Oliver, of Petersburg, Ga., and his 2d wife). She m. (III) Mr. Harris. (See *Early Settlers* of Alabama.) Issue, first marriage:

1. Lucy Woodson[4]; 2. John Daniel[4]; 3. Sarah[4]; 4. Mary[4]; 5. Martha[4]; 6 Susan[4].

(1) LUCY WOODSON[4] WATKINS (b. Petersburg, Ga., 27th February, 1800, d. at "Waverly," 7th July, 1852), m. (9th May, 1825) Col. George H. Young, of "Waverly," Clay county, Miss. Their fine old home, "Waverly," near Columbus, Miss., was a temple of Southern refinement and hospitality. Issue:

    (1) John Watkins[5] Young, d. s. p.

    (2) George Valerius[5] Young, unmarried, lives at "Waverly."

    3) Beverly Daniel[5] Young, C. S. A., died a prisoner in the Civil War at Johnson's Island.

    (4) Anna Josepha[5] Young, m. Alexander Hamilton, of North Carolina. Issue: I. Mary[6], d. y. II. Lucy Young[6], m. Henry C. Long, son of Sherrod Long. Issue: 1. Sue Alyda[7]; 2. Anna Josepha[7]; 3. Mary Elizabeth[7]: 4. Lucy Banks[7], d. y.; 5. Alexander Hamilton[7]. III. George Y[6]., d. y. IV. William Baskerville[6] (twin with George) m. Julia, daughter of Edward Turner Sykes. Issue: 1. Carolyn[7]; 2. Anna Terrell[7]; 3. Alexander[7], d. y. V. Anna Josepha[6], m. H. C. Terrell, of Quincy, Miss. Issue: 1. Elvira[7]; 2. Anna[7]; 3. Henry Clay[7]; 4. Ira[7]; 5. Ellie. VI. Alexander[6], d. y. VII. Sue Alyda[6], d. y.

His children were. 1, James, d. y.; 2, John, died, aged 40; 3, Judge Joseph Philips, of Murfreesboro, Tenn., father of Mrs. Childress and grandfather of Mrs. Gov. John C. Brown, of Tennessee. 4, Eleanor Philips, married Maj. James Neely. parents of the celebrated Methodist divine, P. P. Neely. 5, Elizabeth Philips married Col. Robert Purdy, and 6, Mary Philips married Elisha Williams.

(5) Thomas Erskine[5] Young (———) m. Georgia Butt. Issue: I, Priscilla Young[6] m. T. B. Franklin. Issue: 1, Lilla; 2, Cornell, d. y. II. Sarah Watkins[6] m. Edward Hopkins. Issue: 1, Charles[7]; 2, Thomas Erskine[7]; 3, Annie Cabott[7]; 4, Georgia Proscilla[7]. III. Lucy[6] m. Dr. C. C. Stockard, of Atlanta. Issue, two children: 1, Lucy Vaughn; 2, ———. IV, Valerius[6], unmarried—she lives in Columbus, Miss. V, Anna Alyda[6] m. Henry M. Waddell. Issue: 1, Henry Marsden[7]; 2, Hugh. VI, Moselle[6], d. y. VII, Thomas Erskine[6] m. John S. White—live in Birmingham, Ala. Issue, a daughter: Valley Young[7].

(6) James Hamilton[5] Young (———) m. Emmie, daughter of Hon. David Hubbard, M. C., of Alabama. Issue: I, George[6], d. y. II, William Lowndes[6], d. y. III, Lucy Walker[6]. IV, Emmie Hubbard[6] m. James E. Evans, of Muldon, Miss. Issue: 1, William B[7].

(7) Susan Alyda[5] Young (———) m. (I) Woodford Johnston, and m. (II) Col. Hal. E. Chambers, member of Congress of Confederate States 1861, and also of Congress United States. His father was United States Senator. Issue first marriage (none by second marriage): I, Woodford[6] m. (I), Mr. Carr, of Tennessee, and m. (II) Robert Betts, son of Elisha Betts, of Alabama. Issue (first mar.): 1, James; 2, Alyda; and by the last, Mary Woodford, and twins.

(8) William Lowndes[5] Young (———); unmarried and lives at Waverly.

(9) Sarah Banks Young[5] m. (1865) (second wife) Col. Reuben Reynolds (b. 1835, d. September 4, 1887), C. S. A. Captain of the *Van Dorn Reserves*, and Colonel of the *Eleventh Mississippi Regiment*. Lost an arm in the battle of Petersburg, Va. Prominent lawyer of Aberdeen, Miss. State Senate 1875. The noble wife and mother lives on with her children at the old home. Issue: 1, George Young[6] Reynolds. II, Reuben Oscar[6] Reynolds, prominent young lawyer (d. 1899), married (1897) Nellie, daughter of Walker Fowler. III, Hamilton English[6] Reynolds; IV, Jennie[6] Reynolds; V, Beverly Erskine[6] Reynolds; VI, Houston Watkins[6] Reynolds; VII, Sarah[6] Reynolds.

(10) Lucy Watkins[5] Young ( ) m. Col. James Oliver Banks, of Columbus, Miss., (2nd wife). Issue: I, George Young m. Katherine Yerger, of Jackson, Miss. Issue: I. Lucy Young[7]; II, Lucy Young[7]; III, Wiley Coleman[7]; IV, Ann Josepha[7], student, *Belmont*, Nashville, 1898; V, Reuben Reynolds[7].

(2) JOHN DANIEL[4] WATKINS (b. 27th April, 1801, d. 22nd July, 1890) m. (I) October, 18th 1825, Anna Alyda (b. 14th September, 1806, d. 30th January, 1834) daughter of Judge Joseph Christopher and Ann Elizabeth (De Lancey[*]) Yates (Judge Yates was Governor of New York.) He m. (II) (25th September, 1839) Ellen Augusta Hunt, of New York (died 25th March, 1892). He was the only son, and quite accomplished, his education being completed in New York. He owned the "*Madison Springs*" in Georgia. In 1830, he moved to Lexington, Ga., from New York. Issue: (*1st Mar*.):

(1) John De Lancey[5] Watkins (b. Schenectady, N. Y., 26th August, 1826) m. (I) his cousin, Mary Yates, and m. (II) ———. They live in Schenectady, N. Y. Issue 1st mar.: De Lancey[6] Watkins, and others.

(2) Susan D[5]. Watkins, (b. 1828), d. y.

(3) Joseph Christopher Yates[5] Watkins (b. Lexington, Ga., 6th September, 1831), *d. s. p.*

(4) John[5] Watkins (b. Lexington, Ga., August, 1833), *d. s. p.* Issue, 2d mar. (*Hunt*):

(5) Ann[5] Watkins, (b. 1840, d. 1846).

(6) Daniel[5] Watkins (b. 1842, d. 1846).

(7) Angelina, Griffin[5] Watkins (b. 1844, d. 1846).

(8) Ellen[4] Watkins (b. 1846, d. 1846).
These last four all poisoned by a slave.
(9) Mrs. Georgia Augusta[4] Holmes, of Macon, Ga. (b. 10th December, 1847), who has a daughter, Rosa[7] Watkins.
(10) Daniel Hunt[4] Watkins (b. 1850, d. 1852).

(3) SARAH[4] WATKINS (b. 16 January, 1803, d. 31 January, 1881) m. Petersburg, Ga. (4 February, 1828), John Banks[a], of Columbus, Ga., to which place they moved soon after marriage, and where they long dispensed generous hospitalities from their beautiful home, beloved and respected by all. It was his custom as each son came of age to give him fifteen negroes, four mules and a plantation, though his shelter still was to be the old home, until marriage. Issue:

  (1) George Young[5] Banks m. (I) Sue Shepherd, and had eight children; and (II) Polly Funston, and had daughter Polly. He was a member of the Georgia State Convention 1861, which passed the "Ordinance of Secession." Issue: Mary[6], George[6], and others not known.
  (2) John Troup[5] Banks, d. y.
  (3) Susan Martha[5] Banks, unmarried; lived with Mrs. Peacock.
  (4) Capt. Willis Dunstan[5] Banks, C. S. A., Thirty-ninth Alabama, Deas' Brigade, Hindman's Division; mortally wounded in battle near Atlanta, and died 28th July, 1864.
  (5) Lieutenant Eugene[5] Banks, C. S. A., of the same company and regiment with his brother; killed in battle of "Resaca," Ga., 15th May, 1864.
  (6) Daniel Watkins[5] Banks, killed in siege of Atlanta, while on picket duty, making the *third son killed in battle within three months.* The trio of young heroes dead on the field of honor, and the old parents' hearts breaking at home! Was there *ever* a more pure and glittering sacrifice!
  (7) Edward Simms[5] Banks, of Columbus, Ga., m. Pauline Deloney. Issue: Lucy[6], m. Edward Shepherd, of Wynnton, Ga.
  (8) William Kelley[5] Banks, died aged 35.
  (9) Anne Maria Josephine[5] Banks m. James Gideon Peacock. Issue: I, Sallie; II, Elberta; III, John; IV, James.
  (10) Dr. Elbert Augustus[5] Banks, physician in New York; unmarried, which is to be wondered at, when he takes so much interest in his family lineage, of which he is the noble and unselfish type.
  (11) Sarah Lucy[5] Banks m. Edward E. Yonge, and has: I, Banks[6]; II, Mary Ellis[6]; III, Nettie[6].
  (12) Rockingham Gilmer[5] Banks, of Tallassee, Ala.; State Senate of Alabama, and planter; married Kate ——; no children.

(4) MARY[4] WATKINS (b. 16th January, 1806; d. 18th May, 1818).

(5) MARTHA[4] WATKINS (b. 13th September, 1807; d. 22d October, 1896, in New Orleans), m. Colonel James W. Harris, of Columbus, Miss. (b. 1805; d. 1887), son of Gen. Jeptha V. and Rebecca (Hunt) Harris, of Elbert county, Ga.—" Farm Hill," the family home. With the vivacious charm of the women of her family, the venerable octogenarian was cheerful and most attractive, and considerate of others, to the hour of

---

[a]See Banks Family.

DAVID[1] WATKINS, of Virginia, son of the immigrant (name not known), had son, John[2] Watkins, father of Asa[3] Watkins, who moved to Georgia, and had son John[4] Watkins born Jefferson county, Ga., 1777, m. (1804) Sarah McDonald, and moved to Jefferson county, Miss. Parents of John Watkins, of New Orleans (b. 1806, d. 1898), and of the Rev. William Watkins, for many years faithful Methodist Minister in New Orleans; the father of Dr. Watkins, of Carondelet and St. Andrew streets, New Orleans (1899.)

Mr. John Watkins came to New Orleans 1848. Married (1852) Caroline E. Campbell, of Kentucky, and had one child, Sarah, Mrs. W. W. Divine, mother of Mrs. Wm. H. Allyn, and Mrs. John Watkins Divine.

her death, which came calmly while she was seated listening to hymns sung on a Sabbath evening, by her young grandchildren, in the home of her daughter, Mrs. Mary Guion, of New Orleans (*see Harris Family*). Issue:
(1) Susan Ann⁶ Harris, d. y.
(2) Sarah Watkins⁶ Harris, m. Thomas Bailey, of North Carolina. Issue:
I. Sallie⁷ m. Thomas Hardy. Issue: 1. Mattie⁷ (d. y.); 2. Bailey⁷; 3. Lucile⁷; 4. Lenore⁷; 5. Harris⁷ Hardy.
II. Lucy⁶ m. Baskerville Hardy. One child⁷.
(3) Martha⁶ Watkins Harris, m. Judge Joel M. Acker, of Aberdeen, Miss. Issue:
I. Hon. James M.⁶ m. Anna Cunningham, and has, James⁷.
II. Corinne A.⁶ m. Frank Rogers. Issue: Acker⁷ and Christian⁷.
(5) Col. William Hunt⁶ Harris, C. S. A., of New Orleans, Adjt. General on General Wheeler's staff, m. (I) Emmie Smith, and m. (II) Lilie O. Hanson, of Louisiana. Issue (first marriage):
I. Judson⁶, m. (I) Alice Weeks, and m. (II) Amelia Clute. *Issue 1st mar.*, two children; and several by last. II. James Barton⁶, of N. O., m. (1895) Julia Price. III. Hunt⁶, m. (1896) Minnie Porter, of Key West. IV. Emmie⁶ m. William Frazee. Issue: Mary Lou. V. Jeptha Vining⁶ of Aberdeen, unm. Issue second mar. (*Hanson*): VI. Caldewood⁶. VII. Olivia⁶, VIII, Margaret⁶, IX, Lilie⁶ (b. 1893).
6. Jeptha V.⁶ Harris, Surgeon in Confederate Navy, m. Mollie Perkins. Issue:
I. Jeptha Vining⁶ m. —— Curry. II. Lewis⁶ m. III. Mattie⁶, m. IV. Marion⁶, d. y.
(7) James Watkins⁶ Harris, m. Gertrude Garrard, Jackson, Miss. Issue: (I) Garrard⁶, young lawyer, unm., President Young Men's Business League. II. Isabella⁶; III. Helen⁶; IV. Eva⁶; V. David⁶. Live in Jackson, Miss.
(8) Mary Elizabeth⁶ Harris, m. (I) Dr. James Augustus Lanier, of Mississippi, C. S. A. Surgeon, son of James Lanier, of Courtland, Ala., and m. (II) Lewis Guion, of New Orleans, Lawyer, and Captain C. S. A. *Issue 1st mar.:*
I. James Augustus⁶ Lanier, of Donaldsonville, La., m. Lelia Monnot. Issue: 1, Ernest Monnot⁷; 2, Haskell Du Bose. Issue second mar. (*Guion*): II. Mary Leigh⁶ Guion. III. Carrie Lewis⁶, Guion.
(9) Lucy Harris. m. W. B. Winston, and had: 1, William; 2 Corinne, m.——, and living in Waco, Texas.

(6.) SUSAN⁴ WATKINS, married (1833), Judge Robert Dougherty, of Clark county, Ga; who d. 1868.
They removed to Tuskegee, Ala., 1843, where he rose to eminence at the bar. Was Judge of the 9th Judicial District for eighteen years, until his death. He was a fine type of the American wit and humorist of his day, and at times playing almost boyish pranks upon his relatives and friends. His fun-loving reputation made him a worthy rival of the celebrated Judge Longstreet, of Ga., and many are the anecdotes preserved of his "quips and jests" in the family. Issue, nine children (four dying in childhood):
(1.) William⁶ Dougherty, died in Columbus, Miss., 1880.
(2.) Charles⁶ Dougherty, C. S. A., 3rd. Ala. Reg. Fatally wounded at "*Seven Pines*," and died a prisoner at Fortress Monroe, Va.
(3.) Sarah Banks⁶ Dougherty, married Capt. R. H. Leonard, and lives at Talbotton, Ga.
(4.) Rebecca Carlton⁶ Dougherty, married Col. W. D. Humphries, of Columbus, Miss. Her mother, Mrs. Susan Dougherty, lived with them until her death.
(5.) Lucy Young⁶ Dougherty.
End of descendants of John⁵ Watkins.

DESCENDANTS OF

VII. THOMPSON⁶ WATKINS, of Elbert county, Ga. (b. in Virginia 17th August, 1770), married Nancy, sister of Gen. Benj. Taliaferro, of Virginia and Georgia, and daughter of Zachariah Taliaferro, of Amherst county, Va. They resided a while in Wilks county, Ga., and then removed to Montgomery, Ala. In Wilks county, Ga., their place adjoined Mrs. Watkins' sister, Mrs. Sally (Taliaferro) Harvie,* and a mile or two from Broad river. Issue:

1. Zachariah Taliaferro⁴ Watkins, (   ) married Edna, daughter of Peyton Bibb.— (*See Bibb.*)

2. James Franklin⁴ Watkins, (   ) m. Martha, daughter of Meriwether Marks and his wife, Ann Matthews, granddaughter of Gov. Matthews, of Georgia. Issue:

    1. Rebecca⁵ (only child) married Samuel, son of Joel Matthews. No issue.

VIII. JOSEPH³ WATKINS, (b. in Virginia 17th May, 1772), celebrated planter of Georgia, m. (I) Mary Sayre, of New Jersey, and (II) her sister, Delia Sayre. "Archie Stokes" said Mrs. Mary (Watkins) Saunders, "was called the merchant prince of Petersburg, Ga. He went to New York and there married one of the Misses Sayre. Her four sisters came to Georgia with them. Two of these sisters married, successively, my great uncle, Joseph Watkins, and another married Dr. Elijah Stuart, of Elbert county, and another married Andrew, son of Samuel Rembert." Joseph Watkins left no children to inherit his talents and wealth. His home was near Petersburg, *then a* bustling, thriving tobacco market. "*To-day* it is a wilderness of blackberry bushes, with not even a ruined chimney to mark the spot."

"He was a planter of large means, and in studying the application of mechanics, more for pleasure than for profit, discovered, and made, the first *gin* for upland cotton and had it in successful operation while Eli Whitney, at the house of Mrs. Gen. Nathaniel Greene, in Savannah, Ga.,—puzzled and thwarted—was working at a similar model. Upon hearing of Mr. Watkins' invention, he did the wise thing in going to inspect it in person. He was courteously received, in the old-time Southern style, and shown by the amiable host over the whole plantation, and all its attractive features and improvements delightedly exhibited, and he found the new gin corresponded with his own conception, with the additional idea that one cylinder, studded at right angles with parallel rows of wire teeth to tear the lint from the seed, and another cylinder provided with brushes to sweep it off, and revolving, not above, but on a horizontal plane, would greatly improve his original plan," etc. This was in 1792, and he soon had a success.

"But every one in Georgia regarded Whitney merely as the *improver* and *introducer* of the cotton gin, and not the *inventor*; and Watkins was continually urged to bring counter-suits against Whitney; but, as was said, he had studied the application of mechanics more for amusement than profit, and invariably refused and allowed things to take their own course. Whitney was born in Massachusetts, in 1765. He had been disappointed in gaining the position of private tutor in a private family, for which he had come South, and Mrs. Greene befriended him with the fortunate result to the world.

"All that is here stated regarding Joseph Watkins can, upon demand, be thoroughly substantiated." (See article by Hugh N. Starnes, in the "Southern Bivouac" for December, 1885, on "*The Cotton Gin, its Invention and Effect.*")

NOTE.—Mrs. Sallie Harvie, above was the wife of Daniel, who was the son of John Harvie, of the Shire of Stirling, Scotland, who came to Albemarle county, Va . forty years before the Revolution, and married the daughter of Daniel Gaines, of Virginia. Four sons and five daughters were born to this couple in Virginia. Of these, Daniel (above) weighed nearly 400 pounds, and was stronger than the giant and Revolutionary hero, Peter Francisco. The aggregate weight of the nine brothers and sisters was 2700 pounds.

The children of Daniel Harvie were: 1, Martha m. Dr. Thornton Gilmer; 2, Mary B. m. Peachy R. Gilmer; 3, Nancy m. Thos. L. Gilmer (*two brothers of Governor Gilmer and Mrs. Benajah Bibb, of Montgomery*); 4, Frances m. —— Bostwick, of Kentucky; 5, Daniel, never married; 6, William m. Judith Cosby. Elis. (sister of Daniel) m. James Marks, parents of Meriwether Marks (above).—(See *Governor Gilmer's Early History of Georgia*).

DESCENDANTS OF

IX. ISHAM[3] WATKINS of Georgia (b. 28th Feb. 1774   ) m. Emily, daughter of Gen. Benj. Taliaferro, and had ten children, as follows: (1) Martha[4] m. Robert Bell, near Huntsville, Alabama, several children. (2) Benjamin[4], m. Polly Bell. (3) Betsy[4], m. Thomas Bell, Columbus, Miss. (4) Sarah[4], m. ——— Dismukes, of Davidson county, Tennessee. (5) Albert[4], m. four times, and had a large family. (6) Emily[4], m. ——— Wilson, Elkton, Tenn. (7) Mary[4], m. Henry Bell, of Columbus, Miss. One of her sons, William, was Lieutenant in Mexican war. and lost an arm. (8) Harriet[4], m. (9) Isham Eldridge[4] Watkins, m. daughter of Ben Leflore, and lived in Madison county, Mississippi. It is to be regretted there is no recent data received of Isham Watkins' descendants.

Excursus---Harris.

HENRY[1] HARRIS came from Glamorgan, Wales, to Virginia, and became a Dissenter and Baptist preacher. He obtained, with others (in 1691), a grant, from William and Mary, of ten miles square, on the south bank of James river, some miles above the Great Falls of Richmond. Issue:

EDWARD[2] HARRIS m. ———, and had eight sons and five daughters. Of these, the fourth child, NATHAN[3] HARRIS (b. 1716), m. (1737) Catherine Walton, of Brunswick county, Va. Issue: 1, Walton[4]; 2, Nathan[4]; 3, Isaac[4]; 4, David[4], killed in battle of Augusta, Ga., in Revolution; 5, Elias[4]; 6, Rowland[4]; 7, Herbert[4]; 8, Gideon[4]; 9, Patsy[4]; 10, Jane[4]; 11, Elizabeth[4]; 12, Bowler[4]; 13, Anne[4], and 14, Howell[4]. Of these:

1. WALTON[4] HARRIS (b. Brunswick county, Va., 1739) m. Rebecca Lanier.[o] Issue: 1, Buckner[5]; 2, Sampson[5]; 3, Joel[5] d. y.; 4, Edwin[5] m. Miss Logan (Kentucky branch); 5, Augustin[5] (a large family in Georgia, and father of Judge Iveson L.[6] Harris[o]); 6, Nathan[5] (twice married, and to Mrs. Starnes last); 7, Simeon[5], d. y.; 8, David[5]; 9,

---

[o]John Washington, son of Lawrence and Mildred (Warner) Washington, and also uncle to the President, married Catherine Whiting, of Gloucester county, Virginia (which county was the home of the Warners, Whitings and one line of the Washington family. His children were: Warner, Henry, Mildred, Elizabeth and Catherine. Of these Elizabeth Washington married Thomas Lanier,† and their children were: 1, Richard; 2, Thomas; 3, James; 4, Elizabeth, married ——— Craft, and 5, Sampson Lanier, married Elisabeth Chamberlain of New Kent county, Virginia, and had issue: 1, Lewis, of Scriven county, Georgia; 2, Buckner. of Virginia; 3, Burwell; 4, Winifred, m. Col. Drewry Ledbetter, of Brunswick county, Georgia. and was grandmother of Judge John C. Nicholl, of Savannah, Ga.; 5, Nancy, m. Major Vaughn, of Roanoke. N. C., and 6, Rebecca Lanier, married Walton Harris, of Brunswick county, Virginia.

The Washington descent is not now claimed by all the descendants.

[o]Sidney Lanier, the poet, was son of Robert Sampson Lanier, of this family.

John Lanier (1686), 1482 acres, with Peter Wyche, in Charles City, Surry county.—(Records.)

Sampson Lanier (1718), 150 acres in Surry county.

Lemuel Lanier (1741), two acres on north side of Nottoway river, Surry county, and mentioned in Albemarle Parish, Register, 1742.

Nicholas and Sampson Lanier, Vestry of St. Andrew's parish, Brunswick county, Va., between 1732-36; Thos. Lanier, of Vestry of Cumberland parish, Lunenburg county (now Mecklenburg), after 1747.

Richard and Ann Lanier, a son, William (b. 1768).—(Albemarle Parish Register.)

Louis Lanier m. in Brunswick county. Va. (1752), Martha Speed.

John Lanier in North Carolina, 1764. "His former grant not completed until more particularly mentioned in the warrant."—(N. C. Colonial R cords, VI.)

Robert Lanier, of Granville county, N. C., juror (1769), with James Gancey, Jesse Saunders, Solomon Alston, Samuel Sneed and others.—(Ibid.)

Lewis Lanier, Anson county, N. C. (1788), member of Hillsborough convention.—(Ibid.)

A line of the Violett family is also descended from Thomas Lanier.

Mr. Gideon D. Harris, Columbus, Miss., writes: "The Harris' in Georgia, Alabama, Mississippi, Florida, Louisiana, Tennessee, Kentucky, Arkansas and Texas descend from Nathan. The other seven sons of the first Edward peopled the Middle and Western States." He has a complete genealogy of the descendants of the six sons and six daughters of General Jeptha V. Harris, "of whom the eldest and the youngest were twenty-four years apart to the day." He adds, the "Sampson Harris branch was a family of noted lawyers, three of his sons becoming Judges." He furnishes his own line, and the sons of Nathan Harris for this sketch, as well as a corresponding record to all the above. Acknowledgments are due also Mrs. Jeptha V. Harris, Mrs. Lewis Guion, of New Orleans, and the Family Records of Judge Stephen Willis Harris (deceased), of Huntsville, Ala.

Walton[6] (the Young L. G. Harris line); 10, Elizabeth[6]; 11, Littleton[6], d. y.; 12, Jeptha Vining[6]. Of these:

1. SAMPSON[5] HARRIS m. Susanna Willis, daughter of Stephen and Susanna Willis[*], of a New Kent county, Va., family. Issue: 1, Stephen Willis[6] (b. 1785) m. Sarah Watkins (see Watkins); 2, Thomas W.[6]; 3, Ptolemy T.[6], trustee University of Alabama, 1830; 4, Rebecca[6] m. Mr. Young; 5, Susan[6]; 6 Elizabeth[6], and 7, Catherine[6] (twins). (Early Settlers).

12. GEN. JEPTHA VINING[5] HARRIS, of Athens, Ga., m. (1804) Sarah Hunt. Issue:

I. JAMES WALTON[6] HARRIS, Columbus, Miss. (b. 1st August, 1805), m. Martha, daughter of John and Susan (Daniel) Watkins, of Elbert county, Ga. (See Watkins.)

II. WILLIAM L.[6] HARRIS (b. 1807) m. (1829) Frances Semmes. Issue: Mary R.[7], Sarah Hunt[7], Green[7], Callie[7], Jeptha V.[7], Frances[7], Willie[7] and Regina[7].

III. GEORGE HUNT[6] HARRIS (b. 4th March, 1809) m. (21st May, 1833) Mary Douse of Georgia. Issue: 1, Samuel Douse[7] (b. 1834) m. (1863) Henrietta Williams; 2, Sarah Tallulah[7] (b. 1836) m. (1854) Dr. W. L. Lipscomb; 3. James Walton[7] (b. 1842, d. 1871); 4, Mary Douse[7] (b. 1844) m. (1862) Dr, C. S. W. Price; 5, Gideon Douse[7] Harris (b. June 9, 1846) m. (6th March, 1867) Lizzie Eager, of Mississippi, and had Laura (b. 12th August, 1870), m. (1896) Rev. W. S. Jacobs; Lizzie (b. 25th November, 1874) m. (1893) Wm. E. Waring; Gideon Douse[7] (b. June 26, 1877); George Hunt[7] (b. 14th February, 1880); Edward Strong (b. 28th October, 1883).

IV. ANN E.[6] HARRIS (b. 11th May, 1811) m. Judge George E. Clayton. Issue: Julia[7], Jeptha[7], Almira[7], Fanny[7], Cary[7] and Norma[7].

V. SARAH[6] HARRIS (b. 1814) m. Tinsley W. Rucker, of Georgia Issue: Sarah[7] m. Angus McAlpin; Georgia[7] m. Mr. Hall; Kate[7], Tinsley[7], Jeptha V.[7], and others.

VI. JEPTHA V.[6] HARRIS, of Columbus, Miss. (b. 1st December, 1816) m. Mary, daughter of Willis and Mary (Oliver) Banks, of Georgia. (See Banks and Oliver.)

VII. ELIJAH WILLIS[6] HARRIS (b. 15th August, 1819), m. Irene Taylor of Alabama. Issue: Irene T., m. Albert Ramsey, and had several children.

VIII. REBECCA[6] HARRIS (b. 30th April, 1822), m. William Crawford Bibb, of Alabama.—(See Bibb.)

IX. MARY[6] HARRIS (b. 24th April, 1824), m. William O. Saffold, of Georgia. Issue: Two sons and three daughters, among them, Rebecca.

X. EUGENE[6] HARRIS (b. 16th February, 1826), m. Florine Jones; several children.

XI. SUSAN[6] HARRIS (b. 29th December, 1827), m. Joel Abbott Billups, of Georgia. One daughter, "Loula," who m. Mr. Graham and died without issue.

XII. TALLULAH[6] HARRIS (b. 1st August, 1829), m. (I) Robert Taylor of Georgia, and m. (II) James A. Carleton of Georgia. Several children, of whom Robert Carleton is one.

Mr. C. W. Andrews, of Milledgeville, Ga., son-in-law of Judge Iveson L. Harris, who was son of Augustin and grandson of Walton Harris, has just completed a genealogy of the family, from the progenitor to present date, all from records left by Judge Iveson L. Harris, who had collected more data than any of his family previous to his death.

TALIAFERRO, OF GEORGIA.

ROBERT TALIAFERRO (b. 1635, d. 1700), patent in Gloucester county, Va., 1655, and in 1662, 900 acres, called "Attapotomy," on Poropotank creek, Gloucester, and 6300 acres on Rapp river. Married daughter of Rev. Charles Grymes, of Gloucester, and had five sons: 1. Francis (d. 1710), living in Gloucester 1682; Justice in Essex county 1695; m. Eliza,

---

*Rebecca, daughter of Stephen and Susanna Willis, born in New Kent county, Va., 1739.—(See Peter's Parish Register.)

daughter of Col. John Catlett, of Essex, and had a son, Robert, whose will (1724) had for a crest, a human head.

2. John (d. 1720); Justice of Essex 1695; *m.* Sarah, *dau.* Col. Lawrence Smith, of Gloucester (who came with his father, to that county). Issue: Lawrence (will 1726); John (b. 1687) of "*Snow Creek*," of Spotsylvania and James City county; Charles, Robert, Zacharias, Catharine, Sarah, Mary, Eliz., Richard and William. Of these, Zacharias's will was *p.* in Essex county, 1745.

3. Richard, living (1711) in Richmond county, Va. Richard Taliaferro, 1689, witnessed a deed, York county, with Mathew Ryder, Richard Payne and others.—(*York Records.*)

4. Charles (died 1720), Essex county. John Taliaferro, Francis Conway and John Taliaferro, of "the Mount," his executors. He had at least one son, Charles, who patented 1000 acres in Spotsylvania, 1726.

5. Robert (died 1726), of Essex; *m.* Sarah, also *dau.* of Col. John Catlett, and had Robert, Ann and Elizabeth.

Governor Gilmer in his "*Early Settlers of Georgia*," says of the *name*: "It is from the Latin, *talis* and *ferrum*, to *cut with iron*. Two brothers came to America, and only one left male descendants." Mr. Jefferson, to please Chancellor Wythe, who married Eliz Taliaferro, visited their original home in Italy, and secured their coat-of-arms. (*See Jefferson's letters.*) He had a copper book-plate with the seals of the Taliaferro and Wythe families, made in Paris, 1786. "I sent you, formerly, copies of the documents on the Taliaferro family, which I had received from Mr. Febroni. I now send the originals," September, 1787. Chancellor Wythe's first wife was Anne Lewis; his second, the *dau.* of Richard and Eliza (Eggleston) Taliaferro, of "*Powhatan*," near Williamsburg.

The ancestor of the Georgia family was ZACHARIAS TALIAFERRO, who moved from Williamsburg to Amherst county, Va. His patent there was in 1767.—(*Land Book, 56*). He was Justice. His son GEN. BENJAMIN TALIAFERRO, of Georgia (1764), was captain in the Revolution, and Judge of the Superior Court, Georgia; voted against Yazoo fraud in 1795 while in Legislature. Member of Congress, etc.

His other children were: Zach, Richard, Warner, Burton, Sally, Nancy and Frances. Of these, Nancy married Thompson Watkins (b. 1770), and removed to Georgia, living near their relatives in Oglethorpe county, and had sons: Zach. Watkins; *m.* Edna, *dau.* of Peyton Bibb; and James Watkins, who *m.* Martha, *dau.* of Meriwether Marks, of Alabama, and had a daughter, Rebecca, who *m.* Samuel Matthews. Gen. Benj. Taliaferro, of Georgia, married Martha Meriwether, daughter of David Meriwether. Issue:

1. Major Benj. Taliaferro *m.* Martha (b. 1787), *dau.* of James and Jane (Thompson) Watkins, of Elbert county, Ga. (See *Pictures.*)
2. Emily Taliaferro *m.* Isham Watkins (b. 1774). (See *Watkins.*)
3. Lewis Bourbon (named for King of France) *m.* Betsy Johnson.
4. Martha *m.* William, son of Micajah McGehee ·(*first wife*). His second was Eliza Watkins.
5. David Taliaferro *m.* Mary Barnett.
6. Thornton Taliaferro *m.* (I) Miss Green, and (II) Mrs. Lamar.
7. Margaret *m.* Joseph Green.
8. Nicholas Taliaferro *m.* Malinda Hill.
9. Zach Taliaferro *m.* (II) Miss Cox; one son.

---

*NOTE.—From this it may be seen that Robert H⁴. (b. 1782), son of James and Jane (Thompson) Watkins, had an uncle, Thompson Watkins, who married Nancy, sister of General Taliaferro; another uncle, Isham, married Emily, daughter of General Taliaferro; and a sister, Martha, married Benjamin, son of General Taliaferro; another sister, Eliza, was the second wife of William McGehee, whose first wife was Martha Taliaferro.

The Taliaferro Record goes further back than the battle of Hastings, in which their ancestor so bravely fought.

COLEMAN.

James[1] Coleman, of English descent, married Mary Key, of Cecil county, Maryland, where he settled about 1720. (She was of the same family as the author of the "Star Spangled Banner.") Issue:

DANIEL[2] COLEMAN, of Caroline county, Va. (among others). He was Colonel in the Revolution. His estate on the Mat river, "Concord," where he is buried, is now owned by J. D.[3] Coleman, of Clinton, Miss. Married (I) Miss Childs, and married (II) Martha Cooke, daughter of Hartwell and Ann (Ruffin) Cooke, of "Bremo, Va." Issue, 1st mar.: 1, James D.[3]; 2, Thomas Burbage[3]; 3, Henry[3] 4, Mildred[3]; 5, Sarah[3]; 6, Elizabeth[3]. Issue, 2d mar.: 7, John Hartwell[3]; 8, Ruffin[3]; 9, DANIEL[3]. Of these:

(1) JAMES D.[3] COLEMAN, of Kentucky. m. Miss Warfield, and lived in Lexington. Issue: 1, Nicholas[4]; 2, Lloyd[4]; 3, Polly Ann[4], unm.; 4, Eliza[4] m. Mr. Irvin; 5, Joseph[4] m. Sue Malone, of Alabama, and d. s. p.; 6, Elisha[4], unm. Of these:

    1. NICHOLAS[4] COLEMAN m. Lucy Marshall. He was an eminent lawyer of Vicksburg, and represented that district in Congress. Issue:
        1. FANNIE[5] m. Gov. Randolph, of New Jersey. 2. Lucy[5] m. Dr. Smith, Presbyterian minister, New Orleans. 3.Charles[5] and 4, Harry[5], educated by Dr. Le Roy Broun, Bloomfield Academy, Va., died in service in Civil War. 4. Susan[5] m. Mr. Dickenson, of Yonkers, N. Y. 6. Judge James Coleman, of Vicksburg, m. ——, and had Estelle[6].

    2. LLOYD R[4]. COLEMAN, of New Orleans, president of Traders' and Mechanics' Fire Insurance Co. for many years, and prominent in social and business circles, died 1896. Married Harriet Moore. Issue: 1, Elizabeth Warfield[5], a devoted daughter, and rearing the two children of her brother; 2, Margaret[5], m. Mr. Young and had: Lloyd Coleman, Betty Coleman, Louise Chamberlain, and James Nicholas, all. unm.; 3, Nicholas[5] m. Miss Browning, and had Lloyd, and Browning (daughter); now at school.

(9) DANIEL[2] COLEMAN, of Athens, Ala. Judge of Circuit Court (born in Caroline county, Va., 2 Aug. 1801, d. 4 Nov. 1857), an early settler of Alabama, coming to Mooresville, 1819, and thence to Athens. Resided, with his brother, James, in Kentucky, until he graduated at Transylvania University, where his classmates were Gov. Henry Watkins Collier, and Judge J. J. Ormond, of Alabama. Through influence of Hon. Nich. Davis, he was chosen by the Legislature Judge of the County Court, when 19 years of age. Represented Limestone county, 1829; Circuit Judge, 1835-47; was placed, in 1848, upon Democratic Electoral ticket for State at Large, but declined—also declined election, in 1851, to which he was appointed, to fill vacancy in State Supreme Court, caused by resignation of Judge Parsons. He amassed a large estate, and was deeply interested in educational and religious affairs—devoting much of his time and means to the "Athens Female Institute," and the welfare of the M. E. Church South. Its ministers always found a home with him, and all admired his spotless integrity and piety. His library was one of the most select and extensive in the South. Tall, slender, and with a florid complexion, his manner was grave to austerity. "Had he indulged more ambition, with the strong hold he had upon the public confidence and respect, his public career would have been more varied."—(Garrett's "Public Men of Alabama").

He married Elizabeth Peterson, Northampton county, N. C. (b. 22 May, 1811, d. 15 Feb. 1855), granddaughter of Major Samuel Lockhart, of the Revolution, a woman of much beauty and versatility, and a notable housekeeper. Her home was one of joy and culture. Issue:

    I. James L.[4]; II, Martha, unm.; III, Eliza Lockhart; IV, Daniel; V, John Hartwell (b. 1840), Capt. C. S. A., killed in battle of Murfreesboro (Dec. 31, 1862); VI, Richard Vasser, C. S. A. (b. 1843), Lieutenant of Sharpshooters, killed in battle of Chickamauga, Tenn. (Sept. 20, 1863); VI, Ruffin (b. 1846) unmarried, a physician in Texas; VIII, Franklin (b. 1849), Editor, and in the U. S. Land Office, Huntsville, Ala. Of the first four mentioned,

I, JAMES L.[4] COLEMAN (b. 29 Jan. 1830, d. 1896) Methodist Minister, *m.* Kate Lester, of Giles county, Tenn. Issue: Daniel[5], d. s. p.; Granville[5], of Columbia, Tenn.; Minnie[5], *m.* Wm. Irvine, of Athens, Ala.; Lila[5], unm.; Grace[5], d. s. p.; Richard[5], *m.* Macon, daughter of Gen. W. W. Allen, of Sheffield, Ala., and James[5], unm.

III. ELIZA LOCKHART COLEMAN (b. 10th April, 1836) *m.* (1859) Robert H. Thach, lawyer, Athens, Ala. She has, for many years, been a widow, but by wise forehought and self-sacrificing love has nobly reared her children. Her encouraging companion through all her generous exertions, was her sister, Martha. *Children:* Charles C.[5], Richard[5], d. s. p. in young manhood, and Robert[5]. Of these:

  1. CHARLES COLEMAN[5] THACH (b. March 15, 1860, Athens, Ala.), is a brilliant member of the Faculty of the Polytechnic Institute, Auburn, Ala., in whom the potent influence of distinguished ancestry is nobly exemplified. Married (November 11, 1885) Nelly Stanford (b. 1867), dau. of Prof. Otis D. and Antoinette (Howell) Smith, of Auburn, Ala. Prof. Smith traces his lineage in Connecticut, to 1639, and also to Capt. Gills Dana, and the Knickerbocker family of *Van Deusen*, of New York, who came from North Brabant, Netherland, in 1650. His great-grandfather was. Col. Jonathan Smith, of the Revolution, and member of the Massachusetts Constitutional Convention to adopt the Federal Constitution. He was also of Bacon lineage, of which is also Dr. Bacon, of Yale College, and which goes back to England, 1608. His wife is descended from the Porter, Burwell and Armistead families of Virginia. Issue:

    1. Elizabeth Lockhart[6] (b. April 27, 1887); 2, Otis Dowd[6] (b. 1891); 3, Charles Coleman[6] (b. 1893); 4, Richard Hartwell[6] (b. 1898.)

  2. Richard Hannon[5] Thach (born April 1, 1865; d. Auburn Ala., June 18, 1888.)

  3. Robert H.[5] Thach (b. 9th November, 1866), lawyer Birmingham, Ala.; *m.* Stella, daughter of Col. L. A. and Stella (Tureaud) Briugier, of a distinguished Louisiana family. Children: Robert Gordon (b. December 27, 1891); Stella Mayo (1893.)

IV. DANIEL[4] COLEMAN (b. 7th September 1838), lawyer, Huntsville, Ala. Brave soldier in the Civil War, and of fine literary and social talents. Married Claude, daughter of Francis and Ann E. (Withers) Levert, of Huntsville. Children: 1, Levert[5], now Lieutenant in 5th Artillery, U. S. A.; 2, Verdot[5].

WITHERS.

The ancestor of this line in Virginia was William Withers, of Williamsburg, Va. (b. January, 1731), reared by his uncle, a clergyman in England. He came to Fairfax county (1745) to take possession of land in Stafford county, as heir of Captain John Withers, which lands were sold in 1756 to Samuel Washington. For an extensive genealogy of *Withers* in Virginia, see *Virginia Magazine of History (Vols. VI and VII, 1898–99).* This mentions the arms of Sir Richard Withers, ancestor of the poet, registered 1487 in the *College of Arms. Arg. a chevron gules between three crescents sable; crest, a Rhinosceros or.*

THOMAS WITHERS was clerk to Anthony Walke, in Nansemond county, Va., and afterward private secretary to Lord Dinwiddie, the Governor. He was also a merchant

---

Daniel Coleman (1745) 226 acres in Amelia county.—(Records.)
Hartwell Cocke, of "*Bremo*," Fluvana county, Va., *m.* Ann, daughter of John Ruffin, of Surry county, related to Edmund Ruffin.
Of this Coleman family in Virginia, was Frederic Coleman, M. A.; educator and founder of Concord Academy. Lewis Coleman, M. A., Col. in C. S. A., and professor of Latin, University Virginia; and Judge Richard Coleman, of the Circuit Bench.
The above sketch presents only the lines of James, of Kentucky, and Daniel, of Alabama, and the former not complete.

in Williamsburg. He married *Priscilla Wright*, in Nansemond county, 14th October, 1761, and finally removed to Dinwiddie county, near Petersburg, their home called "*Kingston*." She was a charming and talented woman, and had other ardent admirers than young Withers, among whom was George Booth, of Gloucester county, Va., in whose papers was found, long years after, a gentle negative to his wooing, signed by "*Your humble obedient servant, Priscilla Wright*," beginning "*Worthy Sir*," and written in 1759; and she hoped "he had ere this recovered his usual *equanimity*." A list of some of her descendants, compiled from *Slaughter's Bristol Parish*, and other sources, is given below:

1. Priscilla, m. (1788) John Grammer; 2. William; 3. THOMAS (b. September, 1766; d. 1843); 4. JOHN (b. 1773); 5. David Wright (d. 1821). Of these:

(3) THOMAS WITHERS (b. September, 1766; d. 1843), married (I) Louisa, dau. of Robert and Eliz (Starke) Walker; and m. (II) Eliz., dau. of John Grammer, of Bristol Parish vestry. Issue (*1st mar.*):

    I. William Withers, M. D. (b. 4th December, 1794), m. (1817) Eliz., dau. of Richard Stith.

    II. Ann Eliz. Withers (b. 4th December, 1795), m. (1814) Gen. Wm. H. Broadnax, lawyer.

    III. Robert Withers, M. D., of Tuscaloosa, Ala. (b. 9th November, 1798), m. (1) 1822, Martha Williams, and (II) Mary Withers. Issue 2d mar. (*Grammer*):

    IV. Mary T. Withers, m. Roger Atkinson; and their dau., Eliz. Atkinson, married Bishop Lay, and a dau., Mary Tabb, m. Rev. L. Walke.

    V. Thomas Withers, M. D. (b. 30th July, 1808; d. 1879), never married; vestry of Bristol parish.

    VI. Louisa W. Withers (b. 1810) m. (1832), Rev. Charles Dresser, of Virginia and Illinois. Issue: David W., and Bolling Walker, etc.

    VII. Eliz. Withers (b. 1815), m. (1832) Rev. Thomas Adams.

    VIII. Rev. Edmund Withers (b. October, 1818; d. January, 1879), m. (1845) Clara C. Gilliam. Issue: Thomas, Clara, Robert and Louisa (b. 1862). (*See Slaughter's Bristol Parish*.)

(4) JOHN WITHERS (b. 1773) married Mary Herbert Jones, 2d daughter of Frederick Jones, of Dinwiddie county, Va., whose wife, Susannah Claiborne (b. 1751) was the daughter of Col. Augustine Claiborne* (b. 1721) of Prince William county, and his wife, Mary, daughter of Buller (or Bulwer), Herbert, of Dinwiddie. (See *Claiborne Family*, also *Jones Family Book*.) Issue:

I. SUSANNA CLAIBORNE WITHERS (b. May, 1796) m. (1817), Hon. Clement Comer Clay, Sr., of Alabama (b. Halifax county, Va., 1789, d. Huntsville, Ala., 1860), member Legislature Alabama 1817; of Constitutional Convention 1819; Chief Justice; Speaker 1828; member Congress, 1829, and Governor of Alabama, 1836; U. S. Senator 1837. Their eldest son:

---

*Col. Augustine Claiborne, of "*Windsor*," (b. at "*Sweet Hall*," King William county, Va., 1721, d. 1787), m. Mary, daughter of Bulwer Herbert, and his wife, Mary Stith, Maid of Honor to Queen Anne, and of "*Puddledock*," Petersburg, Va., (son of Lord John Herbert, descendant of the first Earl of Pembroke.) Issue:
I. Mary Herbert, (b. 1744, d. 1775,) m. Gen. Charles Harrison, of the Rev., brother of Gov. Benj. Harrison. II. Herbert, (b. 1746,) m. (I.) Miss Ruffin, and (II.) Mary Brown. III. Thomas, (b. 1747), member Congress 1790, m. Miss Clayton. IV. Augustine, (b. 1748,) m. Martha Jones. V. Anne, (b. 1749,) m. Richard Cocke. VI. Susanna, (b. 29 Nov., 1751,) m. Frederick Jones of Dinwiddie, and had: 1, Augustine; 2, *Mary Herbert*; and 3, Mrs. George Maclin, of Lunenburg county, Va. VII. William, (b. 1758,) m. Miss Ruffin. VIII. Buller, (b. 1765,) m. Patty Ruffin. IX. Richard, (b. 1767,) m. Daughter of Philip Young, of Dinwiddie county. X. Lucy Herbert, (b. 1760.) XI. Elizabeth, (b. 1761,) m. Thomas Peterson. XII. John Herbert, (b. 1762,) m. Mary Gregory. XIII. Sarah, m. Charles Anderson. XIV. Mrs. Thompson, of S. C. XV. Mrs. Ferdenando, (b. 1773.) XVI. Bethurst, (b. 1774.)

1. Clement Claiborne Clay (b. Huntsville, Ala., 1817) member Legislature 1842; U. S. Senate 1854, until the war; Confederate States Senate 1861; confidential agent to the British provinces in 1864; imprisoned in Fortress Monroe with President Davis, 1865, where, his health failing, he died a few years after at his home, "*Wildwood*," Ala. Married (1853) Virginia, dau. of Dr. Peyton Tunstall, of Virginia—a brilliant ornament to two governments, and a remarkable conversationalist. She *m.* (II) Judge Clopton, of Montgomery, Ala.

2. John Withers Clay, editor of *Huntsville Democrat* for forty years, married Mary Lewis, and had William, Mary, Sue, Withers, Jennie and Elodie. When his health failed from paralysis, his bright young daughters, Sue and Jennie, conducted his paper.

3. Hugh Lawson Clay, lawyer. On staff of Gen. E. Kirby Smith in the Civil War; *m.* Celeste Comer. No living issue.

II. WILLIAM T. WITHERS, *m.* (1820) Miss Hawkins, of Tennessee.

III. DOROTHEA WITHERS.

IV. PRISCILLA WITHERS, *m.* William McDowell, of Huntsville, Ala., and had, among others, Mary Eliza, *m.* (1848) DR. CLAUDIUS HENRY MASTIN,* LL. D., of Mobile, b. Huntsville, Ala., 4th June, 1826, d. Mobile ——), graduated University Pennsylvania 1849, and on the staffs of Gens. Bragg, Polk and Beauregard, C. S. A.; son of Francis Turner Mastin (b. 1781) and Ann Elis. Caroline Levert, (b. King William county, Va., 1789), whose mother was Ann Lee Metcalfe, and father, Dr. Claudius Levert, of France, who came to Virginia as surgeon of Count de Rochambeau's fleet, in Revolutionary War. Issue: Caroline Mastin *m.* her cousin, Charles J. Mastin, of Huntsville; 2, William M. Mastin, M. D. (b. 1852), *m.* Margarita Crawford, of Mobile; 3. Mary Herbert Mastin, *m.* Frank Roberts; and 4, C. H. Mastin. (Francis Turner Mastin (above) was son of Francis Y. Mastin, who came to Virginia with Lord Fairfax.

V. Augustus Jones Withers married Mary Woodson, of Alabama.

VI. Ann Eliza Withers *m.* Francis J. Levert, of Alabama, and had Claude, *m.* Capt. Daniel Coleman. (*Ante.*)

VII. Mary D. Withers m. (1858) Dr. Robert Withers, of Alabama.

VIII. Gen. Jones M. Withers, of the C. S. A. Graduate of West Point, and Captain in U. S. Army; resigned about 1854. Editor of *Mobile Tribune*, and Mayor of that city 1858, married Rebecca Forney. Among his children were: Jones; Hattie, m. Daniel Huger; Priscilla, m. Edward Witherspoon, and died young; daughter married Mr. Thomas; also, twin daughters, and others.

IX. Maria Withers, m. Rev. Anastasius Mercos.

CONCLUSION.

The notes and genealogies within have been arranged w'thout regard to the alphabetical order of the names of families, but rather to link together in groups those most nearly related, though it will be seen that members of nearly all have, at some time, intermarried. Had the limits of the volume permitted, many more could, and *should*, have been added. However, the main object of the work will have been attained should the Alabamians and their kin, herein recorded, think it of sufficient value to treasure among their family archives.

---

*Robert Mastin (1727), 1000 acres in Spotsylvania county, Va.   (*Records.*)

ADDENDA.

CANTZON.

[Family Records of Rev. James E. Dunlap (son of William), of Williamsburg county, S. C., Presbyterian minister, sent too late for insertion on page 394.]

CHARLES or KARL K-NUT-SEN, or CANUTSEN, the great Marshal ("*son of Canute*"), died 1470; chosen King of Sweden, 1448, by the *Wigan*, with the title of Charles VIII. His descendants are yet nobles in Sweden, and it is the tradition of the Cantzon (or Knutson) family that he was the great-grandfather of its founder. The *Family Bible*, containing a *Register*, with dates as remote as the Revocation of the Edict of Nantes (1685), and also tracing Dunlap, Blair, and Foster (or Forester) collateral lines to Scotland, was burned with the house of Mr. William B. Dunlap, in 1840. Rewritten by his son, who was familiar with the old Register, and, with other valuable records, stored in a trunk in Marion, S. C., it was again burned during the Civil War. Much priceless data was lost; but from *notes* preserved, and an excellent memory, he again recorded his family history:

CHARLES HAROLD KNUT-SEN, or KANNTSEN, or CANNTSON, a Swedish noble, married the daughter and heiress of Count Robert Lantier, in France, and there founded his family. His son,

JEAN RENÉ² KANNTSON became a Peer of the Realm, and also a political exile. He married Dorcas Daniel, said to be the beautiful daughter of a Hebrew banker of influence, in Paris. Their son,

JEAN JACQUES² KANNTSON or CANNTSON, the Huguenot, fled in exile after the Revocation (1685). He married Margery Witherspoon, sister, it is said, of John Witherspoon, of Princeton College, signer of the Declaration of Independence. He came to America through Philadelphia, after 1730. The exact dates can not be recovered. His son,

DR. JOHN CHARLES RENÉ JACQUES⁴ CANTZON, of South Carolina, called "*The French Doctor*," gave the family name its present spelling, and retaining only *John* in his own. He spoke French fluently and taught it to his children. Married, in Philadelphia, Sarah Dickie, whose mother was a sister of John Witherspoon, President of Princeton College (above). (The name has sometimes been perverted to Dickey.) He came to Lancaster county, S. C., before 1760, probably from one of the lower counties, and Dickie, Witherspoon, Dunlap, Blair, Foster and Harper relatives were settled in the same or adjoining counties. Their children were:
1, William⁵, b. 1765; 2, Moses⁵, b. 1766; 3, John Charles René Jacques⁵, Jr., b. 1768; 4, Mary⁵, who married James Blair, and, 5, Dorcas⁵ (or Margaret), who married Mr. Young. When William, the eldest, ran off to sea, he joined the Revolutionary navy. Moses died s. p. John Charles René Jacques, Jr., married Rachel Foster.* Mrs. Dorcas Young's daughter, Margaret Young, married William B. Dunlap, and their son, the Rev. James E. Dunlap, many years ago fell heir, by primogeniture, to the inheritance of the "*Dunlops of Dunlop*," Scotland. But because of the great legal expense, and, above all, what *he* thought the superior claim in equity of another, he did not urge his rights.

---

* Their son, Henry Foster Cantzon (born 1796), married Miss Paxton, and *not* Miss Rondeau, as is erroneously stated on page 395.

JOHN CHARLES[1] FOSTER, grandfather of Mrs. Rachel Cantson, was from the Scottish borders, and allied with the Dunlops of Ayr, and Kirkland Heights, and also the Fenwick and Philpot families. His son, HENRY FOSTER[2], of South Carolina, the immigrant, came, first, to Pennsylvania, and there married Ann Dunlop (or Dunlap, as it is called in South Carolina), whose ancestry dated from a younger son of Dunlop of Dunlap, Scotland, who came to Lancaster county, Pa., in the reign of George II, and then moved to South Carolina, there naming a county Lancaster, also. Henry Foster served in the Revolution as corporal, 1778, Capt. George Liddell's company, Third Regiment South Carolina Continental troops, Col. William Thompson. His son, JOHN[3] FOSTER, was captain in Lieutenant Colonel Henry Hampton's Regiment of South Carolina Light Dragoons, and was wounded in the battle of Hanging Rock. For *five* months service at this time, he was paid by the United States "*one grown negro.*"—(*Government Records.*)

(Mrs. Lottie B. Foster, widow of Dr. Joseph Foster, of Lancaster, S. C., sends the above notes. Her son, J. Cantson Foster, is a student at the Richmond Virginia Medical College. An ancestor of hers was Donald McDonald, who came to South Carolina from Scotland with his wife, Rebecca, in 1720.)

COLEMAN NOTES.

JOSEPH COLEMAN, 1679, mentioned in York county, Va., Records.

BRISTOL PARISH REGISTER (Parts of Amelia, Prince George, Chesterfield, Dinwiddie and other counties) mentions births of following:

FRANCIS AND MARY COLEMAN, a *daughter*, Amy (b. 1718); William (b. 1733).

DANIEL AND ELIZABETH COLEMAN, a son, Benjamin (b. 1720); Martha (b. 1726), Daniel (b. 1731), Mary (b. 1724).

WILLIAM AND FAITH COLEMAN, a son, Peter (b. 1720).

JOHN AND MARY COLEMAN, a *daughter*, Mary Ligon (b. 1731). The birth of a slave recorded 1726.

WILLIAM AND SARAH COLEMAN, a *daughter* (b. 1728), Martha (b. 1730), William (b. 1732), Sarah (b. 1734).

WILLIAM AND MARGARET COLEMAN, a *daughter*, Anne (b. 1731), Margery Lucas (b. 1733).

WILLIAM AND ELIZABETH COLEMAN, a son, Warner (b. 1732).

JOSEPH AND ELIZABETH COLEMAN, a son, William (b. 1734).

DANIEL COLEMAN (1745) entered 225 acres in Amelia county.—(*Land Book.*)

Robert, Ellis and Joseph Coleman (1748) in Gloucester county, Va.—(*Survey Book.*)

Robert Coleman, of Louisa county, 1787, as was also William and Bartholomew Dandridge, Joseph Watkins, Rd. H. Lee and John Saunders.—(*Virginia Gazette*).

It is greatly desired to locate in origin the different Coleman families of Virginia.

McGEHEE.

Descendants of Thomas McGehee.

Compiled by his grandson, George T. McGehee, and dedicated, with love and honor, to the memory of his mother, and other noble Texas women of 1836-46. Gathered from personal knowledge and the recollections of elder members of the family, and the OLD BIBLE, now in possession of Mrs. Sarah Jane Driskill, of Madison county, Ala., and in her eightieth year.

THOMAS BATTOP McGEHEE, second son of Micajah and Anne (Scott) McGehee, of Oglethorpe county, Ga. (b. in Virginia, 1st December, 1771; d. at the old homestead, Madison county, Ala.), (two miles from the Tennessee line), 18th April, 1832), *m.* (in Oglethorpe county, Ga., 1798) Elizabeth Thornton Gilmer (b. 15th October, 1780). He was six feet tall, of great strength, and, before his death, weighed 350 pounds. They moved to Alabama in 1815, and settled on the main road from Huntsville to Nashville. Like many of the old stock, he had fine judgment, combined with that indomitable energy, which gave them success and distinction wherever their lots were cast. I have often heard my father relate that once, on the occasion of an annual muster at Huntsville, his neighbors concluded to combine a little fun with the military parade. It was widely known that my grandfather had the largest mule, the largest carry-log, the largest kettle, and that he was the largest man in all that region. So they put a pair of shafts in the carry-log, hitched the mule in the shafts, the kettle on top and "Grandpa" in the kettle, and away they went to the muster. He was of a most kind and affable disposition, but would not brook an insult for an instant. On one occasion, at a public gathering, one of the "bullies" of the district offered him an insult, but the words had scarcely left his lips before he landed flat of his back, with "Grandpa" astride him, having reached the dagger from his sword-cane, but before he could make the fatal thrust, friends intervened in time to save the life of the prostrate bully. He was a very successful business man, and at his death was considered a very wealthy man for those times.

He died at the home he had hewn from the native forest in that new country, on April 16, 1832. He is buried on the old homestead, in one hundred yards of the home of his only surviving child.

I remember grandmother well; she was a woman remarkable for her beauty; and excelled in all those virtues which go to make a noble Christian character. She emigrated to Texas in 1840, where most of her children had already preceded her, and died in Bastrop county, September 6, 1846, and is buried in the cemetery at the town of Bastrop.

About 1820 grandfather and grandmother had their portraits painted. I never knew how my father fell heir to them but he did, and with other paintings. which my mother prised very highly, they were brought to Texas in 1835 The Indians captured and destroyed all of them except those of grandfather and grandmother. Before my mother's death she gave them to my youngest brother, and a few weeks ago among a very few articles saved from the burning of his residence those old portraits were among the number. If those silent features could spring into life endowed with all those God-given attributes of mind. memory and speech, what a wonderful history they could give, of long journeys by land, across mighty rivers, through unbroken stretches of primitive forest, hasty flights from the blood-thirsty savages, long weary marches of a young mother and two small children, a return to a home in ruins, of death-bed scenes, of happy brides at the hymeneal altar, of a happy family separated by the cruel necessities of war, the yearning of children's love for a mother and father, the breaking up and separating of a large family, their narrow escape from the flames of a burning house. Oh! if they could only speak and tell us all that has passed before those silent eyes since the painter's brush, near eighty years ago, so faithfully transferred those splendid features to the canvas! But, alas, it can not be; it may be best that they are silent. I often wonder if we shall ever see the like of such people again! Issue, twelve children:

1, Nancy Scott; 2, Mildred Meriwether; 3, John Gilmer; 4, Charles Lewis; 5, Thomas Scott; 6, Thomas Gilmer; 7, Ann Thornton; 8. Francis Micajah; 9. William Blair; 10, Sarah Jane; 11, William Blair, (2nd); 12 Nicholas Abner; (the first seven born in Georgia—the remainder in Alabama). Of these:

I. NANCY SCOTT McGEHEE, (b. 28th July, 1799, d. in Georgia, 9th October, 1812).

II. MILDRED MERIWETHER McGEHEE, (b. 29th September 1801, d. 20th November, 1861, in Texas). m. (I) 26th May, 1822, Dr. Richmond Carroll; Madison county, Ala., (d. March, 1834). She m. (II) 1836, in Alabama, William Acklen, who lived only a few years. In 1859, she went to live with her children in Texas. Issue, (by 1st marriage), one child;

THOMAS McGEHEE.
Born Dec. 1, 1771, died April 18, 1832.

ELIZABETH GILMER McGEHEE.
Born Oct. 15, 1780, died Sept. 6, 1846.

1. **Elizabeth H. Carroll**, m. (in Winchester, Tenn., 16th November, 1840), Joseph Robins, who died in Travis county, Texas, 2nd January, 1879. Issue:

  1. RICHMOND CARROLL ROBINS (b. 17th November, 1842, in Tennessee), m. (April, 1873, in Hays co., Tex.). Hannah Murphy, and had Amanda Ellis., b. 25th December, 1873. Lew, b. 20th June, 1876, d. 20th March, 1899. Mollie, b. 1st October, 1878. William Joseph, d. infant. Kate, b. 20th July, 1893.

  2. SARAH JANE ROBINS (b. 23d April, 1847): m. (27th December, 1866), George Wesley Hanniford, who d. 27th January, 1873. Issue: Henry Carroll, b. 18th December, 1867. Sarah Ellis., b. 5th January, 1870. George Wesley, b. 4th November, 1872. Of these, Henry Carroll Hanniford had Albert Wesley, b. 21st April, 1888; Grace Lee, 22d July. 1890; Andry, 3rd June, 1894, and Henry Coke, b. 14th May, 1896.

  3. JAMES LEWIS ROBINS (b. 10th December, 1850), d. 6th March, 1880.

  4. JOSEPH E. (b. 30th April, 1854), never married.

  5. WILLIAM AMBROSE ROBINS (b. 31st May, 1858, Travis co.) Had Issue: Anna, b. 19th June, 1878, d. 1st January, 1880; Joseph Anthony, b. 16th June, 1881, d. 15th December, 1890; James Wesley, b. 21st March, 1883; Lula Bell, 23rd December, 1884; Lewis Carroll, 1st October, 1886; William Franklin, 25th July, 1889; Mildred Meriwether, 29th November, 1891; Bertha S., 1st September, 1893, John Thomas, 16th June, 1896; Ella May, 1st February, 1899. Issue second marriage: (*Acklen*), one child.

  2. WILLIAM ACKLEN lives in Buda, Hays co., Tex., with a large family, but declines to give his family data.

III. JOHN GILMER MCGEHEE (b. 20th March, 1804, Carroll, co., Ga.; d. 10th September 1838, Texas); m. (May 18, 1827, in Georgia), Sarah Milton Hill, (sister to Thomas J., Wiley and Middleton Hill, who, in the early 40's, moved to Bastrop, Texas, and there and in adjoining counties, have left many descendants.) She m. (II.) September, 1845, Rev. Josiah W. Whipple, a pioneer Methodist preacher of Texas, and died November, 1850. Their only child, Wilber Scott Whipple, was drowned, 1852, in the Colorado river. In 1833 John Gilmer McGehee, with his brother, Thomas G. McGehee (the father of the compiler of these sketches), and a few others, went to Florida, chartered and loaded a schooner with lumber, sailed around the Gulf coast to the mouth of Brazos river, where they found a small settlement at old Velasco. They disposed of their cargo, and prospected the country, then a wilderness, save for a few families on the Brazos and lower Colorado rivers. They soon satisfied themselves of the beauty and fertility of the land, and in the winter of 1833 returned to Alabama, determined to move their families to this land of promise as soon as possible.

John Gilmer commenced immediately to organise a colony of immigrants for Texas. By the fall of 1834 he had a colony of 140 Georgians and Alabamians organised, and in October arrived at San Augustine in East Texas. By January, 1835, they were at Bastrop, their destination and future home. The work of building houses and forts to protect them from Indians, commenced at once. They were not to enjoy their homes in quiet, as the storm was then gathering in the Halls of the Montezumas. The mutterings could be heard. The butcher, Santa Anna, was marshalling his hosts, to sweep these hardy pioneers from the face of Texas soil. His emissaries were among the Indians exciting them to plunder and murder. Every full moon witnessed their forays in the sparsely settled valleys of the Colorado, Brazos and Guadalupe. Early in 1836, it was known that the armies of Mexico were on the march for the Texas border. Organizations were soon formed, and hastened to meet them. John Gilmer was among the first to reach San Antonio, and at the battle of Conception, on 28th of October, 1835, was severely wounded. He soon returned to Bastrop, where he remained with his family and colony, helping all whom his condition would permit. In the latter part of March, 1836, the Alamo was invested and soon fell, all its brave garrison put to death. Wild consternation seized the settlers who had already concentrated in their places of refuge. Almost the entire male population had rushed to the front to meet the invader, and but few, save women and children, were left; among the few was John Gilmer, just recovering from his wound. He immediately bent all his energies to getting what little transportation there was in shape to move these helpless women and children to a place of safety. With only a few hours for preparation and packing, and all surplus household goods discarded, the memorable "Runaway Scrape" commenced. Through rain, mud and cold he hurried these panic-stricken people east. Each day couriers rushed along the roads with the information that the Mexicans were in hot pursuit. Despair and fright seized the people, but the cool head and indomitable energy of the man that had induced many of these people to cast their lots in this, then a distant land, triumphed, and the whole caravan reached the Trinity river, where they were in comparative safety.

The misery and despair of these heart-broken old men, women and children, was soon to be turned into wild and triumphant joy. The 21st day of April had dawned; and before the shadows of its evening sun had died away, the invader had been met, his army vanquished, *utterly* destroyed, its boasted commander a lone fugitive in disguise, who, in a few hours longer, was a cringing captive at the feet of the matchless Houston and his handful of patriots!

After the battle of San Jacinto, John Gilmer led his colony back to Bastrop, settling himself in the beautiful valley of the Colorado river, on a splendid farm, where he died December, 1838, in the full prime of manhood.

Issue: 1, John Thomas; 2, Sarah Elizabeth; 3, Charles Lewis, and 4, Edward Henry. Of these—

1. John Thomas McGehee (b. Alabama, 20th December, 1829), m. (Nov. 1853), Emily Spencer, and both died a few years since, in San Antonio. No positive data concerning them, but there were four sons, and two daughters, one of whom married Mr. Barrett, and was living in San Antonio, but no reply to letters addressed. One or two sons supposed to be in Mexico.

2. Sarah Elizabeth McGehee (b. Alabama, 20th March, 1831, d. 26th Sept. 1836).

3. Charles Lewis McGehee (b. Alabama, 26th Nov. 1832, d. 1853), m. 1852, his cousin, Mary A. E. McGehee. One child; lived a year. She m. (II) D. A. Word.

4. Edward Henry McGehee (b. Texas, 1st April, 1836), lives in Denison, Texas; m. (22d October, 1856), Mary Harrell. Ten children: 1, Wiley Gilmer (b. 10th August, 1857, d. 12th Sept. 1898); 2, Ida May (b. 23d May, 1859); 3, William Edward (b. 4th February, 1861, d. 5th January, 1869); 4, Mary Minerva, twin, with 5, Elizabeth Milton (b. 7th November, 1862); 6, Anna Hubbard (b. 14th July, 1865); 7, George (b. 1st November, 1866, d. 15th December, 1866); 8, Virginia Emily (b. 30th October, 1870); 9, Henry Scott Miller (b. 30th October, 1870); 10, Charles Wayne (b. 17th June, 1880); 11, Charles Abner Blocker (b. 3d August, 1882). Of these—

    5. Elizabeth Milton, m. 17th April, 1882, James C. Morrison. Issue: Ethel, (b. 27th January, 1883); Mary McG. (b. 28th July, 1885); James Clifton (b. 16th July, 1887); Edward Henry (b. 24th July, 1881). Residence, Omaha, Nebraska.

    4. Mary Minerva, m. 4th June, 1884, Napoleon J. Bourgue. Issue: Milton Cassius (b. 26th June, 1888); Armand Napoleon Joseph (b. 2d August, 1893); Ida May (b. 14th July, 1895); Mildred Josephine (b. 11th January, 1897); Virginia Emily (b. 10th September 1898). Residence, St. Joseph, Michigan.

    6. Annie Hubbard, m. 9th February, 1890, W. C. Blevin. Issue: Beryl Brenton Casey (b. 6th November, 1893), and William Maurice (b. 15th February, 1896). Residence, Greenville, Texas.

    7. Virginia Emily (b. 30th October, 1867), m. 4th December, 1890, Walter S. Nevins, of Denison, Texas. Issue: Carmelita McG. (b. 3d December, 1893).

IV. CHARLES LEWIS McGEHEE, of Bastrop (b. 20th July, 1806, d. 1st September, 1850), m. (I), Madison county, Ala., 1830, Sarah V. Acklen, who d. September, 1845. He m. (II) Caroline Rector, who lived but a short time. He m. (III), on his death-bed, Martha Bridges, who is yet alive in some one of the Northern States. He moved to Mississippi after 1830, and to Texas, 1847; was engaged in building the State House at his death. He was a Methodist of warm heart and truly Christian piety. Issue (by *first marriage only*): 1, Mary A. E.; 2, Charles L. and 3, Sarah V. A., as follows:

1. **Mary A. E.** (b. Alabama 13th October, 1835, d. 8th July, 1898), m. (I), 1852, her cousin, Charles L. McGehee, and had William J., who died at one year of age, just a few days before his father. She married (II) 9th June, 1854, David A. Word, of Madison county, Ala. (d. 23d May, 1898). Issue: 1, Mary Ann Trigg (b. 18th July, 1856, d. 16th August, 1857); 2, Kate C. (14th May, 1859); 3, Maud McIver (b. 8th September, 1861); 4, Itasca Lee (b. 20th March, 1866). Of these:

    2. **Kate C.** m. (21st December, 1876) John Robert Polk, of the family to which belonged the President, James K. Polk, of Scotch-Irish descent, and extending back to Robert Bruce. Issue: 1, Iver May, b. 28th October, 1877; 2, Katie Bob, b. 6th February, 1879; 3, Annie Lee, b. October 2, 1881; 4, Headley Word, b. 1st February, 1886; 5, Euphra Clay, b. 27th October, 1888; 6, Alex. Dallas, b. 12th June, 1894.

    3. **Maud McIver** m. (18th April, 1887) Beauregard Davis Sherrell. Issue: 1, Walter Word; 2, Mary Mehala, 16th June, 1889; 3, Robert Bruce, b. 30th November, 1894.

    4. **Itasca Lee** m. (22 April, 1885) Perrian Kerr Williamson. Issue: 1, Blanche Acklen, b. 20th February, 1886; 2, Word, b. 15 July, 1887, d. 16th July, 1888; 3, Stanley, b. 22d November, 1888, d. 8th July, 1889; 4, Moriana, b. 23d July, 1891; 5, Kate Maud, b. 2d Jan., 1894; 6, Jennie, b. 20th January, 1895, d. 15th December, 1897; 7, Milton, b. 15th April,1896.

2. **Charles L.** (b. Alabama, 2d December, 1838) m. 5th October, 1858, Sarah Jane Humphreys. Issue:

    1. Walter Acklen (b. 15th July, 1859, killed, accidentally, while hunting 16th December, 1896) m. (10th March, 1891) Annie L. Fenley, and had: Clarence, b. 20th September, 1892; Charles, b. 24th June, 1894; Walter A., Jr., b. 28th November, 1896.
    2. Clara Lilian (b. 18th July, 1861, d. 12th July, 1862).
    3. Hugh Wallace (b. 4th October, 1864) m. (5th May, 1886) Minnie L. Bagley. Issue: Nora Lilian, b. 23d May, 1890; Roy Wallace, b. 25th February, 1896; Eva Olive, b. 24th December, 1897.
    4. Charles Lewis, Jr. (b. 20th November, 1864) *unmarried*.
    5. Addie Olive (b. 9th July, 1868) m. (16th July, 1890) Roger Byrnes. Issue: Roger H., b. 9th July, 1894; Marie Estelle, b. 1st June, 1898.
    6. Miles Humphreys (b. 17 January, 1874) *unmarried*.
    7. Wade Blakemore (b. 7th March, 1876) *unmarried*.
    8. Clement Roberts (b. 25th May, 1883, d. 17th January, 1888).

3. **Sarah Vance Acklen McGehee** (b. Mississippi, 4th June, 1846, d. 29th June, 1892), m. (2d July, 1867), Charles H. Word, b. Madison county, 22d Ala., April, 1840. Issue:

    1. William Alex. (b. 29th June, 1868, d. 7th November, 1895), m. (18th April, 1895), Mamie Sledge, and had, Lex, b. 25th March, 1896.
    2. Mary Bruce (b. 12th October, 1870), m. (13th May, 1895), Rev. John W. Stovall, of M. E. Ch. South. Issue: Robert, b. 5th September, 1896.
    3. Carl H. (b. 10th February, 1873), *unm.*, Waxahatchee, Texas.
    4. Vance Acklen (b. 21st May, 1875), *unm.*, lives with her father at Kennedy, Texas.

5. Jennie Lynn (b. 31st August, 1877, d. 29th October, 1882); 6. Zena Clara (b. 3d June, 1880, d. 4th November, 1882); 7. Iver Lee (b. 8th November, 1882); 8. Harry Cecil (b. 19th May, 1885).

V. THOMAS SCOTT McGEHEE (b. Oglethorpe county, Ga., 25th December, 1808, d. 9th November, 1809).

VI. THOMAS GILMER McGEHEE (b. Madison county, Ala., 27th September, 1810, d. San Marcos, Texas, 30th November, 1890), m. (I) 9th October, 1832, Minerva (b. December, 1809, died July 9, 1877), daughter of George and Lydia Hunt, Lincoln county, Tenn., of the family of Hunt for whom Huntsville, Ala., was named. (Her father died in the early 30's, and his widow, with three daughters and six sons, moved to Bastrop county, Texas. All are now dead, except the youngest daughter, who married D. O. Oliver (brother to Cousin Scott Oliver Hill), and they have left many descendants).

Ivory miniatures of the young couple painted soon after marriage are preserved in the family, and they were considered the handsomest pair in North Alabama. They soon removed to Talledega, Ala. In 1833, with his brother John, he prospected in Texas, and was so well pleased that, in 1835, he started overland with his wife and infant daughter for Bastrop. They were accompanied by Campbell Taylor, Martin Walker and Mr. Ricks. (These young men married and settled in Bastrop county as useful and honorable citizens.) Thomas G. McGehee was soon connected with "Milam's Colony," assisting in establishing its first office. But he was quickly called to more exciting work. The Indians had now become very troublesome, and as the settlement at Bastrop was the outpost, the hardy pioneers were constantly on the chase to recover their stolen horses or to revenge the death and scalping of a neighbor. Early in 1836 it was known the Mexicans had begun an invasion for their extermination and all available men were hastened to the front. Thomas Gilmer joined Capt. Jesse Billingsley's company, and was kept on duty between the settlements and San Antonio, so that the settlers might be warned of approaching danger. When Santa Anna's army reached San Antonio and besieged the Alamo Thomas G. was in charge of a portion of the company referred to and stationed on the old San Antonio and Nacogdoches road, about five miles east of the present site of New Braunfels. As soon as the first sound of the enemy's cannon came rolling over the hills, he posted a courier to Bastrop to notify the anxious people of the approaching danger. Thomas G., with all the organized companies, were ordered to concentrate on the Brazos river for the purpose of organizing as large a force as possible to resist the invaders. He remained with the army until the battle of San Jacinto, and as soon as possible after Santa Anna's capture, he rejoined his wife and two children, when they returned as far as Washington county, where he remained most of 1836, returning to Bastrop in the fall and settling on a farm some three miles from the town of Bastrop, on the west bank of the Colorado river.

The writer of these sketches believes he will be pardoned for this extended notice by those who may read these family notes and recollections. Thomas G. and Minerva McGehee were his mother and father, and it is natural that he should be more familiar with their early experiences in the trying scenes through which they had to pass for many years after they emigrated to Texas, which for ten or twelve years was territory of Mexico, and an independent republic. Their trials and hardships were no more than hundreds of others experienced.

The writer was a little more than a month old when the news of the fall of the Alamo reached the few settlers at Bastrop. The women and children had been for weeks before this in a state of constant terror caused by the frequent raids of the Indians, coming in the day time and driving off the few old horses left, and threatening them with massacre any moment, or a fate more to be dreaded—prisoners in their brutal hands. I have often heard my mother tell of her experience in these trying times. One evening the Indians in large numbers made their appearance near the stockade where they had all taken refuge. (This stockade was about half an acre in extent, built with timbers set on end in the ground; one side was formed by a high perpendicular bluff overlooking the river.) There were only a few men for defense, mostly old. My mother, then but 21 years old, determined that she and her little daughter, but two years old, and infant son, should never fall into the hands of those savages alive, so she took my sister by the hand, her infant son in her arms and stationed herself near the bluff, determined if they were attacked successfully she would throw herself with her children over this precipice before becoming a captive in savage hands. The Indians soon disappeared in the adjacent hills. It was among such excitement that a courier arrived with the sad news of the fall of the Alamo with all its heroic defenders. All must flee with all possible haste in the direction of East Texas. Can any one wonder at the wild consternation and despair that seized these helpless people? There were a few cool heads among them; one of these was John G. McGehee. Every energy was at once bent in getting together the few remaining animals and old wagons for the march east. My mother was fortunate enough to have a small pair of oxen three years old, "Dick" and "Ben." The only horse, "Old Bill," was ridden by Thomas G., her husband, in the army. She extemporized a conveyance by fitting up a two-wheeled cart, to which she attached Dick and Ben, put in what few things the cart would hold, leaving much of her nice bed clothing, books, paintings, etc., she had brought from Alabama. She, and a small negro girl she owned, walked, and drove the oxen. and the two children were stowed in the cart with the plunder. On they plodded through mud and cold, not knowing what day they might be overtaken by the Mexican cavalry, or set upon by the more hated enemy, the Comanche Indians. The Alamo had fallen, its garrison butchered. Fannin and his men had been foully murdered.

Santa Anna and his victorious hosts were steadily pushing on. Stop for a moment, and let your mind try to grasp the condition of this almost helpless concourse of women and children.

My mother said, afterward, that at times she almost despaired, and gave up all hope of proceeding further. One evening about sundown she had taken a seat on an old rail fence near her camp, in utter despair, her money was exhausted, her scanty supply of provisions almost gone. It seemed there was no ray of hope left. She heard the sound of horses feet coming down the road, she looked up and saw a splendid specimen of young manhood approaching. He stopped as he reached her, and inquired if she was the wife of Thomas G. McGehee; on being told she was, he sprang from his horse, saying his name was Wiley Hill (a cousin), and he was then hurrying to join Houston's army. This meeting, and his kind and encouraging words, were "Balm of Gilead" to my mother's weary heart. Cousin Wiley divided his purse with her and hastened on.

In these incidents, I can not feel I have done my duty if I neglect to mention "old Bill," who carried his rider safely through all these stirring scenes, and died at a good old age, lamented as if one of the family; and old "Dick" and "Ben," who took the wandering cart safely through the "Run-away" episode and landed it back in old Basthrop; also assisting to move the family in 1846, to their final home: my father's "head right," a league of land on the beautiful San Marcos river. If there is a home Beyond, where the faithful dumb brute finds rest, old Bill, Dick and Ben are there, under the green trees, near by the cool brooks, and fanned by the sweet breezes of perpetual spring! Many other stirring incidents, could the writer mention of his early life in the new land, but space forbids.

Issue: nine children, all grown to adult age, and with the exception of two, alive at this writing—1. Anne E. L.; 2. George Thomas; 3. John Francis; 4. Charles M.; 5. Sallie Louisa; 6. William Alfred; 7. Palmyra Amanda Whipple; 8. Alex. David; 9. Edward Anderson. Of these:

I. Ann E. L. McGehee (b. Alabama, 3d Nov., 1833; d. Llano, 3d Nov. 1891) m. (21st Nov., 1850) Milton M. Watkins, who died in Llano, Texas, April, 1885. (See *William Watkins line*.) Issue, nine children, as follows:

1. Isabella Moore Watkins (b. 4th June, 1856) m. (Nov., 1881) Edward Wilkes. One child: Milton C., b. 6th June, 1886.
2. Thomas James Watkins (b. 18th May, 1857; d. 1st Nov., 1892) m. (18th June, 1885) Bettie M. Barlow (d. 25th Dec., 1886). No issue.
3. Samuel Hunt Watkins (b. 25th June, 1860) m. (30th March, 1892) Clara G. Arnold. Issue: 1, Owen Milton, b. 3d March, 1893; 2, Thomas James, b. 15th August, 1895; John Lester, 27th November, 1897.
4. George McGehee Watkins (b. 19th April, 1863) m. (I) (12th Nov., 1891) Kittie Benedict (d. 19th Sept., 1892). One child: George Benedict, b. 13th September, 1892. He m. (II) 16th September, 1896, Lutie McLean. One child, a babe.
5. Lee Davis Watkins (b. 30th Sept., 1865) m. (6th April, 1892) Margaret M. Moore. No issue.
6. Clara May Watkins (b. 30th July, 1870), unm.
7. William Wallace Watkins (b. 12th July, 1872) m. (4th Sept., 1895) Cora Edwards. Issue: 1, Martha Ioline, b. 8th August, 1896; 2, an infant.
8. Lydia Hunt Watkins (b. 26th Sept. 1875; d. 24th Aug., 1876).

II. George Thomas McGehee (b. Bastrop, 5th February, 1836), *author of this sketch*, m. (12th May, 1872) Sarah Cherokee Woods (daughter of Dr. P. C. Woods, who went to Texas 1850; Colonel of a Texas Cavalry Regiment in the Civil War). No issue. He was in the lower house, and not in the Senate of his State, as stated on a previous page. But has retired from politics.

III. John Francis McGehee (b. 1st October, 1838), m. (27th April, 1863), Mary Eliz. Davis. Nine children, as follows:
1. John Hood (b. 18th February, 1864), unm.
2. Kate Ward (b. 17th June, 1866), m. (15th November, 1886), E. L. Thomas. Issue: Roy L., born 12th September, 1887; Sue Hill, b. 24th September, 1889; Mabel, b. 24th November, 1891; Mildred, b. 1st October, 1894.
3. Tallulah Thomas (b. 5th April, 1868), m. (24th October, 1887), Dr. J. A. Beall. Issue: 1, Ollie Banks, b. 24th August, 1888, d. 20th March, 1891; 2, Gladstone, b. 27th June, 1890, d. 14th May, 1892; 3, Annie Marie, b. 26th July, 1892; Cleo Lucile, b. 12th July, 1894.
4. Sallie E., (b. 9th July, 1870), m. (8th February, 1899) P. Orion Beard.
5. Pallie, (b. 25th October, 1872), unm.
6. Albert Scott, (b. 22d June, 1875); m. (31st August, 1896) Clara Roesing. Issue: Lucile, b. 1897; Myrtle, b. 1898.
7. Maud. (b. 9th December, 1877), unm.
8. Lou, (b. 28th September, 1879, d. 4th June, 1881).
9. Mary Davis, (b. 26th October, 1886), at school, Coronal Institute.

IV. Cʜᴀʀʟᴇs Wɪʟʟɪᴀᴍ MᴄGᴇʜᴇᴇ, (b. 6th September, 1841), m. (I) 25th September, 1865, Elizabeth Dixon (d. 12th June, 1890), and m. (II) Mrs. M. E. Sherrod. Issue (*by first mar. only*): 1, Minnie, b. 23d May, 1868, d. 4th October, 1885; Ada, b. 4th December, 1869, d. 15th August, 1870; Jessie, b. 9th October, 1875, m. (9th October, 1896) John O. Tucker. Issue: Infant, who died.

V. Sᴀʀᴀʜ Lᴏᴜɪsᴀ MᴄGᴇʜᴇᴇ, (b. 30th July, 1844), m. (28th November, 1865), Thomas A. Hill, (son of Thomas B. J. and Scott Oliver Hill, who were related to Uncle Edward McGehee). Eight children, of whom:
1. Tye Yates, (b. 29th September, 1867), m. 16th January, 1890) Leila Cole. Issue: 1, Scott Shelby, b. 28th October, 1890; 2, Mary Louisa, b. 18th October, 1892; 3, Cora Itasca, (b. 5th January, 1895). 2, Cap. C. (b. 11th September, 1869), m. (11th January, 1891), Annie Grace; two children; 3, Thomas William, (b. 11th September, 1871), unm.; 4, Scott Pearl, (b. 2d February, 1874), m. (23d December, 1897) Eugene Sparks; infant, b. October 14, 1898; 5, Leila May, (b.

3d May, 1876), *unm.*, lives with her parents; 6, Eddie McGehee, (b. 5th November, 1879), *unm.*, lives with her parents; 7, George Woods, (b. 12th February, 1882, d. 16th August, 1835); 8, Itasca Louisa, (b. 15th June, 1884), at school, Coronal Institute.

VI. WILLIAM ALFRED MCGEHEE. (b. 23d December, 1846, d. 13th December, 1890), graduated M. D. 1878–9, New Orleans, *m.* (8th October, 1874) Julia Vernita Donaldson. Seven children, of whom:
   1. Anna Laura, (b. 9th July, 1875), *m.* (16th October, 1895), Thomas J. Laughlin, one child; 2, Julia Minerva, (b. 23d July, 1877), *m.* (9th November, 1898) Merton Swift, one child; 3, Lucy Lee, (b. 8th May, 1879), *unm.*; 4, Earlie Donaldson, (b. 13th July, 1881, d. 24th June, 1888); 5, Ruth Lindsay, (b. 1st July, 1884), *unm.*; 6, Pallie Hill, (b. 19th March, 1886); 7, Lydia Hunt, (b. 26th May, 1888, d. 4th March, 1890). All of San Marcos, Texas.

VII. PALMYRA AMANDA WHIPPLE MCGEHEE (b. 18 July, 1849) *m.* (4 May, 1869,) Dr. James Oliver (son of Peter Oliver, who came from Mississippi, and was a brother of Cousin Scott Oliver Hill). Dr. Oliver practised in Bastrop until his death, 6 Feb., 1890. Issue: Eight children, of whom:
   1. Minerva A. E. Oliver, (b. 6 January, 1872,) *m.* (19th November, 1891,) W. H. Nelson. Issue: Julia, b. 1892; William Oliver, b. 1894; Pallie, b. 1897; James, an infant.
   2. Peter Micajah Oliver, (b. 7 Dec., 1874; d. 25th June, 1887.)
   3. Thomas Gilmer Oliver (b. 9th Sept., 1876;) in Iowa at present.
   4. Francis Powell Oliver, (b. 7th August, 1878,) now in the Panhandle of Texas.
   5. Sarah Lucinda Scott Oliver, (b. 25th August, 1880,) *unm.*
   6. and 7, James and Samuel, (twins,) b. 29th January, 1884. James died 31st July, 1884; Sammy died 11th August, 1884.
   8. Pallie A. Oliver (b. 18th Nov., 1885; d. 9th January, 1888.)

VIII. Alexander David McGehee, b. 17th October, 1851,) *m.* (17th December, 1876;) Fannie E. Johnson. Seven children, of whom:
   1. Lloyd (b. 13th October, 1877; d. 13th September, 1878;) 2, Lola F., b. 15th September, 1880; 3, Lettie O., b. 17th November, 1882; 4, Hunt C., b. 23d April, 1885; 5, Mary J., b. 13th February, 1889; 6, Alex G., b. 2d October, 1892; 7, Thomas G., b. 9th March, 1895; all, with their parents, in San Marcos, Texas.

IX. Edward Anderson McGehee (b. 16th April, 1855,) *m.* (19th January, 1887) Mary F. Hinsley. Issue:
   1. Thomas Edward (b. 13th January, 1888, d. infant); 2, Lucy F. (b. 4th September, 1889); 3, Mary K., (b. 19th October, 1891).
   Of the nine children of Thomas and Minerva (Hunt) McGehee all are alive but two. He married, secondly, (8th October, 1884;) Mrs. Mary B. McGhee, who is yet living.

VII. ANN THORNTON MCGEHEE, (b. 9th February, 1813, d. 19th August, 1834, in Ala.); *m.* (Montgomery county, Ala., July, 1833;) William Getmer, no issue.

VIII. FRANCIS MICAJAH MCGEHEE, (b. 9th January, 1815; d. 1856 in Texas); *m.* (I) Ann Moore (d. 1847) Madison county, Ala. One child, who died infant. He *m.* (II) Annie Perkins, Mobile, Ala. (d. 1883.) They moved to Bastrop county, Tex., 1847, with Charles L. McGehee. Of nine children, only two are known to be now living: Edward McGehee of Miles City, Montana, and Mrs. C. E. West, McDade, Texas. The eldest son, John McGehee, was in Confederate Army, 8th Texas Cavalry (Terry's Texas Rangers), and died Bowling Green, Ky., 1862. Every exertion to learn more of this family has failed.

IX. WILLIAM BLAIR MCGEHEE (b. 16th May, 1818, d. Alabama, 17th July, 1818).

X. SARAH JANE McGEHEE (b. 20th May, 1820), m. (10th May, 1837) Rev. Ambrose F. Driskill, of the M. E. Church, South, who led an active and useful life in the itinerant ministry, and died in the triumph of faith (17th March, 1875). She is the only one of her father's children now living, and has led a noble, blameless Christian life; is ready when her Master calls, and bids me say to all her large connection that she hopes to meet them in that family mansion in the Beautiful Beyond. She adds her parents were Methodists in faith, and her father's house was the preacher's home, and also preaching place before a church was built. I may say here almost all of these McGehees are Methodists. She lives near the old family residence; P. O., Fisk, Ala.

XI. WILLIAM BLAIR McGEHEE (b. 28 Oct., 1822), went to Bastrop, Texas, with his mother, 1840. Of a splendid physique and much like his father. Mortally wounded (1863) while leading his company in the battle of Crawley's Ridge, Ark. M. (1842) Louisa Morgan, who m. (II) 1866, Thomas H. Jones. She lives with her children. Issue:

1. Mary A. (b. 5 Dec., 1848, d. 27 Dec., 1887) m. (10 April, 1869) James B. Rogers, and had: 1, William, b. 24 Jan., 1871; 2, Mary L., b. 18 Sept., 1873; 3, Edward E., b. July, 1874; 4, Lizzie M., b. 25 Feb., 1876; 5, Nora, b. 13 June, 1878; 6, Maggie, b. 8 Aug., 1881; 7, Thomas M., b. 31 Aug., 1887.

2. Thomas Scott (b. 8 Feb., 1845) m. (29 Dec., 1870) Jennie R. Glenn. Issue: 1, Maud, b. 7 Dec., 1873; 2, May, b. 18 Dec., 1875; 3, Gilmer, b. 20 Oct., 1878; 4, Thomas, b. 9 March, 1880.

3. James H. (b. 8 Nov., 1847) m. (9 March, 1871) Josephine Aiken. Issue: 1, William, b. 27 Feb., 1874; 2, Maggie, b. 3 Oct., 1878; 3, Ethel, b. 30 Aug., 1881; 4, Hiram, b. 12 Sept., 1888; 5, Myrtle, b. Oct., 1892.

4. William Leroy (b. 29 May, 1849) m. (10 Sept., 1874) Caroline E. Denman. Issue: Leroy Moran, b. 1 December, 1875; 2, Ora Lee, b. 8 March, 1878; 3, Morgan Briscoe, born 26 Nov., 1879; 4, Horace Denman, born 9 Oct., 1881; 5, Leon Bell, born 18 Aug., 1884; 6, Mary Lou, b. 10 July, 1885; 7, Noble Page, b. 17 Sept., 1888.

XII. NICHOLAS ABNER McGEHEE, died in Alabama, Oct. 1, 1825. *In conclusion:* There are many McGehees in Texas related to this family. I have not time to hunt them up; and of Oliver and Hill relatives there are scores. In no instance have I, intentionally, left out any of my grandfather's descendants. I am the oldest living male representative of this large family, and if I have herein stimulated any of its members to a higher and nobler life by emulating the lives of the worthy men and women they sprang from, I am a thousand times repaid for the imperfect work given to these sketches.   GEORGE T. McGEHEE.

* San Marcos, Texas, Oct. 1, 1899.

OLIVER.

"The name of Oliver," writes Father Charles Augustus Oliver, Catholic Priest, of Jackson, Miss., "is derived from the Latin words ' *Oliva*', and : '*fer*' (from ' *fero*,' I carry. Therefore, it means "*carrying olives;*" *Olivirri*, in Italian, and *Olivier* in French.

(*From Mr. Dionysius Oliver Hill, of Smithfeld, Texas, and Mr. James McGehee Watkins, of Weimar, Texas.*)

DIONYSIUS OLIVER (page 421), only child of Peter Oliver, of Broad River, Ga., moved to Panola county, Miss., 1839, with his second wife, Sarah McGehee, (widow of Thomas Hill, of Oglethorpe county, Ga.). By his first wife, Lucinda McGehee, he had:

*Two sons of Abner McGehee, of Montgomery, Jefferson and Rev. Lucius McGehee, went to San Antonio, Tex., after the Civil War.

1. Mary[1] (called Martha on page 421), 2. Frank[1], died in Panola county, 3. Sarah Lucinda Scott[1], 4. Peter[1], 5. Dionysius[1], 6. Edward[1] (twin with Dionysius), died 1844 in Panola county, 7. Susan[1], 8. Margaret[1]. Of these:

3. SARAH LUCINDA SCOTT[2] OLIVER (d. 20 May, 1898), educated at the Moravian Institution, Salem, N. C., 1834–8; m. (August, 1840) her cousin Thomas B. J. Hill (d. 6 May, 1873) of Wilks county, Georgia, son of Thomas and Sarah (McGehee) Hill, who was then on his way to Bastrop county, Texas, where they arrived 18 November, 1840. Issue:

    I. Thomas Anderson[3] Hill (b. 8 December, 1841) of Weimer, Texas, m. (1865) Sarah L. McGehee. Eight children. (See McGehee above).

    II. DIONYSIUS OLIVER[3] HILL, of Smithville, Texas (b. 26 October, 1843), m. (25 December, 1866) Mamie Aldridge. Issue:

        1. Susie Blanton[4] m. G. W. Jones (who d. 1897). No issue.

        2. Walton Aldridge[4] (b. 1872, d. 1896) m. Miss Burleson. No issue.

        3. Thomas Oliver[4], unm.

4. PETER[2] OLIVER (b. Georgia about 1812), moved with his father to Mississippi and then to Bastrop county, Texas, in the 40s, with his step-brothers, Thomas B. J., Wiley and Middleton Hill (sons of his aunt and step-mother, Sarah McGehee.) They have all been dead more than thirty years. He married his cousin, Cordelia Ann Hill, and had an only son, Dr. James Dionysius[3] Oliver, of Bastrop county (d. 6 February, 1890), m. (4 May, 1869) Palmyra A. W. McGehee, and had eight childred. (See McGehee above.) Mrs. Oliver lives in San Marcos.

5. DIONYSIUS[2] OLIVER, of Bastrop County, Texas, moved (1839) from Georgia to Panola county, Mississippi, and again, 1850, to Texas, and m. Palmyra Hunt (sister to Mrs. Thomas G. McGehee, of San Marcos), now Mrs. Hubbard. Issue:

    I. Edward Dionysius[3] Oliver, m. Miss Aldredge (sister of Mrs. Dionysius O. Hill). Issue: 1, Leroy[4]; 2, Anna[4]; 3, Susie[4]; 4. Myra[4]; 5, Edward[4]; 6, Cap[4]; and 7, Donivan[4].

    II. Alice Medora[3] Oliver m. John Aldridge (brother of above), several children.

    III. Alexander David[3] Oliver m. Miss Ross, who died, leaving one child. He m. again, but no issue.

    IV. Ida May[3] Oliver m. Mr. Donivan, of Weatherford, Texas. Several children.

7. SUSAN[2] Oliver, m John Robertson, of North Mississippi. Several children.

8. MARGARET[2] OLIVER m. Joseph Phillips, of Holly Springs, Miss. Left one child, Lucinda Scott[3] ,m. Charles Newton, Griffin, Ga. Issue: Four children.

I. MARY[2] OLIVER (above) m. (I) her cousin, Thomas Winfrey Oliver. (See page 341.) She married (II) Rev. J. N. Davis, of Mississippi. Issue: 1, William (killed when a child); 2, Newton; 3, Elizabeth; and 4, Lucinda—nothing known of these.

Excursus—Hill. (For McGehee and Oliver Families.)

THOMAS HILL, of Oglethorpe county, Ga., m. Sarah, daughter of Micajah McGehee, of Broad river. (See McGehee.) His sister, Malinda Hill, also married John McGehee, her brother. Issue: 1. Emaline. 2. Mary. 3. Middleton. 4. Ann. 5. Thomas, B. J. 6. Wiley. Of these:

I. EMALINE HILL, m. her cousin, Thomas Hill, of Oglethorpe county, Ga. Issue: 1. Bettie, m. D. Seay, of South Carolina. 2. Lucinda, m. Ben. Blanton, of Griffin, Ga. 3. Cordelia Ann, m. her cousin, Peter Oliver (ante). 4. Thomas, m. Miss Stratton, of North Mississippi, and moved to Texas, there leaving a family.

II. MARY HILL, m. Thomas Parks, of Newton county, Ga. One son, who died s. p.

III. MIDDLETON HILL (d. 1848), m. Miss Foster, of Alabama, and went to Texas, 1837, and left a large family.

IV. ANN HILL, m. Elisha Strong, and moved to Aberdeen, Miss., and left quite a family.

V. THOMAS B. J. HILL, (d. 6th of May, 1873), m. (1840) Sarah Lucinda Scott Oliver, his cousin and stepsister (ante).

VI. WILEY HILL (d. 1887); joined a company in Montgomery, Ala., 1835, for the Texas revolution, in which he bravely fought. Returning to Georgia, he married (January, 1837) Evaline Hubbard, and settled immediately in Texas, Bastrop county. Issue: 1. Mary, m. John Watson, and had three children. 2. Sarah, m. William Powell, one child. 3. Robert, m. Lucinda Caldwell, four children. 4. Augustus, m. Miss Holmes and had two children. (All from Mr. Dionysius Oliver Hill, of Smithfield, Texas.

Watkins.

COL. THOS. G. WATKINS, of Caldwell, Ky., had two sons and three daughters. The two sons:

1. Judge John D. Watkins, of Minden, La. (b. in Kentucky, 27th September, 1828; d. December 18, 1897). District attorney in Louisiana, 1854; Judge, 1845-69; lieutenant colonel, 1864; Judge Advocate of Court Martial of the Trans-Mississippi Department; State Senate, 1880; elected to Congress, but was counted out by the "Returning Board;" married (1852) Miss M. F. Morrow, of Georgia. Issue: Judge J. T. and L. R. Watkins.

2. Judge Linn Boyd Watkins—named for his mother's cousin, a lieutenant governor of Kentucky; (b. in Caldwell county, Ky, October 9, 1836); went to Minden, La., 1857; admitted to the Bar, 1859, and partnership with his brother, 1860; first lieutenant of cavalry company, Armstrong's brigade, Forrest's corps, in Civil War; afterward on staff of General Jackson, in the Georgia campaign; Judge in 1871; married (October 8, 1884), to a young lady in Red River parish; in 1886 was Associate Justice of Supreme Court, and reappointed by Governor Foster, 1888.

Col. Thos. Watkins was probably descended from John and Edward Watkins, of Cumberland county, Va., whose descendants went to Kentucky in early days.

John P. Watkins, Burnt Corn, Monroe county, planter; student in class of 1864, at the University of Alabama. (See *Watkins family.*) His line has not been completely traced.

ERRATA.

✎ ✎ ✎ ✎

Page 41: Expunge quotation marks under the subject "*Minerals*."

Page 43: Read *was*, and not *were*, after the phrase "*Vox populi*."

Page 62: In the *Booth Note* it was omitted to enumerate *all* the children of William F. and Mary (Fitzgerald) Booth, who moved to Alabama in 1825. These were: 1. Dr. William F. (b. 1796, d. 1858, Quincy, Fla.), *m.* Sarah Gilliam Coe; 2. Sarah Epes (b. 1798), *m.* Sam'l Mitchell; 3. Martha Ann (b. 1800), *m.* James Searcy, Batesville, Ark.; 4. Maria (b. 1802), *m.* Benj. Ward, of Alabama; 5. Charlotte (b. 1804), *m.* (1) Daniel Wade, and (11) Dr. David White, Quincy, Fla.; 6. Elizabeth (b. 1806), *m.* Rev. Jesse Coe; 7. Edward (b. 1808), *unm*; 8. Mary Ann (b. 1810), *m.* (Oct. 18, 1837), A. J. Forman (State Senate of Fla.); 9. Harriet (b. 1812, d. 1858), *m.* 1858, Hudson Muse, Quincy, Fla.; 10. Louisa (b. 1814), *m.* (1) Dr. J. W. Malone, and (11) H. Muse; 11. Caroline (b. 1817), *m.* (1), John Adams, and (11) L. B. Stephens, Quincy, Fla.

Page 113: Read, Smith, for "Smyth."

Page 214: Read, Rousseau for "Rrousseau."

Page 215: Read, Sarah *Epes* Fitzgerald, for "Sarah *Epos*. Fitzgerald."

Page 327: Read, *primus inter pares* for "primis inter pares."

Page 236: Read, *Garber* for "Guitor." (7th line bottom of page).

Page 237: Read, *McKee*, for "Macke" and *Orevecouer et Valué* for "*Orevecouer et Valse*."

Page 241: Read, *pari passu*, for "*pari passee*."

Page 244: Read, *Sampson* Harris, for "*Sampon* Harris."

Page 252: Read, *Anna Josepha* Young, for "*Josephine* Young."

Page 255: Read. I *heard* it; for "I head it," (26th line from bottom of page).

Page 276: For the children of Matthew and Mary (Harrison) Clay, of Deerbrook, Miss., see page 278, and fourth paragraph under head of Green Clay, beginning with "Their children, living, are Matthew Clay," etc. They are, by mistake, placed on this page.

Page 297: Expunge the asterisk to *Winston* (3rd line from the top).

Page 302: Read. *Maritime*, for *Maratime*.

Page 304: Read, R. A. Brock, for "R. A. Brook."

Page 361: Turner Saunders Hancock and Stirling Brown Hancock, sons, also, of William and Eliza J. Hancock, died 1858, of yellow fever, with their mother, all three in six weeks, September and October.

Page 357: Read, Dr. D. D. Saunders, born *26th* February.

Page 358: Read, Mrs. Mary Wheatley Saunders, died *1892*.

Dr. D. D. Saunders, Jr., graduated at the *Medical University of Pennsylvania* (Philadelphia).

Kate Saunders married G. W. Agee in *1892*.

Page 396: Mary, daughter of Col. James Blair, married Alonzo Vortor (and not Mr. Rugeley, as is erroneously stated).

Page 402: Read *Debuam* for "Debuam," and *Hansford* for "Hausford," and *was* Bacon's celebrated Rebel, for "*Mrs.* Bacon's celebrated Rebel."

Page 403: The John Marshall *Note* belongs to page 402; and for "Sir Edwin Landys," read, Sir Edwin Sandys.

Page 409: Read, *Menx* for "Menx."

Page 434: John Bibb, born *1780* (*not* "1789," as stated).

Page 438: Read, Mrs. Frances *Saffold* married (II) Dr. Walter Jackson. Her daughter, Mary Ellen Saffold was married but once. Also Caroline Bibb married Walter Coleman, about *1849* (not 1869).

Page 442: Loula G. Bibb, for "Sarah G.," and John D. Hutcheson for "John S. Hutchinson."

Page 451: Read, *Farrington*, instead of "Fannington."

Page 457: "Charles Thurston" should be *Charles Thruston*.

Page 478: "Davis Lewis" should be *David Lewis*.

Page 482 (*Harris Note*): Read. *W. G. Stanard* for "W. G. Staught."

Pages 519 and 395: It was omitted to state that the other children of Dr. **Joseph Foster**, besides John Cantson, are: Harry, Louise, Gertrude, Carl, Iota, Joseph, Jessie, and one other. Mr. John Foster has also one child, Annie, Mrs. Paul Moore.

An accidental omission on page 412 leaves out the last two children of Isaac Oliver, of Nottoway, who married Mary A. G. Bacon⁴, and had *ten* children. These two are—

9. Anna Oliver *m*. Dr. Robert Watkins, of Eutaw, Ala., and had two children. She is the oldest surviving member of her family, and takes great interest in its annals.

10. Elizabeth T Oliver married Samuel Dunlap. Issue: Four children.

ABBREVIATIONS.

Large Roman numerals indicate *heads* of families; Arabic numbers, children and grandchildren. *Minute* figures, at end of a name, denote the number of generations from the *first* recorded ancestor; *b*. for born; *m*. for married; *d*. for died; *unm*. for unmarried; *dau*. for daughter; will *p*. for will proved. Each succeeding generation is indented (or receded in the margin of the page) from the preceding one.

INDEX.